ST. JAMES
ENCYCLOPEDIA OF
LABOR HISTORY
WORLDWIDE

ST. JAMES
ENCYCLOPEDIA OF
LABOR HISTORY
WORLDWIDE

Major Events in Labor History and Their Impact

VOLUME 1
A–M

With Introductions by

Willie Thompson, Northumbria University
and
Daniel Nelson, University of Akron

Neil Schlager, Editor

PRODUCED BY SCHLAGER GROUP

ST. JAMES
PRESS®

Detroit • New York • San Diego • San Francisco • Cleveland • New Haven, Conn. • Waterville, Maine • London • Munich

St. James Encyclopedia of Labor History Worldwide: Major Events in Labor History and Their Impact

Schlager Group Inc. Staff

Neil Schlager, editor

Vanessa Torrado-Caputo, assistant editor

Project Editor
Margaret Mazurkiewicz

Editorial
Erin Bealmear, Joann Cerrito, Jim Craddock, Stephen Cusack, Miranda H. Ferrara, Peter M. Gareffa, Kristin Hart, Melissa Hill, Carol Schwartz, Christine Tomassini, Michael J. Tyrkus

Permissions
Shalice Shah-Caldwell

Imaging and Multimedia
Robert Duncan, Leitha Etheridge-Sims, Mary Grimes, Lezlie Light, Daniel Newell, David G. Oblender, Christine O'Bryan, Kelly A. Quin

Product Design
Cynthia Baldwin

Manufacturing
Rhonda Williams

Library of Congress Cataloging-in-Publication Data

St. James encyclopedia of labor history worldwide : major events in labor history and their impact / Neil Schlager, editor ; with introductions by Daniel Nelson and Willie Thompson.
    p. cm.
        Includes bibliographical references and index.
        ISBN 1-55862-542-9 (set : alk. paper) — ISBN 1-55862-559-3 (Vol. 1) — ISBN 1-55862-560-7 (Vol. 2)
        1. Labor movement—History—Encyclopedias. 2. Labor unions—History—Encyclopedias. I. Schlager, Neil, 1966-

HD4839.S74 2003
331.8'03—dc21
2003000294

CONTENTS

EDITOR'S NOTE

Overview

Welcome to the *St. James Encyclopedia of Labor History Worldwide*. Our aim is to provide a scholarly, encyclopedic treatment of the labor movement during the past 200 years. The encyclopedia covers 300 key events in labor history, from the struggle to abolish slavery both in the British Empire and in the United States during the 1800s; to the rise of trade unions later in the century; to the often violent clashes between labor and management in the early twentieth century; and to the onset of globalization toward the end of the twentieth century. Throughout the encyclopedia, events are placed in the context of the labor movement as a whole and related to societal change and development worldwide.

Scope and Coverage

The encyclopedia includes 300 events from period from 1800 to 2000. Two-thirds of the articles focus on U.S. labor history and one-third are devoted to international history. Because of this distribution, international events in particular were chosen for their relevance to larger social movements and their impact on development of the labor movement in a country or region. The entries were selected by an advisory board of expert labor historians, whose names and affiliations are listed elsewhere in this frontmatter; more information about the advisers is available in the "Notes on Advisers and Contributors" section at the back of Volume 2. The entries were written by labor historians, freelance writers, librarians, and journalists.

Format of Volumes, Entries

In response to feedback from public and academic librarians, we have arranged the volumes alphabetically by entry title. An alphabetical listing of the entry titles is included in the frontmatter. In addition, readers may also wish to consult the chronological listing of entries elsewhere in the frontmatter as well as the detailed index at the back of Volume 2.

Within each entry, readers will find the following format:

* Entry title, location, and date. Although the location is typically the country where the event occurred, in some cases it refers to the place where an organization or movement was founded.
* Synopsis: Brief overview of the event.
* Event and Its Context: In-depth discussion of the event and its impact.
* Key Players: Brief biographical notes on people who figured prominently in the event.
* Bibliography: List of sources used to compile the entry.
* Additional Resources: Other sources that readers may wish to consult.

In addition, each entry contains a chronology of key events in world history, so that readers may better understand the historical context in which the event occurred. At the end of most entries, readers will find cross references to other entries in the encyclopedia that may be of interest.

Other Features

In addition to the main text, the encyclopedia features two lengthy introductions, one of which discusses international labor history and another that covers U.S. labor history. In addition, users will find a glossary of labor terms; a general chronology consisting of key events in world history combined with important labor events; a reading list covering English-language sources devoted to labor history; and a subject index. The encyclopedia also includes more than 350 photographs as well as nearly 50 sidebars that provide information on other subjects of interest.

Acknowledgements

The editors wish to thank the following individuals for their assistance in preparing the encyclopedia: Judson Knight, who compiled all of the sidebar material in addition to the chronologies; Caryn E. Neumann, who prepared the glossary; and Willie Thompson and Daniel Nelson, who wrote the introductory pieces.

—Neil Schlager
Editor

INTRODUCTION: INTERNATIONAL LABOR, 1800–2000

The worldwide labor movement that was a central social reality of the nineteenth and twentieth centuries was formed from many and diverse sources and traditions. Its development and history coincided with that of the growth and spread of factory industry and of similar forms of capitalist and public enterprise, such as transport, primary production, and the many divisions of labor in societies economically connected to mass markets and advanced public utilities.

This labor movement originated in Europe. However, its spread around the world was determined less by imitation of the European model (although that played its part) as by similar responses from industrial or quasi-industrial workforces to equivalent problems of the workplace and living environment, and above all by conflict with employers.

Given the character of modern production, it was inevitable that organizations of workers aiming to defend their members' interests would emerge sooner or later, unless repressively prevented, but the shape of the labor movement and its precise nature and development were the outcome of contingent circumstances and actions that might well have taken place under other situations. There was nothing inevitable about the structure of more-or-less nationally unified labor unions supporting labor parties, which evolved as the general rule (outside the United States), not only in the original centers of modern industry, but also in what was later to be termed the Third World.

Early Trade Associations

The decades of the late eighteenth and early nineteenth centuries were eras of economic, social, and political transition and upheaval. In Western Europe and Britain, protocapitalist market forces (developing in Britain since the previous century, if not earlier) made growing inroads into traditional standards and practices. Handicraft artisans found themselves increasingly threatened with deskilling, reduced incomes, and tighter subordination to the mercantile elements on whom they were dependent for supply and marketing, and they protested vigorously as a result. The French revolutionary government of 1790 regarded workers' coalitions as troublesome enough to outlaw them under the Le Chapelier law, and at the turn of the century, the Parliament of Britain, where there had already been workers' riots leading to fatalities, reinforced the already existing prohibition against "combinations in restraint of trade" by means of the notorious Combination Acts of 1799 and 1800.

Combinations nevertheless continued, both in Britain and elsewhere. They were feared by the propertied classes, not only on account of their immediate objectives, but for the possibility they could be infected by the democratic virus of the French Revolution, which, although defeated, continued to inspire many at the bottom of the social pyramid.

By the 1820s, with the accelerating penetration of steam-powered machinery into the production process, a further development became apparent—concentrated masses of factory operatives in expanding urban areas. The growing reliance upon coal required new factories to be sited in towns for ease of transport, first by canal and subsequently by railway. The latter generated entire industries, and coal mining also expanded prodigiously.

The Emergence of Modern Labor Movements

In these circumstances, a European labor movement of a more recognizably modern type began to evolve. A new social layer of workers entirely dependent upon minimal subsistence wage payments as their sole source of income, lacking any alternative resources of land or capital, multiplied in the new industrial centers of the United Kingdom, France, Belgium, and Germany. Although divided by age, gender, occupation, and cultural traditions, these workers shared the miseries of overcrowded slums bereft of space, sanitation, clean water, and access to adequate diet or medical care. Plagued by adulterated foodstuffs, alcoholism, crime, violence, and the narcotic substances of the time, they were also subject at unpredictable intervals to a total loss of income, whenever economic depression or an overstocked labor market produced long-term unemployment.

These circumstances, together with memories of the French Revolution—or rather its image of mighty elites overthrown and social equality enforced for all citizens—combined to determine the shape of the European labor movement. Out of that revolution in its later stages had been born the idea of socialism, with its core idea that the enormous productive forces that new technologies were releasing should be collectively owned and operated for the common good rather than private profit. However, it was not predestined that socialism would come to dominate the consciousness of European labor in the nineteenth century, for other options were available. Socialist ideas did not prevail among labor in the United States, and only by the narrowest of margins did they become the accepted mainstream ideology of British labor in the twentieth century. It was even less inevitable that the Marxian variety would emerge as the prominent form of socialism in most European countries, yet by the turn of the century, with the notable exception of Britain, it indeed had.

Marxism and Labor

The Manifesto of the Communist Party (1847), was written by the young revolutionaries Karl Marx and Frederick Engels. The *Manifesto* sketched their vision of historical development, rational and purportedly scientific, which denoted the bourgeoisie as the revolutionary class that through technology and market relations had transformed the world so that the society of universal abundance had moved from the realm of utopia to that of the possible. Having acclaimed the historical role of capital, Marx and Engels went on to condemn its current reality as an obstacle to the great possibilities it had created. They pronounced that it was both necessary and inevitable that the proletariat should displace the bourgeoisie and institute its own rule, making the transition to a society of abundance feasible. Their text thus provided both inspiration and confidence that a historic role awaited the proletariat, indeed the most momentous role of all time—in abolishing capitalism, this social class would abolish itself and all class-based society. Marx's analysis of economic relationships in the first volume of *Capital* (written in 1867, but not published until 1887) was equally important. This analysis claimed to demonstrate how, under the misleading guise of freedom and equality, the wage contract was inherently exploitative, and the wage worker, although not bound like a serf to any individual capitalist, was just as tightly bound to capitalists as a class.

It took time, however, for Marx's influence to make itself felt. After the social and political traumas of early industrialization, which had been marked by massive economic slumps along with intense discontent, the 25 years following the failed European revolutions of 1848 were years of comparative social peace, underpinned by relatively consistent high growth rates both in Britain and the continent (the large-scale construction of railway systems had a lot to do with this). During this period Marx's theoretical impact became evident, and labor organizations that based their programs on his analysis began to emerge.

Challenges to Marx

Marx's theoretical superiority did not go unchallenged. It was contested by representatives of the anarchist movement, particularly the French reformer Pierre Joseph Proudhon, in the 1840s, and Mikhail Bakunin, the Russian revolutionist, in the 1860s. Anarchism established a strong presence among workers in Switzerland, Italy, Spain (especially), and to a lesser extent, France. The movement was attractive principally to independent artisans and small farmers rather than factory workers, a reflection of the different positioning of these classes in relation to the state. A more substantial rival to Marx appeared in Germany. The radical lawyer Ferdinand Lassalle, a brilliant demagogue, admired Marx and claimed he could recite the *Manifesto* by heart. However, Lassalle was the first leader of a successful German workers' movement, the German Workers' Association, which he founded in 1863 in opposition to the exiled Marx. Lassalle supported reform, rather than revolution, and was willing to make deals with the landlord-dominated Prussian state led by Bismarck in opposition to the big capitalists. Given that Prussia was developing into the most industrialized society on the continent, with an attendant growing factory proletariat, and would soon amalgamate with smaller German states in 1866 and 1871 to create the mighty *Kaiserreich,* this workers' movement represented the greatest obstacle to Marx's intellectual hegemony.

Marxism Takes Hold

Lassalle's death in 1864, without any significant political heir, left the field clear for Marx's followers, who succeeded in bringing the rapidly growing German labor movement under their aegis. They absorbed the dead leader's very considerable following, establishing the Social Democratic Party of Germany (SPD) in 1875. It was not, however, historical accidents like Lassalle's death in a duel that determined Marx's ascendancy, but the depth and coherence of his comprehensive theoretical undertaking, which provided a ready-made understanding of the social world and a guide to action.

Marx was the moving spirit behind the establishment of the International Workingmens' Association (IWMA) in 1864. Known as the First International, the IWMA was an attempt to bring together political and trade union movements from a number of European countries to concert their actions, especially against strikebreaking. In reality, although it alarmed a number of governments—particularly after the Paris Commune, the bloody insurrection of 1871 for which the IWMA was in no way responsible—it remained small and marginal. Internal wrangles, above all between the followers of Marx and of Mikhail Bakunin, wrecked the organization and brought about its dissolution in 1874. Matters were very different when a successor organization, the Socialist, or Second

International, was set up in Paris on the centenary of the French Revolution in 1889. By this time, significant labor movements, the majority and most important basing themselves on Marx's ideas, were well established throughout western and central Europe. The Socialist International benefited from the fact that it was a loosely structured organization and that its headquarters in Amsterdam served a coordinating, rather than executive, function. This reduced friction between its constituent parts that a more centralized organization would have found difficult to handle.

The Influence of the SPD

The flagship of the Socialist International was its German component, the SPD, with a million and a half voters. Although it had been outlawed in 1878, and in 1889 was still formally illegal in its own country, the SPD was nonetheless thriving. It was clear that the ban could not long be maintained, and it was lifted in 1890. The SPD was more than a political party, more even than a political-industrial organization. With its multiplicity of journals, its attached women's and youth organizations, its cultural and athletic societies, its cooperative retail network, and of course its mighty trade union arm, it provided an alternative subculture for the working masses. The SPD had rivals in the Catholic and Liberal workers' unions, but these were a pale shadow of its own dominant strength. No other labor movement in Europe could claim this breadth of support combined with depth of cultural penetration.

Historians generally agree that the main consideration behind the hegemony of the SPD in the German workers' movement was that the dominant classes and parties in the state disdained the working class and its organizations and provided no alternative avenues for their political participation. This state of affairs was very different from that prevailing in other parts of western Europe, including the United Kingdom, where labor parties were much less hegemonic among their working classes. There is also general agreement that everywhere the SPD succeeded in establishing itself, the labor movement—although only occasionally imposing formal discrimination upon women—was institutionally misogynist (not unlike other societies of its time and since). How far that attitude toward women retarded its progress is impossible to guess, but probably a good deal.

Labor Movements Outside Western Europe

By the time the International was founded, embryonic labor movements had already been established in North America and the British settlement colonies, and were starting to appear in eastern Europe, Asia, and Latin America, where modern industry was beginning to be introduced. These embryonic organizations were frequently subject to persecution, often clandestine, and sometimes more forcefully revolutionary than their formally Marxist (but generally pacific) counterparts in Western Europe, North America, and Australasia. By the end of the 1890s they had become embedded in the working classes, combining trade union activities and political propagandizing. By the beginning of the twentieth century, trade union organizations were beginning to form in India, and in Japan, socialist ideas, albeit rather eclectic ones strongly influenced by Christianity, were appealing to circles of intellectuals.

Labor in the Twentieth Century

The Early Twentieth Century

At the beginning of the twentieth century, existing labor movements with an orientation toward political action as the long-term solution to labor's problems—with socialism as their ultimate goal—were facing a serious rival in the form of syndicalism (the name is derived from the French word for trade union). This trend of thought regarded political approaches, whether reformist or revolutionary, as inadequate to the vital interests of the workers. Instead, syndicalists envisaged taking direct action to overthrow capitalism. This action would involve the formation of wide-embracing industrial unions, followed by a general strike as the final act leading to the establishment of workers' power. As frustration grew with the existing unions and labor parties in the United States, Western Europe, the United Kingdom, and the British settlement colonies, the influence of syndicalism, taking as its icon the physically powerful male industrial worker, proliferated and strengthened. Its most effective and successful component was the organization called the Industrial Workers of the World (IWW), popularly styled the "Wobblies." The IWW put down strong roots in many trade unions, becoming dominant, for example, among the Welsh miners, produced many notable agitators, and left behind a heritage of labor movement songs and legends.

The years between 1873 and 1914 were a period of long-term economic recession (although never of negative growth) punctuated by short-lived inflationary episodes of boom conditions. This period also saw the introduction and initial development of major new technologies, from electrical apparatus to motor vehicles. Industrial workforces increased in number and spread to new parts of the world, as did workers' organizations and working-class ideologies, along with dramatic working-class struggles. The climax of European imperialism was reached with the partitioning of Africa and "opening" of China. Working classes in the imperial countries, their unions and parties, were inevitably drawn into these developments, for the most part giving them a qualified approval. Increasingly frenetic imperial rivalry brought with it the threat of general European war. The danger was foreseen, and on more than one occasion the Socialist International at its congresses committed its member parties to spare no effort in bringing such armed conflict to a stop. Regrettably, when the long-predicted war finally arrived in 1914, these resolutions were consigned to oblivion, and the International shattered. Various International sections in France, Germany, and Britain, along with labor movements, parties, and trade unions, with few exceptions, enthusiastically gave their governments all the support they could by voting war credits, suppressing strike action, encouraging recruitment, and the like. When the chips were down, each national component of the International, whatever its reservations, viewed its existing national state as the best guarantor of its future.

The Rise of the Bolsheviks

This outcome was to have reverberations for global labor movements and for world politics during the remainder of the twentieth century. Up to that point, the labor mainstream had been more and more accommodating to the realities of capitalist market economies, the concern (in spite of bitter industrial struggles and ceremonial revolutionary rhetoric) being to obtain for labor a tolerable niche in terms of material resources and social opportunity within the structures of a capital-dominated universe. Certainly there were elements like the Wobblies and some small parties who seriously envisaged the total overthrow of the existing state and complete social overturn, but these were marginal groups, either politically or geographically or both. Among the latter were the Russian Bolsheviks, one of the factions of what had been intended to be a unified Russian socialist (Social Democratic and Labor) party, but immediately upon its foundation in 1903 had splintered over policy and organizational issues, reflecting support for or disagreement with the unbending revolutionary will to power of the Bolshevik leader Vladimir Ilich Ulyanov, who had adopted the pseudonym "Lenin."

By the late nineteenth century, capitalist industry was developing strongly in parts of Russia amid the most miserable conditions for its workforce (employers tended to pay minimal wages irregularly, whenever it suited their convenience). Illegal workers' organizations soon sprung up, and these were encouraged and guided by circles of Marxist-influenced intellectuals. These same Marxists promptly fell into bitter disputes regarding the correct interpretation of Marxism and its implications for revolutionary strategy in the Russian Empire. The division in 1903 was a reflection of these disagreements; nevertheless, the Bolsheviks (the name means "majority people") and their principal rivals, the Mensheviks ("minority people") were both part of the International, which vainly struggled to reconcile their differences.

Lenin concluded that the collapse of the International's parties into what he termed "social-patriotism" following the outbreak of World War I took place because leaders at all levels of the European working classes had been seduced and debauched by profits derived from imperial exploitation, but that the murderous European war now in progress would shortly open the eyes of the masses to the way in which they had been deceived. Accordingly, from his place of exile in Switzerland, Lenin set out to establish a new genuinely revolutionary International. In the circumstances it appeared to be a completely harebrained scheme, but the outbreak of revolution in Russia in February and March 1917 transformed realities. Seven months later the Bolsheviks had taken control of the Russian state.

The revolution of October and November 1917 was one of the workers, the only example in history. The Russian workers had transferred their political allegiance to the Bolsheviks, not because of mass conversion to Marxism, but because that party promised an end to the war and the resolution of the urban supply crisis. The Bolsheviks also temporarily won the approval of the peasantry by endorsing their seizure of the landlords' estates, and that of the conscripted soldiers by promising peace. The revolution was contingent on a series of contingent events, a very unlikely outcome in historical perspective, but it set the agenda for most of the remainder of the century. Revolutionaries everywhere, especially Marxist ones, now had what they had previously lacked, a model and a point of reference, as well as the material support of an established state. For the Bolshevik leaders, the revolution in Russia was merely the initial episode in a workers' world revolution that they regarded as imminent, and in the midst of a desperate civil war to retain power, they established in 1919 a new, revolutionary International, the Third (Communist) International, or Comintern.

According to Lenin, the Comintern was to function as the general staff of the world anticapitalist revolution, and its first imperative was to establish Bolshevik-style parties in as many parts of the world as possible. The principal strategy for accomplishing this was to hive off the more revolutionary elements from the existing labor movements and parties and form these into communist parties subject to the discipline of the International, although in a number of countries the Comintern had to settle for amalgamating a number of small radical, left-wing sects to form its communist party.

The Failure of the Global Labor Movement

Overall this strategy was only moderately successful. Although within a few years communist parties made their appearance in most countries and major colonies around the world, Lenin's expectations were not realized, and no new revolution emerged out of these developments. Instead the global labor movement was disastrously and irrevocably split; bitter hatred and rivalry, including bloodshed, became the prevailing relationship between the social democrat and communist contenders for the workers' allegiance. A turning point arrived in Germany in 1919 when the working class there solidly supported the Social Democrat government (it had taken office upon the Kaiser's downfall) in using military elements of the old regime to crush communist revolutionaries led by Rosa Luxemburg and Karl Liebknecht, who were both murdered thereafter. The Bolsheviks/Communists now rejected the Social Democrat name they had accepted up to that point and left it to their constitutionalist labor movement rivals.

The experience of Soviet Russia (from 1924 the Union of Soviet Socialist Republics, or USSR), which emerged from the Revolution and Civil War, demonstrated that whether or not a workers' state was a feasible project, it certainly was not practicable in the circumstances of an isolated and devastated Russia. Even before Lenin's death in 1924, the regime had fallen into the control of a largely unaccountable bureaucracy and the labor organizations reduced to ciphers, their main remit being to exhort their members to intensified production. The world revolution had been expected to make limitless resources available for Soviet Russia's desperately needed reconstruction. When the revolution failed to materialize, Lenin's successors quarreled fiercely among themselves over what should be done. The hitherto unimpressive Josef Stalin took advantage of this to quietly accumulate power through the party's administrative apparatus. He displaced and exiled his main opponent, Leon Trotsky, and by 1929 Stalin had established his own personal dictatorship.

The Interwar Years

The working classes in the developed economies of western Europe and the British white Dominions, where they were most numerous and best organized, preferred in the main to trust their political fortunes to parties that worked within the guidelines of the constitutional politics of representative democracy and to unions that conducted industrial relations according to accepted constraints on the behavior of both sides, stretched though these bounds might be from time to time. The balance on the whole remained in favor of the employers in the 1920s, as chronic recession and high unemployment greatly impeded industrial militancy, and workers had to compromise on the best terms they could get. Their parties also tended on the whole to be weak and on the defensive within imperfectly democratic structures. In the 1930s, the situation worsened, except in Scandinavia (especially Sweden), where social democrat governments and strong union movements were able to establish a regime that combined greater levels of welfare than existed anywhere else in Europe, combined with a centralized system of wage bargaining not too disadvantageous to the unionized workforce.

However, even Scandinavia suffered from the economic hurricane that struck the world in October 1929, beginning with the collapse of the U.S. stock market. Elsewhere in the world the effects were catastrophic, both socially and politically. Italy had already provided an indicator of what was to come, with the total destruction in the 1920s of political democracy and workers' movements. In the 1930s, the political system of fascism, which Italy's elites had pioneered to mobilize terrified lower middle-class masses against the left, spread throughout Europe in even more virulent forms, and analogous types of politics appeared elsewhere around the globe, from Argentina to Japan. The years following 1929 were particularly calamitous for labor movements everywhere except for Scandinavia (less Finland) and the United States.

A considerable part of the disaster was due to the policy laid down by the Comintern as a reflection of developments in the USSR, where the workers of the workers' state were being reduced to near-serf conditions in the breakneck industrialization demanded by Stalin. According to the Comintern, the capitalist world was entering the paroxysms of a final crisis (an analysis superficially confirmed by the crash of the U.S. stock market), and capitalism was ripe for overthrow. Social democracy, allegedly deceiving the workers, was stigmatized as the last obstacle to victorious revolutionary advance ("social fascists" indeed) and targeted as the deadliest enemy of the Communists and proletariat. The real fascists were dismissed as a near irrelevance. The unbridgeable antagonisms and divisions caused by this viewpoint greatly undermined the labor movement everywhere it had once flourished, and in Germany produced unparalleled disaster, contributing in no small measure to the success of Adolph Hitler. Thus abstruse expositions of Marxist theory in the councils of the state and the Comintern produced calamitous consequences for workers on the ground almost everywhere throughout Europe and perhaps further afield. Following these manifest catastrophes, the policy began to be relaxed (although without any admission of fault) and in 1935, at the final congress of the Comintern, it was replaced by the policy of the "Popular Front," a complete reversal that called for antifascist unity among all democrats, not merely among organizations of the working class.

The embryonic labor movements of the Third World were also attacked and repressed during the interwar years. Throughout their colonial sphere from Jamaica to Malaya, and especially in India, the British crushed labor unions and jailed trade unionists (although a general strike in the British Caribbean in 1938 won some concessions). The authoritarian military government in Japan, entering into a project of aggressive military expansion, outlawed what had earlier been a significant labor movement. In China, the workforce organizations of the coastal cities were annihilated and the workers massacred when the nationalist general Chiang Kai-Shek turned against his communist allies. The Communist Party, however, survived by abandoning its urban base and turning itself into a peasant movement, and after many traumatic episodes embedded itself among the villagers of remote northwestern China, where its military forces controlled an extensive territory.

Labor During the Cold War

Most labor movements were destroyed or driven deep underground in the years leading up to World War II and the period of Nazi occupation. With the total defeat of the Axis powers in 1945, however, their situation was transformed. It would hardly be an exaggeration to suggest that in the brief period between the Allied victory and the onset of the Cold War, the world was moving to a labor agenda, and communist parties (on account of their resistance records) were popular with wide sections of the liberated European electorate, as reflected in their votes in the elections of that period. Social Democrats were also popular, and even surviving conservative parties such as the Christian Democrats in Germany and Italy were at pains to distance themselves from unregulated capitalism. A unified world trade union movement, the World Federation of Trade Unions (WFTU), was established in 1945.

Matters changed once the Cold War became an unmistakable reality from 1947, and the developed world was divided into two hostile camps, with the labor movements in the Third World assiduously courted by both sides, with varying outcomes. In 1949 China was swept by communist revolution brought from the countryside to the cities, and its urban labor movements, paralyzed since 1927, came under state control as part of the communist bloc. The same happened to labor movements in eastern Europe, when in 1947 and 1948 the continent became divided between the spheres of the United States and the USSR. Not surprisingly, the international labor movement also split, when trade union centers aligned with the West broke away from the Soviet-dominated WFTU to form the International Confederation of Free Trade Unions (ICFTU) in 1949. In Western countries, such as Italy and France, where significant communist movements survived, the parties and their associated unions and labor organizations became isolated in a political ghetto, although they continued to exercise political leverage in legislatures, to control local authorities, and to carry out the routine union functions of collective bargaining with employers.

The period of the Cold War was also an era of decolonization, as European empires disintegrated around the world. Economic development there, modest though it was by "first world" standards, resulted in the formation and development of trade unions, except in cases where they were forcibly suppressed. The trade unions participated in the independence struggles, although only very occasionally, as in Kenya, were trade union leaders also major political figures. Paradoxically, once independence was achieved, trade unionists, and industrial workers in general, tended to count among the privileged classes of the post-colonial regime, enjoying higher incomes and living standards than the mass of the rural peasantry. During the Chinese Cultural Revolution of 1966–1970, wage demands by urban workers were denounced by the Maoist Red Guards—in a state theoretically led by the working-class vanguard—as "sugar-coated bullets."

Since 1945, where workers' uprisings or even insurrections have occurred, they were directed against the supposed workers' governments of the Soviet bloc, from East Berlin in 1953 (and the less well-known simultaneous industrial unrest in Czechoslovakia), through to the strikes in Poland in 1956, the Hungarian armed insurrection immediately afterwards, and to the mass strikes along the Baltic coastline in 1970, 1975, and finally 1980. Of necessity, these actions, provoked by material, political, and national grievances, were spontaneous and inchoate, for the official trade union organizations were under tight regime control, and represented the government to the workers, not the other way round.

During the 25 years or so following World War II, trade union organizations in Western Europe (even those controlled by communists) and in the Western sphere generally enjoyed unparalleled strength, prosperity, and prestige in what was later referred to as the world "long boom." With a labor market favoring the organized workforce, income levels reached unprecedented heights, and the consumer society blossomed. Governments, even conservative ones, were careful to take account of labor demands and aspirations. Social policy fell into a recognizably social democratic mode. Full employment and welfare characterized Western society during the 1950s and 1960s.

Great changes occurred after the onset of a long-term recession following the fuel crisis of 1973. Although unions in Britain were to overthrow a Conservative government in 1974, and in France the Socialist and Communist Parties entered government in coalition in 1981, the overall trend was toward a triumphant reassertion of neoliberal values, reduced taxation, and curtailed welfare, combined with an intensification of corporate business power. Unions found their membership declining as unemployment rose, business grew more hostile, and governments moved to curb their legal powers. Social democratic parties (and electorates) increasingly accepted the new climate of low taxation, market values, and minimum social intervention by government.

The End of the Cold War and Beyond

In eastern Europe, the peaceful revolt by the Polish workforce beginning in the Gdansk shipyards in 1980, although temporarily suppressed, proved to be the overture to the collapse of the Soviet bloc and the USSR itself. With this collapse went not only the command economy and the all-embracing state ruling ostensibly in the name of the working class, but the entire tradition of the October Revolution (even among the purportedly communist parties that survived). Unregulated market capitalism became the order of the day, and full employment and the basic welfare structure of these states were repudiated. In the less-developed of these countries, including Russia, the living standards of the industrial workforce, despite their now-free trade unions, plunged catastrophically.

At the beginning of twenty-first century, labor movements around the world, whether industrial or political, were not facing happy or promising circumstances. Nevertheless, they still retained very considerable assets—human, material, organizational, and intangible—and the rise of the Workers' Party in Brazil beginning in the 1980s demonstrated that their potential was far from exhausted. Of one thing it was possible to be sure: their future role and success would be determined by how far labor movements succeeded in imaginatively facing up to the new challenges that confronted them—the recomposition of workforces everywhere, the reality of globalization, and the environmental issues that increasingly dominated the beginning of the twenty-first century.

The history of the labor movement is extraordinarily convoluted, with more than its share of tragedy and horror as well as achievement and triumph. This volume is intended to highlight, recount, and explain in context the central episodes of that process and to serve as a reference work for the benefit of scholars, of people who participated, and those of the general public who want to be better informed about this remarkable social and political phenomenon.

—Willie Thompson

INTRODUCTION: LABOR IN THE UNITED STATES, 1800–2000

As the American labor force grew from perhaps three million at the beginning of the nineteenth century to nearly 200 million at the beginning of the twenty-first century, the character of the work it performed changed as dramatically as the numbers. In 1800 most American workers were farmers, farm laborers, or unpaid household workers. Many were bound (as slaves in the southern states and indentured servants in the North). Most of the others were proprietors of family businesses. The majority were of British, German, or African origins. Many workers received housing, food, and goods as part of their pay. A large percentage were unaware of labor market conditions in other states or regions and had no reason to take a greater interest: competition was limited by geography, slow and costly transportation, and seemingly unchanging technologies.

Two hundred years later, farm labor had become insignificant, employees vastly outnumbered the self-employed, bound labor had disappeared, and child and unpaid household labor had declined greatly. Family and other social ties had become less important in finding work or keeping a job, large private and public organizations employed more than a third of all workers and set standards for most of the others, the labor force had become more ethnically diverse, labor productivity and real wages were many times higher, wage contracts and negotiated agreements covering large groups were commonplace, and workplace disputes were subject to a web of laws and regulations. Increasingly American workers competed with workers in Mexico, Southeast Asia, or China.

Technology

The changing character of work was closely related to the classic technological innovations of the nineteenth century. Changes in energy use were particularly influential. Thanks to the availability of numerous waterpower sites in New England and the mid-Atlantic region, American industry developed rapidly after the American Revolution. By the 1820s, the massive, water-powered Walthan Mills of northern Massachusetts and southern New Hampshire were among the largest factories in the world. By midcentury, steam power had become widespread in manufacturing as well as transportation, and steam-powered factories had become the foundation of the industrial economy. The advent of electrical power at the turn of the twentieth century had an even greater impact, making possible the giant manufacturing operations of the early twentieth century; the smaller, more specialized plants that became the rule after the 1920s; the great versatility in machine use that characterized the second half of the twentieth century; and the mechanization of stores, offices, and homes.

Steam and electrical power and related innovations in machine technology not only made it feasible to create large organizations but also gave them an economic advantage over small plants and shops. Workers in the new organizations were wage earners, usually not family members, and often were not even acquainted outside the plant. They rejected payment in kind or in services (company housing and company stores in isolated mining communities became a persistent source of grievances), started and stopped at specific times (the factory bell tower remained a powerful symbol of the new era), and became accustomed to rules defining their responsibilities and behavior. Mechanization was also a stimulus to specialization. Elaborate hierarchies of pay and status grew out of the new ways of work.

The industrial model soon spread to the service sector. Railroad corporations created hierarchical, bureaucratic structures with even stricter lines of authority and more specialized tasks. Insurance companies, department stores, mail-order houses, and large banks followed this pattern, though they typically used simple, hand-operated machines. The growth of regional and national markets (a result of technological innovations in transportation and communication as well as the expanding economy) made the hierarchical, bureaucratic organization profitable even when power-driven machines played little role in production.

Free Labor

Although almost one-fifth of the U.S. population was not free at the beginning of the nineteenth century, the institutions and practices that had made unfree labor economically advantageous in earlier centuries soon came under attack. Indentured servitude was a victim of changing market conditions and falling transport costs. It had barely survived the turmoil surrounding the American and French Revolutions and died in the 1820s as immigrants who financed their own transportation replaced bound servants. Slavery was more entrenched and continued to be profitable to many slave owners through the first half of the century. Northern states abolished slavery with minimal controversy, but southern cotton, rice, and sugar growers remained intransigent. They devised elaborate rationales for slavery and used their political power to thwart reform, foreclosing the possibility of a repetition of the northern experience. Antislavery agitators succeeded in making abolition an increasingly important and contentious political cause. More moderate opponents stressed the ill effects of slavery on free labor. By the end of the 1850s the impasse between proslavery and antislavery groups had produced a political and constitutional crisis that quickly degenerated into war.

The Thirteenth Amendment to the Constitution (1865) formally abolished slavery in the United States, but neither it nor the Reconstruction measures that accompanied it effectively addressed the social and economic legacies of slavery. As a result, the South remained an isolated, economically stagnant region, and most southern workers, white and black, remained significantly poorer and less mobile than workers of other regions until the twentieth century.

Immigration

Most workers who filled nonexecutive positions in the new industrial organizations of the nineteenth century were European immigrants or their children. The rapid growth in the demand for labor (interrupted by periodic economic downturns and mass unemployment, notably in the 1870s, 1890s, and 1930s) attracted a swelling tide of newcomers. At first it included many skilled workers from the British Isles and Germany, but by the latter decades of the century most immigrants were from the economic and technological backwaters of Europe and filled the low-skill jobs that better-situated workers, native and immigrant, scorned. By the early twentieth century more than a million people were arriving each year, the majority from eastern and southern Europe.

An obvious question is why ill-paid American agricultural workers, especially those in the South, did not respond to the opportunities of industrial and service employment. Several factors apparently were involved. The regional tensions between North and South and the post–Civil War isolation of the South discouraged movement to northern industrial centers. Racial prejudice and lifestyle decisions were also important. In the midwestern states, where industry and agriculture developed in close proximity, farm workers were almost as reluctant to take industrial or urban service jobs. Consequently, a paradox emerged: American farm workers seemed content to make a modest living in the country, while European agricultural workers and their U.S.-born children filled new jobs in industry and the services.

Mass immigration was socially disruptive. Immigrants faced many hazards and an uncertain welcome. Apart from the Scandinavians, they became highly concentrated in cities and industrial towns. By the early twentieth century, most large American cities were largely immigrant enclaves. With few exceptions, immigrants and their children made up more than 60 percent of the population, and in extreme cases, such as Milwaukee, the total was over 80 percent. To visitors from the countryside, cities were alien places with a hodgepodge of different languages and mores. It is hardly surprising that observers and analysts bemoaned the effects of immigration and especially the shift from "old" northern and western European to "new" southern and eastern European immigrants.

In the workplace, native-immigrant tensions took various forms. The concentration of immigrants in low-skill jobs created a heightened sense of competition—of immigrants driving out old stock or "old" immigrant workers—and led to efforts to restrict immigrant mobility. One other result of these divisions may have been a lack of solidarity in industrial disputes. The relatively low level of labor organization and the particular character of the American labor movement often have been explained in part as the consequences of a heterogeneous labor force.

The end of traditional immigration during World War I and the low level of immigration during the interwar years eased many of these tensions and encouraged the rise of "melting pot" interpretations of the immigrant experience. World War I also saw the first substantial movement of southern workers to the North and West, a process that seemed to promise a less tumultuous future. In reality, the initial phases of this transition increased the level of unrest and conflict. Part of the problem—repeated in the early years of World War II—was the excessive concentration of war-related manufacturing in a few congested urban areas. The more serious and persistent irritant was racial conflict, with the poorest of the "new" immigrants pitted against African-American migrants from the South. Though the violence waned after 1921, tensions lingered. In most northern cities African-American immigrants were more likely than any immigrant group to live in ethnically homogeneous neighborhoods.

By midcentury most Americans looked back at immigration as a feature of an earlier age and celebrated the ability of American society to absorb millions of outsiders. Yet at the same time, a new cycle of immigration was beginning. It had the same economic origins and many similar effects. Most of the post–World War II immigrants came from Latin America and Asia rather than Europe. By the 1990s the movement of Hispanics into the labor force was reminiscent of the turn-of-the-century influx of eastern Europeans. They settled overwhelmingly in the comparatively vacant Southwest and West, areas that had grown rapidly since World War II. In contrast, the Northeast and Midwest, traditional centers of industrial activity, attracted fewer immigrants. Most of the newcomers were poorly educated and filled low-skill positions, but there were exceptions. Among the Asian immigrants were many well-educated engineers, technicians, and professionals, who quickly rose to important positions, a development that had no nineteenth-century parallel.

Employer Initiatives

Though managers of large organizations had enormous power vis-à-vis their employees, they also were dependent on them. Turnover, absenteeism, indifferent work, and outright sabotage were significant threats to productivity and profits. Conversely, highly motivated employees could enhance a firm's performance. Uncertain about how to respond, nineteenth-century employers experimented widely. A handful introduced elaborate benefits, such as company towns; others devised new forms of "driving" and coercion. Most simply threw up their hands, figuratively, and delegated the management of employees to first-line supervisors, who became responsible for hiring, firing, and other personnel functions. The results were wide variations in wages, working conditions, and discipline; abuses of authority; and high turnover rates. Friction between supervisors and wage earners became a common cause of labor unrest.

Growing public anxiety over industrial conflict resulted in numerous policy initiatives. In the last quarter of the nineteenth century, state governments began to impose restrictions on employers, especially employers of women and children. By 1900 most northern and western states regulated the hiring of children, the hours of labor, health and sanitation, and various working conditions. During the first third of the twentieth century, they tightened regulations, extended some rules to male workers, and introduced workers compensation, the first American social insurance plans. The federal government was slow to act until the 1930s, when it embraced collective bargaining (principally via the Wagner Act of 1935), created a social security system based on old age pensions and unemployment insurance, set minimum wages, defined the workday and workweek, and restricted child labor. Nearly all of this legislation, both state and federal, was designed to set and uphold minimum standards (the "safety net" metaphor of later years was apt) rather than to supercede private decision making or to create a welfare state. It reflected both a distrust of government and a belief that individuals could and should work out better arrangements for themselves.

Many employers also responded to the problems of the new industrial economy. Beginning at the turn of the century, a few of them, mostly large, profitable corporations, introduced policies designed to discourage turnover and improve morale. One example that spread rapidly was the personnel department, which centralized and standardized many of the supervisor's personnel functions. By the 1920's, most large industrial and service corporations had personnel departments whose functions and responsibilities expanded rapidly. Also popular were employee benefit plans that provided medical, educational, recreational, or other services. The employment crisis of the 1930s gave renewed impetus to these activities. The largest employers (often responding to union-organizing campaigns or collective bargaining demands) created even more elaborate benefit programs, and smaller and less generous companies introduced rudimentary programs. The spread of collective bargaining and a more prosperous postwar economy further reinforced this trend. The years from the early 1940s to the mid-1970s would be the heyday of welfare capitalism.

The American Labor Movement

As noted earlier, the growth of industrial and service employment in the nineteenth century introduced new forms of unrest and protest. The years from the 1870s to the 1940s witnessed waves of strikes, which were widely viewed as a perplexing and troubling feature of modern society. Yet strikes were only the most visible examples of the tensions and conflicts that characterized industrial employment. In essence, dissatisfied wage earners could quit and search for more satisfying jobs, or they could try to improve their current jobs through the use of their collective "voice," that is, through protests, complaints, and negotiations. Most workers concluded that quitting was easier than trying to organize and sustain a union, the most obvious form of institutional "voice." Still, the history of organized labor (because it has been carefully documented) is the best available valuable measure of the tensions associated with modern employment and the ability of workers to express themselves.

Nineteenth-Century Unions

The American labor movement began in the early nineteenth century, grew fitfully during the antebellum decades, became an important force during the inflationary prosperity of the 1860s, and flourished during the boom years of the 1880s. The people most likely to organize were "autonomous" workers, those who had substantial independence in the workplace. Most, but not all, were highly skilled and highly paid. In any case, they were indispensable workers who could increase their influence through collective action. Their strategic roles also made employers wary of antagonizing them, another critical factor in union growth. Regardless of their particular jobs, workers were more likely to organize successfully in prosperous times and when they could count on sympathetic public officials. Prosperity and a favorable political climate were critical determinants of union growth; recession conditions and state repression often made organization impossible.

Two groups dominated the nineteenth-century labor movement. Miners were autonomous workers who, though not highly skilled or highly paid, worked alone or in small groups and faced extraordinary hazards. Organization was a way to express a sense of solidarity, increase or maintain wages, reduce the cut-throat competition that characterized their industries, and restrict the entrance of less skilled, lower-wage workers. Miners' unions began in the 1840s, flourished in both anthracite and bituminous coal fields in the 1860s and early 1870s, and emerged in the western "hard rock" industry in the 1870s. After numerous conflicts and setbacks during the recession of the mid-1870s, miners' organizations became stronger than ever. Their success was reflected in the emergence of two powerful unions, the United Mine Workers, formed in 1890, and the Western Federation of Miners, which followed in 1892. They differed in one important respect: the UMW was committed to collective bargaining with the goal of regional or even national contracts, while the WFM favored workplace activism over collective bargaining.

The second group consisted of urban artisans, led by construction workers and industrial workers, such as printers and molders. Having established the legal right to organize in the 1820s and 1830s, they became a powerful force in the rapidly growing cities of the antebellum period. Unions maximized opportunities for some workers and created buffers against excessive competition. They also played an influential role in urban politics, adding a worker's voice to local government deliberations. Citywide coalitions appeared as early as the 1820s, but neither the individual groups nor the coalitions were able to withstand the ups and downs of the economy.

In this turbulent environment, highly skilled workers had obvious advantages. The railroad workers were a notable example. Engineers and other skilled operating employees formed powerful unions in the 1860s and 1870s. The Brotherhood of Locomotive Engineers became the most formidable and exclusive organization of that era. Through collective bargaining, the engineers and the other railroad "brotherhoods" were able to obtain high wages, improved working conditions, and greater security, but they made no effort to organize the vast majority of railroad workers who lacked their advantages. Most railroad managers reluctantly dealt with the skilled groups, though the Burlington Railroad strike of 1888 demonstrated that even the BLE was not invincible.

The limitations of this approach inspired efforts to organize other employees. The notable example was the Knights of Labor, which grew rapidly in the late 1870s and 1880s and briefly became the largest American union. The Knights attempted to organize workers regardless of skill or occupation. Several successful strikes in the mid-1880s created a wave of optimism that the Knights might actually succeed, and membership rose to more than 700,000 in 1886. But employer counterattacks, together with the Knights' organizational shortcomings, brought this activity to an abrupt halt. The Haymarket massacre of 1886, at the height of the Knights' popularity, underlined its vulnerability. By 1890 the Knights of Labor had lost most of its members; it never again enjoyed the kind of success it had experienced in the preceding decade.

In 1893 Eugene V. Debs, an officer of the Brotherhood of Locomotive Firemen, and a handful of followers undertook another campaign to create a more inclusive organization. The American Railway Union, an industrial union of railroad workers, enjoyed a few initial successes but suffered a fatal defeat in the infamous Pullman strike of 1894. The ARU's failure was largely a result of the anti-union policies of the federal government, which so outraged Debs that he henceforth devoted himself to the cause of political change, notably as a candidate of the Socialist Party.

In the meantime, most of the established unions banned together to form a new labor federation, the American Federation of Labor, which took a pragmatic approach to the issues of organizational structure and jurisdiction. Although the AFL initially consisted of craft organizations that were hostile to the Knights of Labor and the American Railway Union, it soon demonstrated sufficient flexibility to become the locus of union activity. Dominated by President Samuel Gompers of the Cigar Makers, the AFL thereafter guided relations between unions and between organized labor and government. It also maintained a staff of organizers who aided individual unions.

In its early years the AFL confronted a strong employer backlash and a deteriorating economy. One of the most powerful AFL organizations, the Amalgamated Association of Iron and Steel Workers, lost a decisive battle against the industry's largest employer, the Carnegie Steel Company, in 1892. The failure of the famous Homestead strike sealed the fate of the Amalgamated Association and unionism in the steel industry until World War I. Other defeats followed as the severe recession of 1893–1897 encouraged employers to reject union contracts and agreements and reduce employment opportunities. The Pullman strike and a 1897 United Mine Workers strike against most of the coal industry illustrated the plight of organized labor.

Twentieth-Century Unions

As the economy recovered, the labor movement began a long period of expansion and growing influence. Autonomous workers groups, led by the coal miners and construction workers, dominated organized labor for the next third of a century. The debate over tactics was decisively resolved in favor of collective bargaining, though a dissenting group, the Industrial Workers of the World, originally an outgrowth of the Western Federation of Miners, rallied critics with some success before World War I. This decision was effectively institutionalized during World War I, when the federal government endorsed collective bargaining as an antidote to wartime unrest. The other major development of this period was the revival of the AFL. Under Gompers, who proved to be a wily and articulate leader, the AFL promoted autonomous worker groups while professing to speak for all industrial workers. Gompers and his allies disavowed socialism and efforts to create an independent political party, policies that led to an erroneous perception (encouraged by their many critics) of indifference or hostility to political action. On the contrary, Gompers closely aligned the AFL with the Democratic Party and created aggressive lobbying organizations.

Labor's political activism seemed to pay off during World War I, when President Woodrow Wilson appointed Gompers to a high post in the mobilization effort and the federal government directly and indirectly encouraged organization. The greatest gains occurred in the railroad industry, which was almost completely organized by 1920. Government efforts to limit unrest and strikes also resulted in inroads in manufacturing, notably in steel, shipbuilding, and munitions. In 1920 union membership totaled five million, twice the prewar level.

These gains proved to be ephemeral. The end of wartime regulations, the defeat of the Democrats in the 1920 national elections, the spread of the anti-union "American Plan" in many industries, and the severe recession of 1920–1922 completely reversed the situation of 1915–1920 and put all unions on the defensive. Membership contracted. The disastrous 1919–1920 steel strike, which restored the open shop in most firms, was only the first of many setbacks. The decline of the coal and railroad industries in the 1920s was an additional blow. By the late 1920s union membership was back to its prewar level. The one positive feature of the postwar decade was the rapid growth of service sector unionism.

The dramatic economic downturn that began in 1929 and continued with varying severity for a decade set the stage for the greatest increase in union membership in American history. Why? Recessions and unemployment typically reduced the appeal of anything likely to provoke employer reprisals. This was true of the 1930s, too. Union membership declined precipitously between 1930 and 1933, as unemployment rose. It also plunged in 1937–1938, when a new recession led to sweeping layoffs. Union growth occurred in 1933–1937 and in the years after 1938, when employment was increasing. Yet even the generally unfavorable economic conditions of the early 1930s had important indirect effects. Harsh economic conditions produced a strong sense of grievance among veteran workers who lost jobs, savings, and status. They also turned many voters against Republican office holders. The 1932 election of Franklin D. Roosevelt, who had strong progressive and activist credentials as governor of New York, proved to be a turning point in the history of the twentieth-century labor movement.

Union growth after 1933 reflected these factors, particularly in the early years. Roosevelt's New Deal was only intermittently pro-union, but it effectively neutralized employer opposition to organization and, with the passage of the Wagner Act in 1935, created a mechanism for peacefully resolving representation conflicts and introducing collective bargaining. Though the goal of the legislation was to foster dispute resolution and increase wages, it indirectly promoted union growth by restricting the employer's ability to harass union members. In the meantime, industrial workers, notably workers in the largest firms in steel and automobile manufacturing, reacted to the new political environment with unprecedented enthusiasm. A wave of organizing in 1933–1934 surprised employers and public officials alike. Defeats in a series of spectacular, violent strikes in 1934 and other setbacks in 1935 seemingly had little effect. One expression of the workers' determination was the growing popularity of the sit-down strike, notably in the Goodyear Tire and Rubber strike of 1936 and the General Motors strike of 1937. Though most sit-downs were union-led, they represented a degree of shop-floor militancy that shocked many employers and not a few outside observers. Another important expression of the changing industrial landscape was the emergence of the Congress of Industrial Organizations, a new federation of unions devoted to aggressive organizing, especially in manufacturing. John L. Lewis, the creator of the CIO, was the veteran president of the United Mine Workers who had presided over the decline of that once formidable organization in the 1920s. Whatever his shortcomings, Lewis grasped the possibilities of the moment. By the end of the decade he was closely identified with both the revival of organized labor and the increasingly bitter relations between the CIO and AFL.

Although the Wagner Act (and other related legislation designed for specific industries) most clearly and explicitly addressed the industrial relations issues of the 1930s, other New Deal measures complemented it. The move to regulate prices and production n the transportation, communications, and energy industries, which dated from the National Industrial Recovery Act of 1933 and continued with a variety of industry-specific measures between 1935 and 1938, created additional opportunities for unions. Regulated corporations had powerful incentives to avoid strikes and cooperate with unions. As a result, about one-third of union membership growth in the 1930s occurred in those industries. If the United Auto Workers and United Steel Workers were symbols of the new militancy in manufacturing, the equally dramatic growth of the Teamsters symbolized the impact of government regulation in the service sector.

Government regulations were more directly responsible for the even more dramatic growth in union membership that occurred during World War II, when aggregate membership rose from 10 million to 15 million members. Most new jobs during the war years were in manufacturing companies that had collective bargaining contracts and, in many cases, union security provisions that required new hires to join unions. War mobilization thus automatically created millions of additional union members, including large numbers of women and African Americans. Organized labor, in turn, opposed strikes, cooperated with the government's wage-and-price-control programs, and promoted the war effort. By 1945 the labor movement had become a respected part of the American establishment.

Postwar Labor

By the mid-1940s full employment, high wages, and optimism about the future, based on a sense that government now had the ability to manage prosperity (together with awareness of the safety net that government had created since the mid-1930s), replaced the depressed conditions of the 1930s. Most workers' experiences in the 1940s and 1950s seemed to confirm the lessons of the New Deal era. With the exception of a few mild recession years, jobs were plentiful, real wages rose, and public and private benefit programs became more generous. The labor movement also continued to grow, but with less dynamism than in the 1940s. Optimists viewed the 1955 merger of the AFL and CIO as a likely stimulus to new gains.

In retrospect, however, those lessons were often misleading. The striking feature of the economy of the 1950s and 1960s was the degree to which the character of work and the characteristics of the labor force changed. Farming and other natural resource industries declined at an accelerated rate, industrial employment leveled and then began to decline, and service industry employment boomed. Formal education became even more critical to success. Married women entered the labor force in unprecedented numbers. Civil rights laws adopted in the early 1960s banned racial and other forms of discrimination in employment decisions.

One other major development also was little noticed at the time: organized labor stopped growing. Contrary to most predictions and popular impressions, the labor movement lost momentum in the 1950s and 1960s and faced a host of obstacles by the 1970s. Three problems, in reverse order of importance, were particularly notable. First were the unions' internal difficulties. Adapting to an expanded membership and larger public presence was inevitably challenging, but it also could be damaging, as two well-publicized incidents suggest. At the end of World War II the CIO included numerous (mostly small) communist-dominated unions. Though the CIO soon expelled them and supported U.S. cold war policies, it was unable to prevent anti-union demagogues from loudly portraying it, and by implication unions in general, as subversive.

Even more harmful was the mounting evidence of union corruption and especially of abuses involving the now giant Teamsters organization. Revelations of Teamster misdeeds led to the U.S. Senate's McClellan Committee investigation of 1957–1958 and the subsequent passage of the Landrum-Griffin Act (1959), designed to protect union members from dishonest officials. Whether the act was warranted or effective was beside the point: the scandals devastated the unions' public image.

A more fundamental cause of union decline was organized labor's association with industries (manufacturing, mining, transportation) that were growing slowly, if at all, and its tardiness in recognizing the overwhelming importance of the service economy in the postwar era. Labor's one significant breakthrough came in the 1970s and early 1980s, when it won collective bargaining rights for most state and municipal employees. By the end of the 1980s unions increasingly were associated with public rather than private employment.

Finally, employer counterattacks grew more effective in the postwar years. Though some employer groups sought to challenge unions directly (for example, in the Taft-Hartley Act of 1947 and state right-to-work legislation), others adopted a more subtle approach, attacking union power in the regulatory agencies and the courts and promoting employment policies that reduced the benefits of membership. These attacks gained momentum during the presidency of Dwight D. Eisenhower. One additional tactic, locating new plants in southern or western states, where there was no tradition of organization, also helped isolate organized workers.

The impact of these varied trends became inescapable in the 1970s, when the economy experienced its most severe downturns since the 1930s. Major recessions in 1973–1975 and 1979–1982 led to thousands of plant closings in traditional industrial areas. Unemployment reached levels that rivaled the 1930s. Productivity declined, and real wages stagnated. Exploiting anxiety over the future of the economy, Republican Ronald Reagan ran successfully for president on a platform that attacked government assistance to the poor and support for collective bargaining. Reagan left no doubt about his intentions when, in 1981, he fired air traffic controllers for striking in violation of federal law.

The experiences of the 1970s created a labor force that was more diverse in composition and overwhelmingly engaged in service occupations. The return of favorable employment conditions in the 1980s was almost entirely a result of service sector growth. Formal education, together with antidiscrimination laws and affirmative action policies, opened high-paying jobs to ethnic and racial minorities, including a growing number of immigrants. At the same time, industry continued its movement into rural areas, especially in the South and West, and unions continued to decline. Indeed, by the mid-1990s, the private sector of the American economy was largely union free.

The decline of organized labor was associated closely with three other ominous developments. The first was a slowing in real-wage increases, especially among low-income workers. The purchasing power of most manufacturing and service employees remained largely unchanged between the 1970s and 1990s, eliminating an important source of social mobility. Second was a gradual decline in welfare capitalism. A new generation of nonunion firms that paid high wages but provided few or no benefits initiated this trend. Other firms followed, arguing that cost reductions were necessary for survival. Other employers reacted to the rising cost of medical insurance and to the lower costs of defined-contribution retirement plans (as opposed to the traditional defined-benefit plans). Even the tight labor market conditions of the mid-1990s to late 1990s, which led to real-wage increases, did not result in expanded benefit programs.

Third was the accelerating globalization of economic activity. The growth of international trade and investment were partly a consequence of the transfer of industrial technology to economically disadvantaged countries. It also was a result of a series of legal and regulatory changes, such as the North American Free Trade Agreement of 1993, which liberalized economic relations between countries and encouraged international activity. These changes had the potential to raise living standards, but their immediate effects were often painful, as employers moved some or all of their operations to lower-wage countries. Already many American manufacturers had moved labor-intensive assembly operations to Mexican border towns to take advantage of lower wages and other low costs. In most cases Mexican employees replaced American workers. And while the Mexican employees earned more than most of their neighbors, their jobs were extremely insecure. Indeed, by 2000 manufacturers were increasingly moving their operations from Mexico to China and other Asian countries, where wages were even lower.

The results of these complex developments were at least superficially contradictory. On the one hand, by the 1990s many workers enjoyed expanded opportunities and high wages. Severe labor shortages in some industries attracted a flood of immigrants and made the United States a magnet for upwardly mobile workers. On the other hand, many other workers, especially those in agriculture or industry or who had little formal education, found that the combination of economic and technological change, a less activist government, and union decline depressed their wages and made their prospects bleak. A recession that began in 2000 created additional uncertainties. At the beginning of the new century the labor force, and American society, were divided in ways that would have seemed unlikely or even impossible only a few decades earlier.

—Daniel Nelson

ADVISERS

Michael Hanagan, PhD
Senior Lecturer
New School University

Alice Kessler-Harris, PhD
R. Gordon Hoxie Professor of
    American History
Columbia University

Andrew H. Lee, PhD
Tamiment Librarian
New York University

Daniel Nelson, PhD
Emeritus Professor of History
University of Akron

Colleen O'Neill, PhD
Assistant Professor of Ethnic
    Studies
California Polytechnic State
    University-San Luis Obispo

Marcel van der Linden, PhD
Research Director
International Institute of Social
    History

Zaragosa Vargas, PhD
Associate Professor of History
University of California, Santa
    Barbara

CONTRIBUTORS

Don Amerman
William Arthur Atkins

Kimberley Barker
Bill Barry
Elizabeth A. Bishop
Lawrence Black
Mary H. Blewett
Timothy G. Borden
Jeffrey Bortz
John Boughton
Valeria Bruschi
William E. Burns
Dieter K. Buse

Robert Cassanello
Olivier Compagnon
Sylvie Contrepois
Richard Croucher

Evan Daniel
Jonathan Darby
Ralph Darlington
Hendrik Defoort
Dennis Deslippe
Thomas Dublin
Linda Dynan

Beth Emmerling
Lisa Ennis

Katrina Ford
Carol Fort
Kimberly F. Frederick
Paul Frisch

Kevin M. Gannon
Roberta Gold
Juan José Gómez Gutiérrez
Tom Goyens

Michael Hanagan
Jennifer Harrison
Jane Holzka
Roger Horowitz
Nik Howard

Lisa Kannenberg
Karla Kelling
Brett Allan King
Steven Koczak

Paul Le Blanc
James G. Lewis
David Lewis-Colman
Darren G. Lilleker

Martin Manning
Soe Tjen Marching
Joseph McCartin
David Lee McMullen
Lee McQueen
Greg Miller
Carl Mirra
Paul Misner

David Nack
Miriam C. Nagel
Daniel Nelson
Caryn E. Neumann
Mitchell Newton-Matza

Melanie Nolan

Jaime Ramon Olivares
Michael J. O'Neal
Melissa Ooten

Lee Ann Paradise
Linda Dailey Paulson
Luca Prono
Sean Purdy

Jonathan Rees
David Renton
Markku Ruotsila

Courtney Q. Shah
Emily Straus

Willie Thompson
Rebecca Tolley-Stokes
Patricia Toucas-Truyen

Marcel van der Linden
Michael T. Van Dyke
Geert Van Goethem
Yanic Viau

Joel Waller
Peter Waterman
Elizabeth Willis

Ronald Young

ST. JAMES ENCYCLOPEDIA OF LABOR HISTORY WORLDWIDE

LIST OF EVENTS

Abolition of Serfdom, Russia
Abolition of Slavery, British Empire
Abolition of Slavery, United States
Act to Encourage Immigration, United States
AFL, CIO Merge, United States
AFL-CIO Expels Key Unions, United States
AFSCME Strike, United States
Age Discrimination in Employment Act, United States
Agriculture Workers Strike, Italy
Alliance for Labor Action, United States
All-India Trade Union Congress, India
Amalgamated Society of Engineers, Great Britain
American Association for Labor Legislation, United States
American Federation of Labor, United States
American Plan, United States
Anarchists Lead Argentine Labor Movement, Argentina
Anthracite Coal Strike, United States
Apex Hosiery Co. v. Leader, United States
Arbitration Act of 1888, United States

Bans on Labor Unions Lifted, Germany
Barcelona Workers' Rebellion, Spain
Battle of the Overpass, United States
Bituminous Coal Strike, United States
Black Codes, United States
Bloody Sunday, Russia
Boston Police Strike, United States
Bracero Program, United States and Mexico
Brotherhood of Locomotive Engineers, United States
Brotherhood of Railroad Trainmen, United States
Brotherhood of Sleeping Car Porters, United States
Bureau of Labor Established, United States
Burlington Railroad Strike, United States
Byrnes Act, United States

Calcutta General Strike, India
Cananéa Strike, Mexico
Carlisle Indian School, United States
Charleroi Confrontation Between Miners and the Military, Belgium
Charter of Amiens, France
Chartist Movement, Great Britain
Chiang Kai-shek Purges Communists, China
Child Labor Amendment, United States
Chinese Exclusion Act, United States
Chinese Rail Workers Strike, United States
Christian Trade Unionists Conference, Switzerland
CIO Anticommunist Drive, United States
CIO Expelled from AFL, United States
CIO Joins, AFL Rejects WFTU, United States
Civil Rights Act of 1964, United States
Civilian Conservation Corps, United States
Clayton Antitrust Act, United States
Clifton-Morenci-Metcalf Strike, United States
Coal Mine Contract Signed, United States
Coalition of Labor Union Women, United States
Colored Farmers' Alliance, United States
Colored National Labor Union, United States
Combination Acts, Great Britain
Committee for Industrial Organization, United States
Commonwealth v. Hunt, United States
Communist Manifesto Published, England
Confederación de Trabajadores de América Latina, Latin America
Confederación Obrera Pan-Americana, Western Hemisphere
Confédération Générale du Travail, France
Congress of Industrial Organizations, United States

Congress of South African Trade Unions, South Africa
Coronado Coal v. UMWA, United States

Davis-Bacon Act, United States
Department of Commerce and Labor, United States
Department of Labor, United States
Dockers' Strike, Great Britain
Dorr Rebellion, United States
Dover Textile Strike, United States

Eight-hour Day Movement, United States
Employee Retirement Income Security Act, United States
Equal Pay Act, United States
Equal Rights Amendment and Protective Legislation, United States
Equal Rights Party, United States
Erdman Act, United States
European Strike Wave, Europe
European Trade Union Confederation, Europe

Factory Act, Great Britain
Factory Girls' Association, United States
Fair Employment Practice Committee, United States
Fair Labor Standards Act, United States
Federal Employees Gain Union Rights, United States
Federation of Organized Trades and Labor Unions of the United States and Canada (FOTLU), United States and Canada
First International, Great Britain
Five-Year Plan, USSR
Foran Act, United States
Forced Labor, Germany
Forced Labor, USSR
Ford-UAW Contract, United States
Ford-UAW SUB Agreement, United States
Free Soil Party, United States
French Labor, World War II, France

CHRONOLOGICAL LIST OF EVENTS

1799-1800 Combination Acts, Great Britain

1799-1827 Owen Model Communities, Great Britain, United States

1800 Gabriel's Rebellion, United States

1811-1813 Luddites Destroy Woolen Machines, Great Britain

1814 Power Loom Invented, United States

1819 Peterloo Massacre, Great Britain

1820s-1850s Ten-Hour Day Movement, United States

1823-1836 Lowell Industrial Experiment, United States

1824 Pawtucket Textile Strike, United States

Repeal of Combination Acts, Great Britain

1825 United Tailoresses Society, United States

1827 Mechanics' Union of Trade Associations, United States

Tailors' Strike, United States

1828 Dover Textile Strike, United States

Workingmen's Party, United States

1831 *Liberator* Founded, United States

1831, 1834 Silk Workers' Revolts, France

1833 General Trades' Union, United States

Factory Act, Great Britain

1834 Abolition of Slavery, British Empire

National Trades Union, United States

1834-1836 Factory Girls' Association, United States

1836 Equal Rights Party, United States

London Workingmen's Association, Great Britain

1838 Chartist Movement, Great Britain

1840 Strikes of Journeymen and Workers, France

1842 *Commonwealth v. Hunt*, United States

Dorr Rebellion, United States

1844 Weavers' Revolt, Silesia

1845-1851 Potato Famine, Ireland

1848 June Days Rebellion, France

Communist Manifesto Published, England

Revolutions in Europe, Europe

1848-1854 Free Soil Party, United States

1851 Amalgamated Society of Engineers, Great Britain

1852 National Typographical Union, United States

1853-1854 Lancashire Textile Strikes, Great Britain

1859 National Union of Iron Molders, United States

Harpers Ferry Raid, United States

1860 Shoemaker's Strike, United States

1860-1879 Molly Maguires, United States

1860s-1900s Eight-hour Day Movement, United States

1861 Abolition of Serfdom, Russia

1861-1869 Bans on Labor Unions Lifted, Germany

1863 Working Women's Protective Union, United States

Brotherhood of Locomotive Engineers, United States

1863-1865 Abolition of Slavery, United States

1864 Strike Ban Lifted, France

Act to Encourage Immigration, United States

First International, Great Britain

1865 European Strike Wave, Europe

1865-1877 Black Codes, United States

1866 National Labor Union, United States

1867 Second Reform Act, Great Britain

Chinese Rail Workers Strike, United States

1867, 1869 St. Crispin Organizations, United States

1868 Charleroi Confrontation Between Miners and the Military, Belgium

Trades Union Congress, Great Britain

Workingman's Benevolent Association, United States

1869 Knights of Labor, United States

Colored National Labor Union, United States

1870 Coal Mine Contract Signed, United States

1871 Trades Union Act, Great Britain

Paris Commune, France

1873 Panic of 1873, United States

1874 Union Label Movement, United States

Tompkins Square Rally, United States

1875-1902 Organized Labor Established, Argentina

1876 Workingmen's Party of the United States, United States

Workers' Congress, Mexico

1877 Railroad Strike of 1877, United States

1878 International Labor Union, United States

1878-1911 Taylor and Scientific Management, United States

Memorial Day Massacre, United States

CIO Expelled From AFL, United States

1938 Confederación de Trabajadores de América Latina, Latin America

Fair Labor Standards Act, United States

Congress of Industrial Organizations, United States

1939 Hatch Act, United States

1940 *Apex Hosiery Co. v. Leader*, United States

1940-1944 French Labor, World War II, France

1941 March on Washington Movement, United States

Ford-UAW Contract, United States

No-strike Pledge, World War II, United States

Fair Employment Practice Committee, United States

1941-1945 World War II Labor Measures, United States

1942 United Steelworkers of America, United States

1942-1964 Bracero Program, United States and Mexico

1945 CIO Joins, AFL Rejects WFTU, United States

World Federation of Trade Unions, France

1945-1946 Strike Wave, United States

1945-1960 Japanese Labor After World War II, Japan

1946 Miners' Strike, South Africa

Perón Elected President, Argentina

Socialist Unity Party of Germany, East Germany

1947 *United States v. United Mine Workers of America*, United States

Taft-Hartley Act, United States

1947-1962 General Agreement on Tariffs and Trade, Worldwide

1948, 1950 General Motors-United Auto Workers Landmark Contracts, United States

1949 International Confederation of Free Trade Unions, Worldwide

1949-1950 CIO Anticommunist Drive, United States

1950 Salt of the Earth Strike, United States

1951 Organización Regional Inter-americana de Trabajadores, Western Hemisphere

1952 Steel Seizure Case, United States

Meany and Reuther Lead AFL, CIO, United States

1953 Calcutta General Strike, India

1954 Guatemalan Coup Orchestrated by CIA, Guatemala

1955 Ford-UAW SUB Agreement, United States

AFL, CIO Merge, United States

1956 Poznan Workers' Riots, Poland

Hungarian Revolution and Workers Councils, Hungary

International Confederation of Arab Trade Unions, Egypt

1957 AFL-CIO Expels Key Unions, United States

1959 Landrum-Griffin Act, United States

1960s Maquiladoras Established, Mexico

1962 Federal Employees Gain Union Rights, United States

1963 Equal Pay Act, United States

1964 Civil Rights Act of 1964, United States

1965-1970 Grape Pickers' Strike, United States

1966 National Organization for Women, United States

1967 Taylor Law, United States

Age Discrimination in Employment Act, United States

1968 General Strike, France

1969 Alliance for Labor Action, United States

Philadelphia Plan, United States

Hot Autumn, Italy

1970 Postal Workers' Strike, United States

Hawaii Collective Bargaining Law, United States

Occupational Safety and Health Act, United States

1970-1973 Popular Unity, Chile

1973 European Trade Union Confederation, Europe

Steelworkers Experimental Agreement, United States

Washington Union Shop Law, United States

1974 Coalition of Labor Union Women, United States

Employee Retirement Income Security Act, United States

1975 AFSCME Strike, Pennsylvania, United States

Navajos Occupy Fairchild Plant, United States

1980 Solidarity Emerges, Poland

1981 PATCO Strike, United States

1985 Congress of South African Trade Unions, South Africa

1985-1986 Hormel Strike, United States

1985-1987 Watsonville Canning Strike, United States

1987 General Motors Introduces Team Concept, United States

1991 USSR Collapse, USSR

1992 North American Free Trade Agreement, North America

Abolition of Serfdom

Russia 1861

Synopsis

From the founding of the Russian nation in 1552 to the middle of the nineteenth century, Russia had been the ultimate imperial power. Russia developed out of the area immediately surrounding Moscow and extended from the Bering Strait to what is now Poland; the Russian czars understandably assumed the nation's invincibility. The Crimean War, however, shattered this assumption. The backward, semimedieval Russian industry could not support a modern war. Armaments produced for the war effort took months to reach the front line because of the lack of modern communications. Moreover the Russian army mainly consisted of relatively inexperienced serf volunteers, men who had joined the army solely to seek their freedom from the land. These severe limitations, combined with the threat of revolution that was the scourge of the European ancient regime after 1848, signaled that radical change was a necessity.

In 1856 Czar Alexander II initiated sweeping social reforms, the most historically important of which was the Emancipation of the Serfs Act, 1861. This act created a new Russian population of people who had expected to become free citizens but instead had become wage slaves. The increase in demands from the people, combined with the repressive response from the successors of Alexander II, paved the way for the revolution that would take place in 1917, 56 years later.

Timeline

1842: In *Sanitary Conditions of the Labouring Population of Great Britain,* British reformer Edwin Chadwick draws attention to the squalor in the nation's mill town slums and shows that working people have a much higher incidence of disease than do the middle and upper classes.

1845: From Ireland to Russia, famine plagues Europe, killing some 2.5 million people.

1851: China's T'ai P'ing ("Great Peace") Rebellion begins under the leadership of schoolmaster Hong Xiuquan, who believes himself the younger brother of Jesus Christ. He mobilizes the peasantry against the Manchu emperors in a civil war that will take 20 to 30 million lives over the next fourteen years.

1853: Crimean War begins in October. The struggle, which will last until February 1856, pits Russia against the combined forces of Great Britain, France, Turkey, and Sardinia–Piedmont. A war noted for the work of Florence Nightingale with the wounded, it is also the first conflict to be documented by photojournalists.

1857: Sepoy Mutiny, an unsuccessful revolt by Indian troops against the British East India Company, begins. As a result of the rebellion, which lasts into 1858, England places India under direct crown rule.

1859: American abolitionist John Brown leads a raid on the federal arsenal at Harpers Ferry, Virginia. His capture and hanging in December heighten the animosities that will spark the Civil War sixteen months later.

1861: Within weeks of Abraham Lincoln's inauguration, the Civil War begins with the shelling of Fort Sumter. Six states secede from the Union, joining South Carolina to form the Confederate States of America (later joined by four other states) and electing Jefferson Davis as president. The first major battle of the war, at Bull Run or Manassas in Virginia, is a Confederate victory.

1861: Italy is unified under Sardinian king Victor Emmanuel II.

1861: Louis Pasteur publishes a paper that introduces the concept of germ theory and refutes spontaneous generation.

1863: President Lincoln issues the Emancipation Proclamation, freeing all slaves in Confederate territories, on 1 January. Thus begins a year that sees the turning point of the Civil War, with decisive Union victories at Gettysburg, Vicksburg, and Chattanooga. Thereafter, the Confederacy is almost perpetually on the defensive, fighting not to win but to avoid losing.

1867: United States purchases Alaska from Russia for $7.2 million.

1871: In the wake of defeat by the Germans, Parisians establish the Commune, a revolutionary government that controls the capital—similar revolts break out in other cities—for about two months. In the end, the Third Republic suppresses the Commune with a brutality exceeding that of the Reign of Terror.

Event and Its Context

Why Reform?

Historians have engaged in a lengthy debate over the reasons behind Russian reform and in particular the ending of feudalism. Some emphasize the triumph of liberalism over authoritarianism, describing Alexander II as the "Czar Liberator." The promotion of liberals Iurii Samarin and Nikolai Miliutin, both staunch advocates of reform, to the czar's cabinet reinforces this perception. The arguments of the liberals in cabinet, however, were usually countered by the arch-conservative majority; therefore, the liberals' influence was at best limited. Furthermore, the majority of commentators insist that the reforms were always going to be limited as Russian czarism constantly resisted any move that would result in a transition to a constitutional monarchy. Therefore, the notion that Russia could become liberal under Alexander II is largely viewed as an exaggeration.

Alexander II, Czar of the Russian Empire. © Bettmann/ Corbis. Reproduced by permission.

Marxist historians put forward an alternative view and point to the economic pressures as driving the reforms. Combined with the drive to modernize Russian industry, many of the czar's advisors agreed that serfdom was uneconomic, labor-intensive, and encouraged the nobility, the serf owners, to eschew change. In contrast, emancipation of the serfs would provide an industrial workforce and encourage the modernization of agriculture in a manner consistent with that adopted across western Europe. Clearly this was part of the effect Alexander II desired, and in light of the debacle in the Crimean War, modernization gained acceptance as a necessity. However, there were alternatives to emancipation that would also reap economic benefits, and Alexander particularly was keen to reject any ideas that permeated from western liberal economies. Therefore, the majority of historians seek alternative explanations for his reforming zeal.

The chief concern highlighted in histories of the period is the fear of revolution. As defeat in the Crimea loomed, on 30 March 1856 the czar made a now famous speech to the nobility of Moscow. In the speech he allayed their fears that he intended to abolish serfdom immediately and ensured serf-owners that they would receive reparations for any economic losses they might incur. However he stressed that reform was inevitable: "But, of course, you yourselves realize that the existing system of serf-owning cannot remain unchanged. It is better to begin abolishing serfdom from above than to wait for it to begin to abolish itself from below."

The need for modernization was thus married to other imperatives. The lessons of France almost a century earlier, the impending collapse of the Habsburg empire as a result of the events of 1848, and the fact that these ideas had permeated Russian society (usually imported by troops who had enjoyed contact with other nations and their peoples) all informed the czar's policy. Thus modernization was not only an imperative for continuing Russia's imperial policy, but also for the survival of czardom itself.

Emancipation by Consensus

The competing demands of the nobility, the czar's power base, and the pressures of modernization meant that emancipation would take some time to be enacted. The 1856 speech can be read as Alexander II, metaphorically, testing the water. It is likely that he hoped the nobility would seize the initiative in their tradition of service to the czar. However, it was soon apparent that the serf-owners were reluctant to unravel the system under which power could be measured "per head." The majority felt that the serfs, who were seen as barbaric, would be unable to become citizens of Russia and so could not be freed from the control of the nobles.

Alexander II used the traditional strategy of his predecessors; on 1 January 1857 he set up a secret commission to investigate how Russian society could be restructured. Indicative of the czar's political predispositions, the commission comprised only a minority of reformers. This meant that their work was carried out with little enthusiasm and that the solutions offered by the commission would favor the serf-owners. The czar became increasingly frustrated with the commission and even introduced advisors from western Europe into his entourage. Alexander II was able to make progress on reforms only by circumventing his own commission.

On 20 November 1857 a directive known as the Nazimov Rescript was issued to the governor general of Vilna. This directive, which had been distributed to all regional governors by 18 December, ordered that provincial assemblies be established to discuss how emancipation of the serfs could be achieved in each of the regions. This allowed each region to offer the most appropriate solutions for the individual circumstances, but parameters on discussions were set. The nobility would be granted full ownership rights over all lands and would retain responsibility for maintaining law and order on their land. The former serfs would be allowed to purchase land and would gain "administrative control" over their lives, which suggested freedom of movement at the very least. D. Bibikov, minister of the interior, made it clear that the directive was compulsory: "The nobility is obliged to execute the will of the Sovereign, who summons them to cooperate in the amelioration of peasant life." As with much that surrounded the reforms of Alexander II, even this order was open to interpretation.

The nobility had vast economic power within czarist Russia, and the emancipation of the serfs posed a threat to this power. Therefore the nobility in areas where land values were highest refused to comply. Their only concession was for the state to offer to buy the serfs from their owners. Alexander had no choice but to implement emancipation himself.

Serf family kneeling at feet of Russian noble. © Hulton/Archive by Getty Images. Reproduced by permission.

By December 1858 the liberals held a majority of the commission. New ideas emerged with full support of the czar, thus enhancing his image as a liberator. A scheme for creating a new rural class, based on communes, was tabled. This would allow former serfs to establish virtually autonomous communities, which would be self-regulating and would have the right to purchase adequate land to provide for its members. The commission also discussed fair terms for purchase and, crucially, initiated the removal of police powers from the serf-owners. The nobles' dissent could not prevent emancipation from becoming law, although it took an additional two years to complete the final drafting, mainly because the commission felt obliged to add further protections for the nobility.

The Emancipation Act became law on 19 February 1861. The 360–page document was highly complex and designed only to inform the bureaucrats. The purpose for this complexity seems clear. The act did little to meet the expectations of the serfs themselves. It offered limited emancipation that was, in reality, subject to the whim of the nobility. The "amelioration of the peasants" actually caused greater hardship for the majority of the rural peasantry.

The Seeds of Revolution

Under the terms of the Emancipation Act, the serfs were granted "the status of free rural inhabitants." However, they were not free citizens of Russia. They were allowed self-administration within the collective responsibility of the commune, but this effectively made them slaves to communal law. Moreover, they were issued passports that restricted their movement. A poll tax that was introduced to secure funding for the state further resulted in economic hardships for the freed serfs.

The most controversial aspect of the act was the land settlement. Initially the serfs remained under their obligations for a two-year period during which the government compiled inventories of land ownership. Government and landowners had to reach agreement over what portions of land would pass into commune ownership before the obligations were annulled. A government-financed scheme awarded the land to a commune and presented the former serfs with a contract that obligated the commune to repay the redemptions over a 49-year period. All payments were higher than was expected because landowners had submitted inflated valuations of their land, often up to twice the market value. This meant that the former serfs were financially tied to the communes. Increased hardship resulted because the peasants lost the use of between 10 and 26 percent of the land they had previously worked. The communes were thus hard-pressed to raise sufficient crops to feed the commune and a surplus to pay off the redemptions. Revolution seemed a far grater threat in 1861 than it had in 1856.

The widespread fear of revolution was an outgrowth of the level of unrest. In 1859 and 1860, when emancipation was within reach, there were only 217 recorded incidents of disorder within 24 months. In 1861, as the ramifications of the act became clear, 1889 incidents were recorded. Though the figure subsided to 849 in 1862, 509 in 1863, and 156 in 1864, nobles recorded that the village communes "seethed with resentment and murderous intent." The serfs' support for the czar, "their little father," was impaired, and many refused to sign the invento-

ries as they felt that a signature was an indication of satisfaction. The nobility were equally dissatisfied. They found it difficult to secure labor for the lands they retained, which led to decreased production and financial difficulties. The latter were compounded by the fact that 62 percent of serfs had been mortgaged. The resulting rift between czar and people would never be completely healed.

Although many of the nobility embraced liberal ideas, it was mainly to counter the growth of radical, revolutionary politics. This outlook did, however, encourage the nobility to demand a greater input into the political process. As an industrial revolution began some serfs did become mobile; however, lingering dissatisfaction and the conditions offered to workers in the mines and steelyards caused further anti-czarist feeling and spawned the assassination of Alexander II in 1882. Over the following 50 years further hardships for the people, a return to repression, and failures in war allowed the newly created dispossessed Russian peasantry to unite in opposition to the czarist regime. The longer czardom survived, the more inevitable revolution became; after the experiences of the 1860s it was purely a matter of when.

Key Players

Alexander II (1818–1881): Czar of the Russian Empire, 1855-1881. Alexander oversaw the emancipation of the serfs and the "great reforms" that transformed Russian society starting in 1857.

Miliutin, Dmitri (1816–1912): As minister of war, Miliutin drafted a report in January 1856 comparing Russia's industry, economy, and military to those of western Europe. He was a keen reformist but a staunch Czarist, and was an influential advisor throughout Alexander II's reign.

Reutern, Mikhail (1820–1890): Reutern, Czar Alexander's minister for finance, was an influential, reforming conservative who spearheaded industrial reform and particularly promoted the forced migration of serfs from the land to the cities.

See also: *Revolutions in Europe; Russian Revolutions.*

BIBLIOGRAPHY

Books

Eklof, Ben, James Bushnell, and Larissa Zakharova. *Russia's Great Reforms: 1855–1881.* Bloomington: Indiana University Press, 1994.

Field, Daniel. *The End of Serfdom: Nobility and Bureaucracy in Russia, 1855–1861.* Cambridge: Harvard University Press, 1976.

Lincoln, W. Bryce. *The Great Reforms.* De Kalb: Northern Illinois University Press, 1990.

Rieber, Alfred J., ed. *The Politics of Autocracy: The Letters of Alexander II to Prince A. I. Bariatinskii, 1857–1864.* Paris: Mouton, 1966.

Venturi, Franco. *The Roots of Revolution.* New York: Knopf, 1960.

Zaionchkovsky, Petr A. *The Abolition of Serfdom in Russia*, edited and translated by Susan Wobst; introduction by Terence Emmons. Gulf Breeze. FL: Academic International Press, 1978.

—Darren G. Lilleker

Abolition of Slavery

British Empire 1834

Synopsis

The British Parliament, under the leadership of Prime Minister Earl Grey's Whig government, abolished slavery in the British Empire in 1833, although the slaves were not actually freed until the following year. This act was the culmination of decades of struggle by British abolitionists as well as by rebellious slaves. The freedom granted to hundreds of thousands of slaves, mostly in the Caribbean, was initially incomplete in that many were put forcibly into apprenticeships. The remaining apprenticeships were abolished in 1838, however, and slaves became free laborers. In many areas, the ex-slaves became poor but independent peasants and were replaced as laborers by people from India working under harsh contracts. British slavery abolition contributed to the dissolution of the sugar plantation economy in the British Caribbean and was a key step in the abolition of African slavery in the Americas.

Timeline

1809: Progressive British industrialist Robert Owen proposes an end to employment of children in his factories. When his partners reject the idea, he forms an alliance with others of like mind, including philosopher Jeremy Bentham.

1813: Jane Austen publishes *Pride and Prejudice*.

1818: Donkin, Hall & Gamble "Preservatory" in London produces the first canned foods.

1824: Ludwig van Beethoven composes his Ninth Symphony.

1829: Greece wins its independence after a seven-year war with Turkey.

1831: Unsuccessful Polish revolt against Russian rule occurs.

1834: British mathematician Charles Babbage completes drawings for the "analytic engine," a forerunner of the modern computer that he never builds.

1834: American inventor Cyrus H. McCormick patents his reaper, a horse-drawn machine for harvesting wheat.

1835: American inventor and painter Samuel F. B. Morse constructs an experimental version of his telegraph, and American inventor Samuel Colt patents his revolver.

1837: Queen Victoria is crowned in England.

Henry Charles Grey. The Library of Congress.

1841: Act of Union joins Upper Canada and Lower Canada, which consist of parts of the present-day provinces of Ontario and Quebec respectively.

1846: American inventor Elias Howe patents his sewing machine.

Event and Its Context

The Revival of Abolitionism

The British abolitionist movement, which had become quiescent after the abolition of the slave trade in the British Empire in 1807, began to revive in the 1820s. Leadership passed from William Wilberforce, abolition's champion for many years, to Zachary Macaulay and Thomas Fowell Buxton. The Society for the Mitigation and Gradual Abolition of Slavery, a new group that incorporated many abolitionist leaders, was the force behind the movement throughout the British Dominions. The group, which was more commonly known as the Anti-Slavery Society, was founded in 1823. Buxton, the parliamentary leader of abolitionism throughout the period, introduced in the House of Commons that year a measure for the gradual abolition of slavery but was outmaneuvered by the government leadership.

Abolitionist pressure led the British government to pass some mild measures of "melioration," such as banning flogging of female slaves and requiring slave families to be kept together rather than broken up by sale. The religious motivations of many antislavery activists are evident in the requirement for religious instruction of slaves and the ban on Sunday markets. Even these weak measures were defeated by the resistance of the West India planters, particularly in those islands where they controlled the institutions of local self-government. It was necessary to coerce the assemblies on self-governing islands such

If freedom means anything to you—freedom from repeated injustices, from public humiliation, freedom to protect your own children from corruption and abuse, freedom indeed to live as a man among men—you will not grudge the price of freedom.

The suppression of slavery demanded the whole of one man's life. To establish a living memorial of that life is the aim of this appeal. Whatever you can give will be welcomed. It is the recognition which remains to be paid to a man who would accept nothing for himself.

Medal supporting the abolition of slavery, 1834. © Hulton/Archive by Getty Images. Reproduced by permission.

as Jamaica, which held about half the British Caribbean slave population, to pass amelioration acts of their own after much foot-dragging. Jamaica, the most populous sugar island, was marked by the most rebellious slaves and the most hard-line planters. The "Crown Colonies," which were governed directly from London, presented much less challenge to amelioration. These colonies included areas taken in the Napoleonic wars, such as Trinidad. In both legislative and crown colonies, however, the British government suffered from a lack of officials free from ties to the planter class to enforce the amelioration program.

Despite the success of the planters in the struggle against amelioration, their overall position had greatly deteriorated since the 18th century. For industrializing Britain, the sugar islands were not nearly as important as either source of wealth or as markets for exports as they had been. The end of the Napoleonic wars in 1815 and the opening up of new areas of sugar cultivation also led to a world decline in the price of sugar. Planters, allied on this issue with some of the Church of England clergy, were also concerned about the increased activity of Methodist and Dissenting missionaries among the slave population, but their steps to limit or end it led to increased opposition on the part of politically influential Methodists and Dissenters in Britain itself.

Whigs and Abolitionists

Slavery and emancipation were important issues in the parliamentary election of 1830, which manifested the strength of antislavery sentiment in many areas of the country and replaced the Tories, generally viewed as sympathetic to slave owners, with the Whigs under the leadership of Prime Minister Earl Grey. In 1831 the new government conceded to abolitionist pressure by freeing slaves who belonged to the crown. Buxton's motion in April for Parliament to take up the question of general

emancipation, however, was stymied by the government's indifference. Grey's son, Henry George Grey, Lord Howick, undersecretary of state for the colonies, who personally supported abolition, announced in Parliament that the government had no plans to carry it through.

A slave revolt on Jamaica around Christmas 1831, known as the "Baptist War," was the largest slave revolt in the history of the British Caribbean and accelerated the movement toward emancipation. The leader of the revolt, Sam Sharpe, based his organization on existing religious groups and tried to keep violence to a minimum. Insurgents included calls for the abolition of slavery in their demands. Far more violence was used in suppressing the short-lived rebellion than the rebels themselves used. The planter-dominated Jamaican government executed 312 rebels, including Sharpe, in addition to those killed in battle. Some planters pointed to the revolt to press for a halt to the abolitionist campaign and the activities of missionaries in the West Indies, but British antislavery forces responded to the Baptist War by blaming the repressive measures of the planters for the revolt and pressing for immediate emancipation. Although most of the Whig leaders, including Grey, did not share the antislavery zeal of the abolitionist forces—indeed, some were absentee slaveowners themselves—the government agreed that the West Indian situation warranted reform. Antislavery activity was rising throughout the country. Buxton responded to the new situation by calling for a vote in the House of Commons on immediate emancipation in May 1832. The motion lost by 162 votes to 90.

The reform bill of 1832, which made the House of Commons more representative of the middle classes and the industrial towns, also had the effect of decreasing the power of the West India interest. In the general election that followed the bill, antislavery campaigners vigorously pressed their cause, distributing pamphlets and placards and breaking up proslavery meetings. Constituency groups required parliamentary candidates to pledge to work against slavery. Following the election, the Baptist missionary William Knibb, a powerful speaker, arrived in Britain from Jamaica and became a star of the antislavery lecture circuit. Knibb, who exposed the cruelties of planters and the religious intolerance and complicity with slavery of the Church of England in Jamaica, was particularly popular among dissenters.

Henry Whitely's *Three Months in Jamaica* (1833) became another important piece of antislavery propaganda of the period.

The Abolition Act

At an 1833 meeting, the new Parliament received antislavery petitions with over a million and a half signatories. Proslavery interests were also active and organized some large demonstrations. However, the weakness of the proslavery side was evident in their inability to use arguments justifying slavery as a positive good, which was the traditional justification based on the supposedly civilizing or Christianizing power of slavery as an institution. Instead, slavery apologists were reduced to a pragmatic argument that emancipation would destroy the West Indian sugar industry and cause untold damage to the British Empire.

The Whig government, although it viewed some form of emancipation as necessary and desirable, was not enthusiastic, and was particularly concerned with safeguarding as much as possible the position of the planters. Some hesitated because slave emancipation seemed an attack on the property rights of slave owners, and property rights were, in the Whig view, to be protected rather than attacked by government. The government-written *King's Speech* that was delivered at the ceremonial opening of Parliament on 15 February contained no reference to emancipation. (King William IV's personal opposition to emancipation also contributed to Whig hesitation.) Outraged, Buxton informed the Whig leaders that he intended to bring in another emancipation bill. The government convinced him to withdraw by promising to bring in their own measure. In March, however, to prod the government further, Buxton had to again threaten to bring in a motion. Government leaders were caught between abolitionists in Britain and the representatives of the West Indian sugar planters and merchants. The planters knew that they could not stop emancipation but were determined to hedge it with such restrictions that it would be emancipation in name only and would preserve preferred British access to the sugar market. A committee representing the "West India Interest" succeeded in blocking an emancipation plan that had been drawn up by Viscount Howick, provoking his resignation. The new colonial secretary, Edward George Geoffrey Smith Stanley, published a moderate plan for emancipation in the *London Times* on 11 May. Three days later, parliamentary debate on slavery began. Buxton presented a new petition with the signatures of 187,000 women.

The government's plan, explicated by Stanley in a speech on 14 May, attempted to balance between the consensus for some form of abolition and the demands of the planters. The plan provided the planters with a loan of 15 million pounds as compensation for their lost property, a sum said to equal 10

William Wilberforce. The Library of Congress.

years' profits. The newly freed slaves would be required to work for three-quarters of their working hours for their former owners as apprentices for 12 years. Slaves under the age of six would be freed immediately. The plan was unacceptable to parliamentary abolitionists. Negotiations produced a compromise. The period of apprenticeship was cut to four years for domestic slaves and six for fieldworkers; the apprenticeships were to be overseen by salaried magistrates sent from Britain rather than by local justices of the peace, who were usually drawn from the planter class. Compensation for planters, however, was increased to 20 million pounds and converted from a loan to an outright grant. Some abolitionists were appalled by the idea of the apprenticeships and compensation for the planters, but the parliamentary abolitionist leadership went along with the idea for the purpose of passing the bill. After it received minor amendments in the House of Lords, the bill passed the Commons on 31 July 1833. Actual emancipation would take place at midnight on 31 July 1834.

Although it was still necessary to obtain the consent of local legislatures in those colonies that possessed them, this was done with little difficulty by the simple device of making the payment of compensation contingent on the local legislature's passing an emancipation act of its own. Despite the widespread fears that had been encouraged by the proslavery interests, emancipation passed without violence (which would later serve as an example for American abolitionists of peaceful emancipation). Many slaves spent the day in church. The day was also recognized with public ceremonies in Britain itself.

The Failure of Apprenticeship

It was the hope of most British abolitionists that the sugar economy of the British West Indies could continue after abolition, with free wage labor and humane conditions replacing slave labor. The apprenticeship system had two main purposes: to ensure continuing social control of the former slaves and to keep a steady labor force on the plantations. The first purpose seemed less important over time as emancipation was accompanied by little violence or social unrest. Maintaining a steady supply of labor, however, proved impossible, as newly freed blacks preferred individual peasant cultivation to the exhausting, dangerous, and painful work of the sugar plantation.

Apprenticeship did not last its full term. The colonial legislatures of Antigua, where planters cooperated to fix wages at a low level, and Bermuda waived apprenticeship in 1833. Both islands were marked by a surplus of labor and a shortage of available land, which narrowed the economic options of the freed slaves. Similar conditions existed on Barbados and St. Kitts, as well as some of the smaller islands. Apprenticeship produced the most strain on the Indian Ocean island of Mauritius, Trinidad, Guyana, and especially Jamaica in the Caribbean. Jamaica, a sugar colony for centuries, suffered from exhausted land and outmoded equipment and physical plant. Jamaican planters compensated for the weakness of their situation relative to more recent colonies by harshly exploiting their apprentices. Jamaica also suffered a shortage of plantation labor and extensive territory that was unsuited for sugar cultivation but was well suited for individual peasant farming. Stories of atrocities in the apprenticeship system, workhouses, and savage punishments meted out to former slaves circulated back to England. Knibb, who had returned to the West Indies contributed to the stories. Abolitionists began to mobilize to abolish apprenticeship. In 1836 Buxton successfully pressed for a Parliamentary inquiry, but its report was inconclusive. Antislavery leaders continued to press the issue, however, and in May 1838 Parliament passed a motion to abolish the apprenticeship system. The colonial legislatures quickly followed suit. British humanitarians subsequently lost interest in the ex-slave colonies, now something of a backwater in the British Empire, although the campaign against the international slave trade continued.

The planters' and the imperial government's solution to the problems posed by the changed labor relations following emancipation was the importation of contract laborers from India (and to a much lesser extent, Chinese and free Africans). These laborers partly filled the gap left by the departure of the freed slaves, and provided the planters with what they believed was a more docile and regimented labor force. This began in Mauritius, where in the 15 years following emancipation Indians virtually replaced Africans as the primary plantation labor force. The period of importation of Indian labor in the British West Indies extended from 1838 to 1917. Indian labor did not solve the problems of the West Indian sugar industry, which were particularly marked after the British Parliament's abolition of the duties on foreign-grown sugar in 1846 and the worldwide economic slowdown of the late 1840s. Cuba, where slavery was not abolished until 1886, became the leading sugar exporter in the Caribbean.

Key Players

Buxton, Thomas Fowell (1786–1845): A brewer and Whig Member of Parliament, Buxton took over the leadership of the British abolitionist movement from William Wilberforce in 1822 and helped to found the British and Foreign Anti-Slavery Society the next year. He was the foremost legislative strategist of the abolitionists. After abolition, he wrote *The African Slave Trade and Its Remedy* (1839), which urged an aggressive British policy to discourage the slave trade in Africa itself. He was also active in the cause of penal reform.

Grey, Charles, Second Earl Grey (1764–1845): Grey was a long-serving Whig politician who became prime minister in 1830. His government carried the great Reform Bill of 1832, extending the British Parliamentary franchise, abolishing slavery, and passing the Factory Act. He resigned as prime minister in 1834.

Grey, Henry Charles, Viscount Howick and Third Earl Grey (1802–1894): The son of Charles Grey served as undersecretary for the colonies, secretary at war (1835–1839), and secretary for war and the colonies (1846–1852). He was a moderate supporter of slave emancipation.

Knibb, William (1803–1845): William Knibb left England for Jamaica in 1824 as a Baptist missionary. Shocked by the cruel treatment of slaves, even by members of his congregation, Knibb became an antislavery activist, and was imprisoned during the suppression of the revolt of 1831, the "Baptist War."

Macaulay, Zachary (1768–1838): The son of a Scottish Presbyterian minister, Macaulay was one of the British abolitionists with practical experience of the slave system, having been a clerk on a Caribbean estate and the governor of the British freed slave colony in Africa, Sierra Leone. A voluminous writer and editor of the *Anti-Slavery Reporter*, he was the father of the historian Thomas Babington Macaulay, who also supported slave emancipation as an MP.

Sharpe, Sam (1801–1832): Sharpe was a leader of a Baptist congregation in Montego Bay, Jamaica, who worked to organize resistance to the planters through religious meetings. After the Baptist War of late 1831, Sharpe was hanged by the victorious whites. He became a national hero of Jamaica.

Stanley, Edward George Geoffrey Smith, 14th Earl of Derby (1799–1869): Stanley served as undersecretary for the colonies (1827–1828), chief secretary for Ireland (1830–1833), and secretary for war and the colonies (1833–1834). Later, as Lord Derby, he was the leader of the Conservative Party and prime minister.

Wilberforce, William (1759–1833): William Wilberforce was the leader of the British abolitionist movement for many years. He was one of the original founders of the Society for Effecting the Abolition of the Slave Trade and served in the House of Commons from 1780 to 1825, largely retiring from active involvement in the antislavery movement around that date. He died a few weeks before the passage of the Abolition Act. A political conservative, Wilberforce also supported repressive policies against British workers including the Combination Acts.

See also: *Abolition of Slavery, United States.*

———————

BIBLIOGRAPHY

Books

Barclay, Oliver. *Thomas Fowell Buxton and the Liberation of Slaves.* York, England: William Sessions Limited, 2001.

Craton, Michael. *Sinews of Empire: A Short History of British Slavery.* Garden City, NY: Anchor Books, 1974.

Newbould, Ian. *Whiggery and Reform, 1830–1841: The Politics of Government.* Stanford, CA: Stanford University Press, 1990.

Parry, J. H., P. M. Sherlock, and A. P. Maingot. *A Short History of the West Indies*, 4th ed. New York: St. Martin's Press, 1987.

Woodward, Llewellyn. *The Age of Reform: England 1815–1870*, 2nd ed. Oxford: Oxford University Press, 1962.

ADDITIONAL RESOURCES

Books

Drescher, Seymour. *Capitalism and Antislavery: British Mobilization in Comparative Perspective.* London: Macmillan, 1986.

———. *Econocide: British Slavery in the Era of Abolition.* Pittsburgh, PA: University of Pittsburgh Press, 1977.

———. *The Mighty Experiment: Free Labor Versus Slavery in British Emancipation.* New York and Oxford: Oxford University Press, 2002.

Williams, Eric. *Capitalism and Slavery.* London: A. Deutsch, 1964.

Periodicals

Kriegel, Abraham. "A Converging of Ethics: Saints and Whigs in British Antislavery." *Journal of British Studies* 26 (1987): 423–450.

—William E. Burns

Abolition of Slavery

United States 1863–1865

Synopsis

By early 1861, just before the beginning of the American Civil War (sometimes also called the War Between the States and the War for Southern Independence), serious economic and ideological differences divided the citizens of the United States. The primary points of contention were slavery and the rights of the states with respect to the federal government. These growing differences also divided the country geographically. Nineteen states, including the industrialized northern states, prohibited slavery, while 15 southern states, whose society depended on agriculture, allowed the ownership of slaves. Seven of those 15 southern states had already withdrawn from the United States and formed the Confederate States of America after Abraham Lincoln was sworn in as president of the United States. Despite the hopes of President Lincoln that the secession would end without conflict, the two regions fought a civil war from 1861 to 1865 that exploited the distinctions between the northern states and the southern states. The primary reason why the war was being fought (at least from the perspective of Lincoln and the people in the northern states) changed during the year 1863 from regaining the unification of the country to the abolition and resulting emancipation of black slaves throughout the United States.

Timeline

1846: Frederick Douglass establishes the abolitionist newspaper *The North Star.*

1849: Harriet Tubman escapes from slavery in Maryland. Over the next eight years, she will undertake at least 20 secret missions into Maryland and Virginia to free more than 300 slaves through the so-called Underground Railroad.

1852: *Uncle Tom's Cabin* by Harriet Beecher Stowe, though far from a literary masterpiece is a great commercial success, with over half a million sales on both sides of the Atlantic. More important, it has an enormous influence on British sentiments with regard to slavery and the brewing American conflict between North and South.

1854: Republican Party is formed by opponents of slavery in Michigan.

1857: In its Dred Scott decision, the U.S. Supreme Court rules that a slave is not a citizen.

1859: American abolitionist John Brown leads a raid on the federal arsenal at Harpers Ferry, Virginia. His capture and hanging in December heighten the animosities that will spark the Civil War 16 months later.

1861: Within weeks of Abraham Lincoln's inauguration, the Civil War begins with the shelling of Fort Sumter. Six states secede from the Union, joining South Carolina to form the Confederate States of America (later joined by four other states) and electing Jefferson Davis as president. The first major battle of the war, at Bull Run or Manassas in Virginia, is a Confederate victory.

1863: President Lincoln issues the Emancipation Proclamation, freeing all slaves in Confederate territories, on 1 January. Thus begins a year that sees the turning point of the Civil War, with decisive Union victories at Gettysburg, Vicksburg, and Chattanooga. Thereafter, the

Group of freed slaves gathering on plantation of Confederate General Thomas F. Drayton during Union occupation of property, Hilton Head, South Carolina. © Corbis. Reproduced by permission.

Confederacy is almost perpetually on the defensive, fighting not to win but to avoid losing.

1865: Civil War ends with the surrender of General Robert E. Lee to General Ulysses S. Grant at Appomattox, Virginia. More than 600,000 men have died, and the South is in ruins, but the Union has been restored.

1865: Ratification of the Thirteenth Amendment to the U.S. Constitution, which prohibits slavery.

1868: Ratification of the Fourteenth Amendment to the U.S. Constitution, which grants civil rights to African Americans.

1870: Fifteenth Amendment, the last of the three post–Civil War amendments to the U.S. Constitution, states that an American citizen cannot be denied the right to vote because of race, color, or previous status as a slave. At this time, the new amendment is treated as law in the South, which is still occupied by federal troops, but after Reconstruction ends in 1877, it will be nearly 90 years before blacks in some southern states gain full voting rights.

Celebration in House of Representatives after Congress passed Thirteenth Amendment. © Hulton/Getty Images. Reproduced by permission.

Event and Its Context

From the colonial years in the late 1770s until 1860, the northern states (the "North") and the southern states (the "South") of the United States had developed socially, economically, and politically into two divergent regions. Although governmental compromises had loosely kept the United States (the "Union") together for many years, the situation quickly reversed itself during the 1860 presidential campaign. The resulting election of Abraham Lincoln as the sixteenth president of the United States was viewed by the South as a threat to slavery and the southern way of life; indeed, it ignited the Civil War. The first two years of the war, 1861 and 1862, were fought primarily by the North to restore the Union. These efforts helped to bring about the later years of the war, 1863–1865, which were fought by the North to emancipate black slaves in the South as well as to restore the Union.

Industrialization Versus Agriculture

Sharp differences between the North and the South, though apparent in the eighteenth century, dramatically increased during the first half of the nineteenth century. By 1860 cotton was the primary southern crop, accounting for the majority of total U.S. exports. The South's plantation system and its critical labor component of slavery were developed as a result of the profitability of cotton, along with the other major crops of sugar cane, tobacco, and rice.

The North, on the other hand, had successfully established itself as an industrial society in the second half of the eighteenth century. Free labor was desperately needed by the northern states for their growing industrial facilities, and that labor came in the form of European immigrants. These immigrants worked in factories, built the railroads of the North, and settled the western part of the United States (the "West") that, at this time, comprised the land immediately west of the Appalachian Mountains. According to 1860 census records, the northern population was several times that of the southern population (approximately 21.9 million in the North and West versus about 5.5 million, plus about 3.9 million slaves, in the South). Because of its expanding industrial base, the North was more dependent on the federal government than the South in order to develop a complex transportation network, consisting mainly of highways, railroads, and canals. Immigrants built the bulk of the transportation infrastructure and at the same time settled along its route throughout the North and West; however, few immigrants settled in the South.

The South rejected industrialization and instead looked to agriculture as its primary business. Almost all manufactured goods necessary for southern society had to be imported either

A page designed for the recording of African American family information features an illustration of conditions before and after emancipation. © Corbis. Reproduced by permission.

Behind the Emancipation Proclamation

President Lincoln had long insisted that the purpose of the war was to preserve the Union, but pressure from a number of sides—most notably from abolitionist leaders—forced him to place a greater emphasis on freeing the slaves. Therefore, in July 1862 he drafted a preliminary version of the Emancipation Proclamation, which freed all slaves in the Confederate states as of 1 January 1863. His cabinet suggested that he not make the proclamation public until the Union had secured a major victory in battle; otherwise, it might appear like a desperate ploy to gain support from antislavery elements. The awaited victory came in September, at the Battle of Antietam in Maryland (which also saw the bloodiest day in American history, 17 September 1862). Soon afterward, Lincoln issued the Emancipation Proclamation.

The proclamation only freed slaves in the South, and therefore, for the remainder of the war, slavery remained legal in Kentucky, Missouri, and other non-Confederate states where slavery was still practiced. (In fact, Ulysses S. Grant owned slaves, whereas Robert E. Lee sold his at the beginning of the war.) The proclamation's greatest significance lay in the fact that it legally freed southern slaves to leave their masters and enlist in the Union army.

By the time of the proclamation, most parts of the Confederate states remained defiant, but some localities had returned to the Union. It was for this reason that the proclamation exempted certain named parishes in Louisiana and counties in Virginia, as well as the entire portion of the latter state that had broken away to become the present-day state of West Virginia. In many another states, there were mountainous regions that had little agriculture, and in such areas (for example, northeast Georgia), popular support for slavery—if not secession—was limited.

Source: John Hope Franklin. *The Emancipation Proclamation.* Garden City, NY: Doubleday, 1963.

—Judson Knight

from the North or from Europe or other trading partners. The South was long dependent on slave labor, while the North was dependent on free labor, and both sides wanted to preserve that comfortable situation in their particular homelands.

Slavery

The immediate cause of the Civil War was slavery, although various factions often stated other reasons. Fifteen southern states, including the 11 states that formed the Confederacy, depended on slave labor to support their economy. Although slavery was not universally practiced in the 19 northern states, only a small proportion of northerners (called abolitionists) actively opposed it. The main debate between the North and the South in the years leading up to the Civil War was whether slavery should be permitted in the new territories and states. The territories included Oregon, Minnesota, New Mexico, and Utah (established between 1840 and 1850), and the newly established states that were in contention were Maine (1820) and Missouri (1821). Opponents of slavery were concerned about its expansion into undetermined territories and slave-free states, mostly because they did not want to compete against slave labor.

Compromise or Conflict

According to the U.S. Constitution, the federal government reserved to the states the right to deal with slavery, so it could not prohibit or otherwise interfere with slavery within the states. Opponents of slavery could legally only prevent its spread. Moderates from both the North and the South hoped to compromise the regional differences by equalizing the power between free and slave states in the U.S. Senate. In 1818 the Senate became balanced with the addition of the state of Alabama to the Union. However, for the next 40 years, many territories in the West and Southwest petitioned for statehood, which constantly disrupted the balance of the Senate. As a result, the North and the South began a desperate struggle over whether territories would enter the Union as free or slave states. They found temporary agreements in the Missouri Compromise of 1821, admitting Missouri as a slave state and Maine as a free state, and later in the Compromise of 1850, admitting California as a free state and allowing territorial governments to decide slavery.

Uncle Tom's Cabin

Uncle Tom's Cabin, an antislavery novel written by Harriet Beecher Stowe, greatly changed public opinion in the North. Stowe wrote the novel in response to the Fugitive Slave Act of 1850, which made it illegal to assist an escaped slave. The story was first published in the abolitionist newspaper *National Era* in 1851 and 1852 and then was published as a novel in 1852, when it quickly sold 300,000 copies. The book exposed many Americans, for the first time, to the horrors of slavery and depicted slaves not as shiftless, carefree characters, but as human beings capable of the same thoughts and emotions as white people. *Uncle Tom's Cabin* was widely read in the United States and abroad and motivated many to join the abolitionist cause. Southern critics tried to minimize the book's depiction of slavery, but in the end Stowe's novel helped many people to voice criticism of slavery and to favor its abolition.

Abraham Lincoln

The slavery issue was in the forefront of all thought during the presidential election year of 1860. The Republican Party had run on an antislavery platform, and during the campaign many southerners had threatened secession from the Union if Abraham Lincoln was elected. Rich, white southerners feared that a Lincoln administration would threaten slavery, their cherished antebellum heritage, and southern society.

On 6 November 1860 Lincoln was elected president of the United States—an event that outraged southern states. At his inauguration, Lincoln declared that he had no intention of ending existing slavery. Southerners decided, however, that secession was a better choice than to remain in the Union and risk compromising their familiar way of life. Therefore, on 20 December 1860 South Carolina seceded, and by 1 February 1861 six more states—Alabama, Florida, Georgia, Louisiana, Mississippi, and Texas—had seceded from the Union as well.

When Lincoln took the oath of office on 4 March 1861, the seven seceded states had already adopted the constitution of the Confederate States of America (the Confederacy) and elected Jefferson Davis as its president. Southern leaders believed that their action was lawful. But northern leaders, including Lincoln, were fiercely against the South's withdrawal from the Union. The president maintained that secession was illegal and that the newly formed Confederacy was not a valid nation.

The North wanted to preserve the Union, and the South wanted the right to establish a country that guaranteed the right to own slaves. Lincoln believed that with governmental compromise, diplomatic efforts, and sufficient time—absent a provocative act—the seceded states might return to the Union. However, this did not happen.

The Civil War Begins

On 12 April 1861 Confederate artillery attacked Fort Sumter in the harbor of Charleston, South Carolina. Immediately following the attack, four more states—Arkansas, North Carolina, Tennessee, and Virginia—severed their ties with the Union. To retain the loyalty of the remaining border states—Delaware, Kentucky, Maryland, and Missouri—President Lincoln insisted that the war was not about abolishing slavery but was rather a war to preserve the Union. His words were not aimed just at southerners but were also addressed to white northerners, who were for the most part not interested in fighting to free slaves or in giving rights to black people.

Lincoln upheld the laws barring blacks from the army, proving to northern whites that their privileges would not be threatened. Still, many blacks wanted to join the fighting and continued to place pressure on federal authorities. Even if Lincoln did not publicly state his beliefs, many blacks believed that this was a war against slavery.

Both sides now prepared for a bloody conflict that they knew would last much longer than either had initially imagined. Early Confederate victories at the First Battle of Bull Run in Manassas, Virginia, and in Missouri at Wilson's Creek, crushed the hopes of the Union to stop the rebellion quickly and without great loss of life. Northern forces soon assembled along the upper Mississippi River and the Ohio River in order to assure unimpeded movement of needed goods throughout the North. Northern forces also established new naval bases—and conquered existing ones—along the southern Atlantic coast in order to block international traders and smugglers who could aid the southern war effort.

From the beginning of the war, President Lincoln insisted that his primary purpose was the restoration of the Union, not the abolition of slavery. As the war continued, however, Lincoln saw that the preservation of the Union depended, in part, on the elimination of slavery. The leaders of the Lincoln administration began to believe that if they stressed the abolition of slavery as a major war objective, then they could prevent France and England from recognizing the Confederacy. Both England and France had abolished slavery and would probably not support a country fighting a war to defend slavery. Furthermore, the abolition of slavery (popularly called "emancipation") might permit the North to demolish the South's war effort, which was strongly supported by slave labor.

Self-emancipation

Self-emancipation presented a problem to the Union army as slaves escaped to various Union states. Because there was no consistent federal policy regarding fugitives, individual commanders made their own decisions. Some put them to work for Union forces, while others wanted to return them to their owners. Since these black people were originally enslaved in the South, someone had to decide whether they would become free or be returned to their southern masters, as was required under the existing fugitive slave laws. Northern general Benjamin F. Butler stated that southern slave owners considered the fugitives their property, and during a state of war, an enemy's property can be legally taken. The Lincoln administration supported Butler's rationale. On 6 August 1861 fugitive slaves were declared to be "contraband of war" if their labor had been used against Union forces. As such, they were declared to be free.

Antislavery Legislation

At the beginning of 1862, Lincoln continued to insist that the Civil War was a fight to save the Union, not to free slaves. However, public opinion in the North began overwhelmingly to favor abolition of slavery. In response, Congress began to pass legislation to end slavery. On 10 April 1862 Congress pledged financial aid to any state that proceeded with gradual emancipation of blacks (along with appropriate compensation to their previous owners). In addition, on 16 April 1862 Congress abolished slavery in the District of Columbia; on 19 June 1862 it prohibited slavery in the territories; and on 17 July 1862 it provided (through the Militia Act) for the employment of blacks in military or naval service.

On 22 July 1862 Lincoln informed his cabinet that he intended to free the slaves in states that were in active rebellion against the Union. However, the members of his cabinet persuaded Lincoln to wait for a northern victory in order to give the announcement more credence. After the Battle of Antietam on 17 September 1862, President Lincoln visited the battlefield, the scene of the single bloodiest day in United States history. With the Union army having emerged victorious at Antietam, Lincoln determined that his announcement was now appropriate.

Emancipation Proclamation

Five days later, on 22 September 1862, Lincoln issued the first proclamation, which marked a major change in Union policy. The proclamation stated that the Confederate states were to surrender by 1 January 1863 or their slaves would be freed. It also announced the Union's intention to enlist black soldiers and sailors. On 1 January 1863 Lincoln issued the Emancipation Proclamation, proclaiming freedom for about 3,120,000 slaves. The stated purpose of the Civil War had now changed, for now the North was not only fighting to preserve the Union, but it was also fighting to end slavery.

Black men rushed to enlist upon hearing about the proclamation. They were accepted into all-black units. By late spring large-scale recruitment through the War Department's Bureau of Colored Troops was under way throughout the North and in all the Union-occupied Confederate states except Tennessee. One of the first of these regiments was the Fifty-fourth Massachusetts Colored Regiment. Their heroism in combat proved the willingness and ability of black soldiers to fight. (By the end of the war, more than 186,000 black soldiers had joined the Union army: 93,000 from the Confederate states, 53,000 from the free states, and 40,000 from the border slave states.) By mid-1864 the war was turning in favor of the North. On 3 March 1865 the Congress prepared for the war's end by establishing the Bureau of Refugees, Freedmen, and Abandoned Lands to oversee the transition from slavery to freedom.

On the morning of 9 April 1865, northern commander Ulysses S. Grant and southern commander Robert E. Lee met at a private home in Appomattox Court House, Virginia. Lee accepted the terms of surrender offered by Grant, and the war was effectively over. Over 600,000 people lost their lives during the war, and property valued at $5 billion was destroyed, but the war assured the freedom of about four million black slaves and the preservation of the United States of America. The final number of about four million liberated slaves included those inhabiting the states in the Confederacy (three million) who were liberated in Lincoln's 1863 Emancipation Proclamation, plus those liberated at war's end who lived outside the Confederacy.

Aftermath of the War

The war caused wide-scale economic destruction to the South. The Confederate states lost two-thirds of their wealth during the war. The loss of slave property through emancipation accounted for much of this, but the economic infrastructure in the South was also severely damaged in other ways. Railroads and industries in the South were destroyed, over one-half of all agricultural machinery was destroyed, and 40 percent of all livestock had been killed. It took the South a full 100 years to return to its prewar state with regard to industry and agriculture. In contrast, the northern economy thrived during and after the war. Between 1861 and 1870 northern wealth increased by 50 percent; while during that same decade southern wealth decreased by 60 percent.

Since Lincoln's proclamation was a war announcement that might be held unconstitutional after the war, both houses of the U.S. Congress passed the Thirteenth Amendment to the Constitution, which abolished slavery forever in the United States, early in 1865. It was ratified by three-fourths of the states and was formally proclaimed in effect on 18 December 1865. With the end of the war, four million former slaves were free to travel throughout the South, although some remained in, or moved to, the North. Black men who fought for the Union felt a strong desire for full U.S. citizenship. Because they had risked their lives in the military, black men argued that they should have the right to vote and live as full members of American society. Instead, the North and the South debated the future of black Americans during the 12 years of Reconstruction following the war.

The Fourteenth Amendment that was passed in June 1865 granted citizenship to all people born or naturalized in the United States. The Fifteenth Amendment, passed in February 1869, guaranteed that no American would be denied the right to vote on the basis of race. Despite ratification of the Fourteenth and Fifteenth Amendments to the Constitution, black Americans failed to win equal rights for many years in much of the postwar South.

Following Reconstruction, blacks were denied the franchise in many states until the Voting Rights Act of 1965. As the nineteenth century closed, they faced a segregated life in the South and hostility across most of the North. The Civil War granted blacks their freedom; however, the battle for black equality had yet to be won.

Key Players

Lincoln, Abraham (1809–1865): Lincoln attended a one-room school for only a few months; the rest of his education came from his avid reading habit. While reading law, he worked in a store, managed a mill, surveyed land, and split rails. In 1834 he went to the Illinois legislature as a Whig and became the party's floor leader. He practiced law in Springfield, Illinois, for the next 20 years, except for a single term (1847–1849) in the Illinois Congress. In 1855 he was an unsuccessful candidate for senator, and the next year he joined the new Republican Party. Lincoln gained national attention in 1858 when, as Republican candidate for senator from Illinois, he engaged in a series of debates with the Democratic candidate but lost the election. Lincoln gained the Republican presidential nomination in 1860. His next five years involved directing the Union's activities in the Civil War against the southern states that had seceded from the union. His inaugural speeches and the Gettysburg Address are considered masterpieces of American oratory. Lincoln demonstrated his mastery of foreign affairs by avoiding war with Great Britain. Often called the "Great Emancipator," Lincoln was the central figure of the Civil War and is regarded by many historians as one of the greatest U.S. presidents. He was fatally shot on 14 April 1865 at Ford's Theater in Washington, D.C.

Stowe, Harriet Beecher (1811–1896): Stowe was an American writer and philanthropist, best recognized for the antislavery novel *Uncle Tom's Cabin.* She attended the seminary at Hartford, Connecticut, which was managed by her sister Catherine, and four years later was employed there as an assistant teacher. Harriet and Catherine later founded the Western Female Institute, another seminary. In 1834 Stowe began her literary career when she won a contest sponsored by the *Western Monthly* magazine, and soon she became a regular contributor to the magazine. Her first book, *The Mayflower,* appeared in 1843. She started to publish her writings in the *Atlantic Monthly* and later in the *Independent* and the *Christian Union.* Stowe published *The Key to Uncle Tom's Cabin* (1853), which contains source material from her earlier book. A second antislavery novel, *Dred: A Tale of the Great Dismal Swamp* (1856), tells the story of a slave rebellion. *The Pearl of Orr's Island* (1862), *Old-Town Folks* (1869), and *Poganuc People* (1878) are loosely based on her husband's childhood memories of life in New England.

See also: *Black Codes; Jim Crow Segregation and Labor.*

BIBLIOGRAPHY

Books

Collier, Christopher, and James Lincoln Collier. *The Civil War, 1860–1866.* New York: Benchmark Books, 1998.

Naden, Corinne J., and Rose Blue. *Why Fight? The Causes of the American Civil War.* Austin, TX: Raintree Steck-Vaughn, 2000.

Wesley, Charles H., and Patricia W. Romero. *Negro Americans in the Civil War: From Slavery to Citizenship.* New York: Publishers Company, 1968.

Other

Chronology of Emancipation during the Civil War [cited 16 November 2002]. <http://www.inform.umd.edu/ARHU/Depts/History/Freedman/chronol.htm>.

Civil War and Emancipation. African American History [cited 16 November 2002]. <http://afroamhistory.about.com/cs/civilwar/>.

The Civil War Years: The Fight for Emancipation [cited 16 November 2002]. <http://www.history.rochester.edu/class/douglass/part4.html>.

Lincoln, Abraham. *The Emancipation Proclamation* [cited 16 November 2002]. <http://americancivilwar.com/eman.html>.

Population of the United States (1860) [cited 16 November 2002]. <http://www.civilwarhome.com/population1860.htm>.

Slavery [cited 16 November 2002]. <http://www.spartacus.schoolnet.co.uk/USAslavery.htm>.

—William Arthur Atkins

Act to Encourage Immigration

United States 1864

Synopsis

The United States Congress's Act to Encourage Immigration legalized and bureaucratized a practice similar to indentured servitude. Under this measure, employers could contract with a foreign laborer to come to the United States and pay for his passage in exchange for up to a year's wages. This practice, legally sanctioned by the federal government in 1864 at the prodding of industrialists and President Abraham Lincoln, met with immediate resistance from the embryonic labor movement of the time. Rather than attracting skilled labor for the formation of new industries, third-party recruiting organizations contracted with unskilled laborers to work for wages substandard to those in the United States. Employers often imported contract laborers in efforts to break strikes during labor disputes. Congress technically repealed the law in 1868, but the practice of importing labor already under contract was not made illegal until the 1885 passage of the Foran Act (also known as the Alien Contract Labor Law). Both the repeal and the outright ban, however, served mainly as symbolic gestures rather than enforceable legislation.

Timeline

1844: Samuel Laing, in a prize-winning essay on Britain's "National Distress," describes conditions in a nation convulsed by the early Industrial Revolution. A third of the population, according to Laing, "hover[s] on the verge of actual starvation"; another third is forced to labor in "crowded factories"; and only the top third "earn[s] high wages, amply sufficient to support them in respectability and comfort."

1849: Elizabeth Blackwell becomes the first woman in the United States to receive a medical degree.

1854: In the United States, the Kansas-Nebraska Act calls for decisions on the legality of slavery to be made through local votes. Instead of reducing divisions, this measure will result in widespread rioting and bloodshed and will only further hasten the looming conflict over slavery and states' rights.

1857: Start of the Sepoy Mutiny, an unsuccessful revolt by Indian troops against the British East India Company. As a result of the rebellion, which lasts into 1858, England places India under direct crown rule.

1860: Louis Pasteur pioneers his method of "pasteurizing" milk by heating it to high temperatures in order to kill harmful microbes.

1862: Victor Hugo's *Les Misérables* depicts injustices in French society, and Ivan Turgenev's *Fathers and Sons* introduces the term *nihilism.*

1864: General William Tecumseh Sherman conducts his Atlanta campaign and his "march to the sea."

1864: Founding of the International Red Cross in Geneva.

1864: George M. Pullman and Ben Field patent their design for a sleeping car with folding upper berths.

1866: Austrian monk Gregor Mendel presents his theories on the laws of heredity. Though his ideas will be forgotten for a time, they are destined to exert enormous influence on biological study in the twentieth century.

1870: Beginning of Franco-Prussian War. German troops sweep over France, Napoleon III is dethroned, and France's Second Empire gives way to the Third Republic.

1873: The gold standard, adopted by Germany in 1871 and eventually taken on by all major nations, spreads to Italy, Belgium, and Switzerland. Though the United States does not officially base the value of its currency on gold until 1900, an unofficial gold standard dates from this period, even as a debate over "bimetallism" creates sharp divisions in American politics.

Event and Its Context

Throughout the colonial and antebellum periods, the United States experienced various degrees of labor shortages. Indentured servitude, mostly of white Europeans, and the African slave trade provided ready sources of labor until the early nineteenth century, when the United States banned the Atlantic slave trade and the demand for indentured servants dropped significantly. During the Civil War, industrialists searched for a way to eradicate the acute shortage of labor that resulted from both conscription and the movement of settlers to western farmlands after the passage of the Homestead Act of 1862. The Republican-controlled Congress favored a measure intended to increase immigration of skilled laborers to northern industrial areas.

Interest groups such as manufacturers, transportation companies, and recruitment agencies sought government support for an increase in immigration from Europe. In 1863 President Lincoln aligned himself with the special interests and asked Congress to stimulate immigration so as to keep war industries afloat. As a result, Congress passed the Act to Encourage Immigration, which Lincoln then signed into law on 4 July 1864. With the blessing of the federal government, middleman organizations such as the American Emigrant Company culled labor markets in European ports to lure laborers to the United States. Recruitment agencies and steamship companies profited wildly from this practice, taking a cut of the laborers' wages for their procurement. In addition, because the foreign laborers often received faulty or outdated information about labor conditions, wage scales, and costs of living, long-term contracts often locked workers into wages that were well below the standards followed in America.

Employers often utilized these imported contract laborers as strikebreakers during times of labor unrest. Because their wages were set before arriving at the job site, these workers could be employed at far lower than the prevailing rates. However, this did not always work out according to the employers' designs. Occasionally, striking workers would reason with, cajole, or threaten the contract laborers to return to their home countries or to join a strike. Industrialists believed that they had few options besides property seizure to compel workers to honor their contracts, and because many workers turned to contract labor out of poverty, prosecution in most cases proved more costly than letting a worker leave. Labor activism also challenged the sanctity of the contracts. Unions took up collections to pay return passage for contract workers. In one example, a group of coal miners imported from northern Britain to West Virginia refused to take up their work and sided with the protesting Americans. Communication among trade unions, particularly between the United States and Great Britain, met with some success in preventing the recruitment of strikebreakers. Yet despite these scattered success stories, the importation of contract labor generally reduced wages and disrupted collective action among striking workers.

Opposition to the contract labor law arose quickly, as workers blamed the practice for unemployment and low wages in the immediate postwar period. Onto this scene arose the reform unionism movement, stressing worker organization across craft divisions instead of more traditional trade unionism. Reform unionism's first nationwide incarnation, the National Labor Union (NLU), solidified during the rapid industrialization surrounding the Civil War. Under pressure from the NLU and trade unions, Congress refused industrialists' pleas to heighten enforcement provisions; they even repealed the law in 1868. However, this law served more as a sop to working-class voters than as an effective tool against the practice of contract labor

Uriah Stephens. The Library of Congress.

importation. The law retracted federal support for encouraging immigration but did not explicitly forbid the practice. Employers, steamship companies, and the American Emigrant Company therefore continued to import contract workers throughout the 1870s and 1880s.

Throughout the turbulent boom and bust cycles of the 1870s, many Americans blamed immigrants for troubled economic times and the increasing problems of urban overcrowding. The expanding labor movement furthered its efforts against imported contract labor into the early 1880s, concentrating the blame on Hungarian and Italian peasants, most of whom had emigrated under their own initiative rather than under a prearranged contract. The Holy Order of the Knights of Labor, founded in 1869, replaced the internally divided NLU as the voice of union reform. One assembly of the Knights, the Window Glass Workers, Local Assembly 300, took the initiative to press Congress for a bill that would prohibit contract labor. Imported skilled tradesmen, mostly from Belgium, had been used as strikebreakers against the local in 1879 and 1880. Martin Foran, a congressman from Ohio and a supporter of the Knights of Labor, proposed a bill in 1884 to forbid the importation of contract labor.

Congress received a flood of petitions in support of the bill, mostly from citizen groups, labor organizations such as the Knights, and state legislatures, that pointed out the economic and humanitarian necessity of the measure. The Knights, reaching the apogee of their influence in the mid-1880s, were not the only source of concern over importation of contract labor. Yet despite the actual practices of importation, the main issue in the congressional debates did not revolve around Belgian glass workers or wage cutting. Rather, an all-too-familiar ethnic rhetoric colored the debate. Lawmakers spoke out about the dangers of allowing eastern and southern European peasants to flood the cities of the United States.

Despite the Knights' philosophy of solidarity across racial, ethnic, and gender lines, a definite resistance to immigration emerged. The resistance stressed the dangers of so-called unassimilable foreigners. Some preferred the Foran Act to an outright ban on immigration from Europe, drawing a distinction between workers who voluntarily chose to immigrate (and could therefore join unions) and those who aligned themselves with capitalists before arriving in America. The Knights therefore did not see a conflict between their stated purpose as the voice of all workers and their efforts to keep out specific workers. This matter had been far more clouded three years previously, when the Knights supported the ban on Chinese immigration because they considered the Chinese to be unassimilable racially and culturally.

Business interests did not bother to protest the Foran Act; they claimed that they did not import contract labor. Recruiting organizations and steamer lines, often run by recent immigrants with little political clout, did the dirty work. In addition, the rising levels of overall immigration demonstrated that no labor shortage would result from such meager limitations. Thus, the bill appealed emotionally—if not rationally—to workers and did not damage business interests. Perhaps more important, the law was nearly impossible to enforce. Immigration officials found oral contracts hard to trace, and immigrants quickly learned how to walk the thin line between contract labor stipulations and the "likely to become a public charge" clause. More importantly, the United States still lacked the administrative capacity to regulate immigration on a national level.

Key Players

Carey, Henry C. (1793–1879): Economic theorist who supported protective tariffs and immigration promotion to bolster the industrial economy. During the Civil War, Carey and his colleagues pressed Congress for the Act to Encourage Immigration and to pave the way for organizations such as the American Emigration Company to recruit laborers abroad.

Foran, Martin (1844–1921): U.S. Congressman from Cleveland, Ohio, former president of the Coopers Union, and editor of the labor newspaper, the *Coopers' Journal*. As a congressman, Foran supported the Knights of Labor in efforts to bring about government-led reform. He introduced a bill in Congress to ban the importation of alien laborers under contract; the bill passed in 1885 with the support of the Knights and many other labor groups.

James, John (1839–1902): James was a miner and trade unionist recruited from Britain as part of a strikebreaking force in West Virginia. When James learned of the strike from the local miners, he and his coworkers refused en masse to take up their work. James acted as spokesman for the group, arguing that their contracts were made under false pretenses and were therefore invalid. James continued to work as a labor activist, writing for the *Workingman's Advocate* and serving as secretary of the Miners' National Association.

Stephens, Uriah (1821–1882): Originally trained as a minister, in 1869 Stephens became cofounder and first grandmaster workman of the Holy Order of the Knights of Labor. He carried the tradition of reform unionism, with a heavy emphasis on Christianity, from the defunct National Labor Union to the Knights. Stephens advocated open membership for all workers to the union, although he clung to the group's heritage as a secret society fashioned after freemasonry. Membership in the Knights swelled after Terence Powderly replaced Stephens as the organization's leader.

Sylvis, William (1828–1869): Sylvis was president and one of the founders of the National Labor Union. Instrumental in the early development of the first organization of its kind in the United States, Sylvis advocated organization across craft and skill levels, including membership for women and African American workers. Sylvis opposed the Act to Encourage Immigration as part of a postwar surge in labor activism. He died shortly after the repeal of the Act to Encourage Immigration.

See also: *Chinese Exclusion Act; Foran Act; Knights of Labor; National Labor Union.*

BIBLIOGRAPHY

Books

Briggs, Vernon M., Jr. *Immigration and American Unionism.* Ithaca, NY: Cornell University Press, 2001.

Erickson, Charlotte. *American Industry and the European Immigrant, 1860–1885.* Cambridge: Harvard University Press, 1957.

Hutchinson, E. P. *Legislative History of American Immigration Policy, 1798–1965.* Philadelphia: University of Pennsylvania Press, 1981.

Rayback, Joseph G. *A History of American Labor.* New York: The Macmillan Company, 1959.

Steinfeld, Robert J. *Coercion, Contract, and Free Labor in the Nineteenth Century.* New York: Cambridge University Press, 2001.

U.S. House of Representatives. *Report on Importation of Contract Laborers.* Washington, DC: Government Printing Office, 1889.

Periodicals

"American Labor Portraits No. 4." *Workingman's Advocate* (29 November 1873): 1.

Grob, Gerald. "Reform Unionism: The National Labor Union." *Journal of Economic History* 14, no. 2 (1954): 126–142.

Other

"Martin Foran." *The Encyclopedia of Cleveland History.* Case Western Reserve University Web site. 2002 [cited 10 August 2002]. <http://ech.cwru.edu/ech-cgi/article.pl?id=FMA1>.

ADDITIONAL RESOURCES

Periodicals

Chomsky, Carol. "Unlocking the Mysteries of Holy Trinity: Spirit, Letter, and History in Statutory Interpretation." *Columbia Law Review* 100, no. 4 (2000): 901–957.

Creamer, Daniel. "Recruiting Contract Laborers for the Amoskeag Mills." *Journal of Economic History* 1, no. 1 (1941): 42–56.

Orth, Samuel P. "The Alien Contract Law and Labor Law." *Political Science Quarterly* 22, no. 1 (1907): 49–60.

—Courtney Q. Shah

AFL, CIO Merge

United States 1955

Synopsis

The merger of the American Federation of Labor (AFL) and the Congress of Industrial Organizations (CIO) formed the AFL-CIO and was the culmination of a process that occurred in each of the two organizations for a number of years. The AFL majority had become more open to organizing efforts among unskilled workers and more tolerant of affiliates organizing along industry-wide rather than craft lines. The CIO majority had become less tolerant of left-wing influences that had played an essential role in the organization of industrial unions among mass production workers during the depression of the 1930s. The convergence derived its distinctive shape from the idiosyncrasies of influential individuals. Larger economic, social, political, and cultural trends, however, were decisive influences. In fact, the merger had multiple meanings in regard to the strength and purpose (internationally as well as nationally) of the U.S. labor movement in the twentieth century.

Timeline

1935: Second phase of New Deal begins with the introduction of social security, farm assistance, and housing and tax reform.

1940: Hitler's troops sweep through Western Europe, annexing Norway and Denmark in April, and in May the Low Countries and France.

1945: On 7 May, Germany surrenders to the Allies.

1951: Julius and Ethel Rosenberg are convicted and sentenced to death for passing U.S. atomic secrets to the Soviets.

1955: Warsaw Pact is signed by the Soviet Union and its satellites in Eastern Europe.

1955: African and Asian nations meet at the Bandung Conference in Indonesia, inaugurating the "non-aligned" movement of Third World countries.

1955: Over the course of the year, a number of key ingredients are added to the pantheon of American culture: the 1955

Chevrolet, the first of many classic models; Tennessee Williams's *Cat on a Hot Tin Roof*; Marilyn Monroe's performance in *The Seven-Year Itch*; Disneyland; and Bill Haley and the Comets' "Rock Around the Clock."

1955: Among the year's deaths are Albert Einstein, Thomas Mann, Dale Carnegie, Cy Young, and James Dean.

1955: Rosa Parks refuses to move from her seat near the front of a public bus in Montgomery, Alabama, and is arrested. The incident touches off a boycott of Montgomery's bus system, led by the Rev. Martin Luther King, Jr., which will last well into 1956. The situation will attract national attention and garner support for the civil rights movement, before Montgomery agrees to desegregate its bus system on 21 December 1956—exactly a year after Parks's brave protest.

1958: First U.S. satellite, *Explorer I*, goes into orbit.

1962: As the Soviets begin a missile buildup in Cuba, for a few tense days in October it appears that World War III is imminent. President Kennedy calls for a Cuban blockade, forcing the Soviets to back down and ultimately diffusing the crisis.

1970: President Nixon sends U.S. troops into Cambodia on 30 April. Five days later, National Guardsmen open fire on antiwar protesters at Kent State University in Ohio. By 24 June antiwar sentiment is so strong that the Senate repeals the Gulf of Tonkin resolution. On 29 June, Nixon orders troops back out of Cambodia.

Event and Its Context

When it began in the 1880s, the AFL had proclaimed in the Marxist-influenced preamble of its constitution: "A struggle is going on in the nations of the civilized world between the oppressors and the oppressed of all countries, a struggle between capital and labor, which must grow in intensity from year to year and work disastrous results to the toiling millions of all nations if not combined for mutual protection and benefit."

When the CIO was launched in the 1930s, breaking away from the conservatized AFL, it had some continuity with this working-class radicalism. The AFL's George Meany later commented of the CIO's founding leader, John L. Lewis, "Frankly, I think John was dreaming of being the leader who led the working class to the control of society."

There was nothing of this in the long 1955 preamble of the merged AFL-CIO, which presented a class-collaborationist posture, with a "pure and simple" focus on wages, hours, and working conditions blended with a pledge of loyalty to the U.S. government, a dash of religion, and an almost explicit commitment to cold war anticommunism. This reflected a deradicalized convergence of the two labor federations, which were united in an embrace of the capitalist status quo, facilitating a unity that had eluded the ranks of organized labor for many years.

Earlier Appeals for Unity

There had been significant currents pressing for unity almost from the moment when the key industrial unions—

George Meany and Walter Reuther shake hands at the AFL and CIO merger convention, 1955. © UPI/Corbis-Bettmann. Reproduced by permission.

spearheaded by United Mine Workers of America leader John L. Lewis, with Sidney Hillman (Amalgamated Clothing Workers of America) and David Dubinsky (International Ladies Garment Workers Union, ILGWU)—broke with central leaders of the AFL to form the CIO. Dubinsky in particular had pressured for eventual reunification and finally pulled the ILGWU out of the CIO. He subsequently returned to the AFL but never abandoned efforts toward unity.

There were others in both federations who at various times took up that call. Even John L. Lewis, when he ceased being CIO president in 1941, eventually followed Dubinsky's trajec-

tory (though very much in his own fashion and for his own purposes), which involved working for AFL-CIO unity while in the CIO, then pulling his union out of the CIO and temporarily back into the AFL under the banner of labor unity.

Another key force for unity (again largely for his own purposes) was David J. McDonald, who in 1952 became head of the United Steelworkers of America (USWA). The USWA, with close to a million members, was rivaled in size only by the United Auto Workers, led by Walter Reuther (a McDonald rival who had become CIO president). From the beginning of his USWA reign, McDonald let it be known that he favored unity and might even lead his union out of the CIO to return to the AFL.

In the face of the powerful CIO challenge and example of organizing mass production workers into strong industrial unions, the AFL had abandoned its dogged opposition to industrial unionism, a development that suggested convergence. Both federations (largely because of the liberal-labor coalition forged during the presidency of Franklin D. Roosevelt) tended toward active support of the Democratic Party. Yet there remained a number of profound differences.

Differences Between the AFL and CIO

Although some in the AFL remained true to more expansive radical traditions, for many "pure-and-simple" unionism had evolved into an exclusive concern for the narrow economic interests of its own members, with a disregard for larger social questions. An approach sometimes called "business unionism" often predominated: not only were union leaders very probusiness (seeking far-reaching accommodations with employers), but they saw the union itself as a business providing services to its paying members. Union representatives were called "business agents," and a notion of hierarchical "business-like" efficiency replaced notions of democratic control by the membership.

Often, rather than unionizing unorganized workers, AFL union leaders sought to "raid" other (often CIO) unions, enticing locals of those unions (often with employer assistance) to switch affiliations (and dues payments). Such raiding and interunion squabbles dramatically undermined the strength and credibility of organized labor. Moreover, many AFL unions had a deeply entrenched policy of excluding nonwhite workers, although it did tolerate an occasional all-black "Jim Crow" union local. Most AFL unions also excluded women.

The CIO seemed to represent a qualitatively different model of unionism. Although CIO unions did not always live up to their reputations as champions of racial and gender equality, those reputations were based not only on official pronouncements but also on serious efforts to include African Americans and other racial minorities, and also women, in the organizations they sought to build. The CIO also had a reputation for greater union democracy and was viewed as conducting a social crusade for a better society. Len De Caux, once editor of the *CIO News*, later gave a sense of this radicalization that had been born of mass strikes, pitched battles, factory takeovers, and hard-won working-class victories during the 1930s. The momentum of such struggles generated "new political attitudes— toward the corporations, toward police and troops, toward local, state, and national government." Many felt the movement should "go on to create a new society with the workers on top to end age-old injustices . . . [and] banish poverty and war."

Essential to building the CIO unions had been members of various left-wing groups including the Communist Party, the Socialist Party, and smaller formations (especially breakaways from the Communist Party influenced in one case by the Russian revolutionary Leon Trotsky and in another case by a rightward-moving oppositionist named Jay Lovestone, who ended up following David Dubinsky back into the AFL). The CIO's radicalism clashed with the relative conservatism of the AFL. There were also more mundane—but no less powerful—

considerations about how a merger would affect existing power relations among unions in each federation. As AFL spokesman George Meany put it, "Each AFL and CIO union is autonomous, and proud, and has officials interested in keeping their jobs."

Momentum for Unity

The fact that Meany had become AFL president in 1952, with Walter Reuther assuming the presidency of the CIO in the same year, helped to open new possibilities for overcoming some of the old organizational antagonisms. No less influential was an underlying evolution of the U.S. labor movement. Both the CIO and the AFL—which were committed to the Democratic Party that had passed the National Labor Relations Act (NLRA) of 1935—had shared a growing acceptance of government intervention into labor relations. The NLRA greatly facilitated the possibility of organizing unions by involving the government in overseeing union recognition elections. In 1947 the Taft-Hartley Act amended the NLRA. Taft-Hartley was a politically restrictive, probusiness, antiradical measure, which further increased government power over organized labor. Although both federations protested vociferously against the Taft-Hartley "slave labor law," they were also prepared to live with it.

The increasingly intimate relationship of both the AFL and CIO leaderships with U.S. foreign policy also contributed to the merger. During World War II both aligned themselves with U.S. government aims in the struggle against the Axis Powers. By the end of the war this also involved, for many, a commitment to establish what some called "the American Century," which included the hegemony of U.S. business interests in the development of the postwar global economy. This collided with the rise of revolutionary sentiments and communist influence during the late 1940s.

AFL conservatives and also those with more left-wing backgrounds (such as ex-socialist Dubinsky of the ILGWU and his ex-communist collaborator, Jay Lovestone) were very much inclined to back U.S. cold war policy. Highly skilled in anticommunist infighting, Lovestone had come to accept Dubinsky's dictum that "trade unionism needs capitalism like a fish needs water." Lovestone sought to defend capitalism globally (with the blessing of AFL leaders) in cooperation with the U.S. State Department. The CIO, however, also embraced cold war anticommunism and in 1949 and 1950 expelled 11 "communist-influenced" unions with a total of a million members. Leaders and operatives of both federations became active, though often covert, participants in U.S. foreign policy activities in various countries.

A key to the deradicalization process was the unprecedented prosperity that made possible a profound improvement in the living conditions of a majority of those who were part of the U.S. working class. "I stand for the profit system; I believe in the profit system. I believe it is a wonderful incentive. I believe in the free enterprise system completely," proclaimed Meany, and such procapitalist rhetoric resonated with a majority of his members. The function of unions, he added, "is merely for us to disagree, if you please, as to what share the workers get, and what share management gets from the wealth produced by the particular enterprise."

The ex-socialist CIO president Walter Reuther was inclined to put forward a similar orientation, although he emphasized government social programs to guarantee decent health, education, and welfare for all: "There are many, many, many things that free enterprise can do better than the government . . . . I'm in favor of General Motors making automobiles. I'm opposed to government doing it, but I know General Motors is not going to meet the medical needs of the old-timers. . . . I only want the government to do the things that you can't do without the government." He added that unions represent "voluntary nongovernmental approaches" to advance the well-being of workers through "collective bargaining" with employers.

Dissension and Unification

Following its expulsion of the 11 "left-led" unions, the CIO—although it maintained the image of a dynamic, socially conscious unionism—was unable to recapture the confident and militant spirit that had characterized it in previous years. Some speculated that it would enter a period of decline and disintegration. This, with the rightward shift in the political atmosphere evidenced by the electoral victory of Republican presidential candidate Dwight D. Eisenhower, increased sentiment within the CIO for unity with the AFL. Although Reuther gave rhetorical support to labor unity, Meany took the initiative to open serious merger talks. Meany dropped the old appeal for CIO unions to "come back to the House of Labor," and instead noted that "the CIO had been in existence for seventeen years [and] was a going concern," and that it would be best to overcome the tendency of the two rival labor federations to strive destructively "for competitive advantage."

Nonetheless, serious differences between the two federations remained. "Perhaps the most graphic symbol of the gulf between the two organizations was the quarters they chose for the winter meetings of their respective Executive Councils," Victor Reuther (Walter's brother and confidant and a prominent labor activist in his own right) later reminisced. He noted that "AFL officials periodically journeyed to Florida to spend several weeks, spending a few hours a day in formal session, and then going to the races or golf course or whatever for the rest of the day." In contrast, the CIO Executive Board usually met in a hotel conference room in some northern industrial city, "never too far removed from industrial workers." He also added, however, that a number of CIO leaders "were tired of the rigors and hardships of trade union life and were tempted by the prospect of being a member of a merged AFL-CIO executive council and of basking in the Florida sun every half-year."

Reuther sought to impose certain conditions for unity that would prevent the CIO, which had no more than four million members by this time, from simply being swallowed by the larger AFL. A few CIO leaders actually opposed unity. Mike Quill of the Transit Workers Union insisted that the progressive social philosophy of the CIO was incompatible with "the AFL's three R's—raiding, racketeering, and racism." Reuther insisted that the industrial union structure of the CIO unions must be maintained, that raiding must be eliminated through creating "rational machinery" for jurisdictional disputes, and that racial discrimination and racketeering must be eliminated from the AFL unions. On Reuther's right, however, was the pressure from United Steelworkers' president David J. McDonald, who

despised Reuther's social-liberal orientation, and whose opportunistic threats to bolt to the AFL undermined Reuther's bargaining position in merger talks.

To make unity possible, however, Meany had to deal with dissension within his own ranks. The chieftain of the United Brotherhood of Carpenters and Joiners, "Big Bill" Hutcheson, had attempted to block unity efforts by resigning in protest from the AFL executive council and threatening to pull his union out of the AFL. Instead of attempting to reach a compromise with Hutcheson, Meany accepted his resignation, which forced the Carpenters to break from Hutcheson's intransigence to stay in the AFL.

No less significant was Meany's willingness to break an old AFL precedent by intervening in the internal affairs of its affiliates. He attacked the gangster-ridden regime of Joseph Ryan in the East Coast International Longshoremen's Union and headed efforts to expel it temporarily from the AFL. In addition, Meany helped to cut across longtime AFL "raiding" operations against CIO unions. He criticized racial exclusion and segregation among AFL unions and gave verbal support to civil rights throughout the country. It was also necessary, according to Meany, for the labor movement to "assume broader responsibilities" than its "traditional and continuing goal of obtaining a higher standard of life for the nation's workers and the American people generally."

With the converging positions, it was possible to hammer out such differences as the historic dividing line between craft unionism and industrial unionism: "The merged federation shall be based on a constitutional recognition that both craft and industrial unions are appropriate, equal and necessary as methods of trade union organization." Big majorities mobilized around support for the merger, which was proclaimed on 5 December 1955 at a unified AFL-CIO convention in New York City. This brought together 94 unions that claimed a total membership of 15 million or 36 percent of the labor force—the high-water mark of organized labor in the United States.

When AFL president Meany triumphantly clasped hands with broadly smiling CIO president Reuther, it was Meany who became the undisputed leader of the AFL-CIO. Many who identified with CIO traditions became dissatisfied with the relative conservatism and complacency of the merged AFL-CIO. However, when Reuther led the UAW in a 1968 breakaway to create the Alliance for Labor Action, intended to "revitalize" the labor movement, the great majority of unions remained in the AFL-CIO. Only in the late 1990s, because of the significant economic and social decline that hit the U.S. working class, did the labor federation tilt in a moderately radical direction, somewhat reminiscent of earlier labor traditions.

Key Players

Meany, George (1894–1980): Son of an Irish-American local president in the United Association of Journeymen and Apprentices of the Plumbing and Pipefitting Industry, Meany himself became a plumber in 1916 and by 1922 was business manager of what had been his father's local. He rose in the New York City Building Trades Council and became president of the New York State Federation of Labor in 1934 and became a labor lobbyist and influential in Democratic Party politics. In 1939 he became secretary-treasurer of the AFL and took over the presidency of the federation in 1952. He played a central role in the merger of the AFL-CIO and served as its president from 1955 until 1979.

Reuther, Walter (1907–1970): Son of a German-American socialist brewery worker, Reuther himself was drawn in the 1930s to radical activism and involvement in organizing the United Auto Workers, one of the most dynamic unions in the new CIO. Associated with the left wing of the fledgling and militant union in the late 1930s, he abandoned the Socialist Party to support the Democratic Party's New Deal coalition. A prominent anticommunist in the 1940s, he helped break left-wing influence in the UAW (of which he became president in 1947) and in the CIO. Reuther served as CIO president from 1952 until the merger with the AFL and remained UAW president until his untimely death.

See also: *American Federation of Labor; CIO Anticommunist Drive; Congress of Industrial Organizations; Taft-Hartley Act.*

BIBLIOGRAPHY

Books

Buhle, Paul. *Taking Care of Business: Samuel Gompers. George Meany, Lane Kirkland, and the Tragedy of American Labor.* New York: Monthly Review Press, 1999.

Dubinsky, David, and A. H. Raskin. *David Dubinsky: A Life with Labor.* New York: Simon and Schuster, 1977.

Dubofsky, Melvin, and Warren Van Tine, eds. *Labor Leaders in America.* Urbana: University of Illinois Press, 1987.

Goldberg, Arthur J. *AFL-CIO: Labor United.* New York: McGraw-Hill Co., 1956.

Goulden, Joseph C. *Meany, The Unchallenged Strong Man of American Labor.* New York: Atheneum, 1972.

Herling, John. *Right to Challenge: People and Power in the Steelworkers Union.* New York: Harper and Row, 1972.

Hinshaw, John, and Paul Le Blanc, eds. *U.S. Labor in the Twentieth Century: Studies in Working-class Struggles and Insurgency.* Amherst, NY: Humanity Books, 2000.

Le Blanc, Paul. *A Short History of the U.S. Working Class, from Colonial Times to the Twenty-First Century.* Amherst, NY: Humanity Books, 2000.

Lichtenstein, Nelson. *Walter Reuther: The Most Dangerous Man in Detroit.* Urbana: University of Illinois Press, 1995.

Madison, Charles A. *American Labor Leaders*, 2nd edition. New York: Frederick Ungar, 1962.

Morgan, Ted. *A Covert Life: Jay Lovestone, Communist, Anti-Communist, and Spymaster.* New York: Random House, 1999.

Preis, Art. *Labor's Giant Step, Twenty Years of the CIO.* New York: Pathfinder Press, 1972.

Quill, Shirley. *Mike Quill Himself, A Memoir.* Greenwich, CT: Devin-Adair, 1985.

Reuther, Victor G. *The Brothers Reuther and the Story of the CIO, A Memoir.* Boston: Houghton Mifflin Co., 1979.

Reuther, Walter P. *Selected Papers.* Edited by Henry M. Christman. New York: Macmillan, 1961.

Robinson, Archie. *George Meany and His Times, A Biography.* New York: Simon and Schuster, 1981.

Taft, Philip. *The AFL from the Death of Gompers to the Merger.* New York: Harper and Brothers, 1959.

Zieger, Robert H. *The CIO, 1935–1955.* Durham: University of North Carolina Press, 1995.

—Paul Le Blanc

AFL-CIO Expels Key Unions

United States 1957

Synopsis

The American Federation of Labor and the Congress of Industrial Organizations (AFL-CIO) unified in 1955, a time when labor leaders were determined that labor would enjoy a good reputation. There were rampant stories of thuggery, corruption, and financial misdeeds in local and national unions throughout the United States. Around that time, two key events changed how unions operated, how government affected union activity, and, ultimately, how the public perceived unions. First, the AFL-CIO altered its constitution to address ethical issues and stem corruption. Second, the federal government created its own body to investigate charges of corruption in unions. Three large unions fell into the crosshairs of both organizations: The International Brotherhood of Teamsters, Chauffeurs, Warehousemen, and Helpers of America (Teamsters); The Bakery and Confectionery Workers International Union; and Laundry Workers Union. All were expelled from the AFL-CIO in 1957.

Timeline

1937: Josef Stalin uses carefully staged show trials in Moscow to eliminate all rivals for leadership. These party purges, however, are only a small part of the death toll now being exacted in a country undergoing forced industrialization, much of it by means of slave labor.

1942: By executive order of the U.S. president, some 120,000 Japanese Americans are placed in West Coast internment camps.

1947: Great Britain's Labour government nationalizes coalmines.

1950: North Korean troops pour into South Korea, starting the Korean War. Initially the communists make impressive gains, but in September the U.S. Marines land at Inchon and liberate Seoul. China responds by sending in its troops.

1954: The French military outpost at Dien Bien Phu falls to the communist Vietminh. France withdraws after decades of trying to suppress revolt; meanwhile, the United States pledges its support for the noncommunist government in the South.

1957: High schools in Little Rock, Arkansas, are integrated with the aid of federal troops.

1957: Soviets launch *Sputnik,* the world's first artificial satellite. This spawns a space race between the two superpowers.

1957: European Economic Community is formed.

1960: When an American U-2 spy plane piloted by Francis Gary Powers is shot down over Soviet skies, an end comes to a short period of warming relations between the two superpowers. By the end of the year, Soviet leader Khrushchev makes a scene at the United Nations, banging his shoe on a desk. As for Powers, he will be freed in a 1962 prisoner exchange.

1962: As the Soviets begin a missile buildup in Cuba, for a few tense days in October it appears that World War III is imminent. U.S. president Kennedy calls for a Cuban blockade, forcing the Soviets to back down and ultimately diffusing the crisis.

1965: In the Soviet Union, the reformer Khrushchev is ousted in favor of the hard-liner Leonid Brezhnev.

1970: Nixon sends U.S. troops into Cambodia on 30 April. Four days later, National Guardsmen open fire on antiwar protesters at Kent State University in Ohio. By 24 June antiwar sentiment is so strong that the Senate repeals the Gulf of Tonkin resolution. On 29 June, Nixon orders troops back out of Cambodia.

Event and Its Context

Corruption in Labor Unions

Labor corruption was not new in the 1950s, when the ethics of unions came into question. "As early as the 1920s, for example, government reports documented a widespread pattern of corruption and racketeering among construction trade unions in New York City," wrote Carl F. Horowitz. He observed that the building trades were traditionally most prone to corrupt practices. During the 1950s union corruption became overt, particularly in the Teamsters. "They all came together in the 1950s: the Teamsters, the mob, the politicians, Las Vegas, the greed," observed author Allen Friedman. "Everyone was a user. Everyone had a scam. And the only ones who would eventually prove to be the losers were the rank and file, though not in the way most people imagined."

With the merger of the American Federation of Labor and the Congress of Industrial Organizations in 1955, labor leaders were determined to make a favorable impression as "good partners in the American economy." George Meany was president of the AFL-CIO. The union constitution allowed any affiliate union to be suspended by a two-thirds vote. The AFL-CIO Executive Council created its Ethical Practices Committee in 1956 to provide further guidelines for union officials and to prevent corruption. One of the six guidelines prohibited union leaders from pleading the Fifth Amendment while testifying before public bodies investigating racketeering. Those who took the Fifth were barred from office. "The adoption of the codes represented a departure in the practices of the general labor movement," wrote Philip Taft. "Heretofore, the affiliated national and international unions jealously guarded their autonomy and would not permit the federation to place any limitation upon their freedom." He noted that the creation of these ethics codes, although seen as necessary, was ultimately ineffective.

The United States Senate laid the foundation for the unions' expulsion with its probe into union activities beginning in January 1957. Senator Joseph McCarthy, best known for his probes of communism in the United States, proposed the creation of a select committee to investigate labor racketeering. Union members viewed the Select Committee on Improper Activities in the Labor or Management Field as not entirely dissimilar from the McCarthy-led House Un-American Activities Committee. Senator John McClellan, an Arkansas Democrat, served as the head of this committee. McCarthy was scheduled to serve on this committee as well, but he died soon after his appointment.

This committee, commonly known as the McClellan committee, opened hearings with the intent of examining charges against union officials. These included dipping into union coffers for personal gain and accepting bribes from employers. Among the notable senators on the committee were Sam Ervin, Barry Goldwater, and John F. Kennedy. Counsel for the committee was Robert F. Kennedy. These hearings were televised live until their conclusion. Since these crimes were typically perpetrated against the rank and file, union members originally supported the hearings, thinking that the government would protect them and their unions. The AFL-CIO, however, took senators to task for using committee proceedings as a means "to harass clean and honest unions and to aid anti-labor employers."

The International Brotherhood of Teamsters, Chauffeurs, Warehousemen, and Helpers of America, more popularly known as the Teamsters, was created in 1903 when the Team Drivers International Union and the Teamsters National Union banded together. The majority of its members were truck drivers. Daniel J. Tobin, a Boston Teamster, was president from 1907 until 1952. The Teamsters attracted the most attention during the hearings. Starting on 26 March 1957, the union's president, Dave Beck, appeared before the committee to answer questions about the misappropriation of union funds. He took the Fifth Amendment throughout his appearance before the committee—purportedly a staggering 117 times in a single session. Beck maintained that he had taken an interest-free loan from the union. Other questions arose regarding the sale of his Seattle home to the union, in which Beck was permitted to live rent-free. Jimmy Hoffa, who was union vice president, also testified. His first appearance before the committee was on 20 August 1957. At the September Teamsters convention, and in the wake of his congressional committee appearance, Beck announced that he would not run for reelection. Hoffa succeeded him as president.

At the conclusion of 270 days of hearings, there were more than 50 volumes of testimony and numerous supplementary reports. The Bakery and Confectionery Workers International Union, among the oldest of the unions, had its own problems. The union's president, James G. Cross, and vice president robbed a local that had been placed under trusteeship. They were also given frequent kickbacks. "The debauching of one of the finer labor organizations is a sordid episode in American labor history," proclaimed Taft.

AFL-CIO Takes Anticorruption Stand

When the AFL-CIO convened in late 1957, one of the first orders of business was to hear from James P. Mitchell, United States labor secretary. He presented the proposed 1958 federal labor legislation, much of it designed to deter corruption, such as making it a felony to accept a union-related bribe. The presidents of the 135 member unions were skeptical but voted unanimously to endorse the legislation in order to protect member unions and their membership. The union leadership noted that they would forcefully contest any legislation that was disguised as protective but would weaken the unions and protections for their members.

The most notable action at this meeting was taken against unions tainted by corruption. The Teamsters, the Bakery and Confectionery Workers International Union, and the Laundry Workers Union were all expelled from the AFL-CIO on 12 December 1957. With this, the AFL-CIO lost about 1.6 million members. The Teamsters alone had an estimated 1.4 million members; the Bakery union, 140,000; and the Laundry Workers, 70,000. It was estimated that the expulsion would cost the AFL-CIO $1 million in lost dues. Meany said in 1957 that the unification of the two unions enabled them to purge the corrupt unions. "AFL-CIO still will be plenty strong. And we can go ahead with organizing the millions of workers still outside unions." In place of the expelled bakers' union, the AFL-CIO chartered a new union that same day. The American Bakery and Confectionery Workers International Union was established with only 95 of the 298 old locals and 50,000 members. Daniel E. Conway was appointed as its president.

These were not the only unions being scrutinized, however. The International Longshoremen's Association was expelled. The United Textile Workers Union had been suspended, but the AFL-CIO lifted its suspension at this same convention after the leadership agreed to clean up its operations. The Distillery Workers were still under a probationary watch, but they later agreed to accept a monitor, as did the Allied Industrial Workers. The president of the Waste Materials Handlers Union was expelled on misconduct charges. The McClellan committee continued to investigate other unions, including the Carpenters, Sheet Metal Workers, and Hod Carriers.

In the wake of government exploration of union activities, legislation was passed to prevent further abuses and corruption. Key among these was the Landrum-Griffin Act, which passed by a vote of 95–2 in the Senate, and 352–52 in the House; it was enacted in April 1959. This strengthened the Taft-Hartley Act and included provisions unfavorable to labor, such as restrictions on picketing and government supervision over the election of union officers. Despite the investigations and expulsion, Hoffa's power catapulted him to mythical proportions. He was often taken to task for his associations with organized crime and reportedly invested union pension funds in businesses with ties to organized crime. Hoffa was later arrested on charges of bribery (involving of one of the McClellan committee attorneys) and obstruction.

"By 1958, the corruption in the Teamsters Union was so obvious," writes Friedman, "that the general public was equally

Dave Beck. © Corbis. Reproduced by permission.

divided in their attitude toward the organization. Those who were not eligible to join primarily saw the union as little more than an organized crime group. Those who were eligible often were thrilled by the tough guy image." This image persisted well past Hoffa's tenure. Despite Meany's pledge to police union corruption, the last recorded meeting of the AFL-CIO Ethical Practices Committee was sometime in December 1959.

Robert F. Kennedy, writing in *The Enemy Within* (his perspective of the committee findings), concluded that union corruption was the exception rather than the rule. "With few exceptions, the men who run our great labor unions in this country are honest, dedicated men."

Key Players

Beck, Dave (1894–1993): Beck was a Teamster throughout his life and is credited both with building the union and for introducing corruption into it. He joined the union in Seattle as a teenaged laundry truck driver. He ascended through the ranks and was elected national president in 1952. He was later AFL-CIO vice president. With the Code of Ethical Practices enacted, the union expelled him in May 1957. He was later convicted of misusing union funds and federal tax evasion. He has the distinction of being the first of five Teamsters presidents to have had severe legal problems. He was one of three who served prison time; a fourth was indicted. Beck was later pardoned, both by the state governor and by President Gerald R. Ford.

Robert Francis Kennedy. National Archives and Records Administration.

Byers, Sam: The president of the Laundry Workers International Union at the time of its expulsion from the AFL-CIO, Byers was reportedly a convicted murderer who had been charged with embezzlement of union funds. He resigned.

Cross, James G.: Cross was head of the Bakery and Confectionery Workers of America at the time of its expulsion from the AFL-CIO. One of the charges against Cross was for doctoring expense accounts, including charging the union for the rental of a hotel room where union executives could play poker.

Hoffa, James Riddle (1913–?): Born in Brazil, Indiana, Hoffa started his union career as a warehouseman in 1932. He was a leader within the Teamsters, first as international vice president. He succeeded Dave Beck as president in 1957. Although he inherited many of Beck's problems, Hoffa created many of his own legal problems for impropriety during his tenure as head of the union. He was the second Teamster head to serve a prison term. Ironically, in 1958 *Newsweek* posed the question "What would make Hoffa vanish?" He disappeared in 1975 and is assumed to have been murdered.

Kennedy, Robert Francis (1925–1968): Chief counsel and staff director for the Senate subcommittee on investigations, Kennedy started his legal career in the Criminal Division of the U.S. Department of Justice. Kennedy was appointed chief counsel to the Senate Select Committee on Improper Activities in the Labor or Management Field (McClellan committee) in 1957. He is best known in this regard for his investigation of the International Brother-

hood of Teamsters, but he also conducted other investigations of labor and management abuses.

McClellan, John Little (1896–1977): Democratic senator from Arkansas, McClellan served as the head of the Senate Select Committee on Improper Activities in the Labor or Management Field. These investigations led to the imprisonment of both Dave Beck and Jimmy Hoffa of the Teamsters Union. He served 35 years as a U.S. senator.

Meany, George (1894–1980): Born in New York City, Meany began his union career as an apprentice plumber in his teens. He was a leader in the New York State Federation of Labor and American Federation of labor. When the AFL merged with the Congress of Industrial Organizations in 1955, he was the first AFL-CIO president. From the start of his union presidency, Meany shouldered the responsibility for rooting out union corruption. He held the post until his retirement in 1979.

See also: *AFL, CIO Merge; International Brotherhood of Teamsters; Landrum-Griffin Act; Taft-Hartley Act.*

BIBLIOGRAPHY

Books

Friedman, Allen, and Ted Schwarz. *Power and Greed: Inside the Teamsters Empire of Corruption.* New York: Watts, 1989.

Murray, R. Emmett. *The Lexicon of Labor.* New York: New Press, 1998.

Sloane, Arthur A. *Hoffa.* Cambridge, MA: MIT Press, 1991.

Taft, Philip. *Organized Labor in American History.* New York: Harper, 1964.

Tompkins, Vincent. *American Decades: 1950–1959.* Detroit: Gale Research, 2001.

Periodicals

Belzer, Michael H., and Richard Hurd. "Government Oversight, Union Democracy, and Labor Racketeering: Lessons from the Teamsters Experience." *Journal of Labor Research* 20, no. 3 (15 July 1999): 343–365.

Hill, Herbert. "Mob Rule: Thieves in the House of Labor." *The Nation,* 27 June 1981.

ADDITIONAL RESOURCES

Dobbs, Farrell. "Threat to the Independence of the Unions," *The Labor Standard.* 1967 (cited 23 January 2003). <http://www.laborstandard.org/Teamsters/Dobbs.htm>.

Horowitz, Carl F. "Union Corruption: Why It Happens, How to Combat It." The National Institute for Labor Relations Research. 1999 (cited 23 January 2003). <http://www.nilrr.org/corruption.htm>.

Rieder, Ross. "Beck, Dave (1894–1993)." HistoryLink. 14 February 2001 (cited 23 January 2003). <http://www.historylink.org/output.CFM?file_ID=2972>.

—Linda Dailey Paulson

Effigy of Dave Beck burns in front of Local 524 Teamsters Building, 1957. AP/Wide World Photos. Reproduced by permission.

AFSCME Strike

United States 1975

Synopsis

In July 1975 some 55,000 members of Council 13 of the American Federation of State, County, and Municipal Employees (AFSCME) walked out on strike against the state of Pennsylvania. The strike lasted four days before the union and the state returned to the bargaining table. The union won a wage increase of 12 percent over three years for state workers. The strike was the first full-blown strike by a union against a state government and exemplified AFSCME's increased militancy after the 1960s.

Timeline

1955: African and Asian nations meet at the Bandung Conference in Indonesia, inaugurating the "non-aligned" movement of Third World countries.

1965: Power failure paralyzes New York City and much of the northeastern United States on 9 November.

1969: Assisted by pilot Michael Collins, astronauts Neil Armstrong and Edwin E. "Buzz" Aldrin become the first men to walk on the Moon (20 July).

1972: On 5 September, Palestinian terrorists kill eleven Israeli athletes and one West German policeman at the Olympic Village in Munich.

1975: Pol Pot's Khmer Rouge launch a campaign of genocide in Cambodia unparalleled in human history. By the time it ends, with the Vietnamese invasion in 1979, they will have slaughtered some 40 percent of the country's population. Cambodia is not the only country to fall to Communist forces this year: the pro-Western governments of South Vietnam and Laos also succumb, while Angola and Mozambique, recently liberated from centuries of Portuguese colonialism, align themselves with the Soviet Bloc.

1975: U.S. *Apollo* and Soviet *Soyuz* spacecraft link up in space.

1975: Two assassination attempts occur on President Ford in September.

1978: Terrorists kidnap and kill former Italian premier Aldo Moro. In Germany, after a failed hijacking on behalf of the Red Army Faction (RAF, better known as the Baader-Meinhof Gang), imprisoned RAF members commit suicide.

1980: In protest of the Soviet invasion of Afghanistan, President Carter keeps U.S. athletes out of the Moscow Olympics.

1985: In a year of notable hijackings by Muslim and Arab terrorists, Shi'ites take a TWA airliner in June, Palestinians hijack the Italian cruise ship *Achille Lauro* in October, and fundamentalists take control of an Egyptian plane in Athens in November.

1995: Bombing of the Alfred P. Murrah Federal Building in Oklahoma City, Oklahoma, kills 168 people. Authorities arrest Timothy McVeigh and Terry Nichols.

Event and Its Context

The Formation of AFSCME

The roots of the American Federation of State, County, and Municipal Employees (AFSCME) extend back to 1932, when a group of white-collar state employees in Wisconsin formed the Wisconsin State Administrative, Clerical, Fiscal, and Technical Employees Association, soon renamed the Wisconsin State Employees Association. This group turned to the American Federation of Labor (AFL) for help in defeating a bill in the state legislature that would have dismantled Wisconsin's competitive civil service system. Soon, similar unions formed in other states, and together they formed a national affiliate union, AFSCME, in 1935. In 1936 AFSCME was granted a separate AFL charter and became a fully independent union under the leadership of Arnold Zander.

Growth of the organization was slow at first. By the end of 1936 AFSCME had about 10,000 members. Ten years later membership was up to about 73,000. After World War II many public employees, like their counterparts in private industry, pressed for higher wages to recoup on some of the sacrifices that they had made during the war years. The climate for organized labor was not favorable, however, for the public had grown increasingly impatient with the large number of postwar strikes in the steel, meatpacking, and other industries. Through the early 1950s AFSCME chapters in many locations were, in the words of one observer, "harassed, coerced, dismissed—or entirely ignored." Nevertheless, AFSCME continued to grow—to 100,000 in 1955, 250,000 in 1965, and 680,000 in 1975. At the beginning of the twenty-first century, the union had 1.3 million members.

A New Militancy

In its early years AFSCME was in no sense a militant union. When Zander assumed the presidency, only 11 states had genuine civil service merit systems rather than political patronage or "spoils" systems. Zander saw the union's role primarily as one of expanding the civil service and strengthening existing state laws governing civil service systems. Although the union never formally renounced the right to strike, it regarded striking as counterproductive and focused its attention on public issues as well as civil service reform.

By the mid-1950s, though, many AFSCME members, particularly those from big cities with a history and tradition of trade unionism, began to agitate for collective bargaining to improve their economic position. In the years that followed they made significant gains. In 1958, under pressure from AFSCME, New York City mayor Robert Wagner issued an executive order recognizing the right of city workers to bargain collectively. President John F. Kennedy's 1961 executive order recognizing the right of federal workers to bargain collectively created a climate much more favorable for AFSCME. Then, at the 1964 AFSCME convention, the union turned to more aggressive leadership. Jerry Wurf, then the director of District Council 37 in New York, was elected president on a platform that promised more energetic organization drives and pursuit of collective bargaining rights. Under Wurf's leadership, AFSCME also became connected with the civil rights movement; it was in Memphis, Tennessee, in 1968 to support an African American sanitation workers' organizational drive when Martin Luther King Jr. was assassinated there. Shortly thereafter Memphis agreed to recognize the workers' union, AFSCME Local 1733.

A Right to Strike

Restrictions on the right of municipal workers to strike date back to the years after the Boston Police Strike of 1919, when many cities, including Philadelphia, passed antistrike ordinances. After World War II nine states, including Pennsylvania, passed antistrike laws similar to the Taft-Hartley Act's prohibition of federal strikes. By 1983, 39 states had outlawed public employee strikes by statute or court opinion. However, some states, beginning with Vermont in 1968 and Pennsylvania in 1970, passed more permissive laws that allowed public-employee strikes under some circumstances. Still, at the beginning of the twenty-first century the majority of collective bargaining agreements contained no-strike clauses, typically because public-sector workers provide vital services that their private-sector counterparts do not.

Despite these restrictions, state and municipal employees struck with some regularity, often paying court-ordered fines for their trouble. According to the Bureau of Labor Statistics, throughout the 1960s there were 85 state work stoppages involving a total of almost 41,000 employees and 1,097 municipal work stoppages involving 657,000 employees. Throughout the 1970s these numbers increased: a total of 288,000 state employees took part in 352 strikes and 1.65 million municipal employees took part in 3,866 strikes. These strikes, though, were generally staged by small, local unions against narrow sectors of the affected states and municipalities.

AFSCME Council 13

One of these strikes, however, was more far-reaching in its effects. It took place in 1975 in Pennsylvania when Council 13, the statewide local of AFSCME, which was organized in 1973 and was at that time the nation's largest state employee union with 70,000 members, became the first public union to walk out en masse against a state government.

The events that led to the AFSCME strike in July 1975 began earlier in the year when Governor Milton Shapp submitted his budget to the state legislature. Claiming tight fiscal conditions, Shapp offered state employees a 3.5 percent salary increase at the expiration of their contract the following year. Given the inflation of the early 1970s, this increase was wholly inadequate for Council 13 executive director Gerald W. McEntee, who believed that Governor Shapp was trying to break the union and who pressed for a double-digit percentage increase. In response to unofficial talk about a possible strike, Shapp directed the preparation of requests for preliminary injunctions for delivery to the courts should a strike materialize.

While negotiations remained at an impasse, the union virtually shut down the state government on 9 June. Planned for that day was a union protest at the state capitol building in Harris-

burg. Union leaders urged members to stay away from work in a show of solidarity. The union demonstrated its clout when 25,000 protesters jammed the steps of the capitol building and flowed into the streets. Newspaper columns about the protest expressed bewilderment, citing gains state employees had made in recent years.

Both sides remained adamant, and at 12:01 A.M. on Tuesday, 1 July, AFSCME Council 13 went out on strike. Though no precise figures are available, it is estimated that at least 55,000 employees, possibly as many as 60,000 including nonunion employees, walked off their jobs.

The Shapp administration sprang into action and was in court before most Pennsylvanians had had their morning coffee. State troopers, armed both with riot gear and an injunction against the strike, actually beat union members to a picketing site on Tuesday morning. The court had already issued an injunction ordering essential state employees—prison guards, security guards for prisoners at mental hospitals, and others—back to work. Also that day, state troopers made 17 arrests on such charges as obstructing highways or state buildings and disorderly conduct, all seemingly for the delight of press photographers. On Wednesday the court limited the number of picketers at the entrances to the capitol complex to 15 and ordered all prison employees and nurses at state hospitals back to work. By the time the strike ended on 4 July, the courts had ordered 28,000 state employees back to work. In all, the Shapp administration requested 11 injunctions and won 10; the 11th was still under consideration when McEntee accepted the administration's promise to bargain in good faith and the strike ended.

Public Response and Outcomes

Council 13 received very little support for the strike. The state legislature remained virtually silent. Governor Shapp won the public relations battle by convincing the public that acceding to the union's wage demands would result in higher taxes and by charging that union members were guilty of vandalism.

Most disappointing to Council 13 was the lukewarm support of private-sector unions. Earlier in the year, several hundred Council 13 delegates had walked out during the Shapp's speech at the Pennsylvania AFL-CIO convention to protest the governor's public discussion of ongoing bargaining talks with AFSCME. AFL-CIO officials, political supporters of Shapp, took offense at the council's actions and, instead of backing the strikers, urged the state labor relations board to invoke the fact-finding provisions of Act 195. AFL-CIO President Harry Boyer offered this tepid comment: "We are in support of the members on strike to receive a decent settlement. It would be decidedly imprudent for me to suggest that either side is right. If the employees feel the need to strike, that is a right they may exercise."

After returning to the bargaining table, Governor Shapp's negotiators offered a 9 percent wage increase over two years. The union responded with a counteroffer calling for a $1,500 across-the-board increase during the second year of the new contract, but later lowered this figure to $1,000. The state accepted, and in the final agreement the parties agreed on an immediate 3.5 percent increase, then increases averaging 2.5 percent beginning 1 January 1976, and 6 percent beginning 1 July 1976.

In response to the strike, Shapp appointed a legislative commission to study the effects of collective bargaining on the state's economy. After 18 months of study, 13 days of public hearings, and 100 witnesses, the commission issued a report that had little impact. It did, however, support antilabor forces in the state legislature in their opposition to the union's claim that it had a right to receive compensation from "employees who, for whatever reason, elect not to support the union through the payment of union dues" but who benefit from gains for which the union fought and paid.

Key Players

McEntee, Gerald (1935–): McEntee was born in Philadelphia and began his labor career as an AFSCME organizer there. He was elected executive director of Council 13 when it was founded in 1973 and international vice president of AFSCME in 1974. He was elected president in 1981 and continued to hold that post in 2002.

Shapp, Milton (1912–1994): Shapp was born Milton Shapiro in Cleveland, Ohio. After serving in the army, he founded a highly successful electronics company and gained a reputation as a hard-headed businessman. As an insurgent Democrat, he was elected governor of Pennsylvania and served from 1971 until 1979.

Wurf, Jerome (1919–1981): Wurf was born in New York City and as a young man was active in the Young People's Socialist League. While working for the Hotel and Restaurant Employees Union in New York in 1947, AFSCME president Arnold Zander hired Wurf as an organizer for the New York district. He rose through the ranks of AFSCME until he was elected president in 1964, a post he held until his death.

Zander, Arnold (1901–1975): Born in Two Rivers, Wisconsin, Zander began his career as a civil engineer with an interest in city planning. His first involvement with labor was as an examiner for the Wisconsin Civil Service Department. In 1934 he became secretary of the Wisconsin State Employees Association and was elected president of AFSCME in 1936.

See also: *Boston Police Strike; Taft-Hartley Act.*

BIBLIOGRAPHY

Books

Bent, Alan Edward, and T. Zane Reeves. *Collective Bargaining in the Public Sector: Labor-Management Relations and Public Policy*. Menlo Park, CA: Benjamin/ Cummings Publishing Company, 1978.

Brutto, Carmen. *The History of Council 13, AFSCME*. Harrisburg, PA: Council 13, AFSCME, 1998.

Kearney, Richard C. *Labor Relations in the Public Sector*. New York: Marcel Dekker, 1984.

Levitan, Sar A., and Alexandra B. Noden. *Working for the Sovereign: Employee Relations in the Federal Government*. Baltimore, MD: Johns Hopkins University Press, 1983.

Other

AFSCME, American Federation of State, County, and Municipal Employees AFL-CIO Home Page. "About AFSCME" [cited 24 October 2002]. <www.afscme.org>.

Jerry and Mildred Keifer Wurf Collection, 1936–1982 [cited 24 October 2002]. <www.reuther.wayne.edu/collections/ hefa_1132.htm>

—Michael J. O'Neal

Age Discrimination in Employment Act

United States 1967

Synopsis

The civil rights movement of the 1960s brought about numerous social changes that transformed America. Government officials began to address the important issue of discrimination in the workplace, focusing their attention on race and gender. During this time, however, two other social groups also gained attention—the middle-aged and elderly. Until that time, age discrimination had never been considered a serious issue. Advances in medical technology had begun to extend the average life expectancy and as a result caused a dramatic shift in America's demographics. With more elderly remaining in the workforce, cases of age discrimination were also on the rise. Indeed, positive policies such as the Social Security Act had inadvertently affected the elderly in a negative way, making it disadvantageous to remain in the workforce. Also, middle-aged employees found themselves losing out to their younger coworkers. Although some states already had laws to prevent age discrimination, no federal law existed. Congress began to discuss the issue in depth and in 1967 passed the Age Discrimination in Employment Act (ADEA). Under the new legislation, the employment rights of Americans 40 years of age and older were officially protected, preventing employers from discriminating against them solely on the basis of their age. ADEA would undergo the amendment process in 1974, further strengthening the rights of the middle-aged and elderly.

Timeline

1947: Great Britain's Labour government nationalizes coal mines.

1952: Among the cultural landmarks of the year are the film *High Noon* and the book *The Invisible Man* by Ralph Ellison.

1957: High schools in Little Rock, Arkansas, are integrated with the aid of federal troops.

1962: As the Soviets begin a missile buildup in Cuba, for a few tense days in October it appears that World War III is imminent. President Kennedy calls for a Cuban blockade, forcing the Soviets to back down and ultimately diffusing the crisis.

1967: Biafra secedes from Nigeria.

1967: Arabs attack Israel, launching the Six-Day War, which results in an Israeli victory. Israel now occupies a number of formerly Arab-held territories, most notably the Old City of Jerusalem. In the years that follow, the Israelis will be forced to give up much of the territory, which stretches to the borders of Egypt. Their continued possession of the Jordan River's West Bank will provide a cause for enduring controversy with their Arab neighbors and with the newly mobilized Palestinian minority.

1967: Racial violence sweeps America's cities, as Harlem, Detroit, Birmingham, and other towns erupt with riots.

1967: The Beatles' *Sgt. Pepper's Lonely Hearts Club Band* tops the list of releases for a year that will long be remembered as a high point of rock history. Among the other great musical events of the year are releases by the Jimi Hendrix Experience, the Doors, and Jefferson Airplane; also, the Monterey Pop Festival marks the debut of Hendrix and Janis Joplin.

1967: Assisted by a team of surgeons, South Africa's Christiaan Barnard performs what is considered the world's first successful human heart transplant, though the patient dies 18 days later.

1972: In June police apprehend five men attempting to burglarize Democratic Party headquarters at the Watergate Hotel in Washington, D.C.

1977: Newly inaugurated U.S. President Jimmy Carter pardons Vietnam draft dodgers.

1982: Israeli troops invade Lebanon in an attack on the Palestine Liberation Organization (PLO).

Event and Its Context

The Roots of Discrimination

Until the twentieth century, the aged received little or no attention in government. They were involved in few political groups or movements and held little lobbying power. Much of this had to do with their small numbers. Because of advances in medicine, however, the life expectancy for Americans climbed dramatically. In turn, so too did the population of people aged 60 and older. Suddenly, the "gray lobby" had grown into a force with the size and power needed to pressure politicians for change. One key issue that the gray lobby wanted to address was employment, specifically retirement.

Before the middle of the nineteenth century, the concept of "retirement" was virtually unheard of. Approximately 70 percent of men aged 65 and over remained in the workforce in 1890. The effect of inflation and the high cost of living prevented early retirement. Over the next 100 years, the percentage of elderly in the workforce would drop significantly, but only because of policy changes. Many of these governmental changes began during the Great Depression.

President Lyndon Baines Johnson. The Library of Congress.

Around 1933, Dr. Francis Townsend began the "Townsend movement" to promote a pension plan for Americans aged 60 and older. Under Townsend's plan, every worker would received $200 per month during retirement. Many in government, however, believed the plan would be unworkable. So, despite its popularity with many senior citizens, Townsend's movement died out. On 14 August 1935, however, President Franklin D. Roosevelt signed the Social Security Act into law as part of the New Deal. This act provided an old-age pension for all retirees aged 65 or older.

Although the benefits of an old-age pension were obvious, the Social Security Act also had an underlying negative effect. Although the act did not force the elderly into retirement by "law," the benefits were reduced for those who opted to continue working after age 65. The loss involved one month's pension for each month of continued employment. This restriction inadvertently strengthened the growing trend of age discrimination. Because of the scarcity of jobs at the time, many wanted the elderly to retire and thus make way for younger workers. Those elderly who wished to continue working not only lost pension benefits as a result of their choice but also faced a hostile job market. They discovered that there were few, if any, laws to protect them against age discrimination.

Like their older peers, middle-aged employees also found themselves the frequent victims of age discrimination. Promotions and advancement opportunities typically went to the younger employees. Because these middle-aged employees were closer to "retirement" age, employers were unwilling to invest in these employees by hiring or training them. In the politically turbulent days of the civil rights movement, the rights of this population were commonly forgotten in favor of a focus on matters of race and gender discrimination. Fortunately, the

Math teacher, Salina, Kansas. AP/Wide World Photos. Reproduced by permission.

middle-aged employees' connection to the growing gray lobby meant they did not go completely ignored. Both age groups would eventually see changes in the law to help them overcome the hurdle of age discrimination.

The Civil Rights Movement: Birth of the ADEA

Although the problem of age discrimination existed in the United States workforce, little was done to address the issue until the late 1960s. One major step, however, involved tackling the problems caused by pension penalties. A 1950 amendment to the Social Security Act allowed people 75 years of age and older to work without loss of their benefits. Another amendment in 1954 lowered the age exemption to 72. Although the amendment protected elderly workers who wished to return to the workplace, it in no way protected their employment rights or guaranteed that they would be able to find work. Age discrimination remained virtually unchecked. According to a study cited in Lawrence Friedman's book *Your Time Will Come: The Law of Age Discrimination and Mandatory Retirement*, of "21,386 job openings listed with state employment offices in 7 cities (1956)—more than half of the jobs were closed to people over a certain age."

As the civil rights movement strengthened during the 1950s and 1960s, the concept of fair employment gained the attention of lawmakers. States began to develop laws that prevented un-

fair hiring practices on the basis of race, gender, and religion. In some states, the laws were extended to consider age discrimination as well. In 1956 new statues eliminated the maximum hiring age for federal employees. Several political changes also contributed to an improved picture regarding employment issues of the aged. These included the Manpower Development and Training Act (1962), the Economic Opportunity Act (1964), and President Lyndon Johnson's executive order of 1964, which prevented age discrimination among federal contractors and subcontractors. However, federal legislation that directly affected age discrimination remained elusive despite the matter being featured in the Civil Rights Act debates of 1964. This was undoubtedly because of Congress's fear that any effort to address anything more than racial discrimination under the Civil Rights Act would cause the legislation to fail. Even so, over the next decade, age discrimination continued to be debated.

Between 1955 and 1965, 21 states plus Puerto Rico and the Virgin Islands passed laws that specifically addressed workplace discrimination on the basis of a person's age. However, in its report *The Older American Worker*, the United States Department of Labor explained that "inadequate funds and staff have limited the effectiveness of these laws in most states. Some have not been implemented at all." This report was a direct result of the Civil Rights Act of 1964, after Congress re-

Oil rig worker, Texas. Getty Images. Reproduced by permission.

quested a labor study on age discrimination. The secretary of labor authorized and then distributed the report to Congress in 1965. The study revealed the increasing prevalence of employees 45 and older in the workforce and projected that this population would soon constitute more than a third of employees. Apprised of the sheer number of workers who would be vulnerable to age discrimination, the United States government gained a renewed interest in creating federal legislation to deal with this problem.

That legislation would come on 23 January 1967, in the form of the Age Discrimination in Employment Act (ADEA). Designed to protect the rights of employees aged 40 and older, ADEA prohibited employers from discriminating against employees on the basis of age in hiring, dismissal, status, compensation, terms, and privileges. The law was interpreted as also applying to the management of employment agencies and labor unions. Some limitations were set on the ADEA: only employees of companies with 25 or more workers in industries that affected commerce were protected under the law. In addition, employees 65 years or older were not covered by the ADEA, which strengthened the retirement age set by the Social Security Act.

The ADEA After 1967

ADEA evolved through several changes after President Johnson signed it into law. Two important amendments came in the 1970s. In 1974 an amendment lowered the company size minimum requirement of 25 employees to 20, and in 1978 another raised the age ceiling from 65 to 70. The 1974 amendment also extended the ADEA to protect local, federal, and state government employees, who were not covered previously. Almost as an afterthought, Congress passed the Age Discrimination Act (ADA) of 1975. This law covered age discrimination for both older and younger workers. However, the ADA was vague as a whole and lacked the teeth of the ADEA.

Key Players

Johnson, Lyndon Baines (1908–1973): U.S. president (1963–1969), Johnson did a great deal for the elderly during his term in the White House, including supporting the ADEA and the Older Americans Act (OAA) of 1965 and issuing an executive order that restricted age discrimination by federal contractors and subcontractors.

Roosevelt, Franklin D. (1882–1945): U.S. president (1933–1945), Roosevelt signed the Social Security Act into law in 1935. The act provided elderly retirees with old-age pensions.

Townsend, Francis E. (1876–1948): Townsend developed the "Townsend plan," which was in many ways the first version of the pension plan. Although his movement failed, it opened the debate about the elderly in the workforce.

See also: *Civil Rights Act of 1964; Social Security Act.*

BIBLIOGRAPHY

Books

Axel, Helen. *Employing Older Americans: Opportunities and Constraints.* New York: The Conference Board, Inc., 1988.

Daniel, Clifton, ed. *Chronicle of the 20th Century.* Mount Kisco, NY: Chronicle Publications, 1987.

Friedman, Lawrence M. *Your Time Will Come: The Law of Age Discrimination and Mandatory Retirement.* New York: Russell Sage Foundation, 1984.

Kendig, William L. *Age Discrimination in Employment.* New York: American Management Associations, 1978.

United States Department of Labor. *The Older American Worker: Age Discrimination in Employment.* Washington: U.S. Government Printing Office, 1965.

Other

United States General Accounting Office. GAO/HRD-90-87BR. *Age Discrimination: Use of Age-specific Provisions in Company Exit Incentive Programs.* February, 1990.

ADDITIONAL RESOURCES

Edelman, Charles D., and Ilene C. Siegler. *Federal Age Discrimination in Employment Law: Slowing Down the Gold Watch.* Charlottesville, VA: The Michie Company, 1978.

—Lee Ann Paradise

Agriculture Workers Strike

Italy 1908

Synopsis

In the early twentieth century, revolutionary syndicalists in the Italian province of Parma established a strong base among dissatisfied agricultural day laborers. After taking control of the chamber of labor in Parma, they succeeded in making the labor movement there more radical and confrontational. In 1907 a successful strike brought a number of gains to the workers. Building on this success, the revolutionary syndicalists launched a major strike in May and June 1908. Neither the workers nor the owners were willing to compromise. In the end, the financial strength and unity of the landowners was too much for the workers and the strike was defeated. In the aftermath of the failed strike, the labor movement in the region lost much of its strength and radical nature.

Timeline

1889: Flooding in Johnstown, Pennsylvania, kills thousands.

1893: Wall Street stock prices plummet on 5 May, precipitating a market collapse on 27 June. In the wake of this debacle, some 600 banks and 15,000 other businesses fail. The nationwide depression will last for four more years.

1898: Bayer introduces a cough suppressant, derived from opium. Its brand name: Heroin.

1902: The *Times Literary Supplement,* a weekly review of literature and scholarship, begins publication in London.

1905: Russian Revolution of 1905 occurs. Following the "bloody Sunday" riots before the Winter Palace in St. Petersburg in January, revolution spreads throughout Russia, in some places spurred on by newly formed workers' councils, or soviets. Among the most memorable incidents of the revolt is the mutiny aboard the battleship *Potemkin.* Suppressed by the czar, the revolution brings an end to liberal reforms, and thus sets the stage for the larger revolution of 1917.

1909: Robert E. Peary and Matthew Henson reach the North Pole.

1909: National Association for the Advancement of Colored People (NAACP) is founded by W. E. B. Du Bois and a number of other prominent black and white intellectuals in New York City.

1909: William Cadbury's *Labour in Portuguese West Africa* draws attention to conditions of slavery in São Tomé and Principe.

1911: Revolution in Mexico, begun the year before, continues with the replacement of the corrupt Porfirio Diaz, president since 1877, by Francisco Madero.

1915: A German submarine sinks the *Lusitania,* killing 1,195, including 128 U.S. citizens. Theretofore, many Americans had been sympathetic toward Germany, but the incident begins to turn the tide of U.S. sentiment toward the Allies.

1919: With the formation of the Third International (Comintern), the Bolshevik government of Russia establishes its control over communist movements worldwide.

Event and Its Context

Revolutionary Syndacalism in Parma

In the years before World War I, there was a struggle within the Italian labor movement between reformist socialists and revolutionary syndicalists. The socialists, who had more widespread support throughout the country, advocated cooperation and compromise with management and the government. They also had the support of the Socialist Party in the Italian parliament. By 1905 the revolutionary syndicalists offered an alternative to the socialists. In contrast to the reformists, the revolutionary syndicalists favored direct action by labor unions. In particular, they advocated the use of the strike.

The revolutionary syndicalists had a stronghold in the province of Parma, where they controlled the chamber of labor. Parma was still largely an agricultural area. In 1901, 67 percent of the population still worked in agriculture, growing wheat, corn, grapes, and tomatoes, and raising cattle and hogs. Whereas the southern hills were dominated by small proprietors, ten-

ant farmers, and sharecroppers, the plains of the province contained large, modern farms worked by both salaried workers and day laborers. By the early twentieth century, many changes had taken place in the province. Agriculture had become more modern with the use of machines and scientific methods. Also, many smaller plots had been consolidated into larger estates, resulting in fewer landowners. At the same time, there were an increasing number of day laborers who would be at the forefront of the labor movement. These changes also resulted in chronic unemployment and high inflation.

This situation led to a change in the leadership of the chamber of labor. More moderate elements gave way to the revolutionary syndicalists. In February 1907 Alceste De Ambris, himself a revolutionary syndicalist, became the secretary of the chamber. Then in March a congress of agricultural workers met and approved a program of minimum wages and maximum hours. They also recommended establishing employment offices to aid workers in finding jobs. The landowners responded with resistance. Furthermore, the owners also began to expand the Parmesean Agrarian Association (AAP), which was designed to protect the interests of the owners.

The 1907 Strike

On 15 May 1907 day laborers and salaried workers went on strike. Workers won this strike when stable hands abandoned some 60,000 head of cattle. On 21 May the two sides signed a three-year contract that generally satisfied the workers' demand for wage increases and limited the number of work hours. In reaction, the owners limited the employment of day laborers, reducing work to a minimum and using more machines. The AAP became stronger and more combative. For their part, the workers also claimed victory in 33 additional minor agitations in 1907. Furthermore, membership in the chamber of labor more than doubled from 13,446 in January 1907 to 28,719 in January 1908.

The 1908 Strike

Agricultural workers in Parma went on strike again in 1908. The immediate cause was a disagreement over certain clauses in the 1907 contract. In August 1907 the AAP had offered to submit the dispute to arbitration. However, the chamber of labor refused, since the revolutionary syndicalists preferred direct action, especially in light of the 1907 labor victory.

At the same time, the owners were looking to crush the unions. To this end they established the Inter-Provincial Federation of Landowners for Parma and other provinces in December 1907. The goal of the organization was to defend the interests of the landowners without the aid of the government. They collected insurance against boycotts and strikes. In general, they planned to defeat revolutionary syndicalism. In addition, owners in Parma formed groups of "free workers" to use as possible strikebreakers. Finally, the owners purchased more machinery to reduce their dependence on day laborers.

The conflict came to a head in February 1908, when a dispute between the owners and the workers prompted the AAP to order a lockout of all day laborers and to employ "free workers" as strikebreakers. In response, the workers began to prepare for a general strike to take place during the May and June harvest. Such a general strike would be difficult to carry out, as the owners were united and had the financial means to combat the strike. In addition, the labor movement was still split between the reformist socialists and the revolutionary syndicalists.

The general strike began on 1 May 1908 and included some 20,000 workers. In the short term, the workers demanded that the owners respect the 1907 contract and also requested small wage increases. Furthermore, they sought to discredit the AAP and strengthen their own union movement. The workers associated with the reformist socialists did not participate directly in the strike, although they did oppose the use of strikebreakers. Nevertheless, their failure to join the work stoppage demonstrates the serious split in the Parma labor movement.

In response to the general strike, the government announced that it would defend the right to work and would attempt to prevent any acts of violence. Authorities also informed the two sides in the dispute that they would maintain a stance of neutrality. To this end, the government brought in army units to maintain order and banned public meetings.

Conflicts soon arose as a result of the strike. Strikers made efforts to prevent the arrival of strikebreakers. They also attempted to stop the landowners from sending their cattle out of the strike zone. If the owners succeeded in removing the cattle, the position of the workers would be greatly weakened. Later, the strikers decided simply to allow the cattle to leave, instead concentrating on a complete stoppage of all work activities. There were also clashes between the police and the owners' "volunteer workers." A substantial number of women also participated in the strike-related activities. For example, many women who sided with the strikers slept along roads so as to keep watch. Some of these women even would lie on the road to prevent the passage of cattle and cavalry.

When no settlement seemed to be in sight, the revolutionary syndicalists sought to extend the strike beyond Parma to other provinces and the entire Po Valley. However, support outside of Parma was weak, and several attempts to spread the agitation failed. Having failed to accomplish this goal, the strikers then attempted to include sharecroppers and socialist workers who had not initially participated in the strike. Once again they failed.

In early June government officials encouraged both sides to accept negotiation. The strikers agreed to talks if they were based on their original demands. The owners also reluctantly agreed to the talks. However, the two sides were far apart and any compromise seemed unlikely. The mayor of Parma attempted to prepare a compromise solution on some issues such as wages and hours and suggested arbitration on other issues. In response, De Ambris recommended that the workers reject this offer. The workers did offer to reopen talks if the owners came up with a more conciliatory proposal. Initially, Lino Carrara, the general council for the AAP, accepted the idea with reservations. Yet once again, the two sides were unable to agree. By 12 June the mayor announced that he would no longer attempt to reconvene the workers and owners. These failed negotiations in early June are indicative of the fact that the struggle had gone beyond a mere economic dispute and had developed into a political problem, with neither side willing to back down and be perceived as the loser in the strike.

On 18 June rumors spread that a trainload of strikebreakers was on the way and would arrive the following morning. The strike leaders encouraged the workers to prevent the arrival of the strikebreakers. On 19 June the train did in fact arrive with about 380 strikebreakers under heavy police escort. In addition, government authorities attempted to clear the square in front of the train station using cavalry troops. Once again, women played a key role, placing themselves on the ground. Soon a violent clash broke out. Government troops pushed the strikers off of the square, but rioting then erupted in the center of the city that lasted most of the day. That night, several thousand workers met and voted to call a general strike for the entire province.

On 20 June conflicts between workers and troops continued. Workers crossed the bridge that connected the working-class district of Oltretorrente with the city center. Their goal was to close any shops that had remained open despite the call for a general strike. Troops pushed the workers back across the bridge into the working-class district, where residents on rooftops threw rocks at them. The troops then went to the headquarters of the chamber of labor, where they broke down the door and arrested numerous workers on the strike committee.

The next day, the violence continued. At this point, the workers seemed to have two options. One was to negotiate with the owners to bring an end to the conflict; the other was to call for a national general strike. The revolutionary syndicalists preferred the latter option. However, they still had little support beyond Parma. In the meantime, the reformist socialists negotiated with the authorities to secure the return of the chamber of labor headquarters, and the strike committee ordered the strikers back to work. When the workers attempted to return to the job on 22 June, the owners declared a five-day lockout. Conceding that they had lost, the workers did not resist. They then returned to work under the terms of the 1907 contract.

As a result of the strike, the revolutionary syndicalists lost much of the support that they had gained in Parma. Leading up to the strike, they had been able to build upon their successes of 1907. After, in light of the failed 1908 strike, many workers grew resentful and suspicious of the labor movement. The membership of the chamber of labor fell dramatically. In January 1908 there had been nearly 29,000 members. By January 1909 there were just over 7,000 members remaining, a clear indication that the strength of the radical labor movement in Parma had greatly decreased.

Key Players

De Ambris, Alceste (1874–1934): De Ambris was a well-known Italian revolutionary syndicalist. In 1907 he became the leader of the chamber of labor in Parma and was influential in radicalizing the labor movement in that province. De Ambris and the chamber played a leading role in the great agricultural strike of 1908. When the strike failed, De Ambris went into exile for a time. He later served as the general secretary of the national Italian Syndicalist Union.

See also: *Red Week, Italy.*

BIBLIOGRAPHY

Books

Horowitz, Daniel. *The Italian Labor Movement.* Cambridge, MA: Harvard University Press, 1963.

Van der Linden, Marcel, and Wayne Thorpe, eds. *Revolutionary Syndicalism: An International Perspective.* Hants, England: Scolar Press, 1990.

Periodicals

Sykes, Thomas. "Revolutionary Syndicalism in the Italian Labor Movement: The Agrarian Strikes of 1907–08 in the Province of Parma." *International Review of Social History* 21, no. 2 (1976): 186–211.

—Ronald Young

Alien Contract Labor Act: *See* **Foran Act.**

Alliance for Labor Action

United States 1969

Synopsis

In late 1968 the International Union, United Automobile, Aerospace and Agricultural Implement Workers of America (UAW), under the leadership of Walter P. Reuther, officially disaffiliated with the American Federation of Labor and Congress of Industrial Organizations (AFL-CIO). The UAW's split with the AFL-CIO developed over several years, during which time a widening rift divided Reuther from George Meany, the AFL-CIO's long-standing president. Political differences and personal rivalries caused the division. Politically, Reuther differed from Meany in his activist vision for the labor federation. Personally, Reuther expected to be the next president of the AFL-CIO, but Meany refused to give up the reins of power despite his advancing age. Reuther criticized what he felt was the AFL-CIO's complacency in domestic politics and acceptance of United States' foreign policy. Early in 1969 the UAW created a pact with the International Brotherhood of Teamsters, Chauffeurs, Warehousemen and Helpers of America to form the Alliance for Labor Action (ALA). The ALA's mission was to gain the support of unorganized workers, students, and liberal intellectuals. Reuther hoped that the ALA would address the issues that—in his opinion—the AFL-CIO did not pursue. The UAW's alliance with the Teamsters, however, was short lived; the ALA ended in 1972.

Timeline

1948: Israel becomes a nation and is immediately attacked by a coalition of Arab countries.

1953: Korean War, a conflict with no clear victors, ends with an armistice establishing an uneasy peace between South Korea and North Korea.

Frank E. Fitzsimmons. © Hulton/Getty Images. Reproduced by permission.

1958: China's Mao Zedong proclaims the Great Leap Forward, a program of enforced rapid industrialization that will end a year later, a miserable failure.

1963: U.S. Supreme Court rules that no municipal, county, or state government may require recitation of the Lord's Prayer or of Bible verses in public schools.

1968: Communist victories in the Tet offensive mark the turning point in the Vietnam War and influence a growing lack of confidence in the war, not only among America's youth, but within the establishment as well.

1968: Dr. Martin Luther King, Jr. is assassinated on 4 April, and Robert Kennedy on 5 June.

1968: Violence erupts at the Democratic National Convention in Chicago.

1968: After Czechoslovakia adopts a more democratic, popular regime, Soviet and Warsaw Pact forces invade to crush the uprising.

1973: Signing of peace accords in Paris in January ends the Vietnam War.

1978: U.S. Senate approves a measure presented by President Carter the year before, to turn the Panama Canal over to Panama by 2000.

1983: Sally Ride becomes the first female U.S. astronaut (the Soviets were ahead by two decades, with Valentina Tereshkova) when she goes into space aboard the shuttle *Challenger.*

Event and Its Context

One of the unions in the Congress of Industrial Organization (CIO), the United Auto Workers (UAW) joined with the

George Meany. The Library of Congress.

American Federation of Labor (AFL) when the two labor federations merged in 1955. UAW president Walter Reuther, who had become the president of the CIO after the death of its president in 1952, served as a facilitator for the merger. Because the AFL was twice the size of the CIO, it was clear that George Meany, president of the AFL, and not Reuther would become president. From the time of the AFL-CIO merger, Reuther and Meany differed politically. Meany backed away from broaching political class struggle, and Reuther believed in activist unions. Their political disagreements, compounded by differences in personal style, eventually led to the UAW's 1968 departure from the AFL-CIO and the formation of the Alliance for Labor Action (ALA).

Tensions over political action began as early as 1964 when the UAW, along with others such as Martin Luther King, Jr., and the Farmers Union, created the Citizens' Crusade Against Poverty. Meant as a supplement to President Lyndon B. Johnson's War on Poverty, the Citizens' Crusade was organized by those leaders, as well as Reuther, who saw the War on Poverty as too modest. Reuther testified at the congressional hearings on the creation of the Office of Equal Opportunity, claiming that Johnson's antipoverty program was inadequate and that more resources were necessary to accomplish its goals. He also met personally with Johnson in an effort to lobby for a Price-Wage Public Review Board and a progressive spending tax. The AFL-CIO's executive council disagreed publicly with Reuther's plan. UAW leadership retaliated by criticizing the AFL-CIO for being inactive politically and socially.

Reuther and the other leaders of the UAW laid out their case against Meany's leadership in a long statement to UAW locals in December 1966 (reprinted in the February 1967 edition of the UAW's newsletter, *Solidarity*.) They cited fundamental trade union differences, such as the need to increase unionization among the unorganized industrial, construction, office, technical, and professional workers. They also laid out

new policy positions and structural reforms for the AFL-CIO, such as the need to develop a national economic wage policy and the need to commit more of the federation's staff resources to working for America's farm and migratory workers. In this letter, the UAW's leaders attacked Meany, claiming that under his leadership, "the AFL-CIO lacks a social vision, dynamic thrust, the crusading spirit that should characterize the progressive, modern labor movement."

Reuther's and other UAW leaders' stances on foreign policy issues also divided them from AFL-CIO leaders. The UAW refused to toe the cold war consensus line on international labor and the Vietnam War. At the 1965 AFL-CIO convention, UAW secretary-treasurer Emil Mazey attacked Johnson's policies in Vietnam, and Reuther's brother Victor accused the AFL-CIO of working along with the CIA in Latin America. In 1966 Reuther opposed Meany's decision to withdraw the American representative to the International Labor Organization, a United Nations agency, after its members elected president a Polish Communist. Unlike Meany, Reuther promoted relations with those in the Eastern Bloc countries. He felt the withdrawal isolated the American labor movement from other "Free World" countries because no other delegations participated in the walkout. Furthermore, Reuther called Meany's actions "undemocratic" because Meany did not consult AFL-CIO affiliates.

Although Reuther had at first supported the Johnson administration's policy in Vietnam, by 1966 he favored greater efforts toward negotiations and a bombing halt. The domestic consequences of the war, the opposition movement, as well as left-wing activists in his union led Reuther into the antiwar camp. The UAW held educational seminars to debate resolutions protesting the continuation of the war. According to Reuther's brother Victor, "Disagreement on the Vietnam War was the final blow in the wedge splitting the UAW and the merged AFL-CIO."

In February 1967 the UAW's executive board voted to withdraw its officers from the AFL-CIO executive council and related committees and institutes. Shortly after the resignations, the UAW presented a program to be considered by the entire American labor movement. It included proposals for internal reform, as well as stressing labor's responsibility within the community for rebuilding inner cities, protecting natural resources, and reducing pollution. In the spring of 1968 the UAW stopped paying the per capita tax on its membership owed to the federation. For this refusal of payment, the AFL-CIO executive council suspended the UAW from the federation. The UAW put the funds in escrow and called for the AFL-CIO to allow for a debate at its December convention to help reexamine the federation's policies and programs. The object of the debate was to determine whether the federation met its responsibilities to "the changing needs of the labor movement and the nation." The UAW sought reform within the AFL-CIO rather than officially departing from the federation, in an effort to avoid a division in the labor movement as the presidential election approached. These attempts at reform were ineffective. Once the election was over, the UAW disaffiliated with the federation.

In July 1968 Reuther and the Teamsters general vice president, Frank Fitzsimmons, announced a pact between the two unions that established the ALA. The ALA was not devised as

Walter Philip Reuther. © Hulton/Getty Images. Reproduced by permission.

a rival federation to the AFL-CIO; rather, the teamsters and the UAW established the organization as a means to coordinate organizing campaigns and political activities. Nevertheless, despite what the ALA claimed, Meany identified it as a dual union and threatened to expel AFL-CIO affiliates that joined it. Under this threat, only two other small organizations enlisted in the ALA.

Even without other major supporters, the ALA had major numbers behind it because the teamsters and the UAW were the two largest unions in North America. Between them they represented almost four million workers and their families. Because of its large membership and its geographic concentration in

such states as Michigan, Ohio, and Indiana, the UAW's departure from the AFL-CIO directly affected the participation level in many city and state councils.

The ALA outlined a far-reaching program designed to deal with what they viewed to be the nation's most critical problems, ranging from union organizing to health care to affordable housing. The ALA committed itself to working with any group willing to help organize the nonunionized workers and to strengthening collective bargaining by embracing the concept of coordinated bargaining. It also took active political stances on international policy issues. For example, the ALA urged the U.S. Senate to vote against the deployment of the antiballistic missile system.

In 1970 the ALA suffered a serious blow to its leadership when Walter Reuther was killed in a plane crash. His absence left a leadership vacuum in the ALA. Although the alliance had always been cochaired by a person from both unions, it had been under the direction of Reuther that the alliance was able to hold together the liberal, idealistic UAW and the corrupt, conservative Teamsters Union. With Reuther's death, the more moderate Leonard Woodcock became president of the UAW, and the more conservative Fitzsimmons took control of the ALA. The alliance was no longer viable. The ALA soon collapsed in January 1972 as a result of economic problems as well as the Teamsters' actions toward the farm workers union in California and endorsement of President Richard Nixon for re-election.

The UAW remained independent of the AFL-CIO for 14 years. The UAW's withdrawal from the AFL-CIO showed the fractures in the Democratic Party's liberal coalition. The departure broke the united front of labor's support for the Vietnam War and its abundant military expenditures. It also ruptured labor's support for the Democratic Party. The ALA, although ultimately a failure, provided an example of activism and served as a critique of mainstream unions and politics.

Key Players

Fitzsimmons, Frank E. (1908–1981): General vice president of the Teamsters, Fitzsimmons managed the union when its president, Jimmy Hoffa, was jailed. In 1969, at Hoffa's behest, Fitzsimmons joined the Teamsters with the United Auto Workers (UAW) to create the Alliance for Labor Action (ALA). Following Hoffa's release from prison in 1971, Fitzsimmons became president of the Teamster Union. His support of Nixon and his union's strikes against the United Farm Workers led to the termination of the ALA.

Meany, George (1894–1980): President of the AFL, Meany oversaw its merger with the CIO in 1955. During Meany's presidency, the AFL-CIO became the most important supporter of the Democratic Party. Conservative in his values and politics, Meany sustained criticism for, among other things, his support of the war in Vietnam and his ambiguous attitude toward women and minorities. Personal and political differences between him and Reuther led to the UAW's withdrawal from the AFL-CIO and the formation of the ALA. Meany remained the president of the AFL-CIO from 1955 until November 1979, when he stepped down at the age of 85. He died within two months after leaving office.

Reuther, Walter Philip (1907–1970): President of the UAW and former president of the CIO, Reuther served as a facilitator for the AFL-CIO merger. His activist vision of unionism brought him into conflict with the more passive style of AFL-CIO president George Meany. Reuther led the UAW out of the labor federation and into the ALA with the teamsters. In 1970 Reuther died in a plane crash. Shortly thereafter the ALA collapsed.

See also: *AFL, CIO Merge.*

BIBLIOGRAPHY

Books

Amberg, Stephen. *The Union Inspiration in American Politics: The Autoworkers and the Making of a Liberal Industrial Order*. Philadelphia: Temple University Press, 1994.

Barnard, John. *Walter Reuther and the Rise of the Auto Workers*. Boston: Little, Brown and Company, 1983.

Comier, Frank and William Eaton. *Reuther*. Englewood Cliffs, NJ: Prentice-Hall, 1970.

Dubofsky, Melvyn, and Warren Van Tine, eds. *Labor Leaders in America*. Urbana: University of Illinois Press, 1987.

Halpern, Martin. *UAW Politics in the Cold War Era*. Albany: State University of New York Press, 1988.

Lichtenstein, Nelson. *The Most Dangerous Man in Detroit: Walter Reuther and the Fate of American Labor*. New York: Basic Books, 1995.

Reuther, Victor G. *The Brothers Reuther and the Story of the UAW*. Boston: Houghton Mifflin Company, 1976.

—Emily Straus

All-India Trade Union Congress

India 1920

Synopsis

The All-India Trade Union Congress (AITUC) was formed in 1920 by leaders of the Indian National Congress and others to provide representation for India at the League of Nations' International Labor Organization (ILO). Although the AITUC was created initially for this specific purpose, it also was a consequence of a growing Indian labor movement. In the late nineteenth century, many Indian workers in various sectors of the economy had begun to organize and protest, in large part in response to the conditions imposed by the British colonial rulers. The Indian labor movement continued to expand in the early twentieth century. As was the case in many parts of the world, there was a particularly dramatic wave of working-class activity in the years immediately following World War I. Between 1917 and 1920, when the AITUC was formed, Indians began to form their first truly modern trade unions. A number of significant strikes accompanied this flurry of organizational activity. It was in this context that the AITUC was formed.

Throughout the 1920s British communists gained a great deal of control over the AITUC, although some opposing factions broke away. By World War II the communists had gained complete control of the federation. They lost some backing when they decided to support the war effort on the side of the British once the Soviet Union entered the war on the Allied side. This caused a split of the AITUC between reformist and revolutionary factions.

Timeline

1906: British Labour Party is founded.

1911: Revolution in Mexico, begun the year before, continues with the replacement of the corrupt Porfirio Diaz, president since 1877, by Francisco Madero.

1916: Battles of Verdun and the Somme are waged on the Western Front. The latter sees the first use of tanks, by the British.

1918: The Second Battle of the Marne in July and August is the last major conflict on the Western Front. In November, Kaiser Wilhelm II abdicates, bringing an end to the war.

1921: As the Allied Reparations Commission calls for payments of 132 billion gold marks, inflation in Germany begins to climb.

1921: Canadian scientists Frederick Banting and Charles Herbert Best isolate insulin, an advance that will alter the lives of diabetics and greatly reduce the number of deaths associated with the disease.

1921: Washington Disarmament Conference limits the tonnage of world navies.

1921: In a controversial U.S. case, Italian-born anarchists Nicola Sacco and Bartolomeo Vanzetti are tried and convicted of armed robbery and murder. Despite numerous protests from around the world, they will be executed six years later.

1924: V. I. Lenin dies, and thus begins a struggle for succession from which Stalin will emerge five years later as the undisputed leader of the Communist Party, and of the Soviet Union.

1928: Penicillin is discovered by Alexander Fleming.

1931: Financial crisis widens in the United States and Europe, which reel from bank failures and climbing unemployment levels. In London, armies of the unemployed riot.

1936: Germany reoccupies the Rhineland, while Italy annexes Ethiopia. Recognizing a commonality of aims, the two totalitarian powers sign the Rome-Berlin Axis Pact. (Japan will join them in 1940.)

Event and Its Context

Early Worker Organization in the Nineteenth Century

The origins of the labor movement in India can be traced back to the second half of the nineteenth century as the British more firmly established their rule and brought changes to the traditional economy. The British emphasized the growing of cash crops for export, which contributed to the growth in the number of poor, landless peasants. In addition, cheap British imports hurt Indian artisans. Further changes included the introduction of a money economy, the construction of railroads, and the expansion of mining. In response, Indians often protested or revolted against the British presence. The biggest and most well-known revolt came in 1857. There were also peasant insurrections in Bengal in 1873. Two years later in 1875, the Deccan Riots were directed at mass evictions and moneylenders.

As many peasants moved to the cities to work in cotton textile mills and others toiled on plantations producing cash crops, the first signs of labor unrest appeared. Long hours, low wages, and poor working conditions sometimes led Indian workers to protest. As early as 1862, railroad workers went on strike. Between 1882 and 1890 there were 25 strikes in India. Early organizational efforts in this period included *jamats*, which were based on caste.

Labor organization continued in the 1880s and 1890s. In 1884 N. H. Lokhande called a meeting of mill workers in Bombay. These workers presented a memorandum to the Factory Commission in hopes of limiting working hours, getting guarantees of days off and rest periods, and implementing regulations regarding child and female labor. In 1889 the workers made similar demands to the governor general in Bombay. Finally, the mill workers repeated their demands again at a mass meeting in Bombay in 1890 that was attended by some 10,000 workers. They then formed the Bombay Millhands Association with Lokhande as president. The association, however, had a very precarious existence and seemed to exist mostly on paper.

Throughout the 1890s, workers in the jute, maritime, printing, and railroad industries all attempted to organize in places such as Bengal, Calcutta, and Goa. At this early stage, however, these groups played more of a social role than carrying out the activities of true trade unions. Also, during the 1890s there were protests against the use of indentured Indian workers laboring in other British colonies such as South Africa.

Increased Worker Organization and Activity in the Twentieth Century

There were more strikes in the first decade of the twentieth century in the railroad and other industries. In 1908 there was a six-day mass strike in Bombay that resulted in street fighting between the workers and authorities. In 1910 philanthropists in Bombay formed a workers' welfare association to help settle disputes between the workers and management and to petition government. In general, however, before World War I, the only true trade unions that appeared in India were among certain upper-level railroad employees and among government employees.

The government passed some labor legislation in the years before the outbreak of World War I, mostly affecting the cotton textile industry. However, this legislation was not in response to worker agitation but rather was a result of pressure from cotton interests in England who felt that a cheap labor supply gave Indian cotton producers an unfair advantage. This pressure from England provided a certain degree of protection for Indian industrial workers. The first Factory Act, passed in 1881, dealt exclusively with child labor. A second Factory Act became law in 1891 under increasing pressure. It was broader than the first act but did not affect all industries. This second act was based on the findings of an 1890 factory commission that found that adult workers generally worked between 11.5 and 12.5 hours per day. Finally, a third Factory Act became effective in 1911, which for the first time fixed the workday for adult males at a maximum of 12 hours and also dealt with some health and safety issues.

As World War I drew to an end, economic and political conditions contributed to the rise of trade unions in India. As prices more than doubled, real wages decreased. In some cases there was even looting because of the poor economic situation. In addition, a famine in 1918–1919 made the situation even worse. At the same time nationalism was on the rise. Many Asians had already become increasingly nationalistic after the 1905 Russo-Japanese War, which showed that an Asian country could defeat a European power. Anti-British feelings were also growing in response to the repressive Rowlatt Acts, which extended wartime emergency measures. Then, in April 1919, British troops killed some 400 Indians at the Jallianwala Bagh massacre, further fueling anti-British sentiments.

Under such conditions, there was a wave of strikes after the war, as was the case in many countries throughout the world. In 1918 the first great strike of cotton mill workers took place in Bombay. By January 1919 more than 100,000 workers were on strike. The strikes continued into 1920, with more than 200 strikes in the first half of the year involving more than one million laborers, many seeking a reduction to a 10-hour workday.

In addition to numerous strikes, workers also began to form more unions. In 1917 weavers in Ahmedabad organized. A plague epidemic had hit the city in 1916 and many workers left. In response, some mill owners offered higher wages to keep workers in Ahmedabad. At the same time, some workers had demanded an additional plague allowance to stay on the job. The employers refused to pay both the plague allowance and the higher wages at the same time, which prompted a workers' strike in December 1917 that lasted 20 days and resulted in a 20 percent raise for the workers. After the plague threat subsided in 1918, the employers attempted to reduce wages, and the workers demanded a 50 percent wage increase. This situation led the employers to lock out the workers in February 1918. Eventually, the two sides agreed to arbitration, which resulted in a 35 percent increase in wages. The aftermath of the Ahmedabad dispute was the formation of the city-wide Ahmedabad Textile Labor Association, one of India's most significant early labor organizations.

Also in 1918, workers in Madras formed the Madras Labor Union. B. P. Wadia and Tiru Vika formed this early union in response to a lockout at the British-owned Buckingham and Carnatic Textile Mills. Others in Madras soon followed suit, including railroad, streetcar, electrical, and other textile workers. In addition, after a strike in 1921 at the Buckingham and Carnatic mills, a number of worker newspapers began to appear, including the English-language *Swanharma*. The Indian Seamen's Union also formed in 1918, and more workers organized in 1919 and 1920. However, at this point, most the unions were in reality strike committees that lived very short lives

In response to union organizing, some employers attempted to prevent the unionization of Indian workers. For example, in 1921 Buckingham and Carnatic Mills filed a suit against the Madras Labor Union for damages suffered due to a strike. The Madras High Court declared that unions were an "illegal conspiracy."

The Creation of the All-India Trade Union Congress

Before 1920 there was no national federation to coordinate union activity in India. This lack of a national organization caused a problem when the International Labor Organization (ILO) had its first conference in 1919. The government of India selected N. M Joshi as a representative without consulting the unions. In response, many unions protested. Joshi in return proposed the creation of an All-India Trade Union Congress to solve the dispute.

At a meeting in early July 1920, labor leaders decided that the Congress should meet in Bombay. They demanded that the government withdraw its nomination of Joshi and that the Congress elect the representative to the ILO. Also in July, workers created a reception committee of 500 members headed by Joseph Baptista, president of the Home Rule League. The reception committee originally scheduled the Congress for August 1920, although they later postponed it until October.

The first session convened on 31 October 1920 with Lala Lajpat Rai as chairman. One hundred and one delegates attended the meeting, as did a number of political leaders and a fraternal delegate from the British Trades Union Congress. The delegates elected Rai as the Congress' new president and as India's representative at the next ILO meeting in Geneva. Upon being elected and participating in a procession of 10,000 people, Rai stated that the goals of the Congress should be to organize, agitate, and educate.

The delegates discussed several resolutions. These included a demand for protection from police interference, the maintenance of an unemployment register, restriction on exporting foodstuffs, compensation for injuries, and health insurance. In addition, the delegates demanded that Indian workers be given some representation in the government, just as employers had representatives on legislative councils. Finally, the Congress delegates urged the government to intervene so as to bring about the end of strikes taking place in Bombay among the streetcar, postal, telegraph, and gas workers of the city. The request reflects the reformist sentiments of the early leaders of the AITUC, who preferred a government settlement to continued worker agitation. Indeed, the early AITUC was not run by workers themselves, but rather by members of the Indian National Congress, some social reformers, and even some employers, giving the federation a limited working-class consciousness. The government, however, declined to interfere, allowing the workers and employers to settle the dispute.

Overall, 64 unions in India were affiliated with the AITUC. The unions had a total membership of more than 140,000. In addition, another 43 unions expressed solidarity and promised future affiliation.

One of the AITUC's main goals once the first meeting was completed was to write a constitution. N. M. Joshi and others began to prepare such a document. In April 1921 they sent off a draft of the constitution to the affiliated unions for comment. The AITUC executive committee approved the new constitution in July. At this point the objective of the AITUC was to coordinate India's labor union in all trades in all provinces so as to promote the social, political, and economic interests of the workers. Yet in reality, the federation had no clear program or principles at this early stage. Rather, its main concern was to act as a nominating body for the ILO, a function that the government of India accepted as belonging to the newly created AITUC. Because Rai was unable to attend the meeting, the AITUC elected Joshi to represent India at the ILO's next meeting.

On 30 November 1921 a second meeting of the AITUC convened at Jharia, the center of the British-dominated coal industry. There was some resistance among the employers, who asked the government to send in a show of force and used hired thugs to intimidate the workers. Nevertheless, the meeting did take place, and the AITUC reported that some 50,000 people attended.

The AITUC Splits Along Ideological Lines

After less than a decade of existence, the AITUC began to splinter along ideological lines. In particular, the split divided the left-leaning, communist-inspired unions and the more conservative, reformist groups. AITUC had been created originally by moderates associated with the Indian National Congress. They did not preach class struggle but rather sought nonviolent, legal means to aid Indian workers. Early AITUC leaders preferred negotiation to strikes. Indeed, most of the original leaders were not workers themselves. Throughout the 1920s, however, communists increasingly gained in importance within the AITUC. Their ideology was, of course, class-based, and they preferred a militant struggle against capitalism and imperialism.

The two factions were able to cooperate to a certain extent until 1928, when the split became more significant. Several issues contributed to the increased division of the AITUC. To some degree, the split was simply a personal struggle for power as individual leaders sought to control the organization. In addition, certain specific issues were a cause of dissension. The two sides differed, for example, over AITUC affiliation with a world labor organization, resulting in a debate in 1928 over the matter. The reformers preferred to belong to the International Federation of Trade Unions (IFTU), whereas the communists argued for membership in the Red International of Labor Unions. Another issue was the 1928 Nehru Report, which was a proposal for a constitution that would give India dominion status and internal self-government. The communists argued that India should fight for complete independence.

By 1928, with the struggle becoming even more personal between some of the key leaders, the communists had become much stronger, both within the AITUC itself and within some of the affiliated unions. For example, they controlled the Great Indian Peninsular (GIP) Railwaymen's Union, with some 45,000 members. In addition, they had played a key role in a number of strikes in that year, increasing their presence in the labor movement. The communists had become particularly powerful in industrial centers such as Bombay. Their influence in the Girni Kamger Union of Bombay especially worried the reformers. The union claimed to have more than 50,000 members, and the communists wanted to admit the union into the AITUC. A union with such a large membership would give the communists an additional 240 delegates to the AITUC and allow them to dominate the federation's decision-making process.

When the AITUC did indeed admit the Girni Kamger Union, the communists came to control the organization. They were able to push through a number of more radical resolutions that the reformers opposed. For example, the AITUC ended its affiliation with the ILO, which the communists considered simply to be a tool of capitalists and imperialists. They did, however, continue the affiliation with the ILO against imperialism. In reaction to these and other decisions, in 1929 some 30 unions withdrew from AITUC and formed their own group known as the All-India Trade Union Federation.

Key Players

Baptista, Joseph: President of the Home Rule League in India, Baptista was influential in the formation of the All-India Trade Union Congress (AITUC). He served as the chairman of the original reception committee that planned the first meeting of the congress.

Joshi, N. M.: One of the key leaders of the AITUC, Joshi had been selected by the government of India as its representative to the ILO. However, the leaders of India's incipient labor movement protested because they had not been consulted. This dispute led to the formation of the AITUC in 1920. Joshi played a significant role in organizing the congress and held important leadership roles until the congress split along ideological lines in the late 1920s.

Rai, Lala Lajpat (1865–1928): Known as the "Lion of the Punjab," Rai was the first president of the AITUC. A lawyer and leading nationalist, Rai was a member of the Indian National Congress. During the 1910s Rai traveled extensively, including trips to the United States, England, and Japan. Upon his return in 1920, he was shocked by the British repression that he witnessed. It was at this point that Rai, a critic of imperialism, joined the AITUC and served as its president. Rai died in 1928, 18 days after being severely beaten by a British officer during a demonstration.

See also: *International Federation of Trade Unions; International Labor Organization; Red International of Labor Unions.*

BIBLIOGRAPHY

Books

Bhargava, P. P. *Trade Union Dynamism.* Jaipur, India: Printwell, 1995.

Goswami, Dharani. *Trade Union Movement in India: Its Growth and Development.* New Delhi, India: People's Publishing House, 1983.

Gupta, Prem Sagar. *A Short History of All-India Trade Union Congress, 1920–1947.* New Delhi, India: AITUC Publication, 1980.

Mehta, B. L. *Trade Union Movement in India.* Delhi, India: Kanishka Publishing House, 1991.

Raman Rao, A. V. *Indian Trade Unions.* Honolulu: University of Hawaii Industrial Relations Center, 1967.

—Ronald Young

Amalgamated Society of Engineers

Great Britain 1851

Synopsis

The formation of the Amalgamated Society of Engineers (ASE) in 1851 was soon seen as a major event in British and world trade union history. Trade unions were in their infancy, but now previously competing unions of skilled workers had united to form a new and larger organization. The ASE became effective, despite the fact that, initially, many potential members had doubts and employers attempted to break it through a lockout. The ASE was one of an influential group of skilled workers' unions that were central to the labor movement between the decline of Chartist political radicalism in the late 1840s and the rise of socialism and the new unionism of the 1880s. It concentrated on developing an effective industrial and political strategy, and its leaders set new standards of administration. The union soon became a symbol of mid-Victorian unionism and controlled its members' terms and conditions of labor until challenged at the end of the nineteenth century. The ASE exported its model by forming numerous foreign branches in North America and the British Empire as its members traveled the world.

Timeline

1831: Unsuccessful Polish revolt against Russian rule is waged.

1837: British inventor Isaac Pitman devises his shorthand system.

1842: Scientific and technological advances include the development of ether and artificial fertilizer; the identification of the Doppler effect (by Austrian physicist Christian Johann Doppler); the foundation of biochemistry as a discipline; and the coining of the word *dinosaur*.

1847: Patenting of the first successful rotary press replaces the old flatbed press, in the United States.

1848: Scottish mathematician and physicist William Thomson, Lord Kelvin, introduces the concept of absolute zero, or the temperature at which molecular motion ceases. This value, -273°C, becomes 0K on his Kelvin scale of absolute temperature.

1852: Immigration from Ireland to the United States reaches its peak.

1852: France's Second Republic ends when Louis Napoleon declares himself Napoleon III, initiating the Second Empire.

1852: American inventor Elisha Graves Otis introduces the "safety" elevator, which has a safety brake to keep it from falling even if the cable holding it is completely cut.

1854: Publication of "The Charge of the Light Brigade" by Alfred Lord Tennyson, and *Walden* by Henry David Thoreau.

1858: British explorer John Hanning Speke locates Lake Victoria, which he correctly identifies as the source of the Nile.

1862: American Richard Gatling invents the first practical machine gun.

Event and Its Context

Context

In 1850 British economy, society, and politics had become more stable. After the onset of the Industrial Revolution, Britain had gone through massive social and political upheaval to become the "workshop of the world," and now prosperity was on the rise for skilled workers, who were the aristocrats of the working class. Skilled engineers, the indispensable mechanics at the forefront of the Industrial Revolution, enjoyed relatively high wages. Cheap imports and large markets were available throughout England's extensive empire, still untroubled by the first Indian uprising of 1858. International competition, which would emerge as an important factor in the last quarter of the nineteenth century, was relatively weak. Politically, Chartism, a political reform movement, was in decline. The ASE reflected this new stability by creating a durable form of trade unionism for the labor aristocracy.

A New Model Union?

The Amalgamated Society of Engineers (ASE) was formed in 1851, when several skilled engineering unions merged. It existed under that name until 1920, when it merged with the Steam Engine Makers and other unions to create the Amalgamated Engineering Union (AEU). The ASE was one of a group of "New Model" unions formed around this time. Sidney and Beatrice Webb, the first historians of British trade unionism, used this term, because, unlike some predecessors, such unions were coordinated nationally and concentrated on industrial rather than political issues.

These craft unions represented small, elite groups of engineers such as millwrights, turners, and fitters. Membership was rigidly restricted to those who had served an apprenticeship; women and less skilled workers were excluded. Thus, unions pushed up the price of skilled labor by restricting its supply. This was maintained by pride in the craft and the rights of artisans, including the right to a democratic voice in the union. They also fiercely defended craft prerogatives in the workshop by maintaining the right to determine how journeymen worked; by accepting only fully apprenticed men as skilled workers (they described others as "illegal"); and by rejecting systematic overtime and piecework. These unions were known as societies and sometimes as clubs. The durability of this tradition is shown by the use of these terms among AEU members until well into the twentieth century.

These societies used forms of mutual insurance to help members and their families through sickness, unemployment, migration, and funerals. The largest was the so-called Old Mechanics, which by 1838 had nearly 3,000 members. The Old Mechanics had tried to enforce minimum pay rates at district level (district rates). Nevertheless, the legality of trade unions

Membership card, Amalgamated Society of Engineers, Machinists, Millwrights, Smiths, and Pattern Makers. © Hulton/Getty Images. Reproduced by permission.

was uncertain, and thus the problem of misappropriation of funds by officials could not be pursued legally. While political agitation was widespread, there was also considerable experimentation in the form and direction of these societies. Consequently, there were many competing societies; they were fluid in form and, because of inadequate coverage, often ineffective and short-lived. The formation of the ASE, however, brought most of these societies together. It consolidated engineering trade unions on a sound basis. It brought a clearer direction and coordination to trade unionism, both in engineering and more widely, so that by the end of the nineteenth century, the ASE enjoyed great prestige among trade unionists. That prestige arose from the organization's national coordination and membership control. Coordination, however, did not mean central control.

Employers Challenge the Old Mechanics

By 1851 technological change had de-skilled some jobs; employers would reclassify a job as "unskilled" and hire "illegal" workers below the district rates. When challenged, they used the law against the societies. A turning point occurred in 1846, when workers conducted a strike at the Jones and Potts Newton-Le-Willows locomotive building works. The strike concerned the employment of illegal workers and was supported by voluntary donations organized by the Old Mechanics. Henry Selby, their general secretary, was arrested along with 26 other members for unlawful conspiracy, a legal action that also threatened trade unionism more generally. Although they were convicted, their convictions were reversed on appeal.

The key point, however, was the defeat of the strike, and some thought that an orderly retreat was required. Others, like William Newton and William Allan, felt that stronger craft controls were needed, which could be achieved only by greater unity. Newton wanted trade protection funds in order to show employers that they had the capacity to win strikes, not simply provide individual benefits. Allan became secretary of a provisional committee intended to form such a society at the beginning of 1851, but many remained opposed. One reason was the high rate of dues, which Allan thought was needed to finance defense of craft prerogatives. Opponents also felt that services to individual members should be the key function of societies and that employers should not be provoked by collective action. Opposition meant there was a real danger that the new society would simply add one more to the already large number of competing "clubs."

ASE began on 6 January 1851 with just 5,000 members, making it smaller than the Old Mechanics in 1850. However, by June 1851, because of extensive publicity by Newton and Allan, there were more than 9,000 members in 100 branches. Several other societies also decided to join the ASE. The publicity had stressed the need to function in a more focused and determined way than societies had done before. Indeed, the ASE could also advance the individual service functions of the old societies. For example, members traveling from one district to another in search of work had always been able to visit members in the new town (if they existed) to help find work or to receive benefits while unemployed. Now there was the prospect of a more comprehensive network. For this reason and to enforce craft prerogatives in every town, ASE elected district committees to consolidate their forces.

The Employers Challenge the ASE: The 1852 Lockout

The ASE built confidence among engineers, which alarmed employers. In December 1851 the ASE instructed members in Lancashire and London to ban piecework and systematic overtime after New Year's Day, 1852. The larger employers locked out many ASE members who tried to implement the ban. As union funds for supporting its members ran out, the dispute became very public, which brought support from other unions. It was not long, however, before all the funds were exhausted. The employers won and required workers to sign their "document," which was a rejection of the union and its rules; many were forced to sign. The ASE was defeated, but, because the dispute involved mostly larger companies, the damage was limited. Also, there was some solace from the fact that international trade union coordination had defeated employers' attempts to import substitute labor from abroad.

Consolidating the ASE

The lockout might have spelled the end for the ASE, and it seemed to confirm arguments that the society would provoke employers into major action. Owing to the work of Newton and Allan and the effectiveness of the union on a local level, the ASE did not collapse and was rebuilt in the following years, and further national confrontations were avoided. The organization's policy was dual; whereas it turned a conciliatory face toward employers and national government, it acted effectively at the local level.

As its key officer, Allan sustained the national organization, maintaining cohesion by informing members through the *Monthly Report* and working tirelessly to support local activists. He tended to be cautious politically and facilitated the emigration of members. The effects were positive, largely because of a buoyant labor demand, and the union retained power and influence in many districts. While Allan insisted that the union's policy was "defense not defiance," members conducted "guerilla" actions locally to defend craft prerogatives. Employers who insisted on systematic overtime, piecework, or too many adult "apprentices" could be sanctioned by the "strike in detail"; district committees would pull their members from these "black" employers' workshops and support them out of the gradually rebuilt local funds. The employers, by comparison, were poorly organized.

The union created a positive image both among its members and more widely in the trade union movement, not least because it proved effective and durable. Nationally, the ASE was well administered and its accounting was transparent. It had a strong reputation for democracy, based on the ideas that the union was elite and exclusive and that each member had inalienable rights. Thus, while there were elements of coordination at the national level, strong rights were accorded to districts and, indeed, to members in general. This model was significant beyond Britain. The ASE was the first union to incorporate Irish branches successfully; wherever groups of members went, it formed branches. British engineers traveled throughout North America and the empire selling their skills. In some countries, such as New Zealand, this had a real impact on local trade unionism.

Key Players

Allan, William (1813–1874): General secretary of the ASE until his death in 1874, Allan was active in the Chartist movement for political reform. Allan was Selsby's successor as general secretary of the Old Mechanics and a solid administrator. Although a poor speaker, he had the necessary reputation for scrupulous honesty.

Newton, William (1822–1876): Architect and propagandist for the ASE, Newton was active in the Chartist movement for political reform. Newton was a talented agitator, writer, and editor, and promoted the new society through his paper *The Operative.*

See also: *Chartist Movement.*

———

BIBLIOGRAPHY

Books

Belchem, John. *Industrialization and the Working Class: The English Experience, 1750–1900.* Brookfield, VT: Gower, 1990.

Croucher, Richard. *Local Autonomy in the ASE, 1889–1914.* Master's thesis, University of Warwick, 1971.

Jefferys, James B. *The Story of the Engineers 1800–1945.* New York: Johnson Reprint, 1970.

Weekes, Brian. *The Amalgamated Society of Engineers, 1880–1914: A Study of Trade Union Government, Politics, and Industrial Society.* Ph.D. Diss., University of Warwick, 1970.

ADDITIONAL RESOURCES

Arrowsmith, James. "The Struggle over Working Time in Nineteenth Century Britain." *Historical Studies in Industrial Relations* 13 (spring 2002): 83–118.

—Richard Croucher

John R. Commons. AP/Wide World Photos. Reproduced by permission.

duty of the democratic state." The AALL reform leaders were motivated primarily by the problem of worker insecurity around incidents such as on-the-job accidents, work-related illnesses, and employer-caused unemployment. The organization dedicated itself to promoting better employee compensation in the United States. The AALL also worked diligently for a national system of compulsory social insurance and protective labor legislation. AALL members, taken as a whole, basically felt that government action was necessary whenever the private business sector failed to meet basic employee needs. As a result of its work, the AALL laid the foundation for many modern social programs now in effect, such as unemployment insurance, workers' compensation, Social Security, and pension insurance.

American Association for Labor Legislation

United States 1905

Synopsis

The American Association of Labor Legislation (AALL) was a pioneering organization that dealt with labor reform and legislation during the late nineteenth century and the beginning of the twentieth century. Its commitment to social welfare is expressed by the slogan that appeared on its 1915 *Review of Labor Legislation* article: "To create a minimum standard of life below which no human being can fall is the most elementary

Timeline

1885: Indian National Congress founded. In the years that follow, the party will take the helm of India's independence movement.

1890: U.S. Congress passes the Sherman Antitrust Act, which in the years that follow will be used to break up large monopolies.

1895: Brothers Auguste and Louis Lumière show the world's first motion picture—*Workers Leaving the Lumière Factory*—at a café in Paris.

1898: United States defeats Spain in the three-month Spanish-American War. As a result, Cuba gains it independence, and the United States purchases Puerto Rico and the Philippines from Spain for $20 million.

1901: U.S. President William McKinley is assassinated by Leon Czolgosz, an anarchist. Vice President Theodore Roosevelt becomes president.

1903: Russia's Social Democratic Party splits into two factions: the moderate Mensheviks and the hard-line Bolsheviks. Despite their names, which in Russian mean "minority" and "majority," respectively, Mensheviks actually outnumber Bolsheviks.

1904: Russo-Japanese War, which lasts into 1905 and results in a resounding Japanese victory, begins. In Russia, the war is followed by the Revolution of 1905, which marks the beginning of the end of czarist rule; meanwhile, Japan is poised to become the first major non-western power of modern times.

1905: Russian Revolution of 1905 occurs. Following the "bloody Sunday" riots before the Winter Palace in St. Petersburg in January, revolution spreads throughout Russia, in some places spurred on by newly formed workers' councils, or soviets. Among the most memorable incidents of the revolt is the mutiny aboard the battleship *Potemkin*. Suppressed by the czar, the revolution brings an end to liberal reforms, and thus sets the stage for the larger revolution of 1917.

1905: Albert Einstein presents his special theory of relativity.

1905: In the industrial Ruhr region in Germany, 200,000 miners go on strike.

1909: National Association for the Advancement of Colored People (NAACP) is founded by W. E. B. Du Bois and a number of other prominent black and white intellectuals in New York City.

1914: On the Western Front, the first battles of the Marne and Ypres establish a line that will more or less hold for the next four years. Exuberance is still high on both sides, but will dissipate as thousands of German, French, and British soldiers sacrifice their lives in battles over a few miles of barbed wire and mud. The Eastern Front is a different story: a German victory over Russia at Tannenberg in August sets the stage for a war in which Russia will enjoy little success, and will eventually descend into chaos that paves the way for the 1917 revolutions.

Event and Its Context

At the beginning of the twentieth century, many social scientists believed that through research, analysis, and reporting, poverty in the United States could be eliminated or at least greatly reduced and social problems reversed. Professionals such as doctors, economists, journalists, political scientists, and sociologists often teamed up to gather and disperse this information. With knowledge provided by such support groups, citizens often pressured politicians to help the poor.

Reform Groups

Concerned citizens found support in a variety of voluntary associations dedicated to the improvement of the lives of American citizens. Among the more popular reform organizations were the National Consumers' League, Women's Trade Union League, Urban League, National Association for the Advancement of Colored People, and American Civil Liberties Union. One of these organizations, the American Association of Labor

Legislation (AALL), worked in the area of labor legislation, at a time when labor unions were making modest, but steady, reforms in the workplace. During its first two years of existence, AALL membership grew to about 2,000 members and was fairly steady from that year on.

Founders and Early Leaders

In 1905 a small group of reform-minded academic economists, including John R. Commons and Richard T. Ely, formed the American Association for Labor Legislation (AALL) in Madison, Wisconsin. The AALL was the U.S. component of the International Association for Labor Legislation, a reform organization headquartered in Europe that promoted consistent labor laws among industrialized countries. During AALL's first few years, Henry W. Farnam, Henry Rogers Seager, William F. Willoughby, John B. Andrews, Adna F. Weber, and Charles Henderson were among its leading core activists.

Ely, Farnam, Seager, and Willoughby served as the AALL's first four presidents, and Weber, Commons, and Andrews served as its first three secretaries. These men all came from academia and thus felt they could rationally and independently deal with labor problems without taking either the side of capital or of labor. Each felt a social and moral duty to improve the condition of workers. These "social environmentalists" were united in the belief that conflicts were increasing between a rapidly developing manufacturing community and employees, who lacked adequate protection in the form of labor laws. As people moved from the country to the city, rural workers were increasingly without labor support, and as more people crowded into urban areas, workers became more dependent on their employers. The AALL leaders were not against the growth of U.S. industry, as one might suspect, but felt such growth must be accomplished in unison with adequate labor protections.

Motivation for Formation

The originators of the AALL were motivated by the problem of worker insecurity: the overwhelming feelings of workers in response to the industrial hazards and adverse conditions in the workplace and what could result financially if they were involved in a serious mishap. Worker insecurity was an even greater problem when one considers the fact that during the nineteenth century insurance in any form was virtually nonexistent except for the wealthy, and existed only in limited quantity and monetary coverage early in the twentieth century.

AALL reformers felt that employers, left to their own devices, would abuse employees through overwork and unnecessary exposure to hazards. The organization's founders shared the belief that a government body should assume responsibility for correcting the social wrongs associated with industrial capitalism, especially the problem of work-related accidents beyond the control of the employee.

General Purpose

During the AALL's early years, the group's purpose, under the direction of Ely and Commons, was the research and publicity of labor legislation and labor conditions in the United States. The AALL also pursued a national movement for compulsory social insurance and protective labor legislation.

As intellectuals and political activists, the AALL's leaders and their associates theorized about the social effects of security legislation, proposed policies, and drafted model bills. They sponsored studies and campaigned vigorously for industrial safety laws, workers' compensation, unemployment insurance, and compulsory health insurance. Staff members compiled summaries and comparative analyses on a wide variety of protective labor legislation.

Switching Directions

By 1909, under the leadership of Andrews and Farnam (and against the wishes of Ely and Commons), this passive group expanded its purpose into policy advocacy while retaining its previous agenda of research and publicity. The much more active AALL began to promote aggressively, lobby for, and coordinate major changes in worker's compensation, occupational health and safety, and child labor laws. It also moved its headquarters from Wisconsin to New York City, primarily because leadership was transitioning to men from eastern universities such as Yale, Columbia, and Princeton. Civic leaders, journalists, academics, social workers, labor leaders, and reform groups generally supported their coordinating efforts.

From 1911 to 1941 the AALL published its quarterly journal, *The American Labor Legislation Review*. The early motto was "Conservation of Human Resources" and, later during World War I, the slogan changed to "Conservation of the workers—sound policy for the state and nation in time of peace—becomes an imperative duty in meeting the acute strain of war."

Social Insurance

In the 1910s, when American hospitals were first developing into modern institutions, the AALL organized the first national conference on "social insurance" or, as it was called then, "workingmen's insurance." These progressive reformers argued for health insurance and appeared to be gaining support in the United States. Opposition from medical interest groups and the entry of the United States into World War I in 1917 hindered the reform effort.

In 1910 the AALL estimated that the annual social and economic cost of sickness in the country's industries exceeded $7.7 million. Frederick Hoffman, in a 1915 report for the U.S. Bureau of Labor Statistics, estimated that out of a total labor force of about 38 million workers, 25,000 had died and about 700,000 had suffered serious injuries as a result of industrial accidents in 1915. In response, the AALL called for government-provided health care and workers' compensation so that job absenteeism could be decreased and work productivity could be increased. On the employer side, the AALL felt that a company that cared about the health and safety of its employees would generate more profits. Such reasoning led to improvements of health and safety laws in the early twentieth century. Many companies, for instance, installed restrooms in their facilities along with drinking fountains, baths, and showers. To assure that workers kept up work efficiency in the afternoon, many companies offered free or minimally priced nutritious meals.

By its second decade, the AALL had made substantial gains and had become a leader in promoting social insurance and protective labor legislation. The expanded goal of the AALL reformers was to prevent workers and their families from falling into poverty as a result of work-related accidents or illnesses. The AALL began to differentiate the working poor (or the "worthy poor" and "unemployed") from the nonworking poor (or the "unworthy poor" and "unemployable"). The organizations stated that the working poor were worthy of help because their condition was based on external problems brought on by working conditions, whereas the nonworking poor were not worthy of help because their condition was based on their own internal problems.

Historian Robert Bremner commented that the popular view shifted from seeing the poor as victims of their own devices to seeing the poor as victims of environmental causes, such as industrial accidents. Although it inadvertently ignored some employees, the AALL campaign to improve industrial safety laws, workers' compensation, and unemployment and health insurance did help most workers in the United States.

During the Great Depression of the 1930s, President Franklin Roosevelt's policies of the New Deal era benefited from the earlier social welfare reform movement that had been so staunchly supported by the AALL. The commitment to worker security in the Progressive Era of the 1920s guided the development of most social welfare legislation, such as the enactment of Social Security in 1935, which was accomplished during the catastrophic unemployment of the depression.

Views and Beliefs

The AALL reformers, as a whole, viewed themselves as independent from both the employer and the employee and serving as expert mediators to both sides of labor issues. Their scientific research showed the world that they were disinterested in promoting either side but were simply developing an unbiased view of labor and management. As a result, members of the AALL felt they were uniquely qualified to lead U.S. public opinion to a more rational and truthful view of the state of labor and management. Worker insecurity, in their view, was an injustice to the individual employee and a threat to the profitability of capitalism.

Outsiders held a wide range of opinions about the organization. Some people believed that the AALL served the interests of capitalists because part of the contributions for its support came from wealthy industrialists such as John D. Rockefeller. Others saw the AALL reformers as independent intellectuals who argued for rational conclusions. Legal scholar Ernst Freund wrote in 1915 that the public should receive unbiased information and that information should come from the disinterested AALL. Some claimed that the AALL was controlled by organized labor. Still others viewed the reformers as aggressive and influential lobbyists who were trying to influence the course of social legislation and reform. Samuel Gompers, the president of the American Federation of Labor, compared the AALL to the local gossip and busybody. Because such attacks came from all sides, little damage was done to the AALL. However, the AALL was forced consistently to defend its stand of neutrality when it came to any form of labor matter.

The difficulty of the situation is emphasized by the example in 1909 when a letter was to go out to both labor and management on a union-label controversy. AALL leaders decided to place the union label on the letter that was to be delivered to union members, but leave it off of the letter that was to go to management. Unfortunately, both versions of the letter eventually ended up in the hands of opposing camps. Such practices provoked criticisms from both sides of labor and management.

Disbandment

In 1941 the AALL disbanded after 36 years of working consistently to improve labor legislation in the four broad areas of working conditions, unemployment, health and safety, and social insurance. Throughout its existence the reformers of the AALL continued to stand by their belief that "good" labor legislation would benefit employees, employers, and the public.

Willoughby, the association's fourth president, described AALL policy when he said that all workers should possess a minimum level of economic security and that the government should assure that the industrial community provides that minimum economic security. Although other organizations were devoted to social welfare reform during the early twentieth century, the AALL was the most prominent one in the two critical areas of protective labor legislation and social insurance. For the most part, its activities were difficult because they professed a policy of prevention, not just relief. For instance, the AALL wanted to prevent poverty, not just lessen its effects.

The greatest contributions and influence of the AALL reformers were in their ability to identify social problems, develop reasonable solutions, and propose model legislation. Although the AALL failed in many of its campaigns, such as its long-term battle (with such opponents as business and labor leaders, insurance companies, fraternal organizations, and physicians) for compulsory health insurance in the 1910s, it did set the course for future social legislation in the United States. Historians of American social policy generally agree that the reformers within the AALL played an important role in social welfare reform during the first half of the twentieth century.

Key Players

Andrews, John B. (1880–1943): Andrews graduated from the University of Wisconsin with a doctorate in economics. In 1914 Andrews wrote the book *A Practical Plan for the Prevention of Unemployment in America.* He was appointed chairman of the Advisory Social Service Committee of the Municipal Lodging House (a New York City publicly funded homeless shelter).

Commons, John R. (1862–1945): Commons studied at Johns Hopkins University. He held teaching posts at Ohio Wesleyan, Oberlin, Indiana, and Syracuse Universities from 1890 to 1901. He became associated with the Industrial Commission and the National Civic federation during this time. Beginning in 1904, Commons held a professorship at the University of Wisconsin. He founded the Wisconsin tradition of institutional economics. He was one of the country's most respected writers and lecturers on political economics, institutional economics, and sociology, having written or edited such books as *The Distribution of Wealth* (1893); *Documentary History of American Industrial Society,* 10 volumes (1910–11); *History of Labour in the United States,* 4 volumes (1918, 1935); *Legal Foundations of Capitalism* (1924); *Institutional Economics* (1934); and *Myself* (1934). Commons helped to found the Wisconsin School of Labor History and was president of the National Consumers' League.

Ely, Richard Theodore (1854–1943): Ely was an innovative researcher and academic with a background in institutional economics. He was a professor of economics at the University of Wisconsin and later at Johns Hopkins University. Ely was one of the founders of the American Economic Association (1885), the Christian Social Union, and the American Association for Agricultural Legislation. Among the books that Ely wrote were *Labor Movement in America* and *Socialism and Social Reform* (1920).

Farnam, Henry W. (1853–1933): Farnam was a professor of economics at Yale University. He wrote *Shakespeare's Economics* (1931) and *Chapters in the History of Social Legislation in the United States to 1860* (1931).

Henderson, Charles Richmond (1848–1915): Henderson was a professor of sociology at the University of Chicago, with a specialty in industrial sociology. He wrote the book *Industrial Insurance in the United States* (1909).

Seager, Henry Rogers (1870–1930): Seager was a professor of economics at Columbia University, with a specialty in political economy. Seager wrote the book *Social Insurance: A Program of Social Reform* (1910).

Weber, Adna Ferrin (1870–?): Weber was a professor of political economy at Columbia University and was the chief statistician at the New York State Department of Labor. Weber wrote the book *The Growth of Cities in the Nineteenth Century: A Study in Statistics* (1899).

Willoughby, William F.: Willoughby was a professor of economics at Princeton University.

See also: *Social Security Act.*

BIBLIOGRAPHY

Books

Fink, Gary M., ed. *Biographical Dictionary of American Labor.* Westport, CT: Greenwood Press, 1984.

Moss, David A. *Socializing Security: Progressive-Era Economists and the Origins of American Social Policy.* Cambridge, MA: Harvard University Press, 1996.

Tone, Andrea. *The Business of Benevolence: Industrial Paternalism in Progressive America.* Ithaca, NY: Cornell University Press, 1997.

—William Arthur Atkins

American Federation of Labor

United States 1886

Synopsis

Trade unions in the United States remained relatively weak throughout the nineteenth century. Only about 2 percent of the total labor force and less than 10 percent of all industrial workers were members of unions. Leaders of the labor movement realized that a national union was needed, but efforts to establish such a union were marked by difficulties. The National Trades' Union, the National Labor Union, the Order of the Knights of Labor, the Cigar Makers' International Union, and the Federation of Organized Trades and Labor Unions of the United States and Canada were all early unions that helped to bring about the establishment of the American Federation of Labor (AFL). Prominent among those working to form a successful national union was Samuel Gompers, a man who persistently pursued activities that would eventually lead to the founding of the AFL in 1886.

Timeline

1866: Winchester repeating rifle is introduced.

1871: Chicago fire causes 250 deaths and $196 million in damage.

1876: General George Armstrong Custer and 264 soldiers are killed by the Sioux at the Little Big Horn River.

1878: Thomas Edison develops a means of cheaply producing and transmitting electric current, which he succeeds in subdividing so as to make it adaptable to household use. The value of shares in gas companies plummets as news of his breakthrough reaches Wall Street.

1882: Agitation against English rule spreads throughout Ireland, culminating with the assassination of chief secretary for Ireland Lord Frederick Cavendish and permanent undersecretary Thomas Burke in Dublin's Phoenix Park. The leader of the nationalist movement is Charles Stewart Parnell, but the use of assassination and terrorism—which Parnell himself has disavowed—makes clear the fact that he does not control all nationalist groups.

1884: Chicago's Home Life Insurance Building, designed by William LeBaron Jenney, becomes the world's first skyscraper.

1886: Bombing at Haymarket Square, Chicago, kills seven policemen and injures numerous others. Eight anarchists are accused and tried; three are imprisoned, one commits suicide, and four are hanged.

1886: The Statue of Liberty is dedicated.

1886: Apache chief Geronimo surrenders to U.S. forces.

1888: The Blizzard of 1888 in the United States kills hundreds and causes more than $25 million in property damage.

1892: Bitter strikes in Australia lead to the closing of ports and mines.

Samuel Gompers. The Library of Congress.

1896: U.S. Supreme Court issues its *Plessy v. Ferguson* decision, which establishes the "separate but equal" doctrine that will be used to justify segregation in the southern United States for the next half-century.

Event and Its Context

Precursors to the AFL

The efforts of several earlier, short-lived national organizations made possible the creation of the American Federation of Labor (AFL). Several precursors of this organization paved the way for its creation.

On 17 May 1834 the *Workingmen's Advocate* of New York City printed an article that told of the benefits of a national union of trade societies in sustaining and promoting the rights of every workingman in the country. The National Trades' Union was born in August 1834 when a convention was called by the General Trades' Union of New York. Delegates from local unions in New York City; Poughkeepsie, New York; Newark, New Jersey; Boston; and Philadelphia were present. The National Trades' Union never possessed more than an advisory capacity; nevertheless, its ideas helped to identify the need for a national trade union in the United States. The economic panic of 1837 ended the National Trades' Union, and no more valid attempts at organizing a national union came until near the end of the Civil War.

The Civil War period strongly boosted unionism. By the end of the war, most large cities had a central labor body that represented organized crafts, such as the molders, stone cutters, hat finishers, machinists, blacksmiths, miners, locomotive engineers, cigar makers, ship carpenters, bricklayers, plasterers, carpenters and joiners, painters, and many others. Union membership was estimated at about 300,000 at this time.

With a strong labor movement developing, delegates from eight trade assemblies met in 1864 in Louisville, Kentucky, with the intention of forming the International Industrial Assembly of North America. They adopted a constitution and generated a general strike fund but could not gain enough support to establish the organization formally. Two years later, in August 1866 in Baltimore, Maryland, the National Labor Union was formed (it actually evolved from the International Industrial Assembly) by agreement of 77 delegates representing local unions, city federations, eight-hour leagues (organizations promoting the eight-hour workday), and national unions.

The delegates elected J. C. C. Whaley of Washington, D.C., as the union's first president. The agenda of the National Labor Union was to promote arbitration (instead of strikes), regulation of apprenticeship, the eight-hour workday, a national labor statistics bureau, a federal labor department, and the abolition of contract prison labor. The union held annual congresses between 1866 and 1872 that were attended by most of the existing labor organizations. Although only in existence for a short time, the union helped to establish the concept of the worker as a viable economic group with national interests. Labor historians generally agree that the National Labor Union was the first "permanent" national association of unions that had a substantial impact on the national labor environment. Most historians also conclude that its failure was due to such factors as its inconsistent organizational characteristics, its preoccupation with politics, and its inadequate perception of the goals of the labor movement.

The Knights of Labor

Between 1873 and 1880 three diverse organizations—one composed solely of skilled workers, another group emphasizing the social reforms of the National Labor Union, and a third one composed of immigrant workers with a socialist intent—prevented any national labor union from being formed. In December 1877, however, the Socialist Labor Party formed as a response to the railroad strikes of 1877 and to the interest in labor politics that was spreading across the country. This union was followed on 1 January 1878 by the founding of the Order of the Knights of Labor (KOL) in Reading, Pennsylvania. The 33 delegates present adopted a constitution that established the general assembly as the authority of the KOL. The KOL became a truly national organization, unlike its predecessors, in that its members joined individually rather than through affiliated unions.

The KOL organized itself around district assemblies (of the KOL) and independent local assemblies. It expressed its intent to serve all workers, both skilled and unskilled, and to be different from craft and trade unions. The KOL recognized the importance of workers in the emerging industrial system and felt that the broader-based labor (industrial) union was better equipped than the small trade (craft) union. The KOL emphasized the solidarity of labor and promoted the idea of a centralized association that would represent the workers in all industries and occupations. Its charter granted the power to elect officers; decide policy matters; make, amend, or repeal laws and regulations; issue charters; decide controversies; and tax

members. Although the KOL only lasted from 1878 to 1886, the organizational structure and policies established during those years are considered the foundation that ultimately formed the American Federation of Labor. Historian Norman J. Ware remarked that the KOL "tried to teach the American wage-earner that he was a wage-earner first and a bricklayer, carpenter, miner, shoemaker, after, that he was a wage-earner first and a Catholic, Protestant, Jew, white, black, Democrat, Republican after."

Gompers and the Cigar Makers

During the late 1870s Samuel Gompers—who would later help to establish the AFL—assisted a small craft union in New York City. In 1875 Gompers was the head of Local 144 in New York City, the largest affiliate to the Cigar Makers' Union (a prominent trade union of skilled workers). Along with Adolph Strasser, president of the Cigar Makers' Union, and Ferdinand Laurrell, Gompers led a movement that eventually held a national convention of cigar makers in 1879. At that time they reestablished the Cigar Makers' International Union, which had grown very weak during the economic panic of 1873. They adopted the popular British trade union system into their new organization and also adopted, with the urging of Gompers, a set of sound and efficient business practices. The leaders of the international had complete authority over the local unions. A membership increase helped to build up a large monetary reserve fund, a system of sickness and death benefits for its members, and a plan for lending money to members who were searching for work. Later, various other national and international trade unions modeled their organizations after this structure. These practical methods adapted well to their struggle for higher wages and shorter workdays.

At this time, growth increased in other craft unions that had survived the depression of 1873. As conditions improved, trade unionists again considered the creation of a national organization. The KOL from Indiana joined with the Terre Haute Amalgamated Labor Union for a conference on 2 August 1881, in Terre Haute, Indiana. With only a few delegates in attendance, they agreed to meet again in Pittsburgh, Pennsylvania. During 15–18 November 1881 the Federation of Organized Trades and Labor Unions of the United States and Canada (FOTLU) was founded at Turner Hall in downtown Pittsburgh. (The name was specifically intended to exclude political labor organizations but to include both skilled and unskilled labor.) Over 100 delegates representing nearly half a million members attended the founding convention. Members from many national and international trade unions attended, including the Typographical Workers, the Iron and Steel Workers, the Glass Workers, the Iron Molders, the Cigar Makers, and the Carpenters. Also represented were the central labor councils of 11 cities, 42 local unions, and 3 district assemblies and 46 local assemblies of the KOL, which at that time was the largest labor organization in the country.

The constitution of the FOTLU was modeled almost entirely from the British Trades Union Congress because most of the member craft unions had been greatly influenced by the British. The wording of the constitution gave control of the FOTLU to the skilled workers rather than the unskilled workers. Gompers was nominated to be president of the FOTLU, along with Richard Powers of the Lake Seaman's Union. The members of the

FOTLU were sharply divided over these two candidates, so for the good of the union they stepped aside. John Jarrett of the Amalgamated Association of Iron and Steel Workers became the president, with Gompers and Powers both serving as vice presidents.

During the next four years the FOTLU and the KOL became rivals. Also during this period, a wave of labor unrest developed as a result of (1) generally unsafe and unhealthy working conditions in the rapidly growing industries of the United States, (2) increased replacement of labor by machines, and (3) increasing numbers of immigrants, especially from the eastern and southern parts of Europe. In 1884 alone, the cigar makers, longshoremen, miners, steel workers, printers, railroad shipmen, and textile workers staged numerous strikes. Without the backing of strong labor unions, most of these strikes were unsuccessful. Workers, however, found that boycotts were effective weapons against abusive employers and discovered that the KOL were eager to help all types of workers by funding the strikes, intervening in disputes, and negotiating with employers.

Within a year of its birth, the FOTLU had been reduced to an insignificant labor organization. Only 19 delegates attended its second convention assembled in Cleveland in November 1882. The strongest trade union, the Amalgamated Association of Iron and Steel Workers, withdrew its support, and only a few unions, namely the International Cigar Makers' Union, the United Brotherhood of Carpenters and Joiners, and the International Typographical Union, showed any serious backing. Gompers was one of the few who remained active in the FOTLU. However, increasing numbers of craft unions began to favor the stronger KOL and to distance themselves from the weakening FOTLU.

The Haymarket Incident

Beginning in 1885, relations between the KOL and the trade unions began to change for the worse. The KOL was expanding rapidly, and many craft unions felt lost within the growing organization. The KOL was also becoming more aggressive in its tactics as it secured more successes in strikes, boycotts, and collective bargaining. The final break between the craft unions and the KOL came in 1886, when the FOTLU called a universal strike for an eight-hour day. The leadership of the KOL opposed the eight-hour workday (although the KOL members favored it, and the public perceived the KOL to be in favor of it) and tried to disrupt the strike. By 1 May 1886 around 350,000 workers were on strike, with some of the most violent actions taking place in Chicago in the form of a bomb explosion at Haymarket Square on 4 May 1886. About 125 workers and police were killed or seriously injured. Although the weak FOTLU had initiated the strike, the strong KOL was seen as publicly supporting the eight-hour day; it received the most negative publicity and public hostility. The entire labor movement suffered as a result of the Haymarket incident. The resulting public outrage ultimately contributed to the dissolution of the KOL.

After the Haymarket incident the KOL continued to be hindered by infighting and by struggles with employers and various trade unions. The situation worsened with the New York Cigar Manufacturers Association announcement of a reduction in wages on 1 January 1886. Progressive Union No. 1 rejected the change, but Local 144 accepted it. The manufacturers ordered a lockout that involved 10,000 workers. The Progressives eventually agreed with the manufacturers. However, when the KOL met on 4 October 1886 in Richmond, Virginia, it admitted the Progressive Cigar Makers' Union and expelled the International Cigar Makers' Union, of which Local 144 was a member. This event, and the activities leading up to it, helped to build a sense of cooperation within the trade unions against the KOL. As a result, Samuel Gompers, head of Local 144, who had regularly opposed the KOL, was selected by the Cigar Makers' Union to oppose the actions of the KOL. The FOTLU condemned the acts instigated by the KOL and often ordered that its unions not support the KOL. Gompers's actions resulted in the gathering of delegates that ultimately formed the AFL and led to the eventual ascendancy of Gompers as its leader.

The Formal Beginnings of the AFL

A committee of the various trade unions announced on 10 November 1886 that a convention would be held in Columbus, Ohio, on 8 December 1886 for the purpose of drawing "the bonds of unity much closer together between all the trades unions of America" by means of "an American federation or alliance of all national and international trades unions." As a result, delegates from various affiliates of both the KOL and the FOTLU as well as from certain unaffiliated unions met to organize a national trade union movement. Delegates hoped that the new national organization would be more enduring than any of its predecessors. In all, 42 delegates from 25 labor organizations assembled, claiming to represent over 315,000 members. The FOTLU itself was also meeting at that same time and decided to merge with the newly formed organization. Thus, the AFL was born in 1886. Gompers was elected unanimously as its founding president (with a salary of $1,000 per year plus travel expenses). After electing Gompers as president, the delegation elected P. F. Fitzpatrick of the iron molders as first vice president; J. W. Smith, of the journeymen tailors as second vice president; P. J. McGuire of the carpenters as secretary; and Gabriel Edmonston, also of the carpenters, as treasurer. This executive council would be responsible for the direction of the new organization.

The initial membership of the AFL was estimated at about 140,000 workers grouped in 25 national unions. Its constitution was based on many features of the earlier FOTLU and had as its three main objectives the protection of jurisdictions, the encouragement of legislation favorable to wage earners, and the assistance to constituent groups in organizing. It was financed initially by a per capita tax of one-half cent per month and by charter fees.

The AFL began as a decentralized organization that recognized the autonomy of each of the national craft unions that were its members. Individual workers were not members of the AFL but only of the affiliated local or national union. The AFL emphasized the organization of skilled workers into craft unions (composed of a single occupation such as carpenters or electricians), as opposed to industrial unions (in which all the workers in a particular industry, such as steel, would belong to one union). The AFL was structured as a loose confederation of autonomous unions, each with exclusive rights to deal with the workers and employers in its own field. Each autonomous union had its own leadership, which was determined by its own specific requirements and needs. The AFL had no powers except those that were authorized by the organizations that composed it.

The AFL concerned itself primarily with organizing skilled workers and with the pursuit of specific, attainable goals such as higher wages and shorter working hours. The AFL renounced identification with any political party or movement and adopted instead the policy of urging its members to support federal, state, and local candidates for public office who were considered friendly to labor, regardless of party affiliation, and to vote against those regarded as hostile. Gompers felt that the primary tactics of the AFL should be (1) lobbying the existing political parties, (2) actively improving the public image of unions, and (3) collective bargaining as the primary way to gain benefits for members. Gompers also believed that the goals of the AFL should come from the members themselves. He believed that the union should work with industry, rather than fight against it, so as to improve the economic state of union members. He believed that as capitalism improves, so does the lot of union members. He held conservative political views and believed that trade unionists should accept America's capitalist economic system.

Conclusion

Opposed to the idea of a labor political party, the AFL was a relatively conservative political force in the labor movement of the late nineteenth and early twentieth centuries. The union, however, did help secure higher wages, shorter workdays, workmen's compensation, additional legislation against child labor, and the exemption of labor from antitrust legislation. At the annual AFL convention in 1893, Gompers was proud to say, "It is noteworthy that while in every previous industrial crisis the trade unions were literally mowed down and swept out of existence, the unions now in existence have manifested, not only the powers of resistance, but of stability and permanency."

Key Players

Gompers, Samuel (1850–1924): Gompers was an American labor leader, who, as president of the American Federation of Labor (AFL), believed in cooperation between management and labor as a means of obtaining labor demands, with the strike used only as a last resort. After only four years of elementary school education in London, Gompers was apprenticed to a London cigar maker. In 1863 he and his family moved to New York City, where he became active in the social clubs, fraternal orders, and labor unions of the Lower East Side. Gompers became a member of the Cigar Maker's International Union in 1864 and 10 years later helped found Local 144 of the international union. He remained a member of the Local 144 for the rest of his life and was elected its president in 1874. In 1881 Gompers was one of the chief founders and the first president of the Federation of Organized Trades and Labor Unions of the United States of America and Canada. When the AFL was founded in 1886, Gompers was elected its founding president and reelected each year afterwards (except in 1895) until his death.

See also: *Federation of Organized Trades and Labor Unions of the United States and Canada (FOTLU); General Trades' Union; Haymarket Riot; Knights of Labor; National Labor Union; National Trades Union.*

BIBLIOGRAPHY

Books

Beard, Mary. *A Short History of the American Labor Movement.* New York: Greenwood Press, Publishers, 1968.

Dulles, Foster Rhea, and Melvyn Dubofsky, eds. *Labor in America: A History.* 5th ed. Arlington Heights, IL: Harlan Davidson, Inc., 1984.

Gompers, Samuel. *Seventy Years of Life and Labor: An Autobiography.* New York: Dutton, 1957.

Harvey, Rowland Hill. *Samuel Gompers, Champion of the Toiling Masses.* Stanford, CA: Stanford University Press, and London: Oxford University Press, 1953.

Kaufman, Stuart Bruce. *Samuel Gompers and the Origins of the American Federation of Labor, 1848–1896.* Westport, CT: Greenwood Press, 1973.

Livesay, Harold C. *Samuel Gompers and Organized Labor in America.* Boston: Little, Brown, 1978.

Lorwin, Lewis Levitzki. *The American Federation of Labor: Policies and Prospects.* Washington, DC: The Brookings Institution, 1933.

—William Arthur Atkins

American Plan

United States 1918–1925

Synopsis

During World War I, Progressive Era labor reforms reached a peak with the establishment of the War Labor Board (WLB) and President Woodrow Wilson's support for collective bargaining. At war's end, however, employers reasserted their power to dismantle the WLB and begin a new round of attacks on organized labor. Using the Red Scare and Palmer Raids as evidence that labor unions were radical and un-American, employers declared that a workplace free from unions—the "open shop"—was the best way to ensure the country's stability and prosperity. To keep an open shop in the 1920s, employers undertook a series of measures that came to be known as the American Plan. In various combinations the American Plan incorporated scientific and personnel management, welfare measures, and outright repression to control the work place, increase productivity, and prevent unionization.

Timeline

1908: Ford Motor Company introduces the Model T.

1913: In New York and Boston, striking garment workers win a pay raise and shorter hours.

1918: Influenza, carried to the furthest corners by returning soldiers, spreads throughout the globe. Over the next two years, it will kill nearly 20 million people—more than the war itself.

1919: With the formation of the Third International (Comintern), the Bolshevik government of Russia establishes its control over communist movements worldwide.

1920: In the United States, the U.S. Department of Justice launches a campaign to track down and deport communists, anarchists, and other radicals, as well as those suspecting of being left-leaning revolutionaries. Raids are also used for the purpose of rooting out and deporting illegal aliens.

1921: In a controversial U.S. case, Italian-born anarchists Nicola Sacco and Bartolomeo Vanzetti are tried and convicted of armed robbery and murder. Despite numerous protests from around the world, they will be executed six years later.

1922: Published this year James Joyce's novel *Ulysses* and T. S. Eliot's poem *The Waste Land* will transform literature and inaugurate the era of modernism.

1923: Notable musical works of the year include George Gershwin's *Rhapsody in Blue* and various songs by Bessie Smith and Jelly Roll Morton.

1924: In the United States, Secretary of the Interior Albert B. Fall, along with oil company executives Harry Sinclair and Edward L. Doheny, is charged with conspiracy and bribery in making fraudulent leases of U.S. Navy oil reserves at Teapot Dome, Wyoming. The resulting Teapot Dome scandal clouds the administration of President Warren G. Harding.

1925: In Tennessee, John T. Scopes is fined for teaching evolution in a public school. There follows a highly publicized trial at which famed attorney Clarence Darrow represents the defense, while the aging Democratic populist William Jennings Bryan argues for the state. The "Scopes Monkey Trial" symbolizes a widening divisions between rural and urban America, and though the court decides in favor of the state, it is clear that the historical tide is turning against the old agrarian order symbolized by Bryan.

1930: Naval disarmament treaty is signed by the United States, Great Britain, France, Italy, and Japan.

1935: Second phase of New Deal begins with the introduction of social security, farm assistance, and housing and tax reform.

Event and Its Context

American workers enjoyed boom times during World War I. The demand for war materiel, coupled with the labor shortage

Alexander Mitchell Palmer. The Library of Congress.

induced by the curtailment of immigration from Europe, led to higher wages in most industries. It also gave workers more bargaining power with their employers, and many joined labor unions to implement this power. Membership in the American Federation of Labor jumped from 2 to 3.2 million between 1914 and 1918. For most of the new members, many of whom were immigrants, it was the first time they had joined the ranks of organized labor.

The federal bureaucracy had already expanded before the war to help ease labor tensions in the country. In March 1913 a reluctant, lame-duck President William Howard Taft established the Department of Labor as he turned over power to Woodrow Wilson, who was elected as a standard-bearer of Progressive era reform. In its initial incarnation, the Department of Labor comprised the Bureau of Labor Statistics, Bureau of Immigration, Bureau of Naturalization, and Children's Bureau. The Bureau of Immigration also served as a de facto employment agency for immigrants seeking work; it found work for 280,000 of them in 1917. After the U.S. entered World War I on 5 April of that year, the agency focused most of its efforts on stabilizing the work force and avoiding strikes that would delay war production.

Frederick Winslow Taylor. The Library of Congress.

100% Americanism

Most employers greatly resented the intrusion of the government into labor relations and complained that the WLB actually spurred workers to undertake frivolous strikes in the hope of a favorable settlement. When World War I ended on 11 November 1918, the WLB was almost immediately abolished under heavy lobbying by business interests, including the National Association of Manufacturers. In the absence of a government mediation service, however, a surge of strikes by some 4.1 million workers took place in 1919. Among the most serious actions were a general strike in Seattle in February 1919 and strikes in the textile, mining, and steel industries. All of them were crushed by employers, often with the assistance of state and local police forces.

As powerful as the outright force against the strikes was the publicity directed at the strikers and their leaders. The media labeled them radical agitators. Although much of the antilabor propaganda was hysterical in its tone, the propaganda also developed a sophisticated message that described all strikes as un-American. This message, which demanded "100% Americanism," linked the current labor unrest with the country's fight against subversives during the war. President Wilson himself, after all, had argued for passage of the Espionage Act of 1917, a law that set forth broad definitions of treason and antiwar activities. The law was later amended to include more drastic penalties under the Sedition Act of 1918. The acts prompted the arrests of approximately 1,500 individuals for opposing the draft, criticizing U.S. policies, and speaking out against the war.

The pattern of antilabor activity continued with the Palmer Raids of 1919–1920. After anarchists sent bombs to government and business leaders in April and May 1919, and another series of bombs exploded in eight American cities on 2 June, Attorney General A. Mitchell Palmer ordered a roundup of suspected communists and anarchists. The roundup began in No-

vember 1919 and lasted until March of the following year. An estimated 6,000 suspects were taken into custody in the Palmer Raids and hundreds of noncitizens were deported, even if they had no criminal record. The raids also precipitated an outpouring of vigilante violence against labor unions and other organizations that were perceived to favor a radical agenda. The orgy of arrests ended only when Palmer predicted unrest for May Day 1920 that failed to materialized.

Scientific Management and Personnel Management

Although Palmer faded from the scene, he had accomplished much of what employers were seeking after World War I. Not only were labor unions branded as radical and un-American in the eyes of much of the public, but a cadre of labor leaders had been arrested and deported as well. Now that most employers had "open shops" that were free from unions, they wanted to maintain the status quo. Over time their efforts to keep an open shop through scientific and personnel management, welfare measures, and outright repression would become known as the "American Plan." The term was first used by the National Association of Manufacturers and the national body of the Chamber of Commerce in 1921 and was soon widely used in the business community.

One crucial aspect of labor relations that was linked to the American Plan was scientific management studies to better control better the work place and increase productivity. The most extensive and widely publicized series of studies took place at Western Electric's (WE) Hawthorne Works in Cicero, Illinois, between 1924 and 1933. Previous scientific management studies that had been pioneered by Frederick Winslow Taylor had emphasized the routinization of tasks to increase efficiency. In contrast, the Hawthorne Plant experiments identified a more complex set of variables that was equally important in improving productivity. The most important conclusion of the experiments pointed to the social interaction among workers and between workers and managers as a significant factor in productivity levels. When worker satisfaction was improved through active participation in structuring the work environment, productivity levels also increased, even if work conditions were worsened.

In an April 1928 study conducted by George Elton Mayo, a research group set up a set of 13 experiments with five women assembly-line workers. Altering the lighting of the work room, rest periods, and the length of the working day and week, the researchers found no specific correlation between the changes and level of productivity, which increased a total of 46 percent over the five years of the subsequent studies. From these observations, the researchers concluded that factors such as increased participation by employees in managing the work place were more important than incentive pay schemes or physical conditions in improving productivity. WE implemented this conclusion by conducting over 10,300 interviews with its employees to discuss their opinions about their work environment in the hope of spurring company-wide productivity increases.

Welfare Capitalism

The Hawthorne Works was also known for its welfare capitalism measures, which provided workers with fringe benefits for free or at reduced costs. Like programs implemented by other large employers, WE's programs in the Hawthorne Works were designed to foster satisfaction and company loyalty among its work force. In addition to offering medical care on site, group insurance at reduced rates, a stock ownership plan, and educational courses after working hours, WE sponsored numerous sports teams and social programs for its employees. WE started a vacation plan as well. During the 1920s other employers widely copied these welfare capitalism measures. U.S. Steel, International Harvester, and the Swift and Armour meat packing firms employed similar lists of programs. Outside of the factory gates, many companies also sponsored charity drives to benefit local YMCAs, churches, and other community organizations. In all, about 5 percent of employers implemented welfare capitalism programs to gain the loyalty of their work force.

There were significant variations in welfare capitalist measures, however. Whereas urban industrial workers were quick to voice resentment over any program that smacked of paternalism, welfare measures in southern textile towns constantly reminded workers of their employers' power. In contrast to industrial communities in the North, where workers sought out their own housing, textile workers typically lived in company-built and -owned housing. Although living in company housing usually saved workers about half the rent they would pay for private housing, it put them at the mercy of their employer, who would eject them if they stopped working. Unlike workers' children in the North, who attended public or parochial schools, children of mill workers in the South often attended schools set up by the mill company. Even after states passed compulsory school attendance laws in the mid-1910s, mill schools were grossly inferior and almost always led students into mill work. Workers in the smaller company towns also experienced the dubious benefit of shopping at stores run by their employers. Although the company stores would willingly extend credit to gainfully employed workers, reformers charged that the device was another means to keep workers subservient to their employers.

Each of these factors of the American Plan changed with the onset of the Great Depression in 1929, with most welfare capitalism measures coming to an abrupt halt as employers faced bankruptcy. After the initial crash, some employers conducted food and clothing drives and lent out parcels of empty land for their employees to grow vegetables. Other companies staggered work schedules so that every employee could work at least a few hours each week. By 1932, however, even these efforts could not sustain workers as other private sources of relief had all but disappeared. With the election of President Franklin D. Roosevelt in 1932, workers began a pivotal reorientation of their loyalties and expectations toward the federal government for assistance. After the upswing in labor unionization in the mid-1930s, many unions also began offering their own recreational and social activities for their members and the community at large. Although corporations continued to use scientific management to study the workplace, by World War II they had been outflanked in the battle for worker loyalty by both labor unions and the federal government.

Key Players

Mayo, George Elton (1880–1949): After working as a professor of philosophy in Australia, Mayo came to the United States in 1922. He became one of the leading exponents on industrial relations theory and joined the Hawthorne Experiments in 1928. The experiments sealed his reputation and he worked the final years of his career in England.

Palmer, Alexander Mitchell (1872–1936): Palmer practiced law after 1893 and worked as a banker before winning a seat from Pennsylvania in the U.S. House of Representatives in 1909. He served in the House until 1915 when he joined the administration of President Woodrow Wilson. He became attorney general in March 1919 and served through 1921, when Wilson's term expired. Palmer returned to his private law practice after he left office.

Taylor, Frederick Winslow (1856–1915): An inventor and industrial manager, Taylor became the best known industrial engineer of his era. In his most famous work, *The Principles of Scientific Management*, published in 1911, Taylor argued that management had to assert full control of the work place to increase productivity.

See also: *American Federation of Labor; National War Labor Board.*

BIBLIOGRAPHY

Books

Brandes, Stuart. *American Welfare Capitalism, 1880–1940.* Chicago: University of Chicago Press, 1976.

Brody, David. "The Rise and Decline of Welfare Capitalism." In *Workers in Industrial America: Essays on the Twentieth-Century Struggle.* New York: Oxford University Press, 1993.

Cohen, Lizabeth. *Making a New Deal: Industrial Workers in Chicago, 1919–1939.* Cambridge: Cambridge University Press, 1990.

Fones-Wolf, Elizabeth A. *Selling Free Enterprise: The Business Assault on Labor and Liberalism, 1945–1960.* Urbana: University of Illinois Press, 1994.

Gillespie, Richard. *Manufacturing Knowledge: A History of the Hawthorne Experiments.* Cambridge: Cambridge University Press, 1991.

Hall, Jacquelyn Dowd, James Leloudis, Robert Korstad, Mary Murphy, Lu Ann Jones, and Christopher B. Daly. *Like a Family: The Making of a Southern Cotton Mill World.* New York: W. W. Norton and Company, 1987.

Schatz, Ronald W. *The Electrical Workers: A History of Labor at General Electric and Westinghouse, 1923–1960.* Urbana: University of Illinois Press, 1983.

Trahair, Richard C. S. *The Humanist Temper: The Life and Work of Elton Mayo.* New Brunswick, NJ: Transaction Books, 1984.

Waring, Stephen P. *Taylorism Transformed: Scientific Management Theory since 1945.* Chapel Hill: University of North Carolina Press, 1991.

—Timothy G. Borden

Anarchists Lead Argentine Labor Movement

Argentina 1900–1910

Synopsis

During the first decade of the 1900s, the tone of the labor movement in Argentina turned dramatically from cooperation to defiance as anarchists took over the leadership roles in union organizations. The militant antigovernment policy of anarchism, in turn, forced the government to change dramatically its attitude toward unions from one of general ambivalence to one of repression. As the waves of general strikes built up during this period, the government employed various repressive measures, such as riot controls and even deportation of militants, to control the defiant nature of the labor movement. By 1910, however, organized labor had clearly gathered strength in Argentina. Because of its revolutionary nature, however, it remained outside of the established political and capitalist structure of the country. The labor movement would remain an outsider until the government and the capitalists needed it to fulfill their continuing industrial aspirations.

Timeline

1899: Aspirin introduced.

1900: Commonwealth of Australia is established.

1900: Sigmund Freud publishes *The Interpretation of Dreams.*

1901: U.S. President William McKinley is assassinated by Leon Czolgosz, an anarchist. Vice President Theodore Roosevelt becomes president.

1904: Russo-Japanese War, which lasts into 1905 and results in a resounding Japanese victory, begins. In Russia, the war is followed by the Revolution of 1905, which marks the beginning of the end of czarist rule; meanwhile, Japan is poised to become the first major non-Western power of modern times.

1907: U.S. markets experience a financial panic.

1911: Turkish-Italian War sees the first use of aircraft as an offensive weapon. Italian victory results in the annexation of Libya.

1913: Two incidents illustrate the increasingly controversial nature of the arts in the new century. Visitors to the 17 February Armory Show in New York City are scandalized by such works as Marcel Duchamp's cubist *Nude Descending a Staircase,* which elicits vehement criticism, and theatergoers at the 29 May debut of Igor Stravinsky's ballet *Le Sacré du Printemps* (*The Rite of Spring*) are so horrified by the new work that a riot ensues.

1914: On 28 June in the town of Sarajevo, then part of the Austro-Hungarian Empire, Serbian nationalist Gavrilo Princip assassinates Austrian Archduke Francis Ferdinand and wife Sophie. In the weeks that follow, Austria declares war on Serbia, and Germany on Russia and France, while Great Britain responds by declaring war

on Germany. By the beginning of August, the lines are drawn, with the Allies (Great Britain, France, Russia, Belgium, Serbia, Montenegro, and Japan) against the Central Powers (Germany, Austria-Hungary, and Turkey).

Event and Its Context

Anarchism in Argentina Prior to 1900

As early as the 1880s, the anarchists in the labor movement in Argentina were unable to compete effectively with the socialists for leadership of the working class because they were divided into two factions. One faction supported the philosophy of Mikhail Bakunin, who emphasized the need for individual action. The other faction supported the philosophy of Pyotr Kropotkin, who supported the collectivist attitude that effective action must be undertaken by groups. The only thing upon which the two factions agreed was rejection of the more traditional methods of the socialists, the leading labor group at that time in Argentina. The socialists wanted to assimilate the worker into the society of Argentina, but the anarchists wanted to destroy the existing society and build a new one in its place.

During the 1890s the collectivist faction won control of the Argentine anarchists. The writings of Antonio Pellicer Paraire provided the anarchists with a basis for collective organization. In 1900 Paraire published a series of articles titled *La Organización Obrera* (The Workers' Organization), in which he emphasized the ineffectiveness of individual action in the overall daily struggle and the long-range revolutionary goals of the anarchist movement. He proposed that every local trade group or factory unit organize *soliedad de resistencia* (a resistance society). The local societies, he proposed, would further unite to form craft federations, which would fight to improve economic and social conditions, and local federations, which would handle all organizational matters.

FORA and UGT

In 1901 the anarchists joined together (temporarily, as would be the trend in the future) with the socialists in establishing the *Federación Obrera Argentina* (Argentina Workers' Federation, FOA). At its second congress in 1902, the socialist affiliates walked out over differences with the anarchists. The anarchists changed the FOA's name to the *Federación Obrera de la República Argentina* (Workers' Federation of the Argentine Republic, FORA). For the next 10 years, the anarchists became the strongest voice for the labor movement, and the socialists regrouped and formed a minority organization called the *Unión General de Trabajadores*, UGT (General Union of Workers) and later reorganized as the Workers' Confederation of the Argentina Region (*Confederación Obrera de la Región Argentina*, CORA).

Under the leadership of the anarchists, the labor movement moved toward creating a radically new society rather than assimilating workers into society, as the socialists had tried to do earlier. The leaders of the anarchist movement felt that violence was justified in the effort to return society to a state that was free of the corruption that they felt controlled the country. The most effective method promoted and used by the anarchists to overthrow the government and to win benefits for the workers was the revolutionary general strike.

Using the inspiration of the Barcelona, Spain, general strike of 1902, the Argentine anarchists began a wave of local and general strikes. The general strikes of 1902 illustrated the difference in the new labor movement (anarchist versus socialist) when the workers of Argentina led a national, unified labor struggle and angrily expressed their growing social and political concerns about the country. The strikes, which were initiated by the workers in the central fruit markets at the ports of Buenos Aires, Rosario, and Bahía Blanca, later led to a general strike against the *Ley de Residencia* (Law of Residence), starting on 23 November 1902. The Law of Residence allowed the government to deport anyone whose activities compromised national security or disturbed the public peace. The city of Buenos Aires was besieged with infantry and cavalry, as factories turned into armed camps. In 1904 workers conducted a general strike in the city of Rosario, which eventually was given the name the "Barcelona of Latin America." That year workers on the sugar plantations of Tucumán also engaged in a general strike. The general strike in 1905, in which factory stoppages joined the massive confrontations of the general strikes, is considered to be the high point of the anarchist influence on the labor movement.

Two of the most successful strikes occurred in 1907 and 1909. In 1907 a general strike organized by the railway engineers' union known as *La Fraternidad* (The Brotherhood) engaged a national outpouring of support from about 93,000 workers. During the entire year of 1907, according to the annual bulletins of the Argentine National Labor Department, 169,107 strikers in Buenos Aires were involved in 231 strikes. The number of strikers during 1907 was enormous compared to 1908, when only 11,561 Buenos Aires strikers were involved in 118 strikes. Then in May 1909, government repression of the workers' marches caused about 12 deaths and more than 100 injuries. To protest the killing of workers by the police, between 200,000 and 300,000 laborers soon conducted a work stoppage in Buenos Aires that lasted for six days. The 1909 strike ended after the government conceded to many of the demands of the workers.

Governmental Response

For the most part the government of Argentina had little sympathy for any type of labor movement, whether it was socialist or anarchist. In a strong position of power, the country's leaders would not even consider that the working class could be on equal status with the ruling class. However, as the anarchists took over the labor movement, created the FORA, and introduced militancy into their actions, the government quickly abandoned its noninterventionist mood toward capital-labor conflicts and adopted forceful and repressive measures to control the labor movement. In response to the 1902 wave of strikes—the first general strikes in Argentine history—the police began to raid union headquarters, use labor spies, imprison workers, and suspend the publication of labor periodicals. When necessary the government declared a state of siege—a declaration of emergency—that permitted it to suspend the normal constitutional guarantees due to its citizens. Often the repression led to bloody conflict as the intervention by the police

Pyotr Alekseyevich Kropotkin. © Hulton-Deutsch Collection/Corbis-Bettmann. Reproduced by permission.

and the army created a toll of dead and injured protesters (along with soldiers). When all else failed, the government resorted to deporting the leaders of the militant movement under the new Law of Residence. During its 60-year history, this law allowed for the expulsion of hundreds (perhaps thousands) of anarchist militants and foreign-born workers, along with some of the more revolutionary Argentine workers.

The government tried to compromise with the labor movement in 1904 when it attempted to approve an eight-hour workday, a regulation of night work, accident insurance, rest on Sunday, regulation of women's work, and the prohibition of child labor. However, both labor and business opposed the proposed law for their own one-sided reasons. In 1907 the government again tried to establish a relationship with the working classes by creating a National Labor Department. However, leaders of the labor movement refused to meet with what it perceived as a corrupt government. The National Labor Department enforced new labor legislation, collected statistics on workers' conditions, and arbitrated industrial disputes (when both sides agreed to such a resolution).

The final conflict between the militant labor movement and the equally forceful government happened seven days before the 25 May 1910 celebration of the Centennial of Argentine Independence. After the failure of communications between labor, business, and government, the government approached the leaders of the anarchist FORA with the hope of avoiding any conflict during the celebrations. The FORA leaders, on the one hand, felt they should call a strike at this time, but, on the other hand, felt that the people might see a strike as opposing the celebration. The socialist CORA decided to go ahead with a strike on 18 May 1910. The FORA then felt obligated to call a general strike on that same day so as to maintain its position of leadership.

The government moved swiftly to stop the organized labor demonstrations. On 13 May 1910 it began to arrest labor leaders, and the next day it declared a state of siege. Union buildings were destroyed and people employed at working-class newspapers were attacked. Thousands of workers were jailed and dozens were deported. Tensions remained high throughout the celebrations, but the government eventually canceled all demonstrations during those days. The situation finally reached a peak on 26 June 1910, when a bomb exploded at an empty theatre. An anarchist was accused of the crime, and within the next two days the government passed the Law of Social Defense (*Ley de Defensa Social*) specifically to destroy the anarchist movement. The law prohibited anarchists from entering the country, propagating their ideas, and holding public meetings. The government quickly removed the leaders of the anarchists from their leadership positions, which weakened the overall labor movement. Workers were left to fend for themselves, as the government promptly eliminated any type of organized labor.

Conclusion

The domination by the anarchists of the labor movement in Argentina ended in May 1910. For almost two years, the FORA existed as an underground organization. In 1914 the FORA merged with the CORA at a congress under the new FORA name: *Federación Obrera Regional Argentina* (Argentine Regional Workers' Federation, FORA). However, in a year the socialist element separated from the FORA, at its ninth congress, after refusing to support the organization's pledge to support anarchist communism. The socialists formed what was called the FORA of the Ninth Congress, and the anarchists formed what was called the FORA of the Fifth Congress (based on the "fifth" meeting that first made the pledge to anarchist communism).

Because the anarchists and the socialists could not unite in a common cause for the working class, the effectiveness of the labor movement remained fragmented. Furthermore, because of their militant nature, labor organizations largely remained outside the established institutional political and capitalist structure of Argentina. The labor movement would remain an outsider until the government and the capitalists needed it to fulfill their industrial aspirations. Such a need would eventually arise, but the labor movement still had years of struggle with which to contend as it grew in an industrializing Argentina.

Key Players

Bakunin, Mikhail Aleksandrovich (1814–1876): Bakunin was a Russian revolutionary of the nineteenth century, both in Russia and Europe. He was best known for his anarchistic philosophy. Bakunin was also a prolific theorist, a devoted atheist, and a radical agitator.

Kropotkin, Pyotr Alekseyevich (1842–1921): Kropotkin was one of Russia's best known anarchists and a prominent ad-

vocate of libertarian socialism. Because of his prominence as an anarchist, he was commonly known as the "Anarchist Prince."

Paraire, Antonio Pellicer (1851–1916): Paraire was a Spanish printer who immigrated to Argentina in 1891. In 1900 Paraire published a series of articles on labor organizations in which he put forward the basic principles for a labor federation.

See also: *Organized Labor Established, Argentina.*

BIBLIOGRAPHY

Books

Alexander, Robert Jackson. *Organized Labor in Latin America.* New York: The Free Press, 1965.
———. *An Introduction to Argentina.* New York: Praeger, 1969.
Baily, Samuel L. *Labor, Nationalism, and Politics in Argentina.* New Brunswick, NJ: Rutgers University Press, 1967.
Munck, Ronaldo. *Argentina from Anarchism to Peronism: Workers, Unions and Politics, 1855–1985.* London: Zed Books Ltd., 1987.

Other

Oved, Yaacov. "The Uniqueness of Anarchism in Argentina." Tel Aviv University [cited 4 December 2002]. <http://www.tau.ac.il/eial/VIII_1/oved.htm>.
Booklist.com. "Michael Bakunin 1814–1876: Biographical Notes." 2001 [cited 4 December 2002]. <http://www.booklist.com/michael_bakunin.html>.
Wikipedia.com. "Peter Kropotkin" [cited 4 December 2002]. <http://www.wikipedia.org/wiki/Peter_Kropotkin>.

—William Arthur Atkins

Anthracite Coal Strike

United States 1902

Synopsis

When the United Mine Workers in Pennsylvania went on strike in 1902, the crisis became serious enough that President Theodore Roosevelt stepped in to arbitrate a settlement. By arranging for labor and management to meet face-to-face, Roosevelt unofficially recognized the union for the first time. He achieved a settlement that satisfied both labor and management. The settlement also increased Roosevelt's popularity and strengthened the presidency.

Timeline

1882: Agitation against English rule spreads throughout Ireland, culminating with the assassination of chief secretary for Ireland Lord Frederick Cavendish and permanent undersecretary Thomas Burke in Dublin's Phoenix Park. The leader of the nationalist movement is Charles Stewart Parnell, but the use of assassination and terrorism—which Parnell himself has disavowed—makes clear the fact that he does not control all nationalist groups.

1887: John Emerich Edward Dalbert-Acton, a leader of the opposition to the papal dogma of infallibility, observes, in a letter to Cambridge University professor Mandell Creighton, that "Power tends to corrupt, and absolute power corrupts absolutely."

1891: Construction of Trans-Siberian Railway begins. Meanwhile, crop failures across Russia lead to widespread starvation.

1895: Guglielmo Marconi pioneers wireless telegraphy, which in the next three decades will make possible the use of radio waves for commercial broadcasts and other applications.

1898: United States defeats Spain in the three-month Spanish-American War. As a result, Cuba gains it independence, and the United States purchases Puerto Rico and the Philippines from Spain for $20 million.

1902: The *Times Literary Supplement,* a weekly review of literature and scholarship, begins publication in London.

1902: Second Anglo-Boer War ends in victory for Great Britain. It is a costly victory, however, resulting in the loss of more British lives (5,774) than any conflict between 1815 and 1914. The war also sees the introduction of concentration camps, used by the British to incarcerate Boer civilians.

1902: English geneticist William Bateson translates Austrian botanist Gregor Mendel's long-forgotten writings, which are destined to have an enormous impact on the study of heredity.

1904: Russo-Japanese War, which lasts into 1905 and results in a resounding Japanese victory, begins. In Russia the war is followed by the Revolution of 1905, which marks the beginning of the end of czarist rule; meanwhile, Japan is poised to become the first major non-Western power of modern times.

1908: Ford Motor Company introduces the Model T.

1912: *Titanic* sinks on its maiden voyage, from Southampton to New York, on 14 April. More than 1,500 people are killed.

Event and Its Context

On Strike

On 12 May 1902, 147,000 anthracite coal miners of the United Mine Workers (UMW) walked off the job in central and

Philander Chase Knox. The Library of Congress.

northeastern Pennsylvania to force the coal mine owners to meet their demands. The walkout left the Northeast and Midwest regions without the anthracite coal used to heat nearly every home, hospital, and business in the winter months. The owners, who also owned the railroads that shipped the coal, and thereby operated the largest industrial monopoly in the United States, refused to meet with John Mitchell, the UMW president. President Theodore Roosevelt believed that allowing the strike to go into autumn might cause wide-scale social unrest and violence and that breaking the strike might trigger the same response. Roosevelt's direct involvement in the arbitration talks—a first in United States history—ended the standoff.

In 1900 the mine owners, under political pressure from Republican leaders fearful of losing the White House, had made concessions that they had opposed to end an earlier strike. They vowed not to do that again. George F. Baer of the Philadelphia and Reading Railroad, and spokesman for the mine owners, took a hard line. "We will not surrender," he publicly declared. "The coal presidents are going to settle this strike, and they will settle it in their own way." In other words, they hoped to break the union.

Attempts at arbitration failed in June. Appeals came into the White House asking for the president to appoint a commission to investigate the issues of the strike. The owners advised against any presidential action. On 8 June, Roosevelt asked the

J. P. Morgan. The Library of Congress.

commissioner of labor, Carroll D. Wright, to report to him about the circumstances of the strike. Two weeks later, Wright reported that a great deal of distrust existed between management and labor and made some suggestions about settlement. When Roosevelt asked whether he should release the report to the public, Attorney General Philander Knox responded that he should not on the grounds that the president had no right to interfere with the strike.

UMW Makes Concessions

During the first three months of the strike, Mitchell made as many concessions as he dared without losing leverage. His initial demands included union recognition, a reduction in the workday from 10 to 8 hours, an equitable system of assessing each miner's output, and an overall wage increase of 10 percent. Mitchell offered to go to arbitration to settle the dispute and was willing to forgo union recognition by the owners in return for his demands. When the bituminous coal miners walked out in sympathy, Mitchell persuaded them to go back to work and pay extra union dues to support their fellow miners. He temporarily kept pump men, engineers, and firemen on the job to prevent the mines from flooding or burning. The owners remained intransigent.

The miners' appeal for public sympathy worked as long as the weather remained warm and there was no violence in the coal fields. Mitchell knew that if Baer tried to break the strike with nonunion labor, there would be bloodshed. An attempt to do so at one mine triggered an outbreak of violence on 30 July. Governor William Stone sent troops to surround the area but informed President Roosevelt that federal assistance was neither necessary nor wanted. Public support for the miners soon began to erode. Mitchell implored the miners to obey the law and retain their determination. Violence subsided for the next two weeks.

In August 18,000 bituminous miners went out on a sympathy strike, joined by 50,000 coal-road workers (workers involved in the railroad transport of coal from the mines) who had nothing to move. The total number of idle workers approached a quarter of a million. At the end of August, Roosevelt inquired of Attorney General Knox if he could proceed against the mine owners for being engaged in a trust. Knox again replied that there were no grounds on which he could act. The Sherman Antitrust Act, he informed Roosevelt, was too narrowly drawn to support such a move. Meanwhile, reports of potential coal shortages in major cities began to surface.

Roosevelt Steps in

By September seven counties in northeastern Pennsylvania were under military surveillance, but the governor had not yet sent in state troops to seize the mines. Republican Party officials began to fret that the issue would hurt them in the upcoming congressional elections. Governor Winthrop Murray Crane of Massachusetts suggested to the president that he invite mine operators and miners to confer with him. Roosevelt, aware that he had no constitutional authority in the matter but believing that the situation called for some type of action, sent telegrams on 1 October to the presidents of the railroads that owned the coals mines and to Mitchell, asking them to come to Washington two days later. Mitchell received permission to bring three UMW district presidents.

On the morning of 3 October, Roosevelt informed the group at the beginning of the conference that he had no "right or duty to intervene in this way upon legal grounds or upon any official relation that I bear to the situation." Because of the situation, Roosevelt stated, he hoped to exert whatever influence he could to end the strike. He asked for an immediate resumption of operations in the mines to avert the potential widespread disaster of a shortage over the coming winter. Mitchell expressed the miners' willingness to have the president name a tribunal to settle the issues. If the owners accepted the tribunal's decision, so would the union. In the afternoon meeting, the owners made clear their refusal to deal with Mitchell and his men because they had provoked violence. They asked the president to dissolve the union as a trust (or illegal monopoly) and urged him to use the military to end the strike. When asked directly, they conceded that they would be willing to leave the strike to the courts of Pennsylvania, a concession that implied their willingness to submit to the authority of a third power. The conference ended with no settlement.

Though the conference itself was a failure, it had great significance. As historian Lewis L. Gould noted, "The president had placed a labor union and the workers it represented on something approaching the same political level as management and capital." Roosevelt established the precedent of presidential involvement in domestic economic crisis. Roosevelt's initiative at this stage of the coal strike proved to be an important contribution to enhancing the power of the presidency.

On 8 October, Mitchell rejected Roosevelt's offer to name an investigating commission if the miners would return to work. With no resolution in hand, Roosevelt ignored Mitchell and began assembling a commission to look into the strike on his behalf. At the same time, he decided that if no solution could be reached through negotiation, he would send in the U.S. Army and have the government operate the mines until the commission reported to him. It was a step he was loathe to take because he thought it "would form an evil precedent," but believed it was his only option in such an emergency.

Before taking such a drastic step, though, Roosevelt agreed to allow Secretary of War Elihu Root to meet with J. P. Morgan. Root, who came to government service from Wall Street, believed that Morgan's banking interests and position on the boards of many of the railroad companies gave him leverage with the mine owners. They returned to Washington together on 13 October with a proposal in which the owners aired their grievances and called for immediate resumption of mining, and for the appointment of a commission whose findings would be effective throughout the anthracite industry for three years. They did not acknowledge the union. They also stated their preferences for how the commission should be comprised: a military officer, a mining engineer, a federal judge from Pennsylvania, a man who was active in the anthracite coal business, and "a man of prominence eminent as a sociologist." They made no accommodation for any representative of organized labor.

Mitchell responded that he would agree to the proposal if the president added two more members of Roosevelt's choosing—a high Catholic official and a member of a union. Morgan's representatives agreed to Bishop John L. Spalding, who was also an industrial scholar, but rejected Edgar E. Clark, chief of the Railway Conductors Union, because he was "a labor man." If Clark were placed in the sociologist's slot, however, they had no objection. They simply did not want a union man appointed as labor's representative so they could claim they avoided any recognition of the union movement. Through this twist of semantics, both sides agreed on the membership of the commission. The miners returned to work on 23 October while the commission conducted its investigation.

On 18 March 1903 the commission submitted its findings to Roosevelt. It offered something for both workers and owners. The miners received a 10 percent increase in pay, a 9-hour working day, and a system of arbitration for job-related disputes. The commission did not offer recognition of the union because to do so, it argued, lay outside its mandate. Other coal-industry practices opposed by the UMW remained in place. The report also issued a strong denunciation of violence and of the boycotting tactics of the UMW. As for Roosevelt, who had been in office only a year when he first intervened in October 1902, his role in ending the strike raised his personal popularity to new heights and helped the Republicans at the polls a few weeks after the workers returned to work.

Elihu Root.

Key Players

Baer, George Frederick (1842–1914): A lawyer and railroad executive, Baer served as legal counsel for the Philadelphia and Reading Railroad, and later was president of the organization that managed all the Reading holdings.

Knox, Philander Chase (1853–1921): As attorney general (1901–1904), Knox proved important in the implementation of Roosevelt's antitrust policy. He served one term as a U.S. senator (1904–1909), and then became secretary of state (1909–1913). He later returned to the Senate (1917–1921).

Mitchell, John (1870–1919): A founding member of the United Mine Workers (1890), Mitchell helped in its first successful national strike (1897) and served as its president (1899–1908), a period in which the union expanded its membership tenfold.

Morgan, J. P. (1837–1913): Morgan built his father's financial firm into the most powerful private banking house in America. Morgan financed the Federal Reserve system in the depression of 1895, developed the railroad system, and formed the U.S. Steel Corporation (1901).

Roosevelt, Theodore (1858–1919): A lifelong civil servant, a war hero, and author, Roosevelt became the youngest president ever upon William McKinley's assassination in 1901.

He strengthened the executive branch through his progressive agenda during his two terms. He ran for a third term in office in 1912 on the Progressive Party ticket but lost.

Root, Elihu (1845–1937): A lawyer by training, Root served as U.S. secretary of war (1899–1904) and secretary of state (1905–1909), and was awarded the Nobel Peace Prize in 1912 for his promotion of international arbitration.

See also: *Sherman Antitrust Act; United Mine Workers of America.*

BIBLIOGRAPHY

Books
Cornell, Robert J. *The Anthracite Coal Strike of 1902.* Washington, DC: Catholic University of America Press, 1957.
Gould, Lewis L. *The Presidency of Theodore Roosevelt.* Lawrence: The University Press of Kansas, 1991.
Morris, Edmund. *Theodore Rex.* New York: Random House, 2001.

Other
Grossman, Jonathan. "The Coal Strike of 1902—Turning Point in U.S. Policy." *Monthly Labor Review* (October 1975). Reprinted on U.S. Department of Labor Web site, history page [cited 30 August 2002]. <http://www.dol.gov/asp/programs/history/coalstrike.htm>.

ADDITIONAL RESOURCES

Books
Gould, Lewis L. *Reform and Regulation: American Politics, 1900–1916.* New York: Wiley, 1978.
Harbaugh, William Henry. *Power and Responsibility: The Life and Times of Theodore Roosevelt.* New York: Farrar, Straus and Cudahy, 1961.
Mowry, George Edwin. *The Era of Theodore Roosevelt and the Birth of Modern America, 1900–1912.* New York: Harper and Row, 1958.
Roosevelt, Theodore. *Autobiography.* New York: Charles Scribner's Sons, 1913.

—James G. Lewis

Anti-Injunction Act: *See* **Norris–La Guardia Act.**

Apex Hosiery Co. v. Leader

United States 1940

Synopsis

In *Apex Hosiery Co. v. Leader*, the U.S. Supreme Court ruled that a labor strike carried out to further the interests of the union conducting it, even if the effect of the strike is to reduce the amount of goods in interstate commerce, is not a violation of the Sherman Antitrust Act. The *Apex* decision was significant because it nullified earlier decisions that had preserved the Sherman Act as a tool against organized labor and because it in effect ratified the Norris–La Guardia Federal Anti-Injunction Act of 1932.

Timeline

1919: With the Third International (Comintern), the Bolshevik government of Russia establishes its control over communist movements worldwide.

1924: In the United States, secretary of the interior Albert B. Fall, along with oil company executives Harry Sinclair and Edward L. Doheny, is charged with conspiracy and bribery in making fraudulent leases of U.S. Navy oil reserves at Teapot Dome, Wyoming. The resulting Teapot Dome scandal clouds the administration of President Warren G. Harding.

1929: The Lateran Treaty between the Catholic Church and Mussolini's regime establishes the Vatican City as an independent political entity.

1935: Germany annexes the Saar region after a plebiscite. In defiance of Versailles, the Nazis reintroduce compulsory military service. The Allies do nothing, and many Western intellectuals maintain that it is only proper for Germany to retake its own territory and begin building up its army again.

1940: Hitler's troops sweep through Western Europe, annexing Norway and Denmark in April, and in May the Low Countries and France. At the same time, Stalin—who in this year arranges the murder of Trotsky in Mexico—takes advantage of the situation to add the Baltic republics (Latvia, Lithuania, and Estonia) to the Soviet empire, where they will remain for more than half a century.

1940: Winston Churchill succeeds Neville Chamberlain as British prime minister in May. A month later, he tells Parliament, "We shall not flag or fail. We shall fight in France, we shall fight on the seas and oceans, we shall fight with growing confidence and growing strength in the air, we shall defend our island, whatever the cost may be. We shall fight on the beaches, we shall fight on the landing grounds, we shall fight in the fields and in the streets, we shall fight in the hills. We shall never surrender." In November, German bombers begin air strikes against Britain.

1940: NBC makes the first official network television broadcast.

1945: At the Yalta Conference in February, Roosevelt, Churchill, and Stalin make plans for Germany after its by now inevitable surrender.

1950: North Korean troops pour into South Korea, starting the Korean War. Initially the communists make impressive gains, but in September, the U.S. Marines land at Inchon and liberate Seoul. China responds by sending in its troops.

1955: African and Asian nations meet at the Bandung Conference in Indonesia, inaugurating the "non-aligned" movement of Third World countries.

Event and Its Context

The Sherman Antitrust Act and Organized Labor

The roots of *Apex Hosiery Co. v. Leader* extended back exactly half a century, to the passage of the Sherman Antitrust Act of 1890. The chief purpose of the Sherman Act was to curb the monopolistic practices of big business, but an unintended side effect of the act was that it became a tool that employers could wield against organized labor. Employers repeatedly argued in court that certain union activities, in particular the secondary boycott, violated the Sherman Act because they restrained interstate commerce. The courts agreed. In a series of landmark cases, including *Danbury Hatters* (1908), *Gompers v. Bucks Stove & Range Co.* (1911), *Duplex Printing Press Company v. Deering* (1921), the *Coronado Coal Company* cases (1922 and 1925), and *Bedford Cut Stone Company v. Journeymen Stone Cutters Association* (1927), the Supreme Court applied the Sherman Act and, later, the Clayton Antitrust Act of 1914 against unions—although it did not always do a very effective job of applying them against monopolistic business practices.

One of these cases, *United Mine Workers v. Coronado Coal Company* (1922), would later be of particular relevance to the *Apex* decision. The owners of the Coronado coal mine, facing stiff competition from nonunion mining companies, attempted to close down the mine and reopen it on a nonunion basis despite the fact that the United Mine Workers had a contract with the company. Operation of the mine came to a halt when the workers struck, occupied the mine, and did considerable damage to it; several nonunion workers were murdered. The company brought suit, charging that the union had violated the Sherman Act. The U.S. Supreme Court initially ruled against the company, reasoning that coal mining in and of itself was not interstate commerce and that therefore the Sherman Act did not apply. In reaching its decision, however, the Court provided Coronado management with a claim in a subsequent suit by stating that the union's actions would have fallen under the Sherman Act if the company had shown that the union intended to monopolize or restrain interstate commerce by eliminating the marketing of nonunion coal.

Accordingly, the company refiled its suit, and when the case reappeared before the Supreme Court in 1925 (as *Coronado Coal Company v. United Mine Workers*), the company ar-

Charles Evans Hughes.

gued that the purpose of the strike was to prevent "scab-dug coal"—that is, nonunion coal—from reaching the market. On this basis the Court ruled in favor of the company, agreeing that the union's activities restrained trade under the Sherman Act. The effect of the second *Coronado* case was to dampen the efforts of the United Mine Workers to organize nonunion mines and, more significantly, to call into question the legality of any strike.

The Norris-La Guardia Act of 1932

One widely used tactic management employed against labor unions during these years was the injunction. Section 20 of the Clayton Act had attempted to prevent the federal courts from enjoining labor union activities, but the courts interpreted the act so narrowly as to render it impotent. Indeed, the courts continued to enjoin union activities so frequently that some states, including Arizona, passed anti-injunction statutes designed to keep the courts out of labor disputes. In *Truax v. Corrigan* (1921), however, the U.S. Supreme Court held that the Arizona statute unconstitutionally deprived employers of property rights in their business without equal protection and due process. Congress, though, was recognizing increasingly the value of effective collective bargaining in modern society. After nearly five years of discussion and debate, Congress passed the Norris-La Guardia Federal Anti-Injunction Act in 1932 to reduce the influence of the courts in labor disputes. The act denied the courts the right to enjoin peaceful picketing, regardless of the purpose of the strike, and it carefully drew up procedures regulating when and under what conditions a court could issue an injunction against a union in a labor dispute.

Although Norris-La Guardia was a victory for organized labor, many observers remained skeptical, fearing that the act would meet with the same fate in the courts as had the Clayton Act. Their fears proved unfounded. In *Milk Wagon Drivers*

Harlan Fiske Stone. The Library of Congress.

Union v. Lake Valley Farm Products (1940) and *United States v. Hutcheson* (1941), the Supreme Court affirmed the right of labor to engage in activities intended to affect the outcome of the collective bargaining process, including strikes, picketing, and secondary boycotts. It was in this context that the *Apex* case appeared on the Court's docket in 1940.

The Nullification of *Coronado*

The last obstacle for labor was the precedent set in the *Coronado* case of 1922 and 1925, particularly as the facts of the *Apex* case were remarkably similar to those of the earlier case. The Apex Hosiery Company was a nonunion shop that produced about $5 million worth of hosiery each year with 80 percent of it shipped in interstate commerce. Of the company's 2,500 workers, only eight were members of the hosiery workers' union. In early 1937 the union pressed the company to recognize it as the bargaining agent for the company's workers and to employ only union members. The company refused, so in May of that year union members, along with members of the hosiery union who worked at other plants in the Philadelphia area, gathered at the Apex plant to renew their demands. When the company again refused, union officials ordered a sit-down strike. The workers seized the plant, wrecked machinery, and prevented the shipment of 130,000 dozen pairs of hosiery valued at about $800,000, despite three requests from the company

that it be allowed to retrieve the goods and ship them to fill orders. The strikers held the plant until an injunction issued by the Third Circuit Court of Appeals forced them out on 23 July.

The company filed suit in district court, and under the provisions of the Sherman Act, the court awarded it treble damages in the amount of $711,932.55. In the days and weeks that followed, other companies, smelling blood, filed similar suits. Three northeastern trucking companies filed suit against the Teamsters union, asking for damages as a result of a strike; the Republic Steel Corporation sued the CIO, asking for $7.5 million in damages as a result of a 1937 strike. The outcome of these and other cases would depend principally on the outcome of the *Apex* case, which was argued on 1–2 April 1940 and decided on 27 May. The question on the minds of both the legal and the labor communities was whether the Court would reaffirm its decision in the *Coronado* cases and hold that the strike, because it restrained interstate commerce, violated the Sherman Antitrust Act.

It is important to note that the validity of the union's demands was not at issue, nor was the lawfulness of the strike. Indeed, the Court deplored the defendants' "lawless invasion of petitioner's plant and destruction of its property by force and violence of the most brutal and wanton character." If the company had wanted simply to seek indemnification for damage to the plant, which was unable to resume even partial operation until 19 August 1937, it could have done so in state court, for the union and its members clearly had violated state civil and criminal laws. The Supreme Court, however, had no authority to enforce state laws. The sole issue the Court was called upon to decide was whether the union had violated antitrust law.

In his majority opinion, Justice Harlan Fiske Stone dismissed the company's suit and held that the union's actions were not a restraint of trade within the meaning of the Sherman Act. Stone reasoned that the very purpose of a labor union was to eliminate nonunion competition: "an elimination of price competition based on differences in labor standards is the objective of any national labor organization. But this effect on competition has not been considered to be the kind of curtailment of price competition prohibited by the Sherman Act." Further, one purpose of any strike is to reduce the amount of goods in circulation; striking and stopping production are the same thing. A union strikes not to conspire to restrain interstate commerce but to win a labor dispute with an employer. If a strike were declared unlawful simply because it diminished the amount of goods in interstate commerce, the Sherman Act would undermine the legality of "practically every strike in modern industry," according to Stone and the Court.

The Court's decision was not unanimous. Chief Justice Charles Hughes wrote a lengthy dissent, with Justices James McReynolds and Owen Roberts joining him. Hughes's dissent turned on the union's refusal to grant the company permission to enter the plant to retrieve already finished goods to fulfill existing orders. This was not merely a stoppage of production; it was, in Hughes's words, a "direct and intentional prevention of interstate commerce in the furtherance of an illegal conspiracy."

The Court in *Apex* did not specifically overrule its decision in the second *Coronado* case. Further, it reaffirmed that labor unions were still governed by antitrust law, although later Courts held this to be true only in cases in which labor unions joined with employers to promote a monopoly. Thus, for example, it remains illegal for a contractor to conspire with a labor union to boycott nonunion subcontractors that the union wishes to organize. Nonetheless, in its 1940–1941 term, the Supreme Court finally joined with Congress in getting the judiciary's hands off of labor disputes. From that point on, secondary boycotts became an effective tool in the hands of labor, and the courts no longer used antitrust law to halt union organizing efforts or to threaten the legality of strikes.

Key Players

Hughes, Charles Evans (1862–1948): Born in Glens Falls, New York, Hughes served as governor of New York from 1907 to 1910, when he was nominated to the Supreme Court by President William Taft. He left the Court in 1916 to run for president, narrowly losing against Woodrow Wilson. From 1921 to 1925 he was secretary of state under presidents Warren Harding and Calvin Coolidge. From 1928 to 1930 he served as a World Court judge, until Coolidge appointed him chief justice of the Supreme Court (1930–1941).

Stone, Harlan Fiske (1872–1946): Stone was born in Chesterfield, New Hampshire. After a long career at the Columbia University law school (1898–1924; dean after 1910), he served briefly as U.S. attorney general before President Calvin Coolidge appointed him to the Supreme Court in 1924. In 1941 President Franklin Roosevelt appointed Stone chief justice, and he served in this capacity until his death.

See also: *Clayton Antitrust Act; Coronado Coal v. UMWA; Gompers v. Bucks Stove; Norris–La Guardia Act; Sherman Antitrust Act; Truax v. Corrigan; United Mine Workers of America.*

BIBLIOGRAPHY

Books

Northrup, Herbert R., and Gordon F. Bloom. *Government and Labor*. Homewood, IL: Richard D. Irwin, 1963.

Taylor, Benjamin J., and Fred Witney. *Labor Relations Law*, 3rd ed. Englewood Cliffs, NJ: Prentice-Hall, 1979.

Periodicals

McNatt, E. B. "Labor Again Menaced by the Sherman Act." *The Southern Economic Journal* 6, no. 2 (1939).

Timbers, Edwin. "The Problems of Union Power and Antitrust Legislation." *Labor Law Journal* 16, no. 9 (1965).

—Michael J. O'Neal

Grover Cleveland. The Library of Congress.

Arbitration Act of 1888

United States 1888

Synopsis

The United States federal government passed the Arbitration Act of 1888 on 1 October 1888 to legislate the government's role in railroad labor disputes, thus setting a precedent for federal arbitration between unions and railroad carriers. The act made provisions for two opportunities to settle issues: voluntary arbitration and a temporary investigative commission. The act states that it is intended "to create boards of arbitration or commission for settling controversies and differences between railroad corporations and other common carriers engaged in interstate and territorial transportation of property or passengers and their employees." The earliest legal sanction of federal mediation in labor relations, the act particularly affected subsequent labor legislation including the Railway Labor Act of 1926 and the National Labor Relations Act (Wagner Act) of 1935. Prompted by a decade of railway strikes, most markedly the Great Railroad Strike of 1877 and the 1885–1886 strike, the new law countered the pattern of escalating violence and disruption established by troops and striking workers. The Arbitration Act of 1888 was superseded by the Erdman Act (1898), Newlands Act (1913), and Adamson Act (1916).

Eugene V. Debs. The Library of Congress.

Timeline

1868: Fourteenth Amendment to the U.S. Constitution, which grants civil rights to African Americans, is ratified.

1873: Financial panic begins in Vienna, and soon spreads to other European financial centers, as well as to the United States.

1878: First commercial telephone exchange opens, in New Haven, Connecticut.

1881: U.S. President James A. Garfield is assassinated in a Washington, D.C., railway station by Charles J. Guiteau.

1886: Bombing at Haymarket Square, Chicago, kills seven policemen and injures numerous others. Eight anarchists are accused and tried; three are imprisoned, one commits suicide, and four are hanged.

1888: With a series of murders in London's seedy Whitechapel district, Jack the Ripper—whose identity remains a subject of debate—becomes the first known serial murder.

1888: The Blizzard of 1888 in the United States kills hundreds, and causes more than $25 million in property damage.

1888: American inventor George Eastman revolutionizes photography by introducing the Kodak camera, which makes it possible for amateur photographers to take satisfactory snapshots.

1888: Serbian-born American electrical engineer Nikola Tesla develops a practical system for generating and transmitting alternating current (AC), which will ultimately—

and after an extremely acrimonious battle—replace Thomas Edison's direct current (DC) in most homes and businesses.

1890: Alfred Thayer Mahan, a U.S. naval officer and historian, publishes *The Influence of Sea Power upon History, 1660–1783,* which demonstrates the decisive role that maritime forces have played in past conflicts. The book will have an enormous impact on world events by encouraging the major powers to develop powerful navies.

1894: Thousands of unemployed American workers—a group named "Coxey's Army" for their leader, Jacob S. Coxey—march on Washington, D.C. A number of such marches on the capital occurred during this period of economic challenges, but Coxey's march was the only one to actually reach its destination.

1898: United States defeats Spain in the three-month Spanish-American War. As a result, Cuba gains it independence, and the United States purchases Puerto Rico and the Philippines from Spain for $20 million.

Event and Its Context

When interceding in escalating strike activity that characterized labor at the end of the nineteenth century, the federal government's policy was to issue injunctions and deploy troops. Federal actions were effective in the National Railroad Strike of 1877 (also known as the Great Railroad Strike), when troops suppressed riots and restored order to suspended railway services and breached mail service, and ended interference with interstate commerce by strikers. Caused by economic depression, stagnant construction growth, and massive reduction of workers' wages, the 1877 strike set legal precedents for the use of force in railroad labor disputes and dictated this method of government intervention in strike resolution in the railroad industry until 1885. Beginning in West Virginia in July, labor disturbances erupted and moved westward, reaching Chicago, Illinois, where railroad yards shut down. Some observers attributed the upheaval to Marxist inspiration and to radical influence within the state. Rail traffic ceased throughout the state. The National Guard and federal troops arrived in Chicago to restore order to the volatile community and to railroad transportation. Once this approach proved unsuccessful as a means of resolving labor conflicts and preserving the continuity of commerce, Congress and President Grover Cleveland explored several legislative measures with the objective of introducing a series of laws aimed specifically at the railroad industry.

H.R. 7479 was introduced in 1886 and called for voluntary arbitration to be settled by a three-man board. When this proved unacceptable, another proposed bill provided either party of the conflict the right to demand arbitration and recommended penalties for noncompliance. Congress passed H.R. 7479, but President Cleveland vetoed it in favor of his plan to appoint a permanent commission with the capacity to settle labor disputes on its own terms, which in turn would be enforced by court injunctions. Congress did not agree to Cleveland's plan and so proposed several alternative bills, one of which, H.R. 8865, became the Arbitration Act. It was similar to Cleveland's proposal and also included stipulations for voluntary arbitration.

Dealing exclusively with railroad labor disputes, the Arbitration Act of 1888 was intended to reduce strike activity, which crippled the nation's commercial activities by stopping rail transportation and other allied industries. Initially opposed to the act, railroad management viewed it as federal intervention in the operation and management of workers. Organized labor favored the act because government intervention would force rail companies to recognize labor unions and negotiate with them regarding working conditions, benefits, and other areas of interest to laborers.

In the matter of voluntary arbitration, the act instructed railroad companies to select an arbitrator, who would then make the second selection. Together, these appointees would select the third member to serve on a board of arbitration. Each member had to be a U.S. citizen and "wholly impartial and disinterested in respect to such differences or controversies." Because arbitration worked only when the two parties were willing to submit to the process, this method of settling disputes was highly ineffective. Either party in a labor dispute (workers or management), the governor of the state in which the disagreement arose, or the president could convene the commission of inquiry.

The flaws of the Arbitration Act were realized immediately when it was first applied, six years after its implementation, to the Pullman Strike of 1894. In solidarity with the Pullman strikers, Eugene V. Debs, head of the American Railway Union (ARU), declared a strike in June that effectively paralyzed rail transport across the nation. Cleveland responded to this nationwide railroad strike by ordering Secretary of War David S. Lamont to deploy the U.S. Army based at Sheridan, Illinois, to Chicago to break the strike. On 12 July 1894 representatives of the Knights of Labor along with Senator James H. Kyle of South Dakota, who in 1894 authored the bill that created Labor Day, pressed Cleveland to invoke the act. Cleveland promised to use the act once the rioting and violence in Chicago ceased. On 26 July 1894 Cleveland appointed three men to the U.S. Strike Commission to investigate the matter. This move put the Arbitration Act to the test.

Authorized as a temporary body, the organizational structure of the U.S. Strike Commission was designed to prevent partisan control by alternating its appointments. When unions and companies could not agree upon appointees, the president could select two commissioners who would serve along with the commissioner of labor in the matter of railroad arbitration. The commission reported their decision to the president. Their recommendations were enforced through public opinion, as the act did not govern awards or penalties. This remains the model for public protection from railway strikes.

The chairman of the U.S. Strike Commission was the U.S. commissioner of labor, Carroll D. Wright. Along with John D. Kernan of New York and Nicholas E. Worthington of Illinois, who also served during the investigation, Wright's report, sent to Cleveland on 14 November 1894, concentrated on the inadequacies of the Arbitration Act rather than on the problems of the Pullman Strike. Favoring the appointment of a permanent railway labor commission modeled after the Interstate Commerce Commission (ICC), the report also called for company compliance with the arbitrators' decisions, protection for workers during investigations, and a law that would persuade unions to unite.

In the course of their investigation, Wright, Kernan, and Worthington heard testimony from 107 subpoenaed witnesses at a U.S. post office in Chicago. Their inquiry began 15 August 1894 and lasted 13 days. They moved to Washington, D.C., on 26 September where they heard testimony from two more witnesses. The commission was relentless in its inquiries and showed impartiality by subjecting George Pullman, Everett St. John, Eugene Debs, and George W. Howard to equally intense questioning.

Although the response to Wright's report did not promote any specific changes in legislation, it revived congressional awareness of the ineffective measures specified in the Arbitration Act. Numerous bills again passed through Congress. The House Committee on Labor advocated H.R. 8556 in 1895. This bill gave equal importance to mediation and conciliation along with arbitration and investigation and was supported by the railroad brotherhoods as well as Commissioner Wright. The House approved the bill, but it failed to pass the Senate. Later in the year another bill, H.R. 268, was approved by the House but not the Senate. A revised version of the bill, which came to be known as the Erdman Act, was eventually passed by both houses and approved by President William McKinley in 1898.

Key Players

Cleveland, Grover: (1837–1908): Born in New Jersey, Cleveland became a lawyer, was elected mayor of Buffalo, New York in 1881, and later became governor of the state. Elected president of the United State twice, Cleveland served from 1885 to 1889 and 1893 to 1897. He tried to regulate railroads by signing the Interstate Commerce Act, vetoed early versions of the Arbitration Act, and sent federal troops to Chicago during the Pullman Strike of 1894.

Debs, Eugene V. (1855–1926): Born in Terre Haute, Indiana, Debs left school at age 15 to work in a railroad engine house and later became a locomotive fireman. He traveled through Oneonta, New York, in 1883 and encouraged local brakemen to form a union, the Brotherhood of Railway Brakemen. Debs served the Brotherhood of Locomotive Firemen in several roles, organized the American Railway Union (ARU) in 1892, and was instrumental in forming the Social Democratic Party, Socialist Labor Party, and Socialist Party of America.

Kernan, John Devereaux (1844–1922): Born in Utica, New York, Kernan studied law in the office of his father, Senator Francis Kernan, after graduating from Seton Hall College in New Jersey. John Kernan was appointed to the first Board of Railroad Commissioners of the state of New York in 1883 and served until 1887. After Kernan left that position, Cleveland appointed him to investigate the Pullman and ARU strike of 1894.

Worthington, Nicholas Ellsworth (1836–1916): Born in Brooke County, Virginia, which is now located in West Virginia, Worthington was elected to the 48th and 49th Congress as a Democrat. He practiced law and was the circuit judge of the 10th judicial district of Illinois in 1891 and was reelected to that role in 1897. He was appointed by

Cleveland as a commissioner to investigate the Pullman and ARU strike of 1894.

Wright, Carroll Davidson (1840–1909): Born in New Hampshire, Wright studied law, quickly ascended the ranks in the U.S. Army during the Civil War. After his admission to the New Hampshire bar in 1865, he passed the Massachusetts bar in 1867 and settled in Reading, Massachusetts. He was appointed chief of the Massachusetts Bureau of Labor and Statistics in 1873. Appointed by President Chester Arthur in 1885, Wright served as the first U.S. commissioner of labor from 1895 to 1905. He was the chairman of the U.S. Strike Commission that investigated and reported on the causes of the Pullman Strike of 1894.

See also: *Erdman Act; Pullman Strike; Railroad Strike; Railway Labor Act; Wagner Act.*

———————

BIBLIOGRAPHY

Books

Gotkin, Joshua Abraham. *The Legislated Adjustment of Labor Disputes: An Empirical Analysis, 1880 to 1894.* Ann Arbor, MI: University Microfilms, 1995.

Lecht, Leonard A. *Experience under Railway Labor Legislation.* New York: Columbia University Press, 1955.

Lindsey, Almont. *The Pullman Strike: The Story of a Unique Experiment and of a Great Labor Upheaval.* Chicago: University of Chicago Press, 1942.

Richardson, William A. *Supplement to the Revised Statutes of the United States*, 2nd ed. Vol. 1, *1874–1891, 43rd–51st Congress*, inclusive. Washington, DC: Government Printing Office, 1891.

U.S. Strike Commission. *Report on the Chicago Strike of June–July, 1894, with Appendices Containing Testimony Proceedings, and Recommendations.* Washington, DC: Government Printing Office, 1895.

—Rebecca Tolley-Stokes

Autunno Caldo: *See* **Hot Autumn.**

B

Bans on Labor Unions Lifted

Germany 1861–1869

Synopsis

Between 1861 and 1869 legislation banning trade unions was revised in parts of the German Federation. This process of reform culminated in the 1869 *Gewerbeordnung,* or industrial code, of the North German Federation, which made trade unions legal throughout most of the German states. This occurred as part of a wave of liberal measures in the German region during the 1860s that granted a variety of political and economic freedoms. Progressive liberals supported the workers' right to organize as part of this wider program of liberal economic reform. They also wished to gain the support of the workers for the liberal cause. However, this aim was not successful, as workers moved away from liberal workers' associations to form independent, working-class political parties. From the mid-1860s unions were formed in many different trades, as workers grasped the opportunity to press their collective demands for better wages and working conditions.

Timeline

1851: Britain's Amalgamated Society of Engineers applies innovative organizational concepts, including large contributions from, and benefits to, members, as well as vigorous use of direct action and collective bargaining.

1856: Gustave Flaubert publishes *Madame Bovary.*

1861: Emancipation of the serfs occurs in Russia.

1862: Victor Hugo's *Les Misérables* depicts injustices in French society, and Ivan Turgenev's *Fathers and Sons* introduces the term *nihilism.*

1863: U.S. President Abraham Lincoln issues the Emancipation Proclamation, freeing all slaves in Confederate territories, on 1 January. Thus begins a year that sees the turning point of the American Civil War, with decisive Union victories at Gettysburg, Vicksburg, and Chattanooga. Thereafter, the Confederacy is almost perpetually on the defensive, fighting not to win, but to avoid losing.

1865: British surgeon Joseph Lister pioneers the use of antiseptic methods in surgery.

1866: Austrian monk Gregor Mendel presents his theories on the laws of heredity. Though his ideas will be forgotten for a time, they are destined to exert enormous influence on biological study in the twentieth century.

1866: Prussia defeats Austria in the Seven Weeks' War. In the next year, the dual monarchy is established in Austria-Hungary.

1867: Meiji Restoration in Japan ends 675 years of rule by the shoguns.

1870: The Franco-Prussian War begins. German troops sweep over France, Napoleon III is dethroned, and France's Second Empire gives way to the Third Republic.

1871: Franco-Prussian War ends with France's surrender of Alsace-Lorraine to Germany, which proclaims itself an empire under Prussian king Wilhelm, crowned Kaiser Wilhelm I.

1873: The gold standard, adopted by Germany in 1871 and eventually taken on by all major nations, spreads to Italy, Belgium, and Switzerland. Though the United States does not officially base the value of its currency on gold until 1900, an unofficial gold standard dates from this period, even as a debate over "bimetallism" creates sharp divisions in American politics.

Event and Its Context

Organization and Repression

In the first half of the nineteenth century, authoritarian governments repressed workers' organizations. In 1794, 1798, and 1816, legislation was passed banning workers from organizing in pursuit of their collective economic interest. The Prussian *Gewerbeordnung* of 1845 prohibited organization among employers or employees and prevented workers from discussing, threatening, or engaging in strike activity. With the 1848 revolution, workers' organizations were briefly tolerated, but from 1849 workers were again being arrested under antiunion laws. In addition to specific antiunion legislation, general laws limited freedom of assembly, organization, and expression. In 1850 the Prussian government passed laws placing tight restrictions on any organizations concerned with public affairs. These could only be established after receiving approval from local police or higher authorities.

Despite these restrictive measures, workers' organizations did exist in the first half of the nineteenth century. Journeymen's brotherhoods, which had traditionally provided traveling journeymen with work and support and had organized strikes, survived into the nineteenth century, although in restricted forms. These provided the basis for the first mass movement of German workers, the Workers' Brotherhood, founded by the journeyman Stefan Born during the 1848 revolution. The first national trade unions were also formed in 1848—the National Printers Association in June and the Association of German Cigar Workers in September. However, with the period of reaction that set in after the defeat of the revolution, independent workers' organizations in the 1850s were repressed, and the trade unions were dissolved. Nevertheless, some forms of labor organization did continue. Cooperative schemes were popular among artisans, and journeymen's organizations existed in many crafts, mainly to provide insurance benefits and other services.

The "New Era"

In the late 1850s a change occurred in the political climate of the region. In most of the German states, the liberal movement underwent a resurgence in response to a relaxation of repression. In Prussia the appointment of Prince Wilhelm as regent in 1858 seemed to offer the promise of progress on issues of political and economic reform, and the revival of political activity across the whole region inaugurated the beginning of a "New Era." The liberal movement was mainly concerned with national unification and the establishment of political and economic freedoms. The workers' right to organize was a part of this process of economic liberalization. While many were opposed to the idea of workers' trade unions, some left-leaning liberals argued in favor of workers' organizations for a variety of reasons. The progressive liberal Hermann Schulze-Delitzch was a strong advocate of workers' cooperatives, and he supported their right to form trade unions. While he did not believe that trade unions could provide any positive economic benefits to workers, he recognized the right of workers to form unions. Schulze-Delitzch believed that the success of liberalism lay in attracting the support of the workers. He was willing to support worker demands to form trade unions in order to win them to the liberal cause. Other liberals argued that trade unions were compatible with a free-market economy and saw them as a way to integrate workers into the existing social and economic system. With this aim in mind, a group of trade unions modeled upon the English example was set up under the patronage of the liberal Progress Party. The Hirsch-Dunck unions, named after their liberal founders, even took part in strikes in 1869–1870.

The Social Democrats

The support of some liberals for trade unions was in contrast to the attitude of the founder of the first independent workers' political party in Germany. The resurgence in political activity had led to the establishment of liberal-led workers' educational associations. However, many workers were dissatisfied with their treatment within these liberal organizations. They found the middle-class sponsors to be condescending, patronizing, and divorced from the concerns of the workers. Most liberals appeared to have no interest in tackling the social problems caused by Germany's rapid industrialization in the 1850s and 1860s. One who rejected alliance with the liberals was Ferdinand Lassalle, who established the General Association of German Working Men (ADAV) in 1863. Lassalle subscribed to the "iron law of wages," which held that the laws of supply and demand prevented workers' wages from ever rising above subsistence levels. The only way to improve the material condition of the workers was through state-initiated, cooperative associations. Therefore, the state had to be captured by the workers through democratic reform and political activity. Lassalle believed trade union activity was completely ineffectual in improving the workers' lot. However, due to the workers' interest in forming trade unions, Lassalle's successor, Johann Baptist von Schweitzer, was more willing to accept them, as long as the ADAV could control them and use them as an opportunity to recruit new members.

In contrast to Lassalle, other strands of socialist thought attached more significance to trade unions. In several of his writings, Karl Marx argued that the trade unions had an important role to play in political revolution. They contributed to the creation of class consciousness among the workers and helped their preparation for the final confrontation with the capitalist system. The International Workingmen's Association, established in London in 1865, regarded trade unions as the basis of the Socialist Party's organization. However, it was clear that trade union activity should be a means to an end—the eventual overthrow of capitalism—rather than an end in itself. The Social Democratic Workers Party was set up by August Bebel and Karl Liebknecht in 1869, in opposition to the ADAV. It allowed the fledgling trade union movement a great deal more autonomy than the ADAV. However, tension between trade unions and socialist political parties was inevitable, given that the unions focused on reform within the existing system, whereas socialism had revolution as its ultimate goal.

Legislative Reform

Against this background of liberal activity and the emergence of a working-class political movement, bans on trade unions were lifted in some German states as part of a raft of liberal economic reforms. Saxony removed the ban on coalitions in 1861, as part of a broader legislative package concerned with economic freedoms. Weimar followed with its own reforms in 1863. The process culminated with the *Gewerbeordnung* of the North German Confederation in 1869. Article 152 of the trade regulations lifted "all prohibitions and penal sanctions against tradesmen, trainees, journeymen and factory hands for concluding agreements or forming associations for the purpose of obtaining improved wages or working conditions." However, the right to form trade unions was not given without strict limits. Article 153 added that "anyone who by the use of physical force, threats, insults or slander compels or seeks to compel others to subscribe to such agreements, shall be liable to three months imprisonment." The wide interpretation of this article made recruiting or picketing very difficult for the unions. In addition, the general laws restricting freedom of association remained unchanged and served as the basis for continued harassment of trade unions after the 1869 reform. In particular, laws prohibiting unions from becoming involved in politics made the relationship between the trade unions and the socialist political parties very sensitive.

The Birth of the Trade Union Movement

As a result of what one historian has termed a legislative revolution from above, workers now had the right to organize to pursue their collective economic interests. In the atmosphere of liberalization, laws against coalitions of workers were applied less stringently, and trade unions were organized even before the bans were lifted. The first to be formed were the General German Cigar Workers Association in 1865 and the German Printers Union in 1866, the same occupational groups who had organized in the 1848 revolution, indicating a degree of continuity between the two periods. As in 1848, the first workers to become unionized in the 1860s tended to be journeymen artisans and skilled workers, rather than unskilled factory workers. This suggests that the craft-based traditions of labor unrest and resistance were important in the development of the modern trade union movement. However, much was new about the labor movement of the 1860s. The confrontation between employers and workers was much more antagonistic in this era than had been the case earlier. Cooperation across skill and craft lines had increased, and industrial action focused upon pay rates and working conditions, rather than the defense of traditional craft customs or rights.

The major result of the lifting of bans on workers' unions was an increase in strike activity. Germany experienced a strike wave in the late 1860s and early 1870s, as the relaxation of laws and favorable economic conditions offered workers a chance to gain concessions from employers. Strikes and trade unions had a symbiotic relationship. Strikes often followed the formation of a trade union within a particular occupation. However, trade unions could also be formed when the experience of a strike encouraged the development of more permanent forms of organization. For example, the 1865 Threepenny Strike in Leipzig over piece-rates led to the formation of the Printers Union. This rise in industrial militancy alienated many liberals, and after the 1860s, a liberal-labor alliance in Germany was impossible, given the deep mistrust and suspicion on both sides.

Key Players

Lassalle, Ferdinand (1825–1864): One of the founders of the German labor movement, Lassalle was opposed to a liberal-labor alliance, due to his mistrust of the middle class, and founded the first workers' political party in Germany. Lassalle was also opposed to trade unionism, as he believed trade unions could not improve conditions for the workers, due to the "iron law of wages." This helped to complicate the relationship between the emerging trade unions and the socialist political parties in Germany.

Schulze-Delitzsch, Hermann (1808–1883): Prussian liberal parliamentarian and social reformer, Schulze-Delitzsch was committed to the alliance of liberalism and labor in Germany in the 1860s. With this aim in mind, he was a key proponent of the right of workers to form trade unions.

Wilhelm I (1797–1888): King of Prussia and later, Emperor of Germany, Wilhelm was appointed as Regent in 1858, due to the mental illness of his brother, Friederich Wilhelm IV, an event that excited liberal hopes of political and economic reform. The resulting resurgence in political activity in the late 1850s and 1860s was the impetus for the lifting of the ban on trade unions in many of the German states.

See also: *First International; Revolutions in Europe.*

BIBLIOGRAPHY

Books

Berger, Stefan. *Social Democracy and the Working Class in Nineteenth- and Twentieth-Century Germany.* New York: Longman, 1999.

Breuilly, John. *Labour and Liberalism in Nineteenth-Century Europe: Essays in Comparative History.* New York: Manchester University Press, 1992.

Kocka, Jurgen. "Craft Traditions and the Labour Movement in Nineteenth Century Germany." In *The Power of the Past: Essays for Eric Hobshawm.* Cambridge, England: Cambridge University Press, 1984.

Moses, John A. *Trade Unionism in Germany from Bismarck to Hitler 1869–1933.* Vol. 1: *1869–1918.* London: George Prior Publishers, 1982.

Schneider, Michael. *A Brief History of the German Trade Unions.* Bonn, Germany: J.H.W. Dietz, 1991.

Sheehan, James J. *German Liberalism in the Nineteenth Century.* Chicago: University of Chicago Press, 1978.

ADDITIONAL RESOURCES

Books

Grebing, Helga. *History of the German Labour Movement.* Leamington Spa, Warwickshire: Berg Publishers, 1985.

Miller, Susanne, and Heinrich Potthoff. *A History of German Social Democracy from 1848 to the Present.* Leamington Spa, Warwickshire: Berg Publishers, 1986.

Sheehan, James J. *German History, 1770–1866.* Oxford, England: Clarendon Press, 1989.

—Katrina Ford

Barcelona Workers' Rebellion

Spain 1909

Synopsis

La Semana Trágica, or the Tragic Week, was a momentous episode in Spanish labor history. In 1909 a general strike was called to protest the sending of conscripted troops to Morocco. This erupted into a week-long insurgency remembered as *la Semana Trágica.* The largely spontaneous violence that followed ended in violent repression. Tortures of anarchists in the fortress of Montjuïc and the execution of Francisco Ferrer y Guardia, an internationally celebrated advocate of rational education, led to worldwide protests and the resignation of the conservative government of Antonio Maura in Madrid. These events also led to a congress of Spanish trade unionists at Seville in 1910, which founded the *Confederación Nacional del Trabajo* (CNT) (National Confederation of Labor).

Timeline

1889: Flooding in Johnstown, Pennsylvania, kills thousands.

1893: Wall Street stock prices plummet on 5 May, precipitating a market collapse on 27 June. In the wake of this debacle, some 600 banks and 15,000 other businesses fail. The nationwide depression will last for four more years.

1898: Bayer introduces a cough suppressant, derived from opium, its brand name: Heroin.

1902: The *Times Literary Supplement,* a weekly review of literature and scholarship, begins publication in London.

1905: Russian Revolution of 1905 begins. Following the "bloody Sunday" riots before the Winter Palace in St.

Petersburg in January, revolution spreads throughout Russia, in some places spurred on by newly formed workers' councils, or soviets. Among the most memorable incidents of the revolt is the mutiny aboard the battleship *Potemkin.* Suppressed by the czar, the revolution brings an end to liberal reforms, and thus sets the stage for the larger revolution of 1917.

1909: Robert E. Peary and Matthew Henson reach the North Pole.

1909: National Association for the Advancement of Colored People (NAACP) is founded by W. E. B. Du Bois and a number of other prominent black and white intellectuals in New York City.

1909: William Cadbury's *Labour in Portuguese West Africa* draws attention to conditions of slavery in São Tomé and Principe.

1911: Revolution in Mexico, begun the year before, continues with the replacement of the corrupt Porfirio Diaz, president since 1877, by Francisco Madero.

1915: A German submarine sinks the *Lusitania,* killing 1,195, including 128 U.S. citizens. Theretofore, many Americans had been sympathetic toward Germany, but the incident begins to turn the tide of U.S. sentiment toward the Allies.

1919: With the formation of the Third International (Comintern), the Bolshevik government of Russia establishes its control over communist movements worldwide.

Event and Its Context

Background

In 1898 Spain took on Morocco as a protectorate after losing the last of its overseas colonies, Cuba, Puerto Rico, and the Philippines. After a general strike in 1902, the Law of Jurisdictions gave military authorities the power to try civilians in military courts. At this time the working class in Catalonia was under the sway of the Radical Party of Alejandro Lerroux y García. His primary goal was reviving the Republican movement, not proletarian revolution. The unions were too weak to challenge the Republicans. Many unions had disbanded or were paper organizations, although their leaders retained contact with each other in the years following the general strike.

By 1907 Barcelona's labor movement recovered sufficiently to hold a local congress. In June a commission composed of metallurgical workers, typesetters, bakers, painters, and store clerks gathered in the union headquarters of the store clerks to lay plans for a municipal federation. The federation, called *Solidaridad Obrera* (Worker Solidarity), was founded on 3 August and two months later began publishing a newspaper by the same name. The new organization grew slowly and managed to capture the interest of workers outside the city. A year later, in September 1908, the union expanded into a regional federation that included 112 labor syndicates throughout Catalonia with a membership of 25,000 workers.

Radical leaders viewed *Solidaridad Obrera* as a competitor for working-class support. However, *Solidaridad Obrera* was a "bread-and-butter" union, dedicated to collective bargaining and meeting immediate demands. Furthermore, the union was politically neutral and claimed that it was not under the "tutelage of any political party or . . . either of the two branches of socialism."

Despite these declarations, the labor federation became a battleground between the socialists and anarchists. The socialists were intent on bringing *Solidaridad Obrera* into the socialist-dominated *Unión General de Trabajo,* the socialist national labor federation (UGT). The anarcho-syndicalists in the union were divided between moderates, who wanted the labor movement to expand via anarchist principles, and militants, who wanted to push the federation towards explicit anarchist goals, that is, expropriation of factories and farms, insurrection, and social revolution.

Military Call-up Sparks Resentment

On 11 July 1909 the Maura ministry announced a call-up of military reserves for active duty in Morocco. Firefights between Moroccan Riff tribesmen and Spanish troops resulted in numerous Spanish casualties. Maura's call-up produced anger among the working class in Barcelona, the main port of embarkation for Morocco. The call-up was especially difficult on the families of Catalan workers who could not afford to lose their only breadwinner to combat. The mobilization created further resentment by the working class and poor because well-off men could avoid service by paying a fee of 1,500 pesetas.

Anarchist militants associated with the revolutionary newspaper *Tierra y Libertad* wanted to turn the strike into an insurrection. The authorities quickly arrested the protesters for inciting crowds to attack the police stations and removed them from the scene almost as soon as the strike began. The socialists, by contrast, fearful of "anarchist turmoil," tried to confine the strike to an antiwar protest.

Two anarchists, José Rodríguez Romero and Miguel Villalobos Morena, organized the Central Committee for a strike on a Saturday night. On Monday morning, strike delegations appeared at the factory gates to greet the workers. Fearing retribution against their properties, the employers closed down the factories.

Spontaneous Uprising Begins

The events surprised everyone. During the week of 26 July, Barcelona experienced a largely spontaneous uprising that received little guidance from the union or Radical leaders. The anarchist historian Anselmo Lorenzo wrote, "What is happening here is amazing. A social revolution has broken out in Barcelona and it has been started by the people. No one instigated it. No one has led it. Neither the Liberals nor Catalan Nationalists, nor Republicans, nor Socialists, nor Anarchists."

The actions of the regional authorities caused the strike to escalated into an insurrection. Historian Benjamin Martin noted, "Civil Governor Osorio y Gallardo had originally proposed letting the protest run its course under close police supervision, but he was overruled by his superior, Juan de la Cierva, Minister of Interior, a rigid law-and-order advocate, who declared martial law under the authority of the commanding general of the military region." According to Juan Benet, "Its declaration aggravated the situation for Luis de Santiago, Captain General of Catalonia, who lacked sufficient military forces owing to the departure of part of his troops for Morocco and the fear of fraternization of the soldiers with the people who were hailing them."

Many soldiers began to fraternize with the protesters and passively observed the depredations of the rebellious throngs. Anarchist, philosopher, and author Murray Bookchin wrote, "The crowds roaming the main street were careful to distinguish between police and soldiers. The latter were wooed with cheers and antiwar appeals whenever they appeared; the police stations, on the other hand, were attacked with ferocity." The crowds blew up the railroad lines leading into the city and temporarily isolated the garrisons from the city. The crowds put up barricades and distributed weapons. Women joined in the revolt, often participating in the actual fighting.

The anarchists anticipated that the uprising would spread outside Catalonia to other anarchist enclaves including Gijón, La Felguera, and La Coruña, and other radical hotspots such as Asturias and Andalusia. Lack of communication between the Barcelona anarchists and the rest of Spain, however, worked to the advantage of the government, which misrepresented the uprising as an exclusively autonomous movement. Thus, the non-Catalan working class and peasantry made no attempt to extend the uprising.

Participants and observers variously viewed the uprising as a protest, insurrection, or revolution. The socialists saw the uprising as an antiwar protest, the anarchists as a social revolution, and the Republicans as a blow against the monarchy. Today, the Tragic Week is most commonly counted as an anticlericalist movement.

Before the week was over, 40 religious schools and churches, convents, and welfare centers were put to the torch together with 12 parish churches, less than half of the city's church buildings. Bookchin postulated that the "widespread damage to clerical institutions was instigated by the Radical politicians who were eager to divert the workers from revolutionary paths into well-grooved anticlerical channels." Author and historian Joan Connelly Ullman agreed and noted that the leaders of Leroux's Radical party sought to defuse the situation by directing rebellious elements into anticlerical activities such as burning and pillaging church buildings.

Rebellion Crushed

Troop reinforcements arrived on 28 July and quickly and severely put down the insurrection. It had lasted one week, from 26 July to 1 August, one day short of a planned national strike by the UGT. Nine policemen and soldiers died and an additional 125 sustained injuries; 104 civilians were killed and 216 wounded. More than 2,500 persons were imprisoned, of whom 1,725 were indicted. Seventeen received death sentences, but only five, including Francisco Ferrer, the anarchist and rational educator, were executed.

Solidaridad Obrera did not organize or officially sponsor the strike, but its headquarters was sequestered by the authorities for having instigated a revolution in league with the French General Confederation of Labor (CGT) and international free-masonry. Union offices and all nonsecular schools and Republican centers were closed down, numerous publications were suspended, and large numbers of labor and political activists were exiled or left Spain to avoid imprisonment.

The excessive harshness with which the rebellion was suppressed stirred considerable disapproval among many of the country's leading political figures. The decision to make an example of Ferrer sent shock waves throughout Spain and the rest of the world. Although Ferrer was previously little known outside of the international anarchist movement, his execution ignited worldwide indignation, similar to that generated by the Haymarket Affair several decades earlier and the Sacco-Vanzetti affair several decades later.

Aftermath

Normalcy returned with the lifting of the martial law and other restrictions following the replacement of the Maura regime by a government headed by Liberal Segismundo Moret. Those convicted of misdeeds during the Tragic Week were granted amnesty, and *Solidaridad Obrera* was permitted to resume its activities.

Because many of the key figures and activists in *Solidaridad Obrera* had fled Barcelona to avoid persecution, the anarchists' representation increased markedly, though not to the point of complete hegemony. The Tragic Week, moreover, gave added impetus to the process of radicalization among labor militants and strengthened their reliance on direct action tactics rather than on the more peaceful tactics of collective bargaining and labor relations. For employers, the Tragic Week confirmed their resolve not to seek peaceful coexistence with unions but to brandish the clenched fist with even more severity than before.

Martin noted, "The congress *Solidaridad Obrera* originally planned for September 1909 finally took place October 30 to November 1 of the following year. By an overwhelming margin the delegates voted to constitute a national body, and the newly formed center held its founding congress in Barcelona during September 1911." Indicative of the influence of French syndicalism, the group initially adopted the name General Confederation of Labor (CGT) but then later changed to the *Confederación Nacional de Trabajo* (National Confederation of Labor, CNT). The founding membership was 140 affiliated locals representing more than 26,000 members.

With increasing militant anarchist influence, the pluralism that had been the distinguishing hallmark of *Solidaridad Obrera* was abandoned as prejudicial to the practice and implementation of direct action. The organization abandoned support for a minimum wage and sponsorship of cooperatives and mutual benefit societies.

Though the official trade union vocabulary was permeated with anarchist jargon, as before, "bread-and-butter" trade unionists were the largest component of the new organization. As a union, the organization required a pragmatic approach to organizing. Thus, anarchists engaged in the day-to-day struggle for trade union demands, and apolitical workers generally acquiesced in the adoption of anarcho-syndicalist policies.

Key Players

Ferrer y Guardia, Francisco (1859–1909): Rationalist educator and founder of the Modern School movement who was opposed to state and religious education, Ferrer supported numerous anarchist causes. He was executed as instigator of the Tragic Week in 1909.

Lerroux y García, Alejandro (1864–1949): Journalist, republican anticlericalist and founder of Spain's Radical Party, Lerroux y García was founder of the periodical *El Radical*. In 1910 he adopted a moderate Republican stance and was appointed governmental deputy in Barcelona by a coalition of Republicans and socialists.

Maura, Antonio (1853–1925): Maura was a lawyer and Conservative prime minister. Before the 1898 crisis, Maura adopted a position of censorship against the practices of the Restoration and formulated a policy intended to avoid the proletarian revolutionary process by instituting a "revolution from above." After the 1909 Tragic Week of Barcelona, Maura was forced to resign.

See also: *General Strike, Catalonia.*

BIBLIOGRAPHY

Books

Anderson, Charles W. *The Political Economy of Modern Spain*. Madison: The University of Wisconsin Press, 1970.

Aranzadi, Dionisio. *Collective Bargaining and Class Conflict in Spain*. London: Weidenfield and Nicholson, 1972.

Bookchin, Murray. *The Spanish Anarchists: The Heroic Years, 1868–1936*. Edinburgh, Scotland/San Francisco: AK Press, 1997.

Buenacasa, Manuel. *El Movimento Obrero Español, 1886–1926*. Barcelona, Spain: Impresos Colta, 1928; Madrid, Spain: EDICAónes Júcar, 1977.

Carr, Raymond. *Spain, 1808–1975*. Oxford: Oxford University Press, 1982.

Esenwein, George R. *Anarchist Ideology and the Working-class Movement in Spain, 1868–1898*. Berkeley: University of California Press, 1989.

Martin, Benjamin. *The Agony of Industrialization: Labor and Industrialization in Spain*. Ithaca, NY: ILR Press, 1990.

Ullman, Joan Connelly. *La Semana Trágica*. Espluges de Llobregat, Spain: Ariel, 1972.

———. *The Tragic Week: A Study of Anticlericalism in Spain, 1875–1912*. Cambridge, MA: Harvard University Press, 1968.

Vicens Vives, Jaime. *An Economic History of Spain*. Translated by Frances López-Morillas. Princeton, NJ: Princeton University Press, 1969.

—Evan Daniel

Battle of the Overpass

United States 1937

Synopsis

Henry Ford, the noted automaker and founder of Ford Motor Company, remained adamant in his antiunion opinion from the first unionizing attempts at his company in 1913. The Industrial Workers of the World (IWW) had attempted to unionize Ford workers; Ford upped wages to $5 a day to appease them. As unions continued trying to get a toehold in the plant, Ford fought back increasingly harder. He went as far as to establish a faux union called the Knights of Dearborn, which was both antiunion and anti-Semitic.

Ford Motor Company was the only one of the so-called Big Three automakers that was not yet unionized by the late 1930s. As a result, employees were being paid about 5 cents less per hour than other industry workers and 10 cents less than Chrysler or General Motors (GM) workers who were represented by the United Auto Workers (UAW). Ford's biggest property was the River Rouge facility in Dearborn, Michigan, which housed some 85,000 to 100,000 workers. It was commonly referred to as either the "Sweat Shop" or "Butcher House" by employees.

The UAW's attempt to organize Ford employees involved in a bloody confrontation with Ford Motor Company henchmen occurred in May 1937. The Battle of the Overpass, as this bloody skirmish became known, precipitated the UAW's focused efforts to organize the River Rouge plant. The incident remains among the most enduring events in the United States' labor movement. The widely publicized accounts and images of the event also served to turn public opinion in favor of the union and made public Ford's brutal reign of fear.

Timeline

1922: Publication of James Joyce's novel *Ulysses* and T. S. Eliot's poem *The Waste Land*—works that will transform literature and inaugurate the era of modernism.

1927: American inventor Philo T. Farnsworth demonstrates a working model of the television, and Belgian astronomer Georges Lemaître proposes the Big Bang Theory.

1932: In German elections, Nazis gain a 37 percent plurality of *Reichstag* seats, raising tensions between the far right and the far left. On a "bloody Sunday" in July, communists in Hamburg attack Nazis with guns, and a fierce battle ensues.

1937: Italy signs the Anti-Comintern Pact, signed by Germany and Japan the preceding year. Like the two others before it, Italy now withdraws from the League of Nations.

1937: Japan attacks China and annexes most of that nation's coastal areas.

1937: Stalin uses carefully staged show trials in Moscow to eliminate all rivals for leadership. These party purges, however, are only a small part of the death toll now being exacted in a country undergoing forced industrialization, much of it by means of slave labor.

Ford workers approach UAW representatives on right, from left, Robert Kanter, Walter P. Reuther, Richard Truman Frankensteen, and J. J. Kennedy, outside Ford Motor Company, Battle of the Overpass, Rouge Plant, Detroit, Michigan. AP/World Wide Photos. Reproduced by permission.

1937: In the middle of an around-the-world flight, Amelia Earhart and her plane disappear somewhere in the Pacific.

1937: Crash of the *Hindenburg* in Lakehurst, New Jersey, kills 36 and ends the brief era when rigid airships promised to be the ocean liners of the skies.

1937: Pablo Picasso paints his famous *Guernica* mural dramatizing the Nationalist bombing of a town in Spain. Thanks to artists and intellectuals such as Picasso and Ernest Hemingway, the Loyalists are winning the battle of hearts and minds, even if they are weaker militarily, and idealistic young men flock from America to join the "Abraham Lincoln Brigade." Yet as George Orwell later reveals in *Homage to Catalonia,* the lines between good and evil are not clear: with its Soviet backing, the Loyalist cause serves as proxy for a totalitarianism every bit as frightening as that of the Nationalists and their German and Italian supporters.

1942: Axis conquests reach their height in the middle of this year. The Nazis control a vast region from Normandy to the suburbs of Stalingrad, and from the Arctic Circle to the edges of the Sahara. To the east, the Japanese "Co-Prosperity Sphere" encompasses territories from China to Burma to the East Indies, stretching deep into the western Pacific.

1947: Establishment of the Marshall Plan assists European nations in recovering from the war.

1952: Among the cultural landmarks of the year are the film *High Noon* and the book *The Invisible Man* by Ralph Ellison.

Event and Its Context

Working in Fear

During the 1930s, fierce battles raged between employers and workers who were trying to unionize. Thuggery seemed endemic to big industry. GM reportedly spent an estimated $1 million during an 18-month period on private detective services specifically to subvert labor activity. In 1935 Carnegie Steel was giving an added $25 per month to its company finks, those employees who informed on employees who were "talking union." Third-party companies such as Pinkerton National Detective Agency supplied private security to corporations throughout the country and thrived in these conditions. Pinker-

Ford workers attack UAW Organizational Director Richard Truman Frankensteen during Battle of the Overpass, Rouge Plant, Detroit, Michigan. AP/World Wide Photos. Reproduced by permission.

ton is said to have made $1.7 million between 1933 and 1936 for providing these types of services.

Among the most blatant employers of these tactics was Ford Motor Company. At its River Rouge facility, there were some 9,000 paid informants on the payroll; hidden microphones placed throughout the plant facilitated eavesdropping on union organizing. "We'll never recognize the United Automobile Workers union," said Henry Ford in 1937.

John Bruggemann, writing in *Social Problems*, described the huge plant as "an incomparable triumph of industrialization . . . a highly refined, scientifically managed model of manufacturing production." In 1937 there were more than 84,100 workers at the River Rouge facility, although some sources give the number as high as 100,000. Henry Ford was seen as a paternalistic employer who adopted an extreme antiunion position, as exemplified by his establishment of the Service Department, the intimidating corporate security force. The environment was compared to a "gigantic concentration camp founded on fear and physical assault." Ford had previously purged the plant of union members or suspected sympathizers.

The UAW had, prior to this particular organizing drive, typically distributed materials to workers in their native languages of Polish, Serbo-Croatian, Hungarian, and Italian. They also purchased prounion advertising on Polish-language radio and billboards throughout the area. Organizers also had support from union members at Chrysler and GM. With the benefit of the Supreme Court decision to uphold the Wagner Act in April 1937, the union decided to accelerate its attempts to organize at Ford Motor Company.

A Wary UAW Plans to Leaflet Ford

Organizers for the UAW carefully conducted strategy meetings well away from the shadow of River Rouge. They decided to select a day on which they would distribute union literature outside the plant. Well before the event, leaders scouted areas around the plant, including a pedestrian bridge, at least twice. This pedestrian overpass adjoined the Rouge River plant with streetcar lines used by employees. It had been constructed to keep traffic on Miller Road flowing at shift changes. This was also the entry to Gate 4 of the Ford Motor Company River Rouge complex, the busiest gate at the plant.

Typically, any literature distribution was governed by city ordinance. The union leaders obtained from the City of Dearborn a permit to distribute literature. The leaflets read "Unionism, Not Fordism." The content was primarily reprinted information from the Wagner Act, which in part provides workers with the legal right to organize without employer interference. About 100 members of the UAW women's auxiliary were also mobilized for this event. The simple plan was to distribute literature at the shift change.

The union leafleteers planned to spread out around the plant perimeter on 26 May 1937, just before the 2 P.M. shift change, making sure they remained on public property. The overpass gave leaders a vantage point from which to observe events. Walter P. Reuther, a union organizer, reportedly had expected some confrontation and had planned accordingly. He "put on his Sunday suit, complete with vest, gold watch and chain." Reuther had invited newspapermen, priests, and local officials to attend as neutral observers.

Reuther's instincts were correct. Someone within the Dearborn Police Department tipped off Henry Ford. Reuther, Richard T. Frankensteen, J. J. Kennedy, and Robert Kantor, all union leaders, went to the overpass a little early to take photos and wait for the leafleteers to arrive. One of the local news photographers had an early deadline and asked to take photos prior to the event.

There to meet the group of four union officials were 35 to 40 members of Ford's Service Department, the company's private police force headed by Harry Bennett. They yelled "This is private property, get the hell out of here!" and immediately began pummeling the union members. The union representatives were not given time to leave or to show their permit. "The men picked me up about eight different times and threw me down on my back on the concrete, kicking me in the face, head, and other parts of my body," Reuther said. "Finally, they threw me down the stairs . . . [and] drove me outside the fence."

Photos document how Frankensteen was attacked, clearly showing how his coat was pulled over his head to prevent him from defending himself. He was reportedly kicked in the head, kidneys, and groin and was kicked repeatedly while on the ground. After being thrown down the stairs, three of the union leaders were able to flag down a reporter's car and were taken to a doctor. Leafleteers in other areas around the plant, and even some who were blocks away from the plant, were beaten.

Ford and African Americans

Henry Ford, by all accounts, was hard to decipher. Unlike his industrial counterparts, Ford was the first to institute a five-day work week and the $5 day. He also hired African Americans well before other automotive companies in Dearborn followed suit. Almost half of all African American autoworkers were employed by Ford; they constituted 12 percent of its workforce and made Ford the largest employer of African Americans in the city.

Although Ford employed African Americans, they had few possible working alternatives compared to white autoworkers given the prejudices of the day. He also made connections with leaders in the community to cement a favorable position. "Thus, it is clear that whatever sense of racial fairness motivated Ford," summarized Bruggemann, "it was secondary to maintaining a cheap, docile and non-unionized labor force. Whether by design or as a convenient by-product, Ford's paternalistic relationship with black Detroit was crucial to his unrivaled leverage against autoworkers."

White employees held the highest paying jobs at the plant, including supervisory positions. Although nonmanagerial jobs were open, there were a disproportionate number of African Americans working in the most difficult and dangerous positions, such as working in the foundry. UAW organizers articulated their intent to erase any race restrictions from union membership. The union's Negro Committee was key in assuring African American participation in unionization of Ford. Photos from the Battle of the Overpass hurt these efforts. These showed African American servicemen involved in the violence, which served to escalate racial tensions among Ford workers.

Bennett and the Service Department

Ford himself was not at the crux of this altercation. Instead that position was occupied by a man who had a reputation as Ford's henchman and enforcer, Harry Bennett, who headed the so-called Service Department. This Ford Motor Company security force had some 3,000 employees, including ex-policemen, convicts, and bouncers. They were also generally responsible for ensuring employee order and productivity. Bennett was undoubtedly the most powerful man at Ford Motor Company other than Ford himself. He ruled by intimidation and violence. Bennett had a network of informers within the various facilities to alert him to problems, including any union talk. These spies also commonly eavesdropped on conversations in public gathering places outside the plant as well.

"At River Rouge he has his own private underworld to terrorize the workers," wrote Benjamin Stolberg in a 1937 article in *The Nation*. "Ford brought into River Rouge the underworld gangs of Detroit and their leaders, who now control the plant. And the man who did this job is the notorious Harry Bennett." Stolberg boldly painted an unflattering picture of the Service Department, calling it an "industrial mafia."

Among the gangsters operating in and around Ford were Angelo Caruso, who was affiliated with the Down River Detroit gang and was present at the Battle of the Overpass, and Chester LaMare, who had a fresh fruit concession at the Rouge. "The fact is that the gangsters are in control of River Rouge today," Stolberg said in that same 1937 article. "And the leading authority on the Michigan vigilante movement among the newspapermen in Detroit told me that even Ford himself is afraid—fantastic as it may sound—of the gangster organization he has reared."

Among those within the company who were opposed to Bennett's reign of terror were Charles Sorenson, Ford production manager, and Edsel Ford, Henry Ford's son. The problem was the depth to which Bennett had insinuated himself with Henry Ford.

Although most attention has been paid to the situation that transpired outside Gate 4, farther down the road the women who were distributing union leaflets were being subjected to similar treatment. Katherine Gelles, commander of the Ladies Auxiliary of UAW Local 174, was among them. As the Service Department beat the women, the Dearborn Police looked on and never intervened. One of the clergy-member observers reported hearing the Ford employees insulting the women by yelling "all manner of vile names usually attributed to women of the streets."

The injuries to union members included skull fractures, broken backs, and internal injuries. The police reportedly impeded ambulances that were attempting to tend to the injured. J. J. Kennedy, one of the union leaders with Reuther and Frankensteen, was beaten badly and died four months later. His death was attributed to his beating.

The treatment of the third-party observers, including those reporters and photographers who documented the event, is also noteworthy. They were subjected to similar treatment at the fists of the Service Department, especially as the Ford thugs tried to take cameras and film from photographers. James "Scotty" Kilpatrick, a photographer with the *Detroit News*, captured the famous sequence of the attack. Kilpatrick secreted his film. When one of the Service Department intimidators demanded his undeveloped film, Kilpatrick handed them blank film. Those photographs that survived the event were distributed throughout the country. The press was filled with accounts of the event, including *Time* magazine, which stated, "Men with queasy stomachs had no place one afternoon last week on the overpass at the No. 4 gate of Henry Ford's great River Rouge plant." The photographs and media accounts contributed to the shift in public opinion to the union's favor.

Bennett was adamant that the Ford Service Department was not involved. He quickly issued a statement insisting the union had instigated the incident by shouting insults at passing workers. The evidence was entirely to the contrary. *Time* was among the publications that refuted Bennett's claims by publishing the photos and an article. In retaliation, Ford pulled all of its advertising from the publication and its sister publication for 70 weeks.

The Battle of the Overpass remains among the most enduring events in the U.S. labor movement. *Crain's Detroit Business* called the event "one of the most compelling moments in labor history." This particular organizing effort, however, failed. The national attention to the event and a hearing about the violence exacted against union organizers at Ford and other antiunion companies stimulated a change in public opinion. Ford remained the only one of the major automakers not to be unionized.

In the four years that followed the Battle of the Overpass, family members and others pressed Ford to halt these sorts of actions. His wife, Clara, threatened to leave him if there was any more bloodshed. After relenting on his antiunion position, Ford said, "Don't ever discredit the power of a woman."

National Labor Relations Board (NLRB) hearings in July found Ford in violation of the Wagner Act. The NLRB described conditions at the River Rouge plant as having "many aspects of a community in which martial law has been declared, and in which a huge military organization . . . has been superimposed upon the regular civil authorities." The NRLB ordered Ford to stop interfering in union organizing efforts. After a major eight-day strike and election, Ford Motor Company recognized the union in May 1941.

Key Players

Bennett, Harry (1892–1979): What little factual information exists about Bennett is no doubt hyperbole. He fought hard to maintain a tough image, but many existing accounts of his personal life are contradictory. He was born in Ann Arbor, Michigan. His father was supposedly killed in a bar

fight when Bennett was a child. His stepfather was an engineering professor. Bennett ran away from home and joined the navy at 16. He was reportedly a boxer and had been a diver. He had, however, studied art, and his first job at Ford in 1917 was in the art department. Henry Ford II fired Bennett in 1945. The younger Ford made it his first order of business when he was appointed to run the company.

Ford, Henry (1863–1947): The founder of Ford Motor Company, Ford was against unionization throughout his life. He is often credited for the advent of the $5 work day, as well as for creating the eight-hour work day. He did not relent on his union stance until his wife, Clara, intervened.

Frankensteen, Richard Truman (1907–1977): Born in Detroit, Frankensteen started his career as an assembly line worker at Dodge. He first became a union representative with the Automotive Industrial Workers Association. Frankensteen was among the union leaders injured in the fighting at the Battle of the Overpass. He was the vice president of the United Auto Workers in 1937.

Reuther, Walter P. (1907–1970): Born in Wheeling, West Virginia, Reuther was an autoworker and labor organizer, the son of German immigrants. His first job was working in a Ford Motor Company plant. He was a founder of both the United Auto Workers and CIO. He participated in the first major Detroit auto strike in 1936. Reuther's ascent to prominence in the union started with the Battle of the Overpass. In the 1950s Reuther served as president of the CIO and was among those in leadership when the union merged with its former rival, the AFL. He continued to be active in union causes and the civil rights movement and tirelessly worked to revive the labor movement throughout the 1960s. Reuther died in an airplane crash.

Sorensen, Charles (1881–1968): Born in Copenhagen, Denmark, Sorensen immigrated to the United States with his family in 1884. He graduated from high school in Buffalo, New York in 1896. He was an apprentice patternmaker and continued his education, taking correspondence courses in drafting and mathematics. He became a Ford Motor Company employee in 1904 as a patternmaker and foundryman. Although Henry Ford did not use formal titles in his plants, Sorensen was in charge of production between 1925 and 1944.

See also: *Industrial Workers of the World; United Automobile Workers; Wagner Act.*

BIBLIOGRAPHY

Books

Bird, Stewart, Dan Georgakas, and Deborah Shaffer. *Solidarity Forever: An Oral History of the IWW.* Chicago: Lake View Press, 1985.

Collier, Peter and David Horowitz. *The Fords: An American Epic.* New York: Summit Books, 1987.

De Caux, Len. *Labor Radical: From the Wobblies to CIO, A Personal History.* Boston: Beacon Press, 1970.

Foner, Philip S. *Women and the American Labor Movement: From World War I to the Present*. New York: The Free Press, 1980.

Lacey, Robert. *Ford, the Men and the Machine*. Boston: Little, Brown, 1986.

Lens, Sidney. *Strikemakers & Strikebreakers*. New York: E.P. Dutton, 1985.

Lichtenstein, Nelson. *The Most Dangerous Man in Detroit: Walter Reuther and the Fate of American Labor*. New York: HarperCollins Publishers, Inc., 1995.

Murray, R. Emmet. *The Lexicon of Labor*. New York: The New Press, 1998.

Nevins, Allan and Frank Ernest Hill. *Ford: Decline and Rebirth, 1933–1962*. New York: Charles Scribner's Sons, 1962.

Reuther, Victor G. *The Brothers Reuther and the Story of the UAW*. Boston: Houghton Mifflin, 1976.

Serrin, William. *The Company and the Union*. New York: Knopf, 1972.

Whitman, Alden, ed. *American Reformers*. New York: The H. W. Wilson Company, 1985.

Periodicals

Bluestone, Irving. "Working-Class Hero—Walter Reuther." *Time* (7 December 1998): 157.

Brueggmann, John. "The Power and Collapse of Paternalism: The Ford Motor Company and Black Workers, 1937–1941." *Social Problems* 47, no. 2 (May 2000): 220.

Other

"Battle of the Overpass." Ford Company Chronology. Henry Ford Museum and Greenfield Village. 30 July 1995 [cited 6 August 2002]. <http://www.hfmgv.org/exhibits/fmc/battle.asp>.

Hansen, Curtis. "The Battle of the Overpass." Wayne State University, Walter P. Reuther Library Exhibits Online. 2001 [cited 6 August 2002]. <http://www.reuther.wayne.edu/exhibits/battle.html>.

Stolberg, Benjamin. "Vigilantism, 1937—Part II." *The Nation*, 21 August 1937 [cited 6 August 2002]. <http://www.newdeal.feri.org/nation/na37145p191.htm>.

—Linda Dailey Paulson

Bituminous Coal Conservation Act: *See* **Guffey Act.**

Bituminous Coal Strike

United States 1897

Synopsis

In 1890 the United Mine Workers of America (UMW), an affiliate of the American Federation of Labor (AFL), formed in

John Mitchell. © Getty Images. Reproduced by permission.

Columbus, Ohio. At that time coal miners around the United States labored in horrendous working conditions. Few miners were represented by labor unions, and because of that the coal owners and operators took advantage of the power they held over the miners. The UMW was a weak and ineffective union during its first six years of existence. On 4 July 1897, however, that situation changed when the union began a national strike of bituminous coal miners in Illinois, Indiana, Ohio, and western Pennsylvania. The successful actions of that strike prompted growth from less than 10,000 members to a strong and powerful union with more than 100,000 members. At this time the UMW-AFL became the largest union in the United States. For the miners, it meant a better life with increased wages and improved working and living conditions.

Timeline

1877: In the face of uncertain results from the popular vote in the presidential election of 1876, the U.S. Electoral Commission awards the presidency to Rutherford B. Hayes despite a slight popular majority for his opponent, Samuel J. Tilden. The election of 1876 will remain the most controversial in American history for the next 124 years, until overshadowed by the race between George W. Bush and Al Gore in 2000.

1882: John D. Rockefeller's Standard Oil trust, first major industrial monopoly, is established.

1887: John Emerich Edward Dalbert-Acton, a leader of the opposition to the papal dogma of infallibility, observes, in a letter to Cambridge University professor Mandell Creighton, that "Power tends to corrupt, and absolute power corrupts absolutely."

Music of the UMWA

On the United Mine Workers of America (UMWA) Web site in 2002, the union offered various musical recordings for sale. Among these was *Coal Mining Women,* a collection of 20 songs about coal mining by female singers and songwriters, which included "Which Side Are You On?" by Florence Reese, "Come All You Coal Miners" by Sarah Gunning, and "Blue Diamond Mines" by Phyllis Boyens.

"Which Side Are You On?" also appeared on *Power* by Bones of Contention, promoted on the UMWA Web site as "a high-energy rock-and-roll band [that] has taken labor music to a new platform." In place of acoustic guitars, Bones of Contention gave old labor songs such as "Sixteen Tons" and "Solidarity Forever" new life with electric guitars and drums.

Source: *United Mine Workers of America.*
<http//www.umwa.org>.

—Judson Knight

1893: Henry Ford builds his first automobile.

1897: Zionist movement is established under the leadership of Theodor Herzl.

1897: English physicist J. J. Thomson identifies the electron, the first subatomic particle to be discovered.

1897: In the midst of a nationwide depression, Mrs. Bradley Martin, daughter of Carnegie Steel magnate Henry Phipps, throws a lavish party at New York's recently opened Waldorf-Astoria Hotel, where she has a suite decorated to look like Versailles. Her 900 guests, dressed in Louis XV period costumes, consume 60 cases of champagne.

1897: News of gold discoveries along the Klondike River in Canada's Yukon Territory sparks a gold rush, and thousands flock to Alaska.

1899: The Second Anglo-Boer War, often known simply as the Boer War begins.

1903: Henry Ford establishes the Ford Motor Company.

1907: At the Second Hague Peace Conference, 46 nations adopt 10 conventions governing the rules of war.

Event and Its Context

Coal miners in the United States were generally not represented by labor organizations in the last half of the nineteenth century; nevertheless, a few unions (with limited membership) did exist. Some of the more prominent unions were the American Miners' Association (founded 1860); the Miners' National Association of the United States of America (founded 1873); the Ohio Miners' Amalgamated Association (founded 1882), which became (in 1883) the Amalgamated Association of Min-

ers of the United States; and the National Federation of Miners and Mine Workers (founded 1885).

The United Mine Workers of America (UMW or sometimes UMWA) was founded in Columbus, Ohio, on 25 January 1890. It was created by the merger of the National Progressive Union of Miners and Mine Laborers and the mine locals under the Knights of Labor Assembly No. 135. John Rae became the UMW's first president and Robert Watchorn its first secretary.

The founding delegates of the UMW adopted a constitution that barred discrimination based on race, religion, or national origin. The newly formed organization was affiliated with the American Federation of Labor (AFL). The UMW was organized primarily to address the following situations that faced coal miners: (1) the intermittent (seasonal) nature of employment within the coal industry, (2) the prevalence of company-owned towns (which were seen as detrimental to workers), and (3) the extreme occupational hazards facing the coal miners. Each of these problems led to numerous strikes and constant efforts to improve conditions by collective bargaining. During the first year of the UMW, only 8,000 miners belonged to the organization, out of a total of about 150,000 coal mine workers nationwide.

In the several years leading up to 1897, these 150,000 workers were producing all the coal that was consumed at home and exported abroad. In the most prosperous year, about 250 million tons of coal was needed. This production amount gave an average of about 200 days per year of employment to the men and boys who worked the mines. If the mines were worked 300 days per year, they would produce at least 125 million tons of coal *more* than could be consumed at home or sold abroad. As a consequence, miners could earn only about two-thirds as much as they could from year-round employment.

Because mining communities were, with few exceptions, isolated from other centers of industry, there was little opportunity for the mineworkers to be employed elsewhere during the extended weeks and months during which the mines were shut down. Bituminous coal cannot be kept stored for long without deteriorating in value and quality, making this problem difficult to remedy. The greatest amount of coal is normally consumed in the winter months, so it follows that more coal must be produced in the winter season than in the summer. Consequently, during these winter months all the mineworkers were steadily employed, whereas in the summer the miners were more likely to be unemployed. This seasonality of coal, plus an oversupply of labor, adversely affected the earnings of mineworkers. Thus, for many years prior to 1897, the tendency of wages was downward.

Company-owned Coal Towns

Miners and their families were very dependent on the coal company, as it permeated most aspects of the lives of miners and their families. Most mine owners owned and operated their own towns. Miners' children attended schools that were built using company funds. Although some homes were privately owned, most families lived in rented company-built houses. Although they were not usually obligated to shop at the company stores, many were forced to out of lack of nearby competition. Some miners complained that the stores charged high prices for poor quality goods. Miners also complained that any increases in wages were met with corresponding price hikes at the company store. In addition to complaints about high prices, miners in the early company towns were not paid in cash. Instead, miners received scrip, a company-issued coin substitute for currency. Each company's scrip was exchangeable for goods at the company store, but only at the company store. If miners protested wages or working conditions, they were often evicted from their (company-owned) houses.

The life of the American miner in the late 1890s was one of hazardous employment, filled with constant danger and compensated with low wages. The average miner was generally overworked and underpaid. Indeed, in the late 1890s wages for coal miners were rarely enough for an average family of three to six people to live on. To keep wages low, mine operators flooded the coalfields with immigrants from mostly eastern and southern Europe. According to statistics given by John Mitchell, then president of the UMW, the minimum wage received by any class of adult mine worker in the bituminous coal mines averaged 26.5 cents per hour, whereas the minimum wage paid to boys averaged 12.5 cents per hour in the late 1890s.

Statistics from 1890 to 1893 reveal that 3.29 out of 1,000 anthracite (hard) coal miners and 2.52 out of every 1,000 bituminous (soft) coal miners were killed on the job each year. American techniques for mining coal yielded more coal per worker than did European methods, but they were far more dangerous, and toward the end of the nineteenth century, the dangers worsened. For this period of time, the British reported that 1.61 out of 1,000 anthracite miners and 1.28 out of 1,000 bituminous miners were killed on the job, around half the rate for U.S. coal miners.

First Strike Led by UMW

During the first decade of its existence, the UMW was primarily a regional union. Most of its support and strength were in the states of Illinois, Indiana, Ohio, and Pennsylvania. The panic of 1893, a general business depression, hit the coal industry especially hard, and wages for miners were reduced between 10 and 30 percent; many lost their jobs. According to a Pennsylvania legislative committee, many miners were living "like sheep in shambles." Strikes were common during these days, although they were rarely successful for the coal workers. In 1899, for example, strikes caused the loss of 2,124,154 worker-days; in 1900 strikes caused the loss of 4,878,102 worker-days. The UMW led its first general strike in the Pennsylvania bituminous coal fields in 1894. The miners became worse off with respect to relations with coal operators when the UMW lost that strike. However, the fortunes of the UMW, and the miners they led, would be reversed in 1897.

By the summer of 1897, the conditions of employment were unbearable and resentment toward the mine owners was tremendous. Having used all of their peaceful means to secure better working conditions and wages, the UMW coal miners decided to suspend operations in all of the states in which bituminous coal was mined. The miners themselves did not know the date that the strike was to take effect. They had instructed the officers of the then weak and struggling UMW, at a convention held in the spring of 1897, to order a stoppage of work at whatever time the officers believed to be most opportune, and which held the greatest possibility of success. (To illustrate the frail-

ties of the UMW at this time, when UMW president Michael Ratchford took office in 1897, there was not enough money in the treasury to call a meeting of the national executive board and the district presidents.)

Independence Day (4 July) in 1897 is remembered as an important date in the history of bituminous coal miners of the United States. A few days before that date, Ratchford, UMW vice president John Mitchell, and other UMW leaders issued a proclamation calling for all men employed in or about the mines in the states of Illinois, Indiana, Ohio, West Virginia, Kentucky, and the western part of Pennsylvania to stop work and to remain idle on and after Independence Day. Even though the membership of the UMW numbered less than 11,000 members, on 4 July 1897 about 110,000 coal miners began the first successful national strike of the bituminous coal mines ever led by the UMW. The union miners walked out of the mines demanding better mining rates and the right of the union to supervise the weighing of the coal mined, along with an increase in wages, decrease in working hours, and the abolition of the company store. Company stores were notorious for charging higher-than-normal prices for their goods, in effect lowering the wages the union owners paid the miners.

Mary Harris "Mother" Jones, a traveling organizer and freelance radical labor leader, arrived in Pittsburgh, Pennsylvania, during the strike to assist 20,000 rather disorganized miners who had struck. She quickly organized and rallied the striking miners with an impassioned speech. Later, a national labor newspaper of the day observed that the miners owed much of their victory to Mother Jones.

On 10 September 1897 a UMW-led strike in Lattimer, Pennsylvania, turned violent when a sheriff and his deputies fired on striking miners who were marching in a peaceful demonstration. The police killed 19 men and wounded another 40 strikers. The Lattimer Massacre, as it was called, helped to spur rapid growth in unionism, especially within the UMW.

Later in September 1897, a conference was held between the representatives of the UMW and the mine owners. The outcome was a partial settlement in which mine workers gained a wage increase that averaged 12 percent. The young UMW had finally won its first national bituminous coal strike. These two strikes by the bituminous coal miners in 1894 and 1897 are considered some of the most bitterly contested strikes of the late nineteenth and early twentieth centuries.

In January 1898 the mineworkers and mine owners met in Chicago and agreed that all future disputes over wages and conditions of employment would be determined by joint conference and conciliation. The meeting also led to an increase of wages for mine workers of another 18 percent and reduced the number of working hours from 10 to 8.

Results of Strikes

The 1897 national bituminous coal strikes achieved several goals. (1) The strikes resulted in securing an "interstate joint conference" in which the bituminous operators and the miners cooperated to stabilize labor costs and to improve wages and working conditions (including the eight-hour workday and a system for settling disputes over interpretations of contracts). In reality, both sides benefited because as mine owners raised employee wages, they also raised the selling price for their coal, resulting in more profits for their companies. (2) The strikes greatly enhanced the power of the UMW, resulting in growth in membership from less than 11,000 to more than 100,000 members (estimates are as high as 115,000). (3) The bituminous coal operators in Pennsylvania, Ohio, Indiana, and Illinois recognized the UMW as the representative of the miners and their bargaining agent.

Under the leadership of John Mitchell, the union grew rapidly with other successful strikes in the bituminous and anthracite coalfields over the following five years. Most important, as a result of the UMW's first successful strike in 1897 and other strikes during this time, the UMW, an affiliate of the AFL, became the largest union in the United States. Labor historians agree that the 1897 strike was one of the greatest struggles in American labor history up to that time and that it marked a turning point in the history of both the UMW and of the broader union movement in America.

Key Players

Jones, Mary Harris ("Mother") (1830–1930): Jones was a schoolteacher who worked in Michigan before settling in Memphis, Tennessee. Like her father, Jones held left-wing political views and was an active member of the Iron Molders' Union. When her husband, George Jones, an iron molder, and her four children died of yellow fever in 1867, Jones moved to Chicago, where she set up a seamstress shop. The 1871 Chicago Fire destroyed her home and business. Jones then became a full-time trade union organizer, specializing in helping miners fight for decent wages, improved working conditions, and an end to child labor. After the formation of the UMW in 1890, Jones became one of its officials. Jones was affectionately called "Mother" Jones by the other trade unionists. In 1905 Jones helped to form the radical labor organization the Industrial Workers of the World (IWW).

Mitchell, John (1870–1919): Mitchell became a coal miner in Braidwood, Illinois, at the age of 12. Three years later Mitchell joined the Knights of Labor. In 1890 he became one of the first members of the UMW. He held several offices in the union, eventually serving as president from 1898 to 1908. Between 1908 and 1915 Mitchell lectured on unionism and held office in the National Civic Federation, a group that sought conciliation between labor and business. From 1915 until his death Mitchell was chairman of the New York State Industrial Commission.

Ratchford, Michael: Ratchford was the fourth president of the United Mine Workers (UMW) of America, serving from 1896 to 1898. During his tenure, UMW membership expanded rapidly. During his presidency, Ratchford called the first meeting of what later was known as the Annual Joint Conference of Coal Miners and Operators of Illinois, Indiana, Ohio, and Western Pennsylvania. Many historians believe that the conference was a major stabilizing factor for the union during the next 30 years. Ratchford resigned the UMW presidency to accept a position on the United States Industrial Commission.

See also: American Federation of Labor; Eight-hour Day Movement; Panic of 1893; United Mine Workers of America.

BIBLIOGRAPHY

Books

Aldrich, Mark. *Safety First: Technology, Labor and Business in the Building of Work Safety, 1870–1939*. Baltimore, MD: Johns Hopkins University Press, 1997.

Dulles, Foster Rhea, and Melvyn Dubofsky. *Labor in America: A History*, 5th ed. Arlington Heights, IL: Harlan Davidson, Inc., 1984.

Farnam, Henry W. *History of Labour in the United States*, Vol. II. New York: Macmillan Company, 1921.

Fishback, Price V. *Soft Coal, Hard Choices: The Economic Welfare of Bituminous Coal Miners, 1890–1930*. Oxford, U.K.: Oxford University Press, 1992.

Goldberg, Arthur J. *AFL-CIO: Labor United*. New York: McGraw-Hill Book Company, 1956.

Lorwin, Lewis L. *The American Federation of Labor: History, Policies, and Prospects*. Washington DC: The Brookings Institution, 1933.

Rayback, Joseph G. *A History of American Labor: Expanded and Updated*. New York: The Macmillan Company, 1959.

—William Arthur Atkins

Black Codes

United States 1865–1877

Synopsis

With the end of the Civil War in 1865, conservative white politicians were concerned about how they would control the southern black population without the institution of slavery. Specifically, they wondered how they could keep blacks continuing to work the plantation system after slavery ended. Although all southern states eventually ratified the Thirteenth Amendment, which outlawed slavery, many southern states and local communities passed laws attempting to control the behavior of African Americans and their ability to engage in gainful employment and earn wages. Collectively these laws became known as the Black Codes, and they were the embodiment of white attempts to curb the civil rights of the former slaves. These laws made it hard for blacks to purchase land in certain areas, move from job to job, assemble even in small groups, or terminate labor contracts. Moreover, the Black Codes restricted blacks from testifying in court. The laws essentially violated the individual rights of African Americans as guaranteed by the Bill of Rights. Radical Republicans in Congress reacted to the Black Codes by passing the Fourteenth Amendment, which granted citizenship rights to African Americans, and passing the 1866 Civil Rights Act. The Black Codes helped inspire Republicans in Congress to intervene in the reconstruction of southern lives and institutions following the Civil War.

Timeline

1851: China's T'ai P'ing ("Great Peace") Rebellion begins under the leadership of schoolmaster Hong Xiuquan, who believes himself the younger brother of Jesus Christ. He mobilizes the peasantry against the Manchu emperors in a civil war that will take 20 to 30 million lives over the next 14 years.

1857: The Sepoy Mutiny, an unsuccessful revolt by Indian troops against the British East India Company, begins. As a result of the rebellion, which lasts into 1858, England places India under direct crown rule.

1863: The world's first subway opens, in London.

1867: Dual monarchy is established in Austria-Hungary.

1867: Maximilian surrenders to Mexican forces under Benito Juarez and is executed. Thus ends Napoleon III's dreams for a new French empire in the New World.

1867: The Dominion of Canada is established.

1867: United States purchases Alaska from Russia for $7.2 million.

1867: Meiji Restoration in Japan ends 675 years of rule by the shoguns.

1867: Karl Marx publishes the first volume of *Das Kapital*.

1871: U.S. troops in the West begin fighting the Apache nation.

1874: As farm wages in Britain plummet, agricultural workers go on strike.

1877: Great Britain's Queen Victoria is proclaimed the empress of India.

1882: The Chinese Exclusion Act, a treaty between the United States and China, provides for restrictions on immigration of Chinese workers.

1884: Chicago's Home Life Insurance Building, designed by William LeBaron Jenney, becomes the world's first skyscraper.

Event and Its Context

Origins

At the close of the Civil War, the status of former slaves was in question on the national, state, and local level. Economically, the South was in disastrous shape, in part because for four years the war had prevented the normal planting, cultivation, and harvesting of crops. Many southerners questioned whether freedmen would return to the plantations to cultivate the land. White southern politicians wanted no interference from Congress regarding how they addressed the status of African Americans during this time. In fact, many southern states passed the Thirteenth Amendment outlawing slavery under the assumption

Andrew Johnson. The Library of Congress.

that the federal government would not attempt to create laws pertaining to the social status of former slaves. President Andrew Johnson, himself a southern politician, was sympathetic to this view and considered Reconstruction and the status of African Americans in the South a matter best settled by the southern states and communities themselves.

Without slavery, white southerners feared that a free black population would reject their authority, especially where labor was concerned. Freedom of movement also posed a problem to southern white politicians during this time. They feared that the black population in the South would be drawn to work in cities and not stay in the rural South, so they looked to legislative measures to force the black population to work on the plantations.

African Americans, however, wanted to negotiate their labor. They did not want to continue to work 16-hour days during harvest season, and they expected southern planters to treat them with dignity and respect. Many other blacks wanted to leave the rural South altogether and try to find employment opportunities in both southern and northern cities. Whites, however, viewed blacks in paternalistic terms, considering them little more than children. While blacks wanted to test their occupational opportunities in the urban centers of the nation, whites demanded that they stay in the rural South where they had always worked. Whites did not believe blacks were capable of making informed decisions as to how best to exercise their labor. Many whites believed that blacks were naturally lazy and shiftless, and they feared that blacks would avoid work without the structure of the slave system. In sum, freed blacks and polit-

Lyman Trumbull. The Library of Congress.

ically powerful whites in the South shared conflicting perceptions of the place of black labor in the South following the Civil War.

Fearful of a future they could neither accurately predict nor effectively control, local communities in the South passed a number of laws in 1865 restricting the movement of African Americans, penalizing them for vagrancy, and limiting their opportunities for land ownership and for participation in skilled urban professions. These laws were intended to keep blacks tied to southern plantations as a source of labor.

Creating the Black Codes

Local laws regarding governance of the newly freed slaves were not widespread, and soon white southerners began to clamor for solutions from their state legislatures. Mississippi and South Carolina were the first states to respond with a series of laws known as Black Codes. Mississippi required all African Americans to carry with them at all times evidence that they were gainfully employed and married, if they were living with a person of the opposite sex. They were also required to prove they had a place to live. If black workers quit their jobs, they could be forced to pay back wages already earned or suffer arrest. White politicians who drafted these measures admitted that they wanted to create laws that were as close to slavery as possible. Most white southerners agreed with these measures. Armistead Burt, a moderate constitutional lawyer from South Carolina, helped draft his state's Black Codes. Ironically, Burt was eventually appointed to the judiciary by Republican administrations later in the 1860s.

In sharp contrast to how vagrancy was interpreted and defined in other parts of the United States, the Black Codes legally defined unemployed blacks as vagrants and thus subjected them to punishment under the law. Northerners rarely directed vagrancy statutes against the unemployed; instead, they typically punished prostitutes and criminals as vagrants. In Mississippi, if African Americans were convicted of vagrancy, they were charged with a fine. However, if they were unable to pay that fine, an employer could pay the fine for them and force the individual to work off the debt, with interest. In other places, reminiscent of the antebellum slave auctions, local law enforcement officials auctioned off blacks who were convicted of vagrancy to employers who placed bids on their labor. Sometimes these prosecutions became festivals. In fact in many places, like Lynchburg, Virginia, and Macon, Georgia, the mayor of the town was the person in charge of arresting the "vagrant," placing him in irons, parading him through the center of town, and then locking him in jail. Louisiana, however, was an exception to this rule. Louisiana law never specified that vagrancy laws were to be applied to blacks; however, in practice the vagrancy law applied only to them. Black Codes also made it illegal for an African American laborer to break a labor contract. Both blacks and whites frequently entered into time-specific contracts, but African Americans, unlike whites, were prevented by law from breaking or renegotiating their contracts. If they did not work their full contract, law enforcement could legally force black workers to complete the work in question or place them in custody.

In cases of legal disputes, blacks could testify in court, but only against other African Americans, and they had to have their case tried before all-white juries. According to some Black Codes, African Americans could not serve on juries at all. In Alabama the law required that black children work for their parents' former masters as apprentices or give their family's former master the option to refuse such work.

The Black Codes also made it difficult, and sometimes impossible, for African Americans to purchase property. In fact, the restrictions were so severe in some areas that blacks were effectively tied to the plantation system as cheap labor.

All aspects of the relationship between employer and employee were detailed in the Black Codes. In South Carolina, Georgia, and Mississippi, politicians went to great lengths to define the obligations servants owed masters and masters owed servants. According to Dan T. Carter, black workers were mandated by law to be "honest, truthful, sober, civil, and diligent." If blacks did not display these virtues when interacting with their employers, they could be prosecuted. Employers also had to be honest and committed to the best interests of their black employees. Technically, employers could also be prosecuted if they committed moral or social transgressions with black employees, yet legal reprisals against white employers rarely occurred. Within these codes, employers were designated as the sole authority in times of disputes between black employees. In South Carolina working conduct was meticulously spelled out. Employers had to specify in contracts how long black workers were to work each day, the amount of pay they were to receive, and the conditions under which they were to work. In fact, the South Carolina legislature went so far as to legislate that em-

Excerpts from Mississippi's "Black Code"

[Various portions of the Laws of Mississippi, adopted in 1865, constituted the state's "Black Code." Among these are the Civil Rights of Freedmen in Mississippi, the Mississippi Vagrant Law, the Penal Laws of Mississippi, and the Mississippi Apprentice Law. Portions of the last of these are excerpted below.]

Sec. 1. . . . It shall be the duty of all sheriffs, justices of the peace, and other civil officers of the several counties in this State, to report to the probate courts of their respective counties semi-annually, at the January and July terms of said courts, all freedmen, free negroes, and mulattoes, under the age of eighteen, in their respective counties, beats or districts, who are orphans, or whose parent or parents have not the means or who refuse to provide for and support said minors; and thereupon it shall be the duty of said probate court to order the clerk of said court to apprentice said minors to some competent and suitable person, on such terms as the court may direct, having a particular care to the interest of said minor: Provided, that the former owner of said minors shall have the preference when, in the opinion of the court, he or she shall be a suitable person for that purpose.

Sec. 2. . . . The said court shall be fully satisfied that the person or persons to whom said minor shall be apprenticed shall be a suitable person to have the charge and care of said minor, and fully to protect the interest of said minor. The said court shall require the said master or mistress to execute bond and security, payable to the State of Mississippi, conditioned that he or she shall furnish said minor with sufficient food and clothing; to treat said minor humanely; furnish medical attention in case of sickness; teach, or cause to be taught, him or her to read and write, if under fifteen

years old, and will conform to any law that may be hereafter passed for the regulation of the duties and relation of master and apprentice . . . .

Sec. 3 . . . .In the management and control of said apprentice, said master or mistress shall have the power to inflict such moderate corporal chastisement as a father or guardian is allowed to inflict on his or her child or ward at common law: Provided, that in no case shall cruel or inhuman punishment be inflicted.

Sec. 4. . . . If any apprentice shall leave the employment of his or her master or mistress, without his or her consent, said master or mistress may pursue and recapture said apprentice, and bring him or her before any justice of the peace of the county, whose duty it shall be to remand said apprentice to the service of his or her master or mistress; and in the event of a refusal on the part of said apprentice so to return, then said justice shall commit said apprentice to the jail of said county, on failure to give bond, to the next term of the county court; and it shall be the duty of said court at the first term thereafter to investigate said case, and if the court shall be of opinion that said apprentice left the employment of his or her master or mistress without good cause, to order him or her to be punished, as provided for the punishment of hired freedmen, as may be from time to time provided for by law for desertion, until he or she shall agree to return to the service of his or her master or mistress: . . . if the court shall believe that said apprentice had good cause to quit his said master or mistress, the court shall discharge said apprentice from said indenture, and also enter a judgment against the master or mistress for not more than one hundred dollars, for the use and benefit of said apprentice. . . .

Source: Paul A. Cimbala and Randall M. Miller, eds. *The Freedmen's Bureau and Reconstruction: Reconsiderations.* New York: Fordham University Press, 1999.

—Judson Knight

ployers could not force their black workers to work in the rain, snow, or other poor environmental conditions, and employers could not terminate old or infirm African Americans. Employers had to continue to assist aged and sick blacks under their supervision.

Additionally, in Mississippi and Florida, the Black Codes defined racial status. Anyone with any black blood was considered black according to the law and subject to the provisions of the Black Codes. Since these laws were targeted at blacks, southern legislators wanted to be sure that no African Americans would try to claim white parentage. These laws also sought to outlaw interracial marriage. In North Carolina a person who performed a marriage for a white and black couple could be fined $500. In Georgia they could not only be fined but could also suffer incarceration. In North Carolina a black man convicted of raping a woman of any race could be hanged, while a white man convicted of rape would be fined and suffer a lashing. In other states the Black Codes restricted African Americans from buying liquor and firearms.

These types of discriminatory laws created constitutional problems for federal officials in the South. Daniel E. Sickles and Alfred H. Terry, military officials serving in the South during this time, voided these laws because they violated the right of equal protection under the law. Southern lawmakers maneuvered around these constitutional problems by voiding the specific legislation that applied to African Americans only. In order to keep the spirit of the legislation, southern politicians rewrote many of the Black Codes to remove the specific references to blacks and replaced them with racially neutral language. Yet in application, these laws strictly applied only to African Americans. In turn, southern courts upheld many of these laws without ever mentioning them as race legislation.

Black Reaction

Even with these laws in place, many southern whites found it difficult to force blacks to abide by them and maintain strict labor discipline. Many southern planters noted that they could pass legislation, but they could not convince blacks to remain on the land and work the plantations. Some African Americans who objected to the laws simply refused to abide by them. Many blacks in Mississippi signed agreements to work on the land in return for removal of the Black Codes. Black politicians of the time frequently made references to the Black Codes as evidence that for all practical purposes, blacks were still not free in the South. Black congressman Josiah Walls observed that these actions by southern whites forced black voters away from identifying with the Democratic Party. As a result, blacks in the South drifted to the Republican Party for solutions and expected the federal government to intervene against state interference in civil liberties.

Republican Reaction

For Republicans in Congress, the Black Codes represented a turning back of the clock on the progress made during the Civil War. Northerners believed that the Civil War was fought in part to establish a system of freed labor in the South. Since the Black Codes were aimed to restrict the labor of African Americans, Republicans felt that this betrayed the true mission of the Civil War.

In reaction to the proliferation of the Black Codes throughout the South, Senator Lyman Trumbull, chair of the Judiciary Committee, drafted two bills, one to create the Freedman's Bureau, and the other, the 1866 Civil Rights Act. Both measures were meant to undo the damage of the Black Codes. The Freedman's Bureau was charged with assisting former slaves in their adjustment to freedom. While handling a myriad of responsibilities, the Freedman's Bureau had the authority to arbitrate labor disputes between blacks and their white employers as well as to negotiate labor contracts on behalf of black workers in the South. The Civil Rights Act of 1866 was meant to nullify the Black Codes and guarantee individual rights and protection to blacks in the South.

President Johnson consistently and emphatically believed that issues of black status were best arbitrated by southern legislatures and were not the responsibility of the federal government. He vetoed both of the measures sponsored by Trumbull. Republicans were shocked by Johnson's reaction and as a result of his vetoes, Republicans in Congress moved to wrest power over Reconstruction away from Johnson and into the hands of Congress. This struggle culminated in Johnson's impeachment trial, which was spearheaded by radical Republicans such as Thaddeus Stevens and Charles Sumner.

Impact and Legacy

Although the Black Codes were a product of southern fears that blacks would refuse to work the land in the South, they also had a national impact. Because of the bitterness of this Reconstruction experience, southern blacks learned to be suspicious of local and state governments and looked to the federal government to offer aid and assistance in disputes with local and regional authorities. Additionally, the Black Codes helped to redefine the national applications of vagrancy laws. Prior to this period, vagrancy laws were primarily used against petty criminals or prostitutes. However, after Reconstruction, northern communities and states began to apply vagrancy laws to workers who organized strikes or union leaders who demanded high wages and better working conditions. Within the South, although many of the Black Codes disappeared, vagrancy laws targeted at blacks were still a very real problem for African Americans well into the twentieth century. The system of convict leasing had its foundation in the Black Codes. Many legal and criminal justice scholars argue that the strained relationship between blacks and the law today has its foundation in these Black Codes, a sad legacy of Reconstruction.

Key Players

Burt, Armistead (1802–1883): Burt was a lawyer and politician from South Carolina and represented his state in Congress from 1843 to 1853. He drafted South Carolina's Black Codes during Reconstruction.

Johnson, Andrew (1808–1875): Johnson was a politician from Tennessee who supported the Union during the Civil War. Abraham Lincoln selected him as his running mate in 1864, and he succeeded to the presidency upon Lincoln's death in 1865. Since Johnson was a long-time Democrat, he frequently clashed with Republicans in Congress and even with his own cabinet. He believed that Reconstruction was a "states' rights" issue, so he refused to interfere with the way southern states treated their black populations. He staunchly refused to use the power of the federal government to rescind the Black Codes.

Kenner, Duncan F. (1813–1887): Kenner was a sugar plantation owner and politician from Louisiana. He served in the Louisiana legislature and the Confederate Congress. He was responsible for drafting Louisiana's Black Codes during Reconstruction.

Sickles, Daniel E. (1825–1914): Sickles was a northern Democrat and served in the Civil War as a general. He periodically served as a representative in Congress for the state of New York both before and after the Civil War. As a federal official during Reconstruction, he suspended the Black Codes of South Carolina.

Stevens, Thaddeus (1792–1868): Stevens was a lawyer and politician. He was a representative from Pennsylvania, first as a Whig and later as a Republican. He was a member of the Radical Republicans who wanted to wrest control of Reconstruction away from the president. Because of issues such as the Black Codes, Stevens spearheaded the attempt to impeach and remove Andrew Johnson from office.

Sumner, Charles (1811–1874): Sumner was a senator from Massachusetts. He was one of the founders of the Free Soil Party and later the Republican Party. He was part of the radical wing of the Republican Party who wanted to control Reconstruction and eliminate the Black Codes in the South.

Terry, Alfred H. (1827–1890): Terry was a Civil War general and lawyer. He overturned the Reconstruction Era vagrancy laws in Virginia because he believed they reinstituted slavery.

Trumbull, Lyman (1813–1896): Trumbull was a senator from Illinois. Although he switched back and forth from Democrat to Republican several times in his career, he was known as a moderate politician. As the chair of the Judiciary Committee, he drafted the Civil Rights Act of 1866 as a way to protect African Americans from the Black Codes and affirm their equal protection under the law.

See also: *Abolition of Slavery, United States.*

BIBLIOGRAPHY

Books

Carter, Dan T. *When the War Was Over: The Failure of Self-Reconstruction in the South, 1865–1867.* Baton Rouge, LA: Louisiana State University Press, 1985.

Foner, Eric. *Reconstruction: America's Unfinished Revolution, 1863-1877.* New York: Harper and Row Publishers, 1988.

Litwack, Leon F. *Been in the Storm So Long: The Aftermath of Slavery.* New York: Vintage Books, 1979.

Rabinowitz, Howard N. *Race Relations in the Urban South, 1865–1890.* New York: Oxford University Press, 1978.

Trefousse, Hans L. *Andrew Johnson: A Biography.* New York: W. W. Norton and Company, 1989.

Wharton, Vernon Lane. *The Negro in Mississippi: 1865–1890.* Chapel Hill, NC: University of North Carolina Press, 1947.

Periodicals

Carter, Dan T. "Fateful Legacy: White Southerners and the Dilemma of Emancipation." *Proceeding of the South Carolina Historical Association* (1977): 49–63.

Oakes, James. "A Failure of Vision: The Collapse of the Freedman's Bureau Courts." *Civil War History* 25 (fall 1979): 66–76.

Richardson, Joe M. "Florida Black Codes." *Florida Historical Quarterly* 47 (summer 1969): 365–379.

Sansing, David G. "The Failure of Johnsonian Reconstruction in Mississippi, 1865–1866." *Journal of Mississippi History* 34 (summer 1972): 373–390.

Sclomowitz, Ralph. "Planter Combinations and Black Labour in the American South, 1865-1880." *Slavery and Abolition* 9 (fall 1988): 72–84.

Sowle, Patrick. "The Abolition of Slavery." *Georgia Historical Quarterly* 52 (spring 1968): 237–255.

—Robert Cassanello

Bloody Sunday

Russia 1905

Synopsis

By the end of 1904, the Russian economy was strained by the country's involvement in the Russo-Japanese War (1904–1905) and from social disruptions persisting since the late nineteenth century. In January 1905 the head of one of the legal (government-recognized) trade unions, Georgy ("Georgii") Apollonovich Gapon, led a peaceful demonstration to the home of Emperor Nicholas II, the Winter Palace in St. Petersburg, hoping to present him with a petition on behalf of the country's workers. Soldiers fired upon the procession; hundreds of people were killed and many more injured. The massacre of innocent men, women, and children outside the palace by imperial security guards was eventually called Bloody Sunday; it was the event that ignited the Russian Revolution of 1905.

Timeline

1885: Indian National Congress is founded. In the years that follow, the party will take the helm of India's independence movement.

1890: U.S. Congress passes the Sherman Antitrust Act, which in the years that follow will be used to break up large monopolies.

1895: Brothers Auguste and Louis Lumière show the world's first motion picture—*Workers Leaving the Lumière Factory*—at a café in Paris.

1898: United States defeats Spain in the three-month Spanish-American War. As a result, Cuba gains it independence, and the United States purchases Puerto Rico and the Philippines from Spain for $20 million.

1901: U.S. President William McKinley is assassinated by Leon Czolgosz, an anarchist. Vice President Theodore Roosevelt becomes president.

1903: Russia's Social Democratic Party splits into two factions: the moderate Mensheviks and the hard-line Bolsheviks. Despite their names, which in Russian mean "minority" and "majority," respectively, Mensheviks actually outnumber Bolsheviks.

1904: The Russo-Japanese War begins. It will last into 1905 and results in a resounding Japanese victory. In Russia, the war is followed by the Revolution of 1905, which marks the beginning of the end of czarist rule; meanwhile, Japan is poised to become the first major non-western power of modern times.

1905: Albert Einstein presents his special theory of relativity.

1905: In the industrial Ruhr region in Germany, 200,000 miners go on strike.

1909: Founding of the National Association for the Advancement of Colored People (NAACP) by W. E. B. Du Bois and a number of other prominent black and white intellectuals in New York City.

1914: On the Western Front, the first battles of the Marne and Ypres establish a line that will more or less hold for the next four years. Exuberance is still high on both sides, but will dissipate as thousands of German, French, and British soldiers sacrifice their lives in battles over a few miles of barbed wire and mud. The Eastern Front is a different story: a German victory over Russia at Tannenberg in August sets the stage for a war in which Russia will enjoy little success, and will eventually descend into chaos that paves the way for the 1917 revolutions.

Strikers and soldiers clash on Bloody Sunday, Narva Gate, St. Petersburg, Russia. © Hulton/Archive by Getty Images. Reproduced by permission.

Event and Its Context

The Bloody Sunday massacre in St. Petersburg is usually identified as the event that precipitated the Russian Revolution of 1905. Historians also cite a series of political events, beginning in 1895, and various labor tensions, which had been building for years, that contributed to the killing of these peaceful workers and their families.

Political History

In 1894 Japan entered into the Sino-Japanese War against China, which it won in 1895. From its victory, Japan gained control of Manchuria, including the valuable warm-water seaports of Port Arthur (today called Lüshun) and Dairen (today called Lüda). However, the Japanese lost Manchuria and the two ports when the French and Germans threatened to take military action against Japan if it kept the territory.

Angered by its loss, Japan took offense when Russia and China formed a joint banking enterprise in Manchuria. Japan became angrier still when China allowed Russia to construct a secondary route for the Trans-Siberian Railway through Mukden, in Manchuria, to Vladivostok (off the coast of the Sea of Japan in Russia) in exchange for a Russian pledge of military aid in the event that China was attacked again by Japan. Japan became even more alienated in 1898 when China gave Russia the Liaoyang Peninsula (along the northeastern coast of China and bordering North Korea) and formal rights to the ports of Dairen and Port Arthur (near the southwestern tip of the peninsula).

Beginning in 1904, Japan fought Russia for control of the two disputed Manchurian ports. Russia was not prepared for the war in that its army was not fully mobile due to long delays in completing the Trans-Siberian Railway. Because of these inefficiencies, Russia was soon losing important battles to Japan.

By the end of 1904, Russia was losing the war; Nicholas II was losing support; new political groups, such as the Bolsheviks and the Mensheviks, were making advances toward more radicalism and liberalism, respectively; and discontent continued to escalate, especially among the lower classes. The Bolsheviks (meaning "majority"), the more radical of the two sections of socialists (Social Democratic Labor Party), were led by Vladimir Lenin and eventually called the Communist Party. The Mensheviks (meaning "minority"), the more conservative section, was led by Julius Martov.

Labor History

The number of Russian industrial workers had dramatically increased from 493,000 in 1866 to 1,405,000 in 1896. Between 1865 and 1890 the number of factory workers grew by 65 percent and the number of miners by 106 percent for a combined 75 percent increase in Russian industrial workers. Many workers had migrated to large cities from depressed rural areas to find better jobs. These new workers, unfamiliar with the work-

Police dispersing striking workers near Putiloff Ironworks, Bloody Sunday, St. Petersburg, Russia. © Hulton/ Getty Images. Reproduced by permission.

ing environment of factories, felt isolated in their new surroundings. Agitators who demanded immediate changes to the political and economic systems, even at the cost of violence, easily swayed these workers. Contributing to these problems was the plight of employers contending with the early stages of industrial development. Drastic expansion of equipment, processes, and the number of workers often left them unable to effectively communicate with their workers, a classic complaint in rapidly industrializing regions.

Disputes between employers and employees often resulted. Strikes became a regular part of Russian work life near the end of the nineteenth century. It was exceedingly difficult for the government to control these disputes because of the enormous size of the country; Russia spread across Europe and Asia, contained about 125 million people, and suffered from poor communications, bad roads, and few railroads. In 1894 some 17,000 workers went on strike, typically demanding shorter work hours and higher pay. Even though unions led most of these strikes, few were well organized. The strikes in 1897 and 1898 occurred mostly in the largest cities such as St. Petersburg and Moscow. A growing unrest among Russian workers was gaining momentum at the beginning of the twentieth century. At that time Russian industrial employees worked, on average, 11-hour weekdays and 10-hour Saturdays. Conditions in the factories were extremely harsh, and little concern was shown for the heath and safety of workers. Attempts by workers to form trade unions were resisted by factory owners. Wages, even for the more skilled classes of workers, were dropping steadily, and the price of basic goods was rising; between October 1903 and October 1904 real wages declined between 20 percent and 25 percent. Housing conditions were also terrible, unemployment was increasing, and, worst of all, working people had no recourse for grievances. Employers could treat workers as they pleased and could usually depend on the support of the authorities and the police to enforce disciplinary actions.

Gapon and the Assembly Union

Paralleling the worker unrest, in 1903 a radical Orthodox priest by the name of Georgy ("Georgii") Apollonovich Gapon began a workers' organization called the Assembly of Russian Factory Workers of St. Petersburg (hereafter called the Assembly union). The Russian *Okhrona* (the secret police) considered the Assembly union a friendly social organization that positively influenced the working people. The union, originally based in a tea and reading room, attracted apolitical and antirevolutionary workers whose influence in the workplace was small.

This situation changed in 1904 when V. K. Plehve, the minister of the interior who had helped Gapon create the union, was assassinated as a result of his repression of revolutionary and liberal ideas and practices within Russia. Workers, seeing that social reform was more possible now, turned to Gapon's movement, which soon began to resemble an independent, reform-minded labor union. Its membership in that year dramatically increased to over 9,000.

A major event of worker discontent was the oil workers' strike in Baku (located on the western coast of the Caspian Sea) in December 1904. It was the first large-scale strike in Russia that did not begin spontaneously but was deliberately organized. It caused unrest in other industrial centers and contribut-

ed to the labor movement in St. Petersburg. At that time the Gapon meetings attracted an enormous number of workers, many of whom made dramatic and inspiring speeches about how workers should no longer stand for the abuses they endured in the workplace. The peaceful movement Gapon had created a short time before was turning into a revolutionary mass movement, whether he liked it or not.

On 3 January 1905 at the Putilov Iron Works plant, a simple firing of four Assembly union workers caused Gapon to call for immediate industrial action. In the next few days over 110,000 workers from numerous factories in St. Petersburg went on strike in a major revolt. Both branches of the social democracy movement—the Bolsheviks and the Mensheviks—supported the strike. Both groups continued to initiate strikes and help bring additional organizations into the labor movement.

The Gapon Petition

In an attempt to resolve the situation, Gapon decided to make a personal appeal to Nicholas II. He apparently believed the czar would correct the evils inflicted on the workers if they were brought directly to his attention. Gapon drew up a petition outlining the workers' sufferings and demands, calling for an eight-hour workday; the freedom to organize trade unions; better working conditions, free medical aid, and higher wages for workers; elections for a constituent assembly by universal, equal, and secret suffrage; freedom of speech, press, association, and religion; and ending the war against Japan. Over 150,000 people signed the petition, and Gapon believed Nicholas would accept.

Bloody Sunday

All of these occurrences led to what would eventually be called Bloody Sunday. On 9 January 1905 (according to the Julian calendar used by Russia at that time, which corresponds with 22 January 1905 on the Gregorian calendar) hundreds of thousands of workers, led by Gapon and accompanied by their wives, children, and parents, walked to the Winter Palace in St. Petersburg, the residence of Russian emperor Nicholas II, to demand more food and better pay and working conditions. The protesters carried religious icons and gonfalons (banners), pictures of Nicholas to show their peaceful intent, and the signed petition. As they marched toward the Winter Palace, they chanted "God save the Czar." At the entrance to the palace they were met by the czar's secret police and the Russian Imperial Guard.

Nicholas was absent at the time; his uncle, Grand Duke Vladimir, commander of the Imperial Guard, gave the order to fire on the crowd. Many hundreds of the demonstrators were killed or wounded (with first newspaper reports placing the numbers in the thousands). A Bolshevik historian later wrote that the approximate number of wounded was 450 to 800 and the number of killed 150 to 200.

Most Russians saw Bloody Sunday as a horrendous event. As news of the massacre spread, a general protest ensued as workers stopped working, businessmen would not open their businesses, and soldiers refused to follow orders. Russia literally could not operate, as the people lost faith in their government and withheld support for Nicholas. A wave of mass political strikes and demonstrations spread across Russia under the slogan "Down with the autocracy!" Bloody Sunday marked the beginning of the Revolution of 1905, which eventually brought about drastic changes in the Russian government.

In 1906 Nicholas attempted to pacify protesters by introducing Russia's first elected legislative assembly, the State Duma. Mass opinion, however, had been radicalized by the massacre and resulting violence. Socialist parties, workers, and peasants continued to protest the imperial regime, which was eventually overthrown in the Russian Revolution of 1917.

Key Players

Gapon, Georgy Apollonovich (1870–1906): Gapon, a radical Russian Orthodox priest and former prison chaplain, began organizing workers' clubs, called the Assembly of Russian Factory Workers of the City of St. Petersburg, in 1903 under the patronage of the imperial police and the Orthodox Church. In January 1905 he, along with workers and their families, marched to the Winter Palace in the hope that the czar would come to their aid. Many unarmed workers and members of their families were shot; Gapon was wounded. After the massacre, Gapon left Russia, then returned illegally less than a year later and resumed contact with the tsarist secret police. He was assigned to help dismantle the workers organizations he had helped build. Gapon was murdered by the secret police in March 1906.

Nicholas II (1868–1918): Czar Nicholas II was the last czar of Russia and the last of the Romanov dynasty. The son of Czar Alexander III, he began his reign by marrying Alexandra, the granddaughter of Queen Victoria of England. In 1894 Nicholas became czar on his father's death and employed the same autocratic rule his father had. During his reign Russia experienced a period of great industrialization and land reform. However, Nicholas was considered a weak and superstitious man who strongly disliked intellectuals and politicians. He was forced to abdicate in 1917 and was murdered, together with his family, by the Bolsheviks the following year.

See also: *Russian Revolutions.*

BIBLIOGRAPHY

Books

Bonnell, Victoria E. *Roots of Rebellion: Workers' Politics and Organizations in St. Petersburg and Moscow, 1900–1914.* Berkeley: University of California Press, 1983.

Pospielovsky, Dimitry. *Russian Police Trade Unionism: Experiment or Provocation?* London: Weidenfield and Nicolson and London School of Economics and Political Science, 1971.

Schwarz, Solomon M. *The Russian Revolution of 1905.* Chicago and London: University of Chicago Press, 1967.

Other

"History: Revolutionary Times." Russianet.ru [cited 7 February 2003]. <http://www.russianet.ru/~oldrn/history/revolution.html>

Rempel, Gerhard. "The Revolution of 1905." Western New England College [cited 7 February 2003]. <http://mars.acnet.wnec.edu/~grempel/courses/russia/lectures/23rev1905.html>

"Russian Revolution 1905." OnWar.com [cited 7 February 2003]. <http://www.onwar.com/aced/data/romeo/russia1905.htm>

"The Twentieth Century, Year After Year: 1905." Radio Voice of Russia [cited 7 February 2003]. <http://www.vor.ru/century/1905.html>

—William Arthur Atkins

Boston Police Strike

United States 1919

Synopsis

To protest poor working conditions and low pay, the Boston police unionized and affiliated with the American Federation of Labor (AFL). Boston police commissioner Edwin U. Curtis, in the belief that the police would take orders from the AFL—thereby hampering discipline—banned the officers from associating with any outside organization. When he suspended several union officials for disobeying his order, the police walked out in the first strike by public safety workers in U.S. history. Poor strike preparations left the city without any protection, and Bostonians quickly ran amok. Assaults, rapes, vandalism, and looting went unpunished as the city struggled to get replacement police in place. Angered by the violence, Massachusetts governor Calvin Coolidge proclaimed, in a remark that would catapult him to the presidency, that no one had the right to strike against the public safety. Striking officers were fired, and the collapse of the strike sounded the death toll for the early police labor movement.

Timeline

1900: China's Boxer Rebellion, which began in the preceding year with attacks on foreigners and Christians, reaches its height. An international contingent of more than 2,000 men arrives to restore order, but only after several tens of thousands have died.

1907: U.S. markets experience a financial panic.

1912: *Titanic* sinks on its maiden voyage, from Southampton to New York, on 14 April. More than 1,500 people are killed.

1915: At the Second Battle of Ypres, the Germans introduce a terrifying new weapon: poison gas.

1917: The intercepted "Zimmermann Telegram" reveals a plot by the German government to draw Mexico into an alliance against the United States in return for a German promise to return the southwestern U.S. territories taken in the Mexican War. Three months later, in response to German threats of unrestricted submarine warfare, the United States on 6 April declares war on Germany.

1919: With the formation of the Third International (Comintern), the Bolshevik government of Russia establishes its control over communist movements worldwide.

1919: Treaty of Versailles is signed by the Allies and Germany but rejected by the U.S. Senate. This is due in part to rancor between President Woodrow Wilson and Republican Senate leaders, and in part to concerns over Wilson's plan to commit the United States to the newly established League of Nations and other international duties. Not until 1921 will Congress formally end U.S. participation in the war, but it will never agree to join the League.

1919: The Eighteenth Amendment, which prohibits the production, sale, distribution, purchase, and consumption of alcohol throughout the United States, is ratified.

1919: In India, Mahatma Gandhi launches his campaign of nonviolent resistance to British rule.

1919: In Italy, a former socialist of the left named Benito Mussolini introduces the world to a new socialism of the right, embodied in an organization known as the "Union for Struggle," or Fasci di Combattimento. Composed primarily of young war veterans discontented with Italy's paltry share of the spoils from the recent world war (if not with their country's lackluster military performance in the conflict), the fascists are known for their black shirts and their penchant for violence. Like their communist counterparts, however, they are incapable of winning an election.

1921: As the Allied Reparations Commission calls for payments of 132 billion gold marks, inflation in Germany begins to climb.

1925: European leaders attempt to secure the peace at the Locarno Conference, which guarantees the boundaries between France and Germany, and Belgium and Germany.

1929: On "Black Friday" in October, prices on the U.S. stock market, which had been climbing wildly for several years, suddenly collapse. Thus begins the first phase of a world economic crisis and depression that will last until the beginning of World War II.

Event and Its Context

In the aftermath of World War I, Americans feared that Bolshevik agents were seeking to duplicate the success of the Russian Revolution. The spirit of tolerance and the desire to push for social justice that had marked progressivism vanished, with Americans coming to view strikes as efforts by "Reds" to subvert the United States. In this climate, the Boston police embarked on a futile effort to remedy years of neglectful treatment by city authorities.

Trouble Brewing

The Boston police, in their dome-shaped helmets and high-necked frock coats with rows of glittering buttons, enjoyed a reputation as one of the most law-abiding forces in the nation and once earned the best pay of all skilled workers in the city. During the war, living costs jumped, but police pay remained static. A new recruit, who had to be 25 years of age, received only $2 a day, the same amount that he would have received in 1854 when the police department was first established. After completing a probationary year and receiving a promotion to patrolman, an officer received a yearly salary of $1,000, which then increased annually until it reached a maximum six years later of $1,400. Out of this pay, well below the government-set subsistence minimum of $1,575 for a family of five, the officer had to provide his own uniform and equipment at a cost by 1919 of more than $200. To further infuriate the police, they suffered poor working conditions. Patrolmen worked a seven-day week with one day off in 15. Day men typically put in 73 hours a week, and night officers worked 85 hours. Day men additionally were required to spend one night a week in the station house on reserve, with two to four men sharing beds in succession with insects so voracious that they ate the leather of the police belts and helmets in the station behind City Hall. No patrolman could leave the city limits without express permission. Running errands for superiors had become part of the job, and, without civil service, promotion hinged on the word of captains who could keep men at the patrolman level indefinitely.

To address their complaints, the Boston police relied on the Boston Social Club, created in 1906 by Police Commissioner Stephen O'Meara as a fraternal organization that crossed precinct boundaries. In 1917 and 1918 city authorities rebuffed representatives of the club when they requested a $200 across-the-board raise and only agreed to grant a pay hike to a small number of officers in May 1919. The officers decided to apply for an AFL charter.

The AFL

Under the leadership of Samuel Gompers and with a membership of about four million in 1919, the relatively business-friendly AFL was not a particularly radical organization. Gompers, who had worked with the U.S. government to prevent strikes during the war, espoused the right of unions to conduct their own affairs without interference from the AFL. In June 1919 the AFL announced that it would grant charters to police unions, and in the next month men began circulating petitions in each of the 19 Boston police districts requesting the formation of an AFL-chartered union. By this time, O'Meara had died and his replacement had no sympathy for the many Irish Americans in the police ranks.

A man who lacked any police experience and who resented the growing Irish American domination of politics that had made him a one-term mayor at the turn of the century, Edwin U. Curtis reacted to the brewing trouble with a mindset based on years of class and ethnic conflict in Boston. Because police powers had been removed from the mayors of Boston as a result of conflicts between the traditionally Democratic mayors and largely Republican state legislature, Curtis answered only to Massachusetts governor Calvin Coolidge. Curtis informed Coolidge of his intent to oppose any police union and asked for support. Rather noncommittally, Coolidge advised Curtis to perform his duties. On 29 July, Curtis stated that an officer could not both belong to a union and perform his duty, as his loyalty would be divided between two masters. By this time, the Boston firefighters and city clerks had affiliated with the AFL and had gained both wage hikes and shorter hours. On 9 August the police officially requested an AFL charter to form a union separate from the Social Club. Six days later, on 15 August, the Boston Police Union was established.

Strike

Although Boston police had many grievances, Curtis's unbending attitude became the principal cause of the strike. On the night before the AFL election, he determined to assert his authority by ordering 1,000 blank dismissal notices to be printed and distributed to station house captains. The plumbers, firefighters, boilermakers, and machinists passed resolutions that if Curtis persisted in his course, the unions would call a sympathy strike. The transportation workers announced that they would refuse to transport strikebreakers, and Boston's city council announced its support for organized labor. On 17 August the Boston Central Labor Union, the coordinating body of all the AFL unions in the city, denounced Curtis for his "tyrannical assumption of autocratic authority" and promised support to the police. The AFL's New England organizer, Frank McCarthy, characterized Curtis's order as an attempt to undermine collective bargaining as well as an attack on the individual rights of police officers. Remaining adamant that the police must surrender the AFL charter, Curtis summoned eight union leaders to his office on 26 August and interrogated 11 more three days later. He intended to suspend the officers immediately. The police threatened to strike if he did so, but Boston mayor Andrew Peters intervened to avoid a showdown. At this point, 90 percent of Boston's 1,544 police officers had joined the new union. Coolidge refused to intervene with the justification that he did not possess direct responsibility over Boston police matters.

To fend off a strike, Peters formed a committee with investment banker James Storrow as its head. The Storrow committee proposed a wage hike and the establishment of a grievance committee. Curtis, infuriated that an outsider would attempt to interfere with the discipline of the police department, declared that the grievance board would result in a state of divided responsibility that would weaken policy and slow action. On 8 September he suspended the union leaders indefinitely. The police held a meeting that evening and voted 1,134 to 2 to strike. The walkout began on 9 September. Aware of antistrike sentiment, Curtis expected that two-thirds of the police would remain on the job, but only 400 patrolmen stayed on duty.

City in Terror

When the police left, Boston began to prepare for the worst. Hospitals established emergency care stations and posted their telephone numbers and locations in the morning newspapers. Fearful of vandalism, many factories, stores, and banks armed their male employees. To replace the striking police, Curtis assigned 225 command officers to patrol and attempted to mobilize 100 Metropolitan Park Police who had been placed at his disposal by Coolidge. In response to their refusal to perform street duty, Curtis suspended 58 of the park police. Substitute

Calvin Coolidge. The Library of Congress.

police also arrived as the railroad assigned 220 men to assist, and 3,142 Bostonians, including a large Harvard University contingent, volunteered for duty. Curtis refused to mobilize the volunteer police or call out the National Guard.

The night of 9 September became one of the most violent in Boston history. Mobs roamed at will across the city, robbing men and raping several women. They smashed windows and looted stores. Firefighters responding to false alarms were pelted with any material at hand. Officers attempting to quell disturbances were generally ineffective. Throughout the night, mobs advanced on small groups of loyal policemen and retreated only at gunpoint.

On 10 September a panic-stricken Mayor Peters called out the National Guard, and the volunteers went into action. Despite these efforts, violence continued for a second night before calm was restored. The strike toll stood at 8 dead, 21 wounded, and 50 injured, with property damages estimated at $350,000.

Defeat

The rioting had destroyed any chance for a police victory. Urged by Gompers to stay at work and perhaps disgusted by the violence, other unions failed to support the police. In a speech, Coolidge declared, "There is no right to strike against the public safety by any body, any time, any where." City leaders dismissed the suspended and striking officers, and by November more than 1,300 new patrolmen were on the beat.

The heavy newspaper coverage given to the rioting ensured that fears of police unionization spread across the nation. Other

Rioters clashing with National Guardsmen called in by Massachusetts Governor Calvin Coolidge during strike by Boston police officers, Boston, Massachusetts. © Bettmann/Corbis. Reproduced by permission.

states subsequently passed laws forbidding the police to unionize and, even when those laws were eventually relaxed, few police showed any enthusiasm for organizing until the 1950s. The failure of the strike ultimately destroyed police attempts to make demands from city governments and solidified repressive managerial tactics in law enforcement administration.

Key Players

Coolidge, Calvin (1872–1933): A lawyer who became a professional Republican politician, the notoriously taciturn Coolidge served as governor of Massachusetts (1918–1920) until selected as Warren Harding's vice president. Ascending to the presidency upon Harding's sudden death in 1923, Coolidge espoused limited government. He declined to run for reelection in 1928 despite his great public popularity.

Curtis, Edwin Upton (1861–1922): Elected mayor of Boston in 1894, the Republican Curtis came from one of Boston's oldest families. He served one uneventful term and then relied on political connections to become a long-standing member of the Metropolitan Park Commission (1896–1916). A Republican governor, Samuel McCall, appointed Curtis police commissioner of Boston in 1918, and he held this position until his death.

Gompers, Samuel (1850–1924): The English-born Gompers founded and led the American Federation of Labor (AFL), an umbrella union for skilled workers. Known for a willingness to work with business and government to reduce industrial tensions and avoid strikes, he was appointed to the National War Labor Board by President Woodrow Wilson during World War I.

See also: American Federation of Labor.

BIBLIOGRAPHY

Books

Russell, Francis. *A City in Terror: The 1919 Boston Police Strike*. New York: Viking, 1975.

Periodicals

Lyons, Richard L. "The Boston Police Strike of 1919." *New England Quarterly* 20 (July 1947): 148–159.

Other

White, Jonathan Randall. "A Triumph of Bureaucracy: The Boston Police Strike and the Ideological Origins of the American Police Structure." Ph.D. diss., Michigan State University, 1982.

ADDITIONAL RESOURCES

Books

Fogelson, Robert M., ed. *The Boston Police Strike: Two Reports*. New York: Arno, 1971.

Harrison, Leonard V. *Police Administration in Boston*. Cambridge, MA: Harvard University Press, 1934.

Other

Koss, Frederick Manuel. "The Boston Police Strike." Ph.D. diss., Boston University, 1960.

—Caryn E. Neumann

Bracero Program

United States and Mexico 1942–1964

Synopsis

The Bracero program was a series of agreements between the government of the United States and Mexico signed between 1942 and 1964. The name of the program comes from the Spanish word *brazo*, or arm. The program started during World War II, when there was a labor shortage in the United States. The U.S. government signed an agreement with the Mexican government to bring in Mexican workers for temporary employment mainly in the agricultural sector.

The two countries renewed the agreement several times in the postwar era, although not without some dispute. The Mexican government wanted more control over wage rates. The United States responded with an "open border policy," in which the government did not attempt to stop illegal immigration. In response, Mexico attempted to prevent its workers from crossing the border into the United States, even sending in the military. When the two countries finally renewed the agreement, the United States implemented Operation Wetback to deport undocumented workers. The Bracero program continued until 1964.

Timeline

1928: At the first Academy Awards ceremony, the best picture is the silent *Wings*.

1933: Newly inaugurated U.S. president Franklin D. Roosevelt launches the first phase of his New Deal to put depression-era America back to work.

1938: The U.S. Fair Labor Standards Act establishes a minimum wage.

1943: At the Casablanca Conference in January, Winston Churchill and Franklin Roosevelt agree on the demand of unconditional surrender for the Axis powers.

1948: Israel becomes a nation and is immediately attacked by a coalition of Arab countries. Despite being outnumbered, Israel will win the war in the following year.

1948: Stalin places a blockade on areas of Berlin controlled by the United States, Great Britain, and France. The Allies respond with an airlift of supplies, which, like the blockade itself, lasts into late 1949.

1949: North Atlantic Treaty Organization (NATO) is established.

1949: The People's Republic of China is established under the leadership of Mao Zedong.

1950: North Korean troops pour into South Korea, starting the Korean War. Initially the communists make impressive gains, but in September the U.S. Marines land at Inchon and liberate Seoul. China responds by sending in its troops.

1950: Senator Joseph McCarthy launches his campaign to root out communist infiltrators.

1955: African and Asian nations meet at the Bandung Conference in Indonesia, inaugurating the "non-aligned" movement of Third World countries.

1960: An American U-2 spy plane piloted by Francis Gary Powers shot down over Soviet skies brings an end to a short period of warming relations between the two superpowers. By the end of the year, Khrushchev makes a scene at the United Nations, banging his shoe on a desk. As for Powers, he will be freed in a 1962 prisoner exchange.

1965: Power failure paralyzes New York City and much of the northeastern United States on 9 November.

1966: In August, Mao Zedong launches the "Great Proletarian Cultural Revolution," which rapidly plunges China into chaos as armed youths plunder the countryside, rooting out suspected foreign collaborators and anti-Chinese elements. Along with rifles and other weapons, these Red Guards are armed with copies of Mao's "Little Red Book."

1967: Arabs attack Israel, launching the Six-Day War, which results in an Israeli victory.

1968: Communist victories in the Tet offensive mark the turning point in the Vietnam War and influence a growing lack of confidence in the war, not only among America's youth, but within the establishment as well.

Event and Its Context

World War II and the Need for Workers

With the outbreak of World War II, labor supply became a key issue in the United States, as many agricultural workers moved into better paying jobs in the defense industry. The situation became even more urgent with the passage of the Selective Service Act in September 1940 and the National Defense Act in March 1941. As a result, growers turned their eyes to Mexico and began asking the government for help. For example, in September 1941 California requested 30,000 Mexican workers. At this point, the national government denied such requests. After Pearl Harbor, however, the federal government began to consider more seriously importing Mexican workers

Migrant farm workers under the Bracero Program. The Library of Congress.

and began to approach informally the Mexican government about the possibility of bringing in Mexican laborers for work on U.S. farms during the war.

The Beginnings of the Bracero Program

In April 1942, under pressure from California beet growers, the Immigration Service formed a committee to study the labor shortage problem. The group produced a plan for recruiting Mexican workers that was approved in May 1942. Then on 1 June 1942 Mexico declared war on the Axis powers. Soon after, the United States approached the Mexican government about

the possibility of importing Mexican labor. On 15 June 1942 George Messersmith, the U.S. ambassador in Mexico, met with Mexican foreign minister Ezequiel Padilla to discuss the issue.

Mexico had also studied the issue prior to the June meeting. In May 1942 the Mexican government had created an interdepartmental committee to consider the advantages and disadvantages of allowing Mexican citizens to go to work in the United States during the war. Following the June meeting, this committee then studied the issue in detail for a month. Although the Mexican committee found a number of negative aspects of the arrangement, it generally approved of the idea of supplying Mexican labor to the United States.

After the June meeting, an agreement between the two countries quickly followed. In July 1942 U.S. Secretary of Agriculture Claude Wickard attended the Inter-American Conference on Agriculture in Mexico City, and while there he approached Mexico about the labor issue. Although some Mexican officials were reluctant, they did agree to begin negotiations, which commenced on 13 July 1942. The talks only lasted 10 days, as on 23 July the two countries reached an accord that formally took effect on 4 August with an exchange of diplomatic notes.

According to the agreement, both U.S. and Mexican officials would screen potential Mexican workers at a recruitment center in Mexico. At first, all those hoping to participate had to go through the Mexico City center, although later centers opened elsewhere in the country. The workers would then be transported to the United States and placed on farms. At the end of their contracted period, they would be returned to Mexico.

Once the two countries signed the agreement, Mexican workers began flowing into the United States. In the last several months of 1942, some 4,000 Mexicans arrived on farms in the United States. The high point of the Bracero program came in 1944, when some 62,000 contracted Mexican workers crossed the border. Between 1942 and 1947 more than 219,000 Mexican came to the United States out of a total of 309,000 foreign workers who arrived in the United States. They worked on farms in 24 different states, although most were concentrated in California. None went to Texas because of discrimination. In all, the braceros earned $205 million between 1942 and 1947.

The Bracero Program in the Post–World War II Era

The period between 1948 and 1951 was a difficult one for the program. Neither side was happy with the existing conditions. For example, in 1951 the United States issued the recommendations of the President's Commission on Migratory Labor. The commission was critical of a number of issues, including the argument that bracero labor was detrimental to the wages and conditions of domestic workers. At the same time, Mexico was unhappy because of claims that some employers did not honor the provisions of the contracts.

Mexican-U.S. relations became especially strained over the issue of undocumented workers who had entered the United States illegally. The low point came in October 1948 with the "El Paso Incident." A group of Mexican workers gathered in Juárez, Mexico, in hopes of becoming braceros. However, the Mexican government did not grant their wish because of a dispute over wages. At the same time, Texas growers eagerly awaited the potential workers on the other side of the border, hoping to transport them to the cotton fields. Then, apparently under pressure from the growers, the INS did not attempt to stop the unauthorized entry of Mexicans for three days. This allowed some 4,000 Mexicans to enter the United States illegally. The incident greatly angered the Mexican government.

Mexico, however, regained an advantage in June 1950 with the outbreak of the Korean War. Once again, workers were needed in the United States. After representatives from both countries met at a conference in Mexico City in January and February 1951, U.S. congressman Allen Ellender introduced an amendment to the Agricultural Act of 1949 that would allow the U.S. government to recruit Mexican workers and guarantee

their contracts. On 13 July 1951 President Truman signed the legislation, which became known as Public Law 78 and served to codify and institutionalize the Bracero program. Then in August 1951 the two countries signed a new agreement similar to the one originally signed in 1942.

The Bracero Program from 1952 to 1959

In general, the period between 1952 and 1959 was one of growth and stabilization of the Bracero program. Amicable negotiations in 1951 and 1952 led to an extension of the program. During this period, some 2.5 million braceros arrived in the United States.

A major conflict that arose in 1954 led to tensions in the relationship between Mexico and the United States. Both countries had concerns. Mexico, for example, was worried about low wages. The United States had concerns about the location of recruitment centers and wages. When neither side was willing to compromise, talks between the two sides were suspended on 15 January 1954. The United States then implemented a program of unilateral recruitment, which led to many illegal border crossings by Mexican workers. Mexico tried to stop this flow of unauthorized workers, which led to several bloody conflicts along the border between workers and Mexican authorities. This situation lasted until early February. In March the two nations reached a new agreement.

The so-called wetbacks (undocumented workers) continued to present a problem for the United States in this period. By 1954 such undocumented workers numbered more than one million, whereas there were just over 300,000 braceros. In the United States, demands increased for ending this illegal immigration. In August 1953 Attorney General Herbert Brownell toured the California-Mexico border region and reported back to President Eisenhower that the undocumented workers posed a major problem. This led to "Operation Wetback" in 1954, a program led by recently retired general Joseph Swing and meant to crack down on undocumented workers. In June and July 1954 California alone detained and deported some 57,000 Mexicans. By 1955 government figures placed the number of undocumented workers at 250,000, and by 1960 at less than 30,000.

The End of the Bracero Program, 1960–1964

The Bracero program came to an end in the early 1960s. Already by the late 1950s, many growers had become unhappy with the way that the Department of Labor was regulating wages, housing, and transportation in the program. At the same time, increasing mechanization reduced the need for manual labor on many farms. Furthermore, the Kennedy administration, which came to office in 1961, opposed an extension of Public Law 78 without amendments. The Bracero program did not fit with his "New Frontier" program, which sought to help domestic workers. Kennedy only reluctantly signed a two-year extension in October 1961 because some growers still depended on bracero labor and because of potential Mexican opposition to ending the program. The U.S. government agreed to extend the program one last time in 1963. Then on 31 December 1964 the new Johnson administration allowed Public Law 78 to expire, and the Bracero program came to an end.

Key Players

Avila Camacho, Manuel (1897–1955): Avila Camacho was president of Mexico from 1940 to 1946. During World War II Avila Camacho sought to cooperate with the United States in programs of hemispheric defense, trade, and agricultural labor. In 1942 he established an interdepartmental committee to study the possibility of sending Mexican agricultural workers to the United States.

Ellender, Allen (1890–1972): Democratic senator from Louisiana from 1937 to 1972 and one of the architects and main supporters of the Bracero program, Ellender was often viewed as a friend of Mexico and defender of Mexican workers in the United States, although he sometimes became frustrated with the pressure applied by the Mexican government. Ellender was responsible for introducing the legislation that would become Public Law 78.

Goldberg, Arthur (1908–1990): Secretary of labor under President Kennedy in 1961–1962 and reflecting the policies of the Kennedy administration, Goldberg sought to reduce the adverse effects of the Bracero program on domestic workers. He attempted to increase the power of the secretary of labor over the program and insisted on making changes to the program that would make the use of bracero labor more unattractive to growers.

Mitchell, James P. (1900–1964): Secretary of labor under President Eisenhower from 1953 until 1961, Mitchell was a strong supporter of domestic farm workers, which often put him at odds with the Bracero program and growers. In 1959 Mitchell issued what was known as the "New Wagner-Peyser Regulations," which guaranteed wages and working standards for domestic farm workers. He also appointed a committee of expert consultants to study wages and the farm labor market, which led him to attempt to limit the use of bracero labor.

Padilla, Ezequiel (1890–1971): Mexican foreign minister from 1940 to 1945, Padilla was a strong supporter of the Bracero program during its early years. He considered it an important opportunity for Mexican workers to earn wages. Furthermore, Padilla was a supporter of inter-American solidarity and considered the supplying of Mexican workers to the United States to be proof of Mexico's dedication to hemispheric cooperation.

Ruiz Cortines, Adolfo (1889–1973): Ruiz Cortines was president of Mexico from 1952 to 1958. In 1952 rumors circulated that the Ruiz Cortines administration would reduce the number of Mexican workers allowed to leave for the United States. His attitude toward immigration would be tested in the 1954 border crisis. At first, his administration sent the military to block the passage of illegal immigrants across the border. He later reversed his policy and instructed government and military officials not to impede illegal border crossings. In his 1954 State of the Union address, Ruiz Cortines deplored the loss of Mexican workers but admitted that it was unavoidable because there were not enough jobs in Mexico.

BIBLIOGRAPHY

Books

Briggs, Vernon M., Jr., Walt Fogel, and Fred H. Schmidt. *The Chicano Worker.* Austin: University of Texas Press, 1977.

Calavita, Kitty. *Inside the State: The Bracero Program, Immigration, and the I.N.S.* New York and London: Routledge, 1992.

Craig, Richard B. *The Bracero Program: Interest Groups and Foreign Policy.* Austin: University of Texas Press, 1971.

Galarza, Ernesto. *Merchants of Labor: The Mexican Bracero Story.* Charlotte, N.C., and Santa Barbara, CA: McNally and Loftin Publishers, 1964.

Kirstein, Peter N. *Anglo over Bracero: A History of the Mexican Worker in the United States from Roosevelt to Nixon.* San Francisco: R and E Research Associates, 1977.

Kiser, George C., and Martha Woody Kiser. *Mexican Workers in the United States: Historical and Political Perspectives.* Albuquerque: University of New Mexico Press, 1979.

—Ronald Young

Brotherhood of Locomotive Engineers

United States 1863

Synopsis

On 8 May 1863, 12 delegates from several regional railroad employee organizations met in Detroit, Michigan, to form the Brotherhood of the Footboard. Later changing its name to the Brotherhood of Locomotive Engineers (BLE), the labor union aimed to create unity among railroad workers, strive for better working conditions, and establish certain social protections for its members. The union's first year saw a number of unauthorized, failed strikes and a lack of solidarity among disgruntled workers who were reportedly more interested in vengeance against their own employers than in creating unity among fellow engineers. Despite this chaotic start and attacks against the BLE leadership, the union instituted constitutional changes and grew to nearly 10,000 members within a decade.

Timeline

1844: Samuel Laing, in a prize-winning essay on Britain's "National Distress," describes conditions in a nation convulsed by the early Industrial Revolution. A third of the population, according to Laing, "hover[s] on the verge of actual starvation"; another third is forced to labor in "crowded factories"; and only the top third "earn[s] high wages, amply sufficient to support them in respectability and comfort."

Group of locomotive engineers and train conductors with United States Military Railroad during American Civil War, Alexandria, Virginia. © Medford Historical Society Collection/Corbis. Reproduced by permission.

1849: Elizabeth Blackwell becomes the first woman in the United States to receive a medical degree.

1854: In the United States, the Kansas-Nebraska Act calls for decisions on the legality of slavery to be made through local votes. Instead of reducing divisions, this measure will result in widespread rioting and bloodshed and will only further hasten the looming conflict over slavery and states' rights.

1857: The Sepoy Mutiny, an unsuccessful revolt by Indian troops against the British East India Company, begins.

As a result of the rebellion, which lasts into 1858, England places India under direct crown rule.

1860: Louis Pasteur pioneers his method of "pasteurizing" milk by heating it to high temperatures in order to kill harmful microbes.

1862: Victor Hugo's *Les Misérables* depicts injustices in French society, and Ivan Turgenev's *Fathers and Sons* introduces the term *nihilism.*

1864: General William Tecumseh Sherman conducts his Atlanta campaign and his "march to the sea."

1864: International Red Cross in Geneva is established.

1864: George M. Pullman and Ben Field patent their design for a sleeping car with folding upper berths.

1866: Austrian monk Gregor Mendel presents his theories on the laws of heredity. Though his ideas will be forgotten for a time, they are destined to exert enormous influence on biological study in the twentieth century.

1870: The Franco-Prussian War begins. German troops sweep over France, Napoleon III is dethroned, and France's Second Empire gives way to the Third Republic.

1873: The gold standard, adopted by Germany in 1871 and eventually taken on by all major nations, spreads to Italy, Belgium, and Switzerland. Though the United States does not officially base the value of its currency on gold until 1900, an unofficial gold standard dates from this period, even as a debate over "bimetallism" creates sharp divisions in American politics.

Event and Its Context

Railroad Grievances Leading to Union

Railroading in nineteenth-century America was a poorly paid, hazardous activity. Locomotive engineers, who spent their days and nights covered in grime and exposed to the elements, were often deprived of sleep, yet they were expected to stay alert so as to avoid accidents. Derailments, collisions, and mechanical problems were constant, and engineers were required to spend their "free" time servicing and maintaining the trains, inspecting, and repairing when necessary every single piece of the engine truck. While the hours were long, engineers were paid not for the time they were on duty, but rather for the actual time they were on a run. In the early 1860s a locomotive engineer could expect to run at least 2,500 miles monthly if he wanted to earn the going rate of $60 per month. Engineers waiting at the end of the line were required to pay their own expenses while waiting for the next train home. Moreover, job security was at management's whim, since railroad managers did not respect the idea of seniority.

The hazards railroad engineers of the time faced were recounted in graphic detail in *Lives of the Engineers, with an Account of Their Principal Works,* the memoirs of British engineer George Stephenson, as written by Samuel Smiles. In 1861 U.S. readers learned of some of the tragedies endured by railroad men, such as the cautious veteran worker whose leg was cut off by a train, or the engineer who was slowly cooked to death on the head of a boiler. In chapters like "A Victim of Low Wages" and "Human Lives v. the Dollar," Stephenson stabbed at the profit-over-people policies of some railroad managers. Accidents, he asserted, should teach managers that the policy of hiring unqualified men for $25 per month "is suicidal to their best interests." He suggested that an additional $10 per month for all switchmen might be "a good investment" if it saved just one worker a year from death or suffering. "Who then shall say that, though he be grimy and greasy, rough and uncouth, given to tobacco-chewing, and sometimes to hard swearing, he is of no consequence to the world?" Stephenson asked.

Miserable working conditions and declining real wages brought organized attempts at protecting the rights of railroad men. In 1854 engineers on the Baltimore and Ohio went on strike for better working conditions; management responded by firing 16 engineers, replacing them with novices. In 1855, following two failed attempts at organization, 68 engineers from 45 railroads in 13 states met in Baltimore, Maryland, to form the National Protective Association of the Brotherhood of Locomotive Engineers of the United States. This organization lasted five years.

In 1862 grievances at the Michigan Central led more directly to the formation of the subsequent BLE. The railroad had hired A. S. Sweet to be superintendent of machinery; he was known for cutting pay to reduce costs. When workers protested, he fired several senior firemen and replaced them with inexperienced ones. Engineers, in solidarity with the firemen, refused to work on the runs where the regulars had been cut. In April 1863, 13 Michigan Central engineers met at the home of Jared C. "Yankee" Thompson in Marshall, Michigan, to plan a strategy. The men signed a circular saying that if one man were fired, the others would quit en masse; any new members would be required to take the same oath. The movement caught on, and eventually a committee representing disgruntled workers from Chicago, Illinois, to Detroit, Michigan, managed to speak to Sweet, who had initially refused to receive them.

When Sweet asked if the men planned to shut down operations, committee member Sam Hill reportedly answered, "We are here as gentlemen, representing gentlemen, and desire to be treated as such." After detailed deliberation, Sweet granted all of their requests. Word of this local victory spread throughout the ranks of railroad workers, and a general meeting was called for in Detroit on 5 May 1863.

Birth of the BLE

May 1863 brought a new era in the organization of American railroad workers. Engineers from several regional railroad organizations convened for a three-day session in the upstairs meeting room of the Old Firemen's Hall in Detroit. Present were 12 delegates from the Michigan Central, Michigan Southern, Grand Trunk, Detroit and Milwaukee, and the Michigan Southern and Northern Indiana railroads. The men drafted a constitution that, according to the union, combined "democratic control with efficient central administration, thus solving the fundamental problem that had wrecked many previous labor organizations." On 8 May the men joined hands and swore allegiance to a pioneer labor union called the "Brotherhood of the Footboard." William D. Robinson was elected chief engineer.

The brotherhood's constitution held that the organization of five new divisions warranted the creation of a "grand division," consisted of one delegate from each division. With 10 divisions as of 1 August 1863, the Grand National Division of the Brotherhood of the Footboard was formed in Detroit on 18 August. Robinson was elevated to the status of "grand chief engineer."

Membership was not for everyone. The locomotive engineers required that a candidate be a "white man, not less than 21 years of age" with at least one year's experience as an engineer. Moreover, the engineer had to be able to read and write and to be "of temperate habits and good moral character." The union's early constitutions dictated a moral code among its members. The 1884 constitution, for example, censured "occasional intoxication" and deemed "habitual intoxication" cause for expulsion; a later rule prohibited membership to saloon owners or anyone "engaged in the sale or traffic of intoxicants." The 1866 constitution threatened with expulsion any behavior "unbecoming to a man." Such ungentlemanly breaches of personal discipline included profane language, fraud, disrespect toward superiors, desertion of families, breaking agreements, drunkenness, "moral offenses," and general misconduct. Sanctions for moral misconduct were issued at the discretion of the local division.

During the first years of the union, the leadership sorted out internal conflict and forged an ethos in which engineers saw that "the problem of one engineer was the problem of all." Several strikes at the local level occurred in 1863, none of which was authorized by the union or carried out following consultations with the leadership. Due to "a lack of unity of interest and effort," all the strikes failed. According to the BLE, many of the men were "overanxious to get even with the roads on which they worked," oblivious to the effects their isolated actions could have on the brotherhood's future.

1864 Convention

A year of turmoil brought many grievances to the union's second convention, which was held on 17 August 1864 in Indianapolis, Indiana. The convention was heavily guarded, given local rumors that the convening railroad men were actually coming to free Confederate soldiers held at a nearby prisoner of war camp; delegates were shadowed by squads of Union soldiers, who also stood outside the convention hall.

Despite the union's growth to 54 divisions, disgruntled members had arrived to blame a year of failed strikes on Grand Chief Robinson and other grand officers. At the time of his leadership, Robinson was not an engineer in active service; with the aid of his detractors, he was forced from power when the union approved a resolution requiring all grand chiefs to be working engineers. Robinson was replaced by Charles Wilson of the New York Central. Delegates to the 1864 convention amended the union's constitution to exclude from membership firemen, machinists, and workers from other crafts. The union's name was officially changed to Grand International Division of the Brotherhood of Locomotive Engineers.

The excluded nonengineers later formed their own railroad unions. The Brotherhood of Conductors (later called the Order of Railway Conductors and Brakemen) was formed in 1869. The Brotherhood of Locomotive Firemen (later the Brotherhood of Locomotive Firemen and Enginemen) appeared in 1873.

As the BLE grew over the next decade, the leaders focused on organizing as a single working unit, correcting internal problems, and projecting an image of the BLE as an effective labor organization. In general, the strike was not a preferred method of negotiation and was used only to enforce core demands. Formally authorized strikes were supported through a special strike fund. In general, the brotherhood defended the economic well-being of its members, negotiating hours, wages, and similar issues.

The union also worked toward greater social protections for its members. Labor observers in 1867 noted that in the brotherhood, as in many other trade unions, "the benefit features, so largely developed in the English societies, appear to a limited extent." One major grievance among workers was their inability to buy insurance to protect their families, given that frequent deaths in the trade caused "locomotive engineer" to be classified as a hazardous occupation. In a first step toward recognizing this issue, the 1866 convention in Boston, Massachusetts, established the Orphans and Widows Fund. The milestone event in the struggle for worker protection came the following year with the establishment of the Locomotive Engineers Mutual Life Insurance Association on 3 December 1867. The insurance plan, modeled after a similar one for New York City police officers, was open exclusively to BLE members. The association, founded at Port Jervis, New York, was operated independently of the union. Some 3,000 of the union's 8,000 members purchased insurance policies that year.

In 1865 the BLE founded its first Canadian division. By 1873 the union had 9,500 members spread over 172 divisions; by 1876 there were 12,000 members spread over 188 divisions throughout North America.

Key Players

Robinson, William D. Robinson (1826–1890): An American locomotive engineer, Robinson was a founding member of the BLE and served as its first chief officer from 1863 to 1864. He was replaced under pressure from enemies who blamed him for the new union's lack of organization and unity of purpose.

Stephenson, George (1781–1848): Stephenson was an English railroad engineer and inventor who pioneered steam engine construction. He served as chief engineer on several railways; the miserable conditions experienced by railroad engineers were recounted in a book of his that reached American readers in 1861.

Wilson, Charles: Wilson, an American locomotive engineer, was a founding member of the BLE and served as its chief officer from 1864 to 1874. Under his leadership the union grew to approximately 10,000 members.

See also: *Brotherhood of Railroad Trainmen.*

BIBLIOGRAPHY

Books

The American Cyclopedia. New York: D. Appleton and Company, 1873–1876.

Smiles, Samuel. *Lives of the Engineers, with an Account of Their Principal Works: Comprising Also a History of Inland Communication in Britain.* Vol. 3, *George and Robert Stephenson.* London: J. Murray, 1861–1862.

Other

History of the Brotherhood of Locomotive Engineers [cited 2 October 2002]. <http://www.ble.org/pr/history/>

Michigan Historic Marker: Railroad Union Birthplace [cited 2 October 2002]. <http://www.michmarkers.com/Pages/L0282.htm>

A "Yellow-Dog" Contract

[In order to keep out unions, corporations in the late nineteenth and early twentieth centuries often compelled employees to sign so-called yellow-dog contracts as a condition for employment. Below is an example of such a contract, with Western Union.]

I, [name] of [city] in consideration of my present reemployment by the Western Union Telegraph Co. hereby promise and agree to and with the said company that I will forthwith abandon any and all membership, connection or affiliation with any organization or society, whether secret or open, which in anywise attempts to regulate the conditions of my services or the payment thereof while in the employment now undertaken. I hereby further agree that I will, while in the employ of said company, render good and faithful service to the best of my ability, and will not in anywise renew or re-enter upon any relations or membership whatsoever in or with any such organizations or society.

Dated . . . . . 1883.Signed . . . . . Address . . . . . (Seal)
Accepted for the Western Union Telegraph Co. . . . . ,
Superintendent

Source: Joel I. Seidman. *The Yellow Dog Contract.* Baltimore: Johns Hopkins Press, 1932.

—Judson Knight

Van Ophem, Marieke. The Iron Horse: The Impact of the Railroads on 19th Century American Society. 1999 [cited 2 October 2002]. <http://odur.let.rug.nl/~usa/E/ironhorse/ironhorse20.htm>.

—Brett Alan King

Brotherhood of Railroad Trainmen

United States 1883

Synopsis

One of the largest of four transportation unions in the United States, the Brotherhood of Railroad Brakemen (BRB) was established on 23 September 1883 by eight railway workers who met in a caboose in Oneonta, New York, in the yards of the Delaware and Hudson Railroad. The organization changed its name to the Brotherhood of Railroad Trainmen (BRT) in 1890 because so many of the members it represented had been promoted from brakemen to conductor or had changed positions since their initial enrollment. Eugene V. Debs, then na-

tional officer of the Brotherhood of Locomotive Firemen and Enginemen, encouraged the eight men to form a national organization of brakemen rather than joining a local chapter already functioning in Albany.

Timeline

1863: The world's first subway opens, in London.

1869: The first U.S. transcontinental railway is completed.

1873: The typewriter is introduced.

1876: Four-stroke cycle gas engine is introduced.

1878: Thomas Edison develops a means of cheaply producing and transmitting electric current, which he succeeds in subdividing so as to make it adaptable to household use. The value of shares in gas companies plummets as news of his breakthrough reaches Wall Street.

1881: In a shootout at the O.K. Corral outside Tombstone, Arizona, Wyatt, Virgil, and Morgan Earp, along with "Doc" Holliday, kill Billy Clanton, Frank McLowry, and Tom McLowry. This breaks up a gang headed by Clanton's brother Ike, who flees Tombstone. The townspeople, however, suspect the Earps and Holliday of murder. During the same year, Sheriff Pat Garrett shoots notorious criminal William Bonney, a.k.a. Billy the Kid, in Fort Sumner, New Mexico.

1883: Brooklyn Bridge is completed.

1883: Foundation of the League of Struggle for the Emancipation of Labor by Marxist political philosopher Georgi Valentinovich Plekhanov marks the formal start of Russia's labor movement. Change still lies far in the future for Russia, however: tellingly, Plekhanov launches the movement in Switzerland.

1883: *Life* magazine begins publication.

1885: Belgium's King Leopold II becomes sovereign of the so-called Congo Free State, which he will rule for a quarter-century virtually as his own private property. The region in Africa, given the name of Zaire in the 1970s (and Congo in 1997), becomes the site of staggering atrocities, including forced labor and genocide, at the hands of Leopold's minions.

1889: Indian Territory in Oklahoma is opened to settlement.

1893: Henry Ford builds his first automobile.

Event and Its Context

Prior to the establishment of the BRB, there were three transportation brotherhoods operating in the United States: Brotherhood of Locomotive Engineers (1863), the Order of Railway Conductors (1868), and the Brotherhood of Locomotive Firemen and Enginemen (1873). All operated as fraternal organizations offering brotherhood and mutual insurance to members. Members also participated in rituals stemming from a Masonic tradition that were similar to those of other fraternal brotherhoods.

Insurance companies refused to offer death or disability coverage to railroad workers because the high incidence of morbidity and mortality would break their business. Mutual insurance organizations such as the BRB formed because the nature of the brakeman's job was so dangerous: crippling injuries, amputations, and accidental death were everyday incidents. At the engineer's signal, both head-end and rear-end brakemen began a precarious trip along their respective sections of the speeding train, leaping from car to car and manually applying and releasing handbrakes on each car. Due to the precarious rocking and shifting of the boxcars, life expectancy for brakemen quite often was less than one year. Brakemen frequently inserted themselves between cars that could quickly come to a halt, crushing their bodies between them. Mishaps also occurred when the job required the brakemen to run over ballast and railroad ties alongside the moving train.

The BRB offered members death insurance benefits of $300 at a time when wages averaged little more than one dollar per day, which was an excellent wage in 1883. Many men were willing to undertake the dangerous conditions to support their families. Nationally, one-third of brakemen were killed in 1883. The insurance appealed to brakemen because as much as 70 percent of men in the position had to expect injury or death.

Beginning in 1887, the steady growth of BRB membership set in motion the organization's evolution from a purely benevolent society to a trade union. Eight men met to discuss their disappointment with the operation of the Capital City Aid Association, which failed to address the current concerns of the brakemen, though it was originally established by brakemen. Those eight men were William Gurney, Daniel Hopkins, Elmer Wessel, H. S. Wilber, Charles J. Woodworth, Union C. Osterhout, Daniel J. McCarty, and Eugene McCarty. The initial meeting in Charles Woodworth's caboose Number 10 in June 1883 spawned a larger meeting in September at Blend Hall in Oneonta, where participants founded the Grand Lodge.

The BRB's goals were simple: promoting unity and improving the welfare of its members. The preamble specifically mentioned protecting each member's family through benevolence and fostering an amiable association between the company and members. The Brotherhood's motto was "Benevolence, Sobriety, and Industry."

The Grand Lodge was originally called the Eugene V. Debs Lodge No. 1, after the man who inspired the formation of the brotherhood. Though formed in Oneonta, the Grand Lodge moved to Chicago in 1884. Additionally, Lodge No. 1 was renamed for Daniel Hopkins, one of its original lodge members and founders. Debs is often credited as the founder of the brotherhood, though he was essentially an organizer. Between the first and second annual conventions held in October 1884 and October 1885, the organization grew from 39 lodges with 900 members to 160 lodges with 4,500 members. That same year the BRB became an international organization when it granted the first Canadian charter to a lodge at Moncton, New Brunswick. In December 1885 the Grand Lodge moved from Chicago to Galesburg, Illinois.

The importance of insurance became so overriding that the insurance department formed in 1885 and increased death coverage to $600. As membership strengthened yearly, the BRB collected more membership dues and increased death disbursements. In 1886 benefits increased to $800 with national membership at 8,000.

The BRB established the *Railroad Brakeman's Journal*, a periodical edited and managed by Ed O'Shea, a charter member of the Galesburg, Illinois, lodge. Printed in Galesburg by the Brotherhood Steam Print, the journal supplied members with information and functioned as an instrument for recruitment. Circulation fluctuated but averaged about 8,000 each month. Issues listed monthly claims that the BRB paid out, as well as recent deaths and injuries and their causes.

In 1890, under the leadership of Stephen E. Wilkinson, the BRB took the name Brotherhood of Railroad Trainmen (BRT) when it expanded to include railroad workers in more than 14 trade classifications. Elected at the 1890 annual meeting in St. Paul, Minnesota, Wilkinson strengthened the BRT's conservative stance as he strongly advocated arbitration and opposed strikes. Wilkinson was one of the first union leaders to negotiate contracts for employees. He put into action a regulated system of promotion for members. A worker hired as a brakeman or a flagman could eventually become a conductor. Conductors held a prestigious position on the train; the train could not physically move without the conductor's command. They controlled the train yet could not direct the engineer's operation of the locomotive.

The BRT did not initially function as a trade union, and brotherhood leaders maintained cordiality with company officials. In this manner, the BRT's comport was similar to its counterpart railway brotherhoods in that it did not fraternize with other labor unions. In fact, there was little cooperation between the four railroad brotherhoods though essentially they functioned as one by ignoring collective bargaining with management and continuing their foci on insurance and welfare benefits of their members. Railroad company officials did not legitimately recognize the organization. BRT members were often discriminated against or fired once management learned of their affiliation.

The Pullman strike of 1894 cost the BRT between $9,000 and $20,000, with the exact number in dispute. Many were purged for supporting the strike and others lost their jobs in the economic depression brought on by the Panic of 1893, which was caused in part by excessive railroad investments and the inability of rail companies to operate efficiently. Effects of the panic were felt nationwide until 1897.

Members who gathered at annual convention in May 1895 at Galesburg expressed their displeasure with Wilkinson's leadership, and he resigned. Patrick H. Morrissey, the next grand master of the BRT, worked toward rebuilding the union after the Pullman strike, as well as cooperating with other railroad unions to form solidarity for its members.

After talks between the major transportation unions during 1968, union presidents announced in August 1968 that they would merge and designate themselves as the United Transportation Union, which was established on 1 January 1969. Eventually merging with the Brotherhood of Locomotive Firemen and Enginemen, the Order of Railway Conductors and Brakemen, and the Switchmen's Union of North America to form the United Transportation Union in 1968, the BRT ceased to exist.

Key Players

Debs, Eugene V. (1855–1926): Born in Terre Haute, Indiana, Debs left school at age 15 to work in a railroad engine house and later became a locomotive fireman. He traveled through Oneonta, New York, in 1883 and encouraged local brakemen to form a union, the BRB. Debs served the Brotherhood of Locomotive Firemen in several roles, organized the American Railway Union (ARU) in 1892, and was instrumental in forming the Social Democratic Party, Socialist Labor Party, and Socialist Party of America.

Morrissey, Patrick Henry (1862–1916): Born in Bloomington, Illinois, to Irish immigrants, Morrissey was initiated to the industry by his father, John, who was a section foreman on the Chicago and Alton Road. Patrick began his railroad career as a call boy while he attended high school. In 1880 he became a full-time employee on the Chicago and Alton, working as a clerk for the roundhouse foreman, a passenger brakeman, freight brakemen, and freight conductor. He became a member of the BRT, holding several offices in the organization, and eventually serving as the second grand master of the BRT (1895–1908). He restored the BRT and reconciled the membership after the Pullman strike in 1894.

Whitney, Alexander Fell (1873–1949): Born in Cedar Falls, Iowa, Whitney left high school in 1888 to become a news agent on the Illinois Central Railroad. He worked as a brakeman on several Midwestern railroads (1890–1901). He joined the G. F. Boynton Lodge 138 of the BRT in 1896 and served the BRT in many roles over the years, eventually becoming its president in 1925.

Wilkinson, Stephen E. (1850–1901): Born in Monroeville, Ohio, Wilkinson served the Union by guarding the railroads during the Civil War. After mustering out he entered service as a switchman on the I.B. and W. Railway, which later became the Philadelphia and Erie Railroad. Known as the "Old Man," he was a charter member and first master of Lodge No. 27, organized in Peoria, Illinois, on 16 August 1884. A delegate at the first annual convention, he was appointed to fill the vacated grand master position of the BRB on 10 July 1885, and was elected grand master at the second annual convention in 1885, a position he held until he resigned on 1 August 1895.

See also: *Brotherhood of Locomotive Engineers; Panic of 1893; Pullman Strike.*

BIBLIOGRAPHY

Books

Fink, Gary M., ed. *Biographical Dictionary of American Labor Leaders*. Westport, CT: Greenwood Press, 1974.

Madison, Charles A. *American Labor Leaders: Personalities and Forces in the Labor Movement*. New York: Harper & Brother Publishers, 1950.

McCaleb, Walter Falvius. *Brotherhood of Railroad Trainmen, with Special Reference to the Life of Alexander F. Whitney*. New York: A. and C. Boni, 1936.

Seidman, Joel Isaac. *The Brotherhood of Railroad Trainmen: The Internal Political Life of a National Union*. New York: Wiley, 1962.

Tallion, Paul Michel. *Culture, Politics, and the Making of the Railroad Brotherhoods, 1863–1916*. Ann Arbor, MI: University Microfilms, 1997.

Periodicals

Simonson, Mark. "Caboose Serves as Reminder of Our Rich Railroad History." [Oneonta] *Daily Star*, 28 February 2000.

ADDITIONAL RESOURCES

Books

Licht, Walter. *Working for the Railroad: The Organization of Work in the Nineteenth Century*. Princeton, NJ: Princeton University Press, 1983.

—Rebecca Tolley-Stokes

Brotherhood of Sleeping Car Porters

United States 1925

Synopsis

Meeting secretly on the night of 25 August 1925 in the Elks Lodge on 129th Street in New York City's Harlem, 500 Pullman porters organized the Brotherhood of Sleeping Car Porters (BSCP), which was to become the first successful African American labor union. The major goals of the newfound union were to win higher wages and shorter working hours and to draw support away from a company union called the Employee Representation Plan (ERP), led by blacks handpicked by the Pullman Company, the porters' employer. In its infancy, the BSCP had a difficult time winning support among the rank and file of Pullman porters, many of whom saw little difference between BSCP and the company union, besides which they were reluctant to risk incurring the company's wrath by organizing. Slowly but surely the new union grew, but winning recognition from the Pullman Company was slow in coming. Finally, on 25 August 1937, a full 12 years after its founding, the BSCP was recognized as the official union of the Pullman porters.

Timeline

1910: Neon lighting is introduced.

1915: A German submarine sinks the *Lusitania,* killing 1,195, including 128 U.S. citizens. Theretofore, many Americans had been sympathetic toward Germany, but the incident begins to turn the tide of U.S. sentiment toward the Allies.

1920: Bolsheviks eliminate the last of their opponents, bringing an end to the Russian Civil War. By then, foreign troops, representing a dozen nations that opposed the communists, have long since returned home.

1922: Inspired by the Bolsheviks' example of imposing revolution by means of a coup, Benito Mussolini leads his blackshirts in an October "March on Rome" and forms a new fascist government.

1923: Conditions in Germany worsen as inflation skyrockets and France, attempting to collect on coal deliveries promised at Versailles, marches into the Ruhr basin. In November an obscure political group known as the National Socialist German Workers' Party attempts to stage a coup, or putsch, in a Munich beer hall. The revolt fails, and in 1924 the party's leader, Adolf Hitler, will receive a prison sentence of five years. He will only serve nine months, however, and the incident will serve to attract attention for him and his party, known as the Nazis.

1925: Wyoming Democrat Nellie Tayloe Ross becomes the first woman governor elected in the United States.

1925: European leaders attempt to secure the peace at the Locarno Conference, which guarantees the boundaries between France and Germany, and Belgium and Germany.

1925: In Tennessee, John T. Scopes is fined for teaching evolution in a public school. There follows a highly publicized trial at which famed attorney Clarence Darrow represents the defense, while the aging Democratic populist William Jennings Bryan argues for the state. The "Scopes Monkey Trial" symbolizes a widening divisions between rural and urban America, and though the court decides in favor of the state, it is clear that the historical tide is turning against the old agrarian order symbolized by Bryan—who dies during the trial.

1925: Released from Landsberg Prison, Adolf Hitler is a national celebrity, widely regarded as an emerging statesman who offers genuine solutions to Germany's problems. This year, he publishes the first volume of *Mein Kampf* (My Struggle), which he dictated in prison to trusted confederate Rudolf Hess. The second and final volume of Hitler's opus, a mixture of autobiography, "history," and racial rant, will appear two years later.

1928: Sixty-five nations sign the Kellogg-Briand Pact, outlawing war.

1930: Naval disarmament treaty is signed by the United States, Great Britain, France, Italy, and Japan.

1935: Italians invade Ethiopia, and the response by the League of Nations—which imposes sanctions but otherwise fails to act—reveals the impotence of that organization.

Event and Its Context

On a balmy evening in late August 1925, some 500 Pullman porters secretly gathered in a Harlem Elks Lodge. There the men, seeking a way to win higher wages and shorter working hours, founded the Brotherhood of Sleeping Car Porters (BSCP). The establishment of the union, a goal of the porters since the early years of the twentieth century, was just the be-

Asa Philip Randolph. Fisk University Library. Reproduced by permission.

ginning of their struggle to bring their employer, the Pullman Company, to the bargaining table. Fully 12 years would pass before the BSCP was able to win Pullman's recognition as the porters' official labor union.

The Pullman Palace Car Company

Founded in 1867 by George Mortimer Pullman, the Pullman Palace Car Company was created to build and operate luxury sleeping cars (under contract to the railroads) to serve well-heeled passengers who routinely traveled long distances on the nation's railways. To meet the needs of their affluent clientele, the company from the outset hired black porters in the belief that the legacy of slavery ensured that blacks as a group would provide the desired degree of subservience as well as a willingness to work long hours for low wages.

In the early years of Pullman sleeping car service, porters fulfilled the company's vision of gracious service: warmly receiving passengers, transporting their luggage to their quarters, making up beds, serving beverages and food, and generally making themselves available at all hours of the day or night to meet passengers' needs. So well did the porters do their jobs that they became known as the "Ambassadors of Hospitality." However, by the 1920s, with more than half a century separating porters from the end of slavery, their willingness to suffer the job's long hours and low wages in silence had grown very thin indeed.

Poor Working Conditions for Porters

Although Pullman porters were still counted among the elite of black labor, thanks to the assurance of steady employment and extensive travel experience, in time porters grew in-

Members of the Brotherhood of Sleeping Car Porters, 1955. © Corbis-Bettmann. Reproduced by permission.

creasingly unhappy with their lot in life. They came to believe that, as Americans, they had the right to live and work on an equal basis with white Americans. The establishment of a company-sanctioned union, called the Employee Representation Plan (ERP), did little to improve life for the porters, for most of its leaders had been handpicked by the Pullman Company. To survive and support their families, most porters relied on tips from passengers, which typically totaled more than their monthly pay from Pullman. Porters' smiles and gracious treatment of sleeping car passengers belied their deplorable working conditions: Hours were long with no overtime, and wages were low.

A. Philip Randolph Selected to Lead the BSCP

A critical element in the eventual success of the BSCP was the porters' selection of A. Philip Randolph to lead the union. Son of a Methodist minister and born in Crescent City, Florida, Randolph had moved to Harlem in 1911. With Chandler Owen, Randolph founded an employment agency, which he used as a vehicle to help organize black workers. Shortly after the United States entered World War I in 1917, Randolph and Owen began publishing a magazine, *The Messenger,* which called for more

positions for blacks in the armed forces and the war industry. Randolph was an inspired choice for the porters since he was not a porter himself and was thus immune from the Pullman Company's threat of firing. For his part, Randolph found himself drawn to the porters' cause. He began educating them about the value of trade unionism and the basics of collective bargaining.

It is impossible to consider seriously the porters' struggle for better working conditions and pay without looking more closely at the "New Negro" movement, of which Randolph was a leading proponent. Upon his arrival in Harlem in 1911, Randolph was dismayed at the widespread lack of self-reliance and independence from white control among African Americans. He was particularly critical of black leaders who were a part of what he called the Old Crowd, "subsidized by the Old Crowd of white Americans—a group which viciously opposes every demand made by organized labor for an opportunity to live a better life." As editor of *The Messenger,* Randolph said blacks badly needed both new tactics and new leaders if they were to claim their rightful place in American society. In Randolph's view, one of the greatest obstacles to winning equal economic opportunity for black workers was the reluctance of white Americans to recognize the moral equality of African Americans.

Slow Growth of the BSCP

Outside of the hard-core porters who had spearheaded formation of the BSCP, the majority of porters were hesitant to join the newly founded union. For many it was hard to see any real difference between the BSCP and the company union, while others feared company reprisals if they agitated for higher pay and better working conditions. For the average porter, the choice between steady—if low—pay and no pay at all was not a hard one. Also giving many porters pause was the black community's goodwill toward the Pullman Company, fueled largely by the company's contributions to black churches.

As president of the BSCP, Randolph was headquartered in New York City, where he was assisted by Ashley Totten and Benjamin McLauren. Outside New York his main lieutenants were Milton P. Webster in Chicago, Illinois, C. L. Dellums in Oakland, California, and E. J. Bradley in St. Louis, Missouri. The union's leaders encountered considerable resistance from porters who were fearful of losing their jobs. The company, fighting the new union with all its resources, was even successful in pressing some porters into spying on the union's strategy sessions. These spies attended meetings and then reported back to the company on what they had seen and heard.

One early recruit to the BSCP was E. D. Nixon, Sr., an Alabama-born sleeping car porter who first heard Randolph speak at a local YWCA in St. Louis. Impressed by Randolph's ambitious goals for the newly formed union, Nixon contributed a dollar to its cause. Shortly thereafter Nixon was summoned by his manager and threatened with firing for having attended the St. Louis meeting. He calmly informed his manager that he not only had attended the meeting but had joined the union as well and would sue the Pullman Company if the threats continued. In later years Nixon became a civil rights activist, playing a major role in the Montgomery, Alabama, bus boycott in the mid-1950s.

Attempts to Increase Wages for Porters

Despite the misgivings of most porters, membership in the BSCP slowly but surely increased. Recognizing the threat posed by the gradually strengthening union, the Pullman Company pulled out all stops in its attempts to undermine the BSCP, launching a wide variety of retaliatory measures, including firings, beatings, and frame-ups. As leader of the BSCP, Randolph used his own bag of tricks to help force the company to the bargaining table. In 1926 he invoked the Watson-Parker Railway Labor Act as a justification for arbitration under the supervision of the Federal Board of Mediation. Although the board recommended arbitration, the company refused to participate, and the effort came to naught. Randolph next sought to get through to the company by attacking porters' reliance on tips to survive. In 1927 he pressed the Interstate Commerce Commission (ICC) to outlaw tipping in interstate travel. Such a ban would have forced Pullman to increase wages, but in the end the ICC decided that it lacked jurisdiction for such a ruling.

Left with few other alternatives, Randolph called for a strike by the BSCP in 1928. But support among porters for such

a work stoppage simply wasn't there. Many feared that other blacks would rush in to fill their jobs in the event of a strike. Randolph also learned through American Federation of Labor (AFL) president William Green that Pullman was rumored to have lined up nearly 5,000 Filipinos to replace striking BSCP members. In the face of this threat, Randolph postponed the strike.

Despite his earlier opposition to the AFL's craft-union stance, Randolph in 1928 applied for an international charter from the labor organization to strengthen BSCP's bargaining position. The AFL turned down the union's bid for an international charter, granting federal charters to individual BSCP locals instead. Although unhappy with the AFL's decision, Randolph and other BSCP officials realized they needed the support of the national labor organization and took what they could get.

Prohibition of Company Unions

After the BSCP's threatened strike of 1928 was aborted, membership in the union dropped sharply. For a time it even appeared that the union would cease to exist. However, the enactment of more favorable labor legislation under President Franklin D. Roosevelt helped to keep the BSCP from extinction. Particularly helpful was passage of the amended Railway Act of 1934, which prohibited company unions. The new legislation spelled the end of the ERP, but the Pullman Company simply responded by replacing the ERP with the Pullman Porters and Maids Protective Association, changing the situation for porters very little, if at all.

Union Receives International Charter from AFL

In 1935 the AFL finally granted the BSCP the international charter it had first sought in 1928. The union officially received the charter at the AFL's convention, which saw a number of other momentous developments. Since the AFL's convention in 1932, Randolph had become increasingly outspoken in his attacks on racism within the labor federation, focusing in particular on federal unions designed for blacks only. He lashed out against racism again at the 1935 convention and had the first of many floor fights with AFL leadership over the issue of discrimination in affiliate unions.

Conflict Within the AFL

The convention also witnessed a fateful clash between the union's mainstream leadership and a dissident group led by John L. Lewis of the United Mine Workers of America. Lewis's group believed strongly that workers should be organized by industry, while the AFL's leadership wanted the unions organized by craft. A heated debate over the issue at the 1935 convention erupted into a fistfight on the convention floor between Lewis and "Big Bill" Hutcheson of the carpenters' union. Lewis won the battle but lost the war. Shortly after the donnybrook, AFL leaders voted to expel industrial unions from the labor federation.

After his expulsion from the AFL, Lewis led industrial unions in the formation of the rival Congress of Industrial Organizations (CIO), an umbrella group for unions organized by industry. Although Randolph had long favored industrial unions, he chose to keep the BSCP within the AFL fold, saying he felt it better positioned the union to fight for equality. Over time competition from the CIO forced the AFL to moderate its stand on racial equality. However, for Randolph and his lieutenants, the AFL's failure to move more quickly on this issue eventually led them to pull the union out of the labor federation in 1938 and join the CIO. When the two national labor organizations finally resolved their differences and merged in 1955 to form the AFL-CIO, Randolph was made a vice president and member of the combined organization's executive council. He was instrumental in persuading the labor organization to throw its support behind the growing movement for civil rights. Still not satisfied that the AFL-CIO was doing all it could do to combat discrimination, Randolph and other black labor leaders in 1960 formed the Negro American Labor Council, for which Randolph served as president from 1960 until 1966.

BSCP Recognized as Official Union for Porters

Twelve years to the day after the union's formation, the BSCP achieved victory in its long struggle to win recognition from the Pullman Company as the official union of its porters. On 25 August 1937 the union and company signed a contract that guaranteed porters improved working conditions and higher pay. This was just the first in a series of contracts negotiated by BSCP over the next few decades. In addition to its work on behalf of porters, the union contributed both its labor and financial support to the growing movement for racial equality, in which Randolph played a central role.

Role of the BSCP in the Civil Rights Movement

With Randolph at its helm, the BSCP played a major role in the civil rights movement throughout the mid-twentieth century. The union-sponsored March on Washington in 1941 was organized to protest governmental hiring practices that excluded blacks from federal employment and federal contracts. It was this type of racial discrimination, Randolph contended, that accounted for the economic disparities between the country's whites and blacks. With this in mind, he urged African Americans from around the country to march on Washington to demand jobs and freedom. The payoff for Randolph's strategy was not long in coming. In June 1941 President Franklin D. Roosevelt signed Executive Order 8802, banning discrimination in hiring by the federal government and defense contractors. Even more impressive was the 1963 March on Washington. Randolph tapped civil rights activist Bayard Rustin as organizer for the march, which successfully—and peacefully—brought together disparate elements of the movement for racial equality. More than a quarter-million people attended the massive 28 August 1963 march, which is perhaps best remembered for Dr. Martin Luther King, Jr.'s stirring "I Have a Dream" speech. Most importantly, the march helped pressure Congress to pass landmark civil rights legislation.

Aftermath

Plagued by ill health in the latter half of the 1960s, Randolph in 1968 stepped down as president of the BSCP and retired from public life. He was succeeded as president by C. L. Dellums, based in Oakland, California, who had long served as the union's vice president. Randolph died in New York City in 1979. The union, acknowledging the decline of the American railroad industry, in 1978 merged with the Brotherhood of Railway and Airline Clerks.

Key Players

Dellums, C. L. (1900–1989): A native of Corsicana, Texas, Dellums moved to California in search of better job opportunities. He was eventually hired as a sleeping car porter and joined with A. Philip Randolph in helping to organize the Brotherhood of Sleeping Car Porters in the mid-1920s. Dellums served for a number of years as a vice president of the union, and he took over as president in 1968 after Randolph stepped down.

Nixon, E. D., Sr. (1899–1987): Nixon, born in Montgomery, Alabama, worked briefly as a baggage handler before he was hired as a sleeping car porter. Impressed with a speech by A. Philip Randolph, he was an early recruit to the Brotherhood of Sleeping Car Porters and headed one of the union's first locals. A dedicated civil rights activist, Nixon played a major role in the Montgomery bus boycott of the mid-1950s.

Randolph, Asa Philip (1889–1979): Randolph worked to organize African American workers, founding a magazine in 1917, *The Messenger,* which called for more jobs for blacks in the armed forces and the defense industry. In the 1920s he was persuaded to help organize Pullman sleeping car porters, who sought shorter hours and higher pay. As a result, he helped found the Brotherhood of Sleeping Car Porters, the first successful African American labor union, which he served as president from 1925 until 1968.

Webster, Milton P. (?–1965): A former sleeping car porter, Webster fought throughout his career to end racial discrimination in organized labor in general and within the defense industry in particular. He played a key role in the early efforts to organize the Brotherhood of Sleeping Car Porters and in 1925 was named the union's first international vice president. He served as a leader of the BSCP until his death in 1965.

See also: *American Federation of Labor; Civil Rights Act of 1964; Congress of Industrial Organizations; March on Washington Movement.*

———————

BIBLIOGRAPHY

Books

Bates, Beth Tompkins. *Pullman Porters and the Rise of Protest Politics in Black America, 1925–1945.* Chapel Hill, NC: University of North Carolina Press, 2001.

"Brotherhood of Sleeping Car Porters." In *Encyclopedia of African-American Culture and History,* edited by Jack Salzman, David Lionel Smith, and Cornel West. New York: Macmillan, 1996.

"E. D. Nixon, Sr." In *Notable Black American Men,* edited by Jessie Carney Smith. Detroit, MI: Gale Research, 1998.

Other

The Evolution and History of the Union. A. Philip Randolph Pullman Porter Museum [cited 22 October 2002]. <http://aphiliprandolphmuseum.com/evo_history4.html>.

The Pullman Porter's Story [cited 22 October 2002]. <http://www/northbysouth.org/2000/Fraternal/pullman1.htm>.

Records of the Brotherhood of Sleeping Car Porters. Series A: Holdings of the Chicago Historical Society and the Newberry Library, 1925–1969 [cited 22 October 2002]. <http://www.lexisnexis.com/academic/guides/ African_American/bscp/bscp3.htm>.

ADDITIONAL RESOURCES

Books

Chateauvert, Melinda. *Marching Together: Women of the Brotherhood of Sleeping Car Porters.* Urbana: University of Illinois Press, 1998.

Harris, William Hamilton. *Keeping the Faith: A. Philip Randolph, Milton P. Webster, and the Brotherhood of Sleeping Car Porters, 1925–1937.* Urbana: University of Illinois Press, 1977.

McKissack, Pat and Frederick McKissack. *A Long Hard Journey: The Story of the Pullman Porter.* New York: Walker, 1989.

—Don Amerman

William Sylvis. © Bettmann Archive. Reproduced by permission.

Bureau of Labor Established

United States 1884

Synopsis

The fight for a federal department of labor began in the late 1800s and spanned almost 50 years. Shortly after the Civil War, William H. Sylvis and the National Labor Union lobbied for a Department of Labor, but Congress was unwilling to create any new cabinet-level departments. When Sylvis died in 1869 and the National Labor Union dissolved in 1873, the movement slumped. In response, a number of states created their own bureaus of labor. Under the leadership of Terence Powderly and the Knights of Labor, some leaders changed their strategy and proposed a national Bureau of Labor, which was created in 1884 and placed under the Department of the Interior.

Timeline

1864: George M. Pullman and Ben Field patent their design for a sleeping car with folding upper berths.

1869: The first U.S. transcontinental railway is completed.

1874: Gold is discovered in the Black Hills of South Dakota.

1877: Great Britain's Queen Victoria is proclaimed the empress of India.

1882: The Chinese Exclusion Act, a treaty between the United States and China, provides for restrictions on immigration of Chinese workers.

1884: At the Berlin Conference on African Affairs, 14 nations (including the United States) discuss colonial expansion in Africa and call for an end to slavery and the slave trade.

1884: Due to isolationist policies, Japan's government had prohibited emigration, but this year it finally lifts the ban and allows citizens to immigrate to Hawaii, where many—having escaped the country illegally—already work as temporary laborers. Thereafter, Japanese will increasingly replace Chinese as workers in the United States, where a treaty limits Chinese immigration.

1884: Chicago's Home Life Insurance Building, designed by William LeBaron Jenney, becomes the world's first skyscraper.

1884: Fabian Society of socialist intellectuals is founded in London. Early members include George Bernard Shaw, London economist Sidney Webb, and writer Beatrice Potter. Webb and Potter later marry and become founding members of the British Labour Party in 1906.

1886: Bombing at Haymarket Square, Chicago, kills seven policemen and injures numerous others. Eight anarchists are accused and tried; three are imprisoned, one commits suicide, and four are hanged.

1890: Congress passes the Sherman Antitrust Act, which in the years that follow will be used to break up large monopolies.

1894: War breaks out between Japan and China. It will end with China's defeat the next year, marking yet another milestone in China's decline and Japan's rise.

Event and Its Context

The development of the Department of Labor can be divided into three periods that correspond with three different labor unions: the National Labor Union, Knights of Labor, and the

American Federation of Labor. As each union waned, it was replaced by another that carried on the struggle for a cabinet-level department to represent the worker. The main concerns for each of these included the expansion of competition through the development of the railroad, the influx of immigrants who worked for lower wages, and the use of labor-saving machinery. Labor leaders hoped that a cabinet-level Department of Labor would stand equally with the powerful business and commerce interests.

Early Efforts to Create a National Department of Labor

The struggle for an executive department of labor began shortly after the close of the Civil War. Although the exact chronology of events is uncertain, the man credited with beginning the movement is William H. Sylvis. Recognized as the nation's leading labor leader, Sylvis advocated the creation of a Department of Labor in speeches and in newspaper articles, such as his letter to the editor of the *Evening Advocate*. Sylvis also took the idea of a department of labor to the National Labor Union. He stressed that the existing government departments protected the wealthy businesses and companies and that there was no department to protect labor. Congress, however, was reluctant to create any new departments and was more concerned with the interests of powerful agriculture and business groups than with labor. Sylvis's leadership carried the movement; when he died in 1869, the movement was unable to continue on without his zeal and leadership.

Without their charismatic leader, labor leaders changed strategies and pushed for state and federal bureaus of labor statistics in the hopes that a bureau would eventually become a department. In 1869 Massachusetts became the first state to create a bureau of labor statistics. Almost immediately the bureau became involved in an argument over whether it was supposed to be a voice for labor or an impartial organization. Its first two directors, Henry K. Oliver and George McNeil, were ardent labor reformers, and their reports expressed their bias. Viewed as too radical by business owners, the new bureau was soon involved in a partisan struggle that severely hindered the organization.

In 1873 the governor of Massachusetts appointed a new director, Republican Carroll Davidson Wright, and instructed him to "make it or bust it." Although Wright had little experience with the labor movement, labor problems, or statistics, he was impartial. Wright changed the direction of the bureau and earned a reputation for objectivity. By 1883, 12 other states had followed Massachusetts' example and created their own bureaus of labor statistics.

The creation of the state bureaus coincided with the evolution of a national department. The depressions of 1868 and 1873 had weakened labor unions and had destroyed the National Labor Union. Realizing their position, labor leaders put aside the idea of a national department and focused on attaining a national bureau. As the economy recovered from the 1873 depression, the federal bureau movement began to gain strength and a new organization, the Knights of Labor, grew and filled the vacuum that had been left by the National Labor Union. As the Knights of Labor gained more power and influence and the election of 1884 approached, both Democrats and Republicans developed platforms that included the creation of a national labor bureau.

Bureau of Labor Created

In 1884 five different congressmen introduced five different bills for the creation of a national labor bureau. Pennsylvania Representative James Hopkins wrote the bill that was accepted by the House committee and finally sent to Congress. The bill passed the House by an impressive margin in a vote of 182 to 19. Most of the opposition to the bill came from the South, where labor was weak. The bill went on to pass easily in the Senate. President Chester Arthur signed the bill into law on 27 June 1884.

The new agency, called the Bureau of Labor, came under the jurisdiction of the Department of the Interior. The president appointed the bureau's head, called a commissioner, for a term of four years with a yearly salary of $3,000. The commissioner's duties included gathering information on labor, its relation to capital, workday hours, wages, and providing for the well-being of workers.

Appointing the first commissioner was much more difficult. Unionists expected President Arthur to appoint a labor leader, and Terence Powderly of the Knights of Labor was the leading choice. When Powderly met with the president, Powderly brought more than 2,500 petitions from labor organizations as well as clippings of newspaper articles that had been published to show support for his candidacy. Pressured by manufacturers who felt Powderly was too radical, President Arthur submitted the name of labor leader John Jarrett for the position. Arthur withdrew Jarrett from consideration after learning that he had criticized Arthur's administration. After six months, Arthur finally settled on Carroll D. Wright of Massachusetts.

Wright and the bureau were immediately popular and successful. Early reports covered a wide range of topics, including convict labor, and were generally well received as was Wright himself. Organized labor supported the bureau and, although they were less enthusiastic about Wright, labor leaders argued for an increased budget. By 1888 the annual budget for the bureau had increased to nearly four times that of the original 1884 budget. Part of the budget increase provided for field agents who were needed to supplement the data gathered by questionnaires. President Grover Cleveland further recommended that the scope of the bureau be expanded to include investigation of labor disputes and arbitration; in 1888 Congress responded by adding these duties to the responsibilities of the bureau.

Efforts for a Cabinet-level Department

In 1888 Wright's term at the head of the bureau came to a close, so President Cleveland offered the job to Powderly. In 1884 Powderly had wanted the position, but by 1888 the Knights of Labor were at its peak and Powderly was unwilling to leave the organization. Instead, Powderly recommended that Cleveland make the existing bureau a cabinet-level department, with the department chief as a cabinet member. Powderly and the Knights of Labor sponsored a bill to create a Department of Labor with cabinet rank. The bill passed both houses, but the cabinet rank was again dropped. Instead of being given cabinet rank, the Department of Labor was made independent of the Department of the Interior. President Cleveland signed the bill on 21 March 1888.

Recognizing Carroll Wright's immense contribution to the Bureau of Labor, President Cleveland appointed him to head the new Department of Labor. The new department's budget was larger, and it had more personnel to support its functions. These functions remained the same as those of the former bureau except that Wright now submitted his reports, which addressed topics such as railroad labor, working women, liquor traffic, insurance, housing, and machinery's impact on labor, directly to the president. Wright also inaugurated a semimonthly bulletin to report the status and findings of the department's various efforts and projects.

During this time period, other interest groups clamored for recognition in the president's cabinet. For instance, business pressed for a Department of Commerce and Industry, and farmers wanted their Bureau of Agriculture to become a department. Interest in a cabinet-level Department of Labor, however, decreased. Wright was opposed to making his position a cabinet position because he wished to avoid partisan politics to promote stability; a cabinet-level commissioner would change with each new presidential administration. Labor organizations were occupied with other problems that were more immediately pressing than the cabinet issue. The Knights of Labor organization was falling apart because of internal and external pressures. The organization that would replace it, Samuel Gompers's American Federation of Labor (AFL), was too new.

In the 1890s business leaders began a movement to create a Department of Commerce and place the Department of Labor under Commerce, again making it a subordinate bureau. Labor had to respond. Gompers, then president of the AFL, made it clear that he would oppose any attempt to subordinate the Department of Labor. The AFL stood firm against any bill other than one for a cabinet-level Department of Labor. Gompers and the AFL, however, faced the very powerful business and industry interests and a conservative Republican Congress that was sympathetic to the proposal. President Theodore Roosevelt also called for the arrangement as put forth in the proposal in his 1901 speech to Congress.

Senator Knute Nelson introduced a commerce bill during the first session of the 57th Congress that proposed the formation of a Department of Commerce and Industries. Opposition from a Democratic minority argued that the independent Department of Labor would be lost. Labor organizations opposed the bill on the grounds that mistrust between labor and business would handicap the organization. President Roosevelt and Republicans, however, felt that labor and commerce had many things in common and that the Department of Labor would benefit from its association with other bureaus. The one concession made was to change the name from the Department of Commerce and Industries to the Department of Commerce and Labor. Despite stubborn opposition from a few, the bill passed easily, and President Roosevelt signed it in 1903.

Roosevelt appointed George B. Cortelyou as the first secretary of Commerce and Labor. Cortelyou proved to be impartial and even won over Gompers to an extent. In 1906 Oscar S. Straus replaced Cortelyou and clashed with Gompers over the issue of immigration. Gompers and the AFL were against immigration because the influx of workers willing to work for wages that were lower than U.S. norms held wages down; Straus opposed rigid restriction and tests for immigrants.

As a result, Gompers and the AFL increased their effort to separate commerce and labor. As early as 1903, the AFL con-

vinced the Democratic Party to adopt a plank advocating the creation of a Department of Labor. From 1903 until 1909 Democrats introduced bills to create a separate Department of Labor, but their efforts met with little success as they were in the minority. In 1910, however, the Democrats won control of both the House and the White House. Further, congressman William B. Wilson, champion of an independent Department of Labor and a former officer of the United Mine Workers, became chairman of the House Committee on Labor. In 1912 a bill introduced by Representative William Sulzer of New York passed.

President William Howard Taft had reservations about the bill and did not want to sign it. Taft, however, knew that a veto would mean nothing because the incoming Democratic president, Woodrow Wilson, had already selected William B. Wilson as the secretary of labor. So, Taft signed the bill creating the Department of Labor on 4 March 1913.

Key Players

Cortelyou, George B. (1862–1940): Cortelyou served as the first head of the Department of Commerce and Labor, postmaster general, and secretary of the treasury. During Cortelyou's term as secretary of treasury, the panic of 1907 brought business to a complete standstill. Cortelyou was an advocate of creating an elastic currency and a central banking system.

Gompers, Samuel (1850–1924): President of the American Federation of Labor for nearly 40 years, Gompers started his career as a cigar maker. The nation's leading trade unionist and labor advocate, Gompers worked for shorter hours, higher wages, workplace safety, and collective bargaining. Gompers organized the Federation of Organized Trades and Labor Unions of the United States and Canada.

Hopkins, James (1832–1904): Born in Pennsylvania, Hopkins practiced law for more than 20 years. He was also active in banking, mining, and manufacturing. He twice served as a Democrat in Congress (1875–1877 and 1883–1885). During his second term he was chairman of the Committee on Labor.

Powderly, Terence (1849–1924): Powderly began work on the railroad at age 13 and became a machinist in 1869. He joined the Machinists' and Blacksmiths' National Union and became its president in 1872. Two years later he joined the secretive Noble Order of the Knights of Labor and served as its president during the organization's peak from 1879 until 1893. Powderly also entered politics, joining the Greenback-Labor Party and serving as the mayor of Scranton, Pennsylvania, from 1878 to 1884, the federal immigration commissioner from 1897 to 1902, and head of the information department of the Bureau of Immigration from 1907 to 1921.

Sylvis, William (1828–1869): An iron molder, Sylvis joined the local the molder's union in 1857 and helped organized the Iron Molders' International Union. He founded the National Labor Union in 1866 and served as its president from 1868 to 1869. One of the most important labor leaders of his day, Sylvis was one of the first to lobby for the creation of a Department of Labor.

Wright, Carroll Davidson (1840–1909): Wright, a statistician, served in the Massachusetts senate from 1872 to 1873, and worked as president of Clark College in Worcester, Massachusetts, from 1902 until 1909. As the U.S. commissioner of labor, he organized the Bureau of Labor Statistics and conducted objective research on various labor problems. He also authored two books: *The Industrial Evolution of the United States* (1887) and *Battles of Labor* (1906).

See also: *American Federation of Labor; Department of Labor; Knights of Labor; Panic of 1873.*

BIBLIOGRAPHY

Books

Lombardi, John. *Labor's Voice in the Cabinet.* New York: AMS Press, 1968.

Other

Grossman, Jonathan. "The Origin of the U.S. Department of Labor" [cited 17 October 2002]. < http://www.dol.gov/asp/programs/history/dolorigabridge.htm >.

ADDITIONAL RESOURCES

Books

Powderly, Terence Vincent. *The Path I Trod.* New York: AMS Press, 1968.

—Lisa A. Ennis

Burlington Railroad Strike

United States 1888

Synopsis

The Burlington Railroad strike of 1888 was one of the most significant labor conflicts of the nineteenth century. It tested the power of one of the most important unions of that era, the Brotherhood of Locomotive Engineers (BLE), and the approach to organization that it exemplified. It also illustrated the problems of confronting large corporations with vast resources and wide influence. The BLE's defeat was a disaster for the strikers that anticipated the problems that unions would face in the following years. In the longer term, it reinforced the unions' tendency to emphasize skilled workers and relatively narrow jurisdictions.

Timeline

1868: Ratification of the Fourteenth Amendment to the U.S. Constitution grants civil rights to African Americans.

1873: Financial panic begins in Vienna, and soon spreads to other European financial centers, as well as to the United States.

1878: The first commercial telephone exchange opens, in New Haven, Connecticut.

1881: U.S. President James A. Garfield is assassinated in a Washington, D.C., railway station by Charles J. Guiteau.

1886: Bombing at Haymarket Square, Chicago, kills seven policemen and injures numerous others. Eight anarchists are accused and tried; three are imprisoned, one commits suicide, and four are hanged.

1888: With a series of murders in London's seedy Whitechapel district, Jack the Ripper—whose identity remains a subject of debate—becomes the first known serial murder.

1888: The Blizzard of 1888 in the United States kills hundreds, and causes more than $25 million in property damage.

1888: American inventor George Eastman revolutionizes photography by introducing the Kodak camera, which makes it possible for amateur photographers to take satisfactory snapshots.

1888: Serbian-born American electrical engineer Nikola Tesla develops a practical system for generating and transmitting alternating current (AC), which will ultimately—and after an extremely acrimonious battle—replace Thomas Edison's direct current (DC) in most homes and businesses.

1890: Alfred Thayer Mahan, a U.S. naval officer and historian, publishes *The Influence of Sea Power upon History, 1660–1783,* which demonstrates the decisive role that maritime forces have played in past conflicts. The book will have an enormous impact on world events by encouraging the major powers to develop powerful navies.

1894: Thousands of unemployed American workers—a group named "Coxey's Army" for their leader, Jacob S. Coxey—march on Washington, D.C. A number of such marches on the capital occurred during this period of economic challenges, but Coxey's march was the only one to actually reach its destination.

1898: United States defeats Spain in the three-month Spanish-American War. As a result, Cuba gains it independence, and the United States purchases Puerto Rico and the Philippines from Spain for $20 million.

Event and Its Context

The Setting

The Burlington Railroad strike of April–May 1888 stood out among the thousands of strikes that marked the mid-1880s. It involved more than 1,000 strikers and 1,500 strikebreakers and guards, making it one of the most serious disputes of that era. It involved one of the largest contemporary firms, with workers in dozens of separate locations. Similarly, replacement workers came from all over the East and Midwest, testament to the regional and even national implications of such disputes. Above all, the Burlington strike was an influence, perhaps a cat-

Chicago Burlington and Quincy Railroad strikers, 1888. The Library of Congress.

alyst, in the creation of an American labor movement. Until that time, unions had represented a hodgepodge of organizational forms, reflecting the varying perspectives and needs of different groups. Some organizations, such as the Brotherhood of Locomotive Engineers (BLE), were elite groups of highly skilled workers. Others, like the miners' unions, embraced everyone who worked in the industry. The most prominent union of the 1880s, the Knights of Labor (KOL), was a conglomerate of different groups. The Burlington strike helped to sort out these approaches. Though the BLE lost decisively—partly because it was unable to attract the support of less-skilled railroad employees and the organizations that represented or sought to represent them, notably the KOL—the legacy of bitterness was so

great that the BLE and other elite groups became even more rigid in their determination to chart their own courses.

Background

In the 1880s the American railroad industry was the foremost exemplar of industrialization and technological innovation. Though only 50 years old, the railroads spanned the continent and, by the end of the 1880s, would connect nearly every community to every other community. Railroading was also one of the preeminent high technology industries of the age. Based on steam power, the great symbol of nineteenth-century industrialization, it introduced a host of new and complex machines and created a vast array of new jobs, including the engineer, who operated the engine and in effect the train, and the fireman, who stoked the boiler and backed up the engineer. Apart from technical skills, the locomotive engineer had to have sound judgment and a sense of social responsibility. Hundreds of people were killed or injured every year because a few engineers lacked the skill, judgment, or maturity to operate their engines safely. Successful engineers thus commanded great respect and earned the highest average wages of all industrial workers. Nevertheless, their lives were difficult. They were often away from home, faced great personal danger, and, as the highest paid railroad employees, were targets of cost-cutting campaigns. In response, engineers sought the support and assistance of other engineers.

The BLE formed in 1864, largely to provide assistance to the families of engineers who were killed in accidents. In the 1870s the organization began to assume economic functions, for example by striking against employers who cut wages. Conflicts over strike policies led to an internal upheaval and the election in 1874 of Peter M. Arthur as president. A cautious leader who emphasized the union's economic role, Arthur promoted collective bargaining but opposed strikes. Between 1874 and 1888 he recruited thousands of new members and negotiated numerous wage agreements with railroads but did not call a single strike.

Arthur was also conservative in another sense. Engineers may have been the aristocrats of rail crews, but they presided over a hierarchy of other workers. A good argument could be made for enlisting all of these employees in a single organization so as to maximize the workers' influence in their dealings with railroad managers. Arthur and a majority of BLE members rejected this argument, scorning any organizational link with nonengineers, even the firemen. In effect, they defined their union in the narrowest possible way. As a consequence the firemen, brakemen, conductors, and ultimately other railroad occupations organized and bargained separately.

Fragmentation did not necessarily mean hostility or lack of cooperation, but the potential existed. In the mid-1880s rivalries developed between the BLE and the KOL, which also enlisted railroad workers and competed successfully on some lines. The BLE pointedly refused to support major KOL strikes in 1886 and 1887. Workers who had lost their jobs when those strikes failed were naturally bitter and often blamed the BLE for their plight.

The other major element in the 1888 conflict was the Burlington Railroad, a notable example of a relatively new phenomenon: the big business corporation. The first large railroad corporations had appeared on the eve of the Civil War. During the boom years of the postwar period, the late 1860s to the early 1870s and 1880s, railroads grew and consolidated through mergers, mostly in the East, and through building into new areas, mostly in the West. The Burlington, which was located strategically between Chicago, the principal rail hub, and the eastern terminals of the new transcontinental railroads, was among the fastest growing of them all. Under a visionary president, Charles E. Perkins, it grew from 1,300 miles of track in 1881 to 7,600 miles in 1901, when Perkins retired. To expand that rapidly, the company had to decentralize decision-making. Regional managers thus had substantial autonomy, including the ability to negotiate labor agreements with employees. Per-

kins had one hard-and-fast rule, however. He would not formally recognize any union or acknowledge the employees' right to belong to such organizations. In normal times local managers were generally cooperative, despite the rule. In a showdown, however, union members knew there would be reprisals.

The Strike Begins

Though the BLE had successfully negotiated an agreement with the Burlington in 1886, two major grievances remained unsettled. First, the company paid lower wages to new hires than to veteran workers. On the surface this was a logical distinction because experience was essential to safe and effective locomotive operations. Burlington managers, however, used the differential to discriminate against experienced employees. When they had to reduce costs, they would lay off the older, higher paid workers and hire novices. At that point the second policy became a problem. The company only promoted from within, and Burlington managers interpreted this policy as a ban on the rehiring of workers who had been laid off. Thus workers who lost their jobs in cost-cutting campaigns could never regain them. Because the Burlington was the only railroad in many Midwestern towns, former Burlington employees had no choice but to leave their homes or leave the industry. The effects were both financially disastrous and humiliating to proud, respected, and comparatively affluent engineers.

By early 1888, militant workers were ready to strike against the company, regardless of BLE policy. A series of misunderstandings and the managers' refusal to settle several minor grievances were the last straw. On 17 February the militants walked away from their engines and appealed for support. Many other engineers and firemen joined them. Burlington operations were paralyzed and Arthur and the head of the firemen's union had no choice but to support the strike. Perkins, surprised and angry, determined to teach the strikers a lesson.

At his direction, the managers did everything in their power to keep the trains running. To fill the strikers' ranks, they suspended the rule against not hiring former employees and outsiders—precisely the rules that had provoked the engineers—and hired new engineers. Some of the new employees were former Burlington workers who were willing to come back under any conditions. Others, apparently a substantial number, were KOL. The Burlington had formerly refused to hire KOL members; then it disregarded union affiliation—another affront to the strikers—and assured the replacement workers that their jobs would be permanent. It even gave them seniority over any of the strikers who eventually returned. By late March, Burlington operations were back at their prestrike level.

Apart from hiring new engineers, the Burlington managers sought to prevent pickets from interfering with train operations. To protect strategic areas such as rail yards, stations, and bridges, management adopted the provocative strategy of employing armed guards. Working through the Pinkerton Detective Agency, a notorious strikebreaking outfit, Burlington hired a small army of thugs and petty criminals to keep the strikers at bay. The strikers understood what was happening, of course, and often confronted the guards. A number of violent altercations left at least four men dead and a much larger number injured. Nevertheless, the guards succeeded in their immediate goal.

The company also persuaded most other railroads to accept Burlington cars, thus thwarting union efforts to organize a boycott. Some rival managers covertly encouraged their employees to refuse to handle Burlington property, but most of them decided that if the BLE won the strike it would be much tougher to deal with in the future. The Burlington managers also obtained a court injunction against the boycott, which made the union as well as the strikers subject to legal reprisals.

By April the strike had failed. Arthur and his counterpart in the firemen's union urged the strikers to return to work to save their jobs and formally called off the strike in January 1889. Still, many strikers refused to go back. Others reapplied but found that there were no openings or that they had been blacklisted. Most of the Burlington strikers never returned to their old jobs. In many small towns along the Burlington line, the divisions and antagonisms created by the 1888 strike lasted for decades.

Results

The Burlington strike had a lasting impact on the labor movement, the practice of industrial relations, and the policies of large corporations. The BLE and its members were the most obvious losers. Despite its strength and resources, the BLE had proven no match for a large, aggressive corporation. The strike had failed in so many ways that it was hard to imagine what the union could do to prevent similar debacles in the future. The most commonly suggested change was to scrap the narrow occupational focus of the BLE in favor of a comprehensive organization. Several years later Eugene V. Debs, vice president of the Fireman's Brotherhood, embraced this approach in his American Railway Union, which had some initial successes. In 1894, however, Debs and the ARU became involved in a conflict with the Pullman Company that escalated into a strike against the major midwestern railroads and ended exactly as the Burlington strike had ended.

In the aftermath of the Burlington strike, Arthur, who had faced considerable internal opposition for failing to support the strikers more effectively, reasserted his original position on strikes and craft unionism. The collapse of the Pullman strike strengthened his position. The brotherhoods went their separate, parallel ways and succeeded in organizing most of the skilled workers who made up the train crews. Other railroad workers had greater difficulty, and the laborers who maintained tracks and performed unskilled jobs remained unorganized until the World War I years. The pattern of the railroad industry, moreover, became roughly the pattern of industry in general.

The strike also affected the Burlington Company. Though it had won the conflict, the financial cost had been enormous. Nor had it ended the union presence. Many of the replacement workers were union members or former members, and few of them were grateful to the company for their jobs. The BLE and other unions quickly revived. The Burlington managers began to realize that their policies were counterproductive. By the turn of the century, they had made peace with the brotherhoods and introduced company welfare plans to inoculate the other employees. Their actions probably helped prevent an ARU-style union from emerging, but they did little to prevent the spread of craft unionism in the industry.

The Burlington strike also helped shape the social reform agenda of the following years. Unions had long bemoaned the effects of strikebreaking but had made little progress against conservative defenses of the rights of property owners. Yet the railroads were so big, their services so vital, and the effects of unrestrained industrial conflict so far-reaching that many people began to question the wisdom of the traditional view. There had been many violent miners' strikes, but they tended to occur in remote rural areas and had little effect on nonparticipants. The violence in railroad strikes was more visible, appalling, and disruptive. As a consequence, the following decades would see a sustained and gradually successful campaign by unions and their allies to restrain and regulate industrial disputes, especially those involving railroad workers.

Key Players

Arthur, Peter M. (1831–1903): Arthur was born in Scotland and immigrated to the United States with his parents in 1842. He obtained his first railroad job at 18 and remained associated with railroad labor for the rest of his life. Active in local unions and then in the Brotherhood of Locomotive Engineers (BLE), he was elected grand chief or president in 1874, a position he retained for the rest of his life. Arthur was a tireless advocate of collective bargaining and of independence from the rest of the labor movement. Under his stewardship, the BLE became one of the most formidable American unions. A Cleveland resident, Arthur was active in civic affairs and a highly successful real estate speculator.

Perkins, Charles E. (1840–1907): Perkins was a New England native with family ties to major business interests. His cousin, John Murray Forbes, was a merchant who took the lead in directing Boston mercantile capital into western railroads and became the principal owner and officer of the Burlington Railroad. Perkins started at the Burlington as a clerk in 1859 but with Forbes's backing, rose rapidly to vice president in 1873 and president in 1881. Under Perkins's leadership, the Burlington expanded rapidly, becoming one of the country's largest and most profitable railroads. Perkins was not inflexible on labor issues but tried to contain union power. His approach became the approach of most rail managers after 1900.

See also: *American Federation of Labor; Brotherhood of Locomotive Engineers; Pullman Strike.*

BIBLIOGRAPHY

Books

McMurry, Donald L. *The Great Burlington Strike of 1888: A Case History in Labor Relations.* Cambridge: Harvard University Press, 1956.

Overton, Richard C. *Burlington Route: A History of the Burlington Lines.* New York: Alfred A. Knopf, 1965.

Richardson, Reed C. *The Locomotive Engineer, 1863–1963: A Century of Railway Labor Relations and Work Rules.* Ann Arbor: University of Michigan Press, 1963.

—Daniel Nelson

James Francis Byrnes. © Archive Photos, Inc. Reproduced by permission.

Byrnes Act

United States 1936

Synopsis

In 1936 Congress enacted the Byrnes Act, also known as the Antistrikebreaker Law, which was authored by Senator James Francis Byrnes of South Carolina. The act made it a federal felony to willfully transport strikebreakers across state lines for the purpose of obstructing or interfering by force or threats with peaceful picketing by employees during any labor controversy affecting wages, hours, or conditions of labor, or the exercise by employees of any of the rights of self-organization or collective bargaining. The legislation responded to over a half century of industrial violence that had been fueled in part by management's persistent use of armed mercenaries to infiltrate, intimidate, threaten, and use violence against laborers to prevent or to break labor strikes.

Timeline

1921: As the Allied Reparations Commission calls for payments of 132 billion gold marks, inflation in Germany begins to climb.

1926: Britain is paralyzed by the general strike.

U.S. Code Title 18, Section 1231: Transportation of Strikebreakers

Whoever willfully transports in interstate or foreign commerce any person who is employed or is to be employed for the purpose of obstructing or interfering by force or threats with

(1) peaceful picketing by employees during any labor controversy affecting wages, hours, or conditions of labor, or

(2) the exercise by employees of any of the rights of self-organization or collective bargaining; or

Whoever is knowingly transported or travels in interstate or foreign commerce for any of the purposes enumerated in this section—

Shall be fined under this title or imprisoned not more than two years, or both. This section shall not apply to common carriers.

Source: *Findlaw: U.S. Code.* http://www.findlaw.com/casecode/uscodes/.

—Judson Knight

1931: Financial crisis widens in the United States and Europe, which reel from bank failures and climbing unemployment levels. In London, armies of the unemployed riot.

1933: Adolf Hitler becomes German chancellor, and the Nazi dictatorship begins.

1936: Germany reoccupies the Rhineland, while Italy annexes Ethiopia. Recognizing a commonality of aims, the two totalitarian powers sign the Rome-Berlin Axis Pact. (Japan will join them in 1940.)

1936: The election of a leftist Popular Front government in Spain in February precipitates an uprising by rightists under the leadership of Francisco Franco. Over the next three years, war will rage between the Loyalists and Franco's Nationalists. The Spanish Civil War will prove to be a lightning rod for the world's tensions, with the Nazis and Fascists supporting the Nationalists, and the Soviets the Loyalists.

1936: Hitler uses the Summer Olympics in Berlin as an opportunity to showcase Nazi power and pageantry, but the real hero of the games is the African American track star Jesse Owens.

1939: Britain and France declare war against Germany after the 1 September invasion of Poland, but little happens in the way of mobilization.

1944: Allies land at Normandy on 6 June, conducting the largest amphibious invasion in history.

1951: Six western European nations form the European Coal and Steel Community, forerunner of the European Economic Community and the later European Union.

Event and Its Context

The Byrnes Act makes it a federal felony to knowingly transport a "strikebreaker" across state lines. The act defines a strikebreaker as a person paid to use force or threats to obstruct or interfere with lawful labor activity. Two types of labor activity are specifically protected against interference by strikebreakers from out of state. First, during labor controversies regarding wages, hours, or working conditions, strikebreakers may not interfere with peaceful picketing activity. Second, at all times, strikebreakers may not interfere with union organizing or collective bargaining activity.

The Byrnes Act prohibits transport only of persons specifically hired to use force or threats against laborers. The uses of "force or threats" prohibited by the act include infiltrating labor strikes, stirring up violence, and motivating popular opinion against striking workers. In the early twentieth century, people who engaged in these prohibited activities often were employed by private detective agencies or were in the private armies of industrial employers. Labor unionists referred to such professional strikebreakers as "goons" or "finks" and distinguished them from "scabs," or nonunion workers who filled jobs that were opened temporarily by labor strikes. Interstate transport of peaceful "scab" replacement workers is not a violation of the Byrnes Act, even when such workers are brought in for the purpose of breaking a labor strike.

Violations of the Byrnes Act are punishable by fines or by imprisonment for up to two years. The Byrnes Act does not apply to transportation common carriers, such as railroads, commercial bus lines, or commercial airlines. Thus, if an employer uses a commercial airline to fly in a group of strikebreakers from out of state to threaten local labor organizers, only the employer—and not the commercial airline—is subject to prosecution under the Byrnes Act, regardless of whether the airline knows why the strikebreakers are traveling across state lines.

Labor Strikes before the Byrnes Act

From the 1890s through the 1930s, the United States economy was repeatedly disrupted by labor strikes, employer lockouts, and horrendous acts of violence perpetrated by labor and management alike. Some of the worst such violence erupted when striking laborers clashed with professional strikebreakers employed by specialized agencies such as the Pinkerton National Detective Agency, Bergoff Detective Bureau, and the Baldwin-Felts Detective Agency.

In 1892 Pinkerton agents clashed with organized labor when, in an effort to halt union organizing, the Carnegie Steel Company locked out 1,100 steelworkers from their jobs at the company's Homestead, Pennsylvania, plant. When 3,000 of the plant's 3,800 workers picketed the plant, plant manager Henry C. Frick called in the Pinkertons. Hundreds of armed agents arrived by barge on the Monongahela River. Thousands of strikers and strike supporters lining the riverbank warned them not to disembark. Shots were fired, and a 14-hour battle ensued. When the Pinkerton agents surrendered, three agents and nine steelworkers were dead. The Pennsylvania National Guard eventually took control of the plant.

In 1914 in Colorado's "Ludlow Massacre," agents from the Baldwin-Felts Detective Agency participated in setting fire to a tent camp that had been established by striking miners who had been evicted from their company-owned homes. The Ludlow fires killed 12 children and seven adults. On 19 May 1920 the "Battle of Matewan, West Virginia," erupted when Baldwin-Felts detectives hired by the local mining company tried to evict striking miners and their families from the Stone Mountain Mine camp. The ensuing gun battle resulted in the deaths of seven detectives, two miners, and the mayor of Matewan.

Neither the Pinkertons nor the Baldwin-Felts agents, however, were as notorious in organized labor circles as was the self-proclaimed "King of the Strikebreakers," Mr. Pearl L. Bergoff, founder of the Bergoff Services Bureau. In 1910, 16 men, women, and children were killed by Bergoff Services Bureau employees who had been hired to break a Philadelphia rapid transitworkers' strike. In 1920 the Bergoff Detective Bureau received $2 million to break just two strikes: the Brooklyn, New York, rapid transit strike and the Erie, Pennsylvania, railroad strike. By 1935 Bergoff boasted in both *Fortune* magazine and *Readers' Digest* that his bureau had undertaken 172 strikebreaking engagements between 1907 and 1934. In fact, the bureau had been hired to break more than 300 strikes during that period, during which its activities were associated with 54 deaths.

Not all labor-related violence was directed against unionists. In 1923, for example, striking miners in Herrin, Illinois, murdered 20 "scab" replacement workers. Nonetheless, lawmakers in the 1930s directed their efforts primarily against the professional strikebreaking agencies. In the early twentieth century, at least 16 states enacted "Pinkerton Laws." These variously prohibited the maintenance of armed forces within the state, required licensure for private detective agencies, barred employment during labor disputes of people who customarily and repeatedly offered themselves for employment in the place of employees involved in labor disputes, required employers to notify job applicants of impending labor unrest, and forbade the transport of armed men into a state. These state laws, however, failed to eliminate the scourge of violent professional strikebreaking.

The Enactment of the Byrnes Act (1935–1936)

On 22 August 1935 Senator James Francis Byrnes (D-SC), a self-described "conservative liberal" and key southern congressional ally of President Franklin Roosevelt, introduced in the U.S. Senate a bill to hinder strikebreaking activities undertaken by private agencies of national scope. Senator Byrnes stated that the bill was specifically targeted against several existing national agencies—namely the Baldwin-Felts Detective Agency and the Bergoff Detective Bureau—that employed "armies of men for the purpose of sending them into various States of the Union to interfere in labor controversies by obstructing and interfering physically with those who are engaged in peaceful picketing." Citing Colorado's Ludlow Massacre and a similar massacre of coal miners in West Virginia, Byrnes asserted that whenever these private agencies "sent their hirelings into the coal mines or into other industrial centers, the result has invariably been to cause bloodshed, and the use of weapons, and physical violence."

Byrnes's antistrikebreaking bill passed the Senate without controversy. In the House of Representatives, John Elvis Miller

(D-AR) introduced the Byrnes bill in May 1936, where it was met with some opposition. The leading opponent, Thomas Lindsay Blanton (D-TX), argued that the Byrnes bill would deprive employers of necessary means to protect their property and the safety of replacement workers against violence and vandalism initiated by striking laborers. To illustrate this point, Blanton argued that the federal government itself had been disrupted recently when carloads of union thugs had beaten up "scab" replacement workers who had been hired to continue building the Supreme Court building in Washington, D.C. during a labor strike. Blanton also argued that the Byrnes bill would render workers who chose not to join unions vulnerable to physical intimidation or retaliation by union thugs. In floor debate, to substantial applause, Vito Marcantonio (R-NY) characterized Blanton's remarks as "the most vicious antilabor speech that has ever been made on the floor of this House."

Robert Fleming Rich (R-PA) further objected that the Byrnes bill would impose liability on transportation companies that innocently hauled strikebreakers from one state to another, although in the Senate, Byrnes had assured the contrary. In response, the House amended the bill to clarify that it would not apply to transportation common carriers.

Despite such individual objections, the Byrnes bill easily passed the House, where most members saw it as a potentially useful tool for moderating a cycle of violence between labor and management that had escalated out of control. Miller, the bill's House sponsor, articulated this viewpoint: "The trouble is that whenever you take men from Arkansas into New York, or from Massachusetts to Arkansas, and they go interfering with the local problems, it is just like waving a red flag in a bull's face."

President Roosevelt signed the bill into law on 24 June 1936.

Efforts to Convict under the Byrnes Act

Although the Byrnes Act has remained in effect since 1936, only a handful of individuals ever have been charged with violating it. Moreover, not a single person has ever been convicted of violating the act.

Shortly after the Byrnes Act became law, criminal prosecutions were brought against Bergoff Detective Bureau, one of its principal intended targets, whose agents had crossed state lines to break strikes. In 1937, however, a federal district judge in Connecticut acquitted these agents, finding that the government had not proved that the agents intended to interfere with peaceful picketing, collective bargaining, or union organizing at the time they crossed state lines.

In 1956 a National Labor Relations Board (NLRB) trial examiner initially determined that the Byrnes Act had been violated when the captain of a shipping vessel docked near Cairo, Illinois, physically attacked four union organizers who refused to leave the vessel after boarding at the invitation of a crewman. Later that year, however, the full NLRB overturned the trial examiner's determination, finding that the union organizers had been trespassing on the vessel and that the captain was within his rights in attempting to remove them.

The dearth of criminal convictions under the Byrnes Act may indicate that the law is ineffective; that is, that it is easily evaded or that it is difficult for prosecutors to prove that an accused strikebreaker crossed state lines specifically to interfere with peaceful picketing, collective bargaining, or union organizing. On the other hand, it may indicate that the law has been highly effective; that is, that the Byrnes Act eliminated the existence of private agencies of national scope that specialize in using force or violence to break labor strikes. Alternatively, the Byrnes Act may have fallen into disuse after the 1935 National Labor Relations Board enabled the government to address "unfair labor practices"—including the use of threat or force against workers, intimidation, and the use of industrial spies—through administrative proceedings rather than through the criminal justice system.

Key Players

Byrnes, James Francis (1879–1972): Byrnes served as a member of both the House of Representatives and the Senate and was associate justice of the Supreme Court, director of economic stabilization under President Roosevelt, director of war mobilization, secretary of state, and ultimately governor of South Carolina. He was the author of the Byrnes Act.

Miller, John Elvis (1888–1981): Democrat representative (1931–1937) and senator (1937–1941), Miller was appointed U.S. district judge for the western district of Arkansas in 1941 and retired in 1967, becoming U.S. senior district judge.

See also: *Homestead Lockout; Ludlow Massacre.*

BIBLIOGRAPHY

Books

Fitch, John. *The Causes of Industrial Unrest.* New York: Harpers, 1924.

Hoxie, Robert Franklin. *Trade Unionism in the United States.* New York: D. Appleton and Company, 1923.

Norwood, Stephen H. *Strikebreaking and Intimidation: Mercenaries and Masculinity in Twentieth-Century America.* Chapel Hill: University of North Carolina Press, 2002.

Periodicals

"Anti-Strikebreaking Legislation—the Effect and Validity of State-Imposed Criminal Sanctions." *University of Pennsylvania Law Review* 115, no. 190 (December 1966).

The Congressional Record: Vol. 79, pp. 14105–14106 (22 August 1935); Vol. 80, pp. 6654–6655 (4 May 1936); Vol. 80, pp. 10218–10222 (19 June 1936).

"Employer Interference with Lawful Union Activity." *Columbia Law Review* 37, no. 816 (1937).

"Legislation: Congress Assails Industrial Thuggery." *University of Pennsylvania Law Review* 85, no. 406 (February 1937): 406–413.

Wolf, Herman. "Strike-Breaker Number One." *The Nation* 141, no. 3671 (13 November 1935): 568.

ADDITIONAL RESOURCES

Other

The Byrnes Foundation. "James Francis Byrnes." 1998 [cited 28 September 2002]. <www.byrnesscholars.org>.

PBS Online. *The American Experience.* "Homestead Strike." 1999 [cited 28 September 2002]. <http://www.pbs.org/wgbh/amex/carnegie/peopleevents/pande04.html>

— Linda Dynan

C

Calcutta General Strike

India 1953

Synopsis

India gained its independence from Great Britain in 1947. In the years that followed, the country faced numerous problems that ranged from extreme poverty to a rapidly growing population. Prime Minister Jawaharlal Nehru attempted to overcome these problems and transform India into a modern, developed country. Among the issues that posed particular problems for India was the situation of the working class. Just as India and Pakistan had split at independence, the Indian labor movement was divided at independence, with four major labor federations competing for the loyalty of the country's workers. Often, these unions and federations resorted to strikes as a means to achieve their goals. In 1953 in particular, there was a wave of strikes in India. Among the most significant was a general strike in the city of Calcutta in July that resulted from increased streetcar fares.

Timeline

1932: Charles A. Lindbergh's baby son is kidnapped and killed, a crime for which Bruno Hauptmann will be charged in 1934, convicted in 1935, and executed in 1936.

1937: Stalin uses carefully staged show trials in Moscow to eliminate all rivals for leadership. These party purges, however, are only a small part of the death toll now being exacted in a country undergoing forced industrialization, much of it by means of slave labor.

1942: Signing of the Declaration of the United Nations occurs in Washington, D.C.

1945: On 7 May, Germany surrenders to the Allied powers. Later in the summer, the new U.S. president, Harry Truman, joins Churchill and Stalin at Potsdam to discuss the reconstruction of Germany. (Churchill is replaced in mid-conference by Clement Attlee as Labour wins control of the British Parliament.)

1947: Establishment of the Marshall Plan is intended to assist European nations in recovering from the war.

1949: Soviets conduct their first successful atomic test. This heightens growing cold war tensions, not least because the sudden acquisition of nuclear capabilities suggests that American spies are passing secrets.

1952: Among the cultural landmarks of the year are the film *High Noon* and the book *The Invisible Man* by Ralph Ellison.

1952: George Jorgenson travels to Copenhagen and returns as Christine Jorgenson. (This is not the first sex-change operation; however, it is the first to attract widespread attention.)

1955: The Warsaw Pact is signed by the Soviet Union and its satellites in Eastern Europe.

1957: Soviets launch *Sputnik,* the world's first artificial satellite. This spawns a space race between the two superpowers.

1962: As the Soviets begin a missile buildup in Cuba, for a few tense days in October it appears that World War III is imminent. President Kennedy calls for a Cuban blockade, forcing the Soviets to back down and ultimately diffusing the crisis.

1967: Racial violence sweeps America's cities, as Harlem, Detroit, Birmingham, and other towns erupt with riots.

Event and Its Context

India After Independence

In August 1947 the independent states of India and Pakistan emerged from British colonial possession. Despite the celebrations that marked India's break from Great Britain, however, the path to independent statehood was not an easy one. Hindu and Muslim leaders had been unable to reach an agreement by which to keep British India unified after independence. After independence, numerous outbreaks of violence erupted in response to ethnic and religious strife that affected the new countries. Hundreds of thousands of people died in the unrest, with millions more forced to move from their ancestral homes. Indeed, an angry Hindu refugee assassinated Mohandas Gandhi.

The person charged with smoothing India's transition to independence was Jawaharlal Nehru. Greatly influenced by the West, the nationalist Nehru sought to facilitate quick transition to a modern and prosperous India upon taking office in 1947. He hoped to achieve economic development for his country while also maintaining a sense of social justice. However, Nehru faced a number of daunting problems that would prove difficult to overcome.

One problem was that India was a large and diverse country. It was divided by geography, language, culture, religion, and caste. Furthermore, India was a predominantly peasant society that continued to practice traditional ways of life and work. It would be difficult to convince many in India to modernize. The country's growing population was another key issue that Nehru had to confront. At independence in 1947, the population was around 400 million and was growing by as many as five million every year. Such a large population contributed to high unemployment in India. By 1951 there were some two million unemployed in the cities and another 15 million in rural areas. High unemployment was exacerbated by widespread illiteracy and a lack of education and training. Furthermore, unemployment reflected and contributed to India's poverty, as low

Jawaharlal Nehru. The Library of Congress.

wages and malnutrition were common throughout the country. Many of the poor lived in India's growing cities, with Calcutta being home to some of the largest and poorest slums.

The Nehru government was forced to design an economic plan to deal with these many issues. Although Nehru left most established industries in private hands, the government came to control public utilities and many new projects, such as steel plants and irrigation systems. To this end, the government created a planning commission in 1950, reflecting the belief that the best way to raise the standard of living in India was to develop industry. The planning commission, chaired by Nehru himself, devised a series of five-year plans. The first five-year plan went into effect in 1951. This first plan was modest and cautious compared to subsequent plans. It emphasized several projects such as agricultural production, transportation, and communications. In general, the first five-year plan was a success, as national income grew faster than the population, food production increased, and output of capital and consumer goods grew. However, despite these impressive gains, India remained poor and unemployment continued to rise. Furthermore, the labor movement continued to agitate.

The Labor Movement in Post-independence India

The period immediately before and after the independence of India in 1947 was marked by much labor activity. In the year

before India achieved its independence from Great Britain, there was a significant amount of labor agitation. In June 1946 a railroad workers' strike was averted at the last minute. In July 1946 post and telegraph workers struck for three weeks to demand wage increases. Some 40,000 teachers also went on strike in Utter Pradesh. There was further agitation among dockworkers, electrical workers, and textile workers in places such as Madras and Bombay.

After independence, the new Indian government inherited a situation of much pent-up labor unrest. Efforts toward a unified labor movement had failed. Instead, most workers and their unions were divided among four main labor federations in India. First was the Indian National Trade Union Congress (INTUC). Formed in May 1947, INTUC was directly linked to the Indian National Congress. INTUC members included some 200 unions with about 575,000 members. Its nucleus was the powerful Textile Labor Association of Ahmedabad and its 55,000 members. INTUC sought to resolve workers' issues peacefully without resorting to the use of strikes.

A second major labor federation from the independence era was the *Hind Mazdoor Sabha*, or Indian Workers' Association. This group was formed by socialists who broke away from the INTUC in 1948. They did so because they felt that INTUC's close association with the Indian National Congress and the government was not in the best interests of the working class. Rather, the goal of the Indian Workers Association was to bring about a socialist state. Often, therefore, this federation was critical of government labor policy. On the other hand, at times the Indian Workers Association collaborated with INTUC and the government when their interests and goals coincided. At its formation, the *Hind Mazdoor Sabha* consisted of 427 unions representing more than 600,000 workers.

United Trade Union Congress, a third federation of trade unions, formed in 1949. This federation generally held left-wing political views and was often critical of the government's labor policy. It called for a socialist state of workers and peasants. It also sought nationalization of industries. The United Trade Union Congress sought to carry out these goals through peaceful and democratic means, using strikes only as a last resort. It had some 250 affiliated unions with nearly 332,000 members.

The fourth major labor federation was the All-India Trade Union Congress, one of the first modern trade associations in India. The oldest of the federations, AITUC was founded in 1920 by leaders of the Indian National Congress. Its purpose was to provide representation for India at the League of Nation's International Labor Organization (ILO). Furthermore, AITUC was an outgrowth of India's growing labor movement in the late nineteenth and early twentieth centuries.

Throughout the 1920s communists gained a great deal of control over the AITUC. By World War II they had gained complete control of the federation. They lost some backing when they decided to support the war effort on the side of the British, which caused AITUC to split between reformist and revolutionary factions. Nevertheless, at independence, AITUC, like some of the other federations, called for a socialist state and nationalization. AITUC was the biggest of the four federations in the late 1940s, with more than 600 member unions and nearly 800,000 members.

Events in Calcutta, July 1953

An example of the unrest in India during 1953 was the result of an increase in streetcar fares in the city of Calcutta during the month of July. On 1 July the city raised the fare for the second-class passage on Calcutta's streetcars. Many of the city's residents refused to pay the higher fare. By 3 July most streetcar service had been suspended as the situation grew violent. On that day, protesters twice attempted to set fire to streetcars. As the disorder increased, demonstrators threw fireworks at police and at a bus, injuring one child.

In response to the growing protests, authorities decided to arrest anyone who refused to pay the fare or leave the vehicle. This reaction in turn prompted a "resistance committee" to erect barricades throughout the city to inhibit streetcar service. Police had arrested some 300 people by the early afternoon even while the protestors threw stones at them. Among those arrested were three members of the West Bengal legislature, including two communists. Although service was restored by 3:00 P.M. to carry rush-hour traffic, there was no streetcar service after 6:30 P.M.. The communist-led "resistance committee" called for a strike to take place the following day to continue the protest.

The *hartal*, or general strike, virtually shut down the city for the next several days. On 5 July several policemen and demonstrators were injured in a number of confrontations. Notable among them was when the West Bengal police fired into a crowd of thousands protesting near the airport. The protestors had barricaded all roads approaching the area and stoned the police. Other demonstrators tried forcibly to prevent passengers from boarding the streetcars. As the police dispersed the crowd, they set fire to a railroad car. Police arrested more than 500 people that day for picketing, throwing bombs, and nonpayment of streetcar fares.

The situation worsened 10 days later when another general strike shut down Calcutta's stores, markets, and restaurants, once again to protest the increased streetcar fares. Protestors again impeded streetcar and bus service, attacking the vehicles with bombs, acid, and stones. Police fired on a crowd at Jadavpur, killing one person and injuring five others. Twelve policemen were injured by stones. Authorities arrested some 250 people on 15 July. Unrest grew that night and early the next morning, as strikers looted, set fires, and attacked police. Overnight, protestors uprooted the streetcar tracks and cut the overhead wires. Police again resorted to the use of force, firing on crowds and using tear gas. The police commissioner prohibited the assembly of five or more people. As tensions mounted, the government called in troops on 16 July to relieve a weary police force. The presence of the troops calmed the situation in the city, although sporadic violence still occurred over the next several days. For example, on the evening of 19 July, police refused to allow the demonstrators to hold a meeting. Protestors responded by barricading roads and breaking streetlights. In addition, the streetcars remained out of service for several days, impeding normal business activities in the city. Finally, by the end of the month, a semblance of order was restored to the city when the government suggested that the streetcar company suspend the fare increase until a tribunal could rule on the issue.

Key Players

Nehru, Jawaharlal (1889–1964): One of the leaders of India's independence movement in the 1930s and 1940s, Nehru became the first prime minister of independent India in 1947. He sought to modernize the country so as to achieve economic and social development. To do so, he implemented a series of five-year plans. Despite some successes, India continued to face numerous problems such as poverty and unemployment. Many of these problems contributed to a strike wave in 1953.

See also: *All-India Trade Union Congress; International Labor Organization.*

BIBLIOGRAPHY

Books

Brecher, Michael. *Nehru: A Political Biography.* London: Oxford University Press, 1959.

Raman Rao, A. V. *Indian Trade Unions.* Honolulu: University of Hawaii Industrial Relations Center, 1967.

Wolpert, Stanley. *A New History of India.* 4th ed. New York and Oxford: Oxford University Press, 1993.

—Ronald Young

Cananéa Strike

Mexico 1906

Synopsis

In the northern Mexican state of Sonora lies a quiet mining town called Cananéa. In 1906 this town witnessed a violent social struggle between labor and American capital. In June 1906 miners employed by Colonel William Greene, owner of the Cananea Consolidated Copper Company, declared a work stoppage in the mines of this usually quiet town. As the workers went on strike over wages and salaries, Greene pleaded with the national government of Porfírio Díaz for help in forcing the striking workers to return to their jobs. The result was catastrophic, as Greene imported American troops from the neighboring American state of Arizona. As the troops were called in, violence broke out, and more than 10 miners were killed in the process. The social turmoil that would later become known as the Mexican Revolution had begun in this small mining town.

Timeline

1886: Bombing at Haymarket Square, Chicago, kills seven policemen and injures numerous others. Eight anarchists are accused and tried; three are imprisoned, one commits suicide, and four are hanged.

Porfírio Díaz. The Library of Congress.

1891: Construction of Trans-Siberian Railway begins. Meanwhile, crop failures across Russia lead to widespread starvation.

1896: Nobel Prize is established.

1902: Second Anglo-Boer War ends in victory for Great Britain. It is a costly victory, however, resulting in the loss of more British lives (5,774) than any conflict between 1815 and 1914. The war also sees the introduction of concentration camps, used by the British to incarcerate Boer civilians.

1904: The ten-hour workday is established in France.

1906: After disputes resulting from the presidential election in Cuba, various Cuban parties invite the United States, under the 1901 Platt Amendment (which limits the terms of Cuban independence), to restore order. American troops begin a three-year occupation of the country.

1906: German neurologist Alois Alzheimer identifies the degenerative brain disorder that today bears his name.

1906: An earthquake, the worst ever to hit a U.S. city, strikes San Francisco on 18 April. It kills some 2,500 people, leaves another 250,000 homeless, and destroys more than $400 million worth of property.

1906: The British Labour Party begins.

1908: The Tunguska region of Siberia experiences a strange explosion, comparable to the detonation of a hydrogen bomb, whose causes will long be a subject of debate. Today many scientists believe that a comet caused the Tunguska event.

1912: *Titanic* sinks on its maiden voyage, from Southampton to New York, on 14 April. More than 1,500 people are killed.

1916: Battles of Verdun and the Somme on the Western Front. The latter sees the first use of tanks, by the British.

Event and Its Context

On 30 September 1899 American capitalist William Greene founded the Cananea Consolidated Copper Company with operations centered in Sonora, Mexico. The Cananea Company was one of Greene's international capitalistic ventures, which focused on agriculture and livestock. Greene's mining operation in Cananéa transformed the small town into a booming mining town. In 1891 Cananéa had a population of 100 villagers. By 1900 the town's population had expanded to over 14,000.

The mining community in Cananéa manifested economic and political inequalities with the emergence of this new operation. It became increasingly evident to many Mexican miners that their American counterparts would receive higher wages and better living conditions. The mining labor force included more than 3,500 men, of which 33 percent were Americans. The American workers held the higher-paying jobs such as camp supervisor. Moreover, when Mexican miners and American miners provided the same labor, the Mexicans received half the pay of the Americans. In Cananéa a common Mexican miner received three pesos a day while the American worker performing the same duties received between six and eight pesos a day. Clearly, the wage discrepancies were problematic for the Mexican workers.

In early 1906 workers clamored for some form of labor organization to redress their grievances against the American company. This association would be led by Manuel Diéguez and Esteban Baca Calderón, two miners who became aggravated by the social conditions of the working class in Sonora. Diéguez and Calderón assumed the leadership of the workers' movement. The miners association—which incidentally was influenced by the radical *Partido Liberal Mexicano* (PLM), whose leader, Ricardo Flores Magón, was exiled in Saint Louis, Missouri, for his radical views—specified certain social changes that needed to be implemented within the mining camps. The workers publicly demanded a minimum daily wage of five pesos; called for an eight hour workday; stated that 75 percent of the work force in the camps must be Mexican; and demanded equal pay for American and Mexican workers. This last demand was instrumental in the strategy of the leadership, which reflected a growing nationalism among the workers. They were manifestly disgruntled with the unfair and at times unequal treatment received by their Mexican colleagues. This sense of nationalism played a major role in the development of the strike. Within days, the association sent a petition to company representatives. After deliberations, the company refused the demands, citing the high comparative wages of the miners. In his response to the workers' demands, Greene intimated that the workers' job security was threatened by the aggressive actions of their leaders. Moreover, company officials in Cananéa increased the workloads of many of their workers in the mines. Once again, the actions of Greene seemed arbitrary and repressive to the Cananéa mining community. In response to the difficult work regimen, Diéguez and Calderón called for a strike. Mexican President Porfírio Díaz sent a telegram to the Sonoran governor stating that a work stoppage would not be tolerated by the national government. Diaz implied that any action taken by the workers would be met with the full force of the national government. Greene was also contemplating alternative forms of labor relations, specifically the deployment of American troops. Clearly, labor relations were intensifying in the northern mining community. On 31 May 1906 the night shift of the mines decided to begin a work stoppage in the camps. These night workers dropped their mining tools and walked out of the mines in an open act of defiance against both Greene and Díaz.

Heeding the call of the night workers for a work stoppage, the other sectors of the mining community joined the strike. On 1 June 1906 these workers walked the streets of Cananéa toward one of the many company stores located in the city. These company stores sold consumer goods at discounted prices to the workers. For many workers, they symbolized the negative influence of the American capitalist culture. Nevertheless, the workers entered the store and looted it. In the process, they set fire to the store and destroyed it. The actions angered the storeowner. Incensed by these actions, the American storeowner opened fire and killed two workers. Other workers throughout the city burned other buildings owned by the Greene interests. The local police forces were losing control of Cananéa and the Greene camps, as 3,500 workers walked the streets and

threatened American interests in the city. Greene was incensed at both the actions of the workers as well as the inactivity of the state governor and Díaz in dealing with the impending crisis. Greene and the American consul in Sonora decided to assume responsibility for dealing with the striking workers. Greene imported a detachment of American Rangers to deal with the crisis. By 3 June 1906 the rioting had stopped and Cananéa was once again in a peaceful state. On the same day, many miners either returned to work or fled into the neighboring hills. The leaders of the striking workers were captured and sent to prison as political agitators.

The actions of the workers in Cananéa were neither historically nor socially isolated. The arbitrary nature of the regime of Porfírio Díaz inspired the actions of the workers. As the workers went on strike in Cananéa, workers in the mining town of Río Blanco in Veracrúz also declared a general work stoppage against the arbitrary powers of the local mill owners. Second, the Cananéa strike must be understood within the context of an intensification of the relationship between foreign capital and the regime of Porfírio Díaz. Díaz had invited foreign capital into Mexico to develop the nation's infrastructure and economy. By the end of Díaz's regime in 1910, American capitalists like William Greene owned close to 75 percent of the Mexican national economy. This elicited a nationalistic response not only from the workers in Cananéa but in other areas of the Mexican working force. This nationalism, first expressed overtly by the workers in Cananéa, proved to be a major force in the development of the Mexican political and social arena over the next few years.

Impact

The events in Cananéa had both short- and long-term ramifications for the Mexican economy and polity. To a large degree, the strike and the ensuing repression shocked the Mexican political system. The Díaz system prided itself on stability and order. The actions of the Cananéa workers undermined this stability by threatening foreign interests. Moreover, within three years opposition leaders such as Francisco I. Madero would be influenced by the actions of the Cananéa workers and the PLM. Madero would become the initial leader of what came to be known as the Mexican Revolution, a social revolution that began in 1910 and lasted 27 years. In the long run, however, the actions of the Cananéa workers indicated a growing nationalism against foreign capital. Workers in the mining community responded to the alliance between American capital and the national elites in Sonora and Mexico City. This alliance symbolized a parasitical relationship for the workers. Díaz's *vende-patria* policies offered fuel to the nationalistic tendencies of the working class. His defense of foreign interests in the labor conflict fed the nationalistic interests of not only the Cananéa workers but, more importantly, the entire working class. The arbitrary actions of the Díaz regime led to its downfall in 1910. Finally, the actions in 1906 indicated a growing awareness by Mexican workers of the impact of industrialization and modernization on their economic system. To a large degree, the economic policies of the past 35 years and the introduction and ubiquity of foreign capital in Mexican territory forced a reevaluation of these policies, especially after 1906. The reevaluations involved deciding whether industrialization provided benefits and goods to the worker or whether industrialization merely increased the intense nationalism of the workers who were charged with carrying out this industrialization. Essentially, the actions of the Cananéa strikers highlighted the danger of rapid industrialization in a society ill-equipped to handle such complex processes.

Key Players

Díaz, Porfírio (1830–1915): President of Mexico from 1876 to 1910, Díaz was instrumental in the pacification of the Cananéa workers. He was toppled in a coup in 1910 and forced to flee the country.

Diéguez, Manuel: Leader of the Cananéa Mining Workers Community, Diéguez was instrumental in calling a general work stoppage in the mining centers. A former miner, Diéguez was imprisoned after the strike.

Greene, Colonel William (1851–1911): American owner of Cananea Consolidated Company, Greene was also owner of numerous multinational enterprises specializing in cattle and agriculture.

BIBLIOGRAPHY

Books

Anderson, Rodney. *Outcasts in their Own Land: Mexican Industrial Workers, 1906–1911.* De Kalb: Northern Illinois University Press, 1976.

Hart, John Mason. *Anarchism and the Mexican Working Class, 1860–1930.* Austin: University of Texas Press, 1978.

Trueba Lara, José Luis. *Cananea, 1906.* Sonora: Gobierno del Estado de Sonora, 1989.

—Jaime Ramon Olivares

Carlisle Indian School

United States 1879

Synopsis

The Carlisle Indian Industrial School, located on the site of an army barracks in Carlisle, Pennsylvania, was founded by Richard Henry Pratt, an army officer who remained the school's driving force until he resigned in 1904. The purpose of the school, the first nonreservation Indian school funded by the federal government, was to "civilize" Native American children by removing them from their reservations, immersing them in the values of white society, and teaching them a trade.

Timeline

1859: Building of the Suez Canal begins.

1864: George M. Pullman and Ben Field patent their design for a sleeping car with folding upper berths.

1869: The first U.S. transcontinental railway is completed.

1871: U.S. troops in the West begin fighting the Apache nation.

1876: General George Armstrong Custer and 264 soldiers are killed by the Sioux at the Little Big Horn River.

1877: Nez Perce leader Chief Joseph surrenders to federal troops.

1879: Thomas Edison invents the incandescent electric light.

1879: Great Britain fights the Zulus in South Africa, bringing an end to the nation founded by Shaka Zulu in 1816.

1879: F. W. Woolworth opens his first department store, in Lancaster, Pennsylvania.

1881: In a shootout at the O.K. Corral outside Tombstone, Arizona, Wyatt, Virgil, and Morgan Earp, along with "Doc" Holliday, kill Billy Clanton, Frank McLowry, and Tom McLowry. This breaks up a gang headed by Clanton's brother Ike, who flees Tombstone. The townspeople, however, suspect the Earps and Holliday of murder. During the same year, Sheriff Pat Garrett shoots notorious criminal William Bonney, a.k.a. Billy the Kid, in Fort Sumner, New Mexico.

1885: Sudanese capital of Khartoum falls to forces under the Mahdi Mohammed Ahmed, whose forces massacre British General Charles "Chinese" Gordon and his garrison just before a British relief expedition reaches the city.

1889: Indian Territory in Oklahoma is opened to settlement.

Event and Its Context

Background

In the years following the Civil War, federal and state authorities wrestled with what was referred to as the "Indian problem." As the nation's borders pressed inexorably westward, federal troops did frequent battle with Native American tribes, usually—but not always—with brutal success. In 1867 General Winfield Hancock led an unsuccessful campaign against the Plains tribes. General Philip Sheridan had more success in the winter of 1868–1869, but the Plains tribes were not broken until the Red River War of 1874–1875. To the north, the government's campaign against the Native Americans led to the disastrous Battle of Little Bighorn in 1876. In the Northwest, General George Crook defeated the Paiutes of northern California and southern Oregon in 1867–1868. In the Southwest, federal troops carried on a running battle with the Apache, often having to pursue them across the Mexican border until the Apache surrendered in the mid-1880s.

As armed conflict began to slow and finally end, the question that remained for the authorities was what to do with the Native American tribes. Some whites advocated preservation and development of a distinct Native American culture on the reservations, whereas others thought that the only way the Native American could survive in a white man's world was to become, in effect, as much like the white man as possible and be assimilated into white culture. Among those who took this position was a young cavalry lieutenant who had taken part in the campaigns of 1867–1868 and 1874–1875, Richard Henry Pratt.

In 1867 Pratt, an officer in the Tenth Cavalry stationed at Fort Sill, Oklahoma, assumed command of a regiment of African American "Buffalo Soldiers" whose task was to keep the Native Americans on the reservations and protect white settlers from raiding parties. During these years (1867–1875) Pratt developed a deep and abiding distrust of the Bureau of Indian Affairs, which he repeatedly harassed with complaints about the pitiful provisions—rancid beef, diseased livestock, poor grain—that the bureau provided for the reservations. These conditions, Pratt believed, made it inevitable that the Native Americans would try to escape the reservations to find game.

In 1875 the government, frustrated with its inability to control the "hostiles," decided to incarcerate 72 Native Americans at Fort Marion in St. Augustine, Florida. These prisoners were in effect hostages held to ensure the good behavior of their kinfolk out west. Appointed as their jailer was Pratt, who, with the help of local women who volunteered their services, taught the Native American prisoners to read. He enforced military discipline, promoted arts and crafts, and even allowed many of the Natives to find work as laborers in the local community. Then in 1878, when Pratt was transferred to the Hampton Institute in Virginia to organize the school's Indian Branch, he persuaded 17 of his Fort Marion prisoners to follow him there and enroll at the school. The Hampton Institute, founded in 1868 by Samuel Chapman Armstrong, was a boarding school for African Americans; its goal was to train "the head, the hearts, and the hands" of students, then return them to their communities where they could become leaders and professionals.

During this period Pratt's educational philosophy began to take shape. In many respects he found the Hampton philosophy consonant with his own, although he believed that the only lasting solution to the Native American problem was assimilation. With this end in view, he began an aggressive campaign to create a Native American school that would be supported with federal funds augmented by donations from wealthy backers, many of whom had vacationed in the St. Augustine area and had expressed support for Pratt's efforts. Those efforts began to bear fruit in 1879, when he received permission from the U.S. Secretary of the Interior to take over a deserted army barracks in Carlisle, Pennsylvania, for this purpose. In September he headed to the Dakota Territory, where he recruited a total of 82 students from the Rosebud and Pine Ridge reservations, overcoming the skepticism of tribal leaders by arguing that only by learning English and the white man's ways could the Indians ever protect their own interests. Meanwhile, two of his former Fort Marion prisoners recruited students from Kiowa and Cheyenne reservations further south. Pratt arrived at the Carlisle train station with his students in the middle of the night on 6 October—only to discover that the provisions he had been promised, including beds, food, and clothing, had not arrived. Pratt immediately turned around to accompany the Kiowa and Cheyenne students to the school; when he returned, the needed provisions, with one exception, still had not appeared. The exception was an organ.

James Francis Thorpe, in football uniform of Carlisle Indian School, 1909. National Archives and Records Administration.

The Carlisle Curriculum

When students arrived at the school in native dress, the staff immediately cut the students' hair. The school provided military uniforms for the boys and Victorian-style dresses for the girls. Pratt and his staff enforced strict military discipline: students were organized into companies with a hierarchy of officers, and they marched to classes and the dining hall. They were forbidden to speak their native languages, so they learned English by total immersion. One can only imagine the sense of dislocation students felt as they left their families and communities and entered this utterly alien environment—though many in later years conceded in autobiographies that after a while they adapted and took pride in their personal accomplishments and in those of the school.

Pratt often expressed his philosophy in a single statement: "Kill the Indian, save the man." A central part of his effort to assimilate nomadic Native Americans into white society was the school's industrial program, which was designed to help the Native Americans enter the U.S. labor force. Like many reservation schools, the Carlisle school followed a "half-day" curriculum. Half of the day was spent on academic subjects such as

Carlisle Indian School. National Archives and Records Administration.

English, writing, arithmetic, drama, and geography. The other half was devoted to industrial education. Thus, every student learned a craft. For the boys, these included industrial crafts such as tinsmithing, construction, carpentry, and farming. The girls learned cooking, sewing, laundry, baking, and similar domestic arts. Students received payment for their work, and the school staff encouraged them to save their earnings. Additionally, the school maintained an extensive printing shop that they used to publish newspapers and magazines. This trained students in printing and gave Pratt—a tireless advocate for the school—the opportunity to promulgate his views and to raise funds.

An important component of the school's industrial program was the so-called outing system. During the summer months students did not return to their reservations. Instead, Pratt continued the process of "detribalizing" them by placing them for hire with non–Native American families. Many worked on farms; some worked at the Wanamakers department store in Philadelphia. Some eventually remained with the families year-round and attended local public schools. For business owners, craftsmen, and farmers, the outing system was a good source of cheap, reliable labor.

Postscript

Until his retirement in 1904, Pratt remained in nearly continual conflict with government officials over Native American policy. He also incurred the enmity of reservation schools in the West, whose superintendents felt that Pratt's school siphoned off scarce funds that they needed. Some people were highly critical of his methods, including Zitkala-sa (Gertrude Simmons Bonnin), a teacher at the Carlisle school who frequently clashed with Pratt over his methods and argued that the school left students suspended between two worlds, ill equipped either to return to their reservations or to enter white society.

By some measures the Carlisle school was a success. During the school's 39-year history more than 10,000 students attended. Every student took music classes and received private instruction, and the school band performed in every presidential inaugural parade during the life of the school. Drama productions at the school attracted large audiences, and original works of art created by the school's students are still highly valued. Sports fans will recognize the name of student Jim Thorpe, who won gold medals in the 1912 Olympics, led the school's football team to winning records against college competition, and went on to a career in professional baseball and in the National Football League. Ironically, though, most of the students who attended Carlisle returned to their reservations rather than entering the white labor force, although some, to Pratt's dismay, joined Buffalo Bill Cody's Wild West Show.

The school's prominence could not ensure its continued existence. In the immediate aftermath of World War I, the Carlisle barracks were returned to the army and became the site of the U.S. Army War College.

Key Players

Bonnin, Gertrude Simmons (orig. Zitkala-sa, 1876–1938): Bonnin was born Zitkala-sa, which means Red Bird in Sioux, in South Dakota and attended a Quaker school in Wabash, Indiana. At the age of 19 she enrolled in Earlham College in Indiana, where she distinguished herself as an orator. After teaching at Carlisle for two years, she published short stories and essays in such magazines as *Atlantic* and *Harper's* and studied at the New England Conservatory of Music in Boston, where she met and married Raymond Bonnin. As Gertrude Bonnin, she became a leading Native American activist, serving as secretary of the Society of American Indians and editor of the *American Indian Magazine*. In 1926 she and her husband organized the National Congress of American Indians.

Pratt, Richard Henry (1840–1924): Pratt was born in Rushford, New York, and grew up in Logansport, Indiana. With the outbreak of the Civil War he joined the Ninth Indiana Infantry, then served as a junior officer in the Eleventh Indiana Cavalry. After briefly trying the hardware business, he returned to the army in 1867 to command a regiment of African American soldiers on the western frontier. After leaving Carlisle in 1904 and retiring from the army as a general, he devoted himself to public discussion of Indian affairs.

Thorpe, James Francis (1888–1953): Born Wa-tho-huck (Bright Path) near Shawnee, Oklahoma, Thorpe was sent to the Carlisle school in 1904. In 1909 he left to play two seasons of minor league baseball, then returned in 1911 to lead the Carlisle football team to an 11–1 record. In 1912 he won gold medals in the pentathlon and decathlon at the Olympics in Stockholm, though he was later stripped of the medals when it was learned that he had played professional baseball. (The medals were returned to his family in 1982.) He played professional baseball and football before being named the first commissioner of the NFL in 1920. In 1950 the Associated Press named him the greatest athlete of the first half of the twentieth century, and he was inducted into the College and Pro Football Halls of Fame.

BIBLIOGRAPHY

Books

Adams, David Wallace. *Education for Extinction: American Indians and the Boarding School Experience, 1875–1928.* Lawrence: University Press of Kansas, 1995.

Coleman, Michael C. *American Indian Children at School, 1850–1930.* Jackson: University of Mississippi Press, 1993.

Pratt, Richard Henry. *Battlefield and Classroom: Four Decades with the American Indian, 1867–1904.* Lincoln: University of Nebraska Press, 1964 (reprint, 1987).

Witmer, Linda F. *The Indian Industrial School, Carlisle, Pennsylvania, 1879–1918.* Carlisle, PA: Cumberland County Historical Society, 1993.

Other

Carlisle Indian Industrial School Web site [cited 3 September 2002]. <www.carlisleindianschool.org>.

—Michael J. O'Neal

Charleroi Confrontation Between Miners and the Military

Belgium 1868

Synopsis

The confrontation in Charleroi, Belgium, is commonly called *la grève [strike] de l'Épine*. Starting in 1867, severe wage cuts resulted in numerous strikes in the coal fields of Charleroi and the Borinage. On 26 March 1868 a coalition of some 3,000 miners assembled and occupied L'Épine, the mine located in Montigny-sur-Sambre. Acting on orders, soldiers charged the crowd, which caused at least 10 casualties and heavily injured some strikers. A widely publicized trial and the intense propaganda of the Brussels section of the First International following the events ensured that, according to Marx, "after the affair of Charleroi, the success of the International in Belgium was assured." For the first time the idea of working-class strength through organization was spread on a large scale in Belgium, which was to host one of the strongest socialist labor movements in the world prior to 1914.

Timeline

1851: China's T'ai P'ing ("Great Peace") Rebellion begins under the leadership of schoolmaster Hong Xiuquan, who believes himself the younger brother of Jesus Christ. He mobilizes the peasantry against the Manchu emperors in a civil war that will take 20 to 30 million lives over the next 14 years.

1857: The Sepoy Mutiny, an unsuccessful revolt by Indian troops against the British East India Company begins. As a result of the rebellion, which lasts into 1858, England places India under direct crown rule.

1863: The world's first subway opens, in London.

1867: Dual monarchy is established in Austria-Hungary.

1867: Maximilian surrenders to Mexican forces under Benito Juarez and is executed. Thus ends Napoleon III's dreams for a new French empire in the New World.

1867: The Dominion of Canada is established.

1867: United States purchases Alaska from Russia for $7.2 million.

1867: Meiji Restoration in Japan ends 675 years of rule by the shoguns.

1867: Karl Marx publishes the first volume of *Das Kapital.*

1871: U.S. troops in the West begin fighting the Apache nation.

1874: As farm wages in Britain plummet, agricultural workers go on strike.

1877: Great Britain's Queen Victoria is proclaimed the empress of India.

1882: The Chinese Exclusion Act, a treaty between the United States and China, provides for restrictions on immigration of Chinese workers.

1884: Chicago's Home Life Insurance Building, designed by William LeBaron Jenney, becomes the world's first skyscraper.

Event and Its Context

Belgium—a territory the size of the state of Maryland—was the second country in the world to industrialize. Industrial production had already outgrown agricultural output by around 1870. Geographically, this process of industrialization was limited to the Walloon provinces, the French-speaking southern part of Belgium, the cotton city of Ghent being the only exception. The main centers of industrialization were Verviers (wool), Liège (metal and coal), Charleroi (iron and coal), and the Borinage (coal). Given the economy's dependence on the import of raw materials and the export of products, it was highly sensitive to competition and economic fluctuations. The presence of a large labor force surplus made low wages the most efficient way to cut production costs and lowered the chances of successful trade union activity. The standard of living of the Belgian industrial workers was the lowest of all the industrialized countries. In the midst of the tremendous changes set off by industrialization, many farmers, members of the middle class, and workers tried to create new forms of solidarity to protect themselves from economic insecurity. The judicial position of all types of workers in this "little paradise of the landlord, the capitalist, and the priest" was extremely poor. The first social legislation dates from 1890, and voting rights were not extended until 1894. General suffrage for men—in the form of one man, one vote—was not introduced until after World War I.

The spectacular expansion of the mining industry during the 1840s and 1850s slowed down considerably in the 1860s. Nevertheless, the number of workers in mining kept growing. Between 1850 and 1875 the number of workers employed in coal mines almost doubled from about 48,000 to nearly 92,000. In 1861 mine owners agreed on a unified exploitation regulation designed to minimize inland competition. This regulation resulted in a deterioration of the working conditions and even made workers responsible for all damages to any material they used. This triggered labor unrest. The first of numerous strikes and conflicts in the 1860s contrasted sharply with the absence of such events during the 1850s. Although it does not imply any direct causal relation between movements of real wages and social agitation, the parallel between increased social unrest and substantial decreases of the real wage index numbers in 1861–1862 and especially 1867–1868 is remarkable. In 1867, for instance, daily wages in the Charleroi basin decreased from 3.05 to 2.79 francs, while the cost of living index went up from 86 to 107. The announcement of yet another wage cut of 5 to 6 percent on 23 March 1868 at the Gouffre mine at Châtelineau set off a wave of strikes in the area.

The far-outnumbered police force of Châtelineau was unable to avoid mutiny. The strikers engaged in a series of destructive acts and "visited" several other mines. On 26 March 1968 some 3,000 men reached l'Épine in Montigny-sur-Sambre, where they stopped work, broke windows, and threw away workbooks that were a symbol of the judicial inferiority of workers because they implied the possibility that workers could not change bosses even if they had complied with all their contractual obligations. The appeal to send troops to l'Épine was answered immediately. The company of 120 men under the command of Major Quenne encircled some 600 miners in the inner court of the mine. When the surrounded miners threatened to destroy the ventilation system, Quenne ordered his men to charge the crowd and force the evacuation of the mine. This resulted in chaos. Strikers fled while throwing stones. The soldiers' bayonets caused at least 10 casualties and left several strikers badly injured. During the next few days, the situation was remarkably calm, and by Monday, 30 March, most miners went back to work without any satisfaction. Some hard-liners kept demanding a raise, but by Wednesday, 1 April, even they gave in and went back to work at the lower wages. Through the fall of 1868 several small partial strikes occurred, but not once did the workers gain anything. In August that year, 22 strikers involved in the episode at l'Épine were put on trial for the destruction of property and the intent to kill soldiers, a charge that even liberal newspapers catalogued as hugely exaggerated. Thanks to a brilliant defense by young liberal lawyers from Brussels, the accused were all acquitted on the plea that the workers' actions had been provoked by an unreasonable cut in wages and that their preliminary imprisonment of five months was in itself adequate punishment.

The mediation of Cesar de Paepe and the Brussels section of the First International—founded in July 1865—inspired these lawyers, who included Paul Janson, to take up this defense. The acquittal of the strikers therefore added immensely to the prestige of the International, which was further stimulated by the organization of and the publicity surrounding the Brussels Congress of the International in September 1868. In the immediate aftermath of the events of March 1868, the Internationalists from Brussels started an intense campaign with propaganda meetings all over the Walloon area. By December 1868 some 156 such meetings had occurred; in the course of 1869 this campaign intensified and 540 meetings, an average of more than 10 a week, took place. By the end of 1869 these activities resulted in the foundation of 70 local sections of the International in the south, and in the Flanders—the northern Dutch-speaking part of Belgium—the International had active sections in Ghent and Antwerp. The Internationalists were mainly concerned with spreading the word that workers should organize in trade unions and cooperatives, for as long as they lacked organization any strike was doomed to fail and would be nothing but a waste of strength and energy. In his pamphlet, "The Belgian Massacres," which was entirely based on a report, "Les Massacres de Seraing," by Eugène Hins of Brussels, Karl Marx even typified a strike as "a blasphemy."

In spite of this theoretical stand, it was precisely in the context of strikes that contact between militants of the International and the workers was established. Moreover, the mushrooming of local sections was mainly due to the spread of the myth that the International had millions of members and inexhaustible resources. Basically the Internationalists tried to create a labor movement by making workers believe that such a movement already existed. The main problem was, of course, how one was to keep workers from going on strike, as they were convinced that strikes must be effective given the support of the "Bank of London," as the International was sometimes called. Although it could cope easily with small and partial strikes, the organization of meetings, and the occasional donation of legal and medical assistance, in April 1869 the International was completely overwhelmed by a new wave of strikes that spread over the whole mining region in the course of a few days. The announcement on 2 April 1869 that all workers would have to work longer to keep their wages set off a strike in the Cockerill factories of Seraing (Liège). To break the strike, management immediately met some of the strikers' demands, only to revoke its promises a few days later. On 9 April all puddlers at Cockerill went on strike, immediately followed by their colleagues in several other factories in the Liège area. That day and again on 10 April 1869 troops charged the crowds, causing three casualties and injuring several others. The International explicitly dissociated itself from the strike and appealed to the strikers to remain calm and serene.

The puddlers maintained the strike until the 21st; on 15 April they were joined by miners all over the Borinage, where another bloody clash between strikers and armed forces occurred at Frameries. The synchronicity and scope of both strikes convinced judicial authorities that this was the work of a revolutionary conspiracy by the International. Authorities arrested several leaders of the International and conducted a large-scale investigation. The attorney general did everything in his power to indict the "bandits," but could not find any proof of such a conspiracy. All of the arrested and incarcerated Internationalists were released after a month. Similar panic reigned again in higher circles following the Paris Commune, but once again no ties could be established to the organizations of the International. By that time the International was disintegrating rapidly. The fact that except for the usual meetings it remained absent during the whole April 1869 episode dealt a fatal blow to the organization's reputation. The regional federations of the International still existed until the early 1870s, but the locals that comprised the organization disappeared as quickly as they had appeared. Exactly how many workers at one time or another belonged to the mostly short-lived organizations of the International is unclear. Historians have estimated between 50,000 and 250,000. However, considering the size of Belgium and the short period in which the International deployed its activity, it is clear that the impact of the International was huge.

The only direct result of the strikes and the confrontations between workers and the military in 1868–1869 was an official inquiry into the working conditions in the mines. The indirect consequences were far reaching, however. Paternalist strategies expanded from merely being considered means of managing the human resources of the factory. Paternalism became a political strategy and was then perceived as the main instrument for countering socialist propaganda. Considering the wages, it was nearly impossible to set up powerful trade unions, and therefore

one of the main objectives of the Internationalists had been the creation of consumer cooperatives. Industrialists responded immediately and created stores that they dubbed "cooperatives"—most of them were company stores—and in 1873 took steps to change the legislation governing cooperatives. Although the record of the First International was far from successful, its approach and accomplishments marked the history of the labor movement in Belgium in a profound way. In 1880 the remaining members of what once was the Ghent local section of the International set up a cooperative *Vooruit* that was to be the backbone and money-maker of the whole socialist labor movement. The success of *Vooruit*, which was often called "the socialist Rochdale" ensured that after another violent confrontation between military and workers in 1886 the formula of the interdependence and unity of political, trade union, and cooperative labor organizations would be copied by Social Democrats and later on by Christian Democrats all over Belgium. According to Georges Haupt, this so-called Belgian socialist model probably had more influence on the formation of European socialist parties than did the organizational model of the German Social Democratic Party.

Key Players

De Paepe, César (1842–1890): De Paepe was a printer and physician. He became a renowned theoretician of international socialism. Positioned "between Marx and Bakunin," he was among the founding members of the Belgian section of the International, dominated the socialist movement in Brussels, and was the driving force behind the establishment of the influential Belgian Labor Party in 1885.

Hins, Eugène (1839–1923): Hins was a teacher and journalist. He published *L'International* and was the general secretary of the Belgian section of the International, organizing the spread of the movement to the Charleroi region and the Borinage. He participated in the Paris Commune and later lived in exile in Russia. In 1900 he returned to Belgium and became a key figure in the Belgian and international freethinkers movement.

See also: *First International; Paris Commune.*

BIBLIOGRAPHY

Books

Dandois, Bernard. *Entre Marx et Bakounine: César de Paepe. Correspondance. Textes de présentation et notes par Bernard Dandois.* Paris: Maspero, 1974.

Devreese, Daisy E. *Documents Relatifs aux Militants Belges de l'Association Internationale des Travailleurs: Correspondance 1865–1872.* Louvain-Brussels: Nauwelaerts, 1986.

Gubin, Eliane. "Libéralisme Économique et paternalisme en Belgique au XIXe Siècle." In *Liberalism and Paternalism in the 19th Century*, edited by E. Aerts, et al. Louvain: University Press, 1990.

Haupt, George. "Socialisme et Syndicalisme. Les Rapports Entre Parti et Syndicat au Plan International. Une

Mutation?" In *Jaurès et la Classe Ouvrière,* edited by M. Rebérioux. Paris: Ed. Ouvrieères, 1981.

Henneaux-Depooter, Louise. *Misères et Luttes Sociales dans le Hainaut, 1860–1869.* Brussels: University Press, 1959.

Mayné, Marc. *Eugène Hins: Une Grande Figure de la Première Internationale en Belgique.* Brussels: Académie Royale de Belgique, 1994.

Oukhow, Catherina. *Documents Relatifs à l'Histoire de la Première Internationale en Wallonie.* Louvain-Brussels: Nauwelaerts, 1967.

Puissant, Jean. *L'Évolution du Mouvement Ouvrier Socialiste dans le Borinage.* Brussels: Académie Royale de Belgique, 1982.

Scholliers, Peter. "The Cost of Living in Nineteenth-century Belgium." In *Studia Historica Oeconomica: Liber Amicorum Herman Van der Wee*, edited by E. Aerts, et al. Louvain: University Press, 1993.

Wouters, Hubert. *Documenten Betreffende de Geschiedenis der Arbeidersbeweging ten Tijde van de Ie Internationale 1866–1880.* 3 vols. Louvain-Paris: Nauwelaerts, 1970–1971.

Periodicals

Devreese, Daisy. E. "Vestiging van het Internationaal Werkliedenverbond in België 1865–1868." *Tijdschrift voor Sociale Geschiedenis.* (1976): 42–56.

ADDITIONAL RESOURCES

Books

Deneckere, Gita. *Sire, Het Volk Mort: Sociaal Protest in België, 1831–1940.* Ghent-Antwerp: AMSAB-Houtekiet, 1997.

Knudsen, Knud. "The Strike History of the First International." In *Internationalism in the Labour Movement, 1830–1940*, edited by F. van Holthoon and M. van der Linden, et. al. Leiden, The Netherlands: Brill, 1988.

Strikwerda, Carl. *A House Divided: Catholics, Socialists, and Flemish Nationalists in Nineteenth Century Belgium.* New York: Rowman & Littlefield, 1997.

—Hendrik Defoort

Charter of Amiens

France 1906

Synopsis

The Charter of Amiens was a statement of anarcho-syndicalist principles adopted overwhelmingly at the annual congress of the major French trade union, the Confédération Générale du Travail (CGT), when it met in the city of Amiens on 8–16 October 1906. The charter quickly attained mythical status, principally for its emphasis on the importance of keeping trade union affairs separate from political parties. A close look at the charter shows that it was less a blanket endorsement of anarcho-syndicalism than an expression of the conflicting strains within French unionism and a realistic reflection of political realities. Within the CGT, support for the charter came from a broad political coalition that spanned left to right and united mainly in opposition to Marxist domination. While revolutionary syndicalists tried to avoid entanglements with the state, one of the chief reasons for the charter's success was a tacit acknowledgement of government legislation that restricted political participation among trade unionists.

Timeline

1886: Bombing at Haymarket Square, Chicago, kills seven policemen and injures numerous others. Eight anarchists are accused and tried; three are imprisoned, one commits suicide, and four are hanged.

1891: Construction of Trans-Siberian Railway begins. Meanwhile, crop failures across Russia lead to widespread starvation.

1896: Nobel Prize is established.

1902: Second Anglo-Boer War ends in victory for Great Britain. It is a costly victory, however, resulting in the loss of more British lives (5,774) than any conflict between 1815 and 1914. The war also sees the introduction of concentration camps, used by the British to incarcerate Boer civilians.

1904: The ten-hour workday is established in France.

1906: After disputes resulting from the presidential election in Cuba, various Cuban parties invite the United States, under the 1901 Platt Amendment (which limits the terms of Cuban independence), to restore order. American troops begin a three-year occupation of the country.

1906: German neurologist Alois Alzheimer identifies the degenerative brain disorder that today bears his name.

1906: An earthquake, the worst ever to hit a U.S. city, strikes San Francisco on 18 April. It kills some 2,500 people, leaves another 250,000 homeless, and destroys more than $400 million worth of property.

1906: The British Labour Party begins.

1908: The Tunguska region of Siberia experiences a strange explosion, comparable to the detonation of a hydrogen bomb, whose causes will long be a subject of debate. Today many scientists believe that a comet caused the Tunguska event.

1912: *Titanic* sinks on its maiden voyage, from Southampton to New York, on 14 April. More than 1,500 people are killed.

1916: Battles of Verdun and the Somme are fought on the Western Front. The latter sees the first use of tanks, by the British.

Event and Its Context

The Charter

Considered a classic statement of anarcho-syndicalist goals, the charter combined an extremely practical trade unionism with a call for revolution, based on a commitment to a new trade union tactic, the general strike. Written by Victor Griffuelhes, general secretary of the CGT, and Emile Pouget, the editor of the CGT's journal, the charter asserted that trade unions had a dual task as engines of social improvement and as tools of social transformation. Engaging in strikes to raise wages and improve working conditions were legitimate goals for radical trade unionists, for separate strikes for immediate demands might converge into a general strike that could bring about a new social order. Trade unions were the best representatives of workers' interests and the most capable of carrying out social revolution. Relations with political parties would only divide the labor movement.

Origins of the Charter

The charter emerged in response to a series of challenges to the anarcho-syndicalist leadership of the CGT. Months in advance of the Amiens meeting, a group of Marxist trade unionists announced their intent to introduce a resolution authorizing CGT leaders to consult with Socialist Party leaders about opportunities for social reform. The Marxists in question were followers of Jules Guesde, a doctrinaire whose talent for dividing movements was as remarkable as his ability to attract loyal followers. Guesde believed in the "iron law of wages" and argued that strikes could not successfully raise wages. Guesde's belief in the futility of demands for raising wages and bettering conditions provided little role for trade unions except to educate and mobilize their members for socialism. Guesde's combination of Marxism and sectarianism had wrecked earlier efforts to create a national trade union movement. Guesde's followers hoped that the creation of a unified Socialist Party in 1905, a party in which they had great influence, might provide a new opportunity to establish socialist control over the trade unions.

The anarcho-syndicalist leadership of the CGT used the fear of Guesdist Marxism to rally conservative trade unionists around their anarcho-syndicalist program. At Amiens, the CGT leadership also faced a challenge from conservative trade unionists who believed that wages and working conditions should be the exclusive concern of the union movement. A group of conservative trade unionists let it be known that they intended to submit a resolution opposing the antimilitarist propaganda carried out in the trade unions by some CGT leaders and by a small coterie of followers of the fiery Gustave Hervé. Conservative trade unionists not only opposed formal connections with political parties but argued that antimilitarism was a brand of politics pursued by the CGT leadership. In the context of the increasing hostility between France and Germany that would shortly yield World War I, antimilitarism was certainly a highly controversial policy, one that attracted opposition among conservative unionists and the liberal politicians sympathetic to the trade union movement and even among many socialists.

The charter was intended to persuade conservative trade unonists that anarcho-syndicalism constituted less of a threat to their everyday trade union practices than Marxist socialism. The charter validated strikes for higher wages that the conservatives saw as the main task of the labor movement. Also to the conservative's taste, the resolution promised no ties to socialist parties. Conservatives dreaded the thought of relations with any Socialist Party, but particularly with one influenced by Jules Guesde. In his address at Amiens, Griffuelhes maintained a distance from the leadership of the antimilitarist campaigns, although he did not condemn them. Syndicalist principles posed no challenge to their day-to-day practices, and conservative trade unionists ultimately came around to support the charter.

Despite his mastery of revolutionary rhetoric, Victor Griffuelhes was an astute politician and went out of his way to court the moderate socialists. In the weeks preceding the congress, for example, Griffuelhes attended a trade union meeting in Carmaux, the electoral bailiwick of the great French moderate socialist, Jean Jaurès. Griffuelhes praised Carmaux as a model of militant class struggle and skillfully suggested that if less dogmatic Jaurèsian socialists were at the helm of the new Socialist Party (instead of the sectarian Guesdists), it might be possible to restore healthy relations with the CGT.

More important considerations led many moderate socialists to endorse the resolution. By insisting on the separation of political parties and trade unions, the Charter countered a growing source of tension and turmoil within the French trade union movement. The legal recognition of trade unions had come very late in France, and French law, chiefly the law of 1884, strictly regulated the conduct of trade unions. Among other restrictions, the law forbade trade unions from dealing with religious or political questions. State authorities had considerable power to enforce this law: indeed until 1901, the authorities possessed the right to dissolve trade unions almost any time they wished to do so.

In the years before 1906, conflicts over the legal status of trade unions emerged most sharply within the *Bourse du Travail* movement affiliated with the CGT. The Bourses were labor exchanges run by the trade union movement; most received subsidies from municipal government. The law of 1884 granted corporate status only to local trade unions. Such legislation greatly weakened the strength of the national organizations vis-à-vis their local branches. Making use of the local strength of French trade unions, the Bourses linked trade unions across occupations within a city or region and exerted a powerful political influence at the local level.

As the influence of the Bourses grew, the organizations came into confrontation with the local and even national government. In many cities, the local Socialist Parties controlled the Bourses. These parties used the Bourses to oppose republican or even moderate socialist municipal governments. When the Bourses became too militant or too overtly political, such as occurred in Paris or Limoges, municipal governments could always use the 1884 law to shut down a local Bourse, a move that often brought a city's trade union movement to a screeching halt. The delegates at Amiens were not hostile to Socialist Parties per se; very likely most of the delegates at Amiens ignored anarchists calls to abstain from elections and voted for Socialist Parties. Yet by 1906, after their experience with the politicization of the Bourses, even many moderate socialists could see the wisdom of avoiding a close relationship with left-wing parties. Moderate socialist support combined with that of the conservatives and anarcho-syndicalists helped to make the final vote for the charter overwhelming, with 830 voting in favor, 8 opposed, and one abstention. The vote made it appear that the charter reflected the will of the broad trade union movement, not just that of a handful of syndicalist militants.

The premiership of Georges Clemenceau (1906–1909) tested these beliefs. A social reformer, Clemeanceau was committed to bringing the CGT to heel. His policy of confrontation helped produce the bloody events of Villeneuve-Saint-Georges (1908). At Villeneuve, CGT leaders could not prevent the overzealous actions of newly unionized building workers. They were unable to launch a general strike to protest the repression of the building workers. Almost all of the CGT leadership was arrested in the action. Faced with the full force of government repression, many syndicalists began to turn to the political order for defense. The speedy decline of militant anarcho-syndicalsm after 1908 reflected the rapidly shifting political coalitions within the trade union movement in the wake of Villeneuve-Saint-Georges. Only a minority had ever been firm believers in the syndicalist creed.

In the years after World War I, the charter was frequently invoked as both socialist and communist political parties began to collaborate more closely with trade union leaders. After World War II it justified the indignation of many unionists when the French Communist Party unofficially took control of the CGT.

Key Players

Griffuelhes, Victor (1874–1922): Trained as a shoemaker, Griffuelhes was politically active in the leatherworking federation before becoming the general secretary of the Confédération Générale du Travail (CGT) (1901–1909). His leadership marked the height of the CGT's commitment to anarcho-syndicalism. He promoted the general strike for an eight-hour day on 1 May 1906. His militant leadership led the CGT into head-on conflict with the government of Georges Clemenceau (1906–1909). Clemenceau's brutal repression forced many trade unionists to reconsider anarcho-syndicalist tactics. Griffuelhes's pupil and successor as head of the CGT, Leon Jouhaux, remained longer in office by avoiding direct confrontations with state power.

Guesde, Jules (1845–1922): Founder of the *Parti Ouvrier* (Labor Party), the first Marxist-Socialist Party in France, Guesde was an indefatigable organizer and propagandist. The highly industrialized French departments of the Nord and Pas-de-Calais became bastions of Guesdest strength. Party organization there resembled that of the German Social Democrats. Unable to impose his own unity on French socialism, Guesde united with Jean Jaurès to from a unified French Socialist Party, the *Section Française de l'Internationale Ouvrière* (French Section of the Worker's International or SFIO) in 1905. Guesde was notorious for his sectarian and uncompromising positions.

Jaurès, Jean (1859-1914): Undoubtedly the most beloved and charismatic of prewar French socialists, Jaurès was an intellectual engaged in reform politics who joined the socialist movement after witnessing the Carmaux mining strike of 1892. His undoubted integrity, eloquence, and willingness to compromise made him a pivotal figure in the creation of a unified French socialist movement. On the eve of World War I he was assassinated by a right-wing extremist.

Pouget, Emile (1860-1931): A longtime anarchist, Pouget became the editor of the CGT newspaper *La Voix du Peuple* in 1900 and assistant secretary in 1901. He was a strong advocate of the antimilitarism. His book (coauthored with Emile Patau), *How We Shall Make the Revolution,* was about as close as CGT theorists ever got to describing their overarching strategy for revolution.

See also: *Confédération Générale du Travail.*

BIBLIOGRAPHY

Books
Hanagan, Michael. "Markets, Industrial Relations and the Law: The United Kingdom and France, 1867–1906." In *European Integration in Social and Historical Pespective, 1850 to the Present.* Edited by Jytte Klausen and Louise A. Tilly. Lanham, MD: Rowman and Littlefield, 1997.
Lefranc, Georges. *Le Mouvement Syndial sous la Troisième République.* Paris: Payot, 1967.
Monatte, Pierre. *Trois Scissions Syndicales.* Paris: Les Éditions Ouvrières, 1958.
Vandervort, Bruce. *Victor Griffuelhes and French Syndicalism, 1895–1922.* Baton Rouge: Louisiana State University Press, 1996.

Periodicals
Turner, Patricia. "Hostile Participants? Working-Class Militancy, Associational Life, and the 'Distinctiveness' of the Prewar French Labor Movement." *The Journal of Modern History* 71 (March 1999): 28–55.

—Michael Hanagan

Chartist Movement

Great Britain 1838–1848

Synopsis

Chartism was a mass movement that emerged in the political disappointments and economic difficulties of the later 1830s and was active until 1848. The movement centered on the People's Charter (May 1838), which made six demands: universal manhood suffrage, annual parliaments, a secret ballot, equal electoral districts, abolition of the property qualification for Members of Parliament (MPs), and payment of MPs. Chartism was the culmination of a well-established tradition of radical politics in both its analysis and strategy. Chartism blamed political corruption and "class legislation" for working-class hardships. It sought to mobilize its supporters and intimidate its opponents by demonstrations of the strength of popular opinion in mass meetings and petitions to Parliament. Chartism proffered three petitions (in 1839, 1842 and 1848); each was rejected. The movement also marked a development in the nature of radical politics in that it was a more exclusively and assertively working-class body. The National Charter Association, established in 1840, and, more controversially, the Chartist Land Plan of 1845, provided the working-class political movement with its first permanent organization. Chartism, confronted by a resolute and effective state and uncertain of its own response, failed to achieve any of its aims but bequeathed a significant legacy of working-class activism.

Timeline

1818: In a decisive defeat of Spanish forces, soldier and statesman Simón Bolívar leads the liberation of New Granada, which includes what is now Colombia, Panama, Venezuela, and Ecuador. With Spanish power now waning, Bolívar becomes president and virtual dictator of the newly created nation of Colombia.

1823: U.S. president James Monroe establishes the Monroe Doctrine, whereby the United States warns European nations not to interfere in the political affairs of the Western Hemisphere.

1830: French troops invade Algeria, and at home, a revolution forces the abdication of Charles V in favor of Louis Philippe, the "Citizen King."

1836: Boer farmers embark on their "Great Trek" into the hinterlands of South Africa, forming the enclaves of Natal, Transvaal, and the Orange Free State.

1837: Coronation of Queen Victoria in England takes place.

1838: The forcible removal of the Cherokee Nation from Georgia to Indian Territory (now Oklahoma) along the "Trail of Tears" begins.

1838: As crops fail, spawning famine in Ireland, Britain imposes the Poor Law. Designed to discourage the indigent from seeking public assistance, the law makes labor in the workhouse worse than any work to be found on the outside, and thus has the effect of stimulating emigration.

1839: England launches the First Opium War against China. The war, which lasts three years, results in the British gaining a free hand to conduct a lucrative opium trade, despite opposition by the Chinese government.

1844: Samuel Laing, in a prize-winning essay on Britain's "National Distress," describes conditions in a nation convulsed by the early Industrial Revolution. A third of the population, according to Laing, "hover[s] on the verge of actual starvation"; another third is forced to labor in "crowded factories"; and only the top third "earn[s] high wages, amply sufficient to support them in respectability and comfort."

1851: Britain's Amalgamated Society of Engineers applies innovative organizational concepts, including large con-

NOT SO *VERY* UNREASONABLE!!! EH?

British Prime Minister John Russell is presented with bill from the Chartist Movement, cartoon from *Punch* magazine. © Hulton/Getty Images. Reproduced by permission.

tributions from, and benefits to, members, as well as vigorous use of direct action and collective bargaining.

Event and Its Context

Origins and Causes

Chartism was not, as portrayed in the past, "hunger politics"—an irrational, untutored response to economic hardship—but economic circumstances were significant in its origins and course. The movement grew as industrialization took hold. Artisanal trades were increasingly subject to market pressures and mechanized competition; although Chartism was not the prerogative of the so-called declining trades, these literate craftsmen formed a significant component of its support. Skilled factory workers also fought to defend their working conditions and retain some control over the labor process. In fact, Chartism provided the umbrella under which a wide cross-section of the working population struggled to defend its status. Chartism peaked at times of economic depression. A slump that began in the late 1830s and peaked in 1842 provided powerful

Chartist demonstration, Blackfriars Bridge, London, England. © Hulton/Getty Images. Reproduced by permission.

momentum for Chartist protest. Chartist activity declined in the mid-1840s as conditions improved, but the economic difficulties of 1847–1948 revived the mass movement.

At the heart of the Chartists' economic grievances, however, there lay a powerful *political* analysis. The labor theory of value (i.e., that the value of a item derives from the labor applied to produce it), which had developed in the 1820s, strengthened the Chartists' sense of exploitation, but the exploitation itself was attributed not to the economic process as such but to the political system. Chartists, as had their radical forebears, blamed their poverty on "Old Corruption, " which was construed as a greedy and self-interested governing elite that taxed the wealth of the "producing classes " to maintain its extravagant and parasitic lifestyle. The 1815 Corn Laws (which placed a duty on imported grain) and the variety of other tariffs on consumption gave this analysis credibility. Up to sixteen percent of working-class incomes went to indirect taxation.

The Chartists, therefore, sought political redress and were strengthened in their demand for political power by the 1832 Reform Bill and its aftermath. This bill, which was brought about in large measure by working-class protest, extended the franchise to the property-owning middle classes while deliberately excluding working-class men from the vote. The bill split the fragile reforming alliance of the middle and working classes and, as intended by its creators, largely recruited the former to

the cause of order and the status quo. The apparent cynicism of this maneuver and the pusillanimity of their erstwhile allies were amply confirmed in Chartist eyes by the behavior of Whig governments after the "great betrayal " of 1832. The 1833 Factory Act disappointed a widespread working-class protest movement by refusing to legislate a 10-hour working day. The 1834 Poor Law, by its provision that any relief must be provided in a workhouse, seemed to punish the poor and rob the state of any legitimizing paternalist role. Attempts to defend living conditions through nonpolitical means failed. Owenite cooperation, represented in the National Equitable Labour Exchange of 1832, proved impractical. The upsurge of trade unionism in the early 1830s, notably the Grand National Consolidated Trades Union (GNCTU) of 1834, collapsed as a result of both its own internal weaknesses and government repression. This repression was exemplified by the transportation of the "Tolpuddle Martyrs " (six agricultural laborers who had attempted to form a branch of the GNCTU) in 1834 and the prosecution of the Glasgow cotton spinners for strike activity in 1838.

In this context, working-class radicalism's critique of "class legislation " and class rule revived. Although the Charter itself was little more than a tabulation of long-established radical demands, the London Workingmen's Association provided the program of the nascent Chartist movement by drafting the six points and publishing the People's Charter in May 1838.

Thomas Attwood's Birmingham Political Union offered significant support and supplied Chartism's core tactic of a national petition. Some 600 radical societies formed in the North and provided strength in depth to the movement. Feargus O'Connor played a leading role and many activists and such leaders as J. R. Stephens switched directly from anti–Poor Law agitation to the wider politics of Chartism. O'Connor's newspaper, the *Northern Star*, was first published in 1837 and sold 50,000 copies weekly at its peak in 1839; it provided propaganda and cohesion to the growing movement, which coalesced in a series of mass meetings that held in Glasgow, Birmingham, Manchester, and elsewhere between May and September 1838. These meetings elected the 53 delegates to the "General Convention of the Industrious Classes, " which convened in February 1839 to oversee strategy and present the Chartist Petition.

The Course of Chartism

Chartism represented a powerful convergence of experience, agitation, and organization, yet it remained rooted in the fallible radical conviction that the strength of mass public opinion could persuade the ruling classes to relinquish their power. The General Convention discussed a variety of "ulterior measures " to be implemented should the petition fail. These included a "Sacred Month " (general strike), a run on banks, and a boycott of hostile traders. The delegates were divided in temperament and tactics, however, and no coherent response emerged when Parliament rejected the petition, with its 1.28 million signatures, in July 1839 by 235 votes to 46. Depleted by arrests and split by the resignation of more moderate, often middle-class, delegates, the convention eventually dissolved itself in September, having first endorsed and then rescinded the general strike tactic.

Some radical Chartists believed that the time had come for insurrection. The most violent response came in Newport, South Wales, where, in November 1839, John Frost led 5000 miners to release imprisoned Chartists. Troops dispersed the attack, killing 24. A rising in Sheffield in January 1840, which had been reported to the authorities, was even less successful. Whether any more concerted action was planned or, at least, hoped for is difficult to determine, but the government's fear of the Chartist threat was demonstrated by its arrest of 543 Chartist leaders between June 1839 and July 1840. This was an effective move that disoriented the movement at a crucial time by robbing Chartism of its local and national leadership and instilling fear of the power of the state.

Chartism regrouped in July 1840 with the foundation of the National Charter Association (NCA), which was intended to provide a permanent leadership and organization. By April 1842, the NCA had 401 branches and some 50,000 subscribing members. The NCA, championed by O'Connor, represented the mainstream of the movement. Traditional historians, influenced by the partisan memoirs of some of O'Connor's opponents, have emphasized at this point a growing rift in the movement between so-called "Physical Force " Chartists and their "Moral Force " adversaries. In reality, the Chartist slogan, "Peaceably if we may, forcibly if we must, " represented the viewpoint of most Chartists and reflected the widespread and well-established radical belief in the justifiability, and perhaps necessity, of working-class self-defense against state oppression.

Similarly, the rhetorical violence of O'Connor and other more "extreme " Chartist leaders echoed the "language of menace " that had been traditionally employed by radical leaders in their attempts to intimidate an entrenched ruling class. William Lovett, founder of the National Association for Promoting the Political and Social Improvement of the People in 1841, emphasized working-class self-improvement; the movement rejected his doctrine not for its object per se but for its implication that the vote had to be earned rather than granted as a right. O'Connor's rejection of any alliance with middle-class groups that were campaigning for parliamentary reform or the repeal of the Corn Laws also reflects Chartism's deep distrust of any compromise that might detract from the integrity of their cause. O'Connor's single-mindedness—or arrogance in the eyes of his critics—did, however, alienate the support of other leaders of Chartism such as Bronterre O'Brien and Henry Hetherington.

In May 1842, the House of Commons rejected the second Chartist petition, which claimed 3.3 million signatures, by 287 votes to 49. The rejection came at a time of severe economic depression. A strike wave, protesting wage cuts, spread from the Midlands to the North and Scotland. (The removal of boiler plugs from steam engines as a means of enforcing the stoppage gave this strike wave its pejorative name, the "Plug Plot.") Though the strikes originated in economic grievances, they took on a political character: some strikers and a delegate conference of trade union leaders in Manchester vowed not to resume work until the Charter was granted. The Conservative Government of Robert Peel responded firmly by arresting approximately 1500 strikers. The strikes petered out by September.

Its second failure and the economic recovery after 1842 hit Chartism hard. O'Connor used this hiatus to promote the Land Plan, which he launched formally in 1845. The plan established a subscription fund to purchase land and provide members, selected by ballot, with smallholdings. By 1851, the plan had accrued only 250 subscribers and was beset by financial and legal difficulties. Though frequently criticized as a sign of O'Connor's eccentricity and incompetence, the plan had greater attraction and relevance to the urban working classes than often credited. Some 70,000 eventually subscribed, drawn by its promise of self-reliance and also by its intended benefit to industrial workers (i.e., that land settlement would reduce pressure on the labor market and raise working-class incomes). The plan at least provided a cause and a focus for Chartism when the movement was at low ebb.

Poor harvests starting in 1846 and a commercial crisis in 1847 provided the conditions for the last upsurge of Chartism. Meetings resumed and the collection of signatures for a third petition commenced. The Chartist Convention, buoyed by the success of the February revolution in France, planned a mass meeting in Kennington Common, south London, to present the petition with its claimed 5.5 million signatures. The authorities, alarmed at the threat of insurrection, recruited 170,000 special constables and deployed 7,000 regular troops. The Chartist leadership, intent on a peaceful meeting, abandoned a planned march on Parliament. Parliament inspected the petition, found that only some 1.5 million signatures were genuine, and rejected it. The government easily suppressed the poorly planned August Chartist rising and arrested approximately 300 participants. Chartism, humiliated in hostile eyes, was at least outfaced and dissolved as a mass movement. In the 1850s, O'Connor lapsed into insanity. Ernest Jones and George Julian Harney sought to move what remained of the movement in a socialist direction, but most former Chartist activists moved into other areas of working-class politics.

Significance and Interpretation

Chartism did not achieve any of its objectives though all (with the exception of annual parliaments) were enacted subsequently. Parliament abolished the property qualification for MPs in 1858, extended the franchise to working-class males in 1867 and 1884, introduced the secret ballot in 1872, redistributed constituencies in 1885, and established payment for MPs in 1911.

Traditionally, the Chartist movement failure was explained by the "premature" and "extreme" nature of its demands and the immaturity of a working-class that had been led astray by unscrupulous demagogues (notably O'Connor) who divided the movement and wrested it from its respectable and rational artisanal roots. The decline of Chartism in times of economic prosperity and its demise as working-class living standards rose after 1850 is seen as confirmation that the movement was essentially an inchoate and reflexive response to economic hardship.

Historians in the 1980s substantially revised this outlook. The modern interpretation of Chartism is as an essentially cohesive and coherent movement that successfully mobilized a disparate working class behind a common program and shared ideology. This view also stresses the breadth and depth of Chartism as well as O'Connor's role as an important organizer and articulator of a mass movement that reached across the trades and localities that were sometimes held to have divided it. It became a very largely working-class movement, reflecting a class identity forged in the economic process and tempered by the politics of the 1830s. It created new forms of working-class self-organization, notably the NCA, and it generated a democratic counter-culture of Chartist schools, temperance societies, burial clubs, and the like. Yet it failed.

Chartism failed essentially because its strategy of change failed. It failed to overawe the ruling elite, and its legitimizing constitutionalism and focus on peaceful means left it powerless when government rejected its demands. The resolution and strength of state repression at key moments ensured that the much-vaunted right of forcible resistance to oppression was both impractical and, to most Chartists, unappealing.

Chartism was also limited by its ideology. The Chartist critique, which was centered on the attack on "Old Corruption" and "class legislation," was undermined by government reforms in the 1840s. The 1842 Mines Act, the 1847 Factory Act (which conceded a 10-hour day), Peel's Free Trade budgets of the 1840s and, most notably, the repeal of the Corn Laws in 1846 all benefited the working class and discredited Chartism's analysis that progress could only be achieved through wholesale political reform. In this respect, the direct legacy of Chartism was slight. In the following decades, working-class activism focused principally on measures of self-help (e.g., trade unionism and friendly societies), and the political agenda concentrated on demands for legal protection. In the second half of the century, as the economy grew and society stabilized, the working class became more integrated into the existing order and more politically reformist in temperament. Indirectly, Chartism had provided a corps of activists who continued to struggle in defense of working-class interests, albeit by different and less radical means.

Key Players

Attwood, Thomas (1783–1859): Attwood, a successful Birmingham banker, believed in currency reform to stimulate trade and supported parliamentary reform to achieve a House of Commons representative of manufacturing interests. A founder of the Birmingham Political Union (BPU) in 1830 and a leading campaigner for reform in the early thirties, Attwood served as MP for Birmingham from 1832 to 1839 but, frustrated by Parliament's continued unwillingness to adopt his ideas, he revived the BPU in 1837 to press for further reform. Though willing to cooperate with the respectable radicalism of the London Working Men's Association, Attwood disliked the "extremism" of other Chartist leaders and withdrew from the reform campaign and political life after the rejection of the first Chartist petition.

Frost, John (1784–1877): A master tailor from Newport, South Wales and supporter of universal manhood suffrage from the early 1830s, Frost was elected a Newport councilor, served as mayor from 1835 to 1837, and as a magistrate until removed by the Home Secretary after he had emerged as one of the most radical delegates to the 1839 General Convention. He was charged with high treason for his leadership role in the Newport Rising and sentenced to death. The sentence was commuted to transportation to Tasmania and Frost lived there and in the United States until finally allowed back to Britain in 1856. He remained an advocate of radical political reform.

Jones, Ernest (1819–1869): An upper-class barrister, Jones became active in Chartist politics in the mid-1840s as an ally of Feargus O'Connor and co-editor of the *Northern Star*. He was imprisoned for two years for sedition in 1848, then on his release, cooperated in left-wing journalism with George Julian Harney, whose socialist politics he shared, before founding the *People's Paper* (1851–1858). Failing to get elected to Parliament, he reverted to the practice of law but continued to work for radical causes (and write novels) until his death.

O'Brien, James Bronterre (1805–1864): Born in Ireland, O'Brien gave up a planned legal career in London to support the radical movement and became one of its more powerful journalists. O'Brien, dubbed the "schoolmaster of Chartism," was unusual in forming a socialist critique of the existing order and advocating a sweeping program of social reform. In the 1840s he diverged with O'Connor on tactics but remained active in the reform campaign (in the Complete Suffrage Union), in journalism, and later in working-class education.

O'Connor, Feargus (1794–1855): O'Connor was a lawyer and Irish Radical MP from 1832 to 1835, when he was unseated for failing the property qualification. He toured the North of England starting in 1835 to oppose the 1834 Poor Law and demand radical political reform and founded the *Northern Star* in 1837, thus playing the principal role in the development of northern Chartism. O'Connor was a powerful orator whose fierce rhetoric belied his opposition to insurrectionary violence. He was sentenced to eighteen months imprisonment in 1840 for seditious libel and was arrested again in 1842. Criticized by some for arrogance and fractiousness, O'Connor was, nevertheless, the most popular leader of Chartism in the 1840s and the key proponent of the failed Land Plan in 1845. He was elected MP for Nottingham in 1847 but suffered serious mental decline in his later years.

Stephens, Joseph Rayner (1805–1879): A nonconformist minister, Stephens was a Tory radical whose belief in the state's paternalist role led him to support the factory reform movement and oppose the 1834 Poor Law. A fiery orator and militant, he was imprisoned in 1839 for sedition but he was never a supporter of Chartism's political analysis and dropped out of the movement. He did, however, remain active in campaigns for child welfare and workers' conditions.

See also: *Factory Act; London Workingmen's Association.*

BIBLIOGRAPHY

Books

Epstein, J. and Thompson, Dorothy, eds. *The Chartist Experience: Studies in Working-Class Radicalism and Culture, 1830–60.* London and Basingstoke: Macmillan Press, 1982.

Thompson, Dorothy. *The Chartists.* New York: Pantheon Books, 1984.

Periodicals

Belchem, John. "Taking Chartism Seriously." *Modern History Review.* (April 1996).

Royle, Edward. "Chartism." *ReFRESH. Recent Findings of Research in Economic and Social History* 2 (spring 1986): 1–4.

Taylor, Miles. "Rethinking the Chartists: Searching for a Synthesis in the Historiography of Chartism." *The Historical Journal* 39, no. 2 (June 1996): 479–495.

ADDITIONAL RESOURCES

Books

Ashton, Owen R., Robert Fyson, and Stephen Roberts, eds. *The Chartist Legacy.* Rendlesham: Merlin Press, 1999.

Briggs, Asa. *Chartist Studies.* London: Macmillan, 1977.

Epstein, James. *The Lion of Freedom: Feargus O'Connor and the Chartist Movement, 1832–1842.* London: Croom Helm, 1982.

Jones, David J. V. *Chartism and the Chartists.* New York: St. Martin's Press, 1975.

———. *The Last Rising: The Newport Insurrection of 1839.* Oxford: Clarendon Press, 1985.

Ward, J. T. *Chartism.* New York: Barnes & Noble Books, 1973.

Periodicals

Pickering, P. A. "'And Your Petitioners, &c.': Chartist Petitioning in Popular Politics, 1838–48." *English Historical Review* 116, no. 466 (April 2001): 368–388.

Stack, D. "William Lovett and the National Association for the Political and Social Improvement of the People." *Historical Journal* (1999).

Other

"Chartism." *Spartacus Educational.* 30 June 2002 [cited 11 July 2002]. <http://www.spartacus.schoolnet.co.uk/chartism.htm>.

—John Boughton

Chiang Kai-shek Purges Communists

China 1927

Synopsis

In April 1927 Chiang Kai-shek and the nationalists in China purged the Chinese Communist Party (CCP) in the city of Shanghai. After the Nationalist Party, or *Guomindang* (GMD), split upon the death of Sun Yat-sen in 1925, Chiang became the leader of its right-wing faction. In 1926 he launched the Northern Expedition against warlord rule in China. While initially the GMD and the communists had cooperated through their United Front, Chiang felt the communists had become too revolutionary. Therefore, as his Northern Expedition approached the city of Shanghai, he decided that, along with business interests, gangsters, and foreigners in the city, he would crack down on the communists and the labor unions controlled by the CCP. This action was part of a broader conflict in Chinese cities in April 1927 that pitted conservative political elements against radicals such as the communists. Chiang's decision led to a bloody purge of the CCP in Shanghai, in which several thousand people died. While this "cleansing of the party," as the nationalists called it, helped to solve the immediate question of whether the communists or the nationalists would control China, it also led to decades of civil war in the country and hundreds of thousands more deaths.

Timeline

1911: In China, revolutionary forces led by Sun Yat-sen bring an end to more than 2,100 years of imperial rule.

1917: On both the Western Front and in the Middle East, the tide of the war begins to turn against the Central Powers. The arrival of U.S. troops, led by General Pershing, in France in June greatly boosts morale and reinforces exhausted Allied forces. Meanwhile, Great Britain scores two major victories against the Ottoman Empire as T.

E. Lawrence leads an Arab revolt in Baghdad in March, and troops under Field Marshal Edmund Allenby take Jerusalem in December.

1922: Inspired by the Bolsheviks' example of imposing revolution by means of a coup, Benito Mussolini leads his blackshirts in an October "March on Rome," and forms a new fascist government.

1924: V. I. Lenin dies, and thus begins a struggle for succession from which Josef Stalin will emerge five years later as the undisputed leader of the Communist Party, and of the Soviet Union.

1927: Stalin arranges to have Trotsky expelled from the Communist Party.

1927: Charles A. Lindbergh makes the first successful solo nonstop flight across the Atlantic and becomes an international hero.

1927: American inventor Philo T. Farnsworth demonstrates a working model of the television, and Belgian astronomer Georges Lemaître proposes the Bang Theory.

1927: *The Jazz Singer,* starring Al Jolson, is the first major motion picture with sound. Within a few years, silent movies will become a thing of the past.

1927: Babe Ruth hits 60 home runs, establishing a record that will stand until 1961.

1930: Naval disarmament treaty is signed by the United States, Great Britain, France, Italy, and Japan.

1932: When Ukrainians refuse to surrender their grain to his commissars, Stalin seals off supplies to the region, creating a manmade famine that will produce a greater death toll than the entirety of World War I.

1937: Japan attacks China, and annexes most of that nation's coastal areas.

Event and Its Context

The City of Shanghai

By the 1920s Shanghai had become the largest and most cosmopolitan city in Asia. The city had been growing in size and importance since the middle of the nineteenth century. After China's humiliating defeat in the Opium War (1839–1842), the British had forced China to open Shanghai and several other "treaty ports" to foreign trade. The city, therefore, had a large foreign presence and was home to many Western financial institutions. Foreigners lived in separate, autonomous districts. The city had also industrialized, and its many factories attracted thousands of migrants from other areas within China. By the 1860s, after the Taiping Rebellion (1851–1864), the city surpassed Guangzhou (Canton) as China's primary commercial center. By 1900 Shanghai was home to more than one million inhabitants. The city also had its share of dance halls, brothels, gambling centers, and opium dens.

The Communists in Shanghai

In addition to being China's main trading city, the Chinese Communist Party (CCP) was formed in Shanghai in 1921. The

Chiang Kai-shek. © Archive Photos. Reproduced by permission.

early CCP was influenced by the events of 1911, in which forces led by Sun Yat-sen overthrew the Qing Dynasty; the CCP cooperated with Sun's Nationalist Party, which was organized in 1912. The May Fourth Movement of 1919 also influenced the CCP. In that year students in Beijing began to protest against the terms of the Versailles Treaty that ended World War I, sparking a national political movement that spread to Shanghai.

The CCP received aid from Soviet advisers. In 1922 the Comintern (the Communist International, which existed from 1919 to 1943) ordered the CCP to cooperate with the *Guomindang* (GMD). Thus, in 1923 the CCP and GMD formed the first United Front. (The two groups united once again when the Japanese invaded Manchuria in 1937.) However, in 1925 Sun Yat-sen died, and his GMD divided into left- and right-wing factions. The left-wing faction, headed by Wang Jing-wei, set up a government at Wuhan in Hubei Province. The right-wing faction was led by Chiang Kai-shek, who in 1926 launched the Northern Expedition against warlord rule in China and sought to unify the country

In the period from 1925 to 1927, the Communist Party in Shanghai grew rapidly, part of a general trend throughout the country following the May Thirtieth Movement of 1925 and the establishment of the United Front. In October 1925 there were just over 1,000 Communist Party members in China's largest city. By April 1927 there were some 13,000. As the CCP in Shanghai grew in strength, it came to dominate many unions and was also influential among student groups. In addition, the CCP had created a paramilitary force known as the Workers' Inspection Corps, which it used to enforce strikes and intimidate foremen in both Chinese and foreign-owned factories. Soon they began to lead uprisings in the city against warlord rule.

In addition to the Communist Party itself in Shanghai, the communist-dominated Shanghai General Labor Union (GLU) played a key role in the city during the events of 1927. The union fought against local authorities, the warlords, foreign powers, and the nationalists. Despite increased repression, the union led a series of strikes in 1926 and 1927. The union's activities were related in part to economic grievances, as inflation was high. In addition, the union leaders were spurred on by the success of Chiang Kai-shek's Northern Expedition and the weakening of Sun Ch'uan-fang, the warlord who controlled the city.

The "Three Armed Uprisings"

As Chiang Kai-shek continued to win military victories, the Shanghai GLU was encouraged by the possible takeover of the city by the GMD. In anticipation of Chiang's arrival, the GLU sought to mobilize the city's workers. In October 1926 the union made its first attempt to overthrow the militarist warlord rule in the city, as Sun Ch'uan-fang was busy elsewhere fighting a rebellious subordinate and the nationalists. The strike was put down, however, and more than 100 workers were arrested. In light of this initial failure, the communists later sent Zhou Enlai to Shanghai to direct the struggle there.

In early 1927 the radicals in Shanghai attempted a second uprising against warlord rule. More demonstrations were planned for February 1927 as Chiang and the nationalists approached Shanghai after defeating Sun Ch'uan-fang's forces, who had blocked his approach. As Chiang neared the city, the communists and the Shanghai GLU decided that the best course of action was to take control of the city first and then welcome Chiang. The communists hoped this would prevent Chiang from establishing hegemony in Shanghai. They began to plan an uprising in the city to achieve this goal, imitating the May Thirtieth Movement.

On 23 February the communists established a special committee to plan the uprising. They also negotiated for support among members of the GMD who were already in the city. The communists proposed that after the uprising, a "citizen's assembly" would ratify a new government for Shanghai. The GMD agreed to the idea of sharing governmental control of the city. However, they objected to the idea of an uprising. As a compromise, the sides agreed to stage a general strike.

This time, the action began with a massive strike of some 350,000 workers, paralyzing the city. The workers posted banners with slogans such as "Hail the Northern Expedition" and "Hail Chiang Kai-shek." However, the strike was not well coordinated, and once again warlord Sun Ch'uan-fang and his supporters crushed the attempted rebellion. There were 20 public decapitations, and authorities mounted the heads on stakes for public display. Some observers and historians have suggested that the nationalists purposely held back from the city to

allow Sun Ch'uan-fang to crack down first on the workers and then on the communists. The communist leadership then sent more workers into the streets, and street fighting took place in late February.

Despite the repression, the union remained intact and even initiated more action. As the nationalists continued their march toward Shanghai, the workers and the communist leaders called for more strikes and demonstrations. Zhou Enlai approved a third uprising for March 1927 that included a simultaneous general strike and armed uprising. On 21 March between 600,000 and 800,000 workers struck in demand for an end to militarist rule of the city. Among the workers who played key roles were the printers, postal workers, and mechanics. Several thousand radicals also formed an armed militia that occupied key sections of the city.

In addition to the general strike and armed uprising, a key to the initial success of the movement was the support of the gangsters from Shanghai's underworld. At a secret Communist Party planning meeting two days before the uprising began, Wang Shouhua, chairman of the GLU, reported to Zhou Enlai that a leading gangster, Du Yuesheng, wanted to cooperate with the radical movement. Du, along with Green Gang patriarch Huang Jinrong, played an important support role. These gangsters supplied money for the communist-backed unions, arranged for the release of arrested workers, shared intelligence about the warlords, and offered protection to individuals trapped in Shanghai's foreign concessions.

With this aid from Shanghai's gangsters, the radicals controlled the city within two days. They succeeded in liberating the city from control by the northern military warlords and disarmed the Chinese police in Shanghai. They occupied police stations, railway stations, an arsenal, courts, and prisons. In most cases, the warlord troops simply abandoned their positions. In fact, some of the defeated warlord troops joined the radicals. However, in some parts of the city, there was heavy fighting. In the Zhabei district, for example, some 200 workers died in the struggle.

The communists and workers set up a provisional municipal government for the city that included members of the Communist Party, the GMD, gangsters, and business interests. There was a 19-man governing council that included five communists, such as GLU chairman Wang Shouhua. On 27 March, Wang was elected as the chairman of the executive committee of the new workers' government. The new provisional government called for better working conditions for the workers and an end to the unequal treaties. They later agreed to leave negotiations to end the treaties to the nationalist government at Wuhan, fearing foreign intervention. The diverse groups represented in the new Shanghai government were the products of their united opposition to warlord rule. Their coalition, however, did not last, as disputes quickly arose over the composition of the provisional government and the arming of workers.

Chiang Kai-shek Purges the Communists and Workers

As early as 22 March 1927, Chiang's force in Shanghai was already 3,000 strong. Chiang himself arrived on 26 March, and he began meeting with members of the GMD, the Shanghai business community, and the gangsters. Chiang and his allies concluded that the changes that the communists and the workers desired were too radical. Indeed, Chiang had decided that both the communists and the left wing of the GMD had become too revolutionary. In exchange for a promise to destroy the radical movement in the city, Shanghai's more conservative elements provided Chiang with large sums of money. It should have come as no surprise to anyone that Chiang decided to move against the radicals, as he had already done so in several other cities in late March.

The gangsters soon decided to turn on the communists and the workers. They did so because they viewed Chiang as a more important backer of their lucrative opium trade than either of the other two groups. Chiang had old ties to the Shanghai gangsters. Now he needed their support in order to take control of the city. For their part, the gangsters, aware of Chiang's military victories, sought protection for their opium business. Thus, in late March, Chiang sent some of his associates to the city to contact the gangsters. They met with some of the key gang leaders and began to plan an anticommunist movement.

The gangsters in turn contacted the authorities in the Shanghai International Settlement and the French Concession. Foreign officials agreed to provide weapons and ammunition to Chiang and the gangsters and to allow them free passage through the International Settlement. Western authorities did not want to see the seizure of foreign settlements in the city, as had happened in other cities, such as when angry Chinese crowds of the anti-imperialist movement attacked the British settlement in Hankou. Foreigners were also frightened by the Nanjing Incident, which they blamed on communists; actually, however, the nationalists were the perpetrators of this series of attacks on foreign civilians. Some foreign officials, such as the Japanese Consul General, thus advised Chiang to crack down on the radical elements in the city.

Soon Chiang's supporters established a rival municipal government and labor union to counter the communists and the GLU. In early April skirmishes began to take place between the rival groups. By 5 April a crackdown on the radicals began, and workers were arrested. Chiang had ordered his general, Bai Chongxi, to force the radicals to surrender their arms. Those who did not were suppressed, and some 3,000 members of the Workers Inspection Corps were defeated. At this point, many world leaders still hoped to avoid a major conflict. Even Stalin sent a message from Moscow, ordering the Chinese communists to disarm. The CCP, however, did not heed Stalin's advice.

In the early morning hours of 12 April 1927, nationalist troops disguised as workers and members of the Green Gang made their move against the workers. After passing through the International Settlement with the aid of foreign authorities, Chiang's supporters entered the Chinese section of the city and rounded up many radical leaders, including Zhou Enlai, who later escaped. Wang Shouhua was not so lucky. Green Gang leader Du Yuesheng invited Wang, who was also a gang member, to dinner, only to have him killed. Many of those captured were sent to General Bai's headquarters, where hundreds were executed.

In response, some 200,000 workers struck the next day. The radicals also protested to the Wuhan government, but to no avail. They were no match for the combined opposition of the GMD and the gangsters. Unlike the May Thirtieth Movement

two years earlier, the Shanghai uprising in 1927 seems not to have had the widespread support from the workers necessary for the uprising's success. Chiang's men shot and killed hundreds more on 13 April amid these protests. The remaining communist and labor leaders fled or went into hiding. Some merged with CCP groups elsewhere in the country. Some, like Zhou Enlai, organized uprisings against the GMD later in the year. However, many were captured and executed in the coming months. The situation of the communists was made worse when in addition to Chiang and his followers, the left wing of the GMD also determined that the communists posed a threat and therefore began to persecute the CCP. In the days after the failure, Zhou Enlai felt the radicals had been unable to communicate to the general population why the uprising was needed and that the average people were simply confused about the events.

Aftermath of the Crackdown

Following his brutal suppression of the communists in Shanghai, Chiang continued his Northern Expedition. By 1928 he had also captured Beijing. Chiang set up a nationalist government at Nanjing, effectively ending the warlord era in China.

After the events of 12 April, the nationalists and the gangsters took control of the labor movement in Shanghai. They formed the Unification Committee for Shanghai Union Organization, which was largely staffed with gangsters. This ruthless organization arrested and executed many suspected radicals in the city. There was some resistance to the new organization among the workers. However, due to the repressive measures used by the gangsters, such resistance was mostly ineffective. Even some members of the GMD disapproved of the gangsters' heavy-handed treatment of the workers, leading them to create the Shanghai Workers' General Association in November 1927. The two new organizations now competed for control of Shanghai's working class.

Key Players

Chiang Kai-shek (1887–1975): After the death of Sun Yat-sen in 1925, Chiang became the principal leader of the Nationalist Party in China. In 1926 he launched the Northern Expedition in an attempt to end warlord rule and unify the country. While initially the nationalists had cooperated with the Chinese Communist Party through the United Front, in 1927 Chiang turned on the communists. He violently attacked the communists and the workers in Shanghai, an act that resulted in thousands of deaths.

Du Yuesheng (1888–1951): Du Yuesheng was a powerful gangster in Shanghai associated with the notorious Green Gang. The primary concern of Du and the other gangsters was the opium trade. Du supported whichever group he felt would both benefit and protect his opium business. At first he supported the communists in their struggle against warlord rule, only to turn on the radicals in support of Chiang Kai-shek.

Sun Ch'uan-fang: Sun Ch'uan-fang was a Chinese warlord who dominated Shanghai and the region around it. Sun's position was greatly weakened by Chiang Kai-shek's Northern Expedition. As Chiang approached the city, the communists and workers took advantage of Sun's decline and took control of the city.

Wang Shouhua: Member of the Communist Party in Shanghai, Wang was also the leader of the city's General Labor Union. He played a key role in planning the 1927 uprising against warlord rule. In the crackdown that followed, the Shanghai gangsters who cooperated with Chiang Kai-shek killed Wang.

Zhou Enlai (1898–1976): Zhou Enlai was a key communist leader in China who eventually became the second most powerful member of the communist government after the 1949 revolution. Zhou had taken part in the May Fourth Movement in 1919. In 1922 he became a member of the CCP. In 1926 he moved to Shanghai. He was influential in organizing the 1927 uprising that was then crushed by Chiang Kai-shek. Zhou narrowly escaped the nationalist crackdown on the communists in the city.

See also: *Shanghai May Fourth Movement; Shanghai May Thirtieth Movement.*

BIBLIOGRAPHY

Books

Harrison, James Pinckney. *The Long March to Power: A History of the Chinese Communist Party, 1921–1972.* New York: Praeger Publishers, 1972.

Isaacs, Harold R. *The Tragedy of the Chinese Revolution.* Stanford, CA: Stanford University Press, 1961.

Perry, Elizabeth. *Shanghai on Strike: The Politics of Chinese Labor.* Stanford, CA: Stanford University Press, 1993.

Stranahan, Patricia. *Underground: The Shanghai Communist Party and the Politics of Survival, 1927–1937.* Lanham, MD: Rowan & Littlefield Publishers, Inc., 1998.

Van de Ven, Hans. *From Friend to Comrade: The Founding of the Chinese Communist Party, 1920–1927.* Berkeley, CA: University of California Press, 1991.

Wakeman, Frederic, Jr. *Policing Shanghai, 1927–1937.* Berkeley, CA: University of California Press, 1995.

—Ronald Young

Child Labor Amendment

United States 1924

Synopsis

Had it ever been enacted, the proposed Twentieth Amendment to the U.S. Constitution would have granted Congress the power to regulate child labor. First proposed in 1922, the amendment was approved by both houses on 2 June 1924. Despite wide popular support, the amendment was only ratified by 28 of the required 36 states before the Fair Labor Standards Act of 1938 made it a moot issue by placing child labor under control of the Department of Labor.

The debate about the amendment touched on concerns about the power of the federal government as opposed to the power of both the local government and the family. Advocates argued that the state had a compelling interest in nurturing children for subsequent citizenship. Opponents argued that the amendment would give Congress power over what ought to be a family decision. Republican presidents Calvin Coolidge and Herbert Hoover each supported the amendment, as did both major political parties. A widely based federation of trade unionists, women's groups, and social reformers campaigned for the amendment. Opposing the amendment, the National Association of Manufacturers (NAM) led a group of organizations representing businesses, religious groups, and anti–big government groups. In the 1920s a decline in the belief that government could solve social problems caused supporters of the amendment to lose momentum. By the time the Great Depression pushed the pendulum in the opposite direction, the amendment was quickly superceded by broadening workplace regulation.

Timeline

1909: Robert E. Peary and Matthew Henson reach the North Pole.

1914: On 28 June in the town of Sarajevo, then part of the Austro-Hungarian Empire, Serbian nationalist Gavrilo Princip assassinates Austrian Archduke Francis Ferdinand and wife Sophie. In the weeks that follow, Austria declares war on Serbia, and Germany on Russia and France, while Great Britain responds by declaring war on Germany. By the beginning of August, the lines are drawn, with the Allies (Great Britain, France, Russia, Belgium, Serbia, Montenegro, and Japan) against the Central Powers (Germany, Austria-Hungary, and Turkey).

1919: Treaty of Versailles is signed by the Allies and Germany but rejected by the U.S. Senate. This is due in part to rancor between President Woodrow Wilson and Republican Senate leaders, and in part to concerns over Wilson's plan to commit the United States to the newly established League of Nations and other international duties. Not until 1921 will Congress formally end U.S. participation in the war, but it will never agree to join the League.

1921: As the Allied Reparations Commission calls for payments of 132 billion gold marks, inflation in Germany begins to climb.

1923: Conditions in Germany worsen as inflation skyrockets and France, attempting to collect on coal deliveries promised at Versailles, marches into the Ruhr basin. In November an obscure political group known as the National Socialist German Workers' Party attempts to stage a coup, or putsch, in a Munich beer hall. The revolt fails, and in 1924 the party's leader, Adolf Hitler, will receive a prison sentence of five years. He will only

Young boy working in Pennsylvania coal mine. AP/Wide World Photos. Reproduced by permission.

serve nine months, however, and the incident will serve to attract attention for him and his party, known as the Nazis.

1924: V. I. Lenin dies, and thus begins a struggle for succession from which Josef Stalin will emerge five years later as the undisputed leader of the Communist Party and of the Soviet Union.

1924: In the United States, Secretary of the Interior Albert B. Fall, along with oil company executives Harry Sinclair and Edward L. Doheny, is charged with conspiracy and bribery in making fraudulent leases of U.S. Navy oil reserves at Teapot Dome, Wyoming. The resulting Teapot Dome scandal clouds the administration of President Warren G. Harding.

1927: Charles A. Lindbergh makes the first successful solo nonstop flight across the Atlantic, and becomes an international hero.

1929: On "Black Friday" in October, prices on the U.S. stock market, which had been climbing wildly for several years, suddenly collapse. Thus begins the first phase of a world economic crisis and depression that will last until the beginning of World War II.

1934: Austrian chancellor Engelbert Dollfuss, who aligns his nation with Mussolini's Italy, establishes a Fascist regime in an attempt to keep Austria out of the Nazi orbit. Austrian Nazis react by assassinating Dollfuss.

Event and Its Context

Background

Before industrialization, few people questioned child labor. Work was considered to be beneficial for all except those whose life circumstances had provided them with the means to have others work for them. Child laborers were central to the Industrial Revolution. Early textile mills employed children because mill owners found them to be both good workers and malleable employees. Yet not all child workers were malleable; children were important to the early trade union movement as both activists and as rank-and-file members. In 1835 children in the textile mills of Paterson, New Jersey, struck for the 64-hour workweek. Regulation of child labor began in states where the textile industry was concentrated. By the middle of the nineteenth century, Massachusetts, New Hampshire, Maine, Pennsylvania, Ohio, and Rhode Island had all passed laws limiting the number of hours that children could work. The Knights of Labor made opposition to child labor part of its program in the 1870s.

Up until a certain point, however, the labor movement had ambivalent feelings about child labor. On the one hand, employment of children depressed wages for adult workers. On the other, given that the wages of adult workers were inadequate to feed a family, child labor was essential to the economy of most working-class families. The development of a family wage, at least in some economic sectors, was a necessary precondition for the labor movement to place strong emphasis on regulating child labor. Throughout the nineteenth century, employers worked their workers too hard for too little remuneration as they built the capital to expand their businesses. An 1891 study conducted by the Illinois Women's Alliance and the Chicago Trades Assembly told of thousands of children under age 14 working for the garment industry in tenement sweatshops. Children in this period also worked in agriculture, in stockyards and slaughter houses, in canning factories, in coal mines, and all manner of occupations, many of them dangerous.

In the late nineteenth and early twentieth centuries, as industrialization entered a new phase of escalating mass production, reformers outside the labor movement developed new arguments against child labor. Chief among these was a rising belief in childhood as a time when one was entitled to the protection of the state. Reformers such as Grace Abbot and Florence Kelley placed child labor at the center of their critique of industrialization. In settlement houses like Jane Addams's Hull House in Chicago and Lillian Wald's Henry Street Settlement in New York, they studied the living and working conditions of the working class as they sought to change these conditions. In 1902 Wald and Kelley organized the New York Child Labor Committee, and in 1904 they helped found the National Child Labor Committee (NCLC). Like most Progressive Era reform efforts, the drive to restrict child labor focused on the state level more than the national level. This made sense because the states were generally more active in regulating industry.

As trade unionists and reformers sought increased state involvement in workplace regulation, business interests argued against it. The business community profited from the low wages it paid to children, but it also opposed state regulation more generally. Business sought support from a larger community that regarded children as the property of their parents. In this viewpoint, parents controlled a child's labor and had the right to put the child to work for the good of the family.

In 1904 with the formation of the NCLC, the movement's focus shifted to the national level. In 1912 the U.S. Children's Bureau was created, and in 1917 Grace Abbot became director of its child labor division. By 1914, 40 states plus Puerto Rico and the District of Columbia had enacted some sort of restriction on child labor. Yet, reformers recognized the limits of these gains. With disparate regulations in the various states, businesses could move to states with less regulation. Enforcement was inconsistent; some states had no public agency charged with enforcement. Increasingly reformers came to advocate national legislation and enforcement by the federal government.

The first such effort came in 1906. Senator Albert J. Beveridge of Indiana proposed a law that would have prohibited interstate transportation of the products of any factory or mine that employed children under the age of 14. Beveridge's law never passed. In 1916 and 1919 reformers pushed Congress to pass child labor laws, each tackling the problem from a different angle. Both times, the Supreme Court found the laws unconstitutional. The 1916 law, patterned on Beveridge's law, regulated interstate commerce in the products of child labor. In *Hammer v. Dagenhart*, the Court found that this interfered with the states' rights to regulate conditions in manufacturing. The 1919 bill placed a 10 percent tax on the net profits of manufacturers that employed children under age 14. Once again, in *Bailey v. Drexel Furniture Company*, the Supreme Court found that the law unconstitutionally regulated local labor laws.

Designing a New Strategy

Following the Court's decision in 1922, efforts began in both houses of the federal legislature for an amendment to give Congress the power to regulate child labor. These efforts responded to pressure from the American Federation of Labor (AFL) and reform groups. The NCLC resolved that there was "no opportunity to secure legislation regulating child labor by the federal authorities under the present Constitution." Samuel Gompers convened a conference on child labor at AFL headquarters in Washington. Organizations represented at the meeting included the U.S. Children's Bureau, the National Council on Jewish Women, the National Education Association, the National Federation of Teachers, the General Federation of Women's Clubs, the National League of Women Voters, the YWCA, the American Association of University Women, the National Women's Christian Temperance Union, and the National Congress of Mothers and Parent-Teacher Associations. Gompers was chosen chairman. Florence Kelley of the National Consumer's League became vice chairman. The group formed the Permanent Conference for the Abolition of Child Labor and agreed that a constitutional amendment would be the best way to get around the Supreme Court's insistence that the Congress had no business regulating child labor.

A constitutional amendment certainly seemed feasible in the climate of the times. The constitution had already been amended four times since 1913. Constitutional amendments had been the strategy used by both women's suffragists and advocates of a national income tax to overrule Supreme Court decisions. The success of the battle for the Eighteenth Amendment (Prohibition) had raised awareness of a constitutional amendment as a strategy for policy change. These factors, added to the victories that child labor reformers had enjoyed in getting states to pass regulatory legislation, led the reformers to have confidence in this new strategy.

An amendment also seemed the only workable solution to a problem that was growing in both size and intensity. A report made by the Children's Bureau in 1923 indicated that few states had reduced their regulation of child labor since the Supreme Court's decision in *Bailey*. Only 13 states had child labor legislation that met the standard of the federal statutes that had been voided by the Court decision. State labor officials themselves wished for federal legislation to set national standards for child labor regulation. More factories had moved to states with less regulation of child labor. Not coincidentally, these states also had less union organization and fewer worker safety regulations.

Once reformers reached a consensus that an amendment was the best strategy, they had only to agree on the wording of the amendment. A battle shaped up between the NCLC and the Permanent Conference. The former group wanted to be sure that the amendment did not interfere with the rights of states to have stricter child labor regulations than the federal government. The latter, which was a broader group, simply wanted to see the U.S. Congress gain the authority to regulate child labor.

The Amendment

Hearings on the amendment took place from 7 February to 8 March 1924. A strong opposition to the amendment emerged under the aegis of the NAM. It included forces that had opposed women's suffrage just a few years previously. On 26 April 1924 the House voted in favor of a resolution for an amendment by a vote of 297 to 69. On 2 June the Senate supported the resolution 61 to 23. The amendment had been the result of a compromise between the NCLC and Permanent Committee and the Senate Judiciary Committee. It was a permissive law, not a regulatory one; it simply empowered Congress to regulate child labor. It was worded quite broadly to allow for a good deal of congressional discretion in the future. The word "child" was dismissed as too vague and replaced with "persons under 18 years of age." The term "labor" was used in preference to "employment" to ensure that children working in family businesses or alongside their parents could be regulated as well as those working for wages of their own.

The proposed amendment had two sections. The first stated simply, "The Congress shall have the power to limit, regulate, and prohibit the labor of persons under 18 years of age." The second clarified this power in terms of existing state regulations as follows: "The power of the several States is unimpaired by this article except that the operation of State laws shall be suspended to the extent necessary to give effect to legislation enacted by the Congress." Thus, the first section was as broad and simple as the Permanent Committee wanted, and the second addressed the issue raised by the NCLC. It clearly permitted states to regulate child labor more intensively than the federal government did.

The Campaign for the Amendment

There was great popular support for regulating child labor, and most politicians recognized it. The fact that this was an election year enabled the passage of the amendment. All three presidential candidates, Calvin Coolidge, John W. Davis, and Robert M. LaFollette, supported it. Six states (Arizona, Arkansas, California, Colorado, Montana, and Wisconsin) ratified the amendment initially. Then the ratifications slowed. There was a second wave of ratifications between 1933 and 1937, part of a general trend toward more active government in that period. Fourteen states ratified the amendment during this period, 11 of which had previously rejected it in at least one legislative house. This brought the total of ratifying states to 20, or 16 shy of the required 36.

Ratification followed a regional pattern. States in the Midwest and West ratified it; only Arkansas and Kentucky did in the South. Both the Central region and the Northeast were very mixed. Neither New York nor Massachusetts ratified it, though both had strong traditions of Progressive reform. This suggests that in some states the issue of state's rights overrode the issue of child labor itself in the debate.

The intensity of the battle in New York was surprising given the state's willingness to regulate working conditions. In 1925 the New York Committee for Ratification of the Child Labor Amendment was formed by the Women's Trade Union League, Consumers' League, and the New York Child Labor Committee. Even with a strong movement pushing for ratification, reformers were unable to win a majority in the state legislature.

Opposition

All across the country the amendment faced a well-organized opposition. That opposition could appeal to states' rights and the general opposition to government regulation that many Americans shared. Some argued that controlling child labor would destroy parental authority. In this view, an alliance between Congress, social workers, and rebellious adolescents threatened to destroy both local government and parental prerogatives.

Another center of opposition was in agriculture. Farmers invoked what one progressive journal sarcastically referred to as "the sacred right of the 17-year-old farmer boy to pick blueberries on the hill." In short, they argued that children's participation in agriculture was a traditional part of a traditional family business. The only problem with this argument was that most children working in agriculture were doing so as underpaid employees, not as family members.

The NAM formed a National Committee for the Rejection of the Twentieth Amendment to lobby against ratification. Their arguments included all of those mentioned above and placed a special emphasis on the issue of local government. "Local" was a codeword for different things in different regions in the 1920s and 1930s. In the South, it meant "segregated." In many regions it meant "anti-Prohibition." Invoking localism, parental authority, and traditional practices was a powerful formula during this time. NAM succeeded in blocking ratification in enough states to prevent the amendment from being approved. It would take the Great Depression to get the federal government to assume power over the issue of child labor.

Key Players

Abbot, Grace (1878–1939): Abbot moved to Chicago from Nebraska in 1907 and became a resident of Hull House. She received a doctorate in political science from the University of Chicago. She directed the Immigrant's Protective League and in 1917 became director of the child labor division of the U.S. Children's Bureau, which she headed from 1921 until 1934. In 1938 she published her two-volume book *The Child and the State*.

Beveridge, Albert Jeremiah (1862–1927): U.S. senator from Indiana (1899–1911), Beveridge supported the policies of Theodore Roosevelt and helped organize the Progressive Party, which ran him as its candidate for governor of Indiana in 1912.

Coolidge, Calvin (1872–1933): The 30th president of the United States (1923–1929), Coolidge presided over a period of what was called "Coolidge prosperity." He favored isolation in foreign policy, government inactivity in the economy, and tax cuts.

Davis, John W. (1873–1955): Representative from West Virginia from 1911 to 1913, Davis resigned to become a federal judge. Later he was ambassador to the Court of St. James's and unsuccessful Democratic Party candidate in 1924.

Gompers, Samuel (1850–1924): Gompers began work as a cigarmaker at age 10, becoming leader of the Cigarmakers' Union by 1877. In 1881 he helped organize the AFL, and he served as its president until 1924.

Kelley, Florence (1859–1932): Kelley translated Friedrich Engels's *The Condition of the Working Class in England* before moving to Hull House in 1891. In 1899 she moved to Henry Street Settlement in New York and became general secretary of the National Consumers League, a position she held until her death. She founded the New York Child Labor Committee with Lillian Wald in 1902 and participated in forming the National Child Labor Committee in 1904. She was a founding member of the National Association for the Advancement of Colored People (NAACP) in 1909 and served as vice president for the National American Woman Suffrage Association.

LaFollette, Robert M. (1855–1925): Known as "Fighting Bob," LaFollette served in the House of Representatives from 1885 to 1891, as governor of Wisconsin from 1900 to 1905, and as U.S. senator from 1905 to 1925. He ran as a Progressive Party candidate for president in 1924. Upon his death in 1925 he was succeeded in the Senate by his son, Robert M. LaFollette Jr.

See also: *American Federation of Labor; Fair Labor Standards Act; National Child Labor Committee.*

BIBLIOGRAPHY

Books

Johnson, Elizabeth Sands. "Child Labor Legislation." In John R. Commmons, et al., *History of Labor in the United States*, 4 vols. New York: Macmillan, 1918–1935.

Johnson, Julia E. *Child Labor*. New York: The H. W. Wilson Company, 1926.

Kyvig, David. *Explicit and Authentic Acts: Amending the U.S. Constitution, 1776–1995*. Lawrence: University Press of Kansas, 1996.

Lumpkin, Katharine, and Dorothy Wolff Douglass. *Child Workers in America*. New York: Robert M. McBride and Company, 1939.

Trattaner, Walter I. *Crusade for the Children*. Chicago: Quadrangle Books, 1970.

Periodicals

Abbot, Grace. "Federal Regulation of Child Labor, 1906–1938." *Social Service Review* 13 (September 1939): 409–430.

Hulett, J. E., Jr. "Propaganda and the Proposed Child Labor Amendment." *Public Opinion Quarterly* 2, no. 1 (1938):105–115.

Sherman, Richard B. "The Rejection of the Child Labor Amendment." *Mid-American* 45 (January 1963): 3–17.

—Jane Holzka

Samuel Gompers. The Library of Congress.

Chinese Exclusion Act

United States 1882

Synopsis

The Chinese Exclusion Act of 1882 was the first law passed in the United States that excluded a people of a specific ethnicity from immigrating to the country. It was the culmination of several decades' worth of agitation on the part of white workers in the United States, as well as violence directed against Chinese workers. The initial time period covered by the statute was 10 years; at the end of that time period, the law was renewed in 1892 for another 10 years, and in 1902 the law was made permanent. The act was not repealed until 1943, after China became an ally of the United States during World War II.

Timeline

1863: The world's first subway opens, in London.

1869: The first U.S. transcontinental railway is completed.

1873: Typewriter is introduced.

1876: Four-stroke cycle gas engine is introduced.

1878: Thomas Edison develops a means of cheaply producing and transmitting electric current, which he succeeds in subdividing so as to make it adaptable to household use. The value of shares in gas companies plummets as news of his breakthrough reaches Wall Street.

1881: In a shootout at the O.K. Corral outside Tombstone, Arizona, Wyatt, Virgil, and Morgan Earp, along with "Doc" Holliday, kill Billy Clanton, Frank McLowry, and Tom McLowry. This breaks up a gang headed by

Clanton's brother Ike, who flees Tombstone. The townspeople, however, suspect the Earps and Holliday of murder. During the same year, Sheriff Pat Garrett shoots notorious criminal William Bonney, a.k.a. Billy the Kid, in Fort Sumner, New Mexico.

1883: Brooklyn Bridge is completed.

1883: Foundation of the League of Struggle for the Emancipation of Labor by Marxist political philosopher Georgi Valentinovich Plekhanov marks the formal start of Russia's labor movement. Change still lies far in the future for Russia, however: tellingly, Plekhanov launches the movement in Switzerland.

1883: *Life* magazine begins publication.

1885: Belgium's King Leopold II becomes sovereign of the so-called Congo Free State, which he will rule for a quarter-century virtually as his own private property. The region in Africa, given the name of Zaire in the 1970s (and Congo 1997), becomes the site of staggering atrocities, including forced labor and genocide, at the hands of Leopold's minions.

1889: Indian Territory in Oklahoma is opened to white settlement.

1893: Henry Ford builds his first automobile.

Event and Its Context

The discovery of gold in California inspired not only American "49ers." Many Chinese peasants had been displaced by the Red Turban Rebellion, and they suffered under extremely high taxes levied by the Qing government to pay indemnities to Western imperialist powers as a result of the First Opium War (1843). This was coupled with hardships caused by the extensive flooding in the rich delta areas and resulted in large numbers of peasants being drawn to the promises held by *Gam Saan* (Gold Mountain) in the United States. The success achieved by early migrants who returned to their villages with the money they made in Hawaii and in the United States spurred more migration to America. Labor recruiters posted circulars in many villages in China, promising high wages. In 1860 a Chinese laborer who made $2 to $3 a month in China could make $30 a month working on the railroad in the United States, plus have clothing and housing provided by the American employers. This wage differential, and the other promised amenities, made immigration to the United States extremely attractive to struggling Chinese peasants.

Some Chinese peasants paid their own way to the United States, as they were able to gather enough money on their own or to borrow from family members or other villagers. A substantial number of Chinese men immigrated to the United States as contract laborers by borrowing money from a broker to cover the cost of transportation, and then paying off that loan plus interest out of earnings in the United States. There is little documentation that Chinese workers were kidnapped or coerced into immigration, so few Chinese immigrants could properly be labeled "coolies" (from the Chinese term *Ku Li,* meaning bonded servant), despite the popular depiction during this time of the typical Chinese laborer. The few who did come to the United States as bonded laborers were banned by law in 1862, in the midst of a war over slavery. In a pattern that would be repeated over and over with the Chinese, however, little distinction was made between bonded and free Chinese laborers; many Americans applied the divisive term to all Chinese workers.

Although some Chinese were initially warmly received in the United States, the increasing numbers of "Celestials" (one of the least objectionable names by which natives of China were known) engendered greater levels of hostility. By 1852 white miners were able to persuade the legislature of California to pass a law levying a tax of $3 per month on "foreign" miners who did not attempt to become citizens. (Chinese immigrants were prevented from applying for naturalization because of the 1790 law that limited those eligible for naturalized citizenship to "white" persons.) This foreign miners' tax remained in force until passage of the Civil Rights Act of 1870. Although this law was mainly aimed at protecting the civil rights of the newly freed African Americans, provisions also were made to prevent the imposition of discriminatory penalties, taxes, licenses, or other exactions, which were initially applied to the Chinese. By the time this occurred, however, the state of California had collected over $5 million through this tax, a sum representing over 25 percent of all state revenue. Most Chinese miners during this early time period worked for themselves in placer mines (the stereotypical mine claim in Gold Rush California), shoveling sand into pans or rockers and then washing it away, looking for the heavier gold particles. Like other miners, however, the Chinese were soon looking for other work as the surface mines quickly played out.

As this was happening, the impetus to construct railroads in California was growing stronger. In 1866 the Central Pacific Railroad began to recruit Chinese laborers to construct a rail line from Sacramento east. According to historian Alexander Saxton, the railroad kept some 10,000 Chinese men employed in boring and blasting the tunnels through the Sierra Nevada, as well as laying track across Nevada and much of Utah. Many of these Chinese laborers remained employed in railroad construction, because after joining the Union Pacific Railroad at Promontory Point in Utah, the Central Pacific built feeder lines north and south in California. Chinese workers who left the railroad construction industry often provided labor on California farms, which were moving from pastoral pursuits into cash crops; the Chinese provided the strong backs for clearing land, digging ditches, building dikes and irrigation systems, and harvesting crops. Chinese workers who could not find work in either of these two fields, or who chose not to, drifted into the cities in the West, where they often found jobs in industries being established in western cities, worked as domestics, or opened laundries. "Chinese laundries" are an American invention, as in patriarchal Chinese society, women were expected to perform household chores such as laundry. In the western portion of the United States, single men comprised a large portion of the population, and the entrepreneurial Chinese saw an opportunity to make money by providing a needed service. Chinese men provided this service because there were so few Chinese women in the United States; only one in every 13 Chinese immigrants was female. To ensure the return of prodigals, the Chinese gov-

Denis Kearney. The Library of Congress.

ernment often kept wives and children at home to help sojourners resist the temptation to become permanent residents in the United States. Chinese custom at the time provided for the patrilineal division of property among all sons, who were in turn responsible for supporting their elderly parents. The immigration of Chinese females was further restricted in 1875, with the enactment of the Page Law that forbade the immigration of Chinese prostitutes. This effectively banned most Chinese females from immigration to the United States, as no effort was made to ascertain whether a particular Chinese female was a prostitute or not; it was simply assumed that all Chinese females who attempted to immigrate to the United States were prostitutes. This law, coupled with antimiscegenation laws that were passed by several states at about the same time, made it extremely difficult for the Chinese to marry and establish families in the United States. Many whites undoubtedly felt that allowing large numbers of Chinese to establish families in the country would encourage their permanent settlement, which they wished to avoid.

In the imaginations of many white Americans, Chinese workers replaced African American slaves on the lowest rung of humanity. Chinese workers were supposed to be living on a diet, consisting of rice and rats, that any self-respecting white man would reject. The imagery that Chinese workers could subsist on fewer rations than white workers remained a part of American labor ideology for an extended period of time. Samuel Gompers utilized this vision in a speech and article published in the *American Federationist*, entitled "Meat v. Rice," to plead the case for permanent Chinese exclusion in 1901. Chinese

Chinese man hanging from branch labeled "Freedom to All," tiger representing Irish workers, and elephant representing republicans hanging from pigtail with signs "20 Years" and "10 Years," an illustration about moratorium on Chinese immigration. © Hulton/Getty Images. Reproduced by permission.

Yick Wo v. Hopkins (1880)

In 1880, two years before the passage of the Chinese Exclusion Act, the city of San Francisco put into law a pair of ordinances, orders no. 1569 and 1587. Passed 26 May and 28 July, respectively, the ordinances provided that all laundry facilities in the city must be of brick or stone, unless the owner had obtained the consent of the city's board of supervisors.

Taken at face value, these did not appear to discriminate against Chinese workers; in other words, they were, in legal terms, "facially neutral." In practice, however, the city applied the laws in a discriminatory fashion. Of 88 applications for exemption filed by non-Chinese laundry owners in the five years after the passage of the ordinances, only one had failed to win approval. By contrast, every single one of the 200 applications submitted by Chinese laundry owners had been denied.

On 24 August 1885 a laundry owner named Yick Wo petitioned California's supreme court, maintaining that he had been deprived of life and liberty. The case eventually went to the U.S. Supreme Court, which delivered its opinion on 10 May 1886. A facially neutral law, the court maintained, is a violation of equal protection when it is operated in such a way as to discriminate in practice against a racial minority. Though the law might be written in such a way as to be neutral on its face, the fact that it is enforced in "an invidiously discriminatory matter" deprives that law of any claim to neutrality. The Court therefore overturned the California court's ruling against Yick Wo.

Source: Tony Mauro. *Illustrated Great Decisions of the Supreme Court*. Washington, DC: CQ Press, 2000.

—Judson Knight

were also imagined as replacing African Americans as laborers in the cotton fields of the American South. At the Cotton States Exhibition held in Memphis in 1869, Cornelius Koopmanschap boasted that he could provide planters with all the labor they needed, directly from China, for as little as $10 or $12 dollars a month. Also in 1869, Chinese laborers were imported to North Adams, Massachusetts, to break a strike of shoemakers there; later in the century, African Americans would often be used for the same purpose. This brief contact with Chinese workers by a small portion of the white working class was kept alive by the daily and labor press and became the impetus for labor's support for the Chinese exclusion legislation when it was introduced. The Chinese worker was, in fact, excluded from consideration for membership from the Knights of Labor, the most egalitarian labor movement in the history of the United States to that point and an organization that readily admitted African Americans. Although the Chinese faced opposition from whites wherever they chose to try to make a living, the opposition was strongest where their numbers were the greatest—namely, in San Francisco, California.

In 1876 the mayor of San Francisco, Andrew Jackson Bryant (1823–1882), decided the time was propitious to settle the Chinese question. The presidential election that fall would be a close one, and the House and the Senate were split between the two parties. Both Democrats and Republicans would be looking for a political issue that could gain them votes. California political leaders quickly jumped on the bandwagon, and in the midst of an economic depression this issue became the leading issue in California politics. The problem with this development for California's white workers, however, was that other issues that concerned them, such as the enforcement of the eight-hour workday, were given short shrift by politicians in the state.

California politicians were not the only beneficiaries of this development, however. In San Francisco the Workingman's Party and its best-known demagogue, Denis Kearney, capitalized on much of the opposition to the Chinese. Kearney's dramatic oratorical style proved to be very popular in the nightly meetings held in empty lots near San Francisco's Chinatown. Kearney was regularly arrested for inciting violence (mainly against the Chinese); just as regularly he was acquitted. The Workingman's Party in California faded into obscurity after 1879, in part because the Democratic Party appropriated its biggest issue, the exclusion of Chinese.

The Democratic Party in California had been able to use the advocacy of the exclusion of Chinese to reestablish the party there, and this strategy was quickly utilized on the national level, as well. The appeal of the exclusion of the Chinese to workingmen, who found their status threatened by the increased importance of industrial capital, led many to abandon the Republican Party and vote Democratic because of this issue. This, of course, prompted many Republican politicians into the advocacy of Chinese exclusion and contributed to the abandonment of the advocacy of equal rights for former slaves.

Key Players

Gompers, Samuel (1850–1924): Gompers was the first president of the American Federation of Labor (1888–1924). Although Gompers himself was an immigrant (a Jew of Dutch parents, born in England), he advocated placing restrictions on all immigrants because he believed that their presence drove down the wages for American workers and immigrants already present in the country. Although unsuccessful in restricting immigration from Europe, Gompers contributed to the successful drive to continue the restriction on immigration from China.

Kearney, Denis (1847–1907): A native of County Cork, Ireland, Kearney rose to prominence in San Francisco in 1877 when he began addressing workers and the unemployed in vacant sand lots in the city during the depression. His speeches quickly devolved from denouncements of the power of monopolies, however, to denunciations of the Chinese. He began most speeches with the words, "The Chinese must go." Kearney helped found the Workingmen's Party (San Francisco, 1878), which was influential in helping form the new California constitution that year, although provisions denying Chinese certain civil liberties were later thrown out by the courts. The popularity of these anti-Chinese laws made the final passage of the Chinese Exclusion Act in 1882 much more palpable to politicians, however.

See also: *American Federation of Labor.*

BIBLIOGRAPHY

Books

Chan, Sucheng, ed. *Entry Denied: Exclusion and the Chinese Community in America, 1882–1943.* Philadelphia: Temple University Press, 1991.

McClain, Charles, ed. *Chinese Immigrants and American Law.* New York: Garland Publishing, 1994.

Saxton, Alexander. *The Indispensable Enemy: Labor and the Anti-Chinese Movement in California.* Berkeley: University of California Press, 1995.

Takaki, Ronald. *A Different Mirror: A History of Multicultural America.* Boston: Little, Brown & Co., 1993.

—Gregory M. Miller

Chinese Rail Workers Strike

United States 1867

Synopsis

Thousands of Chinese immigrant railroad laborers working in California's Sierra Nevada mountain range went on strike against the Central Pacific Railroad in June 1967. They demanded higher wages and a shorter workday and protested the right of overseers to whip them or prohibit them from quitting and seeking alternative employment. While the "Big Four" railroad magnates originally shied away from Chinese labor, "coolies" laboring in severe weather, under cruel working conditions, with pay inferior to that of whites, became the bulk of the western railroad labor force. Amidst a climate of anti-Chinese sentiment, the workers lacked the support of other workers, and the strike failed in one week after the railroad cut off their food supply.

Timeline

1851: China's T'ai P'ing ("Great Peace") Rebellion begins under the leadership of schoolmaster Hong Xiuquan, who believes himself the younger brother of Jesus Christ. He mobilizes the peasantry against the Manchu emperors in a civil war that will take 20 to 30 million lives over the next 14 years.

1857: The Sepoy Mutiny, an unsuccessful revolt by Indian troops against the British East India Company, begins. As a result of the rebellion, which lasts into 1858, England places India under direct crown rule.

1863: The world's first subway opens, in London.

1867: Dual monarchy is established in Austria-Hungary.

1867: Maximilian surrenders to Mexican forces under Benito Juarez and is executed. Thus ends Napoleon III's dreams for a new French empire in the New World.

1867: The Dominion of Canada is established.

1867: United States purchases Alaska from Russia for $7.2 million.

1867: Meiji Restoration in Japan ends 675 years of rule by the shoguns.

1867: Karl Marx publishes the first volume of *Das Kapital.*

1871: U.S. troops in the West begin fighting the Apache nation.

1874: As farm wages in Britain plummet, agricultural workers go on strike.

1877: Great Britain's Queen Victoria is proclaimed the empress of India.

1882: The Chinese Exclusion Act, a treaty between the United States and China, provides for restrictions on immigration of Chinese workers.

1884: Chicago's Home Life Insurance Building, designed by William LeBaron Jenney, becomes the world's first skyscraper.

Event and Its Context

Labor Shortage

In the 1860s, as the Central Pacific (CP) and Union Pacific railroads struggled toward completion of the first transcontinental railroad, management realized the need for a stable workforce. In June 1865 the CP had reached Clipper Gap, at the edge of the Sierra Nevada; cutting through the rock and making the detours necessary for level tracks would be a costly and laborious endeavor. While the railroad offered workers between $1 and $2 daily, European and American workers preferred mining. Men habitually signed on with the CP for free transportation, with nine out of ten abandoning the railroad camps for mining towns after a week's work. Faced with a labor shortage, the railroad reluctantly heeded suggestions by Central Pacific general superintendent Charles Crocker to hire Chinese immigrants. (The idea came from his brother, Judge E. B. Crocker.)

The Chinese in California

Despite evidence of a miniscule Chinese presence in the United States from early colonial times, a Chinese community did not develop until the mid-nineteenth century. Hardships in China and the gold rush in California led Chinese immigrants to strike claims there. In 1849 there were 325 Chinese residents in California; by 1860 there were 34,933. Unable to pay their own passage to America, many Chinese arrived as indentured servants. By 1870 roughly half the Chinese in the United States were working in mining, making up more than a quarter of all miners. The xenophobia meeting the large-scale arrival of Chinese miners led the California state legislature to approve the

Chinese laborers working on the Central Pacific Railroad. © Bettmann/Corbis. Reproduced by permission.

Foreign Miners' Tax law. The Chinese were also required to obtain a license to work in the mines. In 1862 "An Act to Protect Free White Labor Against Competition with Chinese Coolie Labor, and to Discourage the Immigration of the Chinese into the State of California" established a monthly "police tax" for all adults "of the Mongolian race." As mining opportunities declined, more Chinese turned to the railroads to earn a living.

Chinese Workers on Trial

The Crockers' idea to hire so-called coolies to work on the railroad was at first shunned. The "Big Four" entrepreneurs behind construction (Collis P. Huntington, Mark Hopkins, Leland Stanford, and Charles Crocker) debated whether the physically smaller Chinese would deliver the productivity that management required. Averaging a mere 5 feet in height and weighing only 120 pounds, the Chinese were not considered fit for the job. J. H. Strobridge, the Central Pacific's construction superintendent, refused to "boss Chinese. I will not be responsible for work done on the road by Chinese labor." Stanford nonetheless backed Crocker; since 5,000 laborers were needed "for constant and permanent work," the Chinese were given a chance to prove their worth. A trial group of 50 men in basket hats, blue blouses, and floppy, blue cotton pants showed up to fill dump carts. Despite jeering by their Irish counterparts, the men's careful, methodical approach proved successful, and more Chinese were brought on to do all sorts of excavation and construction work. In one observer's words, they were the perfect workers: fast learners and deft performers, "never becoming drunk, or disorderly, or going on a 'strike.'" Railroad agents scoured California towns for Chinese laborers, and by the fall of 1865 some 3,000 were on the payroll.

Inferior Conditions

Whereas Irish workers received room, board, and $2 a day, "Crocker's pets" worked from sunrise to sunset under hazardous conditions for roughly $1 a day and no room or board (this later rose to $35 a month in the face of competitive mining rates). The only special concession was a varied diet of "exotic" Chinese foodstuffs, which the railroad acquired to sell to workers. The Chinese were organized into gangs averaging 20 men, headed by Irish "riding bosses". The "evil-looking, eye-patched" Strobridge drove the men mercilessly. While the Irish got the most prestigious jobs, the Chinese mostly did the backbreaking work. Their toughest obstacle came at a rocky promontory called Cape Horn. There, suspended on ropes from near-vertical cliffs more than a thousand feet over the American River, the Chinese workers chipped through granite, drilled holes to place explosives, and then raced up the lines to avoid the blast. The work became even more dangerous with the advent of nitroglycerin in 1866. Countless workers disappeared in rock slides and avalanches. In winter, workers were ordered to tunnel through the snowy Donner Summit; they lived in shacks under the snow, and snowslides carried away the camps and many men died, their bodies not found until the spring thaw. Such hazards allegedly inspired the phrase "not a Chinaman's chance."

The Chinese Strike

On 25 June 1867 the Chinese workers initiated a strike. Some 2,000 workers (twice that, by some accounts) simultaneously threw down their picks and shovels and "dissolved into a sullen mob, shuffling back to their encampments." The men demanded treatment equal to white workers, including a raise to $40 dollars per month. They asked that the workday above ground be reduced to 10 hours and that work in the tunnels be put at eight. "Eight hours a day good for white men, all the same good for Chinamen," said one. They called for an end to the right of company overseers "to either whip them or restrain them from leaving the road when they desire to seek other employment." When Strobridge's attempts to bully them back to work failed, he telegraphed Charles Crocker.

The news reportedly came as a surprise to Crocker, who assumed worker relations were excellent. He at first believed the strike was "instigated by Chinese gamblers and opium traders." He then blamed agents of the rival Union Pacific for the strike and its demands in order "to keep us in the mountains while they were building the road over the plains." The walkout came amidst the hardest work on the entire stretch of the railroad, a rocky area between Strong's Canyon and Cisco. "This strike of the chinamen is the hardest blow we have had here," wrote E. B. Crocker. "If we get over this without yielding, it will be all right hereafter." He also recognized that if the Chinese were successful in their demands, they would then be in control and their demands would be increased.

Charles Crocker, the only one of the "Big Four" to have direct contact with the job, confronted some of the "leading Chinamen." He asserted that he would not pay them more than $35 per day. The men reportedly smiled, bowed, and said they would tell their compatriots to return to work. The workers, however, remained in their camps.

Among the few accounts of the actual dynamics of the strike are a series of letters from Judge E. B. Crocker to Huntington during these days of conflict. Departing from the idea that the "Big Four" were the sole masterminds behind the transcontinental railroad, David Haward Bain argues in his book *Empire Express* that Judge Crocker was also a pivotal force, a uniting factor in times of crisis.

Breaking the Strike

According to E. B. Crocker, the Chinese were "getting smart." Evoking the law of supply and demand, Crocker advocated flooding the western labor market with recently liberated African American workers from the South. The only "safe way" to counter the Chinese demands was to "inundate this state and Nevada with Freedmen, Chinese, Japanese, all kinds of labor, so that men come to us for work instead of us hunting them up." Just as the poorly paid Chinese laborers kept the Irish workers reminded of their own dispensability, Crocker hoped that "a Negro labor force would tend to keep the Chinese quiet. That," he said, was "the only remedy for strikers."

This proposed strikebreaking strategy was feasible. Earlier that year a man by the name of Yates had approached Stanford with the idea of enlisting government assistance to bring thousands of black freedmen to California. Stanford had reportedly told Yates that there would be railroad work for them. Perfectly timed with the Chinese conflict was a newspaper report that Yates was in Washington, D.C., pitching his idea of organizing 5,000 black workers; he was even identified there as an agent of the Central Pacific. E. B. Crocker and Hopkins urged Huntington, who managed the railroad's affairs in the East, to contact Yates and aid his endeavor.

On 27 June workers along the line from Cisco to Truckee Meadows were on strike. Facing Crocker's threats, the Chinese increased their demands to $45 per month. While the plan to bring in black workers failed, Charles Crocker's refusal to meet Chinese demands took a "cruel but effective" course: the railroad stopped supplying the Chinese with food and other provisions. The railroad agents ignored and isolated the men for a week, so as not to "exhibit anxiety." Charles Crocker then gathered the hungry men to tell them he "would not be dictated to" and that he made the rules. Any workers who wanted to work would, from their wages, pay fines for not working; if they refused, the railroad would withhold June wages. The men tried to negotiate, but Crocker refused to grant even a monthly raise of 25 cents. When most Chinese caved in, a few allegedly threatened to whip those who returned to work and set fire to their camps. Crocker, who was accompanied by Strobridge, the sheriff, and "an armed mob of deputized whites," said anyone trying to harm the laborers would be shot. According to E. B. Crocker, the Chinese were "glad to go to work again."

With no support from other workers, the Chinese strike ended without event, and the men went back to "working hard and steady." Thousands more Chinese were brought on to finish the railroad. In 1868 Central Pacific crews finally broke out of the Sierra Nevada. That same year the United States and China signed the Burlingame Treaty, which assured cheap Asian labor for the American market. Over the next decade an average of 12,000 Chinese immigrated to the United States annually.

Key Players

Crocker, Charles (1822–1888): Crocker was an American financier who acted as general superintendent of the Central Pacific Railroad from 1863 to 1869. He is credited with ensuring that the western stretch of the transcontinental railroad was completed seven years before the U.S. government deadline. In 1871 he became president of the Southern Pacific Railroad of California, which merged with the Central Pacific in 1884.

Crocker, Edwin Bryant (1818–1875): E. B. Crocker was the brother of Charles Crocker and the official attorney of the Central Pacific Railroad. A justice of the California Supreme Court, he was credited with using his legal expertise, political connections, diplomacy, and engineering education to maintain unity among the railroad's "Big Four" associates.

Strobridge, James Harvey (1827–1921): Strobridge, a Vermont native, began working for East Coast railroads at age 16 but went to California during the gold rush. He joined the Central Pacific railroad in 1864 and soon headed the entire construction program, directly overseeing workers. Crocker rehired him in 1877 to oversee the second transcontinental line from Los Angeles to New Orleans.

Stanford, Amasa Leland (1824–1893): Stanford was an American industrialist and politician who, after serving as California governor, financed and promoted the Central Pacific Railroad. He served as its president from 1863 to 1893, during construction of the western link of the transcontinental railroad.

See also: *Chinese Exclusion Act.*

BIBLIOGRAPHY

Books

Ambrose, Stephen E. *Nothing Like It in the World: The Men Who Built the Transcontinental Railroad, 1865–1869.* New York: Simon and Schuster, 2000.

Bain, David Haward. *Empire Express: Building the First Transcontinental Railroad.* New York: Penguin Putnam, 1999.

Chinn, Thomas W., ed. *A History of the Chinese in California: A Syllabus.* San Francisco: Chinese Historical Society of America, 1969.

Elish, Dan. *Transcontinental Railroad: Triumph of a Dream.* Brookfield, CT: Millbrook Press, 1993.

Gale Encyclopedia of U.S. Economic History. Farmington Hills, MI: The Gale Group, 1999.

Rusling, James F. *The Great West and Pacific Coast.* New York: Sheldon & Company, 1877.

Steiner, Stan. *Fusang, the Chinese Who Built America.* New York: Harper & Row, 1979.

Other

An Act to Protect Free White Labor against Competition with Chinese Coolie Labor, and to Discourage the Immigration of the Chinese Into the State of California. 26 April 1862 [cited 5 October 2002]. <http://www.druglibrary.org/schaffer/History/1870/anticoolieact.htm>

Chinese Immigrants and the Building of the Transcontinental Railroad. The Gilder Lehrman Institute of American History. 2001 [cited 5 October 2002]. <http://www.gliah.uh.edu/historyonline/china1.cfm>

Emor, Dawn, and David Bushong. *"The Transcontinental Railroad: Different Faces behind 'The Work of the Age'"* [cited 5 October 2002]. <http://bushong.net/dawn/about/college/ids100/>

"History of Chinese Americans in the United States." Chinese American Data Center [cited 5 October 2002]. <http://members.aol.com/chineseusa/00his.htm>

New Perspectives on the West. Episode Five (1868–1874), "The Grandest Enterprise under God: The Artillery of Heaven." 2001 [cited 5 October 2002]. <http://www.pbs.org/weta/thewest/program/episodes/five/artilleryheaven.htm>

"Rensselaer Alumni Hall of Fame: Edwin Bryant Crocker." Rensselaer Polytechnic Institute, 1996–2002 [cited 5 October 2002]. <http://www.rpi.edu/dept/NewsComm/sub/fame/inductees/edwincrocker.html>

ADDITIONAL RESOURCES

Central Pacific Railroad Photographic History Museum: Transcontinental Railroad & Photography Books in Print [cited 5 October 2002]. <http://cprr.org/Museum/Recent_Books.html>

—Brett Allan King

Christian Trade Unionists Conference

Switzerland 1908

Synopsis

Beginning in the 1880s, Christian trade unions formed in the industrial areas of the Rhine region. At the beginning of the twentieth century, national federations came into being. Delegates of the existing national federations convened in Zurich, Switzerland, on 2–5 August 1908, at the invitation of the Cologne office of the German confederation of Christian unions. They founded an international secretariat housed in Cologne, Germany, under the direction of Adam Stegerwald. Members included all national federations of Christian unions: German, Belgian, Dutch, Austrian, Italian, Swiss, and Polish. France was not represented because the Christian unions there were not yet brought together in such a national federation. Dutch Catholic unions did not join at this time, but the separate Protestant union federation did. A Swedish group was represented initially but dropped out. The make-up of the member federations was predominantly Roman Catholic but with an important Protestant contingent. While textile and agricultural unions formed the largest contingents, an array of other industries also participated Facing their doubly minoritarian position as vindicators of the rights and demands of labor in the church world, while defending Christian ways of life and thought in the world of labor, the delegates sought to strengthen their cause by mutual support and international ties. Delegates elected an international continuation committee consisting of union representatives from Germany, Italy, and the Netherlands. A follow-up meeting convened in Cologne in 1911, but little else transpired in the run-up to World War I. Shortly after the war, however, the International Confederation of Christian Trade Unions took shape.

Timeline

1888: Serbian-born American electrical engineer Nikola Tesla develops a practical system for generating and transmitting alternating current (AC), which will ultimately—and after an extremely acrimonious battle—replace Thomas Edison's direct current (DC) in most homes and businesses.

1893: New Zealand is the first nation in the world to grant the vote to women.

1901: Guglielmo Marconi makes the first successful transmission and reception of a radio signal.

1904: The ten-hour workday is established in France.

1908: An earthquake in southern Italy and Sicily kills some 150,000 people.

1908: The U.S. Supreme Court, in the Danbury Hatters' case, rules that secondary union boycotts (i.e., boycotts of non-union manufacturers' products, organized by a union) are unlawful.

1908: Ford Motor Company introduces the Model T.

1908: Robert S. S. Baden-Powell founds the Boy Scouts in England.

1908: The Tunguska region of Siberia experiences a strange explosion, comparable to the detonation of a hydrogen bomb, whose causes will long be a subject of debate. Today, many scientists believe that a comet caused the Tunguska event.

1911: Turkish-Italian War sees the first use of aircraft as an offensive weapon. Italian victory results in the annexation of Libya.

1915: A German submarine sinks the *Lusitania,* killing 1,195, including 128 U.S. citizens. Theretofore, many Americans had been sympathetic toward Germany, but the incident begins to turn the tide of U.S. sentiment toward the Allies.

1918: The Second Battle of the Marne in July and August is the last major conflict on the Western Front. In November, Kaiser Wilhelm II abdicates, bringing an end to the war.

Event and Its Context

The World of European Labor

The spur to the conference of Christian trade unionists was the clear head start that socialist labor had attained in organizing the industrial workforce in Europe. Christian unionists found it impossible to join socialist unions as long as the latter denigrated religion and pursued class enmity or the dictatorship of the proletariat as their policy. The Christian unions that they founded from the 1880s on appealed to those workers who were not out to identify Christianity with bourgeoisie or capitalism nor to dispossess the owners of productive property. All the same, the confederation's members harbored deep distrust of the economic liberalism (i.e., actually existing capitalism) that erected into natural law the workings of markets and led to drastically unequal benefits for capital and labor. They were deaf, for example, to the blandishments of paternalist employers' associations that promised charity in return for docility. As far as strikes were concerned, Christian unions considered them a last resort but engaged in them often enough to retain the loyalty of their members and to arouse the ire of employers and a good part of respectable churchdom.

Internationally, the new German emperor, Wilhelm II, hosted an international conference on labor legislation in 1890 in Berlin, with little in the way of results. A social Catholic in Switzerland, Kaspar Decurtins, took up the cause and proposed a nongovernmental international conference on the same subject in Zurich in 1897. At this meeting some Christian labor leaders, along with interested socialist and bourgeois participants, met and endorsed certain minimum standards. In the framework of the Second International (founded 1889), the International Secretariat of National Trade Union Centers came into existence in 1901–1902. This was an alliance that Adam Stegerwald in particular wished to emulate and rival.

Roman Catholicism

An internal controversy periodically erupted into public view over the correct interpretation of *Rerum Novarum*, the 1891 encyclical of Pope Leo XIII "on the condition of labor." This authoritative pronouncement, which would attain the status of a veritable "charter" of Catholic social teaching, contained a severe denunciation of materialistic socialism. The encyclical defended private property, including ownership of the means of production, but gave precedence to the human dignity of workers and owners alike, which ownership must serve, making employment and goods available to those who need them. Leo XIII blamed the oppressive conditions that gave rise to socialism on the prevailing economic materialism and individualism of the leading classes.

In a critical clause, the pope allowed that Catholic associations could be formed with a workers-only membership. Taken together with his encouragement for labor legislation to curb the worst abuses, such as child labor and an excessively long work week, and his condoning of strikes when all else failed, Catholic workers took the encyclical as opening the gate to unionism. There had been precedents: of particular note was the endorsement of British-style unionism in 1869 by Bishop Emmanuel Ketteler of Mainz (1811–1877). *Rerum Novarum* came at the right time to spur the development of trade unions in the

1890s. Some institutional support and personal commitment on the part of Catholic politicians, intellectuals, and clergy came to the aid of struggling labor leaders.

Rerum Novarum, however, did not address the details of organizing to vindicate workers' rights. It spelled out the pope's vision to some extent: it depicted a harmonious Catholic utopia. Under the guidance of the church, workers and employers would cooperate to form trade associations that themselves would set standards of humane treatment of labor. The members would then uphold the standards with the backing of state authority, if necessary. Militant trade unions were not really what the pope had in mind, at least not as a part of an ideal Catholic social order. The exception just noted was a concession to prevailing circumstances. In 1903, with the accession of a more reactionary pope, Pius X, the Catholic opponents of trade unions painted all unions, Christian ones included, as enemies of civil peace and destroyers of the social order.

Thus the delegates to the International Conference of 1908 had an additional motive for cohesion: to oppose trends in Catholicism that were hostile to unions. The issue of interconfessionality (Protestants and Catholics in the same labor organization) thus consumed much energy at the conference and explained the Dutch Catholic union's refusal to join. The controversy was a sign of the unresolved issue of the autonomy of labor from the control of the bishops. Catholic trade unionists in general, and the German ones in particular, insisted on their autonomy vis-à-vis church authority, although a positive relationship was important. For purposes of retaining that autonomy, the Protestant component of the German and the international federations was prized by the mostly Catholic leaders. Dutch bishops, however, though recognizing that their nascent unions were to be run by the laity, insisted on separation from parallel Protestant organizations. For Christian trade union activists, the intertwined issues of interconfessionality and relative autonomy from church authority were life-and-death concerns.

The Christian unions had influential backers who made representations to the Vatican that enabled them to escape condemnation, but just barely (encyclical *Singulari Quadam* of 1912). Nevertheless, the matter was extremely controversial, with bishops split for and against unions in general and interconfessional ones in particular. During this crucial period before World War I, when industrialized manufacture became dominant throughout Europe, this Catholic antiunion campaign made it more difficult for the national unions to reach their full potential and hampered organizational efforts at the international level as well.

Subsequent Developments

The period of the greatest growth of the Christian labor movement commenced after 1918. It would lead to the establishment of the International Federation of Christian Trade Unions (IFCTU) with seat in Utrecht (not to be confused with the much more important International Federation of Trade Unions or IFTU). The International Labor Organization (ILO) recognized the Christian union members of the IFCTU. The role of P. J. S. Serrarens was emblematic of the importance of Dutch and Belgian Christian unions, and the French *Confédération Française des Travailleurs Chrétiens* (CFTC) under Jules

Zirnheld assumed a weightier role, especially after 1936. The Italian, German, and Austrian Christian unions fell victim to undemocratic regimes long before World War II.

At the same time, within Catholicism, the official attitude toward trade unions underwent a decisive turn. Since the time of Pope Pius XI (1923–1939), the right of workers to organize for the vindication of their interests and for the common good has been incontrovertibly anchored in Catholic social teaching, as evidenced in the encyclical *Quadragesimo Anno* of 1931. The issue of autonomy vis-à-vis church authority remained problematic, however. Eventually it led, with other trends, to what may be called the secularization of Christian unions and their international confederation in the 1960s and 1970s. As World War II ended, labor leaders in both the Christian and the socialist camps wished to bury the ideological hatchet for the sake of strong unitary structures. Where this took place, as in Germany, Austria, and Italy, the unions' international allegiances went to the successor organization of the IFTU, which was refounded in 1949 as the ICFTU (International Confederation of Free Trade Unions), rather than to the Christian union federation. The further history of the latter organization, with its roots in the 1908 Zurich conference, tended toward meeting the problems of workers in underdeveloped countries and continents. In 1968 the IFCTU became the World Confederation of Labor (WCL), with headquarters in Brussels.

Key Players

Debruyne, René (1868–1941): Debruyne, in his youth a bakery worker, became the first paid staff member of the Christian union association in Ghent in 1896. He was a Belgian delegate to the 1908 conference. From 1904 to 1914 he established the forerunner of the national Confederation of Christian Unions, which he headed from 1920 to 1931. Elected to the chamber of deputies, he retained his seat until 1939.

Eylenbosch, Gustaaf (1856–1939): Eylenbosch, a typesetter and cofounder of the Cotton Workers Union (Ghent, 1886), was a delegate to the 1908 conference. He was secretary of the (Catholic) Democratic League of Belgium, editor of the daily *Het Volk*, the first president of the national Confederation of Christian Unions (1913–1914), and senator after World War I.

Giesberts, Johannes (1865–1938): Giesberts, originally a mechanic and then a labor journalist on the staff of the German Catholic *Volksverein*, gave the keynote address at the 1908 conference; although he gave credit to social democrats for taking the lead in the labor question, he offered a rationale for the need for an alternative to their unions on the Continent. He chaired the continuation committee of the international secretariat. After World War I he became postal minister in the Weimar government.

Pauwels, Henri (1890–1946): Pauwels started work as a mechanic at the age of 14. In 1912 he began Christian trade union organizing among French-speaking (Walloon) Belgians for the Confederation of Christian Unions. As secretary general of this confederation starting in 1921 until he became its president in 1932, he was also much involved at the international level. After World War II Pauwels became president of the International Federation of Christian Trade Unions (IFCTU) and died at age 56 in an airplane accident in Canada.

Serrarens, Petrus Josephus Servatius (1888–1963): Serrarens was head of the Dutch Catholic labor federation and secretary general of the IFCTU (1920–1952) in Utrecht. He served as delegate and technical adviser to ILO conferences starting with the Washington conference in 1919, as member of Parliament (1929–1952), and from 1952 to 1958 was judge on the court of the European Coal and Steel Community.

Stegerwald, Adam (1874–1945): Stegerwald, a cabinetmaker and founder of a Christian woodworkers' union in Bavaria, helped establish the League of Christian Unions in Germany on a national basis and became its secretary general in 1903. He was the prime mover behind the 1908 conference and headed the office of the international secretariat in Cologne (1909–1914). Though favoring a realignment of parties after World War I, he remained in the Center Party while heading the large federation of factory and office worker unions known as the German Labor Federation until the Nazi takeover.

Zirnheld, Jules (1876–1940): Head of a French Christian office workers' union since the turn of the century, Zirnheld returned from German imprisonment to found the national *Confédération Française des Travailleurs Chrétiens* (CFTC) in 1920, which then joined the IFCTU; he was president of the IFCTU from 1936 until his death.

See also: *International Confederation of Free Trade Unions; International Labor Organization; Second International.*

BIBLIOGRAPHY

Books

Bendiner, Burton. *International Labour Affairs: The World Trade Unions and the Multinational Companies.* Oxford: Clarendon Press, 1987.

Brose, Eric Dorn. *Christian Labor and the Politics of Frustration in Imperial Germany.* Washington, DC: Catholic University of America Press, 1985.

The International Labour Organisation: The First Decade. London: Allen and Unwin, 1931.

Kwanten, Godfried. *Cent Ans de Syndicalisme Chrétien, 1886–1986.* Brussels: Confédération des Syndicats Chrétiens, 1986.

Misner, Paul. "The Emergence of an International Organisation of Christian Labour after *Rerum Novarum.*" In *The Church Faces the Modern World: Rerum Novarum and Its Impact,* edited by Paul Furlong and David Curtis. Humberside, UK: Earlsgate, 1994.

———. *Social Catholicism in Europe: From the Onset of Industrialization to the First World War.* New York: Crossroad, 1991.

Pasture, Patrick. *Histoire du Syndicalisme Chrétien International: La Difficile Recherche d'une Troisième Voie.* Paris: Harmattan, 1999.

Schneider, Michael. *Die Christlichen Gewerkschaften, 1894–1933.* Bonn: Neue Gesellschaft, 1982.

Verstraelen, Jules. "L'aspect International." In *150 Ans de Mouvement Ouvrier Chrétien en Europe de l'Ouest, 1789–1939,* edited by S. H. Scholl. Louvain, Belgium: Nauwelaerts, 1966.

Periodicals

"Der Internationale Arbeiterschutz-Kongress in Zürich und sein Einfluss auf die Christliche Arbeiterbewegung in Deutschland." *Jahrbuch der christlichen Gewerkschaften* 2 (1909): 26–42.

Pasture, Patrick. "Internationale vakbondsactie op het KADOC: Archief ICV/WVA." *KADOC Nieuwsbrief* 6 (1999): 11–14.

———. "A Century of International Trade Unionism." *International Review of Social History* 47 (2002): 277–289.

Other

Catholic University of Louvain. 2002 [cited 2 October 2002]. <http://www.kuleuven.ac.be/kadoc>.

—Paul Misner

CIO Anticommunist Drive

United States 1949–1950

Synopsis

In November 1949, at its eleventh annual convention in Cleveland, the Congress of Industrial Organizations (CIO) expelled two member unions—the United Electrical, Radio, and Machine Workers of America and the Farm Equipment Workers—for their alleged disloyalty to the CIO and support for the Communist Party. Within a year, an additional nine affiliates had been expelled. The eleven unions together represented approximately one million members. The expulsions were the culmination of long-simmering tensions that erupted in the context of the developing cold war. The strife within the CIO halted the federation's growth and paved the way for its merger with the American Federation of Labor in 1955.

Timeline

1928: At the first Academy Awards ceremony, the best picture is the silent *Wings.*

1933: Newly inaugurated U.S. president Franklin D. Roosevelt launches the first phase of his New Deal to put depression-era America back to work.

1938: The U.S. Fair Labor Standards Act establishes a minimum wage.

1943: At the Casablanca Conference in January, Winston Churchill and Franklin Roosevelt agree on the demand of unconditional surrender for the Axis powers.

1948: Israel becomes a nation and is immediately attacked by a coalition of Arab countries. Despite being outnumbered, Israel will win the war in the following year.

1948: Stalin places a blockade on areas of Berlin controlled by the United States, Great Britain, and France. The Allies respond with an airlift of supplies, which, like the blockade itself, lasts into late 1949.

1949: The North Atlantic Treaty Organization (NATO) is established.

1949: The People's Republic of China is established under the leadership of Mao Zedong.

1950: North Korean troops pour into South Korea, starting the Korean War. Initially the communists make impressive gains, but in September the U.S. Marines land at Inchon and liberate Seoul. China responds by sending in its troops.

1950: Senator Joseph McCarthy launches his campaign to root out communist infiltrators.

1955: African and Asian nations meet at the Bandung Conference in Indonesia, inaugurating the "non-aligned" movement of Third World countries.

1960: An American U-2 spy plane piloted by Francis Gary Powers shot down over Soviet skies brings an end to a short period of warming relations between the two superpowers. By the end of the year, Khrushchev makes a scene at the United Nations, banging his shoe on a desk. As for Powers, he will be freed in a 1962 prisoner exchange.

Event and Its Context

Communism in the CIO

The Congress of Industrial Organizations (CIO) was an alliance of leftist and centrist elements of the U.S. labor movement. Communism was a source of both inspiration and conflict in the federation from its founding in 1936 until the final expulsion of eleven left-led unions in the 1949–1950 purge. Communist organizers, acknowledged for their skill and dedication, were widely employed and critically important in the early organizing of key CIO affiliates, including the United Electrical Workers (UE), United Automobile Workers (UAW), Transport Workers Union (TWU), United Steel Workers (USW), and International Longshoremen's and Warehousemen's Union (ILWU). Communists often rose to leadership positions within those and other unions, and some held important posts within the CIO. For example, two of the three national officers in the UE, Julius Emspak and James Matles, were communists, although they always denied party membership, and Lee Pressman served as the general counsel to the Steel Workers Organizing Committee and later as the CIO's general counsel.

Still, by the late 1930s the communist presence was creating political conflict within the CIO affiliates, particularly over the issue of communists' support for the Nazi-Soviet Pact of 1939 and what some observers considered their lockstep adherence to the serpentine political line of the Communist Party USA (CPUSA). CIO communists also attracted congressional scrutiny from the Dies Committee (1938–1945) and the House Un-American Activities Committee (1938–1975). But the wartime U.S.-Soviet alliance eased overt tensions. Communist

Harry A. Bridges. The Library of Congress.

unionists' energetic home front efforts were generally applauded, although some in the CIO later charged that communist-led unions, determined to aid the Soviet Union, wrongfully sacrificed their memberships' best interests to the war drive. During World War II, left-wing unionists gained political influence and visibility through their control of CIO Industrial Union Councils (IUCs) in key cities like New York, Detroit, and Los Angeles and in the related CIO Political Action Committees (PACs) organized in 1943 to support President Franklin D. Roosevelt's reelection.

Cold War Pressures on the Left-Center Alliance

After the end of World War II, the CIO initially favored peacetime continuation of the Big Three alliance (the United States, Britain, and the U.S.S.R.), joining the Soviet-sponsored World Federation of Trades Unions. The CIO also sent a friendship delegation to the Soviet Union in 1945, including such staunch anticommunists as Sidney Hillman, James B. Carey, Alan Haywood, and Emil Rieve. But growing tension between the United States and the Soviet Union began to resonate within the CIO; as international accord deteriorated, so too did the truce in the CIO. By 1946 internal conflict had revived in the CIO and within important CIO affiliates. In that year, CIO anticommunists formed the Committee for Renovative Trade Unionism as a vehicle to counter communist influence. Walter

Walter Philip Reuther. © Hulton/Getty Images. Reproduced by permission.

Reuther rode the anticommunism issue to the UAW presidency. In the UE, District One president Harry Block joined Carey, the former UE president, to found the UE Members for Democratic Action (UEMDA). With the Association of Catholic Trade Unionists, UEMDA launched a drive to oust the UE's left-wing leadership.

External pressures also revived, with fresh congressional initiatives culminating in the 1947 passage of the antilabor Taft-Hartley Act, whose Title I, Section 9(h) required all elected union officials to sign affidavits certifying that they were not members of the Communist Party. While the American Federation of Labor (AFL) endorsed Section 9(h), the CIO initially balked, urging noncompliance. Failure to comply, however, barred unions from access to National Labor Relations Board (NLRB) machinery, a provision whose utility in jurisdictional disputes and intraunion conflicts quickly eroded CIO solidarity. Reuther signed in 1947 and used the affidavit to purge his communist opponents in the UAW and to launch raids against locals in noncomplying unions. The affidavit issue sparked an orgy of raiding, since noncomplying unions were kept off NLRB election ballots and thus were unable to defend themselves. The UE alone endured more than 500 raids between 1947 and 1949, when its leaders finally capitulated and signed.

As the chasm widened between the United States and the Soviet Union, the intensifying cold war increasingly politicized the CIO. President Harry Truman vetoed the Taft-Hartley Act, although he understood that his veto would be overturned, and used the gesture to woo labor support. Truman's cold war initiatives—aid to Greece, support for the Marshall Plan—soon became flash points for conflict within the federation and its affiliates, and anticommunist CIO leaders increasingly pressured leftists to abandon their opposition.

The 1948 presidential election marked a turning point in the internal CIO struggle. In December 1947 Henry A. Wallace announced his candidacy for the presidency. Wallace had served as the vice president during Roosevelt's third term and was a quintessential New Deal progressive; moreover, Truman had fired him from his post as the secretary of commerce for advocating peace with the Soviets. CIO leftists supported Wallace; the UE president, Albert Fitzgerald, cochaired Wallace's campaign committee. Wallace initially seemed to tap a pro-peace vein of support, but his campaign was soon eviscerated by withering attacks. He and his leftist supporters were marginalized, and CIO communists were made vulnerable to their opponents within the federation. Although the CIO was officially nonpartisan, since the Roosevelt years it had effectively supported the Democratic Party, and the communist support for Wallace came to be seen as likely to produce a Republican victory. The Wallace campaign thus served to solidify the CIO's initially tepid support for Truman, and Wallace backers became prime targets of CIO ire.

The CIO IUCs and PACs became battlegrounds. CIO president Philip Murray abandoned the restraint that had precluded open attacks on the communists, and in March 1947 the national CIO IUC director, John Brophy, ordered all IUCs to endorse national CIO policy on specific issues or risk losing their CIO endorsement. Harry Bridges, the CIO Pacific Coast regional director, refused to comply and was removed from his post; Pressman, the general counsel, was fired for supporting Wallace. These moves—against CIO employees and specifically CIO-created structures like the IUCs—signaled the beginning of an all-out effort to drive communists entirely out of the CIO, including the communists active in affiliated unions.

The Purge

CIO strategy in the affiliates was to exert heavy pressure on communist leaders and their allies while encouraging anticommunists to oust them, hoping thereby to keep the federation structurally and financially intact. In some instances, the strategy worked. "Red Mike" Quill, the fiery TWU president, denounced his erstwhile allies and purged the TWU. But the largest and most influential of the left-led unions, the UE, remained impervious to assault, successfully repelling a strong, CIO-sanctioned UEMDA challenge at its September 1949 convention. The UE voted to withhold CIO dues until affiliates stopped raiding UE locals; that action opened the UE to direct CIO attack at the November CIO convention. Calling UE "the Communist Party masquerading as a labor union," delegates voted to expel the UE and the small Farm Equipment Workers, which had merged with the UE for protection. Following the UE's expulsion, the CIO chartered a replacement, the International Union of Electrical Workers, and appointed Carey as the president.

The convention amended the CIO constitution, empowering the executive board to hold hearings and expel communist-dominated unions. Ten unions were charged under the new provisions, and hearings were arranged. The unions charged were the American Communications Association; Food, Tobacco, Agricultural, and Allied Workers (FTA); International Fishermen and Allied Workers; International Fur and Leather Workers Union (IFLWU); ILWU; International Union of Mine, Mill, and Smelter Workers; National Union of Maritime Cooks and Stewards; United Furniture Workers (UFW); United Office and

Professional Workers of America; and United Public Workers of America. Again the CIO strategy was to encourage internal "housecleaning," but of the 10 unions, only the UFW complied, earning a reprieve.

The remaining nine unions were subjected to remarkably undemocratic hearings. Anticommunists accused, prosecuted, judged, and sentenced the hapless leftists, denying defense counsel or the right to call witnesses until the IFLWU took the issue to civil court. Evidence was derived from analyzing union publications and comparing political positions to those of the CPUSA. More damaging testimony came from disaffected former communists and allies, who testified to direct links between union leaders and the CPUSA. All nine unions were expelled.

Aftermath and Consequences of Disunion

Expulsion did not end the issue; it merely intensified internecine strife as AFL and CIO affiliates went after the banished unions. The strongest unions—the UE, ILWU, and IFLWU—survived, but as pariahs; others were absorbed by competitors. The USW, for example, absorbed the Mine, Mill, and Smelter Workers after several bitter, racially divisive fights. Some, like the FTA and the Maritime Cooks, were destroyed. All of the expelled unions were additionally subjected to external pressures from governmental agencies and a hostile press. The CIO's momentum fizzled; growth was sluggish, at best. Operation Dixie, the southern organizing drive intended to demonstrate the CIO's post-purge vitality, was a disastrous defeat that paved the way for the CIO's merger with the AFL in 1955.

Scholars differ in their assessment of the CIO's expulsion of its left-wing unions. Early accounts were heavily ideological and starkly partisan. Since the 1980s historians have begun to acknowledge that left-led unions generally were quite well led and notably democratic, often pioneering in organizing previously neglected groups: women, minorities, and white-collar and professional workers. Most now agree that the internecine strife was profoundly detrimental to the CIO and to the U.S. labor movement as a whole. Steve Rosswurm argues that the expulsions hastened bureaucratization; stifled political debate; silenced shop-floor militants; undermined organizing among key groups; chilled the advance of the nascent civil rights movement; and inhibited labor's ability to counter postwar capital mobility. Ronald Filippelli and Mark McColloch call the expulsions "a self-dismemberment... one of the excesses committed in the name of national security during the Cold War." Others acknowledge harmful aspects but nevertheless conclude, as Robert Zieger does, that the expulsions were necessary. Zieger notes, the CIO "opposed Stalinism at home and abroad at a time when many of the left were beguiled by the Soviet mystique," and he concludes that, despite the cost, the CIO still "established new standards of material well-being, personal dignity, and workplace dignity" for working people.

Key Players

Bridges, Harry A. (1901–1990): An Australian, Bridges joined the Industrial Workers of the World in 1921 and became a longshoreman in San Francisco in 1922. He helped to organize a militant local of the International Longshoreman's Association (ILA) in 1933, and rose to prominence as a strike leader. In 1937 he led most of the West Coast ILA locals into the CIO's newly organized International Longshoremen's and Warehousemen's Union (ILWU), and became the CIO West Coast regional director in 1939. A prominent target for anticommunists, Bridges successfully fought off deportation attempts and perjury convictions, but he was unable to avoid expulsion from the CIO during the 1950 purge. In 1960 he negotiated the ILWU's pathbreaking Mechanization and Modernization Agreement, which accepted increased use of machinery in exchange for high pensions and guaranteed pay.

Carey, James B. (1911–1973): Carey attended night school while working in a Philco radio plant. Working for the AFL, he organized the plant and became the president of the National Radio and Allied Trades Council in 1935. When the AFL refused to charter his industrial union, Carey brought his group into the new United Electrical, Radio, and Machine Workers of America (UE) and was elected as the president, holding the office until 1941. He continued to serve as the CIO national secretary, a position he won in 1938. Working with anticommunists in the UE and the Association of Catholic Trade Unionists, Carey sponsored ongoing but ineffective challenges to the leftist UE leadership. In 1949 he quit the UE and became the president of the International Union of Electrical Workers, serving until 1965.

Matles, James J. (1909–1975): Matles emigrated from Romania in 1926 and worked as a machinist in New York City. He held several offices in the International Association of Machinists and the communist-organized Metal Workers Industrial Union in the 1930s. In 1937 he became the director of organization in the newly chartered United Electrical, Radio, and Machine Workers of America (UE), a post he held until 1962, when he was elected as the UE general secretary. As a national UE leader who never admitted to Communist Party membership, Matles came under fire during the anticommunist purge; he endured pressures ranging from congressional inquiries to deportation attempts. Matles was a superb organizer noted for his honesty, intense oratory, and negotiating skills.

Murray, Philip (1886–1952): Murray emigrated from Scotland in 1902 and worked in the mines of western Pennsylvania. He was elected as the president of the United Mine Workers of America (UMWA) District 5 in 1916 and to the executive board in 1919. He was appointed as the chairman of John L. Lewis's Steel Workers Organizing Committee (SWOC) in 1936; when the SWOC became the United Steel Workers in 1942, Murray became the first president. He became the CIO president in 1940; differences with Lewis over support for Franklin D. Roosevelt led to a rift and to Murray's expulsion from the UMWA in 1942. His break with the CIO leftists signaled the beginning of their purge.

Pressman, Lee (1906–1969): Born in New York City of Russian immigrant parents, Pressman earned a law degree from Harvard University in 1929. He served as the general counsel for several New Deal agencies before joining the Steel Workers Organizing Committee in 1936. He later became the general counsel of the United Steel Workers of America and the CIO. Pressman was a prominent CIO communist, and his dismissal in 1948 for supporting Henry Wallace and the Progressive Party was an early act in the developing CIO purge.

Quill, Michael Joseph (1905–1966): Quill emigrated from Ireland in 1926 and worked as a gateman in New York City's subways. He joined *Clan na Gael*, the U.S. affiliate of the Irish Republican Army, and was part of the group's attempt to organize subway workers. Quill founded the Transport Workers Union of America (TWU) with help from the Communist Party USA in 1937, serving as the TWU president from 1936 to 1966. "Red Mike" was elected to the New York City council as a representative from the Bronx in 1937, 1943, and 1945. In 1948 he broke with the Communist Party (his own membership is unconfirmed) over Henry Wallace's presidential campaign; he later testified against CIO communists in the 1950 expulsion hearings and became a CIO vice president in 1950.

Reuther, Walter Philip (1907–1970): A tool and die maker, Reuther organized and became the president of the United Automobile Workers (UAW) Local 174 in 1935. He was elected to the UAW executive board in 1936; became the director of UAW's General Motors department in 1939; and was elected as the first vice president in 1942. In 1946 the anticommunist "Reuther Caucus" gained control of the UAW; Reuther became the president and initiated a purge of UAW leftists. That same year, Reuther was elected to the CIO executive board, where he actively fostered the CIO purge in 1949–1950. He became the CIO president in 1952 and brokered the merger with the American Federation of Labor in 1955, serving as the president of the AFL-CIO Industrial Union Department until 1968, when he led the UAW out of the AFL-CIO.

See also: *AFL, CIO Merge; Congress of Industrial Organizations; Taft-Hartley Act; World Federation of Trade Unions.*

BIBLIOGRAPHY

Books

Buhle, Mari Jo, Paul Buhle, and Dan Georgakas, eds. *Encyclopedia of the American Left.* Urbana: University of Illinois Press, 1992.

Cochran, Bert. *Labor and Communism: The Conflict that Shaped American Unions.* Princeton, NJ: Princeton University Press, 1977.

Filippelli, Ronald L., and Mark McColloch. *Cold War in the Working Class: The Rise and Decline of the United Electrical Workers.* Albany: State University of New York Press, 1995.

Fink, Gary M., ed. *Biographical Dictionary of American Labor.* Westport, CT.: Greenwood Press, 1984.

Freeman, Joshua B. *In Transit: The Transport Workers Union in New York City, 1933–1966.* New York: Oxford University Press, 1989.

Kampelman, Max M. *The Communist Party vs. the CIO: A Study in Power Politics.* New York: Praeger, 1957.

Kelley, Robin D.G. *Hammer and Hoe: Alabama Communists During the Great Depression.* Chapel Hill: University of North Carolina Press, 1990.

Levenstein, Harvey A. *Communism, Anti-Communism, and the CIO.* Westport, CT: Greenwood Press, 1981.

Lichtenstein, Nelson. *Labor's War at Home: The CIO in World War II.* New York: Cambridge University Press, 1982.

———. *Walter Reuther: The Most Dangerous Man in Detroit.* Urbana: University of Illinois Press, 1997.

Rosswurm, Steve, ed. *The CIO's Left-led Unions.* New Brunswick, NJ: Rutgers University Press, 1992.

Schatz, Ronald W. *The Electrical Workers: A History of Labor at General Electric and Westinghouse, 1923–1960.* Urbana: University of Illinois Press, 1983.

Zieger, Robert H. *The CIO, 1935–1955.* Chapel Hill: University of North Carolina Press, 1995.

—Lisa Kannenberg

CIO Expelled from AFL

United States 1937

Synopsis

The Committee for Industrial Organization (later changed to Congress of Industrial Organizations, or CIO) formed within the American Federation of Labor (AFL) in 1935 and was expelled from that organization in 1937. Between 1935 and 1937 the AFL and the CIO engaged in a bitter struggle focused on issues of strategy, timing, and personality. The backdrop of the struggle augmented the intensity of the conflict. In the midst of the Great Depression, working people had every incentive to organize. Facing layoffs, wage cuts, and growing corporate control of work processes, new segments of the workforce turned to unions for representation. President Franklin Roosevelt's New Deal policies facilitated a broader role for trade unions.

In this situation, unions were poised to recruit large numbers of new members and participate in electoral politics on an unprecedented level. AFL vice president John L. Lewis, president of the United Mine Workers of America (UMWA), wanted to shape an organization that could take advantage of these opportunities. President William Green felt that the risks of rapidly organizing unskilled workers outweighed the benefits of attracting greater numbers. The trade union movement grew dramatically during the 1930s and early 1940s as a result of CIO organizing efforts. AFL growth outpaced the CIO's after World War II until the two organizations reunited in 1955.

Teamsters leaders discuss division between AFL and CIO. Front row from left to right: Charles W. Real, Oakland Union; Dave Beck, Seattle, Teamsters International vice president; and John P. McLaughlin, San Francisco, California. © Bettmann/Corbis. Reproduced by permission.

Timeline

1922: Publication of James Joyce's novel *Ulysses* and T. S. Eliot's poem *The Waste Land* will transform literature and inaugurate the era of modernism.

1927: American inventor Philo T. Farnsworth demonstrates a working model of the television, and Belgian astronomer Georges Lemaître proposes the Big Bang Theory.

1932: In German elections, Nazis gain a 37 percent plurality of Reichstag seats, raising tensions between the far right

and the far left. On a "bloody Sunday" in July, Communists in Hamburg attack Nazis with guns, and a fierce battle ensues.

1937: Italy signs the Anti-Comintern Pact, signed by Germany and Japan the preceding year. Like the two others before it, Italy now withdraws from the League of Nations.

1937: Japan attacks China and annexes most of that nation's coastal areas.

1937: Stalin uses carefully staged show trials in Moscow to eliminate all rivals for leadership. These party purges,

Audience of over 7,000 listens as Pacific Coast CIO union director Harry Bridges speaks on the AFL-CIO controversy, Gilmore Stadium, Los Angeles, California. © Bettmann/Corbis. Reproduced by permission.

however, are only a small part of the death toll now being exacted in a country undergoing forced industrialization, much of it by means of slave labor.

1937: In the middle of an around-the-world flight, Amelia Earhart and her plane disappear somewhere in the Pacific.

1937: Crash of the *Hindenburg* in Lakehurst, New Jersey, kills 36 and ends the brief era when rigid airships promised to be the ocean liners of the skies.

1937: Pablo Picasso paints his famous *Guernica* mural dramatizing the Nationalist bombing of a town in Spain. Thanks to artists and intellectuals such as Picasso and

Ernest Hemingway, the Loyalists are winning the battle of hearts and minds, even if they are weaker militarily, and idealistic young men flock from America to join the "Abraham Lincoln Brigade." Yet as George Orwell later reveals in *Homage to Catalonia,* the lines between good and evil are not clear: with its Soviet backing, the Loyalist cause serves as proxy for a totalitarianism every bit as frightening as that of the Nationalists and their German and Italian supporters.

1942: Axis conquests reach their height in the middle of this year. The Nazis control a vast region from Normandy to the suburbs of Stalingrad, and from the Arctic Circle to the edges of the Sahara. To the east, the Japanese "Co-Prosperity Sphere" encompasses territories from China to Burma to the East Indies, stretching deep into the western Pacific.

1947: The Marshall Plan is established to assist European nations in recovering from the war.

1952: Among the cultural landmarks of the year are the film *High Noon* and the book *The Invisible Man* by Ralph Ellison.

Event and Its Context

To Organize the Unorganized

The CIO origin tale features John L. Lewis punching the leader of the Brotherhood of Joiners and Carpenters, William "Big Bill" Hutcheson, during the 1935 AFL convention. By the time the punch occurred, significant changes had already taken place in the nature of production and the type of work done by most members of the U.S. working class. Lewis recognized these changes and was driven to create a new kind of union that would be more inclusive and would pursue broader goals than earlier trade unions. The story of the punch conveys much about the intransigence of the old-line AFL unions as well as something of Lewis's urgency.

By the 1930s mass production of clothing, automobiles, and other consumer goods had replaced smaller scale craft production. Industries such as steel, rubber, mining, textiles, and auto manufacturing required a new kind of worker, one with less skill than the members of the old craft unions who had started the AFL. Yet, this worker was largely without union representation. In 1933 fewer than three million American workers were represented by a union. AFL members were mostly white men who practiced skilled trades, descendents of the mid-nineteenth century first wave of immigrants. In a 2–1 vote at the 1935 convention, these members rejected the move to "establish industrial unions in specific industries, or to set up industrial unions to replace existing national and international unions."

Not all who voted against the resolution to organize by industry opposed the strategy. William Green himself felt that the tactic had some value. At issue was the timing of the move. Lewis wanted to recruit workers by industry right away and quarrel over which craft union had jurisdiction over them later. His goal, as he stated it, was to "organize the unorganized." The old-time AFL leaders worried that such quick growth would overwhelm them with new members. They resisted the idea of organizing workers by industry instead of by craft, but they also resisted the idea of rapid growth.

By refusing to organize the new industrial workers, the AFL lost the opportunity to expand the trade union movement into the most rapidly growing sectors of the economy and ignored a large number of workers. Industrial workers included segments of the population that were not represented in large numbers by the AFL: more recent immigrants, especially Italians and Jews from eastern Europe, larger numbers of African Americans, and women.

With Section 7a of the National Industrial Recovery Act in 1934 and the National Labor Relations Act (also called the Wagner Act) of 1935, the federal government recognized that trade unions were valuable in a mass-production economy. The National Industrial Recovery Act (NRA) was formulated to regulate industry while freeing the federal government from costly antitrust prosecution. It exempted businesses from antitrust legislation in return for adopting federally regulated employment practices. It provided for a maximum 40-hour workweek, set minimum wages, prohibited child labor in many industries, and set prices and controlled levels of production. Section 7a guaranteed workers the right to organize unions and bargain collectively.

Despite opposition to Section 7a, the entire measure passed the Congress on 16 June 1934. Immediately, efforts began to have it voided by Supreme Court decision. In 1935 in *Schechter v. United States*, the Court outlawed the NRA. In the meantime, however, the NRA had meant that many industries paid for the increase in the minimum wage by paying skilled workers a wage closer to the unskilled wage. AFL tradesmen, like all workers, already felt their jobs threatened in the depression. The wage adjustments increased the hostility of AFL members toward unskilled workers.

Before Section 7a was ruled unconstitutional, thousands of new workers were being recruited into federally chartered labor unions. The AFL was overwhelmed with the volume of new union members, which amounted to two million in one year alone.

Schechter dealt a blow to the union movement, but the situation shifted again with the passage of the Wagner Act. The Wagner Act's stated purpose was "to insure a wise distribution of wealth between management and labor, to maintain a full flow of purchasing power, and to prevent recurrent depression." In other words, the Wagner Act recognized that workers were consumers too and that better wages could bolster the economy.

The Wagner Act viewed trade unions as a means to this end. It mandated union recognition and collective bargaining and set up the National Labor Review Board to oversee union elections. Many employers disagreed with the premise that better wages would improve the economy and resisted the Wagner Act's provisions for union recognition. In 1937 the Supreme Court found the Wagner Act constitutional.

Government regulation of trade unionism certainly helped build unions, but more important were the conditions of the Great Depression itself. If skilled workers were threatened by loss of status and income as unskilled workers earned higher wages, unskilled workers were also threatened by job and income loss. Lewis was not the only one frustrated by the AFL's reticence. Furthermore, the NLRA made many of the debates about strategy within the AFL fade in importance. With a government-supervised apparatus by which workers could select union representation, fights between unions about jurisdiction seemed less important.

The Formation of the CIO

A few weeks after the 1935 convention, the Committee for Industrial Organization held its first formal meeting on 9 November 1935. In addition to John L. Lewis as president, the committee was headed by Charles P. Howard, president of the International Typographical Union, as secretary. Other members were Sidney Hillman, president of the Amalgamated Clothing Workers of America; David Dubinsky, president, International Ladies' Garment Workers' Union; Thomas F. McMahon, president, United Textile Workers of America; Harvey C. Freming, president, International Association of Oil Field, Gas Well and Refinery Workers of America; Max Zaritsky, of the United Hatters, Cap and Millinery Workers' International Union; and Thomas H. Brown, president, International Union of Mine, Mill and Smelter Workers.

Originally, the goal of the CIO was to bring more workers under the banner of the AFL. Had the conflict not become a personal battle between Lewis and Green, this might have remained the goal. Both men had started as coal miners and had worked their way up through the UMWA. In terms of their aspirations for the trade union movement, the two had more in common than issues separating them. The biggest difference between them was in temperament and style. Lewis was an inspiring orator to the rank and file. His skill at factional politics often left Green humiliated and unwilling to negotiate. On 23 November 1935 Lewis resigned as vice president of the AFL. He fully publicized his resignation, much to Green's embarrassment.

In its early years, the CIO was so closely identified with John L. Lewis that the two were linked in the public imagination. Lewis was no radical, but he respected the commitment and organizing skills of radicals and made good use of them. His own politics wavered with what he perceived as good for his organization, but he did seem to have a consistent conviction that labor should be a powerful force in the running of the country.

Lewis threw the developing resources of the CIO into a struggle to organize the steel industry by forming the Steel Workers Organizing Committee (SWOC). Steel mills were often located near the coal mines that fueled them. Lewis knew this landscape well and felt that an organized steel industry would be good for the UMWA. Under the NRA, large numbers of steelworkers had joined company sponsored unions. In some cases the company unions served to retard SWOC organizing, in others they offered an organization for SWOC to infiltrate. Steelworkers were anxious to organize. A 1936 article in *The Nation* described the mood in steel towns around Pittsburgh as "Waiting for Lewis."

The leadership of the AFL opposed the organizing drive in steel. The steel drive precipitated a new level of conflict with the CIO. On 3 August 1936 the executive council of the AFL met to discuss charges against the 12 unions that comprised the CIO. The council charged that in participating in the formation of the CIO, the 12 unions had "engaged in fostering, maintaining and supporting this dual movement and of fomenting insurrection within the American Federation of Labor." On 5 August the council voted to suspend 10 of the 12 unions unless they severed their relationship with the CIO. The council did not suspend the International Typographical Union and the Hatters' Cap and Millinery Workers International Union.

Politics and Union Power

In 1936 AFL and CIO representatives got together to form Labor's Non-Partisan League to support Roosevelt in an organization outside the Democratic Party. It was an effort to build an independent political power base for labor as well as to support Roosevelt. CIO influences dominated the new organization, which was staffed mostly by members of Lewis's union (the UMWA) and Sidney Hillman's clothing workers. Against the backdrop of the organizing campaign for steel workers, Lewis argued that support for Roosevelt would challenge the dominance of steel manufacturers and bankers that had caused the Great Depression.

Thus, when Roosevelt won the election, Lewis was prepared to proclaim it a victory for working people. He entered 1937, the second worst year of the depression, confident for labor's future and ready to build the CIO's membership. By the end of 1936 workers had occupied two General Motors Fisher Body plants in Flint, Michigan. In February 1937 they began a sit-down strike in the plants. Workers refused to leave until GM agreed to bargain with the United Auto Workers (UAW), a CIO union. The UAW won the strike and was recognized by GM.

Things looked good for the CIO on several counts. The drive to organize industrialized labor seemed to be proceeding well. The sit-down strike offered a new tactic that would be used in other industries as well. More important, the strategy of allying with the Democratic Party on independent terms seemed to have yielded a role for labor in public policy.

Things looked even better when U.S. Steel signed an agreement with SWOC in March 1937. Organizing efforts then focused on the "little steel" companies: Republic Steel, Youngstown Sheet and Tube, Inland Steel, and Bethlehem Steel. All refused to sign a contract with SWOC. On 26 May 1937 SWOC struck against all except Bethlehem Steel. The strike was one of the most violent in U.S. labor history. It was also a test of both the CIO's political strategy and the new national labor relations system. The strike did not succeed in forcing the little steel companies to the negotiating table. SWOC's defeat forced the CIO to reevaluate its political strategy, as it created a rift between Lewis and Roosevelt.

The Expulsion

After the suspension in the summer of 1936, the CIO unions largely went about the business of building their organization. They did not attend the 1936 AFL convention, which voted to maintain the suspension and endorsed the executive council's authority to judge when the suspended unions deserved to be reinstated. The CIO drives in steel and automobiles created positive publicity for the new national organization. Its position seemed assured as one of two powerful federations of labor, perhaps the stronger of the two.

In March 1937 the AFL executive council ordered all CIO unions expelled from state and city federations of the AFL. Throughout the rest of 1937 and into 1938, leaders of the AFL and the CIO made efforts to bring the two organizations back together. The two organizations met in October 1937 to negotiate the terms of unity. The CIO proposed that the AFL support the organization of workers in mass production only on an industrial basis. The AFL offered to recognize some industrial unions organized by the CIO in exchange for dismantling others and having AFL craft unions take in their members. Each organization strove to look as conciliatory as possible, but neither yielded much of substance. Each wanted to blame the other for the failure to reunite.

Negotiations proceeded until the end of 1937. The AFL remained committed to seeing the CIO disband before its members were readmitted. By late December, at a CIO policy conference, representatives of all 32 affiliated unions adopted Lewis's motion to end the negotiations. In November 1938 the CIO recognized the separation with a formal name change. It became the Congress of Industrial Organizations. It would maintain its independence until 1955, when it merged again with the AFL.

Key Players

Dubinsky, David (1892–1982): As president of the International Ladies' Garment Workers Union for more than 30 years, Dubinsky built the union into a strong, financially stable organization. Throughout his career, Dubinsky retained an interest in social legislation.

Green, William L. (1873–1952): President of the AFL from 1924 to 1952, Green, like John L. Lewis, came from the United Mine Workers of America. Interested in cooperation between labor and management, Green looked to government policy changes to secure a better future for labor. He was a Roosevelt appointee to the Labor Advisory Counsel of the National Recovery Administration.

Hillman, Sidney (1887–1946): Hillman participated in the 1905 revolution in Russia before migrating to New York and becoming a garment worker. In 1914 he became president of the Amalgamated Clothing Workers of America (ACWA) and held that office until his death. Originally a member of the Socialist Party, he became an active Democrat.

Lewis, John L. (1880–1969): A mineworker from Illinois, Lewis became head of the United Mine workers of America (UMWA) in 1920. He resigned from his position as AFL vice president in 1935 to concentrate on building the CIO. Striving to "organize the unorganized," Lewis became one of the most recognized figures in the country. Lewis retired as UMWA president in 1960.

See also: *AFL, CIO Merge; American Federation of Labor; Committee for Industrial Organization; Congress of Industrial Organizations; GM Recognizes UAW; Memorial Day Massacre; National Industrial Recovery Act; U.S. Steel Recognizes the Steel Workers Organizing Committee; Wagner Act.*

BIBLIOGRAPHY

Books

Anderson, Kristi. *The Creation of a Democratic Majority, 1928–1936.* Chicago: University of Chicago Press, 1979.

Bernstein, Irving. *Turbulent Years: A History of the American Worker, 1933–1941.* Boston: Houghton Mifflin, 1970.

Dubofsky, Melvyn, and Warren Van Tine. *John L. Lewis: A Biography.* Chicago and Urbana: University of Illinois Press, 1986.

Dulles, Foster Rhea, and Melvyn Dubofsky. *Labor in America,* 2nd ed. New York: Thomas Y. Crowell, 1960.

Foner, Philip S. *History of the Labor Movement in the United States,* vol. 2. New York: International Publishers, 1955.

Fraser, Steven. *Labor Will Rule: Sidney Hillman and the Rise of American Labor.* New York: The Free Press, 1991.

Galenson, Walter. *The CIO Challenge to the AFL: A History of the American Labor Movement 1935–1941.* Cambridge: Harvard University Press, 1960.

Peis, Arthur. *Labor's Giant Step.* New York: Pathfinder, 1964.

Zieger, Robert H. *John L. Lewis: Labor Leader.* Boston: G. K. Hall, 1988.

———. *The CIO: 1935–1955.* Chapel Hill and London: The University of North Carolina Press, 1995.

—Jane Holzka

CIO Joins, AFL Rejects WFTU

United States 1945

Synopsis

Inspired by the worker militancy of the previous 10 years or more, by state social reformism and liberal internationalism, as well as by the wartime antifascist alliance, the Congress of Industrial Organizations (CIO) committed itself to the founding of the World Federation of Trade Unions (WFTU). The American Federation of Labor (AFL), representing the conservative tradition of "business unionism" and "voluntarism" at home, more inclined to the domination of, than cooperation with, unions abroad, resisted this. Rising cold war divisions internationally led to an early split in the WFTU. The CIO joined the European social-democratic unionists in their withdrawal from the organization and then joined the AFL in the creation of the International Confederation of Free Trade Unions in 1949.

Timeline

1925: In Tennessee, John T. Scopes is fined for teaching evolution in a public school. There follows a highly publicized trial at which famed attorney Clarence Darrow represents the defense, while the aging Democratic populist William Jennings Bryan argues for the state. The "Scopes Monkey Trial" symbolizes a widening divisions between rural and urban America, and though the court decides in favor of the state, it is clear that the historical tide is turning against the old agrarian order symbolized by Bryan—who dies during the trial.

1930: Collectivization of Soviet agriculture begins, and with it one of the greatest crimes of the twentieth century. In the next few years, as Soviet operatives force peasants to give up their lands, millions will die either by direct action, manmade famine, or forced labor. Overseas, however, and particularly among intellectuals and artists of the West, Soviet collectivization and industrialization are regarded as models of progress for the world.

1935: Second phase of New Deal begins with the introduction of social security, farm assistance, and housing and tax reform.

1940: Hitler's troops sweep through western Europe, annexing Norway and Denmark in April, and in May the Low Countries and France. At the same time, Stalin—who in this year arranges the murder of Trotsky in Mexico—takes advantage of the situation to add the Baltic republics (Latvia, Lithuania, and Estonia) to the Soviet empire, where they will remain for more than half a century.

1945: At the Yalta Conference in February, Roosevelt, Churchill, and Stalin make plans for Germany after its by now inevitable surrender.

1945: April sees the death of three leaders: Roosevelt passes away on 12 April; the Italians execute Mussolini and his mistress on 28 April; and Hitler (along with Eva Braun, propaganda minister Josef Goebbels, and Goebbels's family) commits suicide on 30 April.

1945: On 7 May, Germany surrenders to the Allied powers. Later in the summer, the new U.S. president, Harry Truman, joins Churchill and Stalin at Potsdam to discuss the reconstruction of Germany. (Churchill is replaced in mid-conference by Clement Attlee as Labour wins control of Parliament.)

1945: United States drops atomic bombs on the Japanese cities of Hiroshima and Nagasaki in early August, and a month later, on 2 September, Japan surrenders.

1945: The United Nations is established on 24 October.

1950: U.S. Senator Joseph McCarthy launches his campaign to root out communist infiltrators.

1955: African and Asian nations meet at the Bandung Conference in Indonesia, inaugurating the "non-aligned" movement of Third World countries.

1960: Congo, along with several other African nations, becomes independent. But as the province of Katanga secedes, and pro-Soviet prime minister Patrice Lumumba disappears (he is later murdered), the country devolves into civil war. Soon UN troops will arrive to restore order.

Event and Its Context

Labor and Political Economy

The late 1930s and the wartime 1940s saw a dramatic expansion of the U.S. economy and employment. Not only did industry spread to the West Coast and the South, but new generations of immigrants—later including blacks and women—were drawn into the workforce. Under the Keynesian strategy fol-

Sidney Hillman, Atlantic City, New Jersey. AP/Wide World Photos. Reproduced by permission.

lowed by the presidential administrations of Franklin Roosevelt, there was also an expansion of public works and public sector employment. A partially state-sponsored populist culture, reflected even in Hollywood movies, encouraged radicalism that was already present among workers. Dynamism and turbulence in the economy and the reformist, occasionally pro-union, action of the state enabled militant workers and leftist organizers to break away from the conservative and craft traditions of the AFL and form the industrially structured, Democratic Party aligned, and state-oriented CIO.

Internationalism among even the newer and more militant sections of the workers was, however, often combined with a variety of ethnic and religious identities, with racism, and with an Americanism that allowed immigrants not only to defend themselves against but even to pride themselves on being part of the most dynamically developing capitalist country in the world. The result was a "bureaucratic corporatist" and nationalist internationalism expressed not through direct worker solidarity action but through the CIO and the Rooseveltian state. Working-class thinking on international affairs was often colored by concerns for economic and personal safety, grievances against the more privileged, and a belief in American world responsibility. In the mid-1940s a vocal minority of the American working class supported labor internationalism; the majority was either doubtful, unconcerned, or worried by the prospect of continued cooperation with the Soviet Union.

Union

Often compared to the social-democratic unions of western Europe, the CIO shared their social-reformist inclinations but had otherwise a much more socially diverse base and leadership. Although the European unions were largely divided into social-democratic and communist tendencies and organizations, the CIO leadership included communists on the left, socialists in the middle, and liberal democrats on the right. The CIO was then confronted on *its* right by the aggressive business-unionism of the AFL. The CIO, however, also has to be seen as an organization constraining and channeling the militancy of auto, steel, electricity, and other workers. This was much to the chagrin of the left and of the populist John L. Lewis, stormy leader of the militant mineworkers, who led his members first into and then out of the CIO. The CIO was also deeply engaged with both the state and the Democratic Party, which may have increased its influence but decreased its autonomy.

Whereas the "isolationist" AFL was interested in domination of both the Latin American and the world union movement, the CIO became increasingly involved in cooperation with both. In the case of Mexico and then Latin America, this happened, in particular, with Vicente Lombardo Toledano, charismatic leader of the left within the Mexican union movement and then with the *Confederación de Trabajadores de América Latina* (CTAL), which he founded and led. Indeed, the CIO was prepared to treat Latin America as Toledano's sovereign territory.

As the war in Europe drew to a close, the CIO was involved in a burst of international activity that often paralleled and even overlapped that around the creation of the United Nations (1946). Early in 1945 the CIO established an international affairs department. Later that year, it created bilateral committees, such as the Soviet-American, the Anglo-American, and others. These were modeled on the Latin American committee it had created in February 1943. Meanwhile, the CIO took part in the World Trade Union Conference (London, February 1945) and then the founding of the World Federation of Trade Unions (WFTU, Paris, October 1945). The CIO was particularly involved with the colonial department of the WFTU. James Carey, a major CIO figure involved with the WFTU, believed—as did many CIO leaders and trade unionists in general—that the United States could and should oppose colonialism as unethical and unnecessary. Even so, Carey and others felt that the United States had a special responsibility to guide the world toward freedom and participation in the world economy. Blind to their own interventionism, they failed to perceive that the nation as a whole was unwilling to intervene in foreign affairs.

The CIO revealed similar ambiguity about American-Soviet relations. Although some of its leaders were committed to U.S.-Soviet collaboration and defended the Soviet unions, others, like Walter Reuther (who had worked in a Soviet auto plant in the 1930s), became increasingly skeptical about peaceful coexistence with the Soviet Union and the Soviet unions. Tensions between procommunists and anticommunists within the CIO grew when the international communist movement opposed the U.S. Marshall Plan in 1947. An anticommunist wave in the United States, reinforced by the election of Democrat Harry Truman in 1948 (whom U.S. communists had opposed), led to anticommunist purges within the CIO. This set the international stage for its withdrawal from the WFTU and affiliation with the ICFTU (1949) and for the merger with the AFL in 1955. The CIO attempt to create an autonomous social-reformist union leadership failed both nationally and internationally.

The AFL, sharing the aggressive and domineering international orientation of U.S. corporations, linked more with the military and intelligence branches of the U.S. government, had a longer and perhaps more consistent foreign policy than the CIO. Active in pre–World War I efforts to create a trade union international, the AFL was, toward the end of that war, hostile both to "enemy" unions and to the socialist and pacifist inclinations of the European unions more generally. Although AFL leader Samuel Gompers was energetically involved in Wilsonian projects for a League of Nations and an International Labor Organization, he also shared U.S. hostility toward any subordination of the national (American) to the international. This American exceptionalism led to a breach with the International Federation of Trade Unions in 1921 and a concentration on a Pan-American Federation of Labor (1919), which it could both dominate and isolate from the social-democratic Europeans. The breach began to heal a couple of years before World War II.

Hostility toward the CIO at home and social democracy abroad permitted or stimulated the AFL to develop an intimate wartime relationship with the Organization of Strategic Services (OSS). Although this secret service was itself ready to work with social democratic unionists in wartime Europe, it kept its distance from the European and international unions as institutions. This provided the AFL with a separate source of identity and funding in furthering its own agenda against the CIO and the left at home and against the Soviet Union and communism abroad. At the peak of international liberal and socialist optimism, as the war in Europe drew to its conclusion, this certainly helped the AFL to reject the WFTU. The AFL was determined to continue or deepen its alliance with U.S. military and intelligence agencies (particularly the successor of the OSS, the Central Intelligence Agency), in furthering U.S. state, corporate, and union interests in the postwar era. This alliance was to prove rapidly successful at countering the influence of the new International. The AFL spearheaded trade union opposition to the WFTU.

Key Players

Hillman, Sidney (1887–1946): A Jewish labor activist in czarist Russia, Hillman migrated to the United States in 1907. He became a garment worker, a strike leader, and a union leader. In conflict with his old conservative union, he helped create the new Amalgamated Clothing Workers of America and then became a founder of the militant CIO, of which he became first vice president in 1937. Under the reformist and interventionist presidencies of Franklin Roosevelt (1933–1945), Hillman became more and more involved with government and semigovernmental agencies, to the point of becoming the president's union advisor. No left-winger, Hillman was nonetheless prepared to collaborate with communism at home and with the Soviet Union (or Soviet unions) abroad. In both cases this was a matter of a progressive or social-reformist disposition, best expressed by Roosevelt's New Deal, the wartime coalition against fascism, and the founding of the United Nations. Hillman was a convinced union internationalist and played a key conciliating role at the World Trade Union Conference in London in early 1945.

Meany, George (1894–1980): Born into a New York Catholic working-class family, Meany, originally a plumber, worked his way up the union hierarchy, becoming secretary-treasurer of the AFL in 1939. In this position he devoted himself to the AFL's international activities, partly to increase his profile within the federation and partly to increase AFL influence with the U.S. state. He was a member of various national wartime labor boards. Meany's anticommunism was unlimited. He even voted for the Republican candidate, against Roosevelt, in 1944, for this reason. As the process of creating the new WFTU warmed up, Meany, as AFL representative to the 1945 British Trades Union Congress (1945), used the opportunity to denounce the Soviet trade unions and was shouted down for his pains. His anticommunism nonetheless paid off. He became president of the AFL, then of the merged AFL-CIO in 1955. He dominated the national and international policies of the U.S. union movement until his death.

Ross, Michael (1898–1963): Ross was born in London, England. Unusual for a union-official-to-be at that time, he studied economics, later gaining a B.A. in the United States. Active in the British Labour Party, he began a lifetime practice of writing for magazines and newspapers. After immigrating to the United States in 1933, Ross began working for the Roosevelt-era Public Works Administration (1934–1936). After a period as a lecturer, he became a union research director, and during the war he represented his union in Washington. He also served as a labor member on various government wartime committees. In 1945 Ross became director of the CIO international affairs department, serving as its representative to Europe (1953–1955). In 1955 he became assistant director, then director, of the AFL-CIO international affairs department and served until his death.

See also: *AFL, CIO Merge; American Federation of Labor; Confederación de Trabajadores de América Latina; Confederación Obrera Pan-Americana; Congress of Industrial Organizations; International Confederation of Free Trade Unions; World Federation of Trade Unions.*

BIBLIOGRAPHY

Books

Carew, Tony. "A False Dawn: The World Federation of Trade Unions." In *The International Confederation of Free Trade Unions*, edited by Marcel van der Linden. Bern, Germany: Peter Lang, 2000.

Davis, Mike. *Prisoners of the American Dream: Politics and Economy in the History of the U.S. Working Class.* London: Verso, 1986.

Fink, Gary M., ed. *Biographical Dictionary of American Labor Leaders.* Westport, CT: Greenwood Press, 1984.

McShane, Denis. *International Labor and the Origins of the Cold War.* Oxford: Clarendon, 1992.

Silverman, Victor. *Imagining Internationalism in American and British Labor, 1939–1949.* Urbana: Illinois University Press, 2000.

Van Goethem, Geert. "The International Federation of Trade Unions (1919–1945)." In *The International Confederation of Free Trade Unions*, edited by Marcel van der Linden. Bern: Peter Lang, 2000.

Windmuller, John P. *American Labor and the International Labor Movement, 1940–1953.* Cornell International Industrial and Labor Relations Reports, No. 2. Ithaca, NY: Institute of International Industrial and Labor Relations, Cornell University, 1954.

Periodicals

"Special Double Issue: USA—Beyond Trade Union Imperiali$m." *Newsletter of International Labour Studies*, nos. 40–41 (1989): 2–52.

Other

George Meany Memorial Archives. "Collection Title: CIO International Affairs Department. Director's Files, Michael H. S. Ross, 1934–1963" [cited 11 October 2002]. <http://www.georgemeany.org/archives/RG18-006.htm>.

—Peter Waterman

Civil Rights Act of 1964

United States 1964

Synopsis

The Civil Rights Act of 1964, the most significant piece of civil rights legislation since the Civil War, bans discrimination on the basis of race, religion, color, national origin, and gender in the areas of public accommodation, federally funded programs, and employment. The act created the Equal Employment Opportunity Commission to enforce the employment provisions of the act.

Timeline

1944: Allies land at Normandy on 6 June, conducting the largest amphibious invasion in history.

1949: Soviets conduct their first successful atomic test. This heightens growing cold war tensions, not least because the sudden acquisition of nuclear capabilities suggests that American spies are passing secrets.

1954: The French military outpost at Dien Bien Phu falls to the communist Vietminh. France withdraws after decades of trying to suppress revolt; meanwhile, the United States pledges its support for the non-communist government in the south.

Whitney M. Young Jr., Roy Wilkins, A. Philip Randolph, Walter P. Reuther, and Arnold Aronson, Civil Rights March from the Washington Monument to the Lincoln Memorial, Washington, D.C. National Archives at College Park. Reproduced by permission.

1959: Two new leaders appear on the scene in January as General Charles de Gaulle becomes the first president of France's Fifth Republic, and Fidel Castro takes control of Cuba after the collapse of the corrupt Batista regime.

1962: Publication of Rachel Carson's *Silent Spring* heightens Americans' awareness of environmental issues.

1964: On 7 February, in the midst of both a literal and figurative winter in America following Kennedy's assassination, the Beatles arrive at New York's newly renamed JFK Airport. The enthusiasm that greets them is partly the result of a clever marketing campaign—one of the first of its kind—but it also has a great deal to do with the sheer talent and charm exerted by the four. In their 9 February *Ed Sullivan Show* performance, they break a record set seven years earlier by their idol Elvis Presley, with 70 million viewers, or roughly 60 percent of the U.S. audience.

1964: In Mississippi, civil rights workers Andrew Goodman, Michael Schwerner, and Andrew Cheney are murdered.

Twenty-one conspirators are arrested, and seven are convicted by a federal jury.

1964: U.S. Congress approves the Gulf of Tonkin resolution, giving President Johnson broad powers to prosecute the by now rapidly escalating war in Vietnam.

1967: The Beatles' *Sgt. Pepper's Lonely Hearts Club Band* tops the list of releases for a year that will long be remembered as a high point of rock history. Among the other great musical events of the year are releases by the Jimi Hendrix Experience, the Doors, and Jefferson Airplane; also, the Monterey Pop Festival marks the debut of Hendrix and Janis Joplin.

1968: The Reverend Martin Luther King is assassinated on 4 April. Senator Robert F. Kennedy is assassinated on 6 June.

1969: On 20 July, assisted by pilot Michael Collins, astronauts Neil Armstrong and Edwin E. "Buzz" Aldrin become the first men to walk on the Moon.

Crowds of people massed on the Mall and along sides of the Reflecting Pool, Civil Rights March on Washington, Washington, D.C. National Archives and Records Administration.

1974: On 30 July, the House Judiciary Committee adopts three articles of impeachment for President Nixon, but rather than undergo a lengthy trial, Nixon on 8 August becomes the first president in U.S. history to resign. His successor, Gerald Ford, pardons him in September.

1979: After years of unrest, the Shah of Iran leaves the country, and Islamic fundamentalist revolutionaries under the leadership of Ayatollah Ruhollah Khomeini take control. Later in the year, militants seize control of the U.S. embassy in Teheran and take more than 50 Americans hostage.

Event and Its Context

Origins of the Civil Rights Act

The Civil Rights Act emerged as the result of four principal factors. The first was the economic plight of African Americans, who historically had been underrepresented in professional fields and even in jobs that required little or no education. In 1964 the median income of black families was half that of white families, and blacks were only half as likely as whites to work in white-collar jobs as opposed to blue-collar and service jobs.

The second factor was the civil rights movement of the 1950s and early 1960s, which pricked the conscience of the

The Decline in Union Membership Since 1964

According to statistics compiled by the federal government, union membership in almost all of the fifty states decreased between 1964 and 2000. This was equally true in heavily unionized states such as those of the Northeast, and in the strongly non-union Southeast.

For example, in New York, union members constituted 35.5 percent of all non-agricultural workers in 1964. By 1984 the percentage had dropped to 32.3, and by 2000 union workers were just over one-quarter of the non-agricultural workforce—a total drop of about 38 percent.

In Georgia, unions did not constitute nearly as great a presence as they did in New York in 1964: just 11.9 percent of the laboring population outside of agriculture. Twenty years later, this had dropped slightly, to 10.3 percent, but in the next sixteen years, the decline was much sharper. By 2000 only 6.3 percent of the non-farm workforce belonged to unions, a drop of 47 percent.

The greatest declines were in the West, with a 68 percent decrease in both Idaho and Utah. By contrast, the westernmost of all states was the only one out of all 50 in which labor-union membership actually increased: Hawaii had seen a 14 percent growth in the unionized workforce, which represented 21.7 percent of the state's non-agricultural working population in 1964, and 24.6 percent in 2000.

Source: *Special Response Corporation.*
<http://www.specialresponse.com/index.html>.

—Judson Knight

American public. Television brought into American living rooms the bus boycott in Montgomery, Alabama, in 1955, which had been sparked by Rosa Parks's refusal to give up her seat to a white passenger; the sit-ins led by students at North Carolina A&T College to protest segregation at lunch counters in that state in 1960; the 1963 clashes between civil rights demonstrators and police, who brutally dispersed crowds with dogs and fire hoses in Birmingham, Alabama; the 28 August 1963 March on Washington, where 200,000 participants gathered for Martin Luther King's "I have a dream" speech; and, that same year, the federalization of the Alabama National Guard to thwart Governor George Wallace in his effort to block the enrollment of African Americans at the University of Alabama. In response to these momentous events, President John F. Kennedy, who had earlier been lukewarm in his support for civil rights legislation, appeared on national television on 11 June 1963 to make an "appeal to conscience" to the American people and urge the passage of a civil rights law. A week later he sent a sweeping civil rights bill to Congress, legislation that went far beyond bills introduced in 1957 and 1960.

The third factor leading to the passage of the Civil Rights Act was Kennedy's death at the hands of an assassin on 22 November 1963. In the minds of many Americans, including his successor, Lyndon Johnson, a civil rights bill would be the most fitting eulogy to the slain president—which leads to the fourth factor, the political conversion of Johnson. As Senate majority leader from Texas, Johnson had joined many southern members of Congress to oppose civil rights legislation. Indeed, during the Senate debate on the Civil Rights Act, many of Johnson's words would be thrown back in his face. It may never be clear whether Johnson, ever the consummate politician, just wanted to be on the right side of a change that he saw as inevitable, or whether he had a genuine change of heart; ultimately the distinction may be unimportant. What is important is that Johnson became an avid supporter of civil rights, declaring in his first state of the union address, "Let this session of Congress be known as the session which did more for civil rights than the last hundred sessions combined."

The Congressional Debate

Passage of the Civil Rights Act was complex. The Senate debate lasted 80 days and filled 7,000 pages with 10 million words in the Congressional Record. This included the longest filibuster in Senate history and occasioned the rare invocation of an obscure Senate procedure called *cloture*, which put an end to the filibuster and limited debate.

Debate on President Kennedy's bill began in the House of Representatives on 31 January 1964. House leaders from both parties were determined to pass the bill, so they curtailed debate and strong-armed it through on 10 February by a vote of 290 to 130. The bill's first real hurdle should have been the Senate Judiciary Committee, but the committee's chairman, Senator James Eastland of Mississippi, was an opponent of civil rights legislation. To bypass the committee, from which the bill might never have emerged (confirming Woodrow Wilson's wry view that in going to committee, a bill crossed "a parliamentary bridge of sighs to dim dungeons of silence whence it will never return"), Democratic senator Mike Mansfield of Montana introduced it directly to the floor of the Senate. Mansfield's motion met vigorous opposition, even from many supporters of the bill, who squirmed at the notion of violating procedure. The motion, however, passed, and the bill was placed on the Senate's calendar. To ensure bipartisan support, Democrat Hubert Humphrey of Minnesota, the majority whip, and Republican Thomas Kuchel of California, the minority whip, managed the process. Additionally, detailed discussion on the floor of each piece of the bill was assigned to pairs of Democratic and Republican senators.

Predictably, the bill met stiff opposition from most southern senators, who filibustered it. In an unusual move, supporters took part in the filibuster, presenting their case for the bill, interrupting their opponents, and even sharply questioning them. To break the filibuster, Senate leaders concluded that they had to recruit the support of minority leader Everett Dirksen of Illinois, who had reservations about some provisions of the bill. Accordingly, the leadership, with the help of the U.S. attorney general and other members of the Justice Department, negotiated the so-called Mansfield-Dirksen substitute, a compromise bill that softened the House version (by, for example, giving state agencies the opportunity to act before the federal government in cases of employment discrimination) but retained its most crucial features. In the debate that followed the introduction of the substitute bill, southern senators introduced amendment after amendment, all but two of which were defeated. They also called for a record 34 roll-call votes in one day. Their rear-guard action was futile, however, and the Senate overwhelmingly voted to replace the House bill with the Mansfield-Dirksen substitute. On 19 June the Senate passed this version of the bill by a vote of 73 to 27 and then sent it back to the House. With little debate or fanfare the House, by a vote of 289 to 126, passed the Senate version of the bill. President Johnson signed the Civil Rights Act into law the same day, 2 July 1964.

The Major Provisions of the Civil Rights Act

The Civil Rights Act of 1964 consists of 11 titles, the most important of which are Titles II, VI, and VII.

Title II bars discrimination in places of public accommodation, as did the Civil Rights Act of 1875; the earlier act, however, depended for its enforcement powers on the Fourteenth Amendment to the Constitution. Although the amendment guaranteed citizens due process and equal protection under the law, the courts in intervening years had interpreted it to apply only to state action, not to the actions of private citizens or individual business enterprises. In contrast, the teeth of Title II was the power of Congress to regulate commerce granted in Article I, Section 8 of the Constitution, which the courts had been interpreting expansively in recent years. Under Title II, Congress could extend to private action its authority to prohibit discrimination.

Title VI relies on the taxing and spending power of Congress to ban discrimination in federally funded programs. To labor, the most important part of the Civil Rights Act is Title VII, which prohibits discrimination in employment practices by employers, labor unions, and employment agencies based on race, color, religion, national origin, or gender in any industry that affects commerce. Past efforts to eliminate employment discrimination had been piecemeal and ineffective. In 1941 President Franklin Roosevelt, by executive order, created the Fair Employment Practice Committee to combat job discrimination by defense contractors. In 1948 President Harry Truman, again by executive order, created the Fair Employment Board within the Civil Service Commission to promote equal opportunity in federal employment. Johnson himself established the Office of Federal Contract Compliance in the Department of Labor with the goal of putting an end to racial discrimination at the work sites of contractors and subcontractors performing federally funded projects. These efforts, however, tended to be more symbolic than substantive. The Civil Rights Act was the first effort by Congress to bring to bear the full power of the federal government to enforce equal opportunity in employment throughout the economy. Like Title II, Title VII relies on the commerce clause to regulate the actions of private employers rather than being bound by the state action limitation implicit in the Fourteenth Amendment.

Congress vested authority for enforcing Title VII in the Equal Employment Opportunity Commission (EEOC), which began operations on 2 July 1965. In addition, the EEOC enforces the Equal Pay Act of 1963, the Age Discrimination in Employment Act of 1967, the Rehabilitation Act of 1973, the Americans with Disabilities Act of 1990, and the Civil Rights

Act of 1991. With over 2,500 employees in 50 field offices and a budget of approximately $300 million, the EEOC for the 10 years ending with fiscal year (FY) 2001 received an average of just over 59,000 complaints a year, about half of which were found to be without cause. Generally, charges are filed by individuals who believe they have been the victim of discrimination, but individual commissioners can initiate charges. Until 1972 the EEOC had to refer discrimination cases to the U.S. Justice Department, but the law was amended that year to enable the commission itself to bring suit in federal court against employers for violations of the act. Over the same 10-year period, the commission litigated an average of 226 Title VII suits per year; resulting monetary benefits ranged from $7 million in FY 1993 to a peak of $95 million in FY 1997. Generally, the commission's purpose is to resolve cases that have merit through conciliation and alternative dispute resolution. In FY 1992 the commission awarded monetary benefits of $52.5 million, but by FY 2001 that figure had risen to $141.1 million.

The Role of the Courts

As early as the 1940s, the U.S. Supreme Court had heard cases involving employment discrimination. In *Steele v. Louisville and Nashville Railroad* (1944), for example, the Court prohibited unions from practicing racial discrimination, and in *Jones v. Alfred H. Mayer Co.* (1968) it relied on the Civil Rights Act of 1866 to affirm that both blacks and whites have an equal right to contract for work. The Court, however, heard relatively few such cases because whatever protections existed for workers were generally based on state statute, not on the Constitution or federal law.

In the late 1960s the Warren Court allowed lower courts to interpret the 1964 act, but by the early 1970s employment discrimination cases were making their way to the Supreme Court and providing important early tests of the legality not only of the act but of actions taken to implement it. Perhaps one of the most important decisions reached by the Court, then led by Chief Justice Warren Burger, was in *Griggs v. Duke Power Co.* in 1971. African American employees at the Duke Power Co. in North Carolina challenged the company's requirement that both new hires and employees seeking a transfer must have a high school diploma or score a passing grade on an intelligence test. Title VII prohibits any employment practice that discriminates on the basis of race. The power company's requirements adversely affected the employment opportunities of blacks, who faced discrimination in the state's public schools and who graduated from high school at a rate about one-third that of white students. More importantly, the company could not demonstrate a relationship between either the diploma or scores on the intelligence test and job performance. In ruling against the company, the Court noted that employment practices that seem neutral on their face, like those of Duke Power, may have discriminatory effect. Thus, the employees did not have to prove that the *intent* of the company was to discriminate, only that the *consequences* of its actions were discriminatory. With regard to diplomas and intelligence tests, the Court concluded that "the touchstone is business necessity. If an employment practice which operates to exclude Negroes cannot be shown to be related to job performance, the practice is prohibited."

Two years later, in 1973, the Court ruled in *McDonnell Douglas Corp. v. Green* that under Title VII job applicants can make a prima facie case for discrimination by showing that they are members of a racial minority, were denied the job despite adequate qualifications for it, and that the position remained open while the employer sought other applicants with the same qualifications. The Court refined this doctrine in *Hazelwood School District v. United States* (1977), when it held that a prima facie case of discrimination can be made if a statistical comparison of the racial makeup of an employer's workforce, in this case a school faculty, shows an obvious imbalance relative to the racial makeup of the community that supplies that workforce.

Other cases involving the legality of seniority systems had important consequences for labor unions. In *International Brotherhood of Teamsters v. United States* (1977), the Court ruled that a valid seniority system did not violate Title VII, even if the effect of the system is to perpetuate past discrimination against minority truck drivers. In *Firefighters Local Union No. 1784 v. Stotts* (1984) the Court was asked to deal with the collision of seniority systems with affirmative action programs. The Court found that the fire department in Memphis, Tennessee, had violated Title VII, and under court order it instituted an affirmative action plan to hire and promote more blacks to remedy past discrimination. When the city later faced a severe budget deficit, it planned to balance the books by laying off city employees with the least seniority. Stotts, a black firefighter who would have lost his job, filed suit in district court, which enjoined the fire department from adhering strictly to its seniority system. The union appealed to the Supreme Court, and the Burger Court lifted the injunction and once again upheld the legality of a seniority system: "Title VII protects bona fide seniority systems, and it is inappropriate to deny an innocent employee the benefits of his seniority in order to provide a remedy in a pattern or practice [discrimination] suit such as this."

Several other early cases involved affirmative action plans, particularly quotas. One, perhaps the most significant, was *United Steelworkers of America v. Weber* (1979). The Kaiser Aluminum Corporation and the United Steelworkers, in an effort to head off litigation by black employees, voluntarily negotiated an affirmative action plan to correct a gross imbalance in the number of black skilled craftsmen at a Louisiana plant. The program allotted half the slots in a craft training program to blacks until the imbalance was corrected. Weber, who was white, was denied a slot in the training program and filed suit, arguing that he was the victim of racial discrimination under Title VII, which provided that an employer could not be "required" to give preferential treatment to a racial group because of a racial imbalance in the workforce. Weber won in federal court, but the Burger Court overruled the lower court and upheld the legality of the company's affirmative action program. In reaching its decision, the Court noted that the program was not "required," that it was a voluntary program to eliminate segregation. The Court further noted that the legislative history of the act made clear Congress's intent to allow employers to adopt local, voluntary means to improve the economic condition of minorities: "It would be ironic indeed if a law triggered by a Nation's concern over centuries of racial injustice . . . constituted the first legislative prohibition on all voluntary, private, race-conscious efforts to abolish traditional patterns of racial segregation and hierarchy."

Key Players

Burger, Warren (1907–1995): Burger was born in St. Paul, Minnesota. He left the practice of law when President Eisenhower named him assistant attorney general (1953–1955) and then appointed him to the U.S. Court of Appeals (1956–1969). President Nixon appointed him Chief Justice of the Supreme Court in 1969, where he served until 1986.

Dirksen, Everett (1896–1969): Dirksen was born in Pekin, Illinois. He served as an Illinois Republican in the U.S. House of Representatives (1933–1951) until election to the Senate, where he rose to Republican whip in 1957 and Republican leader in 1959. He served in the Senate until his death.

Humphrey, Hubert (1911–1978): Humphrey was born in South Dakota and began his career as a pharmacist. He was mayor of Minneapolis (1946–1949) and a Democratic U.S. senator (1949–1964). In 1964 Lyndon Johnson chose Humphrey as his running mate, and he served as vice president until 1969. In 1968 he narrowly lost the presidential election to Richard Nixon.

Johnson, Lyndon Baines (1908–1973): Johnson, born in Stonewall, Texas, entered Democratic politics when he was elected to the House of Representatives in 1937, where he served until he was elected to the Senate in 1950. He rose to Democratic whip and Senate majority leader until John Kennedy chose him as his vice-presidential running mate in 1960. He assumed the presidency on Kennedy's death in 1963 and was reelected for one term in 1964. His exemplary record in civil rights was undermined by the escalating war in Vietnam, and he chose not to seek reelection in 1968.

Mansfield, Michael (1903–2001): Born in New York City but raised in Montana, Mansfield left a faculty position at Montana State University to serve as a Democrat in the U.S. House of Representatives (1943–1953), then in the Senate (1953–1977), where he was an outspoken critic of the war in Vietnam. President Jimmy Carter appointed him Ambassador Extraordinaire and Plenipotentiary to Japan (1977–1988).

See also: *Age Discrimination in Employment Act; Equal Pay Act; Fair Employment Practice Committee.*

BIBLIOGRAPHY

Books

Burstein, Paul. *Discrimination, Jobs, and Politics: The Struggle for Equal Employment Opportunity in the United States since the New Deal.* Chicago: University of Chicago Press, 1985.

Graham, Hugh Davis. *The Civil Rights Era: Origins and Development of National Policy.* New York: Oxford University Press, 1990.

Modjeska, Lee. *Handling Employment Discrimination Cases.* Rochester, NY: Lawyers Co-operative Pub. Co.; San Francisco, CA: Bancroft-Whitney Co., 1980.

Schwartz, Bernard. *Statutory History of the United States: Civil Rights*, Part II. New York: Chelsea House, 1970.

Sovern, Michael. *Legal Restraints on Racial Discrimination in Employment.* New York: The Twentieth Century Fund, 1966.

Other

Equal Employment Opportunity Commission [cited 31 August 2002]. <http://www.eeoc.gov>.

—Michael J. O'Neal

Civilian Conservation Corps

United States 1933

Synopsis

President Franklin D. Roosevelt established the Civilian Conservation Corps (CCC), originally known as the Emergency Conservation Work program, in 1933 as a means to provide employment for young men in need. This also provided much-needed labor for various public works and conservation projects throughout the United States and its territories.

The United States Departments of War, Labor, Interior, and Agriculture collaborated to create the CCC and keep it running smoothly. Labor leaders objected to the program on several grounds, but by the end of the program in 1942, it had left an indelible legacy.

Timeline

1918: Influenza, carried to the furthest corners by returning soldiers, spreads throughout the globe. Over the next two years, it will kill nearly 20 million people—more than the war itself.

1922: Published this year James Joyce's novel *Ulysses* and T. S. Eliot's poem *The Waste Land* will transform literature and inaugurate the era of modernism.

1928: Penicillin is discovered by Alexander Fleming.

1930: Pluto is discovered.

1933: Hitler becomes German chancellor, and the Nazi dictatorship begins. A month later, the Reichstag building burns, a symbol of the new regime's contempt for democracy. (Though a Dutch communist is punished for the crime, the perpetrators were almost certainly Nazis.) During this year, virtually all aspects of the coming horror are manifested: destruction of Jewish-owned shops and bans on Jewish merchants; elimination of political opposition (including the outlawing of trade unions); opening of the first concentration camps (and the sentencing of the first Jews to them); book-burning; and the establishment of the first racial purity laws.

1933: Germany and Japan withdraw from the League of Nations.

1933: Newly inaugurated U.S. president Franklin D. Roosevelt launches the first phase of his New Deal to put depression-era America back to work.

1933: Twenty-First Amendment repeals Prohibition.

1933: Even as Stalin's manmade famine ravages the Ukraine, the new administration of President Roosevelt formally recognizes the U.S.S.R.

1936: The election of a leftist Popular Front government in Spain in February precipitates an uprising by rightists under the leadership of Francisco Franco. Over the next three years, war will rage between the Loyalists and Franco's Nationalists. The Spanish Civil War will prove to be a lightning rod for the world's tensions, with the Nazis and fascists supporting the Nationalists, and the Soviets the Loyalists.

1938: The U.S. Fair Labor Standards Act establishes a minimum wage.

1943: Worn down by two Russian winters, the Germans begin to fall back. In January the siege of Leningrad (which at more than 800 days is the longest in modern history) is broken, and a month later, the German 6th Army surrenders at Stalingrad.

Event and Its Context

Emergency Conservation Work Program Created

Newly elected president Franklin Delano Roosevelt understood the nation's need for manpower for tasks such as fighting forest fires and creating public structures such as bridges and roadways as well as recreation facilities and parks. Conservation was also a priority throughout the country, especially the prevention of soil erosion. Above all, Roosevelt knew that Americans needed jobs.

Congress passed legislation in 1933 to create the Emergency Conservation Work program, which was designed to address the problem of high unemployment. The program commenced with what one writer quipped "may be an all-time record for bureaucratic speed." The first induction of workers took place at Camp Roosevelt near Luray, Virginia, on 7 April 1933, only 35 days after Roosevelt's inauguration. Four Cabinet departments—Labor, Interior, Agriculture, and War—cooperated in the management of the program, which became popularly known as the Civilian Conservation Corps. Recruitment was the responsibility of the Department of Labor; the army prepared the enrollees for work and supervised the camps; the Interior and Agriculture departments, specifically the Park and Forest services, supervised work projects. The program's first director was Robert Fechner, who was known for his leadership role in organized labor. The CCC was considered the greatest work force mobilization in the nation's history. By July 1933 there were 274,375 young men in 1,300 camps.

Roosevelt was convinced this program would not interfere with routine employment. Labor leaders, however, opposed the program. William Green, president of the American Federation of Labor, said he thought that army involvement would lead to the militarization of American youth. Later, labor leaders objected to vocational training in the camps on the grounds that it would cause too much competition for skilled jobs. Another objection, which originated in the timber industry, was that the CCC work in forestry-related projects would result in lower wages for laborers.

Enrollees participated in projects such as reforestation, road construction, soil conservation, park construction, trail clearing, and flood control projects. Enrollees' varied projects within parks, for example, included constructing bathrooms; installing campground showers, septic and water systems; erecting storage structures; and miscellaneous improvements such as building picnic tables. One observer dubbed the corps "Roosevelt's Tree Army" because the organization planted an estimated three billion trees between 1933 and 1942.

Outside of organized labor, objections to the program were few. Many viewed the CCC as a haven from the Great Depression's economic uncertainties. An estimated 25 percent of all Americans, or 13 million people, were unemployed. Those eligible for enrollment in the CCC were unmarried men between the ages of 18 and 25 (later changed to 17 and 28) whose families were on relief. CCC participants were commonly known as enrollees. Each enrollee was paid $30, between $22 and $25 of which was sent home. That share provided basics such as groceries for the families of the enrollees.

The government paid room and board as well as provided basic supplies. Camps housed about 200 enrollees initially in tents, but soon barracks and buildings housing support offices were erected. Enrollees had clothes, new shoes, and three meals a day. An enrollee from West Virginia said that one of his lasting memories was of seeing the food wasted. Another said that he ate bananas and oranges for the first time at the camp. According to *Smithsonian*, the workers "remember the food with a fondness born in deprivation." The magazine cited Harry Marsanick, an enrollee from Florissant, Missouri, as saying, "Oh, they really fed us, especially breakfast," recalled, "ham and potatoes and sausage, all the eggs you wanted. The kitchen was enough to keep me happy."

A typical enrollee was in his late teens with an eighth-grade education. Most were from humble backgrounds with little work experience. Enrollees reportedly gained weight with regular meals and strenuous work. Camp routine divided days into three eight-hour periods during which enrollees worked, slept, or enjoyed leisure time. There were, however, stories about enrollees in some camps running gambling operations or doing side work.

Enrollees would sign on for six months. Eventually, that was extended to two years. Camp leaders were eligible for longer reenrollment periods. An estimated 5 percent of the original 250,000 enrollees were out of the program within a few months. The majority of these enrollees either refused to work or were absent without leave (AWOL). Those who were AWOL were typically homesick.

Many enrollees learned to read, write, and even type after the CCC instituted educational programs after 1934. An estimated 8,500 enrollees learned to read and write between 1938 and 1939. Even so, critics decried the lack of formal education and called for the addition of vocational training to the program. The camps also taught etiquette and public speaking.

John Collier. The Library of Congress.

Reserve officers with limited ability to discipline the enrollees provided camp supervision. Fines of no more than $3 per month could be assessed as punishment. Disobedient enrollees might also be assigned specific drudge chores. As last resort, they could be dismissed, which resulted in their families losing their relief funds. Those charged with breaking discipline were permitted to appeal up to the corps area commander.

Camps were located in every state plus the territories of Alaska, Hawaii, Puerto Rico, and the Virgin Islands. Each camp cost $6,000 a month in enrollee wages alone, with an additional cost of $8,000 for maintenance and administration. Within two years, the National Park Service estimated forestry and park development in the United States had advanced by 10 to 20 years.

CCC enrollees served when needed as firefighters and were deployed to assist in natural disasters. During flooding of the Ohio River in 1937, the CCC camps in the area assisted with emergency aid. The natural disasters to which they were dispatched included floods in the Mississippi Valley and in Vermont and New York in 1937 as well as various blizzards and hurricanes.

Along with the benefits of the CCC, there were also horrible losses. Three CCC camps located in the Florida Keys were directly in the path of the Labor Day hurricane of 1935, one of the most violent storms on record with winds up to 200 miles per hour. Less than one-third of the 684 corpsmen at those camps were on holiday. The CCC official report listed "44 identified dead, 238 missing or unidentified dead, and 106 injured. Many were literally sandblasted to death, with clothing and skin rasped from their bodies."

Franklin D. Roosevelt sitting at head of Camp Fechner mess table, Civilian Conservation Corps Camp, Big Meadows, Virginia. AP/Wide World Photos. Reproduced by permission.

Diversity in the CCC

A 1933 executive order compelled the CCC to enroll Native Americans, U.S. territory residents, World War I veterans, and "older locally experienced men" to serve as supervisors. An estimated 300,000 African Americans were also enrolled but were in segregated camps under white supervision.

Native American enrollees were not placed in camps but were allowed to return home each night. These enrollees were under the auspices of the Civilian Conservation Corps–Indian Division (CCC-ID). Tribal councils administered projects, typically on reservations because of the dearth of jobs.

One of the beneficiaries of CCC-ID labor was the National Park Service (NPS), which was in a fevered rush to stabilize and maintain various archeological sites throughout the southwest. Working jointly with the Bureau of Indian Affairs (BIA), the NPS provided all-Navajo crews with materials and equipment as well as a supervisor who was a specialist in regional archeology. This particular group was known as the Mobile Unit. The 25 enrollees were based at Chaco Canyon, but for the five years that the unit was active, it worked on some 14 south-

western monuments. The number of Navajo participants within the Mobile Unit numbered 20 in 1938 and dwindled to 10 in 1940.

CCC-ID projects included the restoration of buildings ruined at Chaco Canyon and Aztec Ruins National Monuments and removal of rock at Pueblo Bonito from a fallen cliff. The Mobile Unit's successes earned them a reputation as competent stonemasons.

Although there is little information about women in the CCC, First Lady Eleanor Roosevelt requested that they be given a place within the corps. In addition to those women who served as staff in the camps, typically in secretarial or clerical positions, there were reportedly several all-women camps located near Elmira, New York.

The Broader Scope of Benefits

The larger CCC story is more about good works than problems or controversies. Although just about every Roosevelt New Deal program was fair game for critics, the CCC seemingly escaped the bitterest wrath. Taxpayers could see the fruits of these work programs and benefited from them. They and the participants saw boys transformed into men by hard work and discipline. Educational advisors posted to each camp taught an estimated 40,000 participants to read and write, a task completed after their daily duties. Some enrollees reportedly earned high school diplomas and many learned skills. The CCC-ID, with the aid of Department of Education, sponsored job training starting in 1941.

The CCC was at its top operational capacity in September 1935. There were 502,000 enrollees in 2,514 camps. Raymond Gram Swing, writing in *The Nation* in 1935, called the CCC "the bright jewel of the New Deal. . . . [On] the whole the CCC is liked throughout the breadth of the land, and deservedly so. . . . As a form of relief the CCC has avoided the pitfalls of other relief agencies. And conservation has been both furthered and publicized." By 1942, more than two million young men had participated in the work program. At its peak of operation, more than 500 CCC camps could be found in national, state, and local parks.

As the United States entered World War II, the NPS ended those projects deemed nonessential to the war effort. The program was not truly discontinued until 1942. The Mobile Unit, for example, was disbanded in April 1942. Among the lengthy checklist of completed projects were the planting of more than three billion trees, construction of about 47,000 bridges, and creation of about 800 state parks. The best known legacy of the CCC is located in Catoctin Mountain Park. A camp built there in 1939 became known as Camp David. When President Roosevelt used the camp, he named it Shangrila; President Dwight D. Eisenhower renamed the camp in 1953 in honor of his grandson. Many other CCC-built structures are still standing.

The National Association of CCC Alumni remains active with an estimated 6,500 members in about 120 chapters nationwide as of 2001. The organization has its own museum, the Franklin Delano Roosevelt CCC Museum at Warm Springs, Georgia.

Several contemporary programs, including AmeriCorps and the California Conservation Corps, are modeled on the CCC and contribute to its enduring legacy.

Key Players

Collier, John (1884–1968): Born in Georgia, Collier was a community leader and reformer best known for shaping federal policy on Native Americans. His first career was as a community worker. He was introduced to Native American life while on a trip to Taos, New Mexico. He founded the American Indian Defense Association in 1923 and was active in criticizing the government's legislative proscriptions. Franklin D. Roosevelt appointed Collier commissioner of Indian affairs in April 1933. As such, he admitted Native Americans to New Deal relief programs, including the CCC. He resigned his post in 1945.

Fechner, Robert (1876–1939): Although best remembered for his government work, Fechner had a prior career as an organized labor leader. He was appointed director of the Emergency Conservation Work on 6 April 1933. Under his leadership, the program was effective and was considered a New Deal success story.

Works Progress Administration poster. The Library of Congress.

Murphy, Daniel E.: Successor to Jay B. Nash as director of the CCC-ID, Murphy had previously been the Osage Agency superintendent.

Nash, Jay B.: Nash was appointed first director of the CCC-ID, but he left after one season.

See also: *Stock Market Crash.*

BIBLIOGRAPHY

Books

Biondi, Victor, ed. *American Decades: 1930–1939.* Detroit: Gale Research, 1995.

Graham, Jr., Otis L. and Meghan Wander, eds. *Roosevelt, His Life and Times: An Encyclopedic View.* Boston: G. K. Hall & Co., 1985.

Parman, Donald Lee. *The Indian Civilian Conservation Corps* (typescript of thesis). Norman: University of Oklahoma Press, 1967.

———. *The Navajos and the New Deal.* New Haven, CT: Yale University Press, 1976.

———. *Indians and the American West in the Twentieth Century*. Bloomington: Indiana University Press, 1994.

Phillips, Cabell. *The New York Times Chronicle of American Life: From the Crash to the Blitz, 1929–1939*. New York: Macmillan, 1969.

Prucha, Francis Paul. *The Great Father*. Lincoln: University of Nebraska Press, 1984.

The Reader's Companion to American History. Boston: Houghton Mifflin Co., 1991.

Watkins, T. H. *The Hungry Years: A Narrative History of the Great Depression in America*. New York: Henry Holt and Company, 1999.

Periodicals

Gower, Calvin W. "The CCC Indian Division: Aid for Depressed Americans, 1933–1942." *Minnesota History* 43 (spring 1972): 3–13.

"Is Roosevelt Slipping?" *The New Republic* (14 August 1935).

Jackson, Donald Dale. "They Were Poor, Hungry, and They Built to Last." *Smithsonian* 25, no. 9 (December 1994): 66–78.

McIntosh, Phyllis. "The Corps of Conservation." *National Parks* (September–October 2001): 23.

Meyer, Eugene L. "Camps That Changed Lives; CCC Veterans Work to Preserve Memories." *Washington Post* (27 April 2000): M16.

"Old Beat-up Trucks Represent Something More to CCC Veterans." Knight-Ridder/Tribune News Service (15 November 2001): K5336.

Parman, Donald Lee. "The Indian and the Civilian Conservation Corps." *Pacific Historical Review* 40, no. 1 (1971): 39–56.

Rosen, Jeffrey. "Washington Diarist: Happy Days." *New Republic* 215, no. 20 (11 November 1996): 62.

Other

Aztec Ruins—Administrative History. Chapter 12, Stabilization: The High Cost of Water. National Park Service. 27 February 2001 [cited 6 August 2002]. <http://www.nps.gov/azru/adhi/adhi12d.htm>.

The Civilian Conservation Corps and the National Park Service, 1933–1942: An Administrative History. National Park Service. 4 April 2000 [cited 6 August 2002]. <http://www.cr.nps.gov/history/online_books/ccc/ccc1a.htm>.

The Civilian Conservation Corps. Washington State Parks and Recreation Commission. 1 August 2002 [cited 6 August 2002]. <http://www.parks.wa.gov/civilian.htm>.

"Dusting Off Our Roots: The Dirty 30s." *Countryside & Small Stock Journal*. March–April 2000 [cited 6 August 2002]. <http://www.countrysidemag.com/issues/2_2000.htm>.

Gilbert, Jess and Alice O'Connor. "Leaving the Land Behind: Struggles for Land Reform in U.S. Federal Policy, 1933–1965." Land Tenure Center, University of Wisconsin-Madison. July 1996 [cited 6 August 2002]. <http://www.wisc.edu/ltc/ltc156.html>.

Golden, Randy. "Civilian Conservation Corps." About North Georgia. Summer 2000 [cited 6 August 2002]. <http://ngeorgia.com>.

—Linda Dailey Paulson

Clayton Antitrust Act

United States 1914

Synopsis

In 1914 the U.S. Congress responded to populist antitrust sentiments and deficiencies in the Sherman Antitrust Act of 1890 with a new act. The Clayton Act, authored by Alabama congressman Henry Clayton, outlawed, among other things, anticompetitive mergers and acquisitions, interlocking directorates, and price discrimination. Like the Sherman Act, the Clayton Act made restraint of trade a felony offense punishable by fine and imprisonment. Unlike the Sherman Act, Clayton exempted labor unions and agricultural cooperatives from antimonopoly rules, thus allowing for peaceful strikes and picketing. Nonetheless, although the new legislation formed part of President Woodrow Wilson's New Freedom economic reform program, the bill became so watered down in the Senate that many progressives felt abandoned and Wilson himself lost interest in it.

Timeline

1895: Brothers Auguste and Louis Lumière show the world's first motion picture—*Workers Leaving the Lumière Factory*—at a café in Paris.

1900: China's Boxer Rebellion, which began in the preceding year with attacks on foreigners and Christians, reaches its height. An international contingent of more than 2,000 men arrives to restore order, but only after several tens of thousands have died.

1905: Albert Einstein presents his special theory of relativity.

1910: Revolution breaks out in Mexico.

1915: A German submarine sinks the *Lusitania*, killing 1,195, including 128 U.S. citizens. Theretofore, many Americans had been sympathetic toward Germany, but the incident begins to turn the tide of U.S. sentiment toward the Allies.

1915: Italy enters the war on the side of the Allies, and Bulgaria on that of the Central Powers.

1915: At the Second Battle of Ypres, the Germans introduce a terrifying new weapon: poison gas.

1915: Turkey's solution to its Armenian "problem" becomes the first entry in a long catalogue of genocidal acts undertaken during the twentieth century. Claiming that the Armenians support Russia, the Turks deport some 1.75 million of them to the Mesopotamian desert, where between 600,000 and 1 million perish.

1915: D. W. Griffith's controversial *Birth of a Nation* is the first significant motion picture. As film, it is an enduring work of art, but its positive depiction of the Ku Klux Klan influences a rebirth of the Klan in Stone Mountain, Georgia.

1915: Albert Einstein publishes his General Theory of Relativity.

1917: On both the Western Front and in the Middle East, the tide of the war begins to turn against the Central Powers. The arrival of U.S. troops, led by General Pershing, in France in June greatly boosts morale, and reinforces exhausted Allied forces. Meanwhile, Great Britain scores two major victories against the Ottoman Empire as T. E. Lawrence leads an Arab revolt in Baghdad in March, and troops under Field Marshal Edmund Allenby take Jerusalem in December.

1919: Treaty of Versailles is signed by the Allies and Germany, but rejected by the U.S. Senate. This is due in part to rancor between President Woodrow Wilson and Republican Senate leaders, and in part to concerns over Wilson's plan to commit the United States to the newly established League of Nations and other international duties. Not until 1921 will Congress formally end U.S. participation in the war, but it will never agree to join the League.

Event and Its Context

Curbing Corporate Power

With the advance of industrial capitalism in the late nineteenth century, prominent companies were growing toward monopoly, which created public concern that they would be able to control interstate commerce and prices. In the 1870s and early 1880s, banks and financiers poured huge amounts of capital into rapidly growing industries such as the railroads, mining, and steel. These investments ultimately contributed to a concentration of economic power that was cemented by informal collusion in the form of alleged "gentlemen's agreements." Populist disapproval of the growing power of large corporations, business mergers, and corporate trusts led to the Sherman Antitrust Act of 1890. Drawing legitimacy from the U.S. Congress's power to regulate interstate commerce, this act, which was named after its sponsor, Senator John Sherman, was the federal government's first attempt to thwart monopoly. Section 1 of the act prohibited "every contract, combination in the form of trust or otherwise, or conspiracy, in restraint of trade or commerce among the several States, or with foreign nations." Section 2 made it illegal to "monopolize, or attempt to monopolize, or combine or conspire with any other person or persons, to monopolize any part of the trade or commerce among the several States, or with foreign nations." Violators of either section would be guilty of a felony offense and subject to a fine up to $10 million (if a corporation) or $350,000 (if an individual) and up to three years in prison.

Despite the act's potential as a weapon against corporate power, the government lacked the federal legislation and agencies necessary to make it effective. Moreover, its applicability was for more than a decade weakened by Supreme Court decisions. Those arguing that the Sherman Act was ineffective could point to a post-Sherman period bringing the greatest corporate consolidation in American history. In the five-year fiscal period 1898–1902, there were 1,797 consolidations, 857 of these in 1899 alone. The tide began to change, however, with the launch of President Theodore Roosevelt's "trust-busting"

President Woodrow Wilson. The Library of Congress.

campaigns and a subsequent Supreme Court acknowledgement of the federal government's right to bust the Northern Securities Company. In 1906 Roosevelt filed a federal suit against Standard Oil, which controlled most of the crude oil refined in the United States. The Supreme Court in 1911 found the company in violation of the Sherman Antitrust Act and ordered it to get rid of more than 30 of its primary affiliates. Although the Sherman Act was strengthened during the Taft administration, critics felt it was vague and lacked the juridical teeth to make it effective. Reform would come in 1914, with the founding of the Federal Trade Commission and the passing of the Clayton Antitrust Act.

Wilson's New Freedom

The beginning of the Woodrow Wilson administration in March 1913 brought promises of antimonopoly actions and restoration of free competition. With his "New Freedom" economic reform program, Wilson aimed at banking reform and increased government regulation of business. One part of the new president's economic reform strategy was an interstate trade commission to replace the old Bureau of Corporations; the measure, presented by James Covington of Maryland, passed both houses and was signed into law on 10 September, thus creating the Federal Trade Commission. On 20 November, after successfully defending the Underwood (tariff reform) bill and the

Federal Reserve Bill, Wilson met with leading congressional Democrats to discuss an antitrust act. Wilson's rise to power was accompanied by Democratic control of Congress and a number of southern Democrats in positions of influence. Although the president originally considered reforming and clarifying the Sherman Act, the legislators convinced him to seek a new solution. In January 1914 he announced his antitrust plan before a joint session of Congress. Most of Wilson's antitrust measures, at first reflected in several different bills, were later represented in a single House bill authored by Representative Henry Clayton of Alabama.

The Clayton Act of 1914 outlawed or curtailed several specific business practices considered to be unreasonable attempts to restrain trade or commerce. In the words of Montana senator Thomas J. Walsh, the act was meant "to preserve competition where it exists, to restore it where it is destroyed, and to permit it to spring up in new fields." The act, for example, banned mergers and acquisitions in cases in which the result would reduce competition or lead toward monopoly. Section 2 outlawed price discrimination, thus making it illegal for commodities to be sold to different buyers at different prices (except for cases in which the price discrepancy is the result of transportation or selling costs). Section 3 ruled out exclusive dealing, establishing that producers could not sell to a retailer or wholesaler on the understanding that no other distributor in the trade area would receive similar products and that the purchaser would not deal in products supplied by the seller's competitors.

Violators of both sections would be considered guilty of a felony punishable by a fine of up to $10 million (if a corporation); individuals could be fined up to $350,000 and imprisoned for up to three years.

The act established that corporations could not hold stock in competing companies if the result was to reduce competition substantially. It also outlawed so-called interlocking directorates, prohibiting the same individual from serving on the boards of directors of two or more competing companies having capital surplus and undivided profits greater than $1 million. Moreover, it gave power to the new Federal Trade Commission and the U.S. Justice Department to block any merger that was in violation of antitrust laws.

The Clayton bill saw considerable opposition from many camps. Although huge corporations threatened with dissolution may have seen the bill as dangerous, progressives saw it as weak. Southern Democrats and agrarians, for example, wanted to break all trusts completely. Labor unions took issue with the "combinations in restraint of trade" provisions of the bill for fear their actions would be affected.

Labor and the Clayton Act

By the mid-1890s labor unions had learned to hate the Sherman Antitrust Act, given that its attack on capital could also be turned on labor. This became apparent with the Pullman Strike in 1894. In that year, Cleveland attorney general Richard Olney used the Sherman Act against the American Railway Union and was thus able to imprison the union's president, Eugene Debs, for contempt of court. After labor unions protested language in the Clayton bill that they feared might make unions illegal, Congress amended the act to state that unions were not "illegal combinations or conspiracies in restraint of trade." Labor unions and agricultural cooperatives were thus exempted from the proscriptions of the Sherman Act. Nonviolent labor movements, strikes, boycotts and picket lines would all be legal.

Section 17 of the act specifically declared that antitrust laws would not be applicable to labor organizations. Most significantly, it recognized that "the labor of a human being is not a commodity or article of commerce." Nothing in the antitrust laws, it said, should be understood to prohibit the existence or activities of labor, agricultural, or horticultural activities "instituted for the purposes of mutual help, and not having capital stock or conducted for profit." Moreover, it stated that individual members could not be restrained from carrying out their "legitimate objectives." Samuel Gompers, president of the American Federation of Labor (AFL), hailed the legislation as the Magna Carta of labor, though this original euphoria would soon dissipate with court interpretations that practically nullified labor's expected advances.

Although historians generally attribute passage of the Clayton Antitrust Act to popular antitrust sentiment and the need to address the inadequacies of the Sherman Antitrust Act, some economists believe that congressional approval of the act was also the product of lobbying by interest groups. Because the Clayton Act essentially redistributed wealth among the nation's different economic interest groups and agents, those groups presumably influenced legislators' votes on the act. In the case of Senate voting patterns, although senators from the industrialized New England states (with higher numbers of manufacturing pressure groups) tended to oppose the act, those from the agricultural southern states (with corresponding agrarian interest groups) tended to support it.

With the passage of the Clayton Act, Wilson considered his economic reform package complete. The satisfaction of some of his fellow Democrats was summed up by Alabama congressman Tom Heflin when he declared that "laborers are employed, wages are good, the earth has yielded abundantly, the Democratic Party is in control, God reigns, and all is well with the Republic." Many progressives, agrarians, and labor activists nonetheless considered Wilson's reforms insufficient. The bill's original proponents felt that they had been abandoned, as the bill's strongest measures had been amended and thus rendered harmless.

"When the Clayton bill was first written . . . it was a raging lion with a mouth full of teeth," complained Missouri senator James A. Reed. "It has degenerated to a tabby cat with soft gums, a plaintive mew, and an anemic appearance." Like other antitrust proponents, he considered the amended bill to be a legislative apology to the trusts, "delivered hat in hand, and accompanied by assurances that no discourtesy is intended." Wilson himself complained that Senator Charles Culberson of Texas, chairman of the Judiciary Committee, had worked to water down the bill and had effectively neutralized it. Nonetheless, he lost interest in the bill and did nothing to restore its original force. Congress passed it and he signed it into law on 15 October 1914.

In 1921, in the case of *Duplex Printing Press v. Deering*, the United States Supreme Court essentially gutted the labor provisions of the Clayton Act by ruling that federal courts could enjoin labor unions for actions in restraint of trade.

Key Players

Clayton, Henry De Lamar (1857–1929): Clayton represented Alabama in the House of Representatives from 1897 to 1915. A Democrat, he was the author of the Clayton Antitrust Act of 1914.

Culberson, Charles Allen (1855–1925): A Texas Democrat, Culberson served in the U.S. Senate from 1899 to 1923. He chaired the Senate Committee on the Judiciary from 1899 to 1929. President Wilson accused him of working to weaken the provisions of the Clayton Antitrust Act.

Wilson, Woodrow (1856–1924): Wilson, a Democrat, was the 28th president of the United States, serving from 1913 to1921. His New Freedom program passed economic reforms in the form of banking and antitrust legislation. He complained that the Clayton Antitrust Act was a weak version of the bill he originally supported.

See also: *Pullman Strike.*

BIBLIOGRAPHY

Books

Byrd, Robert C. "The Woodrow Wilson Years: 1913–1920." In *The Senate, 1789–1989*. Washington, DC: Government Printing Office, 1994.

Periodicals

USIA. "Summary of Major U.S. Antitrust Laws." *Economic Perspectives* 4, no. 1 (February 1999).

Other

Bonney, Doug. "The Right to Strike." Kansas City Labor Advocate Online. *Know Your Rights* [cited 17 October 2002]. <http://www.kclabor.org/knowstrike.htm>.

Lucash, Gesmer, and Updegrove, LLC. Web site, ConsortiumInfo.org. The Sherman Antitrust Act of 1890. 2002 [cited 17 October 2002]. <http://www.consortiuminfo.org/antitrust/sherman.shtml>.

Micheloud, Francois. "John D. Rockefeller and the Standard Oil Company. The 1890 Sherman Antitrust Act" [cited 17 October 2002]. <http://www.micheloud.com/FXM/SO/antitrust.htm>.

A Moment in Time Archives. "The South's Revenge: The Amazing Congress of 1912." 24 June 2002 [cited 17 October 2002]. <http://www.ehistory.com/world/amit/display.cfm?amit_id=1258>.

Ramírez, Carlos D., and Christian Eigen-Zucchi. "Why Did the Clayton Act Pass? An Analysis of the Interest Group Hypothesis." Department of Economics, George Mason University. April 1998 [cited 17 October 2002]. <http://www.gmu.edu/departments/economics/working/Papers/98_03.pdf>.

Spartacus Educational. Anti-Trust Act [cited 17 October 2002]. <http://www.spartacus.schoolnet.co.uk/USAtrust.htm>.

—Brett Allan King

Clifton-Morenci-Metcalf Strike

United States 1915

Synopsis

As Americans became increasingly concerned about events in Europe in 1915, domestic labor disputes threatened the stability of the Southwest United States. In 1915 in the Arizona mining towns of Clifton, Morenci, and Metcalf, located close to the border of Arizona and New Mexico, Mexican immigrants and Mexican American miners declared a work stoppage in the mines. Striking over low wages and an unequal wage structure between the two groups, the strikers believed that the American miners in the camps received higher salaries. Moreover, the workers—primarily the Mexican workers—declared a stoppage because of constant abuse imposed upon them by their American bosses. This abuse was a particular problem for the recently arrived workers who had emigrated from Mexico, which was experiencing a social revolution. The Mexican workers had to deal with the constant threat of deportation and imprisonment. The Clifton-Morenci-Metcalf strike proved significant because it illustrated a struggle over issues of identity, class, race, and ethnicity.

Timeline

1895: Brothers Auguste and Louis Lumière show the world's first motion picture—*Workers Leaving the Lumière Factory*—at a café in Paris.

1900: China's Boxer Rebellion, which began in the preceding year with attacks on foreigners and Christians, reaches its height. An international contingent of more than 2,000 men arrives to restore order, but only after several tens of thousands have died.

1905: Albert Einstein presents his special theory of relativity.

1910: Revolution breaks out in Mexico.

1915: A German submarine sinks the *Lusitania*, killing 1,195, including 128 U.S. citizens. Theretofore, many Americans had been sympathetic toward Germany, but the incident begins to turn the tide of U.S. sentiment toward the Allies.

1915: Italy enters the war on the side of the Allies, and Bulgaria on that of the Central Powers.

1915: At the Second Battle of Ypres, the Germans introduce a new weapon: poison gas.

1915: Turkey's solution to its Armenian "problem" becomes the first entry in a long catalogue of genocidal acts undertaken during the twentieth century. Claiming that the Armenians support Russia, the Turks deport some 1.75 million of them to the Mesopotamian desert, where between 600,000 and 1 million perish.

1915: D. W. Griffith's controversial *Birth of a Nation* is the first significant motion picture. As film, it is an enduring work of art, but its positive depiction of the Ku Klux Klan influences a rebirth of the Klan in Stone Mountain, Georgia.

1915: Albert Einstein publishes his General Theory of Relativity.

1917: On both the Western Front and in the Middle East, the tide of the war begins to turn against the Central Powers. The arrival of U.S. troops, led by General Pershing, in France in June greatly boosts morale, and reinforces exhausted Allied forces. Meanwhile, Great Britain scores two major victories against the Ottoman Empire as T. E. Lawrence leads an Arab revolt in Baghdad in March, and troops under Field Marshal Edmund Allenby take Jerusalem in December.

1919: Treaty of Versailles is signed by the Allies and Germany, but rejected by the U.S. Senate. This is due in part to rancor between President Woodrow Wilson and Republican Senate leaders, and in part to concerns over Wilson's plan to commit the United States to the newly established League of Nations and other international duties. Not until 1921 will Congress formally end U.S. participation in the war, but it will never agree to join the League.

Event and Its Context

In the late nineteenth century, the American Southwest underwent a profound change. American capitalist enterprise entered the region in search of profits and revenue. One source of revenue was in the small town of Clifton, Arizona, located a few miles from the New Mexico border on the eastern side of the state. Clifton had developed in the late 1870s upon the discovery of copper in the region. The territorial legislature at the time had mandated an eight-hour workday. The legislature also prohibited union locals, thus inhibiting the creation of any labor movement. By the early twentieth century, the liberal social laws facilitated the entrance of vast amounts of capital into the territory, as an influx of American capitalist enterprises began to populate the region. Among the largest were the Arizona Copper Company, the Detroit Copper Company, and the Shannon Consolidated Copper Company. Initially, the three companies had difficulty finding both skilled and unskilled workers for the mines. Clifton did not have the population base to fulfill the labor needs of the complex mining enterprises. However, the outbreak of a revolution in Mexico in 1910 proved beneficial for the struggling enterprises. Members of the Mexican working class left their native land, which was plagued by unemployment and violence, to seek work in the United States. Many Mexicans immigrated to Texas and California. However, a sizable number of Mexican immigrants ended their trip in Clifton, because of the promises of employment. Unfortunately, many of these workers were unaware that in Clifton as well as the neighboring towns of Morenci and Metcalf, there was an ongoing labor struggle.

Specifically, the miners had established contacts with the Western Federation of Miners (WFM) and the American Federation of Labor (AFL) so as to present a demand for higher wages to the mine owners. For seven and one half hours of work, Mexican workers in the region earned a daily wage of $2.39, whereas their American counterparts performing the same work earned $2.89. The unequal wage structure in the mining camps angered many Mexican and Mexican American workers. They believed that the American corporations were withholding wages so as to boost profits. Moreover, to exacerbate the situation, in 1914 the United States experienced an economic depression that debilitated the copper industry. Given the tense economic and political conditions, in late 1915 the corporations informed the miners that effective immediately, all workers would receive a 10 percent pay reduction. The companies' managements had failed to understand the ramifications of a pay cut at a time when the prices of consumer goods were increasing.

In the few days following the announcement of the cut, Mexican workers met at local town halls to discuss a course of action. In 1915 foreign affairs were in turmoil. The U.S. decision to enter World War I was imminent. The workers aptly perceived that a strike could backfire on them as the public might see the striking workers as selfish and unpatriotic. This labor conflict could become a problem in halting production of the metal, which would be vital in the American war effort. The AFL took the larger view and pleaded with the workers not to go on strike. Samuel Gompers, president of the AFL, had pledged that the affiliates of his labor union would not go on strike during this crucial period. The petition of the workers, in which they asked for higher wages and an end to the disparity between American and Mexican workers, found its way to the National War Labor Board, which was charged with mediating labor disputes. The board decided, after considerable debate, that if a solution was possible in this conflict, it must be dealt with between the workers and the companies.

The companies refused to accede to the demands of the workers. Consequently, on 1 September 1915, 5,000 Mexican miners in Clifton, Morenci, and Metcalf declared a work stoppage. President Woodrow Wilson tried to get his labor representative to meet first with the workers and then with the WFM. Rumors abounded that the government was sending U.S. Army troops to the region to stop the strike. There were also rumors that striking workers would be risking arrest and deportation to Mexico, which was still plagued with unemployment and violence. When peace talks failed, Wilson pleaded with the governor of Arizona, George W. P. Hunt, to aid in the matter. Hunt had the support from the workers because in many recent labor conflicts, he had sided with the workers. Thus he was the ideal mediator in this conflict. With the help of Hunt, in January 1916 the two sides agreed to a compromise in the strike. In return for a pledge to end the strike, the companies agreed to a significant wage increase. By 24 January 1916 workers' salaries in the area had risen as much as 60 percent.

Impact

The strike had both long- and short-term consequences. With the increase in wages to a level equal to that of the Americans, the workers were able to send a message to the companies that equality and fairness should be the mantra of American corporate culture in the Southwest. The success in achieving these aims transformed the nature of the dialogue between workers and the companies. More important, however, is that this was one of the first successful labor mobilizations involving Mexican immigrants in the United States. It showed that Mexicans and their American counterparts could mobilize on a large scale. Essentially, these workers overcame the difficult barriers of race, class, and ethnicity to create a successful labor movement in the American Southwest.

Key Players

Hunt, George W. P. (1859–1934): Governor of the state of Arizona, Hunt was instrumental in the favorable conclusion of the strike. He had the support of the workers in the Clifton-Morenci-Metcalf region and the respect of the mining corporations. Without his mediation, the strike would have proved disastrous not only for the Arizona economy but also for the American economy, which was beginning to mobilize for the war effort.

See also: *American Federation of Labor; National War Labor Board; Western Federation of Miners.*

BIBLIOGRAPHY

Books

Byrkit, James. *Forging the Copper Collar: Arizona Labor Management War of 1901–1921.* Tucson: University of Arizona Press, 1982.

Mellinger, Philip. *Race and Labor in Western Copper: The Fight for Equality, 1896–1918.* Tucson: University of Arizona Press, 1995.

ADDITIONAL RESOURCES

Other

Los Mineros (video). The American Experience: A Galan Production presented by WGBH Boston, 1991.

—Jaime Ramon Olivares

Coal Mine Contract Signed

United States 1870

Synopsis

The first written contract signed between coal miners and coal mine operators had its origins in the first attempt to organize coal miners in the anthracite coalfields of Pennsylvania. The resulting union formed in 1849 but was soon dissolved. Organizational activities resumed in the early 1860s as local unions formed throughout the coalfields of Pennsylvania. During this same period of time, mine owners organized into two operators' unions. In 1867, acting upon a new law establishing an eight-hour workday, John Siney led a movement to enforce

this legislation. The union that formed in 1868 from the consolidation of local unions was named the Workingmen's Benevolent Association, and its first president was Siney. Both miners and owners were now well organized, and disagreements and strikes occurred on a regular basis, especially with regard to the eight-hour day and suspension of work by the operators. A written agreement was eventually reached and signed on 29 July 1870 by the major participants of both sides, the committee of the Anthracite Board of Trade and the committee of the Workingmen's Benevolent Association.

Timeline

1851: Britain's Amalgamated Society of Engineers applies innovative organizational concepts, including large contributions from, and benefits to, members, as well as vigorous use of direct action and collective bargaining.

1853: Crimean War begins in October. The struggle, which will last until February 1856, pits Russia against the combined forces of Great Britain, France, Turkey, and Sardinia-Piedmont. A war noted for the work of Florence Nightingale with the wounded, it is also the first conflict to be documented by photojournalists.

1861: Italy is unified under Sardinian king Victor Emmanuel II.

1864: The International Red Cross is established in Geneva.

1867: Dual monarchy is established in Austria-Hungary.

1871: Franco-Prussian War ends with France's surrender of Alsace-Lorraine to Germany, which proclaims itself an empire under Prussian king Wilhelm, crowned Kaiser Wilhelm I.

1871: U.S. troops in the West begin fighting the Apache nation.

1871: Boss Tweed corruption scandal occurs in New York City.

1871: Chicago fire causes 250 deaths and $196 million in damage.

1873: Financial panic begins in Vienna and soon spreads to other European financial centers as well as to the United States.

1876: Alexander Graham Bell introduces the telephone.

1880: Completed Cologne Cathedral, begun 634 years earlier, with twin spires 515 feet (157 m) high, is the tallest structure in the world, and will remain so until 1889, when it is surpassed by the Eiffel Tower. (The previous record for the world's tallest structure lasted much longer—for about 4,430 years following the building of Cheops's Great Pyramid in c. 2550 B.C.)

Event and Its Context

Anthracite coal, or hard coal, was discovered in eastern and northern Pennsylvania in the late 1790s. The coal industry was slow to develop within these fields primarily because of scarce coal markets and undeveloped transportation routes. Poor working conditions, low wages, and irregular employment characterized miners' jobs during these formative years. However, a commercial market for anthracite coal as a domestic heating source eventually developed. Because of its high efficiency and clean burning qualities, anthracite coal substituted for charcoal. Also, with the building of canals and the improvements to waterways, transporting anthracite coal to such markets as New York City and Philadelphia became less expensive.

First Association: Bates' Union

By 1849 the anthracite coal miners of Pennsylvania in the Schuylkill field, located between the cities of Harrisburg and Allentown, organized under the leadership of Englishman John Bates. The organization that resulted was called Bates' Union, with Bates installed as its first president. With a membership of 5,000 men, the first action by the union was to call a strike in order to counter many years of unreasonable demands by the mine owners. This union is generally considered the first association of miners in the United States, and the strike that followed its creation is considered the first general strike by miners in the United States. Unfortunately for the miners, the strike failed, and they were so discouraged by the defeat that Bates became very unpopular, and the newly established union was dissolved in 1850.

From 1850 to 1868 there were few successful organizational efforts of workers in the anthracite fields of Pennsylvania, and those that succeeded did so only at the local level. At the same time, small, independent operators controlled many of the anthracite mines. One noteworthy local group organized in 1860 when the miners of the Forrestville Improvement Company formed a local union that soon prompted nearby miners to form similar organizations. Because of the increasing demand for coal and the shortage of laborers, especially during the inflationary times of the Civil War, the leaders of these unions were able to secure giant wage increases paid to the miners, since the mine owners were able to sell their coal at extraordinary prices. However, the end of the Civil War reduced the need for coal throughout the reunited nation and, as a result, coal prices plummeted, as did the corresponding wages to miners. The union dissolved after four years of organizing attempts.

Owners and Employees Organize

In response to economic conditions and the actions of coal miners during the Civil War, the mine owners organized in 1867 under two organizations. The Mahoney Valley and Locust Mountain Coal Association organized within the region south of Broad Mountain (located north of Schuylkill County), and the other group, the Anthracite Board of Trade of the Schuylkill Coal Field, formed for the district north of Broad Mountain. Both employer organizations were formed specifically to oppose the demands of coal miners and to work together in order to coordinate worker contracts.

The coal miners saw the mine operators aggressively organize their companies and responded with their own efforts. With wages cut twice since the end of the Civil War, the miners saw their power being diminished. In addition, over a seven-year period in Schuylkill County, problems such as accidents, explosions, fires, and floods contributed to the deaths of 566 miners and the serious injury of another 1,665 workers. With such terrible conditions existing in the mines, the leaders of the local coal unions saw the need to organize under one central union in order to counter more efficiently the actions of the two powerful owner groups.

In 1867 the Pennsylvania legislature enacted a law that made the eight-hour workday legal (beginning on 1 July 1868) so long as there was no agreement between employer and employees that went against the newly established workday length. In order to enforce the new law, the coal miners met in a convention in the early part of 1868 to form the Workingman's Benevolent Association (WBA). This new organization was a combination of the workers in the major coalfields in the region. John Siney, who helped to organize the new union, was elected its first president when it was chartered on 6 April 1868.

The new union consolidated all the local unions of the anthracite coalfields in Pennsylvania, which at its height under Siney's leadership possessed 30,000 members. The WBA drew up a constitution that included a scale of wages and provided for care of sick and disabled miners (along with widows and orphans if a miner should die). Siney, an honest, well-liked man with good organizational skills, was a good choice for the union.

Conflict Arises

The demand by the WBA for the enforcement of the eight-hour day was the first item that engendered conflict between the two sides. The owners refused to obey the law, and a general strike followed in order to show the owners that the miners demanded acceptance of the new law. The miners eventually went back to work without securing all of their demands but with an adequate compromise of a 10 percent wage increase along with the return to the 10-hour workday. Because of this strike, the union leaders learned that they could put a stop to coal production whenever they felt the coal market was being oversupplied. (The overabundance of coal normally reduced coal prices and, as a direct result, reduced miners' wages and their ability to demand their rights and higher benefits.) In fact, union leaders saw that a work stoppage was even more effective when prices and demand for coal were rising. As a result, on 20 April 1869 the executive committee of the WBA, headed by Siney, issued a notice in Pottsville, Pennsylvania, stating that its members would suspend all digging of coal beginning on Monday, 19 May 1869.

The public and the local newspapers denounced the action and demanded that the union resume production of coal. The union leaders ignored the admonishments, knowing that if all else failed, the miners could move to other coalfields, while the owners had to stay at the mines they owned and operated. With the surplus coal almost depleted, the union leaders issued a second notice in Mahoney City, Pennsylvania, on 9 June 1869. They stated that even though the newspapers declared that the union's intention was to raise the price of coal to high levels, they only wished to maintain a healthy market for coal and healthy working conditions for miners. They announced that on 16 June 1869 the union miners would resume all work. The mine owners agreed on a sliding scale (or basis) for wages that varied depending on the location of the mine and on the month that the coal was sold. With a successful conclusion to their strike, the miners went back to work.

Signed Contract Obtained

As a result of further disagreements concerning the issue of a sliding scale for wages, Siney held the first joint meeting of miners and owners at Scranton, Pennsylvania, in 1869. The two sides reached an agreement during this discussion, but not until 29 July 1870 did the committee of the Anthracite Board of Trade and the committee of the Workingman's Benevolent Association formally sign a contract. The agreement stated that throughout the year of 1870, the WBA would not keep members discharged by employers for incompetence, bad workmanship, poor conduct, or any other cause.

On the owners' side, the committee of the Anthracite Board of Trade agreed that no WBA member would be fired as a result of actions or duties required of him by the association. Moreover, WBA members would be assured of work on a regular basis, and wages would be reduced by specified amounts during any month that expenses exceeded gain. A shared structure for determining the sliding scale, or basis, of wages was also part of the agreement. To arrive at the basis figure, representatives of the WBA and the owners were scheduled to meet on the twenty-fifth day of each month. They were bound to select five operators who would, on the twenty-fifth day of the following month, produce a statement confirming the prices of different sizes of coal, and those prices would fix the wage rate (and the basis) for that month.

William Kendrick, J. K. Sigfried, M. P. Fowler, Baird Snyder, and Samuel E. Griscom of the mine operators and owners, and John Siney, George Corbett, George Athey, James Barry, and Robert Weightman of the coal miners' union signed the agreement. This historic agreement is considered the first written contract in the United States signed by a coal miners' union (in this case the Workingman's Benevolent Association) and a coal mine owners' organization (in this case the Anthracite Board of Trade of the Schuylkill Coal Field).

After-effects Weaken the Union

At this time the Workingman's Benevolent Association had a membership of 30,000 of the 35,000 miners in the anthracite coalfields of Pennsylvania. Although the gains it had supported and won were impressive, the WBA suffered losses during an extensive strike in 1875. Failure of the strike forced miners back to work on the operators' terms. The WBA was further weakened by its attempts to organize across ethnic and regional lines. Disagreements erupted among workers from different backgrounds (and corresponding technical abilities and experiences) at a time when mine owners introduced new technology and increased the use of machinery. This led to periods of increased violence, including murder, involving the infamous group known as the "Molly Maguires," which eventually contributed to the end of the WBA. Although eliminated from the union environment, the Workingman's Benevolent Association made a significant contribution to union organization in coal mining, especially with regard to the first employer-employee contract.

From 1875 to the middle of the 1890s, organized labor had virtually no representation in the anthracite fields of Pennsylvania. Attributes such as ethnicity, age, wage levels, and jobs all contributed to the difficulty labor leaders experienced in trying to organize the mineworkers. In addition, the mine owners and the powerful railroad executives, who now controlled many of the coalfields, aggressively opposed them. Although many militant workers attempted strikes during this period, none were successful. The combination of these conditions made the task of organizing by the United Mine Workers an uphill battle. From the earlier pioneering work of the Workingman's Benevolent Association, the United Mine Workers of America eventually organized its first local union in the Schuylkill fields of Pennsylvania in 1894.

Key Players

Siney, John (1831–1879): Siney was born in Ireland and raised in England. Siney learned the basics of organizing labor unions while employed in the Lancashire textile mills of England. He immigrated to the United States in 1863. Siney began to work in the Eagle Colliery in St. Clair, Schuylkill County, Pennsylvania, in 1867, where he participated in his first strike that same year. As president of the Workingman's Benevolent Association (the forerunner of the United Mine Workers union), Siney introduced the first general strike, the first written and signed agreement, the first closed shop, the first board of arbitration, the first system of sick and death benefits, the first official miners' newspaper, and the first effective industrial union in the American coal industry. He helped to pass the Mine Safety Act of 1869 and the Mine Safety Act of 1870, both of which were designed to provide for better regulation and ventilation of mines for the protection of the miners. The requirements contained in these acts, the first mine safety inspection laws in the United States, became the foundation of mine safety legislation for the next century. Siney also conducted the first collective bargaining agreement within the coal mining industry. The Miners' National Association, the first national miners' union in the United States, was formed by Siney in 1873.

See also: *Eight-hour Day Movement; Molly Maguires; United Mine Workers of America; Workingman's Benevolent Association.*

———————

BIBLIOGRAPHY

Books

Fink, Gary M., ed. *Labor Unions.* Westport, CT: Greenwood Press, 1977.

Roy, Andrew. *A History of the Coal Miners of the United States.* Westport, CT: Greenwood Press, 1970.

Taft, Philip. *Organized Labor in American History.* New York: Harper & Row, 1964.

Other

Books on Polish-American History and American Labor [cited 12 October 2002]. <http://www.poles.org/books.html>.

Immigrants in the Coal Region [cited 12 October 2002]. <http://www.amphilsoc.org/library/exhibits/wallace/immigrants.htm>.

John Siney [cited 12 October 2002]. <http://www.spartacus.schoolnet.co.uk/USAsiney.htm>.

Mathews, Tom. *John Siney, St. Claire's Immigrant Son* [cited 12 October 2002]. <http://www.fortunecity.com/victorian/mill/1215/siney.htm>.

A Pictorial Walk through the 20th Century: The Irish in Mining [cited 12 October 2002]. <http://www.msha.gov/century/irish/page6.html>.

United Mine Workers of America—District 25 Papers. [cited 12 October 2002]. <http://www.lib.iup.edu/spec_coll/mg109.html>.

—William Arthur Atkins

Coalition of Labor Union Women

United States 1974

Synopsis

The founding convention of the Coalition of Labor Union Women (CLUW) in Chicago in 1974 brought together activists in industrial, service, government, and skilled trade unions to advocate on behalf of gender equality. CLUW's origins lie in the campaign for the Equal Pay Act of 1963 and the growing demands by rank-and-file women for equality with men in such matters as seniority and job assignments.

The Chicago delegates asserted their identity as feminists and unionists. They called on government, employers, and unions to fight sex discrimination in employment and develop effective comparable worth and pregnancy leave policies. Their alliance with feminists in such groups such as the National Organization for Women (NOW) was weak in the mid-1970s, although the disparate groups united to support the Equal Rights Amendment (ERA). CLUW members defended union grievance and seniority systems in the face of NOW's position that affirmative action should override union practices.

Timeline

1955: African and Asian nations meet at the Bandung Conference in Indonesia, inaugurating the "non-aligned" movement of Third World countries.

1965: Power failure paralyzes New York City and much of the northeastern United States on 9 November.

1969: Assisted by pilot Michael Collins, astronauts Neil Armstrong and Edwin E. "Buzz" Aldrin become the first men to walk on the Moon (20 July).

1972: On 5 September, Palestinian terrorists kill eleven Israeli athletes and one West German policeman at the Olympic Village in Munich.

1975: Pol Pot's Khmer Rouge launch a campaign of genocide in Cambodia unparalleled in human history. By the time it ends, with the Vietnamese invasion in 1979, they will have slaughtered some 40 percent of the country's population. Cambodia is not the only country to fall to communist forces this year: the pro-Western governments of South Vietnam and Laos also succumb, while Angola and Mozambique, recently liberated from centuries of Portuguese colonialism, align themselves with the Soviet Bloc.

1975: U.S. *Apollo* and Soviet *Soyuz* spacecraft link up in space.

1975: Two assassination attempts on President Ford occur in September.

1978: Terrorists kidnap and kill former Italian premier Aldo Moro. In Germany, after a failed hijacking on behalf of the Red Army Faction (RAF, better known as the Baader-Meinhof Gang), imprisoned RAF members commit suicide.

1980: In protest of the Soviet invasion of Afghanistan, President Carter keeps U.S. athletes out of the Moscow Olympics.

1985: In a year of notable hijackings by Muslim and Arab terrorists, Shi'ites take a TWA airliner in June, Palestinians hijack the Italian cruise ship *Achille Lauro* in October, and fundamentalists take control of an Egyptian plane in Athens in November.

1995: Bombing of the Alfred P. Murrah Federal Building in Oklahoma City, Oklahoma, kills 168 people. Authorities arrest Timothy McVeigh and Terry Nichols.

Event and Its Context

Toward Chicago: Union Women Organize for Change

The founding convention of the Coalition of Labor Union Women (CLUW) in Chicago in 1974 marked the establishment of the first bona fide national feminist organization of union women in the United States. The origins of CLUW date back to the early twentieth century, when women workers and reformers came together in such organizations as the Women's Trade Union League to work for passage of protective laws for working women. Beginning in the 1940s the focus of women's issues shifted away from agitating for measures to limit women's working hours and providing them with special employment conditions to attaining equality in the workplace. Union women's embrace of gender equality was a slow, uneven, and often painful process. As a greater number of women moved into the paid workforce, their expectations changed: they sought higher pay, equity with men, and a greater role in their unions. The Equal Pay Act of 1963 was a tangible sign of this changed consciousness; Title VII of the Civil Rights Act of 1964's ban on sex discrimination provided women workers with the legal tool to protest their unequal treatment by employers and their own unions. Some women unionists, such as Myra Wolfgang of the Hotel and Restaurant Employees, never accepted the goal of gender equality but sought to improve women's status in employment and unions.

As a result of their continuing dissatisfaction with union practices, working-class women organized into feminist groups. By the early 1970s women were already meeting to form interunion coalitions. Workers from meatpacking, mining, and Teamster locals in northern Virginia, for example, created Labor for Equal Rights Now, a group founded by Lizzie Corbin, an African American woman. In 1970 a National Rank and File Action Conference attended by 600 unionists drew up a "Declaration of the Rights of Women" and "Proposals for Action." Having pushed their unions to support equality, rank-and-file women joined with older women union leaders who backed gender equality in transforming their unions.

Cross-racial support for gender equality strengthened the emerging feminist movement. Dorothy Haener of the United Automobile Workers (UAW) credited Dollie Lower Robinson, an African American, lawyer, and U.S. Women's Bureau member, with giving her the idea of forming an organization of union feminists along the lines of a civil rights group. African Americans such as Addie Wyatt of the Amalgamated Meat Cutters Union contributed valuable political sophistication gained from their civil rights, community, and church-based activism to working-class feminist organizations.

The immediate steps leading up to the founding CLUW convention was a series of regional workshops across the country in 1973. Union activists organized these workshops in preparation for the Chicago meeting. The 1974 convention was a well-planned event. Organizers, however, did not anticipate the large number of delegates: they expected 500, and more than 1,200 unionists crowded into the hotel ballroom on 12 March 1974 to debate and approve CLUW's policies.

The election of CLUW officers in Chicago set the pattern for the organization's first decade of leadership. Veteran industrial unionists such as Olga Madar of the UAW, CLUW's first president, filled the top spots. Although industrial unions were slowly declining in both their representation of the total work force and their political power, seasoned activists such as Gloria Johnson (International Union of Electrical Workers), Joyce Miller (Amalgamated Clothing Workers), and Caroline Davis (UAW) continued to carry the social unionist banner into battle for gender equality. Younger women workers, energized by second-wave feminism, filled CLUW's ranks. Many of these women were responsible for convincing their labor organizations to back such feminist measures as the Equal Rights Amendment (ERA). Having pushed the older leadership cohort to change their thinking on gender relations, they now joined with them in Chicago to form CLUW.

CLUW as Labor's "Loyal Opposition"

CLUW members criticized organized labor's policies but also rejected solutions that bypassed unions. They displayed admirable agility in maintaining a critical stance toward a union movement to which they were committed by both reminding women unionists of the value of the collective bargaining agreement, union grievance procedures, and union elections, and educating women members on the federal equal employment opportunity (EEO) laws.

CLUW feminists placed most of the blame for inequality with employers who, they charged, gained the most by dividing workers along lines of race, gender, and age. Although they informed women in general about Title VII, CLUW leaders did not promote the filing of charges against unions. Male union leaders had little to worry about from activists regarding disrup-

tive and sudden challenges to union practices. Coalition leaders decried sex discrimination in the building trades, but few members belonged to such unions. They backed efforts by industrial unions such as the International Union of Electrical Workers, Communications Workers, and Automobile Workers to institute Title VII compliance programs and endorsed the filing of supporting briefs by these labor organizations on behalf of their women members. They did not, however, demand the establishment of a counterpart to the AFL-CIO's Department of Civil Rights in providing legal redress to women complainants.

As had women union activists in the 1950s, CLUW members for the most part acted as loyal opposition to organized labor. They challenged labor leaders, but they were not threatening. Most of their platform was predictable. They called on Congress to back school desegregation, childcare funding, national health insurance, and the ERA. On employment issues, they advocated guaranteed collective bargaining rights, improved health-and-safety coverage, an increased minimum wage, and extension of protective labor legislation to all workers. AFL-CIO convention participants in 1975 echoed many of these same demands. Although only 2.6 percent of the convention's delegates were women (women made up around 15 percent of the federation's membership), delegates applied strong pressure for feminist issues. This pressure resulted in the adoption of a six-point program for women that bore a striking resemblance to the coalition's demands. In addition, CLUW members galvanized the federation's executive board to use its clout in backing the ERA. Joyce Miller, CLUW president following Madar's retirement, for example, pressured AFL-CIO president George Meany to change the location of the AFL-CIO's 1977 convention from Florida, where legislators had not ratified the amendment, to Washington, D.C.

CLUW and the National Organization for Women

Since the founding of the National Organization for Women (NOW) in 1966, men and women union leaders had criticized NOW's efforts on behalf of women workers. They charged that NOW did not expend enough resources on economic issues that concerned lower-paid working women. When they did—for example, by advocating strong EEO enforcement—they ignored the valuable role played by labor in educating its members on equality and offering the grievance procedure as a tool to fighting discrimination. The debate over seniority and affirmative action points to the fault lines among CLUW and NOW leaders in the mid-1970s. With the massive layoffs during the economic recession, the EEO Commission, NOW, and other liberal and civil rights organizations proposed that the traditional collective bargaining guarantee of "last-hired, first-fired" be suspended so as to preserve the recent hiring gains of women and minorities. This plan met with scorn from male and female unionists both in leadership and in most rank-and-file positions as undercutting labor's already diminished strength.

NOW and CLUW averted a damaging break over the issue of the Supreme Court's *Franks v. Bowman Transportation* ruling in 1976. The ruling left the traditional seniority system intact but ordered that measures be taken to provide a "rightful-place" remedy (i.e., retroactive seniority to the date of discrimination) for victims of unequal treatment. CLUW and NOW worked together on the ERA and comparable-worth campaigns. For their part, CLUW delegates supported abortion rights at their 1977 convention. With a growing number of women in the workforce, NOW leaders devoted increasing attention to workplace issues such as minimum wage legislation and National Labor Relations Act reform, two items of key importance to organized labor.

CLUW's basic program and relationship to the labor movement changed little in the 1970s and 1980s. Its membership increased steadily, from around 6,000 in the late 1970s to 18,000 members in the mid-1980s. CLUW members tended to be activists, staff members, and office holders within their own international unions. By the late 1970s they could look back with pride over the transformation of the labor movement from that of support for protective laws to a full backing for gender equality. Women comprised an ever-growing share of both the total workforce and its organized sectors, especially in the areas of educational services, medical services, and public administration. In 1956 women had comprised 18.6 percent of all union members; by 1978 they claimed 24.2 percent of total membership. That figure climbed to 37 percent by 1990. Title VII–inspired bans on discrimination increasingly appeared in this period. In 1965 only 28 percent of a representative sample of 400 collective bargaining agreements contained antidiscrimination clauses. In 1970 the figure had jumped to 46 percent; by 1975 it had risen to 74 percent. Although female activists were long accustomed to being marginalized in the feminist and union movements, CLUW's founding marked another step in the transformation of labor's support for protective laws for women to pursuit of gender equality. CLUW further promoted the need of the feminist movement to recognize the central role of workplace concerns and the role of unions in the wider struggle for equality.

Key Players

Johnson, Gloria (1927–): After graduating from Howard University, Johnson found employment in the U.S. Department of Labor and then worked as a staff member of the International Union of Electrical Workers (IUE). She worked for equal pay and pushed the IUE to address "women's issues." Johnson held many leadership positions in CLUW, including serving as president in the 1990s.

Madar, Olga (1926–1996): Madar was the first woman member of the United Automobile Workers (UAW) executive board and the first president of CLUW. She maintained close ties between CLUW and the AFL-CIO.

Wolfgang, Myra (1914–1976): Wolfgang was an international vice president in the Hotel and Restaurant Workers (HERE) union, a founding member of CLUW, and an opponent of the ERA. Although other union activists came to embrace gender equality and mend relations with middle-class feminists, Wolfgang was wary of such goals and alliances, arguing that women workers should defend protective measures.

See also: *Equal Pay Act; Equal Rights Amendment and Protective Legislation; National Organization for Women.*

BIBLIOGRAPHY

Books

Deslippe, Dennis A. *"Rights, Not Roses": Unions and the Rise of Working-Class Feminism, 1945–1980*. Urbana: University of Illinois Press, 2000.
Gabin, Nancy F. *Feminism in the Labor Movement: Women and the United Auto Workers, 1935–1975*. Ithaca, NY: Cornell University Press, 1990.
Milkman, Ruth. "Women Workers, Feminism, and the Labor Movement Since the 1960s." In *Women, Work and Protest: A Century of U.S. Women's Labor History*, edited by Ruth Milkman. New York: Routledge & Kegan-Paul, 1985.
O'Farrell, Brigid, and Joyce L. Kornbluh. *Rocking the Boat: Union Women's Voices, 1915–1975*. New Brunswick, NJ: Rutgers University Press, 1996.

ADDITIONAL RESOURCES

Other

"Step by Step: Building a Feminist Movement, 1941–1977." Joyce Follet, producer; Mimi Omer, coproducer. Close-captioned video. Worthington, MA: Step by Step, 1998.

—Dennis A. Deslippe

Colored Farmers' Alliance

United States 1886

Synopsis

Following the Civil War, some southern African Americans managed to acquire land and establish a degree of economic independence despite many obstacles. In response to Reconstruction Era economic crises, political disenfranchisement, and civil repression, African Americans organized distinctly black institutions including unions, towns, secret self-defense groups, mutual aid societies, businesses, and churches. The Colored Farmers' National Alliance and Cooperative Union (CFA) was founded in Houston County, Texas, on 11 December 1886 to protect African American farmers in the South from falling commodity prices, rising farm costs, and high interest rates. The Southern Farmers' Alliance was founded for similar concerns but barred blacks from joining.

Timeline

1866: The Winchester repeating rifle is introduced.

1871: Chicago fire causes 250 deaths and $196 million in damage.

1876: General George Armstrong Custer and 264 soldiers are killed by the Sioux at the Little Big Horn River.

1878: Thomas Edison develops a means of cheaply producing and transmitting electric current, which he succeeds in subdividing so as to make it adaptable to household use. The value of shares in gas companies plummets as news of his breakthrough reaches Wall Street.

1882: Agitation against English rule spreads throughout Ireland, culminating with the assassination of chief secretary for Ireland Lord Frederick Cavendish and permanent undersecretary Thomas Burke in Dublin's Phoenix Park. The leader of the nationalist movement is Charles Stewart Parnell, but the use of assassination and terrorism—which Parnell himself has disavowed—makes clear the fact that he does not control all nationalist groups.

1884: Chicago's Home Life Insurance Building, designed by William LeBaron Jenney, becomes the world's first skyscraper.

1886: Bombing at Haymarket Square, Chicago, kills seven policemen and injures numerous others. Eight anarchists are accused and tried; three are imprisoned, one commits suicide, and four are hanged.

1886: The Statue of Liberty is dedicated.

1886: Apache chief Geronimo surrenders to U.S. forces.

1888: The Blizzard of 1888 in the United States kills hundreds and causes more than $25 million in property damage.

1892: Bitter strikes in Australia lead to the closing of ports and mines.

1896: U.S. Supreme Court issues its *Plessy v. Ferguson* decision, which establishes the "separate but equal" doctrine that will be used to justify segregation in the southern United States for the next half-century.

Event and Its Context

Because of a hostile environment created by white racial attitudes, the formation and development of the Colored Farmers' Alliance (CFA) remains somewhat cloaked in mystery despite its later large range of influence. Primary sources such as official records, correspondence, diaries, and newspaper articles regarding the membership, activities, and leadership of the CFA are scarce. Thus, information from diverse secondary sources provides much of the historical background of the CFA. Questions remain and have been debated by scholars as to whether the CFA operated as an independent organization or served as a useful political tool of its white leadership and appendage of the Southern Alliance (SA). In 1889 the CFA established the *National Alliance*, a weekly newspaper published in Houston, to educate its membership on basic farm-related issues.

To organize beyond the local level, the organization needed a conduit to white support for financial and political reasons. Richard Manning Humphrey, a white man, was elected general superintendent and served as official spokesman for the group. He served as liaison to the race-restricted SA. Less is known about J. J. Shuffer, who was elected president, and H. S. Spencer, who was elected secretary, except that both were black farmers who owned small tracts of land in east Texas.

Many African Americans who joined the CFA previously had been active in the Knights of Labor or the Grange or the Agricultural Wheel, which were all agricultural unions in the South. Membership of the CFA was set at over a million by *Appleton's Annual Cyclopedia*. The National Colored Alliance, a rival of the CFA led by Andrew J. Carouthers, was founded in Texas at about the same time. The two unions merged in 1890. In 1891 Humphrey estimated the membership at 1.2 million, including 300,000 females, 150,000 males under 21 years of age, and 750,000 adult males. Because of its large membership in every southern state, the CFA became the largest black organization in nineteenth-century America.

Goals of the CFA

Because black farmers suffered from crop liens and the whims of furnishing merchants as much as white farmers, they desired to finance their crops with fair loan terms, to obtain more flexible currency, to benefit from higher commodity prices, and to put an end to spiraling freight rates, among other populist goals. To reach these goals, the CFA created exchanges in the ports of Charleston, North Carolina; Houston, Texas; Mobile, Alabama; New Orleans, Louisiana; and Norfolk, Virginia. Members used the exchanges to buy goods at reduced prices and to obtain loans with which to pay off their mortgages. In this way, the CFA steered black farmers toward a conservative philosophy that encouraged its membership to own their own homes and to pay off debt. Members were also urged to uplift themselves with hard work, sacrifice, and education, a philosophy shared by Booker T. Washington at the turn of the twentieth century. The CFA solicited funds to help sick and disabled members, to provide for longer public school terms, and to found a few academies. Representatives of the CFA convened in St. Louis, Missouri, in December 1889; in Ocala, Florida, in December 1890; and in Cincinnati, Ohio, in May 1891 to resolve internal policies and political issues.

Points of Agreement with the Southern Alliance

The CFA offered support to and received it in kind from the SA on several issues. This support developed more in the interest of political expediency on the part of whites and for survival on the part of African Americans. Both groups advocated the abolition of the Louisiana Lottery, fearing that it would lead farmers further into debt. In 1889 both groups opposed the Conger Lard Bill, which was supported by the Northern Alliance. This bill sought to impose high taxes and strict regulations on the production of vegetable oil over those imposed on the production of animal fats that favored by the Northern Alliance, whose members were mainly dairy farmers. The two Alliances created cooperative business ventures such as the stores and exchanges to foster economic ties between the two organizations. Both groups called for identical reforms including the abolition of national banks, the expansion of currency, and government ownership of railroads. In 1890 the CFA supported the SA's subtreasury plan in the hope that the plan would provide low interest loans for farmers and higher prices for agricultural produce.

Points of Disagreement with the Southern Alliance

Despite having many of the same political and economic interests, the fact remained that members of the SA were still part of the larger white society intent on oppression of all African Americans regardless of their individual economic and occupational status. On several occasions, the SA worked openly for policies that subjugated blacks so as to control their economic and political power.

In 1889 the Georgia chapter of the SA ordered that no land be leased to blacks. SA members preferred that African Americans work for white farmers. Henry Cabot Lodge sponsored the Election Bill, also known as the "Force Bill," which promised federal protection of the voting rights of blacks. The CFA backed the Election Bill in a resolution passed at its 1890 convention in Ocala, while the SA condemned the bill in its publication the *National Economist* and in the *Progressive Farmer*, a North Carolina newspaper. Humphrey, the white spokesperson for the CFA, also opposed the Election Bill. His opposition revealed a significant disconnect with the black members of the CFA.

The SA membership included mostly cotton farmers and landowners, whereas the CFA was composed mostly of cotton pickers and landless tenants. This difference came to the fore when the CFA attempted a cotton pickers' strike in 1891 to demand a minimum wage of $1 per 100 pounds of picked cotton. Conflict over the strike brewed within the CFA because of the fact that Humphrey promoted the strike without proper contingency plans while the black leaders of the organization—Andrew A. Carouthers of the Texas CFA and E. S. Richardson of the Georgia CFA—opposed the strike based on a clearer prediction of the outcome. The SA opposed the strike and denounced the strikers in the *National Economist*. Further, even though the strike was a half-hearted attempt that reflected the apathy and fear of black farm workers, it was suppressed by white violence and intimidation. Of 15 strikers in Arkansas who were killed, nine were lynched.

Impact on Politics

The SA comprised mostly members of the Democratic Party, which had a major platform of white supremacy at that time. Most African Americans were therefore members of the Republican Party. However, dissatisfaction with both major political parties created a desire for a third party by the membership in both Alliances. This desire was driven by the by the CFA membership's disillusionment with the concept of economic and self-help policies. For this reason, the members viewed politics as another avenue for reform. The CFA's call for a third party and its support of radical reform programs caused black Republicans to oppose the efforts of the CFA to organize blacks as a voting bloc. Black populists posed a threat to the political power of black Republicans by drawing black votes away to a populist agenda.

Despite the intraracial opposition, the CFA served as the primary network for the recruitment and development of black populists in the People's Party that was unofficially formed in 1891 and discussed at the Cincinnati convention in May of the same year. The official founding meeting of the People's Party took place in St. Louis in February 1892, where 97 seats were available for representatives of the CFA. The most successful third party in the 1890s, its membership was mostly industrial and included agrarian-based organizations including the Northern, Southern, and Colored Alliances, Knights of Labor, Farmers' Mutual Benefit Association, and the Union Labor Party. The People's Party won a number of state government seats in the South between 1892 and 1896.

Reasons for the Decline of the CFA

The decline of the CFA occurred for several reasons, among them the failure of members to pay dues. The majority of views fall along general themes of some internal conflict among leadership and much external conflict stemming from those who viewed the assertiveness of the CFA as aggression. As the CFA continued to assert itself and gain strength, the resistance and hostility of southern whites also became stronger. Despite the importance of cooperation between white and black farmers to promote progressive change, racism proved to be a consistently divisive and destructive issue. Although white Populists supported the use of the federal machinery to protect the general interests of agrarians, particularly members of the Southern Alliance, these same Populists were vehemently opposed to the use of the same federal machinery to protect the voting rights of black members of the CFA.

When the CFA attempted to change policies or to encourage economic self-determination among its membership, whites in the rural South responded with persistent, determined, and violent opposition and racism. The unsuccessful 1891 cotton pickers' strike marked the beginning of the decline of the CFA due to overwhelmingly violent opposition by white agrarians. By 1892, the CFA appeared finished and unable to recover from internal differences and external terrorism. A more conservative farm club, the Farmers' Improvement Society of Texas, founded in 1890, managed to survive through the first half of the twentieth century by sticking to the original goals of the CFA: adopting improved farming methods and acquiring ownership of their homes. The expansion of the platform of the CFA beyond the self-help philosophy to challenge the entrenched southern caste system contributed to its demise.

During the decline, disenfranchisement of blacks, the enactment of "Jim Crow" legislation, and massive violence and terrorism against blacks escalated. Ultimately, conflicts stemming from efforts by whites to keep blacks in economic and political subjugation contributed not only to the dissolution of the CFA, but to the dissolution of the Populist movement as well. The emphasis of the Populist platform was on land-owning farmers that were threatened by eastern capital. Little attention focused on the needs of landless black farm workers who were caught in the cycle of sharecropping. The tradition of black agrarian radicalism was revived somewhat in the 1930s with the Southern Tenant Farmers' Union and the Alabama Sharecroppers Union, as well as the National Sharecroppers Fund and the National Association for the Advancement of Colored People (NAACP).

Key Players

Humphrey, Richard Manning (1836–1906): Humphrey was a Confederate captain of Irish descent from Clarendon County, South Carolina, who later lived in Lovelady, Texas. He was a schoolteacher and Baptist minister. He sought government office as a member of the Union Labor Party and ran for Congress as a Republican. Humphrey was elected superintendent of the Colored Farmers' Alliance (CFA) and served as the organization's national spokesman.

Shuffer, J. J.: African American landowner in east Texas, in July 1888 Shuffer ordered the establishment of a network of cooperative exchanges in Houston; New Orleans; Mobile; Charleston; and Norfolk. Shuffer was elected president of the CFA.

Spencer, H. J.: African American landowner in east Texas, Spencer served as secretary of the CFA.

See also: *People's Party.*

———————

BIBLIOGRAPHY

Books

Goodwyn, Lawrence. *The Populist Moment: A Short History of the Agrarian Revolt in America.* New York: Oxford University Press, 1978.

Humphrey, Gen. R. M. "History of the Colored Farmers' National Alliance and Co-operative Union." In *The Farmers' Alliance History and Agricultural Digest. American Farmers and The Rise of Agribusiness: Seeds of Struggle.* New York: Arno Press, 1975.

Shapiro, Herbert. "The Populists and the Negro: A Reconsideration." In *The Making of Black America: Essays in Negro Life and History 1. The Origins of Black Americans. Studies in American Negro Life.* New York: Atheneum, 1969

Periodicals

Abramowitz, Jack. "The Negro in the Populist Movement." *Journal of Negro History* 38, no. 3 (July 1953): 257–289.

Dann, Martin. "Black Populism: A Study of the Colored Farmers' Alliance through 1891." *Journal of Ethnic Studies* 2, no. 3 (fall 1974): 58–71.

Holmes, William F. "The Demise of the Colored Farmers' Alliance." *The Journal of Southern History* 41, no. 2 (May 1975).

Miller, Floyd J. "Black Protest and White Leadership: A Note on the Colored Farmers' Alliance." *Phylon* 33, no. 2 (2nd quarter 1972): 169–174.

Other

Ali, Omar. "Preliminary Research for Writing a History of the Colored Farmers Alliance in the Populist Movement: 1886–1896." Columbia University, History Department. 11 May 1998 [cited 19 August 2002]. <http://www.geocities.com/SoHo/Workshop/4275/part1.html>.

ADDITIONAL RESOURCES

Books

Kazin, Michael. *The Populist Persuasion: An American History.* Rev. ed. Ithaca, NY: Cornell University Press, 1998

Periodicals

Crowe, Charles. "Tom Watson, Populists and Blacks Reconsidered." *The Journal of Negro History* 55, no. 2 (April 1970): 99–116.

Saunders, Robert. "Southern Populists and the Negro 1893–1895." *Journal of Negro History* 54, no. 3 (July 1969): 240–261.

Scott, Roy V. "Milton George and the Farmers' Alliance Movement." *The Mississippi Valley Historical Review* 45, no. 1 (June 1958): 90–109.

Other

Petty, Adrienne. "History of the South: The Southern Revolt." Columbia University. Lecture notes. December 1998 [cited 19 August 2002]. <http://www.geocities.com/salika_2000/ap.html>.

—Lee McQueen

Colored National Labor Union

United States 1869

Synopsis

Between the 1820s and the 1860s the overwhelming majority of black workers in Baltimore, Maryland, were free, although some slaves did work alongside freedmen. For the most part, free black workers at this time were not allowed to join white trade unions. Sometimes, however, free blacks working along the industrial East Coast of the United States joined all-black groups such as the American League of Colored Laborers, which was established in New York City in 1850 as one of the first local organizations of black workers.

One such free black man was Isaac Myers, who grew up in Baltimore as the son of poor free parents. By 1841 Myers was apprenticed to James Jackson, a prominent black ship caulker. Within 20 years Myers was working as a skilled caulker and supervising other men in the caulking of clipper ships within the harbor. However, black workers, noticeably in the shipbuilding and maritime industries, were regularly dismissed from their jobs to make room for the growing number of whites looking for work. This unjust, but frequently occurring, situation led Myers and others to organize the Chesapeake Marine Railway and Dry Dock Company. The successful operation of this company eventually led to the establishment of the first national black labor organization, the Colored National Labor Union, in 1869.

Timeline

1849: Harriet Tubman escapes from slavery in Maryland. Over the next eight years, she will undertake at least 20 secret missions into Maryland and Virginia to free more than 300 slaves through the so-called Underground Railroad.

1854: Republican Party is formed by opponents of slavery in Michigan.

1859: American abolitionist John Brown leads a raid on the federal arsenal at Harpers Ferry, Virginia. His capture and hanging in December heighten the animosities that will spark the Civil War 16 months later.

1863: President Lincoln issues the Emancipation Proclamation, freeing all slaves in Confederate territories, on 1 January. Thus begins a year that sees the turning point of the Civil War, with decisive Union victories at Gettysburg, Vicksburg, and Chattanooga. Thereafter, the Confederacy is almost perpetually on the defensive, fighting not to win but to avoid losing.

1865: The Thirteenth Amendment to the U.S. Constitution, which prohibits slavery, is ratified.

1869: The first U.S. transcontinental railway is completed.

1869: Black Friday panic ensues when James Fisk and Jay Gould attempt to control the gold market.

1869: The Suez Canal opens.

1869: Russian chemist Dmitri Mendeleev introduces his periodic table of elements.

1871: Chicago Fire causes 250 deaths and $196 million in damage.

1876: General George Armstrong Custer and 264 soldiers are killed by the Sioux at the Little Big Horn River.

1879: Thomas Edison invents the incandescent electric light.

Event and Its Context

Black Labor Organization Before the CNLU

A number of black labor organizations existed in the northern states and in the cities along the border between the northern and southern states before the U.S. Civil War (1861–1865). Their primary activities were directed toward finding employment and providing education and job training for blacks. These groups included benevolent societies, such as the New York African Society for Mutual Relief (established in 1806); the Negro Convention Movement, which provided annual meetings of black leaders during the 1840s and 1850s; and organizations that promoted worker unity and industrial education, such as the American League of Colored Laborers (established in 1850). Black workers also formed collectives, such as the Waiter Protective Association of New York, to protect themselves from the violence of white workers who felt threatened by black employment, and to engage in unofficial bargaining for wage increases.

The formal unionization of black workers after the Civil War followed two basic means: integration into white unions and the formation of separate black-only labor organizations. Most of the black labor leaders looked toward an affiliation with a white-dominated federation, since, in the words of the black labor leader Isaac Myers in 1868, "Labor organizations are the safeguard of the colored man, but for real success, separate organization is not the real answer. The white and colored mechanics must come together and work together." Such comments reflected popular opinion within black labor unions when Myers imagined the first black national labor organization—the Colored National Labor Union (CNLU).

In the years immediately following the end of the Civil War, the number of northern black labor organizations increased. They concentrated on the usual functions of trade unions. However, the southern black labor organizations, formed after the war, were concerned primarily with the problems of agricultural laborers and the aspects of seeking basic rights for black workers. Strikes in the southern states occurred on a frequent basis as blacks voiced their dissatisfaction with their working conditions. In Savannah, Georgia, for instance, black dockworkers won a strike after the city council imposed an outrageously high poll tax of $19 on all persons employed on the wharves. In Louisiana in 1867, dockworkers in New Orleans pursued a strike for a wage increase to $4 a day, while in the same year a black strike on the levee in Mobile, Alabama, spread to other industries, eventually resulting in one of the largest demonstrations in southern history.

Background and Formation of the CNLU

White workers regularly resorted to actions such as strikes and violence to eliminate black workers from various trades. The CNLU was established as a direct result of one of those incidents. In October 1865 white caulkers from Baltimore, Maryland, along with ship carpenters, went on strike insisting that black caulkers and longshoremen be discharged so that white workers could be employed. The strikers, with the support of the local government and the police, succeeded in discharging black workers who were competing for their jobs.

Myers, one of the workers who had been fired, proposed that the black caulkers form a union in order to collectively purchase and operate a shipyard and railway. The newly formed black cooperative issued stock and raised $10,000 from the black community in and around Baltimore. After securing a six-year mortgage from a ship captain, the cooperative purchased a shipyard and railway and began operations on 12 February 1866. The Chesapeake Marine Railway and Dry Dock Company regularly employed around 300 black workers at an average wage of $3 per day. Within five years the company had obtained numerous government contracts and was able to pay off its debt one year ahead of schedule. The successful cooperative provided black caulkers with plenty of work around the Baltimore docks and ended the practice of white caulkers driving away black competition. The venture was often mentioned as the model used by other black workers in the northern states to solve employment problems.

During this time Myers formed and became the president of the Colored Caulkers' Trades Union Society of Baltimore. By the autumn of 1868, he had begun to think about organizing a national black labor movement that would work together with white labor organizations. He was drawn to the National Labor Union (NLU), which had been established in 1866 in Baltimore and was the first national federation of labor unions to openly acknowledge black workers. The NLU had voiced its eagerness to organize black workers and had declared at its first convention that the labor movement would gain strength when membership was granted without regard to race or nationality.

Black workers, however, continued to find that they were inevitably barred from membership in most white unions. For instance, the cigar-makers' union excluded blacks by constitutional provision, while black carpenters in New Haven, Connecticut, were not admitted to the white carpenters' union. Without any other recourse and in protest at being barred from white unions, black workers decided to form their own national labor organization that would represent local and state unions. According to a news report in the *Baltimore Sun,* approximately 30 blacks met on 20 July 1869 at the Frederick Douglass Institute to discuss Myers's plan to form a national black labor union. The group decided that a national black labor convention would meet in Washington, D.C., in December. During the next several months, local and state meetings were organized to select delegates and to formulate positions on the various topics to be discussed at the upcoming convention.

Historic Conventions for Black Labor

The first statewide convention of black labor took place in Baltimore in 1869. That same year, the NLU had issued a formal invitation to all persons interested in the labor movement regardless of color or sex to attend their annual convention in Philadelphia, Pennsylvania, on 16 August 1869. The NLU had invited nine black delegates. At the statewide black labor convention, Myers was selected to represent the Colored Caulkers' Trades Union Society of Baltimore at the NLU meeting. At this time, Myers stated that black workers did not want to organize separately, but were forced to do so because of their exclusion from existing trade unions.

The NLU congress was the first national labor assembly where blacks were officially present. According to a 19 August 1869 article in the *New York Times,* one highlight of the NLU convention was a speech by Myers in which he expressed the goals of black workers, applauded the white delegates for their racial vision, and declared, "We carry no prejudices. We are willing to forget the wrongs of yesterday and let the dead past bury its dead." The newspaper also reported that Myers extended an invitation to all white delegates to attend the first national black labor convention to be held in Washington, D.C., in December 1869. Although they were recognized as a delegation, the nine black delegates were unsuccessful, at that time, at integrating black workers into the white union.

To fill the gap of black-worker representation in the labor movement, 214 officially accredited black delegates met to establish a confederation of independent black local and state unions: the Colored National Labor Union. On 6 December 1869 Myers called to order a black delegation from 18 states assembled in Union League Hall in Washington, D.C. The assembly was the first black congress in which labor was represented as the majority issue. Northern and southern black leaders collectively stated that only through their own independent union could black workers achieve equal employment opportunities and improved wages.

The delegates elected Myers as the first president of the CNLU and declared Washington, D.C., as the union's headquarters. During the meeting, the delegates stated that the CNLU would be neither a trade union body nor a political class organization, but a black people's assembly that would deal with the critical labor and social needs of all black people. The CNLU was the first national black labor organization founded in the United States.

Development of the CNLU

The new union included all black workers, such as industrial, skilled craftsmen, agricultural, and common laborers, unlike its white counterpart, the NLU, which included only skilled industrial workers. The delegates began developing the CNLU by first establishing a permanent National Bureau of Labor with offices in Washington, D.C. The bureau, composed of the chief officers and a nine-man executive committee, was given the power to collect information about employment opportunities around the country; negotiate with bankers and capitalists for financial assistance in establishing black business ventures; and lobby for legislation in order to achieve equality of employment opportunities.

The three main objectives of the CNLU were: (1) to improve the general condition of black workers; (2) to develop a national system of public education with equal opportunities for blacks; and (3) to attain equality in industry with the elimination of discrimination within trade unions. The CNLU encouraged blacks throughout the country to organize at the state and local levels in order to combine their wealth and information.

The first CNLU convention adjourned on 10 December 1869, with two representatives meeting with President Ulysses S. Grant to inform him of the new organization. After a meeting on 21 February 1870, which formulated plans to organize black workers, Myers began a southern tour for the new black labor federation. His speeches, which were often held for racially mixed audiences, emphasized that for white and black unions to succeed they needed to act together. He conceded, however, that blacks had to unite among themselves first in order to increase their power in the labor community. According to the *New National Era* (the official publication of the CNLU), which reported his speech on 27 April 1870, Myers said that in order for their labor movement to succeed all black workers must join trade unions and establish cooperative associations.

Division over Support for Political Parties

Even during the first year of the CNLU's existence, the Republican Party became a growing facet within the organization. Myers was against political influence within the CNLU, although the union generally supported the Republican Party. At the August 1870 NLU congress, while the newly formed CNLU was still a part of the NLU, the white delegates urged Myers and the other four black delegates to abandon the Republican Party and to unite with them in support of the new National Labor Reform Party.

The majority of NLU members viewed both the Democratic and Republican Parties as enemies of labor, and instead supported the National Labor Reform Party. However, the black delegates, including Myers, had little confidence that white workers would acknowledge black workers as equals in the work place. They felt the Republican Party, although not their ideal political party, was a friend to labor, and especially a friend to black labor. Blacks vividly remembered that the Republican Party, led by President Abraham Lincoln, had won their emancipation only a few years earlier. A bitter fight broke out over differences in support of the Republican and National Labor Reform Parties. Disagreements between blacks and whites eventually made it impossible for the two groups to settle their political differences.

A resolution in favor of supporting the National Labor Reform Party was overwhelmingly passed by a vote of 60 to 5, with all five black delegates voting against the resolution. The black delegates never returned to another convention, and ties with the NLU were soon severed. The effort on the part of the NLU to include blacks within their organization was seen by black labor leaders as only a benevolent gesture after the NLU failed to recognize the specific interests of black workers.

Decline of the CNLU

The second annual CNLU convention took place on 9 January 1871, but delegates from only 10 states were present. President Myers reported on progress made during the previous year. He cited the fact that the local unions established during the year were expanding, but he conceded that the CNLU was hampered by financial difficulties due to lower-than-expected union membership. Myers further stressed that all politics be left out of the convention and the unions themselves. According to a *New National Era* article from 19 January 1871, Myers concluded his remarks by once again emphasizing that unity of black and white labor was essential for the success of both, but that blacks needed to unify within their race first in order for their unions to achieve their own power and be seen as equal to white unions. The delegates elected Frederick Douglass as the CNLU's second president. Against Myers's wishes, the delegation also made a declaration of allegiance to the Republican Party. Myers continued to be active, although less dominant, in the CNLU's activities until the autumn of 1871.

The third CNLU convention was held at Columbia, South Carolina, in October 1871 and was essentially a black Republican convention. In April 1872 the fourth and final meeting convened in New Orleans as a Southern States' Convention, not as the CNLU. During this meeting the delegates consolidated black support for the Republicans for the upcoming presidential election. By this point Myers had disappeared from any leadership role. For the most part the CNLU ceased to exist on 17 May 1874, when the *New National Era,* of which Douglass was the editor, published an article with the title, "The Folly, Tyranny, and Wickedness of Labor Unions."

Lasting Influence of the CNLU

Even though the life of the CNLU was short—less than five years—it greatly influenced the subsequent founding of numerous black labor organizations and led to the eventual incorporation of black workers into previously all-white labor unions.

One of the most significant southern organizations established as a direct result of the CNLU was the Alabama Negro Labor Union (ANLU). James Rapier, the group's founder, promoted the ANLU throughout Alabama, trying to organize as many black workers as possible into the fledgling union. Eventually Rapier organized a state labor convention that met in Montgomery on 2 January 1872, with a total of about 50 black delegates from around the state. The delegates discussed the working conditions of Alabama farmers, promoting desirable areas where blacks could relocate and various state educational opportunities open to blacks. The discussion held during this meeting was used in 1880 before the U.S. Senate Committee on Education and Labor, which was investigating the causes of the Kansas Exodus of 1879 (the movement of southern blacks to the northern border states, especially to the rural areas of Kansas).

While the U.S. Senate Committee on Education and Labor was holding additional hearings in 1882, black workers were actively demonstrating and organizing in order to improve wages and working conditions. In this environment black workers found that the Noble Order of the Knights of Labor (KOL), a labor organization established in Philadelphia in 1869, was actively pursuing black members. Southern blacks—who were exposed to worse working conditions than northern blacks—especially liked the rebellious nature of the KOL. By 1886 about 60,000 blacks were members of the KOL, which held a total membership of about 750,000 members. That same year dissension increased within the KOL as different factions saw conflicting means to improve their working conditions. In December 1886 the American Federation of Labor broke off from the KOL and organized into its own labor union; it continued to exist into the twenty-first century as part of the AFL-CIO.

The decision to integrate white unions with black workers was based on both moralistic and monetary grounds. It was eventually decided to be the moral thing to do, and with increasing numbers of blacks competing for jobs, the inclusion of blacks within membership ranks brought more money into labor unions. Although never without protests from white members, blacks slowly gained inroads to labor organizations. The progress that black workers made during the late nineteenth century, throughout the twentieth century, and into the twenty-first century was in large part due to the pioneering efforts of Myers and his formation of the CNLU, which occurred only a few years after blacks were freed in the United States in 1865.

Key Players

Myers, Isaac (1835–1891): Myers learned the ship-caulking trade and supervised the caulking of clipper ships built in the Baltimore shipyards. After working for a wholesale grocery business, he helped to found a grocery cooperative, but resigned in 1865. Myers returned to the shipyards, but soon lost his job (as did more than 1,000 blacks) due to a strike of white workers. He led a group of black workers to form the Chesapeake Marine Railway and Dry Dock Company and later became the president of the Colored Caulkers' Trades Union Society of Baltimore. From 1870 to 1879 he supervised mail service in the South for the U.S. Post Office. He opened a coal yard in Baltimore; became the editor of a weekly political journal; was appointed as a U.S. gauger from 1882 to 1887; and served as the secretary of the Maryland Republican Campaign Committee in 1888. He was actively involved in many Baltimore business and community organizations.

See also: *Abolition of Slavery, United States; Black Codes; Jim Crow Segregation and Labor; Knights of Labor; National Labor Union.*

BIBLIOGRAPHY

Books

Allen, James S. *Reconstruction: The Battle for Democracy (1865–1876).* New York: International Publishers, 1937.

Department of Research and Investigations of the National Urban League. *Negro Membership in American Labor Unions.* New York: Negro Universities Press, 1969.

Foner, Philip S. *Organized Labor and the Black Worker (1619–1981).* 2d ed. New York: International Publishers, 1982.

Foner, Philip S., and Ronald L. Lewis, eds. *Black Workers: A Documentary History from Colonial Times to the Present.* Philadelphia: Temple University Press, 1989.

Harris, William H. *The Harder We Run: Black Workers Since the Civil War.* New York: Oxford University Press, 1982.

Jaynes, Gerald David. *Branches Without Roots: Genesis of the Black Working Class in the American South, 1862–1882.* New York: Oxford University Press, 1986.

Spero, Sterling D., and Abram L. Harris. *The Black Worker: A Study of the Negro and the Labor Movement.* New York: Columbia University Press, 1931.

Todes, Charlotte. *William H. Sylvis and the National Labor Union.* New York: International Publishers, 1942.

Other

Aguiar, Marian. "Labor Unions in the United States." *Black World News and Views.* Africana.com [cited 5 February 2003]. <http://www.africana.com/Articles/tt_631.htm>.

Isaac Myers, 1835–1891. African American Resource Center. 2000 [cited 5 February 2003]. <http://www.genealogyforum.rootsweb.com/gfaol/resource/AfricanAm/Myers.htm>.

Isaac Myers: In the Business of Leadership. Maryland State Archives. 3 February 1998 [cited 5 February 2003]. <http://www.mdarchives.state.md.us/msa/stagser/s1259/121/6050/html/imyers.html>.

—William Arthur Atkins

William Pitt. © Getty Images. Reproduced by permission.

Combination Acts

Great Britain 1799–1800

Synopsis

Under the conservative leadership of Prime Minister William Pitt the Younger, the British Parliament passed the Combination Acts of 1799 and 1800. These acts were part of the government's reaction against radical workers and the French Revolution; they also expressed the conflicts between owners and workers in many industries. They prohibited all organized activity intended to improve working conditions or wages. They also prohibited organized activities by the masters, but those laws were never enforced. There were other legal weapons available to employers, and most prosecutions of organized labor in the ensuing years took place under other laws. These acts never came close to destroying organized labor in Britain, but they did contribute to government and employers' repression of trade unions. They were repealed in 1824.

Timeline

1775: American Revolution begins with the battles of Lexington and Concord, and delegates from each of the 13 American colonies meet for the Second Continental Congress.

1787: The Constitution of the United States is signed.

1789: French Revolution begins with the storming of the Bastille.

1790: The first U.S. census reports a population of about 3,929,000, including 698,000 slaves.

1793: Eli Whitney patents his cotton gin—a machine that, by making cotton profitable, spurs the expansion of slave labor in the southern United States.

1800: The world's population reaches 870 million.

1800: The United States moves its federal government to Washington, D.C.

1800: British astronomer William Herschel discovers infrared rays, and Italian physicist Alessandro Volta develops the voltaic cell, an early form of battery.

1802: France, under the direction of Napoleon Bonaparte, revokes a 1794 decree emancipating the slaves of Haiti; reintroduces slavery to that colony; and imprisons slave revolt leader Toussaint L'Ouverture.

1803: Administration of U.S. President Thomas Jefferson negotiates the Louisiana Purchase from France, whereby the United States doubles its geographic size, adding some 827,000 square miles (2,144,500 sq km)—all for the price of only $15 million.

1808: U.S. Congress bans the importation of slaves.

William Wilberforce. The Library of Congress.

1810: Revolts begin in South America, initiating the process whereby colonies will win their freedom from Spain and other European colonial powers.

Event and Its Context

Political and Economic Contexts

Increasingly, during the latter part of the eighteenth century, organized workers in certain trades pressed for higher wages and improved working conditions. This activity increase further at beginning of the French revolutionary wars, particularly as food prices increased steeply. Employers increasingly sought the help of the government to limit workers' demands.

At the time, the British government was at war with the French Republic and was extremely wary of domestic revolutionaries, "Jacobins," sympathetic toward France. There had been a great mutiny in the navy in 1797, and the following year a French army landed in Ireland to collaborate with Irish rebels. The government had been moving in the direction of greater repression from the beginning of the war with France in 1793. It suspended *habeas corpus*; broadened the law of treason; banned secret societies through the Unlawful Oaths act of 1797; established tight control over the press with the 1798 Newspa-

per Act; and, with the 1799 Corresponding Societies Act, suppressed political correspondence societies.

The First Combination Act, 1799

The movement that led to the Combination Acts began with a petition to the House of Commons from master millwrights; they complained about an organization (or "combination") of journeymen millwrights in London and the surrounding area. The House of Commons referred the petition to a committee, which was standard practice when a labor dispute was brought to Parliament. The committee suggested repression of the combination and that wages be fixed by local magistrates. The role of local magistrates in the fixing of wages, however, had been shrinking steadily during the eighteenth century.

William Wilberforce, a friend of the prime minister, suggested that Parliament pass a law of general applicability, providing prompt legal recourse for masters when confronted by workers' combinations. The first Combination Act was brought before the House of Commons on 17 June 1799 and passed quickly, receiving the royal assent on 12 July. Also passed on that day was the Corresponding Societies Act, another attack on "subversive" political groups. The act attracted little attention in Parliament, and the only recorded speakers against it were in the House of Commons by Benjamin Hobhouse and in the House of Lords by the Whig leader Lord Holland. There was also little opposition elsewhere. Except for the London calico-printers, workers seemed unaware of the hastily passed bill.

The act of 1799 canceled all previous agreements, written or unwritten, between workers and employers. It forbade workers, on pain of two months hard labor, from combining to press for improvement in wages and working conditions. This was, in fact, a relatively mild penalty by the standards of the time. Workers were also forbidden to encourage other workers to quit or to object to working with anyone else. The act attacked worker solidarity by a fine of ten pounds for anyone caught contributing to the expenses of a person convicted under the acts subject; the person receiving support was liable to a fine of five pounds. The act also made it possible to force defendants to testify against one another. Charges would be brought before one or more magistrates, allowing employers to move quickly against workers without going through a long court process. If convicted, workers were sentenced to two months hard labor. Appeal could be made only to quarter sessions, which met four times in a year. The act confirmed magistrates in their power against employers' combinations but did not enhance them or provide any new means of enforcement.

The Second Combination Act, 1800

After its passage, the act aroused organized working-class opposition. A coordinated campaign led to a flood of petitions to Parliament, protesting the act and demanding its repeal. The petitions were from workers in English cities, including London, Manchester, Liverpool, Leeds, and Nottingham. The petitions were presented to Parliament in June 1800, and the government decided to modify some of the Combination Act's more obnoxious features. The provisions of the final version of the Combination Acts prohibited workers from organizing to increase wages or decrease hours, In response to criticism of the original act, the penalties had to be imposed by at least two magistrates in agreement, and it was required that they not belong to the trade in question. Penalties, however, remained relatively mild—three months imprisonment or two months hard labor. The act went beyond the 1799 act by explicitly forbidding employers' combinations, but these provisions were never enforced. In 1811 the northern trade union leader Gravener Henson carried on a long, ultimately fruitless, campaign to enforce the acts against employers.

The 1800 act also differed from the 1799 act in setting up a system of arbitration—perhaps the last appearance of the old notion that magistrates had a role in setting wages and prices. Both sides of a dispute could nominate an arbitrator, and if the arbitrations did not produce as mutually satisfactory solution in the three days, the dispute would go before a magistrate, though the three-day deadline could be extended by mutual consent. This arbitration procedure was seldom used. The Combination Act of 1800 became law on 29 July.

Effects of the Combination Acts

The legal environment, already tilted heavily against organized labor, was not drastically changed by the combination acts. Also, they did not apply to Scotland, which had a different, even more repressive, legal system. Nevertheless, Scottish magistrates managed to crack down on workers without the benefit of the acts. In England enforcement of the acts and other antiunion laws varied tremendously in different regions and industries, particularly in areas where the magistrates—often rural gentry or Church of England clergy—and masters came from different social backgrounds. The burden of initiating a legal action under the acts lay on the masters, who were varied. In some stable, small-scale artisan industries, masters accepted the existence of trade clubs among their skilled employees. Repression was far greater in large-scale industry, whether it involved factory or contract workers. Given the relatively mild penalties under the acts and the ability of workers to delay the proceedings by appeal to quarter sessions, they were not the best legal tools the masters had. Rather than using the acts themselves, most antiunion legal activity continued use the common law concept of conspiracy or the Elizabethan Statute of Artificers.

The acts did not end workers' combinations by any means. A few kinds of worker organizations were still allowed. Benefit societies, for example, which provided mutual economic assistance for members, were allowed to meet legally, and trade union activity was able to continue under their cloak. Workers could also organize to petition Parliament or to appeal to a local magistrate in a wage dispute. Many trades unions already in existence, such as the wool combers, shipwrights, and tailors, continued relatively unchallenged throughout the period of the acts. New unions also came into existence, and, because they had to work underground illegally, they were often closely allied with radical political groups. Secrecy thus became deeply ingrained in the culture of many unions. The fact that the acts included all trades may have encouraged workers to organize more broadly, rather than each trade battling separately for improved conditions. The acts were repealed in 1824.

Key Players

Fox, Henry Richard Vassal, third Baron Holland (1773–1840): Lord Holland entered the House of Lords in 1796 and was the principal representative there for the Whig party during the late eighteenth and early nineteenth centuries. He supported progressive causes—including the abolition of the slave trade, despite the slave workers on his West Indies plantations. Holland was chancellor of the duchy of Lancaster in Whig cabinets 1830–1834 and 1835–1840.

Henson, Gravener (1785–1852): Henson was a leader of the framework-knitters movement in the Midlands and the author of *History of the Framework-Knitting and Lace Trades* (1831). He tried to bring a legal case against the masters under the Combination Act in 1811, but the magistrates refused to take action. He lobbied Parliament unsuccessfully for legislation that would benefit the framework-knitters in 1812. It was rumored that Henson was connected with the Luddites, and he was imprisoned during the suspension of *habeas corpus* from 1817 to 1818. He presented a new plan to replace the Combination Act in 1824.

Pitt, William, the Younger (1759–1806): Pitt was British prime minister from 1783 to 1801, and again from 1804 to his death in 1806. Although Pitt was initially sympathetic to reform, the reaction against the French Revolution and the necessity of keeping the favor of King George III drove him, often against his will, in a more conservative direction. He is frequently considered the founder of the modern British Conservative Party.

Wilberforce, William (1759–1833): Wilberforce was the leader of the British abolitionist movement for many years. He was an original founder of the Society for the Abolition of the Slave Trade and served in the House of Commons from 1780 to 1825. He retired from active involvement in the antislavery movement around that date. He died a few weeks before the passage of the Abolition Act. A political conservative, Wilberforce also supported repressive policies against British workers including the Combination Acts.

See also: *Repeal of Combination Acts.*

BIBLIOGRAPHY

Ehrman, John. *The Younger Pitt: The Consuming Struggle.* Stanford, CA: Stanford University Press, 1996.

Pelling, Henry. *A History of British Trade Unionism,* 3d ed. New York: Penguin, 1976.

Prothero, Iorwerth. *Artisans and Politics in Early Nineteenth-Century London: John Gast and His Times.* Baton Rouge, LA: Louisiana State University Press, 1979.

Thompson, E. P. *The Making of the English Working Class.* New York: Pantheon Books, 1964.

ADDITIONAL RESOURCES

Aspinall, Arthur. *The Early English Trade Unions: Documents from the Home Office Papers in the Public Record Office.* London: Batchworth, 1949.

Rice, John, ed. *British Trade Unionism, 1750–1850: The Formative Years.* London: Longman, 1988.

Rule, John. *The Labouring Classes in Early Industrial England, 1750-1850.* New York: Longman, 1986.

Trade Unions under the Combination Acts, five pamphlets, 1799-1823. New York: Arno, 1972.

—William E. Burns

Committee for Industrial Organization

United States 1935

Synopsis

The formation of the Committee for Industrial Organization (CIO) was fundamental in the labor movement, as it was the first union group to recognize the need to organize unskilled labor. Historically, unions had typically banded together skilled workers into unions by trade. Existing unions, particularly the American Federation of Labor (AFL), refused to organize unskilled workers, most of whom worked in mass-production industries, such as garment manufacturing and tire making.

With its formation in 1935 as a committee within the AFL, the CIO became a voice in the workplace for underrepresented minorities such as new immigrants, African Americans, and women. CIO representation allowed workers to achieve a more just stake in their workplaces through collective bargaining. Unionized employees were able to change working conditions through grievance procedures, while newly instituted seniority systems assisted in bringing changes to unionized companies' shop floors. Emboldened by their unions, working-class Americans also had a larger say in their own communities. Local political power was often shaped by alliances with prounion entities, especially in company towns. The union also contributed to reshaping class and race dynamics in the United States.

Timeline

1920: League of Nations, based in Geneva, holds its first meetings.

1925: European leaders attempt to secure the peace at the Locarno Conference, which guarantees the boundaries between France and Germany, and Belgium and Germany.

1930: Naval disarmament treaty is signed by the United States, Great Britain, France, Italy, and Japan.

1933: Newly inaugurated U.S. President Franklin D. Roosevelt launches the first phase of his New Deal to put depression-era America back to work.

1935: Germany annexes the Saar region after a plebiscite. In defiance of Versailles, the Nazis reintroduce compulsory military service. The Allies do nothing, and many

western intellectuals maintain that it is only proper for Germany to retake its own territory and begin building up its army again.

1935: Italians invade Ethiopia, and the response by the League of Nations—which imposes sanctions but otherwise fails to act—reveals the impotence of that organization.

1935: Second phase of New Deal begins with the introduction of social security, farm assistance, and housing and tax reform.

1938: The U.S. Fair Labor Standards Act establishes a minimum wage.

1940: Hitler's troops sweep through Western Europe, annexing Norway and Denmark in April, and in May the Low Countries and France. At the same time, Stalin—who in this year arranges the murder of Trotsky in Mexico—takes advantage of the situation to add the Baltic republics (Latvia, Lithuania, and Estonia) to the Soviet empire, where they will remain for more than half a century.

1945: April sees the death of three leaders: Roosevelt passes away on 12 April; the Italians execute Mussolini and his mistress on 28 April; and Hitler (along with Eva Braun, propaganda minister Josef Goebbels, and Goebbels's family) commits suicide on 30 April.

1950: North Korean troops pour into South Korea, starting the Korean War. Initially the communists make impressive gains, but in September the U.S. Marines land at Inchon and liberate Seoul. China responds by sending in its troops.

Event and Its Context

Organizing the Unorganized

The American Federation of Labor (AFL) had been active for some 50 years at the start of the Great Depression. Union membership, whether in the AFL or other national organizations, was almost exclusively restricted to craftsmen, predominantly northern European Protestants. Typically, these individuals were relatively conservative skilled workers who had spent years learning their particular trade. For this and other societal reasons, union members resisted the inclusion of unskilled employees of the mass-production industries in their ranks.

Workers within the automobile, steel, aluminum, and rubber industries, among others, were upset with shop conditions and sought job security as well as organizing assistance from the AFL. Broadly, they sought representation by a single industrial union rather than the traditional craft-based unions, wherein workers were organized according to their specific trade. AFL leaders did not want to charter such industrial unions. By 1934 gains workers in these industries had made in negotiating with their employers had evaporated. The only mass-production unions to have any success during the first years of President Franklin Delano Roosevelt's New Deal administration were the coal and garment unions.

The AFL stance on craft unionism had not changed significantly by 1935. Even with the 1935 passage of the National

Philip Murray. The Library of Congress.

John Llewellyn Lewis. U.S. Information Agency.

Labor Relations Act (NLRA), commonly known as the Wagner Act, labor resisted open membership. The NLRA recognized unions and established basic union-friendly protections for employees nationwide, including provisions barring employers from attempts to intimidate workers forming unions and granting employees the right to strike. But most workers persevered without federal protection.

John L. Lewis, leader of the United Mine Workers (UMW), was intent on organizing these men and women and in 1935 began what can only be characterized as a crusade to gather unrepresented workers into a single industrial union. Lewis was repeatedly frustrated in his attempts to organize workers, specifically within the automobile, iron, and steel industries, under the AFL umbrella. Union leaders continually balked at his calls for organizing mass-production workers and for solidarity.

Despite this, the auto and rubber unions formed their own unions in August and September 1935, respectively. While working to organize the rubber workers, "Lewis insisted that its workers demanded . . . a union structure that encompassed all employees of the industry regardless of job classification or skill," wrote his biographer, Melvyn Dubovsky. Lewis did not oppose craft unions but urged that theories about union structure not be permitted "to obstruct the organization of mass-production workers never before unionized and employed in industries traditionally resistant to craft unionism."

Lewis Delivers a Blow to the AFL

The discussion within the AFL about the merits of industrial unionism came to a head at the 19 October 1935 AFL meeting in Atlantic City, New Jersey. William L. Hutcheson, head of the International Brotherhood of Carpenters, continued to squelch dissent by not allowing young rubber workers who fa-

vored industrial unionism to speak from the floor. He kept bringing up parliamentary procedures to silence the speakers. Lewis reportedly shouted from the floor, "This thing of raising points of order all the time on minor delegates is rather small potatoes." Hutcheson volleyed back, "I was raised on small potatoes. That is why I am so small." Neither he nor Lewis was small in stature.

Tired of his continued interruptions and verbally badgered by Hutcheson, Lewis vaulted over chairs and punched Hutcheson. Fistfights between members of these leaders' respective unions ensued. The next day Lewis convened a breakfast meeting with 40 or 50 advocates of industrial unionism to discuss next steps. He asked several of these union leaders to meet him in Washington, D.C., in three weeks to discuss forming an ad hoc committee. Lewis and others saw time and momentum slipping away. The time was right to organize unskilled workers, and this prompted the founding members and staff to act with urgency. The AFL had not adapted to modern times, leaving a void that could be filled by just about any organization. About two million company unions, independent unions, and non-AFL organizations were active at the time. Interest in unionism was piqued by worker unrest in numerous industries.

Minorities and Unionism

As part of its drive to organize unskilled workers, the CIO also assisted in organizing efforts among other marginalized groups, specifically foreign-born workers, African Americans, and women, who were prohibited from admission to conventional unions. Segregation of African American workers was commonplace throughout American society well into World War II. In some instances African Americans were unwittingly used as scab labor, further alienating them from their white counterparts. The AFL had, at one time, blamed African Americans for creating problems for the union because they had been strikebreakers. Samuel Gompers, head of the AFL in the late 1800s and early 1900s, had suggested removal of race as a condition of membership; the idea was short-lived.

"Were the A.F. of L. leaders imbued with even a semblance of real working class spirit they would take it upon themselves as a first and basic task to defeat the plans of the employers by organizing the Negroes and by mobilizing the whole labor movement behind their elementary demands," wrote William Z. Foster in *The Daily Worker* in 1929. "But they utterly refuse to do this."

Typically, minority employees paid exorbitant union dues—if they were accepted for membership at all. In those rare instances when African Americans were successfully admitted to a union, they were generally relegated to menial tasks. This was true even within the skilled labor unions. Their situation was made worse during the depression; they were "last to be hired, first to be laid off, with least savings from lowest wages, and discriminated against in relief as everywhere else," according to the labor writer Len De Caux.

The situation was not much better for women, black or white. In 1933 some three million women worked. Advocates of their inclusion in unions argued that, if provided the opportunity to join a union, they would. As were African American workers, women were typically relegated to semiskilled jobs and, during strikes, were often targets of company agents, who pressured them to end the strike and to break worker morale. The AFL simply refused to organize women, believing that they "obtained jobs just for 'spending money,'" according to the labor historian Philip S. Foner. "Soon they married and dropped out of the industry. Why, then, should the trade unions tax themselves and expend undue energy attempting to organize women?" The answer, as the CIO found, was that women were themselves tireless organizers. They were enthusiastic volunteers in times of crisis and stood up to physical abuse on the picket lines.

The CIO contended that such discrimination—in matters of race, religion, and gender—were perpetuated in the workplace, allowing employers to continue the cycle of worker exploitation. Ultimately, because of these progressive views, the CIO called itself a "people's movement" as much as a union.

Genesis of the CIO

During an AFL convention in November 1935, Lewis met with the officers of eight unions—including Sidney Hillman, leader of the Amalgamated Clothing Workers of America (ACWA), and David Dubinsky, of the International Ladies Garment Workers Union (ILGWU)—to discuss forming the Committee for Industrial Organization, which they formally founded on 9 November 1935. The other founders were Philip Murray, Tom Kennedy, John Brophy, Charles Howard, Thomas McMahon, Max Zaritsky, Thomas Brown, and Harvey Fremming. Lewis was elected chair. The fledgling group received financial pledges from the UMW, ACWA, and ILGWU, whose memberships, thanks to the Wagner Act, had grown, meaning the CIO could be financially independent of the AFL, even though it would technically remain under the AFL's auspices. The modest initial aim of the CIO was to promote industrial unionism among rubber, auto, steel, and radio workers.

Clearly, each person present at the founding of the CIO had his own reasons for advocating its formation. Howard and Dubinsky saw it as an opportunity to save the AFL from itself. Dubinsky believed that disenfranchised workers who were not welcomed into unions would likely turn to communism. His participation was tempered by caution. Howard, head of the International Typographical Union, participated as an individual rather than with the blessing of his union.

The only action taken at the initial gathering, other than its founding, was to formally state a joint commitment to promoting the organization of workers in mass-production jobs, and to do so without delay. The CIO offices opened on 18 November 1935 across from the UMW headquarters in Washington, D.C. Brophy, who had been active with the UMW, outlined possible activities for the organization and drafted pamphlets about industrial unionism for workers and other union groups.

The organization also hired several staff members. Len De Caux, the editor of the *CIO News,* served as publicist for the organization. Katherine Pollak Ellickson was hired as administrator; she managed the office and assisted with research and other tasks. The first CIO field representatives hired were Adolph Germer and Powers Hapgood. Ironically, they and Brophy had been staunch Lewis foes within the UMW. What happened to make them allies? McAlister Coleman observed, "overnight the magic formula of the words 'industrial unionism' was dissolving ancient grudges."

Lewis was the most important individual within the fledgling CIO. Not only did he have a big voice that resounded within labor circles, but also he was the only founding member with experience in bargaining and negotiating with industries on a par with his AFL counterparts. Further, his own union, the UMW, was considered central to the national industrial economy, which could give the organization leverage in acceptance by industry leaders. Without raw ores and coal for manufacturing goods in times of work stoppages and strikes, industry could be effectively halted nationwide. The CIO was staffed with successful UMW organizers: Germer, Hapgood, Van A. Bittner, and William Mitch. The miners' union was the CIO's major funder. Lewis was not paid; UMW loans made in 1936 and 1937 financed an estimated 83.4 percent of CIO expenses.

Lewis resigned his vice presidency in the AFL on 23 November 1935. This action, according to Walter Galenson, was a "means of dramatizing the split and of driving a further wedge between the AFL and CIO."

Second, perhaps, to Lewis in stature within the CIO was Hillman. He had founded the ACWA in 1914 and is described as being the CIO's "most articulate, decisive and generous supporter." In 1936 CIO member unions, in addition to the UMW, ILGWU, and ACWA, included the United Textile Workers, the United Automobile Workers, and the Amalgamated Association of Iron, Steel, and Tinworkers.

The AFL executives saw the CIO as "a challenge to the supremacy of the American Federal of Labor," wrote Galenson. Although threatened by the CIO, they remained steadfast in their conviction that industrial unionism was a waste of time and resources. Lewis was just as determined to see the CIO succeed. The two organizations butted heads through the next few years. A 1936 strike at Goodyear in Akron, Ohio, is often recognized as the CIO's first real test of effectiveness.

CIO organizers worked tirelessly throughout 1936 to gain union recognition and collective bargaining agreements from executives of leading corporations such as General Motors and U.S. Steel. By fall the AFL tired of the upstarts in what was supposed to be a union committee. At a UMW convention that same year, Lewis said the CIO would not back down from organizing. "[A]ll the members of the Executive Council of the American Federation of Labor will be wearing asbestos suits in hell before [the CIO] is dissolved." The executives took the challenge. The decision was made to suspend the CIO member unions from the AFL. This was soon changed to an expulsion. Lewis was reportedly the only founding member unconcerned about this split.

CIO organizing drives were held throughout 1936 and 1937 in a wide variety of industries. The union courted packinghouse workers, woodworkers, shipbuilders, seamen, and other laborers without union representation. Efforts remained concentrated, however, in the target industries identified at the union's founding: auto, rubber, radio, and steel. By 1937 the CIO had more than 3.7 million members, most of whom were in industrial unions, including maritime workers, white-collar workers, and woodworkers.

In November 1938, with its major unions expelled from the AFL, the CIO officially inaugurated itself as a separate labor federation, in the process changing its name to the Congress of Industrial Organizations. In the next two decades, the CIO would continue its organizing efforts. By the time of the CIO's merger with the AFL in 1955, it included more than five million members. Author Robert Zieger called the creation of the CIO the key episode in addressing the labor issues of the preceding six decades.

Key Players

Dubinsky, David (1892–1982): Dubinsky is best known for his lengthy tenure as president of the International Ladies Garment Workers Union. Dubinksy started working in his family's bakery in Poland at age 11 and first participated in a strike at age 15. In the United States, he became involved in union activity within a ILGWU local. In 1932 he undertook the monumental task of reorganizing the union. He remained active in union politics until his retirement in 1966, after which he served on public and private sector boards until his death in 1982.

Green, William (1873–1952): AFL president at the time of the formation of the CIO, Green was vocal in his opposition to industrial unions. He was the second AFL president since its founding, succeeding Samuel Gompers. Despite his position, he was not a part of the union's inner circle.

Hillman, Sidney (1887–1946): A founder of the CIO and head of the Amalgamated Clothing Workers (ACWA), Hillman was also instrumental in founding the Non-Partisan League within the American Labor Party, the political party that provided union endorsement for Franklin Delano Roosevelt in 1936. He served on the National Defense Advisory Council during World War II.

Hutcheson, William L. "Big Bill" (1874–1953): Head of the International Brotherhood of Carpenters and active in the AFL at the founding of the CIO, Hutcheson is best known

for provoking and then taking a punch thrown by John L. Lewis at the union's national convention.

Lewis, John Llewellyn (1880–1969): The son of a Welsh coal miner who immigrated to the United States, as a young man Lewis worked in various jobs, including coal mining, before becoming a labor organizer. He was United Mine Workers of America (UMW) president and was active in the American Federation of Labor (AFL). Known as a fiery orator, he peppered his addresses with quotations from both the Bible and Shakespeare. He resigned from the AFL to form the Committee for Industrial Organization in 1935, which reorganized in 1938 as the Congress of Industrial Organizations. He served as its president from 1935 to 1940.

Murray, Philip (1886–1952): Born in Scotland, Murray was a leader within the United Mine Workers of America (UMW) and a founding member of the CIO. He was the chairman of the UMW's Steel Workers' Organizing Committee. Murray became the head of the CIO when Lewis resigned in 1940. He is often acknowledged for his work in seeing the union through World War II, a rough period for most unions.

See also: *American Federation of Labor; AFL, CIO Merge; CIO Expelled from AFL; Congress of Industrial Organizations; Wagner Act.*

BIBLIOGRAPHY

Books

Bird, Stewart, Dan Georgakas, and Deborah Shaffer. *Solidarity Forever: An Oral History of the IWW.* Chicago: Lake View Press, 1985.

De Caux, Len. *Labor Radical: From the Wobblies to the CIO, A Personal History.* Boston: Beacon Press, 1970.

Dubinsky, David, and A. H. Raskin. *David Dubinsky: A Life with Labor.* New York: Simon and Schuster, 1977.

Dubovsky, Melvyn, and Warren Van Tine. *John L. Lewis: A Biography.* Champaign: University of Illinois Press, 1986.

Dulles, Foster Rhea, and Melvyn Dubofsky. *Labor in America,* 2nd ed. New York: Thomas Y. Crowell, 1960.

Finley, Joseph E. *The Corrupt Kingdom: The Rise and Fall of the United Mine Workers.* New York: Simon and Schuster, 1972.

Foner, Eric, and John A. Garraty, eds. *The Reader's Companion to American History.* Boston: Houghton Mifflin, 1991.

Foner, Philip S. *History of the Labor Movement in the United States,* vol. 2. New York: International Publishers, 1955.

———. *Women and the American Labor Movement: From World War I to the Present.* New York: Free Press, 1980.

Foner, Philip S., and Ronald L. Lewis, eds. *Black Workers: A Documentary History from Colonial Times to the Present.* Philadelphia: Temple University Press, 1989.

Fraser, Steven. *Labor Will Rule: Sidney Hillman and the Rise of American Labor.* New York: Free Press, 1991.

Galenson, Walter. *The CIO Challenge to the AFL: A History of the American Labor Movement, 1935–1941.* Cambridge: Harvard University Press, 1960.

Lens, Sidney. *Strikemakers and Strikebreakers.* New York: E.P. Dutton, 1985.

Murolo, Priscilla, and A.B. Chitty. *From the Folks Who Brought You the Weekend: A Short Illustrated History of Labor in the United States.* New York: New Press, 2001.

Murray, R. Emmet. *The Lexicon of Labor.* New York: New Press, 1998.

Selvin, David F. *The Thundering Voice of John L. Lewis.* New York: Lothrop, Lee, and Shepard, 1969.

Taft, Philip. *Organized Labor in American History.* New York: Harper and Row, 1964.

Zieger, Robert H. *The CIO: 1935–1955.* Chapel Hill: University of North Carolina Press, 1995.

—Linda Dailey Paulson

Commonwealth v. Hunt

United States 1842

Synopsis

Commonwealth v. Hunt was a significant 1842 Massachusetts court case that considered the right to exist of labor unions. Also at issue was whether such unions had the right to strike, especially for the purpose of establishing a closed shop. Some charged that such labor activities constituted an illegal conspiracy. In both instances the court ruled that not only were trade unions legal, but they had the right to strike for a closed shop. The court also reminded both labor and management that although unions were legal, so must their purposes be legal as well. This was a landmark case occurring in the earlier years of the Industrial Revolution when it appeared that workers might not have very many rights to protect their own interests.

Timeline

1823: U.S. President James Monroe establishes the Monroe Doctrine, whereby the United States warns European nations not to interfere in the political affairs of the Western Hemisphere.

1828: Election of Andrew Jackson as president begins a new era in American history.

1834: American inventor Cyrus H. McCormick patents his reaper, a horse-drawn machine for harvesting wheat.

1836: In Texas's war of independence with Mexico, the defenders of the Alamo, among them Davy Crockett and Jim Bowie, are killed in a siege. Later that year, Texas wins the Battle of San Jacinto and secures its independence.

1838: The forcible removal of the Cherokee Nation from Georgia to Indian Territory (now Oklahoma) along the "Trail of Tears" begins.

1841: Act of Union joins Upper Canada and Lower Canada, which consist of parts of the present-day provinces of Ontario and Quebec, respectively.

1842: Scientific and technological advances include the development of ether and artificial fertilizer; the identification of the Doppler effect (by Austrian physicist Christian Johann Doppler); the foundation of biochemistry as a discipline; and the coining of the word *dinosaur.*

1842: In *Sanitary Conditions of the Labouring Population of Great Britain,* British reformer Edwin Chadwick draws attention to the squalor in the nation's mill town slums and shows that working people have a much higher incidence of disease than do the middle and upper classes.

1842: British forces in the Afghan capital of Kabul are routed, experiencing one of the first major defeats of a European force by a non-European one in modern times.

1844: "Fifty-four-forty or fight" is the rallying cry at the Democratic National Convention, where delegates call for the addition of Oregon to the Union and for the annexation of Texas.

1848: Mexican War ends with the Treaty of Guadalupe Hidalgo, in which Mexico gives up half of its land area, including Texas, California, most of Arizona and New Mexico, and parts of Colorado, Utah, and Nevada. In another treaty, with Great Britain, the United States sets the boundaries of its Oregon Territory.

1852: *Uncle Tom's Cabin* by Harriet Beecher Stowe, though far from a literary masterpiece, is a great commercial success, with over half a million sales on both sides of the Atlantic. More important, it has an enormous influence on British sentiments with regard to slavery and the brewing American conflict between North and South.

Event and Its Context

The impact of the Industrial Revolution includes the advent and increased use of machines that allowed business owners to produce more goods at lower costs. The expansion of machine use was accompanied by the growth of the "outsourcing" system. This was a process by which a skilled craft, such as shoemaking, would be reduced from that of a master shoemaker creating his product to that of dividing the process up into a series of "unskilled" tasks. For example, instead of employing a number of master and journeymen workers, an employer would hire unskilled labor to each perform one aspect of the manufacturing process. This system allowed employers to avoid paying skilled wages because the work was broken up and distributed among those who were not craftsmen but "ordinary" laborers.

The impact of the Industrial Revolution upon workers, especially skilled laborers, was at times devastating, as many saw their craft reduced to either a machine operation or outsourced to unskilled labor. The employers found nothing wrong with these practices: businesses become successful because they outperform the competition; to do that one must be able to find ways to produce goods at the lowest possible cost, thus maximizing profits.

The workers, however, found these practices unfair. For instance, to keep production costs down, in addition to the use of machines and unskilled labor, wage reductions were commonplace. Furthermore, as competition increased, so did the number of hours in the workday, which could range from 12 to 14 hours a day. Another common concern was workplace safety. As industrialism grew, so did the number of disabling and fatal accidents. Workers injured at the workplace had little, if any, protection from such injuries and usually no means of financial compensation should they fall victim to such an occurrence.

As the Industrial Revolution continued, accompanied by a distinct change in the socioeconomic fabric of society, as a natural course of events, people began to band together to protect their interests. Certainly business owners combined to attempt to control the marketplace; the workers also created combinations. The idea of laborers establishing organizations to protect their interests was not new. The earliest such cooperative organizations, called guilds, served a variety of purposes. Some of these purposes were to protect their workplace interests, such as wage scales, bargaining rights, training, and safety. Some also played other roles, including providing educational and financial benefits.

The earliest trade unions centered on skilled crafts such as shoemaking, printing, and hatmaking. In the years following the American Revolution, several strikes of skilled workers occurred. The Philadelphia shoemakers, who organized in 1792, went on strike in 1799. New York printers struck in 1794, as did the cabinetmakers in 1796. The major issues surrounding these strikes were controlling the number of work hours, increasing wages, establishing the closed shop (that is, a business in which only union labor is employed), and putting the training of apprentices under union control.

As the tensions between employers and workers began to grow, employers began to look for ways to keep the labor movement in check. One such method was the use of replacement workers or "scabs" during a strike, usually at a considerably lower wage. The use of scabs to keep a business functioning during a strike was one means to defeat the union because it allowed management to simply wait until the strikers could no longer afford to continue the action.

In the early years of the nineteenth century, employers began to use the court system to challenge labor unions. Employers felt that the formation of unions was both unfair and illegal, and that activities such as strikes deprived business owners of the lawful use of their property. Employers started to claim that labor unions were "conspiracies." In legal terms, a conspiracy is "a combination of two or more persons to commit a criminal or unlawful act, or to commit a lawful act by criminal or unlawful means; or a combination of two or more persons by concerted action to accomplish an unlawful purpose." Employers argued that many union activities caused unnecessary harm to others in that they denied nonunion labor the right to earn a living, for example, in the case of the closed shop.

The first union conspiracy case was tried in Philadelphia in 1806. From that time until 1842, labor unions were charged with conspiracy no less than 17 times. However, the courts tended to be lenient in their punishments, usually levying a fine and threatening much more stern reprisals should the defendants be again found guilty. The labor movement, however, be-

Lemuel Shaw. The Library of Congress.

lieved that the right to engage in collective bargaining, and, thus, protect their own interests was not illegal, especially as there were no precise laws on the books to ban their activities. Laborers clamored to assert their right to demand a say in workplace practices because of the force with which those decisions affected their lives and welfare.

The case of *Commonwealth v. Hunt* arose out of an 1839 strike by the Boston Journeymen Bootmakers' Society. The main issue surrounding the strike involved the closed shop; the Bootmakers attempted to block the use of nonunion labor. Seven union leaders were indicted for creating an "unlawful club" with "unlawful rules." The indictment, however, did not include any accusation of any specific wrongdoing, such as trying to deprive the employer of the lawful use of his business, nor was the union charged with formenting any violence. Prosecutors used the Bootmakers' constitution as evidence of this conspiracy and further charged that the union was depriving a nonmember his legal right to work. The presiding judge, Peter O. Thatcher, already had a reputation for condemning unions as conspiracies. Despite a vigorous defense, the Bootmakers were found guilty of conspiracy in 1840.

In 1842 the case came up on appeal to the Supreme Judicial Court of Massachusetts. In what would become a "celebrated" decision, Chief Justice Lemuel Shaw overturned the ruling of the lower court. First, in addressing the legal rights of unions to exist, Shaw acknowledged that such organizations could have harmful intentions, but that they might also exist for noble ones as well. Whereas past conspiracy rulings were meant to discourage labor activity, Shaw believed that unions were not illegal conspiracies and that they had the right to promote and encourage a higher standard of living for laborers. Shaw saw that labor organizations served a useful purpose by assisting their members in times of hardship and working to improve the overall intellectual and physical well-being of members.

Shaw saw no illegal conspiracies. Unions had the right to exist as long as their purposes and methods were legal. He also held that an entire union could not be held responsible for the actions of a few of its members, a key point in his overturning of the conspiracy charge. Furthermore, he found that unions had the right to strike for a closed shop.

This was certainly far from the end of the conspiracy doctrine as applied to union activities. First of all, this was a state court decision and therefore not binding upon the laws of other states. Second, Shaw's contention that a union's purpose and methods must be legal opened up a whole new dialogue: what constituted a legal purpose or method? What was an illegal purpose or method? Third, conspiracy cases continued to plague labor throughout the rest of the nineteenth century, as did the debate surrounding the legality of the closed shop. Many other state courts applied the principals of Shaw's opinion in their own cases.

Although the conspiracy doctrine was irrevocably changed by the decision in *Commonwealth v. Hunt*, employers looked for other legal means to combat the growing labor movement. Such methods included using court injunctions to curb labor activities; forcing employees to sign "yellow dog contracts" in which a worker agreed not to join a labor union (which was itself upheld by the courts for many years); enacting laws to restrict the use of strikes and boycotts; and the continuing to use

scabs in labor disputes. Despite the existence of such actions, *Commonwealth v. Hunt* still stands as a landmark in U.S. labor law.

Key Players

Shaw, Lemuel (1781–1861): Shaw was the chief justice of the Supreme Judicial Court of Massachusetts; he handed down the infamous ruling in *Commonwealth v. Hunt*. Born and raised in Massachusetts, Shaw was educated at Harvard before embarking on a legal career. He served in several elected posts, including state senator (1821–1822) before assuming the position of chief justice, a post in which he served for 30 years. He was known for recognizing how circumstances were changing as a result of the Industrial Revolution. Many of his decisions were deemed in the public favor. Some of his later decisions were not as popular: he ruled companies were not liable for injuries caused by fellow workers, and refused to free a fugitive slave, as required by federal law.

BIBLIOGRAPHY

Books

Foner, Philip S. *A History of the Labor Movement in the United States.* Vol. 1, *From Colonial Times to the Founding of the American Federation of Labor.* New York: International Publishers, 1962.

Friedman, Lawrence. *A History of American Law.* New York: Touchstone Books, 1985.

Taylor, Benjamin, and Witney, Fred. *U.S. Labor Relations Law.* Englewood Cliffs, NJ: Prentice Hall, 1992.

Zainaldin, Jamil. *Law in Antebellum Society.* New York: Alfred A. Knopf, 1983.

—Mitchell Newton-Matza

Communist Manifesto Published

England 1848

Synopsis

In February 1848 one of the world's most influential documents was published. The *Communist Manifesto,* coauthored by Karl Marx and Frederick Engels, was a statement of the key principles of the Communist League. The league had been established in 1847 by scattered groups of German socialist exiles. In the atmosphere of revolutionary expectation in the late 1840s, the manifesto was intended as a call to arms. However, as copies were coming off the printing press in London, revolution erupted in Paris and soon spread to other major European cities. As a result, the manifesto appeared too late to influence the actions of those involved in the 1848 revolutions. With the eventual victory of reactionary forces and the dissolution of the Communist League, the manifesto seemed to be consigned to oblivion. However, the formation of the International Workingmen's Association in the 1860s and the Paris Commune in 1871 resulted in increased interest in Marx's socialist theories. As the most concise account of Marxist ideas, the *Communist Manifesto* took on new significance until it became one of the most widely read political documents in the world.

Timeline

1824: French engineer Sadi Carnot describes a perfect engine: one in which all energy input is converted to energy output. The ideas in his *Reflections on the Motive Power of Fire* will influence the formulation of the Second Law of Thermodynamics—which shows that such a perfect engine is an impossibility.

1833: British Parliament passes the Slavery Abolition Act, giving freedom to all slaves throughout the British Empire.

1838: As crops fail, spawning famine in Ireland, Britain imposes the Poor Law. Designed to discourage the indigent from seeking public assistance, the law makes labor in the workhouse worse than any work to be found on the outside, and thus has the effect of stimulating emigration.

1842: In *Sanitary Conditions of the Labouring Population of Great Britain,* British reformer Edwin Chadwick draws attention to the squalor in the nation's mill town slums, and shows that working people have a much higher incidence of disease than do the middle and upper classes.

1845: From Ireland to Russia, famine plagues Europe, killing some 2.5 million people.

1846: The Irish potato famine reaches its peak.

1848: Mexican War ends with the Treaty of Guadalupe Hidalgo, in which Mexico gives up half of its land area, including Texas, California, most of Arizona and New Mexico, and parts of Colorado, Utah, and Nevada. In another treaty, with Great Britain, the United States sets the boundaries of its Oregon Territory.

1848: Discovery of gold at Sutter's Mill in California starts a gold rush, which brings a tremendous influx of settlers—and spells the beginning of the end for California's Native Americans.

1848: Women's Rights Convention in Seneca Falls, New York, launches the women's suffrage movement.

1850: German mathematical physicist Rudolf Julius Emanuel Clausius enunciates the Second Law of Thermodynamics, stating that heat cannot pass from a colder body to a warmer one, but only from a warmer to a colder body. This will prove to be one of the most significant principles of physics and chemistry, establishing that a perfectly efficient physical system is impossible, and that all physical systems ultimately succumb to entropy.

1854: In the United States, the Kansas-Nebraska Act calls for decisions on the legality of slavery to be made through

Karl Marx. The Library of Congress.

local votes. Instead of reducing divisions, this measure will result in widespread rioting and bloodshed, and will only further hasten the looming conflict over slavery and states' rights.

1858: In a Springfield, Illinois, speech during his unsuccessful campaign for the Senate against Stephen Douglass, Abraham Lincoln makes a strong case against slavery, maintaining that "this Government cannot endure permanently half-slave and half-free."

Event and Its Context

The Socialist Movement in the 1840s

The most important context for the publication of the *Communist Manifesto* lies in the doctrinal disputes of the 1840s. This was a period of intense intellectual ferment, as a multitude of writers attempted to explain and analyze the problems of modern society. At this stage, Marx was merely one of many socialist writers. Fourier, Saint-Simon, Blanqui, Blanc, Proudhon, Weitling, Owen, and many others had theories on how society might be improved. Some of these theorists already had a substantial following, whereas Marx was an obscure young journalist. However, with his typical intellectual arrogance, Marx believed that he had exposed the misconceptions of the others. By studying the insights of German philosophy, French socialist thought, and British political economy, Marx had not merely produced another socialist theory. Instead, he claimed to have discovered the fundamental principles of modern society, indeed, of the whole of human civilization. With the support of Engels, Marx set out to convince the various socialist groups of the superiority of his ideas.

One such group was the League of the Just, established between 1836 and 1838 by German exiles in Paris. This was a se-

Title page from "Manifesto der kommunistischen Partei," or "Manifesto of the Communist Party," commonly known as the *Communist Manifesto*. © Hulton Archive/ Getty Images. Reproduced by permission.

cret society, influenced by the ideas of German socialist Wilhelm Weitling. Some of its members were involved in an abortive uprising in Paris 1848 and were forced to flee to London. There, Karl Schapper, Joseph Moll, and Heinrich Bauer established another branch of the League of the Just. The group established connections with various members of the labor movement in Britain.

With revolution on the Continent looking increasingly likely, there were advantages in creating an organization to coordinate socialist activity across Europe. Marx had become the center of a small group of German exiles living in Brussels. In 1846 he and Engels established the Communist Correspondence Committees to exchange information and ideas between German, French, and English socialists. Marx also published several pamphlets that attacked the ideas of some of the other socialist theorists. He aimed to wean people away from adherence to what he disparagingly referred to as utopian socialist ideas and convert them to his "scientific" socialism.

The London branch of the League of the Just approached Marx in 1847. Although the Londoners had been in touch with

Marx and Engels, they held important reservations about the group in Brussels. They disagreed with Marx's ideas, and they disliked his intellectual arrogance, especially his attacks on other German socialists. However, the advantages of a compromise outweighed their concerns, and the groups decided to meet to hammer out their differences. A congress convened in London from 2 to 9 June, and the League of the Just became the Communist League. As Marx was unable to attend, Engels represented his position. The statutes of the new organization still reflected the influence of socialist ideas that were at odds with Marx's theories. However, the league's slogan was changed from "All Men are Brothers" to "Workingmen of all Countries, Unite!," a clear indication that Engels was able to make some progress.

A second congress met in London from 29 November to 8 December 1847. This time, Marx attended, and there were heated and lengthy debates as he defended his theories against his critics. The fact that Marx and Engels were given the task of writing up a statement of belief for the Communist League indicates that they were able to persuade their audience. Given the turbulent atmosphere in Europe, the organization needed to recruit people quickly to its cause, and Marx had only a couple of months in which to write the statement. The London leaders sent him a letter in January 1848 threatening to take away the task from him if he did not finish it quickly. In writing the manifesto, Marx used drafts written by Engels, and both their names appeared on the finished document. The first copies were published in London at the end of February 1848.

The Manifesto

The manifesto was an evocative call to revolutionary action. By exposing the true nature of modern society, Marx and Engels hoped to engage their audience in the revolutionary cause of the Communist League. Marx sought to explain the development of modern society in terms of historical materialism, which he and Engels had developed throughout the 1840s. Marx had deduced from his reading of German philosophy, French socialism, and English economics that the basis of society was not ideas, but how the productive forces of that society were organized. This resulted in the claim that "the history of all hitherto existing society is the history of class struggles." Throughout history, social change occurred when the productive forces in society clashed with the conditions of production, resulting in massive social upheaval. This was always to the benefit of one social class at the expense of another. Modern society was the result of a long series of revolutions in the modes of production, of which the bourgeois class was the main beneficiary. The result was the modern industrial age, which had increased the productive capacity of society to unparalleled levels, producing "wonders far surpassing Egyptian pyramids, Roman aqueducts, and Gothic cathedrals."

Nevertheless, these achievements of bourgeois society relied on the oppression of the great majority of people. This resulted in the creation of the proletariat class, whose members were reduced to the level of a mere commodity and "daily and hourly enslaved by the machine." However, as with previous societies, bourgeois society contained within it the seeds of its own destruction. Marx predicted that the economic crises that afflicted Europe in the 1840s would increase in severity and frequency, an indication that modern productive forces were revolting against the constraints of modern conditions of production. In modern society, the capitalist system of production had sharpened class divisions, resulting in the worldwide unification and organization of the proletariat. Thus, it was inevitable that the revolutionary proletariat would overthrow the bourgeoisie and establish a new society in which the conflicting elements of previous societies would be entirely resolved.

The role of the communists was to organize the proletariat to fulfill their destiny as the agents of revolutionary change. Probably heavily influenced by the other leaders of the Communist League, Marx suggested a program for revolutionary change that aimed to instruct those involved in the revolutionary struggle. Given that the manifesto was intended to win over the adherents of the various socialist sects, a large part of the manifesto was also concerned with highlighting the weaknesses of other kinds of socialist thought. Inevitably, Marx wrote with a particular audience in mind, which influenced what he included in the manifesto and the way he presented many of his ideas. However, the manifesto still stands as the most concise and direct example of Marxist theory. Marx was not the first to critique bourgeois capitalism. However, in terms of its systematic explanation, not only of modern society, but also the whole of human history, as well as predicting future developments, the *Communist Manifesto* was outstanding.

The Influence of the Manifesto

The *Communist Manifesto* represents the results of Marx's synthesis of different strands of European intellectual and social thought. By putting this into service for the Communist League, Marx and Engels created a political classic. However, the manifesto had little opportunity to reach the audience for which it was originally intended. The manifesto was supposed to win supporters and shape strategy in the approaching revolutions. However, it came too late to have any influence in 1848. Revolution broke out in Paris at the same time that the *Communist Manifesto* was being published in London. The revolutions quickly spread to the German states, and the members of the Communist League, including Marx and Engels, returned home to participate. However, no coordinated action based on the principles of the manifesto was possible, given that the Communist League consisted of only about 20 members and had little influence on the working-class movement in Europe. In the atmosphere of reaction that followed the defeat of the 1848 revolutions, the socialist movement was forced to retreat. The Communist League itself disintegrated, and it seemed that the manifesto would be destined for oblivion.

However, the establishment of the International Workingmen's Association in 1864 provided the manifesto with another audience. Although it represented a broad range of positions within the labor movement, the First International was an opportunity for Marx to gain exposure for his theories. In 1871 Marx and the International gained notoriety, as the blame for the Paris Commune was laid at their feet. Although this eventually contributed to the dissolution of the International, it raised Marx's profile and stimulated interest in his theories. As a result, a number of new editions of the *Communist Manifesto* in various languages were published in the 1870s. By then, Marx and Engels had admitted that parts of it were outdated but insist-

Excerpts from "Interview With Karl Marx"

[On 5 January 1879, the *Chicago Tribune* ran a lengthy interview with Karl Marx, excerpted below. The identity of the author, "H," was never revealed.]

In a little villa at Haverstock Hill, the northwest portion of London, lives Karl Marx, the cornerstone of modern socialism. . . . His convictions have caused him trouble from the beginning. Judging from the appearance of his home, they certainly have not brought him affluence. . . .

Your correspondent has called upon him twice or thrice, and each time the Doctor was found in his library, with a book in one hand and a cigarette in the other. He must be over seventy years of age. [Marx was sixty.] His physique is well knit, massive, erect. He has the head of a man of intellect, and the features of a cultivated Jew. His hair and beard are long, and iron gray in color. His eyes are glittering black, shaded by a pair of bushy eyebrows. To a stranger he shows extreme caution. A foreigner can generally gain admission; but the ancient-looking German woman [Helene Demuth] who waits upon visitors has instructions to admit none who hail from the Fatherland, unless they bring letters of introduction. . . .

"The reverend gentleman alluded to [the Rev. Joseph Cook of Boston, an anticommunist]," I remarked, "gave an extract from a letter which he said you addressed to the Communists of Paris in 1871. Here it is: `We are as yet but 3,000,000 at most. In twenty years we shall be 50,000,000—100,000,000 perhaps. Then the world will belong to us, for it will be not only Paris, Lyon, Marseilles, which will rise against odious capital, but Berlin, Munich, Dresden, London, Liverpool, Manchester, Brussels, St. Petersburg, New York—in short, the whole world. And before this new insurrection, such as history has not yet known, the past will disappear like a hideous nightmare; for the popular conflagration, kindled at a hundred points at once, will destroy even its memory!' Now, Doctor, I suppose you admit the authorship of that extract?"

"I never wrote a word of it. I never write such melodramatic nonsense. I am very careful what I do write. That was put in *Le Figaro*, over my signature, about that time. There were hundreds of the same kind of letters flying about them. I wrote to the London *Times* and declared they were forgeries; but if I denied everything that has been said and written of me, I would require a score of secretaries."

Source: H. "Interview with Karl Marx." *Chicago Tribune*, 5 January 1879

—Judson Knight

ed that the basic principles remained relevant. As the most concise application of Marx's theories of historical materialism and class struggle, the *Communist Manifesto* became required reading for the worldwide socialist movement.

Key Players

Engels, Frederick (1820–1895): A German socialist, Engels helped write the *Communist Manifesto*, and although he later gave all the credit to Marx, the manifesto should be seen as the result of his close collaboration with Marx during the 1840s.

Marx, Karl (1818–1883): Marx was a German socialist theorist, one of the most influential writers in modern history. Marx's work, including the *Communist Manifesto*, has been the inspiration for millions of people all over the world.

Moll, Joseph (1812–1849): German exile, one of the London leaders of the League of the Just, Moll was sent to Brussels in 1847 to ask for Marx's cooperation in reorganizing the League of the Just.

Schapper, Karl (1812–1870): Schapper was a German exile, one of the London leaders of the League of the Just. Although suspicious of Marx and his ideas, Schapper agreed to join forces with the Brussels socialists, leading to the creation of the Communist League in 1847.

Weitling, Wilhelm (1808–1871): One of the first leaders of the German workers' movement, Weitling influenced the socialist ideas of the League of the Just. Although Marx initially praised Weitling, Marx came to reject his mix of moral socialism and utopian Christian ideas and worked hard to counter the influence of Weitling's ideas.

See also: *First International; June Days Rebellion; Paris Commune; Revolutions in Europe.*

BIBLIOGRAPHY

Books

Cole, G. D. H. *A History of Socialist Thought*. Vol. 1, *Socialist Thought: The Forerunners 1789–1850*. London: Macmillan & Co., 1953.

Lichtheim, George. *Marxism: An Historical and Critical Study*. London: Routledge and Kegan Paul, 1961.

———. *The Origins of Socialism*. London: Weidenfeld and Nicolson, 1969.

Lindemann, Albert S. *A History of European Socialism*. New Haven, CT, and London: Yale University Press, 1983.

McLellan, David. *Karl Marx: His Life and Thought*. London: Macmillan, 1973.

Taylor, A. J. P., ed. *The Communist Manifesto*. Harmondsworth, Middlesex, UK; Penguin Books, 1967.

Other

"Letters of Marx and Engels: 1847" [cited 7 November 2002]. <http://www.marxists.org/archive/marx/works/1847/letters/index.htm>

"Manifesto of the Communist Party." 1987, 2000 [cited 7 November 2002]. <http://www.marxists.org/archive/marx/works/1848/communist-manifesto/index.htm>

ADDITIONAL RESOURCES

Books

Hodges, David Clark. *The Literate Communist: 150 Years of the Communist Manifesto*. New York: Peter Lang, 1999.

Ryazanoff, D., ed. *The Communist Manifesto of Karl Marx and Friedrich Engels*. New York: Russell & Russell Inc., 1963.

Struik, Dirk J. *Birth of the Communist Manifesto*. New York: International Publishers, 1971.

Toews, John E., ed. *The Communist Manifesto by Karl Marx and Frederick Engels with Related Documents*. New York and Boston: Bedford/St. Martin's, 1999.

—Katrina Ford

Confederación de Trabajadores de América Latina

Latin America 1938

Synopsis

In 1938 the fear of communist infiltration of the national labor movements spawned the creation of the multinational *Confederación de Trabajadores de América Latina,* or Confederation of Latin American Workers. Led by the Mexican national labor leader Vicente Lombardo Toledano, the confederation counted on the support of union organizations from 13 Latin American nations. Lombardo and the confederation led Latin American workers on a path toward nationalism and integration among the workers, a track that was untried prior to this confederation. By 1964 the organization was defunct, as it could not overcome the nationalistic tendencies of the rank-and-file members of the international union.

Timeline

1922: Published this year, James Joyce's novel *Ulysses* and T. S. Eliot's poem *The Waste Land* will transform literature and inaugurate the era of modernism.

1927: American inventor Philo T. Farnsworth demonstrates a working model of the television, and Belgian astronomer Georges Lemaître proposes the Bang Theory.

1932: In German elections, Nazis gain a 37 percent plurality of Reichstag seats, raising tensions between the far right and the far left. On a "bloody Sunday" in July, communists in Hamburg attack Nazis with guns, and a fierce battle ensues.

1937: Italy signs the Anti-Comintern Pact, signed by Germany and Japan the preceding year. Like the two others before it, Italy now withdraws from the League of Nations.

1937: Japan attacks China and annexes most of that nation's coastal areas.

1937: Stalin uses carefully staged show trials in Moscow to eliminate all rivals for leadership. These party purges, however, are only a small part of the death toll now being exacted in a country undergoing forced industrialization, much of it by means of slave labor.

1937: In the middle of an around-the-world flight, Amelia Earhart and her plane disappear somewhere in the Pacific.

1937: Crash of the *Hindenburg* in Lakehurst, New Jersey, kills 36 and ends the brief era when rigid airships promised to be the ocean liners of the skies.

1937: Pablo Picasso paints his famous *Guernica* mural dramatizing the Nationalist bombing of a town in Spain. Thanks to artists and intellectuals such as Picasso and Ernest Hemingway, the Loyalists are winning the battle of hearts and minds, even if they are weaker militarily, and idealistic young men flock from America to join the "Abraham Lincoln Brigade." Yet as George Orwell later reveals in *Homage to Catalonia,* the lines between good and evil are not clear: with its Soviet backing, the Loyalist cause serves as proxy for a totalitarianism every bit as frightening as that of the Nationalists and their German and Italian supporters.

1942: Axis conquests reach their height in the middle of this year. The Nazis control a vast region from Normandy to the suburbs of Stalingrad, and from the Arctic Circle to the edges of the Sahara. To the east, the Japanese "Co-Prosperity Sphere" encompasses territories from China to Burma to the East Indies, stretching deep into the western Pacific.

1947: The Marshall Plan is established to assist European nations in recovering from the war.

1952: Among the cultural landmarks of the year are the film *High Noon* and the book *The Invisible Man* by Ralph Ellison.

Event and Its Context

By the late 1930s it was becoming increasingly clear among Latin American leaders that fascism or national socialism was achieving popularity among many workers in the international sector. In the major Latin American nations, fascism was becoming especially prevalent and threatening to union officials. Fascism threatened to replace independent unionism with a state-controlled form of labor representation. Beginning in Mexico, long-time union leader Vicente Lombardo Toledano, with the support of President Lázaro Cárdenas, attempted to create a plan to unite the different national labor groups in Latin America to struggle against the fascist tendencies within many union groups. In Mexico, Cárdenas and Lombardo initiated policies to strengthen the labor movement, each in his own way. Lombardo, an avowed Marxist, wished to establish a dictatorship of the proletariat. Though a Marxist, he was not an internationalist. He believed that Mexico and Latin America could not succumb to a common economic and political reality, as each nation was independent and autonomous. He understood that nationalization of private property might be a problem in a nation that had a long history of supporting the idea

Lázaro Cárdenas. The Library of Congress.

of private property. As leader of the *Confederación de Trabajadores de México* (CTM), Lombardo in 1936 united 6,000 independent unions and 600,000 workers. The CTM served as the voice of the workers against foreign capital, especially in 1938 when Cardenas nationalized the oil industry after a prolonged workers' conflict.

In September 1938 Lombardo created the *Confederación de Trabajadores de América Latina* (CTAL). Armed with his recent successes in Mexico, Lombardo began to communicate with unions throughout Latin America. He wished to create a regional union to ward against fascism and to counter what he saw as an increasing politicization of the workers in many nations. In other words, he believed that many national unions were allying themselves with the major political parties. This was a problem for Lombardo, who feared that such a trend would impinge on the idea of union independence. Thus he was able to garner the support of 13 national unions, including those from Chile, Venezuela, Colombia, and Cuba. Clearly, this labor organization would have distinct ideas about the role of labor within the political and economic systems of Latin America. The union espoused procapitalist ideas. Although its leaders criticized the ideas of capitalism, they also supported the idea of fair capitalism in which labor would control many aspects of the work process. Moreover, in their "Declaration of Principles," the union representatives promoted three fundamental principles. First, they believed that the labor movement should have autonomy from the major political parties that were influential among their respective unions. Lombardo believed that this was key in the development of a truly nationalist, indepen-

Vicente Lombardo Toledano. The Library of Congress.

dent working-class movement. Second, they promoted the ideas of class struggle. Espousing neo-Marxist notions, the confederation believed that workers were involved in a great social struggle against the national elites and foreign capital. Moreover, they believed that unity would be the key weapon in the long run in defeating the alliance of the upper classes and foreigners. Finally, the declaration put forth the idea of an internal proletariat. Each nation contained its own domestic proletariat that served as what Lenin termed the "vanguard of the proletariat," or the leaders of the working-class struggle. Lombardo's philosophy was thus imbued in the principles of the CTAL.

The structure copied that of many communist organizations. Representatives from each nation attended the general assembly. The Central Committee consisted of a president, two vice presidents, a secretary general, and two regional secretaries (ironically, the organization divided Latin America into three regions). The representatives would meet once a year, and the general assembly would convene once every three years. The structure of the organization clearly favored the creation of a class-oriented, regional organization.

By the 1950s the CTAL had competition from several regional labor organizations. Specifically, CTAL contended with the *Organización Regional Internacional Trabajadores* (ORIT)

and the International Confederation of Free Trade Unions (ICFTU), led by Serafino Romualdi. The CTAL lost membership to these unions in part because they favored a free trade union ideology, as opposed to the pro–class struggle ideology of the CTAL. However, the popularity of the CTAL continued as a symbol of the procapitalist and integrationist ideology of the movement, which was intensified as a result of the cold war. The cold war spawned a new anticommunist sentiment within the CTAL, forcing it to abandon its ostensible neocommunist organization to create a new organization based on that of the American Federation of Labor (AFL).

In the 1950s the CTAL was instrumental in a number of foreign policy initiatives pertaining to the cold war. It was ubiquitous in the 1954 Guatemalan Revolution as well as the Cuban Revolution of 1959. However, by the early 1960s, several factors facilitated its influence in the region. First, the CTAL could not contain the nationalism of many union movements in Latin America. Nationalism proved to be a potent force that was difficult to control or deter. This was especially evident after the victory of Fidél Castro in Cuba. Castro advocated a revolutionary ideology for the working classes. Moreover, he advocated the spread of this revolutionary nationalism to other guerilla groups throughout the region. Thus, it became difficult for the CTAL to retain many of its previous supporters. Second, the influence of the cold war proved to be overwhelming to the CTAL leadership. The leadership could not contain the revolutionary zeal of many of their workers within the confines of a passive procapitalist labor union. These two factors facilitated the decline of the union. By 1964 the CTAL was, in terms of support and actions, clearly on the decline. By 1965 the CTAL would be integrated into the larger internationalist movements.

Impact

The emergence of the CTAL signified a fundamental shift in working-class consciousness in Latin America. On the one hand, Lombardo and the leadership promoted the idea of a class-conscious, internationalist bent on the ideology. The CTAL promoted an integrationist policy among the different working-class sectors in Latin America. This marked a clear departure for the labor movements in each country, which for years had supported the idea of a nationalistic, anticapitalist labor movement.

Economic and political realities in the late 1930s forced the working class to shift its approach to an integrationist philosophy. The new ideology connoted cooperation and acceptance. These ideas were difficult for a movement that had yet to attain any sort of cultural identity. Finally, the CTAL and its success provided a challenge to the hegemonic policies of many in the working-class movements, especially within the more urbanized and industrialized sectors. The CTAL was bound to fail in societies with a heavy agrarian population base and low levels of industrialization. This alienated many important groups, particularly the workers within the export sector, who felt that the CTAL was arrogant in pursuing its hegemonic policies.

The CTAL was significant in Latin American labor history in that its approach to state-labor relations influenced future labor relations, which would soon shift to integration and assimilation rather than conflict. Integration into the larger society provided many economic and social benefits to the common worker. In the long run, the CTAL radically transformed the nature of the Latin American working class.

Key Players

Lombardo Toledano, Vicente (1894–1968): Mexican labor leader of the *Confederación de Trabajadores de México* (CTM), Lombardo formed the *Confederación de Trabajadores de América Latina* (CTAL) in 1938 to counter an increasing tendency toward fascism in the regional movements.

Cárdenas, Lázaro (1895–1970): President of Mexico in 1938 at the time of the formation of CTAL, Cárdenas was instrumental in influencing Lombardo to pursue free trade unionism.

See also: *American Federation of Labor; Guatemalan Coup Orchestrated by CIA; International Confederation of Free Trade Unions.*

BIBLIOGRAPHY

Books

Kofas, Jon F. *The Struggle for Legitimacy: Latin American Labor and the United States.* Tempe, AZ: Center for Latin American Studies, Arizona State University, 1992.

Lombardo Toledano, Vicente. *La Confederación de Trabajadores de América Latina ha Concluído su Misión Histórica.* México: Editorial Popular, 1964.

Quintanilla, Obregón Lourdes. *Lombardismo y Sindicatos en América Latina.* México: Distribuciónes Fontamara: Ediciónes Nueva Sociologéa, 1982.

—Jaime Ramon Olivares

Samuel Gompers. The Library of Congress.

Great Depression, led to a period of inactivity during the 1930s. By the end of the 1930s, Latin American labor leaders had created their own federation known as the *Confederación de Trabajadores de América Latina* (CTAL), which did not include the AFL or any other U.S. groups. The PAFL was never revived, and the AFL had little influence in Latin America until it sponsored the formation of the *Confederación Inter-America de Trabajadores* (CIT) in 1948 so as to counter the CTAL.

Confederación Obrera Pan-Americana

Western Hemisphere 1918

Synopsis

In 1918 labor leaders from Mexico and the United States created the *Confederación Obrera Pan-Americana* (COPA), or Pan-American Federation of Labor (PAFL). The goal of the PAFL was to promote and protect the rights of workers throughout the Western Hemisphere, although it was the Mexican and U.S. delegates that generally dominated the federation. In particular, the PAFL reflected the interests and ideology of Samuel Gompers and the American Federation of Labor (AFL). The PAFL held five congresses between 1918 and 1927. However, the death of Gompers and other founders, along with the

Timeline

1898: United States defeats Spain in the three-month Spanish-American War. As a result, Cuba gains it independence, and the United States purchases Puerto Rico and the Philippines from Spain for $20 million.

1903: Russia's Social Democratic Party splits into two factions: the moderate Mensheviks and the hard-line Bolsheviks. Despite their names, which in Russian mean "minority" and "majority," respectively, Mensheviks actually outnumber Bolsheviks.

1910: Revolution breaks out in Mexico and will continue for the next seven years.

1914: On 28 June in the town of Sarajevo, then part of the Austro-Hungarian Empire, Serbian nationalist Gavrilo Princip assassinates Austrian Archduke Francis Ferdinand and wife Sophie. In the weeks that follow, Austria declares war on Serbia, and Germany on Russia and France, while Great Britain responds by declaring war on Germany. By the beginning of August, the lines are drawn, with the Allies (Great Britain, France, Russia, Belgium, Serbia, Montenegro, and Japan) against the Central Powers (Germany, Austria-Hungary, and Turkey).

1916: Battles of Verdun and the Somme are waged on the Western Front. The latter sees the first use of tanks, by the British.

1918: The Bolsheviks execute Czar Nicholas II and his family. Soon civil war breaks out between the communists and their allies, known as the Reds, and their enemies, a collection of anticommunists ranging from democrats to czarists, who are known collectively as the Whites. In March, troops from the United States, Great Britain, and France intervene on the White side.

1918: The Second Battle of the Marne in July and August is the last major conflict on the Western Front. In November, Kaiser Wilhelm II abdicates, bringing an end to the war.

1918: Upheaval sweeps Germany, which for a few weeks in late 1918 and early 1919 seems poised on the verge of communist revolution—or at least a Russian-style communist coup d'etat. But reactionary forces have regained their strength, and the newly organized Freikorps (composed of unemployed soldiers) suppresses the revolts. Even stronger than reaction or revolution, however, is republican sentiment, which opens the way for the creation of a democratic government based at Weimar.

1918: Influenza, carried to the furthest corners by returning soldiers, spreads throughout the globe. Over the next two years, it will kill nearly 20 million people—more than the war itself.

1921: As the Allied Reparations Commission calls for payments of 132 billion gold marks, inflation in Germany begins to climb.

1925: European leaders attempt to secure the peace at the Locarno Conference, which guarantees the boundaries between France and Germany, and Belgium and Germany.

Event and Its Context

The impetus for the formation of the PAFL came from John Murray, a philanthropist from New York City who had moved to California. A socialist, Murray had often aided poor Mexicans in California. He traveled to Mexico before the 1910 revolution and established a friendship with Ricardo Flores Magón of the Liberal Party. Murray again visited Mexico in 1915 in the midst of the revolution. He made contact with Mexico's *Casa del Obrero Mundial,* a revolutionary trade union that had been established in 1912.

After returning to the United States, Murray decided that the time had come for an alliance between the labor movements in the United States and Mexico. To this end, Murray met with Santiago Iglesias, a Spanish-born labor leader in Puerto Rico. Iglesias had worked closely with Samuel Gompers and had been involved with the AFL in Puerto Rico since 1901. Murray and Iglesias met shortly after the 1915 Pan-American Financial and Trade Conference, which laid the foundation for cooperation among large businesses in the Western Hemisphere. Iglesias felt that such cooperation among capitalists could only harm the working class. He therefore proposed a Pan-American labor organization that would serve to protect the interests of the workers.

Iglesias then introduced Murray to Gompers, who had already come in contact with Latin American labor issues through a group of Mexican cigar workers in New York. As Gompers grew in prominence in the AFL, Mexican labor leaders often sought him out. Murray was able to convince Gompers that the AFL should ally itself with the labor movement in Mexico and quickly became Gompers's chief advisor on Mexican affairs. They began planning for the creation of a pan-American labor organization.

In November 1915 Iglesias presented a report on Latin America at the AFL annual convention in San Francisco. He warned that business interests in the region were growing stronger, pointing to the 1915 Pan-American Financial and Trade Conference and to the opening of the Panama Canal. Iglesias proposed that the AFL leadership meet with Latin American labor leaders in Washington, D.C. The convention adopted this proposal.

The next move came in May 1916, when Gompers called for a meeting of the AFL, Mexico's *Casa del Obrero Mundial,* and other Mexican labor organizations. He suggested that the groups meet in El Paso, Texas. After some discussion over dates and location of such a meeting, the groups finally came together in late June and early July 1916 in Washington, D.C. Gompers, Murray, and the AFL executive council met with Mexican labor leaders, headed by Luis Morones, who later would become the leader of the *Confederación Regional Obrera Mexicana* (CROM), Mexico's leading labor organization. The result of the meeting was that the representatives agreed to move forward with the formation of a hemispheric labor federation

In November 1916 Gompers continued to call for a pan-American federation of labor at the AFL annual convention. He asked the delegates for the authority to create a Pan-American Federation of Labor Conference Committee, which would then form the new labor organization. The convention delegates granted this authority and appointed a four-man committee that included Gompers, Murray, Iglesias, and Mexican labor leader Carlos Loveira.

This committee issued a manifesto in February 1917. The manifesto, available in both English and Spanish, addressed the workers of the hemisphere, especially those in Latin America. It asked labor organizations throughout the Americas to send representatives to the conference committee. The manifesto outlined the need for a pan-American federation in light of increasing activities by capitalists without regard for the interests of the masses. Such a labor federation would truly represent the "people" according to the manifesto. The aims outlined by the committee in the manifesto included higher wages, better working conditions and housing, the protection of children, freedom of speech and press, and the right to strike.

When the United States entered World War I, the organization of the new federation had to be put on hold. Gompers, who had come to believe that the war effort was in the best interest of workers, was busy serving on the advisory board for the Council of National Defense. Iglesias had returned to Puerto Rico for an agricultural workers' strike there. Murray went to

Arizona to aid Mexican mine workers who were on strike. Loveira returned to Mexico.

Efforts to create the federation resumed in earnest in April 1918, when some in the United States became increasingly concerned about Mexico's neutrality in the war and possible German influence there. In May 1918 Gompers sent an AFL commission that included Murray and Iglesias to Mexico as part of an effort to improve relations between the two countries. The official purpose was to discuss the formation of the PAFL, although beneath the surface it was hoped that the commission might help convince Mexico to end it neutrality and join the Allies.

When Murray returned to the United States in June 1918, he brought two Mexican labor leaders with him, including Luis Morones of the CROM. The Mexican representatives met with Gompers and set up an international conference scheduled for November 1918 in Laredo, Texas, in order to formally establish the PAFL. In the meantime, they also established a newspaper in San Antonio called *El Obrero Pan-Americano* (*The Pan-American Labor Press*).

The conference opened on 13 November 1918, just two days after the end of World War I. The opening ceremonies took place on the International Bridge that connected Laredo with Nuevo Laredo in Mexico. Seventy-one delegates attended the conference, most from the United States and Mexico, although Guatemala, El Salvador, Costa Rica, and Colombia each sent one representative. The first two days of the conference involved speeches and the selection of committee members. Then delegates moved on to discuss a number of resolutions. There was some tension over the issue of Mexican workers in the United States. The Mexican delegates claimed that Americans discriminated against Mexicans and that border officials treated them poorly. The U.S. delegates responded that Mexicans in the United States did not participate in labor organizations. The two sides decided to set up a committee to further investigate the issue and a permanent headquarters in Washington, D.C. After adopting a constitution and electing officials, the conference concluded on 18 November.

The second PAFL congress took place in New York City in July 1919. Only 26 delegates attended this meeting. They discussed issues such as the peace treaties that ended World War I, the role of U.S. imperialism in the Dominican Republic, a border dispute between Chile and Peru in which Peruvian workers had been expelled from Chile, and the immigration policy of the United States and the AFL. Also, at Gompers's insistence, the delegates resolved that in the future all delegates had to be wage-earning workers. Some of the Latin American representatives were intellectuals; Gompers and the AFL opposed their inclusion. In all, the delegates discussed 30 resolutions, most of which reflected the philosophy of Gompers and the AFL.

The PAFL held several more congresses. The third congress met in Mexico City in January 1921 and the fourth took place in December 1924. Shortly after the fourth congress, however, Gompers died. New AFL president William Green replaced Gompers in the PAFL in 1925. The last PAFL congress was the best attended. This fifth congress took place in Washington, D.C., in July 1927, and 12 countries sent representatives.

PAFL officials scheduled a sixth congress for Havana, Cuba, in January 1930. However, due to the Great Depression, the meeting was postponed a number of times. In August 1931 the AFL announced that it did not have the funds to support a meeting in the immediate future. As the depression continued, no meeting took place.

Then in 1938, Latin American labor leaders formed the *Confederación de Trabajadores de América Latina* (CTAL) in Mexico City. Led by the procommunist Vicente Lombardo Toledano, the group included only Latin American delegates, although the CIO supported the group. In response, the AFL tried to revive the PAFL, fearing its influence in Latin America would decrease. To this end, Iglesias toured a number of Latin American countries. However, Iglesias died in 1939 and the PAFL was never revived.

Key Players

Gompers, Samuel (1850–1924): Born in England, Gompers moved to the United States in 1863. He took up his father's trade as cigar maker. Gompers became involved in the labor movement in the United States, founding the American Federation of Labor (AFL) in 1886 and serving as its president until his death in 1924. Through the AFL, Gompers sought to influence and aid the labor movement in Latin America. To this end, he sponsored the formation of the Pan-American Federation of Labor in 1918.

Iglesias, Santiago (1872–1939): Iglesias was born in Spain, where he served as an apprentice cabinetmaker. At the age of 15, he moved to Cuba, where he soon became involved in union organizing. The Spanish government of colonial Cuba forced him to leave the island because of his involvement in revolutionary activities. Iglesias then moved to Puerto Rico, where he continued his union organizing and was involved in publishing labor newspapers. After meeting Samuel Gompers, he became the AFL organizer in Puerto Rico and Cuba. In 1915 he formed the Puerto Rican Socialist Party. Iglesias was also instrumental in the formation of the PAFL from the beginning. In the 1930s he served as Puerto Rico's resident commissioner to the House of Representatives.

Morones, Luis (1890–1964): An electrical worker, Morones quickly rose to become Mexico's key labor leader by the 1920s. He had been a member of the anarchist *Casa del Obrero Mundial*. In 1918 he formed the *Confederación Regional Obrera Mexicana* (CROM), which became Mexico's leading labor organization. Morones played a significant role in getting Mexican labor to participate in the PAFL. He later served in Mexico's national government, leading to closer ties between labor and the government.

Murray, John: A Quaker and philanthropist from New York City, Murray later moved to California for health reasons. There he aided poor Mexicans who were living in California. Murray became a socialist and worked with a number of radical newspapers. He traveled to Mexico before and again during the Mexican Revolution. He maintained a friendship with the Mexican opposition leader Ricardo Flores Magón and made contact with the *Casa del Obrero*

Mundial, a revolutionary trade union organized in 1912. Upon his return to the United States, Murray sought to create links between workers in the United States and Mexico. He was influential in the formation and activities of the PAFL. Murray later committed suicide after contracting tuberculosis.

See also: *American Federation of Labor; Confederación de Trabajadores de América Latina.*

BIBLIOGRAPHY

Books

Alexander, Robert J. *Organized Labor in Latin America.* New York: The Free Press, 1965.

Levenstein, Harvey A. *Labor Organizations in the United States and Mexico: A History of Their Relations.* Westport, CT: Greenwood Publishing, 1971.

Poblete Troncoso, Moisés, and Ben G. Burnett. *The Rise of the Latin American Labor Movement.* New York: Bookman Associates, 1960.

Snow, Sinclair. *The Pan-American Federation of Labor.* Durham, NC: Duke University Press, 1964.

—Ronald Young

Confédération Générale du Travail

France 1895

Synopsis

In Europe the development and institutionalization of the workers' movement at both national and international levels marked the end of the nineteenth century. In France the first national trade union center, the *Confédération Générale du Travail* (CGT), saw the light of day in 1895 at the end of a long process of transformation of preexisting structures. A gradual clarification of objectives, means, and forms of workers' struggle led to the differentiation of workers' political activities from their union activities and to the creation of distinct organizations to represent each side.

Three factors particularly contributed to the character of the CGT. First, the relatively slow processes of industrialization and urbanization meant that right up to the end of the nineteenth century, the working class was highly dispersed. Second, the force of government repression against the workers' first tentative organizing steps left both deep trauma and, most significantly, initially ruled out a reformist solution. Finally, the separation of managerial from adversarial union functions, established as a result of the 1852 decree on friendly societies, permanently distanced the CGT and indeed the whole of French trade unionism from a strategy of membership services provision.

Timeline

1876: General George Armstrong Custer and 264 soldiers are killed by the Sioux at the Little Big Horn River.

1880: Completion of Cologne Cathedral, begun 634 years earlier. With twin spires 515 feet (157 m) high, it is the tallest structure in the world and will remain so until 1889, when it is surpassed by the Eiffel Tower. (The previous record for the world's tallest structure lasted much longer—for about 4,430 years following the building of Cheops's Great Pyramid in c. 2550 B.C.)

1885: Belgium's King Leopold II becomes sovereign of the so-called Congo Free State, which he will rule for a quarter-century virtually as his own private property. The region in Africa, given the name of Zaire in the 1970s (and Congo in 1997), becomes the site of staggering atrocities, including forced labor and genocide, at the hands of Leopold's minions.

1891: French troops open fire on workers during a 1 May demonstration at Fourmies, where employees of the Sans Pareille factory are striking for an eight-hour workday. Nine people are killed—two of them children—and 60 more are injured.

1894: French army captain Alfred Dreyfus, a Jew, is convicted of treason. Dreyfus will later be cleared of all charges, but the Dreyfus case illustrates—and exacerbates—the increasingly virulent anti-Semitism that pervades France.

1895: German physicist Wilhelm Roentgen discovers X-rays.

1895: Brothers Auguste and Louis Lumière show the world's first motion picture—*Workers Leaving the Lumière Factory*—at a café in Paris.

1895: Guglielmo Marconi pioneers wireless telegraphy, which in the next three decades will make possible the use of radio waves for commercial broadcasts and other applications.

1895: German engineer Rudolf Diesel invents an engine capable of operating on a type of petroleum less highly refined, and therefore less costly, than gasoline.

1898: Marie and Pierre Curie discover the radioactive elements radium and polonium.

1901: U.S. President William McKinley is assassinated by Leon Czolgosz, an anarchist. Vice President Theodore Roosevelt becomes president.

1905: In the industrial Ruhr region in Germany, 200,000 miners go on strike.

Event and Its Context

The creation of the French National Federation of Unions and Work Associations (FNS) in 1886 and then of the National Federation of Labor Exchanges (FNBT) in 1892 were two indispensable stages in the formation of a national union center.

At the beginning, the CGT was a victim of disagreements between its component parts and thus extremely fragile. During

Victor Griffuelhes. © Getty Images. Reproduced by permission.

the organization's first years of existence, it experienced several important modifications to its statutes. As a result, historians often cite 1902 rather than 1895 as its real founding year.

Toward Union Independence

Although the first workers' conferences occurred in the mid-1870s, another 10 years passed before the trade union movement really took on some degree of independence. Even then, the FNS, as formed in 1886, functioned as a simple sounding board for the *Parti ouvrier français* (French Workers' Party) dominated by the followers of Jules Guesde.

The local silk weavers' council called the FNS founding conference in Lyon. Despite moderate opposition, the decision to give the new organization a national and general role passed by 90 votes to 15. The fledgling organization comprised local and regional federations but had to give its core elements, the local councils of different trades, a significant degree of independence. Its statutes declared its opposition to reformism and its support for class struggle and declared the FNS "the sister of all existing socialist workers' federations," which it considered "a friend conducting another wing of the battle with whom we will eventually combine to destroy the common enemy."

At the FNS Montluçon conference in 1887, the collectivist approach inspired by Marx and Engels triumphed over the followers of Proudhon and the utopian socialists. The notion of "bringing capitalism to the edge of disaster" by refusing to work for it prompted the introduction of the idea of a general strike, by which the united workers could overthrow the government and force the building of a new system. At the following year's Bordeaux conference, the FNS adopted the principle of the general strike as the best weapon for emancipation.

In spite of this, the new federation remained strongly subordinate to political action and effectively led a very discrete existence. Much more important was the influence of the National Federation of Labor Exchanges (FNBT). The creation of labor exchanges derived initially from a completely different dynamic than that which had led to the establishment of trade federations. The idea was not new; various proposals for labor exchanges had been discussed in the 1790s. Taken up again by a Paris town councilor, Mesureur, in 1884, it led finally on 3 February 1887 to the opening of an exchange in Paris, followed by openings in Nîmes, Marseille (1888), Saint-Etienne (1889), Toulouse (1890), and so on. By 1892, 14 exchanges existed. Accompanied by a spurt in trade union growth, this rapid development was also partly motivated by a number of republicans, solidly installed in local government, who wished to resolve the "labor question" by establishing social peace. From this perspective, in a period of rising unemployment and increasing strikes, a labor exchange in which the different trades could come together and whereby workers could find work was an essential tool.

Quite naturally, the exchanges decided to link up. A constitutional conference, which brought together a dozen of them, convened at Saint-Etienne in February 1892. It agreed to unify the programs of its various member unions and rejected any involvement of the national or local state in the running of the exchanges. The conference nominated an executive committee made up of one delegate from each exchange to manage the activities of the associated exchanges.

Anarchists and socialists of all persuasions coexisted in this new federation. The anarchists, however, were gathering influence at the time and developed a strategy based on federalism and complete independence from the state and all political parties. The doctrinal differences between the FNBT and the FNS then became irreducible. A strong unifying tendency, however, existed within the FNBT, and its 1893 conference called for a joint conference of labor exchanges and unions to which the FNS was invited. This joint conference took place in Paris in July 1893. It reaffirmed the principle of the general strike and proposed that the two organizations unify more closely.

The Creation of the CGT

One year later, particularly rowdy debates took place at the Nantes conference. The FNBT line passed, by a majority of 65 votes to 37, and imposed a conception of the general strike that rejected the idea of simultaneously conquering state power. A "Workers' National Council" became the umbrella for the two federations and served as a general strike propaganda committee. These organizations had no influence, and it was only really at the Limoges conference in 1895 that the CGT was actually established.

Its founding text gave the CGT the exclusive aim "of uniting workers in struggle on economic issues and in close solidarity to achieve their total emancipation." It asked all present to "keep themselves above all political tendencies." Although not excluding any of the initiatives that had taken place to strengthen workers' organizing efforts to that point, CGT membership would include single trade unions, labor exchanges, local multitrade joint organizations and federations, and national trade federations created to bring together different parts of the same industry or sector and the NFBT.

Different union layers were thus intermingled, and this quickly became a factor that encouraged instability. In addition, relations rapidly deteriorated between the FNBT and the young CGT. Within a year the much weaker CGT was lacking in affiliates. It finally only survived thanks to the support given by the print and railway unions.

For the first seven years following its creation, the CGT barely survived and had very little real influence on events. It was constantly modifying its constitution and was unable to stabilize its leadership. Four general secretaries—Lagailse (1895–1899), Copigneaux (1899–1900), Renaudin (1900–1901), and Guérard (April–November 1901)—followed each other without leaving a mark.

Fernand Pelloutier, the general secretary of the FNBT, was much more influential. Starting in 1895 when he became its leader, he defined the major elements of revolutionary syndicalism and gave the labor exchanges a fourfold purpose: mutual support, education, propaganda, and worker resistance. His premature death coincided with the emergence of two other key figures, Emile Pouget and Victor Griffuelhes. The election of the latter to the head of the CGT in November 1901 marked the victory of revolutionary syndicalism.

As a result, it was possible to settle the issue of trade union unity at the Montpellier CGT conference of 1902. New statutes reaffirmed the desire of the CGT to keep clear of all political activity and required every local union branch to have a double affiliation, both to its local area union and to its national federation. From this point, therefore, the CGT comprised two independent sections: one that included national and isolated union branches of occupational and industrial federations and another that regrouped the labor exchanges and multiunion area, regional, and departmental union organizations.

This created solid foundations for a national union center. The charter that the CGT later adopted at its famous Amiens conference in 1906 made more explicit and deepened the ideas that had been adopted 11 years earlier and subsequently reaffirmed on several occasions, rather than adding anything new.

Key Players

Griffuelhes, Victor (1874–1923): Follower of Blanqui, cobbler, and member of the Leather and Skin Workers' Union, Griffuelhes played a vital role during the early years of the CGT, of which he became secretary general in 1901. An advocate of the replacement of the old skilled unions by industrial federations and a supporter of direct action, he played a key role in writing the Amiens Charter (1906). He resigned his responsibilities in 1909.

Guesde, Jules (1845–1922): Guesde was a journalist. He actively supported the 1871 Commune, earning him a sentence of five years imprisonment and exile. Allowed to return to France in 1876, he then discovered Marxism and fell strongly under the influence of the young German Social Democratic party, launching in 1899 the first French Marxist journal, *Égalité*. Having helped in the passing of collectivism at the 1879 Marseille Workers' Conference, he founded the *Parti ouvrier français* (French Workers' Party) with Paul Lafargue, Marx's son-in-law.

Keufer, Auguste (1851–1924): A typographer who led the print workers' union from 1884 to 1920, above all Keufer

was the leader of the reformist tendency. He participated actively in the founding of the CGT and was its first national treasurer (1895–1896). In addition he sat on the government's advisory National Work Council from its establishment in 1891 and later became its vice chairman.

Pelloutier, Fernand (1867–1901): A journalist and socialist, Pelloutier joined Guesde's French Workers' Party in 1892 but very quickly opposed its leader with his own libertarian conception of the workers' struggle and eventually resigned. With Aristide Briand, he initiated the founding conference of the FNBT and became deputy general secretary in 1894 and then general secretary in 1895. He was one of the principal theoreticians of anarcho-syndicalism.

Pouget, Emile (1860–1931): Anarchist who participated in the 1879 founding of the Paris clerical textile workers' union. In 1889 he published the first edition of *Père Peinard* (Father Indolent), a publication that appeared for 10 years. Elected CGT deputy general secretary in 1901, he was one of the authors of the Amiens Charter (1906) and one of the leading lights of the revolutionary syndicalist movement. An advocate of industrial sabotage, he published the famous study called *Le Sabotage*.

BIBLIOGRAPHY

Books

Bothereau, Robert. *Histoire du Syndicalisme Français*. Paris: PUF, 1946.

Dreyfus, Michel. *Histoire de la CGT*. Paris: Edition complexe, 1995.

Lefranc, Georges. *Histoire du Mouvement Syndical Français*. Paris: Librairie syndicale, 1937.

Louis, Paul. *Histoire du Mouvement Syndical en France, 1789–1918*. Paris: Librairie Valois, 1947.

Pennetier, Claude. *Dictionnaire Biographique du Mouvement Ouvrier Français (Cédérom): Le Maîtron*. Paris: Editions de l'Atelier, 1997.

Reynaud, Jean-Daniel. *Les Syndicats en France*. Paris: Armand Colin, 1975.

Trempé, Rolande. "Renaissance et recomposition du mouvement ouvrier, 1871–1895." In Claude Willard, *La France Ouvrière. Des Origines à 1920*. Paris: Editions sociales, 1993.

ADDITIONAL RESOURCES

Books

Bance, Pierre. *Les Fondateurs de la CGT à l'Épreuve du Droit*. Claix: La pensée sauvage, 1978.

Brécy, Robert. *Le Mouvement Syndical en France. 1871–1921. Essai bibliographique*. Paris: Mouton, 1963.

Dreyfus, Michel. *Les Sources de l'Histoire Ouvrière, Sociale et Industrielle en France: XIXe et XXe Siècles: Guide Documentaire*. Paris: Editions ouvrières, 1987.

Estey, James A. *Revolutionary Syndicalism. An Exposition and a Criticism*. London: P. S. King, 1913.

Jefferys, Steve. *Liberté, Egalité and Fraternité at Work: Changing French Employment Relations and Management.* Basingstoke: Palgrave, 2003.

Levine, Louis. *The French Labor Movement.* Cambridge: Harvard University Press, 1954.

Leroy, Maxime. *La Coutume Ouvrière.* Paris: Giard et Brière, 1913.

Mouriaux, René. *Les Syndicats dans la Société Française.* Paris: Presse Nationale de la Fondation de Sciences Politiques, 1983.

Ridley, Frederick. *Revolutionary Syndicalism in France.* Cambridge: Cambridge University Press, 1970.

Periodicals

Jefferys, Steve. "The Exceptional Centenary of the Confédération générale du Travail, 1895–1995." *Historical Studies in Industrial Relations* 3 (1997): 123–142.

—Sylvie Contrepois

Congress of Industrial Organizations

United States 1938

Synopsis

Formed in 1935 as a group within the American Federation of Labor (AFL), the Committee for Organization (CIO) clashed with its parent organization for the next several years. The leaders of the CIO felt that the organization must begin to recognize the masses of unskilled workers in large industries such as steelmaking and automobile manufacturing, whereas the AFL remained committed to its craft unionism approach, in which only skilled workers were organized. These ideological differences gradually were accompanied by a power struggle between leaders of the two groups. The AFL leadership finally expelled the CIO and its member unions in 1937, opening the way for the CIO to create its own federation. At a constitutional convention held in Pittsburgh from 14 to 18 November 1938, the CIO changed its name to the Congress of Industrial Organizations and took its place as a significant national labor federation.

Timeline

1922: Published this year James Joyce's novel *Ulysses* and T. S. Eliot's poem *The Waste Land* will transform literature and inaugurate the era of modernism.

1927: American inventor Philo T. Farnsworth demonstrates a working model of the television, and Belgian astronomer Georges Lemaître proposes the Big Bang Theory.

1932: In German elections, Nazis gain a 37 percent plurality of Reichstag seats, raising tensions between the far right and the far left. On a "bloody Sunday" in July, communists in Hamburg attack Nazis with guns, and a fierce battle ensues.

1937: Italy signs the Anti-Comintern Pact, signed by Germany and Japan the preceding year. Like the two others before it, Italy now withdraws from the League of Nations.

1937: Japan attacks China and annexes most of that nation's coastal areas.

1937: Stalin uses carefully staged show trials in Moscow to eliminate all rivals for leadership. These party purges, however, are only a small part of the death toll now being exacted in a country undergoing forced industrialization, much of it by means of slave labor.

1937: In the middle of an around-the-world flight, Amelia Earhart and her plane disappear somewhere in the Pacific.

1937: Crash of the *Hindenburg* in Lakehurst, New Jersey, kills 36 and ends the brief era when rigid airships promised to be the ocean liners of the skies.

1937: Pablo Picasso paints his famous *Guernica* mural dramatizing the Nationalist bombing of a town in Spain. Thanks to artists and intellectuals such as Picasso and Ernest Hemingway, the Loyalists are winning the battle of hearts and minds, even if they are weaker militarily, and idealistic young men flock from America to join the "Abraham Lincoln Brigade." Yet as George Orwell later reveals in *Homage to Catalonia,* the lines between good and evil are not clear: with its Soviet backing, the Loyalist cause serves as proxy for a totalitarianism every bit as frightening as that of the Nationalists and their German and Italian supporters.

1942: Axis conquests reach their height in the middle of this year. The Nazis control a vast region from Normandy to the suburbs of Stalingrad, and from the Arctic Circle to the edges of the Sahara. To the east, the Japanese "Co-Prosperity Sphere" encompasses territories from China to Burma to the East Indies, stretching deep into the western Pacific.

1947: The Marshall Plan is established to assist European nations in recovering from the war.

1952: Among the cultural landmarks of the year are the film *High Noon* and the book *The Invisible Man* by Ralph Ellison.

Event and Its Context

Background of the AFL-CIO Split

The American Federation of Labor (AFL) had been butting heads with the Committee for Industrial Organization (CIO) since the formation of the latter in 1935. The CIO was founded as a result of the AFL's failure to organize unskilled workers. Prominent members of AFL member unions, particularly John L. Lewis of the United Mine Workers of America (UMW), thought the time was right to organize under the banner of industrial unionism. This prompted the committee's founding members and its staff to act with an underlying urgency. With

John Lewellyn Lewis addresses 10,000 New England textile workers to open drive to unionize, Lawrence, Massachusetts. © Bettmann/Corbis. Reproduced by permission.

the creation of the CIO, national union membership was no longer restricted to skilled tradesmen or craftsmen. The CIO accepted unskilled workers; furthermore, it assisted in organizing among marginalized groups, specifically new immigrants, African Americans, and women. Union prohibitions against admitting members of these groups were otherwise conventional. "The CIO was clearly the most rigorous, expansive, and inclusive force that the mainstream labor movement had produced in over fifty years," wrote Robert H. Zieger.

The AFL executives, according to Walter Galenson, saw the CIO as "a challenge to the supremacy of the American Federation of Labor." Despite this perceived threat, AFL leaders, including William Green, the organization's president, remained steadfast in their conviction that industrial unionism was a waste of time and resources. Lewis was just as determined to see the CIO succeed.

By the fall of 1936, the AFL tired of the upstarts in what was supposed to be a union committee. At a UMW convention that same year, Lewis said the CIO would not back down from organizing. "[A]ll the members of the Executive Council of the American Federation of Labor will be wearing asbestos suits in hell before that committee [CIO] is dissolved." The executives took the challenge.

Unions Rebuked, then Revoked

Attempts to negotiate a truce between the factions were short-lived. All the CIO unions were expelled from the AFL in March 1937 for "betraying the union cause." CIO founding members Charles Howard and David Dubinksy had hoped for reconciliation with the AFL. Each group wanted to be dominant in the event of a merger. "The issue was no longer, if it ever had been in reality, industrial unionism versus craft unions. It was a contest for power," wrote Rhea Dulles Foster and Melvyn Dubofsky. "The welfare of labor as a whole was sacrificed to the rivalries of stubborn self-willed ambition."

The AFL executive council formally revoked the charters of the UMW; the Mine, Mill, and Smelter Workers; and the Federation of Flat Glass Workers in January 1938. That April, the charters of the Amalgamated Clothing Workers of America (ACWA); the Amalgamated Association of Iron, Steel, and Tinworkers; the United Textile Workers; the United Automobile Workers (UAW); the United Rubber Workers; and the Oil Field Workers were revoked by the AFL. The International Ladies' Garment Workers Union (ILGWU) charter was not.

In its first two years, the CIO had made marked achievements in organizing. It had decided in 1937 to abandon what were considered militant actions, such as sit-down strikes. Instead, its leaders began to rely on legislation from the National Labor Relations Board (NLRB) to gain new contracts. Also, late that same year, Lewis reorganized the union executive office. Many of his family members were given key roles within the union administration. This obviously gave more credence to the statement, "John L. Lewis is the CIO." But he was losing interest in the organization he had helped create and was actually spending more time on UMW activities.

The CIO was moving toward the creation of a new labor federation, thanks to its rift with the AFL. The leaders of the ILGWU were upset. They pointed to promises made by the CIO to "seek every means . . . to compose the rift in the ranks of organized labor." The ILGWU was also concerned about how effectively it could organize in smaller communities, particularly in nonindustrial areas.

In May 1938 the CIO became an independent union. Lewis was reportedly the only founding member unconcerned about this split with the AFL; rather, he saw it as a chance for the unions and their members to chart their own destinies. Two of the founding unions—the ILGWU and the Cap and Millinery Workers—decided to remain with the AFL, which stepped up organizing drives, asserting to workers that it was a conservative alternative to the radical CIO.

The Specter of Communism Provokes an AFL Witch Hunt

John P. Frey, president of the AFL metal trades department, and other AFL members repeatedly rejected attempts to broker a peace with the CIO by making allegations of communists operating within the CIO. The charges were accurate. Communists and sympathizers were indeed active in unions, including the Electrical, Radio, and Machine Workers; the Maritime Union; and the Woodworkers of America. Some rose to top positions within the CIO. Lewis said he could ignore people's politics in exchange for their help in promoting industrial unionism.

Paul W. Ward, writing in the *Nation*, described Frey as the "chief backbiter of the American labor movement," keen on "sabotaging the very unions [he] is supposed to lead." Ward painted Frey as an overwrought fraud, characterizing his speeches before AFL conventions as filled with "vast venom and a stupefying array of irrelevancies. It took hours for Frey to get to the point."

But Frey was persistent and passionate in his diatribes against the CIO. He also testified before the House Un-American Activities Committee, beginning on 13 August 1938. He listed 280 people—all organizers in CIO-affiliated unions—who were members of the Communist Party, thus perpetuating his contention that the CIO was essentially a communist front. President Franklin Delano Roosevelt was incensed that the committee proceedings had turned into little more than Frey's denunciation of the CIO. He demanded Frey's testimony be ended. "There is no menace here in Communism. The great menace in this country is in Nazism and fascism," Roosevelt purportedly said. "The AFL is tory and reactionary, but John L. Lewis is the most progressive, liberal labor leader I've known in my life."

These debates attempted to turn public sentiment against the CIO, regardless of the president's opinion. Publications such as the conservative *News Letter and Wasp*, circulating in San Francisco (*ca.* 19 August 1938), openly said the union's communist ties, no matter how loose, would bring about an end to the CIO. "Americanism will hold sway from now on, due to the co-operation with the A.F.L., of the American Legion and the Americans who have had the courage to fight on in the face of repeated set backs."

Lewis pressed forward with his plan to bring industrial unionism to every worker regardless of how political or popular opinion might cast shadows on his intentions. He remained focused on the single goal of unionizing the nation.

More Unions Affiliate with the CIO

The timing of the break with the AFL was not auspicious. The country was still in a recession and on the brink of a war in Europe. But several unions, many fairly new, did choose to affiliate with the CIO. These included the National Maritime Union; the United Electrical and Radio Workers of America; the American Newspaper Guild; the Transport Workers of America; and the International Woodworkers of America. These unions often faced competition from AFL members unions such as the International Brotherhood of Carpenters, in the case of the woodworkers. Workers in specific niches within industries gravitated to one or the other union.

The CIO held its constitutional convention on 14 November 1938 at Pittsburgh's Islam Grotto. Lee Pressman, an attorney, drafted the constitution. The dues structure decided upon helped the young organization greatly. The CIO charged 5 cents per capita dues. This enabled the creation of an active central organization and, in turn, more resources to use for organization. Lewis was elected president of the new CIO. Philip Murray and Sidney Hillman were elected vice presidents, and James B. Carey was elected secretary.

Union Dues Bring Union Blues

At the time of the convention, the CIO was in poor health, thanks largely to the recession. Dues were not being paid. Employers were still balking at union activity. Organizing in industries such as steel and textiles had slowed appreciably. The UMW remained the CIO's most solvent and stable member union CIO. Of its 4 million members, the CIO collected dues from just a third. The UMW not only paid most of the dues it did collect, it also footed the bill for the CIO staff at $30,000 per month. Overall, it was estimated to be responsible for 43 percent of the CIO funding—83.4 percent between 1936 and 1937—and the CIO also owed the UMW $1.2 million in loans. The ACWA was the other major financial contributor, followed by the ILGWU, which also loaned $100,000 to the union. With the departure of the ILGWU in late 1938, gone, too, was 12.5 percent of the CIO membership. The other stable income source was subscriptions to various CIO publications. Overall, the union was not fiscally healthy.

The union's finances were further complicated by the absence of a budget or cohesive spending plan. Lewis and the UMW controlled the budget; thus, they also dictated the CIO agenda. This led to problems such as ineffective expenditures—for example, drives to organize small groups of workers, such as communications and technical workers. The net to the CIO, in terms of both membership and finances, was negligible.

Additional problems resulted from power struggles within unions, notably the young UAW. Between 1937 and 1940, the UAW split, thanks to personal and ideological differences. Because the union could potentially bring more than a million members into the CIO fold, Lewis and the CIO executives decided to become involved in that specific union's political turmoil. By 1939 two separate UAWs existed: one affiliated with the AFL, the other connected to the CIO. Still, the squabbling continued.

Despite harsh criticism from the AFL, the CIO continued to grow. Its membership passed 2.65 million by 1940. Although CIO members were vocal and dynamic, their numbers would never surpass those of the AFL. Nonetheless, by the time of its 1955 merger with the AFL, the CIO counted five million members.

The AFL experienced a renaissance at the end of the depression. Workers perceived this more established organization as a moderate alternative to the CIO. Unions, including the Teamsters, Machinists, and Carpenters unions, allied with the AFL as a result. The AFL had also softened its hard-line stance on organizing unskilled laborers. Some locals went so far as to adjust membership criteria; most notable among these was the International Brotherhood of Electrical Workers. Unionization in the service industries, such as the hotel and restaurant industries, swelled the AFL ranks even more. AFL membership was about five million by 1940.

Key Players

Carey, James Barron (1911–1973): Born in Philadelphia, Carey worked for the Philco Radio Corporation and Philadelphia Storage Battery Company, where he became involved in unionism. He was president of both the Radio and Allied Trades National Labor Council (1933–1940) and the United Electrical, Radio, and Machine Workers of America (1936–1941). He served as the CIO secretary from 1938 until 1973 and as its secretary and treasurer from 1942 to

1973. He was also involved with the AFL-CIO after the unions merged in 1955.

Dubinsky, David (1892–1982): Dubinsky is best known for his lengthy tenure as president of the ILGWU. He started working in his family's bakery in Poland at age 11 and first participated in a strike at age 15. In the United States he became involved in union activity within a ILGWU local. In 1932 he undertook the monumental task of reorganizing the union. He remained active in union politics until his retirement in 1966, after which he served on public and private sector boards until his death in 1982.

Frey, John Philip (1871–1957): Born in Mankato, Minnesota, Frey was a teenager when he began working, first in a lumber camp, then as a grocery clerk. He became an apprentice iron molder in 1888. He joined the International Molders and Foundry Workers Union in 1893 and quickly ascended to union leadership roles. He became involved in AFL activities beginning in 1909. He was named head of the AFL metal trades department in 1927 and maintained this post until his retirement in 1950. Vocally opposed to industrial unionism, he orchestrated the suspension of all CIO unions from the federation and lobbied against the CIO.

Green, William (1873–1952): Green was vocal in his opposition to the CIO, which was formed while he was president of the AFL—the second since its founding (he succeeded Samuel Gompers). Despite his position, he was not a part of the union's inner circle, as were individuals such as William Hutcheson and Daniel Tobin.

Hillman, Sidney (1887–1946): A founder of the CIO and head of the Amalgamated Clothing Workers, Hillman was also instrumental in the founding the Non-Partisan League of the American Labor Party, the political party that provided union endorsement for President Franklin Delano Roosevelt in 1936. He served on the National Defense Advisory Council during World War II.

Lewis, John Llewellyn (1880–1969): The son of a Welsh coal miner who immigrated to the United States, as a young man Lewis worked in various jobs, including coal mining, before becoming a labor organizer. He was United Mine Workers of America (UMW) president and was active in the American Federation of Labor (AFL). Known as a fiery orator, he peppered his addresses with quotations from both the Bible and Shakespeare. He is said to have read those works in addition to classics such as the *Odyssey* and the *Iliad* and such authors as Oswald Spengler, Karl Marx, and Friedrich Engels as he crossed the country, organizing workers. He resigned from the AFL to form the Committee for Industrial Organization in 1935, which reorganized in 1938 as the Congress of Industrial Organizations. He served as its president from 1935 to 1940.

Murray, Philip (1886–1952): Born in Scotland, Murray was a leader of the United Mine Workers of America (UMW) and a founding member of the CIO. He was the chairman of the UMW's Steel Workers' Organizing Committee. Murray became the head of the CIO when Lewis resigned in 1940. He is often acknowledged for his work in seeing the union through World War II, a rough period for organized labor.

See also: *American Federation of Labor; AFL, CIO Merge; CIO Expelled from AFL; Committee for Industrial Organization; United Automobile Workers; Wagner Act.*

BIBLIOGRAPHY

Books

Bird, Stewart, Dan Georgakas, and Deborah Shaffer. *Solidarity Forever: An Oral History of the IWW.* Chicago: Lake View Press, 1985.

Craft, Donna, and Terrance W. Peck, eds. *Profiles of American Labor Unions.* Detroit: Gale Research, 1998.

De Caux, Len. *Labor Radical: From the Wobblies to CIO, A Personal History.* Boston: Beacon Press, 1970.

Dubinsky, David, and A. Raskin. *David Dubinsky: A Life with Labor.* Simon and Schuster, 1977.

Dubovsky, Melvyn, and Warren Van Tine. *John L. Lewis: A Biography.* Champaign: University of Illinois Press, 1986.

Finley, Joseph E. *The Corrupt Kingdom: The Rise and Fall of the United Mine Workers.* New York: Simon and Schuster, 1972.

Foner, Eric, and John A. Garraty, eds. *The Reader's Companion to American History.* Boston: Houghton Mifflin, 1991.

Foner, Philip S. *History of the Labor Movement in the United States,* vol. 2. New York: International Publishers, 1955.

———. *Women and the American Labor Movement: From World War I to the Present.* New York: Free Press, 1980.

Foner, Philip S., and Ronald L. Lewis, eds. *Black Workers: A Documentary History from Colonial Times to the Present.* Philadelphia: Temple University Press, 1989.

Foster, Rhea Dulles, and Melvyn Dubofsky. *Labor in America,* 2nd ed. New York: Thomas Y. Crowell, 1960.

Fraser, Steven. *Labor Will Rule: Sidney Hillman and the Rise of American Labor.* New York: Free Press, 1991.

Galenson, Walter. *The CIO Challenge to the AFL: A History of the American Labor Movement, 1935–1941.* Cambridge: Harvard University Press, 1960.

Murolo, Priscilla, and A. B. Chitty. *From the Folks Who Brought You the Weekend: A Short Illustrated History of Labor in the United States.* New York: New Press, 2001.

Murray, R. Emmet. *The Lexicon of Labor.* New York: New Press, 1998.

Selvin, David F. *The Thundering Voice of John L. Lewis.* New York: Lothrop, Lee, and Shepard, 1969.

Taft, Philip. *Organized Labor in American History.* New York: Harper and Row, 1964.

Zieger, Robert H. *The CIO, 1935–1955.* Chapel Hill: University of North Carolina Press, 1995.

Periodicals

Ward, Paul W. "Presenting John P. Frey." *Nation* 144, no. 7 (13 February 1937): 176–177.

ADDITIONAL RESOURCES

Le Blanc, Paul. "Congress of Industrial Organizations: Constitutional Convention" (22 January 2003). <http://www.pittsburghaflcio.org/CIO.html>.

—Linda Dailey Paulson

Congress of South African Trade Unions

South Africa 1985

Synopsis

The early 1980s saw a wave of labor organization in South Africa. One result of this flurry of union activity was the creation of the Congress of South African Trade Unions (COSATU) in 1985. Between 1981 and 1985 a number of South African unions and federations negotiated to establish this national labor organization. Although the talks were often difficult and several groups withdrew, labor leaders did succeed in forming the sought-after national congress. In subsequent years COSATU played a major role in the South African labor movement, leading campaigns to raise wages and protest government policies that harm workers.

Timeline

1965: African Americans in the Watts section of Los Angeles riot for six days. Thirty-four people are killed, over 1,000 injured, and fires damage $175 million in property.

1974: In a bout with George Foreman in Zaire, Muhammad Ali becomes only the second man in history (the first was Floyd Patterson) to regain the title of world heavyweight champion.

1979: More than a year after Afghan communists seized control of their nation, Afghanistan is in disarray, and at Christmas, Soviet tanks roll in to restore order, as they once did in East Germany, Poland, Hungary, and Czechoslovakia. This time, however, the task of suppressing the local populace will not prove so easy: little do the Soviets know that they are signing on for a decade-long war from which they will return in defeat.

1982: Israeli troops invade Lebanon in an attack on the Palestine Liberation Organization (PLO).

1985: A new era begins in the USSR as Chernenko dies and is replaced by Mikhail Gorbachev, who at 54 years old is the youngest Soviet leader in decades.

1985: In a year of notable hijackings by Muslim and Arab terrorists, Shi'ites take a TWA airliner in June, Palestinians hijack the Italian cruise ship *Achille Lauro* in October, and fundamentalists take control of an Egyptian plane in Athens in November.

1988: A terrorist bomb aboard a Pan Am 747 explodes over Lockerbie, Scotland, killing 259 people on the plane and 11 more on the ground.

1990: Iraq invades Kuwait, seizing oil reserves, and the United States begins mobilizing for war.

1995: The Aum Shinrikyo cult causes a nerve-gas attack in a Tokyo subway, killing eight people and injuring thousands more.

2002: The Catholic Church is rocked by allegations of sexual molestation carried out by priests.

Event and Its Context

Four Years of Unity Talks

Between 1981 and 1985 South African labor leaders held union talks that resulted in the formation of COSATU. Despite the fact that there was much mistrust and conflict due to differences of interest, politics, organizational methods, and personality, talks began in earnest during August 1981, when more than 100 representatives from 29 unions met in Cape Town. The meeting was convened by the General Workers Union (GWU), and the country's major independent unions attended the meeting. These included the Food and Canning Workers Union (FCWU), the African Food and Canning Workers Union (AFCWU), the South African Allied Workers Union (SAAWU) and the affiliates of the Federation of South African Trade Unions (FOSATU), and the Council of Unions of South Africa (CUSA).

An early test of labor unity came in 1982. When labor organizer Neil Aggett died while in police custody, union leaders called for a protest action. All union members were called to stop work for 30 minutes on 11 February. Some 100,000 workers participated in the protest. It was the first union-organized initiative since the 1950s that mobilized workers throughout the country over an issue not directly related to the workplace.

The second unity summit took place in April 1982. The main topic of discussion was the registration of unions with the government. The antiregistration faction warned that registered unions would be controlled by the government and would end up becoming reformist. The registration faction claimed to be aware of the dangers of co-option and argued in favor of taking advantage of the space opened up by workers' pressure on the state. Despite these disagreements, the labor leaders resolved to continue to work toward a union federation.

The third summit, held in July 1982 in Port Elizabeth, was the most bitter of all. The seven "community" unions put forward seven "non-negotiable" principles as the basis of the new federation. These were nonregistration, shop-floor bargaining, binding federation policy, worker control, nonracialism, participation in community issues, and the rejection of national and international reactionary bodies. Soon a deadlock developed, and it seemed no federation would be formed. However, some labor leaders continued to push for a federation, and a fourth summit to discuss the formation of such an organization convened in Cape Town. This meeting was well attended, drawing large worker delegations that discussed the steps needed to es-

tablish a federation. With one exception, the unions present agreed to participate in the formation of the new federation, and the delegates created a feasibility committee.

A number of problems nearly ended the talks once again. The unions were competing for membership, which sometimes led to accusations and resentment between various organizations. Also, FOSATU felt little pressure to form a new federation, as its affiliates had a rapidly growing membership and were benefiting from the well-organized federation. There was a feeling that unity talks were a waste of time and that those unions wanting unity should simply affiliate to FOSATU. In addition, some union leaders felt that the group of seven community unions were not truly committed to industrial unions.

Despite these problems, some of the union leaders decided to hold one additional meeting. Several unions left the unity talks at this point, but the process continued, and those remaining in the talks, representing about 300,000 workers, committed themselves to forming a new federation. The situation was made more difficult by the growing unrest in South Africa's Black townships. Union leaders and workers argued over how to respond to the increasing national crisis. Many participated in a two-day work stoppage, with some 800,000 workers taking part.

Meanwhile, the practical aspects of launching the federation were progressing smoothly and a draft constitution was circulated for discussion. Another meeting took place at Ipelegeng on 8–9 June 1985. Delegates discussed two main issues: the draft constitution, which proposed a tight federation, and the five unifying principles of nonracialism, one-union-one-industry, worker control, representation on the basis of paid-up membership, and national cooperation. The most hotly debated principle was nonracialism. The Ipelegeng meeting also separated out those unions wanting to be part of the launching congress and those wanting to stay out. There were still differences among the unions moving towards COSATU, but these and other issues were left unresolved, to be debated and ironed out within the new federation. During the final feasibility meeting, delegates discussed a name for the new federation, eventually deciding on the Congress of South African Trade Unions.

The Living-wage Campaign

After its establishment in 1985, COSATU undertook a number of major campaigns. One of COSATU's first activities was to launch the living-wage campaign. Beginning in 1986 the campaign's aim was to unite workers around a common set of demands and to coordinate their struggle to ensure success. Indeed, South African workers did achieve gains in terms of organization, wages, conditions, and benefits, with some of their demands for paid public holidays, education, and training becoming law.

Labor leaders at the first COSATU meeting adopted a resolution called the national minimum living-wage resolution that sought a national minimum living wage. Workers would decide exactly how much the minimum wage would be, and the amount should automatically increase when prices increased. It also included a demand that employers open their books so that workers could understand the profit system. This campaign strengthened COSATU's relationship with community organizations and certain political movements, as all were concerned with ensuring that South African workers and their families earned enough to live a decent life. For example, the campaign had great appeal to South African miners, who traditionally had earned very low wages.

COSATU formally launched the campaign in 1987. The campaign had several key demands, including a living wage for all workers, a 40-hour workweek, job security, six months maternity leave, and the right to decent education and training. In response, the South African government banned rallies and publications and raided labor offices, claiming that the campaign was a communist plot. At the same time, employers instituted lockouts and called in the security forces.

A long strike wave accompanied the living-wage campaign. A December 1986 wage strike continued into 1987. Then railroad and postal workers went on strike. Later in the year, mineworkers embarked on a massive national wage strike, called off after three weeks when employers began dismissing tens of thousands of workers. In subsequent years, the living-wage campaign continued, as COSATU unions extended their demands. South African labor leaders believe that the campaign remains relevant as they attempt to eliminate the wage gap between management and workers, men and women, and between skilled and unskilled workers.

The Campaign Against the Labor Relations Act

A second major COSATU campaign was its movement against the government's Labor Relations Act (LRA). The significant growth in numbers and strength of South Africa's labor unions in the early 1980s threatened apartheid's cheap labor system and the political control of the apartheid regime. In response to labor activities such as COSATU's living wage campaign, in September 1987 P. W. Botha's government amended the LRA. The amendments sought to weaken the growing union movement and undermine the gains made by restricting the right to strike, reversing the gains achieved by the unions, and curbing union activity by threatening punitive damages for strike actions.

COSATU reacted with a campaign to protest the changes. The anti-LRA campaign included lunchtime worker demonstrations, and because of restrictions on the right to protest, members spread their message on trains and buses. COSATU also lodged a formal complaint with the International Labor Organization (ILO), thus making the issue an international one. When the government banned COSATU from engaging in any political activities, labor leaders convened a special congress in which they called for three days of national protest against the LRA. This led to a three-day national strike involving nearly three million workers. Employers retaliated by dismissing thousands of workers.

The government initially agreed to postpone the amendments and to negotiate with workers over specific issues. However, in September 1988 the government passed the Labor Relations Amendment Act (LRAA), and the amendments passed without any changes. The struggle continued, however, and in 1990 workers joined with certain business interests to demand changes from the government. In October 1990 the government signed a labor accord that reversed the 1988 amendments and

set the stage for negotiations on basic rights for farm and domestic workers, an LRA for public sector workers, and a commitment from the government to consult labor and business on key issues concerning them.

Key Players

Barayi, Elijah (1930–1994): Barayi served as the first president of Congress of South African Trade Unions (COSATU). He had been involved in labor and social struggles since the 1950s as a member of the African National Congress. He later was a leader of the National Union of Mineworkers (NUM). He played a key role in the unity talks of the early 1980s that led to the creation of COSATU.

Mufamadi, Fholisani Sydney (1959–): Mufamadi was the first assistant general secretary of COSATU. He was active in the labor movement of the early 1980s in South Africa. He was then influential in organizing COSATU in 1985. After serving for 14 years as one of COSATU's leaders, Mufamadi became the South African minister for provincial affairs and constitutional development.

Naidoo, Jayaseelan (1954–): Starting in the 1970s, Naidoo worked as a teacher and activist in South Africa. In the late 1970s he began working as a union organizer for the Federation of South African Trade Unions (FOSATU). He played a key role in the 1985 establishment of COSATU and was elected its first secretary general, serving in that capacity until 1993. He then was elected to the South African Parliament, and in 1996 Naidoo was given the post of minister for posts, telecommunications, and broadcasting.

BIBLIOGRAPHY

Books

Beck, Roger. *The History of South Africa*. Westport, CT, and London: Greenwood Press, 2000.

James, Wilmont G. *Our Precious Metal: African Labour in South Africa's Gold Industry, 1970–1990*. Bloomington and Indianapolis: Indiana University Press, 1992.

Thompson, Leonard. *A History of South Africa*. New Haven, CT, and London: Yale University Press, 1990.

Wilson, Francis. *Labour in the South African Gold Mines, 1911–1969*. Cambridge, MA: Cambridge University Press, 1972.

Other

Congress of South African Trade Unions Web site (cited 22 November 2002). <http://www.cosatu.org.za/>.

—Ronald Young

Supreme Court Chief Justice William Howard Taft. The Library of Congress.

Coronado Coal v. UMWA

United States 1925

Synopsis

The U.S. Supreme Court heard two separate *Coronado* cases, each of which issued from a violent Arkansas coal strike in 1914. In 1922 the Court ruled that the actions of the strikers did not violate the Sherman Antitrust Act because the plaintiff-company did not show that the strikers intended to impede interstate commerce. The plaintiffs then refiled their petition on the strength of new evidence, and in 1925 the Court reversed its earlier decision and ruled that the strike did in fact violate antitrust law. The *Coronado* doctrine was a major setback to organized labor, for it called into question the legality of any strike that interrupted production of goods that entered interstate commerce.

Timeline

1910: Neon lighting is introduced.

1915: A German submarine sinks the *Lusitania*, killing 1,195, including 128 U.S. citizens. Theretofore, many Ameri-

cans had been sympathetic toward Germany, but the incident begins to turn the tide of U.S. sentiment toward the Allies.

1920: Bolsheviks eliminate the last of their opponents, bringing an end to the Russian Civil War. By then, foreign troops, representing a dozen nations that opposed the communists, have long since returned home.

1922: Inspired by the Bolsheviks' example of imposing revolution by means of a coup, Benito Mussolini leads his blackshirts in an October "March on Rome" and forms a new fascist government.

1923: Conditions in Germany worsen as inflation skyrockets and France, attempting to collect on coal deliveries promised at Versailles, marches into the Ruhr basin. In November an obscure political group known as the National Socialist German Workers' Party attempts to stage a coup, or putsch, in a Munich beer hall. The revolt fails, and in 1924 the party's leader, Adolf Hitler, will receive a prison sentence of five years. He will only serve nine months, however, and the incident will serve to attract attention for him and his party, known as the Nazis.

1925: Wyoming Democrat Nellie Tayloe Ross becomes the first woman governor elected in the United States.

1925: European leaders attempt to secure the peace at the Locarno Conference, which guarantees the boundaries between France and Germany, and Belgium and Germany.

1925: In Tennessee, John T. Scopes is fined for teaching evolution in a public school. There follows a highly publicized trial at which famed attorney Clarence Darrow represents the defense, while the aging Democratic populist William Jennings Bryan argues for the state. The "Scopes Monkey Trial" symbolizes a widening divisions between rural and urban America, and though the court decides in favor of the state, it is clear that the historical tide is turning against the old agrarian order symbolized by Bryan—who dies during the trial.

1925: Released from Landsberg Prison, Adolf Hitler is a national celebrity, widely regarded as an emerging statesman who offers genuine solutions to Germany's problems. This year, he publishes the first volume of *Mein Kampf* (My Struggle), which he dictated in prison to trusted confederate Rudolf Hess. The second and final volume of Hitler's opus, a mixture of autobiography, "history," and racial rant, will appear two years later.

1928: Sixty-five nations sign the Kellogg-Briand Pact, outlawing war.

1930: Naval disarmament treaty signed by the United States, Great Britain, France, Italy, and Japan.

1935: Italians invade Ethiopia, and the response by the League of Nations—which imposes sanctions but otherwise fails to act—reveals the impotence of that organization.

Striking union miners, Lick Creek District, West Virginia. © Getty Images. Reproduced by permission.

Event and Its Context

The Battle in the Coal Mines

The labor dispute began in 1914. The Bache-Denman Coal Company was the principal owner of a number of coal-mining companies in Sebastian County, Arkansas, including the Coronado Coal Company. For years Bache-Denman had operated most of its mines using union labor and in fact had a contract with local District 21 of the United Mine Workers of America (UMWA) that was due to expire on 1 July 1914. Like other unionized companies in the bituminous coal industry, Bache-Denman faced stiff competition from nonunion mines, which

could sell coal at lower prices because they did not have to pay the relatively high wages unionized miners received. The UMWA realized that to survive, it had not only to organize non-union mines but also to ensure that unionized mines remained that way.

Bache-Denman, though, had different ideas. In March 1914 the company decided to close down its unionized mines and re-open them on 6 April on an open, or nonunion, basis. Anticipating trouble in the area's union towns, the company hired guards from a detective agency, armed them with rifles, stretched cable around Prairie Creek Mine No. 4, brought in a number of out-of-state workers, and sent notices to workers in the company's houses that they had to vacate unless they remained in the employ of the company. In response, area miners gathered in protest, disarmed the guards, and shut down the mine, which filled with water when the pumps were stopped.

The company won an injunction against the union miners in federal district court and attempted to reopen the mine first under the protection of U.S. deputy marshals, and then of private guards. Mining operations were about to begin when, on 17 July, a force of union workers and sympathizers armed with guns that had been provided and paid for by District 21 attacked the mine, routed the guards, destroyed property and equipment with dynamite and torches, and even murdered two mine employees.

The Battle in the Courts

Organized labor in the 1920s was reeling. It thought that it had won the right to exert collective economic pressure on employers in the form of strikes, boycotts, and other means with the passage of the Clayton Act of 1914, which stated that union activities did not violate antitrust law. The act, however, granted employers an escape clause in its reference to unions' "lawfully carrying out legitimate objects," for it left it in the judiciary's hands to decide whether union activities were lawful or legitimate in particular cases. In one of the first of these cases, *Duplex Printing Company v. Deering* (1921), the U.S. Supreme Court ruled that the International Association of Machinists' boycott against the Duplex Printing Company violated the Sherman Antitrust Act because it was staged with the specific intent to restrain interstate commerce.

It was in this context that Bache-Denman, through the Coronado Coal Co., brought suit against the United Mine Workers in the District Court for the Western District of Arkansas, alleging that the union destroyed property to consummate a conspiracy to restrain interstate trade. The company claimed damages of $740,000, an amount that would be tripled under Section 7 of the Sherman Act. After prolonged litigation, the Court of Appeals essentially affirmed the district court's judgment of $200,000 against the union, which was then tripled.

The union appealed, and the case came before the U.S. Supreme Court in 1922 as *United Mine Workers of America v. Coronado*. In the "first" *Coronado* case, the union thought it won a victory when the Supreme Court overturned the Court of Appeals and vacated the judgment, ruling that the national union had not authorized the strike and that the local union had not violated the Sherman Act. The Court reasoned that because coal mining as such was not interstate commerce, federal antitrust law did not extend to it.

More important, however, the Court provided the company with grounds for an amended complaint. It noted that the company had failed to provide evidence that the local union's intent was to monopolize or restrain interstate commerce within the meaning of the Sherman Act. It was not enough to show simply that the strike reduced the amount of coal in the marketplace; any strike had that effect. Rather, the company had to show that there was a conspiracy to restrain trade or to suppress competition—that is, to keep *nonunion* coal from entering the marketplace. Virtually inviting the company to amend its complaint, the Court stated that if Bache-Denman could have produced evidence that the local union was part of a conspiracy to eliminate nonunion coal from the market, it would have won the case.

Bache-Denman accepted the Court's invitation and immediately began the search for new evidence. Based on the results of that search, the company amended its complaint and the legal process began again. The case, now *Coronado Coal Co. et al. v. United Mine Workers of America et al.,* the "second" *Coronado* case, again worked its way to the Supreme Court, which heard it on 7 January 1925.

The company's chief new witness was James K. McNamara, who was secretary of Local Union No. 1526 and worked for the Central Coal and Coke Company, a unionized competitor of Bache-Denman. McNamara, one of the leaders of the bloody events of 17 July 1914, was convicted for violating the original injunction against the strike and sentenced to two years in prison. He testified that between the riot in April and the July conflict, he met with Pete Stewart, the president of District 21. During that meeting Stewart said that he had met with UMWA president John P. White and that the two had formed a plan to prevent Bache from producing coal. Later, McNamara himself met with White in Arkansas. During their conversation White said to him, "Stewart told me that they cannot get enough men to operate the mine. If they do that, we must prevent the coal from getting into the market." When asked whether White had said why, McNamara responded, "He said, 'Because if Bache coal, scab dug coal, got into the market it would only be a matter of time until every union operator in that country would have to close down his mine, or scab it, because the union operators could not meet Bache competition.'"

McNamara went on to testify that White instructed him to go back and tell the workers what he had said. He also testified that he heard a speech in which Stewart offered to provide guns and ammunition to all the families in the area and said that "if it was necessary he would sacrifice his own life to prevent Bache getting coal out there."

The company provided other new evidence as well. It entered an extract from the February 1914 convention proceedings of District 21 in which the delegates discussed the dangers of competition from nonunion mines in Colorado, Alabama, and Tennessee. It also brought forward a former president of District 21 who testified that the danger that nonunion coal would force a nonunion wage scale on the workers was a constant subject of discussion among the union's officers and members.

On 25 May, Chief Justice William Howard Taft delivered the opinion of the Court, which had been persuaded by the new evidence. The Court reiterated that the national union was not involved, but in ruling against the local union, the Court found that it had violated the Sherman Antitrust Act: "When the intent of those unlawfully preventing the manufacture or production [of an article of commerce] is . . . to restrain or control the supply entering and moving in interstate commerce, or the price of it in interstate markets, their action is a direct violation of the Anti-Trust Act." The opinion stated that the Court believed that the evidence of the second trial proved that there was intent to restrict the movement of nonunion coal to markets outside of Arkansas.

The Aftermath of *Coronado*

The Court's ruling in the second *Coronado* case had a profound impact on the United Mine Workers. The decision dampened the UMWA's organizing efforts. In the years that followed, many mine operators filed copycat suits against the union, alleging that the union violated the Sherman Act by attempting to suppress competition from nonunion coal; in fact, the UMWA in these years was named as the defendant in antitrust actions more than any other union.

More importantly, the Court's sweeping decision in *Coronado* cast doubt on the legality of virtually any strike. Until *Coronado*, the Court, in such cases as *Danbury Hatters* (1908) and *Gompers v. Bucks Stove and Range Co.* (1911), had applied the Sherman Act primarily to secondary boycotts. In *Coronado*, however, the Court ruled that a strike directly against a company and not involving other business enterprises was unlawful. All a company had to do to show a violation of antitrust law was prove that the union intended to suppress interstate trade.

It was not until 1940 that the Supreme Court nullified the doctrine that it had announced in *Coronado*. The case, *Apex Hosiery Co. v. Leader*, arose in connection with a labor dispute that in many respects resembled *Coronado*. The Apex Hosiery Company refused to accede to the demands of the Philadelphia hosiery workers union that it recognize the union as the workers' bargaining agent. The union called for a strike; workers occupied the plant, and the strike grew violent and destructive. The company filed suit, asking for triple damages under the Sherman Act. The Court ruled in favor of the union and declared finally that union efforts to eliminate nonunion competition by collective economic pressure did not violate the Sherman Antitrust Act.

Key Players

Taft, William Howard (1857–1930): Born in Cincinnati, Ohio, Taft enjoyed a long and distinguished career. Starting in 1892 he was a federal circuit judge until President Theo-

dore Roosevelt appointed him civil governor of the Philippines in 1900, then secretary of war in 1904. Taft was elected president in 1908, but he lost the 1912 election to Woodrow Wilson. In 1913 he joined the Yale law school faculty, which he left in 1921 when President Warren Harding appointed him Chief Justice of the Supreme Court, where he served until a month before his death.

White, John P. (1870–1934): Born in Coal Valley, Illinois, White was head of the Iowa district of the UMWA when, in 1907, he was elected vice president of the national union. Then in 1911 he was elected to succeed Thomas Lewis as president. He served until 1917, when Woodrow Wilson appointed him to the Wartime Federal Fuel Board.

See also: *Apex Hosiery Co. v. Leader; Clayton Antitrust Act; Gompers v. Bucks Stove; United Mine Workers of America.*

BIBLIOGRAPHY

Books

Gregory, Charles O. *Labor and the Law*. New York: W. W. Norton & Co., 1961.

Northrup, Herbert R., and Gordon F. Bloom. *Government and Labor*. Homewood, IL: Richard D. Irwin, 1963.

Taylor, Benjamin J., and Fred Witney. *Labor Relations Law*, 3rd ed. Englewood Cliffs, NJ: Prentice-Hall, 1979.

Other

Apex Hosiery Co. v. Leader, 310 U.S. 409 (1940).

Coronado Coal Co. et al. v. United Mine Workers of America et al., 268 U.S. 295 45 (1925).

United Mine Workers v. Coronado Coal Co., 259 U.S. 344 (1922).

—Michael J. O'Neal

D

Davis-Bacon Act

United States 1931

Synopsis

In 1931 the U.S. Congress passed the Davis-Bacon Act, which is still in effect in modified form. The act requires certain private contractors working on federal construction projects to pay their workers at least locally prevailing wages, as determined by the U.S. Department of Labor (which has used union pay scales as its guide), for the type of work being performed.

The Davis-Bacon Act was enacted to prevent nonlocal contractors from "invading" a region, using cheap labor, and disrupting local wage rates. In 1931 the use of immigrant and African American migrant workers, often far cheaper than local unionized workers, was the primary issue. As a result, some parties then and now have decried the act as a "Jim Crow" law. Since its passage, the Davis-Bacon Act has been a favorite of organized labor, for obvious reasons. In addition, several states have prevailing wage statutes that apply to nonfederal public work.

Timeline

1915: A German submarine sinks the *Lusitania*, killing 1,195, including 128 U.S. citizens. Theretofore, many Americans had been sympathetic toward Germany, but the incident begins to turn the tide of U.S. sentiment toward the Allies.

1920: League of Nations, based in Geneva, holds its first meetings.

1925: European leaders attempt to secure the peace at the Locarno Conference, which guarantees the boundaries between France and Germany, and Belgium and Germany.

1927: Charles A. Lindbergh makes the first successful solo nonstop flight across the Atlantic, and becomes an international hero.

1930: Naval disarmament treaty is signed by the United States, Great Britain, France, Italy, and Japan.

1930: Collectivization of Soviet agriculture begins, and with it one of the greatest crimes of the twentieth century. In the next years, as Soviet operatives force peasants to give up their lands, millions will die either by direct action, manmade famine, or forced labor. Overseas, however, and particularly among intellectuals and artists of the West, Soviet collectivization and industrialization are regarded as models of progress for the world.

1930: Pluto is discovered.

1933: Newly inaugurated U.S. president Franklin D. Roosevelt launches the first phase of his New Deal to put depression-era America back to work.

1935: Second phase of New Deal begins with the introduction of social security, farm assistance, and housing and tax reform.

1940: Hitler's troops sweep through western Europe, annexing Norway and Denmark in April, and in May the Low Countries and France. At the same time, Stalin—who in this year arranges the murder of Trotsky in Mexico—takes advantage of the situation to add the Baltic republics (Latvia, Lithuania, and Estonia) to the Soviet empire, where they will remain for more than half a century.

1945: April sees the death of three leaders: Roosevelt passes away on 12 April; the Italians execute Mussolini and his mistress on 28 April; and Hitler (along with Eva Braun, propaganda minister Josef Goebbels, and Goebbels's family) commits suicide on 30 April.

Event and Its Context

Origins and Ideas: The Prevailing Wage Concept

The Davis-Bacon Act and various related laws, together known as DBRA, comprise the "prevailing wage" law for the federal government. The concepts of a "prevailing wage" and a "living wage" law are related but not identical. The living wage movement is of recent origin, usually manifests itself on a local level, and calls for private companies working with or for the locality in some way to grant some of their workers a higher minimum wage, usually based on the local poverty rate. The prevailing wage is an older concept, usually applies specifically to construction and other public works projects, and requires that workers performing government contracts be paid at least the locally prevailing wage rate for the type of work they are performing.

The first prevailing wage law in the United States was a 1891 Kansas statute, enacted as one of a series of reforms that mainly followed a long-standing American Federation of Labor legislative program. Moral and economic theories were the foundation of many labor reforms of this period. The moral theory held that it was simply wrong to condemn workers to poverty in the name of cutting costs. The economic theory held that treating workers well could be positive economically, as they would then become more productive and better able to contribute to the economy.

The motivation behind the enactment or preservation of prevailing wage laws in particular appears to be multilayered. Many desired to use government's position as a prominent "buyer" of various services to protect local wage standards against the possibility of cheaper, mainly nonunion labor from outside a community being hired to perform a government contract and disrupting local pay scales. As a general rule, governments are legally obligated to award contracts to the "lowest

Robert Low Bacon. AP/Wide World Photos. Reproduced by permission.

qualified bidder," thus making the described situation a distinct possibility, especially in construction, wherein wages tend to be higher, workers more unionized, and nonlabor costs more fixed than in other sectors. Labor also feared that these cheaper out-of-area contractors would be less qualified and do poorer work than local contractors, especially unionized ones. Finally, some worried that the cheaper contractors may be less concerned with worker health and safety, thus indirectly creating an economic drain on the community.

Some have argued that, in many cases, the initial enactment of many of these laws had an at least partially racist intent, as the nonlocal labor at issue, in many places, consisted of African Americans and recent immigrants.

A Brief History of the Davis-Bacon Act

The idea of a national prevailing wage law dates back around the time of the Kansas statute, but it was not considered seriously until 1929, when Republican representative Robert Low Bacon, representing a district on New York's Long Island region, introduced a bill. In Bacon's district, a Veterans' Administration hospital was built in 1926, using nonunion laborers that were directly imported from the South, housed on-site by the contractor, and paid wages that were far beneath the prevailing wages of the community. Many, if not all, of these workers were African American. References to this fact during the 1931 debates on the Davis-Bacon Act are in large part responsible for the act's reputation in some quarters as a kind of "Jim Crow" law.

Bacon originally proposed to enact legislation to apply state wage laws to federal construction projects. New York had had a prevailing wage statute for some time. Bacon's bill failed for several years in a row, apparently because of the prominence of *laissez faire* economic thinking at the time. However, the perception that the Great Depression represented a failure of *laissez faire* economics facilitated a change in American thinking about government regulation of the economy. The depression caused a great deal of wage deflation, and any measure that might inflate wages suddenly seemed rather reasonable. A modified version of Bacon's bill found a Senate sponsor, Republican senator James J. Davis of Pennsylvania, a former secretary of labor. Although the act had other provisions, it was the prevailing wage concept that garnered the most attention.

Debates over the act, compared to more contemporary debates over its efficacy, were in the main relatively mild. The bill was enacted, with little apparent fanfare, on 3 March 1931 (PL 71-798). It was regarded as flawed, in large part because it was read to provide only for the awkward "post-determination" of prevailing wage rates; that is, after a project was completed, the Department of Labor would determine whether prevailing wages had been paid and would then seek redress for workers in those instances in which they had not been fairly compensated according to the terms of the act. Further, the act contained little if any in the way of enforcement or punishment mechanisms. After several attempts, Congress amended Davis-Bacon in 1935 (PL 74-403) into the form in which it has more or less stayed. Around 60 other acts have been enacted to apply the prevailing wage concept to various federal government contracts. Together, these statutes are known as DBRA (Davis-Bacon and Related Acts).

DBRA in the Twenty-first Century

By the early twenty-first century, the Davis-Bacon Act was located in 40 USC 276a *et seq*, and the related acts were found in various places. DBRA has the following main provisions, as described by the United States Department of Labor:

- Covers contractors and subcontractors performing federal construction contracts valued at $2,000 or more

- Requires all covered contractors or subcontractors provide prevailing wages and prevailing benefits for the kind of work being performed in the area in which it is being performed

- Specifies that certain apprentices and trainees can be paid a lower wage

- Requires that covered contractors and subcontractors pay employees weekly and submit various payroll records to the contracting agency

- Establishes various reporting and enforcement requirements and penalties

The Ongoing Controversy

DBRA, the various state prevailing wage laws, and the prevailing wage concept in general have become emotional issues for both sides of the debate. The following summary of the arguments opposed to and in favor of the Davis-Bacon Act is drawn from various sources, but the categories are mainly derived from a 1978 Congressional Research Service report.

Opposed to:

1) *The act was a depression-era measure that has outlived its usefulness.* The wage deflation brought about by the Great Depression has long since passed.

2) *The act interferes with the workings of a free competitive market.* "Pure market" forces should determine the wages for construction projects, government or otherwise. The degree to which prevailing wage determinations tend to rely on union pay scales only makes matters worse.

3) *The act is inflationary.* Prevailing wage laws by their nature push wages beyond market level and thus contribute to inflation, generally as well as in construction.

4) *The act gives an unfair advantage to unionized contractors.* "Open shop" nonunion contractors, used to paying lower wages and operating with more flexibility, will not be able to meet the requirements of the act as well as will unionized contractors and thus are shut out of public works projects.

5) *The act impedes the entry of minority groups into the construction industry.* Some data suggest that minorities are better represented in nonunion construction shops. Favoring unionized shops may therefore result in the exclusion of African American workers. Further, some statements made during the 1931 debates on the Davis-Bacon Act may be read as indicating that the act was intended to give white workers an edge over lower paid African American workers.

In favor of:

1) *The act was more than a depression-era measure, and the need for it has not diminished.* The prevailing wage concept predates the Great Depression. Further, construction workers may make high wages, but their work is seasonal; incomes can be less, or zero, during the off-season. Hence, the higher wages are needed for the well being of the workers, and this is perennial to this industry regardless of depression or other economic circumstances.

2) *The act prevents cutthroat competition and promotes fair competition based on decent labor standards.* Labor is among the easiest places to cut costs on a construction project. The market has already decided upon a fair construction wage. Without a prevailing wage law, the "lowest qualified bidder" principle would allow government in effect to depress artificially the local market wages and would promote contractors that cut costs at the expense of worker health, welfare, and safety.

3) *Paying the prevailing wage is simply a long-established federal government policy,* even on projects to which none of the DBRAs applies.

4) *The act is not inflationary and may in the long run reduce costs* by promoting labor peace, helping to keep up a decent level of productivity, and reducing the "costs" of decreased worker safety.

5) *The act's repeal or weakening could adversely impact apprenticeship programs in the construction industry,* and thus hurt minority groups.

James John Davis. AP/Wide World Photos. Reproduced by permission.

The Impact of the Act

Opinions regarding the impact of the Davis-Bacon Act are as diverse as those regarding its efficacy. The Congressional Research Service once admitted that it was basically impossible to determine exactly the economic impact of the Davis-Bacon Act and that the estimates on both sides of the argument were equally flawed.

The impact of the act, in some areas that are not specifically economic, is clearer. For example, the act has probably helped labor unions (though to what extent is impossible to determine) to maintain a foothold in an era that is hostile to them and their interests. It has probably played a role in maintaining construction wages at a relatively high level.

In the past 10 years or so, prevailing wage requirements have indirectly promoted the use of Project Labor Agreements (PLAs, also called Pre-Hire Agreements, or PHAs) in government construction contracts; such agreements have been common in the private sector for several decades. A PLA is an agreement between a contracting entity, such as a state or municipal government, and local labor organizations to either use union labor, to use contractors that agree to abide by union rules, or contractors that agree to come to terms with local unions over the rules of the project. PLAs are related to Davis-Bacon because they can be a shortcut to abiding by the prevailing wage requirement.

Key Players

Bacon, Robert Low (1860–1919): A Boston native, a Harvard graduate, and a Republican, Bacon represented a House district in the Long Island region of New York State from 1923 until his death. He was a colonel in the United States Army and is buried at Arlington National Cemetery. The Davis-Bacon Act appears to have been his primary achievement in the House.

Davis, James John (1873–1947): Born in South Wales and immigrated to the United States at the age of eight, with his parents, Davis performed a number of blue-collar industrial jobs, eventually moved to Pennsylvania, and served as secretary of labor from 1921 to 1930 under presidents Harding, Coolidge, and Hoover. In 1930, he was elected to the United States Senate as a Republican to fill a seat vacated by death. He served from 1930 to 1945, when he lost a reelection attempt. The Davis-Bacon Act appears to have been his primary achievement in the Senate.

See also: *American Federation of Labor; Jim Crow Segregation and Labor.*

BIBLIOGRAPHY

Books

Belman, Dale, and Paula B. Voos. *Prevailing Wage Laws in Construction: The Costs of Repeal to Wisconsin.* Milwaukee, WI: The Institute for Wisconsin's Future, 1995.

Bernstein, David E. *Only One Place of Redress: African Americans, Labor Regulations, and the Courts, from Reconstruction to the New Deal.* Durham, NC: Duke University Press, 2001.

Gould, John P., and George Bittlingmayer. *The Economics of the Davis-Bacon Act: An Analysis of Prevailing-Wage Laws.* Washington, DC: American Enterprise Institute, 1980.

Thieblot, Armand J. *Prevailing Wage Legislation: The Davis-Bacon Act, State "Little Davis-Bacon" Acts, the Walsh-Healey Act, and the Service Contract Act.* Philadelphia, PA: The Wharton School Industrial Research Unit, 1986.

Periodicals

Goldfarb, Robert S., and John F. Morrall. "The Davis Bacon Act: An Appraisal of Recent Studies." *Industrial and Labor Relations Review* 34 (1981): 191–206.

Griffaton, Michael C. "Prevailing Wage Laws." *Members Only: An Informational Brief Prepared for Members of the Ohio General Assembly by the Legislative Service Commission Staff* 122 (1998): 1–15.

Gujarati, D. N. "The Economics of the Davis-Bacon Act." *The Journal of Business* 40 (1967): 303–316.

Harlin, Kevin. "A Contract for Controversy." *Albany Times Union.* 10 June 2001.

Keyes, William A. "The Minimum Wage and the Davis-Bacon Act: Employment Effects on Minorities and Youth." *Journal of Labor Research* 3 (1982): 399–407.

Moreno, Paul. "An Ambivalent Legacy: Black Americans and the Political Economy of the New Deal." *Independent Review* 6 (2002): 513–531.

Northrul, Herbert R., and Linda E. Alario. "Government-Mandated Project Labor Agreements in Construction, the Institutional Facts and Issues and Key Litigation: Moving Toward Union Monopoly on Federal and State Financed Projects." *Government Union Review* 19 (2000): 1–159.

Pearce, James E. "The Minimum Wage and the Davis-Bacon Act: A Comment." *Journal of Labor Research* 3 (1982): 411–413.

Reynolds, Morgan O. "Understanding Political Pricing of Labor Services: The Davis-Bacon Act." *Journal of Labor Research* 3 (1982): 295–309.

Other

Fulton, Joseph F. *The Davis-Bacon Act: History, Administration, Pro and Con Arguments, and Congressional Proposals* (Report #78-161E). Washington, DC: Congressional Research Service, 1978.

Hughes, Tim. Michigan State AFL-CIO. "HB 4329 and 4383—Attack on Prevailing Wage." Memo to House Employment Relations, Training and Safety Committee. 16 October 2001 [cited 29 September 2002]. <http://www.miaflcio.org/legis/PWTestimony.htm>.

National Center for Policy Analysis. "Davis-Bacon Act Results in Racial Inequities" [cited 29 September 2002]. <http://www.ncpa.org/~ncpa/pd/unions/unionsb.html>.

Philips, Peter. *Kansas and Prevailing Wage Legislation.* Prepared for the Kansas Senate Labor and Industries Committee, February 20, 1998.

United States Congress, House of Representatives. Committee on Education and Labor. *Legislative History of the Davis-Bacon Act.* Washington, DC: Author, 1962.

Whittaker, William G. *The Davis-Bacon Act Suspension of 1971: The Nixon Administration, Organized Labor, and the Prevailing Wage Statute in Federal and Federally Assisted Construction* (Report # 79-249 E). Washington, DC: Congressional Research Service, 1978.

Wial, Howard. *Do Lower Prevailing Wages Reduce Public Construction Costs?* (Briefing Paper 99/2). Harrisburg, PA: Keystone Research Center, 1999.

—Steven Koczak

Dawes Severalty Act: *See* **General Allotment Act.**

Department of Commerce and Labor

United States 1903

Synopsis

The rise of labor unions after the U.S. Civil War led labor activists to seek government protection from business owners. In 1884 the federal government established the Bureau of Labor Statistics to gather data on labor, and four years later made it an independent agency. Businessmen, on the other hand, resented the hodgepodge of state and the federal regulatory bodies and laws and wanted the government to establish an agency to aid commerce. They also wanted the government to help them control or even break labor unions.

Timeline

1883: Foundation of the League of Struggle for the Emancipation of Labor by Marxist political philosopher Georgi Valentinovich Plekhanov marks the formal start of Russia's labor movement. Change still lies far in the future for Russia, however: tellingly, Plekhanov launches the movement in Switzerland.

1893: Henry Ford builds his first automobile.

1899: The Second Anglo-Boer War, often known simply as the Boer War, begins.

1903: Anti-Jewish pogroms break out in Russia.

1903: Henry Ford establishes the Ford Motor Company.

1903: Russia's Social Democratic Party splits into two factions: the moderate Mensheviks and the hard-line Bolsheviks. Despite their names, which in Russian mean "minority" and "majority," respectively, Mensheviks actually outnumber Bolsheviks.

1903: Polish-born French chemist Marie Curie becomes the first woman to be awarded the Nobel Prize.

1903: One of the earliest motion pictures, *The Great Train Robbery,* premieres.

1903: United States assumes control over the Panama Canal Zone, which it will retain until 1979.

1903: Wright brothers make their first flight at Kitty Hawk, North Carolina. Though balloons date back to the eighteenth century and gliders to the nineteenth, Orville Wright's twelve seconds aloft on 17 December marks the birth of practical human flight.

1906: The British Labour Party is established.

1913: Two incidents illustrate the increasingly controversial nature of the arts in the new century. Visitors to the 17 February Armory Show in New York City are scandalized by such works as Marcel Duchamp's cubist *Nude Descending a Staircase,* which elicits vehement criticism, and theatergoers at the 29 May debut of Igor Stravinsky's ballet *Le Sacré du Printemps* (*The Rite of Spring*) are so horrified by the new work that a riot ensues.

Philander Chase Knox. The Library of Congress.

Event and Its Context

In 1903 President Theodore Roosevelt, with the support of conservative Republicans in Congress and prominent businessmen, established the Department of Commerce and Labor to investigate business practices, assure fair trade, address labor issues, and aid commerce. The new department absorbed the independent Department of Labor over the protests of labor leaders. The move set back by another 10 years labor's efforts to gain its own cabinet-level representation in government.

Predecessors to the Department

Banking, industry, railroads, and manufacturing grew at phenomenal rates after the Civil War. The gross national product (the measure of the total value of all goods and services produced in the United States in one year) rose from less than $5 billion in 1850 to $88 billion in 1900. The majority of workers, however, did not share in this wealth. Child labor, long workdays and workweeks, low wages, and hazardous conditions led to labor agitation and the creation of unions in the 1860s and 1870s. After failing to get help from the federal government, unions led by the Knights of Labor turned to state governments to help protect them from growing abuses by corporations.

In 1869 the state of Massachusetts formed a bureau of labor statistics. When its first two commissioners went beyond its mandate of collecting data and began pursuing reform to reme-

President Theodore Roosevelt. The Library of Congress.

dy labor problems, employers protested the bureau's lack of objectivity. Carroll Wright, who had no experience with either statistics or labor problems, took over the bureau. He returned the bureau to impartially gathering statistics and refused to advocate for labor. His work, though, proved so successful that 12 other states formed similar bureaus by 1883. In 1884 Congress established the Bureau of Labor Statistics in the Department of Interior to compile data on national employment levels, wage scales, work hours, and industrial accidents. After rejecting Terence Powderly of the Knights of Labor as being too radical for the post, President Chester A. Arthur appointed Wright as commissioner. Wright carried out his work along the same lines as he had in Massachusetts.

In 1888, after further agitation from labor interests, Congress established an independent Department of Labor but did not give it cabinet-level status. Powderly was offered the position of commissioner but turned it down; Wright continued as commissioner. The department expanded its investigations into railroad labor, industrial education, working women, compulsory life insurance for factory workers, and housing for working people. Through the 1890s, as labor unions continually lost strikes and support among the general public or in state legislatures, paradoxically, the push for federal representation de-

clined, too. Wright opposed a situation in which the head of a Department of Labor would change with every administration, which further hampered efforts by labor to get a voice in the cabinet.

Business Interests Overtake Labor's Needs

The efforts of labor unions since the 1860s to gain cabinet-level representation in the federal government received an inadvertent boost from businessmen. The establishment of the Department of Commerce and Labor was a direct result of the wave of corporate mergers that began in the 1890s and culminated with the creation of the Northern Securities Company in 1902. Overall, between 1898 and 1902, more than 2600 firms were absorbed into other companies as a result of mergers. The railroad mergers that occurred during the 1890s and 1900s left 32 railroad companies controlling 80 percent of the railroad mileage in America by 1910.

The mergers came at the expense of labor. As the companies grew in economic power, in one violent confrontation after another, they sought the destruction of labor unions in order to keep labor costs down. One newspaper warned that the increasing antagonism between trusts and labor might "lead to one of the greatest social and political upheavals that has been witnessed in modern history." The mergers also renewed fears that trusts and holding companies might stifle economic opportunity for the middle class, and that their overvaluation might destabilize the stock market. Similar concerns in the 1870s and 1880s led to the passage of the Interstate Commerce Act in 1887 and the Sherman Antitrust Act in 1890 to fight restraint of trade practiced by the trusts. (Ironically, businesses used the Sherman Act to break strikes on the grounds that unions were in restraint of trade.) The laws proved largely ineffective against businesses, and the public and press clamored for something to be done. President Theodore Roosevelt agreed and began searching for a solution that would be acceptable to both business leaders and the public.

Like many Republicans, Roosevelt did not oppose trusts in general. Instead, he distinguished between "good" trusts, which were deemed socially useful, and "bad" trusts, which injured the public welfare. All but the most radical believed it wrong to break up large corporations. As an alternative, Roosevelt, like many of his party's members, favored publicizing corporate affairs. If the public was informed about corporate activities, citizens could then make appropriate decisions about investment and policy. Possible remedies would reveal themselves after business practices were exposed. In fact, the Republican platform in 1900 had called for a department of commerce, in part to publicize corporate behavior. Roosevelt's predecessor, William McKinley, supported this view and had been contemplating some antitrust actions before he was killed in 1901. Roosevelt differed from McKinley only in how he wanted to handle informing the public, which was by having the president manage the information.

Roosevelt's position, therefore, was not radical at all, but was in line with the conservative wing of the Republican Party. What worried businessmen about Roosevelt was his assertion that national interest was more important than any individual private economic interest. In other words, he believed that the federal government reserved the right to regulate corporations, notwithstanding the Supreme Court ruling in *United States v. E. C. Knight* (1895) that the Sherman Act did not outlaw monopolies of manufacturing. Roosevelt understood the political ramifications of inaction. Not doing anything about corporations would give the Democrats a potent weapon.

Roosevelt consulted with George W. Perkins, who represented business tycoon J. P. Morgan, about corporate regulation before issuing his 1901 "Message to Congress." In the message, Roosevelt pointed out that state laws had not halted the trusts, nor could state action provide adequate regulation of interstate corporations. Consequently, Roosevelt said, the federal government should "assume power of supervision and regulation over all corporations doing an interstate business." Banks were already subject to federal regulation, he noted. Roosevelt argued that a federal law similar to the Interstate Commerce Law could be passed, if Congress was willing to try. If they were not, then he called for a constitutional amendment to confer the power.

Roosevelt also called for a cabinet-level department and secretary of commerce and industries, with jurisdiction over industrial, labor, and merchant-marine matters. This would be one phase of "a comprehensive and far-reaching scheme of constructive statesmanship," in Roosevelt's words, to broaden markets, protect business interests, and solidify the nation's international economic standing. These proposals, he declared, would achieve those goals while "scrupulously safeguarding the rights of wage worker and capitalist, of investor and private citizen, so as to secure equity" between all men in the country. His willingness to equate the rights of laborers to those of businessmen was a clear indication that the challenges facing labor were not understood and would remain subservient to business in the eyes of the government.

Despite the unwillingness of Congress to pass legislation along the lines the president had suggested in 1901, Roosevelt remained undeterred on the issue of trusts. In his next annual message, he declared that corporations "should be managed under public regulation." He spoke out "against misconduct, not against wealth." He repeated his previous call for stronger legislation and a department of commerce. This time Congress responded.

What had transpired between the two messages that Congress would heed this latest message, which did not fundamentally differ from the first? Two events: the Anthracite Coal Strike of 1902 and the Northern Securities antitrust suit. In the autumn of 1902, President Roosevelt had intervened to settle the coal strike fairly through arbitration between the United Mine Workers and the coal mine operators. The strike revealed the economic and political strength of labor unions and the need for cooperation between labor and owners. In the wake of that settlement, the time seemed right for giving both sides representation in the cabinet. The president and many Republicans, however, considered business and commerce to be more important than labor. The cabinet-level department created by Congress reflected those biases.

The unresponsiveness of Congress to the 1901 message prompted the administration to pursue an alternate course of action. U.S. Attorney General Philander Knox filed an antitrust suit against the Northern Securities Company in February 1902 in an effort to assert federal power over trusts. Northern Securities was the result of James J. Hill, E. H. Harriman, and J. P.

Morgan combining their separate railroads to control the railroads in the Northwest. When Knox realized that the various state antitrust lawsuits might not make it to the Supreme Court, he informed Roosevelt that the merger was illegal under the Sherman Act and filed in federal court. After announcing the suit, Morgan met privately with Roosevelt and asked whether they could have their representatives "fix it up." Roosevelt told him that it could not be done. Morgan inquired whether the administration intended to attack his other interests. In keeping with his belief of there being good and bad trusts, Roosevelt informed him he did not, unless it was found they, too, had done something illegal.

Knox had several obstacles to overcome if the suit were to succeed. In 1901 the Justice Department had no permanent office space; its employees worked out of hotel rooms and scattered office spaces near the White House. There existed no antitrust division with appropriately trained legal hands, nor did the department have much control over its own financial resources. Knox served as lead counsel on the case and assembled a team of lawyers to aid him. Roosevelt believed the lawsuit provided the crucial first step in establishing the government's authority.

While the Northern Securities case wound its way through the court system, Knox defined the administration's objectives for dealing with trusts. In a January 1903 letter to the Senate Judiciary Committee, Knox suggested that Congress make it illegal for railroads to give or receive rebates, a practice about which small shippers had long complained and that railroads also wished to eliminate. Knox next asked for the creation of a commission to investigate the operations and conduct of all corporations engaged in interstate and foreign commerce. Third, he encouraged the passage of an antitrust law "aimed at what we certainly know to be unreasonable practices directly restrictive of freedom of commerce." His last recommendation was for a measure to expedite antitrust cases in the court system.

Knox also needed increased appropriations for his department and more personnel to enforce antitrust laws. Congress responded quickly to this with a half a million dollars, and the antitrust division of the Justice Department was established. The bill outlawing rebates faced little opposition, in part because the railroads supported it because they stood to benefit greatly from it. Gathering support for a department of commerce took more effort. Roosevelt's recruitment of George W. Perkins of Morgan's firm to exercise influence on Capitol Hill did not bode well for labor. The president's secretary, George B. Cortelyou, also courted key Republicans.

Creating the Department

In January 1903 the Senate passed the bill that created the Department of Commerce and Labor. The bill contained no language regarding any kind of agency or bureau to investigate and publicize corporations, which had been the reason that Roosevelt had supported creating the department. The House version, however, contained that language and was passed. The conference committee attached an amendment that had been written by Knox that authorized the new commissioner of the bureau of corporations to assemble data that would allow the president to make recommendations to Congress, and make the data public, if he so desired. After the media revealed some embarrassing revelations about executives from Standard Oil encouraging some senators to kill the amendment, the Senate quickly passed the bill. The president signed Department of Commerce and Labor in February 1903.

The department immediately became one of the largest and most complex organizations in the government. Several of the oldest activities that had been overseen by the federal government were gathered together in one place to aid commerce. Labor, however, took a backseat. Over the protests of labor supporters, the Department of Labor was absorbed into the new department and made subordinate. Carroll Wright resigned his position rather than accept the inferior position offered him. The bureau collected information on hours of labor, earnings, and means of promoting the material and social well-being of workers. Constant disagreements between the labor and commerce factions, however, limited the effectiveness of the new department. Much of the debate was over the issue of immigration. Labor supporters called for restrictions on immigration, so as to reduce competition for jobs, whereas business interests opposed the restrictions because immigrant labor helped keep labor costs and wages down.

The department also included:

- The Bureau of Corporations, designed to monitor trusts under the Sherman Act, which prohibited the restraint of trade through the use of unfair methods of competition such as rebates and price-fixing

- The Bureau of Immigration, which enforced the immigration laws

- The Bureau of Navigation, which monitored merchant vessels

- The Lighthouse Board, which maintained lighthouses to facilitate safe navigation

- The Steamboat Inspection Service, which inspected steamships to ensure safe waterborne commerce

- The Bureau of Statistics, which compiled and published statistics on domestic and foreign commerce

- The Coast and Geodetic Survey, which determined the size and shape of the states and coastal areas

- The Bureau of Standards, which ensured the accuracy of measurements

- The Bureau of the Census, which counted the population every 10 years

- The Bureau of the Fisheries, which supervised fisheries and the Alaskan seal-fur trade

George B. Cortelyou, the first secretary of the new Department of Commerce and Labor, was the first of four secretaries, all of whom were either businessmen or financiers, in a 10-year period. Labor unions were unsatisfied with the focus and composition of the department and again began to push for a cabinet-level department to represent only labor. Ten more years of lobbying passed before a Democrat-controlled Congress created a separate Department of Labor in 1913.

After more than 30 years of seeking a cabinet-level department to aid labor in its efforts to combat business, labor supporters had their request granted, and had a seat in the president's cabinet. Ironically, it was the misbehavior of corporations, and not the rise of unions, that led to the department's creation. The Department of Commerce and Labor, however, was established for the benefit of business, was run by businessmen for its first 10 years and served as a poor advocate for the needs of labor.

Key Players

Cortelyou, George B. (1862–1940): Cortelyou was appointed stenographer for President Grover Cleveland in 1895 and then served as personal secretary to McKinley and Roosevelt. In that era, the president's secretary functioned as the modern chief of staff does. As secretary, Cortelyou helped shape the modern presidency. After one year as secretary of commerce and labor (1903–1904), he served as postmaster general (1905–1907), and secretary of the treasury (1907–1909).

Knox, Philander Chase (1853–1921): A corporate lawyer before becoming attorney general (1901–1904), Knox proved important in the implementation of Roosevelt's antitrust policy. He served one term as a U.S. senator (1904–1909) and then became secretary of state (1909–1913). He later returned to the Senate for a second term (1917–1921).

Perkins, George W. (1862–1920): Perkins made New York Life Insurance Company a dominant company before joining J. P. Morgan's firm in March 1901. In addition to managing public relations, he brokered merger deals and cooperated with the Bureau of Corporations, including the deal on behalf of U.S. Steel to avoid an antitrust suit. A firm believer in federal regulation of corporations, Perkins became a major supporter of Roosevelt and was a major financial backer of Roosevelt's 1912 bid for the White House.

Roosevelt, Theodore (1858–1919): A lifelong public servant, war hero, and author, Roosevelt became president upon William McKinley's assassination in 1901. The first president willing to prosecute trusts, he earned the nickname "The Trustbuster," even though Roosevelt's successor filed more suits in four years than Roosevelt did in eight. He ran for a third term of office in 1912 on the Progressive Party ticket but lost.

Wright, Carroll D. (1840–1909): Wright's varied experience included a term (1872–1873) in the Massachusetts senate before his appointment as state commissioner of labor. As U.S. commissioner of labor, he organized the Bureau of Labor Statistics and stimulated objective research on labor problems. From 1902 until his death, he was president of Clark College at Worcester, Massachusetts. His books include *The Industrial Evolution of the United States* (1887) and *Battles of Labor* (1906).

See also: *Anthracite Coal Strike; Department of Labor; Knights of Labor; Sherman Antitrust Act.*

BIBLIOGRAPHY

Books

Cutrona, Cheryl. *The Department of Labor.* Broomall, PA: Chelsea House Publishers, 1988.

Gould, Lewis L. *The Presidency of Theodore Roosevelt*. Lawrence: The University Press of Kansas, 1991.

Griffin, Robert J., Jr. *The Department of Commerce*. Broomall, PA: Chelsea House Publishers, 1991.

Kolko, Gabriel. *The Triumph of Conservatism: A Reinterpretation of American History, 1900–1916*. New York: The Free Press, 1963.

Morris, Edmund. *Theodore Rex*. New York: Random House, 2001.

Other

Grossman, Jonathan. "The Origin of the U.S. Department of Labor." Original publication, *Monthly Labor Review* (March 1973). Available in a modified version [cited 28 August 2002] from U.S. Department of Labor Web site. <http://www.dol.gov/asp/programs/history/dolorigabridge.htm>.

ADDITIONAL RESOURCES

Books

Gould, Lewis L. *Reform and Regulation: American Politics, 1900–1916*. New York: Wiley, 1978.

Lombardi, John. *Labor's Voice in the Cabinet*. New York: Columbia University Press, 1942.

Roosevelt, Theodore. *Autobiography*. New York: Charles Scribner's Sons, 1913.

—James G. Lewis

Samuel Gompers. AP/Wide World Photos. Reproduced by permission.

merce and Labor was divided into the Department of Commerce and the Department of Labor, which included the Bureau of Labor Statistics, formerly the Bureau of Labor; the Bureau of Immigration and Naturalization; and the Children's Bureau. The secretary of labor had the power to "act as a mediator and to appoint commissioners of conciliation in labor disputes."

Department of Labor

United States 1913

Synopsis

On 4 March 1913, only hours before he left office, President William H. Taft signed the legislation (Public Law 426-62) "to Create a Department of Labor" with cabinet status. The first attempts to form such an agency occurred after the Civil War when labor leader William Sylvis called for the creation of a Department of Labor with a secretary chosen from the ranks of working men. Between 1864 and 1900 more than 100 bills and resolutions related to a Department of Labor were introduced unsuccessfully. A Bureau of Labor, without cabinet status, was created on 27 June 1884 with Carroll D. Wright as its first commissioner. Labor leaders continued to lobby for a cabinet-rank department with mixed success. President Grover Cleveland signed a bill on 21 March 1888 that set up a toothless Department of Labor within the Department of Interior. This new department was subordinate again with a Department of Commerce and Labor (1903–1913), established by act on 14 February 1903, consolidating functions that previously had been scattered through several government departments and agencies. By the act of 4 March 1913, the Department of Com-

Timeline

1893: Wall Street stock prices plummet on 5 May, precipitating a market collapse on 27 June. In the wake of this debacle, some 600 banks and 15,000 other businesses fail. The nationwide depression will last for four more years.

1903: Russia's Social Democratic Party splits into two factions: the moderate Mensheviks and the hard-line Bolsheviks. Despite their names, which in Russian mean "minority" and "majority," respectively, Mensheviks actually outnumber Bolsheviks.

1909: Robert E. Peary and Matthew Henson reach the North Pole.

1911: In China, revolutionary forces led by Sun Yat-sen bring an end to more than 2,100 years of imperial rule.

1913: In the month-long Second Balkan War, Bulgaria marches against Serbia and Greece but is defeated by an alliance of those two with Romania. A border dispute between Bulgaria and Turkey soon follows, resulting in the Turkish recapture of Adrianople.

William H. Sylvis. © Corbis. Reproduced by permission.

1913: Two incidents illustrate the increasingly controversial nature of the arts in the new century. Visitors to the 17 February Armory Show in New York City are scandalized by such works as Marcel Duchamp's cubist *Nude Descending a Staircase,* which elicits vehement criticism, and theatergoers at the 29 May debut of Igor Stravinksy's ballet *Le Sacré du Printemps* (*The Rite of Spring*) are so horrified by the new work that a riot ensues.

1913: In New York and Boston, striking garment workers win a pay raise and shorter hours.

1913: Henry Ford develops the first moving assembly line.

1913: Two new amendments are added to the U.S. Constitution: the Sixteenth (income tax) and Seventeenth (popular election of senators). Also, this year sees the passage of a bill creating the U.S. Federal Reserve System.

1915: A German submarine sinks the *Lusitania,* killing 1,195, including 128 U.S. citizens. Theretofore, many Americans had been sympathetic toward Germany, but the incident begins to turn the tide of U.S. sentiment toward the Allies.

1919: With the formation of Third International (Comintern), the Bolshevik government of Russia establishes its control over communist movements worldwide.

1923: Conditions in Germany worsen as inflation skyrockets and France, attempting to collect on coal deliveries promised at Versailles, marches into the Ruhr basin. In November, an obscure political group known as the National Socialist German Workers' Party attempts to stage a coup, or putsch, in a Munich beer hall. The revolt fails, and in 1924 the party's leader, Adolf Hitler, will receive a prison sentence of five years. He will only serve nine months, however, and the incident will serve

to attract attention for him and his party, known as the Nazis.

Event and Its Context

The creation of the U.S. Department of Labor with cabinet status came after a century in which the United States had remained a largely agricultural nation. Unskilled workers fared poorly in the early U.S. economy; they received as little as half the pay of skilled craftsmen, artisans, and mechanics. About 40 percent of the workers in the cities were low-wage laborers and seamstresses in clothing factories and often lived in dismal circumstances. With the rise of factories, children, women, and poor immigrants were commonly employed to run machines.

Rise of Industrialization

The late nineteenth century and the twentieth century witnessed a period of substantial industrial growth, as many Americans left farms and small towns to work in factories. The workplaces were organized for mass production and characterized by a reliance on relatively unskilled labor and low wages. Against this background, the U.S. labor movement expanded, as labor unions gradually developed clout and a series of federal bureaus and agencies were created to deal with the complex issues it caused.

During the era of industrialization in America, between the Civil War and World War I, dangerous and unhealthy working conditions and frequent serious accidents with resulting economic and social losses prompted calls for the government to take action. The initial pressure for government remedies came primarily from labor groups. Investigations by state labor bureaus of dangers to workers' safety and health helped fuel a successful drive by labor for state factory acts in the industrial North, beginning with the Massachusetts Factory Act of 1877. The system of factory inspection that evolved produced significant improvements in the workplace. After 1900, middle- and upper-class Progressives added their support to the movement for government regulation of workers' safety and health. These reformers sought to overcome shortcomings that had developed in factory legislation and enforcement. They also introduced the twin innovations of workers' compensation and administrative rule-making by industrial commissions. To complement these new public initiatives, many corporations established voluntary safety programs. In addition, industrial health received special scientific and public attention in the so-called Progressive Era (1900–1917) and was the subject of several government and private investigations.

The first steps toward legislation and regulation were the investigation of conditions and publication of the results. In response to labor lobbying and public concern for the condition of the working classes, most states had established bureaus of labor statistics. Massachusetts set up the first such bureau in 1869. These bureaus conducted investigations into all facets of labor and industry and published the data in their annual reports. One of their primary concerns was the emerging problem of hazardous industrial working conditions. The bureaus sent questionnaires to employers; interviewed workers; collected descriptive and statistical data on deaths, injuries, and illnesses;

and investigated unhealthy trades. The bureaus' reports also included examples of safe and healthful workplaces. These published accounts constituted a relatively unscientific but often shocking survey of the conditions under which millions of Americans worked. State bureaus helped arouse public opinion to rally behind labor's campaign for protective legislation.

After Massachusetts, states that followed with state inspection bureaus were Rhode Island, a textile manufacturing state, and its Bureau of Industrial Statistics; the New York Bureau of Labor Statistics, which published one of the first large-scale surveys of industrial accidents in a report on workers' compensation; the New Jersey Bureau of Statistics on Labor and Industry, which attempted to produce useful statistics on occupational health; and the Bureau of Industrial Statistics of Pennsylvania, which listed all reported victims of industrial accidents alphabetically by name, with brief descriptions of the cause and nature of the accident, especially those in sweatshops. Ohio also published individual descriptions of serious accidents, some poignant, some repulsive, in the annual reports of its Bureau of Labor Statistics. Wisconsin did not require employers to report workplace accidents to its Bureau of Labor and Industrial Statistics, though some volunteered the information anyway. Minnesota also lacked mandatory reporting of industrial accidents, but, like Pennsylvania, it did list known accidents individually in its reports.

As early as the 1830s, labor groups investigated shop safety and health conditions and published accounts of them but in the 1870s and in the early 1880s, labor groups such as the Knights of Labor were the driving force behind the establishment of state labor statistics bureaus and state factory legislation. Enforcement of the laws gradually came under close scrutiny from historians, social scientists, and even state legislatures. These groups traced the origins of workers' safety and health laws and the history of factory inspection and evaluated the system that had developed. Some looked closely at one state, and others surveyed the national picture. During the Progressive Era, there was considerable interest in investigation and amelioration of hazardous working conditions. President Theodore Roosevelt helped labor interests. He championed the conservation movement, one of his favorite causes; he broadened its scope to include human life. Social reformers helped Roosevelt's cause immeasurably by establishing settlement houses, assisting workers and their families, and entreating employers to eliminate dangerous working conditions and other abuses. Muckraking journalists and others gave nationwide publicity to accidents and unsafe conditions.

In 1884, when Germany became the first country to provide compensation to workers injured in accidents, other countries quickly followed suit. In the United States, however, workers still had to sue their employers for compensation for injuries. It was difficult or almost impossible, under common law principles, to prove to a jury that the employer was at fault, so the size of awards varied enormously. States started to change this, however, partly from pressure by organized labor. By the early 1900s a few states had passed rather weak workmen's compensation laws. These did not hold up in court or were too limited in coverage, such as the one in Maryland, whose 1902 law providing accident compensation regardless of fault was declared unconstitutional by the state supreme court in 1904.

In the early 1900s labor started to support workmen's compensation after years of opposition. Awards were sometimes very large, but workers wanted a safe workplace more than compensation for injuries. Then, in 1908 the U.S. government initiated a rather limited compensation system for its employees that sparked interest at the state level. In 1909 New York, Wisconsin, and Minnesota set up commissions to investigate the question of employers' liability for accidents; eight states followed in 1910, and nine more came aboard in 1911. The reports of these commissions showed that most employers were in favor of workmen's compensation; in May 1911 Wisconsin became the first state to establish a workmen's compensation system. By 1921, 46 jurisdictions had workmen's compensation laws in force.

First Efforts for a Labor Bureau

The origin of the U.S. Department of Labor grew from these struggles, but its development was a long one. The idea for an actual labor bureau began after the Civil War when William Sylvis, the most important labor leader of his day, advocated the creation of a Department of Labor. He protested that there was no department whose "sole object the care and protection of labor." He and his followers petitioned President Andrew Johnson for a secretary of labor, chosen from the ranks of working men, to be labor's voice in the cabinet. Between 1864 and 1900 more than 100 bills and resolutions relating to a Department of Labor were introduced in Congress. In 1867 the House of Representatives created a standing committee on labor, marking the first federal recognition of labor's importance, but the campaign for a national Department of Labor died, temporarily, with the death of Sylvis in 1869.

After several state bureaus of labor were established, beginning in Massachusetts, labor refocused its strategy to create a federal labor department. By the late 1870s and early 1880s, the movement for a U.S. bureau grew as the American economy recovered from the 1873 depression and labor organizations such as the Knights of Labor expanded their political influence.

In the 48th Congress, a bill was introduced to establish a Bureau of Labor to collect information on the subject of working people and the "means of promoting their material, social, intellectual, and moral prosperity." The Senate approved, and President Chester Arthur signed the bill (27 June 1884). The new bureau was placed in the Department of the Interior and, after tense negotiations between labor leaders and President Arthur, Carroll D. Wright of the Massachusetts labor bureau became the first U.S. commissioner of labor, a position he was able to retain into the next administration.

The new Bureau of Labor was a success, and it was supported by organized labor, which lobbied Congress for larger appropriations. President Cleveland recommended a larger staff and budget for the new bureau to facilitate investigation and arbitration of labor disputes. Labor leaders continued to campaign for a more influential "National Department of Labor" with cabinet status. In 1888 a bill for such a purpose, with support from the Knights of Labor, went to committee, which dropped the idea of cabinet rank because the Bureau of Labor did not have enough support in Congress to gain cabinet status. Instead, the Department of Labor would be independent of the Department of Interior. The bill passed with only token opposition. On

21 March 1888 Cleveland signed the bill into law. Carroll Wright headed the new department; he held the post for many years.

The new Department of Labor, even without cabinet status, gained much-needed prestige. Its reports covered subjects ranging from railroad labor, industrial education, and working women to the effect of machinery on labor, labor legislation, compulsory insurance, and housing for working people. In addition, in 1895 the department inaugurated the *Bulletin of Labor*, now the *Monthly Labor Review*.

Beginning in the 1890s, congressmen introduced bills to establish a Department of Commerce in which the existing Department of Labor again would be reduced to a subordinate bureau. Labor leaders strongly opposed this and revived demands for their own "direct representative in the councils of the President." There was little chance of success with the growing power of business and industry against it. When Theodore Roosevelt became president in 1901, he wanted a cabinet officer, to be designated secretary of commerce and industries, to deal with commerce in its broadest sense, including the concerns of labor. The 57th Congress introduced such a bill. The act to create a Department of Commerce and Labor passed with little opposition; President Roosevelt signed it on 14 February 1903 and appointed his private secretary, George B. Cortelyou, as the first secretary of commerce and labor.

Department of Labor Established

That same year, the American Federation of Labor persuaded the Democratic Party to adopt a plank in its platform that pledged "the enactment of a law creating a Department of Labor, represented separately in the President's Cabinet." The Republicans controlled both the White House and Congress in 1903, however, so the chances of such legislation were limited. Still, Democratic congressmen continued to introduce bills for a separate Department of Labor, but none gained sufficient support to pass. Then, in 1910 the Democrats won control of the House, and 15 union members won congressional seats. Congressman William B. Wilson, formerly an officer of the United Mine Workers, became chairman of the House Committee on Labor; he championed creating an independent department. Representative William Sulzer of New York introduced a Department of Labor bill in 1912, which passed the House with little opposition. It almost died in the Senate Committee on Education and Labor, but Senator William Borah (D-Idaho) rescued it and the Senate passed the bill without a record being kept of the votes.

President Taft did not like the bill, as he felt the new department would hinder efficient administration. As a lame duck president, however, Taft was in no position to oppose the legislation. Incoming president Woodrow Wilson had already selected former congressman William B. Wilson as the first secretary of labor, pending Senate confirmation, and his administration had enough support to reenact a similar measure over a last minute Taft "pocket veto." Instead, Taft tried to bargain for the use of antitrust laws against unions, a counterattack against organized labor's support of a "rider" to the Sundry Civil Appropriations Bill, which Taft opposed. The rider prevented money authorized for the Department of Justice from being used to prosecute organizations or individuals who combined for the purpose of bettering conditions of labor.

Taft signed the bill on 4 March 1913. That morning, the *New York Times* reported that the outgoing president might veto the bill, send his reasons to Congress, and give the advocates of the measure a chance to override his veto, if they could. After an early breakfast, with only a few hours before Woodrow Wilson took office, President Taft went to the executive office in the Senate, observed by the incoming president-elect, who arrived at the office before being received in the Senate. During the closing hours of his administration, Taft signed Public Law 426-62, "An Act to Create a Department of Labor." In his message to Congress on 4 March 1913, he wrote, "I sign this bill with considerable hesitation. . . . I forbear, however, to veto this bill, because my motive in doing so would be misunderstood. . . . The purpose of the Department of Labor shall be to foster, promote, and develop the welfare of the wage earners of the United States, to improve their working conditions, and to advance their opportunities for profitable employment."

The first headquarters of the new Department of Labor was across the street from the U.S. Department of the Treasury, on Pennsylvania Avenue, N.W., in Washington, D.C.

Key Players

Gompers, Samuel (1850–1924): One of the most important figures in the U.S. labor movement, Gompers was founder and first president of the American Federation of Labor. He established the pattern of labor's struggles for improved working conditions. Beginning in the 1890s, he revived labor's demand for its own "direct representative in the councils of the President" and for an independent cabinet department. Gompers was the 1988 honoree in the Department of Labor's Hall of Fame.

Powderly, Terence Vincent (1849–1924): Powderly was a labor organizer and head of the Knights of Labor, the first successful trade union organization. He was a recognized spokesman for the "army of the discontented," an official in the Department of Commerce and Labor and, after its creation, a commissioner of conciliation in the Department of Labor. He advised President Cleveland to make the Bureau of Labor a cabinet department.

Sylvis, William H. (1828–1869): Sylvis was a Pennsylvania labor leader and president of the National Labor Union. He advocated the creation of a Department of Labor during the administration of President Andrew Johnson for the "sole object the care and protection of labor."

Wilson, William Bauchop (1862–1934): Wilson was a labor leader who helped organized the United Mine Workers of America, and U.S. congressman (D-Pennsylvania), in which capacity he was chairman of the House Committee on Labor. He was appointed the first secretary of labor by President Wilson shortly after the department's creation in early 1913.

Wright, Carroll Davidson (1840–1909): Wright was chief, Massachusetts Bureau of Statistics of Labor, the first such organization in the world, and the first commissioner of the Department of Labor (without cabinet rank) in the U.S. Department of the Interior.

See also: *Bureau of Labor; Department of Commerce and Labor; Knights of Labor.*

BIBLIOGRAPHY

Books

Grossman, Jonathan. *The Department of Labor.* Praeger
    Library of U.S. Government Departments and Agencies
    Series, no. 37. New York: Praeger, 1973.
Lombardi, John. *Labor's Voice in the Cabinet: A History of
    the Department of Labor from Its Origin to 1921.* New
    York: Columbia University, 1942.
MacLaury, Judson. "Labor, Department of." In *A Historical
    Guide to the U.S. Government*, edited by George T.
    Kurian. New York and Oxford: Oxford University, 1998.
Morris, Richard B. *Government and Labor in Early America.*
    New York: Columbia University, 1946.
Powderly, Terence V. *Thirty Years of Labor.* Revised ed.
    Cleveland, OH: Excelsior, 1890.
Terrell, John U. *The United States Department of Labor: A
    Story of Workers, Unions, and the Economy.* New York:
    Meredith, 1968.

Periodicals

Grossman, Jonathan, "The Origin of the U.S. Department of
    Labor." *Monthly Labor Review* (March 1973): 3–7.
Weinstein, James. "Big Business and the Origins of
    Workmen's Compensation." *Labor History* (spring
    1967): 159–160, 162–170.

Other

MacLaury, Judson. Telephone interview by the author. 30
    August 2002.
Public Law No. 426, Chapter 141. "An Act to Create a
    Department of Labor." U.S. *Statutes at Large.* 62nd
    Congress, Session III. (1912–1913): 736–738.
U.S. Department of Labor. *The Anvil and the Plow: A
    History of the United States Department of Labor,
    1913–1963.* Compiled and edited by O. L. Harvey.
    Washington, DC: U.S. Dept. of Labor, Office of
    Information, Publications, and Reports; for sale by the
    Government Printing Office, 1963.
U.S. Department of Labor. *Reports of the Department of
    Labor, 1913; Report of the Secretary of Labor [William
    B. Wilson] and Reports of the Bureaus.* Washington, DC:
    Government Printing Office, 1914.
U.S. Department of Labor Web site [cited 9 October 2002].
    <http://www.dol.gov/asp/programs/history/main.htm>.

—Martin J. Manning

Dockers' Strike

Great Britain 1889

Synopsis

The London dock strike during the summer of 1889 was a
crucial victory for British trade unionism in two main ways.

First, the strike secured the "dockers' tanner," increasing pay
to six pence per hour, and altered the arbitrary system of hiring
("contracting") men at the dock gates. Second, the strike
marked the advance of "new unionism" or organizing among
less skilled workers and deploying more militant tactics, often
with socialist leaders. Although the advances of new unionism
were soon contested by employers, the breakthrough could not
be reversed. Public support and effective leadership were at the
heart of the strike's success. Moreover, the events of 1889 were
a noteworthy representation of the power and imagery of a burgeoning labor movement and of international solidarity marked
by the dockers marching and demonstrating through the city of
London. Australian dockers lent international support by boosting the strike fund with substantial donations.

Timeline

1869: Black Friday panic ensues when James Fisk and Jay
Gould attempt to control the gold market.

1874: Norwegian physician Arrnauer Gerhard Henrik Hansen
discovers the bacillus that causes leprosy. This marks
the major turning point in the history of an ailment (now
known properly as Hansen's disease) that afflicted humans for thousands of years and was often regarded as
evidence of divine judgment.

1882: Agitation against English rule spreads throughout Ireland, culminating with the assassination of chief secretary for Ireland Lord Frederick Cavendish and permanent undersecretary Thomas Burke in Dublin's Phoenix
Park. The leader of the nationalist movement is Charles
Stewart Parnell, but the use of assassination and terrorism—which Parnell himself has disavowed—makes
clear the fact that he does not control all nationalist
groups.

1885: Belgium's King Leopold II becomes sovereign of the
so-called Congo Free State, which he will rule for a
quarter-century virtually as his own private property.
The region in Africa, given the name of Zaire in the
1970s (and Congo in 1997), becomes the site of staggering atrocities, including forced labor and genocide, at
the hands of Leopold's minions.

1887: John Emerich Edward Dalbert-Acton, a leader of the opposition to the papal dogma of infallibility, observes, in
a letter to Cambridge University professor Mandell
Creighton, that "Power tends to corrupt, and absolute
power corrupts absolutely."

1889: Indian Territory in Oklahoma is opened to white settlement.

1889: Flooding in Johnstown, Pennsylvania, kills thousands.

1889: The 986-foot (300.5-m) Eiffel Tower, part of the Paris
exposition, becomes the tallest structure in the world. It
will remain so until the Chrysler Building surpasses it
in 1930.

1889: Discontented southern farmers merge their farm organizations to form the Southern Alliance.

1891: Construction of Trans-Siberian Railway begins. Meanwhile, crop failures across Russia lead to widespread
starvation.

John Burns addressing group of striking London dockers, London, England. © Hulton/Getty Images. Reproduced by permission.

1895: Guglielmo Marconi pioneers wireless telegraphy, which in the next three decades will make possible the use of radio waves for commercial broadcasts and other applications.

1899: Polish-born German socialist Rosa Luxembourg rejects the argument that working conditions in Europe have improved and that change must come by reforming the existing system. Rather, she calls for an overthrow of the existing power structure by means of violent international revolution.

Event and Its Context

1880s London

London's social and political atmosphere in the second half of the 1880s was quite as hot as the weather in August 1889. Radical social campaigners and journalists such as Andrew Mearns and W. T. Stead and the Jack the Ripper murders of 1888 had focused attention on the social conditions of the East End. Charles Booth published his survey, *The Life and Labour of the People of London*, in 1889. There had been demonstrations organized and led by socialists and riots against unem-

ployment during 1886 and 1887. This culminated in "Bloody Sunday" in November 1887, after which socialist orator John Burns was among those imprisoned. Two strikes also boosted the confidence of the dockers. In London's East End, the previously un-unionized matchgirls of Bryant and May, organized by Annie Besant, a member of the socialist Fabian Society, struck successfully in the summer of 1888. The gas workers, organized by Will Thorne, a member of the Marxist Social Democratic Federation (SDF), also struck in August 1889.

As the British economy faced greater international competition, the economic uncertainty of the docks themselves contributed to conditions that led up to the strike. The West and East India Company, which had built Tilbury dock some 20 miles downstream of the established East End docks in 1886, went bankrupt two years later. Tilbury functioned well below capacity. That London was "overdocked" further reduced the stability of dock employment, but also meant the employers' position was weakened.

The "Dockers' Tanner"

The five-week strike started on 10 August 1889 during a period of high employment. The array of different unions on the docks, including Ben Tillett's tea porters, joined together. At the dock gates, strikers urged the unorganized "casuals" not to sign on for work. The unifying aim was the "dockers' tanner," a rate of six pence an hour. Since an 1872 strike, pay had been at best five pence an hour (for the likes of ship loaders, the stevedores, whose union was formed from the strike), so securing six pence an hour meant an increase of at least 20 percent.

The "contract" system also was a cause of grievances that fueled pressure for reform. Except for more skilled sectors such as stevedores or tugmen, dock work was casual. Employment depended upon ships docking and on workers being awarded a "contract." The laborers would assemble daily at the dock gates, hopeful of work, but dependent upon being selected by contractors and even then guaranteed no more than a few hours' labor and pay.

The hot weather aided the daily mass meetings near the Tower of London. Burns addressed the gatherings in his distinctive white straw hat and led regular marches through the city of London. Contrary to recent unemployed demonstrations and Burns's reputation for ready fists, these marches were notable for their order and discipline, evincing "the dignity of labour." This demeanor proved effective in terms of swinging popular opinion and donations behind the strike as did the exposure of the dockers' cause and their plight. Emblems such as the "dockers' dinner" and "dockers' baby" emphasized the hardship these workers faced with the morality of their cause.

The employers, however, were successful at bringing in nonunion or "blackleg" labor, and after two weeks of striking and rallies the dockers were no nearer to a resolution. Funds were sparse. At the peak of the strike, the strike office was issuing as many as 25,000 food tickets (worth £1250) daily. An unexpected donation from Australian dockers, better organized than their British counterparts, helped to rescue the financial situation. By the end of the strike the Australian contribution amounted to more than £30,000, two-thirds of the total strike funds raised. The new banner of the Stevedores' Union, which pictured Australian and British dockers hand in hand, commemorated this generosity. The contributions meant that Tom Mann's proposal to end the deadlock and the general strike across London was not necessary.

The End of the Strike

The Lord Mayor of London and Cardinal Manning, from a shipping family and concerned at the fate of Catholic strikers, initiated conciliation. The employers conceded the "dockers' tanner" and an increased rate for overtime. Four-hour shifts reduced the impermanence of the contract system. One concession on the part of the union was that blackleg labor might remain employed, but Tillett was effective at convincing the majority to leave.

Clearly decisive in the victory—as much as the unity and fortitude of the dockers, the popular support for their cause, and the radical mood of London—was the leadership of the likes of Tillett, Thorne, Burns, and Mann. All were socialists, connected to the Marxist Social Democratic Federation, and effective organizers. They comprised an eccentric, sectarian group. Much of the influence of these leaders was despite rather than because of the SDF. For them socialism was practical as well as rhetorical; for Mann and Thorne, socialism meant the municipalization of the docks or gasworks under local control. Above all, these leaders epitomized the spirit of new unionism.

The Impact

A dockers' union (the Dock, Wharf, Riverside and General Workers' Union) formed with Tillett as secretary. The new organization had some 30,000 members by November 1889. Other general unions (such as the General Railway Workers' Union) emerged to cater to the needs of unskilled workers. This group also had an effect on other unions, such as the national Miners' Federation of Great Britain, which formed in 1889. The dockers' strike marked the advance of new unionism against the older, exclusive craft unions. Yet there were limits to the change. The dockers' union for instance, though flourishing in Tillett's hometown of Bristol, faced competition elsewhere. Many new unions such as the gasworkers lost members through the 1890s. The older unions, such as the engineers, picked up members in the late 1880s and retained them as well as their influence over the wider movement and Trades Union Congress (TUC). Mann was narrowly defeated in the leadership election for the engineers in 1891. The new, general unions numbered around 200,000, around 12 percent of total union membership. If the new unionism was not all that new, the response to it suggested otherwise. Various legal decisions made in the courts (but not in Parliament) and an employers' counteroffensive, notably the 1897–1898 engineering lockout, indicated that unions still faced an uncertain prospect. With the Liberals heavily defeated in the 1895 general election, traditional sources of political and parliamentary support could no longer be relied upon.

Workers marching in the dockers' victory parade sang "Rule Britannia" and "La Marseillaise" and inspired James Connell to pen the words to "The Red Flag," which was to become in a few years the theme tune of the newly formed Labour Party. The leadership of socialists in the strike, together with the fragility of the trade union advance that it marked, both contributed to the founding of the Labour Representation Committee in 1900.

Key Players

Burns, John (1858–1943): Born in South London, Burns was by trade a skilled engineer. A radical and socialist, keen cricketer and teetotaler, Burns was notorious for powerful oratory and striking appearance at demonstrations. He earned the title "the man with the red flag" after a disturbance in 1886 and during the dock strike was known as "the man in the white straw hat." He represented Battersea on the new London County Council from 1889 to 1907 and was Member of Parliament (MP) for Battersea from 1892 to 1918. As the president of the local government board under the Liberal government (1905–1914) and briefly president of the board of trade (1914), Burns lost much of his earlier support among socialists.

Mann, Tom (1856–1941): Born near Coventry, Mann was, like Will Thorne, close to Engels and Eleanor Marx in the 1880s and, like Burns, a skilled craftsman and Social Democratic Federation (SDF) member. An advocate of the eight-hour workweek and for reform of London government, Mann was also president of the dockers' union until 1893, secretary of the Independent Labour Party (1894–1897), and chief founder of the Workers' Union in 1898. Between 1901 and 1910 he was active among trade unionists and socialists in New Zealand, Australia, and South Africa. He returned to Britain a syndicalist and was chair of the Communist Party (which he joined from the outset in 1920) National Minority Movement, 1924–1932.

Tillett, Ben (1860–1943): Born in Bristol, Tillett joined the circus, then the navy, and was by the 1880s a tea porter in London. The small Tea Operatives Union that Tillett founded in 1887 was at the heart of the dock strike, and Tillett was leader of the dockers' union that emerged after 1889 until its amalgamation into the Transport and General Workers' Union in 1922. Tillett firmly believed that transport workers, particularly dockerworkers, should organize nationally and internationally in the International Federation of Ship Dock and River Workers (which he helped found in 1896) rather than by region or trade. An SDF member in the 1880s, Tillett was Labour MP for North Salford, 1917–1924 and 1929–1931.

See also: *Maritime Strike.*

BIBLIOGRAPHY

Books
Brown, Kenneth Douglas. *John Burns.* London: Royal Historical Society, 1977.
Fishman, W. J. *East End 1888: A Year in a London Borough Among the Laboring Poor.* Philadelphia: Temple University Press, 1979.
Lovell, John Christopher. *Stevedores and Dockers: A Study of Trade Unionism in the Port of London, 1870–1914.* London: Macmillan 1969.
McCarthy, Terry, ed. *The Great Dock Strike, 1889.* London: Weidenfeld and Nicolson in association with the Transport and General Workers' Union, 1988.
Pelling, Henry. *A History of British Trade Unionism.* London: Macmillan, 1963.
Schneer, Jonathan. *Ben Tillett: Portrait of a Labour Leader.* London: Croom Helm, 1982.

—Lawrence Black

Dorr Rebellion

United States 1842

Synopsis

The Dorr Rebellion, named for its leader, Thomas Dorr, was the climax of years of debate in Rhode Island over the question of suffrage. In 1842 the state of Rhode Island had two separate governments and constitutions, each vying for legality and legitimacy. The established government was a product of Rhode Island's 1663 colonial charter, a framework that suffered

increasing criticism for its antiquated provisions regarding suffrage and legislative apportionment. In late 1841 a movement for a reformist "People's Constitution" culminated with the ratification of a new constitution. The following spring, Dorr, elected under the new constitution as the "people's governor," attempted to organize a new state government under the provisions of the insurgents' document. Severe reprisals from the "Charter Government" prompted an attempt by Dorr and his followers to capture the arsenal at Providence. The attack was a singular failure. A few weeks later, after Dorr left the state, the state militia dispersed the remnants of the rebellion from its "headquarters" at the village of Chepachet. Following this victory, the Charter Government continued its repression of "Dorrism" in an attempt to prevent future insurrection. A new constitution for Rhode Island, adopted in 1843 and replacing the 1663 charter, eased some of the complaints regarding suffrage and apportionment that had given rise to the Dorr Rebellion. The insurgency of 1842, however, left its mark on the state's political landscape and continued to be a significant influence upon debates within Rhode Island society in the coming years.

Timeline

1823: U.S. president James Monroe establishes the Monroe Doctrine, whereby the United States warns European nations not to interfere in the political affairs of the Western Hemisphere.

1828: Election of Andrew Jackson as president begins a new era in American history.

1834: American inventor Cyrus H. McCormick patents his reaper, a horse-drawn machine for harvesting wheat.

1836: In Texas's war of independence with Mexico, the defenders of the Alamo, among them Davy Crockett and Jim Bowie, are killed in a siege. Later that year, Texas wins the Battle of San Jacinto and secures its independence.

1838: The forcible removal of the Cherokee Nation from Georgia to Indian Territory (now Oklahoma) along the "Trail of Tears" begins.

1841: Act of Union joins Upper Canada and Lower Canada, which consist of parts of the present-day provinces of Ontario and Quebec, respectively.

1842: Scientific and technological advances include the development of ether and artificial fertilizer; the identification of the Doppler effect (by Austrian physicist Christian Johann Doppler); the foundation of biochemistry as a discipline; and the coining of the word *dinosaur.*

1842: In *Sanitary Conditions of the Labouring Population of Great Britain,* British reformer Edwin Chadwick draws attention to the squalor in the nation's mill town slums and shows that working people have a much higher incidence of disease than do the middle and upper classes.

1842: British forces in the Afghan capital of Kabul are routed, experiencing one of the first major defeats of a European force by a non-European one in modern times.

1844: "Fifty-four-forty or fight" is the rallying cry at the Democratic National Convention, where delegates call for

Dorr Rebellion principals are denounced in a newspaper article titled "The Great Political Car and Last Load of Patriots." The Library of Congress.

the addition of Oregon to the Union and for the annexation of Texas.

1848: Mexican War ends with the Treaty of Guadalupe Hidalgo, in which Mexico gives up half of its land area, including Texas, California, most of Arizona and New Mexico, and parts of Colorado, Utah, and Nevada. In another treaty, with Great Britain, the United States sets the boundaries of its Oregon Territory.

1852: *Uncle Tom's Cabin* by Harriet Beecher Stowe, though far from a literary masterpiece, is a great commercial success, with over half a million sales on both sides of the Atlantic. More important, it has an enormous influence on British sentiments with regard to slavery and the brewing American conflict between North and South.

Event and Its Context

In the 1830s, the "Age of Jackson," with its emphasis on democratic politics and rhetoric that tended toward egalitarianism, Rhode Island was a curious anomaly. Most other states had revised their constitutions in favor of expanded suffrage (primarily the abolition of strict property requirements for voting), but Rhode Island still operated under the charter that had guided its affairs as a British colony. Promulgated in 1663 by the English monarchy, the charter government for Rhode Island was weighted toward the established towns and wealthy landowners who ran the colony's local affairs. Towns that were established after the charter took effect received fewer representatives in the colonial legislature, and the rights of suffrage devolved upon only those who held a large amount of land. Rhode Island was alone among the original 13 states in not replacing its colonial charter with a republican constitution after the Revolutionary War. The charter's continued operation into the early nineteenth century allowed political domination by a small class of wealthy landowners at the expense of the more rapidly growing strata of the state's society. By the early 1800s the advent of a significant textile manufacturing sector concentrated mostly in the northern part of the state meant that the number of artisans, mechanics, and other workingmen who were denied a voice in politics grew steadily. The government defined "freemen" (that is, those who possessed political rights under the 1663 charter) as those holding at least $134 in real estate; other forms of property and assets did not enter into the calculation. The result was disfranchisement of much of the state's nonlandholding male population who would have been able to vote under the guidelines of any other state. Because the charter weighted legislative apportionment in favor of the agricultural towns of southern Rhode Island, home of most of the state's wealthy landowners, there was no immediate likelihood that the legislature would relax the suffrage requirement. By 1800 the northern manufacturing areas were growing quickly and had a higher population than the southern towns, but until legislative apportionment reflected these realities, those who hoped for reform would be disappointed.

Landed interests were a brake on efforts at political reform through the first third of the nineteenth century. Sporadic efforts

for constitutional modification met with inattention and failure until the 1830s, when Jacksonian democratic-style politics surfaced in Rhode Island. In 1833 a sustained effort at reform commenced with a vocal workingmen's presence. The next year, reformers organized the Rhode Island Constitutional Party. Membership in the new organization crossed socioeconomic lines; accompanying the workingmen was a leadership group drawn from the business and professional classes of the northern manufacturing towns, many of whom identified with the emergent Whig party. One of these Whig-leaning professionals was the Providence lawyer Thomas Wilson Dorr, author of the Constitutional Party's public address to the Rhode Island electorate, in which he advanced the principle of "popular constituent sovereignty" or the notion that citizens of a state had the inalienable right to remake their government along republican forms should the existing structure prove undemocratic or corrupt. Displaying its antecedents in the republicanism of the American Revolution, "popular constituent sovereignty" also asserted that the process of establishing a new government need not take place within the established channels of the current political system. This emphasis on popular grassroots mobilization to effect constitutional change would be at the heart of the subsequent events surrounding the question of constitutional reform in the state.

This agitation for reform went to the state legislature, with a minority of representatives (including Dorr and Samuel Atwell) arguing the principles of the Constitutional Party in the face of the landholding majority. The legislature called a constitutional convention for the spring of 1835, but the election of delegates was confined to the same narrow group of landholding "freemen" who voted in the state's regular elections. The convention thus reflected the entrenched landholding interests of Rhode Island and ignored demands for reform, finally adjourning in June without accomplishing anything. The Constitutional Party then found itself unable to advance its aims within the structure of Rhode Island's politics. The system of suffrage and representation established by the 1663 charter was simply too weighted in the favor of the southern towns and the landholding interests for the reformers to gather any momentum in the state's legislature. After the fall elections of 1837, in which Dorr and other Constitutional candidates for state and federal office were defeated, the party collapsed, and Dorr himself despaired of further efforts for reform.

The presidential election of 1840, with its appeals to popular mobilization and broad-based campaigning, helped mobilize another surge of reform activity in Rhode Island. Again, the impetus came from the workingmen of the northern towns, as mechanics and other workers in Providence formed a new, more militant organization for political reform, the Rhode Island Suffrage Association, in the spring of 1840. Quickly, the association established branches throughout the state and began publication of a newspaper, *The New Age and Constitutional Advocate*, to advance its platform. The state legislature tabled a February petition for repeal of the 1663 charter, but throughout 1841, the association maintained a steady reform campaign. Parades, demonstrations, and public meetings continually raised the issues of suffrage and apportionment. The state legislature called a constitutional convention for November, likely hoping that something similar to the abortive meeting of 1835 would ensue. The association, however, had decided to abjure these efforts of the landholders, and—invoking the ideal of popular constituent sovereignty—called for a "people's" constitutional convention to meet in October.

The resulting "People's Constitution" reflected the long-standing grievances of Rhode Island's disenfranchised adult males. It eliminated the landholding requirement for suffrage and outlined a new system of apportionment that reflected more accurately the demographics of the state. The landholders' convention of November, in turn, produced a document that made only token concessions on these issues, and it received less than a majority in a ratification vote. In December a significant majority of Rhode Islanders who would be able to vote under the relaxed requirements of the People's Constitution ratified that document; this included a majority of the "freemen" according to the stricter definitions of the 1663 charter as well. Emboldened by this victory, adherents of the People's Constitution proceeded to establish a governing apparatus and elect Thomas Dorr, who had reentered the reform movement that year, as the "People's Governor."

The "Dorr Rebellion," as it became known, began with Dorr's efforts in May 1842 to organize his new government. At that point, the landholder-controlled state legislature began its implementation of the so-called Algerine law, a repressive measure aimed at wiping out Dorrism. With the arrest of many Dorrite leaders, Dorr himself fled the state. Critics accused him of cowardice, but Dorr argued that he was attempting to garner support for the people's movement in New York and Washington. Returning to Rhode Island a few weeks later, Dorr decided to seize the state arsenal in Providence. On the night of 17 May 1842, Dorr, Seth Luther (a radical carpenter and foremost representative of labor's presence in the movement), and over 300 men marched to the arsenal, which was well defended by the forces of the charter government (including Dorr's father and younger brother). The assault failed, and by morning Dorr's forces had largely dispersed. Later in the day, Dorr learned that most of his government had resigned. Again fleeing the state, Dorr pondered his next move while the remaining supporters of the people's movement encamped at the village of Chepachet. Dorr would return to join these forces, but faced with the prospect of battle with the state militia, Dorr's supporters again decided to disperse. On 27 June, Dorr wrote a letter intended for publication in which he announced what amounted to a surrender, and once again left the state.

Supporters of the charter government, calling themselves the Law and Order Party, moved quickly to suppress the Dorrite movement. The government declared martial law and over the next six weeks, many in the movement were arrested and imprisoned. The Law and Order forces, however, overreached themselves with the severity of this repression, and the legal voters of the state eventually ratified a somewhat more liberal constitution in 1843. After the ratification, Dorr announced that he would return to the state to aid in further reform. On 31 October 1843 he arrived in Providence and was promptly arrested for treason against Rhode Island. Tried, found guilty, and imprisoned, Dorr became a *cause celébre*, and his liberation became a major issue in state politics. Dorr was released in 1845 and died 10 years later, at the age of 49, his health shattered by the circumstances of his confinement.

A final blow to the Dorr Rebellion came in the U.S. Supreme Court's decision in the 1848 case, *Luther v. Borden*, in which Seth Luther sued for damages resulting from a raid conducted by state forces under the Algerine Law. The Court ruled against Luther, arguing that his claim that the People's Constitution was the government in force at the time had no merit. With this judicial invalidation of popular constituent sovereignty, the Dorr Rebellion reached its final conclusion. The issues of suffrage and constitutional reform, however, continued to play a key role in Rhode Island. Many former Dorrites returned to the Democratic Party and Dorrite issues (including the liberation of Dorr from prison) to reclaim power from the state's Whigs. The Dorr Rebellion thus stood firmly within the currents of larger debates over the nature of a democratic polity integral to the political culture of Jacksonian America.

Key Players

Atwell, Samuel Y. (1796–1844): Atwell was a lawyer, representative from the northern Rhode Island town of Glocester, and a persistent voice for constitutional reform in the state legislature. In 1841 he became active in the Rhode Island Suffrage Association and was a key public supporter of Thomas Dorr, a commitment that waned somewhat after passage of the Algerine Law. Atwell was to represent Dorr at his trial for treason but could only join the case very late into the proceedings due to illness.

Dorr, Thomas Wilson (1805–1854): Harvard-educated and trained as a lawyer, Dorr was active in constitutional reform movements in Rhode Island. A member of the state legislature and the constitutional conventions of 1835 and 1841, Dorr became governor under the People's Constitution and led the movement that subsequently bore his name. Imprisoned for treason in 1843, Dorr spent almost two years in solitary confinement. He was released in 1845, had his political rights restored by a sympathetic state legislature in 1851, and died in 1854 from poor health that resulted from his prison term.

Luther, Seth (1795–1863): Originally from Massachusetts, Luther was a carpenter by trade and traveled widely throughout New England. He was actively involved in numerous reform movements and was instrumental in the early 1830s organization of the Massachusetts Working Men's Party and its crusade against child labor in the textile mills. In Providence during the height of the Dorr movement, Luther played a key role in leading worker support for the People's Constitution, even after much of the moderate leadership deserted Dorr in the wake of the charter government's repression under the Algerine Law.

BIBLIOGRAPHY

Books

Dennison, George. *The Dorr War: Republicanism on Trial, 1831–1861.* Lexington, KY: University Press of Kentucky, 1976.

Gettleman, Marvin E. *The Dorr Rebellion: A Study in American Radicalism, 1833–1849.* New York: Random House, 1973.

King, Dan. *The Life and Times of Thomas Wilson Dorr, with Outlines of the Political History of Rhode Island.* Reprint. Freeport, NY: Books for Libraries Press, 1969. (Original work published 1859.)

Mowry, Arthur May. *The Dorr War; Or, the Constitutional Struggle in Rhode Island.* Providence: Preston and Rounds, 1901.

Schlesinger, Arthur M., Jr. *The Age of Jackson.* Boston: Little, Brown, and Company, 1945.

Periodicals

Schuchman, John S. "The Political Background of the Political-Question Doctrine: The Judges and the Dorr War." *American Journal of Legal History* 16 (1972): 111–125.

Wiecek, William. "Popular Sovereignty in the Dorr War: Conservative Counterblast." *Rhode Island History* 32 (1973): 35–51.

Williamson, Chilton. "Rhode Island Since the Dorr War." *New England Quarterly* 28 (1955): 34–50.

Other

Newton, Anne M. "Rebellion in Rhode Island: The Story of the Dorr War." Unpub. M.A. Thesis, Columbia University, 1947.

—Kevin M. Gannon

Dover Textile Strike

United States 1828

Synopsis

In December 1828 the first all-female strike in America took place in Dover, New Hampshire. The strike was the workers' response to the imposition of additional rules for factory employees, which included docking employees 12.5 cents of pay for being late by even one minute, blacklisting to prevent fired women from finding employment in any New England factory, and forbidding any talking between employees while at work.

Timeline

1803: German pharmacist Friedrich Wilhelm Adam Saturner isolates an opium derivative, to which he gives the name *morphine.*

1808: First performances of Beethoven's Fifth and Sixth symphonies are given.

1813: Jane Austen publishes *Pride and Prejudice.*

1818: British surgeon James Blundel performs the first successful blood transfusion.

1823: U.S. president James Monroe establishes the Monroe Doctrine, whereby the United States warns European nations not to interfere in the political affairs of the Western Hemisphere.

1826: Friction or "Lucifer" matches in England are invented.

1828: Election of Andrew Jackson as president begins a new era in American history.

1829: Greece wins its independence after a seven-year war with Turkey.

1831: Unsuccessful Polish revolt against Russian rule takes place.

1834: American inventor Cyrus H. McCormick patents his reaper, a horse-drawn machine for harvesting wheat.

1837: Victoria is crowned in England.

1839: England launches the First Opium War against China. The war, which lasts three years, results in the British gaining a free hand to conduct a lucrative opium trade, despite opposition by the Chinese government.

Event and Its Context

Textile Mill History

The early nineteenth century was a time of rapid growth of American textile mills, particularly in New England. In Dover, New Hampshire, entrepreneur John Williams and nine other investors opened the Dover Cotton Factory on the Cocheco River in 1812.

The demographics of the women who worked in the Cocheco factory were similar to those of women who worked throughout New England in similar factories: they were white, single, American-born women between the ages of 12 and 25. Men worked as overseers. Each woman worked two looms, each 4 feet by 3 feet, simultaneously.

The young women, for the most part from farming families, left their homes and moved into boarding houses near the factory that were often owned by the company. The companies generally engaged the services of an older widow to oversee the boarding homes and ensure that the house rules were followed. The company expected the residents to maintain a strict code of morality and behavior. In the advertisement for female workers in the *Stafford Register* on 12 August 1822, the company asked for intelligent women "to whom constant employment and good encouragement will be given."

Factory work of this kind was considered respectable work for young women in an era in which very few occupations were open to women. This type of work allowed young women to become financially and physically independent from their families. Some of the workers supplemented their families' incomes by sending home part of their weekly salary. Employing women rather than men saved the company money, as women did not have to be paid as much as men.

Daily Life

Rules in the boarding houses were strict and governed many aspects of the women's lives. The rules forbade activities such as card playing, profanity, drinking, and gambling. The residents were required to join a church and attend services. The 10:00 P.M. curfew limited social activities. The factory owners felt it was crucial to maintain control of the women's behavior and a moral and respectable reputation. In that era, women who worked outside of the home were susceptible to charges of immorality. The companies wanted their employees to be above reproach so that they would be able to continue to recruit young women. The women bonded with each other in the boarding houses and experienced a more autonomous life than they had known in their family homes.

Workdays in the factories left little time for anything except work. The hours were very long, ranging from 11 to 14 hours a day, six days a week. From March to October the women worked from 6:30 A.M. to 6:30 P.M. during the Monday through Friday workweek. On Saturdays the workday ended slightly earlier. From November through February the factory bell rang at 4:30 A.M. to wake the girls. At 5:00 A.M. breakfast was served, and at 5:30 work began. Lunch breaks were half an hour. The women generally worked until 6:30 P.M. and dinner was served at the boarding houses at 7:00 P.M. The women earned about $2.00 a week; from this amount the companies took $1.25 for room and board. The companies held back an additional two cents a week and put it into a general "sick fund" to provide money to women who were in need of medical assistance.

The rules in the factory were very strict. The factory owners required the women to sign a work contract titled *Conditions on which help is hired by the Cocheco Manufacturing Company, Dover, New Hampshire,* in which the women agreed to the rules of the company. These rules included the agreement to work for whatever wages the company saw fit to pay and proper deportment at all times. There was to be no cursing, drinking, gambling, smoking, or talking behind the overseers' backs. The factories levied fines on anyone who showed up late for work. If the worker quit with less than two weeks' notice, the company would keep the worker's final two weeks of pay. Workers were not to talk unnecessarily or call out to friends through open windows. There was no reading while at work, and workers were not to throw anything into the river. Talking back to the overseers was forbidden, and if a woman made an enemy of the overseer, she was quickly fired.

Working conditions were dangerous in the textile factory. Women's hands sometimes got stuck in the looms and hair became stuck in the machines, sometimes pulling off their scalps. The long hours and short breaks contributed to these accidents. The ventilation system was poor in the building as was the lighting, which produced additional health hazards.

New Management Demands Lead to Strike

In 1828 the Dover Cotton Factory went bankrupt, and the Cocheco Manufacturing Company became the new owners of the factory. With the switch in ownership there was a change in the rules for the employees. The Cocheco Manufacturing Company would no longer tolerate any talking or fraternization among the female employees during the workday. Any woman who joined a union would be fired. Management imposed fines on women who were so much as one minute late for work. The new owners reduced salaries by five cents a day for the female employees, but salaries for the men remained the same. At the same time, Cocheco raised the production quotas and increased the loom speeds. The women were not willing to tolerate the reduction in their wages, which they believed was meant to make them dependent on their employer in the same way that slaves were dependent upon their masters.

On 30 December 1828 nearly half of the 800 female employees walked out of the Cocheco factory. This was the first time in American history that women had gone on strike. The strikers made banners and signs that they carried with them as they marched around the mill. The women found a band that agreed to lead them as they paraded throughout the town. They exploded two kegs of gunpowder in celebration of the women's spirit of freedom and sense of controlling their own destiny, however short-lived. The women gave spontaneous speeches in which they protested the unfairness of the working conditions, salary reductions, and work increases that the corporation was forcing on them. The *Dover Enquirer* of 30 December 1828 described the strike with rhetoric that revealed its editors' alliance with the factory owners. The paper called the strike "one of the most disgusting scenes ever witnessed." *The National Gazette of Philadelphia,* however, supported the striking women.

Within a matter of days, 600 of the female workers had submitted their grievances to the Cocheco management. These grievances stated the women's belief that the expected increase in productivity was simply being done to line the pockets of the men in charge of the mill. They stated their refusal to work for reduced wages. They outlined their belief that the new expectations of reduced wages and increased output would reduce the women to mere slaves within the factory system. Included in this statement was an explanation of the unfairness of expecting those on the bottom rung of the financial ladder to bear the brunt of an economic downturn while those on the top rungs of the ladder lost nothing.

The company responded by advertising for new, "better behaved" workers to fill the positions that had been vacated by the striking women. Some of the workers returned to the factories, and others were replaced. The only ground that the strikers gained in the strike was the removal of the rule that prohibited talking while working.

According to historian Philip S. Foner in his book *History of the Labor Movement,* in 1829 the management at the factory decided to nail the windows shut in an effort to keep the humidity out of the textiles in the building. This resulted in sweltering temperatures that caused at least one worker to faint. The women went out on strike again, this time winning their demand that the company open the windows.

In February 1834 nearly 800 women went on strike, once again protesting the company's attempt to reduce their wages. The Cocheco Manufacturing Company emulated the textile mills in Lowell, Massachusetts, by cutting workers' wages in response to a tighter economy and fewer profits. In *Women at Work: The Transformation of Work and Community in Lowell, Massachusetts, 1826–1860,* historian Thomas Dublin noted that the management of all of the New England factories formed a close-knit group, paying similar wages and employing similar rules in their factories. The actions in Lowell thus had an impact on the employees of Cocheco Manufacturing in Dover.

The employees at Cocheco, upon hearing about the reduction in their wages, left the factory. They gathered at the local courthouse to give speeches about the inequality of a system that would ask the lowest workers to take a price cut while middle management and the owners took no pay cut at all. They called themselves "factory slaves" and vowed to fight the owners of the mill. To avoid a pay cut, the women went to the newspapers. They hoped to get their stories out to the public so as to engage their support and to women working in other mills, whom they hoped would strike in support of their sisters. *The Dover Gazette* printed the story, going so far as to call the workers "daughters of the republic." The paper reported that the workers were behaving with dignity. These strikers held no parades and no marches with banners.

The Cocheco factory owners placed advertisements in the paper for 500 replacement workers. Those on strike took up collections among themselves for the "contingency fund" to be used by women who wanted to return to their families but did not have the money to do so. In the end the strikers did not gain any concessions, and many took advantage of the contingency fund to return to their homes rather than to go back to work at the factory.

Before long, immigrant women replaced the native-born female workers. The struggle for fair wages, decent work hours, and safe working conditions continued for decades thereafter.

See also: *Factory Girls' Association; Lowell Industrial Experiment.*

BIBLIOGRAPHY

Books

Dublin, Thomas. *Women at Work: The Transformation of Work and Community in Lowell, Massachusetts, 1826–1860*. New York: Columbia University Press, 1979.

Foner, Philip S. *Women and the American Labor Movement: From Colonial Times to the Eve of World War I*. New York: The Free Press, 1979.

Kessler Harris, Alice. *Out to Work: A History of Wage-Earning Women in the United States*. New York: Oxford University Press, 1982.

Morris, Richard B., ed. *A History of the American Worker*. Princeton, NJ: Princeton University Press, 1983.

Sumner, Helen L. *History of Women in Industry in the United States: Report on Condition of Woman and Child Wage-Earners in the United States*, Vol. 9. Washington, DC: Government Printing Office, 1910.

Other

American Textile History Museum. *Cocheco: Print Works Collection*. 2002 [cited 12 September 2002]. <http://www.pbtex.com/html/cocheco_information.html>.

Andres, John B., and Helen Bliss. *History of Women in Trade Unions, 1825 to the Knights of Labor*. Senate Document 645, U.S. Congress, Senate, 61st Congress, 2nd Session, 1922, 10:23–24.

Beaudoin, Cathleen. *A Yarn to Follow: The Dover Cotton Factory 1812–1821*. Dover Public Library [cited 2 August 2002]. <http://www.dover.lib.nh.us/DoverHistory/mill_history%20new.htm>.

Candee, Richard. *The Great Factory at Dover, New Hampshire: The Dover Manufacturing Co. Print Works, 1825*. Old Sturbridge Village Web site [cited 20 September 2002]. <http://www.spnea.org/resources/articles/pdf225.pdf>.

An Industrializing Nation, Interpreting Primary Sources. University of Houston, College of Liberal Arts and Studies, The Gilda Lehrmen Institute of American History [cited 21 September 2002]. <http://www.hfac.uh.edu/gl/us14.htm>.

—Beth Emmerling

E

Eight-hour Day Movement

United States 1860s–1900s

Synopsis

For more than a century, American workers struggled for a shorter workday. Throughout the nineteenth century and almost halfway through the twentieth, an absence of binding federal legislation had many employees dedicating almost the entirety of their waking hours to employers. It was not uncommon for workers to spend between 10 and 16 hours a day on the job without payment for overtime. Beginning in the 1860s, support for the eight-hour movement grew rapidly among average workers. Evolving from the fight for a 10-hour day in the mid-1800s, the demands of American workers had by the 1860s turned to eight hours. The fight for an eight-hour day was replete with labor demands, strikes, repression, and occasional victories. In a few cases, labor's demands were met with a corporate paternalism that established workday hour limits at the company level. More often than not, companies and local authorities quelled strikes for shorter hours with armed violence. Such was the case of the 1886 Haymarket Square incident in Chicago. Gradually, individual states began adopting limits on the workweek. At the national level, the demands of nearly a century of struggle were finally met in 1940, when Congress amended the Fair Labor Standards Act and reduced the federal workweek to 40 hours.

Timeline

1860: South Carolina secedes from the Union.

1865: The ratified Thirteenth Amendment to the U.S. Constitution prohibits slavery.

1870: Fifteenth Amendment, the last of the three post–Civil War amendments to the U.S. Constitution, states that an American citizen cannot be denied the right to vote because of race, color, or previous status as a slave. At this time, the new amendment is treated as law in the South, which is still occupied by federal troops; but after Reconstruction ends in 1877, it will be nearly 90 years before blacks in some southern states gain full voting rights.

1874: As farm wages in Britain plummet, agricultural workers go on strike.

1882: The Chinese Exclusion Act, a treaty between the United States and China, provides for restrictions on immigration of Chinese workers.

1886: Bombing at Haymarket Square, Chicago, kills seven policemen and injures numerous others. Eight anarchists are accused and tried; three are imprisoned, one commits suicide, and four are hanged.

1890: Congress passes the Sherman Antitrust Act, which in the years that follow will be used to break up large monopolies.

1894: Thousands of unemployed American workers—a group named "Coxey's Army" for their leader, Jacob S. Coxey—march on Washington, D.C. A number of such marches on the capital occurred during this period of economic challenges, but Coxey's march was the only one to actually reach its destination.

1899: Polish-born German socialist Rosa Luxembourg rejects the argument that working conditions in Europe have improved and that change must come by reforming the existing system. Rather, she calls for an overthrow of the existing power structure by means of violent international revolution.

1904: The 10-hour workday is established in France.

1907: U.S. markets experience a financial panic.

Event and Its Context

Early Struggles

The struggle toward an eight-hour day began early in the nineteenth century, when workers in both Europe and the United States began demanding a ceiling on the number of hours they had to work. In 1847 English women and children were granted a 10-hour day. In 1848 French workers won a 12-hour day. The first half of the century also saw the birth of the American 10-hour movement, which successfully achieved legislation establishing a 10-hour day in several states. In 1836, after workers in Philadelphia won a 10-hour day, the *National Laborer* declared, "We have no desire to perpetuate the 10-hour system, for we believe that eight hours' daily labor is more than enough for any man to perform." Nonetheless, given that even the 10-hour laws allowed employees to contract for longer hours should they wish, employers applied this "wish" to all workers, firing or blacklisting those who refused to cooperate. Given the pressure of a growing, needy immigrant labor force, leverage for bargaining was on the side of employers. From 1830 to 1860 the average workday in the United States went from 12 hours to 11 hours.

The fight for an eight-hour day in the United States gained force in the mid-nineteenth century. In the 1850s New York trade unions agreed at a mass meeting that "eight hours is a just and sufficient number of hours for any man to work." At the 1864 International Workingmen's Association convention in Europe, representatives stated that a limited workday was "the first step in the direction of the emancipation of the working class." That year, the first American eight-hour organization was formed.

The following decades brought a combination of strikes and occasional legislative victories. One early victory came in

Labor activists, August Spies, Albert Parsons, Louis Lingg, George Engel, and Adolph Fischer. They were convicted of the murder of a policeman in the Haymarket bombing incident of 4 May 1886 and sentenced to death. All were eventually hanged except Lingg, who committed suicide in prison while awaiting execution. © Corbis. Reproduced by permission.

California, where the state legislature yielded to a series of labor actions to pass an eight-hour law on 22 February 1868. That same year, 25,000 mechanics, miners, and other laborers struck for the same right in Pennsylvania. An early legislative victory at the national level came when Congress approved an eight-hour day for federal workers; however, some department heads cut wages proportionally to match the cut in hours. A three-month strike by 100,000 workers in 1872 resulted in an eight-hour day for 10 labor unions. Strikes soon brought the eight-hour day to workers in Philadelphia, Chicago, Jersey City, Buffalo, and Albany. During the depression that followed the stock market crash of 1873, labor activists began to put forth the idea that a shorter workweek could reduce unemployment, with the work spread more equitably among workers. Unfortunately for eight-hour proponents, the dire economic straits facing the country temporarily slowed the momentum of their cause.

Labor Sets an Ultimatum

In October 1884 the national Federation of Organized Trades and Labor Unions approved a resolution calling for a workday of eight hours. Given the failure to date of legislative methods, trade unions and other worker associations set an ulti-

matum: Either workers would get their eight-hour workday limit by 1 May 1866 or they would defend their demands with a general strike. The epicenter of the eight-hour day movement (also known as the "May Day" movement), which claimed 250,000 laborers nationwide by 1886, was Chicago. Most involved in organizing workers was the anarchist-influenced Working People's Association. Numerous eight-hour strikes broke out prior to the 1 May deadline, and thousands of workers in numerous trades won hour limits. Striking workers nationwide united behind the words of J. G. Blanchard's "Eight-Hour Song": "We're summoning our forces from / shipyard, shop, and mill; / Eight hours for work / eight hours for rest / Eight hours for what you will." Nonetheless, a great number of American workers were still working around 100 hours a week. What started out as a peaceful protest on 1 May became a pivotal moment in labor history.

On the 1 May deadline for a national general strike, thousands of workers in Chicago struck with mostly peaceful actions. As the protest continued over several days, tension between police and strikers intensified. On 3 May, when strikers attacked men who crossed a picket line at the McCormick Reaper Works, police opened fire and killed four demonstrators. That night hundreds of enraged protesters took to the streets, demonstrating at Haymarket Square. Just as the rally was concluding, a dynamite bomb exploded and killed a police officer. The police fired on the crowd, killing one protester and wounding others. Four of the eight demonstrators arrested for the bombing were hanged despite scant evidence against them. The Haymarket affair was a rallying cry for a new generation of activists. Lucy Parsons, on the death of her husband, Albert Parsons, called for direct action against the wealthy. Emma Goldman, a young Lithuanian immigrant and anarchist, cited Haymarket Square as her political birthplace. "If it weren't for what happened here in Chicago back in 1886, you'd be working 16 hours a day," writer Studs Terkel recalled telling a young antiunion couple a century later.

As the hysteria surrounding the Haymarket affair died down, demands for an eight-hour day resumed. In the Northwest, lumber workers of the Industrial Workers of the World enforced their eight-hour demands by simply walking off the job after eight hours of work. Advances toward an eight-hour day were nonetheless the exception to a larger trend: when the U.S. government began keeping track of workers' hours in 1890, it discovered that full-time workers in manufacturing spent an average of 100 hours per week on the job. The struggle continued.

On 12 May 1902 some 150,000 anthracite coal miners in Pennsylvania went on strike to demand better wages and shorter hours. Lasting five months, the strike required government intervention due to fears of a coal shortage. Under the leadership of John Mitchell, the United Mine Workers of America won an eight-hour day. In 1906 the eight-hour day was widely adopted in the printing industry. By 1910 the average U.S. workday had dropped to nine hours.

Over the following decade trade union membership doubled to four million, thus giving greater force to workday limit demands. In the 1910s the rising number of women entering the workforce brought improved legal protections. In states including Minnesota, Utah, Oregon, and Massachusetts, governments

Proclamation supporting 8-hour workday, National Eight-hour Law. © Corbis. Reproduced by permission.

cut the 54-hour legal workweek limit to 48 hours. In 1916 the federal Adamson Act gave railroad workers a set 48-hour workweek. In 1918 workers in the nation's meat-packing plants were working 60-hour weeks; President Woodrow Wilson, after appointing a federal negotiator, ordered a workweek of 48 hours. Labor unions found friends in government; by 1919 some federal agencies were headed by union leaders.

International Labor Organization Calls for Eight Hours

With the 1919 founding of the International Labor Organization (ILO), the eight-hour movement took on an increasingly global character. At the ILO General Conference in Washington on 29 October, the first item on the agenda was the application

of the principle of the eight-hour day (or of the 48-hour week). The Hours of Work (Industry) Convention of 1919 obliged ratifying states to limit working hours for public and private industrial enterprise to no more than eight in the day and 48 in the week. A similar workweek was set at the International Labor Convention in Geneva, Switzerland, on 28 November 1919. The convention made the following exceptions to the eight-hour day: exclusively family run businesses, supervisors, management, and "persons employed in a confidential capacity." In cases where shorter days were worked, lost hours could be made up on other days provided the daily eight-hour limit was not exceeded by more than one hour. Moreover, persons working in shifts could work over the limit provided "the average number of hours over a period of three weeks or less does not exceed eight per day and forty-eight per week." The convention entered into force on 13 June 1921. Given that the U.S. Senate refused to ratify the Treaty of Versailles, which created the ILO, the United States could not join the organization.

Corporate Paternalism

Despite sluggish advances by the U.S. government, so-called welfare capitalists within the American business community had been exercising a sort of corporate paternalism that coincided with some of labor's demands.

On 5 January 1914 the Ford Motor Company cut its workday from nine hours to eight and raised workers' pay to $5 a day (double the going rate at other auto plants). Henry Ford extended his industrial philosophy into the homes of his workers on the grounds that conditions at home had a direct influence on efficiency in the factory. Ford's Five-Dollar Day was available to all employees over age 22 who proved they were "sober, saving, steady, industrious" and that their earnings would not be "wasted in riotous living." The plan generated mobs of unemployed workers outside the Ford plant in Detroit; many men thereafter refused to work for less than $5 a day. Ford's "profit-sharing plan" gave workers enough money to buy automobiles of their own, thus bringing money back to the company and dissolving efforts to unionize the Ford factory. Disciplined by overpayment, workers proved more accepting of speedups and other inconveniences. By 1926 Ford was experimenting with the five-day week.

In 1923 the U.S. Steel Corporation followed in Ford's footsteps to establish an eight-hour policy. Building directly on Ford's experiments, Paul Litchfield of Goodyear Tire and W. K. Kellogg of flaked cereal fame undertook six-hour workday initiatives.

Kellogg's was an American pioneer in what would come to be called *timesizing* (cutting hours instead of workers). Starting on 1 December 1930 the Battle Creek, Michigan, company offered a 30-hour workweek option. Company owner W. K. Kellogg, who championed the importance of rest and leisure in achieving productivity, was joined in his belief in a six-hour day by company president Lewis J. Brown, an Englishman highly influenced by Lord William Leverhulme, an English factory owner and the author of *The Six-Hour Day and Other Industrial Questions* (1919). Kellogg reportedly told Battle Creek mayor William Penty, "If we put in four six-hour shifts . . . instead of three eight-hour shifts, this will give work and paychecks to the heads of three hundred more families in Battle Creek." Cutting the workday to six hours, Kellogg's eliminated breaks and abolished bonuses for working unpopular shifts. With a 12.5 percent hourly raise, standard daily pay fell by only 15 percent.

A true 30/40 plan emerged when the 40-hour wage was again reached with a third wage raise in 1935. That year Kellogg's claimed a 39 percent increase over 1929 employment and a 41 percent accident reduction. With the advent of the Great Depression and a growing unemployment rate, workers were happy to share the work and later recalled using their increased leisure time for family activities, sports, socializing, and general community-building. "You weren't all wore out when you got out of work," one Kellogg's worker said. "You

had the energy to do something else." Both the business press and the U.S. government praised the experiment as a great success. On 14 April 1931 Kellogg's made the six-hour day permanent. That year President Herbert Hoover invited Kellogg to Washington to discuss the six-hour day.

The New Deal and the Shorter Workweek

In the United States, real change at the federal level came in 1933 with President Franklin D. Roosevelt's election and subsequent introduction of the New Deal. Given the despair facing American workers after years of economic depression, Roosevelt found support for his break with the capital-friendly policies of his laissez-faire predecessors and his introduction of sweeping economic and social policy changes. During this time labor leaders such as William Green of the American Federation of Labor were calling for the "six-hour day and the five-day week in industry." Some individual business were already experimenting with this formula. On 6 April 1933 the U.S. Senate approved a bill by Senator Hugo Black calling for a 30-hour week; anything over that limit was to be considered overtime. While the business community wasn't completely opposed to the bill, it did protest the wage and hour levels applied to their industries. After business interests convinced him to oppose the bill, Roosevelt argued that his New Deal was a better way of cutting unemployment. The bill was ultimately killed in the House of Representatives, where it lost by a few votes. According to Roosevelt's labor secretary, Frances Perkins, Roosevelt regretted not supporting the Black bill as early as 1935. Doing so, Perkins would write years later, would have brought decades of "tinkering in the right garage" instead of enshrining a 40-hour week.

The United States finally joined the ILO in 1934, and in 1935 former New Hampshire governor John G. Winant, as the organization's assistant director, convinced the ILO conference to commit to the 40-hour workweek as an international standard. In 1938 the Fair Labor Standards Act, in addition to setting a minimum wage and prohibiting child labor, established a workweek limit of 44 hours, albeit with no overtime pay. A century of demand was finally met in 1940, when Congress amended the Fair Labor Standards Act to limit the federal workweek to 40 hours.

Nonetheless, an important but invisible part of the labor force, one virtually ignored throughout the eight-day struggle, was left out of the 40-hour equation. While men saw their work hours outside the home decrease over the last century, the hours women dedicated to unpaid household work remained steady. In 1912–1914 housewives worked an estimated average of 56 hours per week; in the 1970s this average remained around 52 hours.

By the end of the twentieth century, some labor movements and political parties were calling for a 35-hour workweek, an idea with which some center-left European governments experimented. In the United States, the downward trend in labor hours began to reverse in 1969. The eight-hour day was applied inconsistently; California, for example, repealed its state eight-in-a-day law requiring overtime pay for workdays exceeding eight hours. "'Mandatory overtime has become a standard in most sectors of the working class," noted the *Worker's Voice* in 1997. "The fight for the eight-hour day has again become a demand for American workers."

Key Players

Black, Hugo LaFayette (1886–1971): As a member of the U.S. Senate, Black was a fervent supporter of New Deal policies. His depression-era bill calling for a 30-hour workweek was narrowly defeated in Congress. He went on to become an associate justice of the U.S. Supreme Court (1937–1971).

Ford, Henry (1863–1947): Ford, the leading American automaker of the early twentieth century, was a welfare capitalist who drew national attention to his Five-Dollar Day. In 1914 he paid workers double the industry wage for a shorter workday of eight hours. A staunch opponent of labor organizations, Ford vigorously opposed United Auto Worker unionization at his plants.

Kellogg, William Keith (1860–1951): Kellogg turned the Seventh-day Adventist Battle Creek Sanitarium into a food-processing empire based on flaked cereal production. A staunch advocate of rest and leisure as investments in productivity, he gained national attention with a successful 30-hour week option for his employees.

Parsons, Lucy (1853–1942): Parsons was an American anarchist and a key figure in the late nineteenth century revolutionary labor movement. A founder of the IPWA, she helped organized the general strike of 1 May 1866 calling for an eight-hour day. Following the hanging of her husband, Albert Parsons, after the Haymarket affair, she continued her militancy and helped found the IWW in 1905.

See also: *Fair Labor Standards Act; First International; Haymarket Riot; International Labor Organization; Ten-hour Day Movement; United Mine Workers of America.*

BIBLIOGRAPHY

Periodicals

Camara, Musa T. "When Is the 'Real' Labor Day?" *Los Angeles Sentinel,* 6 September 1995.

Hunnicutt, Benjamin Kline. "Kellogg's Six-Hour Day: A Capitalist Vision of Liberation Through Managed Work Reduction." *Business History Review* (autumn 1992).

Lowndes, Joe. "The Life of an Anarchist Labor Organizer." *Free Society* 2, no. 4, 1995.

Meeropol, Michael. "The Overworked American: The Unexpected Decline of Leisure." *Challenge* (July–August 1992).

Other

"American Business and the Beginning of the New Deal Era" [cited 28 January 2003] <www.timen.com/history/newdealeconomics.html>

"Continue the Fight for the 8-Hour Day." *Workers' Voice* [cited 28 January 2003]. <home.earthlink.net/~workersvoice/8hour.html>

"A Curriculum of United States Labor History for Teachers." Go Union Now [cited 28 January 2003]. <www.gounionnow.com/labor_history_curriculum.htm>

"First of May: Remember the 8-hour Work-day Struggle." Think Centre, Singapore. 26 April 2002 [cited 28 January 2003]. <www.thinkcentre.org/article.cfm?ArticleID=708>

"How the Weekend Was Won: Studs Terkel Gives Us All Hell." *Livelyhood.* PBS [cited 28 January 2003]. <www.pbs.org/livelyhood/workday/weekend/studsterkel.html>

Hyde, Philip. "Bibliography of Worktime Economics." *Timesizing Wire.* 1998–2002 [cited 28 January 2003]. <www.timesizing.com/1bibliog.htm>

"International Labor Convention (No. 1) Limiting the Hours of Work in Industrial Undertakings to Eight in the Day and Forty-eight in the Week, 28 November 1919." University of Minnesota Human Rights Library [cited 28 January 2003]. <www1.umn.edu/humanrts/links/ilo1.html>

Miller, Arthur J. "What Ever Happened to the Eight-Hour Day?" *IWW Workers Literature* [cited 28 January 2003]. <www.iww.org>

Sanchez de Lozada, Boris, and Robert Armoush. "Henry Ford and the Five Dollar Day." 1999 [cited 28 January 2003]. <web.bryant.edu/~history/h364proj/summ_99/armoush/index.htm>

Whalen, Kelly. "History Lesson: How the 8-Hour Day Was Won." *Livelyhood.* PBS [cited 28 January 2003]. <www.pbs.org/livelyhood/workday/weekend/8hourday.html>

—Brett Alan King

Employee Retirement Income Security Act

United States 1974

Synopsis

Most laws relating to private sector pensions in the United States are contained in one of two federal statutes: the Internal Revenue Code and the Employee Retirement Income Security Act (ERISA). ERISA was passed in 1974 and has been amended several times. Although ERISA deals with so-called employee welfare plans, including health plans, pension regulations make up the bulk of the law.

ERISA does not require an employer to establish a pension plan, nor does it dictate actual pension benefits. It does, however, subject established pension plans to numerous legal requirements, mainly to ensure that pension plans are used for employee retirement benefits and not exploited by employers. The law is thus part social insurance, part tax law, and part business regulation. ERISA is implemented by several different federal agencies, some of which were created by ERISA itself. Partly because of the law's broad aims and partly because of the complex politics that underlay its enactment, ERISA is a very large and extremely complex law. It was enacted largely as a kind of

Jimmy Hoffa. AP/Wide World Photos. Reproduced by permission.

delayed response to several pension-related scandals, similar to the pension-drenched accounting and business scandals prominent at the beginning of the 2000s and leading to calls for significant changes to ERISA.

Timeline

1955: African and Asian nations meet at the Bandung Conference in Indonesia, inaugurating the "non-aligned" movement of Third World countries.

1965: Power failure paralyzes New York City and much of the northeastern United States on 9 November.

1969: Assisted by pilot Michael Collins, astronauts Neil Armstrong and Edwin E. "Buzz" Aldrin become the first men to walk on the Moon (20 July).

1972: On 5 September, Palestinian terrorists kill eleven Israeli athletes and one West German policeman at the Olympic Village in Munich.

1975: Pol Pot's Khmer Rouge launch a campaign of genocide in Cambodia unparalleled in human history. By the time it ends, with the Vietnamese invasion in 1979, they will have slaughtered some 40 percent of the country's population. Cambodia is not the only country to fall to Communist forces this year: the pro-Western govern-

National League of Cities v. Usery: A Rare Tenth Amendment Challenge

Whereas numerous Supreme Court decisions have spawned new interpretations of well-known constitutional amendments such as the First, Fifth, or Fourteenth, *National League of Cities v. Usery* (1976) was one of the Court's few cases dealing with the Tenth. That amendment, dealing as it does with the reservation of powers by the individual states, presents an arena for contention between forces endorsing a strong national government and those who favor a greater degree of decentralization.

At issue were 1974 congressional amendments to the Fair Labor Standards Act (FLSA), itself a product of the New Deal. Passed in 1938, the FLSA established minimum-wage provisions. It also set the wage scale for overtime, which it defined as anything over 40 hours per week, as one and a half times the regular hourly rate. Starting in 1961, Congress began to amend the act, extending its provisions to include employees in the public as well as the private sectors.

In 1966 employees of state hospitals, institutions, and schools were placed under the act, and in 1974 Congress further amended it, defining "employer" in such a way that the term would include "a public agency." The latter was identified as "the Government of the United States, the government of a State or political subdivision thereof." Thus the wage and hour provisions of the FLSA were extended to include virtually all employees working for states or their political subdivisions.

To state and local governments, and to organizations such as the National League of Cities, the amendment to the FLSA seemed a violation of the Tenth Amendment. Last of the Bill Rights passed in 1791, the Amendment states simply that "The powers not delegated to the United States by the Constitution, nor prohibited to it by the States, are reserved to the States respectively, or to the people."

Together with the National Governors' Conference and various city and state governments, the National League brought legal action in the District Court for the District of Columbia. The named respondent was President Gerald R. Ford's secretary of labor, W. J. Usery, Jr., who would later enjoy great notoriety as the chief negotiator between the owners and the players' union in the 1994 Major League Baseball strike. (Another figure who would later appear in the news, Robert Bork, served as chief defense lawyer in his capacity as solicitor general of the United States.)

By a 5–4 majority, the Court ruled the 1974 amendments to the FLSA unconstitutional. Writing for the majority, William Rehnquist (the future chief justice) maintained that "Insofar as the 1974 amendments operate directly to displace the States' abilities to structure employer-employee relationships in areas of traditional government functions . . . they are not within the authority granted Congress by the Commerce Clause" of the Constitution. Just nine years later, however, the Court's ruling in *Garcia v. San Antonio Metropolitan Transit Authority* (1985), which again involved the commerce power of Congress to impose a minimum wage law on a city, overturned *Usery.*

Source: Tushnet, Mark V. "Why the Supreme Court Overruled *National League of Cities.*" *Vanderbilt Law Review* 47 (October 1994): 1623–55.

—Judson Knight

---

ments of South Vietnam and Laos also succumb, while Angola and Mozambique, recently liberated from centuries of Portuguese colonialism, align themselves with the Soviet Bloc.

1975: U.S. *Apollo* and Soviet *Soyuz* spacecraft link up in space.

1975: Two assassination attempts on President Ford occur in September.

1978: Terrorists kidnap and kill former Italian premier Aldo Moro. In Germany, after a failed hijacking on behalf of the Red Army Faction (RAF, better known as the Baader-Meinhof Gang), imprisoned RAF members commit suicide.

1980: In protest of the Soviet invasion of Afghanistan, President Carter keeps U.S. athletes out of the Moscow Olympics.

1985: In a year of notable hijackings by Muslim and Arab terrorists, Shi'ites take a TWA airliner in June, Palestinians hijack the Italian cruise ship *Achille Lauro* in Octo-

ber, and fundamentalists take control of an Egyptian plane in Athens in November.

1995: Bombing of the Alfred P. Murrah Federal Building in Oklahoma City, Oklahoma, kills 168 people. Authorities arrest Timothy McVeigh and Terry Nichols.

Event and Its Context

The Problem of Superannuation

To better understand ERISA's purposes, enactment, and meaning, it is necessary to review the concept and history of what used to be called "superannuation" and is now called "retirement." Many issues that were contentious when the concept of retirement emerged in the United States remain so today.

Pensions seem to have emerged as a response to various post-Civil War economic and demographic trends that mirrored one another. Various macroeconomic shifts made it increasingly necessary for people to work for others rather than for themselves, and for employment to move from agriculture to industry. It is conventionally argued that older people have been better able to find a place for themselves in agriculture than in industry because of differing value systems. Further, because of changes in birthrates and longevity between the Civil War era and the 1930s, the population was slowly aging—a trend that continues in the twenty-first century. In short, not long ago, most people seem to have died relatively young and worked until they died, mostly in an agricultural environment. Retirement was thus unnecessary. In response to these changes, the concept of an old-age pension slowly developed. The specifics of why or how would be difficult to trace with certainty, but similar concepts had developed earlier in other countries, usually manifesting as pension schemes similar to social security in the United States.

The first recognizable pensions in America were exclusive to Civil War veterans. It remains unclear whether this program consisted of retirement pensions, disability pensions, or both. Despite many administrative problems with the Civil War pension system, the program proved to be popular and lasted long enough to become a philosophical precedent for modern pensions. Most sources agree that, in 1875, the American Express Company established the first private pension plan in American, and that the Baltimore-Ohio Railroad established the second in 1880. This second plan was jointly financed by employer and employee contributions. This is considered an important innovation, because it increases the actuarial soundness of a pension plan and engenders a feeling of forced savings, or deferred compensation. After that, the pension plan quickly became a widespread and important factor in the economy, and it has only continued to grow in size and importance.

The Rise of ERISA

Government regulation and accommodation of pensions date back to the Revenue Acts of 1921 and 1926, which first gave pensions a special tax status and gave the Internal Revenue Service a limited amount of oversight over their management. Other laws were enacted throughout the 1940s, 1950s, and 1960s.

Pension reform began in earnest, however, in the late 1950s in response to a series of major pension-related scandals. One especially important scandal involved Jimmy Hoffa, the widely publicized leader of the Teamsters Union. Another involved the Studebaker car manufacturer. Both labor and management practices illustrated the need for increased federal regulation. Early reforms were enacted in response to a series of specific incidents and not through reasoned and deliberate public policy debate; reform was thus haphazard and episodic.

Although ERISA was the eventual outcome, the initial attempt at reform was the Welfare and Pension Plan Disclosure Act of 1958 (WPPDA, amended in 1962). WPPDA marked several firsts in retirement policy, including reporting requirements and enforcement by the U.S. Department of Labor. The WPPDA, however, was ultimately discredited. Commentators have described its various failings, most notably the lack of effective penalties and enforcement powers. Loopholes allowed certain activities that fell within the letter of the law but violated its clear spirit and intent; Jimmy Hoffa's worst crimes involving the Teamsters pension fund, for example, were committed after WPPDA. In addition, business leaders considered some re-

quirements unrealistic. The extremes of Studebaker's mismanagement of its pension plan led directly to ERISA, though the effect was quite delayed. The scandal prompted President John F. Kennedy, in 1962, to form the Committee on Corporate Pension Funds, charged with investigating the issue and producing a report, which it finally did by 1965.

Private sector pensions were not a common presidential interest, and it remains unclear why Kennedy was interested enough in the pension issue to form the committee in the first place. Regardless of Kennedy's motivations, however, his commission rapidly became mired in complex politics—both labor and business interests stood in the way of pension reform—and even more complex policy details. Their report was thus delayed until 1965, following Kennedy's assassination. By this time, however, the change in administration from Kennedy to Lyndon B. Johnson signaled a loss of presidential interest in the pensions issue. Johnson effectively put the issue on the backburner, concentrating instead on the Great Society, the War on Poverty, and, eventually, the Vietnam War. Private pensions became a congressional matter, and legislators were rapidly mired in the same complex mix of policy details and political interests. New York senator Jacob K. Javits took the lead and is usually credited as the principal author of ERISA.

No action was taken during the administration of Lyndon Johnson, and the issue stretched into the Richard Nixon era. Commentators suggest three reasons why pension reform took so long following the Studebaker scandals. First, the issue had little popular support, and, for the most part, those who were interested had personal stakes in the issue. Second, considerable time and effort were necessary to investigate and sort through many complex details. Third, the Nixon administration took a cautious approach to the issue, and for much of American history, it has been difficult to enact major legislative packages without active presidential support.

Despite these difficulties, by 1974 Congress had no less than three drafts of the pension reform act to consider. One was a U.S. Department of Labor "program bill," another was favored by the House, and yet another by the Senate. Congress still had many competing ideas and interests to sort through. Among the many issues for disagreement, the main points of contention were enforcement, specifically the roles of the Treasury and Labor departments; "vesting" requirements, which would allow an employee to draw retirement benefits upon reaching retirement age, even if no longer working for the employer providing the pension; and "accrual" requirements, which determine how benefits accumulate. From this point, the legislative history of ERISA becomes too arduous to be detailed here. The final product is the Pension Reform Act (PL 93-406), an extremely complex law that reflects many compromises and a long and complex legislative process.

Although ERISA has been amended several times since 1974—most notably by the Revenue Act of 1978 and the Retirement Equity Act of 1984—essentially it has changed little since its initial enactment. The plan does not require employers to establish pension plans, nor does it mandate what benefits are payable. ERISA does, however, provide certain requirements: vesting, benefit accrual, reporting to the government, maintaining the plan's actuarial soundness (these fiduciary requirements typically require the plan's managers to act in a "prudent" manner), and making information available to members of the plan. In general, traditional "defined benefit" plans are more stringently regulated than "defined contribution" plans such as 401(k), which were less popular when ERISA was enacted than they were at the beginning of the twenty-first century, though they were nonetheless subject to ERISA.

By the early 2000s, ERISA had come under the spotlight, with calls for amendment because of pension-related scandals, involving mainly employer mismanagement of employee defined contribution pension plans.

ERISA and Its Place

ERISA appears to have had many impacts on the American pension system, both philosophical and empirical. On the empirical level, pensions have clearly undergone tremendous growth since ERISA. It is difficult to say how much of this is a direct result of the law, but pension growth is undeniable, especially the less-regulated "defined contribution" pension plans. Philosophically, it is commonly argued that ERISA heralded a shift from thinking of pensions as employee rewards from employers for long and faithful service to a form of deferred compensation, to which employees were entitled sooner or later, simply by virtue of having worked.

Without the philosophical shift signaled by ERISA, today's modern economy—in which people increasingly switch jobs, employers, and careers—would not be tenable at all when retirement time arrives. Further, ERISA boosted private sector pensions, which are, in effect, quasipublic carriers that add to the government's social insurance system, though they remain private entities.

Key Players

Hoffa, James ("Jimmy") (1913–?): Hoffa led the International Brotherhood of Teamsters from 1957 to 1971. His is a strange and ambiguous legacy, having brought his union to both immense power and immense corruption. Raids on the Teamsters pension fund, which he either performed or allowed, led indirectly to the enactment of ERISA. He disappeared in 1975, probably at the hands of organized crime, and was declared legally dead in 1982.

Javits, Jacob K. (1904–1986): Javits, a child of immigrant parents, managed to be admitted to the New York State Bar by the age of 23. He served in the U.S. House of Representatives (1947 to 1954) and the U.S. Senate (1957 to 1981). His work in the Senate is what he is mainly remembered for.

BIBLIOGRAPHY

Books

Allen, Everett T., Jr., et al. *Pension Planning: Pensions, Profit Sharing, and Other Deferred Compensation Plans.* Boston: McGraw-Hill, 2003.

Horahan, Edward B., and Ellen A. Hennessy. *ERISA: Fiduciary Responsibility and Prohibited Transactions.* Washington, DC: Tax Management, 2001.

International Labour Conference. *Older Workers: Work and Retirement.* Geneva: International Labour Office, 1979.

Millis, Harry A., and Royal E. Montgomery. *Labor's Risks and Social Insurance.* New York: McGraw-Hill, 1938.

Sahin, Izzet. *Private Pensions and Employee Mobility: A Comprehensive Approach to Pension Policy.* New York: Quorum, 1989.

Sass, Steven A. *The Promise of Private Pensions: The First Hundred Years.* Cambridge, MA: Harvard University Press, 1997.

Schmitt, Ray. *Private Pension Plan Reform: A Summary of the Employee Retirement Income Security Act of 1974 (ERISA, Public Law 93-406).* Washington, DC: Congressional Research Service, 1979.

Skocpol, Theda. *Protecting Soldiers and Mothers: The Political Origins of Social Policy in the United States.* Cambridge, MA: Belknap, 1992.

United States Department of Labor, Pension and Welfare Benefits Administration. *General Information About ERISA / U.S. Department of Labor, Pension and Welfare Benefits Administration.* Washington, DC: The Administration, 1987.

United States Department of Labor, Women's Bureau. *The Retirement Equity Act of 1984: Its Impact on Women.* Washington, DC: U.S. Dept. of Labor, Women's Bureau, 1986.

Wise, David A. *Pensions, Labor, and Individual Choice.* Chicago: University of Chicago Press, 1985.

Woodruff, Alan P. *The ERISA Law Answer Book.* New York: Aspen, 2001.

Periodicals

Geannacopulous, Nick C., and Daniel J. Julius. "Understanding Document Disclosure and Requirements Under ERISA." *Labor Law Journal* 45 (1994): 359–366.

Henle, Peter, and Raymond Schmitt. "Pension Reform: The Long, Hard Road to Enactment." *Monthly Labor Review* (November 1974): 3–12.

Ippolito, Richard A. "The Economic Function of Underfunded Pension Plans." *Journal of Law and Economics* 28 (1985): 611–651.

Langbert, Mitchell. "ERISA: Law, Interests, and Consequences." *Journal of Economic Issues* 17 (1994): 277–289.

———. "Voice Asymmetries in ERISA Litigation." *Journal of Labor Research* 16 (1995): 455–465.

———. "Compliance with ERISA's Disclosure Provisions." *Journal of Labor Research* (spring 1996).

Lizzio, Joseph P. "Who Is Managing Your Retirement Plan?" *USA Today Magazine,* no. 2596 (1995): 41.

Seburn, Patrick W. "Evolution of Employer-Provided Defined Benefit Pensions." *Monthly Labor Review* (December 1991): 16–23.

Sickles, Carlton R. "Introduction: The Significance and Complexity of ERISA." *William and Mary Law Review* 17 (1975): 205–214.

Snarr, Brian B. "Supreme Court Adopts Common Law Definition of Employee for ERISA Purposes." *Compensation and Benefits Review* 24 (1992): 6–7.

Weiler, John J. "Fiduciary Provisions of the Employee Retirement Income Security Act of 1974." *Louisiana Law Review* 36 (1976): 897–927.

ADDITIONAL RESOURCES

Pension Benefit Guaranty Corporation [cited 3 December 2002]. <http://www.pbgc.gov/>.

U.S. Department of Labor [cited 3 December 2002]. <http://www.dol.gov/>.

—Steven Koczak

Equal Pay Act

United States 1963

Synopsis

The passage of the Equal Pay Act of 1963 marked the federal government's legislative foray into safeguarding working women's employment rights. The law itself was weak: it mandated that women doing work "equal" (not "comparable") to men be paid the same as men. It permitted a gradual elimination of wage differentials between men and women and exempted entirely employers with fewer than 25 employees.

The nearly two-decade battle for equal-pay legislation is as important for how it brought together a small group of women active in government, liberal, religious, and labor organizations to advocate for gender equality as it is for the actual law passed. Where once these activists defended protective laws for women workers, after World War II they turned their attention to widening women's employment opportunity. This came about as American women began to think differently about their status in the workplace and at home in the postwar period. As demographic, economic, and technological transformations began to affect women's lives in the 1950s and early 1960s, women workers demanded equality with men in such areas as seniority, job assignment, promotion, and pay.

Women unionists were at the forefront of the equal-pay effort. The law's passage was one of several factors leading to the rise of second-wave feminism after 1965. Union women's experiences in helping pass the law helped create support for feminism in the labor movement.

Timeline

1944: Allies land at Normandy on 6 June, conducting the largest amphibious invasion in history.

1949: Soviets conduct their first successful atomic test. This heightens growing cold war tensions, not least because the sudden acquisition of nuclear capabilities suggests that American spies are passing secrets.

1954: The French military outpost at Dien Bien Phu falls to the communist Vietminh. France withdraws after decades of trying to suppress revolt; meanwhile, the United States pledges its support for the noncommunist government in the south.

1959: Two new leaders appear on the scene in January as General Charles de Gaulle becomes the first president of France's Fifth Republic, and Fidel Castro takes control of Cuba after the collapse of the corrupt Batista regime.

1962: Publication of Rachel Carson's *Silent Spring* heightens Americans' awareness of environmental issues.

1964: On 7 February, in the midst of both a literal and figurative winter in America following Kennedy's assassination, the Beatles arrive at New York's newly renamed JFK Airport. The enthusiasm that greets them is partly the result of a clever marketing campaign—one of the first of its kind—but it also has a great deal to do with the sheer talent and charm exerted by the four. In their 9 February *Ed Sullivan Show* performance, they break a record set seven years earlier by their idol Elvis Presley, with 70 million viewers, or roughly 60 percent of the U.S. audience.

1964: In Mississippi, civil rights workers Andrew Goodman, Michael Schwerner, and Andrew Cheney are murdered. Twenty-one conspirators are arrested, and seven are convicted by a federal jury.

1964: U.S. Congress approves the Gulf of Tonkin resolution, giving President Johnson broad powers to prosecute the by now rapidly escalating war in Vietnam.

1967: The Beatles' *Sgt. Pepper's Lonely Hearts Club Band* tops the list of releases for a year that will long be remembered as a high point of rock history. Among the other great musical events of the year are releases by the Jimi Hendrix Experience, the Doors, and Jefferson Airplane; also, the Monterey Pop Festival marks the debut of Hendrix and Janis Joplin.

1968: The Reverend Martin Luther King is assassinated on 4 April. Senator Robert F. Kennedy is assassinated on 6 June.

1969: On 20 July, assisted by pilot Michael Collins, astronauts Neil Armstrong and Edwin E. "Buzz" Aldrin become the first men to walk on the Moon.

1974: On 30 July, the House Judiciary Committee adopts three articles of impeachment for President Nixon, but rather than undergo a lengthy trial, Nixon on 8 August becomes the first president in U.S. history to resign. His successor, Gerald Ford, pardons him in September.

1979: After years of unrest, the shah of Iran leaves the country, and Islamic fundamentalist revolutionaries under the leadership of Ayatollah Ruhollah Khomeini take control. Later in the year, militants seize control of the U.S. embassy in Teheran and take more than 50 Americans hostage.

Event and Its Context

The Legacy of World War II

Support for a federal equal-pay law for women dates back to the nineteenth century but only took concrete form in the 1940s, as large numbers of women entering the war production workforce demanded that they be paid on a par with men. In general, they were not, but they did take up jobs previously designated as "men's jobs" and destabilized the notion that women were unfit to perform certain kinds of work. "Rosie the Riveter" came to expect more money and greater status in the workplace and union with this new responsibility. At the very least, "Rosies" everywhere wanted to be paid what men, working alongside them, were paid. Male unionists had long supported equal pay, especially in industries where the replacement of men with women loomed large. Some would come to seek an equal-pay law for reasons rooted in union and political principles.

The United Electrical Workers (UEW) was led by such unionists. Fearful of the influx of women workers into an industry already marked by low wages, piece work, and the threat of female substitution, union leaders demanded equal pay in contracts, government administration rulings, and the law. Equal pay had been a collective bargaining goal long before the country's entry into the war in 1941, but UEW officers stepped up their campaign by calling on the government to mandate equal pay through the War Labor Board (WLB). The WLB had issued "General Order no. 16" in 1942, mandating that companies with government contracts institute equal-pay policies. In a 1945 case that introduced the issue of comparable worth for the first time, the WLB ordered General Electric and Westinghouse to raise women workers' pay by four cents an hour and to set aside two cents per hour in a fund for upgrading jobs held by female employees. The war ended soon after the ruling, and the electrical manufacturers for the most part ignored it. As dramatically as they had come into the war plants, women left or, in most cases, were fired. Those fortunate enough to secure employment during the reconversion period took severe pay cuts: women who had earned an average of 85 to 90 cents an hour were now accepting jobs that paid only 45 to 50 cents an hour.

The Early Campaign for a Federal Equal Pay Law

Mary Anderson, the U.S. Women's Bureau director, crafted the first federal equal-pay bill in 1945, confident that the widespread support for equal pay during World War II would carry over into the postwar period. She called for nondiscrimination in wages paid for "comparable work" rather than "equal work." The Women's Bureau explored the possibility of what is now called "comparable worth" in a series of hearings and investigations held in 1945 and 1947. The bureau scuttled its incipient campaign in the face of contention over how best to develop evaluation schemes and job point weights in specific industries. Moreover, equal pay better "fit" the mood of the postwar United States. Equal pay promised individual justice, helped increase economic growth by putting more money in some women's pockets, and reduced potential workplace friction by maintaining occupational sex-segregation. This buttressed the male-defined, family-wage ideology, while comparable worth challenged accepted conventional notions of gender roles and industrial wage policy. Congressional bills continued to use comparable worth terminology, but most supporters quietly abandoned pushing for its application beyond that meaning work of an identical or nearly identical nature.

As reasonable as equal-pay legislation seemed, nearly 20 years passed before Anderson's proposal became law, and yet another decade went by before her call for "equal pay for comparable worth" gained significant support. Frieda Miller, Anderson's successor in the bureau, continued to work for equal

Esther Peterson. AP/Wide World Photos. Reproduced by permission.

pay into the 1950s. She was met, however, by opposition from the business community, conservative legislators, and a withering of public interest in rewarding women for their wartime contribution, an effort that faded from public memory as the nation moved into the 1950s.

Union support for equal-pay legislation came from the Congress of Industrial Organizations (CIO) and its constituent unions, whose representatives testified before Congress that the bill's enactment was a matter of justice to women workers, beneficial to men, and necessary to the nation's well-being. These unions included the United Automobile Workers, United Rubber Workers, the Amalgamated Clothing Workers, and the Communications Workers of America. They viewed equal-pay legislation as a part of their "social union" mission to move beyond workplace issues and advocate for broad social change that valued human rights over property rights. Although social unionism receded in the face of modern business unionism in the 1950s, its rhetoric continued to embolden activists and some union leaders.

The other large labor federation of the period, the American Federation of Labor (AFL), was an organization dominated by skilled trade unions and had little interest in promoting "women's issues." In addition, the AFL objected to the legislation on the grounds that it opposed any schemes that involved the state in either evaluating job performance or setting wage rates. This hostility was rooted in the AFL's voluntaristic strategy, forged at the turn of the century by skilled trade unionists in reaction to debilitating court decisions and antiunion actions of state and federal politicians. Where the CIO saw its role in

President John F. Kennedy signs Equal Pay Act, White House, Washington, D.C. © Bettmann/Corbis. Reproduced by permission.

American society as wide-ranging and active in social reform, the AFL usually confined their efforts to agreements on such things as wages, hours, and training.

AFL leaders, in fact, were neither consistent nor unified in their approach to legislation. Their relationship to the state was both reactive and fluid, subject to change if circumstances warranted. In response to the debilitating effects of the Taft-Hartley Act, they began endorsing political candidates, usually Democrats. By the early 1950s, under the leadership of George Meany, the AFL was lobbying for further expansion of the Social Security program and an increased minimum wage. Shortly after the two federations merged in 1955, the AFL-CIO executive council formally endorsed equal-pay legislation. Thereafter, federation lobbyists Andrew Biemiller and George Riley worked with sympathetic lawmakers to generate interest in the bill.

The real force behind moving equal-pay legislation through Congress came from a loosely formed coalition sponsored by the U.S. Women's Bureau. The so-called Women's Bureau coalition had as its members unionists and those representing liberal interest groups, some of whom had their roots in the progressive movement. These groups included the Women's Trade Union League, the National Consumers League, and the League of Women Voters. Religion-based organizations and business

and professional organizations participated as well, although in a less-concerted fashion. Unionists spearheaded most of the coalition's efforts. This included men, such as David Lasser of the International Union of Electrical Workers (IUE). As head of the union's research department, Lasser conducted several important studies on equal pay and prepared the IUE's president, James Carey, to become a national advocate for the measure.

The campaign for equal pay languished for much of the 1950s. With the arrival of the Eisenhower administration in 1953, the executive branch's support cooled considerably. The new Women's Bureau director, Alice Leopold, angered equal-pay supporters by hinting that the bureau might soften its anti–Equal Rights Amendment (ERA) stance. She left union women and others on tenterhooks by occasionally stating that her office took no position against the amendment. Legislation backers believed that the ERA would negate protective laws for women workers and, perhaps, an equal-pay law. Although she did not abandon federal equal-pay legislation entirely, she failed to provide data on the prevalence of unequal pay scales, information many in Congress requested before backing the bill. More important, Leopold rejected federation overtures to back Edith Green's (D-OR) version of the original Anderson bill; she endorsed instead the conservative bill introduced into the House of Representatives by Frances P. Bolton (R-OH).

Bolton's bill gave enforcement power to administrators in the Wage and Hour Division of the Department of Labor to mediate disputes; they could not issue "cease and desist" orders, as Green authorized the Women's Bureau head to do in her bill. Also, while the Bolton bill provided for the secretary of labor to file suit on the complainants' behalf, it did not include a blacklist provision for guilty employers as did the Green measure.

For the first time, the center of support for equal pay shifted outside government and onto the National Committee on Equal Pay (NCEP), whose executive board was dominated by unionists. Although their support for equal pay never wavered, federation officers did not make the bill's passage a priority. Nor did unions. Most collective bargaining agreements did not reflect a commitment to equal pay: a Bureau of Labor Statistics study completed in the early 1950s found that only one-fifth of the 2,644 bargaining agreements analyzed contained equal-pay clauses.

Still, if Americans did not support equal pay with vigor during this period, they nevertheless were gradually more willing to accept the idea. Changing economic, social, and familial norms progressively destabilized gender relations in the two decades following the war's end. The massive layoffs and demotions of women workers in the 1945–1947 period gave way to a significant rise in the proportion and number of women in the paid labor force beginning in the late 1940s. While younger women starting families after World War II tended to stay at home, the percentage of mothers in the work force with children between the ages of six and seventeen shot up to 41.5 percent in 1963 from 30.3 percent in 1950, a 37 percent increase. As more women went on the payroll at factories, offices, retail stores, and schools, union activists conveyed the idea that working women's rights were a legitimate issue for public debate.

Passage of the Equal Pay Act of 1963

Prospects for passage of an equal-pay law increased significantly following John F. Kennedy's election to the presidency in 1960. The new administration was not only more open to social legislation than the Republicans but included several unionists receptive to "women's issues." Key congressional figures marshaled support for the equal-pay struggle as well. Adam Clayton Powell (D-NY), who replaced the intractable Graham Barden (D-NC) as chair of the important House Education and Labor Committee in 1960, favored equal-pay legislation. Women legislators, in particular, played an important role in convincing colleagues to back equal-pay proposals. Veterans from both parties, such as Bolton, Katharine St. George (R-NY), and Edna Kelly (D-NY), introduced and supported various bills, eventually backing Edith Green's effort.

Esther Peterson, more than anyone, revitalized interest in equal-pay legislation from her post as Women's Bureau head and assistant secretary of labor for President Kennedy. First as a lobbyist for the Amalgamated Clothing Workers, then as the legislative representative of the AFL-CIO's Industrial Union Division (IUD), Peterson was a tenacious promoter of equal pay. She undertook equal-pay studies, urged congressional hearings, and convened meetings with union and NCEP members in her office, agreeing with those present to back the Green bill.

In the end, conservatives in Congress and the business community weakened the measure considerably. The act, modeled on the Fair Employment Standards Act coverage, exempted employers with fewer than 25 employees and permitted a gradual elimination of wage differentials between men and women workers. Unionists were particularly troubled by the replacement of "comparable worth" language with that of "equal work." Since the bill's inception in the mid-1940s, its advocates had insisted that "equal" would mean identical and that slight differences might be used by employers to justify disparate wages. They had long ago scotched the notion that "comparable" should address the relative aspects of positions based on skill, effort, and responsibility, but they still clung to the belief that retaining such language would prevent employer chiseling. Union leaders feared that managers would make minor changes in job elements in order to evade the law.

Labor representatives were in a weak position on this issue. Although they fought off the introduction of "equal" language into the bill, their fuzzy, narrowly construed notion of "comparable" said more about what they opposed than what they sought from legislators. In order to retain the "comparable" language, unionists had to acknowledge that they would have to make job comparisons at individual work sites; they balked, however, at the establishment of a job evaluation system, since it might strengthen management's already considerable control over employment matters. In the end, conservative lawmakers carried the day on the issue. Despite their misgivings in conceding to opponents on this matter, unionists and other NCEP members nevertheless honored Peterson's request to support the measure as being the only bill that had a chance of passage.

Labor leaders were able to intervene at key points to ward off some of the debilitating changes being made to the pending legislation. Unionists helped defeat an attempt by conservatives to include a provision in the bill postponing the effective date of the Equal Pay Act in the case of employees covered by current labor-management contracts until two years after enactment, or until contracts expired. They worried that such an allowance would set a dangerous precedent when they called for examining the minimum wage or maximum hours provisions of the Fair Labor Standards Act.

In the wake of victory, women unionists assessed with pride their important role in the struggle. Activists viewed the act's passage as a confirmation of their place within the labor movement and in the liberal wing of the Democratic Party. Women were in the forefront of bringing the measure to Congress. They had definitively moved from the role traditionally assigned to them of providing auxiliary support to male unionists. Esther Peterson navigated treacherous political waters in convincing hesitant lawmakers that an equal-pay law was necessary. The struggle for a federal equal-pay law was an undertaking that union women would not let others forget during the height of second-wave feminism in the 1970s.

Those gathered in Washington, D.C., to celebrate on 11 June 1964—the date the Equal Pay Act was put into effect—understood the law's limitations but hoped it would serve as a symbolic victory for equality. In its first decade of enforcement, court decisions interpreted the meaning of "equal" pay broadly by refusing to limit the measure to identical jobs. As a result, the government awarded 171,000 employees $84 million in back pay.

The law was one of several signs in the early 1960s that support for gender equality in the workplace was on the rise. John F. Kennedy's President's Commission on the Status of Women, formed in the early 1960s, brought to national scrutiny for the first time the unresolved question of whether protective laws for women workers should be retained in the face of growing support for equality. In the years immediately preceding the emergence of second-wave feminism, new possibilities had begun to emerge, but they moved against the forces of tradition, industrial policy, and the law. Although the unionists and legislators who were most responsible for the Equal Pay Act of 1963 were not, at the time, in favor of jettisoning protective laws for women for the goal of workplace equality, the new law they helped create underscored a shift in working women's sentiment that would manifest itself over the course of the next decade in feminist activism.

Key Players

Anderson, Mary (1872–1964): As head of the U.S. Women's Bureau, Anderson crafted the first federal equal-pay bill in 1945. She called for nondiscrimination in wages paid for "comparable work" rather than merely "equal work."

Lasser, David (1902–1994): In his position as research director of the International Union of Electrical Workers, AFL-CIO, Lasser was a persistent advocate for equal-pay legislation. He conducted several studies on the matter and presented his prepared testimony to Congress in the 1950s and early 1960s.

Peterson, Esther (1906–1997): Peterson is considered by her peers and historians as being the most significant advocate for equal-pay legislation. She served as lobbyist for the Amalgamated Clothing Workers of America, AFL-CIO, staff member of the Industrial Union Department, AFL-CIO, and the director of the U.S. Women's Bureau in the Kennedy Administration.

See also: *Equal Rights Amendment and Protective Legislation; Women in Industry Service.*

BIBLIOGRAPHY

Books

Deslippe, Dennis A. *Rights, Not Roses: Unions and the Rise of Working-Class Feminism, 1945–1980.* Urbana: University of Illinois Press, 2000.

Cobble, Dorothy Sue. "Recapturing Working-Class Feminism: Union Women in the Postwar Era." In *Not June Cleaver: Women and Gender in Postwar America, 1945–1960,* edited by Joanne Meyerowitz. Philadelphia: Temple University Press, 1994.

Gabin, Nancy F. *Feminism in the Labor Movement: Women and the United Auto Workers, 1935–1975.* Ithaca: Cornell University Press, 1990.

Harrison, Cynthia. *On Account of Sex: The Politics of Women's Issues, 1945–1968.* Berkeley: University of California Press, 1988.

Kessler-Harris, Alice. *In Pursuit of Equity: Women, Men, and the Quest for Economic Citizenship in Twentieth-Century America.* New York: Oxford University Press, 2001.

—Dennis A. Deslippe

Equal Rights Amendment and Protective Legislation

United States 1923

Synopsis

After the ratification of the Nineteenth Amendment in 1920, differences arose among women's rights advocates over strategy. One group of social reformers, most notably the National Consumers' League (NCL) and its allies, favored continuation of the 30-year campaign of multifaceted reform including protective legislation for women workers. A smaller group led by Alice Paul and her National Women's Party (NWP) came to embrace a more narrow strategy to achieve gender equality by passing a constitutional amendment to erase all surviving legal impediments to equality, including gender-specific protective legislation. The ensuing debate between proponents of the Equal Rights Amendment (ERA) and opposing reformers came to focus on the issue of protective legislation, increasingly defined by the NWP as discriminatory and a positive harm to women's economic opportunity. At the heart of the debate was the question of "equality vs. difference" in the workplace: was the common goal of equality best served by insuring women access to the same rights and conditions as men, or did substantive equality require that women be treated differently? ERA opponents staked their positions on women's differences, arguing that women's unique maternal functions necessitated special treatment, including in the workplace; ERA proponents advocated equal access on equal terms to all. The debate was marked by extraordinary vituperation; even after passage of the Fair Labor Standards Act (1938) made gender-specific protective legislation moot, the labor and reform movements remained largely opposed to the ERA until the 1970s.

Timeline

1907: At the Second Hague Peace Conference, 46 nations adopt 10 conventions governing the rules of war.

1912: *Titanic* sinks on its maiden voyage, from Southampton to New York, on 14 April. More than 1,500 people are killed.

1917: In Russia, a revolution in March (or February according to the old Russian calendar) forces the abdication of Czar Nicholas II. By July, Alexander Kerensky has formed a democratic socialist government, and continues to fight the Germans, even as starvation and unrest sweep the nation. On 7 November (25 October old style), the Bolsheviks under V. I. Lenin and Leon Trotsky seize power. By 15 December, they have removed Russia from the war by signing the Treaty of Brest-Litovsk with Germany.

1919: With the formation of the Third International (Comintern), the Bolshevik government of Russia establishes its control over communist movements worldwide.

1922: Inspired by the Bolsheviks' example of imposing revolution by means of a coup, Benito Mussolini leads his blackshirts in an October "March on Rome," and forms a new fascist government.

1922: Great Britain establishes the Irish Free State as a dominion of the British Empire.

1922: With the centuries-old Ottoman Empire dissolved, Mustafa Kemal, a.k.a. Atatürk, overthrows the last sultan and establishes the modern Turkish republic.

1922: Union of Soviet Socialist Republics (USSR) is formed.

1922: Published this year James Joyce's novel *Ulysses* and T. S. Eliot's poem *The Waste* Land will transform literature and inaugurate the era of modernism.

1925: European leaders attempt to secure the peace at the Locarno Conference, which guarantees the boundaries between France and Germany, and Belgium and Germany.

1927: Charles A. Lindbergh makes the first successful solo nonstop flight across the Atlantic, and becomes an international hero.

1932: When Ukrainians refuse to surrender their grain to his commissars, Stalin seals off supplies to the region, creating a manmade famine that will produce a greater death toll than the entirety of World War I.

Event and Its Context

Proponents of women's rights in the United States historically linked political and economic rights; indeed, women's exclusion from political life had been premised in part on their status as economic dependents. Late-nineteenth-century advocates argued that the right to labor and to economic independence was a necessary prerequisite of women's political independence. Women's rights advocates thus widely shared the pervasive outrage at horrific conditions of labor under industrial capitalism and at the particular exploitation of women workers. Social reformers and suffrage activists found common cause in support of measures to alleviate workers' distress. Social reformers desired the vote for women as a means of furthering the reform agenda; suffrage advocates viewed protective legislation for women as a useful mechanism to attract working women to the cause. The American Federation of Labor (AFL) came to support protective legislation for women for a variety of reasons. Reluctant to organize women, male unionists viewed state protection as a viable alternative to collective bargaining for women, and they also saw the laws' utility in protecting traditionally male jobs from female competition.

Efforts to regulate conditions of labor in the United States had a history reaching back to the earliest days of the Republic

Florence Kelley. The Library of Congress.

and were generally not gender-specific. Working people fought throughout the nineteenth century to negotiate or legislate limits on the workday for the general welfare. By the 1870s, 13 states had passed either mandatory or nonbinding 10-hour workday statutes. Such attempts to regulate working conditions by exercising state police power, however, were increasingly struck down by the Supreme Court as violations of freedom of contract. The famous *Lochner v. New York* (1905) decision was a critical turning point. The Court in *Lochner* decisively rejected traditional arguments based on general welfare and overturned a New York State law mandating the 10-hour workday for bakers as violating liberty of contract.

Even before *Lochner,* social reformers, often working out of settlement houses like Chicago's Hull House, had begun to pressure state legislatures to pass protective legislation specifically targeting women and children. The Illinois Factory Act of 1893, for example, limited hours for women, prohibited child labor, and regulated sweatshop conditions. Florence Kelley of Hull House was a prime motivator of this legislation. Though the hours limitation for women was struck down in 1895 (*Ritchie v. People*), Kelley carried the fight for protective legislation to the national level from her new post as general secretary of the National Consumers' League (NCL).

After the *Lochner* setback, social reformers began to espouse protective legislation for women as an "entering wedge" to secure general protections that would apply to all. The NCL, in alliance with other reform organizations such as the Women's Trade Union League (WTUL), spearheaded such efforts; the organization won hours limits and night work restric-

Suffragettes picket the White House. The Library of Congress.

tions in 18 states. In 1908 the NCL rose to defend its work when *Muller v. Oregon* threatened to strike down Oregon's 10-hour law for women workers. Kelley recruited Louis Brandeis to argue Oregon's case; the famous "Brandeis Brief" produced by Brandeis and Josephine Goldmark consisted of 110 pages of sociological data justifying hours limitations as necessary to protect women's unique physiology and reproductive functions. Brandeis argued successfully that the state's interest in protecting the health of mothers of the race superceded freedom of contract doctrine. *Muller* served as precedent for state courts to uphold a variety of protective laws for women, including hours limits, night work bans, and minimum wage laws. Frequently, however, such laws effectively restricted access to better-paying night work and reinforced women's relegation to lower-paid, gender-segregated jobs. Consistent with its "opening wedge" strategy, the NCL in *Bunting v. Oregon* (1917) used the same sort of argument advanced in *Muller* to support successfully a maximum hours law for all workers.

Ratification of the Nineteenth Amendment in 1920 spelled the end of the social reform–suffrage coalition. The largest suffrage organization, the National American Woman Suffrage Association (NAWSA), reorganized as the League of Women Voters (LWV) and continued to work on electoral issues. The militant wing, led by the charismatic Alice Paul, reconstituted itself as the National Women's Party (NWP) and devised a new strategy: another constitutional amendment, an Equal Rights Amendment (ERA), to sweep away remaining legal impediments to women's equality. Paul recruited wealthy supporters such as Alva Vanderbilt Belmont to bankroll the effort, thereby opening the party to later accusations of class bias and insensitivity to working-class women.

Initially, Paul explored the possibility of adding language to the ERA specifically to exempt protective legislation. She fa-

vored maintaining such laws and extending the benefits to men. Others in the NWP, however, were adamantly opposed to protective legislation. Harriet Stanton Blatch, daughter of Elizabeth Cady Stanton, and Gail Laughlin, president of the National Federation of Business and Professional Women's Clubs, considered protective legislation inherently discriminatory and restrictive. Laughlin chaired the NWP Lawyers' Committee that drafted the amendment, and her views convinced Paul; the resulting language did not exempt protective legislation from the sweeping ambit of the amendment.

Social reformers were alarmed at the implications. In December 1921 Florence Kelley of the NCL initiated a meeting of women's rights activists to discuss the issue. Representatives from the NWP, the LWV, the WTUL, the Women's Christian Temperance Union (WCTU) and the General Federation of Women's Clubs (GFWC) attended. Kelley formally requested that the ERA language be altered to preserve protective legislation; Paul refused. By mid-1922 the NCL, the LWV, and the WTUL had all publicly announced their opposition to the "blanket equal rights amendment," and the split in the women's rights movement became painfully evident.

In 1923 the NWP took its growing antipathy to protective legislation to a new level. The party filed an *amicus curiae* brief in *Adkins v. Children's Hospital*, arguing against a Washington, D.C., minimum wage law for women. The Court ruled that the D.C. statute was unconstitutional, thereby restoring *Lochner's* freedom of contract standard and jeopardizing existing and future legislation, to the dismay and anger of reformers. The NWP capped the year with a huge conference in November 1923 at Seneca Falls, New York, where the party commemorated the 75th anniversary of the Declaration of Sentiments by officially launching the ERA. The amendment was introduced in Congress on 10 December 1923.

The NWP made opposition to protective legislation for women a key element of its campaign, appealing to women who had been adversely affected by the legislation, particularly professional women and skilled workers who competed directly with men. The NWP's Industrial Council claimed some 400 members who spoke for working women in support of the ERA. The NWP stood nearly alone, however. Only the National Federation of Business and Professional Women's Clubs allied with them, and opponents were legion. Virtually every major women's organization publicly repudiated the ERA. Joining the NCL, the LWV, the WCTU, the WTUL in opposition were the National Association of University Women, the PTA, the YWCA, the National Federation of Federal Employees, the Department of Labor's Women's Bureau, and a host of others.

The Women's Bureau proved to be a formidable opponent. The bureau's director, Mary Anderson, was a former factory worker and long-time proponent of labor legislation with an instinctive distrust of non-working-class feminists of the NWP. Her office, plus her working relationship with both women's reform groups and the trade unions, made her a pivotal figure in the debate. At a 1926 Women's Bureau conference, the NWP forced through a resolution directing the bureau to undertake an investigation to explore the effects of protective legislation. The ensuing investigation was marked by extraordinary conflict as Anderson sought to placate all sides while arriving at conclusions that would support the need for legislation. Indeed, the final report, *The Effects of Labor Legislation on the Employment of Women*, constituted an overwhelming if somewhat suspect endorsement of protective legislation that functioned to define the bureau's stance on the issue through the 1930s. The 1938 passing of the Fair Labor Standards Act finally settled the issue by extending protection to all workers, regardless of gender.

In the end, both sides in the debate proved right: protective legislation did afford the "greatest good to greatest number" as its supporters argued, but it also left women at a disadvantage in significant occupational sectors and functioned to reinforce the gender-segregated workforce with its inherent inequalities. Perhaps the most lasting outcome of the conflict over the ERA and protective legislation was the split in the feminist movement that reverberated through the decades to present, and is still evident in the periodic revival of the "equality v. difference" debate.

Key Players

Kelley, Florence (1859–1932): Born in Philadelphia and raised as a Quaker, Kelley graduated from Cornell University in 1882 and then studied in Zurich, where she became acquainted with European socialism. She was the daughter of William "Pig Iron" Kelley, a 15-term congressman whose career is said to have instructed Kelley in the efficacy of legislative action. A lifelong socialist, Kelley resided at Hull House from 1891 to 1899, where she energetically undertook the investigation of factory conditions and became the first chief factory inspector for Illinois. Kelley served as secretary general of the National Consumers' League from its founding in 1899 until her death in 1932. Perhaps the foremost proponent of protective legislation for women, Kelley quit the NWP over the ERA and became its most adamant opponent.

Paul, Alice (1885–1977): Born to a wealthy Quaker family in Moorestown, New Jersey, Paul attended Quaker schools and graduated from Swarthmore College in 1905. She spent three years in London doing settlement work; while there, she joined the militant wing of the British suffrage movement and was jailed three times. Paul joined the National American Woman Suffrage Association (NAWSA) on her return but, impatient with the group's decorous tactics, left NAWSA in 1913 to form the British-styled Congressional Union, later renamed the National Women's Party (NWP). After the passing of the Nineteenth Amendment, Paul devised the "clean sweep" strategy to remove remaining legal restrictions via an Equal Rights Amendment. She devoted the rest of her life to its enactment.

See also: *Fair Labor Standards Act; Lochner v. New York; Muller v. Oregon.*

BIBLIOGRAPHY

Books

Becker, Susan. *The Origins of the Equal Rights Amendment: American Feminism Between the Wars.* Westport, CT: Greenwood Press, 1981.

Cott, Nancy F. *The Grounding of Modern Feminism.* New Haven, CT: Yale University Press, 1987.

Dye, Nancy Schrom. *As Equals and as Sisters: Feminism, the Labor Movement, and the Women's Trade Union League of New York.* Columbia: University of Missouri Press, 1980.

Fry, Amelia R. "Alice Paul and the ERA." In *Rights of Passage: The Past and Present of the ERA*, edited by Joan Hoff-Wilson. Bloomington: Indiana University Press, 1986.

Kessler-Harris, Alice. *Out to Work: A History of Wage-Earning Women in the United States.* New York: Oxford University Press, 1982.

———. *In Pursuit of Equity: Women, Men, and the Quest for Economic Citizenship in 20th-Century America.* New York: Oxford University Press, 2001.

Lehrer, Susan. *Origins of Protective Labor Legislation for Women, 1905–1925.* Albany: State University of New York Press, 1987.

Newman, Louise Michelle. *White Women's Rights: The Racial Origins of Feminism in the United States.* New York: Oxford University Press, 1999.

O'Connor, Karen. *Women's Organizations' Use of the Courts.* Lexington, MA: Lexington Books, 1980.

Sklar, Katherine Kish. "Why Were Most Politically Active Women Opposed to the ERA in the 1920s?" In *Rights of Passage: The Past and Present of the ERA*, edited by

Joan Hoff-Wilson. Bloomington, IN: Indiana University Press, 1986.

Other

Skaler, Katherine Kish, and Thomas Dublin, eds. "Who Won the Debate over Equal Rights in the 1920s?" In *Women and Social Movements in the United States, 1775–2000.* State University of New York at Binghamton. 2000 [cited 18 November 2002]. <http://www.binghamton.edu/womhist/era/intro.htm>

—Lisa Kannenberg

Equal Rights Party

United States 1836

Synopsis

On 15 September 1836, 93 delegates from throughout the state of New York convened in the western town of Utica and unanimously resolved "to institute a political party separate and distinct from all existing parties or factions in this State." With this declaration, the Equal Rights Party proclaimed its independent political existence. The party proceeded to ratify a Declaration of Rights enunciating its views on several key issues of political economy and nominated candidates for governor and lieutenant governor for the upcoming election. The Utica convention concluded by issuing an "Address to the People" of New York, which echoed the sentiments of the Declaration of Rights and outlined the party's positions on several specific issues particularly salient for the state's working classes. With these actions, the Equal Rights Party—for its brief period of existence—became the political instrument by which a significant portion of New York's laborers were able to leave an imprint upon the state's political landscape.

Timeline

1812: The War of 1812, sparked by U.S. reactions to oppressive British maritime practices undertaken in the wake of the wars against Napoleon, begins in June. It lasts until December 1814.

1820: In the Missouri Compromise, Missouri is admitted to the Union as a slave state, but slavery is prohibited in all portions of the Louisiana Purchase north of 36°30' N.

1828: Election of Andrew Jackson as president begins a new era in American history.

1833: British Parliament passes the Slavery Abolition Act, giving freedom to all slaves throughout the British Empire.

1834: American inventor Cyrus H. McCormick patents his reaper, a horse-drawn machine for harvesting wheat.

1836: Boer farmers embark on their "Great Trek" into the hinterlands of South Africa, forming the enclaves of Natal, Transvaal, and the Orange Free State.

1836: In Texas's war of independence with Mexico, the defenders of the Alamo, among them Davy Crockett and Jim Bowie, are killed in a siege. Later that year, Texas wins the Battle of San Jacinto and secures its independence.

1836: Charles Dickens publishes the earliest installments of *The Pickwick Papers,* his first novel.

1837: An Illinois mob slays abolitionist publisher Elijah P. Lovejoy.

1842: In *Sanitary Conditions of the Labouring Population of Great Britain,* British reformer Edwin Chadwick draws attention to the squalor in the nation's mill town slums, and shows that working people have a much higher incidence of disease than do the middle and upper classes.

1846: American inventor Elias Howe patents his sewing machine.

1848: Discovery of gold at Sutter's Mill in California starts a gold rush, which brings a tremendous influx of settlers—and spells the beginning of the end for California's Native Americans.

Event and Its Context

Background: The Workingmen's Movement

The movement to organize a politically distinct "Workingmen's Party" rose in New York City during the spring of 1829. A mass meeting of "mechanics and others" convened on 23 April to protest against employers who violated the tacit agreement with workers to hold to a 10-hour workday. Among the resolutions approved was a call for another meeting to contemplate a broader array of working men's concerns. Over 6,000 attended this larger gathering, and from it issued the formal actions to lay the foundations for the proposed Workingmen's Party. A "Committee of Fifty" was appointed to create the framework for the new organization, and it issued its report and statement of principles for the Workingmen's Party on 19 October 1829. On 23 October the Workingmen's Party held a formal convention, during which the members nominated a slate of candidates for the state's General Assembly.

Despite these seemingly auspicious beginnings amid a groundswell of support from New York's workers, the Workingmen's Party was from its inception plagued by factionalism that would fragment the organization within a few months after its founding. The party was able to retain its cohesiveness in the 1829 election, during which it polled approximately 6,000 out of the 21,000 votes cast in the city and saw one of its candidates elected to the General Assembly. Shortly afterward, though, it split along three distinct lines. Out of a contentious December meeting emerged three competing factions, divided by distinct ideological differences, all laying claim to the mantle of the Workingmen's Party. This schism meant that the 1830 elections suffered conflicting claims for workers' loyalty, and the result was a cacophony of rival candidates who all performed dismal-

Tammany Hall, New York City. AP/Wide World Photos. Reproduced by permission.

ly at the polls. Despite earlier arguments of the party's leaders that cooperation with the political establishment was the surest way to undermine the separate agenda and goals of the Workingmen's movement, most New York City workers returned to the fold of the Democratic Party after the 1830 elections, given the lack of a legitimate alternative. Thus, the Workingmen's Party as a formal political organization perished less than two years after its founding.

The broader principles and issues that had inspired the formation of the Workingmen's Party would persist, however, and this larger movement found new organizational form in the 1830s. By the middle of the decade, the General Trades' Union

(GTU) of New York City encompassed more than 50 smaller workingmen's organizations. The GTU organized collective action among its member groups in support of a number of important issues for the city's workers, chief among them the drive for a 10-hour day. The preferred tactic was the strike, or the "turn-out." In the mid-1830s the major cities of the eastern seaboard saw an abundance of "turn-outs" by workingmen's groups for the 10-hour day. The workers of New York kept pace with their brethren from other cities, and the GTU took the lead in the local battles over the issue.

The city's employers and wealthier classes argued that this wave of strikes portended social breakdown and economic chaos. The actions of the groups affiliated under the GTU, they argued, violated both individual employers' property rights and the laws of the state in that they constituted conspiracies geared toward unlawful restraint of free trade. The state's conservative judiciary agreed, making this logic the backbone of two significant decisions that struck a major blow at collective action by workers' organizations. New York's Supreme Court, in *People v. Fisher* (1835), declared that a Geneva cordwainers' society injured commerce by striking for higher wages. "Competition is the life of trade," the court asserted. Thus, the cordwainers had a right to refuse to work for certain wages, but once they undertook to prevent others from doing so they interfered with the free flow of trade. This momentous decision encouraged other employers to strike at workingmen's organizations through the judiciary. The climax of this legal crusade came the next year with the prosecution of a New York City society of journeymen tailors for conspiracy to restrain trade. The presiding judge in the trial gave such a strong antilabor charge to the jury, critics accused, that the verdict was virtually preordained. William Cullen Bryant, the editor of the *New York Evening Post*, editorialized that the tailors were found guilty "because they had determined not to work for the wages offered them! . . . If this is not Slavery, we have forgotten its definition." The efforts of the GTU mobilized the city's workers to protest the verdict at a June mass meeting during which the workingmen's organizations would align themselves with dissident members of the state's Democratic party organization to form a new political body.

Background: The Locofocos

By the mid-1830s the state's powerful Democratic Party was also wracked by internal dissent. Divided into the establishment "Tammany" wing (a reference to the control over party apparatus in New York City by the powerful "sachems" of Tammany Hall) and an "antimonopolist" faction, the party split shortly after the 1834 elections over the issue of legislative chartering of incorporations—especially banks. Following the lead of the national Democratic Party during President Andrew Jackson's "war" on the Bank of the United States, the antimonopolists of New York took exception to the state legislature's easy incorporation policies. Arguing that the actions of the mainstream Democrats who controlled the assembly essentially gave legislative sanction to a monopoly of state banks, most of which were unsound and engaged in dangerous speculative practices, the antimonopolists gathered enough support to be able to get Democratic candidates in the 1834 state elections to pledge their opposition to "monopoly" and the lax, corrupt incorporation practices of previous legislative sessions.

Once the elections were over, however, most of the victorious candidates promptly recanted these antimonopoly pledges. The antimonopolists of New York City concluded that stricter measures were necessary to prevent what they saw as rampant corruption and injurious policies issuing from Albany. At a party meeting at Tammany Hall on 29 October 1835, they sought to elect an antimonopolist to the chair and reclaim the state's Democratic Party by nominating a slate of antibank candidates for the upcoming election. Having received advance warning of this attempted insurgency, the Tammany leaders adjourned the meeting early and turned off the gas lamps upon exiting the building. Prepared for this eventuality, the insurgents lit torches with the new "locofoco" matches—thus the nickname bestowed on their movement. In the match-lit confines of Tammany, the Locofoco Democrats proceeded to nominate their antimonopoly candidates to oppose the Tammany Democrats. Their efforts produced about 4,000 votes in the city elections—somewhat disappointing results, but strong enough to convince locofoco leaders that enough support existed to take the next—and radical—step of forming a separate political party. At a meeting at the Military and Civic Hotel in December 1835, the Locofoco leadership—despairing of the mainstream Democratic Party's chances of ever adopting an antibank, antimonopoly platform—agreed to repudiate Tammany Hall's leadership and rename their movement the Equal Rights Party.

The Confluence

The Workingmen's movement and the Locofocos, already allied in principle, became allied in fact in June 1836. Considerable overlap already existed between the two, as several leaders in the GTU had been active in the antimonopoly movement. At the meeting of 13 June 1836, attended by over 27,000 New York City workers to protest the conviction of the journeymen tailors, members heartily approved resolutions to hold a statewide convention at Utica in September to nominate candidates who would overturn the policies of monopoly and the judicial restraint of workers' organizations. The Equal Rights Party, which had already formulated a statement of principles and a citywide organization, voted overwhelmingly to join the workingmen at Utica, as "the objects and measures" of the convention "must necessarily be founded upon the same reforms in government, as are urged by the anti-monopoly democracy."

The Convention and Its Aftermath

The Declaration of Principles adopted by the Utica convention was actually the document framed by the Locofoco leadership the previous year. Although initially it was the statement of Democrats dissenting from the leadership of Tammany Hall, the issues it addressed underscored the confluence of ideologies between the Workingmen's movement and the Locofoco insurgency. The declaration pledged the Equal Rights Party to "unqualified hostility to bank notes and paper money as a circulating medium" exploited by speculators at the expense of the working classes, opposition to "any and all monopolies by legislation," and a warning that "vested rights, or prerogatives by legislation" were "usurpations of the people's sovereign rights" (a direct attack on the judicial doctrines employed against striking workers such as the journeymen tailors).

After the convention adjourned, however, this confluence became divergence. Seeking above all to dislodge the Tammany Democrats from their positions of power within the state government, Locofoco elements of the Equal Rights Party threw their support to candidates of the newly emergent Whigs in addition to the candidates nominated at Utica. Although this strategy dealt the Tammany Democrats a severe blow in the 1836 election, it also fractured the Equal Rights Party by leaving its candidates relatively unsupported. The Equal Rights gubernatorial ticket of Isaac Smith and Moses Jaques received fewer than 4,000 votes statewide. Many of the party's supporters blamed the defeat of its independent nominees on their supporters' shortsighted collusion with the Whigs and an abandonment of Equal Rights principles. Further blows to the party came the following year, in the midst of the Panic of 1837. In a February meeting in Central Park, called to protest conditions of acute economic distress of the New York workers, the Equal Rights speaker blamed the "monstrous banking system" for the depression and argued that "as the currency expands, the loaf contracts." As if to underscore the relevance of this metaphor, members of the crowd urged the looting of warehoused flour, one of the commodities that was in particularly short supply that winter. The riot that followed seemed to discredit fatally the Equal Rights Party as a group of dangerous radicals (despite the fact that not one person arrested during the riot had any connection to the party). Ironically, however, just as the party's organization and reputation crumbled, the larger ideas of the Utica platform were vindicated. With the election of Martin Van Buren to the presidency and the subsequent Panic of 1837, many of the Equal Rights Party's principles found official expression in the hard-money and independent treasury policies of the Van Buren administration. Though the Equal Rights/Locofoco movement seemed to have been defeated in the wake of the flour riots, in actuality, it essentially co-opted the Democratic Party establishment. What seemed on the surface to be a short-lived explosion of worker-based radicalism was actually a more sustained movement that altered the channels of national politics substantially.

Key Players

Byrdsall, Fitzwilliam: One of the earliest active members among the antimonopoly Democrats, Byrdsall quickly became a leader of the Equal Rights movement in the early stages of its organization. He was elected recording secretary of the Equal Rights Party. His history of the party, though clearly biased, is the most thorough primary account of the movement.

Commerford, John (1853–1932): Newspaper editor and prominent leader of the 1830s labor movement in New York City, Commerford served as the second president of the city's General Trades' Union, succeeding Ely Moore. Commerford, especially in the columns of his newspaper, *The Union*, advocated the alliance between the workingmen and the Locofoco insurgency that was endorsed at the Utica convention as the most promising way to meet the reform agenda demanded by labor.

Ming, Alexander: Ming was a New York printer and antimonopoly Democrat until his 1835 defection from the Tammany organization. A prominent member of the Locofoco insurgency and key supporter of the move to create a separate political party, Ming was the Equal Rights Party's candidate for Mayor of New York City in the 1835 election.

See also: *General Trades' Union; Workingmen's Party (1828).*

BIBLIOGRAPHY

Books

Byrdsall, Fitzwilliam. *The History of the Loco-Foco or Equal Rights Party. Its Movements, Conventions and Proceedings. With Short Characteristic Sketches of Its Prominent Men.* New York: Clement and Packard, 1842.

Hugins, Walter. *Jacksonian Democracy and the Working Class: A Study of the New York Workingmen's Movement, 1829–1837.* Palo Alto, CA: Stanford University Press, 1960.

Schlesinger, Arthur M., Jr. *The Age of Jackson.* Boston: Little, Brown, and Company, 1945.

Wilentz, Sean. *Chants Democratic: New York City and the Rise of the American Working Class, 1788–1850.* New York: Oxford University Press, 1984.

Other

Proceedings of the Convention of Mechanics, Farmers, and Working-Men of the State of New-York. n.p. 1836.

ADDITIONAL RESOURCES

Books

Benson, Lee. *The Concept of Jacksonian Democracy: New York as a Test Case.* Princeton: Princeton University Press, 1961.

Fox, Dixon Ryan. *The Decline of Aristocracy in the Politics of New York, 1801–1840.* New York: Columbia University Press, 1919.

Pessen, Edward. *Most Uncommon Jacksonians: The Radical Leaders of the Early Labor Movement.* Albany: State University of New York Press, 1967.

Periodicals

Degler, Carl. "The Locofocos: Urban 'Agrarians'." *Journal of Economic History* 16 (1956): 322–333.

—Kevin M. Gannon

Erdman Act

United States 1898

Synopsis

The Erdman Act, an early step toward the passage of the more comprehensive Railway Labor Act of 1926, was a federal law that attempted to alleviate labor unrest in the railroad industry by requiring mediation of any labor dispute "seriously interrupting or threatening to interrupt" interstate commerce. In the event that mediation failed, the act provided for an arbitration board whose decision would be binding. Additionally, Section 10 of the act prohibited the railroads from requiring as a condition of employment any discriminatory agreements pertaining to union membership.

Timeline

1878: Thomas Edison develops a means of cheaply producing and transmitting electric current, which he succeeds in

Jay Gould. Archive Photos, Inc. Reproduced by permission.

subdividing so as to make it adaptable to household use. The value of shares in gas companies plummets as news of his breakthrough reaches Wall Street.

1883: Foundation of the League of Struggle for the Emancipation of Labor by Marxist political philosopher Georgi Valentinovich Plekhanov marks the formal start of Russia's labor movement. Change still lies far in the future for Russia, however: tellingly, Plekhanov launches the movement in Switzerland.

1888: Serbian-born American electrical engineer Nikola Tesla develops a practical system for generating and transmitting alternating current (AC), which will ultimately—and after an extremely acrimonious battle—replace Thomas Edison's direct current (DC) in most homes and businesses.

1891: French troops open fire on workers during a 1 May demonstration at Fourmies, where employees of the Sans Pareille factory are striking for an eight-hour workday. Nine people are killed—two of them children—and 60 more are injured.

1894: Thomas Edison gives the first public demonstration of his kinetoscope film projector, in New York City.

1898: United States defeats Spain in the three-month Spanish-American War. As a result, Cuba gains it independence, and the United States purchases Puerto Rico and the Philippines from Spain for $20 million.

1898: Chinese "Boxers," a militant group opposed to foreign occupation of their country, organizes.

1898: Marie and Pierre Curie discover the radioactive elements radium and polonium.

1898: Bayer introduces a cough suppressant, derived from opium. Its brand name: Heroin.

1900: China's Boxer Rebellion, which began in the preceding year with attacks on foreigners and Christians, reaches its height. An international contingent of more than 2,000 men arrives to restore order, but only after several tens of thousands have died.

1904: The 10-hour workday is established in France.

1908: An earthquake in southern Italy and Sicily kills some 150,000 people.

Event and Its Context

Background: Railroad Growth and Labor Unrest

The history of organized labor during the nineteenth century is in large part a history of the rail industry. The railroads were the nation's first truly national industry and had a significant impact on interstate commerce. From the end of the Civil War until World War I, the rail industry burgeoned. In 1865, for example, the national rail network consisted of 35,000 miles of track; by 1880 that figure had grown to 93,000 miles; by 1890, 164,000 miles; and by 1916, 254,000 miles. In 1880 there were about 419,000 railroad employees; by 1900 that number had grown to just over 1 million, and by 1916, 1.7 million. Additionally, technical innovations lowered the cost of shipping goods. In 1865 freight rates were about two cents per ton-mile, but by 1900 that figure had fallen to about three-quarters of a cent per ton-mile. In 1880 the annual freight ton-mileage per employee was about 88,000. This figure rose to 101,000 in 1890; 138,000 in 1900; and 215,000 in 1916. By 1916 the railroads were carrying 77 percent of intercity freight and an astounding 98 percent of intercity passenger traffic.

Although this was the "Golden Age" of the rail industry, it was also a period of widespread corruption and discrimination against organized labor. Robber barons whose names remain familiar today—Jim Fisk, Jay Gould, Tom Scott, and Commodore Vanderbilt—manipulated the stock market, engaged in ruinous rate wars, and grew wealthy on the backs of labor. While annual freight ton-mileage was growing briskly, the average real wages of rail workers were virtually stagnant, growing from about $465 per year in 1880 to just $602 in 1890, then declining to $591 in 1900. (These figures are constant 1880 dollars.)

Inevitably, the railroad owners clashed with workers who were struggling to organize to improve their working conditions. One of the most dramatic clashes occurred in 1877. On 17 July in Martinsburg, West Virginia, rail workers who were members of the Trainmen's Union struck to protest their second pay cut that year, refusing to let any trains move until their wages were restored. The strike, which rapidly spread to Baltimore, Pittsburgh, Chicago, St. Louis, and other cities, grew increasingly violent. In Pittsburgh, for example, townspeople set fire to the station house and destroyed 104 locomotives, over 2,100 train cars, and 79 buildings. Eventually, federal troops put down the uprisings, and the Trainmen's Union was temporarily crushed.

Rail workers, however, continued their efforts to form unions and to bargain with their employers. In 1884, with the backing of the Knights of Labor, they brought about a system-wide strike against the Union Pacific railroad; in 1885 they won wage concessions from Jay Gould. More importantly, the Knights' membership rolls swelled—from 50,000 in 1883 to over 700,000 just three years later. Conflict, however, continued. In 1886 the Knights called for a strike against Gould's Southwestern Railroad System, but Gould broke the strike and blacklisted the union's leaders.

Arbitration Act of 1888

In response to this decade of unrest, Congress passed the Arbitration Act of 1888, the first federal labor relations law. The act called for voluntary arbitration of railway labor disputes and for presidential boards to investigate their causes. However, the arbitration provision of this act was never used, and only once—after the famous Pullman strike of 1894—was a board convened to investigate the causes of a dispute.

In 1893 a financial panic shook the world economy. In response, George Pullman, who had invented the railroad sleeper car, fired a third of his workers and cut the wages of those who remained—without, however, lowering prices for food and homes in Pullman, his company town outside of Chicago, where most of his employees lived. Eugene V. Debs, president of the recently formed American Railway Union, tried to negotiate with Pullman, but Pullman rebuffed his efforts, so Debs called for a strike against any railroad that hauled Pullman sleeper cars. The other rail owners backed Pullman by providing replacement workers during the strike, and the administration of President Grover Cleveland sought and won a court injunction against Debs's union. When Debs defied the injunction, he was arrested and sentenced to six months in prison. The U.S. Supreme Court, in *In re Debs* (1895), upheld the injunction. Writing for a unanimous Court, Justice David J. Brewer stated, "The strong arm of the national government may be put forth to brush aside all obstructions to the freedom of interstate commerce of the transportation of the mails." The case demonstrated that injunctions could be used against labor unions and foreshadowed the application of the Sherman Antitrust Act's prohibition of combinations in restraint of trade to thwart the unions.

Under the provisions of the Arbitration Act, President Cleveland appointed a board to investigate the causes of the Pullman strike. In its report, the board upbraided Pullman and the railroad companies: "The policy of both the Pullman Company and the Railway Managers' Association in reference to application to arbitrate, closed the door to all attempts at conciliation and settlement of differences." The board recommended a more sweeping arbitration and conciliation system and urged that the rail lines be forced, if necessary, to recognize organized labor and deal with it. It also recommended the outlawing of "yellow dog contracts," or labor contracts that forced workers to agree not to join a labor union. Cleveland turned over the report to Jacob Erdman, a Democratic congressman from Pennsylvania, who introduced a bill based on the board's recommendations.

Supreme Court Justice John Marshall Harlan. United States Supreme Court.

The Erdman Act

The Erdman Act of 1898, which in effect repealed the Arbitration Act of 1888, mandated that in any case involving wages, hours, or working conditions in the rail industry, the chair of the recently formed Interstate Commerce Commission and the commissioner of labor were to communicate with the parties to try to settle the dispute. If they failed, the case would be turned over to a permanent arbitration board consisting of a railroad company representative, an employee representative, and a third person named jointly by the company and the workers; this was an improvement over the Arbitration Act, which established temporary boards on a case-by-case basis. No employer could discharge an employee pending settlement of a case or for three months thereafter without 30 days' notice; employees could not strike except under the same conditions. The law further called for the expulsion of union members who used force in any labor dispute.

Adair v. United States

In the meantime, Section 10 of the Erdman Act protected the rights of rail workers to organize into unions by prohibiting the signing of yellow dog contracts, blacklisting of union members, and firing of employees solely for membership in a union. A 1908 U.S. Supreme Court case, *Adair v. United States*, challenged the constitutionality of Section 10. Adair, who managed a rail carrier, discharged an employee because the employee was a union member. Adair was subsequently found guilty of violating Section 10 of the Erdman Act. On appeal to the Supreme Court, however, his conviction was overturned, and by a 6–2 vote the Court ruled that Section 10 was unconstitutional for two reasons: (1) it violated the Fifth Amendment's due process clause, and (2) Congress, in passing Section 10, had overstepped its powers under the Constitution's commerce clause.

Writing for the majority, Justice John Harlan stated that the Court could find "no legal or logical connection" between interstate commerce and a worker's membership in a labor union. Section 10, he wrote, was "an invasion of the personal liberty, as well as the right to property" protected by the Fifth Amendment. Constitutional guarantees of freedom of contract gave the government no authority to "compel any person, in the course of his business and against his will, to accept or retain the personal services of another." An employee has the right to quit, and that right "is the same as the right of the employer, for whatever reason, to dispense with the services of such employee." The Court overruled *Adair* in 1949.

Key Players

Cleveland, Grover (1837–1908): Cleveland was the 22nd and 24th president of the United States (1885–1889 and 1893–1897). After being admitted to the New York bar in 1859, he worked his way up in politics and won election as mayor of Buffalo in 1881 and the governorship of New York the next year. Cleveland is principally remembered both for his nonconsecutive terms, his honesty and efficiency, and for reforming the U.S. civil service.

Debs, Eugene V. (1855–1926): Debs, who grew up in Terre Haute, Indiana, was a leading labor organizer in the late nineteenth century. In 1875 he became secretary of the local lodge of the Brotherhood of Locomotive Firemen and rose to national secretary in 1881. He resigned his position in 1893 to organize the American Railway Union. From 1900 to 1920 he ran five times for president as the Socialist Party candidate—the last while serving 10 years in a Georgia prison for his opposition to World War I.

Erdman, Constantine Jacob (1846–1911): After graduating from Pennsylvania College, Erdman studied law and was admitted to the state bar in 1867. In 1874 he was elected district attorney in Allentown, Pennsylvania. He served in the Fourth Regiment of the Pennsylvania National Guard during the rail strike of 1877. He later was elected as a Democrat to Congress, serving two terms from 1893 to 1897. After leaving Congress he was a successful businessman.

Gould, Jay (1836–1892): Born in Roxbury, New York, Gould was a surveyor by training. In the 1860s he began speculating on shares of small railroad companies, and eventually he gained control of the Erie Railroad. His effort to corner the gold market led to the Black Friday panic of 24 September 1869. In the 1870s he gained control of several western railroads; he also owned the *New York World*, most of New York City's elevated railroads, and a large share of Western Union. When he died, he left an estate valued at over $100 million.

Harlan, John Marshall (1833–1911): Harlan was born in Kentucky, where he was active in politics, serving as state attorney general from 1863 to 1867. After two unsuccessful runs for governor in the 1870s, he was active in Rutherford B. Hayes's successful bid for the presidency and was rewarded with an appointment to the U.S. Supreme Court, on which he served from 1877 to 1911.

See also: *Arbitration Act of 1888; Knights of Labor; Pullman Strike; Railway Labor Act.*

BIBLIOGRAPHY

Books

Chandler, Alfred D., Jr. *The Railroads: The Nation's First Big Business.* New York: Harcourt, Brace and World, 1965.

Jensen, Oliver. *Railroads in America.* New York: American Heritage, 1975.

Koretz, Robert F. *Statutory History of the United States: Labor Organization.* New York: Chelsea House, 1970.

Lieberman, Elias. *Unions Before the Bar.* New York: Harper and Row, 1950.

Lindsey, Almont. *The Pullman Strike.* Chicago: University of Chicago Press, 1942.

Salvatore, Nick. *Eugene V. Debs: Citizen and Socialist.* Urbana: University of Illinois Press, 1982.

Stover, John F. *The Life and Decline of the American Railroad.* New York: Oxford University Press, 1970.

Taylor, Benjamin J., and Fred Witney. *Labor Relations Law,* 2nd ed. Englewood Cliffs, NJ: Prentice-Hall, 1971.

—Michael O'Neal

European Strike Wave

Europe 1865

Synopsis

The Industrial Revolution, which began in England in the late 1700s, spread eastward across the European continent and into Russia by the late 1800s. Throughout the nineteenth century, almost every European country industrialized to some degree, and new and old industries passed through various stages of mass production. Products such as clothing, commodities, and food were being mass produced, and urban areas experienced large population gains. According to the census of 1851, for the first time in any large country, one-half of the people in England lived in cities.

As the Industrial Revolution progressed, workers across Europe felt themselves ceding control of wages and working conditions to employers. In addition, semiskilled and unskilled workers who produced goods quickly were rapidly replacing the traditional craftsmen who, before the nineteenth century, had slowly and skillfully turned out individual articles. The working class was being redefined as industrialism increased its size. To combat the new power of industrial employers, employees turned to unions to engage in collective bargaining or, if that failed, to coordinate strikes and even violent protests. The Revolutions of 1848, which occurred throughout the European continent, voiced worker demands for political representation and freedom. The revolutions helped to consolidate support for the labor movement. Such was the situation when the high point of massive strikes hit Europe in 1865.

Timeline

1844: Samuel Laing, in a prize-winning essay on Britain's "National Distress," describes conditions in a nation convulsed by the early Industrial Revolution. A third of the population, according to Laing, "hover[s] on the verge of actual starvation"; another third is forced to labor in "crowded factories"; and only the top third "earn[s] high wages, amply sufficient to support them in respectability and comfort."

1849: Elizabeth Blackwell becomes the first woman in the United States to receive a medical degree.

1854: In the United States, the Kansas-Nebraska Act calls for decisions on the legality of slavery to be made through local votes. Instead of reducing divisions, this measure will result in widespread rioting and bloodshed and will only further hasten the looming conflict over slavery and states' rights.

1857: Sepoy Mutiny, an unsuccessful revolt by Indian troops against the British East India Company, begins. As a result of the rebellion, which lasts into 1858, England places India under direct crown rule.

1860: Louis Pasteur pioneers his method of "pasteurizing" milk by heating it to high temperatures in order to kill harmful microbes.

1862: Victor Hugo's *Les Misérables* depicts injustices in French society, and Ivan Turgenev's *Fathers and Sons* introduces the term *nihilism.*

1864: General William Tecumseh Sherman conducts his Atlanta campaign and his "march to the sea."

1864: International Red Cross in Geneva is established.

1864: George M. Pullman and Ben Field patent their design for a sleeping car with folding upper berths.

1866: Austrian monk Gregor Mendel presents his theories on the laws of heredity. Though his ideas will be forgotten for a time, they are destined to exert enormous influence on biological study in the twentieth century.

1870: Franco-Prussian War begins. German troops sweep over France, Napoleon III is dethroned, and France's Second Empire gives way to the Third Republic.

1873: The gold standard, adopted by Germany in 1871 and eventually taken on by all major nations, spreads to Italy, Belgium, and Switzerland. Though the United States does not officially base the value of its currency on gold until 1900, an unofficial gold standard dates from this period, even as a debate over "bimetallism" creates sharp divisions in American politics.

Robert Owen. © Getty Images. Reproduced by permission.

Event and Its Context

Although it is difficult to date the beginning of the European Industrial Revolution, historians generally agree that it originated in England in the late eighteenth century as a result of a number of technological and social reasons. One key reason was the increase in efficiency of food production that resulted from a series of laws that permitted lands once held by tenant farmers to be transferred to large, private farms worked by a smaller labor force. This action increased urban populations as peasants searched for new jobs. Another reason for industrialization was the control of the English Parliament by the merchants and capitalists and the resulting legislation that favored their interests. A third reason was the invention of the modern steam engine by James Watt, which for the first time made the factory system profitable.

Industrialization spread from Britain to western Europe, especially France, Germany, and Belgium, from the late eighteenth century into the first decades of the nineteenth century. The explosion of the factory-based, machine-driven manufacturers moved through the rest of Europe after 1830. These new industries transformed Europe's old class system into a new class order.

Class Order

Upper-middle class capitalists grew in strength as their wealth and the size of their manufacturing facilities increased. The middle-middle class grew in variety as new professionals, such as scientists and engineers, joined established professionals, such as doctors and lawyers. The lower-middle class also grew as the need increased for such workers as clerks and schoolteachers. The working class experienced the greatest growth, primarily in the numbers of factory workers but also of dock, municipal, and transportation workers. With rural peasants moving to urban areas, the soon-to-be-powerful working class eventually constituted more than 50 percent of the population.

Workers were affected at different times and places as mass production started in the English textile industry and spread to other industries and into eastern Europe. New industrial centers sprang up in such places as Lille, France; Wels, Austria; Barmen, Germany; and Lodz, Poland. The population of Lille, for example, grew from 59,000 in 1804 to 131,800 in 1860.

Industrial Labor and Working Conditions

In the first half of the nineteenth century, two types of workers dominated industrial labor: skilled artisans and craftsmen, and semiskilled and unskilled workers. The metallurgy, shipbuilding, and printing industries, to name a few, employed large numbers of skilled workers, whereas the textile, mining, and railway industries, as examples, employed mostly unskilled workers. However, innovations in many industries reduced the need for skilled workers, replacing then with semiskilled or unskilled workers, resulting in a reduction of the average wage paid per worker.

Whether skilled or unskilled, all workers had to contend with adverse working conditions. The workday was often as many as 16 to 18 hours and averaged 12 to 14 in the factories. The intensity of the work was another factor. The machine determined the pace of work, and even if the worker was not tied to a machine, the work was extremely monotonous and dangerous compared to preindustrial work.

Employers developed complex systems of penalties for dealing with employee discipline problems. Unlike the rural environments from which these workers had only recently come, work hours in the factories and industrial centers were fixed and controlled, independent of the weather, season, and time of day. Industrial discipline often came at the end of a pay period rather than when the infraction had allegedly occurred. Rules were often not published, giving the employer greater leeway when it came to deciding what was punishable. Being more than five minutes late could mean the loss of the entire day's wages. Fines could be levied even for speaking or singing. Any type of protest often led to immediate discharge.

Legislation of the period discriminated against laborers throughout Europe. British law favored employers over workers. For instance, the British Master and Servant Act made the servant (employee) liable to punishment under "criminal" law for breach of contract, whereas the master (employer) was liable only under "civil" law. Under the law, worker strikes were considered a breach of contract, and criminal law could be applied to the protester. In France and Belgium, civil law stated that in a labor dispute, the master was always believed over the employee. Employers often tied workers to the jobs with a *livret* (French for "booklet"). The *livret* was a little notebook in which the employer recorded employee financial obligations. Workers were obligated to continue employment until all obligations were met.

Early Worker Action

Industrialization created new, often bitter, disagreements in the workplace. The larger industrial setting made it apparent that ordinary workingmen no longer had the opportunity to become independent masters and had little chance to improve conditions. New forms of protest, particularly strikes and various political actions, developed as tools of the labor union. Skilled artisans were especially violent throughout this period, as their wages often did not keep pace with steeply rising prices. When machines began to replace human labor, workers reacted by destroying them. The British Parliament passed a law that allowed execution of anyone found guilty of destroying factories or machines. The violent mass action led to the execution of 18 workers from York, England, in 1813. The wave of violence spread to the mainland as uprisings occurred among Lyon, France, silk workers in 1831 and Silesian weavers in 1844. Eventually, protesters learned that it was more effective to attack capitalists with strikes rather than it was to destroy property.

The European transition to industrialism left individuals little recourse against employers. Unable to change repressive work conditions on an individual basis, workers formed labor organizations so as to stand together as a collective force against their powerful employers. Skilled craftsmen were the first to form unions and did so in reaction to rapid wage declines. The favorite tactic of early unions was collective bargaining enforced by strikes or the threat of strikes.

The early labor unions in Europe encountered resistance from employers and governments. In France, for example, the Chapelier Law of 1791 prohibited coalitions aimed at changes in labor conditions. In England, the British Anti-Combination Acts of 1799–1800 illegalized any organization that attempted to change labor conditions. For instance, groups of workers formed to improve wages or hours were considered unlawful conspiracies in restraint of trade. Similar restrictive labor laws were passed in other European countries, and by 1815 most labor organizations in western Europe had lost their legal right to exist.

When confronted with labor problems, employees could change jobs (some immigrated to the United States), petition the employer, or use violence. Such actions were rarely effective. If all else failed, employees occasionally tried to revive traditional workmen's organizations to regulate trade practices. This sometimes included organizing strikes. However, such actions were outlawed as a danger to authority. Suppression by officials sometimes resulted in local revolts. At the end of the eighteenth century (and for many years thereafter), workers had little recourse against employers.

By the end of the Napoleonic wars (1799–1815, between France and a number of European nations), a wave of labor unrest resulted in the repeal of the Combination Acts in Britain. As early as the 1820s, there were several attempts to unite trade associations. The first truly national craft organization was the Grand Union of Operative Spinners, founded in Britain in 1829 by John Doherty. In 1830 this group became the National Association for the Protection of Labor, which was the first such group to involve different trades. At its peak it possessed 100,000 members from among spinners, construction workers, and engineers. It lasted only a short time. Robert Owen, a self-made cotton mill owner, started the Grand National Consolidated Trades Union, which consisted of London craftsmen such as tailors and shoemakers. The organization was weakened by the actions of government officials and eventually dissolved into only a social body. Although these early labor organizations did not survive long, the ill feelings of employees toward employers persisted. These early attempts at labor organizations were short-lived, and employee dissatisfaction continued.

Unions on the European continent were even more repressed. Belgium enforced a ban on all unions and arrested nearly 1,600 workers between 1830 and 1860 and jailed more than half of them. Workers publicized their plight by whatever means they could. A wave of strike activity began in the early nineteenth century. After the worst of the postwar conditions were over, strikes hit England in 1818 and again in 1824 after the repeal of the Combination Acts. The working-class theories of Robert Owen and William King, founder of *The Co-operator*, helped stabilize the labor movement. In 1824 and 1825 some unions were legalized, but it remained illegal for them to act in any way to improve worker conditions. The British government responded to strikes by arresting strike leaders and reinstituting stronger anticoalition laws in 1834. Even so, local unions continued to organize into larger national unions, much under the direction of Doherty and Owen.

In the early 1830s European workers followed suit with strikes similar to those in Britain. By this time economic conditions in Europe were better, giving workers confidence that they could strike. However, unions did not gain a stronghold in Europe until the latter half of the nineteenth century, and only after unskilled workers joined skilled workers en masse within labor unions. Although generally peaceful during this period of time, strikes sometimes became violent.

In 1831 and 1834 the silk workers of Lyon, France held strikes that turned into uprisings. The local government had approved an illegal tariff list (a list of fees that a government would impose on goods) from the silk workers. Employers went to the national government to protest the action and had the list declared invalid. The workers responded with a strike that paralyzed the city for more than a week. Finally, the government called in 20,000 soldiers to restore order. Three years later, in response to a similar tariff list, workers struck again, creating a "battlefield" within the city with more than 200 casualties on both sides. The government's response was to enact strict anticoalition legislation. Workers continued to struggle for their rights, modeling their labor philosophy on such philosophers as François Noël Babeuf (insisting on the common ownership of land and total economic and political equality among citizens) and Louis Blanc (advocating associations of workers funded by the state and controlled by the workers).

Labor's struggle for recognition was fought as much with legislative measures as it was with strikes and revolts. The Mining Act of 1842, the repeal of the Corn Laws in 1846, and the Ten Hour Bill in 1847 helped strengthen unions by providing a more democratic governing body within England. Despite limited advancements in labor legislation, English workers proved that the working class could force capitalists to grant concessions in wages and working conditions. The process was slow and cumbersome, especially given the fragmented nature of the labor movement, which usually performed its (illegal) duties in secrecy.

During this time, workers often protested with food riots, sabotaging of machines, and strikes, often all at once. Sabotage resulted from the fear that machines would eliminate jobs and corresponding job skills. Such sabotage became known as *Luddism*, after Ned Ludd, the leader of rural workers' actions in England. Workers destroyed thousands of power looms in Manchester in the 1820s for that reason. On the mainland, Belgian coal potters destroyed a railway line in 1829 in the Grand Hornu mine, and Parisian printers destroyed mechanical presses in 1830. Thousands of people sabotaged equipment in cities across the European continent.

Gradual Social Reform

In the 1830s and 1840s social reformers argued for laws to relieve the negative impact of industrialization on workers. Official investigations and private surveys investigated workers' health, housing, and labor conditions. England passed a law requiring government factory inspectors in 1833. France enacted a child-labor law in 1841 that prohibited night work for children and factory work for children under the age of eight years, and Austria followed with a similar law the next year. The birth of a "social consciousness" began in Europe at this time. Governments slowly lifted barriers to unions. Resistance from employers, however, made many early labor laws and unions ineffective and ultimately fueled revolutionary movements in Europe. German political philosopher Karl Marx, for example, argued that the exploitation of labor would eventually lead the working classes to overthrow their governments and set up a classless society of shared resources.

One of the largest labor movements in the late 1830s and 1840s was Chartism, which aimed at general suffrage. It began as a "charter" consisting of numerous demands relating to suffrage rights, such as the secret ballot and payments to members of Parliament. By 1839 two million people had signed a petition for enactment of its demands. Rejection of the petition resulted in strikes and riots. Although the Chartist movement failed, the idea that working people had certain fundamental rights was beginning to be broadly accepted in society.

Revolutions of 1848

Legal attempts at economic and political change were defeated during the economic crisis of 1847. The reaction was the European Revolutions of 1848, a series of violent and generally illegal uprisings throughout the continent. Workers and peasants who revolted against developing capitalist practices (which often resulted in greater poverty) began the labor revolutions. Almost all workers, except those from England and Russia, participated in the revolutions, which demanded self-determination from the political and business organizations that dominated them. In France, the revolutions resulted in the abolition of the Chapelier Law, and the French government incorporated labor representatives within its legislative body, created national workshops for the unemployed, and established the *Commission du Luxembourg*, an agency for social affairs. New trade associations possessed the ability to bargain collectively, hold mass demonstrations, and set labor tariffs.

After a few months, however, the government reversed these labor measures, which immediately caused a protest involving more than 100,000 Parisian workers. The French army eventually restored order, but only after 1,500 casualties and more than 3,500 people were deported to Algeria. Other such revolutions occurred in large cities throughout Europe, such as

Berlin and Vienna. Little advancement in labor reform resulted from such actions. The revolutions did, however, frighten the people in power about the growing dangers of the working class, which suffered after many of its leaders were executed, imprisoned, or exiled. Only in England were trade unions allowed to continue to organize. In continental Europe labor reform was effectively eliminated for the time being. However, the revolutions influenced the future course of European government by popularizing liberalism and socialism and rejecting the concept of absolute monarchy.

Economic Advancements During the 1850s and 1860s

Compared to the first half of the century, the 1850s and 1860s were relatively prosperous throughout Europe. Factories increased in size, especially within the metal industries, as railways spread across the continent. As technology advanced, the demand for more semiskilled and unskilled laborers increased. New unions formed in response to the larger, more sophisticated management structures.

The Amalgamated Society of Engineers was one of the first of the new unions based on a strong internal organization, elected and paid administrators, and the use of the strike as a means of last resort. It was formed in 1851 from a group of older local unions and, with 12,000 members, soon became England's largest union. As new English unions formed, employers also started to organize to bargain more effectively with the unions or to fight them when bargaining failed. One important strike was the London Building Workers' strike of 1859, in which employers reacted with lockouts and the suspension of the right to combine on their premises. The strike ended nine months later when a newly passed law guaranteed the right of workers to combine.

The new British unions and the 1848 revolutions influenced labor across the European continent. After loosening traditional ties with the Catholic Church, the French adopted new forms of socialist thought. Two of the more important French movements were the Proudhonism movement—led by Pierre-Joseph Proudhon, who supported voluntary cooperatives—and the Blanquism movement—named after Louis-Auguste Blanqui, who supported revolutionary-type worker actions. In 1857 and 1858 a wave of strikes were held to protest wage cuts. Strike frequency increased even more after 1864 as mutual aid societies vigorously pursued union goals. They were called *Chambres Syndicales* (or trade union rooms), after existing local employers' clubs.

In Germany the *Allgemeiner Deutscher Arbeiterverein* (or General German Worker Association) was organized for the purpose of universal and equal suffrage; the *Hirsch-Duncker* unions (named after Max Hirsch and Franz Duncker) promoted peaceful cooperation of labor and capital; and the *Sozialdemokratische Arbeiterpartei* (or Social-Democratic Labor Party) advocated for universal and equal voting rights. Each group supported the large number of strikes that occurred particularly during 1864–1865.

In other European countries, worker organizations took the form of mutual aid societies, cooperatives, educational societies, and a few trade unions. Most of the organizations, unlike their older counterparts such as guilds and journeymen's organizations, had a liberal outlook and sought out many different types of workers. By 1862 Great Britain had legalized unions so as to encourage peaceful labor relations. By the middle of the 1860s, many regions in Europe were proceeding toward legalizing unions. National unions were founded in Switzerland in 1858, Holland in 1866, and Belgium in 1867, after having organized construction workers, cigar makers, hatters and others.

Miners were relatively slow to organize. They realized the importance of unions and beginning in 1869 held a number of strikes and revolts that affected mining centers and industrial towns in France, Germany, Italy, and the Czech and Austrian parts of the Austrian Empire. A miners' strike, for instance, near Saint-Etienne, France, over control of worker insurance funds resulted in much violence. Thirteen people were killed in what came to be known as the "*massacre de La Ricamarie.*" In Waldenburg, Germany, fighting broke out over the recognition of the *Hirsch-Duncker* miners' unions; in Belgium heavy fighting between the police and rioting Charleroi miners (who were protesting wage reductions) caused six casualties in 1868.

International Workers Association

In September 1864 an organizing group met in St. Martin's Hall in London, England. The meeting helped to increase international contacts between union leaders and revolutionaries. The International Workers Association was founded as a consulting congress based on the agenda established at the 1862 London Exhibition. At the 1862 meeting, French and British workers met with Karl Marx, who called for international worker unity as stated in his *Communist Manifesto* (1848): "Working Men of all Countries, Unite!" As a result, member organizations of the International Workers Association actively initiated strikes throughout the continent. In addition, the International helped to increase international labor contacts, resulting in the spread of a united working-class struggle. Anarchist Mikhail Bakunin led protest movements, especially in Spain and Italy, as groups such as the construction workers and cigar makers fought for worker rights during these positive economic times.

High Point in 1865

This period of union activity, strikes, and uprisings, which peaked in 1865, provided high hopes and great expectations for the future of unions in Europe. The mid-1860s became a formative time for the working class. Unskilled and semiskilled workers began to see that they could be better off working in factories, but they quickly realized that in order to substantially raise their standard of living they needed the unions to represent their interests. Changes in work habits and corresponding changes in home life and religious practices brought about by industrialization were gradually accepted. The time surrounding 1865 also demonstrated the overall weakness of unionism on the continent and the failure of its political activities. This contrasted with the relative strength of unions in England, which used labor campaigns to influence Parliament. British unions had been officially recognized, had campaigned successfully against inequality in legislation and for some social reforms, and had secured a strong national organization. None of these accomplishments had yet to be realized on the European continent. However, inspired by British labor successes, continental unionism continued the successful, although sometimes slow, route to labor recognition by governments and capitalists alike.

By about 1870 the character of industrial society began to noticeably change in western and central Europe (change in eastern Europe was still a long way off). Workers could afford better housing and food. They generally benefited from the ability to obtain more and better material goods. Legislation began to improve the safety and health conditions within factories for the benefit of workers. In fact, the early 1870s in Europe could be likened to the condition of the United States in the early years of the 1800s. Workers continued to demand better working conditions, especially at times of rising or stagnant wages. Although strikes continued (now under a much more educated and knowledgeable workforce), the union-led strike waves of the preceding 40 years had established a new working class in Europe and forever changed the face of working conditions on the European continent.

Key Players

Doherty, John (1797–1854): Doherty moved to Manchester in 1816 and found work as a cotton worker. He led a successful strike of the cotton spinners in 1829. In 1830 Doherty helped found the National Association for the Protection of Labor. He was the editor of the organization's journal, *The Voice of the People.*

Owen, Robert (1771–1858): Owen was a Welsh industrialist and utopian social reformer. Owen has been called the "Father of English Socialism." He formed a model cotton factory community at New Lanark, Scotland, and pioneered cooperative societies. He later made unsuccessful attempts to establish similar settlements at New Harmony, Indiana (1825), and Harmony Hall, Hampshire, in England (1844). He published books including the *New View of Society* (1813). Owens helped to develop early factory legislation, the cooperative movement, and the establishment of infant schools.

See also: *Amalgamated Society of Engineers; Chartist Movement; Combination Acts; June Days Rebellion; Luddites Destroy Woolen Machines; Owen Model Communities; Repeal of Combination Acts; Revolutions in Europe; Silk Workers' Revolts; Weavers' Revolts.*

BIBLIOGRAPHY

Books

Anderson, Eugene, and Pauline R. Anderson. *Political Institutions and Social Change in Continental Europe in the Nineteenth Century.* Berkeley: University of California Press, 1967.

Fay, Charles R. *Life and Labour in the Nineteenth Century.* Cambridge, UK: The University Press, 1947.

Hoerder, Dirk, ed. *Labor Migration in the Atlantic Economies: The European and North American Working Classes During the Period of Industrialization.* Contributions in Labor History, No. 16. Westport, CT: Greenwood Press, 1985.

Sheehan, James J., ed. *Industrialization and Industrial Labor in Nineteenth-century Europe.* Major Issues in History. New York: Wiley, 1973.

Stearns, Peter N. *European Society in Upheaval.* London: Macmillan, 1967.

—William Arthur Atkins

European Trade Union Confederation

Europe 1973

Synopsis

On 8 February 1973, 17 European members of the International Confederation of Free Trade Unions joined to form the European Trade Union Confederation (ETUC). As European nations moved toward greater cooperation and unification, European labor unions also recognized the need for a union federation that represented them at the supranational level and offered a trade union counterbalance to the forces of European economic integration. One of the ETUC's primary tasks was to act as a liaison with the European Economic Community and other pan-European institutions. This European focus created some concern among the international labor community that the ETUC could isolate European labor from the rest of the world. The ETUC would later come to represent some 90 percent of European labor unions and was thus the only central labor union organization recognized as an interlocutor by the European Union.

Timeline

1958: China's Mao Zedong proclaims the Great Leap Forward, a program of enforced rapid industrialization that will end a year later, a miserable failure.

1963: President Kennedy is assassinated in Dallas on 22 November.

1968: Communist victories in the Tet offensive mark the turning point in the Vietnam War, and influence a growing lack of confidence in the war, not only among America's youth, but within the establishment as well.

1973: Signing of peace accords in Paris in January ends the Vietnam War.

1973: As the Watergate scandal grows, White House advisers H. R. Haldeman and John D. Ehrlichman resign, and Nixon fires counsel John Dean. Later, Vice President Spiro Agnew resigns. Then, in the October "Saturday Night Massacre," Attorney General Elliot L. Richardson resigns, and Nixon fires special prosecutor Archibald Cox and Deputy Attorney General William D. Ruckelshaus.

1973: Overthrow of Chile's Salvador Allende, the only freely elected Marxist leader in history, who dies in the presidential palace. According to supporters of the new leader, General Augusto Pinochet, Allende committed suicide, but Allende's supporters maintain that he was killed by Pinochet's troops.

1973: Attacked in October, during their Yom Kippur religious festival, the Israelis defeat the combined forces of Egypt, Syria, Iraq, and Jordan. Three weeks later, Arab nations impose an oil embargo on the United States to punish it for its continued support of Israel.

1973: United States launches Skylab, its first space station.

1973: The twin towers of the World Trade Center in New York City, built at a cost of $750 million, are completed. The 110-story buildings are the world's tallest, but by year's end they will be eclipsed by the Sears Tower in Chicago.

1978: More than 900 members of the People's Temple, led by Jim Jones, kill themselves in Jonestown, Guyana. Also dead is Congressman Leo Ryan, who was visiting the Guyana compound and was presumably murdered.

1983: A Soviet fighter plane shoots down a Korean Air Lines 747 that had strayed into Soviet airspace. All 269 passengers, including 61 Americans (among them U.S. Congressman Larry McDonald), are killed.

1988: A terrorist bomb aboard a Pan Am 747 explodes over Lockerbie, Scotland, killing 259 people on the plane and 11 more on the ground.

Event and Its Context

Toward a European Labor Federation

In the mid-twentieth century, as goals of a Europe united in free trade began to materialize, so did attempts to create a Europe united through the interests of its labor organizations. In 1945 the World Federation of Trade Unions (WFTU) was founded in Paris with the participation of the United States and the Soviet Union, though the cold war and an increasing communist dominance of the executive committee caused noncommunist nations to split and form their own organization. The International Confederation of Free Trade Unions (ICFTU), which defended Western-style social democracy and shunned state-controlled unions, was born in London in 1949. In 1950 came the first in a string of social democratic trade union organizations that would result in the European Trade Union Confederation (ETUC). The European Regional Organisation of the International Confederation of Free Trade Unions (ERO-ICFTU) was founded, with the Belgian union leader Walter Schevenels as its general secretary. Based in Brussels, the confederation included 20 unions from 18 western European countries.

In 1952, when the Treaty of Paris spawned the European Coal and Steel Community (ESCS; the first treaty organization of what would later become the European Union), labor followed with the Trade Union Committee of Twenty-One. This organization included ICFTU-affiliate coal and steel union federations from ECSC member nations. When the Treaty of Rome established the European Economic Community (EC) in 1957, European ICFTU members formed the European Trade Union

Secretariat (ETUS), composed of trade union confederations of the six EC member states (France, Belgium, the Netherlands, Luxembourg, West Germany, and Italy). The ERO-ICFTU was disbanded and the Trade Union Committee of Twenty-One was absorbed by the ETUS, which in 1969 changed its named to the European Confederation of Free Trade Unions (ECFTU). In 1973, after Great Britain, Ireland, and Denmark entered the EC, the ECFTU merged with the Trade Union Committee for the European Free Trade Area (EFTA-TUC). The purpose of the latter organization, which decided to dissolve at its meeting of 9 March 1973, had been to act as a forum for discussion on increasing pan-European trade union cooperation. The fusion of the ECFTU and the EFTA-TUC was ETUC, known in French as the *Confédération Européenne des Syndicats* (CES) and in German as the *Europäischer Gewerkschaftsbund* (EGB).

The birth of the ETUC was not a casual occurrence. As part of a transition period that took into account future expansion of the EC, meetings had been going on for years. The ECFTU and the EFTA-TUC had been in negotiations since 1968. On 1 February 1968, seven national trade confederations from six countries agreed in London to set up an independent Trade Union Committee. The purpose of this committee was to serve as a platform for communication with trade unions in the countries of the EFTA. Between 1969 and 1973 the ECFTU and the EFTA-TUC maintained contact via a liaison committee. In its meeting of 9 March 1973, the executive committee of the EFTA-TUC, given the recent creation of the ETUC, decided to disband the organization

The ETUC Is Born

ETUC was founded on 8 February 1973 by 17 national confederations from 15 countries. Each confederation was affiliated with ICFTU. The organizations met at the first congress held in Brussels on 8–9 February. The federations present represented workers from Norway to Malta, including organizations such as the *Fédération Générale du Travail de Belgique*, the Trade Union Congress, General Workers' Union, *Confederazione Italiana Sindacati Lavoratori*, *Unione Italiana Lavoratori*, *Landsorganisation en i Sverige*, *Landsorganisasjonen i Norge*, *Österreichischer Gewerkschaftsbund*, *Landsorganisationen i Danmark*, *Confédération Générale du Travail-Force Ouvrière*, *Unión General de Trabajadores* (at that time illegal under the Franco dictatorship in Spain), *Confédération Générale du Travail Luxembourgeoise*, and *Deutscher Gewerkschaftsbund*. Soon after the first congress, requests for membership came from more than a dozen other national trade union centers. Particularly interested in membership were 12 Christian trade unions affiliated with the World Confederation of Labour-European Organisation (WCL-EO).

ETUC's main goals, as declared in its constitution, were to protect and strengthen European democracy and to represent and promote the economic, cultural, and social interests of laborers at the European level. The organization broached this task both generally and at the institutional level as it represented workers before bodies such as the EC and the EFTA.

The first ETUC president was Victor Feather of Great Britain, who served from 1973 to 1974 and was then replaced by Germany's Heinz Oskar Vetter (1974–1979). The ETUC's first general secretary was the Belgian Théo Rasschaert, who held this post from 1973 to 1975. The deputy secretary was the Norwegian Kaare Sandegren (1973–1974), followed by Denmark's Peer Carlsen (1974–1976). Alfred Misslin of France served as secretary from 1973 to 1975. The general secretary, secretaries, and staff operated out of at the International Trade Union House (ITUH) in Brussels. Although the ITUC was conceived as a multilingual organization, most of the secretaries and staff did not speak all of the official languages.

The establishment of the ETUC brought concerns among ICFTU members outside Europe that a separate trade union organization for Europe would lead to isolation of the European labor community. In what it saw as a crucial element in the development of European trade unionism, ETUC established 16 industry committees, organized by economic sector and open to all democratic trade unions in the EC nations. Although the ETUC wanted the committees to allow Christian and communist unions to join, this did not happen initially. The International Trade Secretariats (ITS) served a similar function as federations of national unions organized by particular industries or trades, but they were global in nature. The ITS worked closely with the ICFTU, which also grouped its members in regional organizations. One major barrier to coordination was that the ETUC expected the industry committees to be loyal to its European policy objectives. Attempts at formal alliances between the ETUC and the ICFTU failed, largely because of fears of diminished influence by the ITSs.

Although the ETUC's founding members all came from the ICFTU, the ETUC maintained an open recruitment policy. In addition to all of western Europe's social democratic unions, the ETUC accepted many organizations that represented more specialized interests. Its first expansion in May 1974 affiliated the 12 Christian trade unions linked to the World Confederation of Labour (WCL). The WCL European Organisation (WCL-EO), which had been in existence since 1958, dissolved. In practice, affiliation of the Christian unions (despite their Christian-democrat leanings) was not complicated insofar as they shared the ETUC model and a commitment to European integration and pan-European unity of action. As ETUC general secretary Emilio Gabaglio later recalled, affiliating "Communist-leaning" trade unions was "much more complex and protracted, accompanied in every case by procrastination and the need to allow the situation to mature, if not by burning controversy." One exception to this rule was Italy's *Confederazione Generale Italiana del Lavoro* (CGIL). The ETUC accepted the CGIL in July 1974, after it reduced its ties to the WFTU to the level of "associate" member. Over time, the ETUC accepted former communist trade unions—which were gradually distancing themselves from the USSR—and those without any international affiliations.

The ETUC expanded rapidly during its first 12 years, with the number of member confederations growing from 17 to 35, the number of represented countries from 15 to 20, and the number of workers represented from 36 to 41 million. Nonetheless, this expansion appeared to be at the cost of unity. The rapid incorporation of varied ideological currents and organizations working in diverse industrial realities made forging a common voice difficult, and ETUC worked constantly to find common ground among its affiliates. Alleged indifference toward European issues and "seemingly intractable disagree-

ments" among member confederations "long undermined the ETUC's internal authority and external legitimacy." Gradually, the organization's diverse members grew toward political convergence and worked in concert toward the accomplishment of national objectives. In the end, the ETUC survived not as a traditional industrial trade union or "ideological standard-bearer," but as an effective political pressure group.

By the end of the century, ETUC grew to include more than 70 "free, independent and democratic" trade union confederations and European industry federations, representing more than 60 million members in more than 30 countries. It also introduced "observer status" and allowed full membership to several eastern European federations. Its differences with the ICFTU were resolved and the two organizations enjoyed a close working relationship. The ETUC, representing some 90 percent of Europe's unionized workers, became the only representative cross-sectional European trade union organization recognized by the European Union, the Council of Europe, and the EFTA. Nonetheless, despite growing unity of action at the supranational level, union power at the national level experienced gradual erosion, with the balance of power in the European Union remaining on the side of employers and policy-makers.

Key Players

Feather, Victor Grayson Hardie (1908–1976): Lord Feather was a British labor union leader. In 1969 he was appointed general secretary of the Trades Union Congress, which he led in confronting the government over industrial legislation. Feather was a founder of the ETUC and served as its first president from 1973 to 1974.

Rasschaert, Théo: Rasschaert, a Belgian, was first general secretary of the ETUC, serving from 1973 to 1975.

Schevenels, Walter (1894–1966): Schevenels, a Belgian trade union leader, served as general secretary of the European Regional Organisation of the International Confederation of Free Trade Unions from 1951 until his death in 1966. Although he would not live to see the European Trade Union Confederation (ETUC), he was a primary figure in the parent organization from which the ETUC descended.

See also: *International Confederation of Free Trade Unions; World Federation of Trade Unions.*

———————

BIBLIOGRAPHY

Other

Abbott, Keith. "The ETUC: The Growth of a European Pressure Group." IIRA 6th European Congress [cited 24 October 2002]. <http://www.iira2001.org/proceedings/ws1_110.htm>.

European Trade Union Confederation Web Site. About ETUC. "Constitution of the European Trade Union Confederation" [cited 24 October 2002]. <http://www.etuc.org/en/index.cfm?target=/en/about_etuc/constitution.cfm>.

Gobin, Corinne. "Taming the Unions: The Mirage of a Social Europe." *Le Monde Diplomatique*. November

1997 [cited 24 October 2002]. <http://mondediplo.com/
1997/11/europe>.

Hijma, Bouwe. "Inventory of the Archives of the European
Trade Union Confederation (ETUC) and Its Predecessors
(1939–) 1950–1992." International Institute of Social
History [cited 24 October 2002]. <http://www.iisg.nl/
archives/html/e/10748348.html>.

International Labor Organization. "The Social Partners"
[cited 24 October 2002]. <http://www.ilo.org/public/
english/region/eurpro/brussels/social.htm>.

Swedish Trade Union Confederation Web Site. "EU and the
Trade Union." Focus Europe [cited 24 October 2002].
<http://www.lo.se/english/europe/fragor/fraga2a.htm>.

—Brett Allan King

F

Factory Act

Great Britain 1833

Synopsis

In 1833 the British Whig government passed a factory act that applied to textile manufactures. This was the culmination of intensive lobbying on the part of working-class organizations and humanitarian individuals. The act forbade the employment of children under age nine and limited the employment of children under age 13 to nine hours a day and children under 18 to 12 hours. The act also forbade night work for children and set up the first system of factory inspectors. Although a disappointment to those hoping and working for a 10-hour day for all laborers, the Factory Act was the first major state intervention in the conditions of factory labor and set precedents for further factory acts in 1844, 1847, 1850, and 1853.

Timeline

1809: Progressive British industrialist Robert Owen proposes an end to employment of children in his factories. When his partners reject the idea, he forms an alliance with others of like mind, including the philosopher Jeremy Bentham.

1813: Jane Austen publishes *Pride and Prejudice*.

1818: Donkin, Hall & Gamble "Preservatory" in London produces the first canned foods.

1824: Ludwig van Beethoven composes his Ninth Symphony.

1829: Greece wins its independence after a seven-year war with Turkey.

1831: Polish revolt against Russian rule is unsuccessful.

1834: British mathematician Charles Babbage completes drawings for the "analytic engine," a forerunner of the modern computer that he never builds.

1834: American inventor Cyrus H. McCormick patents his reaper, a horse-drawn machine for harvesting wheat.

1835: American inventor and painter Samuel F. B. Morse constructs an experimental version of his telegraph, and American inventor Samuel Colt patents his revolver.

1837: Victoria is crowned in England.

1841: Act of Union joins Upper Canada and Lower Canada, which consist of parts of the present-day provinces of Ontario and Quebec, respectively.

1846: American inventor Elias Howe patents his sewing machine.

Event and Its Context

The Ten Hours Movement

The first few decades of the nineteenth century in Britain saw a movement for the amelioration of factory conditions. These movements became stronger in the early 1830s and brought together workers who were organized into Short Time Committees in the textile districts of the North of England and Scotland. The committees had allies among the landed classes, notably the Tory activist Richard Oastler and a minority of factory owners. In 1830 Oastler's letter to the *Leeds Mercury*, titled "Yorkshire Slavery," compared the lot of child laborers in the Bradford worsted factories unfavorably to that of African slaves in the West Indies, and attracted much attention. Factory reformers usually set their goal as the protection of children from excessive work. There was much greater reluctance to prescribe the hours of labor of adult men, as it was commonly believed that adult men should be free to set their own conditions of work. In practice this usually meant accepting what was offered by the factory management. The interdependency of the different processes in a factory, however, meant that limitation of the hours of children's labor would lead to the limitation of adult hours as well. Supporters of the "Ten Hours Movement" believed that limiting children to 10 hours of work daily would ultimately limit all factory workers to 10 hours. The movement cut across political lines; Tories, Radicals, and Whigs could all be found supporting and opposing it. The Tory Oastler and the Radical working-class leaders of the Short Time Committees reached an agreement, the Fixby Hall Compact of June 1831, in which they agreed to set aside political and sectarian differences to work together on factory issues.

In 1831 Sir John Cam Hobhouse introduced the first bill under the Whig government, which was led by Prime Minister Earl Grey, to limit the hours of children's factory labor. The bill would have extended the prohibition against workdays greater than 12 hours from 16-year-olds to 18-year-olds. The bill received no encouragement from the government, which was committed to laissez-faire principles. Yorkshire employers petitioned Parliament against the bill. Although eventually passed into law, it was so encumbered with amendments put forth by the manufacturers that it had little to no effect. It applied only to cotton textiles and contained no provision for enforcement other than requiring factory managers to keep a record of hours worked.

Sadler's Bill

The following year, Michael Thomas Sadler, a Member of Parliament for Leeds who had been elected as a Tory/Radical fusion candidate, introduced a new bill. Sadler presented a bill in March 1832 that would have prohibited the employment of children under nine in factories, restricted to 10 the hours of children between nine and 18, and forbidden night work to all under age 21. The bill's principal opponent in the House of Commons was John Charles Spencer, Viscount Althorp, who

Earl Charles Grey. The Library of Congress.

expressed his opposition in terms of classical political economy, claiming that the regulation of child labor would lead to unemployment and the loss of manufacturing capacity. The opposition to the bill tried to stall by appointing a parliamentary select committee of enquiry, headed by Sadler, to gather information on factory conditions. The committee included supporters and opponents of factory reform as well as the undecided. It sat between 13 April and 7 August (when Parliament was suspended) and met on 43 days. Supporters of factory reform dominated the list of witnesses heard by the committee. Of the 87 witnesses who spoke for the committee, 60 were themselves workers, including three women. (The manufacturers were also slated to testify, but the committee was suspended with the adjournment of Parliament before it could hear them.) The committee issued a massive report of nearly a thousand folio pages that included accounts of protracted hours, of workers being locked in factories for 48 or more continuous hours, and of children deformed by the requirements of their work or beaten to prevent them from falling asleep. It shocked the press and roused public opinion, and made the passage of some form of factory legislation inevitable.

The factory owners, hastily organized into an "Association of Master Manufacturers," and their allies in Parliament attempted to recoup by having a Royal Commission appointed to investigate factory conditions. The Home Secretary, Lord Melbourne, limited the effectiveness of the new commission as a stalling device by allowing only six weeks for it to make its report. The commission included several Benthamites, including its leading spirit Edwin Chadwick, who were suspicious of humanitarianism. The workers and their allied supporters of reform boycotted the commission and greeted it in the North with massive demonstrations of protest. The commission's report, which attacked the Ten Hours Movement as a front for trade-union agitators, was generally more sympathetic to the factory owners than that of the Parliamentary Select Committee. The

commission report principally warned that the restriction of child labor would lead to the restriction of adult labor, rather than opposing limitations on child labor per se. It supported some legislative action to remedy the worst abuses inflicted on children under the age of 13.

The Factory Act

The parliamentary election of 1832, the first carried out after the great Reform Bill, seemed to hinder the progress of the bill as Sadler was defeated at Leeds by the historian Thomas Babington Macaulay, a Whig opponent of the bill. Leadership of the factory reformers in the House of Commons in the new session passed to Anthony Ashley Cooper, Viscount Ashley, the Tory member of Parliament for Dorsetshire. Cooper, a deeply religious conservative who was strongly opposed to trade unions, had been converted to the cause of factory reform on humanitarian grounds by the report of the parliamentary select committee. He would remain a leader in the cause for many more years. His first move was to reintroduce Sadler's bill to forestall any attempt by manufacturers to preempt the bill with an Eleven Hours Bill of their own. Althorp countered the move by introducing an amendment (along lines suggested by the commission's report) to lower the age for the 10-hour limit from 18 to 13. Cooper withdrew his bill, and the final bill was Althorp's, which was based on the commission's report with some modifications.

The Factory Act in its final form, unlike Hobhouse's bill, applied to all textile manufacturers (with some exceptions for silk). It forbade the employment of children under nine, limited the employment of children under age 13 to nine hours a day and 48 hours a week, and that of children under 18 to 12 hours a day and 69 hours a week. The act also forbade night work for children by restricting the time they could work to the period from 5:30 A.M. to 8:30 P.M., and required children under 13 to attend school for two hours a day. The Factory Act was a disappointment to many supporters of factory reform, including Oastler. Supporters were frustrated that the original goal of the 10-hour workday, as set forth in Sadler's bill, was lost. Many blamed the government for protecting the manufacturers. The act had much more effect, however, than any previous legislation. Not only did it go further than previous acts, but it also provided a force of inspectors empowered to see to its enforcement. It also established a clear precedent for government regulation of working conditions, and it was followed by further legislation in 1844, 1847 (when an actual Ten Hours Bill was passed), 1850, and 1853.

Key Players

Chadwick, Edwin (1800–1890): A follower and friend of the utilitarian philosopher Jeremy Bentham, Chadwick was a leader in the imposition of the new Poor Law of 1834 and sanitary reform.

Cooper, Anthony Ashley, seventh Earl of Shaftesbury (1801–1885): A deeply religious conservative with a strong belief in social reform and the amelioration of the lot of the laboring poor, Cooper led the cause of better factory conditions in the House of Commons until he succeeded his fa-

Anthony Ashley Cooper (Seventh Earl of Shaftsbury). The Library of Congress.

ther as Earl and moved to the House of Lords in 1851. Cooper was also active in many philanthropic causes, chairing the Ragged School Union for 39 years.

Grey, Charles, Earl (1764–1845): Grey was a long-serving Whig politician who became prime minister in 1830. His government carried the abolition of slavery, the Factory Act, and the Great Reform Bill of 1832, which extended the British parliamentary franchise. He resigned as prime minister in 1834.

Hobhouse, Sir John Cam (1786–1869): A long-serving London radical Member of Parliament and a friend of the poet Byron, Hobhouse served as president of the Board of Control from 1835 to 1841 and from 1846 to 1852.

Oastler, Richard (1789–1861): Oastler was for decades a tireless speaker and writer in favor of factory reform and against the Poor Law of 1834. He earned the nickname "The Factory King" and is often considered a founder of the British tradition of conservative social reform.

Sadler, Michael Thomas (1780–1835): A Tory and an opponent of Catholic emancipation, Sadler wrote an attack on Thomas Malthus's population theory, *The Law of Population* (1832), in which he argued that rising income leads to declining fertility. Sadler served in Parliament from 1829 to 1832 as a champion of factory reform and the improvement of conditions of agricultural laborers.

Spencer, John Charles, Viscount Althorp and third Earl of Spencer (1782–1845): Althorp was a Whig politician and supporter of parliamentary reform. He was chancellor of the exchequer from 1830 to 1834, when he retired from politics.

Excerpt from Peter Gaskell, *The Manufacturing Population of England* (1833)

Any man who has stood at twelve o'clock at the single narrow door-way, which serves as the place of exit for the hands employed in the great cotton-mills, must acknowledge, that an uglier set of men and women, of boys and girls, taking them in the mass, it would be impossible to congregate in a smaller compass. Their complexion is sallow and pallid—with a peculiar flatness of feature, caused by the want of a proper quantity of adipose substance to cushion out the cheeks. Their stature low—the average height of four hundred men, measured at different times, and different places, being five feet six inches. Their limbs slender, and playing badly and ungracefully. A very general bowing of the legs. Great numbers of girls and women walking lamely or awkwardly, with raised chests and spinal flexures. Nearly all have flat feet, accompanied with a downtread, differing very widely from the elasticity of action in the foot and ankle, attendant upon perfect formation. Hair thin and straight—many of the men having but little beard, and that in patches of a few hairs, much resembling its growth among the red men of America. A spiritless and dejected air, a sprawling and wide action of the legs, and an appearance, taken as a whole, giving the world but "little assurance of a man," or if so, "most sadly cheated of his fair proportions" . . . .

Factory labour is a species of work, in some respects singularly unfitted for children. Cooped up in a heated atmosphere, debarred the necessary exercise, remaining in one position for a series of hours, one set or system of muscles alone called into activity, it cannot be wondered at—that its effects are injurious to the physical growth of a child. Where the bony system is still imperfect, the vertical position it is compelled to retain, influences its direction; the spinal column bends beneath the weight of the head, bulges out laterally, or is dragged forward by the weight of the parts composing the chest, the pelvis yields beneath the opposing pressure downwards, and the resistance given by the thigh-bones; its capacity is lessened, sometimes more and sometimes less; the legs curve, and the whole body loses height, in consequence of this general yielding and bending of its parts.

Source: Gaskell, Peter. *The Manufacturing Population of England: Its Moral, Social, and Physical Conditions, and the Changes Which Have Arisen from the Use of Steam Machinery; With an Examination of Infant Labour.* London: Baldwin and Cradock, 1833.

—Judson Knight

BIBLIOGRAPHY

Books

Driver, Cecil. *Tory Radical: The Life of Richard Oastler.* New York: Oxford University Press, 1946.

Newbould, Ian. *Whiggery and Reform, 1830–1841: The Politics of Government.* Stanford, CA: Stanford University Press, 1990.

Thompson, E. P. *The Making of the English Working Class.* New York: Pantheon Books, 1964.

Woodward, Llewellyn. *The Age of Reform: England 1815–1870.* 2nd edition. Oxford: Oxford University Press, 1962.

ADDITIONAL RESOURCES

Books

Cowherd, Raymond. *The Humanitarians and the Ten Hour Movement in England.* Boston: Baker Library, 1956.

Henriques, Ursula R. Q. *The Early Factory Acts and Their Enforcement.* London: Historical Association, 1971.

Ward, John Trevor. *The Factory Movement, 1830–1855.* New York: St. Martin's Press, 1962.

—William E. Burns

Factory Girls' Association

United States 1834–1836

Synopsis

Women factory workers at Lowell, Massachusetts, rejected wage cuts in 1834 and again in 1836 by walking off the job. These early "turn outs," as they were called, required the coordination of hundreds of female operatives and drew on both traditional forms of community networks and a newer form of wage labor negotiations to organize the strikes and protect their interests as female wage laborers. Neither strike resulted in long-term worker associations nor succeeded in preventing wage reductions; but the walkouts did disrupt factory production, demonstrating the significance of collective action and revealing the ambiguous position of women in the world of wage labor.

Timeline

1809: Progressive British industrialist Robert Owen proposes an end to employment of children in his factories. When his partners reject the idea, he forms an alliance with others of like mind, including the philosopher Jeremy Bentham.

1813: Jane Austen publishes *Pride and Prejudice.*

1818: Donkin, Hall & Gamble "Preservatory" in London produces the first canned foods.

1824: Ludwig van Beethoven composes his Ninth Symphony.

1829: Greece wins its independence after a seven-year war with Turkey.

1831: Unsuccessful Polish revolt waged against Russian rule.

1834: British mathematician Charles Babbage completes drawings for the "analytic engine," a forerunner of the modern computer that he never builds.

1834: American inventor Cyrus H. McCormick patents his reaper, a horse-drawn machine for harvesting wheat.

1835: American inventor and painter Samuel F. B. Morse constructs an experimental version of his telegraph, and American inventor Samuel Colt patents his revolver.

1837: Victoria is crowned in England.

1841: Act of Union joins Upper Canada and Lower Canada, which consist of parts of the present-day provinces of Ontario and Quebec, respectively.

1846: American inventor Elias Howe patents his sewing machine.

Event and Its Context

The Lowell Factory System

The growth of cotton mills in New England in the early nineteenth century contributed to industrialization in the United States. The Lowell factory system established a new form of organizing textile production, and the young women who migrated from the countryside to work in the factories constituted a workforce and community previously unseen in the United States. Francis Cabot Lowell, backed by financiers Benjamin Gorham, Tracy Jackson, and Uriah Cotting, established the first modern factory system in 1813. The Boston Manufacturing Company handled every aspect of cotton production and was the first factory to do so. Francis Lowell, along with Paul Moody, a mechanic, further modernized the factory system by improving upon the power loom.

Female operatives held a variety of positions inside the factories. Wage scales were based on the skill of the job performed. Women who attended to spinning machines earned less than women weavers, whose more specialized skills returned higher wages. Male operatives at the low end of the wage scale earned approximately five cents more than the highest paid female operative. The male carding and picking workers required strength, but their jobs were considered semiskilled and were among the lowest paid ranks of male workers. Men also worked in the repair shops and mill yards and held all managerial positions in the factories.

From management's perspective, women workers were ideal because they universally received lower wages than male laborers. To attract young women from the surrounding countryside, Lowell and other factory owners promised decent wages as well as boarding houses operated by women, run with strict rules to ensure young women had moral guidance, even though they lived outside the purview of their parents. The Lowell factory system's opportunity for young women to earn wages without damaging their feminine virtue proved to be a successful strategy.

Power loom worker. National Archives and Records Administration.

Boardinghouse rules served not only to protect women but also to protect the interests of the factory owners. Management sought to forge an obedient, efficient workforce and to assuage fears about the potential dangers of urban life for young women. In Lowell, factory managers established a system that protected their young female operatives and punished those who broke the rules. Women who breached tenets of morality or left their employers without the required two weeks' notice were effectively blacklisted from Lowell factories. "Honorable discharge[s]" served as tickets into the factories and the boarding houses. Without such a document, young women found themselves unable to gain employment or housing.

Factory owners wanted a disciplined work force, and company-owned housing helped them achieve this. It also provided a degree of social control over the young women in their employ. In addition to keeping owners' costs down, the rules of the boardinghouses ensured that young women would continue to receive moral guidance. Factory workers were expected to attend church regularly—failure to do so meant receiving a dishonorable discharge, which would also result in their being blacklisted from the Lowell factories. Boardinghouse regulations included a 10:00 P.M. curfew, which was intended to keep young women out of danger and in good shape for a long day's work. So although the young women who sought work in the factories found independence from their parents' households, they found themselves, to a certain extent, charges of the female boardinghouse keepers and factory supervisors.

The majority of female operatives came from propertied farm families and usually made the decision themselves to seek employment at the mills. As Thomas Dublin pointed out, the women who migrated to the Lowell factories tended to come from larger families and be first or second daughters. Unlike their European counterparts, Lowell's female workers went to work to support themselves, not their families. These young women usually worked for a few years before marrying. During this time they earned their own incomes and gained independence form their parents. Although the female operatives worked 12 hours a day, six days a week, the women experienced new social opportunities that were unavailable to them in their rural communities. The newfound social and economic independence of these women altered the rural patriarchal family structure. Young women experienced the freedom of having their own incomes and could spend their money at their own discretion. Despite the long working days, socializing took place in the factory as well as the boarding houses.

The factory workers forged bonds both in the workplace and in the boardinghouses. Management paired new hires to the mills with more experienced workers. Additionally, many of the women migrating to Lowell had a relative already working in the mills who could help the newcomers adjust to their new environment. Even if young women did not have familial connections, the close living and working quarters, along with the system of pairing workers, helped to socialize the new female factory workers. Although familial ties helped forge a sense of community in the factories, women experienced a different social world than the rural ones from which they had come. The young female factory workers might have loosened the bonds of parental control, but society in the Lowell factory systems was regulated by seasoned workers, and pressure to adopt the

perceived urban sophistication of the veteran women workers was part of life in Lowell.

Pairing new factory workers with veteran workers also helped newcomers learn the ropes of the factory work. Letters from factory workers attest to the significance of women working together, looking out for one another, and keeping women within the accepted norms of the social order. Such working conditions also fostered the solidarity that became evident during the strikes of 1834 and 1836.

If accepted norms of behavior and work habits were easily ascertained, the status of women workers in early industrializing United States was more ambiguous. Factory work increased during the 1830s, but other forms of production such as outwork and artisan shops persisted. Women's place in the world of wage labor remained subordinate to men's, and the women were not considered permanent wage earners. These perceptions sat at cross-purposes for female laborers seeking to change their working conditions. They also undermined the female workers' ability to forge strong alliances with male laborers. Most women at the Lowell factories in the 1830s were wage laborers for a relatively short period of time at a particular stage in their lives, yet the fact that so many women banded together to maintain their wage levels illustrates their understanding of the power of workers' alliances. The impermanence of their associations exemplifies the problematic status of female workers in a period where women were not considered a permanent part of the wage labor force.

The subordination of women workers to male workers' interests, as historian Mary Blewett pointed out, sabotaged any real challenge to burgeoning capitalism in the United States. The 1830s produced increasing activism among the working classes, but men's concerns overshadowed women's and ultimately forged an image of the working class based on masculine identity. The Workingmen's Party and arguments for a "workingman's wage" reinforced the laborer as male and did much to render women's labor invisible in the economy. Blewett's examination of the Lynn, Massachusetts, shoemakers' strike in 1860 demonstrated the continued failure of the working class to address the needs of both female and male wage laborers, which resulted in below-living wages for most women and undermined workers' efforts to mitigate employers' control.

The 1834 Turn-out

Early in 1834 the largest factories in Lowell posted notices of reductions in wages for piecework. Women began organizing as soon as the broadsides were posted, even before the agents set the exact numbers for the reduction in wages. The first action taken by the women was to circulate and sign petitions demanding that wage levels remain the same and threatening that the women would not show up for work if wage reductions took place. Female factory workers called meetings, elected representatives, and pledged financial support for operatives who needed money. When a spokeswoman from one of the mills was fired, the turn-out began in earnest. Despite her warning that the other female operatives would walk out if her employment was terminated, the agent dismissed the spokeswoman. She exited the room, followed by all of the other female operatives present. Some 800 women struck, signing petitions that expressed their heritage as "free" women and daughters of liberty.

Within days the strike was over. Inauspicious timing along with the mobility of many of the women meant that those who did not have to, or could not, return to the mills, moved back to their rural homes, bringing the strike to an inauspicious end. New factory workers quickly replaced those on strike during the 1834 turn-out. Many of the women who had not left the area returned to work at the mills. Little is known about the fate of the women who did not have the choice to return to their parents' homes and remained on strike even in the face of ultimate failure.

Although the strike of 1834 was short-lived and failed to preserve operatives' wages, it left a legacy for worker agitation in the future. In addition to their objections to losing wages, the female workers resoundingly rejected managements' paternalistic approach. The petition stated that management's demeanor was "haughty" and "overbearing." The women chafed under this paternal treatment and demanded their rights to maintain their wages levels as well as their dignity.

Labor activism increased during the late 1820s and early 1830s. As the artisan system eroded, wage workers were well aware that action on their part often proved a necessary response to merchant-capitalists. Although the Workingmen's Party experienced a fast demise, the question of where wage labor stood in the republic unsettled workers and capitalists alike. Workers worried that they would be "enslaved," and owners wanted to mold a system that relied on cheap wages to generate the greatest profits.

The Lowell factory girls' strike was not the only one to occur in 1834. In Dover, New Hampshire, female cotton factory workers also turned out in February and March of that year, repudiating factory owners' attempts to lower their wages. In New York female bookbinders took action in 1835. One publication titled their walkouts the "Broomstick strikes" when these women demanded a higher wage for their work. In Philadelphia the Female Improvement Society for the City and County of Philadelphia formed in 1835 to address the needs of the city's seamstresses, milliners, and other textile piece workers. The Female Improvement Society elected special committees to make formal requests for wage increases; one committee petitioned the secretary of war, arguing that insufficient wages were paid to the women who clothed the army. In Philadelphia increases—although slight—did come about from the association's demands.

The 1836 Strike and Formation of the Factory Girls' Association

Although the women strikers in Lowell did not reap rewards from their walkout, they set the stage for future activism. In 1836 Lowell factory managers increased the rents for their boardinghouses. Reacting to this effective decrease in their income, the women chose to strike in protest. They launched the Factory Girls' Association, which boasted 2,500 members. The organization appointed officers and established committees to formally address their position. The association informed the factory agents that correspondence from management would be received only through the officers of the new union.

The rhetoric in 1836 mirrored that of the 1834 turn-out. The women claimed that they were "daughters of freemen," and refused to be "enslaved" by factory management. The strikers eventually found themselves evicted from their boardinghouses, and the strike quickly dwindled to a close, but production remained below prestrike levels. The Lowell strike of 1836 also spurred strikes in Amesbury and Dover, Massachusetts.

The collective action that led to the founding of the female worker organizations failed to create any permanent associations. In the case of Lowell, the impetus to form permanent labor organizations did not exist, for the majority of the women did not face working in the mills for the rest of their lives. The organizing efforts of these women nonetheless made their walkouts more effective, and for a brief time, affected production output. Manufacturers, of course, quickly moved to fire and blacklist strikers, hoping to prevent future organizing among the female operatives. Given the lack of success of the Lowell strikes, smaller manufacturers around New England and other parts of the North followed Lowell's example by reducing wages. The women workers in these other areas also responded by walking out.

The Lowell factory was the first modern factory in the United States. The initial strategy of Cabot Lowell to offer high wages and other incentives to attract the young rural women from neighboring farms proved unsustainable for the factory owners who needed to maximize profits and compete in industry. Textile factories did not emerge in other parts of the country; in New York and Philadelphia "put-out" work prevailed. This system of labor paid women by the article, but the women worked out of their own homes rather than in a factory. The put-out system did not have the overhead costs that were associated with the Lowell factory system, nor could it match the level of production attainable with factory work.

Despite the failure of the strikes, Lowell women engaged themselves in the important debate about wage workers' status in the Jacksonian era. An emerging sense of female working-class consciousness complicated the debate, as it also asserted the importance of women to labor and the nascent labor movement. In the 1840s the legacy of the 1830s turn-outs would help Lowell women organize and agitate for the 10-hour workday. The early strikes carved out a niche for female wage laborers based on their rights as citizens and asserted their value as an important part of the system of production. Although women's wage labor would continue to be overshadowed by a gender system that devalued women's work, the Lowell factory girls' early organization took the important step of entering women into the debate about the future of the laboring classes in the United States.

Key Players

Larcom, Lucy (1824–1893): Larcom was involved in the 1836 strike. Just 12 years old at the time, she had come to Lowell from the rural outskirts of Massachusetts with her mother, who was widowed and was forced to find work to support her children. Larcom published an article in the *Atlantic Monthly* in 1881 describing life in the mills and the magazine, *The Lowell Offering*, which began publication in 1840 and was written by and for the Lowell factory girls. Larcom wrote both for *The Lowell Offering* and *The Operatives' Magazine*.

Robinson, Harriet Jane Hanson (1825–1911): In 1836 Robinson walked out with other female strikers, and management reprimanded her mother, Harriet Hanson, for the failure to prevent her daughter from turning out. Robinson recounted her life in the mills in her book *Loom and Spindle; Or, Life Among the Early Mill Girls.* In addition to discussing the Lowell factory environment, Robinson included in her book some short biographies of her fellow factory workers who wrote for *The Lowell Offering.*

Turner, Elizabeth Emerson (1822–?): Born in Lyme, New Hampshire, Turner moved to Lowell with her family in 1833, after her father lost his property as the result of an illness. Turner began working in the mills at age 11 and began writing for *The Lowell Offering* when she was 18 years old.

See also: *Lowell Industrial Experiment; Workingmen's Party (1828).*

BIBLIOGRAPHY

Books

Andrews, John B., and W. D. P. Bliss. *History of Women in Trade Unions.* New York: Arno Press, 1974.

Baxter, Annette K., and Leon Stein, eds. *Women of Lowell.* New York: Arno Press, 1974.

Bender, Thomas. *Toward an Urban Vision: Ideas and Institutions in Nineteenth Century America.* Baltimore, MD: The Johns Hopkins University Press, 1975.

Boris, Eileen, and Nelson Lichtenstein. *Major Problems in the History of American Workers.* Lexington, MA: D. C. Heath and Company, 1991.

Dublin, Thomas. *Farm to Factory: Women's Letters, 1830–1860.* New York: Columbia University Press, 1981.

———. *Transforming Women's Work: New England Lives in the Industrial Revolution.* Ithaca: Cornell University Press, 1994.

———. *Women at Work: The Transformation of Work and Community in Lowell, Massachusetts, 1826–1860.* New York: Columbia University Press, 1979.

Foner, Philip S., ed. *The Factory Girls.* Urbana: University of Illinois Press, 1977.

———. *History of the Labor Movement in the United States,* vol. 1. 3rd ed. New York: International Publishers, 1962.

———. *From Colonial Times to the Founding of the American Federation of Labor.* New York: International Publishers, 1962.

Kessler-Harris, Alice. *Out to Work: A History of Wage-Earning Women in the United States.* New York: Oxford University Press, 1982.

Stansell, Christine. *City of Women: Sex and Class in New York, 1789–1860.* New York: Knopf Press, Inc., 1986.

Wilentz, Sean. *Chants Democratic: New York City and the Rise of the American Working Class, 1788–1850.* New York: Oxford University Press, 1984.

—Karla Kelling

Fair Employment Practice Committee

United States 1941

Synopsis

On 25 June 1941 President Franklin Roosevelt issued Executive Order 8802, banning employers, unions, and government agencies involved in defense work from discriminating against workers based on race, religion, and national origin. The order established the Committee on Fair Employment Practice (FEPC) to "receive and investigate complaints of discrimination in violation of the provisions" of the order and to "take appropriate steps to redress grievances which it finds to be valid." During its five-year existence, the FEPC worked to end hiring discrimination and unequal working conditions in the defense industry. The FEPC investigated individual complaints, held public and private hearings, sought allies in other government agencies, and cooperated with civil rights groups to achieve compliance with the executive order. Despite these efforts, the FEPC had a limited impact. A small budget, no enforcement powers, employer and union resistance, and conservative political opposition weakened the committee. The FEPC, however, legitimized wartime protest by African Americans, established work as a civil right, and laid the groundwork for government intervention to ensure equal employment opportunity.

Timeline

1921: Washington Disarmament Conference limits the tonnage of world navies.

1925: European leaders attempt to secure the peace at the Locarno Conference, which guarantees the boundaries between France and Germany, and Belgium and Germany.

1931: Financial crisis widens in the United States and Europe, which reel from bank failures and climbing unemployment levels. In London, armies of the unemployed riot.

1936: Germany reoccupies the Rhineland, while Italy annexes Ethiopia. Recognizing a commonality of aims, the two totalitarian powers sign the Rome-Berlin Axis Pact. (Japan will join them in 1940.)

1941: German troops march into the Balkans, conquering Yugoslavia and Greece. (Bulgaria and Romania, along with Hungary, are aligned with the Nazis.)

1941: In a move that takes Stalin by surprise, Hitler sends his troops into the Soviet Union on 22 June. Like his hero Napoleon, Hitler believes that by stunning Russia with a lightning series of brilliant maneuvers, it is possible to gain a quick and relatively painless victory. Early successes seem to prove him right, and he is so confident of victory that he refuses to equip his soldiers with winter clothing.

1941: Japanese bombing of Pearl Harbor on 7 December brings the United States into the war against the Axis. Combined with the attack on the Soviet Union, which makes Stalin an unlikely ally of the Western democracies, the events of 1941 will ultimately turn the tide of the war.

1941: The United States initiates the Manhattan Project to build an atomic bomb and signs the Lend-Lease Act, whereby it provides aid to Great Britain and, later, the Soviet Union.

1941: Great films of the year include *The Maltese Falcon, Sullivan's Travels, Meet John Doe, How Green Was My Valley,* and a work often cited as one of the greatest films of all time: Orson Welles's *Citizen Kane.*

1946: Winston Churchill warns of an "Iron Curtain" spreading across Eastern Europe.

1951: Color television is introduced.

1956: First aerial testing of the hydrogen bomb occurs at Bikini Atoll. The blast is so powerful—the equivalent of 10 million tons of TNT—that it actually results in the infusion of protons to atomic nuclei to create two new elements, einsteinium and fermium, which have atomic numbers of 99 and 100 respectively.

Event and Its Context

Roosevelt issued Executive Order 8802 to address primarily the discrimination African Americans faced in the defense industry. African Americans were largely excluded from the millions of new industry jobs being created in the United States mobilization for war from 1940 to 1941. Many employers with defense contracts refused to hire blacks, often advertising new employment opportunities with "Help Wanted, White" signs. Most employers who hired African Americans segregated them into low-paid, unskilled work. White unionists in the American Federation of Labor (AFL) and the Congress of Industrial Organizations (CIO) often reinforced racial discrimination. Some unions denied blacks access to jobs and promotions by excluding them from membership, by negotiating discriminatory contracts, and by setting up segregated auxiliary locals. Racial bias also pervaded the government agencies responsible for mobilizing the wartime workforce. Agencies that trained workers for skilled defense jobs often excluded African Americans, and the United States Employment Service (USES) accepted race-specific work orders from employers.

Hope for a Fair Workplace

African Americans organized protests against employment discrimination as part of a broader national equal rights campaign that became known as "Double V for Victory," a victory over fascism abroad and against second-class citizenship at home. Groups like the National Association for the Advancement of Colored People (NAACP), the Urban League, and the National Negro Congress sent telegrams, petitions, and delegations to government officials, demanding an end to discrimination in the defense industry. In early 1941 A. Philip Randolph, president of the Brotherhood of Sleeping Car Porters (BSCP), issued a call for African Americans to march on Washington, D.C., to demand equality in employment and in the armed forces. Led primarily by Pullman porters in the BSCP, black communities across the country mobilized for the march under

Franklin Delano Roosevelt. Franklin D. Roosevelt Library.

the auspices of the March on Washington Committee (MOWC). Activists arranged transportation, raised money, and publicized the march. The committee's exclusion of whites and its emphasis on collective and direct action revealed a militant shift in black protest politics during the war. By June the MOWC had chapters in numerous cities, gained the support of leaders in the NAACP and Urban League, and appeared ready to fulfill its promise to bring 100,000 African Americans to the nation's capitol.

Initially, government officials either ignored black protests or responded with token action. Nevertheless, the threat of the MOWC convinced President Franklin Roosevelt to use his authority to eliminate discrimination in the defense industry. After meeting with Randolph and NAACP head Walter White at the White House, Roosevelt agreed to issue an executive order banning discrimination in the defense industry. On 25 June, Roosevelt issued Executive Order 8802, which declared it the "duty of employers and of labor organization . . . to provide for the full and equitable participation of all workers in defense industries, without discrimination because of race, creed, color, or national origin." The order directed government agencies to ensure equal access to training programs for defense production, required defense contracts to include a nondiscrimination provision, and it established the committee on Fair Employment Practice (FEPC) to receive and investigate complaints and redress grievances. During its first year, Roosevelt placed the FEPC in the Office of Production Management's (OPM) Labor Division, and then in the War Production Board (WPB) after he dismantled the OPM in early 1942. Although denied full administrative autonomy, the committee retained some indepen-

A. Philip Randolph. The Library of Congress.

dence in selecting personnel and setting its budget priorities and policies.

African Americans were cautiously optimistic about the order and the creation of the FEPC. The *Chicago Defender* declared that the order was "one of the most significant pronouncements that has been made in the interest of the Negro for more than a century." The order satisfied Randolph and he canceled the march, but he transformed the MOWC into the March on Washington Movement (MOWM) to ensure the FEPC pursued its mandate vigorously. The order, however, contained limitations that concerned black leaders. It did not cover segregation in the armed forces or employment outside the defense industry. Roosevelt even framed the order narrowly as a measure to "encourage full participation in the national defense program," not as a broad commitment to equal opportunity in all work. The FEPC had no enforcement power. It could not issue subpoenas, its directives had no sanctions, and national defense priorities and legal constraints made government officials unwilling to cancel contracts that were in violation of the order. The FEPC also had to function on a meager budget and a small staff during its first year.

Despite these limitations, in its first year the FEPC developed an administrative infrastructure to address discrimination in defense work. By mid-July, Roosevelt had appointed the FEPC's six board members. The committee included two African Americans, BSCP vice president Milton Webster and Chicago alderman Earl Dickerson; two white trade unionists, AFL and CIO presidents William Green and Philip Murray; and two white employers, David Sarnoff of the Radio Corporation of America (RCA) and Mark Ethridge, the Louisville *Courier-Journal* editor and the committee's chair. Later, John Brophy of the CIO and Frank Fenton of the AFL replaced Murray and Green, and Boris Shishkin from the AFL eventually replaced

Fenton. In early 1942 the committee gained an additional member when Malcolm MacLean, Hampton Institute's white president, replaced Ethridge as chair. Ethridge resigned largely because of professional demands in Louisville. The white former governor of the Virgin Islands, Lawrence Cramer, became FEPC executive secretary, and the black dean of the Howard Law School, Howard M. Johnson, became assistant executive secretary. By early 1942 the FEPC had hired a biracial part-time staff of eleven, who had backgrounds in labor, civil rights, academia, law, and the press. The OPM's Labor Division assisted the FEPC in its investigations.

During its first year, the FEPC employed a variety of tactics to break down discrimination in the defense industry. The FEPC publicized the existence of the executive order by distributing thousands of posters to employers and government agencies. The committee also sought to gain the assistance of government agencies with enforcement power. Cramer convinced the War Department, Navy Department, and the Maritime Commission to cooperate with the FEPC. These procurement agencies, which handled most war contracts, agreed to insert nondiscrimination clauses into contracts, supply employment statistics to the FEPC, and treat the committee as a board of appeals by informing the FEPC of discrimination complaints. The FEPC also convinced the USES to notify employers about the government's nondiscrimination policy and inform the FEPC about discriminatory employers. It was not until 1943, however, that the USES issued a policy against discriminatory employment requests. Despite the early promise of cooperation, national defense priorities and racial prejudices made interagency cooperation difficult. Many officials refused to enforce the order, because they worried that FEPC directives would lead to racial conflict in the workplace and disrupt war production. Government agencies often remained hostile to racial change. Some USES officials, particularly in the South, sympathized with discriminatory employers and continued to accept race-specific work requests.

The FEPC took independent action to end discrimination in defense work. In its first year, the committee held a series of public hearings to publicize its existence, focus public attention on discrimination, and put pressure on discriminatory employers and unions. In the fall of 1941 and spring of 1942, the committee held hearings in Los Angeles, Chicago, New York, and Birmingham. In each city, the committee heard evidence of employment discrimination, gathered by its investigators and civil rights groups. Its members also questioned employers and union leaders who agreed to testify about their industry's employment practices. At its Chicago hearing the committee began to issue directives, which included orders to "cease and desist" discriminatory practices. Some employers and unions responded to the public pressure generated by the hearings and abided by the directives. Most ignored them, however, claiming that FEPC directives lacked legal authority and threatened to create racial chaos and disrupt war production. Although the hearings did not significantly alter employment practices, they generated important documentation of discrimination against African Americans, Mexican Americans, Asian Americans, ethnic Europeans, Jews, and Catholics.

The Battle for Control of the FEPC

Toward the end of the first year of the FEPC, Roosevelt faced growing political pressure from both proponents and opponents of the committee. FEPC members and their supporters called for a new executive order to expand the committee's size, jurisdiction, and enforcement power. They wanted independent status in the White House's Office of Emergency Management (OEM), the ability to subpoena witnesses, and a larger budget to hire more staff and set up regional offices. At the same time, opposition to the FEPC intensified, particularly after the Birmingham hearings. The sight of black FEPC members questioning white witnesses, and black workers testifying against white employers and unionists had outraged white southerners, whose votes Roosevelt coveted. Several administration officials, including War Manpower Commission (WMC) director Paul McNutt and budget director Howard D. Smith, also sought to weaken the committee. McNutt believed that, since the FEPC dealt with labor issues, it should be under his authority, and Smith warned Roosevelt about the disruptive effects of an expanded FEPC on war production.

On 30 July, Roosevelt rejected the expansion proposals and transferred the FEPC to McNutt in the WMC. The move shocked FEPC members, who claimed that the president had expressed support for their proposals. Several committee members and many black leaders feared that, under McNutt the agency would lose its independence. Their concerns proved justified. Under McNutt's authority, which lasted until May 1943, the FEPC's budget was reduced, and the much-anticipated hearings on discrimination in the railroad industry were postponed indefinitely. McNutt curtailed the committee's autonomy, requiring his approval before it held any public hearings. The FEPC, however, successfully resisted McNutt's attempt to control the appointment of FEPC field personnel. Dickerson thought the power of appointment was particularly important for black FEPC members, since it was a privilege previously denied black government officials. McNutt's actions triggered the resignations of MacLean, Ethridge, Sarnoff, Cramer, and three lawyers hired for the railroad cases. Civil rights, labor, and liberal groups sent delegations, telegrams, and letters to Washington, D.C., protesting the FEPC's fate, while Randolph's MOWM held "Save FEPC" rallies.

Roosevelt responded to the protests by reorganizing and, in some ways, strengthening the committee. On 27 May 1943 he issued Executive Order 9346, which set up a new FEPC with independent status in the OEM, a fulltime chair and six members, authorization to hold public hearings, and a budget of $500,000, which could be used to set up regional offices. In an agreement with the WMC in the summer, the FEPC assumed primary responsibility for handling discrimination complaints. The WMC was required to assist FEPC investigations and had ten days to resolve complaints it received before sending it to the FEPC. The new FEPC still had weaknesses. Roosevelt rejected the advice of his attorney general, Francis Biddle, and denied the new FEPC enforcement power, and the committee's chair and executive secretary positions continued to be reserved for whites. The White House also sought to ensure the new FEPC took a cautious approach that appeased African Americans, without provoking white workers or political conservatives. The White House refused to reappoint Earl Dickerson,

who had earned a reputation as an "extremist," and presidential aide Marvin McIntyre ordered the new chair, Monsignor Francis J. Haas, to avoid "contentious open hearings." Malcolm Ross, a former National Labor Relations Board member, replaced Haas as chair in October, after Haas resigned to become the bishop of Grand Rapids, Michigan. Webster, Shishkin, and Brophy were joined by two new white members, Sara Southhall of International Harvester and Samuel Zemurray of the United Fruit Company, and by Plummer Bernard Young, a black man who edited the Norfolk *Journal and Guide*.

The End of FEPC

The second FEPC remained active for the next three years and proved more expansive than the first committee. It set up twelve regional offices that over the next three years handled thousands of complaints. In its first year and a half, the second FEPC docketed close to 6,000 discrimination complaints (those that FEPC investigators decided had merit) and resolved nearly 40 percent satisfactorily. The committee heard 12,000 cases, with 40 percent resolved satisfactorily. Public hearings remained a central feature of the committee, which held fifteen from August 1944 to August 1945 and continued to issue directives to employers and companies. A growing number of citizens' groups assisted the second FEPC. In 1942 and 1943, civil rights activists in a number of cities, including Chicago, Cleveland, and Detroit, organized Metropolitan Fair Employment Councils. Often in cooperation with the FEPC, these councils handled complaints of unfair employment practices and pressured employers to hire and upgrade black workers. Two CIO unions—the United Electrical Workers and the United Auto Workers—reached agreements to cooperate with the FEPC. Lawsuits filed by black workers provided leverage to the committee, and, after black workers won a lawsuit against the boilermakers' segregated auxiliary units that denied blacks full union membership, California shipyard companies and the AFL boilermakers union obeyed FEPC directives.

The second committee, with its augmented powers, faced more opposition than its first incarnation. Opponents of the FEPC, primarily southerners, claimed that the committee was communist, caused racial conflict, and would lead to social equality among the races. In late 1943 conservative southern Democrats, in alliance with some Republicans, launched an anti-FEPC campaign that led to the committee's destruction by mid-1946. In December southern congressman John Rankin called for the FEPC to be abolished and referred to its members as a "bunch of crackpots."

In early 1944 the conservative congressional representative Howard W. Smith from Virginia began hearings to determine whether, in several instances, the FEPC had acted illegally in issuing directives. Meanwhile, the Georgia senator Richard Russell attached a successful amendment to a House appropriations bill, designed to destroy the FEPC. The amendment required the elimination of government agencies that had existed for more than a year without congressional funding, a definition that covered the FEPC. Roosevelt had funded the FEPC through the President's Emergency Fund. The FEPC survived the Russell amendment when Congress passed the War Agencies Appropriations Bill, which provided the FEPC with half a million dollars. The next year, Congress slashed the FEPC budget to

$250,000. The FEPC could afford only three of its regional offices and made drastic staff cuts. President Harry Truman further weakened the FEPC when he issued Executive Order 9664, which denied the committee the right to issue directives. At the end of June, the FEPC folded when appropriations ended and liberal Congressmen failed to pass a bill making the FEPC a permanent agency.

Key Players

Bethune, Mary McLeod (1875–1955): One of several black New Dealers, Bethune used her close ties to Eleanor and Franklin Roosevelt to gain political support for an FEPC. In her capacity as president of the National Council of Negro Women, she backed the March on Washington Committee.

Ethridge, Mark (1896–1981): Ethridge, editor of the Louisville *Courier-Journal,* was the FEPC's first chair. Etheridge's cautious approach occasionally clashed with other committee members, in particular Earl Dickerson, who fought for a more activist FEPC.

Haas, Francis J. (1889–1953): Haas became the first chair of the second FEPC, created by Roosevelt in May 1943 through Executive Order 9346. Haas resigned in October 1943 to become bishop in Grand Rapids Michigan.

MacClean, Malcolm (1894–1977): MacClean replaced Etheridge as FEPC chair in early 1942. He resigned at the start of 1943 to enter the navy.

Randolph, A. Philip (1889–1979): As president of the Brotherhood of Sleeping Car Porters, Randolph organized the March on Washington Committee in 1941, which pressed Roosevelt to act against racial discrimination in employment and the armed forces.

Rauh, Joseph (1911–1992): Rauh was the attorney who drafted Executive Order 8802. He became a well known civil rights and labor activist.

Roosevelt, Eleanor (1884–1962): As first lady, Roosevelt became a champion of civil rights for African Americans. Although she tried to convince A. Philip Randolph to cancel his proposed march on Washington, D.C., she supported the goals of the March on Washington Committee.

Roosevelt, Franklin Delano (1882–1945): As U.S. president (1933–1945), Roosevelt gained the political allegiance of many African Americans by supporting civil rights and New Deal programs. In 1941 he issued Executive Order 8802, establishing the Committee on Fair Employment Practice.

Ross, Malcolm (1895–1965): Ross replaced Haas as chair in the fall of 1943. He served as FEPC chair until the committee was dismantled in 1946.

See also: *American Federation of Labor; Congress of Industrial Organizations; March on Washington Movement.*

BIBLIOGRAPHY

Books

Anderson, Jervis. *A. Philip Randolph: A Biographical Portrait.* Berkeley, CA: University of California Press, 1986.

Bates, Beth Tompkins. *Pullman Porters and the Rise of Protest Politics in Black America, 1925–1945.* Chapel Hill, NC: University of North Carolina Press, 2001.

Daniel, Cletus. *Chicano Workers and the Politics of Fairness: The FEPC in the Southwest, 1941–1945.* Austin, TX: University of Texas Press, 1991.

Garfinkel, Herbert. *When Negroes March: The March on Washington Movement in the Organizational Politics for FEPC.* Reprint with a new preface by Lewis M. Killian. New York: Atheneum, 1969.

Hill, Herbert. *Black Labor and the American Legal System: Race, Work, and the Law.* Madison, WI: University of Wisconsin Press, 1985.

Kersten, Andrew Edmund. *Race, Jobs, and the War: The FEPC in the Midwest, 1941–1946.* Urbana, IL: University of Illinois Press, 2000.

Kesselman, Louis. *The Social Politics of FEPC.* Chapel Hill, NC: University of North Carolina Press, 1948.

Moreno, Paul D. *From Direct Action to Affirmative Action: Fair Employment Law and Policy in America, 1933–1972.* Baton Rouge: Louisiana State University Press, 1997.

Pfeffer, Paula F. *A. Philip Randolph, Pioneer of the Civil Rights Movement.* Baton Rouge: Louisiana State University Press, 1990.

Reed, Merl Elwyn. *Seedtime for the Modern Civil Rights Movement: The President's Committee on Fair Employment Practice, 1941–1946.* Baton Rouge: Louisiana State University Press, 1991.

Ruchames, Louis. *Race, Jobs, and Politics: The Story of FEPC.* New York: Columbia University Press, 1953.

Periodicals

Boris, Eileen. "'You Wouldn't Want One of 'Em Dancing With Your Wife': Racialized Bodies on the Job in World War II." *American Quarterly* 50, no. 1 (1998): 77–108.

Harris, William H. "Federal Intervention in Union Discrimination: FEPC and West Coast Shipyards During World War II." *Labor History* 22, no. 3 (1981): 325–347.

Henderson, Alexa B. "FEPC and the Southern Railway Case: An Investigation into the Discriminatory Practices of Railroads During World War II." *Journal of Negro History* 61, no. 2 (1976): 173–187.

Reed, Merl Elwyn. "The FBI, MOWM, and CORE, 1941–1946." *Journal of Black Studies* 21, no. 4 (1991): 465–479.

———. "FEPC and the Federal Agencies in the South." *Journal of Negro History* 65, no. 1 (1980): 43–56.

ADDITIONAL RESOURCES

"Records of the Committee on Fair Employment Practice."
United States National Archives and Records
Administration [accessed 25 November 2002]. <http://
www.archives.gov/>.

—David M. Lewis-Colman

Fair Labor Standards Act

United States 1938

Synopsis

The Wages and Hours Act, later known as the Fair Labor
Standards Act (FLSA), was passed on 25 June 1938. The act
made it the U.S. government's responsibility to set a minimum
wage. Though the law set a relatively low initial minimum
wage of 25 cents an hour, it provided for increases up to 40
cents an hour by 1945. The act also banned child labor in all
businesses engaged in interstate commerce. It established a 44-
hour workweek and mandated the 40-hour week by 23 October
1940. Beyond these minimum hours, the bill institutionalized
overtime payments for additional hours worked. The law did
not cover workers in the public sector or those in agriculture
and service industries. As a result it favored workers employed
in larger businesses and excluded large numbers of women and
minorities.

President Franklin Delano Roosevelt considered the FLSA
among the most important New Deal reforms, second only to
the Social Security Act. More than any other New Deal legislation, the FLSA had its origins in the recognition that workers
were also consumers. Advocates of the bill hoped to give workers the material conditions to consume enough to pull the nation
out of the depression.

Timeline

1923: Conditions in Germany worsen as inflation skyrockets
and France, attempting to collect on coal deliveries
promised at Versailles, marches into the Ruhr basin.

1928: At the first Academy Awards ceremony, the best picture
is the silent *Wings*.

1933: Newly inaugurated U.S. president Franklin D. Roosevelt launches the first phase of his New Deal to put depression-era America back to work.

1935: Second phase of New Deal begins with the introduction
of social security, farm assistance, and housing and tax
reform.

1938: Hitler's troops march into Austria, and Germany proclaims a political union between the two countries.
Later that year, Britain and France, guided by the elder
statesman Mussolini of Italy, agree at Munich to let the

**Sidney Hillman. AP/WideWorld Photos. Reproduced by
permission.**

Germans take a portion of Czechoslovakia. (Germany
will annex the remainder the following year.) After Munich, the die is cast: Hitler justifiably believes that if he
moves to annex further territory in Europe, the Allies
will not react.

1938: In an incident that pointedly illustrates the heightened
tensions of the era, Orson Welles's radio broadcast of
War of the Worlds causes massive panic in the United
States. Despite disclaimers that the program is a mere
dramatization, people believe that Martians actually
have invaded Earth.

1941: Japanese bombing of Pearl Harbor on 7 December
brings the United States into the war against the Axis.
Combined with the attack on the Soviet Union, which
makes Stalin an unlikely ally of the Western democracies, the events of 1941 will ultimately turn the tide of
the war.

1943: To offset the costs of war, the U.S. government introduces income tax withholding—which it claims to be a
temporary measure.

1948: Stalin places a blockade on areas of Berlin controlled by
the United States, Great Britain, and France. The Allies
respond with an airlift of supplies, which, like the blockade itself, lasts into late 1949.

1953: Korean War, a conflict with no clear victors, ends with
an armistice establishing an uneasy peace between
South Korea and North Korea.

Franklin Delano Roosevelt. Franklin D. Roosevelt Library.

Event and Its Context

Background

Organized labor had been advocating a shorter workweek since the mid-nineteenth century. Progressive Era reformers had sought increased government regulation of business. Several changes needed to take place before these policies could be addressed by Congress. First, the brutal conditions of the Great Depression raised sentiment against unregulated business. Second, the formation of the Congress of Industrial Organizations (CIO) and early New Deal legislation had brought a couple of million more workers into trade unions. Third, President Franklin Delano Roosevelt had received crucial support from organized labor in the 1936 election. Legislators took note; labor controlled a growing number of votes, especially in the cities of the nation's industrial core.

Other factors entered into the equation as well. The growth of interstate markets changed many employers' attitudes about federal wage legislation. Whereas earlier employers had resisted any government involvement in setting wages, by the 1930s employers in higher wage regions saw the minimum wage as a tool to prevent capital flight to lower wage regions. Industry and jobs would stop migrating south, they reasoned, when there was one national wage standard. Proponents saw the FLSA as one strategy by which to cut unemployment by reducing the number of hours worked by each individual worker.

Economists debated the potential effects of state intervention in business. Neoclassical economists believed that the market would lift the nation out of the depression without government involvement. In their view, government regulation would

Imada v. City of Hercules (1998): Travel Time and the Fair Labor Standards Act

In 1998 the Ninth U.S. Circuit Court reviewed the case of *Imada v. City of Hercules,* which concerned the matter of pay for travel time. Interpreting the Fair Labor Standards Act (FLSA), passed 60 years earlier, the court found that the FLSA does not require employers to pay employees for time spent traveling—even travel in excess of ordinary commuting time—when that travel is undertaken for the purpose of attending mandatory off-site employee training.

The plaintiffs, led by police officer Dave A. Imada, sued the city of Hercules, California, which had refused to compensate them for travel time in which they performed no official duties. The city paid for actual time spent in training courses and for time spent traveling between the police department and off-site training locations. However, as Imada discovered when he submitted a compensation request for a three-day training course in Pittsburgh, California, the city did not compensate for time spent commuting directly from home to off-site training locations.

Imada and officers sued the city of Hercules under the FLSA, demanding overtime compensation, liquidated damages, and attorney's fees. The district court ruled that the FLSA did not require payment for excess travel time to an off-site location when the activities conducted at that location are essential to the performance of job duties. The court also held that the FLSA did not require payment for time spent travelling overnight to such a training activity in another city. On appeal, the case went to the Ninth Circuit, which upheld the decision of the lower court.

Source: *Imada v. City of Hercules,* U.S. Ninth Circuit Court of Appeals 9715405 (17 March 1998).

—Judson Knight

only delay recovery by raising the operating expenses of business and artificially inflating prices. Some reform economists saw things differently. A more rational economy regulated by the government would offer business both economies of scale and a more predictable climate. The higher wages would stimulate consumption, which would require increased production and ultimately help everybody.

Precursors

The components of the FLSA had separate precursors. Although the notion of a shorter workweek had been a longstanding demand of labor, the notion of a federally regulated minimum wage standard came primarily from outside the labor movement. Calls for state regulation of child labor came originally from the labor movement but had been elaborated by Progressive Era reformers.

For the labor movement, the demand for a shorter workday had always been viewed as a way to decrease unemployment. By the 1840s workers in many skilled trades had won the 10-hour day. The National Labor Union began pushing for an 8-hour day in the 1860s. In 1868 Congress enacted an 8-hour day for federal employees. The 8-hour day became an early goal of the American Federation of Labor (AFL).

From the early twentieth century, the U.S. labor movement pushed several states to pass laws requiring that women and children be paid enough to provide for necessities. Men, presumably, were more likely to be protected by collective bargaining. Samuel Gompers and the early AFL were reluctant to support government regulation of matters that they felt were best resolved at the bargaining table.

William Green, president of the AFL, began promoting a shorter workweek as a means to end the Great Depression during the Hoover administration. The demand was aimed at employers, not regulators. Following AFL tradition, Green hoped to change social policy at the bargaining table rather than in the legislature.

Yet, in the mass-production unions that were to become the membership of the Committee for Industrial Organization (later the Congress of Industrial Organizations, or CIO), there was a growing consensus that legislative action might facilitate bargaining. Senator Hugo L. Black of Alabama and Representative William P. Connery of Massachusetts cosponsored a 30-hour week bill in 1932. They reintroduced the bill in 1933, 1935, and 1937, but never succeeded in getting it passed.

Upon his election, Roosevelt tried to promote recovery by raising wages and reducing hours with the National Industrial Recovery Act (NIRA). The National Industrial Recovery Act stated, "Employers shall comply with the maximum hours of labor, minimum rates of pay, and other conditions of employment, approved or prescribed by the President." These hours were initially defined as follows: most classes of workers were limited to 40 hours a week. Factory and mechanical workers and artisans were limited to 35 hours. Firms with two or fewer employees in towns of fewer than 2,500 residents were exempted as were professionals, executives earning more than $35 per week, employees on emergency maintenance and repair work, and highly skilled workers on continuous processes who would be paid at least time and a third overtime.

In May 1935 the Supreme Court declared that the NRA had exceeded the federal government's power to regulate interstate commerce in its *Schechter vs. United States* decision. With the NRA rendered powerless, the Roosevelt administration set out to create a labor standards bill that would give the federal government power to regulate work conditions by another means. Both the AFL and the CIO had issues with the bill that the Roosevelt administration proposed, but nevertheless it was introduced as the Black-Connery bill in 1937. The bill set no specific minimum wage or maximum hours. It proposed creation of a five-member committee to determine fair labor standards for each industry on a regional basis. It also proposed to exclude goods made by children or under oppressive conditions from interstate commerce.

The Black-Connery bill faced broad opposition. The AFL opposed making wages the subject of government policy, argu-

ing that they should be determined by collective bargaining instead. After extensive debate, the AFL executive council agreed to support the bill if it was limited to industries without effective collective bargaining. President William L. Green ended up supporting the bill, but without the full support of his membership. CIO leaders John L. Lewis and Sidney Hillman supported the bill, though Hillman was not optimistic about it. He worried about the labor movement depending too heavily on the federal government. "Perhaps there is going to be a new law, fixing minimum wages and maximum hours, but we are not going to take a chance on it. We are going to forget about it and go ahead on our own."

Most businessmen preferred the free-market model and opposed state regulation. A few, chiefly those from larger companies, thought that standardized labor practices would provide them an advantage over smaller firms. Regional differences were as important as size. Northern businessmen more readily favored a minimum wage, hoping that it would stop the movement of industry to the lower wage region of the South. For this reason, southern Democrats opposed the law most.

The biggest question remained whether the Supreme Court would accept national regulation of local labor practices, even if they came through the Congress rather than the executive branch.

Passage of the Bill

In this atmosphere it was inevitable that the bill would be highly debated and amended in the Senate. By the time the Senate passed it, the Black-Connery bill did not provide conditions that would raise the purchasing power of the majority of workers. Instead, it raised the minimum standards of the most oppressed workers, provided they fell into the affected categories. At the legislated $16 a week minimum wage, a worker would still not earn the $1,200 a year required for subsistence living.

Minimal as its requirements were, the bill still met with heavy resistance in the South, where it would have actually raised the standards the most. Southern Democrats felt that preserving their region's lower wages was the best way to keep their momentum toward industrialization.

As the bill passed the Senate in greatly amended form, Representative Connery died, leaving it to face the House without its strongest supporter. The committee began debating the exact wage and hour formula. AFL president Green urged the committee toward a lower minimum wage to keep wages a subject for collective bargaining rather than federal policy.

As the Congress debated the bill, American public opinion increasingly grew to favor federal standards for wages and hours. The CIO criticized both the Roosevelt administration and the AFL for the failure to pass the bill. The Democratic Party faced growing criticism for its inability to get the bill passed and create the conditions to end the depression. The 1937 legislative session ended without decisive action.

Early in 1938 Roosevelt redoubled his efforts to get the bill passed. He worked on several fronts at once, lobbying congressmen and appealing directly to public opinion. Labor Secretary Frances Perkins organized a national committee of leaders of business, industry, and labor to support the bill. In an effort to overcome southern opposition, the Labor Department drafted two different versions of the bill. One created national standards; the second proposed a lower minimum wage for the South. After extensive amendment, the bill passed the house by a vote of 314 to 77.

This sent the bill back to the Senate, where it was once again amended. Geographic differentials were not written into the final bill, but the time frame for reaching the 40 hour and 40 cent formula was extended. The compromise bill provided for a Wage and Hour Division of the Labor Department to oversee its implementation and gave that division a good deal of flexibility in enforcement.

Finally, on 27 June 1938 Roosevelt signed the Fair Labor Standards Act. The law did not serve its original goal of providing workers enough buying power to end the depression. It did, however, clearly establish a role for the federal government as regulator of employment practices.

Analysis of the Bill

The FLSA was an intricate piece of social legislation that represented an attempt to balance competing interests and solve many problems. It was created to exceed any existing local law.

Key Players

Black, Hugo L. (1886–1971): Black was Democratic senator from Alabama from 1926 until President Franklin Roosevelt appointed him to the Supreme Court in 1937. Despite a strong belief in federal economic intervention, Black consistently argued that local southern customs should be allowed to continue. During his controversial confirmation hearing, he admitted to being a former member of the Ku Klux Klan but argued that he could be fair to all Americans. Eventually, Black became a defender of civil rights and the first amendment.

Connery, William P. (1888–1937): Democratic representative from Massachusetts from 1923 to 1937, Connery served as chair of the House Labor Committee from the 72nd through 75th congresses.

Green, William L. (1873–1952): President of the American Federation of Labor (AFL) from 1924 to 1952, Green, like John L. Lewis, came from the United Mine Workers of America (UMWA). Interested in cooperation between labor and management, Green looked to government policy changes to secure a better future for labor. He was a Roosevelt appointee to the Labor Advisory Counsel of the National Recovery Administration.

Hillman, Sidney (1887–1946): Hillman participated in the 1905 revolution in Russia before migrating to New York and becoming a garment worker. In 1914 he became president of the Amalgamated Clothing Workers of America (ACWA), which he served until his death. Originally a member of the Socialist Party, he became an active Democrat.

Lewis, John L. (1880–1969): A mine worker from Illinois, Lewis became head of the UMWA in 1920. He resigned from his position as AFL vice president in 1935 to concentrate on building the Committee for Industrial Organization. Striving to "organize the unorganized," Lewis became one of the most recognized figures in the country. Lewis retired as UMWA president in 1960.

Perkins, Frances (1880–1965): Perkins joined the National Consumers' League as a student at Mount Holyoke College. After a stint as a settlement house worker, she studied economics and sociology at the University of Pennsylvania and began a career in social research. She headed the Committee on Safety of the City of New York, which was formed to investigate factory conditions following the Triangle Shirtwaist Factory fire, and she subsequently became a member of the Industrial Commission of the State of New York. Roosevelt appointed her as secretary of labor, in part because she had reform credentials but no connections with organized labor. She became a symbol of government intervention in the economy to many businessmen and was frequently red-baited. She remained secretary of labor until 1945 and later wrote a memoir of her years with Roosevelt entitled *The Roosevelt I Knew*.

Roosevelt, Franklin Delano (1882–1945): Roosevelt was president of the United States from 1933 to 1945 and governor of New York as a Democrat from 1928 until his election as president.

See also: *American Federation of Labor; Congress of Industrial Organizations; Eight-hour Day Movement; National Industrial Recovery Act; Ten-hour Day Movement.*

BIBLIOGRAPHY

Books

Paulson, George E. *A Living Wage for the Forgotten Man: The Quest for Fair Labor Standards, 1933–1941.* London: Associated University Presses, 1996.

Phelps, Orme Wheelock. *The Legislative Background of the Fair Labor Standards Act.* Chicago: University of Chicago Press, 1939.

U.S. Department of Labor, Bureau of Labor Statistics. *Handbook of Labor Statistics.* Washington, DC: 1936.

Periodicals

Boles, Walter E., Jr. "Some Aspects of the Fair Labor Standards Act." *The Southern Economic Journal* 6, no. 4 (1940).

Samuel, Howard D. "Troubled Passage: The Labor Movement and the Fair Labor Standards Act." *Monthly Labor Review* (December 2000).

—Jane Holzka

Fatti di Magio: *See* **Milan Barricade Fights.**

Federal Employees Gain Union Rights

United States 1962

Synopsis

Unionism's existence in the private sector has, for the most part, gone relatively unchallenged by public opinion during its growth in the United States. One of the strongest weapons employees possess is collective bargaining, a process by which an employer and a union representative negotiate for improvements in work conditions and wages. Generally, contemporary Americans support the concept of unionism and collective bargaining. This includes the employee's right to strike.

In the private sector, outside of key industries like transportation, strikes and walkouts rarely cause difficulties to anyone beyond the industry itself. However, the same cannot be said for the public sector. A strike by federal employees can easily cripple a city, state, or even the entire country. The public seldom supports the strikers, no matter how just their cause may be. This resentment stems from the severe disruptions to daily routines and threats to civic well being that can result from a strike. Conducting fair labor negotiations becomes difficult as public pressure mounts on both sides for a consensus to be reached. For these and other reasons, the government actively opposed unionism for federal employees during the nineteenth century and half of the twentieth. Indeed some laws, such as the Sherman Antitrust Act of 1890, were interpreted in ways that hindered organizing among federal workers.

While the government passed legislation to improve the rights of employees in the private sector throughout the first half of the twentieth century, little was done to improve the rights of workers in the public sphere. Collective bargaining remained virtually unheard of for federal employees for more than half the century. Indeed, it was not until 1962 that certain federal employees gained the right to engage in collective bargaining. President John F. Kennedy's Executive Order (EO) 10988 set strict guidelines for federal union activities but set the stage for legislation to come. This landmark EO began the growth of federal unionism, a movement that flourished in the following years.

Timeline

1942: The Declaration of the United Nations is signed in Washington, D.C.

1947: Great Britain's Labour government nationalizes coalmines.

1952: Among the cultural landmarks of the year are the film *High Noon* and the book *The Invisible Man* by Ralph Ellison.

1955: The Warsaw Pact is signed by the Soviet Union and its satellites in eastern Europe.

1958: First U.S. satellite, *Explorer I,* goes into orbit.

1962: As the Soviets begin a missile buildup in Cuba, for a few tense days in October it appears that World War III

President John F. Kennedy. The Library of Congress.

is imminent. President Kennedy calls for a Cuban blockade, forcing the Soviets to back down and ultimately diffusing the crisis.

1962: Marilyn Monroe, who managed to graduate into serious roles after years of playing the sex kitten—only to devolve into drugs and depression—commits suicide.

1962: Publication of Rachel Carson's *Silent Spring* heightens Americans' awareness of environmental issues.

1965: Rev. Martin Luther King, Jr., and more than 2,600 others are arrested in Selma, Alabama. Three weeks later, in New York City, Malcolm X is assassinated.

1967: Arabs attack Israel, launching the Six-Day War, which results in an Israeli victory.

1971: With Supreme Court approval, U.S. communities adopt busing as a means of achieving racial integration in schools.

1977: Punk rock explodes onto the scene in London and New York City.

Event and Its Context

Early History of Federal Unionism

Since very early in American history, federal employees encountered strong opposition to their quest for forming labor organizations. This opposition came not only from their employers but also the general public. Negative public opinion had a large impact on federal employees, since their direct supervisors "worked" for the public and, therefore, made many of their decisions based on political expediency and realities. In particular, the public feared government employees having the right to strike. In private industry a strike only occasionally affected an entire city or population, because it was usually centered on a specific trade or business. However, a strike in the public sector, such as one conducted by teachers or law enforcement officers, could have drastic or even dangerous effects for a community. The public's fear became reality on 9 September 1919, when the Boston police strike resulted in riots and looting on an unprecedented scale. According to Dennis Bechara, in *Unions and Government Employment,* Governor Calvin Coolidge fired all the strikers and refused to rehire them later, stating, "There is no right to strike against the public safety by anybody, anytime, anywhere." His actions received overwhelming public approval.

The 1919 Boston police strike and similar events strengthened the public's belief that allowing federal employees to engage in unionism empowered them too greatly. Because civil employees provide essential public services, they in essence hold a monopoly on those services. Therefore, some people in the nineteenth and early twentieth centuries believed that public servants might blackmail the local, state, and federal government with the threat of strikes, at worst endangering whole communities and at least snarling vital services. Perhaps for this reason, federal employees found themselves unable to fight for their employment rights or engage in collective bargaining for much of this period.

The roots of collective bargaining for federal employees emerged from shaky ground. During the 1800s the whole concept of unionism was under constant attack by employers and the government. In some instances, such as the Philadelphia Cordwainers Conspiracy Cases in 1806, employee groups seeking better wages were found guilty of conspiracy, and their organizations were declared illegal. Poor working conditions and low wages were as prevalent in the public sector as they were in the private. However, while their counterparts in the private sector gained further rights, federal employees found themselves repeatedly hindered in their quest for improved working conditions and compensation. Some public departments actually went so far as to ignore labor laws completely or manipulate them to work in their favor. For example, the Post Office Department ignored the 1888 law requiring a maximum eight-hour workday. Postal workers found themselves facing 56-hour workweeks, including required shifts on Saturday and Sunday. Despite such opposition, federally oriented unions, such as the National Teachers Association (the precursor of today's National Education Association) in 1857 and the National Association of Letter Carriers (NALC) in 1889, did take shape. Unions such as these gained small victories for federal workers. The NALC, for example, sued the federal government as a direct re-

sult of the postal service's abuse of labor laws. In 1893 mail carriers were awarded $3.5 million in overtime claims as a result of their successful lawsuit.

However, further setbacks to federal unionism soon appeared. In 1890 the Sherman Antitrust Act struck a serious blow against collective bargaining in both the private and the public sectors. Originally enacted to regulate interstate trade and prevent the restraint of interstate and foreign trade, the Sherman Antitrust Act was soon expanded to oversee "wrongful" labor practices. Thus, labor unions found themselves under judicial attack and charged with conspiracy to disrupt and restrain trade by encouraging an employee's right to strike. Because federal agencies by their very nature were considered to hold a monopoly on their labor services, federally based unions became a prime target for antitrust "violations." Another setback followed twelve years later, when in 1902 President Theodore Roosevelt issued a gag order preventing all federal employees from lobbying Congress, directly or indirectly, for wage increases or similar legislation. This included lobbying through any association such as a union. Subsequently, presidential gag orders went so far as to prevent postal employees from publicly discussing their work conditions. Employees faced immediate termination if they violated these gag orders.

Pushing Forward but Left Behind

Between 1910 and 1920 several positive legislative changes strengthened the federal union movement. One significant change came with the Lloyd–La Follette Act of 1912. Since 1902 the NALC had been opposing President Roosevelt's gag order. Robert La Follette, a Republican senator from Wisconsin, took interest in their plight. Following a successful political campaign, La Follette's new act passed and repealed President Roosevelt's gag orders of 1902. In addition, the Lloyd–La Follette Act established that federal and postal workers possessed the right to organize unions. This law significantly changed the future rights of federal employees. During the same year, Congress passed the Reilly Eight-in-Ten Hour Act, preventing postal employees from being forced to spread their typical 8-hour shift over a consecutive 10-hour period. In addition, Congress passed the Mann Sunday Closing Act, requiring that post offices remain closed on Sunday. This effectively guaranteed that workers would receive a day off. Forced overtime, typically without pay, was finally moot in all but the rarest cases.

Further progress was made for federal unionism in 1914 with the Clayton Act. This act effectively eliminated the threat of the 1890 Sherman Antitrust Act for unions, determining that antitrust laws were not applicable to labor organizations. According to the Center for the Advancement of Capitalism, "The labor of a human being is not a commodity or article of commerce. Nothing contained in the antitrust laws shall be construed to forbid the existence and operation of labor . . . organizations . . . [nor are they] . . . illegal combinations or conspiracies in restraint of trade under the antitrust laws." Federal and postal unions were now free to conduct strikes without fear of prosecution for antitrust violations. Although considerable governmental pressure remained to prevent strikes, and no legislation supported this right, at the very least employees would no longer be fined or incarcerated because of the Sherman Antitrust Act.

Another step forward came with the Federal Employees Compensation Act of 1916. Until that time workers were not guaranteed any form of compensation for injuries received during the course of their duties. This act was vitally important for postal workers, in addition to other federal employees. Post offices of the time were dangerous and unhealthy. Unsanitary conditions exposed workers to diseases like typhoid, while poor lighting and overcrowding increased the risk of injury. Death and serious injury were common for railway mail service workers as well. Before the Compensation Act, employees were lucky to receive small amounts of money to pay for funerals—and this pittance came only if the family relinquished their right to sue the offending party. Access to compensation and medical benefits greatly improved working conditions and the quality of life for federal employees.

Soon after the Federal Employees Compensation Act became law, Congress passed further legislation aimed at improving working conditions for federal employees. In 1920 the first Civil Service Retirement Act was passed, providing retirement annuities for employees at age 65. Until that time older employees found themselves being ousted from their jobs and facing the prospect of no income. Now employees no longer faced the very real prospect of poverty and destitution in their old age. During the same year, Congress enacted two other bills that provided sick-leave benefits and a wage increase for postal employees. Many of these legislative changes came about due to pressure on Congress for change exerted by unions such as the NALC.

A major step toward collective bargaining came in 1926. Although it focused primarily on interstate railway services, the Railway Labor Act provided the basis for later legislation. Under this act employers were required to engage in collective bargaining and were prohibited from discriminating against union members. In many ways the Railway Labor Act was the inspiration for the Norris–La Guardia Act of 1932 and similar laws to follow. In the case of the Norris–La Guardia Act, legislation supported the rights of employees to organize unions and engage in strikes. Employers were required to take part in collective bargaining or face possible legal sanctions. Finally, the law prohibited federal enforcement of the infamous "yellow dog" agreements, whereby employees gave up their right to be part of a union. This series of legislative measures culminated in 1935 with the passing of the National Labor Relations Act (NLRA).

With the NLRA, or Wagner Act, unions and employees were provided legislative protection from interference, domination, discrimination, and retaliation from and by employers. In addition, employers could no longer refuse to engage in collective bargaining with regard to labor issues such as wages and conditions of employment. With the enactment of this legislation, unionism found its true foothold in the American labor force.

Unfortunately, the Wagner Act did not extend to the public sector, and the rights of federal, state, and local government employees remained unprotected and, in some cases, nonexistent. Indeed, despite the dramatic changes being made for unionism in the private sector, federal organizing was making very little headway. The closest federal workers had come to earning the right to bargain collectively took place in 1917. Naval yard unions began a working relationship with the assistant secretary of the navy, the metal trades department, and President Franklin D. Roosevelt. Because of this close relationship, the unions were allowed to arbitrate employment issues. Even so, union interaction such as this remained extremely rare. However, the seeds for federal unionism had been planted. As unionism grew in the private sector, federal employees looked on and hoped their efforts would bear fruit. Even so, their hopes were not realized until the 1960s, when the Kennedy administration took office.

President Kennedy and Executive Order 10988

According to *Labor News and Views* by the Human Resources Service Center, in 1962 "only about 1% of the federal workforce was organized." This statistic reflected the entire nation's prevailing attitude against unions of federal employees. Many people both in and out of the federal government believed that allowing public employees the right to engage in collective bargaining and strike against their supervisors essentially stripped their democratically elected employers of power. William Shaw explains in his book, *Moral Issues in Business,* "Government power includes the power . . . to fix the terms and conditions of government employment. This power cannot be . . . taken away. . . . [C]ollective bargaining is irreconcilable with the idea of sovereignty." As such, the presence of unionism in the public sector remained minimal. However, that attitude began to change by mid-century. In 1959 Wisconsin enacted legislation allowing collective bargaining in the public sector; the state effectively managed the law through their labor relations board. Based on the Wisconsin experience, the threat to government sovereignty appeared unfounded.

In a bold move, perhaps inspired by the progress made in Wisconsin and the value he placed on public service, President Kennedy signed Executive Order (EO) 10988 into effect on 17 January 1962. Officially titled Employee-Management Cooperation in the Federal Service, the EO essentially replaced the Lloyd-La Follette Act of 1912, and for the first time federal employees were awarded the right to join official unions freely and without fear of reprisal or discrimination from employers. Employee organizations could receive national and exclusive recognition through a nomination process. Once the organization received recognition, from that point forward, federal agencies were required to engage in collective bargaining with representatives of the recognized union. The EO also protected and upheld agreements reached during arbitration. The EO prompted local and state government employees to unionize as well. However, some restrictions to union activities remained, limiting the rights of federal employees. One important restriction prohibited employees from engaging in a strike. In addition, recognized employee organizations were restricted to collective bargaining with regard to work conditions and personnel policies only. Wage issues could not be discussed. Finally, agencies directly involved in national security, such as the FBI and the CIA, were exempted from the EO.

After EO 10988

Despite the restrictions placed on federal employees, President Kennedy's landmark EO removed the barriers to federal unionism. Unions quickly flourished in the public sector. According to a report from the Department of Economics at the University of Washington, the percentage of federal employees associated with bargaining organizations jumped from 24 percent in 1960 to 42 percent in 1976. Moreover, the percentage of local and state employees who belonged to labor organizations jumped from 5 percent in 1960 to 40 percent in 1976. EO 10988 also served as the blueprint for future legislation and spawned further improvements in the working conditions and compensation for federal employees.

In 1969 President Richard M. Nixon signed EO 11491, expanding and modifying President Kennedy's previous order. President Nixon's order attempted to move public collective bargaining practices closer to those seen in the private sector and established official recognition of the bargaining process and grievance procedures. In addition, the order established the Federal Labor Relations Council and the Federal Service Impasse Panel. However, the order retracted the right to use paid time off for labor negotiations set by President Kennedy's previous EO. Use of official time for negotiations was reinstated by the Civil Service Reform Act nine years later in 1978.

After President Kennedy's signing of Executive Order 10988, federal unionism took several positive steps forward. Further advances of the rights of public employees included the establishment of collective bargaining laws for educators and the transformation of the cabinet-level Post Office Department into the quasi-independent United States Postal Service. The trend toward collective bargaining in the public sector continued to grow into the early twenty-first century. Certainly the initial credit for expanding the rights of public-sector workers goes to President Kennedy, who embraced with intellectual idealism the possibility of positive change in federal labor relations offered by the signing of EO 10988 into law.

Key Players

Kennedy, John F. (1917–1963): In 1962, President Kennedy signed Executive Order 10988, thereby allowing federal agencies to engage in collective bargaining. This landmark order changed decades of legislation that had previously weakened federal unionism.

La Follette, Robert M. (1855–1925): A founder of the Progressive movement, Senator La Follette supported the Lloyd-La Follette Act of 1912 in Congress, helping to retract the gag rules set by President Roosevelt's 1902 executive order and providing federal employees the right to organize unions.

Nixon, Richard M. (1913–1994): President Nixon expanded on President Kennedy's 1962 executive order when he signed Executive Order 11491. By doing so, he hoped to change public collective bargaining to match the process used in the private sector.

Roosevelt, Theodore (1858–1919): President Roosevelt issued a gag order in 1902 preventing federal employees from lobbying Congress for wage increases, improved working conditions, or similar concerns. His subsequent executive orders prevented postal employees from discussing their work conditions either publicly or with Congress.

See also: *Boston Police Strike; Clayton Antitrust Act; Eight-hour Day Movement; Lloyd–La Follette Act; Sherman Antitrust Act; Wagner Act.*

BIBLIOGRAPHY

Books
Shaw, William and Vincent Barry. *Moral Issues in Business.* Belmont, CA: Wadsworth Publishing, 1997.

Periodicals
Human Resources Service Center. "Labor Relations in the Federal Government." *Labor News and Views* 3, no. 2 (2002): 2–3.
National Association of Letter Carriers. "10 Great Moments in Letter Carrier History." *NALC Activist* 10, no. 3 (1995).

Other
Bechara, Dennis. *Unions and Government Employment* [cited 28 October 2002]. <http://www.libertyhaven.com/politicsandcurrentevents/unionsandotherorganizations/unionsgovemploy.html>.
"Clayton Antitrust Act, 1914." Center for the Advancement of Capitalism [cited 28 October 2002]. <http://moraldefense.com/Campaigns/Antitrust/Other_Resources/Clayton_Act.htm>.
"Executive Order 10988: Employee-management Cooperation in the Federal Service." University of Michigan [cited 28 October 2002]. <http://www.lib.umich.edu/govdocs/jfkeo/eo/10988.htm>.
"Federal Labor Laws." *Congressional Digest,* 1993 [cited 28 October 2002]. <http://eserver.org/history/us-labor-law.txt>.
"Unions." University of Washington, Department of Economics [cited 28 October 2002]. <http://www.econ.washington.edu/user/Lundberg/443_99/2_25.pdf>.

—Lee Ann Paradise

Federation of Organized Trades and Labor Unions of the United States and Canada (FOTLU)

United States and Canada 1881

Synopsis

The Federation of Organized Trades and Labor Unions of the United States and Canada (FOTLU) was the predecessor of the American Federation of Labor (AFL), which was pro-

First executive council of American Federation of Labor, from top left, Samuel Gompers, W. H. Foster, Charles F. Burgman, Richard Powers, and Alexander C. Rankin. American Federation of Labor was the precursor to the FOTLU. AP/Wide World Photos. Reproduced by permission.

claimed in 1886. FOTLU replaced the National Labor Union (1866–1872), which had been pulled apart by the lure of divergent electoral strategies. FOTLU veered away from electoralism and sought more efficient organization and a more narrow focus than the more expansive labor reform group, the Knights of Labor. There were both socialists and nonsocialists among FOTLU's founding members, yet the Federation as a whole helped to consolidate the trend toward an increasingly nonradical "pure and simple" unionism in the U.S. labor movement.

Timeline

1861: Serfs in Russia are emancipated.

1871: U.S. troops in the West begin fighting the Apache nation.

1874: Gold is discovered in the Black Hills of South Dakota.

1879: F. W. Woolworth opens his first department store, in Lancaster, Pennsylvania.

1881: President James A. Garfield is assassinated in a Washington, D.C., railway station by Charles J. Guiteau.

1881: In a shootout at the O.K. Corral outside Tombstone, Arizona, Wyatt, Virgil, and Morgan Earp, along with "Doc" Holliday, kill Billy Clanton, Frank McLowry, and Tom McLowry. This breaks up a gang headed by Clanton's brother Ike, who flees Tombstone. The townspeople, however, suspect the Earps and Holliday of murder. During the same year, Sheriff Pat Garrett shoots notorious criminal William Bonney, a.k.a. Billy the Kid, in Fort Sumner, New Mexico.

1881: Louis Pasteur develops a method for inoculation against anthrax.

1881: U.S. author Helen Hunt Jackson publishes *A Century of Dishonor,* which discusses government mistreatment of Indian tribes. In the following year, Jackson is appointed to the position of special commissioner to investigate conditions among the Mission Indians of California.

1881: The first major planned "company town," Pullman, Illinois, outside Chicago, is created.

1883: Foundation of the League of Struggle for the Emancipation of Labor by Marxist political philosopher Georgi

Labor Day procession, Pittsburgh, Pennsylvania, 1882. © Bettmann/Corbis. Reproduced by permission.

Valentinovich Plekhanov marks the formal start of Russia's labor movement. Change still lies far in the future for Russia, however: tellingly, Plekhanov launches the movement in Switzerland.

1887: John Emerich Edward Dalbert-Acton, a leader of the opposition to the papal dogma of infallibility, observes, in a letter to Cambridge University professor Mandell Creighton, that "Power tends to corrupt, and absolute power corrupts absolutely."

1891: French troops open fire on workers during a 1 May demonstration at Fourmies, where employees of the Sans Pareille factory are striking for an eight-hour day. Nine people are killed—two of them children—and sixty more are injured.

Event and Its Context

"We have numberless trades unions, trades' assemblies or councils, Knights of Labor and various other local, national, and international unions," declared the call for the national conference that formed FOTLU. "But great as has been the work done by these bodies, there is vastly more that can be done by a combination of all these organizations in a federation of trades."

Forward Steps

The Federation of Organized Trades and Labor Unions came into being in a gymnasium at the Turner Hall in downtown Pittsburgh. The *Turnverein*, or "Turners," were German-American social and athletic societies; many of the pioneers of the American labor movement in this period were German-American, though many others were Irish-American, these being the two largest immigrant groups at the time. In its early incarnation, the federation called in 1882 for the celebration of Labor Day on the first Monday in September. The organization also called for work stoppages and demonstrations on 1 May 1886 in favor of the eight-hour workday (initiating May Day, the international workers' holiday). The AFL and its predecessor, however, are best known for organizing the most durable union federation in U.S. history, providing an effective approach for improving the wages, hours, and working conditions of its members.

Over a hundred delegates attended the founding convention, representing close to half a million members. Represented were eight national and international trade unions: 14 from the Typographical Workers, 10 from the Amalgamated Association of Iron and Steel Workers, 8 from the Molders, 6 from the Glass Workers, 5 from the Cigar Makers, and 5 from the Carpenters. Also represented were the central labor councils of 11 cities, 42 local unions, 3 district assemblies, and 46 local assemblies of the Knights of Labor, which at that time was the largest labor organization in the country. The Knights organized workers into reform struggles, social events, and educational efforts as well as trade union activities. For several years many workers belonged both to the Knights and to the Federation, though eventually the two groups became rivals.

Solidarity and Class Struggle

Those in attendance at the conference included 68 delegates from Pittsburgh, many of whom were members the Knights of Labor, whose membership included both people who were in unions and those who were not. One controversy arose around whether the new Federation should consist exclusively of people who were already members of labor unions. In this period, and for many years afterward, only skilled workers were able to build and sustain trade unions that were organized around a specific craft. A decision to make the Federation an exclusively union organization would restrict its membership to skilled workers. Many delegates agreed with the comments of one that "I wish this Federation broad enough to encompass all working people in its folds." An African American delegate from Pittsburgh explained, "We have in the city of Pittsburgh many men in our organization who have no particular trade, but should not be excluded from the Federation . . . . I speak more particularly of my own people and declare to you that it would be dangerous to skilled mechanics to exclude from this organization the common laborers, who might, in an emergency, be employed in positions they could readily qualify them to fill."

The inclusive spirit of these delegates won the day not only in the selection of a name, but also in the preamble, which was retained in 1886 when the group was reorganized as the American Federation of Labor. The preamble cited the "struggle between capital and labor" and forecast "disastrous results" if the "toiling millions" did not "combine" in the struggle for protection from oppression: "Conforming to the old adage, 'In union there is strength,' the formation of a Federation embracing every trade and labor organization in North America, a union founded upon a basis as broad as the land we live in, is our only hope."

Samuel Gompers of the Cigar Makers Union was nominated to be president of the Federation, but so was Richard Powers of the lake seaman's union. The *Pittsburgh Commercial-Gazette* ran an article explaining the contest in this way: "It is thought that an attempt will be made to capture the organization for Gompers as the representative of the Socialists, and if such an attempt is made, whether it succeeds or not, there will likely be some lively work, as the delegates opposed to Socialism are determined not to be controlled by it." In fact, such internal conflict was side-stepped when both Gompers and Powers withdrew from the race in favor of John Jarrett of the Amalgamated Association of Iron and Steel Workers (with Gompers and Powers both becoming vice presidents). The organization's secretary was Frank K. Foster.

Socialists—those favoring replacement of capitalism by social ownership and democratic control over the economy—were influential in the early Federation, but Gompers later explained that the newspaper allegation of his being part of a socialist conspiracy was a slander based partly on a misunderstanding. "In those early days not more than half a dozen people had grasped the concept that economic organization and control over economic power were the fulcrum which made possible influence and power in all other fields," he later wrote in his autobiography. This was the founding premise on which the AFL was later built, but Gompers noted that the lines between socialists and trade unionists were "very blurred."

The Rise of Pure and Simple Unionism

During the 1880s, Gompers became known not as an advocate of socialism but as an advocate of what became known as "pure and simple trade unionism." This meant the organization of workers into unions that would focus on workplace struggles around issues of higher wages, fewer hours of work, and improved working conditions, with the exclusion of radical social causes, whether socialism or anything else. When asked what the labor movement wanted, Gompers once replied simply, "More." Yet Pennsylvania Federation of Labor president James Maurer has left a record of one of Gompers's many "pure and simple" union speeches in which he contended that the needs and desires of the workingman continue to escalate with gain that is won: "After that he wants two dollars and more time for leisure, and he struggles to get it. Not satisfied with two dollars he wants more; not only two and a quarter, but a nine-hour workday. And so he will keep on getting more and more until he gets it all or the full value of all he produces."

FOTLU included members and some unions that were affiliated with the expansively reformist Knights of Labor, and it was formally on record as favoring close relations with the larger organization. Yet, in the minds of many trade unionists, FOTLU represented "a broad and enduring basis," as secretary Frank Foster put it, for organization because in contrast to the Knights, it drew members together along "the trade line," providing "greater feasibility and . . . economic soundness" in facing "the growing power of associated capital." Rather than relying on lobbying and elections to secure gains, "in the world of economic reform the working classes must depend upon themselves for the enforcement of measures as well as for their conception," as Foster put it. In 1886 FOTLU was reorganized as the American Federation of Labor to advance more effectively this orientation, and soon afterward it surpassed the Knights of Labor as the dominant force in the labor movement.

Key Players

Foster, Frank K. (1854–1909): Active in the International Typographical Union, Foster had also been involved in the eight-hour leagues, the Workingmen's Party of the United States, and the International Labor Union. He turned away from active participation in the Knights of Labor to focus his efforts on the formation of the American Federation of Labor.

Gompers, Samuel (1850–1924): Prominent in the Cigar Makers Union, Gompers became the long-time (1886–1924) and increasingly conservative president of the American Federation of Labor, a spokesman for the "pure and simple union" orientation that was initially developed by his colleague, Adolph Strasser. In his later years Gompers became an outright opponent of socialism (though he never lost his admiration for Karl Marx, whose outlook he viewed as consistent with his own "pure and simple" unionism).

Jarrett, John (1843–1918): Born in Wales, Jarrett became an iron puddler and emigrated to the United States in 1862, where he became a member of the Sons of Vulcan (a predecessor of the steel workers union, established in 1860). Returning to Britain in 1868, he became associated with the cautious trade unionism of John Kane in the Amalgamated

Ironworkers Association. In 1872 Jarrett returned to the United States, where he became a vice president of the Sons of Vulcan and a founder of the Amalgamated Association of Iron and Steel Workers, of which he became president in 1880. While accepting the office of president of FOTLU, he pulled his organization out of it in 1881 when the Federation failed to endorse a high tariff. In 1883 he left the union, and although he continued to support the labor movement for some years, he became a lobbyist for the Tin Plate Association. A longtime supporter of the Republican Party, he was appointed U.S. consul to Birmingham, England in 1889–1892, after which he took a position as employment agent for the Carnegie Steel Company (which had just destroyed the Amalgamated Association of Iron and Steel Workers in the Homestead Steel Strike).

McGuire, Peter J. (1852–1906): An American-born worker who whose initial involvement in socialist politics was as a member of the First International, McGuire left the Socialist Labor Party in the 1880s to become a founder and general secretary of the Brotherhood of Carpenters and Joiners and a founder of the AFL. He is often credited for being involved in the creation both of Labor Day (1882) and May Day (1886), although, as with Gompers, his socialist commitments faded with the passage of time.

See also: *American Federation of Labor; Eight-hour Day Movement; Haymarket Riot; International Labor Union; Knights of Labor.*

BIBLIOGRAPHY

Books

Brooks, Thomas R. *The Road to Dignity, A Century of Conflict: A History of the United Brotherhood of Carpenters and Joiners of America, AFL–CIO, 1881–1981.* New York: Atheneum, 1981.

Commons, John R., et al. *History of Labor in the United States,* Vol. II. New York: Macmillan Co., 1918.

Fink, Gary, ed. *Biographical Dictionary of American Labor.* Westport, CN: Greenwood Press, 1984.

Foner, Philip S. *History of the Labor Movement in the United States,* Vols. 1 and 2. New York: International Publishers, 1947, 1955.

Kaufman, Stuart Bruce. *Samuel Gompers and the Origins of the American Federation of Labor.* Westport, CN: Greenwood Press, 1973.

Gompers, Samuel. *Seventy Years of Life and Labor.* New York: E. P. Dutton Co., 1925.

Mandel, Bernard. *Samuel Gompers.* Yellow Springs, OH: Antioch Press, 1963.

Maurer, James. *It Can Be Done.* New York: Rand School Press, 1938.

—Paul Le Blanc

The International and "The Internationale"

The title of "The Internationale," the hymn of world socialist parties, refers to the First International. French woodworker Eugene Pottier wrote the words to the song after the fall of the Paris Commune in 1871, and in 1888 Pierre Degeyter of the French Workers' Party Choir wrote the music. By then Pottier was dead, but he would be remembered by no less a figure than V. I. Lenin, who called him "one of the great propagandists in song" in a 1913 *Pravda* article commemorating the twenty-fifth anniversary of Pottier and his song. The latter became the Soviet anthem and has been a rallying song for Marxists and non-Marxists alike. One of the most dramatic instances in which it was sung—ironically enough—was during the prodemocracy demonstrations in Tiananmen Square in 1989, when Chinese students sang "The Internationale" over and over. The text in English is as follows:

Arise ye workers from your slumbers / Arise ye criminals of want / For reason in revolt now thunders / and at last ends the age of cant. / Now away with all your superstitions / Servile masses arise, arise! / We'll change henceforth the oldconditions / And spurn the dust to win the prize.

CHORUS: Then come comrades rally / And the last fight let us face / The Internationale / Unites the human race. [repeat]

We peasants, artisans and others, / Enrolled amongst the sons of toil / Let's claim the earth henceforth for brothers / Drive the indolent from the soil / On our flesh for too long has fed the raven / We've too long been the vulture's prey. / But now farewell to spirit craven / The dawn brings in a brighter day.

CHORUS

No savior from on high delivers / No trust we have in prince or peer / Our own right hand the chains must shiver / Chains of hatred, greed and fear / Ere the thieves will out with their booty / And to all give a happier lot / Each at his forge must do his duty / And strike the iron while it's hot.

Source: Peter Miller, *The Internationale* (videorecording). New York City: First Run/Icarus Films, 2000.

—Judson Knight

First International

Great Britain 1864

Synopsis

On 28 September 1864 the International Working Men's Association (IWMA) was established in London. The organization, later known as the "First International," consisted of skilled workers, artisans, and intellectuals and comprised trade unions, cooperatives, and educational associations. It thrived during the years before 1872. In 1876 the organization disbanded, although efforts to revive it continued for decades. The IWMA was the first organization to achieve fairly systematic material labor solidarity across national borders. In addition to its chapters in Great Britain, the organization operated in many countries in Continental Europe, in the United States, and in parts of South America. Within the organization the followers of Mikhail Bakunin, Karl Marx, and Pierre-Joseph Proudhon engaged in heated debates.

Timeline

1844: Samuel Laing, in a prize-winning essay on Britain's "National Distress," describes conditions in a nation convulsed by the early Industrial Revolution. A third of the population, according to Laing, "hover[s] on the verge of actual starvation"; another third is forced to labor in "crowded factories"; and only the top third "earn[s] high wages, amply sufficient to support them in respectability and comfort."

1849: Elizabeth Blackwell becomes the first woman in the United States to receive a medical degree.

1854: In the United States, the Kansas-Nebraska Act calls for decisions on the legality of slavery to be made through local votes. Instead of reducing divisions, this measure will result in widespread rioting and bloodshed and will only further hasten the looming conflict over slavery and states' rights.

1857: Sepoy Mutiny, an unsuccessful revolt by Indian troops against the British East India Company begins. As a result of the rebellion, which lasts into 1858, England places India under direct crown rule.

1860: Louis Pasteur pioneers his method of "pasteurizing" milk by heating it to high temperatures in order to kill harmful microbes.

1862: Victor Hugo's *Les Misérables* depicts injustices in French society, and Ivan Turgenev's *Fathers and Sons* introduces the term *nihilism.*

1864: General William Tecumseh Sherman conducts his Atlanta campaign and his "march to the sea."

1864: International Red Cross in Geneva is established.

1864: George M. Pullman and Ben Field patent their design for a sleeping car with folding upper berths.

1866: Austrian monk Gregor Mendel presents his theories on the laws of heredity. Though his ideas will be forgotten for a time, they are destined to exert enormous influence on biological study in the twentieth century.

1870: Franco-Prussian War begins. German troops sweep over France, Napoleon III is dethroned, and France's Second Empire gives way to the Third Republic.

1873: The gold standard, adopted by Germany in 1871 and eventually taken on by all major nations, spreads to Italy, Belgium, and Switzerland. Though the United States does not officially base the value of its currency on gold until 1900, an unofficial gold standard dates from this period, even as a debate over "bimetallism" creates sharp divisions in American politics.

Event and Its Context

In the mid-nineteenth century the power of Great Britain exceeded that of any other nation: the British ran a worldwide colonial empire and enjoyed the strongest economy on the face of the earth at the time. London was a fairly liberal sanctuary. Political dissidents from many countries sought refuge there. London's labor movement was fairly extensive and well organized. Understandably, therefore, the city was the center of a gradually emerging labor internationalism. One of the first written manifestations of this trend was a document endorsed by the London-based Working Men's Association on 1 November 1836. In this document, entitled *Address to the Belgian Working Classes*, the WMA expressed the conviction "that our interests—nay, the interests of working men in all countries of the world—are identified." The article advised the Belgian "brethren" of the organization "to form, if possible, a union with countries around you," because "a federation of the working classes of Belgium, Holland and the Provinces of the Rhine would form an admirable democracy."

This interest in the formation of international labor alliances intensified after the revolutions of 1848. The movement produced several small organizations with a multinational memberships, such as the "Fraternal Democrats" and the "Communistische Arbeiter-Bildungs-Verein" (Communist Association for the Education of Working Men), a German group that included many non-German members. All of these small organizations shared several common characteristics. Their membership was comparatively small and did not exceed a few hundred. The groups were especially active in London, although not exclusively so. In general, the organizations' members were highly skilled workers and artisans. Their chief objectives were to provide education and information. The internationalism of these organizations was essentially theoretical, or perhaps rather ideological, in nature, and was in practice expressed above all through solidarity protests and manifested in activities designed to support the members' "brethren" in other countries. In addition to promoting solidarity in the labor struggles of the day, these organizations also supported nations that were engaged in the struggle for independence, such as Italy and Poland.

A parallel development that the international organizations promoted was provision of international aid in strikes, notably between England and continental Europe. The aid generally took one or both of two forms:

- Financial aid for strikes in other countries, either "intraoccupational" in the sense of support for workers in the same occupation, or broader in scope. The first variant seems to have been the more common. In 1852 and again in 1862 the London Society of Compositors sent funds to a sister organization in Paris; similarly Paris construction workers aided their London counterparts in 1860. In the 1850s there were even attempts to publish bilingual trade journals.

- Opposition to the use of strikebreakers. During several strikes, British employers tried to import strike breakers from the Continent. The British trade unions, which were only organized to serve city venues at the time, had tremendous difficulty preventing this practice. The enjoyed some rare successes on this front. For example, the London typefounders, during a strike in 1850, approached their colleagues in Paris and convinced them that they should assist in the prevention of recruitment of strikebreakers.

Collaboration between the British and the French unionists rapidly intensified, after a few workers from the French delegation encountered British trade unionists at the 1862 World Exhibition in London. The contacts established at the time proved to be of value a few months later in late January 1863, during the third Polish rebellion against Russian domination in slightly over three decades. London trade unionists were deeply committed to this struggle and invited their French colleagues to send a delegation to a solidarity meeting in their city. The French accepted the invitation. On 22 July 1863 the meeting took place as scheduled, and the copperplate engraver Henri Louis Tolain spoke on behalf of "the Paris workers." The next day the London Trades Council received the French delegation. In their welcoming speeches, both sides expressed a desire to work together more closely. The meeting participants decided that the London contingent would send an address to the Paris unions to propose an international labor association.

George Odger, the secretary of the Trades Council, wrote the text, which was published in December 1863 and entitled *To the Workmen of France from the Working Men of England*. The address comprised three elements. The first was a general appeal for international consultation between workers from different countries to promote peace and freedom. Second, it urged a simultaneous signature-gathering campaign in England and France for a petition to support the Polish insurgents. Third—between the two other items—the address noted trade union problems and suggested that a "fraternity of peoples" might aid in the struggle to alleviate the difficulties of laborers' "social condition." The appeal stated that attempts by organized labor to reduce the length of the work week or increase wages were often met my employers' threats to recruit laborers from Germany, Belgium, and France. The address placed the blame for the harm caused by this clearly on a lack of "regular and systematic" communications among their worker "brethren" from different countries. The proposed solution included effecting communications among laborers in different countries and a leveling out of wages among them. This, it was hoped, would prevent employers from engaging in "avaricious bargaining" intended to reduce the condition of all workers to that of the lowest echelon by playing them off against one another.

The French response to this earnest appeal reached London eight months later, after the repression of the Polish uprising. On 18 September 1864 a gathering convened at St. Martin's Hall in London, where in addition to the large turnout of London workers, substantial groups of French, Italian, Swiss, Polish, and German citizens were present. The Paris delegation consisted of Tolain, the *passementier* Antoine Limousin, and the bronzefounder Blaise Perrachon. Labor advocates at Paris workshops had collected 25 centime contributions for months to pay for their journeys to the meeting. The chairman that evening was Professor Edward Spencer Beesly. Also sitting on the stage in silence was the German emigrant, Dr. Karl Marx, who had been invited to attend by the preparatory committee. After a performance by a choir of German workers, delivery of the addresses and some debate, the attendees officially established the International Working Men's Association (IWMA). The provisional Central Committee, which consisted of 32 members of different nationalities (which included both Marx and Odger) was charged with drafting the articles of association and rules of procedure.

Although Marx was clearly influential in the new organization, the IWMA never became "Marxist," despite frequent allegations to this effect. The organization suffered from too many ideological factions and the contrasts between factions were too severe to allow any one philosophy to dominate. Many of the British adherents regarded themselves not as socialists but as politically concerned trade unionists at best. Among the French adherents, Pierre-Joseph Proudhon was highly influential. This educated typographer had argued that property arose from blood, theft, and violence ("Property is theft"), that the state was the "gendarme and bailiff" of an unjust society, and that the future society should be based on a "reciprocity of services" (mutualism) of free farmers, artisans, and workers. Other members of the IWMA, however, were drawn to the insurrectionist ideas of Louis-Auguste Blanqui or the republican nationalism of Guiseppe Mazzini.

The Central Committee (which later became known as the General Council) adopted the articles of association on 1 November 1864 after a period of squabbling over the content of the document. An "Address to the Working Class" that was written by Marx and adopted with very minor amendments did not indicate that the IWMA had embraced "Marxist" principles. Admittedly, the preamble to the articles of association stated that "the economical subjection of the man of labour to the monopoliser of the means of labour" is the cause of "all social misery, mental degradation, and political dependence" and that economic emancipation is the supreme objective, "to which every political movement ought to be subordinate as a means." These considerations, however, were rather vague and could be interpreted in various ways.

In the years that followed, the IWMA leadership organized international congresses in Lausanne (1867), Brussels (1868), and Basel (1869). Participants at the congresses debated a great many controversial issues, such as the Polish question, strikes as battle strategies, the importance of producer cooperatives, attitudes toward the state, and the merits of inheritance law. The influence of the Proudhonists diminished with each successive congress. This decline culminated in a sense with the anti-Proudhonist decision at the Basel congress to include land nationalization in the program. Internal dissent did not end with this measure. The anarchist outlook of Mikhail Bakunin gradually gained influence and conflicted increasingly with Marx's communist ideologies. The philosophical differences between the factions concerned both theoretical positions and organizational practices. Bakunin opposed participation in elections and the struggle for social reforms, as this would instill in workers the illusion that they might be able to improve their predicament without concerted social revolution. Marx, however, believed that parliamentary struggle and social reforms could enhance

class consciousness among workers and thus help to bring the revolution closer. The affiliated IMWA chapters in Spain, Italy, Swiss Jura, Belgium, and the Netherlands were inclined to support Bakunin, while those from Germany and German-speaking Switzerland tended to side with Marx.

The debate between Marxists and Bakuninists basically paralleled the disintegration of the IWMA. The heated debates did not mask the declining involvement of the two most important countries in the organization. The French movement had figured prominently in the Paris Commune of 1871 and had been virtually neutralized because of the severe repression that had followed. The British progressively lost interest as well. To make matters worse, the IWMA was already on very shaky financial and organizational ground. According to countless legends, the IWMA had many hundreds of thousands or even millions of members, vast sums of money, and a formidable secret political power. In reality, however, the organization was hard pressed to pay the rent for its London office and included at most a few thousand individual members.

The organization's internal conflicts peaked at the congress in The Hague in 1872. Bakunin and his ally James Guillaume were expelled in a move that alienated much of the remaining support. The transfer of the headquarters to New York (which was virtually inaccessible to the European constituency for all practical intents and purposes) meant that the days of the organization were numbered. Although the IWMA was not officially disbanded until the Philadelphia congress in 1876, its fate had been sealed four years earlier. Opponents to the exclusion of Bakunin and Guillaume did not acknowledge the decisions taken at The Hague congress and regarded their "antiauthoritarian International" (established that same year in St. Imier) as the legitimate successor to the failed association. The first congress of this new organization to be held in Geneva in 1873 was announced as the sixth congress of the IWMA. The new group was probably more influential among European workers than what was left of the old IWMA, and it certainly did not consist exclusively of Bakuninists. Even this International, however, which still convened congresses in 1874 (Brussels), 1876 (Bern), and 1877 (Verviers), collapsed. What remained was an anarchist international that survived into the twentieth century with ever-dwindling support.

The heyday of the IWMA spanned approximately five or six years. The failure of the efforts to revive the organization in the 1870s and 1880s indicated that it had become obsolete. Three factors appear to have undermined the IWMA. First, the organization lost the most important of its original *raisons d'être*. In the beginning the British trade unions and their Continental sister organizations had been local and too weak as individual, independent entities to stop the import of strike breakers from other countries. When the local unions expanded and began to form national confederations, however, they became progressively more able to control their labor markets on their own merits, without the assistance of unionist organizations based in other countries. The interest of these local groups in the IWMA therefore diminished accordingly. The earliest sign of this process was in Britain, where the Trades Union Council (TUC) was established in 1868. Almost simultaneously, the labor movement obtained some form of state recognition. In 1867 the Reform Act extended the franchise. In 1871 the Trade

Union Act came into force and had the effect of improving the legal status of the unions. In 1876 an Amending Act followed. Similar developments occurred in other North Atlantic countries, though with some delay. After Switzerland (1880) and Canada (1883), most other countries in the region followed within a few decades.

Another difficulty arose in the early 1870s, when the upward trend of capitalism was reversed in a slowdown of economic growth. The years up to about 1895 may be described as a period of retarded economic growth with stagnation and recession in a complex economic relationship. A gap appeared in British economic growth; the German and American economies were in a severe crisis; and the French economy of the 1880s was in serious trouble. Third, after the Franco-Prussian War of 1870–1871, the working classes entered into a closer relationship with their nation-states. Nationalist and chauvinist attitudes spread into ever-expanding social strata.

This combination of factors resulted in the undermining of the IWMA, as was apparent from its decline after 1872. What followed was a transitional period in which the old form of internationalism crumbled away. Although a new form was destined to emerge, it was still no further along at that point than the earliest embryonic stage. New forms of international labor organizations such as the International Trade Secretariats would emerge in the 1890s.

Key Players

Bakunin, Mikhail (1814–1876): Bakunin was a Russian aristocrat and revolutionary anarchist and founder of the International Alliance of Socialist Democracy (1864–1874). His writings include *Statism and Anarchy* (1873).

Marx, Karl (1818–1883): Marx was a German communist theoretician. His writings published during his lifetime include *The Poverty of Philosophy. Reply to The Philosophy of Poverty of Mr. Proudhon* (*Misère de la Philosophie. Réponse à La Philosophie de la misère de M. Proudhon*; 1847); *A Contribution to the Critique of Political Economy* (*Zur Kritik der politischen Ökonomie*; 1859); and *Capital* (*Das Kapital*), Volume I (1867).

Odger, George (1813?–1877): British shoemaker and trade unionist, cofounder of the London Trades Council in 1860; ran unsuccessfully for parliament five times, 1868–1874.

Proudhon, Pierre-Joseph (1809–1865): Proudhon was a French typographer and socialist and member of the National Assembly, 1848–1849. He imprisoned several times. His publications include *What is Property?* (*Qu'est-ce que la propriété?*; 1840) and *System of Economic Contradictions or Philosophy of Poverty* (*Système des contradictions économiques ou Philosophie de la misère*; 1846).

Tolain, Henri Louis (1828–1897): French copperplate engraver, Proudhonist, and secretary/correspondent of the IWMA starting in 1865, Tolain was elected deputy in 1870, opposed the Paris Commune of 1871, and was elected senator in 1876, 1882, and 1891.

See also: *Paris Commune; Red International of Labor Unions; Revolutions in Europe; Second International.*

BIBLIOGRAPHY

Books

Archer, Julian P.W. *The First International in France 1864–1872: Its Origins, Theories, and Impact.* Lanham, MD: University Press of America, 1997.

Bernstein, Samuel. *The First International in America.* New York: Kelley, 1962.

Collins, Henry, and Chimen Abramsky. *Karl Marx and the British Labour Movement, Years of the First International.* London: Macmillan, 1965.

The General Council of the First International, 1864–1872, Minutes. 5 vols. Moscow: Progress, 1963–1969).

Gerth, H., ed. and tran. *The First International: Minutes of the Hague Congress of 1872.* With Related Documents. Madison: University of Wisconsin Press, 1958.

Guillaume, James. *L'Internationale. Documents et souvenirs.* 4 vols. Paris: Société Nouvelle de Librairie d'Edition, 1905–1910. Partial reprint, Geneva: Grounauer, 1980.

Katz, Henryk. *The Emancipation of Labor, A History of the First International.* New York: Greenwood Press, 1992.

La Première Internationale. 3 vols. Paris: Colin, 1958-1963.

La Première Internationale. L'Institution, l'implantation, le rayonnement. Paris: CNRS, 1968.

Lehning, Arthur. *From Buonarroti to Bakunin: Studies in International Socialism.* Leiden, The Netherlands: E. J. Brill, 1970.

Mins, L. E., ed. *Founding of the First International: A Documentary Record.* New York: International Publishers, 1937.

Morgan, Roger. *The German Social Democrats and the First International 1864–1872.* Cambridge: Cambridge University Press, 1965.

Nicolaevsky, Boris I. "Secret Societies and the First International." In *The Revolutionary Internationals 1684–1943*, edited by Milorad M. Drachkovitch. Stanford, CA: Stanford University Press, 1966: 36–56.

Prothero, Iorwerth. *Radical Artisans in England and France, 1830–1870.* Cambridge: Cambridge University Press, 1997.

—Marcel van der Linden

Five-Year Plan

USSR 1927

Synopsis

The Five-Year Plans were programs of economic development instituted in the USSR by Joseph Stalin. The first, announced in 1927, began thorough industrialization under state planning and collectivized agricultural production. Despite successes on paper, the state planning suffered from mismanagement, investment was often squandered on grand projects, and the human cost was immense. In spite of these problems, Stalin managed to transform backward Russia into the modern, industrial power that was the USSR, an achievement that, for many, proves the benefits of planning under a socialist government.

Timeline

1911: In China, revolutionary forces led by Sun Yat-sen bring an end to more than 2,100 years of imperial rule.

1917: On both the Western Front and in the Middle East, the tide of the war begins to turn against the Central Powers. The arrival of U.S. troops, led by General Pershing, in France in June greatly boosts morale and reinforces exhausted Allied forces. Meanwhile, Great Britain scores two major victories against the Ottoman Empire as T. E. Lawrence leads an Arab revolt in Baghdad in March, and troops under Field Marshal Edmund Allenby take Jerusalem in December.

1922: Inspired by the Bolsheviks' example of imposing revolution by means of a coup, Benito Mussolini leads his blackshirts in an October "March on Rome" and forms a new Fascist government.

1924: V. I. Lenin dies, and thus begins a struggle for succession from which Josef Stalin will emerge five years later as the undisputed leader of the Communist Party and of the Soviet Union.

1927: Stalin arranges to have Trotsky expelled from the Communist Party.

1927: Charles A. Lindbergh makes the first successful solo nonstop flight across the Atlantic, and becomes an international hero.

1927: American inventor Philo T. Farnsworth demonstrates a working model of the television, and Belgian astronomer Georges Lemaître proposes the Bang Theory.

1927: *The Jazz Singer,* starring Al Jolson, is the first major motion picture with sound. Within a few years, silent movies will become a thing of the past.

1927: Babe Ruth hits sixty home runs, establishing a record that will stand until 1961.

1930: Naval disarmament treaty is signed by the United States, Great Britain, France, Italy, and Japan.

1932: When Ukrainians refuse to surrender their grain to his commissars, Stalin seals off supplies to the region, creating a manmade famine that will produce a greater death toll than the entirety of World War I.

1937: Japan attacks China and annexes most of that nation's coastal areas.

Event and Its Context

Planning: The Early Stages

The Russia inherited by the Bolsheviks in 1917 was economically backward; industry was underdeveloped and agricultural production was in crisis. These conditions were exacerbat-

Joseph Stalin. © Corbis-Bettmann. Reproduced by permission.

ed by civil war. If Vladimir Lenin was to establish the socialist state, as he had claimed on 8 November 1917, it had to be done almost literally from nothing with very weak raw materials. The years of famine, when masses had died of starvation and disease and others resorted to cannibalism, had exacted a high cost on the Russian people.

Lenin made some attempts to restructure society. War communism segregated the people into exploiters and exploited with the former becoming the slaves to the new system. Propaganda tried to establish a new "socialist" popular culture, however, both the nation and the Communist Party (CPSU), the new name for the Bolsheviks, were deeply divided. The combination of Marxist economic theory and czarist repression drove the nation forward and defined the character of the USSR.

Lenin's new government attempted economic reforms, based on the state ownership model. Widespread demonstrations that culminated in a revolt at the Kronstadt naval base in March 1921, the center of Bolshevik power in 1917, encouraged Lenin to alter his course. At the Tenth Congress in 1921, the Central Committee of the CPSU endorsed the New Economic Policy (NEP), which was designed to "[build] socialism with capitalist hands." The policy combined the artificial creation of a market economy, nationalization of small-scale enterprises, and integration of these businesses into the market. The

Nikolai Bukharin. The Library of Congress.

reforms and the taxes levied against small holders were instituted unequally across Russia, and a number of unscrupulous local bureaucrats prospered illegally. As Lenin's health deteriorated, however, political progress slowed and the factions within the CPSU battled for power.

Lenin's preferred successor was Leon Trotsky, who seemed more responsive to the effects of policy. Trotsky himself failed, however, to present Lenin's case to the Twelfth Party Congress in April 1923. This allowed Joseph Stalin to become general secretary. This marked the triumph of "socialism in one country" over Trotsky's theory of "permanent revolution." Stalin created a power base for himself prior to reorienting the NEP.

Socialism by Force

Under the NEP, the majority of Russian people were left without interference. The state did little to enforce progress toward socialism. Everyone, it appeared, subscribed to Bukharin's notion that the USSR should "creep at a snail's pace towards socialism"—everyone, that is, except Stalin. He allowed the lack of urgency to continue only until he had secured his position over the CPSU. By the time Stalin inaugurated the First Five-Year Plan in February 1928, he had the mechanisms in place to control both the party and society. A secret police force, OGPU, maintained order by fear. This organization, the largest employer in the USSR, had access to all parts of the USSR and all levels of society. As Stalin unveiled his plans for remolding society, OGPU officers were deployed to ensure compliance. This marked the start of the modernization of Russia and the beginning of Soviet totalitarianism.

The practical aims of Stalin's plans were to increase industrial production, including consumer goods, by 250 percent and to increase agricultural production by 130 percent. The means

to achieve this was to convert the entire Russian labor force, both rural and urban, into employees of state-controlled enterprises. There were, however, further and more far-reaching objectives toward which Stalin aimed. The first was modernization, an aspect of which was the removal of all conservative elements from Soviet society. The chief target was the *kulaks*, the smallholders who clung possessively to land gained from the czarist reforms. Stalin saw these as a reactionary people and a major obstacle to progress. The aim for the USSR to overtake Western Europe and the United States in industrial production and economic growth encompassed Stalin's goals of modernization and growth. Historian Adam Ulam suggested that this reflected Stalin's obsession with personal greatness. Ulam argued that Stalin saw himself as a modern incarnation of Ivan the Terrible or Peter the Great, and he therefore tried to be both architect and manager of the reformation and rebuilding of Soviet Russia.

The major obstacle to success was Stalin's limited knowledge of economics or how to achieve sustainable growth. His response to failure was irrational accusations and brutal repression. This was first evidenced by his destruction of the kulaks. The fact that 96 percent of Russian land was in kulak ownership meant that they were clearly an obstruction to the collectivization of agriculture. Opposition to Stalin's orders was widespread and attacks upon officials, the slaughter of livestock, and burning of crops was common. These tactics were met, however, with severe brutality. Thousands were killed and thousands more were transported to concentration camps. The inefficient management of collective farms, the lack of skilled or enthusiastic labor, and bad harvests in 1931–33, however, led to widespread famine. Estimates of the deaths range from five to 50 million between 1928 and 1933.

In the long term, the record of collectivization is mixed. Crop production increased: in 1940 it was 80 percent greater than in 1913. The collective farms, which employed and housed up to 75 million people, were also able to feed the population of the USSR throughout World War II, which was crucial to the war effort. Furthermore the increased production allowed substantial amounts to be exported, which provided extra capital for industrial development. On the negative side of the balance sheet, apart from the human cost, collectivization was detrimental to Russian agriculture. Livestock production decreased as husbandry skills became marginalized, which made meat a luxury item. The size of the collective farms caused inefficiency, and the fact that the workers owned none of their output was a disincentive to hard work and to attentiveness to tasks. Although collectivization solved some of the problems of Russian agriculture, largely these successes were only achieved in an atmosphere of fear and disenchantment.

Industrial development required massive investment. The targets set were too high and therefore unrealistic, but industries such as machine production and the manufacture of electrical goods showed great successes. The chief problems were caused by Stalin's desire to outstrip the West. Grand projects, such as the metallurgical center at Magnitogorsk, were costly and detracted investment from more needy areas. Therefore in attempting to build the "socialist utopia" as an example to the nonsocialist world, Stalin caused a decline in the standard of living, maintained food shortages, and pursued his economic aims regardless of the cost in hardship.

Industry was transformed and by 1932–33 the unskilled laborers that had been drafted into the urban production centers were skilled craftsmen. The USSR achieved growth in manufacture and engineering, without massive human cost, and was soon self-sufficient. By 1933, in response to Hitler's ascendance in Germany, Soviet industry made an easy transition to arms production. This was facilitated by massive increases in the production and quality of coal, pig iron, and steel under the second and third five-year plans. The goal of transforming backward Russia into a great industrial nation had been achieved.

Planning, Successes, and Failures

The transition in Soviet industry did, however, result in social problems, though the number of workers purged as wreckers in the wake of unmet goals often obscures the social disturbances. The high turnover of labor between the collective farms and industry led thousands of people to become rootless within the new USSR, and workers often moved from city to collective in search of better wages. Stalin introduced incentives for effort by recasting wage scales and he turned a coal miner named Stakhanov, who had achieved 14 times the output of his peers, into a cultural icon: a shining example of the "new Soviet man." This led to greater stability as workers competed against each other for higher wages and so remained in one place and established a good range of skills instead of drifting between different trades. Fear, rather than Stalin's incentives, however, was the primary motivation that made workers remain in one trade and work harder.

Despite the repressive nature of the USSR under Stalin, the plans were applauded by a variety of commentators from Western nations. As the Wall Street Crash caused economic depression to sweep the United States and Europe, the USSR stood prosperous and immune from danger. *Agitprop,* the Soviet propaganda department, organized guided tours to introduce Soviet planning techniques to the world. Two British economists and social theorists, John Maynard Keynes and G. D. H. Cole, both extolled the benefits of planning for Western Europe. Thus the Soviet example gained an influential audience of sympathizers. Nazi Germany and the European Economic Community both benefited from the influence of those who had analyzed the Soviet model, though their versions were heavily adapted and Stalin was seldom given credit for the ideas. Had the transformation of the USSR not involved such a high human cost, Stalinism arguably would have stood as an example to the world. Unfortunately, because of the tactics employed, planning and state control became discredited as synonymous with totalitarianism and repression. That is perhaps the lasting legacy of Stalinism.

Key Players

Bukharin, Nikolai (1888–1938): An ally of Lenin but seen to be on the right of the Communist Party under Stalin, Bukharin heavily criticized Stalin's planning and was eventually dismissed from the party. As a focal point for opposition to Stalin, Bukarin was arrested, charged with treason and executed.

Djugashvili, Iosif Visarionovich (Stalin; 1879–1953): A revolutionary guerrilla (1905–1917), Stalin became a trusted servant of the Bolshevik leaders. He succeeded Lenin as leader of the Soviet Union and redesigned Marxist-Leninism as socialism in a single country.

See also: *Forced Labor: Soviet Union; Russian Revolutions.*

BIBLIOGRAPHY

Books

Carr, E. H. *A History of Soviet Russia, 1917–1929.* Harmondsworth: Penguin, 1966.

Conquest, Robert. *The Great Terror: A Reassessment.* London: Pimlico, 1992.

———. *The Harvest of Sorrow: Soviet Collectivization and the Terror-famine.* London: Hutchinson, 1986.

Nove, Alec. *The Soviet Economic System.* London: Allen & Unwin, 1977.

———. *An Economic History of the USSR, 1917–1991.* London: Penguin, 1992.

Radzinsky, Edvard. *Stalin.* London: Sceptre, 1997.

Shukman, Harold. *Stalin.* London: Sutton, 2000.

Ulam, Adam. *Stalin.* London: Allen Lane, 1973.

Periodicals

Millar, James R. and Alec Nove. "A Debate on Collectivization: Was Stalin Really Necessary?" *Problems in Communism* 25 (July–August 1976): 49–62.

—Darren G. Lilleker

Foran Act

United States 1885

Synopsis

The Foran Act, also known as the Alien Contract Labor Act, prohibited the use of contract labor in the United States. The law was part of a broader trend of restrictive immigration legislation that began to appear in the 1880s. Prior to this period, immigration to the United States had been largely open. As the number of immigrants grew dramatically in the late 1800s, groups such as nativists and labor unions began to call for a reduction in the flow of foreigners into the United States. One of the targets of those who opposed immigration was the contract labor system. In this system, employers offered a contract to potential workers so as to induce them to come to the United States. The contract system was generally carried out by paid agents who recruited workers and often provided their passage to the United States. Many in the United States had come to believe that such contract workers threatened the jobs of native workers because the immigrants were willing to work for lower wages. In reality, however, employers in the United States used relatively few contract laborers. In general, immigrants still came to the country as long as there were general possibilities for a job. Those who did come on contracts were often skilled workers from countries such as England or Germany. Despite this reality, however, Congress bowed to pressure and implemented the Foran Act to prohibit contract labor.

Timeline

1866: Winchester repeating rifle is introduced.

1871: Chicago fire causes 250 deaths and $196 million in damage.

1876: General George Armstrong Custer and 264 soldiers are killed by the Sioux at the Little Big Horn River.

1878: Thomas Edison develops a means of cheaply producing and transmitting electric current, which he succeeds in subdividing so as to make it adaptable to household use. The value of shares in gas companies plummets as news of his breakthrough reaches Wall Street.

1882: Agitation against English rule spreads throughout Ireland, culminating with the assassination of chief secretary for Ireland Lord Frederick Cavendish and permanent undersecretary Thomas Burke in Dublin's Phoenix Park. The leader of the nationalist movement is Charles Stewart Parnell, but the use of assassination and terrorism—which Parnell himself has disavowed—makes clear the fact that he does not control all nationalist groups.

1884: Chicago's Home Life Insurance Building, designed by William LeBaron Jenney, becomes the world's first skyscraper.

1886: Bombing at Haymarket Square, Chicago, kills seven policemen and injures numerous others. Eight anarchists are accused and tried; three are imprisoned, one commits suicide, and four are hanged.

1886: Statue of Liberty is dedicated.

1886: Apache chief Geronimo surrenders to U.S. forces.

1888: The Blizzard of 1888 in the United States kills hundreds and causes more than $25 million in property damage.

1892: Bitter strikes in Australia lead to the closing of ports and mines.

1896: U.S. Supreme Court issues its *Plessy v. Ferguson* decision, which establishes the "separate but equal" doctrine that will be used to justify segregation in the southern United States for the next half-century.

Event and Its Context

The Growth of Anti-immigrant Sentiments in the United States

In 1886 the Statue of Liberty was dedicated as a monument to the immigrants who had come to the United States. Ironical-

ly, it was during the decade of the 1880s that the federal government began to place restrictions on the growing number of immigrants arriving in the United States from around the world. Before the 1880s immigration had been largely free and open. By the 1920s it had become severely restricted.

A number of groups opposed immigration. The nativist movement that arose in the 1880s included groups ranging from lower-class workers afraid of losing their jobs to elite intellectuals who had "scientific" theories to justify exclusion of certain groups. Many in the United States saw the new immigrants as a threat to the unity of the country. Nativists assumed that most immigrants were radical anarchists or syndicalists who would subvert American ideals. Although most immigrants were not radicals as many feared, the nativists had just enough "evidence" to create fear, including the Molly Maguire conspiracy in the 1870s and the Haymarket Affair bombing in Chicago in 1886.

Some of those who opposed immigration were overtly nativist, such as the American Protective Association, which had more than 100,000 members in the 1880s and 1890s. This organization attacked Catholicism, thus directing fears toward the large numbers of southern European immigrants. The labor movement also was concerned with the influx of immigrants to U.S. shores. In the 1880s, for example, the Knights of Labor, led by Terence V. Powderly—himself a second-generation Irish-American—opposed immigrants who might take jobs away from American workers. Later, Samuel Gompers and the American Federation of Labor (AFL) would also take an anti-immigrant stance, expressing particular concern over the large numbers of unskilled workers.

An academic and literary elite also opposed immigration. They disliked foreign culture and ethnic groups. They often used the social sciences to create theories on race that espoused the superiority of Anglo-Saxons. These intellectuals deemed other groups "unfit" to participate in U.S. life, as they were seen to be inferior physically, culturally, and socially. These immigration opponents sometimes formed groups such as the Immigration Restriction League of Boston.

The Creation of Restrictive Immigration Legislation

Early immigration legislation was largely uncoordinated. Congress slowly restricted the formerly open door to immigrants. There was no overall plan. Rather, the federal government passed individual laws in response to specific demands and situations.

The first general immigration law was passed in 1882. This legislation was aimed at the day-to-day receiving of immigrants in the United States. It implemented a 50-cent head tax to finance immigration centers. The law excluded certain groups from immigration, including "idiots," "lunatics," and criminals. It also prohibited anyone who would become a public charge. This provision would be at the heart of much future immigration policy that did not allow entrance for strictly economic reasons. Also enacted in 1882 was the Chinese Exclusion Act, which banned immigrants from China. Anti-Chinese sentiment had been growing, particularly in the West, as more and more Chinese immigrants settled in the United States in search of economic opportunity.

Congress and the Foran Act

The Foran Act was the next important piece of restrictive immigration legislation. As organized labor grew, groups such as the Knights of Labor had become especially concerned with the use of contract labor, fearing that such workers would steal jobs from native workers. Under this system, U.S. employers sought out foreign workers by offering them a contract before leaving their country of origin. Because of the logistics involved, the employers generally did not do the recruiting themselves. Rather, they hired and paid agents to find the workers. Often the agent was an immigrant who had been in the United States long enough to have learned English and established contacts with employers. The agents then secured workers, either by traveling abroad themselves, or, more commonly, through yet another agent in a foreign country. In addition, these agents might also serve as a sort of overseer for the workers that they brought to the United States.

Nativists and mass opinion felt that U.S. industries used large numbers of contract workers from southern and eastern Europe for cheap labor and as strikebreakers. In reality, there was actually relatively little use of contract labor after the Civil War, as most industrialists viewed it as too unreliable. Furthermore, it was rarely necessary for employers actually to have to offer concrete contracts to potential immigrants. A broad assurance that jobs would be available was usually enough to attract immigrants. When contract workers were used, they were usually skilled workers from Great Britain or Germany that were brought in for particular jobs or to introduce new techniques and processes. Strikebreakers were generally voluntary immigrants. Yet Congress responded to demands and passed legislation to prohibit contract labor. This early legislation set a precedent for future laws that addressed the concern that immigrants were taking jobs from American workers.

During the first session of the 48th Congress, which met from 1883 to 1885, legislators received many petitions regarding the effects of mass immigration on native labor. In particular, many of the petitions took the form of an attack on the contract labor system. This was not the first time such criticisms had been made. An 1864 act was repealed in 1868 because it was seen as encouraging such contract labor. By the 1880s it had become a key issue used by anti-immigration groups. Thus, Congress received more than 50 petitions from individual citizens, state legislatures, labor organizations, and the Chicago Board of Trade asking the government to take action against contract labor.

In response, several members of Congress sponsored bills against contract labor. Martin A. Foran of Ohio submitted the first on 8 January 1884. On 14 January, Thomas Ferrell of New Jersey proposed a similar bill that would prohibit contract labor. Finally, on 4 April, James George of Mississippi sponsored yet another anti-contract labor bill. The Foran bill had the most success. It was reported out by the Committee on Labor and then brought up in the House of Representatives on 19 June. After amendment, the bill passed by a vote of 102–17. The Senate then debated the bill but took no immediate action.

In the second session of the 49th Congress, the Senate once again brought up the Foran bill. After several days of debate, the Senate amended the bill and passed it on 18 February 1885. The House then accepted the amendment and the president approved the bill. On 26 February 1885 the bill officially became the Alien Contract Labor Act, sometimes known simply as the Foran Act.

The Contents of the Foran Act

The Foran Act contained five sections. The first section of the act prohibited individuals or companies in the United States from formally contracting foreign workers prior to immigration and from paying their passage or assisting in any way. Section two voided all such contracts. Section three stated that the government would levy a $1,000 fine per violation on anyone found violating section one. The fine would be paid by the contractor. Section four called for a fine on ship masters who knowingly transported such contract laborers. The fine would be up to $500 per passenger, along with up to six months in jail. Section five provided for some exceptions to the ban on contract workers, allowing certain groups such as workers who possessed skills that could not be found in the United States.

Despite its attempt to eliminate contract labor, the Foran Act was difficult to enforce. For one, the simple fact that actual contract labor was rare meant that the law did little to reduce immigration. Furthermore, knowing that contracts were illegal, employers and their agents could simply make general offers of work without an actual contract. In addition, immigrants soon learned, often because of coaching by the agents, that they simply should never tell immigration officials that they had any sort of labor contract. Later legislation attempted to solve these problems with the Foran Act.

Immigration Restriction After the Foran Act

The Foran Act was certainly not the last piece of restrictive immigration legislation. An 1891 law gave the federal government more complete control over immigration and created the Bureau of Immigration. It also set up Ellis Island to process immigrants and further excluded certain groups, including paupers, polygamists, and those with contagious diseases. A 1903 law also prohibited the entrance of anarchists, epileptics, and prostitutes.

The 1917 Immigration Act codified much of the earlier legislation. It raised the head tax to $8 and implemented a literacy test. There were also more exclusions, including almost all Asians. Then in 1921 a law placed an annual limit on the number of immigrants who could enter the United States. There were national quotas for each country, based on the 1910 census. In 1924 the Johnson-Reed Act further reduced the number of immigrants allowed in any given year. Now the national quotas were based on the 1890 census, which gave more slots to northern Europeans, reduced the number of southern Europeans who could enter the country, and excluded all Asians. Thus, by the 1920s the process begun in the 1880s to restrict immigration was mostly complete.

Key Players

Foran, Martin A. (1844–1921): Foran served as a Democratic representative from Ohio in the House of Representatives from 1883 until 1889. He introduced the bill that became the Alien Contract Labor Act of 1885, also known as the Foran Act.

See also: *American Federation of Labor; Chinese Exclusion Act; Haymarket Riot; Knights of Labor; Molly Maguires.*

BIBLIOGRAPHY

Books

Garis, Roy. *Immigration Restriction: A Study of the Opposition and Regulation of Immigration in the United States.* New York: Macmillan Company, 1928.

Hutchinson, E. P. *Legislative History of American Immigration Policy, 1798–1965.* Philadelphia: University of Pennsylvania Press, 1981.

Jones, Maldwyn Allen. *American Immigration.* Chicago: University of Chicago Press, 1960.

Purcell, L. Edward. *Immigration.* Phoenix: Oryx Press, 1995.

Periodicals

Peck, Gunther. "Reinventing Free Labor: Immigrant *Padrones* and Contract Laborers in North America, 1885–1925." *The Journal of American History* 83, no. 3 (1996): 848–871.

—Ronald Young

Forced Labor

Germany 1933–1945

Synopsis

By 1945 there were several million foreign laborers working in slave conditions in the German economy. The emergence of forced labor was the product of three distinct factors: first, the defeat of the free-labor movement in 1933, which had profound consequences for the condition of all labor, "native" as well as "foreign"; second, the wartime capture of foreign labor, especially Slav workers, millions of whom were set to work in the maintenance of the German war effort; and third, the particular conditions of racial minorities, especially the Jews of Germany, Poland, and Russia. Hundreds of thousands of Jews were forced to work in slave conditions, while many others would be killed more quickly in the Holocaust.

Timeline

1918: The Second Battle of the Marne in July and August is the last major conflict on the Western Front. In November, Kaiser Wilhelm II abdicates, bringing an end to the war. Soon after the surrender, upheaval sweeps Germany, which for a few weeks in late 1918 and early 1919 seems poised on the verge of communist revolution.

1921: As the Allied Reparations Commission calls for payments of 132 billion gold marks, inflation in Germany begins to climb.

1923: Conditions in Germany worsen as inflation skyrockets and France, attempting to collect on coal deliveries promised at Versailles, marches into the Ruhr basin. In November an obscure political group known as the National Socialist German Workers' Party attempts to stage a coup, or putsch, in a Munich beer hall. The revolt fails, and in 1924 the party's leader, Adolf Hitler, will receive a prison sentence of five years. He will only serve nine months, however, and the incident will serve to attract attention for him and his party, known as the Nazis.

1925: Released from Landsberg Prison, Adolf Hitler is a national celebrity, widely regarded as an emerging statesman who offers genuine solutions to Germany's problems. This year, he publishes the first volume of *Mein Kampf* (My Struggle), which he dictated in prison to trusted confederate Rudolf Hess. The second and final volume of Hitler's opus, a mixture of autobiography, "history," and racial rant, will appear two years later.

1933: Hitler becomes German chancellor, and the Nazi dictatorship begins. A month later, the Reichstag building burns, a symbol of the new regime's contempt for democracy. (Though a Dutch communist is punished for the crime, the perpetrators were almost certainly Nazis.) During this year, virtually all aspects of the coming horror are manifested: destruction of Jewish-owned shops and bans on Jewish merchants; elimination of political opposition (including the outlawing of trade unions); opening of the first concentration camps (and the sentencing of the first Jews to them); book-burning; and the establishment of the first racial purity laws.

1936: Hitler uses the Summer Olympics in Berlin as an opportunity to showcase Nazi power and pageantry, but the real hero of the games is the African American track star Jesse Owens.

1942: At the Wannsee Conference, Nazi leaders formulate the "final solution to the Jewish question": a systematic campaign of genocide on a massive scale. By the time the Holocaust ends, along with the war itself, the Nazis will have killed some 6 million Jews, and as many as 6 million other victims in their death camps and slave-labor camps.

1945: April sees the death of three leaders: Roosevelt passes away on 12 April; the Italians execute Mussolini and his mistress on 28 April; and Hitler (along with Eva Braun, propaganda minister Josef Goebbels, and Goebbels's family) commits suicide on 30 April.

1946: At the Nuremberg trials, 12 Nazi leaders are sentenced to death and seven others to prison.

1947: The Marshall Plan is established to assist European nations in recovering from the war.

1948: War results in the formation of a Jewish state in Israel.

1952: West Germany agrees to pay Israel reparations of $822 million for Nazi crimes against the Jewish people.

Prisoners working on rifle production line, SS-owned munitions factory, Dachau, Germany. USHMM Photo Archives.

Event and Its Context

The Catastrophe of 1933

There was no history of forced labor in Germany. Instead, in the 50 years leading up to 1933, German workers had enjoyed some of the best working conditions in Europe. The German chancellor, Prince Otto von Bismarck, passed laws that covered accident, sickness, and old age insurance as early as the 1880s. Industrial tribunals were established in the 1890s, along with laws restricting the working day of women (11 hours) and minors (10 hours). State insurance had initially been accompanied by repressive legislation against the left, but the victory of the German Social Democratic Party (SPD) in the 1890 elections sped the demise of anti-socialist laws. By the mid-1890s German workers were able to organize with relative freedom, and the labor movement progressed rapidly. By 1914 the Social Democrats claimed more than one million members and over 13,000 elected councilors. Following the 1918 revolution, the state granted the eight-hour working day. All employers of more than 50 people were compelled to recognize workers' councils. Meanwhile, Social Democrats organized libraries and walking clubs, consumer cooperatives and burial societies. By the mid-1920s one-fifth of all German families were members

of a cooperative. Between 1918 and 1933 the SPD was the largest party in the Weimar parliament. The position of the workers' movement appeared to be secure.

From the 1930s onward, however, German life was transformed by the rise of Adolf Hitler's National Socialist German Workers Party (NSDAP), better known as the Nazis. The ideology of the Nazis portrayed the threat of Bolshevism (meaning both the communists and the socialists) as the greatest obstacle to the revival of the German nation. The leaders of the German socialist parties were aware of the threat and the need for unity. In the last free elections, held in November 1932, German left-wing groups secured a combined vote of 13 million, larger than the 11.7 million of the NSDAP. What the socialist parties lacked, however, was any sort of program of joint action. In its absence, German politics witnessed a rapid succession of governing coalitions, each more right-wing than the last. The defeat of a Catholic-socialist coalition in the winter of 1930 was followed by the legal destruction of the SPD Prussian state government in spring 1932. On 30 January 1933 Adolf Hitler took power. Within four months, both the left parties and the trade unions were banned.

Under Nazi rule, German workers lost the freedoms they had enjoyed. The labor press and unions were destroyed. The

Women prisoners working in straw-shoeplaiting workshop, Ravensbrück concentration camp.

regime attempted to compensate for their losses through the creation of a network of organizations that claimed to protect the rights of workers. The German Labor Front (DAF) played a key role in orchestrating sports events and affordable holidays. Parks, showers, and common rooms were built in the largest factories. The DAF also administered the remnants of the workers' councils. Yet the removal of political freedoms contributed to a general worsening of working conditions. Between 1932 and 1938 wages fell by some 3 percent. Meanwhile the cost of living rose by 5 percent, food prices by 19.5 percent, and average hours of work per week by 15 percent. Managers at a power station in Baden forced their workers onto a 104-hour week. The intensity of labor also increased, with the government claiming an increased productivity of 11 percent in the same period. The profits of I. G. Farben rose from 74 million Reichmarks in 1933 to 240 million in 1939.

The condition of German labor from 1933 to 1939 has been a matter of surprising controversy among historians. The earliest trend was to emphasize the extraordinary defeat suffered by German labor; the most important task was to rescue the neglected history of those "Aryan" German workers who resisted the regime, most going on to suffer capture and death. The sec-

ond wave of historians tended to rebel against this model. For example, David Schoenbaum maintains that Nazi society was a revolutionary order. The destruction of old patterns of ruling was followed by a "social revolution," in which the people were told constantly that they were the ones who governed. "Interpreted social reality . . . reflected a society united like no other in recent German history," notes Schoenbaum.

A different account appears in the work of the socialist historian Tim Mason. His thesis is that the regime did not successfully integrate the working class and was thus uncertain when it came to imposing economic sacrifices to secure rearmament. In this sense, the most important aspect of regime policy was the continuous fear that Germany would return to the revolutionary days of 1918. In the late 1930s, Mason argues, the economy boomed and the balance tilted yet further toward labor: "Class conflict remained endemic in Nazi Germany." Growing labor shortages slowed military preparations and may even have influenced the character of Nazi foreign policy, including Hitler's belief in a *blitzkrieg*. Historians have criticized Mason's account, with some, such as Ian Kershaw, suggesting that Mason's argument tends to downplay the role of the German state in formulating policy on its own terms.

A Firsthand Account of Slave Labor in a Nazi Concentration Camp

[A French citizen born in 1920, future pastor Aimé Bonifas was neither Jewish nor a member of any of the other groups targeted by the Nazis for incarceration in slave-labor and death camps. He did, however, aid the French Resistance, and he attempted to escape from Nazi-controlled France. Following his capture, he was interned in a series of camps, including the forced-labor facility at Mackenrode, where the events described in the following passage took place.]

". . . We were laying the roadbed for a new railway. We were urged on because the approaching winter freezes might hamper or interrupt our work. It seemed that this railroad was of some military significance. . . .

"Each morning we had to walk eight kilometers to our job, and, of course, each evening, eight kilometers back to the camp. Our worn-out shoes alone would have made this march painful, but our exhaustion made it torturous. The roadbed for this section of the future railroad ran across open fields. Each one of us was assigned a definite work quota. Each day, working as a team of two, we were required to load a certain number of tip trucks with 25 to 30 cubic meters of earth. This demand was unreasonable, for the ground was so hard and stony that first we had to break it with a pick. We were digging our own graves in the German earth! I could still swing my pick fairly well, but many of my friends were noticeably weakening. What would happen to them if we should be forced to spend another winter here? We were so famished that once again our hunger became an obsession. It was absolutely essential to relax our pace, but we were watched too closely. Strange as it may seem, some worked rapidly just to make trouble for others. . . . I had observed that some prisoners—poor intimidated fellows, robots of the System—killed themselves with work when they could have limited their output. We marked them well, for by increasing production norms, they involuntarily became our enemies. They worked to their own detriment, and most of them did not last long.

Source: Aimé Bonifas. *Prisoner 20-801: A French National in the Nazi Labor Camps.* Translated by Claude R. Foster, Jr. and Mildred M. Van Sice. Carbondale: Southern Illinois University Press, 1987.

—Judson Knight

Foreign Labor

One strength of Mason's account is that it connects the experience of German labor between 1933 and 1939 to the wartime conditions experienced by non-German labor. According to Mason, terror had became an indispensable means of "education" in the daily lives of workers, "the ultimate and most important guarantee of the survival of the economic and political system of dominance. . . . Only one further step could follow after the workers had been totally reified: the destruction of human beings in the production process for the sake of production. This fate was reserved for the foreign state laborers." It has been estimated that, by December 1941, there were 4 million foreigners working in German fields and factories. This number then rose to 7.6 million by August 1944. Meanwhile, an equivalent number of foreign workers were laboring on behalf of Germany in their own countries, in state farms, in military construction work, and in menial jobs in German military camps. The man responsible for this whole operation was Fritz Sauckel, the plenipotentiary general for labor allocation, whose staff reported to the office of the Four Year Plan.

The reasons for using vast numbers of foreign workers related both to the pre-war conditions of labor and to the nature of the war itself. The 1939–1945 war was a total conflict in which some 50 million people died. It was a contest of armies and of whole economies. The largest industrial powers battered each other into submission. Conscription was widespread. Nearly 40 percent of all German industrial workers had become soldiers by 1944. Meanwhile, the war was becoming increasingly unpopular with "ordinary Germans," notes C. R. Browning. Following the German defeat at Stalingrad in winter 1942–1943, it became obvious that Hitler was leading his nation to defeat. During the first half of 1944, roughly 2,000 German workers were arrested each month for labor discipline offences.

Outsiders were expected to do all of the dirty and unskilled jobs. According to Stefan Berger, "German workers profited from the deployment of foreign labor and often experienced it as an opportunity for upward social mobility." There is also evidence of popular racism against Jews and Slavs, as happened during the 1943 bombing raids, when "German workers abused and maltreated the foreigners as objects of their anger and revenge," writes Berger. The attitude of the regime toward foreign slave labor was complex. On the one hand, such workers were needed if Germany was going to win the war. On the other hand, their very presence seemed to upset the Nazi hierarchy of approved races, for which the war was being fought. In line with the official ideology of the regime, therefore, decrees were passed that controlled every aspect of the foreign workers' lives. The living standards of foreign workers were strictly ordered according to racial hierarchy. In one Krupp cast steel plant, "Western" male workers received 91 percent of the wages earned by German males; "Eastern" males were paid 41 percent, and "Eastern" females received just 37 percent. Miscegenation became a capital offence. Foreign slave workers were subject to routine beatings and denied medical care. They were inadequately clothed, housed, and fed.

Labor and the Holocaust

The most extreme forms of popular German racism were associated with the Jewish Holocaust. Yet once again historians have disagreed in explaining this process. The most common view has portrayed the Holocaust as the inevitable consequences of state policy. In this account, Hitler long planned the murder of the Jews and embarked on the practice of murder as soon as the world's attention was diverted by war. Such "intentionalism" was challenged in the 1970s by "structuralist," or "functionalist," accounts that emphasized long-term factors such as the monopolistic nature of the German war economy or the peculiar structures of political authority employed by the regime. In this model, Hitler was a "lazy" dictator ruling over a deliberately complex structure of bureaucratic misrule. The disorder of the political regime encouraged interdepartmental competition and eased the path to murder. The most recent trend has been for compromise, emphasizing both the extent of the regime's ideological racism and the conjuncture that made killing more likely.

We can distinguish roughly three stages in the Holocaust. In the first period, 1933 to 1939, the regime set about establishing many legal differences between the Jewish and the non-Jewish population of Germany. The outbreaks of violence took place on the initiative of the local state. The full apparatus of the regime was not yet mobilized. In the second period, 1939 to 1941, the Nazi state was radicalized by war. Nazi leaders faced the question of how to treat non-German Jews, such as the large Jewish population of occupied Poland. These men and women were rapidly separated into ghettos or sent to labor camps. In the third period, 1941 to 1944, the German state suffered military defeat. Concentration camps were rapidly converted into death camps, and the ghettos were cleared. In the bizarre logic of the Nazis, the wasting of resources on the Holocaust was seen as an extension of the military struggle against "Russian Bolshevism." Finally, as Russian troops counterattacked, it became impossible to sustain the apparatus of state murder. At this stage, the camps were closed, and many of the inmates were murdered in a final frenzy of killing.

On 26 October 1939 Governor Frank decreed compulsory labor for the "Jewish Population of the General Government" (of Poland). All Jews between the ages of 15 and 60 would be subject to compulsory daily labor. Initially, such labor consisted of digging rivers or canals, erecting dams, breaking stones, or laying roads. Later there was also some allowance for specific tasks in the ghettos, such as the maintenance of communal kitchens, health care, finance, and internal security.

By the time of the Wannsee conference on 20 January 1942, leading Nazis such as Adolf Eichmann and Reinhard Heydrich seem to have rejected the previous policy as too moderate. The Jews of the ghettos were simply not dying quickly enough. "In pursuance of the final solution, the Jews will be conscripted for labor in the east under appropriate supervision. Large labor gangs will be formed from those fit for work, with the sexes separated, which will be sent to those areas for road construction and undoubtedly a large number of them will drop out through natural wastage. The remainder who survive—and they will certainly be those who have the greatest powers of endurance—will have to be dealt with accordingly. For, if released, they would, as a natural selection of the fittest, form a germ cell from which the Jewish race could regenerate itself."

This statement was an early sign of the shift from a policy of slave labor to one of mass killing. Yet not all authorities were willing to accept this change. In September 1942 there was a brief contest between different wings of the Nazi state over future policy. The military commanders in Poland were determined that war production continue, arguing that, of the one million workers employed on military production in Poland, roughly one-third of them were Jews, including 100,000 skilled workers. If the ghettos were destroyed, "a serious drop in production would occur in the armaments industry of between 25 and 100 percent. There would be a 25 percent reduction in the performance of the motor vehicles repair workshops," and so on. In response, Himmler agreed that some Jews could be deported to special work camps. "However, one day the Jews must disappear from there, too, in accordance with the Führer's wishes."

The ghettos were finally destroyed in spring 1943. When labor camps were established in the East, the Jews were not used there as a reserve army of skilled labor; that role fell to a minority of Poles. Daniel Goldhagen illustrates this point with reference to the Lipowa camp in Lublin. It had been founded in December 1939 as a concentration camp and later evolved to receive Jews extracted from the Lublin ghetto. In theory, Lipowa specialized in making shoes. Yet "the *skills* of skilled laborers went for the most part unused, meaning that the Germans squandered a great portion of the labor power of these workers, who under normal circumstances would have been highly valued and very productive," remarks Goldhagen. For two years, these workers were unused. There was a brief period of activity in spring 1943, then in November the camp population was killed. Even in huge industrial complexes like Auschwitz, the only role of Jews was to die.

It seems, therefore, that the policy of exterminating enemies through work—*Vernichtung durch Arbeit*—belongs to the middle stages of the Holocaust. The utility of Jewish labor declined when the leaders of the Nazi state decided that millions of people had to be killed more quickly. Different policies were then adopted, including mass shootings, the deployment of special gassing vans, and finally the use of gas chambers. Mason describes "a straight line" running "from the factory community to the factory-as-concentration-camp. The various intervening steps were a necessary consequence of the dissolution of the trade unions and a precondition for conducting a war of expansion." His point is simply that the process that began with the destruction of German labor culminated in the experience of the death camps at Auschwitz, Sobibor, and Treblinka.

Key Players

Eichmann, Adolf (1906–1962): An official in the Reich Central Security Office (RSHA), Eichmann took responsibility for the "Jewish Affairs" desk, which sent Jews to camps such as Auschwitz. He was captured by Israeli agents and tried in 1961.

Heydrich, Reinhard (1904–1942): Head of the Secret Police (Gestapo) and RSHA, Heydrich was charged with implementing the Holocaust. He was killed by Czech Partisans.

BIBLIOGRAPHY

Books

Berger, Stefan. *Social Democracy and the Working Class in the Nineteenth Century and Twentieth Century Germany.* New York: Longman, 1999.

Bracher, Karl Dietrich. *The German Dictatorship, Structure and Effects of National Socialism.* New York: Praeger, 1970.

Broszat, Martin *The Hitler State: The Foundation of the Internal Structures of the Third Reich.* New York: Longman, 1981.

Browning, C. R. *Ordinary Men: Reserve Police Battalion 101 and the Final Solution in Poland.* New York: HarperCollins, 1992.

Dawidowicz, L. *The War Against the Jews, 1933–1945.* New York: Bantam, 1986.

Finkelstein, Norman G., and Ruth Bettina Birn Finkelstein. *A Nation on Trial: The Goldhagen Thesis and Historical Truth.* New York: Metropolitan Books, 1998.

Gluckstein, Donny. *The Nazis, Capitalism and the Working Class.* London: Bookmarks, 1999.

Goldhagen, Daniel Jonah. *Hitler's Willing Executioners: Ordinary Germans and the Holocaust.* New York: Knopf, 1996.

Hilberg, Raul. *The Destruction of the European Jews.* New Haven, CT: Yale University Press, 2002.

Kershaw, Ian. *The Nazi Dictatorship: Problems and Perspectives of Interpretation.* New York: Oxford University Press, 2000.

Mason, Timothy W. *Social Policy in the Third Reich: The Working Class and the National Community.* Providence, RI: Berg, 1993.

Merson, Allen. *Communist Resistance in Nazi Germany.* Atlantic Highlands, NJ: Humanities Press, 1986.

Noakes, Jeremy, and Geoffrey Pridham. *Nazism 1919–1945: A History in Documents and Eyewitness Accounts.* New York: Schocken, 1990.

Novick, Peter. *The Holocaust in American Life.* Boston: Houghton Mifflin, 1999.

Renton, Dave, *Fascism: Theory and Practice.* Sterling, VA: Pluto, 1999.

Schoenbaum, David. *Hitler's Social Revolution: Class and Status in Nazi Germany, 1933–1939.* New York: Doubleday, 1966.

—David Renton

Forced Labor

USSR 1930s

Synopsis

The effects of the Russian Civil War and later miscalculations within the newly founded Union of Soviet Socialist Republics (USSR) government of Vladimir Lenin left Joseph Stalin, the new leader of the USSR, with an impending agricultural crisis and a crumbling Russian industrial economy. Instead of giving the peasants economic incentives to raise production, Stalin chose a policy in 1928 that forced them into state-owned collective farms. Stalin resorted to slave and forced labor in order to provide food and materials to the rapidly industrializing Soviet cities.

Excerpt from a 1947 AFL Statement on Slave Labor in the Soviet Union

[The statement excerpted in the following paragraphs appeared in its entirety in the January 1947 issue of *International Free Trade Union News,* a publication of the Free Trade Union of the American Federation of Labor (AFL). Two years later, the AFL included the editorial in documents it presented to the United Nations (UN) as part of an effort to urge UN condemnation of Soviet slave-labor practices.]

About a quarter of a century ago it seemed as if the complete extinction of the last remnants of slavery throughout the world might not be far off. Slavery had been outlawed by international conventions and its abolition in those backward countries where it still existed was, apparently, only a question of time.

However, the rise of totalitarianism brought about a complete reversal of this historical trend. During the last 20 years the world has witnessed the reintroduction of slavery on a gigantic scale. The wide-spread use of forced labor by the modern dictatorships and those under their influence is, indeed, nothing but a reappearance of slavery under a different name. This reversion to servitude—and that is what it is, in the literal sense of the word—is one of the principal characteristics of modern totalitarianism and totalitarian tendencies.

The process of creating huge forced labor armies began in Russia under the first Five-Year Plan. Since that time, slave labor has become a regular and integral factor of the Russian economy as it has developed under subsequent Five-Year Plans. A net of so-called corrective labor camps has been gradually extended all over the Soviet Union. Various estimates of the number of the inmates of these camps have been made, but the figure of 10,000,000—not including prisoners of war and other deported non-Soviet citizens—seems to be not exaggerated. . . .

Free labor has always opposed slave labor in any form or under any pretext. Slave labor anywhere in the world adversely affects the standards of free labor everywhere. Moreover, each highly centralized political system based on slavery engenders aggressive policies, since it tends to enslave new populations in order to satisfy its need for an additional supply of forced labor. Furthermore, such a system tends to resort to conquest as a means of acquiring sources of wealth which it cannot create fast enough because of the notoriously low productivity of slave labor.

There is really an "irrepressible conflict" between free labor and every system of forced labor. To those who excuse the Soviet methods on the ground that such practices serve the aims of socialism, the reply can only be that the founders of the socialist doctrine proclaimed it as a path for workers' liberation, and not their enslavement.

Source: *Slave Labor in Russia: The Case Presented by the American Federation of Labor to the United Nations.* Washington, DC: American Federation of Labor, 1949.

—Judson Knight

On 7 November 1929 Stalin formally unleashed a new revolution, the so-called Great Industrialization Drive, for the total collectivization of the Russian peasants. The country's grain-producing areas were to be collectivized at once. From then on, peasants and small landowners were not allowed to own the land or to profit from crop sales. The government dealt ruthlessly with those who resisted this policy. Some were executed, but millions of others were forced to labor on farms where all the produce was taken to cities; others were driven to the peripheries of the Soviet Empire to form an enormous, expendable slave labor force. Stalin's actions in the 1930s caused a depression and the suffering and death of millions of innocent people.

Timeline

1917: On 7 November (25 October old style), the Bolsheviks under V. I. Lenin and Leon Trotsky seize power in Russia. By 15 December they have removed Russia from the war by signing the Treaty of Brest-Litovsk with Germany.

1920: Bolsheviks eliminate the last of their opponents, bringing an end to the Russian Civil War. By then, foreign troops, representing a dozen nations that opposed the communists, have long since returned home.

1924: V. I. Lenin dies, and thus begins a struggle for succession from which Josef Stalin will emerge five years later as the undisputed leader of the Communist Party and of the Soviet Union.

1927: Stalin arranges to have Trotsky expelled from the Communist Party.

1933: Even as Stalin's manmade famine rages in the Ukraine, the new administration of President Roosevelt formally recognizes the USSR.

1936: Germany reoccupies the Rhineland, while Italy annexes Ethiopia. Recognizing a commonality of aims, the two totalitarian powers sign the Rome-Berlin Axis Pact. (Japan will join them in 1940.)

1937: Stalin uses carefully staged show trials in Moscow to eliminate all rivals for leadership. These party purges, however, are only a small part of the death toll now being exacted in a country undergoing forced industrialization, much of it by means of slave labor.

1937: Pablo Picasso paints his famous *Guernica* mural dramatizing the Nationalist bombing of a town in Spain. Thanks to artists and intellectuals such as Picasso and Ernest Hemingway, the Loyalists are winning the battle of hearts and minds, even if they are weaker militarily, and idealistic young men flock from America to join the "Abraham Lincoln Brigade." Yet as George Orwell later reveals in *Homage to Catalonia,* the lines between good and evil are not clear: with its Soviet backing, the Loyalist cause serves as proxy for a totalitarianism every bit as frightening as that of the Nationalists and their German and Italian supporters.

1939: After years of loudly denouncing one another (and quietly cooperating), the Nazis and Soviets sign a non-aggression pact in August. This clears the way for the Nazi invasion of Poland and for Soviet action against Finland. (Stalin also helps himself to a large portion of Poland.)

1941: In a move that takes Stalin by surprise, Hitler sends his troops into the Soviet Union on 22 June. Like his hero Napoleon, Hitler believes that by stunning Russia with a lightning series of brilliant maneuvers, it is possible to gain a quick and relatively painless victory. Early successes seem to prove him right, and he is so confident of victory that he refuses to equip his soldiers with winter clothing.

1948: Stalin places a blockade on areas of Berlin controlled by the United States, Great Britain, and France. The Allies respond with an airlift of supplies, which, like the blockade itself, lasts into late 1949. Also in 1948, communists seize control of Czechoslovakia, adding yet another Soviet-aligned government to a growing sphere of Soviet influence in Eastern Europe.

1953: Stalin dies.

Event and Its Context

The Russian Revolution of 1917 was followed by a massive peasant revolution in which the land ownership of Russia was divided into more than 24 million individual holdings. The system ran against the professed political aim of the Union of Soviet Socialist Republics (USSR) and impeded any comprehensive industrialization. This soon changed. From the time of USSR leader Vladimir Lenin's death in 1924 until 1929, Stalin succeeded in eliminating his political opponents and established himself as the supreme leader of the USSR.

Declining Agricultural and Industrial Production

During this time, the Soviet economy had serious problems, most notably a declining rate of economic growth and an inadequate peasant-produced grain supply. Later, inflation and huge shortages, especially of food and raw industrial materials, began to plague the country. By the beginning of 1928, rationing was necessary as agricultural production and procurement failed to meet demand. At this time, Stalin decided that the country's New Economic Policy (NEP)—introduced in 1921 by Lenin to facilitate postwar economic recovery by encouraging limited private enterprise and peasant individualism—was not working. Prewar levels of industrial and agricultural production had been achieved with NEP, but further advancements in industry were hindered by a constant shortage of grain for the cities and for export. According to historian Anna M. Pankratova, the practice of small-scale peasant farming could not possibly reach the productivity levels that were needed for a highly industrialized country.

Stalin and his Communist Party followers wanted rapid industrial development and socialization of agriculture. Stalin realized that the Soviet economy was 50 to 100 years behind the industrialized countries of the world, and he was determined to make up this difference in 10 years. Stalin thus rejected the concept of individual farming and a prosperous peasantry and replaced it with collectivization: a coercive, controlling system of production and taxation. Stalin told his 15th Party Congress of December 1927, "The solution lies in the transition from small, divided peasant farms to large, united farms based on the social exploitation of the land, in the transition to the collective exploitation of the land on the basis of a new, higher technology. There is no other solution." This period, commonly called the Great Industrialization Drive, brought economic and social upheaval that became a major turning point in modern Soviet history.

Milovan Djilas, a wartime observer of Stalin, once said, "He was one of those rare and terrible dogmatists capable of destroying nine tenths of the human race to 'make happy' the remaining tenth." Unfortunately for millions of peasants of the Soviet Union, Djilas's prediction came true.

Collectivization

Stalin decided that "collectivization" was the solution. Collectivization was an attempt to modernize the Soviet industrial system rapidly by nationalizing all businesses and factories, forcing peasants off of private lands and into *kolkhozes* (agricultural communes operated by the government), eliminating the *kulaks* (well-off peasants) by mobilizing the middle-class and poor peasants against them, and fixing prices of all food and wages. The backbone of Stalin's philosophy was what he called "pumping" the peasantry but that quickly became "purging" the peasantry. By the fall of 1929, Stalin believed he had sufficient state power to overcome any peasant resistance. Rejecting capitalism, in the spring of 1929 Stalin proceeded with his policy of complete socialism with his first Five-Year Plan (FYP).

Stalin's objective was to unite Soviet agriculture and some 50 major Soviet industries. Stalin needed, first, to solve the grain crisis to provide the necessary agricultural products for the cities and for export. To achieve this objective, Stalin moved forward with a comprehensive 1,700-page document that detailed a program of rapid industrial development and agricultural control, which would run from 1 October 1928 to 31 December 1932. By mobilizing the entire Soviet nation in a military-style operation and bringing millions more people, especially women, into the workforce, Stalin planned to create a highly industrialized socialist country that could compete effectively with the developed nations of the world. This would require that all Soviet workers increase efficiency and restrict consumption, a plan that placed tremendous hardships on the working masses.

Stalin concentrated his efforts on heavy industries in specially constructed industrial manufacturing complexes, many of them in the mineral-rich Ural Mountains and the undeveloped Siberian wastelands. Each business or factory was assigned an annual goal. The government invested nearly all of its resources in the heavy industries, rather than the light industries such as consumption goods. Nearly 1,500 major industrial concerns were constructed during this period, including motor, aircraft, tank and tractor, machine tools, electrical, and chemical industries.

Soviet central planners assumed total control of production and distribution. All elements of competition were eliminated with the formation of a system of industrial ministries whose single responsibility was the production of certain groups of products. Most rights of industrial workers were removed. People could not leave their jobs to find better ones; internal passports limited relocation; unauthorized absenteeism was punished with dismissal; and unions (the ones that were not made illegal) became disciplinarians against the workers.

The goals developed by communist planners were not based on realistic values and prices but on material balances. FYP goals were regularly increased irrespective of economic realities. The workforce labored to the limits of it physical capabilities and was expected to produce more as goals were increased. By the end of 1932, the wage level was down about 49 percent from 1928, and the standard of living had eroded severely in just four years.

From the start of his rule, Stalin thought that the allegedly richer class of peasants, the kulaks, constituted a threat to his plans. *Kulak* means a wealthy peasant (literally "fist" in Russian, but when applied to peasants it means "grasping peasant"). Because kulaks were profiting from their better farming techniques, Stalin felt they might develop into a political force that might try to take control of the food supply and resist his political monopoly. When Stalin began his drive for "collectivization" in 1929, he deliberately tried to eliminate the kulaks as a class, confiscating their lands and property and transporting millions of them to slave labor camps all over Russia. Stalin targeted any peasant who even slightly resembled a well-to-do kulak.

Kulaks were usually prominent members of the Russian villages (such as landowners, political leaders, and clergy) who owned their own livestock and homes and often employed hired hands. Kulaks comprised about 4 percent of the population and produced the majority of surplus agricultural products. Poorer peasants comprised more than 65 percent of the population but seldom produced any surplus. Stalinist *dekulakization* became a common term for the annihilation of the kulaks. If the kulaks were unwilling to join the collective process, then they were subjected to arrest from the state police. By the end of 1929, nearly all peasants labeled kulaks were killed or relocated to Siberian slave labor camps with their families.

Altering the First FYP

The first FYP was designed as a gradual transformation to collective farming in which the state would produce materials and food in parallel with strictly controlled private production. Party leaders and Stalin believed that the system would produce sufficient agricultural products to sustain a major industrialization program. The wealthier and more productive kulaks would be forced to contribute over half of the national agricultural quota. In addition, the several million acres of large-scale state farms (*sovkhozy*) and voluntary collective farms (*kolkhozy*) worked by the poorer peasants would provide the other half of the quota. By June 1929 one million peasant households had joined 57,000 collectives, representing less than 4 percent of the total population. Continuing grain shortfalls necessitated the import of about 250,000 tons of grain that year.

With a rapid build-up of industrialization in the cities, the success of the first FYP was in jeopardy as cities faced food shortages, rationing, and a breakdown of discipline. As the Soviet economy worsened in late 1929, the authorities relied increasingly on force to cope with the crisis. Penalties spurred the peasants to increase production. Some resisted with violence such as rioting, starting fires, and shooting officials.

Forced Collectivization

Stalin's reaction to the poor results in 1929 was to make a momentous decision that would affect the lives of millions of Soviet citizens: he ordered the acceleration of the collectivization of the peasants. To help speed industrialization, Stalin wanted greater production of food from the peasants, who formed approximately 75 percent of the Russian population. Stalin sent armed government officials to seize the peasants' produce. Those peasants who resisted were labeled kulaks and convicted of terrorist acts. Hundreds of thousands of previously law-abiding people were taken off their land, an act that crippled Soviet agriculture for many decades to come.

Pressure increased from Stalin as he forced more than 20 percent of the peasants to join the collective farms by January 1930. Stalin had declared that the most important areas of Soviet grain production, such as Russia's traditional breadbasket, the Ukraine, along with the North Caucasus and the Lower and Middle Volga, would be turned over to collective farms within two years. Stalin also reiterated that no kulaks would be allowed to join the collectives, as their presence would be a negative influence on the socializing objectives of the collectives. The kulaks were divided into three groups: (1) the most militant members would be arrested and either shot or sent to the Gulag and their families deported; (2) the less violent resistors would be deported to hostile regions where the land was unproductive; and (3) the poorer kulaks would be dumped, after confiscation of their property, onto less productive land outside the collective farms.

In 1930 Stalin widened his elimination of all potential sources of local resistance by rounding up peasants from all over the USSR. Hundreds of thousands of peasant families resisted the military police. Though there was some open rebellion at first, most of the affected population eventually complied. The threat of slave labor became the primary mode of discipline. Many people simply refused to work in the collective farms. Stalin's response was to let them starve. The farmers reacted by destroying farm equipment, burning fields, and slaughtering livestock to prevent them from being used by Stalin's forces. By the end of 1930, Soviet farmers had slaughtered a quarter of the nation's cattle, sheep, and goats, and a third of the pigs (and by the end of 1933 had slaughtered nearly half of all livestock).

Stalin decided to stop peasant hostilities by setting impossible grain delivery quotas, especially in troublesome areas such as the Ukraine. In 1932 the Soviets increased the grain procurement quota by 44 percent. They were aware that this extraordinarily high quota would result in grain shortages for the Soviet citizens. Stalin—whose main goal was to force farmers to collectivize—instigated the famine that struck the Soviet Union in 1933, caused by low agricultural yields in 1932 and government seizures of scarce crops. Millions of people died from this man-made famine. Peasants who remained on their farms were forced to work for the state. Some 30 to 50 percent of all produce was turned over to the government in payment of rent and taxes.

Yields of the collectives continued to decline in 1933. Since the kulaks had been eliminated, Stalin had to blame others for agriculture problems. Stalin shifted the blame onto the technical personnel and supervisors of the collective farms. He accused them of sabotaging machines and grain harvests, squandering property, undermining labor discipline, and similar actions. The Soviet leadership began to persecute these people, precipitating a mass political purge during the second half of the 1930s.

By 1936, 90 percent of the peasantry had been collectivized and the centuries-old rural way of life had been destroyed. Crop failures caused continuing shortages. The four years from 1937 to 1940 were called "The Purge Era."

Gulag

The idea of exploiting forced and slave labor for the industrialization drive developed at the beginning of the first FYP. Paralleling the Soviet plans for industrialization, the empire of slave labor camps later known as the *Gulag* became a major sector of the socialist economy. The word *Gulag* is an acronym for Chief Administration of Corrective Labor Camps, (*Glavnoe Upravlenie ispravitelno-tru-dovykh LAGerey*). The Gulag was loosely defined as the network of Stalinist labor camps that stretched some 9,600 kilometers (6,000 miles) across the Soviet Union, from the Russian lands around Moscow to the east wastelands of Kolyma. In the strictest sense, the Gulag was the chief administrative body that oversaw the running of the system of corrective labor camps, detention centers, and prisons. For instance, a Gulag camp was set up at the ancient monastery on Solovetsky Island in the White Sea, where its slaves were used for logging.

The Gulag ruthlessly exploited the slave labor of political and other prisoners that basically industrialized the Soviet Union during this time. Most of the forced laborers were innocent Soviet citizens who were accused of crimes against the state. The need for a compulsory labor force seemed to be a contributing factor (although never officially recognized as such) in the number of arrests and deportations carried out by the security police. A law enacted on 7 August 1932 allowed children as young as 12 to be convicted of capital offenses and sent to a labor camp. By many estimates, the camps held between 100,000 and 200,000 prisoners in the early 1920s (less than one-fifth of 1 percent of the total population). Their numbers swelled starting with the first FYP in 1930, and by the end of the 1930s the population of the Gulag camps was near 10 million, with annual death rates of 10 to 30 percent.

In 1930 Stalin's mass deportations of kulaks provided a major influx of new slave labor. Between 1933 and 1935 peasants made up about 70 percent of the Gulag population. From 1936 to 1938 Gulag numbers swelled when victims of mass arrests were sent to the camps. People from all walks of life and religious persuasions were sent to the camps, from doctors and government officials to Baptists, one of the banned religious groups. No one in the Soviet Union was immune, regardless of ethnicity or nationality. Foreigners were also viewed as a threat. In 1940 Stalin seized the Baltic nations of Lithuania, Estonia, Latvia, and Moldavia; many of the citizens of these areas were immediately deported to the Gulag.

Slave laborers cut timber, mined gold, and harvested many of the untapped resources of Siberia. Trees were felled in the upper reaches of the Ob in western Siberia, and coal mining was performed in Vorkuta and Karaganda in Central Asia. Construction work was the most common form of labor. Most of this labor was done by brute force and without mechanization in subzero temperatures that could last for eight months of the year. Gangs of laborers from the Gulag also built the Moscow subway and major industrial complexes such as the steel mills at Magnitogorsk. The White Sea-Baltic Canal was dug in only 20 months by forced laborers often using only their bare hands. Approximately 60,000 Gulag prisoners died during that project.

Probably the most notorious camp was Kolyma, located in eastern Siberia. Gold and other ores were mined there under horrendous conditions: for every ton of gold mined, as many as 1,000 prisoners died. Kolyma was one of the best-documented Gulag camps, with a high concentration of writers and intellectuals. Surrounded by trackless forests and mountains, escape was nearly impossible. Most of the year Kolyma was cut off from the rest of the country by the extreme temperatures, which often plummeted to minus 51°C (minus 60°F). Recent estimates put the number of people who died at Kolyma at a staggering 3 to 6 million.

The result of the ensuing war-like operation of the government against its citizens was an estimated 10 million men, women, and children gunned down, and 10 to 11 million more transported to North European Russia, Siberia, and Central Asia, where a third went into concentration camps, a third into internal exile, and a third were executed or died in transit.

Conclusion

Stalin believed that the Soviet Union had to industrialize rapidly to strengthen the communist regime and enable the country to defend itself against foreign enemies. Forced labor was common in old Russia, but the extent to which it was employed in the Stalin era has few parallels in human history. Stalin's plan achieved industrialization, but the price in worsened living conditions and lost lives was great. Independent analysts seem to concur that gross industrial output expanded from 1928 to 1950 by almost four times at United States prices and about 4.7 times at Soviet 1926–1927 prices. The expansion of the output of producers' goods increased about 8.8 times during the same period, and consumer goods approximately doubled. In contrast, farm output increased percentage-wise only about as much as did the population.

The Great Industrialization Drive, which was realized by exploiting millions of slaves and forced laborers throughout the countryside, resulted in the near collapse of Soviet agriculture and the deaths of millions of peasants from famine. As many as 10 million people were dispossessed and deported during the 1930s. Perhaps most of these people were not killed but instead imprisoned, exiled, or forced to work the land or the floors of the factories. Certainly millions starved or froze to death, or were shot inside and outside the labor camps.

The exact number of people intentionally killed during the 1930s within the Soviet Union may never be known. However, when Winston Churchill asked Stalin in 1945 at the Potsdam conference how many deaths and deportations had resulted from the collectivization process, Stalin showed Churchill his 10 fingers, indicating around 10 million people.

Key Players

Stalin, Joseph (1879–1953): The general secretary (1922–1953) of the Communist Party of the Union of Sovi-

et Socialist Republics (USSR), Stalin established the USSR as a modern economic and military power that rivaled the United States during the cold war period. He helped repel Hitler's German armies in World War II but rivaled Hitler in the brutality of his genocidal policies. Stalin developed the features that characterized the Soviet regime and shaped the direction of eastern Europe after World War II ended in 1945. His chief theoretical work, *Marxism and the National Question*, was published in 1913.

See also: *Five-Year Plan; Russian Revolutions.*

BIBLIOGRAPHY

Books

Blackwell, William L. *The Industrialization of Russia: An Historical Perspective.* New York: Thomas Y. Crowell Company, 1970.

Blackwell, William L., ed. *Russian Economic Development from Peter the Great to Stalin.* New York: New Viewpoints, 1974.

Blassingame, Wyatt. *Joseph Stalin and Communist Russia.* Champaign, IL: Garrard Publishing Company, 1971.

Conquest, Robert. *Kolyma: The Arctic Death Camps.* New York: The Viking Press, 1978.

Filtzer, Donald. *Soviet Workers and Stalinist Industrialization: The Formation of Modern Soviet Production Relations, 1928–1941.* Armonk, NY: M. E. Sharpe, Inc., 1986.

Gregory, R., ed. *Behind the Facade of Stalin's Command Economy: Evidence from the Soviet State and Party Archives.* Stanford, CA: Hoover Institution Press, 2001.

Other

Open Society Archives at Central European University. "Forced Labor Camps Online Exhibition" [cited 5 December 2002]. <http://www.osa.ceu.hu/gulag/>.

—William Arthur Atkins

Ford-UAW Contract

United States 1941

Synopsis

By 1941 the United Automobile Workers (UAW) had been successful in establishing union representation at all automotive plants in the United States except for the Ford Motor Company. Henry Ford, the company's founder, was vehemently antiunion, and his position appeared firmly entrenched. Newly enacted federal labor legislation, the National Labor Relations Act (also known as the Wagner Act) of 1935, ran counter to Ford's

Ford Motor Company employees leave Detroit plant at end of workday. AP/Wide World Photos. Reproduced by permission.

modus operandi. Between 1937 and 1941 almost every plant Ford operated had been brought up on charges before the National Labor Relations Board (NLRB), the body charged with enforcing the 1935 law. The situation came to a head in 1941 after years of litigation and clear signs the company could be in financial peril if it did not submit to collective bargaining. The NLRB called an election for 21 May 1941 at all the Ford plants in Dearborn, Michigan, in which the UAW-CIO (Congress of Industrial Organizations) had won the right to represent workers. This election paved the way for successful labor negotiations between the parties and an excellent contract for Ford union members.

Timeline

1921: Washington Disarmament Conference limits the tonnage of world navies.

1925: European leaders attempt to secure the peace at the Locarno Conference, which guarantees the boundaries between France and Germany, and Belgium and Germany.

1931: Financial crisis widens in the United States and Europe, which reel from bank failures and climbing unemployment levels. In London, armies of the unemployed riot.

1936: Germany reoccupies the Rhineland, while Italy annexes Ethiopia. Recognizing a commonality of aims, the two totalitarian powers sign the Rome-Berlin Axis Pact. (Japan will join them in 1940.)

1941: German troops march into the Balkans, conquering Yugoslavia and Greece. (Bulgaria and Romania, along with Hungary, are aligned with the Nazis.)

1941: In a move that takes Stalin by surprise, Hitler sends his troops into the Soviet Union on 22 June. Like his hero Napoleon, Hitler believes that by stunning Russia with a lightning series of brilliant maneuvers, it is possible to gain a quick and relatively painless victory. Early successes seem to prove him right, and he is so confident of victory that he refuses to equip his soldiers with winter clothing.

1941: Japanese bombing of Pearl Harbor on 7 December brings the United States into the war against the Axis.

Ford Motor Company assembly line, Edgewater, New Jersey. AP/Wide World Photos. Reproduced by permission.

Combined with the attack on the Soviet Union, which makes Stalin an unlikely ally of the Western democracies, the events of 1941 will ultimately turn the tide of the war.

1941: The United States initiates the Manhattan Project to build an atomic bomb and signs the Lend-Lease Act, whereby it provides aid to Great Britain and, later, the Soviet Union.

1941: Great films of the year include *The Maltese Falcon, Sullivan's Travels, Meet John Doe, How Green Was My Valley,* and a work often cited as one of the greatest films of all time: Orson Welles's *Citizen Kane.*

1946: Winston Churchill warns of an "Iron Curtain" spreading across Eastern Europe.

1951: Color television is introduced.

1956: First aerial test of the hydrogen bomb takes place at Bikini Atoll. The blast is so powerful—the equivalent of 10 million tons of TNT—that it actually results in the infusion of protons to atomic nuclei to create two new elements, einsteinium and fermium, which have atomic numbers of 99 and 100, respectively.

Event and Its Context

Henry Ford's Antiunion Stance

By 1941 the United Automobile Workers (UAW) had been successful in establishing unions at all automotive plants in the United States except for one, the Ford Motor Company. Major manufacturers like Chrysler and General Motors had union contracts, as did others in the industry. The union and its members had struggled through hard-fought battles, including violent strikes, to organize these blue-collar workers. Only Ford had no contract with the UAW.

Henry Ford, the founder of Ford Motor Company, had remained entrenched and unapologetic in his antiunion opinions ever since the Industrial Workers of the World (IWW) tried to organize the company in 1913. Ford had a lengthy, well-documented history of antipathy toward labor organizations. He went so far as to establish a faux union called the Knights of Dearborn, an organization that was both antiunion and anti-Semitic. Ford was keen on pointing out that the wages of his employees were higher than wages provided by unionized plants, which was a fallacy. The company claimed its hourly wage as 90 cents per hour, yet Chrysler and General Motors were paying $1 per hour on average.

The Battle of the Overpass

No other event embodies Ford's antiunion stance more clearly than the Battle of the Overpass, a bloody confrontation between UAW leaders and Ford Motor Company henchmen in May 1937. The event occurred in Dearborn, the location of Ford's vast River Rouge industrial complex. The overpass spanned Miller Road and was a public thoroughfare. Ford henchmen approached four union leaders who had a permit to distribute literature. Taken by surprise and greatly outnumbered, the four men—Walter Reuther, Richard Frankensteen, J. J. Kennedy, and Robert Kantor—were severely beaten and then thrown down the stairs to the pavement below. Members of the union's women's auxiliary were verbally harassed and physically attacked while Dearborn police officers stood idly by. Fortunately, no lives were lost, but many people were injured.

Ford's Service Department

The widely publicized accounts and images of the event turned public opinion in favor of the union and shed the glare of publicity on Ford's brutal reign of fear, the overseer of which was Harry Bennett. Bennett developed a reputation as Ford's henchman and headed the so-called Service Department. This Ford Motor Company security force had some 3,000 employees, including ex-policemen, convicts, and bouncers. They were also generally responsible for ensuring employee order and productivity, which they achieved through threats, fear, and intimidation.

Bennett was undoubtedly the most powerful man at Ford Motor Company besides Ford himself. He ruled through intimidation and violence. His opinions regarding unionism were firmly in line with those of his employer. Bennett had a network of informers within the various facilities to alert him to problems, including any union talk. These spies also commonly eavesdropped on conversation in public gathering places outside the plant.

The Battle of the Overpass was perhaps the most flagrant violation of the Wagner Act that the manufacturer had in its lengthy, conspicuous, antilabor record.

Problems Within the UAW

For their part, the unions were beset by internal factionalism. Bennett decided to capitalize on this and take a different tack with the union. He found the perfect patsy in Homer Martin, a preacher who was viewed as a moderate within the UAW's Detroit local. Since 1938 there had been division within the local leadership with the moderate Martin on one side and fiery young unionists such as Reuther and Frankensteen on the other. Bennett shepherded Martin to a private meeting with him and Ford at the plant. They convinced Martin to engage in secret negotiations designed to force the union to retreat.

These negotiations led to a pact in December 1938, and an announcement was made about the agreements in the pact, none of which were in writing. The keystone of the pact was that the UAW consented to drop all legal actions against Ford. These actions were pivotal to developing any meaningful labor contracts with Ford, whether present or future. Not only would negating the legal actions save Ford from participating in labor negotiations, but the company also stood to save a great deal of money. Reuther was incensed and openly called Martin a traitor. From this point forward, Reuther and other leaders in the UAW distrusted Martin and Ford alike.

Some thought Martin wanted to destroy the UAW, though in retrospect, other observers note that Martin was attempting to do his best for the union. "His long career shows that he was honest and highminded, and though he was much too confiding, he tried hard to assure himself of Ford's good faith," writes Allan Nevins. Moreover, both Martin and Ford ". . . hoped that a settlement would prevent further violence like that of the Rouge overpass."

Martin's handling of the negotiations with Ford served only to split the union further, however. Labor leaders who agreed with Reuther's position affiliated with the CIO, while those sympathetic to Martin formed a new UAW that affiliated with the American Federation of Labor (AFL). Martin placed union negotiations with Ford in even further peril.

Bennett knew the UAW-AFL was short of cash. He had already been successful in plying Martin superficially; now he felt it was time to get out the checkbook. He offered Martin two generous accounts and a completely furnished home. Martin not only took the payoff but also wrote an effusive letter of thanks to Bennett. Now Ford Motor Company had the UAW-AFL under its control, complete with evidence of all that had transpired.

The AFL-affiliated union did gain some rank-and-file support, but the UAW-CIO was keen to organize the company and eliminate forever all Ford-endorsed violence. In early 1940 the union gained additional assistance from the CIO in its continuing efforts to organize Ford employees. The United States Supreme Court further helped organizing efforts at the Rouge. The justices refused to review an NLRB decision ordering 22 workers who had been fired to be reinstated with back pay. These men reportedly returned to work wearing union buttons. Sporadic sit-down strikes occurred after this, but there was no clear management direction on how to handle the union.

The head of the local organization was Michael F. Widman, a staff member of the CIO. By December 1940 there were 14,000 union members. In 1941 the pressure asserted by the UAW-CIO intensified. Leafleting outside the plant was common, and workers were openly wearing union badges. Religious leaders sympathetic to the UAW provided support to the workers, as did personnel in other local organizations. By mid-February 1941 Rouge workers were joining the union. The motor building, for example, was 95 percent union. Local leaders were optimistic at the prospects.

The Strike

The UAW-CIO asked the NLRB to hold an election at Ford to determine which union would represent workers at the plant. The company stalled. The entire UAW grievance committee, consisting of eight men, was fired 1 April 1941. Immediately the workers decided to strike, though there was no endorsement or call from the union to initiate the work stoppage. An estimated 1,500 steelworkers in the Rouge rolling mill shut down their operations, and other workers quickly followed suit. Work was halted instantly in three buildings in the complex. Soon the entire plant, with the exception of the foundry, was closed. The union ultimately endorsed the action.

Strikers 50,000 strong picketed and blockaded the Rouge. One organizer describes the moment as heady, with workers singing and cheering, "a wonderful experience, to walk out along with all those men determined on one thing, through Gate Four [the main entrance]." The observer continued, "No supervisor, no officer of the Ford Motor Company, neither Harry Bennett nor any service man, dared say us nay."

Unfortunately, Ford's Service Department was still inside the plant, as were an estimated 1,000 to 2,500 African American workers recruited to assist the thuggish security force. Although the strikebreakers were promised safety, these recruits engaged in questionable conduct, according to author Robert Lacey. Some of them reportedly "smuggled in alcohol and started drunken races through the plant machinery, driving new cars. Valuable drafting-room blueprints were used by the strikebreakers as mattresses." Other accounts confirm this and other damage to the plant at the hands of the scabs. Some African Americans left the plant at the insistence of the NAACP, but many company loyalists stayed to oppose the strikers.

Ford wanted Bennett to handle the situation alone, but Bennett was not even talking to the UAW-CIO. Both Henry Ford and his only son, Edsel, were in poor health at the time of the crisis. Edsel had been on vacation but returned early when he heard that Bennett was mobilizing the Service Department. Edsel refused to assist and insisted that his father assume full responsibility for the negotiations.

Fistfights broke out in the plant, and some of the men started using iron shafts as weapons. An estimated 150 people were injured in fights on 2–3 April. A local radio station aired encouragement for the strikers and broadcast regular updates. Ford wanted any means used to extract the striking workers. The company appealed to the state and federal governments for assistance. Michigan governor Murray Van Wagoner managed to keep negotiations active for 10 days. The strike was settled on 11 April, and work resumed on 13 April. Ford agreed to reinstate five of the eight men fired and to begin grievance proceed-

ings; any disputes that could not be resolved would be sent to mediation. Additionally, the newest NLRB hearings against Ford were suspended, and Ford agreed to an election.

The Election and Its Aftermath

Ford had little choice but to agree to these terms. The company had been involved in the courts on a variety of labor issues for years. Clearly, if the company did not submit to collective bargaining with the union, it was sure to be deluged with even more unflattering publicity. Ford's market share had plummeted, thanks in no small part to a UAW boycott. (This drop has also been attributed to Ford's political views, including his involvement with Adolf Hitler.) The company stood to lose valuable defense contracts as labor continued to pressure the government to punish the company for its failures to adhere to national labor laws and policies. Ford had lost a $10 million contract for this very reason in early 1941. The company had no option but to acquiesce.

The NLRB called the election for 21 May 1941 at all of Ford's Dearborn plants. An estimated 78,000 ballots were cast at the Rouge alone. The UAW-CIO won the election at the Rouge with 70 percent of the vote and won just as decisively at the company's Lincoln manufacturing plant. Only 2.5 percent (1,958) of all the workers who cast ballots voted "no union." Another 34 ballots were left blank. When the results were announced, Bennett is said to have quipped that it was "a great victory for the Communist Party, Governor Murray Van Wagoner and the NLRB." In a statement issued by I. A. Capizzi, Ford's general counsel, he said it was unfortunate that Ford would have to deal with communists. "The NLRB is . . . [like] the so-called courts by which the Communist, Nazi, and Fascist partners purge the men who resist their tyrannies. It is a dictatorial concept imported from Europe."

Negotiations commenced on 1 June 1941 in Detroit; they were moved to Pittsburgh and then to Washington, D.C. Capizzi was the lead negotiator for the company, while Philip Murray, president of the CIO, led the UAW delegation. By 18 June 1941 Ford was being pressed to come to some agreement, but he obstinately refused to sign. He was railing, saying he would close the plant if he had to. His wife, Clara, was upset about the years of violence and bloodshed and was particularly concerned about the influence Bennett had exerted over her husband and son. That night Clara gave Henry Ford an ultimatum, threatening to leave their marriage if he didn't agree to the contract.

The UAW was ultimately able to secure better contractual terms with Ford than had been possible with other employers. Wages were increased as promised, with increased pay for night shift workers and time-and-a-half provided for overtime pay. An estimated 4,000 workers who had been dismissed for union activity were rehired with back pay. Notably, all members of the Service Department were now required to wear uniforms on the job. The union was also provided with a closed shop and a checkoff. Ford also agreed to affix the union label to its cars. The contract was considered a model and the most liberal of its day. Ford ordered Bennett to sign the contract, which he did on 20 June 1941.

After relenting on his antiunion position, Ford gave the entire credit for his change of heart to his wife. "Mrs. Ford was horrified. . . . She insisted that I sign what she called a peace agreement. . . . I felt her vision and judgement were better than mine," he said. "Don't ever discredit the power of a woman."

Nevins, however, says there were other tangible concerns weighing heavily on Ford. "He realized that if he let labor troubles paralyze his great plant just as it flung itself into the defense effort, the people [of the United States] would condemn him." Moreover, he knew that the more deeply the NLRB delved into the many complaints against his company, the more customer distrust, damaging evidence, and compromising headlines he would have to face.

Key Players

Bennett, Harry (1892–1979): Born in Ann Arbor, Michigan, Bennett was the head of the Ford Service Department, a covert group of employees whose tasks included suppressing union activity. Bennett cultivated a tough reputation that he relished. He ran away from home and joined the navy at age 16. He was reportedly a boxer and had been a diver. He had also, however, studied art, and his first job at Ford in 1917 was in the art department. He continually was at odds with the union, particularly the UAW. Henry Ford II, Edsel's son, fired Bennett in 1945. The younger Ford made it his first order of business when he was appointed to run the company.

Ford, Edsel (1893–1943): The heir apparent to Ford Motor Company, Edsel was Henry Ford's only son and the president of Ford Motor Company. His father's control was palpable, as he was majority stockholder. The father-son relationship was fraught with difficulty. Edsel finally stood up to his father during the strike that precipitated the NLRB election, demanding that the union be negotiated with immediately. He died of stomach cancer.

Ford, Henry (1863–1947): The founder of Ford Motor Company, Ford fought unionization throughout his life. He did not relent on his antiunion stance until his wife, Clara, intervened during the 1941 negotiations with the UAW. Ford is often credited for his contributions to American labor and manufacturing, as well as for creating the eight-hour workday.

Frankensteen, Richard Truman (1907–1977): Born in Detroit, Michigan, Frankensteen started his career as an assembly-line worker at Dodge. He first became a union representative with the Automotive Industrial Workers Association. Frankensteen was among the union leaders injured in the fighting at the Battle of the Overpass. He was the vice president of the UAW in 1937.

Martin, Warren Homer (1901–1968): A preacher who was also a UAW leader in the AFL-affiliated union, Martin placed union negotiations with Ford in peril. He was considered a moderate but quickly succumbed to Harry Bennett's wiles and Ford's gifts. Martin continued to lead the UAW-AFL until he was forced from office in April 1940.

Murray, Philip (1886–1952): Born in Scotland, Murray was a leader within the United Mine Workers of America and was a founding member of the CIO. Murray became the head of the CIO in 1940. He was the chief negotiator for the UAW in its contract with Ford.

Reuther, Walter P. (1907–1970): Born in Wheeling, West Virginia, and the son of German immigrants, Reuther was an autoworker and labor organizer. His first job was working in a Ford Motor Company plant. He was a founder of both the UAW and the CIO. He participated in the first major Detroit auto strike in 1936. Reuther's ascent to prominence in the union started with the Battle of the Overpass.

Sorensen, Charles (1881–1968): Born in Copenhagen, Denmark, Sorensen immigrated to the United States with his family in 1884. He was in charge of production at the Ford Motor Company between 1925 and 1944. Sorensen and Bennett were locked in a power struggle throughout most of the 1930s. They agreed with their employer's view of unions, however. He was able to keep Bennett at bay until Henry Ford II assumed control of the company.

Van Wagoner, Murray Delos (1898–1986): Born in Michigan, Van Wagoner was educated at the University of Michigan. He was trained as a civil engineer but entered politics. He served as state highway commissioner (1933–1940) and was Michigan governor at the time of the union-organizing drive and elections at Ford Motor Company. He is credited with mediating the strike that ultimately laid the groundwork for the NLRB elections to be held at Ford's Dearborn plants.

See also: *American Federation of Labor; Battle of the Overpass; Congress of Industrial Organizations; United Automobile Workers; Wagner Act.*

BIBLIOGRAPHY

Books

Collier, Peter, and David Horowitz. *The Fords: An American Epic.* New York: Summit Books, 1987.

Galenson, Walter. *The CIO Challenge to the AFL: A History of the American Labor Movement, 1935–1941.* Cambridge, MA: Harvard University Press, 1960.

Lacey, Robert. *Ford: The Men and the Machine.* Boston, MA: Little, Brown, 1986.

Murray, R. Emmet. *The Lexicon of Labor.* New York: The New Press, 1998.

Nevins, Allan, and Frank Ernest Hill. *Ford.* 3 vols. New York: Charles Scribner's Sons, 1962.

Reuther, Victor G. *The Brothers Reuther and the Story of the UAW: A Memoir.* Boston, MA: Houghton Mifflin, 1976.

Taft, Philip. *Organized Labor in American History.* New York: Harper & Row, 1964.

Other

Hansen, Curtis. "The Battle of the Overpass." Walter P. Reuther Library, Wayne State University [cited 4 November 2002]. <http://www.reuther.wayne.edu/exhibits/battle.html>.

Stolberg, Benjamin. "Vigilantism, 1937-Part II." *The Nation* (21 August 1937) [cited 4 November 2002]. <http://newdeal.feri.org/nation/na37145p191.htm>

—Linda Dailey Paulson

Ford-UAW SUB Agreement

United States 1955

Synopsis

In the early 1950s, the United Auto Workers (UAW) under President Walter Reuther began to inject the issue of a guaranteed annual wage into contract talks with the "Big Three" auto makers. Throughout the auto industry's history, its workers had suffered economic setbacks when plants were shut down for annual model changes or during times of slack demand. Without unemployment insurance or other social safety net measures, workers were plunged into periods of insecurity and poverty, often without warning. To provide more economic security for workers, Reuther argued that employers should be required to pay a guaranteed wage to their employees throughout the year. Although Reuther was never able to gain such an agreement in collective bargaining talks with the Big Three, the UAW's contract with the Ford Motor Company in 1955 produced the industry's first supplemental unemployment benefits (SUB) provision. Under the contract, Ford agreed to pay five cents per worker per hour into a fund that would be paid to laid-off workers in the amount of $25 for up to 26 weeks. Combined with government-provided unemployment payments, the SUB meant that workers would receive 65 percent of their regular pay through a half year of unemployment. Later contract negotiations in the auto industry raised the unemployment compensation to 95 percent of take-home pay for up to a year.

Timeline

1935: Second phase of New Deal begins with the introduction of social security, farm assistance, and housing and tax reform.

1940: Hitler's troops sweep through Western Europe, annexing Norway and Denmark in April, and in May the Low Countries and France.

1945: On 7 May, Germany surrenders to the Allies.

1951: Julius and Ethel Rosenberg are convicted and sentenced to death for passing U.S. atomic secrets to the Soviets.

1955: The Warsaw Pact is signed by the Soviet Union and its satellites in Eastern Europe.

1955: African and Asian nations meet at the Bandung Conference in Indonesia, inaugurating the "non-aligned" movement of Third World countries.

1955: Over the course of the year, a number of key ingredients are added to the pantheon of American culture: the 1955 Chevrolet, the first of many classic models; Tennessee Williams's *Cat on a Hot Tin Roof*; Marilyn Monroe's performance in *The Seven-Year Itch*; Disneyland; and Bill Haley and the Comets' "Rock Around the Clock."

1955: Among the year's deaths are Albert Einstein, Thomas Mann, Dale Carnegie, Cy Young, and James Dean.

1955: Rosa Parks refuses to move from her seat near the front of a public bus in Montgomery, Alabama, and is arrested. The incident touches off a boycott of Montgomery's

Henry Ford II. AP/Wide World Photos. Reproduced with permission.

bus system, led by the Rev. Martin Luther King, Jr., which will last well into 1956. The situation will attract national attention and garner support for the civil rights movement, before Montgomery agrees to desegregate its bus system on 21 December 1956—exactly a year after Parks's brave protest.

1958: First U.S. satellite, *Explorer I,* goes into orbit.

1962: As the Soviets begin a missile buildup in Cuba, for a few tense days in October it appears that World War III is imminent. President Kennedy calls for a Cuban blockade, forcing the Soviets to back down and ultimately diffusing the crisis.

1970: President Nixon sends U.S. troops into Cambodia on 30 April. Five days later, National Guardsmen open fire on antiwar protesters at Kent State University in Ohio. By 24 June antiwar sentiment is so strong that the Senate repeals the Gulf of Tonkin resolution. On 29 June, Nixon orders troops back out of Cambodia.

Event and Its Context

While the relatively high wages in the United States attracted millions of immigrant workers to the country in the late nine-

Worker on production line, Ford Motor Company factory. © Hulton/Getty Images. Reproduced by permission.

teenth and early twentieth centuries, unemployment remained a constant worry for American workers. American manufacturers made great strides in technological and administrative developments to maximize the continuous operating capacities of their firms, yet closures for product changes, seasonal maintenance, and downturns in the economy all contributed to the irregularity of industrial employment. The automobile industry typified these patterns. Although auto workers earned some of the highest wages among American industrial workers, most of them faced regular periods of unemployment as plants closed for retooling, product changeovers, or slumping automobile sales. Even after the industry settled into an oligopoly by the 1920s dominated by the Big Three—General Motors (GM), the

Ford Motor Company, and the Chrysler Corporation—auto makers were forced to curtail their employment abruptly during the recession of 1921–1922 and the onset of the Great Depression in 1929.

Unemployment Insurance and a Guaranteed Annual Wage

Progressive Era reformers pointed to the unemployment insurance measures in most of the industrialized countries in Europe as examples for the United States to follow. In Great Britain most labor unions had instituted programs to collect payments from their members to be disbursed during periods of unemployment. After the British government established a

Ford Motor Company's Rouge Plant, Dearborn, Michigan. © Hulton/Getty Images. Reproduced by permission.

state-run unemployment compensation program in 1911, it joined the other European countries that maintained such a program to supplement private unemployment compensation programs. In contrast, both public and private efforts in the United States to ameliorate the distress of unemployment lagged far behind those found in European programs. By 1929 only eight states had enacted any form of unemployment insurance; there was no such federal program in existence. Some trade unions had instituted unemployment relief programs out of funds paid into by their members, but the lengthy economic downturn after 1929 demonstrated the shortcomings of such efforts. Prior to 1933, only 38 companies had inaugurated their own private unemployment insurance plans. Typically, only large corporations such as Eastman Kodak, General Electric, Procter and Gamble, and J. I. Case could afford to fund such schemes, which usually took in 5 percent of an employee's earnings up to one year and matched them with the employer's contribution.

With unemployment reaching 25 percent on the national level and exceeding 50 percent in many industrial communities by 1932, voluntary unemployment assistance proved woefully inadequate to ameliorate the misery of the Great Depression. Elected on a New Deal platform to address the country's eco-

nomic problems, President Franklin D. Roosevelt formulated a number of measures to provide relief and recovery. The 1935 Social Security Act, which established a national pension system, also created a federally supervised unemployment insurance program. Under the act, the federal government took in funds from a payroll tax that it then provided to states to administer to unemployment insurance programs under their own guidelines for recipients.

In the private sector, labor unions also focused on unemployment issues through efforts to organize industrial workers and demand improved wages and benefits, job security, and seniority provisions in collective bargaining. Among the most dynamic labor unions of the era was the International Union, United Automobile, Aerospace and Agricultural Implement Workers of America, or the United Auto Workers union (UAW). After organizing the Big Three between 1937 and 1941, the union became one of the foremost advocates of unemployment relief efforts, particularly through the leadership of Walter P. Reuther. Elected president of the UAW in 1946, Reuther had made headlines during World War II for his "500 Planes a Day" plan for industrial production and emerged from the war as a national spokesman for the labor agenda. One of

Williamson v. Lee Optical and the Death Knell of Substantive Due Process

In the 1955 case of *Williamson v. Lee Optical* (348 U.S. 483), the Supreme Court established limits on interpretation of the "due process" clause in the Fourteenth Amendment. The amendment, ratified in 1868 primarily to protect the civil rights of recently freed slaves from potential infringements by the states, was first tested in 1873. Significantly, that first major due process clause case involved not slaves, but slaughterhouse workers in Louisiana, and ever since the slaughterhouse cases, legal actions involving workers had often involved reference to the clause. Not that the clause, as handled by the Court, was always the friend of labor: for half a century following *Chicago, Milwaukee and St. Paul R.R. Co. v. Minnesota* (1890), the legal concept of "substantive due process" protected businesses against encroachments by government and unions.

During the New Deal years, the implementation of national economic policies began to challenge the idea of substantive due process. In 1955, with *Williamson v. Lee Optical*, the Court was in the midst of a paradigm shift in its views on that concept: gone were the days, as Justice William O. Douglas said, when the Court would use substantive due process on behalf of business people such as the appellee in this case. Instead, a day was dawning when the concept would be applied in favor of other constituencies.

At issue in *Williamson* was an Oklahoma law that prohibited persons other than licensed optometrists and ophthalmologists from fitting lenses for eyeglasses. Though the services of an optician—defined by the Court as "an artisan qualified to grind lenses, fill prescriptions, and fit frames"—would be cheaper, the laws required that this service only be performed by optometrists and ophthalmologists, who are medical doctors and whose services are accordingly more expensive. Lee Optical filed a suit in district court, which found the Oklahoma law unconstitutional under the due process clause. The state, in the person of Attorney General Mac Q. Williamson, appealed, and the case ultimately went before the U.S. Supreme Court.

The unanimous opinion, written by Douglas, announced that "The day is gone when this Court uses the Due Process Clause of the Fourteenth Amendment to strike down state laws . . . because they are unwise, improvident, or out of harmony with a particular school of thought." As for the specific due process questions at issue in *Williamson*, Douglas wrote that these were "answered in principle" by *Roschen v. Ward* (1929), in which the Court upheld a New York law preventing the sale of eyeglasses at a retail outlet without the supervision of a licensed physician or optometrist. The Court at that time had placed its confidence in professionals to uphold the intent of the law: "wherever the requirements of the Act stop, there can be no doubt that the presence and superintendence of the specialist tend to diminish an evil."

It is interesting to note that both *Griswold v. Connecticut* (1965) and *Roe v. Wade* (1973) make mention of *Williamson* in several places. These two cases, the former involving birth control and the latter abortion, were landmarks not only with regard to personal freedom in sexual matters, but in their "new" application of sub-stantive due process. *Williamson*, while seemingly striking the final blow against substantive due process in its business application, came at a time when the concept was finding new life in relation to privacy and personal freedom.

Source: Leonard W. Levy, editor in chief, *Encyclopedia of the American Constitution.* New York: Macmillan, 1986.

—Judson Knight

Reuther's priorities was the establishment of a guaranteed annual wage (GAW) for workers to safeguard them from unemployment during economic downturns. It was not until 10 years into Reuther's term as president, however, that the union finally took steps to implement a GAW provision in its 1955 collective bargaining sessions with the Ford Motor Company.

Ford Motor Company and the UAW

Relations between Ford and the UAW in the 1930s and 1940s had been intensely bitter. Ford was the last of the Big Three auto makers to be organized by the UAW, in large part because of the opposition of its founder, Henry Ford, to labor unions. Ford's antiunion outlook stemmed from his rugged individualism—which stood in direct contrast to a union's collective aims—and was manifested in his employment of virulently antiunion subordinates. The company's service department under Ford lieutenant Harry Bennett was notorious for its violent tactics against the UAW, especially the Battle of the Overpass at Ford's Rouge Plant in Dearborn, Michigan, on 26 May 1937. After Reuther and Richard Frankensteen, another UAW leader, were beaten up by Bennett's thugs, a public uproar tarnished Ford's image at a time when the other major auto manufacturers had already signed agreements with the union. Ford resisted unionization until June 1941, when the company suddenly reversed its course and entered into collective bargaining with the UAW. Although the reasons for the decision remain unclear, some have suggested that Ford's wife, Clara, insisted that the company unionize to avoid further violence. Ford signed its first collective bargaining agreement with the UAW in June 1941.

Ford's grandson, Henry Ford II, assumed leadership of the company in 1945 and attempted to repair labor relations between the company and the UAW. In a nationally publicized speech before the Society of Automotive Engineers in Detroit in January 1946, Ford called for an era of cooperation between management and labor. In an abrupt turnaround from the elder Ford's stance, Henry Ford II's administration soon became the most receptive among the Big Three to the UAW's collective bargaining platform. In September 1949 the company became the first major automobile producer to set up a pension plan for workers. UAW members at Ford could expect a monthly pension of $100 per month upon retirement at age 65 with 30 years of service. The UAW secured similar agreements for workers at Chrysler and GM within a year. In addition to the pension agreements, the UAW successfully negotiated for cost-of-living adjustments beginning with its 1948 contract with GM, which also included a partially paid health insurance plan for GM workers covered by the UAW's agreements.

Postwar Collective Bargaining

As in the debates over unemployment insurance during the Progressive Era, social reformers had also advocated a guaranteed income to alleviate economic insecurity for workers. Reform efforts had few tangible results; although Congress passed an Employment Act in 1946 that declared the federal government responsible for fostering full employment in the nation, the law had only symbolic importance. As the Republican Party eclipsed its Democratic rivals during the early years of the cold war, it was obvious that any extensions of Roosevelt's New Deal or even President Harry Truman's more limited Fair Deal programs would be hard-fought battles.

With the continued prosperity of the American economy through the 1950s, Reuther sensed that the time was right to use collective bargaining as a tool in the campaign for a guaranteed annual wage (GAW) for workers. Reuther never stopped advocating greater government involvement in industrial planning to achieve a guaranteed annual wage in the 1950s, but his most tangible success on the issue came with the UAW's contract with Ford in 1955. By that date negotiations with the Big Three had settled into a fairly predictable pattern; as the largest and most profitable company, GM was usually the target of the biggest requests for wage hikes, whereas Ford, considered the most progressive of the major auto makers in terms of its willingness to negotiate benefits issues, was usually the first to receive requests for new company-funded programs such as pensions.

Before bringing the GAW demand to Ford in the 1955 talks, Reuther first conducted a public relations campaign to highlight the issue. Backed by an array of statistics from the UAW's Research Department, led by Nat Weinberg, Reuther attempted to prove first that employers could afford to pay the GAW and that such a measure would create economic and social stability for the entire nation. Reuther also believed that a GAW policy would force manufacturers to plan their production schedules with more efficiency so as to avoid layoffs. The GAW campaign, then, had both a pragmatic side rooted in economic analysis and a moral dimension oriented toward social welfare.

In the first round of the 1955 talks, Ford's chief bargaining agent, John Bugas, initially rejected Reuther's call for a GAW. Instead, Bugas offered to initiate an interest-free loan program for employees based on their company stock holdings that they had purchased through a stock option program. Reuther countered that the loan program was too complicated and avoided the primary issue of helping laid off workers. After more grandstanding, the UAW and Ford worked out a compromise agreement that fell short of the GAW that Reuther envisioned. Instead, Ford agreed to place five cents per employee per hour

worked into a trust fund. Under a new supplemental unemployment benefits (SUB) program, the trust fund would be dispersed to laid off workers in the amount of $25 for up to 26 weeks. When the SUB payments were added to state unemployment compensation disbursements, it translated into approximately 65 percent of a worker's regular take-home pay. In the subsequent 12 years, four new contracts at Ford increased the SUB to 95 percent of take-home pay and expanded the payment period to a full year. Once Ford had established SUB as part of its benefits package under the UAW contract, the other auto makers had little choice but to follow suit. For industries covered by union contracts, the SUB provision became a standard item in collective bargaining by the early 1960s.

To Reuther's admirers, the SUB agreement demonstrated the labor movement's ability to work constructively with management for the benefit of both parties through collective bargaining. To his critics, the SUB scheme was evidence of how far the union movement had strayed from its responsibility to help all members of society by restructuring the economic and political status quo. Yet the UAW remained one of the foremost advocates of public policies to improve the economic status of all Americans. By the early twenty-first century, the UAW had been a leader in the fight to expand SUB to include workers on family leave; to extend unemployment benefits to victims of domestic violence who had to terminate their employment; to make part-time workers eligible for unemployment benefits; and to exempt unemployment benefits from federal income tax requirements.

Key Players

Ford, Henry II (1917–1987): President of the Ford Motor Company from 1946 to 1960 and chairman of the board from 1960 to 1980, Ford gained a reputation as the most receptive of the Big Three's leaders to collective bargaining talks with labor unions.

Reuther, Walter Philip (1907–1970): President of the UAW from 1946 until his death in 1970 and one of the most influential labor leaders of his era, Reuther was a national spokesman on labor, civil rights, and other political issues and used his leadership to promote a liberal social agenda that culminated in the Great Society programs of the 1960s.

Weinberg, Nat (1914–1985): Head of the UAW's Research Department from 1947 to 1974, when he retired, Weinberg also served as the director of special projects and economic analysis for the UAW from 1957 until his retirement and was a leading advocate of social reforms in the United States and abroad.

See also: *Battle of the Overpass; Ford-UAW Contract; GM Recognizes UAW; GM-UAW Landmark Contracts; Social Security Act.*

BIBLIOGRAPHY

Books

Boyle, Kevin. *The UAW and the Heyday of American Liberalism.* Ithaca, NY: Cornell University Press, 1995.

Salmon Portland Chase. The Library of Congress.

Carew, Anthony. *Walter Reuther*. Manchester, United Kingdom: Manchester University Press, 1993.

Chinoy, Ely. *Automobile Workers and the American Dream*. 1955. Reprint, Urbana: University of Illinois Press, 1992.

Lacey, Robert. *Ford: The Men and the Machine*. New York: Ballantine Books, 1987.

Lichtenstein, Nelson. *The Most Dangerous Man in America: Walter Reuther and the Fate of American Labor*. New York: Basic Books, 1995.

Zieger, Robert. *The CIO, 1935–1955*. Chapel Hill: University of North Carolina Press, 1995.

—Timothy G. Borden

Free Soil Party

United States 1848–1854

Synopsis

Launched in 1848, the Free Soil Party sought to prohibit slavery in new U.S. territories acquired in the Mexican War. An upstart third party in the 1848 election, the Free Soilers made a promising showing with Martin Van Buren as their presidential candidate. Eleven Free Soilers also won congressional seats, but the party was unable to forge a strong, unified rival to the two major parties. Although short-lived, the Free Soilers had an impact on the two major political parties, the Whigs and Democrats, and made the expansion of slavery a national political issue. When the Free Soil Party dissolved in 1854 to join the newly formed Republican Party, its members allied with a party whose platform supported their commitment to prohibit the extension of slavery while maintaining the Union.

Timeline

1850: U.S. Congress passes a series of laws, known collectively as the Compromise of 1850, to address growing divisions over slavery and the disposition of territories acquired in the Mexican War.

1851: Herman Melville publishes *Moby Dick*.

1852: Emigration from Ireland to the United States reaches its peak.

1852: *Uncle Tom's Cabin* by Harriet Beecher Stowe, though far from a literary masterpiece, is a great commercial success, with over half a million sales on both sides of the Atlantic. More important, it has an enormous influence on British sentiments with regard to slavery and the brewing American conflict between North and South.

1853: Commodore Matthew Perry arrives in Japan, and the United States forces the Japanese to permit American trade.

1854: Republican Party is formed by opponents of slavery in Michigan.

1854: "The Charge of the Light Brigade" by Alfred Lord Tennyson and *Walden* by Henry David Thoreau are published.

1855: *Leaves of Grass* by Walt Whitman is published.

1857: In its Dred Scott decision, the U.S. Supreme Court rules that a slave is not a citizen.

1858: In a Springfield, Illinois, speech during his unsuccessful campaign for the Senate against Stephen Douglass, Abraham Lincoln makes a strong case against slavery, maintaining that "this Government cannot endure permanently half-slave and half-free."

1859: American abolitionist John Brown leads a raid on the federal arsenal at Harpers Ferry, Virginia. His capture and hanging in December heighten the animosities that will spark the Civil War sixteen months later.

1859: Retired American railroad conductor Edwin L. Drake drills the first successful oil well in the United States, at Titusville, Pennsylvania.

Event and Its Context

Tensions over the Expansion of Slavery

The Mexican War brought the question of the expansion of slavery to the forefront in politics. The Treaty of Guadalupe Hidalgo, signed in 1848, added 500,000 square miles of land to the United States and stimulated the debate. Stephen Douglas, an Illinois senator, proposed popular sovereignty, which would allow residents of the territories to decide for themselves whether to allow slavery in their region. The plan's ambiguity as to whether territories could decide on the issue at any time or only upon statehood threw the plan into debate. John C. Calhoun, the veteran South Carolina politician, had argued that territories were under congressional authority, and therefore slaveholders could rightfully transport their property to any new territory. He further contended that the territories could only vote on whether to be free or slave upon statehood.

Northerners who were disillusioned with their parties' evasion of the issue of extension of slavery encouraged the formation of the Free Soil Party. In 1848, Salmon P. Chase called a convention in Columbus, Ohio. A leader in the weak Liberty Party, Chase, with other party members, hoped to build a stronger rival party to the Whigs and Democrats that could gain national support for their antiextension platform. The People's Convention brought together Conscience Whigs, Barnburner Democrats, and Liberty Party members. Fraught with internal discord from its beginning, the Free Soil Party nonetheless embarked on a national campaign to rally support. The party was particularly successful in states such as Ohio and Wisconsin. Chase, active in the antislavery movement since the early 1830s, was largely responsible for the party's platform, which articulated a constitutional argument against the federal government's involvement in slavery. Chase argued that slavery was a state issue based on state laws alone, and the constitution prohibited federal intervention. Furthermore, the platform resolved that the founding fathers had sought to limit slavery; therefore, and act of Congress should prevent slavery in the new territories. More broadly, the platform demanded cheap postage, the elimination of unnecessary government offices, river and harbor improvements, and the elimination of the national debt. The party platform concluded with the inscription on the party banner, which read, "Free Soil, Free Speech, Free Labor, and Free Men."

Chase and the Free Soil Party helped convince northerners that slave power controlled the federal government so that it protected slaveholders' interests above all others. Political events of the time seemed to confirm the threat of slave power. The failure of the Wilmot Proviso in the Senate served as one example of southern power in Congress. First introduced in 1846 by Pennsylvania congressman David Wilmot, the amendment banned slavery from any territory that the United States might gain from Mexico. The House of Representatives, which was dominated at the time by northerners, passed the Wilmot Proviso on several occasions, but the southern-controlled Senate repeatedly vetoed it, revealing sectional tensions within Congress.

Free labor ideology was a significant part of the Free Soil campaign. Northerners argued that wage laborers chose their own employers and working conditions. Moreover, the market economy offered mobility, and wage earning was a stage in the process of becoming one's own boss. This reasoning protected republican values, although its logic was problematic and based on white racism. The majority of white northerners wanted to keep all African Americans from the western territories and worried that slaves would not only undermine free white laborers, but that the slave population would grow and eventually compete for jobs. Slaveholders rebuffed the free labor argu-

President Martin Van Buren. The Library of Congress.

ment, defending the system of slavery as a benevolent one that provided for the slave from the "cradle to the grave." The slaveholders argued that this was preferable to the condition of the northern wage laborers who endured precarious living conditions and suffered at the whim of the market and employers and received no compensation when their working days were finished.

Van Buren Takes the Helm

In the presidential election of 1848, both the Whigs and Democrats faced the problem of finding candidates with national appeal. The Democrats nominated Lewis Cass who supported popular sovereignty, and the Whigs nominated General Zachary Taylor, who had made no public statement on the issue of slavery in new territories. Both parties attempted to avoid the issue, but the Free Soil Party's platform in support of the Wilmot Proviso made antiextension part of the national election. With Martin Van Buren as their presidential candidate and Charles Francis Adams running as vice president, Free Soilers hoped to attract both Democrats and Whigs who were disillusioned with their own parties. Embroiled in bitter rivalry within the Democratic Party, disheartened with Polk, and virulently opposed to Lewis Cass, Van Buren accepted the Free Soil nomination. He was convinced that southern influence posed a threat to northerners, and, ironically, after a history of avoiding the issue of slavery, became the presidential nominee for the antiextension party.

Aware that they needed to campaign on more than the Wilmot Proviso, the Free Soil Party sought to attract midwesterners and working-class men from the Democratic Party by promoting federal funds to improve rivers and harbors in the Midwest. Free Soilers counted on appealing to white northerners who saw their settlement in western territories threatened by southern

Charles Sumner. National Archives and Records Administration.

slaveholders. Zachary Taylor won the presidency in 1848, but Van Buren earned 10 percent of the electoral vote, which was a substantial achievement for the nascent party. Despite Van Buren's modest success, he failed to carry a single state.

After the 1848 presidential election, Free Soilers focused on state and local elections and gained 11 seats in Congress. Free Soilers also had some success winning state legislature elections, but political maneuvering to win elections, along with tenuous alliances with Whigs and Democrats to gain some level of power, caused friction within the Free Soil Party. Joshua Giddings and Charles Sumner wanted to retain the Free Soil Party's independence and chafed at Chase's suspect alliance with the Democrats that was designed to win a seat in the Senate. Chase, on the other hand, believed that forging alliances was the only way to achieve the party's political objectives. Van Buren, still a Democrat at heart, never thought of the third party as a permanent solution but viewed it as a way to redirect the Democratic Party. These divisions continued to undermine party cohesion and resulted in fierce battles between Giddings and Chase in Ohio, which greatly weakened the party in that state.

African Americans resoundingly rejected the Free Soil's racist platform. Frederick Douglass, Henry Garnett, and other prominent black abolitionists denounced the party's defense of whites' rights rather than equal rights for all. Many African Americans reluctantly supported the party, however. Some Free Soilers were abolitionists, but for political expediency they focused on containment rather than abolition. In Ohio, Chase and Giddings vigorously lobbied to repeal the state's black codes.

Their success in passing the repeal gave some African Americans hope that Free Soil might benefit blacks in the long run.

Compromises and Alliances

The Compromise of 1850 further exacerbated the problems of Free Soilers. The omnibus bill, which had been created originally by Kentucky Senator Henry Clay, passed Congress piecemeal. The compromise strengthened the 1793 Fugitive Slave Law to allow slaveholders more latitude in the capture of runaway slaves in the North. It also outlawed the slave trade in the nation's capital, although slavery remained legal. Additionally, California was admitted as a free state, and the rest of the land gained from Mexico was organized into two territories, New Mexico and Utah, which would decide to enter as a free slave states by popular sovereignty at the time of statehood. Although the Fugitive Slave Law outraged northerners, the compromise temporarily placated regional conflict.

In the 1852 election, Free Soilers, now calling themselves Free Democrats, ran John P. Hale for president and George Julian for vice president. Franklin Pierce, the Democratic presidential nominee, won the election with more than half the popular vote. Hale only managed 5 percent of the vote—half of what Van Buren had received in 1848. Free Soil was still feeling the results of the Compromise of 1850 and could not find many faithful converts from the two major parties. The two-party system seemed entrenched, and the United States was not ready to accommodate a third, sectional party.

The Kansas-Nebraska Act of 1854 further elevated sectional tensions. The ambitious Stephen Douglas bargained to organize the territories of Kansas and Nebraska. Submitting to pressure from southern congressmen, Douglas replaced a prohibition clause with popular sovereignty, which annulled the Missouri Compromise. Northern outrage exposed problems with the second party system; sectional divisions between the North and South were becoming more rigid. The Republicans emerged as a party of the North in 1854 and quickly garnered support from northern Whigs, Democrats, and Free Soilers. The North was poised to support a sectional political party.

The Free Soil Party's brief existence influenced U.S. politics by exposing divisions within the major parties. Although unable to challenge the two-party system, Free Soil agitation kept the issue of antiextension in public debate, and as events of the antebellum era unfolded, slavery became a significant national issue both economically and politically.

Key Players

Chase, Salmon Portland (1808–1873): Chase was an Ohio attorney who became a Whig city councilman in 1840 and joined the Liberty Party in 1841. Chase helped establish the Free Soil Party in 1848 and served in the Senate from 1849 to 1855, when he became governor of Ohio. He served as secretary of the treasury in Lincoln's cabinet until his appointment as chief justice of the U.S. Supreme Court in 1864.

Giddings, Joshua Reed (1795–1864): An Ohio attorney, Giddings became a state house representative in 1826. He was elected to Congress as a Whig in 1838, and in 1848, he was elected as a Free Soiler. Giddings continued his tenure as a Republican congressman until 1859. In 1861, Lincoln appointed him consul general to the British North American Provinces where he served until his death.

Hale, John Parker (1806–1873): A New Hampshire attorney, Hale was elected to the House in 1832, served as attorney general (1834–1841), and then returned to Congress (1843–1845). Hale refused to vote on the annexation of Texas. He won a seat in the Senate in 1846 as an independent Democrat and remained in the Senate until 1853. In 1852, he ran a failed presidential campaign for the Free Soil Party.

Sumner, Charles (1811–1874): A Massachusetts attorney who declined Whig nomination to Congress in 1846, Sumner helped found the Free Soil Party but lost his bid for a congressional seat that year. Elected to the Senate in 1851, Sumner became a Republican in 1854 and held his Senate seat until his death in 1874. During Reconstruction, Sumner was part of the "Radical Republicans," who were instrumental in advocating universal suffrage for African American men and the passage of the Civil Rights Bill.

Van Buren, Martin (1782–1862): A New York lawyer, Van Buren was elected to the Senate in 1821. Known as "the Little Magician" for his evasiveness, Van Buren rode Jackson's coattails to the presidency in 1836. Van Buren reluctantly accepted the New York Barnburner Democrats' nomination for president on the Free Soil ticket in 1848. He hoped the Barnburners' desertion from the Democratic Party would precipitate the party's redesign.

See also: *Abolition of Slavery, United States.*

BIBLIOGRAPHY

Books

Bilotta, James D. *Race and the Rise of the Republican Party, 1848–1865.* New York: P. Lang, 1992.

Blue, Frederick J. *The Free Soilers: Third Party Politics, 1848–54.* Urbana: University of Illinois Press, 1973.

Foner, Eric. *Free Soil, Free Labor, Free Men: The Ideology of the Republican Party Before the Civil War.* Oxford: Oxford University Press, 1995.

Holt, Michael F. *The Political Crisis of the 1850s.* New York: John Wiley & Sons, Inc., 1978.

Mayfield, John. *Rehearsal for Republicanism: Free Soil and the Politics of Anti-Slavery.* Port Washington, NY: Kennikat Press, 1980.

Smith, Theodore Clarke. *The Liberty and Free Soil Parties in the Northwest.* New York: Russell & Russell, 1967.

—Karla Kelling

Front Populaire: *See* **Popular Front.**

French Labor, World War II

France 1940–1944

Synopsis

In 1940 the German forces of Adolph Hitler's Third Reich occupied France, and the Third Republic collapsed. The puppet Vichy regime dissolved French labor unions, forced collaboration with the Nazis, and deported Jewish workers to Germany. France was divided into free and occupied zones. In 1942 the pro-Hitler regime of Marshal Pétain made French labor available to the German invaders, and French youth were forced into mandatory labor service. From the beginning of the occupation, workers of the disbanded trade unions played a key role in the growing French resistance movement. Starting with individual acts of sabotage against Nazi installations, the French populace developed a network of resistance movements. A strike by Paris police and subway workers preceded the liberation of Paris in August of 1944. The postliberation government restored the labor unions and established the Fourth Republic.

Timeline

1921: As the Allied Reparations Commission calls for payments of 132 billion gold marks, inflation in Germany begins to climb.

1925: Released from Landsberg Prison, Adolf Hitler is a national celebrity, widely regarded as an emerging statesman who offers genuine solutions to Germany's problems. This year, he publishes the first volume of *Mein Kampf* (My Struggle), which he dictated in prison to trusted confederate Rudolf Hess. The second and final volume of Hitler's opus, a mixture of autobiography, "history," and racial rant, will appear two years later.

1931: Financial crisis widens in the United States and Europe, which reel from bank failures and climbing unemployment levels. In London, armies of the unemployed riot.

1936: The election of a leftist Popular Front government in Spain in February precipitates an uprising by rightists under the leadership of Francisco Franco. Over the next three years, war will rage between the Loyalists and Franco's Nationalists. The Spanish Civil War will prove to be a lightning rod for the world's tensions, with the Nazis and Fascists supporting the Nationalists, and the Soviets the Loyalists.

1941: The United States initiates the Manhattan Project to build an atomic bomb and signs the Lend-Lease Act, whereby it provides aid to Great Britain and, later, the Soviet Union.

1942: By executive order of the U.S. president, some 120,000 Japanese Americans are placed in West Coast internment camps.

1943: To offset the costs of war, the U.S. government introduces income tax withholding—which it claims to be a temporary measure.

1944: International Monetary Fund and World Bank is created at Bretton Woods Conference.

Marshal Henri-Philippe Pétain. AP/Wide World Photos. Reproduced by permission.

1945: At the Yalta Conference in February, Roosevelt, Churchill, and Stalin make plans for Germany after its by now inevitable surrender.

1950: United States begins developing the hydrogen bomb.

1955: Over the course of the year, a number of key items are added to the pantheon of American culture: the 1955 Chevrolet, the first of many classic models; Tennessee Williams's *Cat on a Hot Tin Roof*; Marilyn Monroe's performance in *The Seven-Year Itch*; Disneyland; and Bill Haley and the Comets' "Rock Around the Clock."

1961: U.S. President Eisenhower steps down, warning of a "military-industrial complex" in his farewell speech, and 43-year-old John F. Kennedy becomes the youngest elected president in U.S. history. Three months later, he launches an unsuccessful invasion of Cuba at the Bay of Pigs.

Event and Its Context

Labor at Its Pinnacle

French labor unions in the years immediately prior to the Nazi invasion were perhaps at one of the most privileged points in French political and labor history. The first-ever socialist government, led by Prime Minister Léon Blum, had been elected in 1936. The Popular Front of 1936–1938 undertook major

reforms. After a wave of demonstrations and strikes, organized labor won a major battle with the Matignon Agreement of 1936. The agreement, which became law in 1937, established a social safety network (paid holidays and pensions), a 40-hour workweek, and a framework of industrial relations that recognized the right to internal and local representation and to collective bargaining. The new law also paved the way for the minister of labor to make collective agreements binding on all employers, regardless of their employer association affiliations.

Nazi Occupation and Collapse of the Third Republic

French labor's gains came to an abrupt end with the Nazi invasion of May 1940, which displaced millions of civilians. The German Army occupied Paris on 14 June 1940. Although some members of the French armed forces refused to surrender and fled to continue to fight from exile, Marshal Henri-Philippe Pétain signed an armistice with the Germans on 22 June. The Third Republic collapsed, and on 10 July the parliament granted full powers to Pétain as head of state. France was divided into free and occupied zones, and the collaborationist government set up its provisional capital at Vichy. The Pétain government was authoritarian, corporatist, and discriminatory (particularly against Jews), substituting the fascist *Travail, Famille, Patrie* (Work, Family, Fatherland) for the republican trinity of *Liberté, Egalité, Fraternité* (Liberty, Equality, Fraternity). Pétain and Hitler met in the town of Montoire on 24 October 1940, thus officially beginning French collaboration with Nazi Germany. That month the overtly fascist Vichy government, on its own initiative and without prodding from Germany, ordered Jewish ID cards and forced Jewish businesses to identify themselves as such. Meanwhile, General Charles de Gaulle, in a BBC radio address to his compatriots from London on 18 June 1940, called for resistance to the occupation and for the French to keep fighting on the side of the Allies, because "whatever happens, the flame of the French resistance must not and shall not die."

Labor and Leftists Under Attack

Once Pétain became head of state, he immediately attacked his political opponents. In July 1940 came the prohibition of political parties and in August the dissolution of the labor unions. The communist *Confédération Générale du Travail* (CGT) and the French Christian Workers' Confederation (CFTC) were banned. The new regime, beginning in 1942, began to make French laborers available to the Germans. Young men were rounded up for mandatory labor service (*Service du Travail Obligatoire*, STO). Some 75,000 Jews were murdered after deportation to Auschwitz (mostly in the summer of 1942). A similar number of non-Jewish French citizens died in Germany or occupied Poland as POWs, concentration camp inmates, and workers drafted for Germany industry.

The militia hunted down the men who avoided STO (as well as Jews, members of the Resistance, and anyone else opposing the regime). The *Milice*, Vichy's version of the German SS, boasted 150,000 militia members who fought alongside the Nazis. As in Germany, they swore allegiance to the head of state and uttered the oath, "I swear to fight against democracy, against Gaullist insurrection and against Jewish leprosy." Likewise, the Legion of French Volunteers against Bolshevism joined Axis forces on the eastern front. For the next four years, the French worked and lived in dire conditions.

French worker threading coal drill with American threading machine made available under Marshall Plan, Lorraine, France. AP/Wide World Photos. Reproduced by permission.

As a leftist of Jewish origin, former prime minister Léon Blum was an immediate target of the Vichy government, which arrested him in 1940. In his war-guilt trial at Riom in February 1942, Blum defended his labor policy. He told his accusers that the Matignon Agreements were, apart from a means of stimulating demand for goods and services, a necessary price to pay to end strikes. His powerful defense made the Vichy government uneasy and so irked the Germans that the hearings were suspended and he was sent back to prison. U.S. troops freed him from a German concentration camp in 1945.

Worker Resistance

Opposition began almost as soon as the occupation, with a few thousand active insurgents in December 1940. At first, isolated individuals sabotaged Nazi installations. As the Gestapo began rounding up socialists and communists, many former trade unionists fled to forests or unoccupied zones and gradually formed into units of internal resistance, which were based on geographical location and political beliefs. As a new French army formed in French North Africa (liberated in November 1942), internal resistance groups known as *Maquis* joined into

France's General Confederation of Labor

Among the French labor organizations shut down in 1940 by the Nazis and the collaborationist Vichy regime was the General Confederation of Labor, or *Confédération Générale du Travail* (CGT). At that time the largest French labor federation, the CGT has had a bumpy history of alternating turns toward moderation and radicalism.

Founded in 1895, the CGT in 1902 merged with the syndicalist Federation of Labor Exchanges *(Fédération des Bourses du Travail)*. In the next few years, it experienced considerable internal conflict between socialists, syndicalists, and others, before the syndicalists took control in 1906. Membership declined thereafter until socialist Léon Jouhaux took the leadership in 1909.

Jouhaux would remain at the helm of the CGT until 1947, presiding over some of its most trying years. During World War I the newly moderate CGT supported the French war effort, and in 1921 it expelled all of its communist, syndicalist, and anarchist unions. The latter responded by forming the Unitary General Confederation of Labor *(Confédération Générale du Travail Unitaire,* or CGTU), which fell under Soviet control.

At a time when anarchists and syndicalists—and, for that matter, labor unionists—were fodder for Stalin's slave-labor camps, communists in democratic countries were under orders to make common cause with friendly leftists, including anarchists, syndicalists, and even trade unionists and liberals. This set the blueprint for the Popular Front strategy, which in the French labor movement was reflected by the merging of the CGT and CGTU in 1936. After the Nazi/Vichy interregnum of 1940–44, French labor became increasingly dominated by communists, who were no longer required to maintain the illusion of the Popular Front. By 1945 their power in the CGT was sufficient that one of their own, Benôit Frachon, became co-secretary-general with Jouhaux.

Jouhaux, having had enough of the communists, departed the CGT with a large body of moderate socialists to form the *Force Ouvrière* (Workers' Force) in 1947. He helped found the anticommunist International Confederation of Free Trade Unions in 1949, and in 1951 received the Nobel Peace Prize. As for the CGT, it continued to be aligned with the French Communist Party and the communist-infiltrated World Federation of Trade Unions. From the late 1970s onward, its membership began to decline dramatically.

Source: Tony Judt. *Marxism and the French Left: Studies in Labour and Politics in France, 1830–1981.* New York: Clarendon Press, 1986.

—Judson Knight

a network that gained increasing popular support. With 6 percent of the French population made up of foreigners, many thousands of immigrants were also active in the struggle.

One important resistance group was the *Armée Secret* (oriented toward the Socialist Party), whose primary objective was the execution of traitors and Gestapo agents. The group's second goal was to cut railway lines so as to derail enemy trains. It also aimed to cut enemy telegraphic installations. To stop production at key factories or groups of factories, the group defended cutting high-tension networks and engaging in industrial sabotage. In January 1941 radical Socialist Party members formed the *Comité d'Action Socialiste.*

Although the French Communist Party (PCF) leadership was originally stalled by the German-Soviet nonaggression pact, thousands of rank-and-file party members and trade union militants (more interested in revolutionary struggle than in defending the status quo of the republic) were taking up arms against the Nazis and their French collaborators. The PCF leadership, which viewed the conflict as being between French and German imperialisms, often had these party dissidents assassinated by the *Organisation Secrete.* When Germany attacked the Soviet Union in 1941, however, the PCF adopted an overtly anti-German stance. That year, the *Francs Tireurs Partisans* (Partisan Snipers, FTP) resistance movement formed, comprising mainly trade unionists who were tied to the PCF. The FTP engaged in sabotage of industry and infrastructure. The group, led by Charles Tillon, later formed the military wing of the *Front National,* which appeared in May 1942.

Members of the PCF/FTP and the CGT had been pioneers in late-nineteenth-century revolutionary syndicalism and thus had a history of revolutionary activity. FTP units in rural areas were practically isolated from PCF leadership. Their grassroots political activities often put them further left than the PCF (which nonetheless advocated resistance through direct action and sabotage). In the Haute-Vienne area of Vichy France, FTP Maquis actively involved local peasants and encouraged local political activity (thus defying PCF leadership). Stealing dynamite from mines, local units blew up bridges, railroads, and telephone lines. They also targeted the hay bailing machines that peasants used before shipping hay. The Maquis fought the wartime black market by setting price ceilings and fined those who violated them. Following the dissolution of the Comintern in 1943, the PCF's Stalinist leadership dealt the ultimate blow to rank-and-file militants: they joined the (right-leaning) Gaullist *Conseil National de la Resistance* (National Resistance Council, CNR).

National Resistance Council

Jean Moulin, General de Gaulle's envoy to occupied France, arrived in the spring of 1943 to unite key resistance groups into the CNR. The CNR charter, published on 15 March 1944, demanded economic and social reforms for postliberation France. It demanded independent trade unions, universal suffrage, and equality for all citizens (as well as rights for colonial citizens). It demanded social security, a minimum wage, and worker participation in management. The CNR served as the base of the provisional government of the French Republic.

Massive Strikes and the Liberation of Paris

On 10 August 1944 striking railroad workers paralyzed the country. On Tuesday, 15 August, Paris police and metro workers went on strike, thus setting off a series of strikes and mass insurrection. On Wednesday, 16 August, postal workers struck. On Thursday, Radio Paris halted transmissions. On Friday, PTT (Post, Telephone, and Telegraph) workers went on strike and there was no edition of the pro-Vichy press; walls of Paris were covered with posters and notices proclaiming a general mobilization calling for insurrection. On Saturday, 19 August, the first combat of the insurrection began, and Pétain fled Vichy under German escort. Days of street fighting followed. Although many working-class militants wanted class insurrection against both the Nazis and the employing class, the PCF stated that the struggle should be limited to stopping fascism.

On 25 August 1944 General Leclerc and his troops liberated Paris. French and Allied forces that had aided in freeing Paris retook the rest of France and continued on to fight the Nazis until the Germans surrendered the following year. The Vichy government was replaced, and on 31 August the provisional government transferred to Paris, where it attempted to comply with the CNR charter by granting universal suffrage, improved social security, and nationalization of key industries. Labor returned to the national scene. The *Confédération Générale des Cadres* (CGC), which appeared in 1944, was a moderate, largely apolitical union representing the upper echelon of white-collar workers. In 1945 the *Conseil National du Patronat Français* (CNPF), the main employers' association, was established. The constitution of 1946 recognized the rights of all individuals to defend their rights and demands through union activity and to join the union of their choice.

Key Players

Blum, Léon (1872–1950): Blum was the leader of French socialism who, in 1936, led the Popular Front coalition of communists and radical and moderate socialists to national power. His short-lived government oversaw numerous advances for labor. His Jewish roots made him a special target of the Vichy government, which imprisoned him from 1940 until the end of the war.

De Gaulle, Charles André Joseph Marie (1890–1970): General and leader of the Free French movement who was the symbol of resistance outside of France, De Gaulle urged the French to continue fighting on the side of the Allies. He served as president of the provisional government in 1945, resigning in 1946. He later became the first president of the Fifth Republic (1959–1969).

Pétain, Henri-Philippe (1856–1951): Marshal Pétain, a French hero of World War I, was prime minister of the pro-Nazi government of Vichy, France (1940–1944). His alliance with Adolf Hitler entailed forced French labor. The Allied victory of 1945 brought him a death sentence, which was later commuted to life imprisonment.

Tillon, Charles (1897–1993): Tillon was a life-long militant in the French Communist Party (PCF). The PCF was dissolved in September 1939, and in June 1941 Tillon led the clandestine *Francs Tireurs Partisans* (FTP) in guerilla resistance against the Vichy government as chief of the national military committee.

See also: *Confédération Générale du Travail; Popular Front.*

BIBLIOGRAPHY

Periodicals

Jenkins, Gareth. "The Forgotten Fighters." *Socialist Review*, no. 187 (1995).

Other

"Biography: Leon Blum." The World at War [cited 22 October 2002]. <http://worldatwar.net/biography/b/blum/>.

Callaghan, John. "Globalisation: The End of Social Democracy?" [cited 22 October 2002]. <http://www.essex.ac.uk/ecpr/jointsessions/turin/papers/ws11/callaghan.pdf>.

"Chronology of the Liberation." The Paris Pages. 2001 [cited 22 October 2002]. <http://www.paris.org/Expos/Liberation/chronoA.html>.

"From the French Revolution to Today." John F. Kennedy Catholic School, Hertfordshire (UK) [cited 22 October 2002]. <http://www.jfk.herts.sch.uk/class/french/ks5/hist1_gb.html>.

Lagrou, Pieter. "Representations of War in Western Europe, 1939–1945" [cited 22 October 2002]. <http://www.oslo2000.uio.no/program/papers/s20/s20-lagrou.pdf>.

Reshef, Yonatan. "The Evolution of IR/HRM in France." University of Alberta (Canada) Web site [cited 22 October 2002]. <http://courses.bus.ualberta.ca/orga417-reshef/france.htm>.

"Tillon, Charles." *Biographies des Contemporains*. Web site of Charles de Gaulle.org. [cited 22 October 2002]. <http://www.charles-de-gaulle.org/degaulle/biographies/tillon.htm>.

—Brett Allan King

G

Gabriel's Rebellion

United States 1800

Synopsis

Gabriel, a slave born on a plantation near Richmond, was a blacksmith who could read and write. Inspired by an earlier successful rebellion on Haiti, he masterminded the first U.S. slave rebellion in 1800. Using the communication network fostered by social and religious gatherings, Gabriel and his supporters spread the plans for a mass uprising in which the slaves planned to march into Richmond and take control of weaponry from the arsenal then attack the whites of the city. Weather and betrayal foiled the plot, and Gabriel and more than 40 other slaves were hanged for their part in the uprising. Ultimately, the rebellion contributed to the process of questioning the basic assumptions about slave capabilities and prerogatives that eventually lent force to abolitionist arguments.

Timeline

1775: American Revolution begins with the battles of Lexington and Concord, and delegates from each of the 13 American colonies meet for the Second Continental Congress.

1787: Constitution of the United States is signed.

1789: French Revolution begins with the storming of the Bastille.

1790: The first U.S. census reports a population of about 3,929,000, including 698,000 slaves.

1793: Eli Whitney patents his cotton gin—a machine that, by making cotton profitable, spurs the expansion of slave labor in the southern United States.

1800: The world's population reaches 870 million.

1800: The United States moves its federal government to Washington, D.C.

1800: British astronomer William Herschel discovers infrared rays, and Italian physicist Alessandro Volta develops the voltaic cell, an early form of battery.

1802: France, under the direction of Napoleon Bonaparte, revokes a 1794 decree emancipating the slaves of Haiti; reintroduces slavery to that colony; and imprisons slave revolt leader Toussaint L'Ouverture.

1803: Administration of President Thomas Jefferson negotiates the Louisiana Purchase from France, whereby the United States doubles its geographic size, adding some 827,000 square miles (2,144,500 sq km)—all for the price of only $15 million.

1808: U.S. Congress bans the importation of slaves.

1810: Revolts begin in South America, initiating the process whereby colonies will win their freedom from Spain and other European colonial powers.

Event and Its Context

The Economic Climate

In a period of revolution—in America, France, Ireland, and Haiti—the first slave rebellion, led by Gabriel, deserves special attention, for it brought the elements of organization into the most backward workplace: the plantations of Virginia.

Gabriel was born a slave in 1776 on the tobacco plantation of Thomas Prosser, in Henrico County, southwest of Richmond, Virginia. By the age of 10, he was trained, along with his brother Solomon, as a blacksmith and, remarkably, had learned to read and write. His great physical strength, his artisan status, and his literacy mingled with an intense desire to free the slaves made him a natural leader.

In 1798, Thomas Prosser died and the control of the plantation passed to his son, Thomas Henry Prosser, just as a period of economic hardship struck the plantation economy. Prosser responded in disparate ways: by cruelly driving his slaves while allowing some of the skilled artisans like Gabriel to self-hire themselves out in Richmond for wages. Even though the Virginia legislature had passed laws to restrict the hiring of slaves, the laws were seldom enforced because local merchants relied on skilled self-hire slaves, who worked more cheaply than white tradesmen.

The period of 1780–1800 was a time of dramatic change in Richmond, as it became the center of a thriving regional economy. Plantations, which had once been isolated and self-sufficient entities, now shipped and bought commodities from Richmond. Slaves transported these good back and forth from the plantations while other blacks, both slave and free, had positions as boatmen guiding wooden skiffs on the regional rivers and canals. These boatmen were so important that, during the rebellion, Governor James Monroe was reluctant to ship weapons to outlying areas on the skiffs because he feared that the pilots would turn over the weapons to the rebels.

As a growing urban area, Richmond had a significant African American population. According to the federal census in 1800, slaves constituted 47 percent of Virginia's population, with a higher percentage in the Richmond area. Within the city, 20 percent of blacks were free. This created a large community in which slaves, free blacks and poor whites lived, worked, worshipped, and even socialized together. Extensive communication networks proliferated among the slaves; individual slaves and those attending mass meetings such as religious services or social events relayed news and messages.

Coming to Leadership

Gabriel gained prominence in 1799, when he and Solomon tried to steal a pig from a nearby tenant farmer named Absolom

349

Denmark Vesey

In the same year that Gabriel Prosser led and died in his famous revolt, another slave bought his freedom from his master. This was Denmark Vesey of Charleston, South Carolina. About thirty-three years old at the time of gaining his freedom, Vesey then worked for many years as a carpenter, but he became so troubled by the fact that so many around him were still in chains that eventually he organized a revolt.

By 1822 Vesey had enlisted some 9,000 slaves in a complex network of information cells. They planned to attack several cities in South Carolina at once in a revolt that would have certainly been a history-making event— if it had occurred. Instead, several slaves who were privy to information concerning the planned uprising informed their masters, and Vesey and the other conspirators were arrested.

At the prospect of imprisonment and torture, one of Vesey's lieutenants, Peter Poyas, is said to have instructed his men, "Do not open your lips. Die silent as you shall see me do." In the end, only one of the co-conspirators gave any information to the authorities. Vesey, Poyas, and the others were hanged on 2 July 1822.

Source: David Robertson, *Denmark Vesey.* New York: Alfred A. Knopf, 1999.

—Judson Knight

Johnson. When Johnson caught the brothers, he fought with Gabriel, who beat him and also bit off part of Johnson's left ear. Gabriel was "tried" in the Oyer and Terminer court, where disputes were heard without a jury, and was sentenced to 39 lashes; in addition, his left thumb was branded.

With this notoriety, Gabriel began to organize for the rebellion in the spring of 1800. If there were a good time for such a dangerous plan, the year of 1800 provided it. The state of Virginia was seething with the presidential campaign between native son Thomas Jefferson and John Adams in a campaign to define the "life, liberty and the pursuit of happiness" promised by the American Revolution. Gabriel even hoped—incorrectly, as it turned out—that Governor Monroe might be sympathetic to a movement by the slaves to free themselves.

A possible naval war with France and disputes with Native Americans on the state's borders distracted the government. During the summer of 1800, as part of his evaluation of the state's military preparedness, Governor Monroe compelled the county militias to collect all weapons and turn them in for reconditioning to the Richmond penitentiary, which was temporarily transformed into an arsenal. At the same time, the state purchased 4,000 new muskets, which were also stored in the arsenal. This prompted Gabriel to focus on this building as he planned his rebellion. Visiting Richmond on Sundays, he gained access to the keys with the intention of arming the rebellious slaves.

One inspiration for Gabriel was the successful rebellion of the slaves on the island of St. Domingue, which had been led by a coachman named Toussaint; always able to find *l'overature*, or the opening, it became his historical surname. On 1 August 1789, after hearing of the events in France, the slaves rose up in a rebellion that was brutally put down by the authorities after the rebels burned 6000 coffee estates and 200 sugar plantations. Several years later, the rebels were more successful and, assisted by Spanish military, they drove out the French troops, repelled counter-attacks by the French and British, and established the continent's first black government.

Toussaint L'Overature established a civilian government on the island, called Haiti, with uniform currency and courts of law. Emigrants from Haiti, both white and black, came to Virginia to spread the word of this successful slave rebellion and black government.

The Campaign

Gabriel traveled the countryside in the spring of 1800 to gather recruits for the rebellion. Some slaves joined for simple revenge against cruel owners, and others were attracted by a plan to seize the state treasury. In general, the simple the desire for freedom roused to action the slaves, free blacks, and even some free whites. Gabriel often spoke of creating a silk flag bearing the motto "Death or Liberty," as an echo of both Patrick Henry and of the Whiskey Rebellion, which had raged across the frontiers of Virginia in 1790.

Supported by his brother Solomon and by Jack Ditcher, the recruiting expanded. Another of Prosser's slaves, named Ben, and Ben Woolfolk, both of whom would subsequently turn on the rebellion in exchange for mercy, joined the campaign.

Although not a religious visionary in the manner of Nat Turner, Gabriel used religious gatherings for organizing, as slaves gathered to practice a religion that combined elements of African worship with religious practices of the Great Awakening. Although white religion often preached submission to the slave owner, the slaves' practices emphasized the vengeful stories of the Old Testament in which oppressed tribes either rose up or fled their masters. A favorite passage at these meetings was Leviticus 26:8: "And five of you shall chase an hundred, and an hundred of you shall put ten thousand to flight: and your enemies shall fall before you by the sword."

The rebels indeed began to gather swords, breaking plowshares in half so that blacksmiths like Gabriel and Solomon could sharpen them and add handles.

Gabriel set 30 August 1800 as the date for the rebellion. The slaves were to gather at Brook Bridge, about six miles outside Richmond, and march toward the city. The plan called for the slaves to kill all whites encountered along the way to protect the secrecy of their movement, although the plans allowed sparing white Quakers, Methodist, French, and other abolitionists.

When the slaves entered Richmond, the plans called for the rebels to divide into three columns: one would set fires in the warehouse district, called Rocketts, to divert the attention of the whites while the rest of the rebels seized the arsenal and captured the weapons. As they returned from Rocketts, the armed rebels would then attack the whites and spread the word. They hoped to incite similar slave rebellions in Norfolk and Petersburg, which had been drawn into the communications network over the summer. There was also some hope that the rebellion would be joined by poor whites in Richmond and by the Catawba Indians, who lived on the frontiers, and even a distant possibility that the French might provide military assistance.

Two factors defeated the rebellion. A torrential rainstorm hit the area in the afternoon, washing out bridges and making it impossible for the rebels to travel from Henrico County into Richmond. At twilight, Gabriel decided to postpone the rebellion for one day, so the slaves tried to return to their plantations undiscovered.

More important, in late morning on 30 August, two slaves of Mosby Shepherd named Pharaoh and Tom confessed to their master about the planned rebellion. Shepherd frantically worked to get a message to Governor Monroe, who then raised the militia to patrol the area around the Prosser plantation. Patrols covered the countryside, picking up any suspected conspirators; within several days, more than 30 slaves had been jailed in Richmond. A series of "trials" began in the Oyer and Terminer Court on 11 September. To reward their loyalty to their master, Shepherd freed both Tom and Pharaoh after the rebellion was crushed.

The Aftermath

Gabriel escaped. Governor Monroe issued a warrant for his arrest, with a bounty of $300. The warrant described Gabriel as "a Negro of brown complexion about 6 feet 3 or 4 inches high, a bony face, well made and very active, has two or three scars on his head, his hair is very short . . . . He can read and write and perhaps will forge himself a pass, or certificate of his freedom."

After hiding out in Richmond for a week, Gabriel escaped down the Chickahominy River toward Norfolk. He swam out to the schooner *Mary* in the middle of the river, hoping to convince her captain, a former plantation overseer named Richardson Taylor, to carry him out of the country. Lured by the bounty, however, two men on the *Mary*, a slave named Isham and a free black named Billy, alerted authorities when the boat docked in Norfolk. Gabriel was captured and brought back to Richmond in chains.

The authorities interviewed Gabriel but postponed his execution in the hope that he would identify other conspirators. The rebel leader refused and was hanged alone on the Richmond gallows at 15th and Broad Streets on 10 October 1800. According to legend, his last words were, "I have nothing more to offer than what General Washington would have had to offer, had he been taken by the British and put to trial by them. I have adventured my life in endeavoring to obtain the liberty of my countrymen, and am willing to sacrifice to their cause; and I beg as a favour, that I may be immediately led to execution. I know that you have pre-determined to shed my blood, why then all this mockery of a trial?"

Eventually more than 70 slaves were tried and 44 were hanged, often near to plantations as a public spectacle intended to intimidate the other slaves. Some rebels were "transported," or sold south, and a few were declared innocent. By Virginia law, the state had to compensate the owners for executed or transported slaves, so the owners received the enormous sum,

for the time, of $8,900. It is impossible to determine a final count of slaves who participated in Gabriel's rebellion; figures range from 200 to 5,000.

The Legacy

The consequences of Gabriel's rebellion were extraordinary, depending upon which side one supports. The white ruling class became watchful for signs of other uprisings, even though many officials publicly claimed that the slaves were too ignorant to organize themselves. States expanded their police and spy systems and even permitted private patrols to cover the countryside. Thomas Jefferson, who owned 185 slaves, used money and favors to bribe some slaves to act as spies; other slave owners publicly offered freedom to slaves who betrayed plans for rebellion. The government tightened the Black Codes, especially to prohibit slaves from learning to read and write.

For slaves, resistance to slavery took both individual and collective forms. Individual acts such as sabotage, murder, or running away were paralleled by successive generations of slave rebels, most famously Denmark Vesey and Nat Turner, who learned of Gabriel's rebellion from oral history. The goal of seizing weapons and arming the slaves for a rebellion, of course, was the dream of John Brown as he made his raid on Harpers Ferry.

The rebellion encouraged the abolitionists, both north and south, but also alarmed many of them, as the vision of slaves, armed and rising, was as frightening as the institution of slavery itself.

Ultimately, the slave uprisings challenged the myths of the happy and submissive slave, loyal to the plantation, and of the ignorant African, for whom slavery was a step up in civilization. Under pressure from southern historians who supported the life of the Confederacy, several more generations passed before the strength and courage of rebels like Gabriel were recognized and celebrated.

Key Players

Gabriel (1776–1800): An educated blacksmith slave, Gabriel led Virginia's largest slave rebellion in August 1800. Touring the countryside, he roused hundreds of slaves to join an invasion of Richmond, but was defeated by a heavy rainstorm that made roads impassable and by slaves who informed their masters of his plans. He was hanged on 10 October 1800.

See also: *Abolition of Slavery, United States; Harper's Ferry Raid.*

BIBLIOGRAPHY

Books

Aptheker, Herbert. *American Negro Slave Revolts.* New York: Columbia University Press, 1943.

Bontemps, Arna. *Black Thunder.* New York: Macmillan, 1936.

Egerton, Douglas. *Gabriel's Rebellion: The Virginia Slave Conspiracies of 1800 and 1802.* Chapel Hill: University of North Carolina Press, 1993.

John L. Lewis. AP/Wide World Photos. Reproduced by permission.

Sidbury, James. *Ploughshares into Swords: Race, Rebellion, and Identity in Gabriel's Virginia, 1730–1810.* (New York: Cambridge University Press, 1997)

Periodicals

Tang, Joyce. "Enslaved African Rebellions in Virginia." *Journal of Black Studies* 27, no. 5 (1997): 598–614.

—Bill Barry

Gallup Coal Strike

United States 1933–1934

Synopsis

In August 1933 miners in Gallup, New Mexico, walked out on strike against the coal producers. Although the strike began peacefully, the state governor declared martial law and used National Guard troops to seal off the town for five months. The strike ended in early 1934 when the miners and the coal companies reached a settlement, although not all of the miners returned to work. In the aftermath of the strike, a riot erupted on 4 April 1935, and after a sensational trial union members were convicted for the murder of the county sheriff and two other men.

Timeline

1919: With the formation of the Third International (Comintern), the Bolshevik government of Russia establishes its control over Communist movements worldwide.

1924: In the United States, Secretary of the Interior Albert B. Fall, along with oil company executives Harry Sinclair and Edward L. Doheny, is charged with conspiracy and bribery in making fraudulent leases of U.S. Navy oil reserves at Teapot Dome, Wyoming. The resulting Teapot Dome scandal clouds the administration of President Warren G. Harding.

1929: On "Black Friday" in October, prices on the U.S. stock market, which had been climbing wildly for several years, suddenly collapse. Thus begins the first phase of a world economic crisis and depression that will last until the beginning of World War II.

1931: Financial crisis widens in the United States and Europe, which reel from bank failures and climbing unemployment levels. In London, armies of the unemployed riot.

1934: Austrian chancellor Engelbert Dollfuss, who aligns his nation with Mussolini's Italy, establishes a fascist regime in an attempt to keep Austria out of the Nazi orbit. Austrian Nazis react by assassinating Dollfuss.

1934: Dionne sisters, the first quintuplets to survive beyond infancy, are born in Canada.

1937: Japan attacks China, and annexes most of that nation's coastal areas.

1939: After years of loudly denouncing one another (and quietly cooperating), the Nazis and Soviets sign a non-aggression pact in August. This clears the way for the Nazi invasion of Poland, and for Soviet action against Finland. (Stalin also helps himself to a large portion of Poland.)

1942: Axis conquests reach their height in the middle of this year. The Nazis control a vast region from Normandy to the suburbs of Stalingrad, and from the Arctic Circle to the edges of the Sahara. To the east, the Japanese "Co-Prosperity Sphere" encompasses territories from China to Burma to the East Indies, stretching deep into the western Pacific.

1945: April sees the death of three leaders: Roosevelt passes away on 12 April; the Italians execute Mussolini and his mistress on 28 April; and Hitler (along with Eva Braun, propaganda minister Josef Goebbels, and Goebbels's family) commits suicide on 30 April.

1949: North Atlantic Treaty Organization (NATO) is established.

Event and Its Context

A Frontier Coal Town

Gallup, New Mexico, was founded in the nineteenth century along the westward route of the Atlantic and Pacific Railroad by rail workers who stayed behind to mine the rich coalfields of McKinley County. These twin interests—coal and railroading—were reflected in Gallup's geography, for the main street in town, Railroad Avenue, ran parallel to Coal Avenue one block south. For many of Gallup's citizens, these streets symbolized the deep cultural and racial divisions that would threaten to tear the community apart in the mid-1930s, for they formed the boundaries that divided the moneyed, Anglo district that controlled the railroads and mines from the poorer neighborhoods, home mostly to Mexican immigrants who descended daily into the mines.

Despite the hardships of mining, the people of Gallup, even many of the miners themselves, had always been ambivalent about labor unions. Unions were "eastern," but Gallup saw itself as a frontier town that did not need unions. Unions carried a foreign, even communist, taint; indeed, a Gallup resident could turn onto Railroad Avenue and follow the fabled Route 66 to Chicago and the offices of the Industrial Workers of the World (IWW, the "Wobblies"), a radical labor organization that had led strikes in the coal mines of the Rockies and the lumber camps of the Pacific Northwest. Militant IWW unionists, such as William Haywood of the Western Federation of Miners and socialist Eugene V. Debs, would have been alien figures to the citizens of this dusty western coal town that prided itself on not being like "uppity" Albuquerque to the east.

Nevertheless, in 1917 the United Mine Workers (UMW) succeeded in negotiating a labor contract with one of Gallup's big coal companies, the Victor American Fuel Company. The town's other big mine, run by the Gallup American Coal Company, was not unionized, so the UMW called a strike. Gallup American responded by bringing in strikebreakers, primarily Mexicans, and allowed them to build adobe houses and shacks on its land on the town's western edge in a district that came to be known as *Chihuahuaita*. This community, which eventually housed about a hundred families, would become the epicenter of the controversy that led to violence in 1935.

The UMWA Versus the National Miners Union

By the mid-1930s, John L. Lewis had been president of the UMW for over a decade. Faced with declining membership throughout the 1920s, he seized on the National Industrial Recovery Act of 1933, with its encouragement of organized labor, to launch a major membership drive and rebuild the UMW into a large and powerful union. Although the UMW had been representing some of the miners in Gallup since 1917, in the spring of 1933 the rival National Miners Union (NMU) won recognition by the Gallup miners. As a result of grievances over recent wage cuts and the low wages paid for "deadwork," or nonmining maintenance work, the union called a strike. On 29 August 1933 Gallup American workers climbed out of their mines. In sympathy, workers in the other mines followed suit, and picket lines formed at each of the five major mines in town. The NMU claimed that 970 out of about 1,000 workers had joined the union and walked the picket lines.

Response to the strike forms a case study on how simple fear can affect political decisions. State politicians and local business leaders were nervous. It was the decade not only of the Great Depression but of "Red scares" as economic distress opened the way for the Communist Party, a fringe element in the 1920s, to move closer to the mainstream of American politics and invigorate organized labor. That the NMU was markedly more radical than the UMW was confirmed by a local assistant administrator of the National Recovery Administration, who declared that the NMU was "linked to the Communist Party." Everyone from Governor Arthur Seligman to the Gallup American Legion post feared the influence of communism in the town's affairs. Memories were still fresh of 1928, when martial law had been declared in response to a strike in Colfax County, New Mexico, led by the radical Wobblies.

Seligman had considerable assistance in deciding how to respond to the strike. Lewis, who had been chafing under the NMU's recent organizing victory and had been watching closely as events unfolded, contacted the governor and offered his help. In his telegram he reminded the governor of the ties between the NMU and the Communist Party and wrote, "The policy ought to be for the mine operators in Gallup to make an agreement directly with the UMW and encourage a union which is committed to upholding of American institutions." At the same time the McKinley County sheriff, Gallup's mayor, and several local mine managers sent telegrams predicting "bloodshed and probable loss of life and damage to property." Accordingly, the strike had been under way for just one day, without violence, when Seligman declared martial law and called in the National Guard.

Temporary Truce

In the weeks and months that followed, tensions ran high. Children walked to and from school under the eyes of 300 armed troops. Checkpoints and search warrants became commonplace. Some union leaders were jailed for violating curfew. A "mass gathering ordinance" required a permit for meetings of five or more people; because permits were routinely denied to strikers, the union held meetings across the border in Arizona and picketers strung themselves out along the roads in groups of three or four. The UMW offered membership to those who crossed the picket lines, so technically they were not "scabs," but because many of them were Mexican, racial slurs directed against them were common. Children who had formerly crossed the divide to play together no longer did so. American Communist Party publications enflamed the situation by calling the strike a victory for "the new proletarian spirit created by the Depression in America."

Seligman died suddenly on 25 September, leaving his successor, vice governor Andrew Hockenhull, with a dilemma: National Guard units were costing the state $80,000 a day, but if he withdrew them and the mines shut down, the state would lose sizable tax revenues. Determined to relieve the town from martial law, he dispatched prominent representatives to Gallup to resolve the strike. Finally, the parties worked out a settlement that increased the miners' wages from $4.48 to $4.70 per day. The companies agreed to rehire about 100 of the 400 miners who were still out on strike, though they later reneged on that pledge. The jailed union leaders agreed to leave the state. Finally, on 31 January 1934, Hockenhull lifted martial law, but the peace was uneasy.

The Aftermath

Gallup had survived coal strikes before, but it was the aftermath of this strike that remained seared on the town's consciousness for decades. Despite the new wage agreement, many miners did not return to work, for although the smaller mines adhered to the wage agreement, Gallup American did not and remained closed. Animosities festered as some members of the community thought that the miners were acting unreasonably in turning down work paying nearly five dollars a day during the Great Depression. The plight of the striking miners, many of whom were blacklisted by the companies, deteriorated when at about this time the NMU dissolved at the national level. The Gallup local struggled on under local leadership, but in the spring of 1935 it faced a decision: either continue as a weak local union or join the UMW. A meeting convened on the morning of 3 April 1935 to discuss the details of a merger with the UMW, but many of the union's members arrived with another issue on their minds.

The issue was the fate of Chihuahuaita. Since 1917 the miners who lived there had paid a modest ground rent of 10 to 15 dollars a year. In 1935 workers who continued to strike occupied most of the homes. For the companies' part, one way to finally break the strike would be to force these miners out of their homes. Accordingly, Gallup American sold about 110 acres of Chihuahuaita to state senator Clarence Vogel, who then offered to sell lots back to the striking miners on a payment plan of $10 to $15 *a month*. Worse, any buyer who defaulted on a single payment would forfeit all payments made to that point. In the meantime, Vogel introduced a bill in the legislature that would have made it easier to foreclose on defaulting debtors. In the eyes of many people, the scheme was a thinly disguised attempt to break the strike with the collusion of a state legislator.

In time Vogel served eviction notices on three residents. When they failed to vacate, they were jailed. The NMU came to their defense, and discussion of the issue was heated during the meeting of 3 April 1935. On 4 April a bitterly angry crowd gathered in town in an effort to free the men. Gunfire erupted, and the sheriff and two other persons lay dead in the streets. One hundred eighty union members were arrested, 48 were jailed, 14 were arraigned, and 10—all Mexican—were bound over on murder charges.

In October 1935 those 10 were tried in an atmosphere rife with charges of "agitation," "communism," "Bolshevism," "radicalism," and "anarchism." Although all were acquitted of capital murder, the jury found three of the men guilty of second-degree murder. Despite a clemency recommendation, the judge sentenced them to 45 years at hard labor. On appeal, the conviction of one of the three was overturned in 1937. Under pressure from the UMW, Governor John E. Miles pardoned the remaining two in 1939. Few observers today are prepared to say who really shot the sheriff.

Key Players

Hockenhull, Andrew (1877–1974): Hockenhull was serving as vice governor of New Mexico when Governor Arthur

Seligman died in 1933. He then served out the rest of the term before being defeated for reelection.

Lewis, John L. (1880–1969): Lewis was born in Lucas, Iowa, and went to work in the coal mines at age 16. He worked his way up through the ranks of the United Mine Workers until he become vice president in 1917 and acting president in 1919. In 1920 he was elected president, a post he held until 1960.

Seligman, Arthur (1871–1933): Seligman served briefly as governor of New Mexico. He took office in 1931 but died while in office in 1933.

See also: *Industrial Workers of the World; National Industrial Recovery Act; United Mine Workers of America; Western Federation of Miners.*

BIBLIOGRAPHY

Books

Rubenstein, Harry R. "Destruction of the National Miners' Union." In *Labor in New Mexico: Unions, Strikes and Social History Since 1881*, edited by Robert Kern. Albuquerque: University of New Mexico Press, 1977.

Stuart, Gary. *Gallup 14*. Albuquerque: University of New Mexico Press, 2000.

Other

O'Neill, Bill. "Gallup's Worst Day—April 4, 1935." Master's thesis. New Mexico State University, 1978.

State of New Mexico v. Ochoa, et al. 41 N.M. 589; 72 P2d 609.

—Michael J. O'Neal

General Agreement on Tariffs and Trade

Worldwide 1947–1962

Synopsis

The General Agreement on Tariffs and Trade (GATT) was created after World War II as one of three international organizations intended to oversee postwar economic relations; the other two were the International Monetary Fund and the World Bank. The idea of such an organization first originated with a Preparatory Committee, established in February 1946 by the United Nations Economic Council, to develop an agenda and proposals for an international conference on trade and employment. This resulted in a charter for a proposed International Trade Organization (ITO), which was supported by the United States. More bilateral negotiations culminated in a draft charter, which was amended in successive conferences held in 1946–1948 in London, New York, Geneva, and Havana. The latter gave its name to the final version, created there in March 1948, but key countries objected to parts of the ITO charter and the organization was never established. However, 23 countries agreed to sign the GATT, which was finalized in Geneva in October 1947, the same month that President Harry Truman used his authority under the Reciprocal Trade Agreements Act (RTAA) to join GATT. In 1962 President John F. Kennedy signed the U.S. Trade Expansion Act (Public Law 87-794); Section 235.2(b) which authorized the president to enter into trade agreements with other countries and established the post of special representative for trade negotiations in the executive office.

Timeline

1937: In the middle of an around-the-world flight, Amelia Earhart and her plane disappear somewhere in the Pacific.

1942: The women's military services are established in the United States.

1947: Great Britain's Labour government nationalizes coalmines.

1948: Israel becomes a nation.

1949: North Atlantic Treaty Organization (NATO) is established.

1950: North Korean troops pour into South Korea, starting the Korean War. Initially, the communists make impressive gains, but in September the U.S. Marines land at Inchon and liberate Seoul. China responds by sending in its troops.

1951: Julius and Ethel Rosenberg are convicted and sentenced to death for passing U.S. atomic secrets to the Soviets.

1954: The French military outpost at Dien Bien Phu falls to the communist Vietminh. France withdraws after decades of trying to suppress revolt; meanwhile, the United States pledges its support for the noncommunist government in the South.

1956: Elvis Presley appears on Ed Sullivan's *Toast of the Town,* where he performs "Hound Dog" and "Love Me Tender" before a mostly female audience. Nationwide, 54 million people watch the performance, setting a new record.

1961: President Eisenhower steps down, warning of a "military-industrial complex" in his farewell speech, and 43-year-old John F. Kennedy becomes the youngest elected president in U.S. history. Three months later, he launches an unsuccessful invasion of Cuba at the Bay of Pigs.

1962: As the Soviets begin a missile buildup in Cuba, for a few tense days in October it appears that World War III is imminent. President Kennedy calls for a Cuban blockade, forcing the Soviets to back down and ultimately diffusing the crisis.

1962: Publication of Rachel Carson's *Silent Spring* heightens Americans' awareness of environmental issues.

Cordell Hull. U.S. Signal Corp.

1965: Rev. Martin Luther King, Jr., and more than 2,600 others are arrested in Selma, Alabama. Three weeks later, in New York City, Malcolm X is assassinated.

1967: Arabs attack Israel, launching the Six-Day War, which results in an Israeli victory.

Event and Its Context

The passage of the British Corn Laws in 1832 and their repeal in 1846 led to free trade in corn and to the Cobden-Chevalier Treaty (1860). This agreement reduced tariffs throughout Europe. Problems with tariff regulation have always been an unavoidable factor in trade policy, as have concerns about labor standards and their impact on international economic competition. The development of international labor standards in the nineteenth century and the creation of the International Labor Organization (ILO) in 1919 were centrally related to commercial considerations. The Treaty of Versailles, which created the ILO, recognized that the "failure of any nation to adopt humane conditions of labor is an obstacle in the way of other nations which desire to improve the conditions in their own countries."

The Tariff Act of 1930 (also called the Smoot-Hawley Tariff Act after the two legislators who sponsored it) raised tariff rates on most articles imported by the United States, triggering comparable tariff increases by U.S. trading partners. Since its passage, Smoot-Hawley has been amended by subsequent legislation, beginning with the 1934 U.S. Reciprocal Trade Agreements Act, which amended the Tariff Act of 1930. The Reciprocal Trade Agreements Act delegated to the U.S. president the power to enter into reciprocal agreements to lower tariffs.

At the United Nations Monetary and Financial Conference in Bretton Woods, New Hampshire, in July 1944, 44 countries met and agreed on a global fixed-rate foreign exchange system. This system laid the groundwork for the International Monetary Fund, the World Bank, and the GATT, which were founded in 1944–1945. An International Trade Organization (ITO), with much support from U.S. Department of State officials, became a highly acclaimed institution for the implementation of bilateral negotiations conducted with the British. The organization was to be part of the postwar economic order because, by 1945, the United States had entered into 32 bilateral agreements reducing tariffs. The results of the bilateral negotiations were published in a pamphlet, *Proposals for Expansion of World Trade and Employment*, the first version of U.S. plans. The United States expanded this document into a draft charter and amended it in successive conferences between 1946 and 1948. The conferences convened in London, New York, Geneva, and Havana; the latter city gave its name to the final version, Havana (or Habana) Charter, in March 1948. The organization was never established, although it did address the impact of labor standards on competition. The draft of the charter stated that "the members recognize that unfair labor conditions, particularly in production for export, create difficulties in international trade and, accordingly, each member shall take whatever action may be feasible and appropriate to eliminate such conditions within its territory."

Twenty-three countries agreed to sign the GATT, which had already been finalized in Geneva on 30 October 1947. The Protocol of Provisional Application of the GATT was not signed as a separate document but as an attachment to the Final Act of the United Nations Conference on Trade and Employment, which was signed the same day. This provisional agreement allowed each of the participating countries to maintain escape clauses to protect its domestic producers. With the failure of the U.S. Congress to approve the ITO, there was new interest in GATT as a more permanent framework for tariff reductions. GATT represented the first successful postwar multilateral codification of the principles of free trade. The signatories pledged therein to conduct their trade on a multilateral basis without favor to particular countries, to reduce or abolish trade barriers and quotas, and to discuss tariff levels as well as exceptions at successive rounds of negotiations.

On 16 December 1947 President Harry Truman issued Proclamation 2761A, "Carrying Out General Agreements on Tariffs and Trade Concluded at Geneva, October 30, 1947," which provisionally made the agreement effective for the United States on 1 January 1948. A series of trade negotiations, or rounds, were convened during the postwar years to stimulate international trade through reduced tariff barriers. In 1949 the second round, negotiated in Annecy, France, achieved 5,000 tariff cuts. In 1950–1951 the third round, negotiated in Torquay, England, achieved 8,700 tariff cuts. In 1956 the fourth GATT round, in Geneva, achieved tariff cuts covering $2,500 million in trade. In 1960–1962 the fifth GATT round, negotiated in Geneva and named the Dillon Round for the chief U.S. trade negotiator, Under Secretary of State Douglas Dillon, achieved 4,400 tariff cuts. This last round marked the first time that the European Economic Community negotiated as an entity for individual member countries.

The Democratic administration of John F. Kennedy fostered a more active trade policy. Kennedy convinced Congress to pass the Trade Expansion Act (TEA) to stimulate American growth, reduce the American balance of payments deficit, and strengthen economic relations with other countries. On 11 October 1962 President Kennedy signed this legislation (Public Law No. 87-794), which authorized the president, under Section 235.2(b), to enter into trade agreements with other countries and established the post of special representative for trade negotiations in the executive office.

In the period immediately following the Trade Expansion and official U.S. entry into GATT, three additional GATT rounds ensued. The sixth GATT round (1963–1967) was named the Kennedy Round after President Kennedy. The seventh was named the Tokyo Round (1973–1979), and the eighth the Uruguay Round (1986–1994).

In April 1994 the Uruguay Round ended with 111 countries signing an agreement in Marrakesh, Morocco, to establish the World Trade Organization (WTO), an intergovernmental organization with a firmer legal foundation than its predecessor. Governing the WTO are a number of legal texts, most notably the GATT, the General Agreement on Trade in Services, and the agreement on Trade-Related Aspects of Intellectual Property Rights.

Key Players

Clayton, William Lockhart (1880–1966): Clayton was a cotton merchant who served on the War Industries Board during World War I. In 1945 he headed the U.S. economic delegation to the Potsdam Conference. In 1947, the same year he helped negotiate GATT, he was instrumental in drafting the Marshall Plan. He was also instrumental in the creation of the International Trade Organization.

Dillon, Douglas (1909–2003): Dillon was a securities trader who was named U.S. ambassador to France in 1953 by President Eisenhower. In 1958 Dillon became undersecretary of state for economic affairs and was influential in creating the Inter-American Development Bank. In 1961 President Kennedy appointed him secretary of the Treasury. From 1960 to 1962 he was chief U.S. trade negotiator at the fifth GATT round, also known as the Dillon Round, in Geneva.

Herter, Christian Archibald (1895–1966): Herter was governor of Massachusetts and a U.S. congressman. His Herter Committee report initiated proposals for the Marshall Plan. Herter was U.S. secretary of state (1959–1961). In 1962, President Kennedy appointed Herter to be the first to fill the position of special U.S. representative for trade negotiations.

Hull, Cordell (1871–1955): Hull was a Tennessee congressman and U.S. senator who advocated low tariffs to stimulate world trade. In 1933 he was appointed secretary of state. In this role, he was responsible for the Reciprocal Trade Agreements (1934) that delegated to the U.S. president the power to enter into reciprocal agreements to lower tariffs.

See also: *International Labor Organization.*

BIBLIOGRAPHY

Books

Curzon, Gerard. *Multilateral Commercial Diplomacy.* New York and Washington: Frederick A. Praeger, 1965.

Dam, Kenneth W. *The GATT: Law and International Economic Organization.* Chicago and London: University of Chicago, 1970.

Evans, John W. *Kennedy Round in American Trade Policy.* Cambridge, MA: Harvard University, 1971.

U.S. Congressional Budget Office. *The GATT Negotiations and U.S. Trade Policy.* Report prepared for the Subcommittee on International Trade, Senate Committee on Finance. Washington, DC: GPO, 1987.

Other

Rehberg, Jeanne. "GATT/WTO Research." Law Library Resource Xchange. 3 September 2001 [cited 15 October 2002]. <http://www.llrx.com/features/wto2.htm>.

ADDITIONAL RESOURCES

Books

Applebaum, Harvey M., and Lyn M. Schlitt. *The GATT, the WTO, and the Uruguay Round Agreements Act: Understanding the Fundamental Changes.* Commercial Law and Practice Course Handbook Series, no. A-722. New York: Practicing Law Institute, 1995.

Belford, J., ed. and comp. *Law and Practice Under the GATT and Other Trading Agreements—The European Community: The Single Market.* New York: Oceana Publications, 1990.

Bhala, Raj, and Kevin Kennedy. *World Trade Law: The GATT-WTO System, Regional Arrangements, and U.S. Law.* Charlottesville, VA: LEXIS Law Publishing, 1999. With supplements.

Dennin, Joseph F., ed. *GATT Reports/ WTO Reports.* Law and Practice of the World Trade Organization. Dobbs Ferry, NY: Oceana, 1995.

GATT Analytical Index: Guide to GATT Law and Practice. 2 vols. Updated 6th ed. Geneva: WTO and Bernan Press, 1995.

Hoekman, Bernard M., and Michel M. Kostecki. *The Political Economy of the World Trading System: The WTO and Beyond.* 2nd ed. Oxford, U.K., and New York: Oxford University Press, 2001.

Jackson, John H. *The World Trade Organization: Constitution and Jurisprudence.* Chatham House Papers. London: Royal Institute of International Affairs, 1998.

———. *The World Trading System: Law and Policy of International Economic Relations.* 2nd ed. Cambridge, MA: MIT Press, 1997.

Kunz, Diane B. *Butter and Guns: America's Cold War Economic Diplomacy.* New York and London: Free Press, 1997.

Petersmann, Ernst-Ulrich. *The GATT/WTO Dispute Settlement System: International Law, International Organizations, and Dispute Settlement.* London: Kluwer Law International, 1997.

Preeg, Ernest H. *Traders in a Brave New World: The Uruguay Round and the Future of the International Trading System.* Chicago: University of Chicago Press, 1995.

Trebilcock, Michael J., and Robert Howse. *The Regulation of International Trade.* 2nd ed. London and New York: Routledge, 1999.

—Martin J. Manning

General Allotment Act

United States 1887

Synopsis

The General Allotment Act, or Dawes Severalty Act, was passed by the U.S. Congress and signed by President Grover Cleveland in 1887 to give formally (or "allot") land to individual Native Americans. This federal policy would replace the existing communal tribal landholdings that historically had been a part of Native American culture with individual ownership of land. The allotments were usually 65 hectares (160 acres). U.S. Senator Henry Laurens Dawes sponsored the bill that intended to incorporate tribal members into the "civilized" white man's world, a world declared to be based on freedom, individualism, opportunity, and progress. The act stated that allotments could only be sold after a statutory period of 25 years, and all surplus lands not allotted to the Native Americans were open to public sale. Within a few decades following the passage of the act, whites owned the vast majority of what had been tribal land. The act was designed to absorb Native Americans into the society of the United States but instead contributed to the further decline of their populations, customs, and well-being.

Timeline

1867: United States purchases Alaska from Russia for $7.2 million.

1872: The title of Claude Monet's painting *Impression: Sunrise* gives a name to a new movement in art.

1877: Peter Ilych Tchaikovsky's ballet *Swan Lake* debuts.

1880: Cologne Cathedral, begun 634 years earlier, is completed. With twin spires 515 feet (157 m) high, it is the tallest structure in the world, and will remain so until 1889, when it is surpassed by the Eiffel Tower. (The previous record for the world's tallest structure lasted much longer—for about 4,430 years following the building of Cheops's Great Pyramid in c. 2550 B.C.)

Henry Laurens Dawes. © Bettmann/Corbis. Reproduced by permission.

1883: Brooklyn Bridge is completed.

1885: German engineer Karl Friedrich Benz builds the first true automobile.

1887: Heinrich Hertz proves the existence of electromagnetic waves, which are propagated at the speed of light.

1887: Thomas Edison invents the first motor-driven phonograph.

1887: John Emerich Edward Dalbert-Acton, a leader of the opposition to the papal dogma of infallibility, observes, in a letter to Cambridge University professor Mandell Creighton, that "Power tends to corrupt, and absolute power corrupts absolutely."

1889: The 986-foot (300.5-m) Eiffel Tower, part of the Paris exposition, becomes the tallest structure in the world. It will remain so until the Chrysler Building surpasses it in 1930.

1893: Henry Ford builds his first automobile.

1897: In the midst of a nationwide depression, Mrs. Bradley Martin, daughter of Carnegie Steel magnate Henry Phipps, throws a lavish party at New York's recently opened Waldorf-Astoria Hotel, where she has a suite decorated to look like Versailles. Her 900 guests, dressed in Louis XV period costumes, consume sixty cases of champagne.

Event and Its Context

As early as 1792 President George Washington's secretary of war, Henry Knox, stated that individual ownership of land by Native Americans would help convert them to a "civilized" lifestyle. Lewis Cass, U.S. secretary of war in 1831, and T. Hartley Crawford, U.S. commissioner of Indian affairs in 1838, continued to emphasize the adoption of "severalty in property" (that is, individual ownership of land) as a way to eliminate the tribalism of the Native Americans and to incorporate them into the white man's way of life.

Local and regional laws and treaties emphasizing individual ownership of land for Native Americans were common in the early years of the United States. By 1885 the government had thousands of these "lands-in-severalty" agreements for various tribes. The predominant attitude of American leaders during this period can be summed up with the words of Carl Schurz, U.S. secretary of the interior in 1877: "The enjoyment and pride of the individual ownership of property [is] one of the most effective civilizing agencies."

Winning the Battle, Losing the War

Before 1870 many Native American lands had been guaranteed to remain under the control of the various tribes within the United States. However, unscrupulous whites (sometimes in the official guise of government bodies) had frequently violated these treaties whenever anything of value was found on or under these lands.

A famous example of this treaty-breaking practice occurred in the Black Hills of South Dakota when white miners were lured to the area in the early 1870s by rumors of valuable minerals. When disputes erupted between the miners and the Native Americans, the federal government tried to buy the land from the tribes. The Native Americans—who had been guaranteed the land by the Treaty of 1868—refused the offer. In 1876 the Seventh Cavalry Regiment, under the leadership of George Armstrong Custer, entered the land, only to be massacred by warriors from the Sioux and Northern Cheyenne tribes. Although they won the battle, the Native Americans eventually lost the war as they were killed, imprisoned, ejected from the country, or evicted to the Indian Territory (now called Oklahoma).

1865–1880

The years following the Civil War (1861–1865) brought the first concerted effort to force private land ownership upon the Native Americans. They possessed little power by the end of the 1870s and posed little threat to white settlers in the West. Native American treaties to which the federal government had formerly agreed were rarely honored.

Some humanitarian organizations tried to force the government to support existing treaties, maintain the tribes' customs and lifestyles, assure the tribes' right to hold community land, and to protect individual Native Americans against white confrontations. A few organizations, such as the Boston Indian Citizenship Association, which included Massachusetts governor John Davis Long, poet and novelist Helen Hunt Jackson (originally from Massachusetts), and Massachusetts senator Henry L. Dawes, formed with the purpose of helping the Native Americans. Jackson had written the book, *A Century of Dishonor*, that rejected U.S.–Native American policy. Other noted organizations that generally sided with the Native Americans were the Indian Defence Association, the Woman's National Indian Association, and the Indian Rights Association. Dr. Thomas A. Bland, editor of *The Council Fire*, regularly voiced his opinions against allotment in severalty. Even though such organizations were against dividing up land in severalty, they often had their own agendas, such as Christianizing and educating the tribes in the ways of the white man.

Reformers tried to incorporate Native Americans into mainstream America. During the 1870s such organizations attempted to speed up the assimilation of Native Americans by white society. An important part of the assimilation was the transfer of tribal land ownership to individual ownership. A popular theory of the time held that Native Americans would be assimilated more quickly if they were owners of land and encouraged to pursue civilized agricultural pursuits as opposed to their traditional pursuits, such as hunting, fishing, and gathering. Alice Fletcher, a prominent ethnographer (a scientist who studies the customs of cultures) and leader of a Boston group called Friends of the Indians, felt that private land ownership by the Indians would allow the Native American to be a free person without any need for a tribe to secure his future.

Allotment in Severalty

The policy of allotment of land in severalty would divide up all Native American lands so that individuals would own individual parcels. Major John Wesley Powell, leader of the Bureau of Ethnology within the Smithsonian Institution and an authority on Native Americans, said that creating individual property for Native Americans was necessary for them to advance along with the rest of the country.

During the Lake Mohonk Conference, an annual symposium of the Friends of the Indian, participants concluded that the organization of Native Americans in tribes was one of the major factors that prevented them from achieving a "civilized" culture. Conference attendees felt every action should be taken to eliminate tribal organizations. The editor of the *Christian Union* urged the rejection of the tribal system because it had only led to barbarism over the years. General S. C. Armstrong, principal of the Hampton Normal School, which educated Native Americans, recommended that if an allotment could not be obtained voluntarily, then it should be done without tribal consent. Armstrong felt, as did many whites, that the white man must save the Native Americans, because they could not save themselves.

Dawes and the General Allotment Act

Although Henry Dawes was originally against any type of rapid and forced allotment, he still was in favor of slowly and voluntarily assimilating Native Americans into the American way of life. Without strong convictions, Dawes conceded to the greedy landgrabbers and went along with the majority opinion when the General Allotment Act became national legislation in 1887. The new plan to rescue Native Americans from extinction actually contributed to the elimination of the tribes by parceling out communally owned reservation land to individuals. The law basically provided for the following:

- Transfer of 160 acres to each family head, 80 acres to each single person over 18 years of age and to each orphan under 18, and 40 acres to each single person under 18

- Holding of all transferred lands in governmental trust for 25 years, during which time it could not be sold or mortgaged

- A period of four years in which Native Americans could make their land selections; failure to select land would result in the choice being made by the government

- Citizenship granted to any Native American who abandoned his tribe and adopted the "civilized" way

Objectives

The declared objectives of the General Allotment Act were to enable the Native Americans to become self-supporting farmers and to be assimilated into the culture of the whites. The government hoped to incorporate the Native Americans into the labor market and make them productive members of society, that is, "civilized taxpayers." However, the act's underlying purpose was to release land to such groups as homesteaders, land companies, and the railroads, and to resettle Native Americans from valuable lands to much-less productive ones.

The act had an underlying goal to individualize and absorb the Native Americans by ending tribal land ownership and replacing it with private, individually owned land. The act was basically a plan to make the Native Americans independent farmers and ranchers by making them individual landholders. It also was intended to break up the reservations where the tribes could shut themselves off from contact with the rest of the country. The intent of the law was to loosen tribal bonds so as to bring the Native Americans under U.S. laws and eventually make them citizens.

The Native American View

The results of the General Allotment Act were less than satisfactory for the Native Americans. It provided for each head of a Native American family to be given 160 acres of farmland or 320 acres of grazing land. The remaining tribal lands were to be declared "surplus" and opened up for whites. Tribal land ownership and tribes themselves were intended to simply disappear. Before the act, the tribes held approximately 150 million acres of land. Within 20 years, two-thirds of their land was gone and the reservation system was nearly destroyed. Whites soon controlled the land that had been allotted to individual Native Americans, who lost much of their land and received inadequate payment for the land they relinquished. Moreover, because most Native Americans were unfamiliar with managing money, the money that they did receive for their land was often quickly spent. Few historians judged the act as successful from the Native American point of view.

The Allotment Act turned out to be a gigantic disaster. In addition to losing their "surplus" tribal land, many Native American families lost their allotted land as well, despite the government's 25-year period of trusteeship. Hundreds of thousands of acres that were left over after the selection of the individual 160-acre allotments were then sold cheaply to land-hungry or land-speculating whites. The Native Americans, then landless and still resisting assimilation, reached their lowest population numbers soon after the turn of the twentieth century.

The White View

Most whites considered the General Allotment Act to be the "Indian Emancipation Act" and felt the "Indian problem" would soon end. Land-hungry citizens of the western states eagerly awaited the passing of the act because excess land that was not needed for the allotment would be opened up for sale. This process resulted in the gain to white men of approximately 90 million acres of tribal land between 1887 and 1934 through the sale of surplus lands and purchases of original allotments.

Several circumstances contributed to the transfer of allotments from Native Americans to whites. The Burke Act of 1906 authorized allotments to be taken out of trust if the individual owner was declared incompetent to manage his own land. When an allotment was taken out of trust, the land became for the first time subject to state and local taxes. It was often sold at a tax sale several years later for unpaid taxes, often without the knowledge of the Native American owner.

Act Administration

The administration of the General Allotment Act failed to help the Native Americans adjust to their new circumstances. The administrators did not consider Native American education and welfare. Many tribal historians feel that the originators of the act failed to consider the possibility that some Native Americans would be unable to farm their allotment because of age, lack of experience, physical disability, or other such circumstance.

The misapplication by the act's administrators was primarily responsible for the unsuccessful result of the General Allotment Act, which was the United States' first systematic effort to provide for Indian welfare. The Native Americans for the most part evolved from a poor land-owning minority to an even poorer landless minority.

Many historians of the American West concur that the policy of breaking up Native American lands into individual allotments had its origin in the General Allotment Act, which was forced through Congress by the combined efforts of land-hungry westerners and moralistic easterners. The injustices thus perpetrated were not corrected to any noticeable degree until the administration of President Franklin D. Roosevelt, when reforms were begun with the Indian Reorganization Act of 1934.

Key Players

Dawes, Henry Laurens (1816–1903): Dawes graduated from Yale College in 1839. He became a teacher and edited the newspapers *Greenfield Gazette* and the *North Adams Transcript*. He later studied law, was admitted to the bar in 1842, and began to practice law in North Adams, Massachusetts. During the late 1840s and mid-1850s, Dawes was a member of the Massachusetts House of Representatives, the Massachusetts Senate, and the Massachusetts constitutional convention. He was also a district attorney for the western district of Massachusetts. Dawes was a Republican member of the U.S. House of Representatives from 1857 to 1875, where he served as the chairman on the Committee of Elections, Committee of Appropriations, and Committee of Ways and Means. Dawes was a Republican member of the U.S. Senate from 1875 to 1893, where he served as

chairman for the Committee on Public Buildings and Grounds and the Committee on Indian Affairs. Dawes served as the chairman of the commission created to administer the tribal affairs of the five "civilized" Tribes of Native Americans in the Indian Territory from 1893 to 1903.

BIBLIOGRAPHY

Books

Bruchey, Stuart, ed. *The Rape of Indian Lands*. New York: Arno Press, 1979.

Otis, D.S. *The Dawes Act and the Allotment of Indian Lands*. Norman: University of Oklahoma Press, 1973.

Washburn, Wilcomb E. *The Assault on Indian Tribalism: The General Allotment Law (Dawes Act) of 1887*. Philadelphia: J. B. Lippincott Company, 1975.

—William Arthur Atkins

General Motors Introduces Team Concept

United States 1987

Synopsis

General Motors (GM) introduced the team concept of labor management into the Van Nuys, California, Camaro and Firebird assembly plant in May 1987 in the hopes it would boost production. At the time, GM was facing triple troubles: (1) sagging sales due to foreign and domestic competition; (2) a mobilized Van Nuys United Auto Workers (UAW) Local union with a mission to keep the plant open and a threatened boycott of GM in the Los Angeles market if it did not—plus the Local was hotly divided on the team concept as the solution; and (3) the threat of a general UAW strike if GM did not agree to a new three-year contract that included job guarantees and other benefits that the UAW had just won from Ford. In the end, GM and the UAW did sign a three-year contract, during which time the plant operated under the team concept. The plant was eventually closed in 1992.

Timeline

1967: The Beatles' *Sgt. Pepper's Lonely Hearts Club Band* tops the list of releases for a year that will long be remembered as a high point of rock history. Among the other great musical events of the year are releases by the Jimi Hendrix Experience, the Doors, and Jefferson Airplane; also, the Monterey Pop Festival marks the debut of Hendrix and Janis Joplin.

1972: In June police apprehend five men attempting to burglarize Democratic Party headquarters at the Watergate Hotel in Washington, D.C.

1977: Newly inaugurated U.S. President Jimmy Carter pardons Vietnam draft dodgers.

1980: In protest of the Soviet invasion of Afghanistan, President Carter keeps U.S. athletes out of the Moscow Olympics. Earlier, at the Winter Games in Lake Placid, New York, the U.S. hockey team scored a historic—and, in the view of many, a symbolic—victory over the Soviets.

1983: Sally Ride becomes the first female U.S. astronaut (the Soviets were ahead by two decades, with Valentina Tereshkova) when she goes into space aboard the shuttle *Challenger.*

1986: In November, the scandal variously known as Iran-Contra, Irangate, and Contragate breaks, when it is revealed that the Reagan administration agreed to sell arms to Iran in exchange for hostages, and to divert the funds from the arms sales to support the anti-Sandinista Contras in Nicaragua.

1987: Iran-Contra hearings continue for much of the year, making a household name of such figures as Oliver North and his secretary, Fawn Hall.

1987: By a narrow margin, the Senate votes to reject Robert H. Bork, Reagan's nominee to take the recently vacated seat of Lewis Powell on the U.S. Supreme Court.

1990: Though the Internet (originally the Arpanet) has existed for twenty-one years, it has not been very user-friendly, and has remained the province of defense personnel and other specialists. This year, however, sees the beginnings of the World Wide Web, which will make the Net accessible to a broad range of users over the coming years.

1992: Trouble begins after the Yugoslav Federation breaks up in January. Soon Yugoslavia, now dominated by Serbia, is at war in several former Yugoslav republics, and in September, the United Nations expels Yugoslavia.

1997: On 31 August, Princess Diana is killed in a Paris car crash along with two others. Her state funeral is as much a public event, watched by millions of mourners the world over, as her wedding to Prince Charles sixteen years earlier had been. The day after her funeral, another beloved figure, 87-year-old Mother Teresa, dies.

2000: In the most disputed presidential election in U.S. history, Democrats demand a recount after initial tabulation of votes in Florida shows a narrow victory for Republican candidate George W. Bush. The battle goes on for five weeks, and involves numerous recounts and court injunctions, until the U.S. Supreme Court puts an end to recounts and declares Bush the winner.

Event and Its Context

Background of the Van Nuys GM Plant

To understand how GM got into the difficulties it faced in 1987, one has to look at the history of the Van Nuys plant. GM opened the Van Nuys plant on a vacant piece of land in 1947.

J. Lane Kirkland. The Library of Congress.

At the time, the largely white San Fernando Valley suburb north of Los Angeles had a relatively small available workforce, but by 1982, when an organized campaign formed to prevent the plant from closing, an entire working class, with new ethnic demographics, had grown up around the plant. There were 5,000 workers at the GM Van Nuys assembly plant; 2,500 were Latino and 750 were African American.

The auto assembly industry in California went through a period of growth, followed by rapid decline, between the opening of the Van Nuys plant in 1947 and the threatened closing of it in 1982. At peak production in 1978, between GM, Ford, and Mack Truck there were six assembly plants in California employing nearly 25,000 workers. By the next year, the oil crisis in the United States had taken its toll on the American auto industry. California, one of the largest centers for production outside of Detroit, was hit hard.

By 1982 the GM Van Nuys plant was the only one of the six assembly plants that remained in operation, and GM was hinting that it also might be closed. The UAW Local 645 union hall, located across the street from the plant, was in November 1982 the birthplace of the campaign to keep GM Van Nuys open. The strategy for the movement was based on a broad united front between the workers and the community aimed at getting a long-term commitment from GM to keep the Van Nuys plant open. Its chief tactic was the threat of a boycott of GM throughout Los Angeles, a major GM market, if the plant closed.

One of GM's arguments against the California plant was the high cost of shipping parts to that location. GM was looking to cost cutting and consolidation to become more competitive in a tight market. Placing assembly operations close to parts manufacturing in the Midwest would allow reduction of inventories. GM figured to save tens of millions of dollars with such a move. An effective boycott in California, on the other hand, would certainly, at least in part, offset those savings.

The Campaign and GM's Response

At the start, the campaign organizers clashed with the union ranks. Organizers had to overcome dissent among some of the union members, who challenged them to declare whether they were communists, socialists, or "Americans." Also, throughout the action, its leaders were in conflict with the leadership of the UAW International, which generally saw as inevitable that plants would be closed to make American-made automobiles competitive with imports.

To be effective, the organizers had to get the attention of the media. On 14 May 1983 famed labor leader Cesar Chavez appeared as a speaker at a rally in Los Angeles. The *Los Angeles Times* Metro section headline the next day read, "Boycott by UAW of GM Threatened." Chavez, president of the United Farm Workers, had run a successful boycott against California grape growers a decade earlier.

For a boycott to be effective, the campaign would have to include a diverse coalition of leaders and groups representing all the communities within the greater Los Angeles area. The 40,000 African American residents of the area were an important population to the campaign. The Latino groups were not a single homogenous entity in the region, but Latinos comprised 50 percent of the local union and thus represented another important faction. Campaign leaders approached the Los Angeles Chamber of Commerce to represent the business community. A Chamber of Commerce report cited the GM plant as a "vital and integral part of the San Fernando community since its opening in 1947." If the plant closed, 5,000 jobs at GM would be lost; moreover, some observers estimated that the closure would also result in the loss of 35,000 nonmanufacturing jobs and closure of 514 retail establishments.

The campaign became a coalition by the end of 1983. The local union enlisted the support of religious, political, and business leaders who agreed that GM had an obligation to the community and noted that the plant had generated a good profit for GM over the years of its operation. The coalition would target GM's $2.3 billion in sales a year in Los Angeles County for a boycott, if necessary.

GM's president, F. James McDonald, agreed to a face-to-face meeting with the leaders of the coalition in January 1984. The factions had established ground rules for the meeting: a half hour for GM's presentation, a half hour for the coalition leaders, and a half hour for free discussion. It did not work that way. McDonald made a long prepared slide presentation, then concluded: "If the local leadership of the union cooperates with us, tries to cut down absenteeism, raises quality and productivity and creates a more positive labor-relations climate there is still hope."

The coalition members were not happy. A succession of speakers that included college professors, legislators, and clergy expressed their disappointment at the "canned" presentation that went too long and provided for no free discussion. McDonald was caught off guard. He agreed when pressed that the plant would be kept open for two years, but he would not promise three years.

Shortly after the meeting with McDonald, GM brought a new manager, Ernest Schaefer, to the Van Nuys plant. Schaefer started his own campaign to open up dialog with the workers. By December 1985 he was spreading the word that a Japanese-style management system called team concept would help to save the plant. A good example of team concept was available at the GM/Toyota joint venture, known as New United Motor Manufacturing, Inc. (NUMMI), operating in Fremont, California.

The Team Concept Comes to Van Nuys

The team concept had been advocated years earlier by Walter Reuther, then UAW chairman, as a way to improve job satisfaction. In the team concept, workers—four to seven or more, depending on the specifics of the particular assembly—operate together in groups on entire sections of a car under one leader instead of doing a single repetitive task. The team is expected to handle problems such as defects as they arise. If necessary, they can even stop the assembly line to correct a problem.

Introduction of the team concept at the Van Nuys plant was a challenge. The local UAW members were split on the idea, and very heated contests resulted. The split was evident in the election of a union president in favor of the team concept, while the chairman of bargaining lobbied against it. Schaefer, however, pressed on and met with small groups to advocate for the concept. He hinted that the team concept was the only answer to keeping the plant open. In May 1987 the team concept officially started at Van Nuys.

By the end of September 1987 the Van Nuys plant was 1,500 cars behind its production schedule. Schaefer publicly blamed the shortfall on the complicated design of the new 1988 models that the plant had begun manufacturing in August, not on the team concept that he considered essential to survival of the American auto industry. To the workers, however, Schaefer pointed out that GM was losing customers to Ford and other car manufacturers because they were stopping the assembly line too often. This was not a good time for GM to be falling behind. Negotiations had begun earlier in September 1987 in Detroit on a new contract between GM and the UAW.

Ford was also negotiating with the UAW and settled first with the UAW on a three-year contract that included job guarantees. There was much speculation that GM would not be able to meet the same demands from the union because Ford had a competitive advantage over GM in that Ford bought a larger percentage of its parts (which, in general, was less costly than manufacturing them). Many in Van Nuys were expecting a strike. Schaefer admitted that workers were concerned. Evidence of this included the fact that disability leaves were on the increase at the Van Nuys plant. Workers on disability leave are paid during a strike. No strike materialized, however.

General Motors settled with the UAW under terms that were very similar to those negotiated with Ford. The three-year agreement included a commitment not to close any plants during the term of the contract, except for those that had been announced before the agreement. Although there had been suggestions that the Van Nuys plant would be closed, no official announcement of a closure had been made. The plant would remain open and would function under the team concept for three more years. In exchange for the job security program, GM got a commitment from the UAW to join in efforts to improve production output and quality. The Ford contract contained a similar clause.

The GM Van Nuys assembly plant closed on 27 August 1992 after 45 years of operation, during which it had assembled 6.3 million vehicles. The GM/Toyota joint venture continued to operate profitably in Fremont.

Key Players

Chavez, Cesar (1927–1993): Chavez was the founder and president of the National Farm Workers Association, which later became the United Farm Workers of America, AFL-CIO. He focused on nonviolent tactics to win better pay and safer conditions for farm workers. He was born in Yuma, Arizona, but spent most of his life working in the fields of California.

Kirkland, J. Lane (1922–1999): Kirkland was president of the American Federation of Labor–Congress of Industrial Organizations (AFL-CIO) from 1979 to1995.

McDonald, F. James: A native of Saginaw, Michigan, McDonald was president of General Motors between February 1981 and August 1987.

Reuther, Walter (1907–1970): Reuther led the first major auto strike in Detroit, Michigan, in 1936. He was elected president of the United Auto Workers (UAW) in 1946. He was elected president of the CIO in 1952 and helped engineer the merger of the AFL and CIO, but in 1968 he led the UAW out of the federation. Reuther died in a plane crash in Michigan in 1970.

Schaefer, Ernest: Schaefer was plant manager of GM's Fiero plant from 1982 to 1985, at which point he became plant manager at GM's Van Nuys plant.

See also: *GM Recognizes UAW; Grape Pickers' Strike.*

BIBLIOGRAPHY

Books

Mann, Eric. *Taking on General Motors: A Case Study of the Campaign to Keep GM Van Nuys Open.* Los Angeles: Institute of Industrial Relations Publication, University of California, Los Angeles, 1987.

Periodicals

Apodaca, Patrice. "End of Road for GM's Van Nuys Plant." *The Los Angeles Times*, 28 August 1992.

Crouch, Gregory. "GM Losing Sales to Ford Due to Production Delays at Van Nuys Plant." *The Los Angeles Times*, 19 September 1987.

"GM's Bootstrap Battle: The Factory-floor View." *U.S. News & World Report*, 21 September 1987, pp. 52–53.

"GM–UAW Settlement." Developments in Industrial Relations, *Monthly Labor Review* (December 1987).

Mann, Eric. "L.A. Could Lose Valley Auto Plant GM Drives a Hard Bargain." *The Los Angeles Times*, 26 January 1986.

"Team Concept: GM Plant Chief Says New Work Rules Will Benefit Company Despite Slow Start." *The Los Angeles Times* (Valley Edition), 29 September 1987.

Weinstein, Henry. "'Team Concept' Foe Wins UAW Van Nuys Vote." *The Los Angeles Times*, 5 June 1987.

ADDITIONAL RESOURCES

Books

Katz, Harry C. and Richard W. Hurd. *Rekindling the Movement: Labor's Quest for Relevance in the 21st Century.* Ithaca, NY: Cornell University Press, 2001.

Lichtenstein, Nelson. *State of the Union: A Century of American Labor.* Princeton, NJ: Princeton University Press, 2001.

Periodicals

"The Reindustrialization of America." *Business Week* (special issue), 20 April 1987.

—M. C. Nagel

General Motors Recognizes United Auto Workers

United States 1937

Synopsis

The sit-down strike came to prominence in America in 1937, and no industry was affected by this ingenious new tactic as much as the automobile industry. The Flint, Michigan, sit-down strike, which lasted from 30 December 1936 to 11 February 1937, was the most important strike of the year. Aimed at the heart of General Motors, the largest industrial corporation in the world, the strike set the company on the path to recognizing a single industrial union as the representative for all its hourly line workers.

The 44-day strike in Flint followed on the heels of a few smaller sit-down strikes, such as the one that occurred in the middle of December at the Kelsey-Hayes wheel-producing plant on the west side of Detroit. But the Flint strike galvanized the country and the world because of its boldness, its potential for violence, and the dramatic intercession of Michigan's governor Frank Murphy and the president of the Committee for Industrial Organization (CIO), John L. Lewis, in the settlement talks. After Flint, the relationship between management and labor in modern American industry would never be the same.

Timeline

1922: Published this year James Joyce's novel *Ulysses* and T. S. Eliot's poem *The Waste Land* will transform literature and inaugurate the era of modernism.

United Auto Workers sit-down strike, General Motors plant, Flint, Michigan, 1937. © UPI/Corbis-Bettmann. Reproduced by permission.

1927: American inventor Philo T. Farnsworth demonstrates a working model of the television, and Belgian astronomer Georges Lemaître proposes the Big Bang Theory.

1932: In German elections, Nazis gain a 37 percent plurality of Reichstag seats, raising tensions between the far right and the far left. On a "bloody Sunday" in July, communists in Hamburg attack Nazis with guns, and a fierce battle ensues.

1937: Italy signs the Anti-Comintern Pact, signed by Germany and Japan the preceding year. Like the two others before it, Italy now withdraws from the League of Nations.

1937: Japan attacks China and annexes most of that nation's coastal areas.

1937: Stalin uses carefully staged show trials in Moscow to eliminate all rivals for leadership. These party purges, however, are only a small part of the death toll now being exacted in a country undergoing forced industrialization, much of it by means of slave labor.

1937: In the middle of an around-the-world flight, Amelia Earhart and her plane disappear somewhere in the Pacific.

1937: Crash of the *Hindenburg* in Lakehurst, New Jersey, kills 36 and ends the brief era when rigid airships promised to be the ocean liners of the skies.

1937: Pablo Picasso paints his famous *Guernica* mural dramatizing the Nationalist bombing of a town in Spain. Thanks to artists and intellectuals such as Picasso and Ernest Hemingway, the Loyalists are winning the battle of hearts and minds, even if they are weaker militarily, and idealistic young men flock from America to join the "Abraham Lincoln Brigade." Yet as George Orwell later reveals in *Homage to Catalonia,* the lines between good and evil are not clear: with its Soviet backing, the Loyalist cause serves as proxy for a totalitarianism every bit as frightening as that of the Nationalists and their German and Italian supporters.

1942: Axis conquests reach their height in the middle of this year. The Nazis control a vast region from Normandy to the suburbs of Stalingrad, and from the Arctic Circle

Striking workers, Chevrolet Parts Plant No. 9, Flint, Michigan, 1937. © UPI/Corbis-Bettmann. Reproduced by permission.

to the edges of the Sahara. To the east, the Japanese "Co-Prosperity Sphere" encompasses territories from China to Burma to the East Indies, stretching deep into the western Pacific.

1947: Marshall Plan is established to assist European nations in recovering from the war.

1952: Among the cultural landmarks of the year are the film *High Noon* and the book *The Invisible Man* by Ralph Ellison.

Event and Its Context

Every American industry was hit hard during the Great Depression, including the profitable automobile industry. For General Motors, the largest and richest industrial corporation in the world, the depression did not threaten its existence, but it did prompt belt-tightening measures, including seasonal layoffs and greater efficiency goals during production cycles. This meant that the already insecure labor force was subjected to working conditions that pushed them to the limits of their endurance and caused them to entertain radical notions about how they might improve their lot. Many workers were forced to borrow from the company during layoff periods and pay back their debt later on wages that averaged around 70 cents an hour. All workers were susceptible to threats of being fired on the spot for any reason, and the turnover rate in the mid-1930s was entirely unacceptable by modern standards.

In late 1935 the Committee for Industrial Organization (later the Congress of Industrial Organizations) was formed under the leadership of United Mine Workers president John L. Lewis to provide more effective representation for beleaguered industrial workers. The older American Federation of Labor (AFL) was showing itself unsuited to the challenges of a new industrial America on account of its historic orientation toward skilled workers and tradesmen and because of a leadership that had become conservative over the years. Nevertheless, the nascent United Auto Workers (UAW) remained a member of the AFL throughout the early 1930s because the AFL was the only legitimate and powerful parent organization with which the UAW could affiliate.

With the passage of the National Labor Relations (Wagner) Act in 1935, however, the rights of labor were expanded to such a degree that the more radical and progressive elements within the American labor movement were encouraged. Going well beyond the mere right to bargain collectively that had been stipulated in Section 7(a) of the 1930 National Industrial Recovery Act, the Wagner Act banned all company interference with workers' rights to organize. It also forbade any attempt by a company to control a labor organization, to discriminate against workers because of their union activities, and to refuse to bargain with employee representatives. To protect against potential chaos and labor anarchy, though, the act also endorsed the principle of majority rule.

Most large companies believed that the U.S. Supreme Court would eventually strike down the Wagner Act as unconstitutional, and General Motors was no exception. Nevertheless, the Wagner Act and the elections of 1936 (which provided a mandate for Roosevelt's New Deal programs and made Democrat Frank Murphy governor of Michigan) provided a new impetus to labor organizers who wanted to go after the larger industries. Key people within the UAW, like Homer Martin, began to harshly criticize AFL leadership in 1935 for their failure to support large-scale organization in the auto industry. They pointed to the successes in the Cleveland Fisher Body strike of 1934 and in the Toledo Chevrolet strike of 1935 as evidence that General Motors was vulnerable when key plants were shut down. They also began to talk to leaders in the CIO about the possibility of switching allegiances.

Things moved quickly on this front. At the August 1935 AFL convention in Detroit, UAW progressives tried to take over the proceedings with their roster of complaints, but the old guard maintained its control. Over the next six months, UAW membership plummeted and the power of the progressives and radicals grew. At the 27 April 1936 convention, progressives were able to take over the key leadership positions; Homer Martin was elected the first president of the now independent UAW. On 2 July the transition was complete when Martin aligned the UAW with the CIO and broke all AFL ties. The CIO, in turn, promised its full support in the effort to organize autoworkers.

Soon thereafter, the reenergized UAW sent Wyndham Mortimer to Flint to try to gain a toehold in the heart of General Motors territory. Finding fewer than 100 union members among a workforce of 40,000 and an extensive network of company spies making sure that that number didn't rise, Mortimer resorted to holding secret meetings in random places. Slowly, the union grew. In October a young and persuasive organizer from Toledo named Bob Travis replaced Mortimer, and the pace of organization accelerated.

Throughout November and December, short and lightly publicized sit-downs occurred at several GM plants, such as Bendix Products and Kelsey-Hayes, setting the stage for the larger strike to come—while at Flint, the workers became more and more anxious. Travis, though, wanted to delay the strike until the beginning of the New Year so the men would get their Christmas bonuses. The union would also have the advantage then of Frank Murphy occupying the governor's chair. Moreover, Travis wanted to make sure the union was strong enough to pull off a different kind of strike than most of the men were

familiar with—namely, a sit-down strike. For such a radical action to succeed, every precaution had to be taken.

The sit-down method of striking was a European innovation in the early part of the twentieth century, but by the 1930s radicals and labor leaders in America had become knowledgeable about its potential for stalling the engines of industry. It was more effective than the usual method of picketing outside the factory because it prevented scabs from carrying out production. The use of scabs had always given the company an edge in negotiations. The technique of the sit-down strike is for the workers inside the plant to barricade all entrances and make sure the line is shut down along its entire length. When accused of violating the property rights of the company, proponents of the sit-down tactic answered that the employees were merely protecting the means of their own livelihood—and, by extension, their own material possessions. The U.S. Supreme Court denied the validity of this argument in 1941, but by then the tactic was no longer necessary. Most of American heavy industry had been unionized.

Although Travis wanted to wait until the new year to pull the strike, the company forced his hand. On the afternoon of 30 December 1936, two trucks pulled up to the docks of the Fisher 1 plant to take away the huge dies used there to cast car bodies. When Travis heard this, he ordered the plant shut down immediately, and the trucks were sent away empty. If they had been able to transfer the dies to another plant, the importance of any strike at Fisher 1 would have been dramatically decreased. The Fisher 2 plant shut down at the same time to avoid further company shenanigans, and the strike was on.

When the men in Fisher 1 and Fisher 2 barricaded themselves in the plants on the evening of 30 December, the company initially was stymied. It made a few feeble attempts to force the men out by turning off the heat in the plants, but these were unsuccessful due to the company's worries about the damage burst water pipes might do. Then, on 2 January, Judge Edward D. Black granted GM an injunction against the strike, and Sheriff Wolcott, the city's chief law enforcement officer, delivered it to the men at Fisher 1. This injunction was quickly invalidated, however, when UAW attorneys discovered that Black held over $200,000 in General Motors stock.

In the first days of the new year, townspeople in Flint who opposed the strike began to make plans for vigilante action, and city leaders mobilized the police force for an invasion of the plants. Meanwhile, the strikers inside the plants prepared themselves for the inevitable. Leaders assigned them to a variety of committees and platoons—including surveillance, cleanup, exercise, and defense—with each man pulling a six-hour shift every day. Discipline was the primary concern of the leaders, for they knew their stay was unlikely to be peaceful.

The attack came on 11 January in what was later referred to as the "Battle of Bulls Run." Squadrons of Flint police wearing riot gear and carrying tear gas guns advanced on the smaller Fisher 2 plant in the center of town as darkness fell, only to be turned back by a barrage of high-powered water hoses and one-pound door hinges. Additionally, a strong wind blew the tear gas back in the attackers' faces. Only when the battle was lost did the police resort to real bullets and cause the only serious injuries of the night; 14 strike supporters were injured.

On 12 January, Governor Frank Murphy came to Flint to try to calm the situation. He called in the National Guard, not to evict the strikers but to protect them from the city authorities, and he ordered both sides to the bargaining table. A few days later, Murphy thought he had a settlement, but everything was scuttled when the union discovered that GM officials were negotiating at the same time with a large vigilante group calling itself the Flint Alliance.

Throughout the rest of January, an uneasy truce prevailed in Flint. GM president Alfred Sloan refused to negotiate further, claiming the UAW had no rights under the law because they had not enrolled a majority of GM employees in the union, as the Wagner Act required. He also persisted in claiming that the strike should be settled on a plant-by-plant instead of company-wide basis. The union, for its part, insisted on the latter, while also hardening its position on exclusive bargaining rights. It claimed the company had illegally hindered its organizational efforts and that the sit-down was the workers' only alternative. By the beginning of February, Flint was a powder keg.

The union made the first move to break the stalemate. In a bold and ingenious stroke, it took over the huge Chevrolet 4 plant on 1 February by employing a diversionary tactic that threw the company off balance. A false plan for taking over the smaller Chevrolet 9 plant was leaked to company spies; company forces were subsequently massed at Chevrolet 9 while a relatively small group of men shut down the larger plant. Because Chevrolet 4 supplied the engines for every Chevrolet car in the country, the union had, in effect, paralyzed a significant portion of the mighty General Motors. The union was crucially assisted in the takeover by the Women's Emergency Brigade, a small group of militant women, led by 23-year-old Genora Johnson, who placed themselves between the plant and the police at Chevrolet 9.

On the same day, 1 February, a second injunction was granted against the strike, which placed Murphy in an awkward position. He had a legal duty to carry out the injunction, by force if necessary, and yet his greatest desire was to bring the conflict to a peaceful end. In an atmosphere of mass demonstrations by strike supporters and constant threats of vigilante action by strike opponents, he decided to ignore the injunction for the time being. In desperation, he called on President Franklin D. Roosevelt to order GM to the bargaining table, which Roosevelt did. The company, now weakened further by sympathy strikes in Detroit, Cleveland, Kansas City, and Wisconsin, agreed to talk. Roosevelt also asked Lewis to enter the talks at this point to represent the UAW. After a week of tense and sometimes emotional bargaining, Murphy and Lewis were able to bring the two sides to an agreement on 11 February. Not a single life was lost in the 44 days of the strike.

The contract General Motors signed gave the UAW sole bargaining rights in 17 of its struck plants for six months. The company also agreed to rehire all workers who had been fired for union activities and to begin negotiations on wages and working conditions. During the six-month period, the UAW was easily able to sign up a majority of GM workers, which fulfilled the requirement of the Wagner Act for majority rule. As a result, the UAW was established as the sole representative for all.

Almost immediately, sit-down strikes spread to Chrysler and Dodge in Detroit and to other industries and smaller businesses across the country. In all, 1937 saw over 150 sit-down strikes nationwide. More than 130,000 workers took part; more than 100 of these strikes occurred in the Detroit area alone. Ford was the last of the Big Three auto makers to resist the UAW, finally agreeing on the eve of World War II to a union shop agreement. There was an air of inevitability about this, however, as the wide-scale transformation of modern American industry, begun at Flint four years earlier, had proceeded unabated.

In retrospect, it is possible to see 1937 as the most crucial year in the history of organized industrial labor in the United States. The transformation that occurred during that year was helped along by Roosevelt's New Deal policies, by the passage of the Wagner Act, and by the actions of a few conscientious leaders like Frank Murphy. But the workers themselves deserve the most credit, as they put their livelihoods on the line in order to gain their objectives.

Key Players

Johnson, Genora (1913–1995): Founder and leader of both the Women's Auxiliary and the Women's Emergency Brigade, Johnson was in the forefront of those women's groups that supported the efforts of the sit-down strikers through activities, both tedious and dangerous. Her radical efforts were supported by her devotion to the Socialist Party, which she joined at the age of 16.

Lewis, John L. (1880–1969): President of the United Mine Workers from 1920 to 1960, Lewis broke his union away from the American Federation of Labor in 1935 and formed the Committee of Industrial Organization (CIO). An aggressive, dramatic, and frequently cantankerous personality, Lewis antagonized some of the most powerful individuals in American politics and labor over the course of his long career, yet his contributions to the fierce and radical nature of American labor during the middle of the twentieth century brought about positive changes in the lives of thousands of laborers.

Murphy, Frank (1890–1949): Murphy was elected governor of Michigan in 1936 on the coattails of Franklin Roosevelt's overwhelming reelection to the U.S. presidency. A lifelong supporter of the rights of labor, Murphy served as mayor of Detroit from 1930 to 1933. When his reelection campaign for governor failed (largely due to his actions during the Flint sit-down strike), he was appointed attorney general of the United States and then a member of the U.S. Supreme Court by President Roosevelt.

Travis, Robert (1906–1979): Travis was a key player in the 1935 Toledo Chevrolet strike and rose rapidly as an organizer after that. He was sent to Flint in the late fall of 1937 to take over leadership of organizational activities from Wyndham Mortimer. It was well known among UAW leaders that Travis's political sympathies were with the Socialist Party, yet he was more of a grassroots organizer than a politico, and his greatest gift was an ability to gain the trust of working men and women.

See also: *American Federation of Labor; Committee for Industrial Organization; Ford-UAW Contract; National Industrial Recovery Act; Wagner Act.*

BIBLIOGRAPHY

Books

Fine, Sidney. *Sit-Down: The General Motors Strike of 1936–1937.* Ann Arbor: University of Michigan Press, 1969.

Kraus, Henry. *The Many and the Few: A Chronicle of the Dynamic Auto Workers.* Los Angeles: Plantin Press, 1947.

Mortimer, Wyndham. *Organize! My Life as a Union Man.* Boston: Beacon Press, 1971.

ADDITIONAL RESOURCES

Books

Reuther, Victor. *The Brothers Reuther and the Story of the UAW: A Memoir.* Boston: Houghton Mifflin, 1976.

Dollinger, Sol, and Genora Johnson. *Not Automatic: Women and the Left in the Forging of the Auto Workers Union.* New York: Monthly Review Press, 2000.

Other

"Remembering the Flint Sit-Down Strike, 1936–1937." [cited 6 November 2002]. <www.historicalvoices.org/flint>

—Michael Van Dyke

General Motors-United Auto Workers Landmark Contracts

United States 1948, 1950

Synopsis

The collective bargaining agreements between General Motors (GM) and the United Automobile Workers union (UAW) in 1948 and 1950 established the framework that characterized U.S. labor relations through the 1980s. Although the UAW had previously tried to gain a voice in production and investment decisions in its negotiations with GM, the 1948 and 1950 agreements limited its collective bargaining demands to wage and benefits issues in contract talks. The resulting arrangement, labeled the "Treaty of Detroit" by *Fortune* magazine in 1950, linked wage hikes to the rate of inflation through cost-of-living adjustments and increases in productivity and established a pension plan and health insurance plan for workers. Although this collective bargaining achievement created a stable atmosphere of industrial relations from the early 1950s onward, it fell apart in the corporate restructuring and antiunion efforts of the federal government in the 1980s.

Timeline

1928: At the first Academy Awards ceremony, best picture is the silent *Wings.*

1933: Newly inaugurated U.S. president Franklin D. Roosevelt launches the first phase of his New Deal to put depression-era America back to work.

1938: The U.S. Fair Labor Standards Act establishes a minimum wage.

1943: At the Casablanca Conference in January, Winston Churchill and Franklin Roosevelt agree on the demand of unconditional surrender for the Axis powers.

1948: Israel becomes a nation and is immediately attacked by a coalition of Arab countries. Despite being outnumbered, Israel will win the war in the following year.

1948: Stalin places a blockade on areas of Berlin controlled by the United States, Great Britain, and France. The Allies respond with an airlift of supplies, which, like the blockade itself, lasts into late 1949.

1949: North Atlantic Treaty Organization (NATO) is established.

1949: People's Republic of China under the leadership of Mao Zedong is established.

1950: North Korean troops pour into South Korea, starting the Korean War. Initially the communists make impressive gains, but in September the U.S. Marines land at Inchon and liberate Seoul. China responds by sending in its troops.

1950: Senator Joseph McCarthy launches his campaign to root out communist infiltrators.

1955: African and Asian nations meet at the Bandung Conference in Indonesia, inaugurating the "non-aligned" movement of Third World countries.

1960: An American U-2 spy plane piloted by Francis Gary Powers is shot down over Soviet skies brings an end to a short period of warming relations between the two superpowers. By the end of the year, Khrushchev makes a scene at the United Nations, banging his shoe on a desk. As for Powers, he will be freed in a 1962 prisoner exchange.

Event and Its Context

The International Union, United Automobile, Aerospace and Agricultural Implement Workers of America—commonly known as the United Auto Workers (UAW)—was the leading industrial union in North America from the time of its founding in 1935. The fastest-growing union in the 1930s and 1940s, the UAW had about a quarter million active members in 1940, about a third of whom worked for General Motors, the Ford Motor Company, or the Chrysler Corporation. The UAW reached an early peak of 1.5 million members during World War II.

The UAW's initial success depended on its ability to use the collective bargaining framework established by such New

Deal measures as the Wagner Act, Fair Labor Standards Act, and the National Labor Relations Board (NRLB). While labor union membership expanded greatly during World War II, however, the UAW's leadership juggled the competing demands of a restive rank-and-file and its no-strike pledge that it had offered the federal government during the war. Power struggles within the union between its political left and right wings also characterized the UAW's wartime experience. Although both wings generally followed a liberal social agenda and advocated greater government oversight of the economy, the right wing had taken an anticommunist stance that angered the left wing. The right-wing caucus under Walter P. Reuther finally gained control of the UAW when he was elected to office in 1946. Reuther soon purged the UAW of any official who refused to disavow his or her communist ties—a step mandated by the Taft-Hartley Act of 1947—and he remained international president of the UAW until his death in a plane accident in 1970.

Reuther faced a number of challenges when he assumed the leadership of the UAW. Although its membership had declined from its wartime high as the nation's industries reconverted to the production of consumer goods, the UAW included approximately 900,000 members in the immediate postwar era. With the mountain of shop-floor grievances and fears of unemployment, concerns over inflation added to the tense atmosphere between the UAW and its collective bargaining counterparts.

Labor Relations in the Auto Industry

The UAW's most important round of postwar negotiations came with the largest of the Big Three auto makers, General Motors (GM), headed by President Charles E. Wilson and Chairman of the Board Alfred P. Sloan, Jr. President of General Motors from 1923 to 1937 and chairman of the board from 1937 to 1946, Sloan had been responsible for rationalizing the administration and production schedule of the company in the 1920s. GM had been chaotically managed under its founder, William C. Durant, who incorporated the company in 1908. After Durant's final ouster in 1920, Sloan implemented unyielding financial and administrative controls that led the company to produce a then-record corporate profit of $235 million in 1927. Like that of its competitors, GM's sales plummeted during the initial years of the Great Depression. Yet it managed to increase its overall market share to become the nation's largest auto maker after 1930, a position it still held at the start of the twenty-first century.

One legacy of Durant that survived his ouster was his vision of GM fostering an age of mass consumerism through installment buying and credit programs for car buyers. With a range of cars from the economic Chevrolet to the luxurious Cadillac and annual style changes to keep consumers eager for new cars, GM's approach set the standard for mass marketing of consumer items. Having survived a fall in sales between 1929 and 1933, the company took a tough stance in the face of a labor force that was being courted by the fledgling UAW. The union finally organized GM, but only after a bitter series of sit-down strikes during 1936 and 1937. Although World War II brought a truce in labor relations, many expected a new wave of strikes to rock the automobile industry as they had after World War I. The largest and most profitable of the Big Three auto makers,

President Ronald W. Reagan. The Library of Congress.

GM wanted to move aggressively to reconvert its factories from military to consumer production in 1945. One major obstacle to GMs postwar expansion plans, then, was the uncertainty of its labor contracts with the UAW.

Mass Production, Mass Consumption

Just as GM had reshaped American society along mass consumption lines, so too did the UAW have ambitious plans for remaking the country after the war. Chief among the union's desires was to achieve greater economic security for its members through collective bargaining. Although the most obvious goal under this agenda was to gain higher wages for workers, a slew of other proposals joined its collective bargaining priorities in the 1940s. As indicated by a May 1947 survey (later included in Ely Chinoy's landmark 1955 book, *Auto Workers and the American Dream*) that was published by *Fortune*, despite the postwar economic expansion in America, one-fourth of workers were worried about keeping their jobs, and an overwhelming two-thirds believed it unlikely that they would ever earn enough money to be able to retire at the age of 65. Workers were also worried about inflation eroding their earning power, especially after President Harry Truman allowed the Office of Price Administration to be dismantled in 1946 after heavy corporate lobbying. In contrast to the state activism of the New Deal years, the administration now appeared to be stepping aside from active management of the economy, despite public support for such measures. The union's leaders believed that by setting an economic benchmark through its contracts, they had found the best way to gain higher wages and improved benefits for their members and, by extension, for other workers who would benefit from the improved standards that union contracts introduced to the economy at large.

In the first collective bargaining negotiations after World War II, Reuther suffered a serious setback to his reputation during a failed strike effort against GM that lasted from November

Alfred Pritchard Sloan, Jr. The Library of Congress.

1945 to March 1946. Aware of the public's support of price controls to stem inflationary pressures, Reuther coupled the UAW's demand for a 30 percent wage increase during contract talks with a pledge by GM not to increase the final cost of its automobiles. Objecting to what they viewed as an unnecessary and counterproductive intrusion by the union into managerial prerogatives, GM's officials rejected Reuther's program outright. The ensuring 113-day strike made Reuther a nationally known labor leader, but it did little to achieve the UAW's goals. In the end the union settled for a wage increase and some minor changes in the final contract.

Hoping to avoid the prolonged wrangling of the 1946 talks, GM introduced a new factor into the March 1948 collective bargaining negotiations. Eager to stabilize its work force to ensure a steady and profitable stream of vehicles leaving its factories, GM President Charles E. Wilson offered to link future wage adjustments to the national Consumer Price Index, determined by the federal government's Bureau of Labor Statistics. The idea came to be popularly known as a cost-of-living adjustment (COLA). Wilson also put forth the idea of linking general boosts in wage rates to increases in worker productivity, a concept he labeled an "annual improvement factor." The UAW countered with demands for a pension program and a guaranteed 40-hour workweek in addition to wage hikes. After two months of negotiations, the resulting two-year contract generally followed what GM had initially offered, with the annual improvement factor pegged at 2 percent annually and a COLA to be adjusted quarterly. Although the union's leaders were disappointed over their failure to expand the contract beyond wage and benefits issues, the COLA agreement was the first that an industrial union ever achieved in a collective bargaining agreement.

The Treaty of Detroit

The 1948 contract proved to be a model for the 1950 collective bargaining sessions. The May 1950 agreement between the UAW and GM, publicized as the "Treaty of Detroit" by *Fortune* magazine, essentially drew the lines of collective bargaining for the next generation. In exchange for improved wages and benefits—including cost-of-living adjustments, pensions beginning at $125 per month, and health care provisions paid in half by GM—the company retained all managerial prerogatives, including production and investment decisions. Over five years, the contract guaranteed a 20 percent rise in wages for GM members covered by UAW contracts. The arrangement allowed the company to enjoy a measure of stability in its work force; with a five-year contract in place, GM could implement long-range plans without the fear of labor disruptions. In exchange, auto workers expanded their wage and benefits packages in succeeding years. Reuther's goal of taking the UAW into managerial affairs would not be realized during his lifetime, but the agreement did signify that GM had accepted unionization as a permanent condition of its labor force.

Additional wage and benefit gains—not only at GM but among all auto companies and other heavy industrial manufacturers—followed in succeeding years. The collective bargaining agreement with Ford in 1955 introduced supplemental unemployment benefits (SUB). When combined with government unemployment compensation, the SUB provision allowed laid-off workers to collect up to 65 percent of their regular take-home pay. Contract talks with Chrysler in 1964 produced the first early retirement provisions, another advance in the wages and benefits enjoyed by UAW members. From 1950 onward, then, collective bargaining achieved the security and stability that would have seemed impossible during the tumult of the 1930s. Together with gradual increases in regular wages and COLA, SUB, health insurance, and pension contributions from employers, the standard of living for UAW members approximately doubled during Reuther's tenure in office through 1970. Following the pattern established by UAW contracts, other labor unions also successfully bargained for COLA provisions, pensions, and health care plans; by the time of Reuther's death, more than half of all collective bargaining agreements in the United States contained a COLA agreement and more than one-third provided for pensions.

The UAW and Labor Liberalism

Throughout his career, Reuther maintained that the Treaty of Detroit and its succeeding agreements demonstrated the pragmatism necessary for the survival of the labor movement. If the union had not delivered higher wages and improved benefits to its membership, it would have been far less able to engage in any of the other broad-based public policy projects that Reuther and other labor leaders championed. The list of contributions that Reuther and the UAW made to American liberalism from the 1940s onward is indeed impressive. In addition to being a major funding source for various civil rights groups, the UAW was also a major supporter of the historic 1963 March on Washington, a pivotal moment in the modern civil rights movement. The UAW's leadership also had a major voice in President Lyndon Johnson's War on Poverty and Great Society programs of the late 1960s, helped to enact student loan programs and Medicaid and Medicare, and consistently lobbied to raise the minimum wage. To Reuther's supporters, these accomplishments proved that the UAW retained its commitment to a broad-based social and economic agenda that went far beyond the collective bargaining table.

Critics of Reuther's career have claimed that the UAW's collective bargaining agreements in 1948 and 1950 set the stage for generations of union complacency. Although the UAW expanded contract talks to include COLAs, pensions, health insurance, SUB, early retirement provisions, and other benefits for its members, it failed to restructure the American economy in any fundamental way. Reuther's attempt to secure wage hikes while forcing GM to hold the line on its auto prices in 1946 marked the last time the UAW demanded a significant say in the management of its bargaining partners. From that failed attempt onward, the UAW would confine itself to negotiating over wages and benefits in contract talks. Because it did not restructure the political or economic landscapes of America through the Treaty of Detroit, the union remained vulnerable to the changes that eventually voided the agreement and brought back another period of uncertainty for its members during the 1970s and 1980s.

Indeed, all of these gains were possible because the American automobile industry, like most other sectors of the economy, shared in almost uninterrupted growth from the postwar era through the oil crisis of 1973 and 1974. Faced with little foreign competition, increasingly affluent consumers, and a stable labor force, American auto makers enjoyed a golden age of expansion and profitability. Concentrating on annual style revisions for larger, more profitable models instead of technological innovation or the introduction of smaller, more fuel-efficient cars, the industry was caught off guard by the abrupt change in consumer demands in the 1970s.

Dismantling the Treaty of Detroit

The economic restructuring of America's industrial landscape after the oil price shocks of 1973–1974 and the deep recession and "stagflation" after 1978 significantly curtailed the pattern established by the Treaty of Detroit. A sharp reduction in employment by the Big Three followed the declining sales of domestic autos in the late 1970s. UAW membership dropped from 1.5 million in 1979 to 1 million in 1983 and then to about 750,000 in 1992. Although competition from German and Japanese auto makers was often cited as the primary reason for the drop in the sales of American-made automobiles, the Big Three had contributed to their own dilemma by ignoring consumer demands for quality and fuel efficiency in their products. Under pressure to cut their operating costs, automobile manufacturers entered into contract discussions with the UAW in the 1980s determined to curtail the collective bargaining arrangement that had guided the industry for two generations.

Concession bargaining took various forms in the late 1970s and 1980s. One example drew the union into a closer working relationship with management in 1979 when the UAW's participation in the government bailout of the Chrysler Corporation helped to bring the auto maker back from bankruptcy. Given the economic changes that transformed the American economy in the 1980s, however, the UAW joined many other unions in concession bargaining in the hopes of saving the jobs of its mem-

Charles Erwin Wilson. The Library of Congress.

bers. Typically, the UAW was forced to limit or concede its demands for increases in SUB, COLA, and wage increases.

The union also confronted a hostile environment under the administration of President Ronald Reagan from 1980 to 1988. Eager to implement his vision of a free-market economy unencumbered by labor unions, Reagan set about dismantling the labor relations framework that had been in place since the New Deal. The president used his power to end a strike by the Professional Air Traffic Controllers Organization by breaking up the union in 1981, a clear indication of his administration's approach to labor relations. Reagan also appointed a slate of officials with antiunion perspectives to government posts, including the NLRB. With the federal government subsequently issuing a series of antilabor decisions through the NLRB, labor leaders also spoke of a breakdown of the labor relations bureaucracy that had been in place since the 1950s. Although the Treaty of Detroit survived in terms of the benefits maintained by auto workers, it was no longer the model for industrial labor relations in the United States.

Key Players

Chinoy, Ely (1921–1975): A professor in sociology at Smith College, Chinoy authored *Automobile Workers and the American Dream* in 1955. The book detailed the rising consumer aspirations of the increasingly affluent working class in America and is considered one of the most important sociological studies of its era.

Reagan, Ronald W. (1911–): President of the United States from 1980 to 1988, Reagan lived up to his reputation as a free-market advocate who wanted to curtail federal regulation of the economy. In addition to firing the members of the federal air traffic controllers over their refusal to end a strike in 1981, Reagan staffed the National Labor Relations Board with officials who shared his free-market antiunion beliefs. Union membership declined during Reagan's two terms in office, and the pattern of labor relations established under the Treaty of Detroit was curtailed.

Reuther, Walter Philip (1907–1970): Reuther was president of the UAW from 1946 until his death in 1970. In addition to making the UAW into one of the largest and most powerful labor unions in the United States, Reuther helped to define a cooperative model of labor relations between his union and its collective bargaining partners beginning with the Treaty of Detroit in 1950. Reuther was also a major figure in the modern civil rights movement and other liberal social causes.

Sloan, Alfred Pritchard, Jr. (1875–1966): President of General Motors from 1923 to 1937 and chairman of the board from 1937 to 1946, Sloan was responsible for rationalizing the administration and production schedule of the company.

Wilson, Charles Erwin (1890–1961): President of General Motors from 1941 to 1952, Wilson was trained as an engineer and after a legendary career in the automobile industry served as secretary of defense from 1953 to 1957.

See also: *Fair Labor Standards Act; Ford-UAW Contract; Ford-UAW SUB Agreement; GM Recognizes UAW; PATCO Strike; Wagner Act.*

BIBLIOGRAPHY

Books

Boyle, Kevin. *The UAW and the Heyday of American Liberalism*. Ithaca, NY: Cornell University Press, 1995.

Carew, Anthony. *Walter Reuther*. Manchester, England: Manchester University Press, 1993.

Chinoy, Ely. *Automobile Workers and the American Dream*. 1955. Reprint, Urbana: University of Illinois Press, 1992.

Freeland, Robert. *The Struggle for Control of the Modern Corporation: Organizational Change at General Motors, 1924–1970*. New York: Cambridge University Press, 2000.

Goode, Bill. *Infighting in the UAW: The 1946 Election and the Ascendancy of Walter Reuther*. Westport, CT: Greenwood Press, 1994.

Harris, Howell J. *The Right to Manage: Industrial Relations Policies of American Business in the 1940s*. Madison: University of Wisconsin Press, 1982.

Keller, Maryann. *Rude Awakening: The Rise, Fall, and Struggle for Recovery of General Motors*. New York: William Morrow and Company, 1989.

Lichtenstein, Nelson. *The Most Dangerous Man in America: Walter Reuther and the Fate of American Labor*. New York: Basic Books, 1995.

Sloan, Alfred P. *My Years with General Motors*. Garden City, NY: Doubleday and Company, 1963.

Zieger, Robert. *The CIO, 1935–1955*. Chapel Hill: University of North Carolina Press, 1995.

—Timothy G. Borden

General Strike

France 1968

Synopsis

Significant protests by students and workers on an international scale marked 1968. In France these protests took on an exceptional character. Involving at their height between 7 and 10 million strikers and 150 million working days lost, the May-June strikes were the largest ever recorded.

In addition to these figures, 1968 also had the social, cultural and political impact of an earthquake. Bruno Groppo remarked, "For any French person, 1968 immediately evokes the May events: so close a linguistic association of the year and the month that one automatically and instinctively says 'May 1968'." As a result this movement occupies so important a place in the French collective memory that it has ended up by obscuring the other events of this critical year.

Familiarity does not always imply clarity, and it is difficult with hindsight to retrace the coherence of the events. Their singularity lies in the conjunction of two major crises on behalf of students and workers that did not merge. At the end of nearly two months of often violent demonstrations, these events led to an overwhelming victory by the Right in parliamentary elections. Whether the revolution was unattainable, betrayed, or failed is often debated. The French May 1968 has been the subject of many interpretations and is still analyzed more as a societal phenomenon than as a classic labor conflict.

Timeline

1948: Israel becomes a nation and is immediately attacked by a coalition of Arab countries.

1953: Korean War, a conflict with no clear victors, ends with an armistice establishing an uneasy peace between South Korea and North Korea.

1958: China's Mao Zedong proclaims the Great Leap Forward, a program of enforced rapid industrialization that will end a year later, a miserable failure.

1963: U.S. Supreme Court rules that no municipal, county, or state government may require recitation of the Lord's Prayer or of Bible verses in public schools.

1968: Communist victories in the Tet offensive mark the turning point in the Vietnam War and influence a growing lack of confidence in the war, not only among America's youth, but within the establishment as well.

1968: Dr. Martin Luther King, Jr., is assassinated on 4 April, and Robert Kennedy on 5 June.

1968: Violence erupts at the Democratic National Convention in Chicago.

1968: After Czechoslovakia adopts a more democratic, popular regime, Soviet and Warsaw Pact forces invade to crush the uprising.

1973: Signing of peace accords in Paris in January ends the Vietnam War.

1978: U.S. Senate approves a measure presented by President Carter the year before, to turn the Panama Canal over to Panama by 2000.

1983: Sally Ride becomes the first female U.S. astronaut (the Soviets were ahead by two decades, with Valentina Tereshkova) when she goes into space aboard the shuttle *Challenger*.

Event and Its Context

A sudden and uncontrollable explosion, the May movement had its origins in the processes of accelerated economic and social modernization that affected the industrialized world in the aftermath of World War II. An exceptional level of growth culminated from the increase in working hours, an intensification of work, and the widespread existence of low pay. Throughout the 1960s this situation heightened social tensions. Several important strikes occurred, in particular a huge miners' strike in 1963.

The year 1968 continued the ambient agitation of the times and opened with a wave of disputes involving engineering workers. The level of the protests pressured the government for the first time in 15 years to grant a legal permit to the traditional 1 May march.

Despite being strongly mobilized on the eve of the "May events," the working class, however, only played a secondary role in triggering them. For the first time in history, students moved to the front rank of the social struggle. Considerably transformed by the early beginnings of mass access to secondary and higher education, swollen by the demographic boom, influenced by changing values and the development of a mass consumption society, they started to levy totally unexpected demands.

Students Trigger a General Strike

The May events began at the University of Nanterre. Built in 1964 on an army training ground surrounded by shanty towns, it housed no less than 11,000 students. From 1967 the university was the source of a growing series of conflicts over such issues as sexual freedoms and victimizations of certain students in the exams.

Confronted by a wave of protest demonstrations that had been fueled by the 22 March Movement—a united front with anarchist leadership that began at Nanterre on 22 March 1968 following a demonstration against the arrest of a student suspected of involvement in terrorism—the university dean decided on 2 May to suspend all classes.

The following day the students responded by organizing a meeting in the Sorbonne courtyard in central Paris. The police intervened, at first peacefully, but the situation deteriorated and by the end of the day violent confrontations occurred between some 2,000 students and about 1,500 police. For the first time in the history of the university, the police had orders to enter the Sorbonne and to evacuate it using force. The confrontation left 72 students wounded, 600 detained for questioning, and 13 arrested. The rector of Paris University then decided, three weeks before the exams, to close the Sorbonne and Censier buildings.

Daniel Cohn-Bendit. © Archive Photos, Inc. Reproduced by permission.

From this point, student and lecturer demonstrations multiplied in Paris and elsewhere in France, each time being suppressed by the police. United in response to the immediate events, the student movement was nonetheless deeply divided. Two main tendencies appeared. Some believed it was hopeless to try to change the university system and called on students to rejoin the working class to help rekindle its "revolutionary flame." Others struggled for a democratic reform of the educational system that would bring it closer to real life and modernize teaching methods.

On 10 May the Paris police erected barricades. At the end of a night of street battles with the forces of law and order, there were 367 wounded and over 5,000 arrests. The shock provoked in public opinion by that night's police brutality prompted the workers' trade union confederations, which until then had been bystanders, to act. The next day the Confédération générale du travail (CGT), the CFDT, and the teachers' union (FEN) called for a 24-hour general strike. The *Force Ouvrière* (FO) union joined the call shortly afterwards. On 13 May marches took place all over France to inspire action for a variety of causes, including amnesty for sentenced demonstrators, trade union and political freedoms, democratic reform of education for workers, full employment, and transformation of the economic system "by and for the people." The Paris demonstration brought together 800,000 behind a banner urging solidarity between students, teachers, and workers. The Sorbonne reopened its doors the same day, but it was too late. The student movement continued with a new intensity, and the workers' strike movement took off.

Workers Take Up the Baton

By mid-May the CGT and the CFDT were already involved in their own struggles. Several regional actions for jobs, against cuts in purchasing power, and over Social Security took place

Police rushing student demonstrators, University District, Paris, France. AP/Wide World Photos. Reproduced by permission.

in the West on 8 May, in the Loire on the 10th, and in the North-Calais and Moselle on the 11th. Some demonstrations had brought together, according to the local press, "crowds not seen since the Liberation."

On 14 May the Nantes Sud-Aviation workers occupied their factory. They were followed on the 15th by workers at Renault Cléon, then by the Kléber-Colombes workers at Elbeuf, by the Roclaine workers at Saint-Etienne-du-Rouvray, and at the Odéon Theatre in Paris. The movement continued to spread over the following days. Authorities counted two million strikers on 18 May and six million on 10 May. In turn, teachers and civil servants stopped work on 21 May. From this date all public services with the exception of the emergency services were paralyzed.

Despite tensions and divisions, the common platform that had been agreed between the CGT and CFDT on 10 January 1966 held up. It had five points: improving purchasing power and living and working conditions; the defense and extension of trade union rights at firm level; cuts in unproductive expenditure in favor of more public investment in housing, education,

and health; guarantees for the right to work through introducing new industries; and fiscal reform. The protesters, however, failed to establish a national strike committee. Each confederation, for its own reasons, emphasized the "self-direction" of the movement. In practice, the strike revealed an extreme diversity both between sectors and between one firm and another. In this context, the negotiations proposed by the government received a mixed reception with some factions viewing them as a necessity and others as a betrayal.

The Grenelle Negotiations

Although matters were following the same pattern as the 1936 *Matignon* agreements (agreements between the government, employers unions, and labor unions that outlined numerous workers' rights), the government nonetheless carefully avoided using the same symbols. It was therefore in the offices of the Ministry of Social Issues, based in the Rue de Grenelle, and not at the prime minister's Matignon offices, that the negotiations began at 3 P.M. on 25 May. On the agenda were wages, working hours, pensions, jobs, and trade union rights.

French workers and university students marching through the boulevards of Paris, France. © Hulton/Archive by Getty Images. Reproduced by permission.

The parties reached agreement rapidly on raising the hourly national minimum wage to three francs. The discussions on wages proved more difficult: the government refused to consider adopting a sliding scale. On 27 May, at the end of a second night of negotiations, the participants agreed to a statement without signatures. The statement included several important points: a 35 percent increase in the national minimum wage (known as the SMIG), abolition of the lower SMIG rates outside of Paris, increases in the lowest wages, an increase of 56 percent to bring the agricultural minimum wage in line with the SMIG, commitment to a process of reducing real working hours, recognition of firm-based trade union organization, and 50 percent compensation or repayment in full for days on strike. On the other hand, the government rejected a discussion of the abolition of the 21 August 1967 Social Security decrees. These involved suppressing the joint management elections, an increase in deductions, and cuts in benefits of three billion francs.

The Grenelle text went to the strikers later on 27 May and provoked a very strong reaction. Over the following days the strike continued at its highest level. There was no more public transport, no more petrol, the streets of Paris were empty, and workers either occupied their factories or stayed at home.

Several signs revealed that government power was virtually falling apart. Several new strategies broached on the political arena. The noncommunist left mobilized around Pierre Mendès-France, more or less openly supported by the CFDT and FO, and around François Mitterrand. On 28 May, Mitterrand called for the creation of a provisional government. At the end of the day several tens of thousands of people met at the Charléty stadium for a meeting that had considerable political repercussions.

The Situation Turns

The Ministerial Council meeting scheduled for 10 A.M. on 19 May was canceled at the last minute. The French president, General Charles De Gaulle, had just secretly left Paris for Baden-Baden, Germany, where he met General Massu to seek the support of the army. Judging that there was no one in power, the CFDT invited Pierre Mendès-France to take over the government.

The next day, however, De Gaulle returned to give a speech that reversed the course of events. He announced his decision to remain as head of state. He noted that the prime minister would also stay in office and then dissolved the National Assembly. More than one million Gaullists demonstrated that evening in Paris and elsewhere in France with slogans such as "communism will not pass," "drain the Sorbonne," and "Mitterrand, it's failed."

During the night the oil companies resupplied the stations. Tens of thousands of Parisians left the capital for the Whitson holiday. Adapting to the new climate, the unions focused on factional and company negotiations to try and obtain the best possible agreements. Only the national student union, UNEF, called for demonstrations against the "election-treachery," but it met with little success.

The decline of the strike movement continued slowly until 17 June, when work resumed at Renault. Factional negotiations produced agreements in a majority of trade sectors that were better than the terms that had been decided at Grenelle, particularly relative to wages. In higher education the Edgar Faure reform introduced autonomy for the universities and some joint management.

The election campaign that opened on 10 June gradually eclipsed the industrial struggle. The elections of 23 and 30 June 1968 confirmed the victory of the Right and gave the Gaullist UDR political party 50 seats more than an absolute majority in the National Assembly. Although according to many observers this showed the electorate's rejection of the May excesses, it nonetheless was not a landslide: the change in voters' preferences were well below those that later occurred in June 1981, when the Left finally took power.

Various Interpretations

The May–June 1968 events have been the object of many analyses in an abundant literature. Beyond issues of historical detail, the controversies have centered on the nature and significance of the movement. A range of views exists between those who affirm its incidental and superficial character and those who proclaim its depth and its necessity. Other differences concern how far it can be seen as having national or international origins. Some analyses name it a "French problem," whereas others situate the national case within a world crisis of civilization or of capitalism.

French sociologists have played a particularly important role in this debate, from the very beginning proposing analytical frameworks that have been used continually since. Sociologist Raymond Aron treated the events as a psychodrama, as a great letting off of steam, or as a frenzy. If he recognized the existence of common problems in the developed industrial societies and among student youth, he believed that the crisis owed its particular intensity in France to a specific situation. In particular structural factors, such as the weakness of the mediating institutions, the maintenance of a revolutionary tradition based on the myth of the general strike, and—in the university world—the distance that traditionally existed between the teachers and the taught, contributed to the vehemence of the day. On a more basic level, worker discontent arose from wage restraint and rising employment.

In the view of Michel Crozier, the 1968 events were essentially a cultural crisis. Commensurate with the bureaucratic rigidities and centralism of French culture, the strikes and demonstrations reflected a deeply repressed rejection of change. Nonetheless, in mimicking the achievement of a total revolution, the May actors could have exorcized definitively the revolutionary myth and opened the way to a different method of conducting change.

Alain Touraine, for his part, saw the strikes as a reaction to the contradiction that opposes changing current technical and cultural realities to past organizational and institutional traditions. He also developed his thinking about the evolution of class consciousness, which prompted him to interpret 1968 as a struggle for the conquest of political power that was led by a manual working class that wished to achieve a greater share of the fruits of growth.

Finally, Henri Lefebvre called for a renewal of a Marxist analytical framework. He was largely interested in the students' situation, which, for him, revealed factors common to all age groups. He showed how 1968 marked the arrival of new actors on the employment relations scene (such as managers and scientific professionals), and how this push shook the society's superstructures and put the invention of new forms of social life on the agenda.

Other authors have subsequently tried to explicate and theorize the new elements introduced by May 1968. Jean Capdeveille and René Mouriaux underlined its ambiguity. They saw several similarities with the more significant revolutionary moments of the nineteenth century: the violence of the demonstrations and, more generally, their political character; the nearly insurrectional dimension of the paralysis of most public services; the scale and spread of the movement in certain provisional cities and towns; and the omnipresent symbolic references to working-class history. Yet other of its characteristics projected its participants forward toward the twenty-first century, especially the calls for lifestyle liberation and gender equality, the aspirations for greater quality of life, criticisms of the consumer society, and heightened demands concerning citizenship.

A major renewal of the forms of social protest accompanied the emergence of new social issues. In particular, the incomplete and conflicting combination of the student spirit with a mobilization of wage earners had an impact on most of France's subsequent large social movements.

At the same time, May 1968 represented a critical turning point in the development of the media coverage of conflicts. The radio station Europe 1 reported directly on the student demonstrations, and television covered the night of the barricades. Manipulators and countermanipulators challenged each other all through the events, the reporting of which itself finally became an essential component of the turmoil.

Whether a fake or a failed revolution, the May 1968 movement nonetheless represented a real ideological earthquake. It incontestably marked the starting points of a broadening of the social movement and of an end to the hegemony of the manual working class. As a result, it considerably altered the political and social picture and brought about major institutional changes.

Key Players

Cohn-Bendit, Daniel (1945–): Sociology student at Nanterre, leader of the anarchist 22 March movement, Cohn-Bendit has an important place in the events of May-June 1968. Arrested and served with an exclusion order for his role in the student movement, he was expelled from France on 24 May 1968. Subsequently, in the 1980s and 1990s, he was an active member of the German Green Party.

Fouque, Antoinette (1936–):A psychoanalyst and one of the founders of the French Women's Liberation Movement (MLF), Fouque created the group Psychoanalysis and Politics, then became publisher of *Des femmes*.

Geismar, Alain (1939–): Far left activist, representative of the university lecturers' union (SNESUP) during the May events, Geismar subsequently became the leader of the Proletarian Left (GP, a Maoist organization that espouses self-

criticism and the building of a New Popular Resistance that included an embryonic armed struggle) and was imprisoned for "reforming a dissolved organization" in 1970. In the 1990s he served in various ministerial posts.

Krivine, Alain (1941–): Krivine was the founder in 1966 of the Revolutionary Communist Youth that was dissolved by the government in June 1968. In 1969 he founded the Communist League (which was dissolved in 1973) and then in 1974 the Revolutionary Communist League (LCR), of which he remained general secretary as of 2003.

Sauvaget, Jacques (1943–): Vice president of the French students' union (UNEF), Sauvaget was pushed to the front page by the events. He was the only leader to give up his positions as early as the autumn of 1968. After a period in the far left he joined and became active in the Socialist Party.

See also: *Confédération Générale du Travail.*

BIBLIOGRAPHY

Books

Aron, Raymond. *La révolution Introuvable*. Paris: Fayard, 1968.

Capdevielle, Jacques and René Mouriaux. *Mai 1968, L'entre Deux de la Modernité. Histoire de Trente Ans*. Paris: PNFSP, 1988.

Crozier, Michel. *La société bloquée*. Paris: Seuil, 1970.

Dubois, Pierre, R. Dulong, Claude Durand, Sabine Erbès-Seguin, and D. Vidal. *Grèves Revendicatives ou Grèves politiques? Acteurs, Pratiques, sens du Mouvement de Mai*. Paris: Anthropos, 1971.

Lefebvre, Henri. *L'irruption de Nanterre au Sommet*. Paris: Anthropos, 1968.

Mouriaux, René, Annick Percheron, Antoine Prost, and Danièle Tartakowsky. *1968: Exploration du Mai Français*. Paris: L'Harmattan, 1992.

Salvaresi, Elisabeth. *Mai en Héritage, 14 Portraits, 490 Itinéraires*. Paris: Syros Alternatives, 1988.

Tartakowsky, Danielle. Les Événements de Mai. In *La France ouvrière, de 1968 à nos Jours*, edited by Claude Willard. Paris: Editions de l'Atelier, 1995.

Touraine, Alain. *Le Mouvement de Mai ou le Communisme Utopique*. Paris: Le Seuil, 1968.

Weber, Henri. *Que Reste-t-il de Mai 1968? Essai sur les Interprétations des Événements*. Paris: Seuil, 1998.

Periodicals

Bénéton, Philippe and Jean Touchard. "Les Interprétations de la Crise de Mai-Juin 1968." *Revue française de Science Politique* (June 1970) : 503–543.

ADDITIONAL RESOURCES

Books

Bensaïd, Daniel and Henri Weber. *Mai 1968: Une Répétition générale*. Paris: Maspero, 1968.

Club Jean-Moulin. *Que Faire de la Révolution de Mai?* Paris: Le Seuil, 1968.

De Gaulle, Charles. *Lettres, Notes et Carnets. Juillet 1966–Avril 1969*. Paris: Plon, 1987.

Fohlen, Claude. *Mai 68: Révolution ou Psychodrame?* Paris: PUF, 1973.

Gretton, John. *Students and Workers: An Analytical Account of Dissent in France, May-June '68*. London: MacDonald and Co., 1969.

Mémoires de 1968. Guide des Sources d'une Histoire à Faire. Paris: Verdier, 1993.

Mendès-France, Pierre. *Pour Préparer l'Avenir*. Paris: Denoël, 1968.

Paillat, Claude. *Archives Secrètes. 1968/69: Les Coulisses d'une Année Terrible*. Paris: Denoël, 1969.

Pompidou, Georges. *Le Nœud Gordien*. Paris: Plon, 1974.

Quattrocchi, Angelo and Tom Nairn. *The Beginning of the End: France, May 1968; What Happened, Why It Happened*. London: Panther Books, 1968.

Rochet, Waldeck. *Les Enseignements de Mai–Juin 1968*. Paris: Les Editions Sociales, 1968..

Sauvageot, Jacques, Alain Geismar, Daniel Cohn-Bendit, and Jean-Pierre Duteuil. *La Révolte Étudiante*. Paris: Le Seuil, 1968.

Séguy, Georges. *Le Mai de la CGT*. Paris: Julliard, 1972.

Singer, Daniel. *Prelude to Revolution: France in May 1968*. New York: Hill and Wang, 1970.

Tariq, Ali and Susan Watkins. *1968, Marching in the Streets*. New York: Free Press, 1998.

UNEF-SNE-Sup. *Le Livre Noir des Journées de Mai*. Paris: Le Seuil, 1968.

Wylie, Laurence, Franklin D. Chu, and Mary Terral. *France: The Events of May-June 1968. A Critical Bibliography*. Pittsburgh, PA: Center for West European Studies, 1973.

Periodicals

CFDT. "Position et Action de la CFDT au Cours des Événements de Mai–Juin 1968." *Syndicalisme*. Special edition no. 1266A (November).

—Sylvie Contrepois

General Strike

Spain 1890

Synopsis

At the founding of the Socialist (Second) International in Paris in July 1889, delegates passed a resolution to make 1 May a universal day of action for the eight-hour workday and approved a host of measures intended to improve working conditions. The choice of this date was meant to recall the bloody events that occurred during the general strike in Chicago in May 1886 (the "Haymarket Massacre"), which resulted in the execution of the "Chicago Martyrs." In Catalonia, one of Spain's most industrialized regions, the International's resolution led to widespread mobilization. More important, a significant proportion of Catalan workers faced uncompromising employers and military repression as they embarked on an unlimited general strike.

Timeline

1870: Franco-Prussian War begins. German troops sweep over France, Napoleon III is dethroned, and France's Second Empire gives way to the Third Republic.

1876: Four-stroke cycle gas engine is introduced.

1880: South Africa's Boers declare an independent republic, precipitating the short First Anglo-Boer War.

1883: Foundation of the League of Struggle for the Emancipation of Labor by Marxist political philosopher Georgi Valentinovich Plekhanov marks the formal start of Russia's labor movement. Change still lies far in the future for Russia, however: tellingly, Plekhanov launches the movement in Switzerland.

1886: Bombing at Haymarket Square, Chicago, kills seven policemen and injures numerous others. Eight anarchists are accused and tried; three are imprisoned, one commits suicide, and four are hanged.

1888: Serbian-born American electrical engineer Nikola Tesla develops a practical system for generating and transmitting alternating current (AC), which will ultimately—and after an extremely acrimonious battle—replace Thomas Edison's direct current (DC) in most homes and businesses.

1890: U.S. Congress passes the Sherman Antitrust Act, which in the years that follow will be used to break up large monopolies.

1890: Police arrest and kill Sioux chief Sitting Bull, and two weeks later, federal troops kill over 200 Sioux at Wounded Knee.

1890: Alfred Thayer Mahan, a U.S. naval officer and historian, publishes *The Influence of Sea Power Upon History, 1660–1783*, which demonstrates the decisive role that maritime forces have played in past conflicts. The book will have an enormous impact on world events by encouraging the major powers to develop powerful navies.

1893: Henry Ford builds his first automobile.

1896: First modern Olympic Games are held in Athens.

1900: Commonwealth of Australia is established.

Event and Its Context

The Labor Movement in Restoration Spain

In mid-nineteenth-century Spain, industrialization remained a regional phenomenon mainly limited to Asturias and the Basque Country (mining and metallurgy), and Catalonia (textiles). The First Republic, proclaimed in 1873 in the wake of the Revolution of 1868, was overturned in 1874 and was followed by the Bourbon Restoration under Alfonso XII (constitution of 1876). Universal suffrage for men and freedom of worship, expression, and association, granted under the republic, were suspended. The new two-chamber monarchist regime instituted limited suffrage. The Conservative party leader, Antonio Cánovas del Castillo, instituted the *turno pacífico*, an artificial brand of bipartisanship whereby the Liberals and the Conservatives took turns at the helm, through the *caciquismo*, a vote-catching system that enabled the swaying of electoral choices. The ascension to power of the Liberal Práxedes Mateo Sagasta in 1881 brought about merely superficial changes to the Spanish political landscape. One notable exception was a greater tolerance of labor organizations.

Catalan trade unions, the first of which had appeared in 1840, were 80,000 members strong when they were outlawed by Espartero's military regime in 1855. Following the Revolution of 1868, all three textile industry unions (spinners, weavers, and day laborers) merged to form *Tres Classes de Vapor* (1869), the largest union in nineteenth-century Catalonia. The International Workingmen's Association was set up in Spain.

During the 1880s, Catalan trade unionism evolved along two distinct paths. The first saw the founding, in 1881, of the Workers' Federation of the Spanish Region (FTRE), an anarcho-syndicalist organization close to Mikhail Bakunin, which advocated the creation of legal unions as a prerequisite to the establishment of a classless society, and, on the other side, an individualist, radical form of anarchism influenced by Pyotr Kropotkin, the Russian revolutionary and philosopher, and bent on propaganda and clandestine action. The second path was that taken by a socialist trade unionism with Marxist but noninsurrectionist leanings. It was embodied by the Workers' General Union (UGT), founded in Barcelona in 1888 by Pablo Iglesias Posse at the same time as the Spanish Socialist Workers' Party (PSOE). However, the possibility of fostering widespread, labor party-sponsored unionism was preempted by limitations on the freedom of association imposed under Restoration. Rather, the prevailing context allowed insurrectionist movements to take root.

As of 1886, the high number of firings and the intensifying exploitation of workers brought about by the economic downturn stimulated labor mobilization in parallel to the rise of Catalan nationalism under the impetus of Liberal leader Valentí Almirall. Such was the setting for the 1 May celebrations in 1890 in Catalonia.

A General Rehearsal: The Strike for Solidarity with Workers of Manresa

The labor conflict in Manresa in March 1890 provided workers with the opportunity to put their capacity for mobilization to the test. On 20 March the directors of textile factory *Els Dolors* refused to concede to the wage demands of their employees. Workers immediately called a strike. Eighteen of the city's factories enforced a preemptive lock-out in an attempt to curb the movement's expansion. On 26 March the leaders of *Tres Classes de Vapor*, Esteve Vidal and Antoni Sagués, proclaimed a Catalonia-wide strike in a show of solidarity with the Manresa workers. More than 50,000 strikers expressed their support, most notably in Barcelona, Berga, and Vilanova i la Geltrú. On 12 April the parties reached an agreement calling for the 70-hour workweek, a 12 percent wage increase, and the cre-

ation of a permanent mixed commission. Faced with the employers' refusal to implement this agreement, workers once again brandished the threat of strike action on 20 April. However, a timely intervention by the civil governor of the province of Barcelona led to the enforcement of the terms of the agreement, thereby putting an end to this "magnificent general rehearsal" for 1 May 1890.

On this occasion, labor considered three forms of mobilization. First, the Socialist Center of Barcelona, directed by Antonio García Quejido, recommended a massive action devoid of any precise ideological line and augmented by claims addressed to the political authorities. Labor organizations in favor of this course of action agreed, on 22 April, to organize a peaceful gathering and protest. Second, the anarchists advocated spontaneous actions and refused to beg the authorities for rights. Following a meeting of more than 3,000 persons held in Barcelona's Tivoli theater on 20 April, participants pondered a general strike to bring about the eight-hour workday. Third, poised between the socialists and the anarchists, the brand of "pure-and-simple" or so-called possibilist trade unionism advocated by *Tres Classes de Vapor*, was defined by a strategy of "caution and peace, slow and gradual, yet pacifist and solid progress." Finally, on 27 April the union joined with the socialists' program. Thanks to effective propaganda, the workers' increasing enthusiasm in the last week of April contrasted sharply with the panic that spread among the bourgeoisie, cultivated by alarmist press coverage. The civil governor mobilized troops to anticipated trouble spots, namely Barcelona, Manresa, and Granollers.

1 May 1890

In practical terms, the workers' main demand was the limitation of the workday to eight hours for adults. A more radical redistribution of the day ("eight hours of work, eight hours of education and leisure time, and eight hours of rest") was their goal. Many saw the protest as the catalyst for a social revolution by means of an unlimited general strike that would crush bourgeois society. On the morning of 1 May, the working class and its supporters throughout Barcelona heeded the call for a general strike. The resulting mood in the city was festive: all the shops were closed, and thoroughfares were clear of streetcars and carriages. Authorities in several Catalan towns expected protests in front of municipal and provincial headquarters.

At a meeting at the Tivoli theater at 10:00 A.M., Antonio García Quejido and Toribio Reoyo addressed a packed house. A peaceful demonstration of about 25,000 people followed, ending at *Plaça del Palau*, the seat of civil governor Luis Antúnez Monzón, who met with an official delegation led by García Quejido. The demonstration ended peacefully. In the rest of Catalonia, other gatherings took place. Some 5,000 people marched in Mataró, 4,000 in Badalona, 4,000 in Vilanova i la Geltrú, 2,500 in Olot, and 2,000 in Sallent as well Reus, Valls, and other towns. In Barcelona several small demonstrations occurred during the course of the day. At a gathering of 200 workers, the leaders issued a call for an unlimited strike. The anarchist strategy managed to impose itself.

The General Strike Continues

Despite the condemnation of the Socialist Center of Barcelona, the general strike continued on 2 May. At approximately

5:00 P.M., the civil governor transferred his powers to the military governor Ramon Blanco, who declared a state of war and deployed 9,000 soldiers in Barcelona, plus the *guardias civiles* and troops deployed in other parts of Catalonia.

On 3 May a few factories tried in vain to reopen their doors. The strike remained widespread in Barcelona, Manresa, Reus, Terrassa, and Sabadell. In the Catalan capital, attempts to reestablish streetcar service provoked riots. Police charges and arrests were widespread. The next day, negotiations began between employers and union representatives under pressure from General Blanco. Sector-based agreements permitted a gradual return to work: masons and shoemakers obtained the eight-hour workday and double pay for overtime, textile whiteners got closed shops, and the bakers of Gràcia got sleeping mattresses. On 6 May the workers went back to work *en masse*. According to press reports, by 8 May only 23 factories were still on strike in Barcelona and 81 had reopened. In spite of the release of many prisoners by General Blanco, about 100 people remained jailed. On 12 May the strike actions were for the most part over.

A Merely Symbolic Gain

The mass protests of 1 May 1890 were in the end only somewhat successful: workers' demands were only temporarily or partially recognized by employers. However, 1 May made it possible for the Catalan labor movement to regroup with the "social question" at center stage as a public priority. Anarchist strategy seemed to be legitimized with the gain of the eight-hour workday in certain sectors as the consequence of the unlimited general strike. However, later attempts at general strikes, on 1 May 1891, 1892, and 1893, failed. Many anarchists thus left the trade union organizations and turned to "direct action" or "propaganda by the deed." From 1893 to 1897 Barcelona became the "City of Bombs" as a cycle of anarchist attacks and crackdowns by the authorities ensued. Brutal and indiscriminate repression inspired an international campaign of solidarity. Through it all, the labor movement continued to grow.

Despite the introduction in 1890 of universal suffrage for men, the question of political representation of labor remained unsolved: the *turno pacífico* was maintained and unions remained illegal. In addition to social tensions came the loss to the United States, in 1898, of Cuba and the Philippines, the last vestiges of the colonial empire and important markets for manufactured products.

In the years after 1890, anarchism began to dominate the labor movement in Catalonia. Because of low membership numbers, the socialist UGT moved its headquarters from Barcelona to Madrid in 1899. The increasingly moderate *Tres Classes de Vapor* disappeared during World War I. For the general strike of 1902, trade unionism and anarchism began a reconciliation of sorts. The development of anarcho-syndicalism led to the founding of the National Confederation of Labor (CNT) in 1910.

Key Players

García Quejido, Antonio (1856–1927): García Quejido was a typographer, trade union activist, socialist, and member of the Printing Craft Association. In 1879 he participated in founding the Spanish Socialist Workers' Party (PSOE). In 1888 he cofounded the Workers General Union (UGT), over which he initially presided. He was leader of the Socialist Center of Barcelona and a coorganizer of the 1 May 1890 actions. After World War I he left the PSOE and participated in founding the Communist Party of Spain (PCE).

Reoyo, Toribio: Typographer, trade union activist, and socialist, Reoyo was a member of the Printing Craft Association and president of the Typographic Society of Barcelona. He was an activist in the PSOE and UGT, which he cofounded in 1888, and director of the Mataró's newspaper *La República Social* (1896–1898) and secretary general of the Spanish Typographic Federation as well as the UGT (1897–1899).

Sagués, Antoni: Typographer, trade union activist, and socialist, Sagués as a member of the textile union *Tres Classes de Vapor*, of which he was president as of 1887. He cofounded the Spanish Social Democratic Labor Party (1881) and was signatory of the Manresa labor contract in March 1890. He also cofounded the moderately left-wing Socialist Opportunist Party (1890).

Vidal, Esteve: Vidal was a textile worker, trade union activist, and secretary of *Tres Classes de Vapor* in 1890. In reaction to the lock-out decreed by Manresa's employers, he organized and led a general strike of the textile sector in Barcelona in March 1890 in solidarity.

See also: *Haymarket Riot; Second International.*

BIBLIOGRAPHY

Books

Anguera, Pere. "El primer de Maig." In *Història, política, societat i cultura del Països Catalans*, vol. 7: *La Consolidació del món burgès*, edited by Pere Anguera. Barcelona, Spain: Enclopèdia Catalana, 1996.

Carasa, Pedro. "La Restauración monárquica." In *Historia de España, Siglo XX, 1875–1939*, edited by Ángel Bahamonde. Madrid, Spain: Cátedra, 2000.

Ferrer, Joaquim. *El primer "1r. de Maig" a Catalunya.* Barcelona, Spain: La Llar del Llibre, 1986 (1972).

Martínez de Sas, María Teresa, and Pelai Pagès i Blanch, eds. *Diccionari biogràfic del moviment obrer als Països Catalans.* Barcelona. Spain: Edicions Universitat de Barcelona, Publicacions de l'Abadia de Montserrat, 2000.

Termes, Josep. *Història de Catalunya*, vol. 7: *De la Revolució de Setembre a la fi de la Guerra Civil (1868–1939)*. Barcelona, Spain: Edicions 62, 1987.

Periodicals

Ballester, David, and Manuel Vicente. "El primer de maig a Barcelona. Vuit hores de treball, d'instruccó i de descans." *L'Avenç* 137 (May 1990): 12.

ADDITIONAL RESOURCES

Books

Álvarez Junco, José. *La ideología del anarquismo español, 1868–1910.* Madrid, Spain: Siglo XXI, 1976.

Hobsbawm, Eric. "Birth of a Holiday. The 1st of May." In *Uncommon People. Resistance, Rebellion and Jazz.* London: Weidenfeld and Nicholson, 1998.

Mir, Conxita, ed. *Actituds polítiques i control social a la Catalunya de la Restauració (1875–1923).* Lleida, Spain: Virgili i Pagès, Institut d'Estudis Ilerdencs, 1989.

Núñez Florencio, Rafael. *El terrorismo anarquista, 1888–1909.* Madrid, Spain: Siglo XXI, 1983.

Other

Diccionari de Sindicats, Sindicalistes i de la Història del Moviment Obrer de Catalunya (dels orígens fins l'any 1939). Vilanova i la Geltrú (Spain). 2000 [cited 1 October 2002]. <http://www.terra.es/personal7/perefer/index.htm>.

Ripoll, Xavier. *Història del moviment obrer a Catalunya.* 2002 [cited 1 October 2002]. <http://www.geocities.com/xripoll/obrer.html>.

—Yanic Viau

1818: Donkin, Hall & Gamble "Preservatory" in London produces the first canned foods.

1824: Ludwig van Beethoven composes his Ninth Symphony.

1829: Greece wins its independence after a seven-year war with Turkey.

1831: Unsuccessful Polish revolt takes place against Russian rule.

1834: British mathematician Charles Babbage completes drawings for the "analytic engine," a forerunner of the modern computer that he never builds.

1834: American inventor Cyrus H. McCormick patents his reaper, a horse-drawn machine for harvesting wheat.

1835: American inventor and painter Samuel F. B. Morse constructs an experimental version of his telegraph, and American inventor Samuel Colt patents his revolver.

1837: Coronation of Queen Victoria in England takes place.

1841: Act of Union joins Upper Canada and Lower Canada, which consist of parts of the present-day provinces of Ontario and Quebec, respectively.

1846: American inventor Elias Howe patents his sewing machine.

General Trades' Union

United States 1833

Synopsis

From 1800 to 1840 dramatic changes occurred within the U.S. economy primarily in response to the Industrial Revolution. Thousands of skilled craftsmen and artisans, the bulk of nonfarm workers before the nineteenth century, were increasingly unemployed (or were given reduced wages) as industries became larger and more mechanized and used more unskilled and semiskilled workers. As factories became larger, employers became more detached from their greater numbers of employees. Employers, as a result, became less concerned with the individual worker. Because large-scale production of goods reduced the need for skilled artisans and craftsmen, these men joined unions so as to preserve their heritage and to join together to fight for their common good. As a result, trade union interest grew in popularity during this time.

The General Trades' Union formed in New York City in 1833 with the purpose of uniting under one organization all of the trade societies of New York. The goal of this central union was better coordination between the various trade unions in the New York City area, conflict resolution with employers, and maintenance of a fund for striking laborers.

Timeline

1809: Progressive British industrialist Robert Owen proposes an end to employment of children in his factories. When his partners reject the idea, he forms an alliance with others of like mind, including the philosopher Jeremy Bentham.

1813: Jane Austen publishes *Pride and Prejudice.*

Event and Its Context

Before the 1830s, skilled artisans and craftsmen formed the majority of U.S. nonfarm workers. They were generally independent from the organizations that bought their finished goods and produced for a limited local market and for limited profits. These highly skilled people worked in small, independent shops and learned their trades by advancing from apprentice to journeyman to master artisan in such traditional occupations as butchers, carpenters, and tailors. These craftsmen were extremely independent and immensely proud of the quality of their finished products.

The Factory System

Beginning as early as the 1780s, and even more so after 1825, the system that had used artisans and craftsmen began to deteriorate. It eventually collapsed as a side effect of rapid industrial development in the New England states, especially in New York City. Equipped with new machinery, large supplies of raw materials, and increasing numbers of cheap immigrant and rural migrant laborers, many merchants performed assembly work of their finished goods in early "sweatshops." The beginning of the factory system resulted in skilled workers making smaller wages and being less in demand. With the labor market demanding ever-greater quantities of produced products, the result was a loss of status and independence for these artisans and craftsmen.

Larger consumer markets opened up as transportation systems such as railroads, waterways, and roadways expanded throughout the country. Technological advancements allowed more variety and quantity of goods to reach more customers from the East coast to the Ohio Valley. The New England states led this advancement. The steam engine contributed to the progress and encouraged factories to increase operations. Merchant and craft entrepreneurs bought large amounts of raw materials and hired out simpler jobs to low-skilled, low-paid workers who were mainly women and immigrants. The increased demand for finished goods could be met by hiring large numbers of unskilled workers for low wages, thus replacing the skilled worker. Low-skilled workers took over more and more of the skilled workers' activities during the first half of the nineteenth century.

In the 1830s the general factory worker began to outnumber the craftsmen and artisans. In addition, the craftsmen and artisans who had previously worked independently from home or from small, local shops were more likely required to work for a company outside the home, and were for the first time in their lives at the direction of a boss.

Interest in Trade Unions

Trade union interest in the United States grew in popularity in the second and third decades of the nineteenth century. Unskilled and semiskilled workers who ran the new machinery and equipment inside the new factories and manufacturing facilities often replaced skilled craftsmen and tradesmen. The mass-produced finished goods that were manufactured by machines and unskilled laborers were rapidly replacing the hand-made articles once produced by skilled craftsmen.

The process was gradual as different products transferred from craft to factory production at different rates. In New York City that transition occurred mainly during the first half of the nineteenth century. For example, before the 1830s shoe craftsmen hand made a pair of shoes from start to finish. Beginning in the 1830s, low-skilled laborers began to make everything but the final shoe assembly. The displaced artisans fiercely opposed each transition, from the early ones in the 1830s, such as the bakers, printers, and cordwainers (artisans who dealt in goods such as shoes, hats, coats, and purses), to those several decades later, such as the butchers and luxury furniture makers.

Workers Organize in Response

Skilled workers who were disgruntled with the decreasing employment opportunities and declining wages began the first period of mass union-building in the United States during the early nineteenth century. These professionals tried to prevent the collapse of their craft system and to preserve their earlier status. In the early 1830s attempts at trade union activity occurred in the country's northern seaport cities, especially in large cities such as New York City and Philadelphia. This union activity often resulted in strikes over reductions of wages and job skills and sometimes culminated in violence and arrests. For instance, shoebinders in Massachusetts struck in 1831 and, because of their success, struck again in 1833. The Boston Ship Carpenters demanded a 10-hour workday when they struck in 1832.

By the mid-1830s workers in many industries and communities had organized. These precursors of the modern trade union were called trade guilds or societies. By 1828 many of these professionals had joined organizations that lobbied for reform and equality for employees. The rapid development of the unions led to a movement for a closer association so as to better promote their common aims. As employers became larger and more powerful, the small trade societies needed to do likewise and become larger trade unions for their mutual benefit and protection. When the U.S. labor movement began around 1830, three demands motivated workers to form unions: (1) the 10-hour workday, (2) education for workers, and (3) wages in legal tender, or coin money, instead of the banks' paper money.

The General Trades' Union

The first large trade union, the General Trades' Union (GTU), organized in New York City on 14 August 1833. The purpose of this central union was to encourage closer cooperation between the many trade unions already in existence in the New York City area, provide coordinated assistance during conflicts with employers, and create a fund to assist striking laborers. From the start the GTU was a very public organization. It celebrated its creation with a public parade displaying its new emblem, the GTU banner bearing a likeness of Archimedes lifting a mountain with a lever. The GTU made it known that it was a new type of organization dedicated solely to the advancement and protection of journeymen wage earners from various crafts.

The General Trades' Union linked all the trade societies of New York in one organization. Wage earners for the first time united as a "band of brothers" allied against the business capitalists and entrepreneur-owners. Ely Moore, a journeyman printer, was elected as its first president. Moore was a strong organizer, effective administrator, and eloquent speaker for union activities. John Commerford, a cabinet and chairmaker, became its second president, replacing Moore in 1834 (when he left to become president of the newly formed National Trades' Union). Commerford asserted that the skilled craftsmen were only seen as commodities to the employers. The GTU newspaper, *The Union*, declared that workers must "preserve the inheritance for which their fathers have fought."

The GTU spread across many cities along the eastern seaboard, including Baltimore, Boston, Cincinnati, Newark, Philadelphia, and Washington, D.C. By 1835 well-organized networks of trade unions developed in New York City and Philadelphia. One year later the number of unions in the network had grown to 13, with 52 local societies in New York, 53 in Philadelphia, 23 in Baltimore, and 16 in Boston. Together, these GTU chapters represented the beginning of an active industrial American laboring class that was organized against harsh employer conditions. These trade unions helped to bring about a dramatic social transformation for the working class.

New York City

The most important of these new central trade unions, the GTU in New York City, eventually unionized nearly two-thirds of the city's male artisans. GTU president Ely Moore spoke to the GTU in 1833 and emphasized the core beliefs of the trade union, with emphasis on words such as "artisans," "laborers," "workingmen," "producing classes," "journeymen," "mechanics," and "brothers."

The GTU of New York City initiated one of the first strikes in the United States. A fierce disagreement between journeymen and employers occurred over higher wages and quickly spread to other craftsmen. After a month of striking throughout New York City, the employers met the strikers' demands. In another strike, carpenters in New York struck to drive home their demand for wages to be set at $1.75 day (a 25-cent raise). Successful in their demands, they quickly struck again for $2 a day. This newfound power, eventually known as collective bargaining, became the motivation for craftsmen all over New York City to unite.

National Trades Union

Cooperation among various cities was clearly as advantageous as cooperation within one city. In 1834 the GTU of New York City issued an invitation to trade unions in other cities to form a national organization. Trade unions in New York City, Brooklyn, Boston, Philadelphia, Newark, and Poughkeepsie met in New York City, sending a total of 30 delegates representing approximately 21,000 members.

The GTU founded the National Trades Union (NTU) in New York City on 3 December 1834. The delegates elected Ely Moore, the president of the New York City GTU, as its first president. The NTU was the first attempt at a national labor federation. Its major goals were to (1) suggest measures to the various unions to promote the moral and intellectual interests and welfare of the working classes, (2) publish and disseminate information to members, (3) promote the establishment of GTUs throughout the United States, and (4) unite the efforts of the country's working classes.

By 1836 membership of the NTU numbered 300,000, which represented between 20 and 33 percent of all urban workers in those areas. By 1837, however, the NTU was eliminated, likely a combination of the declining wages and unemployment caused by an economic downturn (called the "Panic of 1837") and friction between groups within the union. During this time the unions had less power because reduced demand for workers enabled employers to dictate wages. Workers fled the unions, fearing employer retaliation. Although short-lived, the NTU was the first concerted effort to establish a national federation of trade unions. It established the precedent for future national labor organizations and proved that the labor movement of the 1830s did have strength. Perhaps its greatest accomplishment was uniting labor leaders from various parts of the country and thus providing a sense of common purpose and support to the laboring community. The NTU basically encouraged workers in the belief that improvements, such as the change from the 12- to a 10-hour workday, were necessary in the workplace.

Impact on Subsequent Labor Organizing

The union activities of the GTU represented the beginning of an active industrial American working class. It was found to enable workers to stand up for their economic rights during a period of dramatic social reform. Even though the depression of 1837 eliminated the early advances of labor reform, the 1830s union movement in New York and other port cities was significant because of its concerted attack on the powerful industrial system. John Commerford summed up the thoughts of labor: "Men would be judged by their labor's worth, as productive citizens, and not be reduced to a dependent class, 'the willing tools of other men.'"

Key Players

Commerford, John (1830–1874): Commerford was a cabinet and chairmaker in Brooklyn, New York. He lived and worked in New York City for many years. Commerford was president of the New York Chairmakers' and Gilder' Union society. He was the leader of the United Working Men's Association in 1834, and the president of the Free Trade Association in 1842. Commerford ran for the U.S. Congress on the Lower East Side of New York on various third party tickets including the Republican in 1860.

Moore, Ely (1798–1861): Moore studied medicine and eventually became a printer. He was elected as a Jacksonian to the 24th Congress and was reelected as a Democrat to the 25th (1835–1839). Moore was the political editor of the *New York Evening Post* from 1838 to 1839 and president of the board of trade and surveyor of the port of New York City from 1839 to 1845. President James Polk appointed Moore as United States marshal for the southern district of New York in 1845. Moore became owner and editor of the *Warren Journal* of Belvidere, New Jersey, then agent for the Miami and other Native American tribes in Kansas in 1853. He was appointed register of the United States land office in Lecompton, Kansas, from 1855 to 1860.

See also: *National Trades Union.*

BIBLIOGRAPHY

Books

Austin, Aleine. *The Labor Story: A Popular History of American Labor 1786–1949*. New York: Coward-McCann, Inc., 1949.

Dulles, Foster Rhea. *Labor in America: A History*. New York: Thomas Y. Crowell Company, 1949.

Fink, Gary M., ed. *Biographical Dictionary of American Labor*. Westport, CT: Greenwood Press, 1974.

———. *Labor Unions*. Westport, CT: Greenwood Press, 1977.

Frisch, Michael H., and Daniel J. Walkowitz, eds. *Working-Class America: Essays on Labor, Community, and American Society*. Urbana: University of Illinois Press, 1983.

Schlesinger, Arthur M., Jr. *The Age of Jackson*. New York: Little Brown & Company, 1945.

Other

Greenberg, Joshua R. Home Page. "Struggling Downward: Unionism and Masculinity in 1830s New York City." [cited 19 September 2002]. <http://home.earthlink.net/~knorseth/struggling.html>.

Kaster, Gregory L. "Workers and Men: Labor Discourse and the Gendered Construction of Class, 1827–1860." Gustavus Adolphus College. [cited 19 September 2002]. <http://www2.h-net.msu.edu/~shear/s2000.d/ab/KasterGreg.htm>.

Lause, Mark. "Extent of Unionism." *American Labor History: Early Labor Reform*. Department of Humanities and Social Sciences, University College, University of Cincinnati. [cited 19 September 2002]. <http://www.geocities.com/CollegePark/Quad/6460/AmLabHist/1830.html>.

Ricker, Ben. "U.S. Labor History 1830–1910." Impact of "Free Trade" Issue. *Confluence* 7, no. 3 (summer 2001).

St. Louis Indymedia Center [cited 19 September 2002].
<http://www.stlimc.org/local/confluence/Confluence_
SUMMER-v7.3_22/SUM01_laborhist1.html>.

—William Arthur Atkins

German Revolution

Germany 1918–1919

Synopsis

At the end of a lost world war, Germany's divided labor movement attained political power. The reluctant revolutionaries, however, achieved limited gains for working people because of each leading group's different priorities, methods, and relations to bourgeois parties. The revolution attained a republican form of state, parliamentary democracy, women's suffrage, an eight-hour day workday, and some social reforms. Differences over the pace of change, conflicts on new forms versus representation such as workers' councils, and finally engagement in civil war divided labor even more than had the international conflict. The revolution attained few institutional alterations, and most of the social gains were lost within five years.

Friedrich Ebert. The Library of Congress.

Timeline

1907: Great Britain, France, and Russia form the Triple Entente, which will form the core of the Allies in World War I—even as the Triple Alliance of Germany, Austria, and Italy, signed in 1882, will constitute the basis for the Central Powers. (Italy, however, will opt to side with the Allies.)

1914: On 28 June in the town of Sarajevo, then part of the Austro-Hungarian Empire, Serbian nationalist Gavrilo Princip assassinates Austrian Archduke Francis Ferdinand and his wife, Sophie. In the weeks that follow, Austria declares war on Serbia, and Germany on Russia and France, while Great Britain responds by declaring war on Germany. By the beginning of August, the lines are drawn, with the Allies (Great Britain, France, Russia, Belgium, Serbia, Montenegro, and Japan) against the Central Powers (Germany, Austria-Hungary, and Turkey).

1917: In Russia, a revolution in March (or February according to the old Russian calendar) forces the abdication of Czar Nicholas II. By July, Alexander Kerensky has formed a democratic socialist government, and continues to fight the Germans, even as starvation and unrest sweep the nation. On 7 November (25 October old style) the Bolsheviks under V. I. Lenin and Leon Trotsky seize power. By 15 December they have removed Russia from the war by signing the Treaty of Brest-Litovsk with Germany.

1918: The Bolsheviks execute Czar Nicholas II and his family. Soon civil war breaks out between the communists and their allies, known as the Reds, and their enemies, a collection of anticommunists ranging from democrats to czarists, who are known collectively as the Whites. In March troops from the United States, Great Britain, and France intervene on the White side.

1918: The Second Battle of the Marne in July and August is the last major conflict on the Western Front. In November, Kaiser Wilhelm II abdicates, bringing an end to the war.

1918: Influenza, carried to the furthest corners by returning soldiers, spreads throughout the globe. Over the next two years, it will kill nearly 20 million people—more than the war itself.

1919: With the formation of the Third International (Comintern), the Bolshevik government of Russia establishes its control over communist movements worldwide.

1919: Treaty of Versailles is signed by the Allies and Germany, but rejected by the U.S. Senate. This is due in part to rancor between President Woodrow Wilson and Republican Senate leaders, and in part to concerns over Wilson's plan to commit the United States to the newly established League of Nations and other international duties. Not until 1921 will Congress formally end U.S. participation in the war, but it will never agree to join the League.

1919: In Italy a former socialist of the left named Benito Mussolini introduces the world to a new socialism of the right, embodied in an organization known as the "Union for Struggle," or Fasci di Combattimento. Composed primarily of young war veterans discontented with Italy's paltry share of the spoils from the recent world war (if not with their country's lackluster military performance in the conflict), the fascists are known for their black shirts and their penchant for violence.

1921: As the Allied Reparations Commission calls for payments of 132 billion gold marks, inflation in Germany begins to climb.

1923: Conditions in Germany worsen as inflation skyrockets and France, attempting to collect on coal deliveries promised at Versailles, marches into the Ruhr basin. In November an obscure political group known as the National Socialist German Workers' Party attempts to stage a coup, or putsch, in a Munich beer hall. The revolt fails, and in 1924 the party's leader, Adolf Hitler, will receive a prison sentence of five years. He will only serve nine months, however, and the incident will serve to attract attention for him and his party, known as the Nazis.

1927: Stalin arranges to have Trotsky expelled from the Communist Party.

Event and Its Context

The German labor movement—the world's largest before World War I with one million members in the Social Democratic Party (SPD) and two and a half million trade union members—split into three major factions by 1918. The largest, the so-called majority SPD, supported the war effort while agitating for political and social reforms.

Led by Friedrich Ebert and Philipp Scheidemann, the main labor party simultaneously agitated for peace and for responsible parliamentary government while opposing the social policies of the imperial regime. The SPD supported the regime's supposedly defensive war effort by repeatedly voting for war credits. In 1917 the SPD participated in an informal opposition alliance with liberals and Catholics that advocated parliamentary government and moderate war aims. In October 1918 the SPD joined in a coalition government that tried to negotiate peace and institute political reforms such as ending the three-class suffrage and making the monarch and the military directly responsible to parliament.

The Independent Social Democratic Party (USPD), which split from the SPD to set up its own caucus in 1916 and then created a separate party in 1917, resolutely opposed the war. Led by Hugo Haase, some Independents fostered revolution and others demanded change through parliamentary means. The USPD obtained a large enough following to challenge the SPD for the leadership of labor by 1918.

The Spartacists, a radical faction of the Independents led by Rosa Luxemburg and Karl Liebknecht, sought direct mass action, but mostly had to agitate secretly against the war and against the tactics of the SPD from jail. This group could claim only a tiny following until the Russian Revolution of 1917 gave their approach some plausibility.

The trade union federation under reformer Carl Legien supported the war effort; however, by 1918 many metalworkers and some politicized women and youth moved to the militant

Announcement of Berlin Revolution, in *Vorwärts,* organ of Social-Democratic Party, 1918. © Hulton/Getty Images. Reproduced by permission.

stance of the Independents and Spartacists. The union leaders opposed strikes during wartime, but in January 1918 the munitions workers struck to oppose the continued war and inflation.

New, spontaneous antiwar organizations emerged in late October and early November 1918 when the war had obviously been lost. These councils of workers and soldiers, created partly in imitation of the soviets of the Russian Revolution, drastically altered the political landscape. The first councils prevented a desperate naval sortie, took power in northern coastal cities, and under the local leader of the Independents, Kurt Eisner, initiated the actual revolution of 1918–1919 by overthrowing the Wittelsbach dynasty in Bavaria. A few days later, on 9 November 1918, the Hohenzollern monarchy of Wilhelm II was deposed in Berlin.

The SPD and the USPD formed provisional coalition governments throughout Germany and gained the support of the workers' and soldiers' councils. The dual authority system of political parties and councils did not function well. SPD and union members attained control of most councils and labor's previous political and union leaders maneuvered them out of power. Labor's political leaders, especially the coheads of the Berlin government, Ebert and Haase, looked to parliamentary compromise rather than radical social change in a moment of

Rosa Luxemburg. The Library of Congress.

opportunity. Thus the main institutional bulwarks of the old society (the Prussian officers' corps, the conservative civil service, and the huge monopoly industries) were hardly affected by the revolution. The trade union leaders allied with big business (the so-called Stinnes-Legien agreement of November 1918 for mutual recognition), which further undercut the possibility of social change. Ebert and Haase worked with the old military to fulfill the stringent terms of the Allied armistice. Ebert secretly allied himself with General Wilhelm Groener to attain a power base and thus hindered a transformation of the military. Scheidemann and Haase recruited Count von Brockdorff-Rantzau from the aristocratic diplomatic corps to prepare for negotiations with the Allies on the assumption that their task included maintaining Germany as a great power state. National concerns triumphed over the social interests of labor.

Early in the revolution, moderation and compromises on behalf of national values set the parameters for minimal institutional alteration. Instead, national elections to a constituent assembly in mid-January 1919 sought and gained legitimization. The SPD obtained 37 percent of the vote and the Independents took 14 percent, but the SPD allied with the liberals and Catholics as they had since 1917. During the crucial months of November and December 1918, the Independents shifted indecisively between radicalism and moderation, between advocating that power be invested in the councils and accepting parliamentary compromise. When SPD had to decide just before Christmas 1918 whether the use of military force was justified in putting down a revolt of marines, the Independent leaders resigned from the main coalition government in Berlin, though they tried to use regional bases in Bremen, Braunschweig, and Bavaria to foster council-based democratization and socialization.

In Berlin, then in other cities, the clashes between the moderate, reformist SPD and the more radical factions among the

Junkers and Bolsheviks, Nazis and Soviets

When a Russian revolutionary named V. I. Lenin attracted the support of imperial German leaders who saw him as the key to taking Russia out of World War I, this began a quarter-century of alliances between Russian communists and the German Right: first Kaiser Wilhelm and the Junkers, and later the Nazis. Throughout those decades, of course, both sides were vocal in denouncing one another, but their actions told quite a different story.

It was the Kaiser's men, after all, who smuggled Lenin back into Russia from Switzerland in 1917—in a sealed railroad car, so that none of his dangerous talk of revolution would infect workers in German-held lands along the way. Lenin returned the favor a few months later, after his Bolsheviks took power, when they signed the Treaty of Brest-Litovsk that ended the war on the eastern front.

Lenin had long been impressed with the workings of the imperial German state, which was in turn influenced by aspects of the authoritarian czarist model. During World War I, the Germans placed production under direct control of the military and gave their system a name Lenin would later appropriate: "war socialism." Later, he would write in *On "Left" Infantilism and the Petty Bourgeois Spirit,* "Yes: learn from the Germans!" History, he said, had played a "strange trick" by producing "two separate halves of socialism, side by side, like two chickens in one shell."

The German "war socialism" that so impressed Lenin was exemplified by the brutality of General Erich von Ludendorff, whose troops broke up a strike by some 400,000 men in January 1918 and sent the workers to the front in "labor battalions." Thus was born twentieth-century totalitarian slave labor, to be used so effectively by Lenin, Stalin, and Hitler.

Surprisingly, there is little evidence of networking between Russian and German communists during the short-lived German communist revolutions of 1918–1919. In part this was because the Bolsheviks were just then consolidating their power; but it probably also had something to do with the fact that Rosa Luxemburg was among Lenin's most outspoken detractors, a critic of the authoritarian, elitist system she saw developing in Bolshevik Russia.

Later, in the Weimar years, Junkers and other conservative elements often made common cause with Soviet-aligned leftists to destabilize the democratic regime. When this destabilization paid off with the rise of the Nazis, Hitler and Stalin admired and imitated one another's methods. This commonality of aims became manifest with the Non-Aggression Pact of August 1939, but fortunately for the rest of the world, Stalin's trust in Hitler turned out to be misplaced. As Nazi tanks rolled into Russia on 22 June 1941, a quarter-century of German and Soviet cooperation came to an end.

Source: Paul Johnson. *Modern Times: The World from the Twenties to the Nineties.* New York: HarperPerennial, 1992.

—Judson Knight

Independents and Spartacists turned to civil war after the Independents left the coalition government. In early January 1919 the Spartacists held a congress and formed themselves into the Communist Party of Germany. One faction, which included Liebknecht, attempted an uprising against the Ebert government. The SPD unleashed the old military and brutal volunteer troops (*Freikorps*) against the action. Luxemburg and Liebknecht were among those murdered during this so-called Spartacist uprising.

The week-long street fighting in Berlin and the move of the national government to Weimar left many mental scars among the middle class, who organized "self-defense" organizations and paramilitary groups. The Weimar national assembly, however, created a modern democratic constitution for Germany with some social rights such as collective bargaining and unemployment support. Parts of the labor movement continued to seek a greater social transformation via strikes and regional governments based on councils. The Ebert and Scheidemann-led coalition of SPD, liberals, and Catholics employed the military and repressed in turn each council or Independent challenge: Bremen in February, Braunschweig in March, Bavaria in May. From February to May the Bavarian scene had become ever more chaotic with the assassination of Eisner, then the formation of a council, and finally the formation of an anarchist regime. The moderate forces of social democracy and trade unionism had restored law and order against the councils and radical elements of labor; by 1920, however, putsches from parts of the old elite on the right and the new Communist Party on the far left were challenging the moderates.

In the process of demobilizing the millions in the German army and navy under Allied armistice and then Versailles Treaty terms, working women were shunted aside and men were given preference for jobs held before conscription. The labor leaders allowed high wage settlements in the public sector and fostered unionism in private industry, all of which fueled the inflation that had been started by wartime financing and debt. The trade union movement expanded rapidly until it reached nearly eight million during the hyperinflation era. With the loss of the eight-hour day in late 1923 and the so-called rationalization of industry, however, the gains of the revolutionary era mostly disappeared. Because society had been prepared neither for democracy nor especially for a lost war, many workers saw the revolution as a failure to attain the socialization that had been demanded by the prewar labor movement. Among the middle class and the old elite, the revolutionary era provided the resentment that fueled the myths that labor, its councils, or Jewish-Bolshevik conspiracies had stabbed the back of an allegedly victorious army. Certainly, many refused to accept that laboring people should have an equal say in public affairs and in the work world, attitudes which paved the way for fascism.

German society had been altered by the war and the subsequent revolutionary events. For the first time labor leaders achieved and exercised political power. With it they established parliamentary government. But the society—like labor—became more divided, and in the end the revolution provided no solid base for democracy or the defense of long-term labor interests.

Key Players

Ebert, Friedrich (1871–1925): As cohead of the German Social Democratic Party (1913–1918), leader of the national government (1918–1919), and president of the republic (1919–1925), Ebert moved increasingly toward the middle of the political landscape as national values replaced social ones. During the world war he employed his influence against the leftist radicals within the party and later utilized the military against the Spartacists and council governments. He became president of the Weimar Republic in February 1919.

Eisner, Kurt (1867–1919): This long-haired, bearded Jewish journalist appeared to embody the stereotype that anti-Semites despised. Moving from the right of the SPD to the Independents in his opposition to war, Eisner utilized the war weariness of the Bavarian populace to overthrow the monarchy in Munich on 7 November 1918. He advocated the continuation of council authority but lost electoral support and was assassinated as he was about to hand over power to the SPD.

Haase, Hugo (1864–1919): As cohead of the German Social Democratic Party (1911–1916) and leader of the Independent Social Democratic Party (1917–1919), Haase opposed imperialism and war. He sought compromise solutions and advocated a combination of parliamentary and council government. Ebert consistently outmaneuvered Haase, who could not unify the various factions among the Independents. He was assassinated in November 1919.

Legien, Carl (1861–1920): Legien organized the federation of trade unions in 1892 and helped expand them into a powerful social force. During the world war he supported the imperial regime and in November 1918 reached an agreement with Hugo Stinnes from the federation of industry. Legien opposed the council movement but strongly supported the republic and its parliamentary government against the putsch of reactionaries in March 1920.

Liebknecht, Karl (1871–1919): An antimilitary labor lawyer, Liebnecht led the SPD youth movement for a short time. His advocacy of radical tactics alienated him from the SPD leadership but he courageously opposed war credits beginning in 1914 and broke with caucus unity. By 1915 he spoke publicly against war, and in May 1916 he was arrested. He agitated against the war and the moderate policies of the SPD via the Spartacist league. After release from jail in October 1918, he refused to participate in the coalition government of Ebert and Haase and reluctantly supported the January uprising against the national government. He was murdered by volunteer (*Freikorps*) troops in January 1919.

Luxemburg, Rosa (1870–1919): A superb agitator and writer, Luxemburg became an outspoken radical in opposition to imperialism and in favor of mass strikes. Her radical tactics isolated her within the SPD and immediately upon the outbreak of the war, she attacked the leadership's approach. As a Spartacist faction leader she wrote against the war from jail. After her release she advocated council government. A feisty journalist and speaker, she advocated a revolutionary course against the SPD-USPD regime and helped found the Communist Party in January 1919. Soon after she was murdered by troops crushing the radical left revolt.

See also: *Russian Revolutions.*

BIBLIOGRAPHY

Books

Bessel, Richard. *Germany after the First World War.* Oxford: Clarendon Press, 1993.

Feldman, Gerald D. *The Great Disorder: Politics, Economics and Society in the German Inflation, 1914–1924.* Oxford: Oxford University Press, 1993.

Morgan, David. *The Socialist Left and the German Revolution.* Ithaca: Cornell University Press, 1975.

Winkler, Heinrich August. "Revolution by Consensus? Germany 1918–19." In *The Problem of Revolution in Germany, 1789-1989,* edited by Reinhard Rürup. Oxford: Berg, 2000, 93–108.

Periodicals

Buse, Dieter K. "Ebert and the German Crisis, 1917–1920." *Central European History* V (1972): 234–55.

—Dieter K. Buse

Gompers v. Bucks Stove

United States 1911

Synopsis

In *Gompers v. Bucks Stove and Range Company,* the U.S. Supreme Court upheld the ruling of a lower court enjoining the American Federation of Labor from including the Bucks Stove and Range Company on its "unfair" and "We Don't Patronize" lists and from thereby promoting an illegal secondary boycott. Additionally, the Court overturned a ruling by the lower court sentencing AFL president Samuel Gompers and two of his associates to jail terms for contempt for violating the terms of the injunction. The *Bucks Stove* decision was a setback to organized labor's efforts to develop legal means, including boycotts, to press its demands.

Timeline

1891: Construction of Trans-Siberian Railway begins. Meanwhile, crop failures across Russia lead to widespread starvation.

1896: First modern Olympic Games are held in Athens.

1901: U.S. President William McKinley is assassinated by Leon Czolgosz, an anarchist. Vice President Theodore Roosevelt becomes president.

1904: Russo-Japanese War, which lasts into 1905 and results in a resounding Japanese victory, begins. In Russia the war is followed by the Revolution of 1905, which marks the beginning of the end of czarist rule; meanwhile, Japan is poised to become the first major non-Western power of modern times.

1911: Turkish-Italian War sees the first use of aircraft as an offensive weapon. Italian victory results in the annexation of Libya.

1911: In China revolutionary forces led by Sun Yat-sen bring an end to more than 2,100 years of imperial rule.

1911: Revolution in Mexico, begun the year before, continues with the replacement of the corrupt Porfirio Diaz, president since 1877, by Francisco Madero.

1911: Ernest Rutherford at the University of Manchester correctly posits that the atom contains a positively charged nucleus surrounded by negatively charged electrons. (Discovery of the protons that give the nucleus its positive charge, and of the neutrons that, along with protons, contribute to its mass, still lies in the future.)

1911: Norwegian explorer Roald Amundsen and his team of four other Norwegians are the first men to reach the South Pole, on 14 December. A month later, a group of British explorers led by Robert F. Scott will reach the Pole, only to die of starvation soon afterward.

1915: A German submarine sinks the *Lusitania,* killing 1,195, including 128 U.S. citizens. Theretofore, many Americans had been sympathetic toward Germany, but the incident begins to turn the tide of U.S. sentiment toward the Allies.

1919: With the formation of the Third International (Comintern), the Bolshevik government of Russia establishes its control over communist movements worldwide.

1919: Treaty of Versailles is signed by the Allies and Germany but rejected by the U.S. Senate. This is due in part to rancor between President Woodrow Wilson and Republican Senate leaders, and in part to concerns over Wilson's plan to commit the United States to the newly established League of Nations and other international duties. Not until 1921 will Congress formally end U.S. participation in the war, but it will never agree to join the league.

Event and Its Context

Background of the Case

The *Bucks Stove* decision is one of a sequence of events that charted the difficult road that was traveled by organized labor in the early decades of the twentieth century, particularly in a court system that seemed more sympathetic to the wishes of employers than to the needs of labor. Of particular relevance to a full understanding of the case are the passage of the Sherman Antitrust Act in 1890, the U.S. Supreme Court's decision in the so-called *Danbury Hatters* case of 1908, and, following *Bucks Stove,* the passage of the Clayton Act in 1914.

Sherman Antitrust Act

In the late nineteenth and early twentieth centuries, the public and legislators were observing with alarm the growing economic power of corporations, trusts, pools, trade associations, and similar business combinations whose purpose was to stifle competition. Business leaders in such industries as oil, sugar, whiskey, tobacco, and industrial machinery were learning that by cooperating rather than competing, they could eliminate smaller competitors, control output and the supply of products, establish market territories, raise prices to maximize profits, and impose penalties on members who violated the anticompetitive policies of the combination. The result was an industrial system that denied freedom of entry to the smaller competitor—or that drove the competitor out of business.

To curb the predatory monopolistic practices of corporations and trusts, Congress passed the Sherman Antitrust Act in 1890. Section 1 of the act made illegal "Every contract, combination, . . . or conspiracy, in restraint of trade or commerce among the several States." The act, however, failed specifically to mention labor unions, leaving it an open question whether Congress intended unions to be subject to the act and whether their activities in some circumstances could be construed as "combinations . . . in restraint of trade or commerce." A federal court in Louisiana offered an early answer to this question in 1893, when, in *United States v. Workingmen's Amalgamated Council*, it applied the act to a group of New Orleans unions that had gone out on strike in support of the local draymen's union. In issuing an injunction against the unions—a tool employers frequently sought and won in their efforts to thwart organized labor during these years—the court declared that the intent of Congress was to "include combinations of labor, as well as capital; in fact, all combinations in restraint of commerce, without reference to the character of the persons who entered into them." Similarly, a federal court in *United States v. Agler* (1897), ruling on a suit brought in the wake of the Pullman railroad strike of 1894, asserted its authority under the Sherman Act to "apply the restraining power of the law for the purpose of checking and arresting all lawless interference with . . . the peaceful and orderly conduct of railroad business between the States."

Danbury Hatters

A major blow to organized labor was the U.S. Supreme Court's 1908 decision in the landmark *Danbury Hatters* case; officially, the case was *Loewe v. Lawlor*, but it took on the name of the location of the Loewe and Company hat factory in Danbury, Connecticut. In 1902 the United Hatters of North America—a 9,000-member union and an affiliate of the American Federation of Labor (AFL) since the 1896 merger of the International Trade Association of Hat Finishers of America and the National Hat Makers' Association of the United States—attempted to organize workers at the Loewe plant. The union's recent successes had included organizing 70 out of 82 firms in the felt hat industry, but these firms operated at a competitive disadvantage because they had to sell their products at a higher price than those that used nonunion labor. These nonunion shops, in fact, were threatening the very existence of the union, which was in danger of collapsing unless it could organize every shop in the felt hat industry. The union trained its sights on Loewe, but when it asked the company to recognize it as the bargaining agent for the company's workers and to hire only union workers, Loewe refused. In response, the union called about 250 workers out on strike.

Samuel Gompers. The Library of Congress.

The strike did not have its desired effect, for the company was able to conduct business using nonunion workers and the number of strikers constituted only a small percentage of the firm's workforce. In desperation, the union adopted a different tactic: it called for a nationwide boycott. The union pressured retailers and wholesalers to stop carrying Loewe hats, and it urged the public not to buy from any store that sold the company's products. The boycott gathered steam when the union obtained the support of the AFL, which publicized the boycott in pamphlets, union newspapers, and the public press. Many retailers and wholesalers, fearing that they too would become the targets of a boycott, stopped doing business with Loewe. So successful was the boycott that the company claimed that in one year it lost $85,000.

Accordingly, the company sued the union and its members in 1903, alleging a violation of the Sherman Act. After the circuit court of appeals ruled in the union's favor, the company appealed to the U.S. Supreme Court. Five years after the initial suit, the Court overturned the court of appeals and ruled that the union's activities, particularly its use of a secondary boycott, were in fact a restraint of trade within the meaning of the Sherman Act. The Court held that the union met the definition of "combination" and acted "in restraint of trade or commerce among the several states" in the manner intended by the act, which "prohibits any combination whatever to secure action which essentially obstructs the free flow of commerce between the States, or restricts in that regard, the liberty of a trader to engage in business."

Thus, the *Danbury Hatters* case removed from labor's hands one of its most effective tools, the "secondary boycott," or pressure on one firm to persuade it to stop doing business with another firm. The decision also established the principle that individual union members, not just union officials and the union itself, were jointly liable to pay any judgment levied

Joseph R. Lamar. Supreme Court of the United States.

against the union in successful antitrust suits. It was not until the passage of the Taft-Hartley Act in 1947 that successful litigants were able to collect damage awards only from union funds.

The *Bucks Stove* Case

If the *Danbury Hatters* decision was a sharp blow to labor, the *Bucks Stove* decision three years later could be characterized as nearly a knockout punch. The Bucks Stove and Range Company, whose president, J. W. Van Cleave, was also president of the American Manufacturers' Association, had a dispute with the company's workers over hours. In connection with this dispute, Bucks Stove refused to recognize the Molders and Foundry Workers Union of North America, another affiliate of the AFL, as the workers' bargaining agent. Accordingly, the AFL, publisher of the *American Federationist* newspaper, placed the company's name on the paper's "unfair" and "We Don't Patronize" lists. As had the hatters union, the AFL pressured retailers not to carry the company's products and threatened to boycott those that did. It also urged the public not to buy Bucks Stove products. The union's actions were successful, and sales at the company dropped.

In response the company filed suit against the officers of the AFL, including its president, Samuel Gompers; its vice president, John Mitchell, who was also president of the United Mine Workers; and Frank Morrison, the AFL secretary who ran the newspaper. The company sought a temporary injunction against the boycott, which the Court of Appeals for the District of Columbia granted on 8 December 1907 and made permanent on 23 March 1908. The defendants appealed, but before a decision was reached on the appeal, the company began contempt proceedings, alleging that Gompers, Mitchell, and Morrison had violated the injunction and continued to include the company's name on its "unfair" and "We Don't Patronize" lists and to pub-

licize the boycott in speeches, editorials, and other publications. Company representatives alleged that the three had deliberately rushed publication of an issue of the newspaper containing the boycott lists so that it would be distributed before the effective date of the injunction. On 23 December the court found the three men guilty of contempt and sentenced them to jail. They appealed to the U.S. Supreme Court, which heard the case on 27 and 30 January 1911 and rendered its decision on 15 May.

Justice Joseph R. Lamar delivered the majority opinion. Much of the opinion concerned the contempt-of-court issue, and on technical and procedural grounds the Court dismissed the charges against the three men. The Court reasoned that the matter should have been handled as a separate civil proceeding in which the plaintiff sought damages from the union officials. Instead, the lower court treated it as a criminal proceeding and ordered the men jailed rather than fined, which would have been a more appropriate penalty. The more far-reaching, though briefer, part of the decision was that bearing on whether the Sherman Act was applicable to the case. The Court, citing *Loewe v. Lawlor*, declared that it was and that any boycott or blacklist promoted by printed matter or by words violated the act. In an assault not just on labor but on free speech and freedom on the press, the Court noted that the use of its "protective and restraining powers" were intended to "extend to every device whereby property is irreparably damaged or commerce is illegally restrained. To hold that the restraint of trade under the Sherman antitrust act . . . could be enjoined but that the means through which the restraint was accomplished could not be enjoined, would be to render the law impotent."

Thus, any boycott that restrained trade within the meaning of the Sherman Act was against the law, and any union official or member who took part in such a boycott, either by spoken words or in print, was breaking the law. In reaching its decision the Court pointed to the "vast power" of labor unions, with their "multitudes of members." It distinguished between the "right of speech" of a single individual and the "verbal acts" of a multitude that can come under court scrutiny as much as "the use of any other force whereby property is unlawfully damaged." In following this line of reasoning, the Court continued to do what many earlier courts had done: to define as "property" not just tangible items such as plant and equipment but, more expansively, to include intangibles such as the right to trade. Accordingly, any "property" that faced "irreparable damage" such as lost profits because of the activities of a labor union could be protected by the courts through the issuance of an injunction.

The Court's decision was not without precedent. Similar cases had come before lower courts in several states, including Massachusetts, Georgia, Minnesota, Missouri, Michigan, and New Jersey. These courts had concluded that the use of letters, circulars, and other printed matter constituted a means by which a boycott could be unlawfully continued and could be enjoined.

The Clayton Act of 1914

Discussion of the Clayton Act is relevant to *Bucks Stove* in that its passage constituted a kind of postscript to the decision. After their defeat in *Danbury Hatters*, the labor unions concluded that the judiciary was no ally and that they had to support candidates for elective office who were sympathetic to their goals. Thus, the unions became markedly more politically active than they had been previously. In the 1908 and 1910 congressional elections, the unions closely questioned Democratic and Republican candidates and concluded that their best hope lay with the Democratic Party. In the wake of the *Bucks Stove* setback, the unions redoubled their efforts to elect supporters to office. In 1912 they actively supported Woodrow Wilson in his successful quest for the presidency, based on campaign pledges he made that were endorsed by the AFL. With Wilson in the White House and the Democrats controlling both the legislative and executive branches of government for the first time in two decades, the unions called in their markers and pressed for legislation that would protect their interests.

Congress responded in 1914 by passing the Clayton Act. The Clayton Act, like the Sherman Act before it, was an antitrust law, but Section 6 tried to fill the gap the Sherman Act had left regarding labor unions that had led to court decisions such as that in *Bucks Stove*. It declared "that the labor of a human being is not a commodity or article of commerce. Nothing contained in the anti-trust laws shall be construed to forbid the existence and operation of labor . . . organizations . . . or to forbid or restrain individual members of such organizations, from lawfully carrying out the legitimate objects thereof; nor shall such organizations . . . be held or construed to be illegal combinations or conspiracies in restraint of trade, under the anti-trust laws."

Labor was jubilant, for it felt that finally the federal government recognized the right of labor organizations not just to exist but to engage in concerted economic action to press their demands. As it turned out, this jubilation was premature, for in the years that followed, the courts, adopting their own view of what constituted "*lawfully* carrying out the *legitimate* objects thereof," rendered the Clayton Act worthless to labor. Labor had to wait until 1932 and the passage of the Norris-La Guardia Act to see a law that would succeed in reducing the influence of the courts in labor disputes.

Key Players

Gompers, Samuel (1850–1924): Gompers was born to Dutch-Jewish immigrants in London, where he began his working life at age 10 as a cigar maker. He immigrated to the United States in 1863 and in 1886 was elected vice president of the Cigarmakers' International Union. That year he was a founder of the American Federation of Labor (AFL) and served as its president from 1886 to 1895, then from 1896 to 1924. In 1919 Gompers was appointed to the American delegation at the Paris Peace Conference following World War I. His autobiography, *Seventy Years of Life and Labor*, was published in 1925.

Lamar, Joseph R. (1857–1916): Lamar, who was born in Elbert County, Georgia, served in the Georgia legislature from 1886 to 1889 and on the Georgia Supreme Court from 1904 to 1906. In 1911 President William Howard Taft appointed Lamar to the U.S. Supreme Court, where he served until his death.

Mitchell, John (1870–1919): Mitchell was born in Braidwood, Illinois, and worked in the coal mines beginning at age 12. He rose through the ranks of the United Mine Workers of America (UMWA) until he was elected vice president in

1898. He became acting president that year and served as president until 1908. Under his leadership the UMWA's membership grew from 34,000 to 300,000. He also served as vice president of the AFL from 1899 to 1913.

Morrison, Frank (1859–1949): Morrison was born in Frankton, Ontario, Canada, and began his working life as a printer. While employed as a printer in Chicago, he studied law and was admitted to the Illinois bar in 1895. In 1896 he was elected secretary of the AFL and served in that post until 1935. From 1936 until his retirement in 1939 he was secretary-treasurer of the AFL. During World War I he chaired the wages and hours subcommittee of the Committee on Labor of the Advisory Commission of the Council of National Defense.

See also: *American Federation of Labor; Clayton Antitrust Act; Norris-La Guardia Act.*

BIBLIOGRAPHY

Books

Madison, Charles A. *American Labor Leaders: Personalities and Forces in the Labor Movement.* New York: Frederick Unger Publishing, 1962.

Northrup, Herbert R., and Gordon F. Bloom. *Government and Labor.* Homewood, IL: Richard D. Irwin, 1963.

Taylor, Benjamin J., and Fred Witney. *Labor Relations Law,* 3rd ed. Englewood Cliffs, NJ: Prentice-Hall, 1979.

Other

Loewe v. Lawlor, 208 U.S. 274 (*Danbury Hatters*).

Gompers v. Bucks Stove and Range Company, 221 U.S. 418.

—Michael J. O'Neal

Goodyear Strike

United States 1936

Synopsis

The Goodyear Strike of February and March 1936 in Akron, Ohio, was an unplanned protest that demonstrated the potential of organized labor in the mass production industries of that era. The strike was a consequence of improving economic conditions and efforts by Goodyear managers to eliminate policies, especially the six-hour day, that they had introduced during the depressed years of the early 1930s. Worker protests against such changes led to sit-down strikes, another product of the depression era, and finally a full-scale strike starting on 18 February. The strikers successfully mobilized allies in and out of the labor movement and countered efforts by the company, the company union, city officials, and the business community

Goodyear Tire and Rubber Company Factory, Akron, Ohio. AP/Wide World Photos. Reproduced by permission.

to break the strike. The ultimate settlement, approved on 21 March, addressed the workers' grievances but did not formally recognize the union. Nevertheless, it was a significant victory for organized labor, an indication that there could be no return to the past, and a stimulus to additional organizing and collective bargaining.

Timeline

1921: As the Allied Reparations Commission calls for payments of 132 billion gold marks, inflation in Germany begins to climb.

1926: Britain is paralyzed by the General Strike.

1931: Financial crisis widens in the United States and Europe, which reel from bank failures and climbing unemployment levels. In London, armies of the unemployed riot.

1933: Hitler becomes German chancellor, and the Nazi dictatorship begins.

1936: Germany reoccupies the Rhineland, while Italy annexes Ethiopia. Recognizing a commonality of aims, the two totalitarian powers sign the Rome-Berlin Axis Pact. (Japan will join them in 1940.)

1936: The election of a leftist Popular Front government in Spain in February precipitates an uprising by rightists under the leadership of Francisco Franco. Over the next three years, war will rage between the Loyalists and Franco's Nationalists. The Spanish Civil War will prove to be a lightning rod for the world's tensions, with the Nazis and Fascists supporting the Nationalists, and the Soviets the Loyalists.

1936: Hitler uses the Summer Olympics in Berlin as an opportunity to showcase Nazi power and pageantry, but the real hero of the Games is the African American track star Jesse Owens.

1939: Britain and France declare war against Germany after the 1 September invasion of Poland, but little happens in the way of mobilization.

1944: Allies land at Normandy on 6 June, conducting the largest amphibious invasion in history.

1951: Six western European nations form the European Coal and Steel Community, forerunner of the European Economic Community and the later European Union.

Event and Its Context

The Goodyear Tire and Rubber Company strike of February–March 1936 was a major contributor to the turbulent labor history of the 1930s and a symbolic turning point in American industrial relations. Paradoxically, the formal results of the strike were unimpressive: the strikers went back to work with minor concessions, the union modestly improved its position in the plant, and the managers insisted that nothing had changed. In fact, almost everything at Goodyear and in the industry had changed. The workers showed that they could hold out against a powerful corporation and the company union movement suffered a dramatic defeat. The new Committee for Industrial Organization (CIO) gained a degree of legitimacy, and the sit-down movement, the most prominent symbol of 1930s militancy, spread to other plants and industries. In retrospect, the Goodyear strike marked the end of the spontaneous worker rebellions of the National Recovery Administration (NRA) years and the beginning of more systematic union organizing that would culminate in World War II.

Goodyear employees, like millions of other industrial employees, had taken advantage of Section 7a of the National Industrial Recovery Act (1933; NIRA) to create a local union that embraced a majority of employees at the vast Akron, Ohio, complex by late 1933. Local union president John D. House and other officers soon discovered, however, that it was easier to create an organization than to sustain it. They and their followers faced several formidable obstacles: the Goodyear managers were hostile and resolutely opposed to a formal contract; the workers expected immediate, tangible concessions; the American Federation of Labor, which had chartered the locals as directly affiliated, federal locals, was bereft of leaders and suspicious of the workers' instinctive preference for an industrial union (one that embraced all the workers in the industry, as opposed to a craft union or the various hybrids that reserved a special place for the more highly skilled workers); and the federal government was incapable of enforcing Section 7a.

There were also several distinctive features of the Goodyear situation. Though Goodyear managers were antiunion, they were not reactionaries. The company had long been a champion of advanced personnel management and provided various financial, social, and educational benefits to employees. In 1919 it had created the Industrial Assembly, one of the most famous and successful company unions. The principal architect of this action was the company president, Paul W. Litchfield, who was viewed and viewed himself as a sensitive and innovator manager. Litchfield thought of Goodyear as a seamless continuum of jobs from the executive suite to the shop floor; employees could rise as far as their abilities would take them. As proof, he pointed to his chief lieutenants, all of whom had risen from lowly positions. Yet the depression had temporarily interrupted this process, and the union, if successful, would permanently disrupt it.

A second distinctive feature of the strike setting was the presence of thousands of other rubber workers, employees of two other major tire firms, a half dozen secondary tire firms, and a dozen or more small companies that manufactured other rubber products. Together they made the industry one of the most geographically concentrated in the United States; as a result, Akron was virtually a one-industry city. After Congress passed the NIRA, the Akron locals recruited nearly 30,000 members. The B.F. Goodrich local was the largest, with more than 7,000 members; Goodyear was second with more than 6,000; and Firestone was third with 5,000. By virtue of his leadership of the Goodrich local, Sherman A. Dalrymple, a soft-spoken, unpretentious West Virginian, became the best-known union leader in the industry.

The unions that emerged in the secondary tire firms were also formidable. They had several significant advantages: their employers were less powerful and confident, were unable to finance expensive welfare plans to ward off organizers, and might not even survive a prolonged strike. Cautious but generally cooperative relationships often resulted. An example of what could happen if the employer was not cooperative occurred at the General Tire and Rubber Company in early 1934. During the early months of the year, the General Tire managers, who otherwise had had good relations with the local, rejected demands for a signed agreement and recognition. Frustrated, union activists decided on a bold strategy. They would strike but instead of trying to close the plant from outside, inviting conventional strike-breaking techniques, they would remain inside and occupy it. On the night of 19–20 June, the General local staged the first important sit-down strike, a planned, rehearsed maneuver that surprised the management, emboldened the workers, and set the stage for the successful conventional strike that followed. The eventual settlement included a written agreement and de facto union recognition. Other workers were impressed.

The Sit-Downs

By the winter of 1935 the depression seemed to be waning. Tire sales were rising, employment was gradually increasing, and the demise of the NRA seemingly invited a return to pre-depression normality. The NRA may have been legally toothless, but its power to publicize abuses had restrained large corporations in cities like Akron with watchful citizens and aggressive newspapers. Goodyear managers, for example, had met routinely with union leaders in Akron but just as routinely mobilized police and vigilante groups to attack union activists in smaller, out-of-the way communities like Gadsden, Alabama. By this point, however, the NRA influence had been eliminated. Litchfield signaled the change in late 1935 by announcing piece rate cuts and an end to the six-hour day, which had been introduced in 1931 to share the available work. The other manufacturers made similar announcements. Henceforth the Akron factories would operate on eight-hour shifts.

How would the workers react? By that time the local was much weaker. (With the formation of the United Rubber Workers [URW] in September 1935, the Goodyear federal local became URW Local 2.) Its failure to win a contract or even to challenge the company directly in 1934 and 1935 had demoralized its members, most of whom had stopped paying dues. The new URW under president Sherman Dalrymple, the former president of the B.F. Goodrich local, was almost penniless. As a result the Industrial Assembly orchestrated the most significant protests, a development that should have alerted Litchfield to a basic flaw in his logic. He had assumed that workers would willingly trade lower rates and longer hours for higher total earnings, but his proposals had a different meaning to many Goodyear employees. After five years of sporadic work and lingering poverty, longer hours meant fewer jobs and new rounds of layoffs. They demanded the retention of the six-hour day.

When Litchfield, together with the managers of the other Akron companies, moved to implement the longer workday, the workers responded with sit-down strikes. In January and early February, there were major sit-downs at Goodyear, Firestone, and B.F. Goodrich that forced the managers to close their plants. In each case the URW locals defended the strikers, won reinstatements, and even obtained a few concessions. The locals started to revive. At Goodyear, the sit-downs had another, equally important effect. Though the Industrial Assembly had taken the lead in opposing the eight-hour day, it refused to defend the strikers. Closely identified with the high seniority, relatively secure workers who viewed the sit-downs as irresponsible and disruptive, it cast its lot with management. URW Local 2 thus emerged as the only steadfast defender of the protesters.

The sit-downs culminated in mid-February. A sit-down by Goodyear fourth shift tire builders—the men slated for immediate layoff—sparked sympathetic sit-downs by workers on other shifts, which shut down the entire complex for several days and widened the gap between the Industrial Assembly and the union. President House of Local 2 called an emergency union meeting for the night of 18 February. After several hours of fiery speeches, one of the local's firebrands jumped on the stage, seized a flag, and called for the others to follow him to the plant gate. Despite subzero temperatures, the pickets remained at the gates through the night and turned away first shift workers the following morning. The strike had begun.

The Strike: Union Resources

The strike was a spontaneous and, given the fierce winter storm that accompanied it, ill-timed challenge to a major corporation. Yet it was not a desperate or foolhardy act. A year earlier the local had prepared for a major strike then backed down. Though most of its members were inactive by 1936, the leaders remained. They implemented the earlier plans and by 20 February, had set up a headquarters and dining hall, issued appeals for financial assistance, recruited picket teams, created a relief system for needy families, and established close contacts with the other rubber locals and the URW. Their ties to other unions ensured that they would have sufficient funds and picket line reinforcements. House and Dalrymple worked well together. They also attracted the attention of John L. Lewis and the staff of his new CIO. Lewis sent funds and organizers to Akron. Veteran organizer Adolph Germer became a close advisor to House and Dalrymple. Other CIO operatives wrote news releases and radio scripts and helped with public events. The conflict became the first major CIO strike.

The strike organization's first major challenge was the Non-Strikers, an impromptu antiunion group, closely linked to the Industrial Assembly, that appeared on 19 February and demanded an immediate return to work. The Non-Strikers insisted that the sheriff enforce an injunction prohibiting pickets from blocking the gates, even if it meant a violent confrontation with the strikers. When strike leaders blocked the streets outside the plant with thousands of sympathizers on the appointed day, 24 February, the sheriff and the police backed down, the picket line held, and the plant remained closed. The Non-Strikers and the Industrial Assembly never recovered. The company union became the first casualty of the strike.

The strike organization's second and more difficult assignment was to sustain public support for a negotiated settlement. This became more difficult as the conflict began to hurt the merchants and professionals who depended on the company and its employees. One of the last dramatic episodes in the strike was the appearance of a "Law and Order League" that was designed to enlist a broad spectrum of outsiders and force the union to capitulate. Created by a former mayor and other business leaders, it failed because the union once again refused to be intimidated. Nevertheless, the Law and Order League was an indication of a growing restiveness. To counter this trend the strike leaders used rallies, public demonstrations, and frequent radio speeches to emphasize their reasonableness. CIO leaders made their greatest contributions as orators, writers, and publicists. Most observers believed they won "the battle of the airwaves."

By mid-March the strikers had defeated the Non-Strikers, ensured the neutrality of local officials, and preserved a large measure of public support. They still had to negotiate a settlement.

Negotiations

In a 19 February statement to the Industrial Assembly, Litchfield agreed to preserve the six-hour day and call off the rate cuts, eliminating the workers' most serious grievances. Thereafter, the overriding substantive issue was union recognition. On that point the Goodyear managers were inflexible and unyielding. Litchfield insisted that only the Industrial Assembly represented Goodyear employees; his more pragmatic subordinates acknowledged that the Assembly was dead but were no less emphatic in rejecting any type of formal union recognition. Their goal was an informal, preferably unwritten arrangement whereby supervisors would negotiate specific problems with union representatives. This was essentially what they had done since mid-1933. Together with Litchfield's announced concessions, this arrangement would re-create the conditions of 1934 and early 1935, conditions that had been unsatisfactory to the management and the union, and would likely lead to more conflicts. URW and CIO leaders were aware of the pitfalls of such an agreement and were determined to come away with more. Explaining to workers who had had no paychecks for a month why they should continue to hold out for something less than formal recognition, however, became increasingly difficult.

Serious negotiations began on 5 March and continued for two weeks as negotiators tried to find a formula that would avoid a formal contract and yet grant the union the equivalent of a contract. Litchfield continued to be uncooperative, publicly rejecting on several occasions what his representatives had conceded in private. Ultimately, however, the negotiators found circuitous ways of spelling out concessions and the union's role without specifically recognizing the union. On 21 March the exhausted strikers finally agreed to this arrangement. On paper the agreement was at best a modest union victory. Yet, as the federal mediator concluded, the union had in fact realized "the main objectives of the strike . . . [and] additional benefits as well."

Results and Implications

The strike had proven to be a high-stakes gamble for Goodyear as well as the union. By 21 March Litchfield's plan for increasing profits had failed, the Industrial Assembly had died, and Local 2 and the URW were stronger than ever. Equally important were the less obvious effects. Goodyear supervisors were demoralized by the union "victory." Shop floor discipline declined, and the sit-down, hitherto a response to important policy changes, became an almost daily occurrence between late March 1936 and early 1937. After mid-1937, when the Supreme Court upheld the Wagner Act and the power of the National Labor Relations Board (NLRB), the company became subject to extended litigation for its refusal to sign a contract with Local 2. The continuing turmoil contributed to the company's poor economic performance in the late 1930s.

In contrast, Local 2, the URW, and the CIO had been tested, had survived, and were poised for additional gains. The strike became part of the legend of "labor on the march." It also demonstrated that an informally organized, decentralized union such as the URW could hold its own in a contest with a powerful corporation, a lesson that most other union leaders conveniently overlooked. In the late 1930s the URW, like other industrial unions, campaigned for formal recognition and collective bargaining contracts. It negotiated agreements with most of the smaller tire companies in 1936–1937, Firestone in 1937, B.F. Goodrich in 1938, and finally, Goodyear in 1941, after Litchfield had retired from the presidency. Yet the URW retained much of the spirit of 1936. Even at the peak of its power, it had little bureaucracy and a high degree of local autonomy.

The broader repercussions of the strike were also significant. The sit-down strike soon spread to other mass production industries and became a nationwide phenomenon in 1937. The CIO became more visible in the following months, rallying other industrial workers and scoring several dramatic breakthroughs. Its agreements with General Motors and U. S. Steel in early 1937 reinforced the notion of the signed contract as the primary objective of union activity, a goal that the NLRB soon made official policy. Indirectly at least, the Goodyear strike also contributed to the antiunion backlash that grew rapidly after 1937. In Akron the sit-down strikes and the simultaneous "decentralization" of the industry (i.e., the transfer of jobs to outlying communities) cost organized labor much of its public support. By 1937, the city administration was generally hostile and the public increasingly divided between union members and nonmembers. Similar divisions appeared in other industrial communities and in the country generally. Yet because of the simultaneous movement for collective bargaining agreements, this shift had only a modest impact on union membership. Most of what had been achieved in Akron and in other industrial communities continued to be part of a new industrial landscape that persisted for a third of a century.

Key Players

Dalrymple, Sherman H. (1889–1962): Dalrymple was a West Virginia farmer who sought his fortune in the industrial city of Akron. Quiet, likeable, scrupulously honest, and a World War I hero, he embodied the qualities that rubber workers sought in their leaders. Dalrymple served as president of the giant B. F. Goodrich local from 1933 to 1935 and as president of the URW from 1935 to 1945. Three months after the Goodyear strike, he was nearly beaten to death in Gadsden, Alabama, while trying to organize the Goodyear plant there.

House, John D. (1904–1988): A Georgian who came to Akron in the early 1920s in search of a better job, House became a tire builder at Goodyear and took advantage of the company's programs for ambitious employees. The depression destroyed his prospects, however, and he became an enthusiastic union supporter. House served as president of Local 2 until 1940, then as a CIO and URW organizer.

Litchfield, Paul W. (1875–1962): Litchfield was a Massachusetts Institute of Technology graduate who took a job at Goodyear just as the tire industry entered a period of explosive growth. As factory manager, he presided over the company's dramatic expansion and introduced advanced personnel programs to retain qualified workers. A financial crisis in 1920 led to his elevation to the company presidency. During the following decade he consolidated Goodyear's position as the leading tire maker and an innovator in industrial management. Strongly antiunion, Litchfield fought the URW through the 1930s.

See also: *Committee for Industrial Organization; National Industrial Recovery Act.*

BIBLIOGRAPHY

Books

Bernstein, Irving. *Turbulent Years: A History of the American Worker, 1933–1941.* Boston: Houghton Mifflin, 1970.
Nelson, Daniel. *American Rubber Workers and Organized Labor, 1900-1941.* Princeton, NJ: Princeton University Press, 1988.
Roberts, Harold S. *The Rubber Workers.* New York: Harper & Brothers, 1944.
Zieger, Robert. *The CIO, 1935–1955.* Chapel Hill: University of North Carolina Press, 1995.

—Daniel Nelson

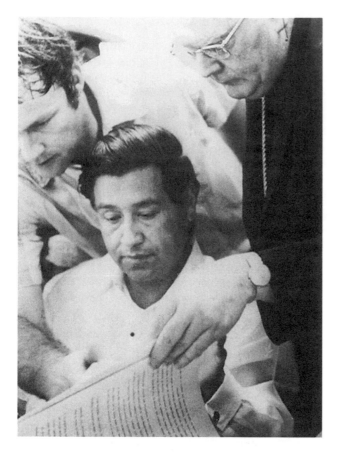

Cesar Chavez looking over proposed union contracts. AP/ Wide World Photos. Reproduced by permission.

Grape Pickers' Strike

United States 1965–1970

Synopsis

During the years before 1965, the agricultural unions—the Agricultural Workers Organizing Committee (AWOC) and National Farm Workers Association (NFWA)—sought recognition from grape growers and hoped to enter into contracts by fair negotiations as guaranteed by collective bargaining rights. Because farm laborers were excluded from coverage under the provisions of the 1935 National Labor Relations Act, or Wagner Act, they sought to be legally protected in the workplace by unions as were the majority of workers in other industries throughout the United States. The push by union leaders to have farm workers fairly represented and under contract reached its apex after 1965.

With growers' failure to recognize the unions, the California farmworkers initiated a strike against grape growers. These strikes, between 1965 and 1970, ultimately unified the two primary agricultural unions and demonstrated the effective power of boycotts. These actions also publicized to the American public the substandard, often dangerous, working conditions in the fields. In addition to representation and fair wages, the unions sought decent working conditions. These included a ban on pes-

ticide use while workers were in the fields, clean drinking water, and basic health benefits. By the time the strikes were officially halted by the United Farm Workers in 1973, they had also helped to change conditions in the fields for laborers, although significant improvements of working conditions were comparatively slow to come.

Timeline

1945: On 7 May, Germany surrenders, marking the end of World War II.

1950: Senator Joseph McCarthy launches his campaign to root out communist infiltrators.

1955: Rosa Parks refuses to move from her seat near the front of a public bus in Montgomery, Alabama, and is arrested. The incident touches off a boycott of Montgomery's bus system, led by the Rev. Martin Luther King, Jr., which will last well into 1956.

1960: An American U-2 spy plane piloted by Francis Gary Powers shot down over Soviet skies brings an end to a short period of warming relations between the two superpowers. By the end of the year, Khrushchev makes a scene at the United Nations, banging his shoe on a desk. As for Powers, he will be freed in a 1962 prisoner exchange.

1965: Power failure paralyzes New York City and much of the northeastern United States on 9 November.

1966: In August, Mao Zedong launches the "Great Proletarian Cultural Revolution," which rapidly plunges China into chaos as armed youths plunder the countryside, rooting out suspected foreign collaborators and anti-Chinese elements. Along with rifles and other weapons, these Red Guards are armed with copies of Mao's "Little Red Book."

1967: Arabs attack Israel, launching the Six-Day War, which results in an Israeli victory.

1968: Communist victories in the Tet offensive mark the turning point in the Vietnam War and influence a growing lack of confidence in the war, not only among America's youth, but within the establishment as well.

1969: On 20 July, assisted by pilot Michael Collins, astronauts Neil Armstrong and Edwin E. "Buzz" Aldrin become the first men to walk on the Moon.

1970: Gamal Abdel Nasser, father of Arab nationalism and mentor of younger leaders such as Libya's Muammar al-Qaddafi, dies.

1975: Two assassination attempts on President Ford occur in September.

1980: In protest of the Soviet invasion of Afghanistan, President Carter keeps U.S. athletes out of the Moscow Olympics. Earlier, at the Winter Games in Lake Placid, New York, the U.S. hockey team scored a historic— and, in the view of many, a symbolic—victory over the Soviets.

Cesar Chavez leading UFW grape protest, 1969. AP/Wide World Photos. Reproduced by permission.

Event and Its Context

Preceding the strikes, complex issues had simmered for decades, notably those concerning racial tensions and immigration. Racial tensions existed not only between employers and field workers, but also among the workers, starting with the first Chinese and Japanese recruited to farm in the state. During the Great Depression of the 1930s, those able to continue farming were flooded with workers—poor whites and African Americans escaping areas with no job prospects. Beginning in 1942, growers began the controversial use of *braceros,* or guest workers from Mexico. Since 1900, four unions had attempted to unionize agricultural workers. The grape strikes in the 1960s

were not the first ones in the state. Among preceding actions was a 1938 Kern County strike that moved into the cotton fields.

Wage Disparities

Clearly, wage disparity precipitated the strike. Grapes, particularly table grapes, are a labor-intensive crop and a perishable commodity. Trouble erupted in May 1965, when braceros were paid $1.40 per hour while seasonal workers earned between $1.20 and $1.25. A box bonus added about 30 or 35 cents per hour on average.

The first grapes to ripen were in the far south of the state, in an area known as the Coachella Valley. Typically, workers

Cesar Chavez (front row left, in leather jacket) and Walter Reuther (center, in suit) leading a group of United Farm Workers Union picketers, Delano, California, 1965. © Bettmann/Corbis. Reproduced by permission.

moved frequently as they followed the harvest throughout the state. The Filipino workers were considered the most skilled of these grape workers, and those who worked in the vineyards were affiliated with AWOC, an AFL-CIO affiliate formed in February 1959. When wages were disputed at the start of the 1965 season, Larry Itliong, an AWOC organizer, eventually got Coachella Valley growers to agree to a wage increase.

As the seasonal workers followed the harvest, growers in other regions continued favoring the braceros with higher hourly wages, and the others continued to demand $1.40 per hour and 25 cents per box. By now, the harvest had moved to Delano,

California. The growers in Delano did not respond to Itliong's request to discuss the issues by 8 September, resulting in a strike by the Filipino workers. There were about 3,500 grape workers in Delano at the time. About 1,000 people walked off the job or picketed. The growers refused to negotiate.

The independent NFWA, another agricultural labor union organizing in the area, consisted of about 1,200 members, almost all of them Mexican Americans. The union's founder was Cesar Chavez. Eight days into the grape strike, Chavez called his union together to discuss whether they should support the AWOC strike. The NFWA first asked for recognition and contracts. With no answer, the NFWA joined the strike. Marshall Ganz, a labor organizer who would later dissect the events of the strike, called this "the beginning of the grape strike . . . [but] more as the first step in the birth of a farmworkers movement." From the outset, Chavez—inspired by a deep respect for the Indian leader Mohandas K. Gandhi, his own religious training, and the American civil rights movement—insisted on a nonviolent strike.

State officials concluded that the strike was indeed a labor dispute and prevented growers from hiring either braceros or workers referred by the farm labor office. At the time, grape growers ranged from corporate operations such as Di Giorgio Corporation and Schenley Industries to resident growers, who also owned vineyards in the region. Growers hired strikebreakers, and union members went to shape-ups (early morning dayworker selection by labor contractors), distributed leaflets, and asked laborers to honor the Delano strike.

During the first months of the 1965 strike, local sheriffs and state police tracked the picketers, and intimidation became common. Despite Chavez's peaceful resistance, violence was also common. Growers and their foremen carried through on threats with fists, dogs, and automobiles. In one case, growers sprayed the strikers with pesticides, temporarily blinding them for days.

Pesticide use was one of the primary union concerns. "You can smell the poison sometimes in Delano," Chavez told Peter Matthiessen, author of *Sal Si Puedes: Cesar Chavez and the New American Revolution*. "It's very, very strong. Workers can't begin to comprehend the dangers of these sprays; most of them look so innocent. I'm determined to do battle against the growers on this." Nevertheless, Mattheissen noted that Chavez was initially reluctant to press this issue, which would become central in late 1968.

Grape loading points for distribution were picketed as well. Sympathetic union members such as dockworkers also supported the strike by refusing to handle Delano grape shipments. Additional support came from other unions—notably the United Automobile Workers—as well as churches and college students. Caravans brought needed supplies into Delano. Additional alliances were forged with civil rights groups such as the Congress of Racial Equality, the Student Nonviolent Coordinating Committee, and other left-wing organizations.

On 18 December 1965 the NFWA called additional attention to the situation through a consumer boycott of Schenley products. Because the company's products included beverages consumed and given as gifts at the holidays—scotch, bourbon, and wines—the union hoped to dent sales and attract attention to the workers' plight. It helped little.

The support of the church was pivotal in the success of the strike from its start. The farmworkers, many of them Catholic, saw the support of clergy and nuns as an endorsement of the strike. Religious images, such as the Virgin of Guadalupe, were often carried in marches. The church, however, was not united in its opinion. Most of the growers were Catholic, too. As pointed out by John Gregory Dunne in *Delano: The Story of the California Grape Strike*, "Most of the financial support for the Church came from the Anglos, while the Mexicans made up the bulk of the parishioners." This formed a rift within the church.

Even the priests were polarized and frequently spoke out against each other's opinions. With the encouragement of Bishop Hugh Donohoe, on 16 March 1966 the church issued a formal position on farm labor, asking for legislation that would include farmworkers under the National Labor Relations Act.

The Nation Learns About Delano

It was not until 1966 that national attention was focused on the situation in Delano. In March 1966 the U.S. Senate Subcommittee on Migrant Labor, headed by New Jersey Senator Harrison Williams, conducted hearings throughout the state to better understand the issues of those working in the fields. The vocal presence of Senator Robert F. Kennedy and his call for farmworkers' collective bargaining rights drew media and public attention.

To coincide with Lent, Chavez and supporters made *La Peregrination* (The Pilgrimage) to Sacramento. The more than 230-mile protest march sought to elicit support from Governor Pat Brown. Ganz states there were three main objectives: "to win support for the strike, . . . to pressure Democratic Governor Edmund G. Brown, who was up for election that year and concerned about Mexican American voters, [and] to gain public support for the Schenley Boycott by demonstrating the injustice of the farmworkers' plight." As the march progressed, word reached Chavez that Brown was in Palm Springs vacationing as a guest of the entertainer Frank Sinatra. Union representatives were sent to Palm Springs as was a telegram requesting an audience with Brown. It went unanswered. As the march reached Sacramento, Chavez was contacted by a Schenley Industries representative seeking a contract. Chavez left to negotiate and returned just as the group reached the state capital. Schenley Industries had agreed to recognize the NFWA in Delano.

Di Giorgio Corporation indicated its willingness to unionize, but negotiations broke off in April 1966. A consumer boycott of the company's various food products was announced to put pressure on the firm. Di Giorgio consented to an election but allowed the Teamsters to be placed on the union ballot as well, much to the chagrin of Chavez, who was wary of that union's involvement. They had already been expelled from membership under the AFL-CIO umbrella. Just before the election, the AWOC and NFWA merged on 22 August and became the United Farm Workers Organizing Committee (UFWOC), AFL-CIO. Despite victory in these elections, there was still no contract.

Continuing to seek contracts, the UFWOC launched a strike against Giumarra Vineyards Corporation, then California's largest table grape grower. Yet another consumer grape boycott was launched in August 1967 to assist in that strike. When nonunion growers began to "borrow" union labels to place on grape boxes, a strike was announced against all California table grapes. Union organizers were sent throughout the United States and Canada to spread the word. Meanwhile, the boycott was working; grapes were rotting in warehouses and growers were taking a financial hit. Support abroad bolstered the strikers. "A lot of people adhered to the boycott, and it had a real dramatic impact on the grape industry in California," said economist Kevin McGee in a 2001 article.

Frank Bardacke, writing in *The Nation* in 1993, observed that boycotts might not have been the optimal union priority during this era. "Ultimately, it interfered with organizing in the fields. . . . From the point of view of building the boycott, it was a genius decision. But from the point of view of spreading the union among farmworkers themselves, it was a disaster."

During the winter of 1968–1969, thanks to a back problem, Chavez was physically unable to lead the union. He worked from bed, sending out letters to growers, calling for negotiations to avoid a third boycott year. In early 1968, as the union continued to seek contracts, he decided to launch a fast to draw attention to his continued commitment to nonviolence. He broke his 25-day fast at an Easter Sunday mass with family members and Robert F. Kennedy at his side.

With Richard M. Nixon, a Californian, in the White House, union leaders had hoped issues important to farmworkers might be heard. Members of the Senate Subcommittee on Migratory Labor, including Edward Kennedy and Walter Mondale, sided with the union, entering into the record on 11 October 1968 a point-by-point rebuttal to each of the growers' claims about conditions of farmworkers. This document concluded, "The grape strikers do not ask for pity or charity, only their rights. They are not rejoicing in the boycott. It is tragic that the grape industry will not talk with representatives of their employees."

Boycotts Effective in Securing Contracts

Grapes were also an issue in the presidential elections in 1968. Every Democratic candidate, including eventual nominee Hubert H. Humphrey, supported the boycott, while Nixon defiantly and openly provided grapes at campaign events. California's governor, Ronald Reagan, who had been elected in 1967, served as a celebrity spokesperson for the growers. He frequently called the boycott "immoral." By 1969 the growers were claiming damages of about $25 million thanks to the boycotts. The growers launched a $2 million public relations campaign to bolster their position and increase grape consumption. Nixon ordered the Department of Defense to purchase grapes to be shipped to military personnel in Vietnam and Europe, drawing the wrath of antiwar protestors. In 1969 the government bought 11 million pounds of fresh grapes—eight pounds for each service member in Vietnam, or six times the volume purchased in 1967. Reagan appeared on television in 1969 in support of the growers.

In May 1970 the stalemate between growers and union representatives was broken when the two leading Delano growers signed contracts with the union. Ultimately, in July 1970, 26 Delano growers signed three-year UFWOC contracts, giving 10,000 workers union representation. This placed 75 percent of the state's table grapes under contract. The wages for workers had increased from $1.10 per hour to a contracted $1.80 per hour. In addition, this contract initially gave a 20-cents-per-box bonus to workers and required growers to contribute to the union health plan on behalf of each worker. The hourly wage rates were scheduled to increase to $1.95, and then to $2.05 in 1972. The boycott continued despite this so-called victory. The union still sought contracts with grape growers in other parts of the state.

The price of this contract was high for union members who had been on strike for five years. Almost all of them—an estimated 95 percent—lost their homes and cars. Now the difficult work began for the union: seeing that the growers would adhere

to the contracts. Eventually, the union brought the entire California table grape industry under contract, successfully unionizing some 70,000 workers. The UFWOC became the United Farm Workers in 1972 and remained an active voice for farmworkers into the twenty-first century.

Chavez did not call an official end to the grape strike until fall 1973. By then an estimated 17 million Americans had stopped consuming table grapes and continued to actively boycott them and related products. It was not until 1975, with the passage of the California Agricultural Labor Relations Act, that California farmworkers were given the legal right to organize.

Although conditions in the fields purportedly improved for workers since the 1960s, there remained vociferous calls for reform. Similar boycott tactics were implemented against various growers, even specific corporate farming operations.

Key Players

Chavez, Cesar Estrada (1927–1993): Born in Arizona, Chavez first became active in the Community Service Organization in California in 1952 with the encouragement of Father Donald McConnell and Fred Ross. He served as its general director between 1958 and 1962. He left to organize grape workers and formed the National Farm Workers Association in 1962.

Giumarra, John G., Jr.: The third generation of the California agricultural Giumarra family, John G. Giumarra had graduated in 1965 from Stanford University Law School and was practicing business, labor, and real estate law in Orange County, California, when he was asked to return to help the family business. Giumarra Vineyards was the target of union organizing throughout the 1960s. Giumarra was one of the growers at the fore of publicly opposing the union during the grape strikes. He cited the period between 1970 and 1973 as the most turbulent of his career.

Huerta, Dolores Fernandez (1930–): A native of New Mexico, Huerta grew up in Stockton, California. She earned a teaching degree and taught elementary school. While living in Stockton in the mid-1950s, she became active with the Community Service Organization. She met Cesar Chavez there, and they formed the National Farm Workers Association, which later became the UFW. She remained an active labor organizer and negotiated the key 1970 contract that ended the Delano grape strikes. She served as vice president of the UFW between 1970 and 1973.

Itliong, Larry (1913–1977): Born in the Philippines, Itliong immigrated to the United States as a teenager. He started his lifelong career as a union organizer' while working in the fishing and canning industries in the northwestern United States. He was a staff member of the AWOC and assistant director and national boycott coordinator of the UFWOC. Itliong resigned from union work in 1971.

BIBLIOGRAPHY

Books

Del Castillo, Richard Griswold, and Richard A. Garcia. *Cesar Chavez: A Triumph of Spirit.* Norman: University of Oklahoma Press, 1995.

"Dolores Huerta." In *Hispanic American Biography: A–K,* edited by Rob Nagel and Sharon Rose, eds. New York: International Thomson, 1995.

Dunne, John Gregory. *Delano: The Story of the California Grape Strike.* New York: Farrar, Straus, and Giroux, 1967.

Ferriss, Susan, and Ricardo Sandoval. *A Fight in the Fields: Cesar Chavez and the Farmworkers Movement.* New York: Harcourt Brace, 1997.

Kushner, Sam. *Long Road to Delano: A Century of Farmworkers' Struggle.* New York: International Publishers, 1975.

London, Joan, and Henry Anderson. *So Shall Ye Reap.* New York: Crowell, 1970.

Matthiessen, Peter. *Sal Si Puedes (Escape if You Can): Cesar Chavez and the New American Revolution.* Berkeley: University of California Press, 2000.

Sosnick, Stephen H. *Hired Hands: Seasonal Farm Workers in the United States.* Santa Barbara, CA: McNally and Loftin, 1978.

Terzian, James P., and Kathryn Cramer. *Mighty Hard Road: The Story of Cesar Chavez.* Garden City, NY: Doubleday, 1970.

Periodicals

Bacon, David. "Josefina Flores: A Veteran of the War in the Fields." *Dollars and Sense* 231 (September 2000).

Bardacke, Frank. "Cesar's Ghost: Decline and Fall of the U.F.W." *The Nation* 254 (26 July 1993).

Barr, Evan T. "Sour Grapes: Cesar Chavez Twenty Years Later." *The New Republic* 193 (25 November 1985).

"Big UFWOC Delano Victory." *California AFL-CIO News* (31 July 1970).

Carnal, Jim. "Head of Giumarra Vineyards Influential in California, U.S. Politics." *Knight-Ridder/Tribune Business News* (9 October 1995).

Ganz, Marshall. "Resources and Resourcefulness: Strategic Capacity in the Unionization of California Agriculture, 1959–1966." *The American Journal of Sociology* 105 (January 2000): 1003.

Mulholland, Megan. "Unions Use Boycotts to Get Their Message Across." *Knight-Ridder/Tribune Business News* (22 July 2001).

"Threatened by Fasts, Foes, Chavez Held His Peace." *National Catholic Reporter* (7 May 1993).

"Union: Grape Boycott, Round Three." *Time* (19 August 1985).

ADDITIONAL RESOURCES

Other

United Farm Workers of America website [cited 22 November 2002]. <http://www.ufw.org/>.

—Linda Dailey Paulson

William Z. Foster. The Library of Congress.

Great Steel Strike

United States 1919–1920

Synopsis

The National Committee for Organizing Iron and Steel Workers, led by John Fitzpatrick of the Chicago Federation of Labor and a former Industrial Workers of the World (IWW) organizer named William Z. Foster, began a campaign to unionize American steelworkers during World War I. Taking advantage of a wartime labor shortage, the campaign signed up thousands of mostly less skilled workers. When the war ended, Fitzpatrick and Foster demanded a hearing with Elbert Gary, chairman of the United States Steel Corporation and the informal leader of the industry. When Gary refused to meet with them, pressure from the rank and file forced a strike.

The strike began on 22 September 1919. The two main issues were union recognition and shorter working hours. (Many steelworkers still worked a 10- or 12-hour day at this time.) Approximately 250,000 steel workers heeded the strike call that first day. The industry used a mixture of brute force and propaganda to pressure employees to go back to work. When the administration of President Woodrow Wilson chose not to force arbitration, the walkout was as good as dead. The committee formally ended the strike on 8 January 1920, although production had returned to normal levels weeks before.

Criminal Syndicalism Acts

As with the era of McCarthyism in the 1950s, the Red Scare of the late 1910s and early 1920s followed a world war. In both cases, the spread of communism attended the conclusion of international hostilities. Yet by the late 1940s, the appeal of communist doctrine had largely faded in Europe and North America, and few nations succumbed willingly to communist takeover. By contrast, in the years immediately following the Bolshevik coup in Russia, it seemed the world was on fire for revolution. Throughout the United States, workers demanded greater rights and appeared willing to take those rights by force.

Fearful of such an uprising, Idaho in 1917 passed a criminal syndicalism law, which in turn became the model for those of other states. California's, adopted in 1919, defined criminal syndicalism as "any doctrine or precept advocating, teaching, or aiding and abetting the commission of crime, sabotage . . . or unlawful acts of force . . . as a means of accomplishing a change in industrial ownership . . . or effecting any political change." The California law, in accordance with the Idaho model, defined participation in criminal syndicalism as "a felony . . . punishable by imprisonment."

In the heyday of the Red Scare, from 1917 to 1920, no fewer than 22 states and territories adopted criminal syndicalism laws, and the legislatures of eight others considered doing so. *Whitney v. California* (1927) brought the constitutionality of the California statute before the U.S. Supreme Court, which ruled that advocating violence against the state constitutes such a clear danger that the state may outlaw such advocacy. By the 1930s, however—during a period of widespread American sympathy for communism in the wake of the Great Depression—most criminal syndicalism laws had fallen into disuse.

The Court overturned its *Whitney* ruling once and for all with *Brandenburg v. Ohio* (1969), which concerned a 50-year-old Ohio criminal syndicalism law that was still in effect. Interestingly, the appellant in this case was neither a unionist nor a radical—or at least not a radical of the left, though as a Ku Klux Klansman, Brandenburg was certainly a radical of the right. In a filmed speech to Klansmen, he had threatened that if the federal government "continues to suppress the white, Caucasian race, it's possible that there might be some revengeance [sic] taken."

Source: Leonard W. Levy, editor in chief. *Encyclopedia of the American Constitution*. New York: Macmillan, 1986.

—Judson Knight

Timeline

1900: China's Boxer Rebellion, which began in the preceding year with attacks on foreigners and Christians, reaches its height. An international contingent of more than 2,000 men arrives to restore order, but only after several tens of thousands have died.

1907: U.S. markets experience a financial panic.

1912: *Titanic* sinks on its maiden voyage, from Southampton to New York, on 14 April. More than 1,500 people are killed.

1915: At the Second Battle of Ypres, the Germans introduce a new weapon: poison gas.

1917: The intercepted "Zimmermann Telegram" reveals a plot by the German government to draw Mexico into an alliance against the United States in return for a German promise to return the southwestern U.S. territories taken in the Mexican War. Three months later, in response to German threats of unrestricted submarine warfare, the United States on 6 April declares war on Germany.

1919: With the formation of the Third International (Comintern), the Bolshevik government of Russia establishes its control over communist movements worldwide.

1919: Treaty of Versailles is signed by the Allies and Germany but rejected by the U.S. Senate. This is due in part to rancor between President Woodrow Wilson and Republican Senate leaders, and in part to concerns over Wilson's plan to commit the United States to the newly established League of Nations and other international duties. Not until 1921 will Congress formally end U.S. participation in the war, but it will never agree to join the League.

1919: The Eighteenth Amendment, which prohibits the production, sale, distribution, purchase, and consumption of alcohol throughout the United States is ratified.

1919: In India, Mahatma Gandhi launches his campaign of nonviolent resistance to British rule.

1919: In Italy, a former socialist of the left named Benito Mussolini introduces the world to a new socialism of the right, embodied in an organization known as the "Union for Struggle," or Fasci di Combattimento. Composed primarily of young war veterans discontented with Italy's paltry share of the spoils from the recent world war (if not with their country's lackluster military performance in the conflict), the fascists are known for their black shirts and their penchant for violence.

1921: As the Allied Reparations Commission calls for payments of 132 billion gold marks, inflation in Germany begins to climb.

1925: European leaders attempt to secure the peace at the Locarno Conference, which guarantees the boundaries between France and Germany, and Belgium and Germany.

1929: On "Black Friday" in October, prices on the U.S. stock market, which had been climbing wildly for several years, suddenly collapse. Thus begins the first phase of a world economic crisis and depression that will last until the beginning of World War II.

Event and Its Context

The steel industry was the most antiunion industry in America. Carnegie Steel had delivered a devastating blow to steel unionism during the Homestead lockout of 1892. U.S. Steel completed the process of neutralizing the union presence in the industry during a strike in 1909. But World War I changed the balance in the labor-management relationship because it spurred the interest of the government in maintaining production. When labor strife hit a war industry, the Wilson administration forced management into arbitration, sometimes even into collective bargaining. Organized labor regained a foothold in the steel industry by taking advantage of the war emergency.

At the beginning of the war, Fitzpatrick and Foster led an organizing campaign in the Chicago stockyards. The campaign succeeded in bringing packinghouse workers many benefits because of federally mandated wartime arbitration. Their next target was steel. The drive was national in scope because Fitzpatrick's Chicago Federation of Labor convinced the normally conservative president of the American Federation of Labor, Samuel Gompers, to go along. The National Committee was a voluntary body representing 24 unions with steel industry interests, including the blacksmith, boilermaker, electrical worker, and machinist unions. Unlike in other strikes, the unions involved deferred to the decisions made by the committee so as to guarantee unity. The unions also pooled organizing resources, which was practically unheard-of in the labor movement up to that time. These changes in practice indicate the importance of organizing the steel industry to the entire union movement. The National Committee's campaign was the first sustained effort to organize steelworkers in decades.

During the war, the National Committee had great success signing up less skilled workers who had never had a home in the steel industry's existing unions. Immigrants responded particularly well to the organizing drive. The National Committee equated unionism with democracy in its rhetoric, and immigrants who wanted to show themselves American saw joining the union as a way to do so. The steel industry tolerated this organizing activity during the war for fear of government intervention and fear that work stoppages would prevent firms from making huge wartime profits. Furthermore, any lockout during the war would have led to charges that management was unpatriotic, so the steel industry bided its time.

The organizing drive continued after the war ended, but now management and its allies felt freer to oppose the effort. It had many weapons with which to accomplish this goal. Spies in the mills, blacklists, and exercising control of local governments in steel towns were among their most effective methods. Yet the union ranks continued to grow. After the strike began, armed policemen, state troopers, and even the federal army were mobilized on management's side.

The National Committee wanted to take time to build its organization, but impatient steelworkers forced it to act more quickly. On 25 May 1919 steelworkers from throughout the Midwest met at a general conference in Pittsburgh. Despite calls for caution, the committee realized that its membership demanded action. On 20 July the National Committee issued 12 demands. Besides union recognition and shorter hours, the demands included one day's rest in seven, a wage increase, dues checkoff, and the abolition of company unions. When Elbert Gary refused to meet with committee representatives, Gompers, who had been deeply involved with the government war effort, got President Wilson to approach Gary on their behalf. Despite pressure from the president, Gary still refused to meet any representative of any union. At this point the National Committee set the strike date of 22 September.

U.S. Steel and the rest of the industry was determined to fight the committee no matter the cost. Steel executives had an almost visceral hatred of organized labor because of the costs it imposed on production and the notion that collective bargaining violated a basic tenet of American capitalism—the idea that men should rise and fall as individuals rather than as part of a collective entity. Elbert Gary repeatedly stated that U.S. Steel did not bargain with unions "as such" but that his door was always open to any individual worker who had a complaint. He never suggested that a single worker ever took him up on this offer. A few firms, notably Bethlehem Steel, had instituted company unions during the war, but only to avoid government-imposed recognition of outside trade unions. Now that the government no longer needed steel for the war effort, the industry wanted to roll back wages and eradicate independent trade unions from American mills. In the weeks following the Armistice, steel companies fired many union leaders in the process of lowering their payrolls from bloated wartime levels.

Steelmakers thought they would have no trouble beating back the National Committee's drive because they believed the vast majority of steelworkers supported them. Many steel executives received a rude awakening when the strike came. Approximately half the steelworkers in America stayed home the first day. This was almost twice the number of employees who had joined the union by that time. However, the effectiveness of the walkout varied widely. Gary, Indiana, for example, was almost completely dormant on 22 September. Managers at the Colorado Fuel and Iron Company in Pueblo, Colorado, had expected the strike to bypass them because they thought their company union had addressed all of the union's concerns, but that mill had to shut down too. However, in the Lehigh Valley of Pennsylvania and in Birmingham, Alabama, the strike had little or no effect. In the Pittsburgh district, some mills shut entirely, while others were unaffected.

The steel companies and their allies fought the strike with three successful strategies. First, they used repression to prevent the strikers from meeting and to break their will to fight. For example, the day before the strike began, mounted police officers in North Clairton, Pennsylvania, broke up a strike rally, beating the strikers with clubs as the rode through the crowd. In Allegheny County, Pennsylvania (which includes Pittsburgh), Sheriff William S. Haddock banned meetings of three or more people in any outside public place and deputized 5,000 men to enforce the order; the men were paid and armed by local steel firms.

The steel producers also deliberately inflamed racial and ethnic tensions in the workforce. For example, a spy in Chicago received instructions from the U.S. Steel subsidiary there to aggravate tensions between the Italians and the Serbians with the goal of getting one group to go back to work before the other. U.S. Steel paid African Americans in Gary, Indiana, to march through the streets rather than to make steel, anticipating that the mere prospect of a black person taking their job would be enough to convince white strikers to return to work. The strike, in fact, proved an opening for large numbers of African Americans to keep good steel jobs on a permanent basis for the first time.

Last, the industry encouraged the media to attack the politics of the strike and its organizers. Most of these attacks centered on William Z. Foster, whose previous career with the IWW gave the National Committee's enemies an easy way to make the campaign seem dangerously radical. Labor organizers had known of Foster's radical past. He had even offered to resign his position before the strike began to avoid it becoming an issue, but Gompers and the National Committee supported him anyway because of his success in the Chicago stockyards. Unfortunately for the committee, a reporter for the industry trade journal *Iron Age* heard about Foster's previous affiliation and even found an old pamphlet he wrote. The pamphlet, entitled "Syndicalism," was an extreme left-wing tract filled with denunciations of the capitalist order. Even though the pamphlet had been out of print for years, copies soon poured into steel towns. Despite the reasonableness of the National Committee's demands, the public and the steelworkers themselves began to consider whether the strike was part of a left-wing master plan. The attacks on Foster proved particularly effective, as the strike coincided almost exactly with the first Red Scare in the country at large. Foster eventually became the leader of the American Communist Party.

The National Committee's best hope for winning anything from the strike would have come from government intervention. Hearings by the Senate Committee on Education and Labor led nowhere. Therefore, union hopes centered on President Wilson's previously scheduled Industrial Conference, which began on 6 October. The high-level meeting comprised 57 delegates representing the public, organized labor, and industry. It was supposed to improve the climate that had led to so many labor disputes in 1919, but it quickly became bogged down by the steel strike. At the beginning of the conference, the labor group immediately introduced a series of resolutions designed to force arbitration of the dispute on terms favorable to the National Committee. Gary attended the conference, strangely enough, as a member of the public delegation, even though he had refused to meet with some of the labor leaders at the conference just a few months before. When forced to confront the existence of the strike, Gary merely repeated his philosophical opposition to trade unionism. Because the conference had no power, nothing was resolved, and because the Wilson administration did not want to antagonize the steel industry in its quest for broader industrial peace, it did not interfere in the dispute again. With all hope of reaching a favorable settlement gone, striking workers gradually returned to their jobs in increasing numbers all across the country.

The Amalgamated Association of Iron, Steel, and Tin Workers ordered its members back to work in early November. The Amalgamated Association, though much weaker, was still the largest union in the steel industry. In 1919 its few locals had as members approximately 5,000 skilled workers, employed mostly in a small number of midwestern specialty steelmakers. When the less skilled men in the National Committee struck,

many Amalgamated Association members came out in sympathy with them. This violated the labor contracts at union mills. When these union employers threatened to cease dealing with the union entirely, Amalgamated president Michael Tighe felt compelled to protect his organization. Although the union might have been expected to help the committee financially, at least, it offered little support of any kind to the strike—although, to be fair, other unions did not offer much support either. The Amalgamated Association's behavior during the strike helps explain how Tighe earned the nickname "Grandmother."

By December 1919 the number of strikers had dropped by two-thirds, and steel production had returned to 50 or 60 percent of normal. Nevertheless, the representatives of the National Committee voted to continue the strike. By 8 January 1920, however, the strike remained effective in only a few places, so the committee voted to end the walkout. Some union leaders immediately planned another organizing campaign, but when the Amalgamated Association withdrew from the National Committee all hopes at a revival disappeared. No unionists were willing to violate that union's jurisdiction. The Amalgamated Association wanted to be the dominant voice in any subsequent union drive, but it lacked the will to undertake the kind of effort necessary to conquer this citadel of antiunionism. Even the passage of section 7(a) of the National Industrial Recovery Act in 1933 did not inspire the Amalgamated Association to take initiative.

Even though labor lost the 1919 strike, one positive development grew out of the dispute. During the strike, the Interchurch World Movement, a Protestant group committed to the liberal ideas of the Social Gospel movement, began an investigation of the steel industry and the conditions that led to the strike. Their report, released on 28 July 1920, did much to justify labor's lost cause. In its coverage of the report, the press seized on the existence of the continued existence of the 12-hour workday even though that issue made up only an eighth of the document. Following its playbook, the industry and its paid operatives attacked the Interchurch Movement and its report as dangerously radical. Nevertheless, the report inspired follow-up reports in the press and a volume of the Interchurch movement's field studies. Even though interest in the report tailed off, it led to pressure from both Congress and the administration of President Warren Harding to end the 12-hour day once and for all. Although most of the steel industry, in particular Elbert Gary, resisted the move, Gary changed his mind after he received a personal letter from President Harding in 1923 that threatened the industry with legislation if it did not make this change on its own. This decision made the steel industry the last major industry in the United States to eliminate the 12-hour day. If the 1919 strike had not occurred, the will to force that change would not have emerged as soon as it did.

The steel industry remained largely nonunion until the Steel Workers Organizing Committee took control of the Amalgamated Association and won major victories in the late 1930s.

Key Players

Fitzpatrick, John (1871–1946): Fitzpatrick was the Chicago Federation of Labor president. In addition to his work that led to the 1919 steel strike, he organized a successful effort to organize the Chicago stockyards.

Foster, William Z. (1881–1961): Former Industrial Workers of the World organizer and coleader of the Chicago stockyards campaign with Fitzpatrick, Foster went on to lead the American Communist Party.

Gary, Elbert (1846–1927): Gary was an Illinois state judge and, later, first president of the United States Steel Corporation. The size of his company and his intense opposition to trade unions made him the natural leader of steel industry forces during the strike.

Gompers, Samuel (1850–1924): American Federation of Labor president, Gompers thought his support for World War I would translate into help from the Wilson administration. The government's response to the steel strike dashed these hopes.

Tighe, Michael (1858–1940): President of the nearly inoperative Amalgamated Association of Iron, Steel, and Tin Workers, Tighe decided to have his skilled members cross picket lines as soon as the strike looked unwinnable.

See also: *American Federation of Labor; Homestead Lockout; Industrial Workers of the World; U.S. Steel Recognizes Steel Workers Organizing Committee.*

BIBLIOGRAPHY

Books

Brody, David. *Labor in Crisis: The Steel Strike of 1919.* Urbana: University of Illinois, 1987.

Foster, William Z. *The Great Steel Strike and Its Lessons.* New York: B.W. Huebsch, 1920.

Interchurch World Movement. *Public Opinion and the Steel Strike.* New York: Harcourt, Brace, and Howe, 1921.

———. *Report on the Steel Strike of 1919.* New York: Harcourt, Brace, and Howe, 1920.

Periodicals

Hill, Charles. "Fighting the Twelve-Hour Day in the American Steel Industry." *Labor History* 15 (winter 1974): 19–35.

—Jonathan Rees

Guatemalan Coup Orchestrated by CIA

Guatemala 1954

Synopsis

In 1954 the Central Intelligence Agency (CIA) orchestrated the overthrow of Guatemala's democratically elected president,

Jacóbo Arbenz Guzman. The Library of Congress.

Jacóbo Arbenz. After World War II American leaders were committed to preventing the Soviet Union from spreading communism across the globe. This concern generated much of U.S. policy toward Guatemala during the 1950s. Historians debate whether the intervention in Guatemala was an overzealous attempt to stop the flow of communism or a calculated action to protect American business interests in the region.

Timeline

1935: Second phase of New Deal begins with the introduction of social security, farm assistance, and housing and tax reform.

1940: Hitler's troops sweep through Western Europe, annexing Norway and Denmark in April, and in May the Low Countries and France.

1945: On 7 May, Germany surrenders to the Allies.

1951: Julius and Ethel Rosenberg are convicted and sentenced to death for passing U.S. atomic secrets to the Soviets.

1955: Warsaw Pact is signed by the Soviet Union and its satellites in Eastern Europe.

1955: African and Asian nations meet at the Bandung Conference in Indonesia, inaugurating the "non-aligned" movement of Third World countries.

1955: Over the course of the year, a number of key ingredients are added to the pantheon of American culture: the 1955

Chevrolet, the first of many classic models; Tennessee Williams's *Cat on a Hot Tin Roof*; Marilyn Monroe's performance in *The Seven-Year Itch*; Disneyland; and Bill Haley and the Comets' "Rock Around the Clock."

1955: Among the year's deaths are Albert Einstein, Thomas Mann, Dale Carnegie, Cy Young, and James Dean.

1955: Rosa Parks refuses to move from her seat near the front of a public bus in Montgomery, Alabama, and is arrested. The incident touches off a boycott of Montgomery's bus system, led by the Rev. Martin Luther King, Jr., which will last well into 1956. The situation will attract national attention and garner support for the civil rights movement, before Montgomery agrees to desegregate its bus system on 21 December 1956—exactly a year after Parks's brave protest.

1958: First U.S. satellite, *Explorer I,* goes into orbit.

1962: As the Soviets begin a missile buildup in Cuba, for a few tense days in October it appears that World War III is imminent. President Kennedy calls for a Cuban blockade, forcing the Soviets to back down and ultimately diffusing the crisis.

1970: President Nixon sends U.S. troops into Cambodia on 30 April. Five days later, National Guardsmen open fire on antiwar protesters at Kent State University in Ohio. By 24 June antiwar sentiment is so strong that the Senate repeals the Gulf of Tonkin resolution. On 29 June, Nixon orders troops back out of Cambodia.

Event and Its Context

Fears of communist infiltration in Guatemala date back to 1944, when a student revolt ended the dictatorship of Jorge Ubico Castañeda. During Ubico's rule, 2 percent of the population controlled more than 60 percent of the land, most of which was held by the American company United Fruit. The company also held a monopoly over the nation's banana, utility, and railroad industries and controlled the country's shipping center and activities at Puerto Barrios. Secretary of State John Foster Dulles negotiated this favorable arrangement while doing legal work at the firm of Sullivan and Cromwell in the 1930s. Following the defeat of Ubico's government, Guatemala's first elected president, Juan Jose Arevalo, threatened to reverse these profitable trade agreements.

Part of the threat of the reversal entailed mild land reform measures and the 1947 Labor Code, which gave nonunion workers the right to organize, to bargain for increased wages, and to strike. These activities had been forbidden under Ubico's dictatorship. Given that United Fruit employed more than 40,000 workers, such reforms unsettled the company's management. The fruit conglomerate reportedly funded a CIA coup of the Guatemalan government, code named Operation Fortune. The Truman administration eventually aborted the operation.

With the change of leadership in both the United States and Guatemala in the early 1950s, plans for a coup heated up. In 1951 Jacóbo Arbenz Guzman defeated Arevalo in the presidential race, and the new leader promised to implement agrarian reforms. Meanwhile, the incoming Eisenhower administration was bristling with confidence in its ability to thwart communism after successful operations in the Middle East. Arbenz's pledge to nationalize all arable land coupled with the close ties of the newly appointed secretary of sate, John Foster Dulles, to United Fruit provided fertile soil for the development of a plot for another coup. That scheme came to pass in 1954 after Arbenz passed Decree 900, which called for the government seizure of all uncultivated land. Although United Fruit owned more than 40 percent of the arable land in Guatemala, it cultivated only 10 percent of it. Arbenz seized 200,000 of the company's unused acres and offered the company $127,000, an amount equal to United Fruit's own estimate of the land's value for tax purposes. U.S. officials viewed the offer, which was well below market values, as an underhanded political maneuver. To U.S. observers, Arbenz appeared to be a Marxist dupe. As Eisenhower explained in his memoirs, the land measure constituted a "discriminatory and unfair seizure," clearly the work of "a puppet manipulated by Communists."

Dulles underscored the president's accusation, characterizing Arbenz as a ruthless communist. These charges proved difficult to sustain. Shortly after assuming office, Arbenz vowed to transform Guatemala from its depleted economic condition into a modern capitalist state. Many of his programs resembled the free-market economics praised by American leaders, such as constructing a highway to compete against United Fruit's transportation monopoly. As it became increasingly clear that Arbenz was not a communist, U.S. policymakers instead charged that Arbenz tolerated Marxist penetration in his government. Communists held four seats in the 51-member Guatemalan Congress, and 26 out of 350 administrators in the National Agrarian Department were socialists. Nevertheless, the toppling of Arbenz appears to have been motivated largely by his policies toward United Fruit, rather than by his sympathetic stance toward communism.

According to Schlesinger and Kinser's highly regarded study, *Bitter Fruit: The Story of the American Coup in Guatemala,* each of the U.S. officials involved in the overthrow of Arbenz had connections to United Fruit. Not only did Dulles once serve as the company's counsel, he also invested in United Fruit. Another major shareholder, John Moors Cabot, was appointed assistant secretary of state for inter-American affairs at the time of the overthrow. Cabot's brother had once been president of the fruit company. Senator Henry Cabot Lodge, a significant stockholder, was U.S. ambassador to the United Nations. Finally, CIA director Walter Bedell Smith was seeking employment with the company during the plot and was later appointed to its board of directors.

The intricate connection between Washington, D.C., and United Fruit helps explain why the United States removed Arbenz from office. For example, E. Howard Hunt, a key U.S. agent in Guatemala during the coup who was later embroiled in the Watergate scandal, expressed some resentment that his duties appeared to be more missionary actions for United Fruit than a legitimate instance of fighting communism. It is interesting to note that Eisenhower acknowledged in his memoirs that Arbenz's land expropriation did not prove that he was a communist.

Agrarian reform was not an adequately alarming pretext to justify Arbenz's removal. The *Alfhem* incident provided the needed justification. Arbenz had ordered a shipment of weapons from communist Czechoslovakia, which sailed into Guatemala aboard the *Alfhem* in May 1954, under the watchful eyes of restless CIA agents. Secretary of State Dulles overstated the significance of the weapons shipment, telling reporters that the weapons were part of a larger strategy to create a communist base at the Panama Canal. Reports soon appeared in U.S. newspapers regarding Guatemala's design to spread communism throughout Central America. Missing from these reports was the fact that the U.S. had initiated an arms embargo against Guatemala before the shipment had arrived. Such restrictions led Guatemala's foreign minister to suspect that America was searching for an incident to rationalize its planned invasion. That the coup was already planned before the arms shipment confirms this suspicion.

Armed with a reason to remove Arbenz, the CIA launched Operation PBSUCCESS in June 1954. Bombings accompanied fabricated radio reports that a massive internal uprising was taking place. In reality, the United States relied on outside forces, particularly Nicaraguan dictator Anastasio Somoza, to organize what was very much an external invasion. The air assault and psychological warfare successfully undermined Arbenz, who fled to Mexico City in July. The United States installed Castillo Armas to replace the democratically elected Arbenz.

Castillo Armas cancelled Decree 900 and returned all of the confiscated land to United Fruit. The authoritarian regime soon outlawed more than 500 labor organizations, including the Banana Workers' Federation, from which seven labor leaders were missing under questionable circumstances. Castillo Armas also prevented almost 75 percent of the population from voting and formed the National Committee of Defense against Communism at the request of the CIA. The group prevented the formation of political parties, blocked newspaper stories, and burned books. Dostoyevsky's works, Victor Hugo's writings, and those of Miguel Angel Asturias, a Nobel-prize recipient who had chastised United Fruit, were among the books set ablaze. Despite Armas's record on human rights, U.S. leaders initially supported his regime.

Critics across the globe felt differently about Castillo Armas's rule. The British Labor Party described U.S. actions as a naked act of aggression, and anti-American protests swept across Latin America. Che Guevara was among these protestors. He had traveled to Guatemala in the hope of witnessing Arbenz's reforms. Instead he watched as the CIA dismantled Guatemala's social progress. According to Guevara's wife, it was the Guatemalan experience that inspired him to take up arms against "Yankee imperialism." Guevara fled to Mexico City, where he met Fidel Castro. The two men traveled to Cuba to overthrow the government in 1959.

Key Players

Arbenz Guzman, Jacóbo (1913–1971): Arbenz served as a Guatemalan military officer for much of his adult life. He was also a strong advocate of agrarian reform and served as Guatemala's president from 15 March 1951 to 27 June 1954, when he fled to Mexico. He later moved to Europe.

Castillo Armas, Carlos (1914–1957) Armas was Guatemala's head of state from 1954 to 1957, when he was assassinated by military opponents. He was commander of Guatemala's Forth Military zone in the 1940s before assuming leadership of the nation under the National Democratic Movement Party. His brief rule was characterized by antidemocratic measures.

Dulles, John Foster (1889–1959): Dulles served as secretary of state under President Dwight D. Eisenhower. In this capacity, he held great influence in foreign policy decisions. He died of cancer in 1959 shortly after resigning his post. His accomplishments include facilitating the Southeast Treaty Organization (SEATO) and receiving the Medal of Freedom.

Eisenhower, Dwight David (1890–1969): Eisenhower served as president of the United States from 1952 to 1961. His foreign policy focused on the containment of communism, but he would later warn of undue corporate influence on American diplomacy, which he called the "military-industrial complex."

Nixon, Richard Milhous (1913–1994): Nixon served as vice president of the United States under Eisenhower. He later became president during the Vietnam War, and his presidency was marred by the infamous Watergate scandal.

See also: *United Fruit Company Strike.*

BIBLIOGRAPHY

Books

Blum, William. "Guatemala 1953–1954: While the World Watched." In *Killing Hope: U.S. Military and CIA Interventions Since World War II,* edited by William Blum. Monroe, ME: Common Courage, 1995.

Schlesinger, Stephen, and Stephen Kinzer. *Bitter Fruit: The Story of the American Coup in Guatemala.* Cambridge, MA: Harvard University Press, 1999.

—Carl Mirra

Guffey Act

United States 1935

Synopsis

The Guffey Act, also called the Guffey-Snyder Act and, more formally, the Bituminous Coal Conservation Act, was passed by the U.S. Congress to stabilize the coal industry. The act fixed minimum prices for coal and attempted to bring order to the wages, working conditions, and hours of coal workers. It also protected the rights of coal workers to organize and bar-

George Sutherland. Collection of the Supreme Court of the United States.

gain collectively. The act came under fire as unconstitutional congressional interference in private commerce, and in 1936, in *Carter v. Carter Coal Co.*, the U.S. Supreme Court declared the act unconstitutional.

Timeline

1920: League of Nations, based in Geneva, holds its first meetings.

1925: European leaders attempt to secure the peace at the Locarno Conference, which guarantees the boundaries between France and Germany, and Belgium and Germany.

1930: Naval disarmament treaty is signed by the United States, Great Britain, France, Italy, and Japan.

1933: Newly inaugurated U.S. President Franklin D. Roosevelt launches the first phase of his New Deal to put depression-era America back to work.

1935: Germany annexes the Saar region after a plebiscite. In defiance of Versailles, the Nazis reintroduce compulsory military service. The Allies do nothing, and many western intellectuals maintain that it is only proper for Germany to retake its own territory and begin building up its army again.

1935: Italians invade Ethiopia, and the response by the League of Nations—which imposes sanctions but otherwise fails to act—reveals the impotence of that organization.

1935: Second phase of New Deal begins with the introduction of social security, farm assistance, and housing and tax reform.

1938: The U.S. Fair Labor Standards Act establishes a minimum wage.

1940: Hitler's troops sweep through Western Europe, annexing Norway and Denmark in April, and in May the Low Countries and France. At the same time, Stalin—who in this year arranges the murder of Trotsky in Mexico—takes advantage of the situation to add the Baltic republics (Latvia, Lithuania, and Estonia) to the Soviet empire, where they will remain for more than half a century.

1945: April sees the death of three leaders: Roosevelt passes away on 12 April; the Italians execute Mussolini and his mistress on 28 April; and Hitler (along with Eva Braun, propaganda minister Josef Goebbels, and Goebbels's family) commits suicide on 30 April.

1950: North Korean troops pour into South Korea, starting the Korean War. Initially the communists make impressive gains, but in September the U.S. Marines land at Inchon and liberate Seoul. China responds by sending in its troops.

Event and Its Context

Background

The Guffey Act and the *Carter* case that issued from it represented a collision of at least three social, political, and economic trends in the mid-1930s.

The first of these was the condition of the coal industry itself. Coal mining since the 1920s had been regarded as a "sick" industry. Profits were declining, and mine closures were frequent. The industry was plagued by frequent strikes as miners attempted, often with violence, to ameliorate the squalid, dangerous, and unhealthful conditions in which they lived and worked. In 1921 the number of men employed in coal mining peaked at over 832,000; by 1933 that number had declined to just over 523,000. In 1923 the average annual earnings of workers in the bituminous (soft) coal industry were $1,917; by 1932 that figure had declined to $937. The number of mines in operation declined from a peak of 9,311 in 1923 to 5,555 in 1933. Total industry production declined from a peak of $1.506 billion in 1923 to just $625 million in 1932, although production recovered to $822 million in 1935 and $954 million in 1936. In the meantime, the retail price of coal was increasing in real dollars; using 1926 as a base year of 100, the price was 112.1 in 1933 and 116.8 in 1934. Given conditions in the coal mines and the importance of coal to both industry and the public, Congress was under increasing pressure to regulate the coal industry.

The second trend was the New Deal of President Franklin D. Roosevelt, a set of legislative initiatives enacted to curb the effects of the Great Depression and to protect organized labor. The National Industrial Recovery Act (NIRA) of 1933 recognized the right of workers to bargaining collectively, but that law was declared unconstitutional in 1935. After labor unrest in 1934, when half a million workers in a range of industries went on strike, the administration tried again in 1935 with the Wagner Act, more formally the National Labor Relations Act (NLRA), which established the National Labor Relations Board (NLRB) to supervise union elections and stop unfair labor practices. The question on the minds of many observers was whether the Wagner Act would meet with the same fate as the NIRA in the courts.

The third trend, then, was the response of the judiciary to New Deal legislation. During these years the U.S. Supreme Court under Chief Justice Charles Hughes was sharply split between supporters of the New Deal—justices Louis Brandeis, Benjamin Cardozo, Harlan Stone, and Owen Roberts—and the so-called Four Horsemen, a conservative bloc comprising justices Willis Van Devanter, James McReynolds, George Sutherland, and Pierce Butler. These justices adopted a strict construction of the commerce clause of the Constitution—the theoretical underpinning of most New Deal legislation—and a laissez-faire view of government's role in the economy. Frequently able to forge majorities, they invalidated a number of important facets of the New Deal, including the NIRA. What Roosevelt regarded as the recalcitrance of the Court led him to devise a "court-packing" plan in 1937 that would have increased the size of the Court and created a majority that would neutralize the Four Horsemen. Although that plan met with resistance and was never enacted, the Court did take a remarkably more liberal turn after 1937 in response to the threat and to the overwhelming support the president received in his 1936 reelection. This about-face eventually affected the Court's view of the Wagner Act, but in the meantime it had to deal with the Guffey Act.

The Bituminous Coal Conservation Act

The Bituminous Coal Conservation Act, popularly known as the Guffey Act after its Senate sponsor, Joseph Guffey of Pennsylvania, was passed in 1935. Section 1 of the act detailed the circumstances that, Congress believed, made the act necessary: that mining and distribution of coal were "affected with a national public interest"; that coal played an important part in industrial activity, transportation, and the "health and comfort of the people"; that coal had to be conserved and economically produced; that coal had to be supplied consistently and at a reasonable price; and that rational relations among the public, producers, and workers were necessary.

The Guffey Act established the Bituminous Coal Code, which divided the coal industry into 23 districts, each with a board that established minimum prices within its district to help stabilize wages, working conditions, and hours. From labor's standpoint, the most important part of the code was Part 3, which gave miners the right to organize and bargain collectively through representatives of their own choosing and without interference from employers. It also gave them the right to peaceably assemble and to select their own check-weighmen. It created a presidentially appointed labor board under the Department of Labor to adjudicate disputes. Further, the act provided a formula for wages and hours. When producers of more than two-thirds of the national average tonnage of coal and more than half of the mine workers agreed on hours, that agree-

ment would be accepted throughout the industry; similarly, within each district, if producers of more than two-thirds of the coal and the majority of workers in the district agreed on wages, those wages would be accepted by all firms and workers in that district. Finally, the act imposed a federal excise tax on all coal production, 90 percent of which would be rebated to firms that adopted the code.

Carter v. Carter Coal Company

Immediately, coal producers attacked the constitutionality of the act and filed suits in the U.S. Court of Appeals for the District of Columbia and the Circuit Court of Appeals for the Sixth Circuit. These suits were consolidated and brought before the Supreme Court as *Carter v. Carter Coal Co.*, which the Court heard on 11–12 March and decided on 18 May 1936.

The core question was whether Congress had exceeded its authority under the commerce clause of the Constitution. Justice Sutherland, who delivered the opinion of the Court, undertook a lengthy examination of this question, citing, for example, Justice Joseph Story, who in 1816 "laid down the cardinal rule" that the federal government can claim no powers that are not actually and expressly granted by the Constitution. Going back farther, he noted that the "determination of the Framers Convention . . . to preserve complete and unimpaired state self-government in all matters not committed to the general government is one of the plainest facts which emerges from the history of their deliberations."

Sutherland went on to examine the history of the word *commerce* as it applied to the commerce clause. He reasoned that while the Constitution grants to Congress the power to regulate interstate commerce—the transportation, purchase, sale, and exchange of commodities between the citizens of the states—it does not grant the power to regulate that which is not commerce. So the next question was whether manufacturing (and by extension, mining) is "commerce." Citing a number of earlier cases, including the recent *Schechter Poultry Corp. v. United States* (1935), Sutherland declared that it was not. The commerce clause gave Congress the power to regulate the *exchange* of goods between the states but not the power to regulate the *manufacture* or *production* of those goods, even if they are intended for interstate commerce.

Accordingly, Sutherland concluded, mining is not commerce. Mining, like manufacture or agriculture, is a strictly local activity. It brings the subject matter of commerce into existence, but in and of itself it is not commerce. On this basis, the Court, with justices Cardozo, Brandeis, and Stone dissenting, declared the Guffey Act unconstitutional. "Beneficent aims," the Court concluded, "however great or well directed can never serve in lieu of constitutional power."

The Aftermath

Labor was troubled by the anticipated impact of this decision on the recently passed Wagner Act, which applied to the 10 million workers in manufacturing. If the *Carter* doctrine held, then the protections labor gained under the Wagner Act would certainly be invalidated. But when the Wagner Act was tested in 1937, in *NLRB v. Jones and Laughlin Steel Corporation*, the Court upheld it and affirmed the authority of Congress to intervene in the labor relations of manufacturing and protect the rights of strikers, even if the effect of a strike was to impede interstate commerce.

As it turned out, then, the *Carter* decision was the last gasp of those who wanted to curb the involvement of the federal government in labor issues. Just a year after striking down the Guffey Act as an unconstitutional congressional foray into matters of local interest, the Court affirmed both the right of employees to organize and bargain collectively and the power of Congress to protect that right by outlawing unfair labor practices. Under the protection of the Wagner Act, union membership in the United States increased from about four million in 1935 to 16 million in 1948. Membership in the United Mine Workers of America, which had fallen by two-thirds during the 1920s, exploded until virtually all mines were organized and the union claimed 500,000 members.

Key Players

Butler, Pierce (1866–1939): Butler was born near Northfield, Minnesota, and practiced law for 25 years, gaining expertise in railroad law, before President Warren Harding appointed him to the Supreme Court (1923–1939).

Guffey, Joseph F. (1870–1959): Guffey was born in Guffey's Landing, Pennsylvania, and was president of several oil companies before being elected as a Democrat to the Senate (1935–1947), where he was a strong backer of New Deal legislation.

McReynolds, James Clark (1862–1946): McReynolds was born in Elkton, Kentucky, and began his judicial career as an assistant U.S. attorney general (1903–1907) and as a federal prosecutor. President Woodrow Wilson appointed him attorney general (1913–1914) and to the Supreme Court (1914–1941), where he wrote over 100 dissenting opinions.

Sutherland, George (1862–1942): Sutherland was born in England but came to the United States at age two. He served in Utah's first legislature and in the House of Representatives (1901–1903) and the Senate (1905–1917). President Warren Harding appointed him to the Supreme Court (1922–1938).

Van Devanter, Willis (1859–1941): Born in Marion, Indiana, Van Devanter was appointed assistant U.S. attorney general (1897–1903) and federal judge (1903–1910). He was appointed to the Supreme Court (1910–1937) by President William Howard Taft.

See also: *National Industrial Recovery Act; United Mine Workers of America; Wagner Act.*

BIBLIOGRAPHY

Books

Badger, Anthony. *The New Deal: The Depression Years, 1933–1940.* New York: Hill and Wang, 1989.

Mason, Alpheus Thomas, and William M. Beaney. *American Constitutional Law: Introductory Essays and Selected Cases.* Englewood Cliffs, NJ: Prentice-Hall, 1978.

Taylor, Benjamin J., and Fred Witney. *Labor Relations Law,* 3rd ed. Englewood Cliffs, NJ: Prentice-Hall, 1979.

U.S. Department of Commerce. *Historical Statistics of the United States: Colonial Times to 1970.* Washington, DC: Government Printing Office, 1976.

Other

Carter v. Carter Coal Co., 298 U.S. 238 [cited 13 February 2003]. <http://print.westlaw.com/delivery.html>.

—Michael J. O'Neal

H

Harpers Ferry Raid

United States 1859

Synopsis

On Sunday evening, 16 October 1859, the abolitionist John Brown and a band of supporters raided the U.S. arsenal at Harpers Ferry, Virginia. Brown's purpose was to strike a decisive blow against slavery and to embolden slaves to rise up and revolt. The raiders managed to seize control of the arsenal, but on Tuesday morning federal troops stormed it and captured several prisoners, including Brown. Later that month he was tried and convicted of treason, and on 2 December he was hanged. The notoriety of the Harpers Ferry raid further polarized the nation over the slavery issue and propelled the North and South closer to civil war.

Timeline

1839: England launches the First Opium War against China. The war, which lasts three years, results in the British gaining a free hand to conduct a lucrative opium trade, despite opposition by the Chinese government.

1844: American artist and inventor Samuel F. B. Morse successfully sends the first message via telegraph: a series of dots and dashes that conveys the phrase, "What hath God wrought?," across a circuit between Baltimore, Maryland, and Washington, D.C.

1849: Harriet Tubman escapes from slavery in Maryland. Over the next eight years, she will undertake at least 20 secret missions into Maryland and Virginia to free more than 300 slaves through the so-called Underground Railroad.

1852: *Uncle Tom's Cabin* by Harriet Beecher Stowe, though far from a literary masterpiece, is a great commercial success, with over half a million sales on both sides of the Atlantic. More important, it has an enormous influence on British sentiments with regard to slavery and the brewing American conflict between North and South.

1855: *Leaves of Grass* by Walt Whitman is published.

1859: Building of the Suez Canal begins.

1859: Charles Darwin publishes *On the Origin of Species by Means of Natural Selection,* sparking enormous controversy with an account of humankind's origins that differs markedly from the Bible.

1859: Retired American railroad conductor Edwin L. Drake drills the first successful oil well in the United States, at Titusville, Pennsylvania.

1861: Within weeks of Abraham Lincoln's inauguration, the U.S. Civil War begins with the shelling of Fort Sumter.

Six states secede from the Union, joining South Carolina to form the Confederate States of America (later joined by four other states) and electing Jefferson Davis as president. The first major battle of the war, at Bull Run or Manassas in Virginia, is a Confederate victory.

1865: U.S. Civil War ends with the surrender of General Robert E. Lee to General Ulysses S. Grant at Appomattox, Virginia. More than 600,000 men have died and the South is in ruins, but the Union has been restored.

1869: The first U.S. transcontinental railway is completed.

Event and Its Context

The Development of an Abolitionist

John Brown was born in Connecticut on 9 May 1800, and during his childhood and early manhood he developed a deep and abiding hatred of slavery. By the 1830s he was a successful tanner, but the depression of 1837 wiped out his modest wealth, which he had intended to use to finance an antislavery campaign. Throughout the 1840s his attitude toward slavery hardened, and he came to believe that only armed resistance—not speeches, protests, and petitions—would bring down the institution of slavery.

A turning point in Brown's life was the passage of the Kansas-Nebraska Act in 1854. Plans to organize Nebraska as a territory met with opposition from the South because under the terms of the Missouri Compromise of 1820, Nebraska would be a free state. Accordingly, the area was organized as two territories, Nebraska and Kansas, and each would determine whether it wanted to be a free or a slave state—in effect repealing the Missouri Compromise. Kansas immediately turned into a battleground over slavery. Proslavery settlers were rushing into Kansas, while northern abolitionist groups were financing the settlement of "free-soilers." In 1855 a proslavery legislature was elected, but free-soilers refused to recognize it and established their own shadow government. Meanwhile, border ruffians from Missouri were launching raids into Kansas, where they burned homes and murdered antislavery settlers.

In the midst of this chaos, Brown arrived in Kansas on 6 October 1855. Convinced that decisive action had to be taken, particularly after a force of 2,000 Missourians sacked and burned Lawrence, the free-state capital of Kansas, he organized a small troop of men, including four of his sons who had settled in Kansas. On the night of 24 May 1856, Brown led them to Pottawotamie Creek, where he directed the execution of five leaders of raids on free-staters. His actions helped plunge the state into a bloody conflict that ended only with the intervention of federal troops. Brown escaped to spend the next three years collecting money from abolitionists to aid runaway slaves. To accomplish his aims, however, he needed weapons such as those produced at the arsenal at Harpers Ferry, Virginia.

U.S. Marines storm engine house, after it was captured by abolitionist John Brown, Harpers Ferry. © Getty Images. Reproduced by permission.

Preparation and Plans

Some historians have described Brown as a "madman," and the popular conception of the Harpers Ferry raid was that it was little more than a desperate, ragtag effort to lash out at the slave system. In many respects, though, the raid was carefully planned and became the first step in a strategic campaign to bring about the collapse of slavery. Brown needed a dramatic way to galvanize a response both from slaves, who he believed would flee their plantations and join him, and from northern abolitionists, who he was convinced would send men and arms in the belief that an attack on slavery had begun in earnest. Using the Virginia mountains as a base, he planned to send small bands of men to local plantations to persuade slaves to join him. Once slavery collapsed locally, slave owners in surrounding counties would feel increasingly insecure about their ability to defend their "property" and would sell their slaves farther south. This process would repeat itself throughout Virginia, then throughout an ever-expanding area of the South, with Brown and his men following. Eventually, Brown believed, the nation's nearly four million slaves would be freed by an orderly, disciplined revolution—one governed not by a thirst for

blood but by a "Provisional Constitution" written to ensure honorable and restrained conduct by his supporters.

To accomplish his goals, Brown needed arms and money. Much of the money came from the so-called Secret Six, a group that included some of New England's foremost abolitionists: Gerrit Smith, a millionaire philanthropist and a member of Congress from New York; Theodore Parker, a Unitarian minister who hid runaway slaves in his Boston home; Franklin B. Sanborn, an educator and later Brown's biographer; Dr. Samuel Gridley Howe, coeditor of an abolitionist newspaper with his wife, Julia Ward Howe; George Luther Steams, a wealthy businessman; and Thomas Wentworth Higginson, also a Unitarian minister. Even Henry David Thoreau contributed money to Brown's cause, though no evidence shows that he knew of the raid. The arms, Brown concluded, would come from the Harpers Ferry Arsenal, which had been created by George Washington in 1794 and continued to produce weapons until it was destroyed at the outbreak of the Civil War.

Abolitionist John Brown portrayed in the "Tragic Prelude Mural." National Archives and Records Administration.

The Raid on Harpers Ferry

In the summer of 1859, Brown took up residence on a Maryland farm near Harpers Ferry, where he trained a group of 21 men in military maneuvers; among them were his sons, Oliver, Owen, and Watson. There he tried to maintain an air of normalcy to allay the growing suspicions of neighbors. Originally the raid was scheduled for 24 October, but Brown feared exposure of his plans, so on the night of 16 October the men launched their assault on the arsenal and took a number of watchmen prisoner, including Lewis Washington, the great-grandnephew of George Washington. In spite of his planning, though, Brown made two serious tactical errors. One was to allow a train that had stopped at Harpers Ferry to proceed to Baltimore; Brown expressed concern both for the passengers and for those awaiting them. When the train arrived in Baltimore, those aboard notified the authorities of what they had seen, and the government dispatched federal troops from Washington, D.C. The other mistake was to await the arrival of a wagonful of guns that two of the raiders were to bring from Brown's Maryland farmhouse. The men were delayed, but Brown insisted on waiting for them rather than taking the opportunity to flee.

By the morning of 17 October, local militia had surrounded the arsenal. During the day, at least three citizens, including the

The Saga of Dred Scott

In the famous Dred Scott case, or *Scott v. Sanford* (1857), the U.S. Supreme Court ruled that a slave was not a citizen, and was therefore ineligible to bring a suit in a federal court. Furthermore, as a slave, the Court ruled, Scott was the personal property of his owner. Therefore, the fact that he had lived in free territory did not make him a free man.

Born in Virginia in about 1799, Scott moved to St. Louis with his first masters, the Peter Blow family. There he married another slave, Harriet Robinson, in 1830, and together they had two children. Sold to Dr. John Emerson, a military surgeon, Scott (sometimes accompanied by his family) spent the next 12 years on the go with the doctor, whose work often took him out of slave territory and into free states. When Emerson died in 1843, his widow, Irene, attempted to hire out Dred, Harriet, and their children to other families.

Then, in 1846, Scott did something that, for an illiterate slave, represented both great resourcefulness and great courage: he sued his mistress in the St. Louis Circuit Court, demanding freedom for himself and his family. The court, not surprisingly, ruled in favor of Mrs. Emerson. Scott refiled the suit, whereupon a jury—much more surprisingly, given the time and the place—held that the Scotts deserved to be freed, based on their former residence in free territory.

Mrs. Emerson appealed the case to the Missouri Supreme Court, which struck down the decision of the Circuit Court in 1852. The next year, Scott, with the support of several abolitionist lawyers, filed a new suit in the U.S. Federal Court at St. Louis. By now Mrs. Emerson had turned over responsibility for her husband's estate to her brother, John Sanford, who served as the respondent in the famous case that made its way to the U.S. Supreme Court.

The Dred Scott story has several ironic twists at the end. Just after the Supreme Court ruled that Scott did not own himself, Mrs. Emerson remarried, and since her new husband opposed slavery, she returned the Scotts to the Blows, who released them. Sadly, however, Scott was dying of tuberculosis, and passed away in 1858. Like most slaves, he was buried in an unmarked grave, but on the centennial of the famous case, admirers placed a plaque on the final resting place of the man who had forced an unjust system to spell out the extent of its injustice.

Source: Fehrenbacher, Don Edward. *The Dred Scott Case: Its Significance in American Law and Politics.* New York: Oxford University Press, 1978.

—Judson Knight

John Brown's Fort. From this position he tried to negotiate the release of the prisoners in exchange for the freedom of the raiders, but without success. By this time, townspeople were enjoying an unofficial holiday, much of it spent in the saloons. When Colonel Robert E. Lee arrived with federal troops, his first action was to close the saloons and restore some order. Then at 6:30 on the morning of 18 October, Lee's troops stormed the engine house, and the raid ended as quickly as it had begun. Among Brown's men, 10 were killed, including two of Brown's sons; two escaped but were caught and brought back for trial; five escaped and were never caught; and five, including Brown, were captured and imprisoned.

Reactions to the Harpers Ferry Raid

Many Northerners were deeply disturbed by Brown's execution. They had been impressed by his dignity and eloquence during his trial, his almost quiet insistence that slavery was an evil that had to be ended. In cities throughout the North, people held memorials and gathered in churches to pay tribute to Brown as a fallen martyr and to condemn his hanging. The city of Albany, New York, fired a hundred-gun salute in his honor; businesses and government offices were closed on 2 December in Akron, Ohio. An outpouring of songs, poems, essays, and public addresses flowed from sympathizers. Henry Wadsworth Longfellow wrote in his journal that day, "This will be a great day in our history; the date of a new Revolution—quite as much needed as the old one."

Reaction was markedly different through much of the South. The South had long feared a slave revolt, and those fears were enflamed by the Harpers Ferry raid, led, many felt, by a dangerous fanatic. In the weeks and months that followed the raid, the South was rife with rumor and speculation. The governor of Virginia received letters and telegrams claiming that bands of antislavery marauders were invading the state; reports circulated that armed men from Kansas were on their way to Virginia to rescue Brown. Crowds publicly burned books that were critical of the South; suspicious people were jailed or run out of town; anytime a house caught fire, rumors flew that the slave revolt had begun. Calls for secession from the Union grew louder.

Brown's raid fostered a new militancy among abolitionists. Many abandoned the belief that slavery could be ended by moral suasion. Pacifists were fired by determination and anger and began to accept that force was the only solution. As Frederick Douglass wrote in the November 1859 issue of the *Liberator,* "Moral considerations have long since been exhausted upon Slaveholders. It is in vain to reason with them. . . . Slavery is a system of brute force. It shields itself behind might, rather than right. It must be met with its own weapons."

After the Civil War, Storer College, a school for African Americans, was established at Harpers Ferry. Later, the college became the site of the Second Niagara Movement, a precursor of the National Association for the Advancement of Colored People. John Brown's Fort stands now in the Harpers Ferry National Historical Park, near where it originally stood.

Key Players

Douglass, Frederick (1817–1895): Born a slave in Tuckahoe, Maryland, Douglass later was able to buy his freedom and

mayor of Harpers Ferry, were killed in sporadic gunfire. Brown, his escape routes cut off, selected nine prisoners and moved with them to the arsenal's fire-engine house, later known as became the leading African American spokesman against slavery, both as a lecturer and as editor of abolitionist newspapers. In 1845 he published his autobiography, later titled *Life and Times of Frederick Douglass*.

Higginson, Thomas Wentworth (1823–1911): Born in Cambridge, Massachusetts, Higginson was a Unitarian minister and an active abolitionist. During the Civil War he commanded an African American regiment of the Union Army. He is most remembered for inspiring and supporting Emily Dickinson, and he edited a collection of her poetry after her death.

Howe, Samuel Gridley (1801–1876): Born in Boston, Howe was a physician and active social reformer, lending his support to education for the blind, humane treatment for the mentally ill, prison reform, abolition, and the Underground Railroad. With his wife, Julia Ward Howe, he edited the abolitionist newspaper *Commonwealth*.

Lee, Robert E. (1807–1870): Lee was born in Westmoreland Country, Virginia, and attended West Point. He opposed secession but resigned from the U.S. Army to join the Confederate Army. He commanded troops at Second Bull Run, Antietam, Fredericksburg, Chancellorsville, and Gettysburg before surrendering to Ulysses S. Grant at Appomattox Courthouse in 1865.

Smith, Gerrit (1797–1874): Born in Utica, New York, Smith managed an inherited family fortune. He opposed the Fugitive Slave Act, and after 1835 his house was a stop on the Underground Railroad. He served one term in the U.S. House of Representatives (1853–1855). After the Civil War, he opposed voting rights for African Americans.

See also: *Abolition of Slavery: United States*

BIBLIOGRAPHY

Books

Frederickson, George M. *The Inner Civil War*. New York: Harper and Row, 1965.

Morison, Samuel Eliot. *The Oxford History of the American People*. New York: Oxford University Press, 1965.

Stavis, Barrie. *John Brown: The Sword and the Word*. New York: A.S. Barnes and Co., 1970.

Stewart, James Brewer. *Holy Warriors: The Abolitionists and American Slavery*. New York: Hill and Wang, 1986.

Other

"West Virginia History: Articles on John Brown." West Virginia Archives and History [cited 21 September 2002]. <www.wvculture.org/history/jbrown.html>.

—Michael J. O'Neal

Hatch Act

United States 1939

Synopsis

The 1939 Hatch Act places certain restrictions on executive and federal employees in regard to their participation in political activities. Certain employees of local and state government also fall under the restrictions that are codified by this law. In addition, the act prohibits federal agencies and specific types of employees from engaging in political activities of a partisan nature. Although this act became an official law after its introduction in 1939, the law is based on an executive order that had been set down by President Thomas Jefferson in 1801. The nonpartisanship principles of this act were developed not only to protect the government from its employees, but also to protect its employees from government, particularly those in government who hold positions of authority. Since its inception, the Hatch Act has been upheld in the Supreme Court, and attempts to amend it have been vetoed twice. In 1993 President Bill Clinton signed the Hatch Act Reform Amendments, loosening the law with regard to most federal and District of Columbia employees engaging in political management or campaigns. However, restrictions remain under Public Law 103–94, and the protections offered under the Hatch Act remain fully in effect.

Timeline

1919: With the formation of the Third International (Comintern), the Bolshevik government of Russia establishes its control over communist movements worldwide.

1924: In the United States, secretary of the interior Albert B. Fall, along with oil company executives Harry Sinclair and Edward L. Doheny, is charged with conspiracy and bribery in making fraudulent leases of U.S. Navy oil reserves at Teapot Dome, Wyoming. The resulting Teapot Dome scandal clouds the administration of President Warren G. Harding.

1929: The Lateran Treaty between the Catholic Church and Mussolini's regime establishes the Vatican City as an independent political entity.

1935: Germany annexes the Saar region after a plebiscite. In defiance of Versailles, the Nazis reintroduce compulsory military service. The Allies do nothing, and many Western intellectuals maintain that it is only proper for Germany to retake its own territory and begin building up its army again.

1940: Hitler's troops sweep through Western Europe, annexing Norway and Denmark in April, and in May the Low Countries and France. At the same time, Stalin—who in this year arranges the murder of Trotsky in Mexico—takes advantage of the situation to add the Baltic republics (Latvia, Lithuania, and Estonia) to the Soviet empire, where they will remain for more than half a century.

1940: Winston Churchill succeeds Neville Chamberlain as British prime minister in May. A month later, he tells

Carl A. Hatch. AP/Wide World Photos. Reproduced by permission.

Parliament, "We shall not flag or fail. We shall fight in France, we shall fight on the seas and oceans, we shall fight with growing confidence and growing strength in the air, we shall defend our island, whatever the cost may be. We shall fight on the beaches, we shall fight on the landing grounds, we shall fight in the fields and in the streets, we shall fight in the hills. We shall never surrender." In November, German bombers begin air strikes against Britain.

1940: NBC makes the first official network television broadcast.

1945: At the Yalta Conference in February, Roosevelt, Churchill, and Stalin make plans for Germany after its by now inevitable surrender.

1950: North Korean troops pour into South Korea, starting the Korean War. Initially the communists make impressive gains, but in September, the U.S. Marines land at Inchon and liberate Seoul. China responds by sending in its troops.

1955: African and Asian nations meet at the Bandung Conference in Indonesia, inaugurating the "non-aligned" movement of Third World countries.

Event and Its Context

Early History

Very early in the history of the United States government, politicians recognized the risks associated with government employees taking part in partisan activities. In 1801 President Thomas Jefferson delivered an executive order regarding the need for the nonpartisanship of federal employees as discussed by the Office of Personnel Management in its book, *The United States Civil Service Commission, Biography of an Ideal: A History of the Federal Civil Service.* Although Jefferson's order was not meant to curb voting rights of federal employees, he stated that "it is expected that [a federal employee] will not attempt to influence the votes of others nor take any part in the business of electioneering, that being inconsistent with the spirit of the Constitution and [the employee's] duties to it."

Jefferson's executive order was in no way meant to restrict the rights of government employees, but rather to protect them from coercion stemming from partisanship. In addition, he considered the government to be a public trust that needed protection from the abuse of government officials. Presidents following Jefferson continued this effort to protect the civil service from partisanship. One such protection was the development of the federal merit system in 1883 as part of the Civil Service Reform Act. This act restricted officers and employees of the United States government from soliciting or receiving political contributions from one another. President Theodore Roosevelt continued this trend in 1907. As discussed in Robert E. Moffit's article, "Gutting the Hatch Act," Roosevelt signed an executive order that "required federal employees to take no active part in political management or in political campaigns."

The fear of partisan coercion of federal employees was not unfounded. During the Great Depression (1929–1941), several cases of partisan abuse and intimidation came to light in the federal government, including the case of Kentucky government employees who found their jobs threatened by a senator who was seeking reelection. It became evident that additional laws to protect federal workers were required to prevent abuses of power.

The 1939 Hatch Act

In 1939 Senator Carl Hatch, a Democrat from New Mexico, spearheaded the effort to create laws intended to protect federal employees from partisan intimidation. Already an advocate for such issues as antiracketeering controls and a federal minimum wage law, Hatch also wished to protect the electoral process from abuse. Hatch authored and sponsored the "Act to Prevent Pernicious Political Activity," as it was originally named. Later renamed the Hatch Political Activities Act, or "Hatch Act," the proposed legislation restricted the partisan political activities of federal and District of Columbia government employees, as well as the employees of state and local agencies that were federally funded either fully or in part. The Hatch Act also extended restrictions that had been laid out by the Civil Service Reform Act of 1883 to include almost all employees of the executive branch of the federal government. Senator Hatch believed that the restrictions would serve to protect federal employees, maintain the public's trust in the electoral system's fairness, and provide an equitable work environment.

Later in 1939, the Democratic majorities of the House and Congress passed the Hatch Act, and President Franklin D. Roosevelt then signed it into statute as Public Law 252. From that time until 1978, the Civil Service Commission undertook the responsibility for enforcement of the Hatch Act. The act in no way prevented federal employees from exercising their right to vote. It did, however, provide the legislative teeth necessary to protect employees from any undue arm-twisting with regard to the political process. As stated by Moffit in his 1993 article, "Most federal employees understand this, and that is why most federal employees have little or no desire to become actively involved in partisan politics." In return for the restrictions placed upon them, federal employees were, and are, provided with a level of job security that is unmatched in the private sector. Indeed, the popular phrase, "I'm Hatched," about which the late historian Marjorie Fribourg often wrote, was coined by civil servants who were pleased to avoid the complications and pressure that could arise from taking a public political stand.

The Hatch Act Before 1993

One positive, although likely unforeseen, consequence of the Hatch Act was evident soon after it became law. During World War II the act protected the government and its employees from outside manipulation in a politically troubled and chaotic era. As Ellen Schrecker stated in her book *The Age of McCarthyism*, "The 1939 Hatch Act barred Communists, Nazis, and other totalitarians from government employment." By doing so, the public trust remained uninfluenced by radical elements.

However, since its inception in 1939, the Hatch Act has occasionally come under attack. For example, the American Civil Liberties Union (ACLU) claimed that the Hatch Act is unconstitutional because it restricts the political rights of federal employees. Despite this, the Supreme Court upheld the constitutionality of the act in 1947 and 1973. In addition, both President Gerald Ford and President George Bush vetoed amendment bills in 1976 and 1990, respectively. The only significant change to the Hatch Act before 1993 came with the Civil Service Reform Act of 1978. This act transferred the authority of the Civil Service Commission to the Merit Systems Protection Board (MSPB). Since that time, all investigative and prosecutorial functions have been handled by the MSPB's Office of Special Counsel (OSC).

As the U.S. government changed and grew from 1939 onward, new possibilities for Hatch Act infringement arose. The sheer size of the federal government by the 1990s inspired several officials to debate whether it was time to make some changes to the Hatch Act. The addition of new federal, state, and local agencies meant that there were further opportunities for partisan pressure to arise. In 1993 the debates came to a head, and the Hatch Act underwent the amendment process.

The 1993 Hatch Act Amendments

Senator John Glenn sponsored the Hatch Act Amendments of 1993, which would allow federal employees to become more involved in partisan political activities. This took place on the heels of a similar bill, the Federal Employees Political Activities Act, which had already passed the House. Later, President Bill Clinton signed the Hatch Act Amendments of 1993 into Public Law (P.L. 103–94), thereby loosening, for some, the restrictions laid out by the Hatch Act. The amendments did not, however, dismiss the Hatch Act restrictions that would protect the federal employees and the public trust.

Under the Hatch Act (as per the amendments), most federal, state, and local government employees are prohibited from using their authority to influence, either positively or negatively, the election process; fundraising for or receiving political contributions; pursuing public office candidacy in partisan elections; and engaging in partisan campaigning or management activities.

Employees found guilty of these or other Hatch Act violations can be either suspended (30-day minimum) or removed from office depending on the severity of the violation. The OSC has been diligent in upholding the law and does not take infractions of the Hatch Act lightly. On 16 December 2000 Michael

M. Hash, acting administrator of the Health Care Financing Administration, resigned as part of a settlement with the OSC after he hosted a political fundraiser at his home in violation of the federal law (albeit unknowingly at the time). On 12 July 2002 the OSC sought disciplinary action against Alan White, director of investigative operations at the Pentagon's Defense Investigative Services, for three Hatch Act violations during his Republican candidacy for the Fairfax County, Virginia, school board.

Conclusion

The Hatch Act continues to protect federal employees and the public trust from partisan manipulation and intimidation. Throughout its history, the law has been maintained and enforced with little change to its original precepts.

Key Players

Clinton, William J. (1946–): Clinton is the U.S. president (1993–2001) who signed the Hatch Act Reform Amendments, or P.L. 103–94, on 6 October 1993. The amendments allow certain federal employees to participate in political management or campaigns.

Glenn, John H. (1921–): Glenn is the Democratic senator from Ohio who sponsored the Hatch Act Amendments of 1993 to loosen the law with regard to federal employees.

Hatch, Carl A. (1889–1963): Hatch was the Democratic senator from New Mexico who introduced the "Act to Prevent Pernicious Political Activity" to protect civil servants from partisan pressures. The act would later become the 1939 Hatch Act.

Jefferson, Thomas (1743–1826): Jefferson was the U.S. president (1801–1809) who issued an executive order in 1801 to stop the partisan activities of government employees. This executive order later became the foundation of the Hatch Act in 1939.

Roosevelt, Franklin D. (1882–1945): Roosevelt was the U.S. president (1933–1945) who signed the Hatch Act into statute after Congress passed it in 1939.

BIBLIOGRAPHY

Books

Office of Personnel Management. *The United States Civil Service Commission, Biography of an Ideal: A History of the Federal Civil Service*. Washington, DC: The Office of Personnel Management, 1977.

Schrecker, Ellen. *The Age of McCarthyism: A Brief History with Documents*. Boston: St. Martin's Press, 1994.

Periodicals

Ballard, Tanya N. "Caught in the Hatch [Legal Briefs]." *Government Executive Magazine* (12 July 2002).

Moffit, Robert E. "Gutting the Hatch Act: Congress's Plan to Re-politicize the Civil Service." *The Heritage Foundation Issues Bulletin* 180 (6 July 1993).

———. "Personnel Is Policy: Why the New President Must Take Control of the Executive Branch." *The Heritage Foundation Backgrounder* 1403 (8 January 2001).

Other

Schwemle, Barbara L. *Hatch Act Amendments: Political Activity and the Civil Service*. Doc. #87153. 1996 [accessed 12 December 2002]. <http://fas.org/irp/crs/87-153.htm>.

United States Office of Special Council. Political Activity (Hatch Act). 2002 [accessed 12 December 2002]. <http://www.osc.gov/hatchact.htm>.

U.S. Public Law 103–94, 103rd Cong., 1st sess., 6 October 1993. *Hatch Act Reform Amendments of 1993*.

U.S. Public Law 252, 76th Cong., 1st sess., 2 August 1939. *Hatch Political Activities Act*.

ADDITIONAL RESOURCES

Books

Bolton, John R. *The Hatch Act: A Civil Libertarian Defense*. Washington, DC: American Enterprise Institute for Public Policy Research, 1976.

Periodicals

Vaughn, Robert G. "Restrictions on the Political Activities of Public Employees: The Hatch Act and Beyond." *George Washington Law Review* 44 (1976): 516–553.

—Lee Ann Paradise

Hawaii Collective Bargaining Law

United States 1970

Synopsis

Unionization of the public employees of Hawaii reached its peak in the early 1970s with the passage of the state's collective bargaining law for public employees. In 1970, when the Hawaii state legislature enacted the Hawaii Public Employment Relations Act, the state of Hawaii became the first of the United States to allow its public employees the right to strike. At that time, the state and county public employees were among the lowest paid and least stable workers; their employment and wages were generally at the mercy of politics. Eventually, however, they were granted the right to bargain collectively for contracts and to file grievances as do private sector workers.

Timeline

1950: North Korean troops pour into South Korea, starting the Korean War.

1955: The Warsaw Pact is signed by the Soviet Union and its satellites in eastern Europe.

1959: Alaska and Hawaii are added to the Union.

1965: Rev. Martin Luther King, Jr., and more than 2,600 others are arrested in Selma, Alabama. Three weeks later, in New York City, Malcolm X is assassinated.

1967: Arabs attack Israel, launching the Six-Day War, which results in an Israeli victory.

1970: After 32 months of civil war in Nigeria, Biafran secessionists surrender in January.

1970: Nixon sends U.S. troops into Cambodia on 30 April. Four days later, National Guardsmen open fire on antiwar protesters at Kent State University in Ohio. By 24 June antiwar sentiment is so strong that the Senate repeals the Gulf of Tonkin resolution. On 29 June, Nixon orders troops back out of Cambodia.

1970: Gamal Abdel Nasser, father of Arab nationalism and mentor of younger leaders such as Libya's Muammar al-Qaddafi, dies.

1973: Signing of peace accords in Paris in January ends the Vietnam War.

1975: Pol Pot's Khmer Rouge launch a campaign of genocide in Cambodia.

1980: In protest of the Soviet invasion of Afghanistan, President Carter keeps U.S. athletes out of the Moscow Olympics.

1985: A new era begins in the USSR as Konstantin Chernenko dies, and is replaced by Mikhail Gorbachev, who at 54 years old is the youngest Soviet leader in decades.

Event and Its Context

Before Union Organization

In 1935 President Franklin D. Roosevelt, as part of his New Deal legislation, signed the National Labor Relations Act (NLRA, commonly called the Wagner Act), which gave workers the legal right to organize unions. The NLRA, revised principally in 1947 and 1959, covers only the private employee sector and explicitly excludes the public employee sector. Although public employees are generally covered under separate legislation at federal, state, and local levels, the NLRA eventually had a major influence on most public sector labor legislation, including that in the state of Hawaii.

During the depression years of the 1930s, times were difficult for Hawaii's public workers. Republicans with a probusiness bias dominated the territorial legislature, and public workers worked six days a week with diminishing wages and benefits. In 1932 and again in 1933, the legislature cut salaries of the public employees by 10 percent. Soon thereafter, the government eliminated 229 public jobs, about 10 percent of the entire public workforce.

Hawaii Government Employees Association

As a result of this action, two Board of Water Supply (BWS) workers, Daniel Ainoa and Edward Morgan, decided to organize the BWS employees. When Frederick Ohrt, the general manager of the BWS, heard of the plan, he liked the idea because he hoped that the union would strengthen his department. Ohrt even suggested (to the surprise of Ainoa and Morgan) that they expand the idea to include all government workers and contacted other department heads about bringing their employ-

ees into the union. The managers of departments including Fire, Planning, Territorial Tax Office, and the Parks Board sent representatives to an organizational meeting at the Library of Hawaii in 1934. The representatives appointed Charles Welsh as the constitutional chairman. Welsh then appointed a committee to draft the new organization's constitution. The representatives met again in the first half of 1935 and adopted the constitution along with the union's new name, the Hawaiian Government Employees Association (HGEA), and formally established the union on 11 September 1936.

In the decade after its founding, the HGEA lobbied for such legislation as the Civil Service Act and the Hawaiian Standard Classification law. In addition, the Hawaii Employee Relations Act, the Hawaiian version of the Wagner Act (informally called the "Little Wagner Act"), became law in 1945, but only gave workers in the private sector the right to organize and to bargain collectively. Hawaii enacted this legislation because the federal Wagner Act only applied to the states of the Union, and not to territories such as Alaska and Hawaii.

Thinking that the new HGEA lacked strength and unity in the early 1950s, the Republican-dominated legislature continued to reduce public employee benefits, specifically reducing vacation and sick leave, lowering salary rates, and freezing wages. The public employees, allied with a determined HGEA, launched a voter registration drive and threw their support behind the reform-minded Democratic Party. More than 9,200 members of the HGEA switched to the prolabor Democratic Party. This action helped the Democrats take control of both houses of the territorial legislature. In fact, the *Hawaii Times* newspaper reported on 4 November 1954 that the HGEA was a deciding factor in the outcome of the landslide Democratic victory.

Democrats made good on their election promises in the 1955 legislature by restoring the holiday and sick leave benefits that had been abolished in 1953. They unfroze public worker salaries and in 1957 gave public employees the right to take coffee breaks. Still, the public employees had no collective bargaining and had to visit the state capitol on a regular basis to request improvements in working conditions and increased wages.

Hawaii became a state in 1959. By the 1960s the labor-management system for the Hawaii public employees was similar to that in the other 49 states in that it was slowly evolving fragments of different laws. The slowness in applying collective bargaining to the public sector was due to the following principle reasons:

- Unions had difficulty organizing because the government was considered sovereign (supreme), and its public employees generally could not take action against their employer without the employer's consent.

- Elected government officials legally could not delegate their responsibilities to others, and because government employees were responsible only to the voters (according to the U.S. democratic system), the idea of being responsible to a trade union was not supported.

- Adoption of collective bargaining principles that had been developed by the private sector was often difficult and reflected the complexities of the political system.

- Government-wide classifications and working conditions that were mandated by legislation and applied to public employees contributed to difficulties in collective bargaining.

- Problems involving the lack of a right to strike for public employees were an obstacle to the growth of unions and collective bargaining.

By the late 1960s there was a growing recognition (and eventual acceptance) in some state governments that strikes would happen in the public sector whether they were legal or not. Leaders of some state governments agreed that it was best to regulate the process rather than to try to stop it. The greatest resistance in labor laws for the public sector related to the question of whether public employees should have the right to strike. Limitations were imposed in large part because of the public safety concerns related to essential public employees such as firefighters and police. The argument in favor of the right to strike for public sector employees was that the collective bargaining process was impossible without the possibility of strikes: without cause for concern about a shutdown, employers have no incentive to compromise and negotiate in good faith.

Hawaii Public Employment Relations Act

The HGEA lobbied for greater worker benefits both before and after statehood was achieved in 1959. In 1961, under the leadership of Charles Kendall, the government created a state-subsidized medical insurance program and an "Equal Pay for Equal Work" law (designed to make pay scales uniform throughout the state).

The HGEA emphasized the idea of collective bargaining in the late 1960s, after first lobbying the legislature in 1949 to allow public employees to choose an organization as their sole bargaining agent. At the historic 1970 legislative session, lawmakers submitted 15 bills on public sector collective bargaining. At that session the legislature, after amending Article XII of the state constitution, passed the Hawaii Public Employment Relations Act, which established the right of public employees to organize for bargaining collectively. It required public employers to negotiate and enter into written agreements with exclusive bargaining representatives on matters of wages, hours, and other conditions of work.

The Hawaii Public Employment Relations Act of 1970 made the rights of public employees in the state parallel to those of employees in the private sector. As of 2003, the right of Hawaii's public employees, along with its private employees, to collective bargaining was stated in Article XIII of the state constitution:

- Private Employees (Section 1): Persons in private employment shall have the right to organize for the purpose of collective bargaining.

- Public Employees (Section 2): Persons in public employment shall have the right to organize for the purpose of collective bargaining as provided by law.

At the beginning of the twenty-first century, only two states had statutes granting all public employees the limited right to strike. Hawaii was technically the first state to provide by state law the legal right for public employees to strike, though Pennsylvania enacted a similar statute in the same month just a few days after the Hawaii law was passed. The innovative laws of both Pennsylvania and Hawaii provide a mechanism for dispute resolution that could lawfully end in a strike. However, both states permit public workers to strike only after the parties have adhered strictly to the impasse provisions of the law.

The Hawaiian mechanism that eventually allows strikes by public employees is a complicated one. The Hawaii law, which applies to all public employees, provides a limited right to strike when all of the following conditions are met:

- There must be no danger to the public health or safety.
- The employees involved must be in a unit certified by the Public Employment Relations Board.
- The employee unit must not be one for which arbitration is required to resolve interest disputes.
- The parties must have exhausted good-faith mediation and fact-finding efforts to resolve the dispute.
- If an unfair labor practice exists, the parties must have exhausted all proceedings under the statutes.
- Sixty days must have elapsed since the fact-finding report was made public.
- The union must file a 10-day written notice of its intent to engage in a work stoppage.

The Hawaii Public Employment Relations Board is authorized to decide whether these prerequisites have been met and to set requirements to avoid or remove imminent or present dangers found in a situation that may lead to a work stoppage. After the Hawaii Public Employment Relations Act was passed, few strikes occurred because of the act's complicated requirements pertaining to work stoppages.

Conclusion

The 1970 Hawaiian law was benchmark legislation at the time. It remained controversial. After 1994 the Hawaii legislature replaced the right to strike (except for teachers, professors, and sanitation workers) with binding arbitration after about 20,000 clerical and white-collar professional employees of the state and its four counties (represented by the HGEA) conducted the first strike in that union's 60-year history. However, after a series of arbitration losses in the first few years of the 2000s, the state of Hawaii returned the right to strike and has removed binding arbitration (for all but police, firefighters, prison guards, and nurses).

Currently, the HGEA is affiliated with the American Federation of State, County, and Municipal Employees (AFSCME). The AFCSME represents more than 1.3 million public employees and health care workers throughout the United States. It is the largest affiliate of the American Federation of Labor-Congress of Industrial Organizations (AFL-CIO).

With the state of Hawaii leading the way for other states to follow, state and local legislation grew considerably with respect to collective bargaining. Forty of the 50 states have some type of legislation to protect the right of public employees both to organize and to bargain collectively. Twenty-six states have adopted a comprehensive collective bargaining-labor relations policy for all public employees. Ten other states have adopted collective bargaining policies that cover only certain public employees. Four more states have established an alternative "meet-and-confer" policy, which is a weaker form of collective bargaining. It places no obligation on the employer either to negotiate or to sign a contract. Finally, only 10 states (Arizona, Arkansas, Colorado, Louisiana, Mississippi, North Carolina, South Carolina, Utah, Virginia, and West Virginia) currently do not have any legislation whatsoever granting collective bargaining rights to their public employees. At the end of 1998, 6.9 million workers at all levels of government were unionized, comprising 37.5 percent of total government employment.

Key Players

Ainoa, Daniel: With Edward Morgan, Ainoa, an employee at the Hawaii Board of Water Supply (BWS), initiated the first organizational meeting for Hawaiian state public employees.

Kendall, Charles: Kendall was a leader of the Hawaiian Government Employees Association (HGEA) and helped to lobby the state congress for additional state employee benefits in the late 1950s and 1960s.

Morgan, Edward: With Ainoa, Morgan initiated the first public employee organizational meeting for Hawaiian state workers. Morgan was an employee of the Hawaii BWS.

Ohrt, Frederick: Ohrt was the manager of the BWS, a Hawaii state department. He helped Daniel Ainoa and Edward Morgan establish the Hawaiian Government Employees Association (HGEA).

Welsh, Charles: Welsh was appointed the constitutional chairman of the HGEA in 1934.

See also: *Wagner Act.*

BIBLIOGRAPHY

Books

Beechert, Edward D. *Working in Hawaii: A Labor History.* Honolulu: University of Hawaii Press, 1985.

Flynn, Ralph J. *Public Work, Public Workers.* Washington, DC: The New Republic Book Company, Inc., 1975.

Herman, E. Edward, Alfred Kuhn, and Ronald L. Seeber. *Collective Bargaining and Labor Relations*, 2nd ed. Englewood Cliffs, NJ: Prentice-Hall, 1987.

Weitzman, J. *The Scope of Bargaining in Public Employment.* New York: Praeger Publishers, 1975.

Other

Center for Labor Education and Research, University of Hawaii (CLEAR), University of Hawaii, West Oahu. "A Brief History of Labor in Hawai'i" [cited 6 December 2002]. <http://homepages.uhwo.hawaii.edu/~clear/Lhistory.html>.

———. "Hawai'i Public Employment Relations Act: HRS, Chapter 89, Collective Bargaining in Public Employment" [cited 6 December 2002]. <http://homepages.uhwo.hawaii.edu/~clear/HRS89.html>.

———. "HRS Chapter 377, Hawai'i Employment Relations Act [as of July 2000]." July 2000 [cited 6 December 2002]. <http://homepages.uhwo.hawaii.edu/~clear/HRS377.html>.

Gould, William B. "Industrial Relations in the Public Sector: U.S.A." Italian Labor Law Online [cited 6 December 2002]. <http://www.dirittodellavoro.it/miscellanea/atti/israele/0037-u~1.pdf>.

Hanham, Robert O. "Collective Bargaining and Public Employee Unionism in West Virginia" [cited 6 December 2002]. <http://www.polsci.wvu.edu/ipa/par/report_9_4.html>.

Hawaii Government Employee Association. "Two-Year Wage Freeze." *HGEA/AFSCME News and Announcements.* 10 January 2000 [cited 6 December 2002]. <http://www.hgea.org/news/special/wagefreeze.html>.

Smyser, A. A. "Public Worker Bargaining Veteran Gives Some Advice." Hawaii's World, *Honolulu Star-Bulletin*, 18 May 2000 [cited 6 December 2002]. <http://starbulletin.com/2000/05/18/editorial/smyser.html>.

State of Hawaii. "State Constitution: The Constitution of the State of Hawaii-As Amended and in Force January 1, 2000, Article XIII, Organization; Collective Bargaining" [cited 6 December 2002]. <http://www.state.hi.us/lrb/con/conart13.html>.

—William Arthur Atkins

Hawes-Cooper Act

United States 1929

Synopsis

In the early 1900s, most prisons were involved in selling on the open market products made by inmates. The money earned from these sales was most often used to finance the prison itself. However, manufacturers, employers, and labor leaders in the open market argued that they could not compete with the prisons, which had a free labor force that could not strike. State governments could outlaw the sale of convict-made goods from their own state, but they had no control over the sale of prison-made goods imported from other states. The passage of the Hawes-Cooper Convict Labor Act in 1929 allowed states to remove the interstate commerce nature of prison-made goods and to prohibit the sale of such goods in their state, even if the goods were produced in another state.

Timeline

1914: On the Western Front, the first battles of the Marne and Ypres establish a line that will more or less hold for the next four years.

1919: Treaty of Versailles is signed by the Allies and Germany, but rejected by the U.S. Senate. This is due in part to rancor between President Woodrow Wilson and Republican Senate leaders, and in part to concerns over Wilson's plan to commit the United States to the newly established League of Nations and other international duties. Not until 1921 will Congress formally end U.S. participation in the war, but it will never agree to join the League.

1924: In the United States, Secretary of the Interior Albert B. Fall, along with oil company executives Harry Sinclair and Edward L. Doheny, is charged with conspiracy and bribery in making fraudulent leases of U.S. Navy oil reserves at Teapot Dome, Wyoming. The resulting Teapot Dome scandal clouds the administration of President Warren G. Harding.

1927: Charles A. Lindbergh makes the first successful solo nonstop flight across the Atlantic and becomes an international hero.

1929: The Lateran Treaty between the Catholic Church and Mussolini's regime establishes the Vatican City as an independent political entity.

1929: On "Black Friday" in October, prices on the U.S. stock market, which had been climbing wildly for several years, suddenly collapse. Thus begins the first phase of a world economic crisis and depression that will last until the beginning of World War II.

1929: Edwin Hubble proposes a model of an ever-expanding universe.

1931: Financial crisis widens in the United States and Europe, which reel from bank failures and climbing unemployment levels. In London, armies of the unemployed riot.

1933: Newly inaugurated U.S. president Franklin D. Roosevelt launches the first phase of his New Deal to put depression-era America back to work.

1935: Second phase of New Deal begins with the introduction of social security, farm assistance, and housing and tax reform.

1941: Japanese bombing of Pearl Harbor on 7 December brings the United States into the war against the Axis. Combined with the attack on the Soviet Union, which makes Stalin an unlikely ally of the Western democracies, the events of 1941 will ultimately turn the tide of the war.

1944: Creation of International Monetary Fund and World Bank at Bretton Woods Conference.

Event and Its Context

Passed on 19 January 1929, with an effective date of 1934, the Hawes-Cooper Act stated that all goods produced wholly or in part by convict labor "transported into any State or Territory of the United States and remaining therein for use, consumption, sale, or storage, shall upon arrival and delivery in such State or Territory be subject to the operation and effect of the laws of such State or Territory," thus allowing individual states to prohibit the sale of goods made by convicts on the open market whether those goods had been made within or outside of

their state. The Hawes-Cooper Act was the product of cooperation between organized labor and business, and stemmed from the competition between the prisons and the free market.

Prisons used five different systems of labor: the lease system, contract system, piece-price system, public account system, and state use or state account system. In the lease system, prisoners were literally leased to another party who paid the prison for the use of the prisoners. A number of prisons supported themselves using the contract system, which took the revenue made by selling convict-manufactured goods to pay the prison's operating costs. The piece-price system was similar to the contract system, except the contractors provided the raw materials while the prisons provided the labor. The public account system was like the piece-price system, except the state provided the raw materials. Finally, in the state use or state account system, the goods produced were only sold to the manufacturing institution of other state institutions.

With each of these labor systems, the production and sale of convict-produced goods proved a serious competitor in the open market. Prison-made goods were cheaper to produce and sold for less. Prisons were in a unique position to cheaply and efficiently produce such items as brooms, brushes, shoes, iron moldings, and cigars. Besides the free labor, prisons also had low overhead. For instance, taxes paid for lighting, heating, and water whether the prisoners were working or sleeping. Free-market employers felt they had few options for competing with prison labor. Their choices included lowering the quality of work or abandoning the area of competition.

State governments could control the products made in their home state, but they had a harder time controlling the items brought in from other states. Before the passage of the Hawes-Cooper Act, individual states could not prevent the sale of convict-made goods from other states. Hawes-Cooper made convict-produced goods subject to the laws of the state in which the items were sold. Thus, if an individual state outlawed the sale of prison goods in their state, then the sale of prison-produced goods imported from neighboring states also would be prohibited. This feature made the Hawes-Cooper Act an enabling act: it let individual states decide whether to permit the sale of prison goods on the open market.

In 1932, two years before the Hawes-Cooper Act went into effect, a Department of Labor study found that of 158,947 convicts in 104 prisons, 82,276 (or 52 percent) were involved in some sort of manufacturing. The majority of the 104 prisons (42 percent) used the state-use labor system. About 38 percent of the goods, worth more than $28 million, were destined for the open market: 40 percent of these products were sold in the state where the goods were manufactured, while the remaining 60 percent were sent to markets out of the state where the goods were made.

Most of the convicts involved in making goods received no wages; for inmates who were paid, the wage was approximately 2 to 15 cents per day. The Department of Labor study also produced a list of the industries most affected by prison labor; the top prison industries included making shirts, pants, binding twine, chairs, and farm, garden, and dairy items. In the open market, businesses suffered not only because of the volume of items prisons produced but also because their specialization in making a particular item could threaten a regular business.

Most prison officials opposed the Hawes-Cooper Act. One of the most cited arguments against Hawes-Cooper was that its passage would leave prisoners idle. The American Prison Association stated that idleness destroyed the inmates' physical, mental, moral, and spiritual well-being. Others pointed out that some prisons used the proceeds from their manufacturing to support themselves, thus lessening the tax burden on citizens.

The enforcement of the Hawes-Cooper Act caused a financial crisis in a number of prisons. The cost of supervising and disciplining idle prisoners proved more expensive and many prisons lost a valuable source of income for the prisons' upkeep and staffing. In 1935 President Franklin D. Roosevelt created the Prison Industries Reorganizing Administration to foster state cooperation through a national program to give inmates meaningful work.

The constitutionality of the Hawes-Cooper Act was challenged in *Whitfield v. Ohio* (1936), but the U.S. Supreme Court upheld Hawes-Cooper by stating that free labor could not compete "with enforced and unpaid or underpaid convict labor." Other legislative acts followed Hawes-Cooper, including the Ashurst-Sumners Act (1935), Walsh-Healey Act (1936), Sumners-Ashurst Act (1940), and Comprehensive Crime Control Act (1984), which encouraged prison manufacturing to help control the cost of incarceration.

Key Players

Cooper, John Gordon (1872–1955): Cooper immigrated to the United States from England in 1880 and settled in Youngstown, Ohio. He attended public schools and worked in steel mills and for the Pennsylvania Railroad Company. A Republican, Cooper served as a member of the Ohio State House of Representatives from 1910 until 1912. In 1915 he was elected to Congress, where he served until 1937.

Hawes, Harry Bartow (1869–1947): Hawes was born in Kentucky and attended Washington University School of Law in St. Louis, Missouri. He represented Hawaii during its annexation and served as the president of the St. Louis police board from 1898 until 1904. Hawes also served as a state representative for Missouri (1916–1917). During World War I he served with the Military Intelligence Department of the General Staff and later was assigned to the U.S. embassy in Madrid. A Democrat, in 1921 he was elected to Congress and served until 1926, when he resigned to take a Senate seat. He served in the Senate until his retirement in 1933.

BIBLIOGRAPHY

Books

Commons, John R., and John B. Andrews. *Principles of Labor Legislation.* New York: Augustus M. Kelley, 1967.

Convict Labor: Model Amendments to Solve Prison Labor Competition. Washington, DC: American Federation of Labor, 1930.

Hallett, Michael A. "Hawes-Cooper Act." In *Encyclopedia of American Prisons,* edited by Marilyn D. McShane and Frank P. Williams III. New York: Garland Publishing, 1996.

—Lisa A. Ennis

Haymarket Riot

United States 1886

Synopsis

The Haymarket Riot, which is also often referred to as the *Haymarket Massacre* or the *Haymarket Incident,* was a radical labor protest meeting on 4 May 1886 in Chicago, Illinois, that turned deadly. Although the assembly began peacefully, an unknown person threw a dynamite bomb when the police began to raid the meeting. While the identity of the bomb thrower has never been determined, hysteria over the event, which had been organized by anarchists, was sufficient to secure the conviction of eight people for murder and conspiracy, despite little or no evidence to prove the charges brought against them. Four men were eventually hanged for a crime they did not commit.

Timeline

1866: The Winchester repeating rifle is introduced.

1871: Chicago fire causes 250 deaths and $196 million in damage.

1876: General George Armstrong Custer and 264 soldiers are killed by the Sioux at the Little Big Horn River.

1878: Thomas Edison develops a means of cheaply producing and transmitting electric current, which he succeeds in subdividing so as to make it adaptable to household use. The value of shares in gas companies plummets as news of his breakthrough reaches Wall Street.

1882: Agitation against English rule spreads throughout Ireland, culminating with the assassination of chief secretary for Ireland Lord Frederick Cavendish and permanent undersecretary Thomas Burke in Dublin's Phoenix Park. The leader of the nationalist movement is Charles Stewart Parnell, but the use of assassination and terrorism—which Parnell himself has disavowed—makes clear the fact that he does not control all nationalist groups.

1884: Chicago's Home Life Insurance Building, designed by William LeBaron Jenney, becomes the world's first skyscraper.

1886: The Statue of Liberty is dedicated.

1886: Apache chief Geronimo surrenders to U.S. forces.

Haymarket Riot, 1886. The Library of Congress.

1888: The Blizzard of 1888 in the United States kills hundreds and causes more than $25 million in property damage.

1892: Bitter strikes in Australia lead to the closing of ports and mines.

1896: U.S. Supreme Court issues its *Plessy v. Ferguson* decision, which establishes the "separate but equal" doctrine that will be used to justify segregation in the southern United States for the next half-century.

Event and Its Context

Origins of the Haymarket Riot

The Haymarket Riot grew out of a long string of circumstances that eventually culminated in an unfortunate incident. At issue were several key points: the continued growth of the Industrial Revolution and its impact on society, the movement for the eight-hour workday, worker dissatisfaction, suppression of labor activities by various government authorities, and the growth of radicalism in the United States. Each of these topics played an important role in labor unrest as the climate in the country between workers and the state reached fever pitch. Re-

Tom Mooney

It was a sequence of events that mirrored the Haymarket incident thirty years earlier: an explosion in the middle of a large crowd in a major American urban center, followed by the arrest of radicals on questionable charges. This time, the city was San Francisco, and the date was 22 July 1916, where at 2:06 P.M. a bomb exploded on Market Street. Ten people died in the blast, which critically injured 40 others. Within hours, authorities had arrested labor leader Tom Mooney, his wife Rena, another radical named Warren K. Billings, and two others. The other three would be cleared, but Mooney and Billings would spend years in prison—all on the flimsiest of evidence.

Though the United States had not yet entered the war in Europe, signs of the coming U.S. involvement were clear. Hence the purpose of the parade, in which more than 50,000 people marched: to drum up support for the war effort. Though many conservative workers supported the war, radicals in the United States, like their counterparts in Europe, opposed it. In their view, the war was simply an instrument of capitalist interests, who were only too willing to send the working men of the world to die in battle against their brothers from other lands. In the week prior to the parade, a pamphlet ostensibly put out by a radical group circulated in San Francisco. "We are going to use a little direct action on the 22nd," it promised, "to show that militarism can't be forced on us and our children without a violent protest."

After the explosion, caused by a bomb concealed in a suitcase, the people of San Francisco were eager for vengeance, and District Attorney Charles Fickert aimed to give it to them. Politically aligned with United Railroads, which had provided him with a secret fund of $100,000—a staggering sum in those days—Fickert hired private investigator Martin Swanson. The latter had long been tracking Mooney and Billings, as well as anarchists Emma Goldman and Alexander Berkman. Later it would be revealed that Swanson, acting on behalf of the city, coached witnesses to present false testimony.

Despite revelations of corruption in the prosecution's case, the court convicted Mooney and Billings of first-degree murder and sentenced them to death. California's governor commuted these to life sentences in 1917, and 22 years later, in January 1939, Mooney received a full pardon. Billings was released in 1942, having served more than 25 years.

Source: Curt Gentry. *Frame-Up: The Incredible Case of Tom Mooney and Warren Billings.* New York: Norton, 1967.

—Judson Knight

gardless of who might have been at fault in a labor struggle, each moment of violent upheaval had serious consequences.

During the post-Civil War era, there were periods of labor upheaval both in Chicago and across the nation. Such incidents revolved around many issues, including, among others, job security, wages, occupational safety, and, especially, the eight-hour day. It was this last issue that was particularly important as the Industrial Revolution truly swept over America. Not only were skilled craftsmen seeing their professions disappear in the face of machines operated by unskilled labor, but the length of hours in the workday lengthened and could range from ten to twelve and even longer in some specific instances.

The movement for the eight-hour day, led by Ira Steward, was organized and launched in Baltimore, Maryland, in 1866. Stewart argued that paying laborers poor wages and forcing them to work inordinately long hours hurt both the workers and the economy. Proponents of the eight-hour day theorized that by limiting the number of daily work hours and paying a decent wage, people would have time on their hands and money in their pockets, thus providing them with the opportunity to spend discretionary funds and help expand the economy. However, the idea of the eight-hour day did not immediately resonate with the populace. States such as Illinois enacted an eight-hour day for specific occupations, but the lack of enforcement made the law weak to the point of uselessness. Loopholes in the law also allowed for easy evasion of compliance; since eight hours was considered to be the legal work day, an employer could bargain with his employees to work longer periods of time.

Chicago experienced several labor upheavals in the post-Civil War era, some of which had as their basis the question of the eight-hour day. There was an eight-hour movement and strike in 1867, another massive strike in 1873, and, of course, the Haymarket Riot in 1886. It was the concept of the eight-hour day that inspired the leaders of the Chicago labor movement to become more involved in politics. Andrew C. Cameron, a member of the Chicago Trades Assembly, helped create Eight-Hour Leagues in Chicago. In 1866 this movement actually had the support of prominent Illinois politicians, including then-governor Richard J. Oglesby, Attorney General Robert Ingersoll, and many of Chicago's aldermen. But the lack of enforcement and loopholes in the Illinois law prompted the labor movement to action. On 1 May 1867 workers went out on strike, began marching, and subsequently began rioting. While the movement then died down for a while, the action on the part of the workers prompted the city of Chicago to create an eight-hour day for city workers.

Another issue that presaged the Haymarket Riot was the growth of radicalism. Such extreme groups included socialists, communists, anarchists, and anarcho-communists, all of which had divisive internal factions as well. To many Americans these ideas, some of them based on the writings and influence of Karl Marx, were appalling and anti-American, regardless of whether or not the platform urged peaceful change in the social and economic fabric of society. Furthermore, the foreign-born bore the brunt of the blame for the introduction of these beliefs to the United States, for many Americans were convinced that no true, native-born U.S. citizen would subscribe to revolutionary ideals of any sort. Many of the foreign-born radicals worked with labor movement leaders to promote a prolabor agenda, a move that often caused these more moderate, mainstream individuals to be branded as "radical" themselves.

Police Actions at the McCormick Reaper Works

Such was the sociopolitical environment in which the Haymarket Riot occurred. On 1 May 1886 the drive for the eight-hour day gained momentum when more than 40,000 workers went on strike, with the main issue being ten hours pay for eight hours of work. Many Chicago workers, such as furniture workers and clothing cutters, had in fact won such concessions from their employers. But the eight-hour day was anything but universal, and this strike was another attempt to win the valued concession.

The strike continued for a few more days, including demonstrations at the McCormick Reaper Works, where relations between management and labor were already extremely tense. The company's management was attempting to use strikebreakers, and when the striking workers attacked these "scabs," police fired into the crowd, killing several strikers. Captain John Bonfield, a man universally despised within the labor movement, led the attacking police. The outrage over the shootings prompted many of the strikers to call for action, including the taking up of arms.

The Meeting in Haymarket Square

While many members of the labor movement were calling for immediate direct action, a group of anarchists suggested holding protest meetings. August Spies, who witnessed the scene at the McCormick plant, called for just such a meeting at Haymarket Square, which was immediately west of the Chicago loop, to take place the next day, 4 May. One of the meeting's most important purposes was to protest against Bonfield and police brutality. Other anarchists—such as Albert Parsons, Michael Schwab, and Samuel Fielden—showed up to make speeches. Also in attendance was the highly popular and charismatic Chicago mayor, Carter Harrison. Harrison was well-known for his strong support of labor, especially for his championing of the eight-hour day.

However, tensions surrounding the meeting were running high. Many people feared another violent confrontation. Harrison himself had nearly 200 riot-trained police, again led by Bonfield, on standby. The meeting itself, however, did not appear to pose any threat to civilized society. To begin with, only about 1,200 people showed up, and most of them left when it began to rain. Harrison was satisfied with the peaceful tone of the meeting, which merely consisted of speeches. At 10:30 A.M. Harrison left the meeting, but before departing he warned the police to stay clear, since there obviously was no danger being posed to either citizens or property.

The Riot

As soon as Bonfield learned that Harrison had left, he and the police moved in to break up the remainder of the meeting. At this point someone threw a dynamite bomb into the front of the police charge, the first time in which dynamite was used in such a way. The explosion killed one person, Mathias Degan. The other police began to open fire on the meeting, starting a full-scale riot that resulted in several more deaths. Seven police in all were killed, and between 60 and 70 were wounded.

The hysteria that followed the riot hit huge proportions as all types of radical were arrested, many without actually being charged. The labor movement was branded as lawless and violent, and many people called for swift justice, especially against foreign-born radicals. Harrison was forced to take drastic measures as he put a restraint on gatherings and crowds, fearing another outbreak of violence. Eight people in all were arrested and charged with the murder of Degan: Spies, Parsons, Schwab, Fielden, Louis Lingg, George Engel, Adolph Fischer, and Oscar Neebe. The last four people on this list were not even present at the time of the incident, and those who were there were on the stage, in plain view of the entire crowd. The identity of the bomb thrower was never determined.

Trial of the Haymarket Defendants

The trial began in an atmosphere of hysteria on 15 June 1886. Presiding over the trial was Judge Joseph E. Gary. Gary had a reputation as an impartial judge, but his behavior during the trial proved otherwise. The prosecutor was the state's attorney for Cook County, Illinois, Julius S. Grinnell, who helped fuel the hysteria by allowing the police unusual liberties in the seizure and collection of evidence.

The eight defendants stood accused of conspiracy and murder even though several of them were not even present at the time of the incident. The fact that their political views were radical and that they were part of the labor movement made them suspect. Nevertheless, the problem facing the prosecution was proving not only that one of the accused threw the bomb, but also that the group provoked the incident through their speeches and words. In Gary's eyes, however, the prosecution had no need to prove these connections.

The jury deliberations took a mere three hours, and the verdicts were not a surprise. Seven of the defendants were condemned to death by hanging, with only Oscar Neebe receiving a prison sentence of 15 years. Lucy Parsons, the wife of Albert, began working immediately to have their convictions overturned. Cries for clemency rose across the country, as people became aware of the circumstances of the convictions and were outraged at what they called a miscarriage of justice.

Outcomes of the Sentencing

Both the Illinois Supreme Court and the U.S. Supreme Court rejected appeals. Many people looked to Governor Oglesby for clemency. Even Judge Gary asked the governor to commute the sentences of Fielden and Schwab, since they asked for mercy, a request that Oglesby honored by commuting their sentences to life in prison. As for the remaining defendants, however, since they had not requested mercy, Oglesby by law could not commute their sentences. Lingg escaped execution by committing suicide in his jail cell. A friend of his smuggled a dynamite cap into the jail, and in a moment of dark irony, Lingg placed the cap in his mouth and set it off.

Various officials involved with the trial and upcoming execution received threats against their persons. Further anonymous threats of murder and bombings were made, but none were carried out. The execution of Parsons, Spies, Engel, and Fischer took place on 11 November 1887. Lucy Parsons and her two children attempted to visit Albert prior to his execution. They were not only not allowed to visit Albert, but they were also strip-searched and placed in separate jail cells. Prior to the execution each condemned man made brief, proanarchist statements such as "Hurray for Anarchy!" News reports of the time noted that upon springing the trap door under the gallows, the fall did not break the necks of the accused; it took nearly eight minutes for the last of the men to strangle to death.

In what was the largest funeral in Chicago history up to that time, the men were buried at Waldheim Cemetery (now Forest Home Cemetery in Forest Park, Illinois, just outside the city limits). The issue of the Haymarket Riot and subsequent trial and execution divided not just the city but the nation. In June 1893 Governor John Peter Altgeld pardoned the remaining three defendants in what was considered a very controversial move, especially since Altgeld openly called the trial unfair. As for Carter Harrison, the Haymarket Riot ruined his political career. He was later assassinated, though the assassin was a disgruntled job seeker, not a radical from within the labor movement.

Laws Resulting from the Haymarket Riot

Two laws were enacted in 1887 in the wake of the Haymarket Riot, the Cole Anti-Boycott law and the Merritt Conspiracy law. The Cole law prevented people from conspiring to issue a blacklist or to boycott. The Merritt law, however, was far more controversial. Since part of the problem at the trial was demonstrating that the defendants instigated the violence, this law made any group as a whole or group of individuals responsible for the actions of any of the other group members, regardless of any knowledge of their activities. The only proof required was the appearance of cooperation and complicity. While the Cole law lasted into the twentieth century, modified by amendments and court decisions, the Merritt law was repealed in 1891.

Aftermath of the Riot

The labor movement, especially its radical connections, suffered as a result of the Haymarket Riot. Several years later, in 1894, Chicago experienced another labor upheaval with the Pullman Strike. As for the memory of the "Haymarket Martyrs," on 3 May 1998 their gravesite was made a National Historic Landmark. The anarchist groups present considered this move an outrage, since the condemned men were executed by the state for their beliefs rather than for any actual crime. Regardless, because of the work of the Illinois Labor History Society, the gravesite has a place of honor.

Key Players

Altgeld, John Peter (1847–1902): Born in Germany, Altgeld joined the Democratic Party in the United States. His support of issues having to do with social justice and equality caused him to be branded a radical in many quarters. He rose to prominence within the Democratic Party, but he lost a great deal of his power and respect when he pardoned the remaining Haymarket defendants. His tract outlining his reasons for the pardon was in print as of 2003.

Engel, George (1836–1887): A German-born socialist, like Schwab, Engel was orphaned at a young age. He settled in Chicago in 1874 and soon created his newspaper, *Der An-*

archist. He and his wife eventually ran a toy shop. He was not present at Haymarket Square when the bomb exploded, yet he was convicted for the action.

Fielden, Samuel (1846–?): A British-born socialist, Fielden championed the cause of labor. He arrived in Chicago in 1871, eventually joining the American Group of the International Working People's Association.

Fischer, Adolph (1858–1887): A German-born socialist, Fischer worked several jobs in various locations before moving to Chicago in 1883, where he worked for the *Arbeiter-Zeitung,* a German-language newspaper. A believer in direct action, he wanted to encourage people to show up to the Haymarket meeting with arms, a call that Spies eliminated from printed materials. Fischer truly believed he was dying for his cause when he was executed for taking part in the Haymarket Riot.

Lingg, Louis (1870–1887): Youngest of the eight accused, Lingg was born in Germany and came to the United States in 1885. An outspoken advocate of anarchist violence, he was a bomb maker who took his own life before the state could execute him.

Neebe, Oscar (1850–1915): Neebe was born in New York City and educated in Germany. Although he lived in several locations, he settled in Chicago, where he joined the socialist movement. He was not present at Haymarket, nor was he aware that such a meeting was planned. He was accused because at the time of the incident he was on the board of directors of the Socialist Publishing Company, which published the radical publication *Arbeiter-Zeitung.*

Parsons, Albert Richard (1848–1887): Parsons was one of the Haymarket protest meeting organizers and speakers. Born in Alabama and raised in Texas, Parsons fought on the Confederate side of the Civil War, a move he later regretted, turning to more radical views in the post–Civil War years. He married his wife Lucy in 1872, moving then to Chicago in 1873. Parsons continued to work as a labor agitator, spreading his views through his newspaper, *The Alarm.* After delivering his speech at the Haymarket protest meeting, he left and was at a local beer hall when the bomb exploded. He left Chicago after the incident but returned to stand trial with the others accused.

Parsons, Lucy (?–1942): Wife of Haymarket martyr Albert Parsons. Her background is unclear, although it is assumed she was a descendent of both slaves and Indians. She was a staunch advocate of anarchy and worked for and supported a number of causes connected with social rights and equality.

Schwab, Michael (1853–?): Born in Germany and orphaned before he was a teenager, Schwab made his living as a bookbinder. He became a socialist and first went to Chicago in 1879. He began to work for the *Arbeiter-Zeitung.* He was granted clemency for his conviction in the Haymarket affair and was eventually pardoned by Governor Altgeld.

Spies, August (1855–1887): Born in Germany, Spies first went to Chicago in 1873 but then spent some time traveling around the country. He became a socialist and began working on behalf of the labor movement. Upon witnessing the violence at the McCormick Reaper Works, he called for the protest meeting to take place at Haymarket Square on 4 May. He was arrested the following day at the offices of the *Arbeiter-Zeitung*.

See also: *Eight-hour Day Movement; Pullman Strike.*

BIBLIOGRAPHY

Books

Adelman, William. *Haymarket Revisited.* Chicago, IL: Illinois Labor History Society, 1976.

Avrich, Paul. *The Haymarket Tragedy.* Princeton, NJ: Princeton University Press, 1984.

Brecher, Jeremy. *Strike!* Boston, MA: South End Press, 1972.

Miller, Donald L. *City of the Century: The Epic of Chicago and the Making of America.* New York: Simon & Schuster, 1996.

Zlotnik, Harold. *Toys of Desperation: A Haymarket Mural in Verse.* Interlaken, NY: Hearts of the Lake Publishing, 1987.

—Mitchell Newton-Matza

Herrin Massacre

United States 1922

Synopsis

On 21–22 June 1922 a coal miners' strike near the small town of Herrin in southern Illinois erupted in deadly violence. Twenty-three men were killed in the strike; all but two were strikebreakers. Along with the Chicago Battle of the Viaduct during the great railroad strike of 1877 (30 fatalities), the Homestead strike of 1892 (18), and the Ludlow Massacre in 1914 (19), the Herrin Massacre was among the deadliest single incidents of strike violence in American history. Despite impassioned cries for blood in the nation's press, no one was ever punished for any strike-related activities. A look at the causes of the massacre, its authors, and the failed efforts to punish them casts important light on the character of U.S. industrial relations during this period.

In the late nineteenth and early twentieth centuries, the United States was well known for high levels of labor violence. In large-scale strike actions, such as the great railroad strike of 1877 or the American Railway Union strike of 1894, the U.S. federal government intervened forcefully, often at the command of the judiciary. But most labor violence occurred at the local level, and here the federal and even state governments were notable for their absence. Local-level strike conflicts often dissolved into violent encounters between unionized strikers and employers' private police forces. Much attention has been

given to cases where employers triumphed; less attention has been devoted to the frequent cases where they were defeated. Indeed, the lack of a national police force and the local election of police authorities gave considerable advantages to working-class groups such as coal miners, who were often concentrated in large numbers in rural areas where they had experience in using weapons. At Herrin, the fact that hundreds of armed miners were able to besiege 50 armed strikebreakers for two days without any interference and slaughter them without any retribution illustrates the remarkably limited character of U.S. federal and state intervention in many local class conflicts during the era of high industrialization.

Timeline

1907: At the Second Hague Peace Conference, 46 nations adopt 10 conventions governing the rules of war.

1912: *Titanic* sinks on its maiden voyage, from Southampton to New York, on 14 April. More than 1,500 people are killed.

1917: In Russia, a revolution in March (or February according to the old Russian calendar) forces the abdication of Czar Nicholas II. By July, Alexander Kerensky has formed a democratic socialist government, and continues to fight the Germans, even as starvation and unrest sweep the nation. On 7 November (25 October old style), the Bolsheviks under V. I. Lenin and Leon Trotsky seize power. By 15 December, they have removed Russia from the war by signing the Treaty of Brest-Litovsk with Germany.

1919: With the formation of the Third International (Comintern), the Bolshevik government of Russia establishes its control over communist movements worldwide.

1922: Inspired by the Bolsheviks' example of imposing revolution by means of a coup, Benito Mussolini leads his blackshirts in an October "March on Rome," and forms a new fascist government.

1922: Great Britain establishes the Irish Free State as a dominion of the British Empire.

1922: With the centuries-old Ottoman Empire dissolved, Mustafa Kemal, a.k.a. Atatürk, overthrows the last sultan and establishes the modern Turkish republic.

1922: Union of Soviet Socialist Republics (USSR) is formed.

1922: Published this year James Joyce's novel *Ulysses* and T. S. Eliot's poem *The Waste* Land will transform literature and inaugurate the era of modernism.

1925: European leaders attempt to secure the peace at the Locarno Conference, which guarantees the boundaries between France and Germany, and Belgium and Germany.

1927: Charles A. Lindbergh makes the first successful solo nonstop flight across the Atlantic, and becomes an international hero.

1932: When Ukrainians refuse to surrender their grain to his commissars, Stalin seals off supplies to the region, creating a manmade famine that will produce a greater death toll than the entirety of World War I.

Event and Its Context

Roots of the Massacre

The Herrin Massacre was the culmination of a long history of violence in the Illinois coalfields in general and in those of Franklin and Williamson Counties in particular. Violent encounters between armed strikers and strikebreakers had produced fatalities in the central-southern Illinois coalfields in Pana and Virden in 1899. In southern Illinois, earlier struggles had clearly foreshadowed the events of 1922. In September 1899 in two separate incidents, five African American strikebreakers and the wife of a strikebreaker were killed by armed strikers in Carterville. In 1904–1905 strikebreakers in the company town of Zeigler were besieged by hundreds of armed miners. Barricaded in a fortified Zeigler, the employers and their armed retainers successfully resisted strikers' armed forays. However, three successive coal-mining disasters between 1905 and 1908, which killed 51, 26, and 3 men, respectively, ended the attempt to run a nonunion mine in the area. Company officials privately alleged that striking miners caused the disasters, but there can be no question of the negligence of the mine's owner who, while spending large sums to secure his mines, neglected elementary rules of mine safety.

In earlier strikes, as in the Herrin Massacre, private armies of strikebreakers and union members confronted one another. Local authorities struggled to get out of the way. County sheriffs were not anxious to act against the miners who elected them, nor were they eager to call in state authorities who would require their cooperation. Without reliable local contacts, the state's efforts to intervene in strike conflicts could not succeed. The inactivity of local authorities favored violent actions among a mining population that was well armed and well organized—and violence succeeded. In the wake of the Pana-Virden and Carterville strikes, management retreated and gave up efforts to dig non-union coal. In the Carterville as in the Herrin shootings, southern Illinois juries refused to convict miners accused of killing strikebreakers.

Mining violence was not a product of left-wing radicalism. Although southern Illinois was not as conservative as many claimed, it was no seedbed of left-wing militancy. In the early 1920s, radical groups such as the Industrial Workers of the World, the Socialist Labor Party, and the newly founded American Communist Party had a foothold among Italian miners and an even smaller following among native whites. These native whites, who composed the majority of the labor force in the larger mining towns, came from local farming populations but traced their origin to migration in the first half of the nineteenth century from rural Kentucky or Tennessee. As a heritage of the Civil War, the rural population voted Republican, but it espoused a militant Protestant fundamentalism retained by many of its sons who entered the mines. The religious revivals that periodically swept Protestant communities threatened relations with immigrant workers who were predominantly Italian, Lithuanian, and Polish Catholics. The Ku Klux Klan had a greater appeal to the mass of Franklin and Williamson County natives than radical leftist groups.

The Herrin Massacre

The Herrin Massacre was not caused by doctrines of class struggle but emerged from a fierce local class conflict. The

William J. Lester. ©Bettmann/Corbis. Reproduced by permission.

proximate cause of the massacre was the attempt of the Southern Illinois Coal Company (SICC) to run a mine whose workers were not members of the United Mine Workers of America (UMWA) during the middle of a national coal strike. Larger issues of trust and betrayal were involved and strongly promoted violence. Following in the wake of a great wave of wildcat strikes in 1919, the 1922 national strike was a bitter conflict. Broad support for the strike expressed Illinois miners' deep discontent with the cooperation of their union with employers and the government during World War I and efforts to preserve this cooperation into the postwar era. Local mining officials were on the defensive and anxious to defend their militant reputation. Local officials of UMWA District 12, comprising all Illinois coal miners, had agreed to permit the owner of the SICC, William J. Lester, to open a strip mine in Williamson County during the 1922 strike with the proviso that he would not load or ship the coal to market until the strike was over. Giving employment to a few miners when many thousands of miners were on strike was a controversial policy. Allegations of corruption arose after the massacre and are not to be dismissed, but the local officials' deal with the SICC had been well known.

Unfortunately, as the strike wore on, Lester found himself hard pressed to pay debts incurred by his start-up costs—and this at a time when he was accumulating large quantities of coal that could be sold for high prices. Finally greed triumphed, and on 13 June 1922 Lester fired his UMWA workers and announced that he would run the mine with members of the Steam Shovelmen's Union.

In southern Illinois, Lester's actions were condemned universally. Responsible authorities on the scene such as Colonel Samuel Hunter, the personnel officer of the Illinois adjutant general, worked for compromise. The national UMWA leadership was less conciliatory. At the time, District 12's chief, Frank Farrington, was locked in a bitter conflict with the

Investigators of Herrin Massacre, from left, attorney general Edward J. Brundage, chief investigator J. G. Glasser, and assistant attorney general C. W. Kiddekauf. © Bettmann/Corbis. Reproduced by permission.

UMWA president, John L. Lewis, and Lewis was probably not sorry to see the District 12 leadership embarrassed by the local officials' deal with Lester. In any case, Lewis's telegram to a local miners' leader that the Steam Shovelmen's Union was an "outlaw organization" and that its members should be seen as "common strikebreakers" undoubtedly exacerbated tensions on the eve of the massacre. Regardless, Lester's public violation of his commitment and subsequent conduct were almost bound to produce violence. Having charted a dangerous course of action, he took no half measures. Lester and his mine manager, C. K. McDowell, openly expressed their contempt for the UMWA. Lester's strikebreakers and mine guards, imported from Chicago, antagonized everyone, closing off local farm roads around the mine, bullying neighboring farmers, and even giving short shrift to local policemen.

While the mine guards' attitudes toward the police were unwise, they reflected justified suspicions. Whatever else they were, in Williamson County the police were not the agents of a bourgeois state. In the coming elections, the county sheriff was running for county treasurer and was determined not to an-

tagonize coal miners and their family members, who constituted an overwhelming majority of the electorate. The sheriff's position became nearly impossible when on 21 June hundreds of miners at an open-air meeting finally decided to take immediate action. When local coal miners raided hardware stores for arms, when convoys of armed miners clogged Herrin's streets, and when the mine manager made frantic calls to the sheriff's office, the sheriff disappeared.

On the morning of the second day of the siege, the strikebreakers' situation was desperate—the number of armed strikers was increasing rapidly, outnumbering the armed strikebreakers by at least ten to one. The strikebreakers' better aim had made their position much worse. Embattled strikebreakers and mine police killed one of the besieging miners and fatally wounded another, but their supplies began to run out. Finally, under great pressure, Lester accepted a truce, agreeing not to export coal; in exchange, the embattled strikebreakers would be allowed to depart. While state authorities in the person of Colonel Hunter were reassured by the truce, little attention was given to the actual details of the surrender. Under the most charitable interpretation, local UMWA officials made only half-hearted efforts to oversee the agreement.

With no help forthcoming that morning, the surrounded strikebreakers gave up and triumphant miners immediately began to dynamite the mine and its equipment. No responsible public or trade union official was present and authorized to accept the surrender of those who had already fatally wounded two strikers. As the strikebreakers were marched out of the mine, they were attacked by members of the crowd. Badly beaten, the hated mine manager, McDowell, was taken away to a nearby grove and killed with three bullets. Women and children from the mining community joined the crowd mocking the parade of surrendered men. Small groups of strikebreakers were whisked out of sight to be killed. Survivors were forced to run across a field separated from an adjacent wood by a barbed-wire fence; there, the real butchery began. Almost all of the strikebreakers were injured; 18 were killed that afternoon and 2 more died later of injuries. In addition, the driver of a truck carrying strikebreakers had also been killed on 21 June. After the massacre the sheriff appeared in time to collect the wounded and the dead.

The Herrin Massacre captured national headlines and provoked angry indignation throughout the country. The Illinois legislature commissioned its own investigation. The legal system was prodigal with indictments. Outrage was almost universal—except in Williamson and Franklin Counties. When a judge set bail for some of the defendants, Herrin's citizens lined up to subscribe. The Illinois miners' union paid for fans to cool the eight defendants denied bail during the hot southern Illinois summer. A union local donated a Victrola and miners' wives prepared home-cooked meals for imprisoned miners. Local juries would not convict union men. It would be 50 years before another coal company attempted to mine non-union coal in southern Illinois.

Key Players

Lester, William J. (1889–1935): Trained as a civil engineer, Lester was involved in a string of failed mining projects after the Herrin Massacre. He finally established a practice as a consulting engineer in Indiana.

Lewis, John L. (1880–1969): Lewis was president of the United Mine Workers of America (UMWA) from 1919 to 1960. Between 1919 and 1932, Lewis's dictatorial rule almost destroyed the UMWA. But faced with the crisis of the 1930s, Lewis became one of America's greatest national labor leaders, founding the Congress of Industrial Organizations and helping to unionize millions of American workers. His creation of the UMWA welfare and retirement fund in 1946 was an outstanding accomplishment, greatly benefiting those coal miners with sufficient seniority to resist the shrinking of the mining workforce.

See also: *Pullman Strike; Railroad Strike of 1877; United Mine Workers of America.*

BIBLIOGRAPHY

Books

Angle, Paul M. *Bloody Williamson: A Chapter in American Lawlessness.* Urbana: University of Illinois Press, 1992.

Friedman, Gerald. *State-making and Labor Movements: France and the United States, 1876–1914.* Ithaca, NY: Cornell University Press, 1998.

Parker, Chatland. *The Herrin Massacre.* Marion, IL: Williamson County Historical Society, 1979.

Other

Westra, Curt. "The Herrin Massacre." 15 August 1999 [cited 5 January 2003]. <http://www.geocities.com/Heartland/7847/massacre.htm>.

—Michael Hanagan

Homestead Lockout

United States 1892

Synopsis

Besides being one of the most violent episodes in American labor history, the importance of the Homestead lockout derives from two factors: the fame of the men who ran Carnegie Steel and the effect that it had on the Amalgamated Association, thought to be the strongest union of its day. In early 1892 the Carnegie Steel Company built a fence around its Homestead, Pennsylvania, mill. When its contract with the Amalgamated Association of Iron and Steel Workers expired on 29 June 1892, Carnegie Steel management locked out the 3,800 employees who worked there. On the morning of 6 July, two barges carrying 300 Pinkerton agents sailed up the Monongahela River toward Homestead to protect the new nonunion workers whom Carnegie Steel planned to hire to return the mill to operation. Tipped off about their arrival, a mob met the barges and started a gun battle that lasted all day. Ten people died in the fighting, including three detectives and seven townspeople. After the Pinkertons surrendered, the crowd marched the survivors through the streets of Homestead, beating and kicking them. The agents escaped by rail that night under sheriff's custody.

On 10 July the governor of Pennsylvania called in 8,500 Pennsylvania National Guardsmen, who quickly restored order. This allowed management to bring in replacement workers. On 17 November 1892, 300 of the locked-out workers successfully reapplied for work at the mill on a nonunion basis. On 20 November the remaining union members voted to return to work.

Timeline

1872: The Crédit Mobilier affair, in which several officials in the administration of President Ulysses S. Grant are accused of receiving stock in exchange for favors, is the first of many scandals that are to plague Grant's second term.

Attempted assassination of steel factory owner Henry Clay Frick during Homestead strike, Homestead, Pennsylvania, 1892. © Bettmann/Corbis. Reproduced by permission.

1877: In the face of uncertain results from the popular vote in the presidential election of 1876, the U.S. Electoral Commission awards the presidency to Rutherford B. Hayes despite a slight popular majority for his opponent, Samuel J. Tilden. The election of 1876 will remain the most controversial in American history for the next 124 years, until overshadowed by the race between George W. Bush and Al Gore in 2000.

1882: Agitation against English rule spreads throughout Ireland, culminating with the assassination of chief secretary for Ireland Lord Frederick Cavendish and permanent undersecretary Thomas Burke in Dublin's Phoenix Park. The leader of the nationalist movement is Charles Stewart Parnell, but the use of assassination and terrorism—which Parnell himself has disavowed—makes clear the fact that he does not control all nationalist groups.

1885: German engineer Karl Friedrich Benz builds the first true automobile.

1888: Serbian-born American electrical engineer Nikola Tesla develops a practical system for generating and transmit-

ting alternating current (AC), which will ultimately—and after an extremely acrimonious battle—replace Thomas Edison's direct current (DC) in most homes and businesses.

1890: U.S. Congress passes the Sherman Antitrust Act, which in the years that follow will be used to break up large monopolies.

1891: French troops open fire on workers during a 1 May demonstration at Fourmies, where employees of the Sans Pareille factory are striking for an eight-hour workday. Nine people are killed—two of them children—and sixty more are injured.

1893: Henry Ford builds his first automobile.

1893: New Zealand is the first nation in the world to grant the vote to women.

1894: French army captain Alfred Dreyfus, a Jew, is convicted of treason. Dreyfus will later be cleared of all charges, but the Dreyfus case illustrates—and exacerbates—the increasingly virulent anti-Semitism that pervades France.

1896: First modern Olympic Games are held in Athens.

1900: The first zeppelin is test-flown.

Event and Its Context

The man whose name and reputation will forever be linked with events at Homestead is Andrew Carnegie. Before he became the greatest philanthropist of his generation, Andrew Carnegie was a model for poor and middle-class Americans who wanted to move up in the world. Born in Dunfermline, Scotland, in 1835 to a master weaver and the daughter of a cobbler, Carnegie and his family immigrated to the United States in 1848 because of the difficulties that the rise of the English factory system created for his father's career. Because the senior Carnegie was unable to support the family in America, Andrew went to work in a series of menial jobs. While employed as a telegraph messenger, he caught the eye of Thomas Scott, the superintendent of the Pennsylvania Railroad. Impressed by Carnegie's work ethic, Scott gave him a new job with the railroad and helped him make successful investments in a number of different industries. Carnegie moved from investor to full-time steel magnate in 1863, and by 1892 Carnegie Steel was the largest steel producer in the world.

Although the Homestead lockout was a complete triumph for Carnegie Steel and entirely eliminated the union from its mills, it hurt Carnegie by damaging his popularity with ordinary Americans. In 1886 Carnegie had written two essays for *Forum* magazine that seemed to support trade unions. Often-quoted parts of these articles paint Carnegie as far more liberal on labor questions at that time than any of his business contemporaries. For instance, in "An Employer's View of the Labor Question," he wrote, "My experience has been that trade-unions, upon the whole are beneficial to both labor and capital." In "Results of the Labor Struggle," Carnegie explained, "There is an unwritten law among the best workmen: 'Thou shalt not take thy neighbor's job.' No wise employer will lightly lose his old employees." Industrialists never wrote this sort of thing in the late nineteenth century. The two *Forum* essays made Carnegie a hero to the working classes. After the violence, much of the public thought Carnegie a hypocrite.

Carnegie's views on labor were self-serving, however. He wrote the *Forum* essays at a time when he had an overwhelming technological advantage in the industry. At that time, it paid for him to recognize the Amalgamated Association because this ensured that he would not have to shut down production when his nonunion competitors faced strikes. Because his superior technology could produce steel at a substantially cheaper price than other firms, he could afford the high union wages that this strategy required. By 1892, however, this situation had changed drastically. Because Carnegie's nonunion competitors had caught up to him in steel-making technology, the entire industry faced depression caused by overproduction. To make matters worse, Carnegie Steel's competitors could now undersell him because they paid lower wages. This is why Carnegie determined that the union had to go, despite the words he had written six years earlier.

When the lockout began, Carnegie was at his castle in Scotland. The man in charge in Pennsylvania was his lieutenant,

Henry Clay Frick. Frick began his career in the coal business. He organized the Henry Clay Frick Coke Company in 1871, and the business quickly grew, selling all the coal it could produce, mostly to the rapidly growing steel industry. By 1880 Frick dominated the coal industry in western Pennsylvania. When Carnegie decided that his firm should be vertically integrated so as to protect his supply of coal, he began to buy up stock in Frick's company. Although Carnegie controlled approximately 50 percent of Frick's firm by the mid-1880s, Frick continued to run it himself. In 1889 Carnegie brought in Frick as a partner and named him chairman of Carnegie Steel. Frick already had a reputation for breaking trade unions in his company's coal fields. In a famous 1887 coal strike, Frick employed permanent replacement workers and Pinkerton guards to protect them.

During the lockout, Frick became famous for something other than producing coal and subduing unions. On 23 July 1892 an anarchist named Alexander Berkman appeared at Frick's downtown Pittsburgh office. Although Berkman appeared nervous, he was allowed to see the industrialist, at which time he shot and stabbed Frick. Despite being seriously wounded, Frick helped wrestle Berkman to the floor and hold him there until the police came. Then, while still in his office, a doctor removed a bullet from Frick's neck and back. Frick received no anesthesia. He finished his day's work before leaving for home in an ambulance. Even though Berkman had no ties to the Amalgamated Association, the public connected the assassination and the labor dispute. By creating sympathy for an unsympathetic figure, this incident helped dissolve what little public support remained for the union.

Although Carnegie was not in Pittsburgh to implement strategy during the strike (he had informally "retired" from business a few years before), he approved of Frick's tactics at the time. Only when the press and the public began to attack Carnegie for going back on the words in his *Forum* essays did he begin to change his mind. Criticism of Carnegie's role in events at Homestead was so rancorous that some towns for which he offered to build libraries actually turned him down with the lockout as the reason. Therefore, it is not surprising that over the years Carnegie increasingly began to distance himself from events at Homestead and even expressed his regret for the violence. Rather than defend the aspects of his earlier writings that supported his later policies, however, Carnegie misrepresented the facts so that he appeared to still believe in the ideas in the *Forum* essays that had once made him so popular with labor. Whether this constituted deliberate deception or merely self-delusion, the deception suggests that Carnegie was motivated by guilt.

Historians also consider the Homestead lockout to have been an important event in American labor history because of its negative effect on the Amalgamated Association of Iron and Steel Workers. The role of the dispute in the collapse of the union, however, has been greatly overstated. Although widely perceived as the strongest labor union in the country at that time, the power of the Amalgamated Association had begun a precipitous decline in power in the years preceding Homestead.

To understand the weakness of the Amalgamated Association, it is important to consider the difference between iron and steel production. Iron and Bessemer steel were almost perfect substitutes for one another in the late nineteenth century. Therefore, the two products competed against one another. The first modern steel plants built in the 1870s and 1880s used the Bessemer process. Essentially, this technology replaced skilled iron puddlers, who had to make many informed decisions to remove impurities from molten slag, with an automatic system that used blown air to remove the impurities. Whereas it took up to two years to learn puddling, with the new process, a common laborer could become a skilled steelworker in as little as six to eight weeks. If labor savings were not enough to get producers and consumers to switch from iron to steel, the Bessemer process produced higher quality product than could the iron mills. Steel was more durable than iron when used for railroad rails, the industry's most popular product during this era. Because of this new technology, steel manufacturers hired many new workers, particularly immigrants, who had no experience in the iron industry. Unfortunately for the Amalgamated Association, it had always concentrated its organizing efforts on highly skilled puddlers. Less-skilled workers tended to view the union with contempt. The increased demand for less-skilled labor damaged the long-term viability of the organization.

Although strong in the iron industry, the Amalgamated Association was never able to organize even half the steelworkers in the Pittsburgh district, which was the union's strongest venue. As early as 1885, the signing of the union scale was irrelevant to most steel firms across the industry because they already ran nonunion. Steelmakers avoided the union by building entirely new mills and keeping the Amalgamated out. In this manner, they outflanked the skilled workers who had once wielded a considerable amount of power on the shop floor. When the Amalgamated Association reached its peak membership in 1891, only 25 percent of steelworkers eligible for Amalgamated membership nationwide were in the union. Even at Homestead, a few months before the strike less than 400 of the 2,000 workers at the plant who were eligible to join the union were actually members.

After 1889 the situation of the Amalgamated Association changed dramatically for the worse. In 1891 the union had 24,068 members, but by 1893 that figure had dropped by almost half to 13,613. Yet these numbers obscure a sharper drop in employment in the iron and steel sector of the industry. While employment in that sector of the economy decreased, the tin plate sector of the industry increased sharply. Tin plate is steel rolled into thin sheets and dipped in tin. Its primary uses were for cans and as roofing material. In 1890 the United States was completely dependent upon Wales for its tin plate; it produced virtually none of its own. High duties on tin plate passed as part of McKinley Tariff of 1890 caused imports of Welsh tin plate to drop sharply and jump-started a domestic tin plate industry. In the first quarter year of operations after the tariff took effect on 1 July 1891, United States manufacturers produced 826,922 pounds of tin plate. In each of the next two quarters, production nearly doubled to more than three million pounds. By 1896 American tin plate production exceeded imports from Wales for the first time. Without the tariff, this industry would not have existed in the United States.

The skilled labor that made this increase in production possible came from Wales. Thousand of Welshmen joined the Amalgamated Association in the early 1890s because of the strong tradition of trade unionism in their home country. Many Amalgamated members who were not Welsh had been displaced from nonunion rolling mills. Growth in employment for tin workers compensated for shrinking membership rolls in other sectors of the industry. If tin plate production had not taken off when it did, the decline in the Amalgamated Association's membership would have occurred earlier and been more pronounced than indicated by the total membership numbers.

In the iron and tin plate sectors of the industry, the skills possessed by Amalgamated Association members were indispensable to the production process. This was not true in the technologically advanced steel-producing sector. Because steel was by far the fastest growing segment of the industry, the Amalgamated Association would have been in serious decline even if Homestead had never occurred.

The other problem with the argument that the Homestead lockout destroyed the Amalgamated Association is that Carnegie Steel was not the first or the last firm to oust the union. In addition to losing ground as new steel manufacturers opened non union shops, Amalgamated conducted series of failed strikes in the late 1880s and early 1890s that could have crippled the organization regardless of these other losses. Under the weight of increased competition, iron and steel manufacturers across the United States moved to cut back on their labor costs by running nonunion with increasing frequency. By exploiting their lower labor costs, these firms increased the pressure on Carnegie Steel to jettison the union.

In 1892 the conflict between management and the union spread throughout the industry. Virtually every firm in both the iron and steel sectors of the industry found the Amalgamated Association scale unacceptable and refused to sign. Most companies that had previously signed the scale refused that year. In fact, manufacturers from every sector of the industry and every region of the country began to propose deep wage cuts even before the union first proposed its scale. Many steel manufacturers in addition to Carnegie Steel took on the union in the summer of 1892 because companies throughout the industry perceived the Amalgamated Association as vulnerable. In the struggle that followed, steelmakers across the country managed to banish Amalgamated permanently from their facilities. By August there were more nonunion mills up and running across the country than at any time in the previous 20 years. Approximately 70,000 steelworkers were out of work that summer. Even so, the struggle between labor and management at Homestead attracted all the attention.

After the lockout, the Amalgamated Association still had many members in sectors of the industry that still required skilled labor (such as tin plate production). When United States Steel formed in 1901, it completed the work that Carnegie Steel began by beating the Amalgamated Association in two disputes, a strike in 1901 and a lockout in 1909. Only then was the Amalgamated Association completely subdued. The iron and steel industry remained largely nonunion until the Steel Workers Organizing Committee found success in the late 1930s.

Key Players

Carnegie, Andrew (1835–1919): Carnegie was an industrialist and philanthropist whose rags-to-riches life was a model of success for countless Americans. His role in the Homestead lockout severely damaged his reputation.

Frick, Henry Clay (1849–1919): Coal baron, notorious opponent of organized labor, and art collector, Frick organized Carnegie Steel's campaign to destroy the Amalgamated Association in its mills but later broke with Carnegie in part over public revulsion to his tactics.

McLuckie, John (1852–?): Former steel worker and burgess (mayor) of Homestead who led the town's resistance to the lockout. His opposition to Carnegie Steel destroyed his political career.

See also: *U.S. Steel Recognizes the Steel Workers Organizing Committee.*

BIBLIOGRAPHY

Books

Burgoyne, Arthur. *The Homestead Strike of 1892*. Pittsburgh, PA: University Press, 1979. (Originally published by the Rawthorne Engraving and Printing Company, 1893).

Demarest, David, Jr. *"The River Ran Red": Homestead 1892*. Pittsburgh, PA: University of Pittsburgh Press, 1992.

Krause, Paul. *The Battle for Homestead, 1880–1892: Politics, Culture and Steel*. Pittsburgh, PA: University of Pittsburgh Press, 1992.

Wolff, Leon. *Lockout*. New York: Harper & Row, 1965.

Periodicals

Rees, Jonathan. "Homestead in Context: Andrew Carnegie and the Decline of the Amalgamated Association of Iron and Steel Workers." *Pennsylvania History* 64 (autumn 1997): 509–533.

Other

Levy Industrial. Rivers of Steel National Heritage Area Web site [cited 27 August 2002]. <http://www.riversofsteel.com/>.

—Jonathan Rees

Hormel Strike

United States 1985–1986

Synopsis

On 19 August 1985 Local P-9 of the United Food and Commercial Workers (UFCW) went on strike against Geo. A. Hormel and Company's Austin, Minnesota, flagship plant. The strike attracted widespread support among rank-and-file workers in the U.S. labor movement despite the reluctance of the

UFCW to endorse its objectives. In January 1986 Hormel reopened the plant with strikebreakers, leading P-9 to widen its efforts to secure support from other workers. In April 1986 the UFCW terminated its support for the strike, removed the local union officers, and ended the strike by signing a contract very similar to the one P-9 had rejected when it walked out. Most strikers never regained their jobs.

Timeline

1965: African Americans in the Watts section of Los Angeles riot for six days. Thirty-four people are killed, over 1,000 injured, and fires damage $175 million in property.

1974: In a bout with George Foreman in Zaire, Muhammad Ali becomes only the second man in history (the first was Floyd Patterson) to regain the title of world heavyweight champion.

1979: More than a year after Afghan communists seized control of their nation, Afghanistan is in disarray, and at Christmas, Soviet tanks roll in to restore order, as they once did in East Germany, Poland, Hungary, and Czechoslovakia. This time, however, the task of suppressing the local populace will not prove so easy: little do the Soviets know that they are signing on for a decade-long war from which they will return in defeat.

1982: Israeli troops invade Lebanon in an attack on the Palestine Liberation Organization (PLO).

1985: A new era begins in the USSR as Chernenko dies and is replaced by Mikhail Gorbachev, who at 54 years old is the youngest Soviet leader in decades.

1985: In a year of notable hijackings by Muslim and Arab terrorists, Shi'ites take a TWA airliner in June, Palestinians hijack the Italian cruise ship *Achille Lauro* in October, and fundamentalists take control of an Egyptian plane in Athens in November.

1988: A terrorist bomb aboard a Pan Am 747 explodes over Lockerbie, Scotland, killing 259 people on the plane and 11 more on the ground.

1990: Iraq invades Kuwait, seizing oil reserves, and the United States begins mobilizing for war.

1995: The Aum Shinrikyo cult causes a nerve-gas attack in a Tokyo subway, killing eight people and injuring thousands more.

2002: The Catholic Church is rocked by allegations of sexual molestation carried out by priests.

Event and Its Context

The 1985–1986 strike by Local P-9 at Hormel's Austin, Minnesota, plant was the most visible of a wave of local meatpacking strikes during the 1980s that sought, unsuccessfully, to halt the unraveling of unionism in that industry. In a strike that lasted from August 1985 to June 1986, Local P-9 transfixed the labor movement—and occasionally the nation—with its dramatic struggle against contract concessions. The strike also divided packinghouse workers inside the United Food and Commercial Workers (UFCW), as P-9 refused to accept the decisions of the international union, which disagreed with P-9's strategy.

Declining Real Income and Stability

The strike was provoked by the decision by Hormel's management to terminate the 1940 guaranteed annual wage agreement that had made the company's Austin employees the highest-paid workers in the meatpacking industry. For almost four decades Austin packinghouse workers received a guaranteed wage calculated on a 38-hour week, regardless of the hours actually worked. In addition, the workers collected incentive earnings that grew from 41 percent of the base wage in 1947 to 68 percent in 1956. As a result, the Austin workers earned on average $120 for a 35-hour week in 1956, compared to $87 for a 40-hour week in Iowa packinghouses. The hourly wage was pegged to the rates paid under union contracts in the major packing companies; it was incentive pay that made Hormel's Austin employees the wealthiest packinghouse workers in the country.

Under company pressure, the Austin local started granting concessions in 1963 in the form of higher production schedules that reduced incentive earnings. This erosion in earning levels continued throughout the 1960s and 1970s. In 1978, in order to exact a commitment from Hormel to build a new plant in Austin, the local union agreed to abandon the incentive system and not to strike for three years after the completion of the new facility. The new plant (which opened in 1982) also disrupted long-established work habits and rhythms. The massive retirement of experienced workers and the hiring of new employees added to the disruption on the shop floor.

The Hormel workers who led P-9's struggle in the 1980s generally were hired in the late 1960s, and had grown up in Austin under conditions of steadily rising income and stable employment for their parents, who generally worked at Hormel. Like many of their supporters, the P-9 president James V. Guyette and business agent Peter Winkels were second-generation Hormel workers who had started their employment in the late 1960s. However, this cohort experienced declining real income almost from the moment they were hired, and in an environment where pattern bargaining seemingly provided little assistance. When Guyette and his supporters took control of the local in the 1980s, the master agreements were disappearing from the industry and the UFCW was negotiating concessionary contracts. In fact, their main experience with pattern bargaining hurt Austin workers. As a result of concessions to companies under national agreements, an arbitrator held that Hormel could unilaterally cut hourly pay by $1.69, in accordance with a contract provision that tied the P-9 workers' wages to master agreement rates.

The P-9 Strike and Strategy

The road to the strike began in September 1984 when P-9 refused to go along with other Hormel local unions in signing a contract that accepted the arbitrator's decision and lowered wages to $9 an hour from $10.69. P-9's leaders maintained that the need to resist concessions and regain the $10.69 level outweighed the need to cooperate with other local unions. They ar-

gued that since their plant was one of the most modern in the industry, they should try for a high wage and act as an upward force on national pay levels. P-9's decision was based on the apparent collapse of pattern bargaining as a means of increasing—or even maintaining—the living standards of packinghouse workers. But their decision went against traditions in meatpacking of cooperation between local unions, and many local union officials in the meatpacking industry disagreed with P-9's position.

While the P-9 strike that began in August 1985 reflected resistance to the concessionary pressures typical in meatpacking, particular local concerns significantly fueled the militancy and direction of its struggle. Hormel's final proposal eliminated major contractual provisions that had been secured by the union in the 1930s: a guaranteed annual wage, one year's notice prior to layoffs, and job placement in accordance with seniority. The contract also provided for a two-tier wage system, a 30 percent reduction in pensions, and a common labor wage of $9.25 with no increases over three years, and it eliminated maternity benefits.

With the UFCW unenthusiastic about the local union's approach, P-9's leaders looked elsewhere for assistance with their strike. They decided to hire Ray Rogers of Corporate Campaign, Inc., who had helped several local strikes, to act as an adviser to P-9's efforts. A skilled organizer, Rogers helped to structure the local union's strategy of reaching out to other workers and finding other points of pressure against Hormel. By the time P-9 walked out in September, it had a well-organized infrastructure that would spread support for the strike within Austin and among midwestern workers.

P-9's methods bore considerable resemblance to forms of working-class solidarity in the organizing drives of the 1930s and 1940s. P-9's members dispatched informational pickets to other packinghouses, distributing information on their strike and establishing personal relationships between rank-and-file packinghouse workers. Union members handed out thousands of leaflets about their struggle to working-class residents in towns throughout the Midwest. An educational committee trained more than 100 P-9 members in public speaking and dispatched them to speak at union meetings throughout the United States and Canada.

P-9 also devoted considerable energy to involving the families of Hormel workers. The local kept its large hall open 24 hours a day, seven days a week, serving basic meals in the basement and distributing free food weekly to union families. A Santa's workshop organized before Christmas in 1985 made hundreds of toys for the strikers' children. A toolbox committee run by workers and their spouses handled the union members' financial, legal, and emotional problems. While Rogers coordinated the union's strike activities, much of the initiative, energy, and resources actually came from the Austin United Support Group, an organization of P-9 spouses that had been established in 1984. P-9 also aggressively reached out to workers in other, unrelated trades to ask for their moral and material support.

Division and Defeat

Opposition from the UFCW, high unemployment in the Midwest, and the hostile political climate for labor doomed P-9's resistance. In January 1986 Hormel reopened the plant with new employees and, with the aid of the Minnesota National Guard, stymied P-9's efforts to block entrances to the facility. The UFCW refused to sanction P-9's request to use roving pickets to halt production at other Hormel plants. Nevertheless, more than 500 workers respected P-9 pickets at Ottumwa, Iowa, and were promptly suspended. Without support from the international, however, this tactic was doomed. In Fremont, Nebraska, local UFCW officials instructed union members to cross P-9's picket lines; only a handful of workers stayed out. By February 1986 the strike was no longer effective. Slowly, P-9 union members started to trickle back into Austin even though the local remained on strike, until almost 400 had joined the plant's 1,000 new employees. As the strike unraveled, public recriminations between P-9 and the UFCW reached a crescendo, including a vitriolic clash between Lewie Anderson, the UFCW Packinghouse Division head, and Guyette on the ABC television show *Nightline*.

In April the UFCW president, William Wynn, decided the international union would settle the dispute on its own. The UFCW removed P-9's officers, terminated strike benefits, and signed a contract with Hormel (based on a settlement reached in the Oscar Mayer plants) for a $10 per hour base wage with an increase to $10.70 in three years. Aside from wages, the Austin agreement was very close to the terms demanded by Hormel when P-9 struck in August 1985. It eliminated two key contractual provisions that had been in the Austin agreements since 1940: a guaranteed annual wage and a 52-week notice prior to any layoffs. The four-year contract also terminated the common expiration dates achieved under the Amalgamated, and contained no language requiring Hormel to rehire the 850 P-9 members still out of work. Fewer than 100 of the P-9 members who refused to cross union picket lines ever regained their jobs.

Key Players

Anderson, Lewie: Director of the Packinghouse Division of the United Food and Commercial Workers and a former packinghouse worker, Anderson was the key figure in the UFCW's efforts to curtail the Hormel strike.

Guyette, James V.: President of Local P-9 during the 1985 to 1986 strike, Guyette began work at Hormel in 1968, was elected as P-9's president in 1994, and was removed from office by the UFCW.

Rogers, Ray: President of Corporate Campaign, Inc., Rogers was hired by Local P-9 to coordinate its efforts to involve retired Hormel workers, spouses, and other workers in Minnesota and nationwide to support the P-9 strike.

Winkels, Peter: Winkels was the business agent for Local P-9 during the 1985 strike. The son and grandson of former Hormel workers, he commenced work at Hormel in 1968. He was elected as P-9's business agent in the same election as Guyette became the president, and was removed from office by the UFCW.

BIBLIOGRAPHY

Books

Green, Hardy. *On Strike at Hormel: The Struggle for a Democratic Labor Movement.* Philadelphia: Temple University Press, 1990.

Horowitz, Roger. *Negro and White, Unite and Fight! A Social History of Industrial Unionism in Meatpacking, 1930–1990.* Urbana: University of Illinois Press, 1997.

Rachleff, Peter. *Hard-pressed in the Heartland: The Hormel Strike and the Future of the Labor Movement.* Boston: South End Press, 1993.

Schleuning, Neala J. *Women, Community, and the Hormel Strike of 1985–1986.* Westport, CT: Greenwood Press, 1994.

Other

Koppel, Barbara. *American Dream.* 1990. Movie documentary.

—Roger Horowitz

Hot Autumn

Italy 1969

Synopsis

The fall of 1969 in Italy was popularly called "hot autumn" (or in Italian, *autunno caldo*). During this time severe conflicts between workers and the capitalists (and the government) culminated in a period of labor militancy that involved Italian workers, students, the unemployed, and the general citizenry. Tensions over demands from management, built up during the preceding two years, had peaked at this time, leading to a high degree of worker unrest. Workers increasingly violated no-strike contract clauses, chanting their slogan: "Better Wages, Shorter Hours."

At the same time, student unrest paralleled the violence of Italian workers. The situation was further complicated by a government that was split between its three major parties: the coalition of the center-left Christian-Democrat Party (DC or *Democrazia Cristiana*); the left-wing Italian Socialist Party (PSI or *Partito Socialista Italiano*); and the Italian Communist Party (PCI or *Partito Communista Italiano*). In addition, the three national union confederations were weakened by the militaristic demands of their members. The labor confederations were: (1) the Italian General Confederation of Labor (CGIL or *Confederazione Generale Italiana del Lavora*), made up of communists, socialists, activists of the New Left tradition, and independent leftists; (2) the Italian Confederation of Workers' Unions (CISL or *Confederazione Italiana Sindacati Lavoratori*), made up of members and supporters of the Christian Democratic Party, independent Catholics, independent leftists, and some socialists; and (3) the Italian Union of Labor (UIL or *Unione Italiana del Lavoro*), made up of socialists, social democrats, and republicans.

Timeline

1954: The French military outpost at Dien Bien Phu falls to the communist Vietminh.

1959: Vice President Richard Nixon and Soviet leader Nikita Khrushchev engage in their famous "kitchen debate" in Moscow.

1964: On 7 February, in the midst of both a literal and figurative winter in America following Kennedy's assassination, the Beatles arrive at New York's newly renamed JFK Airport.

1966: In August, Mao Zedong launches the "Great Proletarian Cultural Revolution," which rapidly plunges China into chaos as armed youths plunder the countryside, rooting out suspected foreign collaborators and anti-Chinese elements.

1969: Richard M. Nixon sworn in as president of the United States. In June he pulls 25,000 troops from Vietnam. From this point, America is no longer trying to win the war but is trying to keep from losing it.

1969: Assisted by pilot Michael Collins, astronauts Neil Armstrong and Edwin E. "Buzz" Aldrin on 20 July become the first men to walk on the Moon.

1969: Some 400,000 people attend the Woodstock Music and Arts Festival in August. Also in the world of popular culture, the year is notable for several outstanding movies: *Midnight Cowboy, Butch Cassidy and the Sundance Kid,* and *Easy Rider.*

1969: At the orders of Charles Manson, members of his "Family" kill seven adults and one unborn child (Sharon Tate's) in a pair of grisly L.A. murders. Other crimes are also in the news: authorities learn that in March 1968, an army platoon led by Lieutenant William Calley massacred 567 villagers in the South Vietnamese hamlet of Mylai.

1969: U.S. Department of Defense puts its Arpanet, forerunner of the Internet, online.

1972: In June, police apprehend five men attempting to burglarize Democratic Party headquarters at the Watergate Hotel in Washington, D.C.

1974: On 30 July the House Judiciary Committee adopts three articles of impeachment against President Nixon, but rather than undergo a lengthy trial, Nixon on 8 August becomes the first president in U.S. history to resign.

1979: After years of unrest, the Shah of Iran leaves the country, and Islamic fundamentalist revolutionaries under the leadership of Ayatollah Ruhollah Khomeini take control.

Event and Its Context

The events that led to Italy's "hot autumn" of 1969 had their origin in the employee-employer relations of the early 1960s. In the aftermath of World War II (which ended in 1945), Italian trade unionization began a steady expansion. As a result, the stronger unions learned more effective techniques of mobilization and organization for the new mass manufacturing industries (such as metalworking, chemicals, textiles, and construction). By 1962 the first noticeable volume of employee conflict occurred, which led to an increased frequency and duration of strikes. These strikes were a direct response to the repressive conditions that existed in factories, including exile departments (which limited troublesome employees to certain areas), blacklisting, and political surveillance. According to Italy's Central Institute of Statistics (ISTAT or *Istituto Centrale di Statistica*), strikes steadily increased during the early 1960s, and labor began to make wage gains in 1962 because of such strikes.

Student Protests and Government Divisions

Student protests paralleled worker protests during this time period. Herbert Marcuse (who criticized the consumer society in *One Dimensional Man*), various leftist magazines, several dissenting Catholic groups, and dramatic world events (including the Vietnam War) strengthened unrest on campuses throughout Italy. By 1968 revolutionary student-based organizations developed in response to such conflicts as: (1) overcrowding (the number of students had grown from 268,000 in 1960 to over 450,000 in 1968, but few new buildings had been built); (2) disputes with lecturers who had gained their positions under fascism; (3) rejection of communism (especially the Italian Communist Party); and (4) general lack of student reforms. Many students spoke to workers, which had a great influence on the dramatic increase of worker strikes and violence in the second half of 1969.

For five years a center-left majority, based on the alliance between the center-left Christian-Democrat Party and the left-wing Socialist Party, had governed Italy. The coalition government remained in power for the first half of 1969 under pressure of employee strikes and student protests. These troubles mirrored the attitude of *"contestazione"* (or skepticism about traditional values) that had been developing over the past year.

The Christian-Democrats and the socialists had their own ideas as to how the government should deal with a rapidly changing society. Both parties were trying—in different ways that often clashed—to become more open-minded toward the communists. They recognized a need for increased attention to the Communist Party because the communists had a history in local administration and in labor union affairs. During these turbulent times, the government struggled internally with its own problems as different factions, such as the Republican Party (PRI) and the Unitarian Socialist Party (PSU), split from the major parties. A new government formed around these new divisions and old parties.

Worker Demands

An increase in protests and strikes began in the first half of 1968 because of a shortage of labor, which helped workers to win economic concessions (especially wages) from companies. During this time, the three unions were, for the most part, out of touch with their members. They were unable to control their combatant members, as moderate demands in 1968 turned into violent confrontations with employers and the police during the fall of 1968. Workers lengthened strikes and broadened demands with such tactics as overtaking factories, organizing slowdowns, setting up militant picket lines and roadblocks, and demonstrating through cities. Although the unions were initially outside this labor movement, they eventually conceded that it was better to join than to oppose the movement.

The early months of 1969 continued the trends of 1968. Industrial unrest and social discontent originated in a series of small strikes that turned into widespread strike action. In early April protests occurred in Battipaglia, southeast of Salerno, when a threatened factory closing caused a riot that ended with the shooting death of two people.

The workers demanded many things that were already standard in other countries, such as an end to compulsory overtime and some control over the work environment. Italian workers also made unique demands, most notably the equality of the working class, which did not want to be divided by wages, job categories, regional origins, sex, and age. Employees desired pay raises and fringe benefits to be equal, the number of job categories to be reduced, and some worker control over category definitions. The movement called for a 40-hour workweek; the abolition of piecework, other incentive systems, and compulsory overtime; and the ability to hold union assemblies inside the workplace on company time and to bargain (and strike if necessary) even after a contract had been signed.

Over time, more workers were drawn into the struggle. Workers at this time were socialist (or anticapitalist). They did not necessarily want to collaborate with management in operating the business or to compromise with management in labor and economic policies. Strikes and collective bargaining were their preferred means to achieve concessions. Radical union members wanted to gain control of businesses, but the majority of workers only expected to gain power at the expense of the capitalists.

Unions: Pension System and Salary Cages

During the time that workers were demanding better conditions, labor confederations campaigned to reform the pension system and to abolish regional salary. The pension issue in early 1968 aroused worker anger because the government controlled the nationwide pension system, and a new pension law was viewed as providing little improvement. The government ignored these protests until the three labor confederations staged a strike in November 1968 that received unified worker support. In February 1969 the Italian government agreed to a new pension law that provided 74 percent of the average of the last several years' salaries to all workers who had worked at least 40 years. The issue of regional salary differentials progressed slowly from early 1968 to March 1969 as state-owned industries, then small- and medium-sized businesses, and finally the large private corporations signed agreements to equalize wage differences over the next few years.

Both issues (pensions and regional equalization), although seemingly resolved, spurred further organization of workers. This was especially notable among semiskilled and unskilled workers and among workers from regions that had not participated in past union activities. In spite of disagreements, workers from industry, office, agriculture, and engineering sectors united during the momentous year of 1969. Although that camaraderie decreased in later years, 1969 was pivotal for labor rights. Indeed, according to Italy's ISTAT, strikes peaked in 1969 when the volume of strikes was almost twice as great as during any other single year since 1950.

Defensive Employers

When workers began to voice their demands, employers took a defensive posture. They resorted to repressive tactics such as individual and mass layoffs. They often called in police to confront demonstrators and relied on local governments for additional support. Between September and December 1969, about 13,000 Italians were arrested or charged with labor-related incidents. Leaders of companies such as Confindustria and Intersind realized that their traditional business environments were in jeopardy. As a result, they resisted conceding to demands in the areas of work conditions, company-level bargaining, and control over the organization of labor. Sometimes the actions of companies backfired, as happened with Fiat, which suspended 35,000 employees who rejected company policies. The workers' solidarity increased in response. For example, in spite of ratifying a new contract, metal and mechanical workers in state-controlled factories voted to support metal workers in private industry until an equal contract was signed.

The Hot Autumn of 1969

In the fall of 1969, national and local strikes occurred throughout Italy. The wave began with a wildcat strike in the Fiat Mirafiori works on 1 September. Only 800 workers struck, but the numbers were sufficient to halt production of vital parts. Management suspended around 30,000 workers until the strikers returned to work. Violent strikes broke out later at Alfa Romeo and Pirelli. Rioting took place in many towns, the most serious in Reggio Calabria, where many thousands of people fought against government troops. The number of strikes had multiplied fourfold during 1968 and 1969. The key revolts were centered in the factories, and by the autumn of 1969 many union leaders had lost control. Workers made strategy decisions at impromptu meetings or over a cup of coffee in the lunchroom.

More than 5.5 million workers—more than 25 percent of the labor force—walked off the job during 1969. Strikes caused 520 million worker-hours to be lost, a figure not seen since the 1940s. Dissatisfaction with social conditions was the underlying cause of the extensive strikes of the autumn of 1969. It was especially noticeable in northern industrial towns, where thousands of relocated southern workers put a strain on housing and public services. The direct cause of the strikes, however, was the negotiation of a number of collective wage agreements that became due.

Negotiations opened in the middle of October for contract renewals for 1.25 million workers in state and private metalworking industries, but were quickly broken off. Later that month, additional negotiations stopped, and more strikes continued. The strikers demanded pay increases of as much as 35 percent and contract clauses covering the rights of employees during working hours and holidays.

On 19 November 1969, 20 million citizens united in a nationwide general strike to demand reforms from the government. At the end of November, 150,000 metal and mechanical workers marched on Rome. The outcome of these strikes during the "hot autumn" of 1969 was a victory for the labor movement.

In fact, the labor unions considered the victory to be one of the most significant events of their entire history.

Labor legislation was passed as a result of the 1969 strikes, as the government wanted to show that it was amenable to labor reform. On 20 May 1970 the Statutes of the Laboratories (*Statuto dei Laboratori*) granted a series of individual and collective labor rights, including the right to organize, the right to hold union assemblies during working hours, and the right of shop-floor union representatives to take time off to perform union tasks. The bill also promoted subsequent trade union stability. Most important, the new law recognized the right of organized labor to act in the workplace.

The contracts won in 1969 and 1970 usually had several things in common:

- Reduction of the workweek to 40 hours
- Significant wage gains that were largely equal across categories
- Limits on overtime
- Additional worker holidays
- Equal treatment for sick or injured white- and blue-collar workers
- Right to hold up to 10 hours of annual assemblies on company time in plants with over 15 workers
- Recognition of union representatives in the factories
- Expansion of decentralized bargaining
- Formalization of "unity-of-action" agreements among the labor confederations
- Acknowledgement of eight hours a month with pay for representatives to perform union duties
- Concession to post union notices on designated bulletin boards
- Ratification by the rank-and-file of union contracts
- Concession of the right of workers to a written management explanation (and to defend themselves) for any disciplinary action

Historical Analysis and Consequences

Italian historian Alessandro Pizzorno felt that the "hot autumn" of 1969 came about because unrepresented groups of semiskilled workers finally brought attention to themselves with strikes and violence. Other scholars have advanced different explanations for the militancy. Most agree that the deliberate wage restraint in the mid-1960s by employers was the conduit for worker strikes and violence a few years later.

BIBLIOGRAPHY

Books

Barkan, Joanne. *Visions of Emancipation: The Italian Workers' Movement Since 1945*. New York: Praeger Publishers, 1985.

Golden, Miriam. *Labor Divided: Austerity and Working-Class Politics in Contemporary Italy*. Ithaca, NY, and London: Cornell University Press, 1988.

Horowitz, Daniel L. *The Italian Labor Movement*. Cambridge, MA: Harvard University Press, 1963.

Neufeld, Maurice F. *Italy: School for Awakening Countries*. Ithaca, NY: Cayuga Press, 1961.

Roberts, David D. *The Syndicalist Tradition and Italian Fascism*. Chapel Hill: The University of North Carolina Press, 1979.

Other

Behan, Tom. "What Socialists Say: Italy in the 1970s—The Strategy of Tension." Socialist Worker Page [cited 24 October 2002]. <http://www.socialistworker.co.uk/1760/sw176018.htm>.

European Foundation for the Improvement of Living and Working Conditions. "Autunno Caldo (Hot Autumn)" [cited 24 October 2002]. <http://www.eurofound.eu.int/emire/ITALY/HOTAUTUMN-IT.html>.

———. "Fascism and the Establishment—Italy: The Stratergy [sic] of Tension" [cited 24 October 2002]. <http://flag.blackened.net/revolt/freeearth/fe3_italy.html>.

Media '68. "The Long Italian '68." 1968: A World Revolution. February 1998 [cited 24 October 2002]. <http://www.media68.com/eng/italy/italy.htm>.

—William Arthur Atkins

Hungarian Revolution and Workers Councils

Hungary 1956

Synopsis

In October 1956 a popular uprising in Hungary liquidated the Stalinist bureaucracy that had ruled the country since 1949. Imre Nagy, a reformist Communist Party member, became the head of a new government, supported by popular grass-roots organizations including the workers' and revolutionary councils.

The councils pursued a program of national independence from the Soviet Union and workers' self-management in the factories. They also established coordinating bodies that took control of regions, cities, and productive centres. For critical left-wing militants on both sides of the Iron Curtain, the experience meant a new form of direct democracy. The councils' heterogeneous social composition and unclear political platform, however, caused fears in the USSR leadership about their shift toward nationalist and pro-Western positions. When the Hungarian government withdrew from the Warsaw Pact at the councils' requests, the USSR's Red Army occupied the country, arrested Nagy, and placed a puppet government in office.

Timeline

1936: Germany reoccupies the Rhineland, while Italy annexes Ethiopia. Recognizing a commonality of aims, the two totalitarian powers sign the Rome-Berlin Axis Pact. (Japan will join them in 1940.)

1941: Japanese bombing of Pearl Harbor on 7 December brings the United States into the war against the Axis. Combined with the attack on the Soviet Union, which makes Stalin an unlikely ally of the Western democracies, the events of 1941 will ultimately turn the tide of the war.

1946: Winston Churchill warns of an "Iron Curtain" spreading across Eastern Europe.

1951: Julius and Ethel Rosenberg are convicted and sentenced to death for passing U.S. atomic secrets to the Soviets.

1953: The people of East Berlin revolt against communist rule, but the uprising is suppressed by Soviet and East German tanks.

1956: Elvis Presley appears on Ed Sullivan's *Toast of the Town,* where he performs "Hound Dog" and "Love Me Tender" before a mostly female audience. Nationwide, 54 million people watch the performance, setting a new record.

1956: By now firmly established as the Soviet leader, Nikita Khrushchev denounces the crimes of his predecessor and mentor, Josef Stalin.

1956: First aerial testing of the hydrogen bomb at Bikini Atoll. The blast is so powerful—the equivalent of 10 million tons of TNT—that it actually results in the infusion of protons to atomic nuclei to create two new elements, einsteinium and fermium, which have atomic numbers of 99 and 100, respectively.

1956: Egypt seizes control of the Suez Canal, and Israel attacks Egypt on the Sinai Peninsula. Britain and France intervene against Egypt and only relent under U.S. pressure.

1961: President Eisenhower steps down, warning of a "military-industrial complex" in his farewell speech, and 43-year-old John F. Kennedy becomes the youngest elected president in U.S. history. Three months later, he launches an unsuccessful invasion of Cuba at the Bay of Pigs.

1966: In August, Mao Zedong launches the "Great Proletarian Cultural Revolution," which rapidly plunges China into chaos as armed youths plunder the countryside, rooting out suspected foreign collaborators and anti-Chinese elements. Along with rifles and other weapons, these Red Guards are armed with copies of Mao's "Little Red Book."

1971: East Pakistan declares its independence, as the new nation of Bangladesh, from West Pakistan (now simply known as Pakistan); civil war, exacerbated by famine and a cholera epidemic in Bangladesh, ensues.

Event and Its Context

The Revolution

In 1956 the Twentieth Congress of the Soviet Union Communist Party denounced Stalin's crimes and personality cult,

Janos Kádár. The Library of Congress.

and a wave of changes stalked the Eastern bloc. In Hungary, Matyas Rákosi, the Stalinist chairman of the Hungarian Workers' Party, had to resign after being accused of imposing draconian economic measures on the workers and practising state terrorism against dissidents. Rákosi was replaced by Erno Gerö, who was, however, unable to cope with the increasing political agitation. On 22 October 1956 the Petöfi Circle, a student debate club within the Young Communist Organization, called for a demonstration in Budapest. Demands included the replacement of Gerö by Imre Nagy; better labor conditions, free elections, freedom of speech, the suppression of compulsory study of Russian, the withdrawal of the Soviet troops, and political neutrality.

Workers from industrial areas of Budapest joined the students. Riots started and the demonstrators occupied government and party buildings, newspapers, and radio stations. The army hesitated: some of the units passed to the demonstrators' side, and others remained in the barracks or deserted. On 24 October a Hungarian Workers' Party meeting dismissed Gerö and nominated Nagy as prime minister, and elected Janos Kádár, another communist who was critical of Stalinism, to be the party's chairman. Almost at the same time, Soviet troops formally entered Budapest to "restore order," and gained full control of the city.

Imre Nagy. The Library of Congress.

On 27 October, Nagy formed a coalition government of communists and noncommunists that freed political prisoners, dissolved the state security police, and initiated negotiations with the Soviets. The Soviets withdrew from Budapest on 28 October with no apparent objections to the course that the Hungarian government had taken, as the agreements indicated that Hungary would respect its commercial and military agreements with the Soviet Union and the peoples' democracies. However, on 1 November, Nagy declared neutrality and Hungary withdrew from the Warsaw Pact. Then, Kádár and the other communist members of the cabinet resigned after accusing Nagy of losing control of the situation to nationalists and reactionaries. On 4 November the Red Army entered Budapest again, and a new pro-Soviet government, headed by Kádár, took power. Nagy sought refuge in the Yugoslav Embassy and agreed to go into exile. However, as he left the embassy, he was arrested. He was executed in 1958.

The Agents of the Revolution: Revolutionary and Workers' Councils

After Nagy took power, revolutionary councils and workers' councils formed throughout Hungary to support the revolution. These organizations worked together very closely by means of territorial councils in the provinces and industrial areas. The nature of the workers' and revolutionary councils varied with regard to their social composition, their activities, and their objectives.

The workers' councils were based in factories, mines, and other centers of production. The councils comprised all the workers in the case of a small factory, whereas in bigger ones, the elected representatives attended the council. Despite their original lack of coordination, all workers' councils dismissed the much-hated Rákosian "factory triangles" (composed of the director of the factory, the party secretary, and the trade union representative) and campaigned for the end of centralized economy, direct control of the companies, reform of the trade unions, and better labor conditions.

Whereas the workers' councils focused on trade union demands, the revolutionary councils had a broader political scope. Their focus was not the industrial areas but state administration, the army, the universities, the media, and other social and government institutions. The revolutionary councils wholeheartedly supported the workers' councils and demanded neutrality, free elections, freedom of speech, cessation of Warsaw Pact membership, and the withdrawal of the Soviets.

The Coordination of the Councils and the Second Soviet Intervention

Starting on 25 October, territorial councils, also called central or national councils, formed across Hungary. These groups were particularly active in industrial areas such as Debrecen, Dunapentele, Györ, and Budapest's XI and XIII districts, and in the Csepel iron and steel complex. One of the most active territorial councils was the Transdanubian National Council (TNC), a coordinating body of revolutionary and workers' councils based in Györ that controlled all of western Hungary.

The army and the police assisted with the founding of the TNC after demonstrators in Györ pulled down Soviet emblems and called for Western military intervention. One of the TNC's leading members was Béla Kóvacs, the former chairman of the Smallholders Party (an antifascist political force that had acted as a satellite of the communists from 1949). Kóvacs joined Nagy's government on 27 October, as did Petöfi Party member István Bivó, who was the ideologue of the Budapest Central Council.

After the second Soviet intervention on 4 November, the TNC was isolated from the capital and neutralized. The Central Workers' Council, an association of the Ujpest Revolutionary Council, and the workers' councils of Csepel and the XI and XIII districts, which counted on the support of the students' and intellectuals' councils, however, offered further resistance in Budapest. The Central Workers' Council refused to recognise Kádár's government and pursued a program of democratization and national independence. Demands included the return of Nagy to office; free elections "with the participation of all parties which recognise the Socialist conquests and collective property of the means of production"; and Hungary's withdrawal from the Warsaw Pact, to be substituted by bilateral treaties with the USSR and the peoples' democracies.

On 12 November, with Budapest paralyzed by strikes, Kádár issued a decree that limited the activity of the revolutionary councils to a consultative role and declared workers' councils illegal beyond single factories. Meanwhile, organized groups of Kádárist workers began to appear in the factories, and students and intellectuals continued to demand the return of Nagy and the withdrawal of the Soviets. These internal divisions, together with repression, soon finished any effective opposition to Kádár. By January most of the territorial and revolutionary councils had dissolved and the new government had gained full control of the country.

Two Views of the Hungarian Revolution

The majority view in the West presented the councils' experience as a spontaneous exercise of democracy. For example, Balasz Nagy, a former member of the Budapest's Central Council, claimed from exile in France that "the Hungarian Revolution essentially meant a workers' struggle" against Stalinist tyranny and the cold war status quo. Meanwhile, those in the Soviet bloc and the Western communist parties regarded the event as a counterrevolution carried out by demagogic, nationalist, and populist forces that had infiltrated the councils, taking advantage of the workers' anger against Rákosi and his period of Stalinist terror. "Pasionaria," the head of the Spanish Communist Party, compared the Hungarian revolution with Franco's fascist rebellion in Spain and the Red Army with the International Brigades. In her view, "The sectarian swanky behaviour of the leaders of the Hungarian Workers' Party . . . helped the Fascists to set off the counter-revolutionary terror."

Other Western communist leaders offered a similar interpretation. However, they could not halt dissident interpretations within their own organizations. So far the Soviet Union had been the main reference point for the bulk of the European left. The repression of the Hungarian revolution (which many people in the West regarded as a real socialist experience), however, also marked the definitive dethronement of the Soviet Union as the standard-bearer of radical virtue.

Key Players

Bivó, Itsván (1911–1979): Historian, sociologist, and politician, during the 1930s Bivó opposed Admiral Miklós Horthy's pro-Nazi dictatorship and became a representative of the so-called Populist Movement, a 1930s sociological trend that sought for a third way between Hungarian nationalism and Bolshevism. In 1956 Bivó became a leading figure of the Petöfi Party and was nominated as minister of state in Nagy's cabinet. He was arrested in 1957 and sentenced to life imprisonment.

Kádár, Janos (1912–1989): Kádár joined the Communist Party in 1931 and became a leading member of the Hungarian inland clandestine communist organization. He served as minister of interior during Rákosi's rule until he was purged in 1950. Nagy freed and rehabilitated him in 1954, and they worked together against Rákosi until 1 November 1956. Kádár took power three days later and remained the Hungarian leader until 1988.

Nagy, Imre (1896–1958): Politician, scholar, a lifelong socialist militant, Nagy fought with the Bolsheviks during the Russian Civil War and returned to Hungary in 1922. He went on exile in 1928 and became a member of the Hungarian communist leadership in Moscow. After World War II Nagy returned to Hungary and occupied different positions in the government, the parliament, and the party. He was elected prime minister from 1953 to 1955, coexisting with Rákosi until the latter expelled him from the party. Nagy returned to power for a brief period during the 1956 revolution. After the Soviet intervention, he was deported to Romany, judged, and executed in 1958.

Rákosi, Matyas (1892–1971): A politician, Rákosi was a founding member of the Hungarian Communist Party and participated in Bela Kun's government during the 1919 revolution. After Kun's fall, Rákosi went into exile, but he returned to Hungary in 1924 to lead the underground communist organization. He was arrested in 1925 and remained in prison until 1940, when he went into exile in Moscow; he remained there until 1945. In 1948 Rákosi was elected chairman of the Hungarian Workers' Party and became prime minister in 1952. After the 1956 uprising, he went into exile in the USSR. He was expelled from the party in 1962.

See also: *Poznan Workers' Riots.*

BIBLIOGRAPHY

Books

Berecz, János. *1956: Contrarrevolución en Hungría, Palabras y Armas.* Budapest, Hungary: Tesys, 1988.

Fejtö, François. *Hongria 1956, Socialisme I Llibertat.* Barcelona, Spain: Edició de Materials, 1966.

Halász, Zoltán. *Historia de Hungría.* Budapest, Hungary: Corvina, 1973.

Hungría Informe de la Comisión Especial de las Naciones Unidas. Buenos Aires, Brazil: Ágora, 1957.

Kádár, Jaános. *Algunas Enseñanzas Sobre la Construcción del Socialismo en Hungría.* Budapest, Hungary: Budapress, 1981.

———. *Socialismo y Democracia en Hungría: Discursos, Artículos y Entrevistas, 1957–1982.* Budapest, Hungary: Corvina Kiadó, 1984.

Mercier, Louis. *La Revolución Popular Húngara, Hechos y Documentos.* Buenos Aires, Brazil: Editorial Reconstruir, 1957.

Nagy, Balasz. *La Formación del Consejo Central Obrero de Budapest, 1956.* Barcelona, Spain: Crítica Comunista, 1981.

Periodicals

Ibárruri, Dolores. "No Podemos ser Neutrales Frente al Fascismo." *Mundo Obrero* 25, no. 10 (November–December 1956).

Ruiz de Azúa, Estíbaliz. *Hungría 1956.* Historia 16, Cuadernos del Mundo Actual, Grupo 16. Madrid, Spain: 1994.

—Juan José Gómez Gutiérrez

I

Indonesian Communist Party and Trade Unions Suppressed

Indonesia 1927–1966

Synopsis

The Indonesian Communist Party (PKI) was formed in 1920. Because of its opposition to Dutch imperialism, the PKI suffered much hostility from the colonial government. The PKI fomented revolutions in Java in November 1926 and in Sumatra in January 1927. Soon after, the Indonesian government outlawed the PKI and exiled some of its leaders. The PKI was reestablished on 21 October 1945. In November 1946 the *Sentral Organisasi Buruh Seluruh Indonesia* or the All-Indonesia Organization of Trade Unions (SOBSI), which embraced communist ideology, was founded. On 11 August 1948 Sardjono-Alimin Musso, one of the exiled communist leaders, returned from the Soviet Union. He tried to enlarge the PKI by including other socialist parties under its umbrella. This led to the communist rebellion in Madiun in 1948. In this rebellion, Musso was killed. In July 1950 Dipa Nusantara Aidit, another exiled communist, returned to Indonesia and in 1951 assumed leadership of the organization. Sensing a threat from the PKI, the United States began to support a military dictatorship over Indonesian communists in the early 1960s. The killing of six generals by an Indonesian Army faction on 30 October 1965 led to the mass murder of PKI supporters and destroyed the Communist Party and trade unions in Indonesia.

Timeline

1925: Released from Landsberg Prison, Adolf Hitler is a national celebrity, widely regarded as an emerging statesman who offers genuine solutions to Germany's problems. This year, he publishes the first volume of *Mein Kampf* (My Struggle), which he dictated in prison to trusted confederate Rudolf Hess. The second and final volume of Hitler's opus, a mixture of autobiography, "history," and racial rant, will appear two years later.

1936: Hitler uses the Summer Olympics in Berlin as an opportunity to showcase Nazi power and pageantry, but the real hero of the games is the African American track star Jesse Owens.

1942: At the Wannsee Conference, Nazi leaders formulate the "final solution to the Jewish question": a systematic campaign of genocide on a massive scale. By the time the Holocaust ends, along with the war itself, the Nazis will have killed some 6 million Jews, and as many as 6 million other victims in their death camps and slave-labor camps.

1945: April sees the death of three leaders: Roosevelt passes away on 12 April; the Italians execute Mussolini and his mistress on 28 April; and Hitler (along with Eva Braun, propaganda minister Josef Goebbels, and Goebbels's family) commits suicide on 30 April.

1947: The Marshall Plan is established to assist European nations in recovering from the war.

1948: Israel becomes a nation and is immediately attacked by a coalition of Arab countries. Despite being outnumbered, Israel will win the war in the following year—as it will win many another war against larger forces mobilized by its hostile neighbors.

1955: The Warsaw Pact is signed by the Soviet Union and its satellites in eastern Europe.

1955: African and Asian nations meet at the Bandung Conference in Indonesia, inaugurating the "non-aligned" movement of Third World countries.

1956: By now firmly established as the Soviet leader, Nikita Khrushchev denounces the crimes of his predecessor and mentor, Josef Stalin.

1956: First aerial testing of the hydrogen bomb at Bikini Atoll creates a blast so powerful—the equivalent of 10 million tons of TNT—that it actually results in the infusion of protons to atomic nuclei to create two new elements, einsteinium and fermium, which have atomic numbers of 99 and 100, respectively.

1961: Almost overnight in August, East Germany builds the Berlin Wall, ostensibly to protect against invasion from West Berlin, but in fact to prevent East Berliners from escaping.

1968: After Czechoslovakia adopts a more democratic, popular regime, Soviet and Warsaw Pact forces invade to crush the uprising.

1971: Taiwan is ousted from the United Nations so that China can take its place, both in the General Assembly and as a permanent member of the Security Council. In the next year, President Nixon will make an unprecedented visit to China, where he meets with an aging Mao.

Event and Its Context

Background

Indonesia, which had been known as the archipelago or the Dutch East Indies, was colonized by the Dutch from 1596 until 1945. During this period, the Dutch cultivated spices and crops for export back to their own country and demanded high taxes from the peasants. The Dutch also established business enterprises that exploited the peasants and laborers in the production of export crops and mining. An example of this was the management and exploitation of the archipelago's oil resources by Royal Dutch Shell.

Although the Soeharto regime often associated Indonesians of Chinese descent with the PKI or communism in general in

Indonesian President Soeharto. AP/Wide World Photos. Reproduced by permission.

Indonesia, the Indonesian communist party was in fact established by Europeans and Indonesian Muslims. Movements such as the Social Democratic Association of the Indies (ISDV) and *Sarekat Islam* (Islamic Union) spurred the growth of a Communist Party in Indonesia. ISDV was a Communist Party founded by some young Dutch activists; *Sarekat Islam* was established by local Javanese in order to protect Javanese merchants from the more powerful non-Javanese traders. Although *Sarekat Islam* did not espouse anything like an orthodox Marxist ideology, some of this movement's ideas were in fact quite similar to the classical Marxism that formed the ideological background of the ISDV.

The PKI was founded in 1920 with the support of ISDV and *Sarekat Islam*. The main aims of the PKI were to challenge the imperialism and capitalism of the Dutch government by building trade unions and to promote the importance of political consciousness among the peasants. Nevertheless, during the next six and a half years, the PKI and *Sarekat Islam* often had ideological disagreements. *Sarekat Islam* was becoming more religious rather than nationalistic, and the efforts of the PKI to expand its membership base had offended some members of *Sarekat Islam*.

PKI Outlawed, Reestablished

Because of its openly nationalist and socialist ideologies, the PKI had to face increasing levels of repression from the Dutch government, which led to the communist revolutions in 1926 and 1927. The Dutch colonial authorities easily sup-

pressed these revolutions. Soon after, the PKI was outlawed. The former members of PKI, however, continued their underground activities in opposition to the colonial government. The declaration of Indonesian independence on 17 August 1945, with Soekarno as the first president, brought a wind of positive change to left-wing political movements in Indonesia. On 21 October 1945 the PKI was reestablished. Some of the members of the PKI also took part in establishing the *Sentral Organisasi Buruh Seluruh Indonesia*, or the All-Indonesia Organization of Trade Unions (SOBSI), to foster solidarity among workers in opposing the Dutch capitalism in Indonesia. Although the members of SOBSI were not exclusively communists, the organization had a leftist ideology.

On his return from exile in 1948, Musso became the new leader of the PKI and immediately started to assimilate other communist parties into the PKI. These actions led to a communist rebellion, which started on 18 September 1948 in Madiun, during which members of the PKI opposed the army and other groups that had tried to challenge the PKI's ideology. Soekarno, suspecting Musso of being a traitor who wanted to overthrow his government, quickly sent his troops to recapture Madiun. Musso died in battle at the end of October, along with thousands of PKI members.

From 1948 until 1951 the activities of Indonesian communists were very irregular and unorganized. In 1950 some women were able to organize themselves and establish a communist group called *Gerwis*. One of the most important leaders during this period was an Indonesian of Chinese descent, Tan Ling Djie.

The arrival of Aidit, who became the leader of the PKI in 1951, brought a new phase to the party. Aidit was much more careful in preparing his plans. He adopted Marxism-Leninism and tried to adapt this ideology to the sociopolitical context of Indonesia. Between January 1951 and March 1954 the number of full members of the PKI increased tenfold. By August 1965, with more than 20 million members and active supporters, the PKI had become the largest communist party in the world outside Russia and China. Aidit was also supportive of the women's movement and women's participation in the party.

Aidit noticed that although Indonesia had declared its independence, the workers were still exploited by Dutch enterprises, which remained in control of the Indonesian economy. Exports and imports were also controlled by foreign companies. According to Aidit, some feudal remnants had to be abolished in Indonesia. Such feudalism facilitated monopoly of ownership of land and increased the poverty of the peasants, thus constraining the development of the Indonesian economy and society.

Revitalized PKI Attacks Outside Interests

In December 1957 workers and peasants attacked Dutch factories, plantations, and banks. Workers of SOBSI seized the Dutch bakeries and banks in Java and in Sumatra. When the Indonesian government was able to take over the Dutch businesses at the end of 1950s, the PKI started to criticize American imperialism in Indonesia.

Meanwhile, Soekarno had grown less and less attentive to the peasants. Instead, he was busy with his own political career.

Muslim student protesters, Jakarta, Indonesia. © Hulton/Getty Images. Reproduced by permission.

To combine and control the competing ideologies in Indonesia, Soekarno instituted "Guided Democracy" and his concept of *Nasionalisme, Agama dan Komunisme* or Nationalism, Religion and Communism (NASAKOM) in July 1959. This concept sought to combine the three central pillars of nationalism, religion, and communism into one ideological platform. PKI leaders supported this and became closer to Soekarno. This loyalty to Soekarno made the PKI leaders less critical of the first Indonesian president.

In late 1964 and 1965, when fierce clashes between peasants and landowners occurred in Java and Sumatra, the PKI leaders did not devote much attention to the peasants. Instead, these leaders urged the peasants and workers not to be impatient and pleaded with the people to support the government of Soekarno.

In the meantime, the actions and growth of the communist movement in Indonesia had attracted the attention of the United States. Starting in 1957, the American government began to mobilize enormous financial resources to aid antileftist forces in Asia. The CIA began to undertake surveillance of Indonesian communists in the early 1960s.

Massacre of Generals

The murder of six generals on 30 September 1965, led by a faction of the Indonesian Army under the command of Lt.

Col. Untung, eventually brought about the mass murder of communists in Indonesia. Another general who was also on the list of those to be murdered, Abdul Haris Nasution, managed to escape, but his daughter was killed. The news spread that the PKI had planned the murders and that the generals had been tortured and sexually molested by communist women before being executed. This accusation, combined with a list of Indonesian communists provided by the CIA, led Soeharto to destroy the PKI. It is surprising that Soeharto, who was also a general at that time, was not among those murdered by Lt. Col. Untung's faction. This fact has raised some suspicion as to whether the murders were in fact initiated by Soeharto as part of his plan to take over Soekarno's government.

On 6 October 1965 Soekarno called for national unity to bring about an end to the violence and civil war. Soeharto's people became uncontrollable in killing communist supporters. PKI leaders asked the members to remain calm. When thousands of peasants, workers, and communist supporters had been killed within a few months following the murders of 30 September, the PKI leaders still did not fight back but awaited Soekarno's orders. Finally, on 24 November 1965 the army captured and murdered Aidit. About two million people were killed, and hundreds of thousands more were imprisoned without trial during the brutal hunting of the communist supporters and peasants that lasted until the end of 1966. Some communist

447

women were raped repeatedly, and many were murdered. The mass murder was so severe that it created sanitation problems in East Java as some rivers were reddened by blood and clogged with corpses.

On 11 March 1966 Soekarno gave Soeharto some power to take whatever steps were necessary to stop the chaos in Indonesia and demanded personal protection from Soeharto. Soeharto's gate to the presidency was then wide open. In September 1966 Indonesia rejoined the United Nations. In 1967 Soeharto became the second Indonesian president. He broke the relationship with Beijing, developed friendly relationships with Western countries, and welcomed American investors. The communist people and their families remained subject to strict control under Soeharto's rule, which was known as the "New Order period." The left-wing movement in Indonesia was crushed, and the government welcomed capitalist investment. Laborers and peasants became depoliticized, and school textbooks contained stories of cruelty and betrayal perpetrated by communists against the Indonesian populace.

Key Players

Aidit, Dipa Nusantara (1923–1965): Aidit became the chairman of the Indonesian Communist Party (PKI) in 1951. Under his leadership, the PKI became one of the largest communist parties in the world. Aidit was killed during the military coup in 1965.

Musso, Sardjono-Alimin (1897–1948): Musso led the PKI in the 1920s and at the end of 1940s. He was a strong supporter of Stalin and the Communist International in Moscow. He was executed by the Republic of Indonesia army in the wake of the Madiun rebellion at the end of 1948.

Soeharto (1921–): Born in the Yogyakarta region of Central Java in 1921, Soeharto became the second Indonesian president in 1967. He led the liquidation of the PKI and millions of its members and supporters. After seizing the presidency from Soekarno, Soeharto ruled the country until 1998.

Soekarno (1901–1970): Soekarno was born on 6 June 1901 in Blitar, East Java. He was the first president of Indonesia. He was close to Aidit and some communist leaders during Aidit's period. After the military coup, Soekarno was forced to give up his presidency to Soeharto. Soekarno died in political exile.

BIBLIOGRAPHY

Books

Corsino, MacArthur. *A Communist Revolutionary Movement as an International State-Actor: The Case of the PKI-Aidit.* Singapore: Institute of Southeast Asian Studies, 1982.

Edman, Peter. *"Communism a la Aidit:" The Indonesian Communist Party Under D. N. Aidit, 1950–1965.* Townsville, Queensland, N.Z.: Centre for Southeast Asian Studies, James Cook University of North Queensland, 1987.

Hindley, Donald. *The Communist Party of Indonesia, 1951–1963.* Berkeley: University of California Press, 1964.

McVey, Ruth. *The Rise of Indonesian Communism.* Ithaca, NY: Indonesia Project, Southeast Asia Program, Cornell University Press, 1965.

McVey, Ruth, and Benedict Anderson. *Preliminary Analysis of the October 1, 1965 Coup in Indonesia: Interm Report,* 3rd ed. Ithaca, NY: Southeast Asia Program, Cornell University Press, 1990.

McVey, Ruth, and Harry J. Benda, eds. *The Communist Uprisings of 1926–1927 in Indonesia: Key Documents.* Ithaca, NY: Southeast Asia Program, Cornell University Press, 1960.

Swift, Ann. *The Road to Madiun: The Indonesian Communist Uprising of 1948.* Ithaca, NY: Southeast Asia Program, Cornell University Press, 1989.

Törnquist, Olle. *Dilemmas of Third-World Communism: The Destruction of the PKI in Indonesia.* London: Zed Books, 1984.

Other

Anderson, Benedict, and Ruth McVey. "What Happened in Indonesia?" *The New York Review of Books.* 1 June 1978 [cited 11 October 2002]. <http://www.nybooks.com/articles/8144>.

Poulgrain, Greg. "Who Plotted the 1965 Coup?" *Inside Indonesia,* no. 57, January–March 1999 [cited 11 October 2002]. <http://www.serve.com/inside/edit57/poulg.htm>.

—Soe Tjen Marching

Industrial Workers of Africa

South Africa 1917

Synopsis

In 1917 militant workers of the International Socialist League formed the Industrial Workers of Africa (IWA), the first union for black workers in South African history. The anarchist union, based on the model of the Industrial Workers of the World (IWW), aimed to abolish the capitalist system and defend workers' rights. At a time of bloody battles between labor and the white capitalist class, the IWA helped form a leftist block that for a time managed to pull the middle-class African National Congress further left. When the white supremacist government repressed striking workers in June 1918, the IWA called for a general strike; the strike was called off and some leaders were arrested. A dock workers' strike in 1919 also failed, but it set the foundation for greater cooperation among workers in the sector. The union had a profound effect on both militant leftist white workers and workers of color and eventually spread its internationalist, antiracist militancy to the working class of neighboring countries.

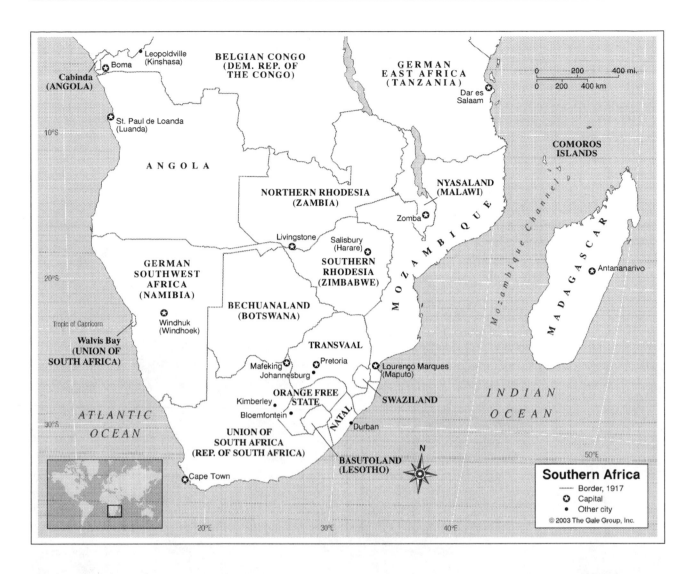

Southern Africa
- - - - - Border, 1917
✪ Capital
• Other city
© 2003 The Gale Group, Inc.

Timeline

1897: The Zionist movement is established under the leadership of Theodor Herzl.

1902: Second Anglo-Boer War ends in victory for Great Britain. It is a costly victory, however, resulting in the loss of more British lives (5,774) than any conflict between 1815 and 1914. The war also sees the introduction of concentration camps, used by the British to incarcerate Boer civilians.

1905: Russian Revolution of 1905 occurs. Following the "bloody Sunday" riots before the Winter Palace in St. Petersburg in January, revolution spreads throughout Russia, in some places spurred on by newly formed workers' councils, or soviets. Among the most memorable incidents of the revolt is the mutiny aboard the battleship *Potemkin.* Suppressed by the czar, the revolution brings an end to liberal reforms and thus sets the stage for the larger revolutions of 1917.

1911: In China, revolutionary forces led by Sun Yat-sen bring an end to more than 2,100 years of imperial rule.

1915: A German submarine sinks the *Lusitania,* killing 1,195, including 128 U.S. citizens. Theretofore, many Americans had been sympathetic toward Germany, but the incident begins to turn the tide of U.S. sentiment toward the Allies.

1917: The intercepted "Zimmermann Telegram" reveals a plot by the German government to draw Mexico into an alliance against the United States in return for a German promise to return the southwestern U.S. territories taken in the Mexican War. Three months later on 6 April, in response to German threats of unrestricted submarine warfare, the United States declares war on Germany.

1917: On both the Western Front and in the Middle East, the tide of the war begins to turn against the Central Powers. The arrival of U.S. troops, led by General Pershing, in France in June greatly boosts morale and reinforces exhausted Allied forces. Meanwhile, Great Britain scores two major victories against the Ottoman Empire as T. E. Lawrence leads an Arab revolt in Baghdad in March, and troops under Field Marshal Edmund Allenby take Jerusalem in December.

449

Workers arrive for work at sugar refinery, Natal, South Africa. © Hulton/Getty Images. Reproduced by permission.

1919: With the formation of the Third International (Comintern), the Bolshevik government of Russia establishes its control over communist movements worldwide.

1923: Conditions in Germany worsen as inflation skyrockets and France, attempting to collect on coal deliveries promised at Versailles, marches into the Ruhr basin. In November an obscure political group known as the National Socialist German Workers' Party attempts to stage a coup, or putsch, in a Munich beer hall. The revolt fails, and in 1924 the party's leader, Adolf Hitler, will receive a prison sentence of five years. He will only serve nine months, however, and the incident will serve

to attract attention for him and his party, known as the Nazis.

1927: Stalin arranges to have Trotsky expelled from the Communist Party.

Event and Its Context

Industrialism in South Africa

The seed of industrialism—and resulting industrial unionism—in South Africa was planted with the 1867 discovery of

Nightmare in the Belgian Congo

By the end of the 1880s, the three most significant slave-based societies of modern times—New World systems that, like Greece and Rome, were built on slave labor—all had outlawed slavery. First was the United States in 1865, then Cuba 20 years later. When slavery in Brazil ended in 1887, optimists seemed justified in believing that the institution was finished. The reality was less cheering, and in fact the coming century would see the rebirth of slavery in ghastly form under the auspices of totalitarian governments in Germany, Russia, and elsewhere.

Even in the same year Cuba outlawed slavery, the practice gained new and terrible life in the heart of Africa. Promising to protect the people of the Congo from Arab slave-traders, King Leopold of Belgium in 1885 assumed control over the vast country, which he proceeded to turn into his personal colony. Over the next 23 years, Leopold ruled the absurdly named "Congo Free State" with almost unimaginable cruelty.

The Belgian Congo, an area 75 times as large as Belgium itself, was rich in natural resources and treasures, which Leopold exploited by using slave laborers. Overseers set impossibly high quotas for workers, and when the latter failed to meet them, would cut off their hands. Leopold's operatives also kidnapped women and children, and in the latter days of Leopold's rule, resorted to wholesale slaughter of populations that failed to produce. In the end, they killed about half the Congo's population of 20 million before the Belgian government forced Leopold to turn over control of the colony in 1908. Leopold himself never set foot in the Congo.

Source: Adam Hochschild. *King Leopold's Ghost: A Story of Greed, Terror, and Heroism in Colonial Africa.* Boston: Houghton Mifflin, 1998.

—Judson Knight

diamonds at Kimberley. The appearance of mines, which increased after the discovery of gold on the Witwatersrand in 1886, drastically changed the way black Africans earned their livelihood. Moreover, the arrival of hundreds of thousands of European, American, and Australian workers formed new cities like Johannesburg almost overnight. In 1886 Johannesburg housed some 3,000 prospectors; by 1913 it had 250,000. South Africa in the early twentieth century was clearly a multicultural society, including black Africans, whites, "Coloureds" (i.e., racially mixed), and a considerable population of Indian origin. Indigenous Africans were not able to opt out of the changes brought by the economic model shift; the 1913 Land Act forced native peoples off the land they occupied and used for sustenance. New legislation forced them to migrate to white-controlled urban centers to work as miners so that they could pay taxes to the white-controlled government. Moreover, black workers travelling outside demarcated areas were required to carry passes. Given the increasing violation of the rights and

freedoms of Africans, a coalition of tribal chiefs and religious leaders founded the African National Congress (ANC) in 1912.

IWW Influence

Socialists organizing in twentieth-century South Africa envisioned an important role for anarchists and revolutionary syndicalists. Two such groups appeared in Johannesburg in 1910: the Socialist Labour Party (SLP; in March) and a branch of the Industrial Workers of the World (IWW; in June). Although the IWW, founded in 1905, was best known for its success among workers in the United States, its influence was also felt among workers in South Africa, Namibia, Zambia, and Zimbabwe (then Rhodesia). In the Union of South Africa, founded as a British colony in 1910 and ruled by a white supremacist government, IWW goals and organizational practices had a particularly important influence on the radical press and early labor movement. Although the South African branch of the IWW was all but dead by 1914, the IWW model in the 1910s spawned at least five South African unions dedicated to organizing workers of color. The most renowned of these was the Industrial Workers of Africa (IWA), founded in 1917 as the region's first-ever union for black workers. The union's motto was *Sifuna Zonke!* ("We want everything!").

The black trade union movement was more than 20 years in the making. In 1896, when mine managers lowered the wages of black mineworkers, the workers responded with the first recorded strike of black workers in the sector. In 1913 parts of the African labor force joined a general strike by white miners that forced South Africa's "Randlords" to the bargaining table; for many white leftist militants, the 1913 strike underscored the need for cooperation with and organization of native workers. As the real earning power of wages continued to decline, the miners' discontent spread to other industrial sectors. In addition to lower wages, the native African workers suffered miserable working conditions and the humiliation of the pass law, which required blacks to carry an "internal passport." By the 1910s, as radical socialist ideals were mobilizing white workers, some organizers saw the need for a strong, militant labor union composed of Africans.

The IWA found its roots in the International Socialist League (ISL), which espoused IWW-style revolutionary syndicalism and the abolition of racist oppression in South Africa. The ISL was founded in 1915 by militant white workers who opposed World War I and the conservative, racist policies of the all-white South African Labour Party and supporting craft unions. In the 1910s the ISL was South Africa's largest, most important revolutionary socialist group. From the beginning, the league attracted black workers with talk of "One Big Union" that would break "the bounds of craft and race and sex," to bring on the "lockout of the capitalist class." An October 1915 editorial in the ISL's weekly publication, *The International*, stressed the need of internationalism to bring "fullest rights" to the working class and the oppressed black population, declaring that "by dealing resolutely in consonance with socialist principles with the native question, it will succeed in shaking South African capitalism to its foundation."

The ISL, in addition to reaching out to existing black organizations such as the ANC, began organizing black and mixed-race workers in 1917. March brought the formation of the Indian Workers Industrial Union in Durban. In 1918 the diamond mining town of Kimberley saw the league found a horse drivers' union and a Clothing Workers Industrial Union (which later spread to Johannesburg). In Cape Town that year, the Industrial Socialist League (an ISL sister organization founded in 1918) formed a Sweet and Jam Workers Industrial Union.

Founding of the IWA

On 19 July 1917 a group of Africans and white radicals heeded a call in Johannesburg to discuss "matters of common interest between white and native workers," namely capitalism and class struggle. The meetings, held in a small room behind the general store on the corner of Fox and McLaren Streets, were led by international socialists (including local IWW founder Andrew Dunbar). The laborers discussed the need for unionization of African workers as a means of earning higher wages and abolishing the pass system. The meeting was deemed successful enough to spawn weekly study meetings. Given police scrutiny, the meetings were kept discreet. As one worker said, "We are treated by *sjambok* [whip] and gaol, that is why you see this hall is not full." Nonetheless, on 27 September an all-African committee converted the study groups of fewer than 200 participants into a union called the Industrial Workers of Africa. It was the first black trade union in South African history.

That month the IWA issued its manifesto, "Listen, Workers, Listen!" Addressed to "Workers of the Bantu race," it asked black workers why they lived in slavery, why they must carry passes—under penalty of imprisonment—to move about, why they were jailed for refusing to work, why they were herded "like cattle into compounds." The answer: "Because you are toilers of the earth," whom the government and police wanted to squeeze for profit. The manifesto called for unity among all workers to break "the bonds and chains of the capitalist" and to shed ethnic identities such as Basuto, Zulu, or Shangaan in favor of a common bond: that of laborer.

IWA Actions

Soon thereafter, Talbot Williams of the African Peoples Organization adopted IWA and IWW principles in a speech calling for black laborers to organize. In 1918 the International Socialist League held the first May Day rally geared mainly toward workers of color; one of the speakers was IWA member T. W. Thibedi. That year saw black and white workers carrying out unprecedented strikes across South Africa, with "capitalists and workers . . . at war everywhere in every country."

Although the main African nationalist group of the time, the ANC, was generally regarded by labor as a "sleepy" petit-bourgeois organization molded to the wishes of liberal whites, IWA militants such as Hamilton Kraai and Rueben Cetiwe carved out a leftist, prolabor bloc that pushed the organization further left. In solidarity with 152 striking African municipal workers jailed in June 1918, the ANC declared a mass rally of black workers on 10 June. Acting on an IWA initiative, a committee of Industrial Workers, International Socialists, and congressmen began organizing for a general strike on 2 July. The workers were to demand a raise of one shilling per day and for the "Africa which they deserved."

The strike was a failure. Weak organization led to its cancellation, though thousands of miners who had not been notified of the cancellation came out anyway. The government arrested a handful of International Socialist, IWA, and ANC activists, making it the first time in South African history that black and white activists were indicted jointly for political activities. Although there was not enough evidence to convict the activists, the struggle was abandoned in July after the conservative faction regained control over the ANC.

Kraai and Cetiwe, who had lost their jobs because of the trial, moved to Cape Town to start an IWA branch there. Thibedi stayed in Johannesburg, where he revived the IWA with several hundred members and supporters. In Cape Town the IWA militants helped organize a dock workers strike, whereby more than 2,000 laborers demanded higher wages and an end to food exports, which they blamed as the cause of inflation. The strike joined the IWA with the local Industrial Commercial Union and the (white) National Union of Railways and Harbour Servants in an action supported by the Industrial Socialist League. The strike ultimately failed, but it served as a basis for further cooperation among dock workers.

By 1921 the bulk of South Africa's revolutionary syndicalists had converted to Leninism and formed the Communist Party of South Africa. The IWA merged that year with the Industrial and Commercial Union and several other black unions to form the Industrial and Commercial Workers' Union of South Africa, a massive black trade union led by Clements Kadalie; peaking in 1927 at 100,000 workers throughout southern Africa, the movement saw its demise in the 1930s.

Key Players

Cetiwe, Rueben: Cetiwe, a South African, was a key African militant in the Industrial Workers of Africa (IWA). He was central to the March 1919 campaign against South Africa's pass laws.

Dunbar, Andrew (1879–1964): Dunbar, who immigrated from Scotland to South Africa in 1906, was a blacksmith and socialist organizer. In 1909 he led 2,500 strikers against the Natal railways. He held membership in the South African Labour Party, the Socialist League, the Socialist Party, and the IWW. He founded the IWW in South Africa and became its general secretary.

Kraai, Hamilton: Kraai, a South African, was a warehouse employee and a key African militant in the IWA. He was central to the March 1919 campaign against the pass laws.

Thibedi, Thomas "T. W.": A South African member of the International Socialist League, Thibedi helped found the IWA in 1917. He headed the Johannesburg branch of the IWA starting in 1918.

See also: *Miners' Strike, 1922: South Africa; Miners' Strike, 1946: South Africa.*

BIBLIOGRAPHY

Books

van der Walt, Lucien. *The IWW, Revolutionary Syndicalism and Working Class Struggle in South Africa, 1910–1921.* Durban, South Africa: Zabalaza Books, n.d.

Other

A-Infos. "Workers Solidarity Federation (South Africa) Dissolves." 26 September 1999 [cited 2 October 2002]. <http://www.ainfos.ca/99/sep/ainfos00224.html>.

Anarchist: People of Color. Chapter Four: "The Development of Socialism in Africa" [cited 2 October 2002]. <http://www.illegalvoices.org/apoc/books/aa/ch4.html>.

Comparative Studies on South Africa, Asia, and the Middle East. Illinois State University History Department [cited 2 October 2002]. <http://www.history.ilstu.edu/mtavakol/cssaame/issues/V19-1/>.

"Fifty Fighting Years." The Communist Party of South Africa 1921–1971 [cited 2 October 2002]. <http://www.sacp.org.za/docs/history/fifty1.html>.

Hirson, Baruch. "The General Strike of 1922." *Turmoil in South Africa, 1918–1922* [cited 2 October 2002]. <http://www.revolutionary-history.co.uk/supplem/Hirson/1922.html>.

Limb, Peter. "Secrecy, Solidarity, and Survival: Political Tactics and Glasnost in the Early History and Historiography of the ANC." Paper delivered at the Biennial Conference of the South African Historical Society. 11–14 July 1999 [cited 2 October 2002]. <http://www.lib.msu.edu/limb/a-z/az.secrecy.html>.

Mbeki, Govan. "The Struggle for Liberation in South Africa, 1992" [cited 2 October 2002]. <http://www.anc.org.za/books/liberation.html>.

Simons, Jack, and Ray Simons. "Class and Colour in South Africa, 1850–1950." 11 September 1968 [cited 2 October 2002]. <http://www.anc.org.za/books/ccsa.html>.

South African Anarchism [cited 2 October 2002]. <http://struggle.ws/africa/safrica.html>.

"South African Police 1917–1922." Institute of Commonwealth Studies Home Page [cited 2 October 2002]. <http://www.aim25.ac.uk/cgi-bin/search2?coll_id=4896&inst_id=16>.

van der Walt, Lucien. "Fight for Africa, Which you Deserve." The Industrial Workers of Africa in South Africa, 1917–1921 [cited 2 October 2002]. <http://flag.blackened.net/revolt/africa/safrica/iwa_history.html>.

———. "A History of the IWW in South Africa." *Bread & Roses* 7 [cited 2 October 2002]. <http://www.iww.org.uk/br/br7southafrica.htm>.

———. "The IWW, Revolutionary Syndicalism and Working Class Struggle in South Africa, 1910–1921" [cited 2 October 2002]. <http://www.zabalaza.net/pdfs/sapams/iww&revsyndic.pdf>.

—Brett Alan King

Industrial Workers of the World

United States 1905

Synopsis

At the turn of the twentieth century American laborers had been generally unionized by organizations such as the Knights of Labor and smaller organizations. The most formidable union was the 25-year-old American Federation of Labor (AFL), but it still excluded many workers from membership. Typical working conditions, particularly in industrial workplaces, were poor and dangerous. Unskilled workers, often seen as interchangeable, replaceable commodities, were at peril.

The goal of the Industrial Workers of the World (IWW) was to organize all United States workers into "one big union." Unlike other unions of the day, this union's creators did not care about race, gender, or ethnic background. What they wanted was an end to capitalism with just, equitable working conditions for all working-class people. The IWW also espoused concepts that were alien in blue-collar America, chiefly an eight-hour work day and a 40-hour week.

The creation of the IWW set into motion a vocal debate about the value of work and workers in the United States. It also drew attention to the importance of marginalized workers—African Americans, new immigrants, women, and unskilled laborers—in the national economy.

Timeline

1885: Indian National Congress is established. In the years that follow, the party will take the helm of India's independence movement.

1890: U.S. Congress passes the Sherman Antitrust Act, which in the years that follow will be used to break up large monopolies.

1895: Brothers Auguste and Louis Lumière show the world's first motion picture—*Workers Leaving the Lumière Factory*—at a café in Paris.

1898: United States defeats Spain in the three-month Spanish-American War. As a result, Cuba gains it independence, and the United States purchases Puerto Rico and the Philippines from Spain for $20 million.

1901: U.S. President William McKinley is assassinated by Leon Czolgosz, an anarchist. Vice President Theodore Roosevelt becomes president.

1903: Russia's Social Democratic Party splits into two factions: the moderate Mensheviks and the hard-line Bolsheviks. Despite their names, which in Russian mean "minority" and "majority," respectively, Mensheviks actually outnumber Bolsheviks.

1904: Russo-Japanese War, which lasts into 1905 and results in a resounding Japanese victory, begins. In Russia, the war is followed by the Revolution of 1905, which marks the beginning of the end of czarist rule; meanwhile, Japan is poised to become the first major non-western power of modern times.

Frank Tannenbaum of the Industrial Workers of the World addressing a crowd of strikers, Union Square, New York City.

1905: Russian Revolution of 1905 occurs. Following the "bloody Sunday" riots before the Winter Palace in St. Petersburg in January, revolution spreads throughout Russia, in some places spurred on by newly formed workers' councils, or soviets. Among the most memorable incidents of the revolt is the mutiny aboard the battleship *Potemkin*. Suppressed by the czar, the revolution brings an end to liberal reforms, and thus sets the stage for the larger revolution of 1917.

1905: Albert Einstein presents his special theory of relativity.

1905: In the industrial Ruhr region in Germany, 200,000 miners go on strike.

1909: National Association for the Advancement of Colored People (NAACP) is founded by W. E. B. Du Bois and a number of other prominent black and white intellectuals in New York City.

1914: On the Western Front, the first battles of the Marne and Ypres establish a line that will more or less hold for the next four years. Exuberance is still high on both sides, but will dissipate as thousands of German, French, and British soldiers sacrifice their lives in battles over a few miles of barbed wire and mud. The Eastern Front is a different story: a German victory over Russia at Tannenberg in August sets the stage for a war in which Russia will enjoy little success, and will eventually descend into chaos that paves the way for the 1917 revolutions.

Event and Its Context

Alternative to AFL Sought

At its founding, the IWW was one of three key labor organizations. The others were the AFL and the Socialist Party of America. Those who were ignored by the AFL—such as immigrants, minorities, and unskilled workers, and those disenchanted with the organization—typically gravitated to either the Socialist Party or IWW. The socialists were a political party rather than a labor union, but labor was one of the party's key platforms.

A significant contrast existed between the unionism of the AFL and that proposed by the IWW. The AFL was keen on organizing skilled workers by their specific craft. The IWW accepted all workers and planned to organize them by industry. The IWW fomented subversion of capitalism, whereas the AFL worked within the capitalist system.

A prime reason for the formation of "one big union" was to overcome the fragmentation caused by the divisions of trades into smaller unions. The IWW, in one of its informational pamphlets, gave the example of 56 unions in the 1903 Chicago packing house industry alone. The IWW advocated one single union for workers, not fragmented by craft, race, or gender. As a result, the IWW openly accepted workers who had been snubbed by the AFL. The AFL also represented only about 5 percent of American workers. Among those industries targeted by early IWW organizers were mining, timber, and shipping industries.

Another factor that contributed to the genesis of the IWW was that there had been no solidarity among existing radical groups. William "Big Bill" Haywood was the head of the Western Federation of Miners (WFM), which had survived the violent Colorado mine strikes. It was in that bloody string of confrontations that the idea of creating a single large union was born. Haywood thought there had to be a way to unite disenfranchised radicals from various active organizations in the United States. He saw it as an opportunity to unite not just those who promoted trade unionism, but politicians and activists as well. Others agreed with him.

The Continental Congress of the Working Class

Acting on a 1904 mandate from the WFM, Haywood contacted various radical leaders to ask for their support in the creation of a single union. Also in 1904 six labor leaders gathered in Chicago to discuss how to launch a new, progressive union movement based in that city. At this meeting, they decided to invite 30 different prominent radicals—including socialists and reformers—to meet in Chicago on 2 January 1905.

The agenda of this "secret conference" was "to discuss ways and means of uniting the working people of America on correct revolutionary principles." The 20 participants created an Industrial Union Manifesto. They extended an invitation to those who supported the concepts outlined in the document and who were intent on realizing them to join them for another meeting Chicago in June. Their hope was to create a new labor organization.

Brand's Hall in Chicago was the meeting place on 27 June 1905 for an estimated 200 delegates who had responded to the invitation. Attendees at the founding meeting of the Industrial Workers of the World held vastly differing viewpoints. The crowd consisted predominantly of socialists, anarchists, and radical trade unionists. Noted labor historian Melvyn A. Dubofsky called the gathering "a weird congregation of individuals and organizations." Workers from Haywood's WFM, in fact, formed the core of the gathering, which was attended by representatives of about 43 other labor organizations.

Haywood called the gathering "the Continental Congress of the working-class." In his opening address, he said the meeting would serve "to confederate the workers of this country into a

Eugene Victor Debs. The Library of Congress.

working-class movement that shall have for its purpose the emancipation of the working-class from the slave bondage of capitalism." Haywood articulated the aims of the new organization as granting the working class possession of "economic power, the means of life, in control of the machinery of production and distribution, without regard to the capitalist masters." The IWW preamble is often viewed less as a charter for a union than as a call for class warfare. It clearly stated that workers and employers had no common ground.

On the speakers' platform with Haywood were Eugene Debs, leader of the Socialist Party, Daniel De Leon, a Marxist considered by some the father of Industrial Unionism, and Mother Mary Jones, an organizer for the United Mine Workers of America. Other speakers at the conference who were key in founding the IWW were Lucy Parsons, an anarchist widow, and Father Thomas Hagerty, a Catholic priest friendly to labor. The delegates elected Charles O. Sherman, from the WFM, as the first IWW president. The Chicago meeting lasted until 8 July 1905.

In a 10 July 1905 address in Minneapolis, De Leon called the creation of the IWW "an epoch in the annals of the labor movement of America . . . a turning point in the history of the land." The text of this address—"The Preamble of the I.W.W.," which explained the organization and its ideals—was later reissued as a pamphlet under the title "Socialist Reconstruction of Society." Haywood reportedly wrote De Leon and lauded the content as "clear and convincing. I wish that a copy of it could be placed in the hands of every man and woman of the working class in this country."

Preamble to the Industrial Workers of the World Constitution

The working class and the employing class have nothing in common. There can be no peace so long as hunger and want are found among millions of the working people and the few, who make up the employing class, have all the good things of life.

Between these two classes a struggle must go on until the workers of the world organize as a class, take possession of the means of production, abolish the wage system, and live in harmony with the Earth.

We find that the centering of the management of industries into fewer and fewer hands makes the trade unions unable to cope with the ever growing power of the employing class. The trade unions foster a state of affairs which allows one set of workers to be pitted against another set of workers in the same industry, thereby helping defeat one another in wage wars. Moreover, the trade unions aid the employing class to mislead the workers into the belief that the working class have interests in common with their employers.

These conditions can be changed and the interest of the working class upheld only by an organization formed in such a way that all its members in any one industry, or in all industries if necessary, cease work whenever a strike or lockout is on in any department thereof, thus making an injury to one an injury to all.

Instead of the conservative motto, "A fair day's wage for a fair day's work," we must inscribe on our banner the revolutionary watchword, "Abolition of the wage system."

It is the historic mission of the working class to do away with capitalism. The army of production must be organized, not only for everyday struggle with capitalists, but also to carry on production when capitalism shall have been overthrown. By organizing industrially we are forming the structure of the new society within the shell of the old.

Source: *Industrial Workers of the World: A Union for All Workers.* <http://www.iww.org>.

—Judson Knight

One important principle of the IWW was direct action. Often, this is interpreted as going hand-in-hand with violence. However, direct action is worker-initiated, unmediated negotiation. As defined in early IWW literature, "The worker on the job shall tell the boss when and where he shall work, how long and for what wages and under what conditions." In addition to direct action, the tools IWW members commonly used to educate and encourage workers to rally against employers included propaganda that the organization published in pamphlets, newspapers, and magazines. They also instigated boycotts and strikes.

Women and the IWW

At this time there were indeed women working in a variety of professions. Women were commonly employed as teachers and in the textile mills, laundry operations, and other factories throughout the United States. Despite this, the AFL did not allow women in its ranks. Mother Jones, one of the prime forces in the creation of the IWW, was certainly familiar with the plight of working women.

Jones gathered and organized women to participate in mining strikes. She frequently went into workplaces to record conditions as well as to organize. She once observed women working in breweries as being "condemned to slave daily in the wash-room in wet shoes and wet clothes, surrounded with foul-mouthed, brutal foremen." Jones noted the prevalence of rheumatism and consumption among women workers, and the overbearing power of the foreman over the workers' minute-to-minute activities, including time allotted to bathroom breaks. The women, many of whom had no parents or other support system, often had to feed, clothe, and shelter themselves on a weekly salary of three dollars.

Mother Jones's presence on the dais at the 1905 convention was no mistake, nor was that of Parsons. The IWW was the first union to discuss housework and to recognize that women had jobs both inside and outside the home. The IWW was also the first union to organize domestics and sex workers. One of its earliest organizing efforts was in the textile industry. An estimated half of that industry's workers were women. Parsons edited *The Liberator*, an IWW paper, which enabled her to publicize issues of importance to women. Considered radical at the time, these positions included supporting a woman's right to divorce and to gain access to birth control. In addition to advocating for women, Parsons also lobbied for inclusion of Mexican migrant workers and other minorities in the IWW.

Politics Divides Philosophy

The IWW would become known as an anarchist-syndicalist trade union. Syndicalism encompasses both politics and economics. Its adherents believe that workers should control the means and processes of production and like anarchists believe in the abolishment of any form of state. Syndicalists advocate direct industrial action. The IWW was formed by leaders with diverse and often conflicting radical opinions, which from its inception contributed to problems and ultimately to its demise. One need only look at the IWW leadership to see how diverse the ideologies within the group must have been: Haywood espoused syndicalism, De Leon was a Marxist, Mother Jones was a staunch trade unionist, Lucy Parsons advocated anarchism, and Debs insisted on nonviolence.

Even in the 1900s, Americans thought of anarchism and socialism as synonymous. As explained by Stewart Bird, "Wobblies,"—as the union members were known—"were attracted to those anarchist currents that stress non-authoritarian structures such as cooperatives, collectives, federations, innovative schools, and decentralized industrial unions. They were hostile to more individualistic anarchists with whom they often had bitter disputes. They also came to a total rejection of Marxism-Leninism."

The primary ideological division was between Marxists and the anarchists and syndicalists. The Marxists were typically involved in either the Socialist Party of America or the Socialist Labor Party. Because its members held common views and they were founded the same year, the Socialist Party was closely allied with the IWW. Some of the leading socialists within the United States were keen on affecting change from within the AFL rather than a new organization. Neither organization, however, sent formal representatives to the founding convention.

In 1906 there was conflict about how politics fit into the union platform. There were those who thought democracy would trump direct action in bringing about meaningful change. There was also a core within the union, however, that thought direct action could be the "embryo of the new society and the revolutionary instrument for achieving it," according to Patrick Renshaw. The goal was to instigate strikes that would eventually escalate into a single, national general strike that would topple capitalism. The IWW majority was vociferously opposed to political action, which engendered controversy. The first point of contention between the Socialist Labor Party and the IWW surfaced in 1906 when the IWW started advocating the deletion of political rhetoric from the organization's preamble.

The political infighting and ideological differences may be moot, as Renshaw observed, "mainly because the Wobblies failed in their revolutionary aims." At the time, the key debate was which faction would prevail within the union. The question was one of political power: If there was to be revolution in the United States, who would lead it? Given world events—notably the coming revolution in Russia—it was reasonable for those within either the SLP or IWW to believe that united workers might be able to affect sweeping societal changes. They hoped they might be able to bring about a revolution against capitalists in the United States.

By 1908 politics were considered no longer essential to the union agenda. Because De Leon espoused Marxism and advocated political action, he and his supporters were essentially expelled from the IWW in 1908. At the 1908 convention De Leon was not seated as a delegate. He and those allied with him walked out. The union transformed into essentially a militant union that was known for prounion propaganda distributed through lectures, debates, newsletters, newspapers, and pamphlets, and for agitating strikes. Later in its existence, Samuel Gompers, then president of the AFL, was among those who spoke openly against the union by decrying the IWW as "destructive in theory and practice." While this infighting persisted, precious little organizing occurred.

The IWW suffered even from its nicknames. There are numerous explanations as to how the term wobblies originated. Among the most plausible is that it was derived from the wobble saw. The union was often incorrectly called the International Workers of the World. Wits played on the acronym to create derogatory monikers such as "I Won't Work" or "I Want Whiskey."

The IWW also inspired numerous writers who portrayed the union favorably. Upton Sinclair is thought to have been the first to do so in a play called *Singing Jailbirds*. Among others who wrote about the IWW were John Dos Passos, Eugene O'Neill, Theodore Dreiser, and William Carlos Williams.

The IWW typically had an estimated 150,000 members at any given time, although numbers would swell appreciably during strikes. Estimates run as high as one million workers who were members at some time between 1905 and 1915. The IWW called approximately 150 strikes during its heyday. Although the union did organize in other parts of the world, it was strongest in the United States. IWW organizers happily courted workers typically snubbed by the AFL. The IWW had its greatest successes within agriculture and textile industry.

Key Players

Debs, Eugene Victor (1855–1926): A life-long unionist, Debs was born in Terre Haute, Indiana. He was an official in the Brotherhood of Locomotive Firemen (BLF) and the American Railway Union (ARU) before helping to found the Industrial Workers of the World (IWW). He became a Socialist Party presidential candidate. Debs left the union because its values clashed with his. He espoused nonviolence. Debs was later seen as a dangerous wildcard and was feared by union leaders.

Hagerty, Father Thomas J.: A Catholic priest friendly to labor, Hagerty was one of the IWW founders who wrote the union's preamble. He was editor of the *Voice of Labor*, the publication of the American Labor Union. He has been described as "a big black-bearded scholarly man." He worked as an organizer during a six-year leave from his church duties.

Haywood, William Dudley (1869–1928): Haywood was a labor leader and radical who was best known for his part in the founding of the IWW. He was born in Salt Lake City, Utah, and became a miner and union member as a teen. He was first involved with the Western Federation of Miners (WFM). His experiences in the Colorado mine strikes between 1903 and 1905 reinforced his belief that it was essential for the future of working people in the United States to form a single national union. After the 1905 convention, Haywood became the country's best-known labor radical.

Jones, Mother Mary Harris (1830–1930): Born in Cork, Ireland, Jones immigrated in 1838 to Toronto. She was a dressmaker, wife, and mother. After the deaths of her husband and children in a yellow fever epidemic, she started a career as a labor organizer among the miners. She was present at the founding of the IWW but later distanced herself from the organization, perhaps because she found the Wobblies too radical.

Parsons, Lucy González (1853–1942): Although much of her early life is not well known, Lucy González married Albert Parsons in 1871. Upon moving to Chicago, they both became active in politics including the Workingmen's Party (WPUSA) and Socialist Labor Party. Widowed by her husband's execution in 1887 following the Haymarket Riots, Parsons was an anarchist who was instrumental in the founding the IWW.

See also: *American Federation of Labor; Knights of Labor; Socialist Party of America; Syndicalist Movement; Western Federation of Miners.*

BIBLIOGRAPHY

Books

Bird, Stewart, Dan Georgakas, and Deborah Shaffer. *Solidarity Forever: An Oral History of the IWW.* Chicago: Lake View Press, 1985.

De Leon, Daniel. *Socialist Reconstruction of Society.* New York: Socialist Labor Party, 1912..

Dubofsky, Melvyn A. *Big Bill Haywood.* New York: St. Martin's Press, 1987.

Murolo, Priscilla and A. B. Chitty. *From the Folks Who Brought You the Weekend: A Short, Illustrated History of Labor in the United States.* New York: The New Press, 2001.

Murray, R. Emmet. *The Lexicon of Labor.* New York: The New Press, 1998.

Renshaw, Patrick. *The Wobblies: The Story of Syndicalism in the United States.* Garden City, NY: Doubleday & Co., Inc., 1967.

Taft, Philip. *Organized Labor in American History.* New York: Harper & Row, Publishers, 1964.

Periodicals

IWW. *One Big Union of the I.W.W.* (pamphlet) Chicago: International Workers of the World, (n.d.).

Other

"Eugene V. Debs: A Union Leader." Eugene V. Debs Foundation Web Site [cited 7 August 2002]. <http://www.eugenevdebs.com/pages/uleadr.html#>.

LeFevre, William. "In the Shadow of I.W.W." Wayne State University, Walter P. Reuther Library. 2001 [cited 7 August 2002]. <http://www.reuther.wayne.edu/exhibits/iww.html>.

Industrial Workers of the World Web Site [cited 7 August 2002]. <http://www.iww.org>.

—Linda Dailey Paulson

International Brotherhood of Teamsters, Chauffeurs, Warehousemen, and Helpers of America: *See* **Teamsters Union.**

International Conference on Arab Trade Unions

Egypt 1956

Synopsis

Foundation of the International Confederation of Arab Trade Unions (ICATU) in 1956 was one means by which the Egyptian state pursued an ideological commitment to organized labor in the Arabic-speaking region while integrating an active trade union movement into an evolving corporatist state. The state's commitment to organized labor varied over time and differed in the various parts of the Arab world; much of this variation can be attributed to changing Egyptian policies in the region.

A militant workers' movement undermined the British colonial presence in Egypt and Egypt's monarchy. Industrialization had increased union memberships, which almost tripled between 1947 and 1953. In particular, growth in the textile, tobacco, and sugar industries resulted in emergence of strong labor interests in those industries. Most of the strikes at the time were organized against these three industries.

Union-led strikes contributed to Egypt's 1952 military coup. With the founding of ICATU, the Egyptian Federation of Free Workers disbanded. Founded in 1956, the ICATU continued to work closely with the American Federation of Labor (AFL), the International Labor Organization (ILO), and the International Confederation of Free Trade Unions (ICFTU), thus positioning trans-Arab trade unionism against the World Federation of Trade Unions (WFTU), which had been operating from the USSR.

Timeline

1936: Germany reoccupies the Rhineland, while Italy annexes Ethiopia. Recognizing a commonality of aims, the two totalitarian powers sign the Rome-Berlin Axis Pact. (Japan will join them in 1940.)

1941: Japanese bombing of Pearl Harbor on 7 December brings the United States into the war against the Axis. Combined with the attack on the Soviet Union, which makes Stalin an unlikely ally of the Western democracies, the events of 1941 will ultimately turn the tide of the war.

1946: Winston Churchill warns of an "Iron Curtain" spreading across Eastern Europe.

1951: Julius and Ethel Rosenberg are convicted and sentenced to death for passing U.S. atomic secrets to the Soviets.

1953: The people of East Berlin revolt against communist rule, but the uprising is suppressed by Soviet and East German tanks.

1956: Elvis Presley appears on Ed Sullivan's *Toast of the Town,* where he performs "Hound Dog" and "Love Me Tender" before a mostly female audience. Nationwide, 54 million people watch the performance, setting a new record.

1956: By now firmly established as the Soviet leader, Nikita Khrushchev denounces the crimes of his predecessor and mentor, Josef Stalin.

1956: First aerial testing of the hydrogen bomb at Bikini Atoll makes a blast so powerful—the equivalent of 10 million tons of TNT—that it actually results in the infusion of protons to atomic nuclei to create two new elements, einsteinium and fermium, which have atomic numbers of 99 and 100, respectively.

1956: Egypt seizes control of the Suez Canal, and Israel attacks Egypt on the Sinai Peninsula. Britain and France intervene against Egypt and only relent under U.S. pressure.

1961: President Eisenhower steps down, warning of a "military-industrial complex" in his farewell speech, and 43-year-old John F. Kennedy becomes the youngest elected president in U.S. history. Three months later, he launches an unsuccessful invasion of Cuba at the Bay of Pigs.

1966: In August, Mao Zedong launches the "Great Proletarian Cultural Revolution," which rapidly plunges China into chaos as armed youths plunder the countryside, rooting out suspected foreign collaborators and anti-Chinese elements. Along with rifles and other weapons, these Red Guards are armed with copies of Mao's "Little Red Book."

1971: East Pakistan declares its independence, as the new nation of Bangladesh, from West Pakistan (now simply known as Pakistan); civil war, exacerbated by famine and a cholera epidemic in Bangladesh, ensues.

Event and Its Context

Labor Unions and Egypt's State

Egypt's labor movement has been described in terms of "state corporatism." Some date Egyptian labor's corporatism before the Free Officers' Revolutionary Command Council of 1952. The 1942 trade union laws legalized unions while binding them with "highly restrictive and destabilizing" requirements.

With the 1952 Free Officers' revolution, also known as the July Revolution, state political parties—the Liberation Rally, the National Union, and the Arab Socialist Union—mobilized the nation while maintaining public discipline. Potentially disruptive groups, including students and workers, were closely watched by the government. The integration of Egypt's leftist opposition into a "structured system of control" is credited as one of the most significant political achievements of the administration of Gamal Abdel Nasser.

Yet in 1952 laws 317, 318, and 319 responded to the pluralist trade unions' needs to control industrial conflict, increase workers' take-home pay, and increase productivity. The founding of ICATU emphasized a close allegiance between organized labor and the state. In what has been identified as a "bargain," Egypt's unionists remained legal so long as they formed a single confederation, for which the government chose leaders.

The July Revolution had little effect on the number of grievances. Raucous since the industry's growth during World War II, a textile federation conference in 1956 demanded doubling the minimum wage and creating a wage council. Of 21 collective agreements concluded between unions and employers in Egypt during the 1950s, 19 were in the oil industry.

Limitations of Corporatism

Formal corporatism emerged under the Revolutionary Command Council (RCC) with the 1952 labor union laws, which under the pressure of national emergency forbade strikes as conciliation and arbitration were in effect. The Egyptian state came to govern the internal affairs of unions that predated the

laws, even given their independent status. Unions were required to allocate a third of their annual budgets to social welfare and health activities. Even though these laws permitted pluralism and enabled establishment of a nationwide labor federation, and even though union shops and union dues contributed to labor unions' financial independence and security, closed shop provisions embarrassed Egyptian delegations to International Labor Organization conferences.

The 1959 comprehensive labor code strengthened unions at the national level but weakened them at the plant level and in Egypt's governorates. Law 91 reorganized the labor movement along industrial lines into 65 federations. The Labor Bureau's employees, in an effort to sabotage the law's implementation, refused to accept the registration papers of the influential oil and textile workers' unions. Union membership declined between 1956 and the end of the decade.

Corporatism is essentially an economic contract; workers saw no need to organize as long as the government provided basic needs. In 1955 an All Egypt Trade Union Congress was founded, and half of all members of the Egyptian labor unions were brought into the new federation. In the years that followed, the government arrested those Egyptians, including communists, whom they suspected of ideological commitments beyond the nation-state. Within two years, the trade union congress changed its name to the Egyptian Federation of Labor and then again to the United Arab Republic Federation of Labor following the union with Syria in 1962. Following the enactment of the 1964 trade union law, the organization became known as the General Federation of Labor.

Corporatism's Origins

Corporatism also dates from 1964 with presidential decree no. 62 and its parallel ministerial decrees. These decrees permitted only one general union to represent workers in related, similar, or associated branches of production, which trimmed the number of labor unions to just 27. Workers in establishments employing 50 or more were able to form union committees, but only one committee could represent each establishment.

The Ministry of Labor was established in 1961. With strict controls imposed on union finances, unions became agencies for promoting cooperation and industrial development, ushering in a corporatist era for Egypt's unions. After 1964 the ministry was responsible for international labor relations, labor inspection, wage and labor relations, as well as education, statistics, and government affairs.

The ICATU and Egypt's Influence in the Arab World

Egyptian representatives attended the conference that led to the announcement of the WFTU. At the conference, a strong Arab presence counteracted the influence of Israel's national union, the General Organization of Hebrew Workers in the Land of Israel (known as Histadrut), founded in 1920. The ICATU followed general trends in postcolonial Arab popular consciousness.

Although the ICATU's independent international role came to an end with Fathi Kamil's removal as general secretary in 1959, the institution continued to extend Egypt's political influence in the Arabic-speaking Middle East. In a demonstration of the Arab world's spontaneous anger following the 1967 defeat to Israel in the Six Days War, the ICATU called on all Arab states to join an incipient petroleum export embargo, urging workers to destroy industrial infrastructure in any Arab nation that refused to comply.

By 1967 all Arab national trade union federations except those in Yemen, Tunis, and Saudi Arabia belonged to the ICATU. As the leading regional partner for the WFTU in the Arab world, the ICATU extended the influence of Egypt's government policies into the region. This is particularly visible with reference to ICATU alliances in Palestine—where the ICATU advocates Palestinian autonomy within the Camp David framework—and in the Arab Gulf states, where the ICATU supports underground unions and underrepresented foreign workers (including numerous Egyptians).

Ongoing occupation inhibits trade union activities in Palestinian territories, as union officials' international and local travel requires authorization. Although formally unaffiliated with international labor organizations, the Israeli-occupied West Bank territories of the Palestine General Federation of Trade Unions (PGFTU) attend ICATU meetings and participate as an observer in the WFTU. The GFTU secretary general has been permitted to attend international meetings, such as those of the International Labor Organization (ILO) and the WFTU. However, the Israeli occupying authority also provided these and other GFTU-affiliated individuals with official identity cards that prohibit their entry into East Jerusalem, where a GFTU office is located.

Egypt's peace agreement with Israel as decreed in the Camp David accords of 1978 divided the ICATU—which followed Egyptian foreign policy—from the Egyptian Trade Union Federation (ETUF), which refused to meet with the Histadrut. Following Camp David, the IACTU excluded the ETUF from its meetings. ETUF representatives questioned to what extent ICATU statements in support of the Palestinian cause alleviate the suffering of the stateless.

In the Arab Gulf region, Bahrainis have lived under a state of emergency since 1975. In this legal environment, Bahrain's Ministry of Labor and Social Affairs' Order No. 9 served as the legal basis for a general workers' committee, to be selected by major establishment's workers representatives. This committee is the alternative to underground trade unions in Bahrain. It protects the government from repeated censure by the Arab Labor Organization (ALO) and the ICATU. From the underground, the Bahrain Workers Union—which is affiliated with the ICATU—denounced the order as "a publicity stunt designed to foil the ALO's resolution relating to the violation of union rights in Bahrain."

Elsewhere in the Arab Gulf region, the ICATU supports Egyptian citizens against local corporatist unions. The ICATU/WFTU affiliate in Kuwait, the Kuwait Trade Union Federation (KTUF), continues under the burden of ILO criticism regarding inclusion issues. Although foreign citizens constitute more than 80 percent of Kuwait's work force, they are only 10 percent of the unionized work force. Kuwaiti law stipulates that any new union must include at least 100 workers, of whom at least 15 must be local citizens. Both the ILO and the International Confederation of Free Trade Unions (ICFTU) have criticized this requirement because it discourages unions in sectors such as the construction industry and the domestic servant sector, which employ few citizens. A new draft labor law grants pervasive oversight powers that further erode union independence.

Elsewhere in the Arab World, the ICATU supports local corporatist unions. Surprisingly, the Egyptian-based IACTU also functions in a corporatist manner even in Iraq, Egypt's rival in the Arab world. Iraq's Trade Union Organization Law of 1987 established a government-controlled trade union, the Iraqi General Federation of Trade Unions (IGFTU), as the sole legal trade federation. The Ba'th Party uses the IGFTU to promote party principles and policies among union members. The IGFTU is affiliated with both the ICATU and the WFTU. Iraq's labor law uses penal sanctions to restrict the right to strike. Workers in private and mixed enterprises, but not public employees or workers in state enterprises, have the right to join local union committees. The committees are affiliated with individual trade unions, which in turn belong to the IGFTU.

Discussion

In the ahistorical world of international relations specialists, trade unions enjoy institutional protection with legal regulations and constraints. To the left, social democratic electoral politics subordinate the international to the national level, fixing attention on western Europe. The ICATU figures in Egyptian national politics, as well as regional and international concerns. The ICATU has dropped from the map of contemporary Arab labor history. Magisterial histories of Egypt's labor movement—the Arab world's most significantly—fail to grant the ICATU more than mere acknowledgement, if they mention it at all.

Key Players

'Abd al Fatah, Muhammed Tawfiq: 'Abd al Fatah was former director of the Ministry of Labor and Social Affairs central administration. He supported the Egyptian Free Officers' opposition to the idea of a single, hierarchical confederation of Egyptian labor unions after the 1956 war and is credited with April 1959 passage of Law 91, the Unified Labor Code, which provided for the reorganization of Egypt's labor movement into 65 federations along industrial lines, united to the ICATU.

Darwish, Youssef (1910–): Darwish was an independent Egyptian lawyer and union advocate.

Fahim, Ahmed (?–1969): Identified with the left, Fahim was president of textile workers' federation and vice president of the General Federation of Egyptian Trade Unions. While he was second president of ICATU, his tenure was extended when union elections were suspended after the 1967 war.

Kamil, Fathi: Noncommunist leader of the General Federation of Egyptian Trade Unions disbanded by the Egyptian Ministry of the Interior in 1953, Kamil was elected general secretary of the Permanent Congress that preceded the ICATU. He resigned before the 1959 ICATU elections.

Salama, Mohammad Abdel-Latif (also known as Anwar Salama) (1921–): Affiliated with International Petroleum Workers' Federation, Salama was first executive for the

Egyptian Workers' Federation (EWF) at its foundation in January 1957. He resigned as confederation president in February 1958.

al-Sawi, Al Sawi Ahmed: President of the Combined Joint Task Force (CJTF), al-Sawi was reported to have received Liberation Rally compensation for leading the transport workers' strike as part of the July 1952 Revolution.

Al Shafi'I, Husayn Mahmoud (1918–): Al Shafi'l was allegedly affiliated to the Muslim Brotherhood preceding the 1952 revolution and member of the Free Officers' Revolutionary Command Council. Following the revolution, he served as vice president and secretary general of the Arab Socialist Union.

Tu'ayma, Ahmed 'Abd Allah: Director of trade union affairs for the Revolutionary Command Council's Liberation Rally, Tu'ayma coordinated with the Permanent Congress of Egyptian Trade Unions.

'Uqayli, Mohamed Ahmed (1943–): President of the Cairo taxi drivers' local, member of the Permanent Congress of Egyptian Trade Unions during the strike by Cairo transport workers during the July 1952 Revolution, 'Uqayli was considered supportive of the Egyptian state's Labor Bureau.

See also: *American Federation of Labor; International Confederation of Free Trade Unions; International Labor Organization; World Federation of Trade Unions.*

BIBLIOGRAPHY

Books

Abbas, Ra'ouf (Ra'ouf Abbas Hamad). *Al-hariaka al-ummaliya fi Misr, 1899–1952.* Cairo, Egypt: Darl al-Kitab Al-Arabli, 1967.

Beinin, Joel. *Was the Red Flag Flying There? Marxist Politics and the Arab-Israeli Conflict in Egypt and Israel, 1948–1965.* Berkeley: University of California Press, 1990.

Beinin, Joel, and Zachary Lockman. *Workers on the Nile: Nationalism, Communism, Islam, and the Egyptian Working Class, 1882–1954.* Princeton, NJ: Princeton University Press, 1987.

Bianchi, Robert. *Unruly Corporatism: Associational Life in Twentieth-century Egypt.* New York: Oxford University Press, 1989.

Cohen, Robin. "Theorising International Labour." In *International Labour and the Third World: The Making of a New Working Class,* edited by Rosalind Boyd, Robin Cohen, and Peter Gutkind. Aldershot, U.K.: Avebury, 1987.

Goldberg, Ellis. "Reading from Left to Right: The Social History of Egyptian Labor." In *The Social History of Labor in the Middle East,* edited by Ellis Jay Goldberg. Boulder, CO: Westview Press, 1996.

Izz al-Din, Amin. *Tarikh al-Tabaqa al-Amila al-misriya,* 3 volumes. Cairo, Egypt: Dar al-kitab al-arabi and Dar al-Shaab, 1967, 1970, 1972.

Mansour, Mohamed B. *The Development of the Industrial Relations System in Egypt.* Ph.D. Dissertation, Graduate School of Business Administration, New York University, 1972.

Posusney, Marsha Pripstein. *Labor and the State in Egypt: Workers, Unions and Economic Restructuring.* New York: Columbia University Press, 1997.

Periodicals

Bianchi, Robert. "The Corporatization of the Egyptian Labor Movement." *The Middle East Journal* 40, no. 3 (summer 1986): 429–444.

Binder, Leonard. "The Allure of the Egyptian Left." *Asian and African Studies* 14 (1980): 20–34.

Cross, Peter. "British Attitudes to Sudanese Labour: The Foreign Office Records as Sources for Social History." *British Journal of Middle Eastern Studies* 24, no. 2 (November 1997): 217–260.

Daoudi, M. S., and M. S. Dajani. "The 1967 Oil Embargo Revisited." *Journal of Palestine Studies* 13, no. 2 (winter 1984): 65–90.

Khalaf, 'Abd ul Hadi. "Labor Movements in Bahrain." *MERIP Reports,* no. 132 (May 1985): 24–29.

"On the Brink: A MEES Commentary on the Current MidEast Crisis and Its Repercussions on the Oil Situation." *Middle East Economic Survey* 19, no. 30 (26 May 1967): 1–14.

U.S. Department of State. "Country Reports on Human Rights Practices for 1990, 'Israel and the Occupied Territories.'" *Journal of Palestine Studies* 20, no. 3 (spring 1991): 98–111.

—Elizabeth Bishop

International Confederation of Free Trade Unions

Worldwide 1949

Synopsis

After abandoning the World Federation of Trade Unions (WFTU) to the communist states, the anticommunist unions, their allies, and clients (in the colonies or semicolonies), as well as the social-democratic, social-reformist, and business unions (with their allies and clients), created a new international confederation: the International Confederation of Free Trade Unions (ICFTU). Formed as the cold war peaked in 1949, the new organization shared with the West the epithet "free." Although the ICFTU was a product of the cold war, it was also a child of long-standing tensions between "pure and simple unionists," "reformists," and "revolutionaries" within the international labor movement. It was also, more directly, a child of the hot labor movement war that began after World War I and the creation of the Soviet-controlled Communist International and Profintern (or the Red International of Labor Unions). Hamstrung by tensions between major members, largely self-

Irving Brown (right), AFL-CIO European representative; U Thant, acting secretary general of United Nations; and Omer Becu, general secretary of the International Confederation of Free Trade Unions, New York City. AP/Wide World Photos. Reproduced by permission.

confined to international labor diplomacy and a community of interstate agencies, the ICFTU later lost the high profile it had attained at its dramatic founding.

Timeline

1931: Financial crisis widens in the United States and Europe, which reel from bank failures and climbing unemployment levels. In London, armies of the unemployed riot.

1935: Second phase of New Deal begins with the introduction of social security, farm assistance, and housing and tax reform.

1940: Hitler's troops sweep through Western Europe, annexing Norway and Denmark in April, and in May the Low Countries and France.

1945: On 7 May, Germany surrenders to the Allied powers in World War II.

1950: United States begins developing hydrogen bomb.

1950: North Korean troops pour into South Korea, starting the Korean War. Initially, the communists make impressive gains, but in September the U.S. Marines land at Inchon and liberate Seoul. China responds by sending in its troops.

1950: Senator Joseph McCarthy launches his campaign to root out communist infiltrators.

1955: Over the course of the year, a number of key ingredients are added to the pantheon of American culture: the 1955 Chevrolet, the first of many classic models; Tennessee

Williams's *Cat on a Hot Tin Roof*; Marilyn Monroe's performance in *The Seven-Year Itch*; Disneyland; and Bill Haley and the Comets' "Rock Around the Clock."

1960: An American U-2 spy plane piloted by Francis Gary Powers shot down over Soviet skies brings an end to a short period of warming relations between the two superpowers. By the end of the year, Khrushchev makes a scene at the United Nations, banging his shoe on a desk. As for Powers, he will be freed in a 1962 prisoner exchange.

1965: Rev. Martin Luther King, Jr., and more than 2,600 others are arrested in Selma, Alabama. Three weeks later, in New York City, Malcolm X is assassinated.

Event and Its Context

The coincidence of the creation of the ICFTU in 1949, at a high point in the cold war, has often led commentators to reduce the organization to this fact alone. The split in the World Federation of Trade Unions (WFTU; ostensibly over acceptance/rejection of the U.S. Marshall Plan offer to rebuild a war-devastated Europe) also must be understood in terms of working-class nationalism/internationalism, of competing labor and socialist ideologies (within the West itself), and of the universal state-dependence of trade unionism during most of the twentieth century. To this must be added the old conflict between international unionism as a relationship between national union centers and as an industrial/occupational relationship. Given

Adler, the Feinberg Law, and Free Speech in the Work Place

Passed in 1949, New York State's Feinberg Law was a product of post-World War II fears concerning the spread of communism. It was designed to aid in the enforcement of two earlier laws, one passed in 1917—during an earlier "Red Scare," brought on by the victory of communism in Russia and the spread of communist sympathies among workers in the United States—and the other in 1939. The 1917 statute designated "the utterance of any treasonable or seditious word or words or the doing of any treasonable or seditious act" an offense for which an employee of the state's public school systems could be dismissed. The 1939 law made any person who called for the overthrow of the government by force, or who published material advocating such overthrow, or who organized or joined any society advocating such overthrow, ineligible for employment in the state's civil service or educational systems.

Under the Feinberg Law, the State Board of Regents was charged with implementing rules to govern dismissal and ineligibility requirements stemming from violations of the two earlier statutes. Likewise, the board was required to identify all subversive organizations operating in the state, and to establish rules whereby membership in any such organization was grounds for disqualification or dismissal from any job in the state's public school system. Though it applied to the state as a whole, the Feinberg Law was in fact directed toward that part of the state most likely to draw radicals: New York City.

During the next several years, hundreds of teachers in the city either resigned or were fired. Among those was Irving Adler, who along with others brought a declaratory judgment calling for the implementation of the Feinberg Law to be declared unconstitutional. Adler's case went to the U.S. Supreme Court, which in *Adler et al. v. Board of Education of City of New York* (1952) found nothing unconstitutional in the Feinberg Law.

Delivering the Court's opinion, Justice Minton held that the classroom is a "sensitive place," and that the teacher "shapes the attitude of young minds." Justices Frankfurter and Douglas dissented, with Justice Black concurring in Douglas's dissent. According to Douglas, "I have not been able to accept the recent doctrine that a citizen who enters the public service can be forced to sacrifice his civil rights."

Four years later, in 1956, New York's education commissioner issued a new order making it possible for persons who had formerly—but not currently—been members of subversive organizations to retain their jobs. With its decision in *Keyishian v. Board of Regents* (1967), the U.S. Supreme Court invalidated the 1917 and 1939 laws, and in effect overruled *Adler.*

Source: James D. Folts. *History of the University of the State of New York and the State Education Department, 1784–1996* (1996). <http://unix2.nysed.gov>.

—Judson Knight

that the International Trade Secretariats (ITS) were the oldest internationals, that they were closer to the unions and workers they represented, and that they had a higher practical and lower "political" or "ideological" profile, the foundation of the ICFTU (which recognized the autonomy of the ITS) had labor motives enough for its creation.

On the other hand, the split in the WFTU and the creation of the ICFTU were also, inevitably, an effect of the cold war between the liberal-democratic and capitalist West and the communist eastern bloc. At that time the West was dominated in many ways by the United States, which had been vastly strengthened by the war. The economically devastated communist bloc was relatively weak. An authoritarian and militaristic party-state—to which the unions were subordinate—and an ideology of proletarian rule and internationalism (for which wartime success and antiimperial movements still provided considerable attraction) attempted to compensate for this weakness.

The major tension in the creation of the ICFTU was between the United States and the western European unions. ICFTU member unions in the colonies and in newly independent countries long remained in a marginal and dependent position. A U.S. culture of unfettered freedom of enterprise; of military interventionism; and of hostility to communism, to social democracy, and even to liberalism, had by 1949 deeply influenced its trade union movement. In Europe the devastated capitalist economies were mostly prepared for a settlement with social democracy and the trade union movements and for the creation of the so-called welfare state, thus providing the labor movement with feelings of both protection and power.

At the moment of creation of the ICFTU, however, a common interest in social-reformism and in anticommunism (which, for the United States, was primarily a symbolic threat, as opposed to the political threat it represented for western Europeans) permitted participants to overcome differing orientations toward colonialism. The United States and its unions had no interest in formal colonialism and preserved their domination of, for example, Latin American unions in neocolonial ways. Meanwhile the European unions often shared the colonial attitudes of their states (and societies), with the British Trades Union Congress providing labor advisers to the colonial authorities and the French still having union affiliates in their increasingly restive overseas territories.

The point of accord between the western unions and the western states and between the European and the American unions was in the use of the word "free" to characterize the new international. This term was variously applied to favored liberal-democratic capitalist states or societies, to union-state relations that were bipartite or tripartite rather than state-controlled, and to union-member relations based on democratic procedures. Insofar as political liberty was here privileged above other terms in the democratic trinity (economic equality, social solidarity), this skewed the ICFTU, the ITS, and regional organizations in a particular political direction. Sharing the word with states and corporations allowed the new confederation to subordinate the other values to that of "freedom," which it narrowly defined as opposition to communism or radical nationalism, both of which had some attraction to labor in the Third World.

The increasing integration of the western trade union internationals into western capitalist states and societies, their varied compromises with corporate capitalism, their distance from the worker members of their national affiliates, and their focus on international and regional agencies were concealed at the founding of the ICFTU. This resulted from the western unions' recent escape from the communist embrace in 1949 and their continuing competition with both the WFTU and nationalist regional organizations such as the Organization of African Trade Union Unity, which lasted until the collapse of both the communist and the radical nationalist projects some 50 years later. At the moment of victory, however, the ICFTU was simultaneously confronted by the threat of a neoliberalized, globalized, and networked capitalism, for which its previous experience had ill-prepared it. Like its immediate predecessor and longtime competitor, the WFTU, the ICFTU represented both the extent and limits of a bureaucratic and corporatist notion of labor internationalism.

Key Players

Brown, Irving (1911–1989): A backroom specialist of U.S. international unionism, Brown is better known to international labor specialists than international union activists. Apparently marginal to the work of the ICFTU and even the AFL-CIO, Brown was the leading *eminence grise* of western union internationalism. He represented the clandestine, even criminal, fringe of cold war unionism in the West. Born into a trade union family in New York City, he became a communist and then left the party together with his friend and mentor, Jay Lovestone. Both spent the rest of their lives operating in the same clandestine international mode, but allied internationally with the U.S. government and corporations against communism, radical nationalism, and the left. After Brown worked in the union movement and participated in wartime government boards, the AFL's Free Trade Union Committee sent him to Europe. Starting by 1949, the Central Intelligence Agency funded Brown's activities. Fighting to wipe out communist dockers' unions in France and Italy, he collaborated with the Marseilles Mafia and thus with what became later infamous as the "French Connection." Some suggest that he not only used the drug trade to fund his activities but even ran drugs himself. In the 1960s Brown shifted his efforts to Africa and became director of the AFL-CIO's state- and corporation-funded African American Labor Center. No task was too humble for him: Brown even presented "dockers toilets" to Nigerian unions (which in practice were handed over to and later reserved for use by senior officers in the Ports Authority). In 1962–1967 he was director of the ICFTU United Nations Office in New York. He returned to Europe in 1973 to lead the U.S. campaign against détente in the international trade union movement, became director of international affairs for the AFL-CIO in 1986, and a senior adviser to its president in 1986.

Narayanan, P. P. (1923–1996): Narayanan, whose family emigrated from India when he was 14, was a leading figure within the Malayan Union of Plantation Workers and participated in the founding congress of the ICFTU. He became president of the ICFTU's Asian Regional Organization in 1960 and in 1975 the president of the ICFTU—the first in that office from the "developing world." He continued in this position until 1992. Narayanan's rise to prominence within the Malayan (later Malaysian) unions was a result of support from the British Trade Union Adviser, himself from the British trade union movement. As in other colonies, seconded British union officers collaborated with the local authorities—in this case with the Special Branch—in seeking out progovernment trade union leaders who would promote anticommunist unionism (limited to "reasonable" objectives). This was not an unusual background for the Third World unionists who became prominent within the ICFTU at either regional or international levels during the cold war.

Oldenbroek, Jacobus (1898–1970): Oldenbroek is one of many Dutch/Belgian unionists to have played a major role in international unionism. Long active in the Dutch social-democratic unions and then in the International Transport Workers Federation, he collaborated closely with the U.S. Office of Strategic Services during World War II. Like most of the International Trade Secretariat leaders, he was a bitter critic of the World Federation of Trade Unions (WFTU), which wanted to turn these oldest and most resilient international union bodies into subordinate trade departments. Although the U.S. unions were suspicious of or hostile to most European social-democrats, Oldenbroek's background encouraged them to support him in becoming the first general secretary of the ICFTU. He later lost this support and resigned from his post in 1960.

See also: *Red International of Labor Unions; World Federation of Trade Unions.*

BIBLIOGRAPHY

Books

Buschak, Willy. "The Meaning of the Word 'Free' in Trade Union History." In *The Past and Future of International Trade Unionism: International Conference, Ghent (Belgium), May 19–20, 2000*, edited by Bart de Wilde. Ghent, Belgium: AMSAB Institute of Social History, 2001.

Carew, Anthony. "Ideology and International Trade Unionism." In *The Past and Future of International Trade Unionism: International Conference, Ghent (Belgium), May 19–20, 2000*, edited by Bart de Wilde. Ghent, Belgium: AMSAB Institute of Social History, 2001.

Dass, Arokia. *Not Beyond Repair: Reflections of a Malaysian Trade Unionist*. Hong Kong: Asia Monitor Resource Centre, 1991.

De Wilde, Bart, ed. *The Past and Future of International Trade Unionism: International Conference, Ghent (Belgium), May 19–20, 2000*. Ghent, Belgium: AMSAB Institute of Social History, 2001.

Van der Linden, Marcel, ed. *The International Confederation of Free Trade Unions*. Berne, Switzerland: Peter Lang, 2000.

Waterman, Peter. "Dockworker Unionism: Workers of the Docks Unite?" In *Division and Unity Amongst Nigerian Workers: Lagos Port Unions, 1940s–60s*. The Hague: Institute of Social Studies, 1982.

Periodicals

Valentine, Douglas. "The French Connection Revisited: The CIA, Irving Brown and Drug Smuggling." *CovertAction Quarterly* 67 (1999): 61–64.

Waterman, Peter. "The Problematic Past and Uncertain Future of the International Confederation of Free Trade Unions." *International Labor and Working Class History* 59 (2001): 125–132.

—Peter Waterman

International Federation of Miners

Belgium 1890

Synopsis

On 20–23 May 1890 an international congress of coal miners convened in Jolimont, Belgium. This congress led to the founding of the International Federation of Miners (IFM), one of the first international trade secretariats. Among the key issues debated at Jolimont were the eight-hour workday; the international strike; and calls for the coordinated international restructuring of output to stabilize prices, wages, and employment (the so-called Lewy Plan). Initially the British unions dominated the organization, but their hegemony weakened once the United Mine Workers of America joined in 1904 and the German unions began to consolidate.

Timeline

1870: Franco-Prussian War begins. German troops sweep over France, Napoleon III is dethroned, and France's Second Empire gives way to the Third Republic.

1876: Four-stroke cycle gas engine is introduced.

1880: South Africa's Boers declare an independent republic, precipitating the short First Anglo-Boer War.

1883: Foundation of the League of Struggle for the Emancipation of Labor by Marxist political philosopher Georgi Valentinovich Plekhanov marks the formal start of Russia's labor movement. Change still lies far in the future for Russia, however: tellingly, Plekhanov launches the movement in Switzerland.

1886: Bombing at Haymarket Square, Chicago, kills seven policemen and injures numerous others. Eight anarchists

are accused and tried; three are imprisoned, one commits suicide, and four are hanged.

1888: Serbian-born American electrical engineer Nikola Tesla develops a practical system for generating and transmitting alternating current (AC), which will ultimately—and after an extremely acrimonious battle—replace Thomas Edison's direct current (DC) in most homes and businesses.

1890: U.S. Congress passes the Sherman Antitrust Act, which in the years that follow will be used to break up large monopolies.

1890: Police arrest and kill Sioux chief Sitting Bull, and two weeks later, federal troops kill over 200 Sioux at Wounded Knee.

1890: Alfred Thayer Mahan, a U.S. naval officer and historian, publishes *The Influence of Sea Power Upon History, 1660–1783,* which demonstrates the decisive role that maritime forces have played in past conflicts. The book will have an enormous impact on world events by encouraging the major powers to develop powerful navies.

1893: Henry Ford builds his first automobile.

1896: First modern Olympic Games are held in Athens.

1900: Commonwealth of Australia is established.

Event and Its Context

At the end of the 1880s, the western European and British trade union movement began to grow rapidly. Against the backdrop of improved economic growth, many workers became more militant. This militancy came to the fore in a series of major strikes, including those by London's dockers and Germany's Ruhr miners in 1889. In the period 1887 to 1892, trade union membership doubled in Britain and tripled in France. In Germany, more strikes took place in 1889–1890 than in the previous five years.

The coal miners' unions benefited from this development. They too began to grow, and, increasingly, to collaborate at the national level, the British unions in particular. The British unions were significantly larger than their western European counterparts. Because wages and working conditions on the Continent were less favorable than those in the United Kingdom, both British and Continental miners had an interest in international collaboration. Improved transportation had created an international coal market, and so miners in various countries became one another's competitors. The British therefore wanted international collaboration because strong Continental trade unions would drive up wages in mainland Europe and so weaken the threat from western European mining companies; Continental miners favored collaboration in the hope of benefiting from British support in their struggle to strengthen the unions and achieve a better standard of living.

When on 14 July 1889—exactly 100 years to the day since the storming of the Bastille—two international labor congresses (those of the Possibilists and the Socialists) opened simultaneously in Paris, miners from various countries naturally participated. On the margins of the main congresses, they organized

James Keir Hardie addressing crowd, Trafalgar Square, London, England. © Hulton/Getty Images. Reproduced by permission.

their own meeting in which Belgian, British, French, and German delegates resolved to hold a politically independent international miners' congress in the near future.

William Crawford, secretary of the British Miners' National Union, assumed responsibility for organizing this congress. Eventually, on 20 May 1890 over 100 delegates from five countries descended on the offices of the consumer cooperative in Jolimont, a small town in Belgium. Thirty-six British trade unionists representing a total of 340,000 members were present, along with 50 Belgian, seven French, five German and one Austrian delegate, who together represented around 65,000 members.

This, the first-ever International Miners' Congress, took place in a context of repression and police surveillance. The group's leaders decided to hold all discussions in public because they feared that police spies were present in the hall. There were persistent rumors that the Belgian government wanted to deport the British and German delegates. The delegates to the congress, however, received an enthusiastic welcome from the local townsfolk. The correspondent for the Lon-

don *Times* wrote, "The miners and their families from many miles around came to see and welcome the delegates. Many were unable to gain admittance. The hall was packed to a dangerous extent."

Thomas Burt, one of the main leaders of the miners of northern England, opened the congress with a speech. It was followed by one and a half days of reports from the various mining districts of England, Wales, Scotland, Saxony, Westphalia, Bohemia, Wallonia, and France. These served once again to illustrate the fact that British miners were much better off than their Continental colleagues. Delegates then went on to conduct lengthy debates on key strategic issues. On the final day of the congress, 23 May, those present unanimously resolved to set up an International Federation of Miners (IFM). The statutes of the new organization were to be drawn up at a subsequent congress set to convene on 1 April 1891.

This second congress took place in Paris. Delegates failed to reach agreement on the voting procedure to be used. The powerful British unions favored a procedure in which the voting power of representatives would reflect the number of union members they represented; naturally, this would have left Continental unions with a purely symbolic influence within the IFM. The weak Continental trade unions therefore favored a procedure in which voting reflected the number of nationalities. It was not until 1892, at the third congress in London, that the factions reached agreement. The British delegates won the day after threatening to pull out of the federation. Delegates created an international committee to prepare the groundwork for the annual congresses; the committee was structured to vote based on nationalities.

The statutes approved in 1892 formulated not only the federation's principal aim—"To bring together the Nationalities of the World"—but also certain specific demands, such as a reduction in the number of hours of underground labor "from bank to bank" and an improvement in mine safety by appointing inspectors to be selected by the miners and paid by the state.

The eight-hour workday was a central issue at the earliest IFM congresses, partly because it split the British delegation. This was clear as early as the 1890 congress. The Miners' Federation of Great Britain (MFGB) strongly favored statutory regulations, and miners' delegates from the North of England argued that working hours were not a matter for the state but for the unions and that self-help was much to be preferred to state-help. The Continental unionists, whose organizations were much too weak to enforce an eight-hour workday on their own, supported the MFGB. A large majority eventually approved a resolution calling for a statutory eight-hour workday, even though it was opposed by nine delegates from Durham, Northumberland, and Yorkshire.

Building on this resolution, Keir Hardie, leader of the Scottish miners, wanted the congress to go even further. He put forward a resolution urging the congress to issue an ultimatum to the various national governments: either they promise before 1 May 1891 to introduce an eight-hour workday or the IFM would call an international miners' strike. French and Belgian delegates, in addition to the Scottish contingent, supported the resolution. The English delegates protested, however, because Hardie had submitted the resolution without prior consultation. The German delegates pointed out that it would be impossible for them to offer their support as this would mean violating German law and exposing themselves to the risk of imprisonment on their return. They would therefore abstain from voting. When the Welsh delegation said it too lacked the authority to make such an important decision, Hardie withdrew his proposal. Instead, the delegates resolved to include the issue on the agenda of the next congress, in advance of which "all nationalities and districts shall have the question fully laid before the men."

The issue of a statutory eight-hour day was on the agenda of all 24 congresses held by the IFM before the outbreak of World War I in 1914. These agendas gradually became longer and focused more on specific occupational problems. Peter Rütters summarized the issues raised at these congresses:

- Working conditions: eight-hour working day and a weekly hour cap, a living wage, holiday entitlement, sanctions imposed by employers, openness about deductions from gross pay, eviction from company houses

- Health and safety: mine inspections, prohibition of child and female labor in mines, hygiene, medical care, hookworm diseases

- Labor relations: collective bargaining and arbitration, right of association

- Social security: employer liability in the event of accidents, invalidity benefits and pensions, health insurance, minimum level of benefit

- Regulation of production: international regulation of production (the so-called Lewy System), coal extraction based on demand; state control/nationalization of mines

One important problem was the close-knit nature of national coal markets. The rapid growth in output at British and German mines ensured that strikes elsewhere would fail. Starting in 1893, Belgian and French delegates therefore tried to win IFM support for the Lewy Plan to regulate European coal production. The Lewy Plan envisaged setting up an international coal cartel in which trade unions, mine owners, and governments would participate; the cartel would set output levels for the various countries and thereby stabilize wages, prices, and the market. The proposal, however, attracted little sympathy.

The domination by British miners continued for several decades but weakened slightly in the course of time. First, Continental trade unions, particularly in Germany, gradually grew and consolidated. Second, the United Mine Workers of America joined the IFM in 1904, after months of correspondence and a visit to the United States from six of the organization's representatives. The UMWA had been founded in 1890 and, after a difficult start, experienced rapid expansion in the late 1890s. By just after 1900 it had around a quarter of a million members. Two UMWA delegates, John Mitchell and William Dodds—the president and secretary of the UMWA—attended the IFM congress in Paris in 1904, the first time the UMWA had sent delegates to an IFM congress. They promised generous financial support to the organization. U.S. competition in the international coal market and the rapid growth in European migration to North America were important reasons for forging transatlantic contacts.

The IFM's organizational structure remained weak for a long time. It had little in the way of an administrative apparatus, and it had just two officials, namely a secretary and a treasurer (both were British until 1914). Coordination was relatively easy because so few countries were members, but the IFM had only a modest regular income. If funds were needed for specific activities, members—especially the MFGB—helped out with ad hoc contributions. The organizations affiliated with the IFM retained full autonomy, and the IFM was unable to make any independent decisions. The annual congresses continued to be its principal activity. Nonetheless, the IFM was one of the first effective international trade secretariats, and apart from during the two world wars, when it was either dissolved or its activities were restricted, it has been in continuous existence to the present day.

Key Players

Burt, Thomas (1837–1922): Burt was a British miner; secretary of the Northumberland Miners' Mutual Confident Association, 1865–1913; liberal Member of Parliament, 1874–1918; and president of the International Peace League, 1882–1914.

Crawford, William (1833–1890): Crawford was a British miner; secretary of the Miners' National Association, 1877–1890; liberal Member of Parliament, 1885–1890.

Hardie, James Keir (1856–1915): Hardie was a British miner; cofounder of the Scottish Miners' Federation in 1886; chairman of the Independent Labour Party, 1893–1900; founder and editor of *The Miner*, 1887, and subsequently of the *Labour Leader*; leader of the Labour Party in the House of Commons, 1906–1908.

See also: *Dockers' Strike; Miners' Strike, Germany; United Mine Workers of America.*

BIBLIOGRAPHY

Books

Herrmann, Karl Georg. *Die Geschichte des Internationalen Bergarbeiterverbandes, 1890–1939.* Frankfurt am Main and New York: Campus Verlag, 1994.

Lazorchick, Daniel C. *Miners' International Federation. An International Labor Study.* Washington, DC: U.S. Department of Labor, 1962.

Rütters, Peter. *Der Internationale Bergarbeiterverband, 1890 bis 1993. Entwicklung und Politik.* Cologne, Germany: Bund-Verlag, 1995.

—Marcel van der Linden

International Federation of Trade Unions

Netherlands 1919

Synopsis

One consequence of World War I was the splitting of the trade union movement of various nations into three camps, with two representing the countries involved in the combat and one neutral. After the armistice, the wounds of the war years ostensibly healed very rapidly. Already in February 1919, when peace negotiations in Versailles, France, were still in full flow, representatives from the three blocks met for a conference in Bern, Switzerland. The representatives reached agreement on the need for a new international of labor organizations to be the instrument by which the social struggle would be internationalized. This new and ambitious international trade union, the International Federation of Trade Unions (IFTU), was established formally a few months later in Amsterdam, Netherlands, the city to which it would always remain connected.

Timeline

1900: China's Boxer Rebellion, which began in the preceding year with attacks on foreigners and Christians, reaches its height. An international contingent of more than 2,000 men arrives to restore order, but only after several tens of thousands have died.

1907: U.S. markets experience a financial panic.

1912: *Titanic* sinks on its maiden voyage, from Southampton to New York, on 14 April. More than 1,500 people are killed.

1915: At the Second Battle of Ypres, the Germans introduce a terrifying new weapon: poison gas.

1917: The intercepted "Zimmermann Telegram" reveals a plot by the German government to draw Mexico into an alliance against the United States in return for a German promise to return the southwestern U.S. territories taken in the Mexican War. Three months later, in response to German threats of unrestricted submarine warfare, the United States on 6 April declares war on Germany.

1919: With the formation of the Third International (Comintern), the Bolshevik government of Russia establishes its control over Communist movements worldwide.

1919: Treaty of Versailles is signed by the Allies and Germany but rejected by the U.S. Senate. This is due in part to rancor between President Woodrow Wilson and Republican Senate leaders, and in part to concerns over Wilson's plan to commit the United States to the newly established League of Nations and other international duties. Not until 1921 will Congress formally end U.S. participation in the war, but it will never agree to join the League.

1919: The Eighteenth Amendment, which prohibits the production, sale, distribution, purchase, and consumption of alcohol throughout the United States, is ratified.

1919: In India, Mahatma Gandhi launches his campaign of nonviolent resistance to British rule.

1919: In Italy, a former socialist of the left named Benito Mussolini introduces the world to a new socialism of the right, embodied in an organization known as the "Union for Struggle," or Fasci di Combattimento. Composed primarily of young war veterans discontented with Italy's paltry share of the spoils from the recent world war (if not with their country's lackluster military performance in the conflict), the fascists are known for their black shirts and their penchant for violence.

1921: As the Allied Reparations Commission calls for payments of 132 billion gold marks, inflation in Germany begins to climb.

1925: European leaders attempt to secure the peace at the Locarno Conference, which guarantees the boundaries between France and Germany, and Belgium and Germany.

1929: On "Black Friday" in October, prices on the U.S. stock market, which had been climbing wildly for several years, suddenly collapse. Thus begins the first phase of a world economic crisis and depression that will last until the beginning of World War II.

Event and Its Context

From relatively early on in the development of the labor movement, economic and political zealots had driven trade unions toward forging international contacts. Even so, it was not until the founding of the Second International in 1889 that international associations for this purpose came into being. The first international trade unions were umbrella organizations of national industrial unions, the so-called International Trades Secretariats. As of 1914, there were 28 such groups. Beginning in 1901, national trade union federations commenced to undertake steps toward international cooperation. At the suggestion of the Danes and with the support of the strong German labor movement, the International Secretariat of National Trade Union Centers (IS) was founded. The founders' aim was to limit the activities of the organization to the exchange of information and the encouragement of personal contacts during its congresses. The purpose of this explicit decision to confine the terrain of the labor international to purely trade union affairs was the avoidance of divisive political debate, something that had come to dominate the political International. This strategy, however, proved unsuccessful, owing to the participation of syndicalist groups with action-oriented and politically inspired programs. The IS thus became the theater of confrontation between the German reformist and the French syndicalistic models. In addition to the French and German organizations, the other members of the IS also were drawn mainly from continental Europe. The British Trades Union Congress (TUC) remained absent, thus leaving the matter of international contacts to the much smaller General Federation of Trade Unions (GFTU). In 1911 the IS significantly expanded its sphere of influence thanks to the addition of the American Federation of Labor (AFL) to its ranks.

The advent of World War I meant an immediate end to any possibility of a unified international labor movement, which split into three camps: a neutral camp that included the Netherlands and (until 1917) the United States; an Axis powers camp whose main member was Germany; and the Allied camp with France, Great Britain, and as of 1917, the United States. Until the American entry into the war, AFL president Samuel Gompers tried to act as mediator between the various camps, but from the moment that the United States joined the Allies, the AFL traded its traditional position of pacifism for one of unadulterated patriotism. Domestically as well as on the world stage, Gompers became a prominent advocate of the war. He would subsequently refuse any contact with the German labor movement, which he accused of having sold out to Kaiserist militarism.

Accession of the AFL to the Allied camp had the immediate effect that a proposal formulated by Gompers, which had already been written at the beginning of the war, to organize an international trade union congress concurrent with the peace conference, indeed struck a common chord. In 1918 the notion that the world of labor would have an important contribution to make to peace negotiations was generally accepted. Meanwhile, Gompers endeavored to dampen the inclination within the Allied camp to favor negotiated peace. With this aim in mind, the AFL sent two delegations to Europe. The first had little effect. The second, led by Gompers himself, was successful in having its views accepted during the inter-Allied conference held in London in September 1918. This conference mandated that Gompers, together with the Briton Arthur Henderson, the Frenchman Albert Thomas, and the Belgian Emile Vandervelde, must organize an international labor conference to be held at the same place and during the same timeframe as the coming peace conference.

The idea that peace negotiators would come together in a city where socialists of all plumage would also be present was anathema to many in diplomatic and governmental circles. Gompers's assurance that he had no intention of meeting with political groups of any shade fell on deaf ears, though it was made known to him that the powers-that-be had no objection to a labor conference convening in another city. This opened the way for Henderson, who wished to organize a meeting of all socialist organizations—labor unions as well as parties—at the earliest opportunity. To this end he contacted organizations from all camps and succeeded in arranging a conference of socialist parties and unions at Bern in February 1919. The American AFL, the British GFTU, and the Belgian labor movement refused to attend, but the British TUC and the French *Confédération Generale du Travail* (CGT) did participate along with delegations from 17 other countries. This conference put forward a broad program of social reforms. The principal demands were the freedom of association, the eight-hour workday, a minimum wage, unemployment insurance, and the protection of women and children in the workplace. This program was to serve as the touchstone for labor's representatives to the Versailles peace conference, which was then already in progress. Gompers, however, rejected the Bern program, and, as chairman of the Commission on International Labor Legislation of the peace conference, followed his own course. This commission nonetheless booked important gains, which were more or less in keeping with the demands formulated in Bern. Furthermore, the participants made provisions for the organization of an International Labor Congress to be held in Washington in the autumn of 1919 and the establishment of an International Labor Organization (ILO) as an agency of the League of Nations, wherein unions and employers would be represented on equal footing. For Gompers this was an affirmation of his policies, for which he had already gained general recognition in his own country. At that time more than ever he wished to assume leadership of the international labor movement, and he planned—in the name of the AFL—to send out invitations for the founding congress of a new trade union international. In Bern, however, Léon Jouhaux of France and Jan Oudegeest of the Netherlands took on precisely the same task. This pair succeeded in reconciling the rival British organizations, the TUC and the GFTU, and also persuaded the German labor movement to neutralize remaining aversions to its participation by offering a public apology for its wartime stance. For the AFL there remained no other choice than to resign itself to this state of affairs, and Gompers accepted the invitation to take part in the founding congress of the International Federation of Trade Unions (IFTU) from 28 July to 2 August 1919 in Amsterdam.

Coming to Amsterdam were delegates from 14 countries representing nearly 18 million union members. Gompers was there on behalf of the AFL as well as the Pan-American Federation of Labor (established 7 July 1919), which drew its members from both North and South America. This founding congress would be Gompers's swansong on the international stage. The congress reaffirmed the Bern program and rejected the results of Versailles. The European trade union leaders wanted an action-oriented international with a strong political agenda. Although the trade union international had declared itself independent of the Socialist International, which for that matter had not yet been redrawn, the IFTU in principle oriented itself only toward organizations of socialist bent. The Dutchmen Edo Fimmen and Jan Oudegeest became the organization's general secretaries, and the Briton W. A. Appleton became chairman. The AFL, fearful of losing its independence and the connection with radical socialist groups, would not take part.

The "Amsterdam International" came to have quite an eventful history. After the radical early years when internationalism seemed to offer hitherto unknown possibilities for the development of social legislation, there occurred a fairly rapid change in climate. In most countries the trade union movement came under increasing pressure, lost many members, and faced a communist-inspired dissident opposition and splinter movements within its own ranks. Amsterdam found itself in a crisis that originated in differences of political opinion, power struggles between leading officers and structures, and having to operate with a paucity of means as well. Calm would not return until 1928. By that time the IFTU had rid itself of its most extreme elements and had traded socialist radicalism for a program of pragmatic reform. This change cleared the way for AFL membership, but in the end their accession took place only in 1937, concurrent with an escalation in the AFL's conflict with the Congress of Industrial Organizations (CIO). The IFTU moved to London during World War II and, in 1945, made way for the World Federation of Trade Unions, a united labor movement that included communist organizations. The World Federation soon fell victim to the cold war and dissolved in 1949. That same year, the noncommunist unions would band together to establish the International Confederation of Free Trade Unions.

Key Players

Fimmen, Edo (1881–1942): Fimmen was a Dutch trade-union leader who in 1919 became general secretary of the International Transportworkers Federation (ITF) and of the International Federation of Trade Unions (IFTU). He combined both functions until 1923, when a dispute with the IFTU executive over possible cooperation with communist organizations forced Fimmen to resign. Thereafter he concentrated wholly on the ITF, where he was an active campaigner against fascism and Nazism.

Jouhaux, Léon (1879–1954): French trade union leader, Jouhaux was general secretary of the French *Confédération Generale du Travail* (CGT; 1909–1947) and vice president of the IFTU (1919–1945). After World War II, with American backing, he became founder and chairman of Force Ouvrière. He received the Nobel Peace Prize in 1951.

Oudegeest, Jan (1870–1950): Dutch labor leader and socialist politician, first chairman of the Dutch trade union central, NVV, and general secretary of the IFTU (1919–1927), Oudegeest was also secretary of the employees group within the International Labor Organization (ILO; 1919–1928).

After his international trade union career, he became chairman of the Dutch Socialist Party.

See also: *American Federation of Labor; International Labor Organization; Second International; World Federation of Trade Unions.*

————————

BIBLIOGRAPHY

Books

Milner, Susan. *The Dilemmas of Internationalism, French Syndicalism and the International Labour Movement, 1900–1914.* Oxford, UK: Berg, 1990.

Taft, Philip. *The AFL in the Time of Gompers.* New York: Harper, 1957.

Van Goethem, Geert. "Conflicting Interests: The International Federation of Trade Unions (1919–1945)." In *The International Confederation of Free Trade Unions*, edited by A. Carew, M. Dreyfus, G. Van Goethem, R. Gumbrell-McCormick, and Marcel van der Linden. Bern, Switzerland: Peter Lang, 2000.

ADDITIONAL RESOURCES

Bush, Gary. *Political Role of International Trade Unions.* New York: St. Martin's Press, 1983.

Radosh, Ronald. *American Labor and the United States Foreign Policy: The Cold War and the Unions from Gompers to Lovestone.* New York: Random House, 1969.

Reinalda, Bob, ed. *The International Transportworkers Federation, 1914–1945: The Fimmen Era.* Amsterdam: Stichting Beheer IISG, 1997.

—Geert Van Goethem

International Labor Organization

France 1919

Synopsis

Throughout World War I, the leaders of the American Federation of Labor (AFL) recommended that the international recognition of certain specified labor rights be included in the war aims of the Allied and Associated Powers and as a special clause in the eventual peace treaty. This AFL advocacy contributed to the appointment of a special Commission on International Labor Legislation at the Paris peace conference, of which Samuel Gompers, the AFL president, was elected chairman. Between February and April 1919, this commission drafted a charter of legally enforceable labor rights' principles that incorporated most of the AFL's wartime recommendations. This

Samuel Gompers (with hands in pockets) walks with other union officials, 1919.

charter became part of the constitution for the new International Labor Organization (ILO) that the peace conference created as a special agency of the League of Nations under the Treaty of Versailles.

1900: China's Boxer Rebellion, which began in the preceding year with attacks on foreigners and Christians, reaches its height. An international contingent of more than 2,000 men arrives to restore order, but only after several tens of thousands have died.

1907: U.S. markets experience a financial panic.

1912: *Titanic* sinks on its maiden voyage, from Southampton to New York, on 14 April. More than 1,500 people are killed.

1915: At the Second Battle of Ypres, the Germans introduce a new weapon: poison gas.

1917: The intercepted "Zimmermann Telegram" reveals a plot by the German government to draw Mexico into an alliance against the United States in return for a German promise to return the southwestern U.S. territories taken in the Mexican War. Three months later, in response to German threats of unrestricted submarine warfare, the United States on 6 April declares war on Germany.

1919: With the formation of the Third International (Comintern), the Bolshevik government of Russia establishes its control over communist movements worldwide.

1919: The Eighteenth Amendment, which prohibits the production, sale, distribution, purchase, and consumption of alcohol throughout the United States, is ratified.

1919: In India, Mahatma Gandhi launches his campaign of nonviolent resistance to British rule.

1919: In Italy, a former socialist of the left named Benito Mussolini introduces the world to a new socialism of the right, embodied in an organization known as the "Union for Struggle," or Fasci di Combattimento. Composed primarily of young war veterans discontented with Italy's paltry share of the spoils from the recent world war (if not with their country's lackluster military performance in the conflict), the fascists are known for their black shirts and their penchant for violence.

1921: As the Allied Reparations Commission calls for payments of 132 billion gold marks, inflation in Germany begins to climb.

1925: European leaders attempt to secure the peace at the Locarno Conference, which guarantees the boundaries between France and Germany, and Belgium and Germany.

1929: On "Black Friday" in October, prices on the U.S. stock market, which had been climbing wildly for several years, suddenly collapse. Thus begins the first phase of a world economic crisis and depression that will last until the beginning of World War II.

Event and Its Context

Wartime Campaigns for a Labor Clause

The AFL issued three successively more detailed war aims statements during World War I. The last and most complete statement, presented to an Inter-Allied Labour and Socialist Conference in September 1918, became the basis for the Paris peace conference's deliberations on international labor legislation. The statement called upon the international labor movement to endorse the Fourteen Points peace program of U.S. president Woodrow Wilson and proposed the addition of a detailed list of specifically labor-related war aims designed to remove the economic causes of war.

At the top of Gompers's 1918 list was the demand that recognized representatives of labor be allowed to participate in the deliberations of the peace conference. In addition, Gompers proposed the arrangement of a parallel, periodically convened advisory labor conference that would be independent of the political, plenary peace conference. Gompers also called for the establishment of an international association of nations to work for the maintenance of peace not only through the peaceful arbitration of disputes between nation-states but also through removing the social and economic causes of strife. This organization—the League of Nations—would promote the concept that labor should never again be regarded or treated as a commodity. The association would also strive to guarantee essential labor rights, including the eight-hour workday; freedom of speech, of press, and of assembly; trial by jury; the abolition of involuntary servitude; and the right of seamen to disembark when in port. Key among these efforts would be work toward the abolition, as far as was practicable, of all protectionist impediments to international commerce.

The AFL plan was predicated on the pursuit of economic benefits only. The plan aspired to regulate labor conditions on the basis of voluntary labor-employer negotiations that were to be guided by the basic principles incorporated in the peace treaty. The AFL did not aspire to nor approve of the creation of any new national or international structures of legislation or compulsion. This limited vision of international labor legislation was intimately related to Gompers's long-standing fight both against socialist theory and practice and for a type of labor unionism that was conceived in strictly crafts-union and economic terms.

President Woodrow Wilson supported the AFL's antisocialist rationale and endorsed the AFL program on that basis.

At the November 1917 AFL convention, Wilson assured the delegates that his peace aims included the advancement of labor rights. Later he included in his drafts for the League of Nations Covenant provisions for the maintenance of fair and humane conditions of labor and for the creation of a new international organization. Wilson, like Gompers, was interested in using such provisions as antisocialist and anticommunist tools, which were as much aimed at strengthening the crafts-unionist AFL against its more radical syndicalist and socialist challengers at home and abroad as they were at the advancement of labor's economic and industrial position. Wilson wanted a social reformist dimension for the projected League of Nations, which he intended after the war to use in the elaboration of his previous social reform legislation. Major liberal and nonrevolutionary socialist politicians and publicists agreed on the necessity of such a League of Nations, and they too tended to give their support to the AFL's plan, even though some of them disagreed with Gompers's overt antisocialism.

The Inter-Allied Labour and Socialist Conference endorsed the AFL plan, but the positions of the AFL and President Wilson differed profoundly from the aspirations of the European protagonists for an international labor agency. Wartime European calls for a peace treaty labor clause were predicated on the pursuit either of an international labor legislature with coercive powers or on the issuance of certain legally binding labor standards that were to be incorporated into national legislation. The Bern Conference of January 1919 formalized recommendations for such a legally binding set of standards and enunciated the goal of an eventual abolition of capitalism. Attendees also proposed, for the meantime, a program considerably more radical than the AFL's. This program included the AFL propositions and such additional demands as guarantees for elementary education, freedom of emigration, unemployment and sickness insurance, and a built-in role or power of veto for the International Federation of Trade Unions in the coming international labor agency.

Wartime debate on the nature of future international labor legislation and organization revolved around the juxtaposition of these two sets of goals, one collectivist and political, the other voluntary and economic. The Bern program provided the blueprint for most of the drafts that British and continental European delegates brought to the Paris Peace Conference, and the Americans remained committed to Gompers's and Wilson's more limited vision.

The Commission on International Labour Legislation

In January 1919 the Paris Peace Conference formed a special Commission on International Labour Legislation. Apart from the Commission on the League of Nations, chaired by President Wilson, the labor commission was the only one of the peace conference's commissions to report directly to the plenary peace conference. Wilson appointed Gompers as the head of the American delegation, and on the suggestion of British delegates, Gompers became the commission chairman. Between 1 February and 28 April 1919, the labor commission debated various European and American drafts for a charter for the new international labour agency and tried to come to an agreement on the guiding principles of the projected organization. These deliberations were marked throughout by a tug of war between the

American voluntarist position and the European collectivist position. Agreement eluded the members of the commission until late April, when (in Gompers's absence) Arthur Balfour, former Conservative prime minister of Great Britain, and Sir Robert Borden, prime minister of Canada, served as mediators and drafters of a compromise labor clause.

The structure of the new organization was agreed upon even without Balfour's intervention. This was relatively easy because Gompers had never intended to preside over the creation of a permanent organization and was not particularly interested in its details. He had envisioned periodic labor conferences only but had to acquiesce to European demands for a permanent Labor Office as well. The activities of Gompers and the rest of the American delegation centered therefore on establishing several limits upon the authority of these two dimensions of the new International Labor Organization.

The Americans managed to restrict the permanent Labor Office to the preparation of recommended legislation, the gathering of labor statistics, and the conduct of propaganda for the advancement of labor legislation. For the periodic conferences, they sought to stipulate that only labor and employer representatives could take part in its activities, but in the end they had to settle for a tripartite system of representation in which governments would have two votes and labor and employer delegations one vote each. The conferees agreed that the annual ILO meeting could hear complaints and petitions from labor or employee organizations whenever either one of these felt that noncompliance with a specific ILO recommendation had occurred. In such cases the ILO could remonstrate with a member nation's government and ask for compliance, but it had no powers of coercion. In case of noncompliance, specific labor rights issues could also be referred to the International Court of Justice, another constituent of the League of Nations. On Gompers's insistence, however, it was stipulated that nothing in the ILO's recommendations would be so construed as to challenge recognized hemispheric arrangements such as the Monroe Doctrine or to put into question the supremacy of national constitutions.

The institutional structure of the new organization was thus a compromise between the voluntarist AFL position and the collectivist European position. Hedged with safeguards against central compulsion, in principle it was based on intimate government participation in the regulation of labor and industrial conditions that the AFL had opposed.

Even when the structure of the ILO was agreed upon, it proved exceedingly difficult to fashion the contents of the organization's charter or "General Principles" (Article 427 of the Versailles Treaty). The charter specified the areas in which the Labor Office could propose and the annual ILO conference enact recommendations and conventions for labor legislation. Because these specifications would relate directly to the purposes of the organization, it was a foregone conclusion that they would generate much debate and dissension. Gompers would have preferred simply to issue the AFL list of labor rights and to ask each ILO member to recognize, implement, and maintain them inviolate in their national legislation. The European members of the commission, on the other hand, insisted that national legislatures be obligated legally to incorporate these labor rights. Moreover, the Europeans fought for a broader statement of labor rights that would have included such items from the

Bern Conference agenda as unemployment and health insurance. As far as Gompers was concerned, these latter rights were not labor rights but politically contentious issues that should not be included in any labor clauses.

After mediation by Balfour and Borden, the committee agreed to retain the bulk of the AFL's list of guaranteed labor rights. The charter affirmed the right of unionization as well the principle of an adequate wage, the eight-hour workday and weekly rest, the goal of abolition of child labor, equal remuneration for men and women for work of equal value, equitable treatment of immigrant laborers, and inspection of industrial conditions. The AFL's core demand that labor not be treated as a commodity or article of commerce, however, was changed to read that labor not be regarded "merely" as a commodity or an article of commerce. The agreement further specified that all ILO members should "endeavor" to apply the labor rights indicated, and only inasmuch as "their special circumstances will permit." The list of labor rights was designated a "guide" only. The charter omitted mention of social insurance and unemployment benefits as labor rights, nor did the final version include original AFL demands for seamen's rights, trial by jury, abolition of involuntary servitude, or freedom of speech and assembly. To satisfy Gompers's repeated demands, the charter included the stipulation that no member nation would have to accept ILO recommendations that would have established labor rights or conditions less beneficial to that country's workers than were already established by national legislation.

The ILO constitution and charter were presented to the plenary peace conference on 28 April 1919, and they were accepted as Part XIII, Articles 387–427, of the Versailles Peace Treaty.

The ILO: Turning Point for Labor

The creation of the ILO marked a major turning point in international labor action. It constituted the first attempt to provide legally binding and enforceable international principles for the regulation of conditions of labor, contracts, and other societal questions of interest to labor. It created the first permanent, internationally recognized bureaucracy engaged in the preparation of labor legislation worldwide and in the creation of a world popular opinion conducive to further advancement of labor's cause. In many cases, the incorporation of the ILO charter into the national legislation of its member states marked the first acceptance of collective bargaining and coequality of labor unions in decisions affecting their interests. The principle of tripartite decision-making in labor and industrial matters was thus internationally recognized for the first time. Moreover, the ILO was carried over to the United Nations and continued its efforts as one of that organization's specialized agencies, only with a revised, more radical and broader charter that was set out in the Philadelphia Declaration of 1944. Thus, the deliberations of the labor commission in 1919 and the AFL war aims manifestoes of 1914–1918 ushered in an entirely new era in the defense and advancement of labor rights.

The vehement and prolonged criticism to which the ILO was immediately subjected by American and European conservatives attested to the radical nature of the departure. In the 1919–1920 debates over the ratification of the League of Nations Covenant, political and religious conservatives on both sides of the Atlantic almost invariably portrayed the ILO as the most objectionable, most collectivist, and most intrusive aspect of the new world organization. In the United States these conservatives managed to prevent American membership both in the League of Nations and, until 1934, in the ILO. Their passionate opposition to the ILO and to its charter left a legacy of increased suspicion of the AFL, of equating the League of Nations with international socialism, and of perceiving of the AFL as an accomplice thereto. The AFL tried to counteract and disprove this impression by stressing its fight in Paris for a noncollectivist ILO and its opposition to international communism, but it had only limited success.

Yet Gompers and other AFL leaders were themselves far from satisfied with the final nature of the ILO. Gompers was so concerned about the modifications to the charter that Arthur Balfour managed to insert in his absence that he appealed to President Wilson for some official statement to assure the American labor movement that the AFL's interests would indeed be served by the organization. Only with the help of this assurance was it possible for Gompers to stave off an incipient rebellion in the AFL and to acquire official AFL endorsement of the ILO and the League of Nations itself. Andrew Furuseth, the president of the American Seamen's Union, led AFL rebellion. Furuseth's opposition to the ILO was essentially a severe version of the same anticollectivist critique for which Gompers himself had stood. Furuseth, however, was unconvinced that Gompers had managed to keep the ILO from becoming a coercive supranational legislature.

European protagonists for international labor legislation tended to be dissatisfied with the ILO for the opposite reasons. They disapproved of the way in which both Balfour and Gompers had managed to delete all the substantive proposals of the Bern Conference from the ILO Charter. On the whole, however, European labor and socialist activists tended to argue that once the ILO was in operation and their countries bound to implement its principles, it would be possible for them to radicalize the organization from the inside, possibly to revise its charter and to point its activities in directions more to their liking. To an extent, this was later effected.

The American labor movement, on the other hand, did not benefit directly from the ILO. American nonmembership in the League of Nations meant that the provisions for labor legislation set out by the ILO could not be automatically incorporated into U.S. legislation. Also, in the aftermath of World War I, a marked shift toward the right took place in American society and politics, and this further conspired against the full implementation of the principles of the ILO charter. There was thus little immediate benefit from the ILO to American workers.

Regardless of the manifest difficulties in translating ILO recommendations into national legislation, the incorporation of a labor clause in the Treaty of Versailles and the Covenant of the League of Nations was by no means an inconsequential event. The new organization could potentially effect far-reaching reforms in labor conditions throughout the world, not least because its charter had expressly kept open the possibility of future elaboration of the organization's competence and aims. In the history of the labor movement the charter was also a powerful testimony to the combined strength of labor, socialists, and advanced liberals who, despite their differences in

principle on many ideological and practical points, had pooled their efforts in 1914–1919 and had managed to inject into the corpus of international law the concept of recognized and enforceable labor rights.

Key Players

Gompers, Samuel (1850–1924): President of the American Federation of Labor from 1881 to 1924, Gompers was born in England and in 1863 immigrated to the United States, where he joined the cigar-makers' union and played a central role in the creation of the AFL. During World World I, Gompers also served as a member of the Council of National Defense, in the American Alliance for Labor and Democracy, and in various other consultative posts set up by the government.

Furuseth, Andrew (1854–1938): President of the International Seamen's Union of America from 1908 to 1936 and a leading American labor critic of the ILO, the Norwegian-born Furuseth was a veteran advocate of the rights of all who worked for merchant marines, and he played a crucial role in the passage of the 1915 Seamen's Act. He represented the radical pole of voluntarist and anti-collectivist labor effort for which the AFL as a whole stood in a more moderated way.

See also: *American Federation of Labor; International Federation of Trade Unions.*

BIBLIOGRAPHY

Books

Alcock, Antony. *History of the International Labour Office.* London: Macmillan, 1971.

Gompers, Samuel. *Seventy Years Life and Labour: An Autobiography*, 2 vols. New York: A. M. Kelley, 1957.

Mayer, Arno J. *Politics and Diplomacy of Peacemaking: Containment and Counterrevolution at Versailles, 1918–1919.* New York: Knopf, 1967.

Radosh, Ronald. *American Labor and United States Foreign Policy.* New York: Random House, 1969.

Ruotsila, Markku. *British and American Anticommunism Before the Cold War.* London: Frank Cass, 2001.

Shotwell, James T., ed. *The Origins of the International Labor Organization*, 2 vols. New York: Columbia University Press, 1934.

———. *At the Paris Peace Conference.* New York: Macmillan, 1937.

Periodicals

Ruotsila, Markku. "The Great Charter for the Liberty of the Workingman: Labour, Liberals and the Creation of the ILO." *Labour History Review* 67 (April 2002): 29–48.

Other

Barnes, George N. *History of the International Labour Office.* London: Williams and Norgate Limited, 1926.

Follows, J. W. *Antecedents of the International Labour Organisation.* Oxford: Clarendon Press, 1951.

Foner, Philip. *The AFL in the Progressive Era, 1910–1915.* New York: International Publishers, 1980.

Galenson, Walter. *The International Labor Organization: An American View.* Madison: University of Wisconsin Press, 1981.

Larson, Simeon. *Labor and Foreign Policy: Gompers, the AFL and the First World War.* Rutherford, NJ: Fairleigh Dickinson University Press, 1975.

—Markku Ruotsila

International Labor Union

United States 1878

Synopsis

The International Labor Union (ILU) was an alliance of U.S. radical labor activists with Marxist-influenced socialists. The ILU was seen as an attempted successor of the National Labor Union (1866–1872), but one that would avoid the diffuse reformism (particularly the allure of "greenback" monetary reform schemes and premature electoralism) that had contributed to the latter's decline. Although the ILU enjoyed only limited success, it was a direct forerunner of the Federation of Organized Trades and Labor Unions, which in turn was the first incarnation of the American Federation of Labor. The ILU differed from those organizations in that they consisted predominantly of skilled workers organized into craft unions, whereas the ILU was the first major labor organization in the U.S. to focus on organizing unskilled workers on an industrial basis.

Timeline

1858: British explorer John Hanning Speke locates Lake Victoria, which he correctly identifies as the source of the Nile.

1863: The world's first subway opens, in London.

1868: Congressional efforts to impeach President Andrew Johnson prove unsuccessful, but they do result in his removal from any direct influence on Reconstruction policy and ensure his replacement by Ulysses S. Grant as the Republican presidential candidate later that year.

1871: Boss Tweed corruption scandal occurs in New York City.

1874: As farm wages in Britain plummet, agricultural workers go on strike.

1876: General George Armstrong Custer and 264 soldiers are killed by the Sioux at the Little Big Horn River.

1878: Russo-Turkish War, begun in 1877, ends with the defeat of Turkey, which ceases to be an important power in Europe. The Treaty of San Stefano concluding the war is revised by the Congress of Berlin, which realigns the balance of power in southeastern Europe.

1878: First commercial telephone exchange opens, in New Haven, Connecticut.

1878: Thomas Edison develops a means of cheaply producing and transmitting electric current, which he succeeds in subdividing so as to make it adaptable to household use. The value of shares in gas companies plummets as news of his breakthrough reaches Wall Street.

1882: The Chinese Exclusion Act, a treaty between the United States and China, provides for restrictions on immigration of Chinese workers.

1884: Due to isolationist policies, Japan's government had prohibited emigration, but this year it finally lifts the ban and allows citizens to immigrate to Hawaii, where many—having escaped the country illegally—already work as temporary laborers. Thereafter, Japanese will increasingly replace Chinese as workers in the United States, where a treaty limits Chinese immigration.

1888: With a series of murders in London's seedy Whitechapel district, Jack the Ripper—whose identity remains a subject of debate—becomes the first known serial murder.

Event and Its Context

The ILU was initiated by participants in the International Workingmen's Association (First International) who had been involved in the formation of the Workingmen's Party of the United States (WPUS). In late 1877 the WPUS had changed its name to the Socialist Labor Party (SLP) and embarked on a course of electoral action. Believing this electoral course was premature, ILU organizers chose a path of union organizing for the purpose of building a more practical form of working-class action.

Radical Program for Labor Organizing

The radicalism of the ILU was written into its program, which declared, "The wage system is a despotism under which the wage-worker is forced to sell his labor at such price and under such conditions as the employer of labor shall dictate." This strategic orientation asserted that "as the wealth of the world is distributed through the wage system, its better distribution must come through higher wages and better opportunities, until wages shall represent the earnings and not the necessities of labor; thus melting profit upon labor out of existence, and making cooperation, or self-employed labor, the natural and logical step from wages slavery to free labor." The perspective was expressed in terms of revolutionary democracy: "The victory over 'divine-right' rulership must be supplemented by a victory over property-rights rulers; for there can be no government of the people, by the people, and for the people, where the many are dependent upon the few for an existence."

The practical objectives enumerated in the program included reduction of hours of labor, higher wages, workplace inspection, abolition of child and convict labor, occupational health and safety, establish labor bureaus, labor education (through labor press, lectures), employment of a general organizer, and the final abolition of the wage system. The ILU program concluded with an emphasis on the need to organize unions. As ILU President George McNeill asserted, the ILU offered "a plan by which the unorganized masses and local unions can become affiliated." Carl Speyer, who became ILU general secretary, later explained that the ILU should function "chiefly to organize the unskilled laborers," because "to induce mechanics [i.e., skilled workers] to join us would be interfering with the Trade Unions who regard the International Labor Union as an associate." As Samuel Gompers, who became involved in the ILU's organizing efforts, explained, its goal "was to get the yet unorganized into trade unions, thus build up trade organizations, and prepare the way for the national amalgamation of all organizations."

Vision and Reality

Within the labor movement the response to the ILU program was generally positive. The influential *National Labor Tribune* commented that "the consummation of this comprehensive plan will be pregnant with results of the most lasting importance to the wage-workers in America, particularly, and generally throughout the civilized world of manufacturers," and lauded the plan as "eminently practical."

SLP national secretary Philip Van Patten was less effusive. "The International Labor Union is far from perfect, and is unfortunately afflicted with a narrow-minded management," he wrote. He noted that "its plans and its platform, however, are good," and urged socialists to participate in, and help "purify" it. In fact, SLP members such as Albert Parsons and George Schilling were centrally involved and served on the ILU provisional central committee along with George Gunton, J. P. McDonnell (who edited the weekly *Labor Standard*, which became an ILU mainstay), George McNeill, Friedrich Sorge, Ira Steward, and Otto Weydemeyer.

In all, 18 states were represented on the provisional steering committee, and the ILU's breadth of vision was nothing if not expansive. As George McNeill put it, the organization sought "to band together Jew, Greek, Irishman, American, English and German, and all nationalities in a grand labor brotherhood" for the purpose of struggling "until freedom shall be achieved for all." Yet Gompers later noted that the ILU "failed of its national purpose and became an organization of textile workers . . . chiefly in New Jersey, New York and Massachusetts."

Nonetheless, in its first year, the ILU's membership rose from 700 to 8,000. The efforts to organize the unskilled textile workers, however, was hampered by the fact, as Gompers put it, that "there was more spirit than organization or money," Strikes led by the ILU organizers were broken by hunger. The result was rapid decline. By 1880 the ILU had only eight branches with a total of 1,500 members, and by1881 it had collapsed into a single branch that lingered on until 1887, by which time most of those associated with the ILU had long departed for more fruitful organizing efforts.

Legacy

The agitation of the ILU had an immediate effect of preparing the ground for the organization of a number of local assemblies of the Knights of Labor in some of the areas in which the trade union efforts had failed. The ideas, experience, and cadres of the ILU were also absorbed, to a large extent, in the later formation of the Federation of Organized Trades and Labor Unions and the American Federation of Labor (AFL). The failure to organize unskilled workers on an industrial basis also influenced future leaders of the AFL and contributed to making that body incline toward a more exclusive focus on skilled workers in craft unions.

Key Players

Gompers, Samuel (1850–1924): Prominent in the Cigar Makers Union, Gompers became the long-time (1886–1924) and increasingly conservative president of the American Federation of Labor, a spokesman for the "pure and simple union" orientation initially developed by his colleague Adolph Strasser. In his later years he became an outright opponent of socialism (though never lost his admiration for Karl Marx, whose outlook he viewed as consistent with his own "pure and simple" unionism).

Gunton, George (1847–1919): British-born textile worker, Gunton became associated with Ira Steward's eight-hour movement and spent a number of years in labor reform efforts. He published *Wealth and Progress* (1887), based on Steward's unpublished writings, and then became editor of the magazine Social Economist, whose name was later changed to *Gunton's Magazine*. In later years he severed connections with the labor movement and, according to Selig Perlman, "became one of the best-known defenders of the trusts."

McDonnell, J. P. (1840–1906): An Irish revolutionary, ex-Fenian, and former secretary to Karl Marx in the First International, McDonnell became prominent in socialist and labor politics upon his arrival in the United States in the 1870s. He remained editor of the *Labor Standard* after it disaffiliated from the WPUS, was prominent in various labor reform efforts, and became the leader of the New Jersey Federation of Trades and Labor Unions from its founding in 1883 until his death in 1906.

McNeill, George E. (1837–1906): A lifelong labor activist, author, and editor of a number of works (including the 1887 classic, *The Labor Movement: The Problem of To-Day*), McNeill was a leading activist in the eight-hour leagues, the Knights of Labor (and was author of its declaration of principles), and the American Federation of Labor (AFL). He lobbied for various labor reforms, served as deputy director of the Massachusetts Bureau of Labor Statistics (1869–1873), edited and served on the editorial staff of a number of labor newspapers, ran unsuccessfully for mayor on the United Labor Party ticket in 1886, and represented the AFL at the1897 British Trade Union Congress.

Parsons, Albert (1848–1887): Parsons was a Confederate war veteran in Texas who fell in love with and married a woman of color (Lucy Gonzales, at least partly African American, perhaps also Indian and Mexican). Parsons subsequently became a Radical Republican; with the collapse of Reconstruction in Texas, he fled with his wife to Chicago where they both become active in radical labor activities. Active in Typographical Workers Union, he was blacklisted after 1877, at which time he became a full-time labor and socialist activist. Editor of the revolutionary paper *The Alarm* in the 1880s and a leader of the radical wing of the eight-hour movement, he was victimized as one of the Haymarket martyrs and executed in 1887.

Schilling, George (1850–1938): Initially a cooper by trade, active in socialist politics for many years (running for mayor of Chicago on the Socialist Labor Party ticket in 1881), Schilling was also involved in the Knights of Labor, the eight-hour movement, and the Chicago Trades and Labor Assembly. He was prominent in the defense of the Haymarket defendants. In the 1890s he became an aide to Democratic governor John Peter Altgeld (under whom he served as secretary of the Illinois Labor Department), and was active in Chicago's "single-tax" club.

Sorge, Friedrich (1827–1906): Sorge was a music teacher who emigrated to the United States after the defeat of the 1848 Revolution in Germany. He joined the Communist Club in New York City in 1858, conducted an extensive correspondence with Marx and Engels, and became a central figure in the North American sections of the First International. After its dissolution, he was a founder of the WPUS, then left it to help build the International Labor Union. In the 1890s Sorge wrote a classic history, *Labor Movement in the United States*, which was serialized in the German Marxist journal *Neue Zeit*.

Speyer, Carl (1845–?): German-born leader of the New York City furniture workers, Speyer was a member of the General Council of the First International and a founding member of the Workingmen's Party of the United States in 1876. In the same year he helped to reorganize the Trades and Labor Council in New York. In the 1880s he edited the journal of the Brotherhood of Carpenters.

Steward, Ira (1831–1883): A machinist and member of Machinists and Blacksmiths International Union, Steward was a pioneer in arguing and agitating for the eight-hour workday. In his union he secured passage of a resolution for the eight-hour day in 1863 and became a tireless advocate of workday reduction. He gave speeches and lectures, wrote articles and pamphlets, and helped to organize 10-hour and eight-hour leagues dedicated to that goal. Sorge helped secure passage of an effective 10-hour law for women and children in Massachusetts. He believed that a reduction in hours of labor would ultimately bring about a redistribution of wealth and also allow workers more time to press for other reforms.

Otto, Weydemeyer: Son of Joseph Weydemeyer (a hero of the 1848 Revolution in Germany and of the Civil War in the United States), and like his father close to Karl Marx, Otto Weydemeyer was a leading member of the International Workingmen's Association (the First International). He was the first to translate into English portions of *Capital*, which was initially published as a series of articles in the *Labor Standard*, then as a pamphlet for U.S. workers.

See also: *American Federation of Labor; Federation of Organized Trades and Labor Unions of the United States and Canada (FOTLU); First International; Knights of Labor; Workingmen's Party of the United States.*

BIBLIOGRAPHY

Books

Buhel, Mary Jo, Paul Buhle, Dan Georgakas, eds. *Encyclopedia of the American Left*. Urbana, IL: University of Illinois Press, 1992.

Commons, John R., et al. *History of Labor in the United States*, Vol. 2. New York: Macmillan, 1918.

Fink, Gary, ed. *Biographical Dictionary of American Labor*. Westport, CT: Greenwood Press, 1984.

Foner, Philip S. *History of the Labor Movement in the United States*, Vol. 1. New York: International Publishers, 1947.

Gompers, Samuel. *Seventy Years of Life and Labor*. New York: E. P. Dutton Co., 1925.

Kaufman, Stuart Bruce. *Samuel Gompers and the Origins of the American Federation of Labor*. Westport, CT: Greenwood Press, 1973.

Mandel, Bernard. *Samuel Gompers*. Yellow Springs, OH: Antioch Press, 1963.

Montgomery, David. *Beyond Equality: Labor and the Radical Republicans, 1862–1872*. New York: Alfred A. Knopf, 1967.

Sorge, Friedrich A. *Labor Movement in the United States*. Edited by Philip S. Foner and Brewster Chamberlin. Westport, CT: Greenwood Press, 1977.

—Paul Le Blanc

International Ladies Garment Workers Union

United States 1900

Synopsis

The International Ladies Garment Workers Union (ILGWU) was one of the most radical and colorful labor organizations in the early decades of the twentieth century. Although the union embraced workers from a variety of ethnic and racial backgrounds, a decisive element in its composition was the wave of eastern European Jewish immigrants who flooded into the United States from the 1880s through the 1920s. Especially important in the union's founding and evolution were dedicated socialists and anarchists who articulated the vision of a better world to be achieved through the collective struggle of workers against their own oppressors. The ILGWU embraced all workers—regardless of specific occupation or skill level—in the women's garment industry and was one of the few unions in the American Federation of Labor of that time to be organized on an industrial rather than craft basis.

Timeline

1880: The completed Cologne Cathedral, begun 634 years earlier. With twin spires 515 feet (157 m) high, is the tallest structure in the world, and will remain so until 1889, when it is surpassed by the Eiffel Tower. (The previous record for the world's tallest structure lasted much longer—for about 4,430 years following the building of Cheops's Great Pyramid in c. 2550 B.C.)

1885: Sudanese capital of Khartoum falls to forces under the Mahdi Mohammed Ahmed, whose forces massacre British General Charles "Chinese" Gordon and his garrison just before a British relief expedition reaches the city.

1890: U.S. Congress passes the Sherman Antitrust Act, which in the years that follow will be used to break up large monopolies.

1893: Wall Street stock prices plummet on 5 May, precipitating a market collapse on 27 June. In the wake of this debacle, some 600 banks and 15,000 other businesses fail. The nationwide depression will last for four more years.

1898: United States defeats Spain in the three-month Spanish-American War. As a result, Cuba gains it independence, and the United States purchases Puerto Rico and the Philippines from Spain for $20 million.

1900: China's Boxer Rebellion, which began in the preceding year with attacks on foreigners and Christians, reaches its height. An international contingent of more than 2,000 men arrives to restore order, but only after several tens of thousands have died.

1900: The Commonwealth of Australia is established.

1900: The first zeppelin is test-flown.

1900: Sigmund Freud publishes *The Interpretation of Dreams.*

1900: German physicist Max Planck develops Planck's constant, a cornerstone of quantum theory.

1903: Henry Ford establishes the Ford Motor Company.

1907: U.S. markets experience a financial panic.

1910: Neon lighting is introduced.

Event and Its Context

In the final years of the nineteenth century, a variety of developments in the women's clothing industry culminated in the emergence of a widely perceived need for a unified organization of workers in that industry. There were almost 84,000 workers in women's garment shops in 32 states. There was a decades-long accumulation of political and trade union experience among many of these workers and a proliferation of local unions with strong organization, especially among many of the cloakmakers.

The United Brotherhood of Cloakmakers' Union No. 1 of New York and Vicinity issued a call on 11 March 1900 for a national convention of garment workers to take place in New York City on 3 June 1900. The call asserted that "to improve our condition, we must have not only local unions, but also a well-organized national union for all America."

Social, Economic, and Political Ferment

The relative moderation in the wording of the cloakmakers' call gives little sense of the realities leading up to it. These in-

Abraham Cahan. The Library of Congress.

cluded sweeping changes in U.S. society that had been generated by rapid industrialization in the decades following the Civil War, the dramatic process of decomposition and recomposition within the U.S. working class and its organizations, and the turbulence and ferment among garment workers in particular.

Between 1860 and 1880 the number of shops in the women's clothing industry rose from 188 to 562, the value of the products produced increased from $7 million to $32 million, and the number of workers increased from about 5,700 to more than 25,000. The workforce was largely immigrant, shifting increasingly after 1880 from Irish and German to eastern European Jewish, as well as Italian, Bohemian, Polish, Russian, Syrian, and others. Female participation in the workforce was high (26,000 women as opposed to 13,000 men in 1890), though increasing numbers of men found employment in this industry. "And the children are called in from play to drive and drudge beside their elders," wrote one observer from this period. "The load falls upon the ones least able to bear it—upon the backs of the little children at the base of the labor pyramid."

Much of the work in this period was done in the home, with contractors providing raw materials and gathering finished products from those laboring in small, poorly lit, poorly ventilated apartments in the tenement buildings of urban slums. Increasingly, however, the work was done in small garment shops. Ambitious entrepreneurs (often immigrants themselves) signed contracts with larger manufacturers to produce clothing goods. Business startup required a relatively small outlay of capital ($50 would be sufficient), and the source of cheap labor provided was the immigrants who were flooding into the cities. Sewing machines were cheap and could be bought on the installment plan or even rented, and they were small enough to be installed easily in the room of a tenement house. The foot-power of the immigrant sewers ran the machines, and the workers could be secured at makeshift labor exchanges such as New York City's "Pig Market." Space could be rented in tenement buildings and apartments converted into miniature factories.

Good profits could be made by paying the garment workers in these cramped and unsanitary "sweatshops" as little as possible (ranging from $3 to $12 per week), making them work as long and intensively as possible (generally 84 hours per week), compelling them to buy or rent their own machines, supply their own needles and thread, and even requiring that they pay a fee for the privilege of securing a job in the shop. The larger manufacturers played off these "sweatshop" contractors against each other, by utilizing the inferior pay and conditions of the sweatshop workers to force down the somewhat better wages and conditions of their own employees, and increasing the hours of work (which tended to fluctuate around 60 hours per week) in the larger shops.

The occupational structure in the women's garment industry of this period was complex. There were cloakmakers, dressmakers, waistmakers, hatmakers, those making underwear, knitgoods workers, embroiderers, and more. The four basic occupational divisions that came to dominate the industry were seen as constituting four basic crafts. The *cloakmakers* made outerwear such as overcoats and capes (which required somewhat greater skill than other clothing), were predominantly male, and tended to be among the most volatile, radical, and militant of the workers in the industry. The *cutters*, also predominantly male, were the most highly paid and highly skilled, with a reputation for being the practical-minded elite in the industry's labor force. (A significant number of cutters were native-born Americans or Americanized Irishmen, Germans, and Jews). The *pressers* were especially muscular, thanks to the strength needed to handle the heavy irons required to press the various garments being produced, and were commonly seen as being interested in more down-to-earth matters. The great majority of women workers in the industry were concentrated among the *dressmakers* and were eventually seen by many as being the most idealistic and radical element in the workforce.

A very high percentage of the garment workers were youthful, close to half being under the age of 31. As many as 80 percent were eastern and southern European immigrants, with a majority being Jewish and a large minority being Italian. Although religion was a significant ideological and cultural element among these workers, radical secular ideologies—particularly various currents of socialist and anarchist thought—had a powerful impact among them as well. Particularly in New York City, a strong labor-radical subculture flourished among Jewish immigrant workers. Key figures in this subculture were men who became leading figures in the socialist movement such as Abraham Cahan, editor of various left-wing publications (the last and most famous being the *Jewish Daily Forward*), and labor lawyers Morris Hillquit and Meyer London, the scholar Isaac Hourwich, and others who were des-

tined to have, as a consequence, a profound influence in the rising Jewish-American sector of the labor movement.

The Long March to Unionization

The earliest unionizing efforts among "modern" garment workers were loosely affiliated with the Knights of Labor in the 1880s, but hit-or-miss organizational efforts did not yield any permanent organization. One AFL affiliate, the United Garment Workers, was a relatively conservative and in many areas a corrupt organization. Tending toward an exclusive focus on such skilled workers as tailors and cutters, the organization's president once confessed a "lack of confidence in the possibility of organizing these people," meaning new immigrants, political radicals, Jews, women, unskilled workers. Such an attitude made the United Garment Workers increasingly irrelevant in the face of dramatically shifting economic and social realities that were reshaping the industry. (In 1914 Sidney Hillman and others would be compelled to lead a mass breakaway from the United Garment Workers to form the Amalgamated Clothing Workers of America.)

By the end of the 1880s clusters of socialist and anarchist activists were forming cadres that would produce more sustained effort among workers to "educate, agitate, and organize" around the trade union idea. In the early 1890s such developments were beginning to bear fruit. Cahan, Hillquit, and others (at this time associated with the Socialist Labor Party) organized the United Hebrew Trades in New York, rallied radicals around Abraham Bisno (who later became a leading figure in the ILGWU) in Chicago, and organized the Workers Education Society. Philadelphia anarchists organized the Jewish Federation of Labor. All of these new groups gave special attention to organizing garment workers. A number of militant strikes and vibrant local unions resulted, particularly among the cloakmakers.

In the forefront of organizing efforts in New York was the charismatic Joseph Barondess, who became the leader of the Operators and Cloakmakers Union, whose membership rose from 2,800 to 7,000 during the tumultuous and victorious strikes of 1890. In 1892 Barondess established the International Cloak Makers Union of America, which became part of the AFL.

The fragile new union soon succumbed to employer assaults combined with factional turmoil. The Chicago affiliate, led by Abraham Bisno, was crushed when it supported the ill-fated Pullman Strike led by Eugene V. Debs's American Railway Union. The Philadelphia cloakmakers moved back and forth between the AFL and Knights of Labor. Under the sectarian leadership of Daniel De Leon, the Socialist Labor Party organized its own union federation, the Socialist Trades and Labor Unions (STLA), which made demands on the union's loyalties. Future ILGWU leader Benjamin Schlesinger and Joseph Schlossberg, who was later prominent in the Industrial Workers of the World and later the Amalgamated Clothing Workers of America, were leading figures in the STLA. Conflicts between anarchists (with whom Barondess formed an alliance) and socialists also took their toll.

As the International fell apart, Barondess regrouped his New York forces into the United Brotherhood of Cloakmakers' Union No. 1 of New York and Vicinity. "In addition to political difficulties there was the difficulty of maintaining internal discipline," Louis Levine, official historian of the ILGWU, later recounted. "The members of the union regarded the paid officers with suspicion as 'job holders.' On the other hand, the paid officials were not too respectful of the 'rank-and-file.'" Tensions and conflicts in Barondess's organization came to be overshadowed, however, by objective realities. Between 1890 and 1900 the number of garment industry establishments had grown from 1,224 to 2,701, the value of products rose from $68 million to $159 million, and the number of workers grew from 39,149 to 83,739. More and more garment workers meant an expansion of the oppressive conditions to which they were subjected. The need to organize the unorganized—to protect the situation of those in unions being no less than the moral imperative to help those who were not—became clear to all.

Birth and Evolution

On 3 June 1900, in response to the call from Cloakmakers' Union No. 1, 11 delegates representing seven local unions with 2,000 members met at New York City's Labor Lyceum to establish an industrial union of all crafts and occupations within the women's garment trades. The new organization was called the International Ladies Garment Workers Union (ILGWU) and within 20 days was granted a charter from the American Federation of Labor. Starting with only $30 in its treasury and no funds to pay its officers and organizers, it nonetheless grew dramatically to 9 locals and 4000 members within a year, and then to 51 locals and almost 10,000 members (of whom 3,500 were women) by 1903.

From the beginning, the ILGWU represented a curious blend of conservatism and radicalism as reflected in different ways in all of its leaders. Although trade union moderate Barondess was decisive in its founding, the similarly decisive layers of socialists in the union prevented his ascension to leadership of the ILGWU. The first president and secretary-treasurer of the union were the relatively undistinguished Herman Grossman and Bernard Braff. The union took its place unambiguously in the left wing of the AFL, favoring industrial unionism, independent political action on the part of the labor movement, and association with the new Socialist Party of America, founded in 1901 by Eugene V. Debs, Morris Hillquit, and others. In 1903 Socialist Party partisan Benjamin Schlesinger became president of the union only to be dislodged in a factional struggle that ultimately brought in the more conservative team of James McCauley and John Dyche as president and secretary-treasurer. Yet Schlesinger was manager of the powerful New York Joint Board of Cloakmakers (and become ILGWU president again in 1914).

Dyche came to be known as the "Jewish Gompers," a former socialist who favored "pure and simple" unionism, and was the major power in the leadership (the presidency going to the ideologically compatible Abraham Rosenberg). Dyche was challenged not only by the left-wing faction of his own union, but also by a decision of the rival Industrial Workers of the World (IWW) to organize garment workers. The IWW insurgents were led from 1905 to 1907 by Morris Sigman, who subsequently rejoined the ILGWU and become its secretary-treasurer in 1914 and its relatively conservative president in 1923. In 1928 Schlesinger returned to help facilitate a transition

to the leadership of a young socialist trade unionist named David Dubinsky, who, while championing industrial unionism (and helping to launch the CIO in the 1930s), also embraced the Democratic Party. Dubinsky maintained a nostalgic attachment to shreds of socialist rhetoric, though he also insisted, "Trade unionism needs capitalism like a fish needs water."

The different blends of radical and conservative elements in the makeup of the various leaders of the ILGWU were only one aspect of the union's story. Its idealism, hard-fought strikes, and the militancy of its membership, plus the strength of its organization, allowed the ILGWU to help many thousands of garment workers to leave behind the worst of the sweatshop conditions and secure qualitatively better lives. This situation was not decisively reversed until the final decades of the twentieth century, which brought dramatic erosion of union gains as a side effect of the restructuring of the global economy.

Key Players

Barondess, Joseph (1867–1928): Barondess came from Russia to the United States in 1888 and quickly assumed leadership among his fellow garment workers for many years. Despite left-wing associations, he gravitated toward more moderate currents in the American Federation of Labor. Later in life, he went into the insurance business and became involved in civic and Zionist activities.

Bisno, Abraham (1866–1929): Working in the garment trades from the time his family arrived in the United States from Russia in 1881, Bisno became involved in anarchist and socialist currents in Chicago and union organizing efforts. Prominent among union leaders in the Chicago garment workers, he became a founder and leader of the ILGWU, though he was often "too militant" for the organization's top leadership. He left the ILGWU in 1917 and went into real estate but maintained his labor and radical sympathies.

Cahan, Abraham (1860–1951): After coming to the United States from Russia in 1882, Cahan became part of the socialist movement and an eloquent pioneer in Yiddish-language literature. For many years the editor of the profoundly influential mass-circulation *Jewish Daily Forward*, Cahan exercised immense influence among the leadership and membership of the ILGWU.

Dyche, John A. (1867–1938): Emigrating from Russia to England, and then to the United States in 1901, Dyche began as a socialist critical of outside "meddlers" in the labor movement. Dyche was hostile to trade union militancy and left-wing influence, knowledgeable about the garment industry, and inclined to collaborate with employers to secure the best deal for his members. He was ILGWU secretary-treasurer from 1903 until 1914.

Hillquit, Morris (1869–1933): Arriving in the United States from Latvia in 1886, Hillquit evolved from garment worker to a prominent labor lawyer. A leading organizer of the United Hebrew Trades in the 1880s, he became an influential force in the ILGWU. He was active in the Socialist Labor Party and helped lead a revolt against SLP leader Daniel De Leon. Hillquit became a founding member and central leader of the Socialist Party of America.

Schlesinger, Benjamin (1876–1932): A Lithuanian immigrant who arrived in the United States in 1891, Schlesinger became involved with the Socialist Labor Party and as an activist among garment workers, then with the *Jewish Daily Forward* and the Socialist Party of America. He was a capable organizer and leader of the ILGWU, for which he served as president in 1903–1904, 1914–1923, and 1928–1932.

Sigman, Morris (1880–1931): Going from Russia to England in 1901 and then to the United States a year later, Sigman got a job as a cloak presser and soon became a leading activist in the Industrial Workers of the World. He first challenged the ILGWU then switched over to it in 1907. He allied himself with socialists in the union and became secretary-treasurer in 1914, first vice president in 1920, and president in 1923, a position he held for five years during a "civil war" that broke Communist Party influence in the union.

See also: *American Federation of Labor; Industrial Workers of the World; Socialist Party of America; Knights of Labor; Protocol of Peace.*

BIBLIOGRAPHY

Books

Bisno, Abraham. *Abraham Bison, Union Pioneer.* Madison: University of Wisconsin Press, 1967.

Epstein, Melech. *Jewish Labor in U.S.A., 1882–1952.* New York: KTAV Publishing House, 1969.

———. *Profiles of Eleven.* Lanham, MD: University Press of America, 1987.

Fraser, Steven. *Labor Will Rule: Sidney Hillman and the Rise of American Labor.* New York: Free Press, 1991.

Hardy, Jack. *The Clothing Workers, A Study of the Conditions and Struggles in the Needle Trades.* New York: International Publishers, 1935.

Laslett, John. *Labor and the Left: A Study of Socialist and Radical Influences in the American Labor Movement, 1881–1924.* New York: Basic Books, 1970.

Levine, Louis. *The Women's Garment Workers: A History of the International Ladies Garment Workers Union.* New York: B.W. Huebsch, 1924.

Stein, Leon, ed. *Out of the Sweatshop: The Struggle for Industrial Democracy.* New York: Quadrangle/New York Times, 1977.

Stolberg, Benjamin. *Tailor's Progress: The Story of a Famous Union and the Men Who Made It.* Garden City, NY: Doubleday, Doran and Co., 1944.

Tyler, Gus. *Look for the Union Label: A History of the International Ladies' Garment Workers Union.* Armonk, NY: M. E. Sharpe, 1995.

—Paul Le Blanc

International Transport Workers' Federation

Europe 1896

Synopsis

In 1896 maritime workers from unions from several European countries formed an organization that would eventually become known as the International Transport Workers' Federation (ITF). Although the ITF would later incorporate laborers in other transportation industries, such as railroad and streetcar workers, seamen and dockworkers initially formed the ITF. In response to the conditions endured by workers in their unions, leaders of several of the British maritime trade unions began to call for an international federation. Strikes in places such as London and Rotterdam inspired these union leaders to create such an organization. After much initial enthusiasm, however, the ITF fell into a period of decline that resulted from its inability to win a strike in Hamburg, Germany. After the failed Hamburg strike, the British leaders lost much of their power. German union leaders took control of the ITF and moved its headquarters to Hamburg. Although the German leadership succeeded in improving the organization of the ITF, the federation once again fell into a period of inactivity during World War I.

Timeline

1876: General George Armstrong Custer and 264 soldiers are killed by the Sioux at the Little Big Horn River.

1880: Completed Cologne Cathedral, begun 634 years earlier, with twin spires 515 feet (157 m) high, is the tallest structure in the world and will remain so until 1889, when it is surpassed by the Eiffel Tower. (The previous record for the world's tallest structure lasted much longer—for about 4,430 years following the building of Cheops's Great Pyramid in c. 2550 B.C.)

1885: Belgium's King Leopold II becomes sovereign of the so-called Congo Free State, which he will rule for a quarter-century virtually as his own private property. The region in Africa, given the name of Zaire in the 1970s (and Congo in 1997), becomes the site of staggering atrocities, including forced labor and genocide, at the hands of Leopold's minions.

1891: French troops open fire on workers during a 1 May demonstration at Fourmies, where employees of the Sans Pareille factory are striking for an eight-hour workday. Nine people are killed—two of them children—and 60 more are injured.

1894: French army captain Alfred Dreyfus, a Jew, is convicted of treason. Dreyfus will later be cleared of all charges, but the Dreyfus case illustrates—and exacerbates—the increasingly virulent anti-Semitism that pervades France.

1895: German physicist Wilhelm Roentgen discovers X-rays.

1895: Brothers Auguste and Louis Lumière show the world's first motion picture—*Workers Leaving the Lumière Factory*—at a café in Paris.

1895: Guglielmo Marconi pioneers wireless telegraphy, which in the next three decades will make possible the use of radio waves for commercial broadcasts and other applications.

1895: German engineer Rudolf Diesel invents an engine capable of operating on a type of petroleum less highly refined, and therefore less costly, than gasoline.

1898: Marie and Pierre Curie discover the radioactive elements radium and polonium.

1901: U.S. president William McKinley is assassinated by Leon Czolgosz, an anarchist. Vice President Theodore Roosevelt becomes president.

1905: In the industrial Ruhr region in Germany, 200,000 miners go on strike.

Event and Its Context

Early Organization of Maritime Workers

The ITF originated as an outgrowth of the early organization of British seamen and dockworkers in the late nineteenth century. Working conditions for these transport workers were often very poor. Seamen and firemen on steamships were often subject to harsh discipline, cramped accommodations, and poor food. It was not uncommon for them to be cheated of their wages. For their part, dockworkers generally received low pay.

In particular, the 1889 Great London Dock Strike served as an inspiration for future organization and activity of British maritime workers. The strike closed the city's docks, and the employers eventually gave in to the demands of the workers, in part because the strikers had financial support from Australian workers. Two of the strike's leaders later helped to create the ITF. Ben Tillet helped to organize unskilled dockworkers, and socialist labor leader Tom Mann also lent support to the strike. In part because of the activities of these two men, the London dockworkers organized a strong union and committed themselves to class struggle.

Another key leader of the early organizational activities was John Havelock Wilson, who led a British seamen's union. Originally, Wilson was more traditional in his views of labor organization, believing that his union should play more of a social role rather than lead a class struggle. He also only allowed seamen and not the other related trades, and was hostile to foreigners. Wilson, however, later changed his views and began to organize workers who were not seamen and who were not British. Thus, in 1890 he changed the name of his union to the Amalgamated Seamen's Union of Great Britain, Ireland, and Other Nations. This new organization had branches in northern and western Europe, Istanbul, the Suez Canal, and Malta. Indeed, 25 percent of the members were non-British. However, the union was not successful and soon ceased to exist.

The Rotterdam Strike and the Birth of the ITF

In 1896 Wilson revived his idea of an international federation of sea and dockworkers. In May several British sailors in

Liverpool informed Wilson of a Dutch dock strike in Rotterdam, Netherlands. They reported that they had been told that if they did not break the strike, they would be fired. In Rotterdam the largest employer in the port attempted to establish a fixed weekly wage that would effectively cut earnings by 25 percent. Furthermore, extra money earned through piecework would only be paid once a year. In response, the maritime workers in the city went on strike.

Upset by this situation, Wilson began a campaign to support the strike and even traveled to Rotterdam, where he found the entire port on strike. The situation was tense, and the government had called in the military to keep order. Upon his arrival, Wilson found about 40 British ships in Rotterdam. He succeeded in convincing British crews not to handle cargo in the Dutch port. He also requested that British dockworkers boycott ships that had been loaded in Rotterdam by strikebreakers. He even set up a branch of his own union in Rotterdam.

The Rotterdam strike inspired Wilson to continue his efforts to form an international organization of transport workers. Thus, Wilson and others began to consider the idea of calling an international meeting to establish such a group. They used the meeting of the Socialist International in London in June 1896 as the basis for their meeting. In June 1896 labor leaders including Wilson, Mann, and Tillet met in London to discuss a possible international federation of seamen and dockworkers. To this end they formed the International Federation of Ship, Dock, and River Industries. They set up a provisional central council, with Mann as president and Tillet as secretary. Mann and Wilson later traveled to Rotterdam and Antwerp, Belgium, to convince the continental unions to join the federation.

These labor leaders met again in London on 27 July in what is sometimes considered to be the first meeting of the ITF. Delegates from Great Britain, Sweden, Belgium, Holland, France, Germany, and the United States attended. Two days later they held another meeting in which leaders of the maritime workers heard reports from 87 ports throughout Europe. They then drew up demands for the shipping and port employers.

ITF leaders often had a difficult time when they attempted to intervene in the labor movements in other countries. Mann and Wilson were both banned in Belgium. In 1896 Tillet was arrested in Antwerp. Then Mann was arrested and deported during the 1896–1897 dock strike in Hamburg.

The Hamburg Dock Strike and the Decline of the ITF

The 1896 dock strike in Hamburg highlighted the contrast between the optimism of the leaders in international solidarity and the reality of the situation. In response to poor conditions, the Association of Port Workers in Hamburg first made demands on the employers in November 1896. Although management did make a few concessions, the workers were not satisfied. On 21 November the stevedores walked off the job, later followed by other dockworkers and the seamen. By the end of the first week of the strike, some 8,000 workers in Hamburg were on strike. The owners refused mediation, and the workers turned down a government proposal to return to work while an inquiry was made into conditions at the port. The employers had modest success in their attempts to bring in strikebreakers. Finally, after 11 weeks, the striking workers returned to work because of the threat of starvation in the winter months. Although they did gain some concessions, the strike was mostly a defeat for the dockworkers. However, a government inquiry later confirmed many of the workers' complaints, and changes followed.

The fact that the ITF had been unable to stop the flow of strikebreakers during the Hamburg strike led many to question the effectiveness of the organization. At the 1898 meeting in London, at which the name was officially changed to the International Federation of Transport Workers, there were many calls for organizational changes. Yet the ITF soon entered a period plagued by problems and ineffectiveness. After the initial enthusiasm and activity of the early years, several issues caused the ITF to decline. The discontent was especially evident at the meetings in 1900 at Paris and in 1902 at Stockholm. At both meetings, there were complaints about the ITF's lack of activity and the disorganization of the leaders based in London.

The London leaders responded that there was not enough money, which in fact was one of the key problems. The leaders were all volunteers who had to earn a living from their jobs. Tom Mann had even tried to run a pub in London. At the 1900 Paris meeting, the union contributions to the federation were cut in half, worsening an already precarious financial situation. The situation was so bad that when Mann was offered the chance to go to Australia to work as a union organizer, he jumped at the chance and left in 1901.

German Unions Take Control

The defeat of the Hamburg strike hurt morale and lessened the appeal of the federation. Many national federations turned increasingly inward. This prompted many to call for more and better organization. In particular, a conflict arose between the Germans and the British. Although the British leaders continued their idealistic call for action, the Germans felt that the federation must first build up its organizational strength before embarking on strikes and other activities. In light of this conflict, a new all-German central council was selected at the 1904 meeting at Amsterdam, with Hermann Juchade as the new president. The headquarters of the ITF was also moved to Hamburg.

When the Germans took over control of the federation, the federation's policy changed such that it stressed a buildup of organizational strength and nonintervention in national disputes. This new attitude did, in fact, succeed in attracting new members to the ITF. Among those who joined the ranks of the ITF were more European maritime workers, railroad workers from Italy, the International Longshoremen's Association, and the International Seamen's Union of America. In 1907 the ITF had 150,000 members. By 1907 that number had increased to about 500,000. By the start of World War I, the ITF had more than one million members.

Despite this growth in membership, the internal conflicts did not disappear. Many within the federation criticized the German leadership for a lack of actual activity. In particular, many Italian, French, and British labor leaders wanted to see less organizing and more direct action. The point became moot, however, with the outbreak of World War I. During the war the ITF largely fell into a period of inactivity. It would not be until after the war that the federation would regain its strength and expand its membership.

Key Players

Mann, Tom (1856–1941): Known for being an inspirational orator, Mann was a key leader of the British maritime workers. Largely self-educated, Mann had started working the mines at age 10. He was jailed during his involvement in the labor movement. A key player in the 1889 London dock strike, he was later selected as the first president of the ITF upon its formation in 1896.

Tillet, Ben (1860–1943): A London dockworker, Tillet served as the leader of his dockers' union for 30 years. Like Mann, he spent time in jail for his labor activities. He was a leader of the London dock strike in 1889. Influential in the creation of the ITF, he served as the first secretary of the organization. Later, he became a Member of Parliament for the Labor Party.

Wilson, John Havelock (1858–1928): British labor leader who was influential in organizing maritime workers. Wilson took many of the first steps toward creating the ITF by organizing workers beyond England in a single union. After the formation of the ITF, he continued to attempt to attract unions and workers to the federation.

See also: *Dockers' Strike.*

BIBLIOGRAPHY

Books

International Transport Workers' Federation. *Solidarity: The First 100 Years of the International Transport Workers' Federation.* London: Pluto Press, 1996.

Reinalda, Bob, ed. *The International Transportworkers Federation, 1914–1945: The Edo Fimmen Era.* Amsterdam: Stichting Beheer IISG, 1997.

—Ronald Young

International Workingmen's Association: *See* **First International.**

Interstate Commerce Commission

United States 1887

Synopsis

The U.S. Congress created the Interstate Commerce Commission (ICC) in 1887 as the first independent regulatory agency of the federal government. The ICC was a response to mounting public protests over perceived malpractices and abuses of the railroad industry. The Interstate Commerce Commission Act, which stated that it would promote interstate commerce within the United States, drafted the organization's char-

Thomas McIntyre Cooley. © The Granger Collection, New York. Reproduced by permission.

ter. The commission would use the rules and regulations of the act to assure fair interactions between the various transportation carriers and the public, apply impartial technical expertise to the regulation of commerce situations, and discourage monopolies. The ICC's first cases involved the railroad industry and were specifically concerned with preventing the railroads from charging excessive rates and engaging in discriminatory practices.

Timeline

1867: United States purchases Alaska from Russia for $7.2 million.

1872: The title of Claude Monet's painting *Impression: Sunrise* gives a name to a new movement in art.

1877: Peter Ilych Tchaikovsky's ballet *Swan Lake* debuts.

1880: Completed Cologne Cathedral, begun 634 years earlier, with twin spires 515 feet (157 m) high, is the tallest structure in the world, and will remain so until 1889, when it is surpassed by the Eiffel Tower. (The previous record for the world's tallest structure lasted much longer—for about 4,430 years following the building of Cheops's Great Pyramid in c. 2550 B.C.)

1883: Brooklyn Bridge is completed.

1885: German engineer Karl Friedrich Benz builds the first true automobile.

1887: Heinrich Hertz proves the existence of electromagnetic waves, which are propagated at the speed of light.

1887: Thomas Edison invents the first motor-driven phonograph.

1887: John Emerich Edward Dalbert-Acton, a leader of the opposition to the papal dogma of infallibility, observes, in a letter to Cambridge University professor Mandell Creighton, that "Power tends to corrupt, and absolute power corrupts absolutely."

1889: The 986-foot (300.5-m) Eiffel Tower, part of the Paris exposition, becomes the tallest structure in the world. It will remain so until the Chrysler Building surpasses it in 1930.

1893: Henry Ford builds his first automobile.

1897: In the midst of a nationwide depression, Mrs. Bradley Martin, daughter of Carnegie Steel magnate Henry Phipps, throws a lavish party at New York's recently opened Waldorf-Astoria Hotel, where she has a suite decorated to look like Versailles. Her 900 guests, dressed in Louis XV period costumes, consume sixty cases of champagne.

Event and Its Context

The first railroad company in the United States was the Baltimore and Ohio, which operated a 13-mile (21-km) rail in Maryland beginning in 1830. By 1850, 9,000 miles (14,500 km) of tracks were crisscrossing a country that was quickly being settled. At a time when the Industrial Revolution was taking hold, railroads provided a fast, convenient way to send and receive raw and finished materials such as timber and furniture, as well as to transport people and livestock. Railroads revolutionized the transportation system and had a significant impact on both the economy and society. With this enormous change, however, came problems with respect to the way that railroads operated their businesses.

The Golden Age

In the nineteenth century, the U.S. railroad industry developed at an unheard of pace. Initially, each privately owned railroad company held a monopoly in the market that it served. Eventually, as the railroad companies expanded into each other's markets, strong competition resulted. After the Civil War (1861–1865), railroads developed networks on lands that were often given to them by state or territorial governments. Towns competed against each other to attract railroads. Historians call the years around 1865 the "golden age" of railroads because the network grew from 30,000 miles (48,380 km) in 1860 to a peak of 254,000 miles (409,650 km) in 1916. On 10 May 1869 at Promontory Point in the Utah Territory, the "Golden Spike" joined the Union Pacific and Central Pacific railroads, signifying completion of the first transcontinental railroad.

To that time the rail system had been constructed with little regard to standards of operation. Railroad owners belatedly realized that efficient conduct of the national freight routes required standardization. Executives standardized the important aspects of their business; for example, the rail gauge was set at

U.S. Military Railroads engine No. 137, 1888. National Archives and Records Administration.

4 feet, 8.5 inches, and the industry agreed to implement four time zones (instead of 54) to improve the scheduling of arrivals and departures.

The railroads did not, however, apply standardization to rates, a task seen as nearly impossible because rates reflected the cargo's weight and distance traveled. The handling of heavy products such as lumber required more expenditure than lighter products such as cotton, but rates for heavy items were set low because of their relatively low worth. In addition, expenses for loading and unloading were the same for short-haul and long-haul shipments, which made it more difficult to set equitable rates. Areas with less demand, such as the still-developing western lands, had the same fixed costs as did high-demand areas, such as the eastern seaboard. The railroads also set low rates for areas where they hoped for economic growth, but set rates high in areas where businesses could afford to pay such prices.

Further, railroads might have no competition in certain areas (resulting in a monopoly) whereas in other areas there might be competition from several companies. For instance, in the 1880s the Trunk Line faced no competition between Chicago and St. Louis, while in the northeast it competed with the New York Central, Erie, Pennsylvania, Grand Trunk, and Balti-

more and Ohio lines. Railroads often based rates on the "value" of traffic, rather than on its "cost." Such "value-pricing" was logical for the railroads, but shippers, who were most concerned with rates and service, viewed it as economically illogical. Neither approach was applied on a consistent basis, and this greatly frustrated shippers.

To maintain rates when competition was strong, companies formed agreements, commonly called "pools," in which rails were assigned to member railroads. For example, from 1870 to 1885 an Iowa Pool between the Chicago, the North Western, Burlington & Quincy, and the Rock Island railroads gave each member a 45 percent stake in passenger and a 50 percent stake in freight income for their particular section of track, with the remaining monies equally divided. Railroads liked pools but preferred acquisitions to reduce competition. For example, the Pennsylvania railroad grew by buying 600 different railroads and leasing out the remaining lines. Railroad consolidation peaked around the beginning of the twentieth century when one-sixth of total rails were acquired. As a result, the danger of monopolies from these growing corporations became apparent.

Railroad owners realized their dominance in transportation. They sometimes raised freight rates beyond what the market would bear. Executives argued that they were exempt from state regulation because they moved goods across state lines in interstate commerce. Railroad executives stated, therefore, that individual states could not legally act against their industry.

Protesters

The American consumer called for action to correct injustices emanating from the railroads, such as unfair political influence, unreasonable rates, and illegal stock manipulation. Farmers and merchants protested to their elected representatives that they were treated unfairly by the railroads. These protests accomplished little. The railroads already had agreements with friendly politicians or ignored and sometimes replaced politicians who opposed them. One grassroots organization that challenged the power of the railroads was "The Grange." Oliver Kelley and six associates founded the National Grange of the Patrons of Husbandry in 1867 for social and educational purposes, not to deal with railroads. Supported by farmers and merchants, however, the Grange rapidly grew in importance in its new fight against railroad abuses. The Grange employed tactics such as holding back crops from the market until railroads agreed to lower freight rates.

Farmers, merchants, and consumers could not agree on how to eliminate the unfair practices that were commonly used. Railroads were spread across the country so investigations of abuses were difficult to conduct. Individual railroads had monopolies in parts of the country but faced intense competition in others. This added to the problem of determining equitable railroad charges, costs, and profits.

Government Regulation

Many of the protesters wanted public ownership of railroads; others demanded stabilizing pools or increased competition. Many thought that government regulation would force railroads to compete fairly and eliminate abuses. Without any clear solution, regulation became the popular way to establish fair railroad practices.

Four states had established railroad commissions prior to 1860, and more were formed over the next two decades. The New England states created the first commissions, but midwestern states later created stronger commissions to battle railroad overdevelopment and consumer discontent. The state of Illinois, beginning around 1869, set the model for surrounding states and eventually set the standard nationwide by establishing maximum rates.

The efforts of the Grange were well coordinated, and, with the help of newspapers, its efforts began to succeed. The movement helped to strengthen the political position of farmers, who now formed a cohesive group that effectively communicated its demands. The Grange elected members to several midwestern legislatures during the mid-1870s, and these leaders passed uniform "Granger" laws to manage railroad regulations and set maximum railroad rates. The railroads countered by raising rates in areas in which there was no commission. For the most part, the state laws that were enacted to regulate the railroad industry (and to protect its customers) were largely ineffectual.

The railroads soon challenged state regulations. In 1876 the Supreme Court case of *Munn v. Illinois* questioned the validity of an Illinois law that set maximum rates for grain storage when the Chicago warehouse of Munn and Scott was found guilty of

violating the law. The company protested the ruling, saying its property was being taken without due process of law. The Court upheld the Granger law, and ruled that the warehouse business in general operated in such a way as to justify public control and that any private utility devoted to public use could be publicly regulated. The railroads thus learned that they affected the public interest and, as a result, could only charge reasonable amounts for their services. The consequence of this case was the setting of a precedent that states have the right to regulate interstate commerce.

In 1886 a Supreme Court decision on *Wabash, St. Louis, and Pacific Railway Company v. Illinois* declared that states are not legally able to control any commerce that crosses state boundaries. This Court ruling reversed previous legislation when it denied the right of Illinois to regulate interstate rates between itself and New York. It concluded that only the commerce clause of the U.S. Constitution could regulate interstate commerce. This ruling, plus the inadequacy of state regulation and the weakening of the *Munn* ruling, led the public to demand federal regulation. The primary effect of the *Wabash* decision was the creation of the Interstate Commerce Commission.

Farmers, merchants, manufacturers, and producers were in favor of federal regulation of the railroads. Farmers worked through the Grange to secure state laws regulating rates and create commissions to enforce them. Most laws were eventually repealed but were important precedents for future federal legislation. Merchants spoke through pressure groups to demand railroad regulation. In 1873 New York merchants established the New York Cheap Transportation Association, which identified over 6,000 discriminatory contracts within the New York Central railroad. Manufacturers and producers also called for federal regulation. Independent oil producers, for example, were often left out of the rebates offered to their giant competitors such as Standard Oil. The independents tried repeatedly to pass legislation to outlaw pooling, rebates, and discrimination.

Interstate Commerce Act

Federal regulation officially began on 4 February 1887, when President Cleveland signed the Interstate Commerce Act into law. This created the first independent regulatory commission, the Interstate Commerce Commission (ICC). It had several functions:

- Ban "special rates" that the railroads arranged among themselves
- Outlaw discriminatory rate setting
- Set guidelines for how railroads could do business
- Prevent monopolies by promoting competition
- Require railroads to submit annual reports to the ICC

The act itself, however, was imprecise in its wording. The act made pooling illegal but failed to mention other discriminatory practices. The act stated that rates were to be "reasonable and just," and the railroads took advantage of the vague phrasing by responding subjectively. The act also outlawed long- and short-haul abuse but only under certain circumstances, and thus it was ambiguous as to what constituted a short- or a long-haul. The act authorized the commission to investigate any railroad engaged in interstate commerce. If a railroad ignored the ICC, however, the commission had to petition the appropriate circuit court to rule on the matter.

Ultimately the ICC's power would depend on its commissioners and the court system. The commission was a five-person committee with all members nominated by the president. The first commission chairman was Thomas Cooley, a University of Michigan law professor and Michigan Supreme Court justice. Cooley rejected unlimited state interference with private property but accepted state regulation of profits where competition had been eliminated.

Cleveland's second appointee was William Morrison, a former Illinois congressman who was known for his attacks on protective tariffs. He was seen as honest but with little railroad knowledge. Augustus Schoonmaker, a New York lawyer, was the third appointee. Schoonmaker also had little railroad experience but was viewed as a man of character. The fourth appointee was Aldace Walker, a railroad lawyer and Vermont senator who opposed railroads. The fifth appointee was Walter Bragg, who had helped to develop the concept of the ICC while he was president of the Alabama railroad commission.

The effectiveness of the fledgling ICC was limited by a lack of enforcement power, by the Supreme Court's interpretation of its power, and by the vague language of the original act. As the country's first regulatory agency, the ICC staff also lacked the necessary experience to set effective interstate standards. Historians generally agree that in the beginning years of the ICC, it failed to maintain a proper balance between the powerful railroads and the public so as to ensure moderate profits and adequate service at a reasonable cost. Many experts agree that the ICC was contaminated both internally and externally by the people it was trying to regulate: the railroad executives.

Though the ICC was not particularly effective in curbing the unfair practices of the railroads, the precedent for federal regulation had been set. Later legislation such as the Sherman and Clayton Antitrust Acts had more of an effect on large businesses. The latter bill created the Federal Trade Commission, which is the major regulatory body of monopolies today.

Key Players

Cooley, Thomas McIntyre (1824–1898): Cooley turned to the practice of law after a successful career as a city clerk, newspaper editor, and circuit court commissioner. He was appointed in 1857 to compile the original statutes of the state of Michigan and in 1864 to the Michigan Supreme Court. At the same time Cooley was also a professor and the first dean of the University of Michigan's fledgling law department (now the University of Michigan Law School). Cooley authored numerous articles on legal subjects and wrote several full-length works on constitutional limitations. He also wrote a benchmark opinion that is still quoted today with regard to the separation of powers among the three branches of government.

Kelley, Oliver Hudson (1826–1913): Kelley, along with William Saunders, Aaron B. Grosh, William M. Ireland, John R. Thompson, Francis McDowell, and John Trimble (assisted by Caroline Hall), founded the National Grange of the Patrons of Husbandry. Today, they are called the "Seven Founders of the Order of the Patrons of Husband-

ry." After the Civil War, when farmers suffered a lack of organization, Kelley contacted President Andrew Johnson with a proposal to organize farmers into what he called a "Secret Society of Agriculturists." Kelley was later appointed as an agent of the Department of Agriculture. As part of Reconstruction, Kelley proceeded in the South to form farmers into the Grange, a name that borrowed from large English farms. The seven founders determined that the organization must serve both the political and social needs of farm families. Women could join on an equal basis because the founders felt that their participation was important to the success of their organization. Their organizing tactics were successful, and the Grange movement spread rapidly across the country.

See also: *Clayton Antitrust Act.*

BIBLIOGRAPHY

Books

Hoogenboom, Ari Arthur, and Olive Hoogenboom. *A History of the ICC: From Panacea to Palliative.* New York: Norton, 1976.

Kirkland, Edward C. *Industry Comes of Age: Business, Labor, and Public Policy, 1860–1897.* New York: Holt, Rhinehart, and Winston 1962.

Stone, Richard D. *The Interstate Commerce Commission and the Railroad Industry: A History of Regulatory Policy.* New York: Praeger, 1991.

Stover, John F. *American Railroads.* Chicago: University of Chicago Press, 1997.

Other

"1880 Train." Black Hills Central Railroad [cited 11 August, 2002]. <http://www.1880train.com>.

"A Trip through Railroad History." TomorrowsRailroads.org. [cited 11 August, 2002]. <http://www.tomorrowsrailroads.org/index.asp>.

—William Arthur Atkins

IWW Copper Strike

United States 1917

Synopsis

On 27 June 1917 the Industrial Workers of the World (IWW, or "wobblies") began a wartime strike at Bisbee, Arizona, demanding shorter hours, higher wages, and better working conditions for copper miners there. The mining companies rejected IWW demands; within three days roughly 80 percent of underground workers had stopped work, threatening to put the mines out of business. Both the "wobblies" and company supporters reportedly used threats and intimidation in the conflict. In a community with a tradition of hostility toward unionization, local authorities denounced the IWW "terrorists" and "German sympathizers" and quickly organized to crush the strike. This pivotal event in Arizona labor history ended on 12 July, when an armed posse headed by the local sheriff illegally forced nearly 1,200 IWW members, sympathizers, and "agitators" into cattle cars and deported them into the desert.

Timeline

1897: The Zionist movement is established under the leadership of Theodor Herzl.

1902: Second Anglo-Boer War ends in victory for Great Britain. It is a costly victory, however, resulting in the loss of more British lives (5,774) than any conflict between 1815 and 1914. The war also sees the introduction of concentration camps, used by the British to incarcerate Boer civilians.

1905: Russian Revolution of 1905 occurs. Following the "bloody Sunday" riots before the Winter Palace in St. Petersburg in January, revolution spreads throughout Russia, in some places spurred on by newly formed workers' councils, or soviets. Among the most memorable incidents of the revolt is the mutiny aboard the battleship *Potemkin.* Suppressed by the czar, the revolution brings an end to liberal reforms and thus sets the stage for the larger revolutions of 1917.

1911: In China, revolutionary forces led by Sun Yat-sen bring an end to more than 2,100 years of imperial rule.

1915: A German submarine sinks the *Lusitania,* killing 1,195, including 128 U.S. citizens. Theretofore, many Americans had been sympathetic toward Germany, but the incident begins to turn the tide of U.S. sentiment toward the Allies.

1917: The intercepted "Zimmermann Telegram" reveals a plot by the German government to draw Mexico into an alliance against the United States in return for a German promise to return the southwestern U.S. territories taken in the Mexican War. Three months later on 6 April, in response to German threats of unrestricted submarine warfare, the United States declares war on Germany.

1917: On both the Western Front and in the Middle East, the tide of the war begins to turn against the Central Powers. The arrival of U.S. troops, led by General Pershing, in France in June greatly boosts morale and reinforces exhausted Allied forces. Meanwhile, Great Britain scores two major victories against the Ottoman Empire as T. E. Lawrence leads an Arab revolt in Baghdad in March, and troops under Field Marshal Edmund Allenby take Jerusalem in December.

1919: With the formation of the Third International (Comintern), the Bolshevik government of Russia establishes its control over communist movements worldwide.

1923: Conditions in Germany worsen as inflation skyrockets and France, attempting to collect on coal deliveries

promised at Versailles, marches into the Ruhr basin. In November an obscure political group known as the National Socialist German Workers' Party attempts to stage a coup, or putsch, in a Munich beer hall. The revolt fails, and in 1924 the party's leader, Adolf Hitler, will receive a prison sentence of five years. He will only serve nine months, however, and the incident will serve to attract attention for him and his party, known as the Nazis.

1927: Stalin arranges to have Trotsky expelled from the Communist Party.

Event and Its Context

Statewide Strikes

In the early summer of 1917, with United States soldiers fighting in Europe and national industry geared toward the war effort, widespread strikes hit the copper districts of Arizona. While ordinary citizens of the country were being asked to make sacrifices, copper companies answering to eastern stockholders gleaned tremendous profits for providing "essential war metal" during World War I. The price of copper had gone from 13.5 cents a pound at the outbreak of the war in 1914 to 37 cents a pound by March 1917. At the same time, miners, who worked around the clock, saw the purchasing power of their wages decline. Moreover, many laborers saw war as essentially capitalistic, with its ultimate consequence the pitting of working men against one another. The four districts, which included towns such as Bisbee, Jerome, Ajo, Globe, Miami, Clifton, and Morenci, accounted for about 28 percent of total U.S. copper output. After three months of partial or total shutdown (and diminished production thereafter), mining activity showed an output deficit of 100 million pounds of copper.

Worker Demands

According to the 1918 report of the secretary of labor, workers in the region made three claims, all of which were rejected by the companies. First, workers generally considered the copper industry to be autocratic, with the companies ultimately dictating the conditions of employment. They wanted direct dealing between companies and unions. While some grievance committees were established, workers generally mistrusted them because resolution of all conflicts sat with the company. Lacking an appropriate negotiating mechanism, "workers were given the alternative of submission or strike." Second, workers wanted "the power to secure industrial justice." They sought the right to organize into unions that would give them the same bargaining power as companies and provide them with protection from abuse. They did not demand a closed shop but rather sought protection from discrimination against union members. The companies denied any such discrimination but refused verification by outside observers. Finally, miners insisted that "the right and the power to obtain just treatment were in themselves basic conditions of employment." While there were specific grievances regarding hours, wages, and working conditions, these were considered secondary to the larger power relationship between labor and capital. The workers declared that their just treatment should not depend on the benevolence or the whim of employers.

Bisbee Mining Conditions

Up until 26 June, roughly 4,500 miners worked underground in the Warren district. Three companies controlled the mining in the district: the Phelps Dodge Corporation, the Calumet and Arizona Mining Company, and the Shattuck Arizona Copper Company. While most of the miners were of European origin, other ethnic groups were present, albeit subject to residential and labor restrictions. Chinese workers, for example, were not allowed to stay in town. According to the *Journal of Arizona History,* the Mexican population lived separately from the Anglo population and was not allowed to work underground "and therefore could be used as strikebreakers." Southern European workers were allowed in the mines but also received lower-paying jobs. These underrepresented workers proved to be of special interest to the IWW, which was particularly successful in recruiting Bisbee's Mexican workers after several months of organization there.

Since its founding in 1905, the IWW had never recruited more than 5 percent of trade unionists in the United States. Nonetheless, its ideas of industrial sabotage and slowdowns were of definite concern to capital. The "wobblies" considered the Western Federation of Miners (WFM) to be a puppet of capital and accused the union of wanting to tie up all miners for three years with a 75-cent reduction in daily pay. The IWW demanded better wages and shorter hours for miners "whether war has been declared or not. It not only wants them but it is going to get them."

Bisbee Prepares for IWW Strike

Although not all miners in the Warren district had voted by the afternoon of 26 June, a committee representing the metal mining branch of the IWW (Metal Mine Workers Union No. 800) presented mine operators with a list of seven demands. The union demanded that mandatory physical examinations of miners be abolished; that two men be employed to work on machines; and that two men work together in all areas. Fourth, it demanded the discontinuance of all blasting in the mines during shifts. The fifth demand called for the abolition of all bonus and contract work. The sixth was for the abolishment of a sliding scale pegged to the market price of copper; all men working underground would receive a minimum flat rate of $6.00 per shift, while all "top men" would receive $5.50 per shift. Finally, the union demanded that no discrimination be shown "against members of any organization." If their demands were not met, they would go on strike within a matter of hours.

According to the antiunion *Bisbee Daily Review,* which was owned by Phelps Dodge, "the companies took no cognizance to the demands nor of the committee." Managers of all three major mining companies issued statements denouncing a nationwide conspiracy by enemies of the United States bent on paralyzing the flow of copper needed by the war effort. They called on workers, whom they asserted did not really support the IWW, to ignore the strike.

On the evening of 26 June, six IWW speakers addressed a crowd of union members and onlookers in the city park and urged the men to walk out the next day. In the hour-long address, the speakers reportedly promised relief to striking miners and their families. According to the *Daily Review,* the crowd was "unenthusiastic" and "hardly one of the speakers was known to the crowd."

That same day, Cochise County sheriff Harry C. Wheeler told the town daily that he would "call upon and deputize, if necessary, every able-bodied loyal American in Cochise County to assist me in preserving peace and order." Shortly thereafter, he requested the aid of federal troops. Given the ongoing conflict in Europe and the drafting into federal service of many of the state militia, the county lacked its usual troops. On suggestion of the governor, the secretary of war sent an experienced army officer to Bisbee to ascertain the need for troop intervention; following investigations on 30 June and 2 July, the officer reported that "everything was peaceable" and that there was no need for troops.

Bisbee had a history of organized resistance to unionization. When WFM organizers worked to form a Bisbee local in the early 1900s, they were confronted by a determined coalition of antiunion business leaders and fraternal societies. The antiunion citizens' alliance centered on the *Bisbee Daily Review,* which the mining companies used as their mouthpiece. The alliance included company officials, the local Episcopal priest, the owner of the company store, and the manager of the company-owned Bank of Bisbee. Unionization also met resistance from the Bisbee Industrial Association, supposedly made up of miners to "reestablish conditions as they were prior to the entrance of the WFM." The union claimed the association, which refused to release membership information, was a creation of the Copper Queen Mining Company. In addition to forceful ejection of organizers, union opponents employed spies to gather information to intimidate and blacklist prounion miners. Some 1,200 miners were fired between 1906 and 1907. Nonetheless, the WFM managed to establish Local No. 106 in Bisbee on 9 February 1907.

The Strike Begins

The strike began at midnight on 27 June 1917. According to procompany forces, "the usual tactics of threat and intimidation invariably associated with IWW disturbances were used." For the first three days of the strike, some 80 percent of underground workers reportedly stopped work. Members of the mechanical trades, however, were reported not to support the strike. After the third day, though, miners gradually started going back to work, with roughly half of them at work on 11 July. Tensions rose with rumors of pro-German infiltration and plans to blow up the post office and other Bisbee landmarks. The citizens of the Warren mining district decided that "nothing short of drastic action would eliminate undesirable troublemakers."

On 6 July about 500 citizens of Globe, Arizona, met in the federal building there to pass a resolution declaring the IWW a public enemy of the United States. "Terrorism in this community must and shall cease," said the resolution. The citizens group opposed any mediation between the IWW and mine owners and promised to suppress any public assemblies where "treasonable, incendiary or threatening" speeches were made. It called for deputizing citizens to restore the peace and banning all "wobblies" from working in the district.

Vigilantes Take Bisbee

On 12 July, Wheeler, having made no new request for federal troops, officially announced the formation of a sheriff's posse of 1,200 men in Bisbee and 1,000 in nearby Douglas. He described these men as "all loyal Americans" and charged them to arrest "all those strange men who have congregated here from other parts and sections for the purpose of harassing and intimidating all men who desire to pursue their daily toil." The strikers were to be charged for vagrancy, treason, and disturbing the peace. "This is no labor trouble," he declared, but "a direct attempt to embarrass the government of the United States." According to the *Daily Review,* the time had come to "bruise the head of the serpent. The policies of peace had failed. The Mexicans were beginning to parade by the hundreds."

On the night of 11 July, the Bisbee Citizens' Association and Bisbee Loyalty League had met to agree formally on deportation of the "wobblies." Present at the meeting were officials and managers of the Copper Queen Consolidated Mining Company (Phelps Dodge Corporation, Copper Queen Division) and the Calumet and Arizona Mining Company. Without consulting the United States attorney in Arizona, their own legal advisers, or state and county law officers, they formally agreed at around midnight to deport the strikers. By 2:00 A.M., the sheriff had deputized 1,200 men, ordering them to report at various points at 4:00 A.M. Assembled citizens who were unarmed were given revolvers and rifles and told to shoot "only in self-defense." Each man wore a "badge," a white handkerchief wrapped around his arm. In a special 6:30 A.M. newspaper printing, the mayor issued a proclamation warning all women and children off the streets. In the face of frequent raids by the guerilla revolutionary leader Pancho Villa from across the nearby Mexican border, the government had equipped one smelter with a siren, to be used only in the case of invasion; the siren sounded early on the morning of 12 July.

Sheriff Wheeler and roughly 2,000 armed citizens (3,000, according to the *Daily Review*), calling themselves the Citizens' Protective League, marched toward the center of town. Along the way each of the five armed bands surrounded, questioned, and arrested "every strange man on the streets." Twenty-five armed citizens surrounded and arrested the 50 pickets at the mouth of the Copper Queen mine. Within about an hour, four bands, each with hundreds of prisoners, simultaneously reached the town center. Vigilantes reportedly entered restaurants and other establishments asking nonminers if they were "with or against" the striking men. Cooks and waiters who said they could not be against people they had been serving for years, and anyone else expressing any sympathy for the workers, were arrested. As the prisoners marched, hundreds of rifles were leveled at their heads from all sides. By 8:30 A.M. the prisoners had been ushered to the train depot, where a fifth squad had assembled several hundred more prisoners. All the men were then ordered to march down the railroad tracks toward Warren, about four miles away; approximately 300 "wobblies" detained at Lowell merged with the march.

In addition to the 167 American deportees, a segregated deportee list showed some three dozen nationalities present. The most affected group was the Mexicans, with 229 prisoners. Other prominent nationalities were Serbians (82), Finns (76), Irish (67), and British (32). Despite talk of German infiltration, only 20 Germans were arrested.

Once in Warren, the prisoners were forced into the baseball stadium, where a special train of cattle cars was rolled in to deport them. According to the *Los Angeles Times,* several prisoners attempted to deliver speeches on IWW principles and called on the crowd to stand with them, "but their voices were lost in the jeers of the crowd of spectators." The vigilantes had managed to round up 1,186 IWW "agitators and sympathizers" and force them, single file, up runways into the cattle cars, at least one of which was filled with sheep dung. Three female strikers were also arrested but were not loaded onto the train. In addition to the IWW newcomers, several prominent citizens of Bisbee and Lowell who had voiced support for them were also herded into the cars. One of those was William B. Cleary, a Bisbee attorney well known throughout the state.

The strikebreakers banned use of the local communications offices at Bisbee and Douglas, censoring interstate telephone and telegraph connections in order to prevent any knowledge of the deportation reaching the outside world. Governor Campbell wired General Parker at Fort Sam Houston in San Antonio, Texas, with a copy to General Green at Douglas, Arizona, requesting military intervention in the crisis; he then learned by telephone that the men had been slated for illegal deportation to New Mexico. The governor denounced the deportations but stated he could not declare martial law because without federal troops he was powerless to act.

There were two casualties that day. One "wobbly," James Brew, hiding out inside a house, reportedly shot and killed a deputy, Orson P. McRae, after declaring he would not be taken without a fight. Vigilantes with McRae then shot Brew.

Mass Deportation

The special train left Warren at noon, carrying the prisoners and more than 200 armed guards to Columbus, New Mexico, where they arrived at about 9 P.M. Local officials denied their disembarkation and arrested F. B. King, division superintendent of the El Paso and Southwestern Railway, for transporting them there. King was released when he agreed to remove the men from Columbus. The train then backtracked to the station at the nearby desert town of Hermanas, New Mexico, where the guards left the "wobblies" to their own luck. For two days the men were left without sufficient food, water, or shelter. When their plight came to the attention of the War Department on 14 July, they were escorted by troops back to Columbus, where they were "maintained by the government" until mid-September.

Back in Bisbee, authorities placed guards on all roads to keep out returnees. They established a kangaroo court to try anyone who returned from Columbus and anyone else considered disloyal to mining interests. Any property-owning deportees (773) who returned were given a deadline to leave town and were forced to sell their property to the mining companies under company terms. Gunmen accompanied them at all times.

The President's Mediation Commission later denounced the deportation as "wholly illegal and without authority in law, either State or Federal," and recommended that any such future occurrences be made a federal offense.

Key Players

Campbell, Thomas E. (1878–1944): Campbell was Arizona's second governor, serving in 1917 at the time of the Bisbee strike and then again from 1919 to 1923. He was the state's first native-born governor and the first Republican to serve.

Wheeler, Harry C. (1875–?): Sheriff of Cochise County, Arizona, from 1912 to 1917, a hero to some, a corporate puppet to others, Wheeler led some 2,000 armed vigilantes to break the IWW strike at Bisbee in July 1917.

See also: *Clifton-Morenci-Metcalf Strike; Industrial Workers of the World; Western Federation of Miners.*

BIBLIOGRAPHY

Periodicals

"Citizens of Globe Brand I.W.W. Enemy to Nation." *Bisbee Daily Review,* 7 July 1917.

"Deported I.W.W.'s, Barred from New Mexico, Return to Arizona." *Los Angeles Times,* 13 July 1917.

McBride, James D. "Gaining a Foothold in the Paradise of Capitalism: The Western Federation of Miners and The Unionization of Bisbee." *Journal of Arizona History* 23 (autumn 1982).

"Military Intervention Is Asked by Governor, Dumping of I.W.W. on Neighboring State Called Illegal by Campbell." *Los Angeles Times,* 13 July 1917.

"Statements of Managers," *Bisbee Daily Review,* 27 June 1917.

"The Great Wobbly Drive." *Bisbee Daily Review,* 13 July 1917.

Watson, Fred. "Recollections of a Bisbee Deportee: Still on Strike!" *Journal of Arizona History* 18 (summer 1977).

Other

Arizona Chapter of the American Mining Congress. *Deportations from Bisbee and a Resume of Other Troubles in Arizona* [cited 28 October 2002]. <http://digital.library.arizona.edu/bisbee/docs2/deport.php>. [UA Special Collections H9791 B621 A51]

Bonnand, Sheila. *Historical Context of the Bisbee Deportation.* 1997 [cited 28 October 2002]. <http://digital.library.arizona.edu/bisbee/main/history.php>.

"Do You Want a Contract?" [cited 28 October 2002]. <http://digital.library.arizona.edu/bisbee/docs/115.php>.

Mining Conditions in Bisbee, Arizona [cited 28 October 2002]. <http://digital.library.arizona.edu/bisbee/docs2/mincon.php>. [UA Special Collections L9791 B62 Pam.15]

President's Mediation Commission. *Report on the Bisbee Deportations.* Washington, DC: Government Printing Office, 1917. [UA Special Collections H9791 B621 U58r].

"Sheriff Announces He Will Use Force to Prevent Any Disorders During Trouble." *Bisbee Daily Review.* 27 June 1917 [cited 28 October 2002]. <http://digital.library.arizona.edu/bisbee/docs2/bd627she.php>.

"Sheriff Calls Americans to Help Oust Disturbers." *Los Angeles Times.* 13 July 1917 [cited 28 October 2002]. <http://digital.library.arizona.edu/bisbee/docs2/la713she.php>.

The Sheriffs of Cochise County 1881–2000 [cited 28 October 2002]. <http://www.cityoftombstone.com/SheriffsofCC.htm>.

Sixth Annual Report of the Secretary of Labor for the Fiscal Year Ended June 30, 1918. Washington, DC: Government Printing Office, 1919 [cited 28 October 2002]. <http://digital.library.arizona.edu/bisbee/docs2/dlrep.php>. [UA Special Collections H9791 B621 U58].

ADDITIONAL RESOURCES

Other

The Bisbee Deportation of 1917 [cited 28 October 2002]. <http://digital.library.arizona.edu/bisbee/>.

—Brett Allan King

J

Japanese Labor After World War II

Japan 1945–1960

Synopsis

Post–World War II Japan faced a monumental struggle between labor and management. American postwar occupation goals included democratization to be achieved, in part, by the fostering of unionism. Management control of production and of the workplace in general eroded until the Mitsui Miike coal mine strike of 1959–1960. Management threats to discontinue safety precautions that been in place at the mine prompted the massive action, which lasted for more than nine months and involved 10,000 picketers a day and solidarity demonstrations by more than 300,000 workers across Japan. Ultimately, management reasserted its formerly eroded levels of control in a mediated settlement that addressed other worker concerns but not the safety issues. Historians are split on whether the resolution constituted a defeat or a victory for labor when viewed through the lens of Japan's future economic successes in the world marketplace.

Timeline

1932: A "Bonus Army" of unemployed veterans marches on Washington, D.C. Many leave after Congress refuses their demands for payment of bonuses for wartime service, but others are forcibly removed by General Douglas MacArthur's troops. Also participating are two other figures destined to gain notoriety in the next world war: majors Dwight D. Eisenhower and George S. Patton.

1937: In the middle of an around-the-world flight, Amelia Earhart and her plane disappear somewhere in the Pacific.

1942: The women's military services in the United States are established.

1947: Great Britain's Labour government nationalizes coalmines.

1948: Israel becomes a nation.

1949: North Atlantic Treaty Organization (NATO) is established.

1950: North Korean troops pour into South Korea, starting the Korean War. Initially, the communists make impressive gains, but in September the U.S. Marines land at Inchon and liberate Seoul. China responds by sending in its troops.

1951: Julius and Ethel Rosenberg are convicted and sentenced to death for passing U.S. atomic secrets to the Soviets.

1954: The French military outpost at Dien Bien Phu falls to the communist Vietminh. France withdraws after decades of trying to suppress revolt; meanwhile, the United States pledges its support for the noncommunist government in the South.

1956: Elvis Presley appears on Ed Sullivan's *Toast of the Town,* where he performs "Hound Dog" and "Love Me Tender" before a mostly female audience. Nationwide, 54 million people watch the performance, setting a new record.

1961: President Eisenhower steps down, warning of a "military-industrial complex" in his farewell speech, and 43-year-old John F. Kennedy becomes the youngest elected president in U.S. history. Three months later, he launches an unsuccessful invasion of Cuba at the Bay of Pigs.

Event and Its Context

The Chaotic Aftermath of War

In the aftermath of World War II, Japan as a nation lay low militarily, politically, and economically. Destruction, food shortages, and poverty were rife. On the other hand, in the same period the Japanese working class displayed moments of great vibrancy and power. This strength had a dual cause: the disaffection caused by the ravages of war, which stoked the rebellion that was to erupt once the war was over, and the early occupation policy of encouraging union growth in Japan as a means to stimulate the development of Japanese democracy.

Japan's contemporary political economy can best be understood by grasping the crucial historical forms that industrial relations in Japan assumed in the 15 years from 1945 to 1960. This requires an accurate outline of events during the immediate postwar period to discern its relationship with the economic process, which effectively led to the defeat of Japanese industrial unionism in 1960. The strike at the Mitsui Miike coal mines on Kyushu in the southwestern island of Japan was a key event in this process.

The war and the American occupation were two crucial factors that stimulated the growth of Japanese trade unionism in the post–World War II period. Another factor was the tradition of and familiarity with both the concept and the practice of trade unionism in Japan, which dates to at least the 1890s.

A disastrous war for Japan and its leaders produced a crisis of legitimacy for the imperial system. Defeat, occupation, and economic and institutional chaos all impressed upon ordinary Japanese people the eminent contestability and incompetence of the established forces in Japan. Initially pushed and prompted by the new occupying force to form unions and assert their own claims, workers became far more assertive in this period. The release of thousands of political prisoners only added to the sense of freedom and liberation that must have been a heady brew, particularly given the collapse of the oppressive authoritarian regime under the emperor. Japanese leadership was under the spotlight, and a democratic backlash for all the repression and authoritarian control that had been meted out during the bleak war years was long overdue.

Democratization from Above and Below

Democratization, called for and implemented from above by the Americans, was not only imposed from on high by the occupying forces. The Japanese masses eagerly adopted it as a slogan and a practice. Ironically kick-started by revolts of Chinese forced laborers at the Mitsubishi Bibai coal mines and then later by revolts of Korean forced laborers at the Yubari coal mines on Hokkaido, this spirit of working-class self-empowerment soon led to demands such as those developed by the Democracy Study Group at the *Yomiuri Shimbun*. In some cases, it resulted in seizure of production control by the workers, as happened famously in the case of the *Yomiuri* itself.

A Revolutionary Situation

Some experts contend that in this period (particularly in 1946) a revolutionary situation existed in Japan. The Supreme Command for Allied Powers (SCAP) eliminated the possibility of revolution. Thenceforth Japanese working-class self-confidence and autonomy were to be steadily restricted and eroded. One scholar estimated that there were close to 50 production takeovers involving at least 30,000 workers per month in the spring of 1946. These figures fell to roughly 25 such takeovers per month with between 5,000 and 6,000 participants in early 1947. SCAP condemned production control, and the conservative Japanese government quickly suppressed any further takeovers and outlawed the general strike planned by Zento (the All-Japan Union Council for Joint Action in Labor Disputes) for 1 February 1947.

Production control may have declined, but labor offensives continued, most notably in the "October Struggle" of the Congress of Industrial Unions of Japan in 1946. This action involved close to 100 strikes and 180,000 workers throughout the country. Such offensives achieved many gains, including a degree of control in the organization and pace of the production process and a high level of wage (and other forms of) equality between white- and blue-collar workers, which had not existed before. In some cases, unions determined wage decisions as well as promotions, the pace of work, and the parceling out of job assignments. There were even shop committees that decided overtime assignments and employee transfers. Labor asserted a high degree of control, which it had earned because of the substantial clout it wielded in council deliberations and collective bargaining. It was a powerful force and often held the upper hand in the workplace.

The Conservative Counteroffensive

Labor's power began to wane in early 1947, given the assistance of the Americans. The conservative prime minister Yoshida Shigeru expressed his attitude toward striking unionists in his New Year's speech in which he denounced strikers as "lawless scum." This class hatred manifested by the conservative leader indicated the seriousness with which the threat of worker hegemony was viewed at this time. With the authority and power of SCAP behind it, management began to engineer its comeback and to regain the "right to manage" that had been lost over the preceding year and a half.

Nikkeiren, the Japan Federation of Employers' Organizations, which was formed in April 1948, was at the center of this push. One commentator on the period argued that Nikkeiren was the crucial ingredient that gave the period from 1948 to 1960 its singular character, namely the struggle and ultimate success of Japanese management to reassert its hegemony in the workplace. Nikkeiren was, for example, heavily involved in breaking the Toho Film strike in 1948. The objective was to break the union and its control, as the people drafted to help with film production appear to have known very little about filmmaking. The intervention of 1,800 armed police on 19 August 1948, supported in turn by hundreds of American troops, a number of whom were in armored cars, heralded the beginning of the end for the dispute, despite the fact it lasted an additional two months. Unsurprisingly, the workers were defeated. Many other disputes went a similar way, with the underlying motif being the reassertion of control by management in the workplace.

The Mitsui Miike Coal Mine Dispute and the End of Union-led Industrial Relations

The coal strike at the Mitsui Miike mine in Kyushu was clearly the most important dispute in the postwar era up to that time. It was arguably even more significant than the failure of the "Suto-ken Suto" (the Public Sector Worker Strike for the Right to Strike) of 1974. As one scholar explained, the power of the action grew from a mix of shop-floor control, study groups, and community organizations involving miners' wives and local residents. The labor offensives at Miike from 1953 to 1960 reversed the arbitrariness and favoritism habitually practiced by mine supervisors and gave concrete substance to the union principle of "democratization."

The defeat of the 1959–1960 strike at Miike marked the most fundamental turning point in postwar Japanese industrial relations and—equally controversially—in the nation's political economy. The strike's meaning is heavily contested in the academic literature. Some scholars regard it as the inevitable demise of an old and decrepit form of warring politics and industrial relations, inaugurating a brilliant and harmonious new social contract between moderate unions and management that helped catapult Japan to the advanced guard in the comity of industrial nations. Others argue that the event was a severe defeat for independent working-class unionism and thereby for democracy, autonomy, and safety in the workplace. This is sometimes construed as an historic defeat of the working class in Japan, which opened the gate for the increasing hegemony of management-controlled, so-called yellow unions, which have dominated the landscape of Japanese industrial relations to the present.

The dispute at Miike was truly on an epic scale, lasting for 282 days in total. By July 1960, some 10,000 people, a mixture of workers, wives, and sympathizers, picketed the mine every day. Massive demonstrations also took place: nearly 300,000 total unionists from all over Japan showed up at Miike at the height of the dispute between March and July 1960 to show solidarity with the miners. This conflict coincided with the massive popular movement to resist the renewal of the Security Treaty with the United States. The strike itself was a reaction to the dismissal of union officials at Miike by a management that was scrapping to reestablish its right to manage. A precursor to today's "radical restructuring" or "reform" in Japan and Britain, it was management's attempt to improve productivity by defeating the power of the union in the workplace. The Miike union was considered the most powerful union in Japan, so management failure could not be countenanced, as there were bound to be national repercussions for management control arising from such a scenario.

Eventually, after much struggle, one murder (of Kubo Kiyoshi by management-hired thugs), and mediation, the dispute came to a settlement. The original aim of the striking workers was to protect the safety procedures that had been in place prior to the struggle. Although relief and retraining measures for workers were included in the package that ended the strike, it actually constituted a big defeat, as the settlement package did not cede the safety measures that had originally triggered the action. The death and injury statistics from Miike in the following years illustrate the loss. In 1959, under the first union-controlled safety system, one worker died in an accident and more than 3,600 sustained injuries. Two years later, during the first year of rationalization under the second union that cooperated with management, 16 people died and more than 4,200 sustained injuries. The following year in 1962, 15 workers died and 3,855 were injured. In 1963, however, 458 workers were killed in the worst mine disaster of Japan's postwar history.

Conclusion

The impact of this defeat was inestimable. It heralded a revolution in labor-management relations away from the union-led system of the immediate postwar era and toward the management-dominated "new common sense" of the later postwar years. The tension between narrow economic rationality (that is, the overriding goal of productivity) and the broader concerns of safety and autonomy in the workplace, choice, quality of life, and democracy within and beyond the workplace defined much of the debate about Japanese politics, economy, and society that took place subsequently at all levels of society.

If the productivity- and enterprise-oriented culture of early twenty-first century Japan had not been so stark and narrow, it might have had better resources upon which to draw in the face of the recession, deflation, and an imbalanced economic system facing the country. Some measure of union independence might have presented resources for the development of a much richer Japanese model of economy and politics. On the other hand, Japan's ambition and the narrow focus of its enterprise orientation helped lift the country to the top of the world's economic rankings. Japan still grapples with the resolution of this conflict.

Key Players

Kubo, Kiyoshi (1928–1960): The worker Kiyoshi Kubo was murdered by right wing thugs during the Miike dispute.

Nakayama, Ichiro (1898–1980): Nakayama studied at Tokyo University of Commerce (formerly Hitotsubashi University) under Fukuda Tokuzo, one of the members of the Social Policy Study Association. He also studied in Germany under Joseph Schumpeter at the University of Bonn. Nakayama was one of the mediators in the Miike dispute, as he was based in the Central Labor Relations Commission of the time.

Ota, Kaoru (1912–1998): Born 1 January 1912 in Okayama Prefecture, Ota was chairman of the left-wing union Sohyo (the General Council of Trade Unions of Japan) from 1958 up to 1966, in which capacity he was involved in the intricate negotiations for mediation during the Miike dispute.

Yoshida, Shigeru (1878–1967): Yoshida was one of the most important prime ministers of postwar Japan and arguably the most influential.

See also: *Japanese Labor Unions Dissolved.*

BIBLIOGRAPHY

Books

Dower, John. *Empire and Aftermath: Yoshida Shigeru and the Japanese Experience, 1878–1954.* Harvard East Asian Monographs. Cambridge, MA: Harvard University Press, 1988. (Original work published 1979.)

Gordon, Andrew. *The Evolution of Labor Relations in Japan: Heavy Industry, 1953–1955.* Cambridge, MA: Harvard University Press, 1985.

———, ed. *Postwar Japan as History.* Berkeley: University of California Press, 1993.

———. *The Wages of Affluence: Labor and Management in Postwar Japan.* Cambridge, MA: Harvard University Press, 1998.

Kawanishi, Hirosuke, ed. *The Human Face of Industrial Conflict in Postwar Japan.* London and New York: Kegan Paul International, 1999.

Kinzley, W. Dean. *Industrial Harmony in Modern Japan: the Invention of a Tradition.* London: Routledge, 1991.

Moore, Joe. *Japanese Workers and the Struggle for Power, 1945–1947.* Madison: University of Wisconsin Press, 1983.

—Nik Howard

Japanese Labor Unions Dissolved

Japan 1936–1940

Synopsis

The early liberalism of the Japanese labor movement of the 1920s fell victim to internal and external pressures. Internally, the infighting between socialist, communist, and fifth column quasifascist factions undermined the unity of the movement and left it open to the ravages of an increasingly militarist and nationalist imperial government. Prewar mobilization spurred the bureaucracy to insinuate control over business, labor, and production. This effort culminated in the 1940 dissolution of the All-Japan Federation of Labor, or *Sodomei,* an act that coincided with the advent of the *Sanpo,* or Industrial Patriotic Societ, state-controlled organizations that brought mainly labor but also management under their umbrella.

Timeline

1919: With the formation of the Third International (Comintern), the Bolshevik government of Russia establishes its control over communist movements worldwide.

1924: In the United States, secretary of the interior Albert B. Fall, along with oil company executives Harry Sinclair and Edward L. Doheny, is charged with conspiracy and bribery in making fraudulent leases of U.S. Navy oil reserves at Teapot Dome, Wyoming. The resulting Teapot Dome scandal clouds the administration of President Warren G. Harding.

1929: The Lateran Treaty between the Catholic Church and Mussolini's regime establishes the Vatican City as an independent political entity.

1935: Germany annexes the Saar region after a plebiscite. In defiance of Versailles, the Nazis reintroduce compulsory military service. The Allies do nothing, and many Western intellectuals maintain that it is only proper for Germany to retake its own territory and begin building up its army again.

1940: Hitler's troops sweep through Western Europe, annexing Norway and Denmark in April, and in May the Low Countries and France. At the same time, Stalin—who in this year arranges the murder of Trotsky in Mexico—takes advantage of the situation to add the Baltic republics (Latvia, Lithuania, and Estonia) to the Soviet empire, where they will remain for more than half a century.

1940: Winston Churchill succeeds Neville Chamberlain as British prime minister in May. A month later, he tells Parliament, "We shall not flag or fail. We shall fight in France, we shall fight on the seas and oceans, we shall fight with growing confidence and growing strength in the air, we shall defend our island, whatever the cost may be. We shall fight on the beaches, we shall fight on the landing grounds, we shall fight in the fields and in the streets, we shall fight in the hills. We shall never surrender." In November, German bombers begin air strikes against Britain.

1940: NBC makes the first official network television broadcast.

1945: At the Yalta Conference in February, Roosevelt, Churchill, and Stalin make plans for Germany after its by now inevitable surrender.

1950: North Korean troops pour into South Korea, starting the Korean War. Initially the communists make impressive gains, but in September, the U.S. Marines land at Inchon and liberate Seoul. China responds by sending in its troops.

1955: African and Asian nations meet at the Bandung Conference in Indonesia, inaugurating the "non-aligned" movement of Third World countries.

Event and Its Context

Setting the Scene: The Depression, Nationalism, and War

The piecemeal dissolution of the Japanese labor movement in the 1930s was an outgrowth of the feverish and dense military-nationalist atmosphere of the Japanese social, political, and historical context from the late 1920s onwards. The demise of the labor movement must be seen as the grim, sorry, yet not inevitable consequence of these conditions. The most important immediate causes of this Japanese descent into what scholars have called the "dark valley" were the depression, which manifested itself in Japan earlier than in the West; the mobilization for war; and the reactionary momentum caused by the beginning of what one commentator termed the "Fourteen Years' War" (1931–1945). The more long-range causes underpinning these destructive political and economic forces included the military build-up that started in the 1920s; the lapsing of the Anglo-Japanese alliance and the perceived unfairness of the new dispensation in the form of the Washington conference of 1921–1922, exacerbated by the London naval conference of 1930; and imperialist competition for economic control of or access to markets in an increasingly politically disunited, fragmenting, and unstable China (spurred by its long history of foreign imperial intervention). The final contribution was the general grievance with the self-serving political and diplomatic agenda of the leading Western imperial powers both on the part of Japanese elites and among wide swathes of the Japanese population at large.

A Failure of Democracy in Japan

One of the domestic causes of the shift toward a more nationalist or military outlook arose, however, from the failure of a budding Japanese democratic movement (or Taisho democracy) to plant sufficiently deep roots, especially when the relatively liberal winds of change appeared to favor it in the 1920s. There was a powerful residue of conservative, nationalist, and authoritarian strength, even at the height of the Taisho democracy (exemplified by the achievement of universal male suffrage in 1925, at the same time as the passing of the new repressive Peace Preservation Law). One distinguished academic advanced the theory that the Taisho era gathered the ambivalent forces of democracy and imperial loyalism under the broad umbrella of "imperial democracy," two strands that are closely intertwined ideologically in Japanese traditions of *Odo*, the Righteous Kingly Way. This outlook constitutes an important step forward in the literature. It suggests that the democratic movement at this time had the potential to run aground or to be deflected toward nationalism or right-wing populism, which in fact did begin to insinuate itself into the rhetoric of many sections of the labor movement.

The Strategic and Ideological Failure of Japanese Labor Unionism

A deeper malaise developed apace in the 1930s, namely the defensive yet ultimately myopic and suicidal tendency on the part of Japanese unionism to extricate itself from its historical relation to politics and socialism. The approach at that time was instead to adapt gradually to the ever-shifting yet increasingly nationalistically charged reality in Japan. This took the form of assertions of patriotism, proclamations of the righteousness of the war in Manchuria or later in China proper, and so on. This tendency had its origins in the mid-1920s in Akamatsu Katsumaro's theory of "realist socialism," which became what historian Stephen Large called "the 'new' ideology of the Sodomei in 1924." Even before the change in direction, the *Sodomei* (more properly, *Nihon Rodo Sodomei*, or the All-Japan General Federation of Labor) was a rather bureaucratic and conservative organization that was then governed by three *oyakata* or feudal heads. These labor *oyakata* each had factions in the Sodomei, which enabled them to control the policies and orientation of the union or at least to exert a form of metaphorical subinfeudation (or the subletting of land by a feudal tenant or vassal to another, who becomes the vassal) whereby they controlled union policies in the areas around Tokyo.

In the early to mid-1920s, however, both anarchists and communists attempted to win control of the Sodomei. This achieved only the decline and eventual defeat of anarchism in the Sodomei and later caused the serious splits between reformist, gradualist socialists, and the revolutionary communists of the Sodomei. The effects of this kind of infighting in dividing the left and the labor movement more generally are tragically self-evident. These divisions undermined working-class and labor unity and in turn left the labor movement more exposed to pressure from Japanism and patriotism in subsequent decades. The capitulation that this ultimately represented—for example, in the policy of "sound unionism," which was increasingly bereft of any expression of resistance to the state or socialist politics in the 1930s and 1940s—was a dire outcome of the weaknesses of the movement in the 1920s.

The Military and the Logic of War

The Manchurian incident, in which the Japanese army occupied the Chinese province of Manchuria in 1931, was a crucial turning point in the power configuration of prewar Japanese politics. It may be seen as a military assault on the top level of Japan's complex and informal prewar power structure. The outbreak of war had a political and economic logic and a dark potential of its own that would, in time, suggest, to Japanese elites in the bureaucracy and the military especially, a new mode of organizing the Japanese state. It was, in addition, a clear signal that Japan's foreign policy would be from that time forth much more self-assertive, power-oriented, and expansionist. It heralded, therefore, the ambition of military elements (sometimes in combination with civilian right-wing groups outside the government or, more frequently, simply within the confines of the establishment) to flex their muscles on both the international and the domestic front.

Consequences of the Early Failure to Resist

The impact on the labor movement of this growth in militarism and nationalism in the mid-to-late 1920s cannot be underestimated. The attacks upon, and the rounding up of, communists by the Japanese government in the late 1920s were a presentiment of things to come. Repressive state activities further narrowed political freedom of expression and were a loss for all Japanese people. The failure to contest, organize against, and defeat the growing strength of the authoritarian or incipient totalitarian trends in Japan at this time only made it harder for

resistance to succeed later on. By 1931–1932, the military and the civilian right wing—in a climate of terror and assassination—clearly had momentum on their side. By 1933 leaders of the labor movement had issued statements of support for the takeover in Manchuria. Former leading communists such as Sano Manabu and Nabeyama Sadachika had shocked their comrades with a retraction of their communist allegiance and their confession of national socialism under the *Tenno* (emperor). In addition, by the early 1930s Akamatsu Katsumaro had once more reiterated the ideological basis of his commitment to "realist socialism" by explaining that "'scientific Japanism' rested simply on the proposition that for socialism to flourish in Japan, it would have to be combined with Japanese nationalism" (Large, 1981). This was a dangerous position for any working-class movement, for it asserted the primacy of emperor and nation over class.

Social Policy

In the 1920s, before the army occupied Manchuria, social policy legislation and initiatives pursued by the Home Ministry bureaucrats represented a relatively liberal phase in Japanese public policy. This changed beginning in the early 1930s with the failure of laissez-faire capitalism to deal with the world economic and political crises. Since the Meiji period (1868–1912), Japan had had a state-led, top-down political-economic orientation. With the perception that the more totalitarian states were coping much better with the challenges of the depression, Japan's bureaucrats more and more looked for suitable or instructive models for Japan that also fitted in with their sense of the trends of the times.

In departing from the more liberal social policy that had prevailed until the 1930s, one crucial model from which the Japanese bureaucracy learned was that of Nazi Germany. Some scholars have argued that this was more extensive than has previously been thought; some have referred to the system that prevailed in Japan at this time as a variety of fascism called "imperial fascism." Certain Japanese bureaucrats, such as Minami Iwao, were influenced in their selection of policies by their study of the Nazi Labor Front in Germany in 1934. Minami was fascinated by its "Strength through Joy" program, the intention of which was to raise the morale of workers by holding inexpensive entertainment for them and sponsoring group travel. In 1936 Minami finished his plan, which he called the "Policy for the Adjustment of Labor-Capital Relations." This formed the core of the Social Bureau of the Home Ministry's "Japanese labor union bill" as well as the plan for the "industrial patriotic" movement that was to follow.

The plan may have been more Nazi-inspired than it might seem at first glance. The plan would dissolve all unions and employers' associations. Like the Nazi Labor Front, it intended to rescind past collective agreements and allow managers to represent workers on the plant discussion councils (which often remained in the form of the existing factory councils of the large companies). The proposal would also delimit the power of employers. In short, it extended the arm of the bureaucratic state into the running of private companies and subordinated private capital to the interests and preferences of a dictatorial military state.

497

Steps Toward Dissolution

With parliamentary government on the back burner starting in 1932, the tide of authoritarian bureaucratic and military government continued fundamentally unchecked. Under the Hirota cabinet of 1936, labor took a step backward. Hirota Koki had come to power as prime minister in the wake of the 26 February incident (an attempted coup d'etat by young officers in right-wing military elements) of the same year. Although labor and the socialist party had not been involved in the February event, Hirota decided to use the martial law directive that had been imposed during the revolt to ban May Day demonstrations so as to maintain "public order." The remonstrations of the leaders of organized labor fell on deaf ears.

In September 1936 Hirota dissolved the General Federation of Work in Japanese Government Enterprises. The majority of the unions of this federation were located in military arsenals. Because of this, the War Ministry, which was overtly opposed to labor unions in these kinds of military-related workplaces, had initiated the order to disband, as it regarded unions as barriers to the military's plans to take over industrial production for war purposes. Naturally, the labor movement was upset about this order and feared that the next step would be the outlawing of all labor unions. The war minister firmly denied this assertion. As nothing could be done to prevent the dissolution of the federation, on 23 September 1936 it became the first moderate labor organization in Japan to be suppressed directly. This was a crucial moment in the struggle for the existence of independent unions in Japan.

The New Order

Historians disagree as to the extent to which the Nazi Labor Front inspired the Japanese bureaucrats (and in particular Minami Iwao) in their formulation of the *Sangyo Hokoku Kai* (or *Sanpo*, meaning Industrial Patriotic Society). Some have argued that there is a common ideological and organizational core among the two labor systems that included a classless national community. Both cultures replaced unions with universal plant advisory councils, and both espoused the "organic harmony and unity of an industrial 'shop community' based on mythic village, folk, or family models." Totally rejecting laissez-faire liberalism or ideas of class struggle, the ideology embraced a corporate view of the enterprise as a "functional community where each member, equal before the Emperor, had a vocation (*shokubun*), and where labor and capital fused together into a 'single body' (*ittai*)."

The rationale for launching the Sanpo program was the increased social unrest that gripped Japan in 1937 and 1938. The worry was that the strife would feed communist agitation and sow confusion. Although the employers would lose a certain degree of autonomy in this process of ever-encroaching state management (despite the reassurances of the bureaucrats), the resistance from business was not all in vain. Employers managed to water down some aspects of the bureaucrats' far-reaching plans, and thus they did not lose as much as labor did in the process.

The socialist Aso Hisashi assessed the working-class disillusionment with socialism as an opening for the possibility that Prime Minister Konoe Fumimaro's New Order of the late 1930s and early 1940s might furnish a route by which to implement socialism from above. In 1934 Aso seems to have flirted with the idea of bringing socialism to Japan at the muzzle of the army's gun, as he felt then that the army could be a "progressive" force. Konoe had links to certain ultranationalists in the civilian bureaucracy and the military and a hawkish foreign policy. Given Aso's prior political predilections, it thus comes as no surprise that at the end of the 1930s he began to put his trust in Konoe to transform the Japanese political landscape. This was not a change in tactics on Aso's part, but rather a similar approach to that of Akamatsu of jumping on board a Japanist train and steaming in the direction of the conservative, authoritarian, or even so-called radical right.

One concrete way in which Aso supported Konoe during his first tenure as prime minister (1937–1939) was to support the National Mobilization Bill of 1938. Aso and his supporters in the Shakai Taishuto (or Social Masses Party) saw in Konoe the definite contours of a progressive and thus had been very vocal in backing this bill, which granted extensive wartime powers. Another labor leader, Nishio Suehiro, while advocating the strengthening of the National Mobilization Bill in the Diet, once caused a stir when he waxed lyrical about the march of totalitarianism and how it represented the wave of the future, and how individualism would become a relic of the past. In his enthusiasm, he added, "Prince Konoe should lead Japan . . . like Hitler, Mussolini or Stalin!" The problem was not his pro-totalitarian attitude but his assumption that Japan might learn from Stalin; Nishio was eventually expelled from the Diet for this unconscionable faux pas.

The jury is still out on whether Japan turned fascist in this period. The Japanese context may well be so removed from the Nazi and fascist institutions and ideologies that it is impossible to place prewar Japanese systems in quite the same box. The comparison between Japanese "fascism" and these others political systems dissolves in the face of the relative domestic benignity of the Japanese case. One of the unique features of Japanese is that it wreaked most of its violence and death abroad as a byproduct of the aggressive expansionism at the core of the Japanese Empire. The sociologist Bai Gao considers fascism an influential variable in the transformation of Japanese capitalism before and during the war. Although he believes that Japan was fascist, he also believes that Japan borrowed policies from Nazi Germany. This makes Japan a coconspirator in the international march of fascism, but it does not follow from this that fascism is necessarily the best label for Japan domestically during this period.

The Dissolution

The New Order and the Sanpo were intended to harmonize labor-management relations to create a climate of industrial peace in which war production would remain on course and uninterrupted. The only leader who seemed to be concerned about the New Order was Matsuoka Komakichi. He was attentive to the possibility that the unions might be pressured into dissolving their independent existence to become a kind of Labor Front. Matsuoka realized that Sanpo constituted a real threat to the existence of autonomous trade unionism and to the Sodomei, of which he was an important leader. Matsuoka did all that he possibly could without actively resisting or reinvigorating the link to socialist politics. There was no leverage he or any other labor organization could bring to bear without actively fighting for their independence in a wider political struggle for the independent interests of the working class. Matsuoka and the other labor leaders instead had passively latched onto an accommodation to the politics of patriotism after the occupation of Manchuria.

It would be inaccurate to say that Sanpo forced the final dissolution of the labor movement in Japan. In fact, both organized and unorganized workers flocked to the Sanpo of their own will (although it is difficult to say whether that will was exactly free). The extent to which the unions had been won over is apparent in one indication of these leaders' attitudes. All of the moderates (the labor leaders Nishio, Matsuoka, and Aso) believed that Sanpo could be accepted and that it might improve the conditions of the workers. Thus there was no contradiction for them between abiding by Japan's unique national polity, emperor worship, and cultural myths on the one hand and gaining real advances for the working classes on the other. Even Matsuoka, who otherwise did not wish to dissolve these well-established autonomous organizations of the working class, was willing to adhere to a formula of dual membership in a union and in Sanpo. The pressure to dissolve the unions, both from above in requests from the state and from below or within, however, was tangible. The Sodomei could not staunch the flow of its members and member unions that were all the while leaving in droves for the Sanpo.

Finally, the Social Masses Party, which might have been expected to remain firm, dissolved itself and entered the Sanpo. This left the Sodomei on its own, striving to maintain its independence, without support from inside or outside. It was, as Stephen Large put it, in these depressing circumstances that the Sodomei central committee decided to dissolve the federation on 8 July 1940.

Conclusion

How did the Japanese labor movement come to this sorry pass? What essentially undercut the potential for the labor movement to develop along a truly democratic path was its failure to remain in contact with its organic political twin, the socialist party movement. The old adage about strength lying in unity is a sober note to finish on, especially when both the communists and the socialists were at loggerheads and handed the momentum to the forces of the establishment to divide and hence puncture their combined power. The communists were picked off and the socialists conformed, and this marked the beginning of the end for the labor movement and the socialists. Even if they had all stood solid together, victory still was not assured, as the opposition loomed large and powerful. Disunity among the labor factions became the chief weapon of the opposing forces of the military and the bureaucracy. Ideological prostration and organizational infighting compromised the intellectual and spiritual as well as the material unity of the Japanese working class. The only road after this was a slow and painful ideological and organizational death. In 1940 the Sodomei experienced the demise of what had become a barely warm corpse, so desperately had it lunged toward the onrushing Japanist express.

Key Players

Aso, Hisashi (1891–1940): Aso was an intellectual in the Shinjinkai (the New Man Society), which was based at Tokyo Imperial University, under the watchful eye of its patron, the famous intellectual Yoshino Sakuzo. Later he made his way into the Japanese labor movement.

Hirota, Koki (1878–1948): Hirota was prime minister from 9 March 1936 until 2 February 1937.

Konoe, Fumimaro (1891–1945): A prince of the noble Fujiwara clan and prime minister from 4 June 1937 until 5 January 1939 and again from 22 July 1940 until 18 October 1941, Konoe was a charismatic leader, famous for his brain trust (called the Showa Research Association), in which many intellectuals and bureaucrats participated.

Matsuoka, Komakichi (1888–1958): A worker leader in the Yuaikai (the Friendly Society, Japan's first lasting national labor federation), who had worked his way up to the top, Matsuoka had been at the Muroran Steel Works, where he had some *kokata*, or feudal subordinates.

Minami, Iwao: A key bureaucrat in the Home Ministry, Minami was originally a labor manager before he became a bureaucrat and an advocate of Nazi programs following a visit to Germany. His book *Germany on the Rise* was published in 1938.

Nishio, Suehiro (1891–1981): Nishio was a grand old man of the Sodomei. He was a worker leader, like Matsuoka.

Suzuki, Bunji (1885–1946): Suzuki was the founder of the Yuaikai, which developed from a 15-man group into a national organization of 30,000 members in eight years, laying the groundwork for potentially building a strong, long-lasting, and successful union movement in the post–World War I era.

BIBLIOGRAPHY

Books

Ayusawa, Iwao F. *A History of Labor in Modern Japan.* Honolulu: East-West Center Press, Hawaii University, 1966.

Gao, Bai. *Economic Ideology and Japanese Industrial Policy: Developmentalism from 1931 to 1965.* Cambridge, MA: Cambridge University Press, 1997.

Garon, Sheldon M. *The State and Labor in Modern Japan.* Berkeley: University of California Press, 1987.

Gordon, Andrew. *Labor and Imperial Democracy in Prewar Japan.* Berkeley: University of California Press, 1991.

Hane, Mikiso. *Modern Japan: A Historical Survey.* Boulder, CO: Westview Press, 1992.

Hirst, Margaret E. *Life of Friedrich List and Selections from His Writings.* London: Smith, Elder & Co., 1909.

Johnson, Chalmers A. *MITI and The Japanese Miracle: The Growth of Industrial Policy, 1925–1975.* Tokyo: Charles E. Tuttle Co., 1982.

———. *Japan: Who Governs? The Rise of the Developmental State.* New York and London: W. W. Norton & Company, 1995.

Large, Stephen S. *Organized Workers and Socialist Politics in Interwar Japan*. Cambridge, MA: Cambridge University Press, 1981.

List, Friedrich. *The National System of Political Economy*. Translated by Sampson S. Lloyd. Longmans, 1885.

Nakane, Chie. *Japanese Society*. Berkeley: University of California Press, 1970.

Niimura, Satoshi. "Modernization and the Studies of Adam Smith in Japan During and After World War II: Kazuo Okouchi, Zenya Takashima and Yoshihiko Uchida." In *Economic Thought and Modernization in Japan*, edited by Sugihara Shiro and Tanaka Toshihiro. Northampton, MA: Edward Elgar, 1998.

Van Wolferen, Karel. *The Enigma of Japanese Power: People and Politics in a Stateless Nation*. New York: Vintage Books, Random House, 1990.

—Nik Howard

Jim Crow Segregation and Labor

United States 1880–1964

Synopsis

After the end of Reconstruction in 1877, southern states and local communities began to enact laws known as segregation or "Jim Crow" laws. These measures separated the races in public accommodations. Rather than passing one sweeping law, local and state legislators in the South passed a series of laws between 1881 and 1910 that required separate accommodations for blacks and whites in public spaces. These laws were indicative of the hardening of the philosophy of white supremacy throughout the South during this time.

C. Vann Woodward, a scholar of the New South, recognized that after slavery former slaves voluntarily chose to separate themselves from white southern society. This practice became de facto segregation, or segregation by custom. By the 1880s, however, the first generation of African Americans born outside of slavery entered adulthood, and they were the first of their race to test the bounds of de facto segregation by engaging themselves in the all-white public sphere. In order to maintain a rigid practice of white supremacy, southern white politicians began to codify segregation within the legal system. Thus began the transition from de facto to de jure segregation.

Although there were no segregation laws that applied to labor specifically, segregation and the emergence of a rigidly defined, biracial South had a tremendous impact on the way black and white workers organized, interacted with each other, and dealt with management.

Timeline

1877: In the face of uncertain results from the popular vote in the presidential election of 1876, the U.S. Electoral Commission awards the presidency to Rutherford B. Hayes despite a slight popular majority for his opponent, Samuel J. Tilden. The election of 1876 will remain the most controversial in American history for the next 124 years, until overshadowed by the race between George W. Bush and Al Gore in 2000.

1877: In part as a quid pro quo demanded by southern legislators in return for their support of the Republican Hayes over the Democrat Tilden, the new president agrees to end the period of martial law in the South known as Reconstruction.

1884: At the Berlin Conference on African Affairs, fourteen nations (including the United States) discuss colonial expansion in Africa, and call for an end to slavery and the slave trade.

1889: Discontented southern farmers merge their farm organizations to form the Southern Alliance.

1896: U.S. Supreme Court issues its *Plessy v. Ferguson* decision, which establishes the "separate but equal" doctrine that will be used to justify segregation in the southern United States for the next half-century.

1909: National Association for the Advancement of Colored People (NAACP) is founded by W. E. B. Du Bois and a number of other prominent black and white intellectuals in New York City.

1915: D. W. Griffith's controversial *Birth of a Nation* is the first significant motion picture. As film, it is an enduring work of art, but its positive depiction of the Ku Klux Klan influences a rebirth of the Klan in Stone Mountain, Georgia.

1936: Hitler uses the Summer Olympics in Berlin as an opportunity to showcase Nazi power and pageantry, but the real hero of the games is the African American track star Jesse Owens.

1947: Jackie Robinson joins the Brooklyn Dodgers, becoming the first African American player in Major League Baseball.

1949: Apartheid is institutionalized in South Africa.

1954: In *Brown v. Board of Education of Topeka*, the U.S. Supreme Court unanimously strikes down racial segregation in public schools.

1955: Rosa Parks refuses to move from her seat near the front of a public bus in Montgomery, Alabama, and is arrested. The incident touches off a boycott of Montgomery's bus system, led by the Rev. Martin Luther King, Jr., which will last well into 1956. The situation will attract national attention and garner support for the civil-rights movement, before Montgomery agrees to desegregate its bus system on 21 December 1956—exactly a year after Parks's brave protest.

1957: Integration of high schools in Little Rock, Arkansas, is accomplished with the aid of federal troops.

Dr. and Mrs. Charles Atkins read segregation sign in Santa Fe Depot, Oklahoma City, Oklahoma. AP/World Wide Photos. Reproduced by permission.

Event and Its Context

Origins of Segregation

Segregation, or "Jim Crow" laws, originated in the post-Reconstruction South. The first state to enact any such segregation law was Tennessee. This law was actually directed toward railway transportation. In 1881 the Tennessee legislature passed a law requiring that railroad companies provide distinct and separate accommodations for black and white passengers in first class. This law mandated railroads to provide these accommodations, divided by partition, while maintaining the same amenities for each section. Thus was born the policy of "separate but equal." Soon other states and local communities in the South passed similar legislation concerning first railroads and then other aspects of public life. By 1896 the United States Supreme Court ruled in the *Plessy v. Ferguson* case that the "separate but equal" doctrine was constitutional. Although these laws never applied to labor directly, they affirmed white attempts to stratify southern life on the basis of race.

The Farmer's Alliance

The Farmer's Alliance was a labor union that had made significant political inroads into southern politics by the 1890s, when these segregation laws were being drafted. The Alliancemen, as they were known, were instrumental in passing segregation laws in Alabama, Arkansas, Georgia, and Kentucky. Politicians who were also Alliancemen sided with southern Democrats and supported "Jim Crow" segregation legislation for two reasons. First, they genuinely hated the railroads and believed that "Jim Crow" facilities hurt the railroad owners economically. Second, they believed that racial segregation was inevitable.

"Jim Crow" and the Workplace

The movement to mandate separate public spheres for blacks and whites gradually crept into the workplace. Before 1900 whites and African Americans frequently worked side by side in trade as well as in unskilled positions. During this time the South was becoming more industrialized, however, and factory owners were complicit in extending "Jim Crow" into the workplace.

Initially, factory owners and management throughout the South segregated the work place by providing "Jim Crow" housing for their black employees. As industries grew throughout the South, employers began to designate certain occupations for white labor only and other, less desirable, positions exclusively for black labor. Positions that required domestic or manual labor were "racialized" occupations. In places like Mississippi, local whites referred to these occupations as "nigger" work, or reserved for blacks only. Typically, many of these positions were in the service industry, including household domestics, which reinforced notions of white hegemony, since these positions placed blacks in roles subordinate to whites. Other positions involved manual labor and usually required hard or possibly dangerous work. Southern whites believed that black workers could be pushed harder than white labor and were more expendable when there was danger involved.

Factory owners had a monetary stake in creating "Jim Crow" positions throughout the South. By making certain positions exclusively black, management then drove the wages for those positions down well below equivalent white wages. Additionally, since certain jobs were reserved for whites, management reinforced an impression of racial status for white labor, keeping them tied to "Jim Crow" and making interracial cooperation between blacks and whites unlikely.

Service workers on the railroads, who were African American almost without exception, often found themselves relegated to substandard sections of the train during breaks, meals, and sleep periods. They were not allowed to mingle with whites during their free time. They could neither purchase nor eat their meals in the dining car; instead, they had to eat their food in the baggage car. Additionally, they had the responsibility of removing black passengers who tried to ride in the first-class cars reserved for whites. As a result of these unfair labor practices, they faced reprisals from the African American community. These workers were often called "Uncle Toms" because they were perceived as complicit in enforcing "Jim Crow" regulations.

Interracial Unionism

Since the 1960s historians have debated the amount of cooperation in labor organizing between white and black labor. Herbert Gutman was the first scholar to question the role interracial cooperation played in the labor movement. Gutman looked to the letters of Richard L. Davis, who was an Ohio coalminer and union official with the United Mine Workers in the 1890s. Gutman believed that labor scholars had overlooked the role black labor played within the labor movement and suggested that black and white labor cooperated more frequently than previously thought.

By the 1980s labor scholars were challenging Gutman's assertions. Herbert Hill, former labor secretary for the National Association for the Advancement of Colored People, argued that the experience of Richard Davis represented an aberration in labor history. He explained that interracial cooperation between black and white labor was sporadic at best and represented the exception, not the rule. Instead, he noted that craft and unskilled labor unions had a history of systematically excluding black labor and other workers of color. Hill noted that the history of unionism in America represented a firm acceptance of "Jim Crow" practices rather than a challenge to segregation and discrimination in the workplace.

Scholars since Hill have noted that, although many labor unions professed a commitment to interracial unionism, "Jim Crow" represented too great an obstacle for white workers to overcome in order to embrace racial cooperation. Daniel Letwin, in his examination of black and white mine workers in Alabama, believed that labor unions in that state encouraged cooperation and solidarity across racial lines, but white workers were unwilling to challenge a segregated occupational sphere to enact progressive social change.

Black Organizing and Biracial Unionism

Black labor unions in the United States have followed a path similar to the history of "Jim Crow." After the Civil War, some local labor unions accepted black members, yet many would not. With the creation of the National Labor Union in 1866, the labor movement finally spoke with a national voice, and although they welcomed black craft workers, they made it clear that African American workers would have to adhere strictly to organizational ideology. Typically this ideology neglected race concerns that black workers wanted to address. This position within the labor movement led black craft workers to form the National Negro Labor Union in 1869. The practice of black workers organizing separately from whites continued throughout the "Jim Crow" period. Even with the creation of other national labor organizations—such as the American Federation of Labor (AFL), the Knights of Labor, and the Congress of Industrial Organizations (CIO), all of which were founded with the intention of equally representing all labor—black workers were mostly ignored or required to organize in separate branches.

In order to create a voice for black labor, many African American workers organized independent unions to challenge the hegemony of white supremacy within the labor movement and society in general. Black workers organized all-black unions like the Brotherhood of Sleeping Car Porters and Maids in 1925 as a means to combat labor issues that white unions refused to address. Other black and white workers participated in biracial unionism and organized in segregated divisions within specific local branches. Although the national chapter of the AFL had allowed black workers to participate in national conferences by the end of World War I, and southern states like Florida encouraged black workers to engage in biracial unionism, the state chapter refused to allow black workers to participate in the state conference. They could not even enter the building where the meeting was being held for fear that black workers might begin thinking that they were socially equal to whites. In short, white labor refused to allow black labor to participate with whites on an equal basis.

Even though some African American workers were not officially organized in unions, they still found ways to protest segregation. During World War I the federal government created the National War Labor Board (NWLB). The purpose of the NWLB was to investigate grievances that workers had with management during the war years in order to avoid crippling strikes that might hamper the war effort. Although white labor typically demanded higher wages, standardized hours, or better working conditions, black workers typically demanded that the NWLB investigate issues related to racial discrimination. Black workers for the New Orleans streetcar company, for example, demanded higher wages, which the NWLB recommended, yet the board also adhered to the "Jim Crow" scale of wages restricted to black labor in the South. Maids, who worked for several southern railway companies, filed numerous complaints with the U.S. Department of Labor's Division of Negro Economics. One complaint alleged that they were segregated from white washroom facilities and instead had to utilize a sandbox instead of an actual bathroom. Other blacks who worked for the railroads told stories of how railroad management demanded that they work in skilled positions but paid them unskilled wages. Like the NWLB, the Division of Negro Economics could do little more than request that these companies stop such discriminatory practices, but whether they did or not was completely up to the discretion of the company's management. Yet, black workers still mobilized and protested their treatment in the face of segregation, even without the protection of a labor union.

As a result of the practice of segregated unions and organizing, management typically used black workers as scab labor to break strikes and other labor actions initiated by whites. As long as white and black labor regarded race and labor issues differently, the chance for real biracial cooperation was nonexistent; therefore, management used race as a wedge between the two groups, effectively limiting gains that a united labor movement might otherwise have made.

Michael K. Honey, in his study of labor organizing in Memphis, Tennessee, during the New Deal era, noted that black workers were encouraged to engage in biracial organizing. As happened in other attempts to organize biracially, however, black and white workers were interested in different issues. Black workers in Memphis wanted to address issues related to segregation, while white workers refused to address the topic at all. As black workers participated in these biracial efforts, they gained experience in leadership roles and social organizing that a later generation translated into grassroots, civil rights organizing and activism after World War II. In addition, black workers created connections with liberal whites, who were amenable to black demands to end segregation. Thus, although black workers could not address segregation within segregated unions, they learned how to engage the local community politically in issues of segregation and discrimination.

March on Washington 1941

The March on Washington in 1941 was the first time black labor organizers promoted a successful national campaign against discrimination in the workplace. A. Phillip Randolph, president of the Brotherhood of Sleeping Car Porters, wanted to address low wages and discrimination within the war industries. He and other black labor leaders around the country planned a march on Washington during the summer of 1941. President Franklin D. Roosevelt and his administration feared the reaction an event like this could have on the image of the United States during the war and moved to stop the march. Through Executive Order 8802, the president created the Fair Employment Practices Committee (FEPC). The FEPC investigated complaints of racial discrimination and had the power to recommend that the government withhold or withdraw federally funded defense contracts from companies engaging in such discrimination. This measure was enough to convince march organizers to call off the protest.

Although the executive order was a triumph for black labor leaders, the victory was incomplete. The FEPC did not have the authority actually to punish employers whom they deemed guilty of racial discrimination. In fact, the committee was afraid to commit to any policy that might disrupt the production of war goods. The committee had the power only to submit recommendations to the federal government. Additionally, the measure was never intended to be a challenge to segregation in the workplace or a challenge to "Jim Crow" occupations. White southern politicians and segregationists protested the FEPC's authority to investigate claims of discrimination and finally satisfied themselves that the FEPC was not challenging segregation. Before black labor leaders could bask in the glow of victory, some acknowledged that African American unions still had to fight segregation and agitate for access to jobs traditionally reserved for whites. In fact, the gains from the proposed march on Washington were hollow ones; however, the events that transpired subsequent to its cancellation convinced black union leaders that organization and activity could lead to important changes for African American workers.

Civil Rights Act of 1964

The Civil Rights Act of 1964 had its origins in the 1963 "March on Washington for Jobs and Freedom." This event was coorganized by A. Philip Randolph, Martin Luther King, Jr., Roy Wilkins, and other civil rights activists. Although the purpose of this march was more broadly based than the one planned in 1941, civil rights leaders still demanded that the federal government address discrimination and segregation in the workplace. After the march, President John F. Kennedy supported a bill in Congress to guarantee civil rights for all Americans. Segregationists in Congress stalled his bill for the rest of his presidency. After Kennedy's death, President Lyndon B. Johnson spearheaded passage of the Civil Rights Bill. Unlike Kennedy, popular sympathy was with Johnson, owing to the violent death of four young girls in the infamous Birmingham, Alabama, church bombing.

The Civil Rights Act of 1964 made its way through Congress in the face of protest from southern segregationists and conservative Republicans like Senator Barry Goldwater. It passed, however, and President Johnson signed it into law on 2 July 1964. The Civil Rights Act created the Equal Employment Opportunity Commission (EEOC). The EEOC has the authority to investigate, arbitrate, and recommend judicial prosecution of employers found guilty of discrimination based on race, sex, or ethnic background. A great deal of the overt discrimination in the workplace has been hampered or stopped entirely by the creation of the EEOC and the investigations it has initiated.

Key Players

Gutman, Herbert (1928–1985): Gutman, father of American working-class history, challenged conventional labor historians by examining the experience of workers instead of unions and other institutions. In 1969 in he wrote a seminal article that questioned the important role blacks played in the labor movement. Although labor scholars have since proven that his assertions were exaggerated, he was the first labor historian to interject race into the labor question.

Johnson, Lyndon B. (1908–1973): Johnson was president for more than half of the 1960s. Like his predecessor, John F. Kennedy, he was committed to publicly addressing racial discrimination and segregation. He was instrumental in Congress's finally passing the Civil Rights Act of 1964. The Civil Rights Act created the Equal Employment Opportunity Commission that investigated cases of racial discrimination in the workplace.

Randolph, A. Philip (1889–1979): Randolph was editor of the black newspaper *The Messenger*. He also founded the Brotherhood of Sleeping Car Porters and helped organize the 1941 and 1963 Marches on Washington.

Roosevelt, Franklin D. (1882–1945): Roosevelt was president from 1932 to 1945 and is the only president to serve more than two terms. His presidency encompassed the depres-

sion and World War II years. Although he was sympathetic to African Americans, he never publicly challenged segregation or racism. As a result of trying to avert the 1941 March on Washington, he initiated Executive Order 8802, which created the Fair Employment Practices Committee that investigated racial discrimination in war industries.

See also: *Black Codes; Brotherhood of Sleeping Car Porters; Civil Rights Act of 1964; Fair Employment Practice Committee; March on Washington Movement; National Labor Union; National War Labor Board.*

BIBLIOGRAPHY

Books

Arnesen, Eric. *Brotherhoods of Color: Black Railroad Workers and the Struggle for Equality.* Cambridge, MA: Harvard University Press, 2001.

Ayers, Edward L. *The Promise of the New South: Life After Reconstruction.* New York: Oxford University Press, 1992.

Gutman, Herbert. *Power and Culture: Essays on the American Working Class.* New York: Pantheon Books, 1987.

Honey, Michael K. *Southern Labor and Black Civil Rights: Organizing Memphis Workers.* Urbana, IL: University of Illinois Press, 1993.

Letwin, Daniel. *The Challenge of Interracial Unionism: Alabama Coal Miners, 1878–1921.* Chapel Hill, NC: University of North Carolina Press, 1998.

Weaver, Robert C. *Negro Labor: A National Problem.* New York: Harcourt Brace and Company, 1946.

Woodward, C. Vann. *The Strange Career of Jim Crow.* New York: Oxford University Press, 1955.

Periodicals

Arnesen, Eric. "Following the Color Line of Labor: Black Workers and the Labor Movement before 1930." *Radical History Review* 55 (1993): 53–87.

———. "Up from Exclusion: Black and White Workers, Race, and the State of Labor History." *Reviews in American History* 26 (March 1998): 146–174.

Boston, Michael. "No Gold for Jim Crow's Retirement: The Abolition of Segregated Unionism at Houston's Hughes Tool Company." *Southwestern Historical Quarterly* 101 (spring 1998): 496–521.

Hill, Herbert. "Myth-Making as Labor History: Herbert Gutman and the United Mine Workers of America." *International Journal of Politics, Culture, and Society* 2 (spring 1978): 132–200.

Honey, Michael K. "Fighting on Two Fronts: Black Trade Unionists in Memphis in the Jim Crow Era." *Labor's Heritage* 4 (fall 1992): 50–68.

—Robert Cassanello

Johnson-Reed Act: *See* **National Origins Act.**

June Days Rebellion

France 1848

Synopsis

In June 1848 civil war broke out in Paris. Although the fighting only lasted for four days, it was one of the bloodiest conflicts in France in the nineteenth century, with thousands killed and injured. The fighting occurred between the forces defending the Second Republic and a minority who believed that the new government was betraying the principles of the February revolution from earlier that year. The failure of the insurrection signaled the defeat of the movement for radical social and political change and the victory of the conservative reaction to the 1848 revolution. Brutal repression had alienated a large part of the lower classes from the republican government. Most observers were horrified by the violence and bloodshed and wanted a return to law and order. This helps to explain the widespread popularity of Louis Napoleon Bonaparte and his landslide victory in the December 1848 presidential elections. In the June Days rebellion lies the triumph of Bonapartism, which led to the eventual downfall of the Second Republic.

Timeline

1824: French engineer Sadi Carnot describes a perfect engine: one in which all energy input is converted to energy output. The ideas in his *Reflections on the Motive Power of Fire* will influence the formulation of the Second Law of Thermodynamics—which shows that such a perfect engine is an impossibility.

1833: British Parliament passes the Slavery Abolition Act, giving freedom to all slaves throughout the British Empire.

1838: As crops fail, spawning famine in Ireland, Britain imposes the Poor Law. Designed to discourage the indigent from seeking public assistance, the law makes labor in the workhouse worse than any work to be found on the outside, and thus has the effect of stimulating emigration.

1842: In *Sanitary Conditions of the Labouring Population of Great Britain,* British reformer Edwin Chadwick draws attention to the squalor in the nation's mill town slums, and shows that working people have a much higher incidence of disease than do the middle and upper classes.

1845: From Ireland to Russia, famine plagues Europe, killing some 2.5 million people.

1846: The Irish potato famine reaches its height.

1848: Mexican War ends with the Treaty of Guadalupe Hidalgo, in which Mexico gives up half of its land area, including Texas, California, most of Arizona and New Mexico, and parts of Colorado, Utah, and Nevada. In another treaty, with Great Britain, the United States sets the boundaries of its Oregon Territory.

1848: Discovery of gold at Sutter's Mill in California starts a gold rush, which brings a tremendous influx of settlers—and spells the beginning of the end for California's Native Americans.

1848: Women's Rights Convention in Seneca Falls, New York, launches the women's suffrage movement.

1850: German mathematical physicist Rudolf Julius Emanuel Clausius enunciates the Second Law of Thermodynamics, stating that heat cannot pass from a colder body to a warmer one, but only from a warmer to a colder body. This will prove to be one of the most significant principles of physics and chemistry, establishing that a perfectly efficient physical system is impossible, and that all physical systems ultimately succumb to entropy.

1854: In the United States, the Kansas-Nebraska Act calls for decisions on the legality of slavery to be made through local votes. Instead of reducing divisions, this measure will result in widespread rioting and bloodshed, and will only further hasten the looming conflict over slavery and states' rights.

1858: In a Springfield, Illinois, speech during his unsuccessful campaign for the Senate against Stephen Douglass, Abraham Lincoln makes a strong case against slavery, maintaining that "this Government cannot endure permanently half-slave and half-free."

Event and Its Context

The February Revolution

The June Days had their roots in the expectations of radical social reform that had been raised by the February revolution. Starting in 1847, a concerted campaign for reform included demands for political freedoms and a limited extension of the suffrage. The campaign for limited reform gathered momentum, mobilizing the lower classes of Paris. The large crowds that gathered in Paris in late February 1848 espoused radical republican, and even socialist, ideas. Following two days of fighting on the barricades in the streets of Paris, King Louis-Phillippe abdicated, and on 24 February a new provisional government took office. Although the majority of the members were moderate republicans, the government also included the socialist Louis Blanc. Their presence indicated the influence of the armed crowds, which at that point virtually controlled the streets of Paris. Such direct democracy had been far from the minds of those who had initiated the campaign for reform.

First Months of the Second Republic

The provisional government tried to placate the radicals. France became a republic, and many political and social reforms were passed. These included universal male suffrage, freedom of the press, and freedom of assembly and association. After decades of repression, there was an explosion of newspapers and political clubs, which discussed all kinds of radical ideas. It was proving a difficult task to pacify the masses. Given a taste of power, the lower orders were unwilling to return to being passive observers of the political process. Some people clearly saw the overthrow of the July Monarchy as the beginning of a process of radical change that would fundamentally transform France's social structures. (*July Monarchy* refers to the Restoration government of France, 1830–1848. It was charged with preserving the principles of the French Revolution, which began in July 1789, while simultaneously restoring and maintaining civil order.)

Of particular concern to Parisian workers was the issue of the organization of work. The Luxembourg Commission was set up to investigate the problems of Parisian workers and to suggest solutions. The government published a decree that "guaranteed labor to all citizens," which raised expectations of concrete reforms in the sphere of work and production. This decree was hastily drafted in response to pressing petitions from workers for social welfare measures from the government. France was in the midst of a severe economic crisis, exacerbated by the political uncertainty caused by the revolution. In the following months, unemployment in Paris rose to 50–60 percent. With no financial support for themselves or their families, desperate people expected the government that they had put into power to provide assistance. In response, the provisional government set up the National Workshops. This was intended to provide those without work with an income and employment on public works schemes. By June nearly 117,000 workers were earning one or two francs a day, much lower than the average daily wage of three to four francs. Even this small amount was a drain on the meager resources of the state, and the National Workshops became ammunition for conservative opponents of reform.

The Conservative Reaction

The first national elections of the Second Republic were held in April and returned a moderate government. Of the 900 elected members of the Constituent Assembly, only 34 were working class. Only 10 percent could be described as radical republicans, and one third were monarchists of various kinds. The provisional government was dissolved, and a new executive commission was chosen to lead the Assembly. The radicals and socialists were dismayed at the outcome of the elections, and they feared that the reforms of the previous two months were in danger of being overturned. The government was growing increasingly anxious at the continuing political agitation and unrest amongst the masses. The compromise between radical and moderate elements that had created the revolution was falling apart as the desire for political and social order prompted many to take a much more conservative stance.

The events of 15 May seemed to confirm the worst fears of many moderate republicans. In chaotic scenes, a crowd invaded the Assembly. Although originally organized as a demonstration of support for Polish democrats, it developed into an attempted coup, with the invaders dismissing the Assembly and trying to set up a new provisional government. Although those responsible were easily arrested, the whole incident horrified the moderates in government and provided support for reactionary measures against working-class agitation. It was becoming apparent that the radical forces unleashed in February were not prepared to relinquish control of the political arena quietly. The

attitude of the executive commission became much less conciliatory, and several laws were passed circumscribing the freedom of the press and freedom of association. The Luxembourg Commission was terminated, ending any hope of significant labor reforms. General Louis Eugène Cavaignac, the new minister of war, recalled troops to Paris. The tension between the government and militant workers who wished to continue down the path of political and social reform was developing into naked hostility.

It became apparent that the National Workshops were next on the reactionary agenda. Conservative observers regarded them as a source of radical agitation, when in fact to that point they had been effective in curbing working-class radicalism. On 21 June, following weeks of rumors and uncertainty, the government passed a decree announcing that all members of the workshops aged 18–24 had to join the army, and older members were to go to public works projects in the provinces. Those who would not go by choice would be taken by force. The government was clearing Paris of the National Workshops and its troublesome working-class population.

Civil War

Civil war was the issue that finally sparked the confrontation between the government and radicals after weeks of tension. On 22 June a large demonstration protested against the decree. The next day, 23 June, barricades started going up, and fighting with government forces started around midday. Although their specific motivations in fighting remain unclear, those who returned to the barricades probably saw the decree as a final betrayal of the principles for which they had fought in February. The revolutionaries regarded the revolution as their victory and therefore expected the new government to address their social and economic grievances. When this did not occur, they tried to wrest back control of the revolutionary process through armed force.

Contemporary reports and later analysis characterized the insurrection as a class conflict between workers and the bourgeoisie. However, only certain sections of the working class were mobilized against the government. From analysis of those later arrested by the government, it appears that most of the insurgents were workers from the building, metalworking, transport, and clothing trades. Estimates of the numbers of insurgents range from 10,000 to 50,000 out of a population of approximately 200,000 working-class males in Paris. The last minute decision of the government to continue paying those enrolled in the National Workshops throughout the four days of the rebellion may have helped to prevent many workers from taking up arms against the Republic. Others probably decided that limited reforms were preferable to renewed bloodshed. Many working-class people also fought in defense of the government, particularly in the *gardes mobile* forces.

Initially, the insurgents controlled a large part of Paris and almost all of the eastern working-class suburbs. General Cavaignac was slow to deploy his troops, which gave the rebels a chance to establish themselves in several key positions. The Constituent Assembly, horrified by the threat, surrendered dictatorial powers to Cavaignac. Despite the initial success of the insurgents, they faced a numerically superior, more organized force, and Cavaignac used artillery against the barricades. In

February the monarchy had capitulated easily, but the Republic was able to amass more support in the form of committed troops. By 26 June the insurrection was defeated, and government forces were mopping up the remains of resistance. This meant arresting virtually every working man on the street under suspicion of being a rebel. In four days of intense street fighting, 4,000 casualties occurred on both sides and 1,500 people were killed. Observers reported atrocities during the hunt for suspects and were appalled at the violence and bloodshed.

Consequences

With the defeat of the June insurrection, the working-class movement in Paris was crushed. In the days following the defeat of the rebels, approximately 15,000 Parisians were arrested. Of these, 4,500 were jailed or transported to Algeria as punishment for their part in the insurrection. No prominent radical or socialist leaders supported the insurgents. Men such as Louis Blanc were trapped between defending reforms from conservative opponents and preventing the far left from damaging the cause in a futile attempt to continue the revolution. They could do nothing but look on in dismay as the June insurrection completely isolated the radical cause from the political mainstream. Nevertheless, in the conservative backlash that followed, Louis Blanc was blamed for instigating the revolt and was forced to flee to England to avoid imprisonment.

Following the June Days, Cavaignac became the head of the Republic. The conservative reaction to the revolution had triumphed, and the government overturned some of the freedoms that had been gained in February. The bloodshed served as an example of the terrors unleashed by political and social reform. The brutal repression of the largely working-class uprising alienated the very people who had created the republic. Therefore, in the long term, the June days signaled a defeat for the Second Republic itself. Large sections of the population turned to Bonapartism, which resulted in the victory of Louis Napoleon Bonaparte in the December presidential elections. This eventually led to the establishment of the Second Empire and a long period of oppression for the French labor movement.

Key Players

Blanc, Louis (1811–1882): Blanc was a French socialist theorist and author of *Organisation du Travail*. Following the February revolution, Blanc became a member of the provisional government and headed the Luxembourg Commission. However, as the atmosphere of the Republic turned increasingly reactionary, Blanc lost his position. Although he had not supported the June Days revolt, he was forced into exile in England.

Blanqui, Louis-August (1805–1881): French revolutionary socialist, Blanqui played an influential role in the radical movement after the February revolution. He led the attempted coup on 15 March, which alienated the moderate republicans from the radicals and led to the June Days rebellion.

Cavaignac, Louis Eugène (1802–1857): French army general, Cavaignac was in charge of the defeat of the June Days rebellion. After this, he served as head of state until the election of Louis Napoleon Bonaparte as president in December. Under his regime, the Republic pursued its repression of the workers' movement, while simultaneously preserving some of the democratic aspects of the February revolution.

See also: *Revolutions in Europe.*

BIBLIOGRAPHY

Books

Magraw, Roger. *France 1815–1914: The Bourgeois Century*. London: Oxford, 1983.

Price, Roger. *The Second French Republic: A Social History*. Ithaca, NY: Cornell University Press, 1972.

Rude, George. *The Crowd in History: A Study of Popular Disturbances in France and England, 1730–1848*. New York: Wiley, 1964.

Tilly, Charles, and Lee, Lynn H. "The People of June, 1848." In *Revolution and Reaction: 1848 and the Second French Republic*, edited by Roger Price. London: Croom Helm, 1975.

Traugott, Mark. *Armies of the Poor: Determinants of Working-class Participation in the Parisian Insurrection of June 1848*. Princeton, NJ: Princeton University Press, 1985.

ADDITIONAL RESOURCES

Books

Amann, Peter H. *Revolution and Mass Democracy: The Paris Club Movement in 1848*. Princeton, NJ: Princeton University Press, 1975.

Merriman, John M. *The Agony of the Republic: The Repression of the Left in Revolutionary France 1848–1851*. New Haven, CT: Yale University Press, 1978.

Smith, William C. *Second Empire and Commune: France 1848–1871*. 2nd ed. London & New York: Longman, 1996.

—Katrina Ford

K

Keating-Owen Act

United States 1916

Synopsis

In 1916 Congress passed the Keating-Owen Act, which regulated the hours and wages of child labor and prohibited interstate transportation of products made in violation of the act. Although reformers hailed the bill as a major step toward alleviating the evils of child labor, manufacturers maintained that in passing the bill Congress had exceed its powers under the commerce clause of the U.S. Constitution. In 1918 the U.S. Supreme Court agreed, holding in *Hammer v. Dagenhart* that the federal act was unconstitutional.

Timeline

1898: United States defeats Spain in the three-month Spanish-American War. As a result, Cuba gains it independence, and the United States purchases Puerto Rico and the Philippines from Spain for $20 million.

1903: Russia's Social Democratic Party splits into two factions: the moderate Mensheviks and the hard-line Bolsheviks. Despite their names, which in Russian mean "minority" and "majority," respectively, Mensheviks actually outnumber Bolsheviks.

1910: Revolution breaks out in Mexico and will continue for the next seven years.

1914: On 28 June in the town of Sarajevo, then part of the Austro-Hungarian Empire, Serbian nationalist Gavrilo Princip assassinates Austrian Archduke Francis Ferdinand and wife Sophie. In the weeks that follow, Austria declares war on Serbia, and Germany on Russia and France, while Great Britain responds by declaring war on Germany. By the beginning of August, the lines are drawn, with the Allies (Great Britain, France, Russia, Belgium, Serbia, Montenegro, and Japan) against the Central Powers (Germany, Austria-Hungary, and Turkey).

1916: Battles of Verdun and the Somme are fought on the Western Front. The latter sees the first use of tanks, by the British.

1918: The Bolsheviks execute Czar Nicholas II and his family. Soon civil war breaks out between the communists and their allies, known as the Reds, and their enemies, a collection of anticommunists ranging from democrats to czarists, who are known collectively as the Whites. In March, troops from the United States, Great Britain, and France intervene on the White side.

1918: The Second Battle of the Marne in July and August is the last major conflict on the Western Front. In November, Kaiser Wilhelm II abdicates, bringing an end to the war.

1918: Upheaval sweeps Germany, which for a few weeks in late 1918 and early 1919 seems poised on the verge of communist revolution—or at least a Russian-style communist coup d'etat. But reactionary forces have regained their strength, and the newly organized Freikorps (composed of unemployed soldiers) suppresses the revolts. Even stronger than reaction or revolution, however, is republican sentiment, which opens the way for the creation of a democratic government based at Weimar.

1918: Influenza, carried to the furthest corners by returning soldiers, spreads throughout the globe. Over the next two years, it will kill nearly 20 million people—more than the war itself.

1921: As the Allied Reparations Commission calls for payments of 132 billion gold marks, inflation in Germany begins to climb.

1925: European leaders attempt to secure the peace at the Locarno Conference, which guarantees the boundaries between France and Germany, and Belgium and Germany.

Event and Its Context

The Child Labor Problem

In 1900 the United States was a different nation than it had been just 50 years earlier. The Industrial Revolution, improvements in technology, the expansion of the railroad system, immigration, and the westward sweep of America created a powerful industrial nation, but one that was also rent by grave social and economic injustices.

One of these injustices was child labor. The factory system, with its emphasis on simple, repetitive processes and its seemingly insatiable demand for unskilled labor—and rationalized by a spirit of Social Darwinism and the prevailing laissez-faire economic spirit of the times—provided fertile ground for the exploitation of children. In 1870 the Census Bureau first started collecting information about the employment of children. By 1900 a startling one in six children between the ages of 10 and 15, or about 1.75 million, was gainfully employed. About 60 percent of these children were employed in farming, and 16 percent, or about 280,000, were employed in manufacturing. The remaining 24 percent worked in personal and domestic service, street trades, and the like. Nearly all of these children, whose numbers by 1910 had risen to 1.99 million, were from the bottom rungs of the economic ladder: they were the sons and daughters of recent immigrants, the growing urban working classes, and those who depended on the southern cotton mills for their survival.

As early as the mid-nineteenth century, humanitarian reformers tried to end child labor by pressing for state and local

Children strip stems from tobacco leaves, New York City Tenement House Tobacco Strippers. The Library of Congress.

legislation to limit the workday for children to 10 hours, but these laws were rarely enforced. It was not until the early twentieth century and the Progressive Era that serious efforts at reform took shape. Under the leadership of reformer Edgar Gardner Murphy, the National Child Labor Committee was formed in 1904. During Theodore Roosevelt's second term, the committee was successful in getting two-thirds of the states to pass reform legislation or to strengthen existing laws; by 1914 all but two of the 48 states had done so. On the federal level, reformers found a congressional supporter in Senator Albert Beveridge, a popular, flamboyant figure who championed a variety of social causes and who, in January 1907, harangued the Senate for three days in an effort to end "child slavery." His bill to this end, however, met with opposition largely based on uncertainty about the extent of congressional power to pass federal legislation that would interfere with economic activity within the states, particularly when that legislation would be designed to deal with what was essentially a moral problem.

The Turning Point: 1913

A turning point occurred in 1913. That year the U.S. Supreme Court upheld the constitutionality of the Mann Act, the famous "white slavery" act that made it a federal crime to transport prostitutes over state lines. The significance of the decision was that the Supreme Court affirmed that the commerce clause of the Constitution gave Congress the power "to occupy, by legislation, the whole field of interstate commerce" and that it could do so for the purpose of protecting health, morals, or welfare.

Emboldened by this Court decision and believing that progressive public opinion had turned against child labor, the National Child Labor Committee decided to focus its efforts on federal legislation. In April 1913 five bills were submitted to Congress, including the resurrected Beveridge bill. Other matters took precedence, however, and it was not until February 1914 that serious debate began on the most promising of these bills. The bill sponsored by Representative A. Mitchell Palmer from Pennsylvania and Senator Robert L. Owen from Oklahoma called for a minimum wage and an eight-hour workday for children aged 14 through 16. Opposition from southern cotton mill owners surfaced immediately. They argued that stiff competition and thin profit margins forced them to require 11- and 12-hour shifts. More fundamentally, they objected to federal intervention in what they perceived as a state matter, and they ar-

Children work in cotton field with their parents. The Library of Congress.

gued that local lawmakers were in a better position to pass regulations that would take into account local conditions. Congress adjourned in early 1915, however, before the bill could come to a vote.

Later that year Colorado representative Edward Keating replaced Palmer as House sponsor of the bill, now known as the Keating-Owen bill. They reintroduced the bill in the 64th Congress. In early 1916 hearings began before the House Committee on Labor and the Senate Committee on Interstate Commerce. In addition to limiting working hours and prohibiting employment of children aged 13 and under, the bill would give authorities police power to remove illegal child laborers from

factories, mills, and mines. Further, manufacturers who illegally used child labor would see their products banned from interstate commerce. Again southern mill owners rose in opposition, choosing North Carolina Governor W. W. Kitchin to represent them before Congress. Kitchin's arguments were the same as the mill owners' had been in 1914–1915: federal regulation of child labor would harm southern mill owners and that in passing such a law, Congress would exceed its powers by invading the jurisdiction of the states. Over well-organized opposition, however, the House passed the bill in February by a vote of 337 to 46, and in August the Senate passed it 52 to 12. On 1 September 1916 President Woodrow Wilson, before a large gathering, signed the bill into law.

Challenge to the Keating-Owen Act

The southern mill owners needed a figurehead to test the constitutionality of the act. They found one in the Dagenhart family, a father and two sons who worked for a small cotton mill in North Carolina. The circumstances were ideal, for the older son was 15 and under North Carolina law could work for up to 11 hours a day at piece rates; thus, an eight-hour day would cut his earnings. The younger son was 13, and under the Keating-Owen Act he could not work in the mill at all. In the name of the father, Roland Dagenhart, the mill owners filed suit in district court to enjoin enforcement of the act. After the district court held that the act was unconstitutional and enjoined its enforcement, U.S. Attorney W. C. Hammer appealed the ruling to the U.S. Supreme Court, which heard *Hammer v. Dagenhart* in 1918.

Hammer made two fundamental arguments. The first was that the power of Congress to regulate interstate commerce, as specified in the Constitution, encompassed the power to regulate the interstate transportation of goods. The Court itself had upheld congressional power to regulate the interstate transportation of impure food and of prostitutes. The second argument was that Congress had the power to prohibit the transportation of goods made by children because those goods unfairly competed with the presumably more expensive goods that were made lawfully, without child labor, in other states.

In a blow to opponents of child labor, the Court, by a vote of 5 to 4, rejected these arguments, declared the Keating-Owen Act unconstitutional, and affirmed the injunction. Justice William Rufus Day delivered the opinion of the majority. In rejecting Hammer's first argument, Day wrote that the power of Congress to regulate interstate commerce extended only to such commerce that had evil results. The Keating-Owen Act did not apply to the movement of goods in interstate commerce but simply regulated the conditions under which those goods were made. The goods in question, unlike impure food and prostitutes, were not harmful or illegal; the fact that they were intended for interstate commerce did not bring their production under federal control. The means of production, the Court held, were subject only to local regulation.

In disposing of Hammer's second argument, the Court reasoned that the commerce clause did not give Congress the power to pass laws designed to equalize economic conditions between the states. Nor could it require the states to exercise their police power to regulate local trade or manufacture. Were the Court to recognize such a power, it would contravene the Tenth Amendment to the Constitution, which reserves those powers not granted to Congress for the states.

Predictably, it was Oliver Wendell Holmes, Jr., with the concurrence of Justices McKenna, Brandeis, and Clarke, who took a different view. In his dissent, Holmes pointed out that without the Constitution, no manufacturer in any state would be able to ship its goods across state lines without the permission of those other states; therefore, the Constitution of course authorizes Congress to regulate the interstate shipment of goods. Holmes also reaffirmed the evils of child labor: "If there is any matter upon which civilized countries have agreed—far more unanimously than they have with regard to intoxicants and some other matters over which this country is now emotionally aroused—it is the evil of premature and excessive child labor."

Postscript

In 1933 Congress passed the National Industrial Recovery Act, and in 1938, the Fair Labor Standards Act—both of which contained provisions that restricted child labor. Once again these provisions were tested, but in 1941, in *United States v. Darby Lumber Co.*, the Court repudiated its 1918 ruling, upholding the constitutionality of the acts and the power of Congress under the commerce clause to regulate interstate commerce. Justice Holmes's 1918 dissent became the law of the land.

Key Players

Beveridge, Albert J. (1862–1927): Born in Lorain, Ohio, Beveridge was a lawyer who served as a Republican from 1899 to 1911 in the Senate, where he avidly supported antitrust and child labor legislation. He published *The Life of John Marshall* in 1916.

Day, William Rufus (1849–1923): Born in Ravenna, Ohio, Day was secretary of state under William McKinley and helped to negotiate the treaty that ended the Spanish-American War. Theodore Roosevelt appointed him to the Supreme Court, where he served from 1903 to 1922.

Holmes, Oliver Wendell, Jr. (1841–1935): Holmes was born in Boston, was seriously wounded three times in the Civil War, and practiced law before serving on the Massachusetts Supreme Court (1882–1902; chief justice 1899–1902). Theodore Roosevelt nominated him to the Supreme Court (1902–1932), where he became known as the "Great Dissenter" for the power of his frequent dissenting opinions.

Keating, Edward (1875–1965): Keating was born on a farm near Kansas City, Kansas. He began his career as a journalist and eventually became editor of the *Rocky Mountain News*. He was elected as a Democrat from Colorado to the House of Representatives and served from 1913 to 1919.

Owen, Robert Latham (1856–1947): Owen, part Cherokee, was born in Lynchburg, Virginia. In later life he became active in tribal affairs in the Indian Territory, and he played an important role in the congressional act that granted citizenship to Native Americans there. When Oklahoma became a state, he won a seat in the Senate (1907–1925), where he sponsored progressive labor legislation.

See also: *Fair Labor Standards Act; National Child Labor Committee; National Industrial Recovery Act.*

BIBLIOGRAPHY

Books

Hindman, Hugh. *Child Labor: An American History*. Armonk, NY: M. E. Sharpe, 2002.

Hobbs, Sandy, Jim McKechnie, and Michael Lavalette. *Child Labor: A World History Companion*. Santa Barbara, CA: ABC-CLIO, 1999.

Langhorne, Elizabeth Dabney, and Lewis Otey. *The Beginnings of Child Labor Legislation in Certain States: A Comparative Study*. Manchester, NH: Ayer, 1974.

Wood, Stephen B. *Constitutional Politics in the Progressive Era: Child Labor and the Law*. Chicago: University of Chicago Press, 1968.

Other

Hammer v. Dagenhart, 247 U.S. 251 (1918).
United States v. Darby Lumber Co., 312 U.S. 100 (1941).

—Michael J. O'Neal

Knights Break Color Line

United States 1886

Synopsis

Late-nineteenth-century America experienced a hardening of racial lines that was reflected in the American working class, including white craftsmen who excluded African American workers. The unskilled workers, who included nearly all African American wage earners, were unorganized before the Noble and Holy Order of the Knights of Labor brought them into the largest labor organization in Gilded Age America. African Americans accounted for about 60,000 of the over 700,000 members at the Order's zenith in 1886. Race became the defining issue at the general assembly in Richmond, Virginia, in 1886. At that time the Order embraced its motto—"An injury to one is the concern of all"—by boycotting a white-owned hotel that refused to lodge an African American delegate from New York City. The organization then selected this same delegate to introduce its leader, Grand Master Workman Terence Powderly, at the opening of the convention. After the Knights declined to insignificance, their legacy of interracial cooperation found life in new labor organizations.

Timeline

1866: The Winchester repeating rifle is introduced.

1871: Chicago fire causes 250 deaths and $196 million in damage.

1876: General George Armstrong Custer and 264 soldiers are killed by the Sioux at the Little Big Horn River.

1878: Thomas Edison develops a means of cheaply producing and transmitting electric current, which he succeeds in subdividing so as to make it adaptable to household use. The value of shares in gas companies plummets as news of his breakthrough reaches Wall Street.

1882: Agitation against English rule spreads throughout Ireland, culminating with the assassination of chief secretary for Ireland Lord Frederick Cavendish and permanent undersecretary Thomas Burke in Dublin's Phoenix Park. The leader of the nationalist movement is Charles Stewart Parnell, but the use of assassination and terrorism—which Parnell himself has disavowed—makes clear the fact that he does not control all nationalist groups.

Terence Vincent Powderly. The Library of Congress.

1884: Chicago's Home Life Insurance Building, designed by William LeBaron Jenney, becomes the world's first skyscraper.

1886: Bombing at Haymarket Square, Chicago, kills seven policemen and injures numerous others. Eight anarchists are accused and tried; three are imprisoned, one commits suicide, and four are hanged.

1886: The Statue of Liberty is dedicated.

1886: Apache chief Geronimo surrenders to U.S. forces.

1888: The Blizzard of 1888 in the United States kills hundreds and causes more than $25 million in property damage.

1892: Bitter strikes in Australia lead to the closing of ports and mines.

1896: U.S. Supreme Court issues its *Plessy v. Ferguson* decision, which establishes the "separate but equal" doctrine that will be used to justify segregation in the southern United States for the next half-century.

Event and Its Context

The adoption of the Thirteenth Amendment to the U.S. Constitution abolished the institution of slavery, but the end of Reconstruction in 1877 brought to a close the short-lived attempts at racial justice. The white majority denied African Americans freedom and equality by various means. De facto racial segregation was practiced, to varying degrees, throughout America, but the South added a plethora of restrictions, such as vagrancy laws, poll taxes, and segregation laws, coupled with intimidation and violence, to isolate and exploit African Americans.

Frank J. Ferrell, standing at left. The Library of Congress.

The Knights' Racial Ideology

At the same time that African Americans, especially in the South, suffered from racial segregation, American workers began to feel a loss of opportunity and equality caused by the consolidation of capital in post-Civil War era. On 28 December 1869 a band of skilled garment cutters led by Uriah Stephens, organized Local Assembly No. 1 of the Noble and Holy Order of the Knights of Labor, a labor organization that emphasized education and cooperation as means to escape the wage system. Wage earners, especially skilled workers during the early years of the Gilded Age, embraced a mix of cultural, political, and economic values that historians refer to as the concept of the producing classes. They revered the freedom, egalitarianism, dignity of labor, and rewards of self-improvement as concepts and principles that defined the American republic. Skilled workers saw themselves as valued citizens who contributed to the welfare of their communities. Citizenship and work were intertwined. On the other hand, workers, who had fought recently for the Union in a war that had saved the republic and abolished slavery, decried the consolidation of capital and its concomitant power that dictated to labor and treated wage earners as wage slaves.

The Knights' leadership set the tone for its ideological and strategic perspectives towards African American workers. Stephens, the first grand master workman, grew up as a Quaker and trained for the Baptist ministry. He was a staunch abolitionist who supported the Republicans' first two presidential candidates—John Fremont and Abraham Lincoln—and saw African Americans as equal in the economic sphere, but not as social equals. Stephens condoned segregated labor organizations.

Terence V. Powderly, the Knights' second grand master workman, believed abolitionism and organized labor were two revolutionary movements that supported the freedom of toilers. He recognized African Americans and whites as equal in the field of production and argued that poor whites were held back by their refusal to join together with African Americans for the betterment of all producers. Although Powderly had no problem on principles with the racial integration of Knights' local assemblies, he believed it more practical, especially in the South, to maintain segregated assemblies until such time as education might break down the barriers of prejudice. The paramount concern to Powderly was the advancement of workers and not racial equality, a social question that he believed would by remedied with time.

Organizing African American Workers

Most black wage earners resided in the South, where the Order's white leaders tended to be more liberal on racial matters than were the rank-and-file white members. Some white leaders hailed from the North, some were Republicans, and others were Democrats who were enlightened on racial issues. The Knights' policy of accepting African Americans as economic equals while maintaining the social superiority of whites caused tension. On the local assembly level, whites maintained a policy of separate locals for black and white workers. Locals, in turn, belonged to district assemblies that usually had both black and white local assemblies. District Assembly 92 of Richmond was the only all-black district assembly, a situation that gave the African American local assemblies more representation at the state and general assemblies. Black locals at Savannah, Georgia, and Pensacola and Petersburg, Florida, also tried to form African American district assemblies, but they were thwarted by white-led district assemblies. Though local assemblies were nearly always segregated, the racial integration of district, state, and general assemblies provided leadership opportunities for African American Knights.

White union organizers formed the initial African American Knights' local assemblies in the South. The indifference and insensitivity shown by some white organizers, however, led to their replacement by African American organizers. The use of black organizers received support from white state assemblies in the South, as whites realized the importance of bringing black wage earners, who might otherwise be competitors, into the Order.

In 1885 the Knights' successful labor strikes against railroads controlled by financier Jay Gould brought a flood of new members into the Order. When the Order suffered some major defeats in late 1885 and 1886, membership reached its zenith and went into a rapid decline. While white workers left the Knights, African American wage earners continued to join the Knights because they believed the Order represented the best hope for their desperate plight. Unskilled African American wage earners, who resided in large cities and smaller industrial

towns in the North, founded local assemblies of waiters, hod carriers, laborers, teamsters, and dockworkers. Although southern cities also had black local assemblies, including women's locals of domestic workers, most African Americans resided in the rural South, where they suffered the indignities of racial segregation, hard labor for meager earnings, and debt peonage that tied them to their white employers.

When the Knights attempted to organize southern agricultural workers, they encountered determined and sometimes violent opposition from white planters and farmers. In one of the largest strikes engaged in by southern Knights, thousands of sugarcane workers struck during the 1887 fall harvest. Planters appealed to Louisiana's governor for assistance from the state militia, which joined with local sheriffs' posses to shoot strikers; they killed at least 30 African Americans. The strike was crushed and the local Knights destroyed.

The Richmond Convention

The Knights' general assembly in 1886 drew 658 delegates to Richmond, the former capital of the Confederacy. New York City's District Assembly 49 (Home Club), a large, politicized body, sent 60 delegates, including Frank J. Ferrell, an African American. The New York delegation made room reservations at the Merchants Hotel but voted to cancel them before leaving New York City when the proprietor refused to admit any blacks. The entire delegation, motivated by the Knights' motto—"an injury to one is the concern of all"—stayed in tents they had brought or boarded with African American families. These Knights further challenged Richmond's racial practices when Ferrell accompanied them to an evening's entertainment at the theater, where he became the first black in the city's history to occupy an orchestra seat rather than the gallery seats designated for blacks.

Master Workman J. E. Quinn of District Assembly 49 approached Powderly to request that Ferrell introduce Virginia governor Fitzhugh Lee to the convention. Powderly thought this proposal would needlessly insult Richmond's social mores, so a compromise was reached. Governor Lee welcomed the Knights' delegates, followed by Ferrell, whose introduction of Powderly mentioned the Knights' dedication to the abolition of distinctions based on color. The convention ended with a picnic attended by a few thousand of the city's African Americans, making it the largest racially integrated social event in Richmond up to that time. The Richmond convention created consternation among local whites and became a national sensation. Southern newspapers blasted the Knights for forcing social equality upon the host city, while the African American press, along with many labor and Northern newspapers, praised the Knights' actions and principles.

The Legacy of Racial Inclusion

The Knights admitted African American members at a time when blacks increasingly experienced the degradation and limited opportunities fostered by legal and de facto segregation. The actions of the Knights at the Richmond general assembly in 1886 showed congruence with the Order's motto and earned the allegiance of many African Americans. Lost strikes and the rise of antilabor sentiments rendered them an insignificant labor organization by the early 1890, but their influence as a biracial movement carried forward in the North and South. After racially integrated local assemblies of coal miners in the Midwest passed from existence, the principle of racial inclusion went with these miners into the nascent United Mine Workers. Coal miners in West Virginia organized racially integrated unions, and the same situation existed in Birmingham, Alabama, with coal and iron ore miners.

Key Players

Ferrell, Frank J.: Ferrell, an engineer and member of District Assembly 49, was the only black in the 60-man New York City delegation sent to the Knights' 1886 convention. He registered six patents for steam boiler parts in the 1890s.

Powderly, Terence Vincent (1849–1924): Powderly, a machinist, joined the Knights in 1876 and served as a leader in the Scranton, Pennsylvania, local and district assemblies. He succeeded Uriah Stephens, the Knights' founder, to the office of grand master workman in 1879 and held the post until defeated in 1893. In 1878 he was elected on the Greenback Labor party ticket to three two-year terms as the mayor of Scranton.

See also: *Jim Crow Segregation and Labor; Knights of Labor.*

BIBLIOGRAPHY

Books

Brier, Stephen. "Interracial Organizing in the West Virginia Coal Industry: Participation of Black Mine Workers in the Knights of Labor and the United Mine Workers, 1880–1894." In *Essays in Southern Labor History: Selected Papers, Southern Labor History Conference, 1976,* edited by Gary M. Fink and Merl E. Reed. Westport, CT: Greenwood Press, 1977.

Foner, Philip S. *Organized Labor and the Black Worker, 1619–1981.* 2nd ed. New York: International Publishers, 1982.

Foner, Philip S., and Ronald L. Lewis, eds. *Black Workers: A Documentary History from Colonial Times to the Present.* Vol. 3, *The Black Worker During the Era of the Knights of Labor.* Philadelphia: Temple University Press, 1989.

McLaurin, Melton A. *The Knights of Labor in the South.* Westport, CT: Greenwood Press, 1978.

Spero, Sterling D., and Abram L. Harris. *The Black Worker: The Negro and the Labor Movement.* New York: Columbia University Press, 1931.

Periodicals

Kessler, Sidney H. "The Organization of Negroes in the Knights of Labor." *Journal of Negro History* 37 (July 1952): 248–275.

Miner, Claudia. "The 1886 Convention of the Knights of Labor." *Phylon* 44, no. 2 (1983): 147–59.

Worthman, Paul B. "Black Workers and Labor Unions in Birmingham, Alabama, 1897–1904." *Labor History* 10 (summer 1969): 375–407.

ADDITIONAL RESOURCES

Books

Grob, Gerald. *Workers and Utopia: A Study of Ideological Conflict in the American Labor Movement, 1865–1900.* Evanston, IL: Northwestern University Press, 1961.

Rachleff, Peter J. *Black Labor in the South: Richmond, Virginia, 1865–1890.* Philadelphia: Temple University Press, 1984.

Ware, Norman. *The Labor Movement in the United States, 1860–1895: A Study in Democracy* (reprint ed.). Gloucester, MA: Peter Smith, 1959.

—Paul A. Frisch

Knights of Labor

United States 1869

Synopsis

The Noble and Holy Order of the Knights of Labor began in 1869 as a small, secret organization of Philadelphia garment cutters. After dropping the oath of secrecy in 1882, membership grew from around 20,000 to 111,000 in 1885. The order's motto, "An injury to one is the concern of all," was fitting for the first national labor union that recruited all producers (workers and employers) as well as the unskilled, African Americans, and women, none of whom had been previously organized. Ideologically, in its early years, the Knights opposed the wage system, still believing that its cooperative efforts would allow workers to escape wage slavery. After a successful strike against the Wabash railroad, the Knights' membership swelled to 111,000 in 1885, and new recruits began to demand better wages and working conditions rather than long-range reform. By 1886 membership exceeded 700,000, but it declined precipitously to 250,000 in 1887, after unsuccessful strikes and the loss of skilled workers in unions affiliated with the American Federation of Labor (1886). By the late 1890s the Knights ceased to be an effective labor organization.

Timeline

1860: Louis Pasteur pioneers his method of "pasteurizing" milk by heating it to high temperatures in order to kill harmful microbes.

1861: Within weeks of Abraham Lincoln's inauguration, the U.S. Civil War begins with the shelling of Fort Sumter. Six states secede from the Union, joining South Carolina to form the Confederate States of America (later joined by four other states) and electing Jefferson Davis as president. The first major battle of the war, at Bull Run or Manassas in Virginia, is a Confederate victory.

1865: U.S. Civil War ends with the surrender of General Robert E. Lee to General Ulysses S. Grant at Appomattox, Virginia. More than 600,000 men have died, and the South is in ruins, but the Union has been restored.

Women delegates of Knights of Labor. © Corbis. Reproduced by permission.

1870: Fifteenth Amendment, the last of the three post-Civil War amendments to the U.S. Constitution, states that an American citizen cannot be denied the right to vote because of race, color, or previous status as a slave. At this time, the new amendment is treated as law in the South, which is still occupied by federal troops; but after Reconstruction ends in 1877, it will be nearly 90 years before blacks in some southern states gain full voting rights.

1873: Financial panic begins in Vienna and soon spreads to other European financial centers, as well as to the United States.

1877: In the face of uncertain results from the popular vote in the presidential election of 1876, the U.S. Electoral Commission awards the presidency to Rutherford B. Hayes despite a slight popular majority for his opponent, Samuel J. Tilden. The election of 1876 will remain the most controversial in American history for the next 124 years, until overshadowed by the race between George W. Bush and Al Gore in 2000.

1877: In part as a quid pro quo demanded by southern legislators in return for their support of the Republican Hayes over the Democrat Tilden, the new president agrees to end the period of martial law in the South known as Reconstruction.

1881: U.S. President James A. Garfield is assassinated in a Washington, D.C., railway station by Charles J. Guiteau.

1881: In a shootout at the O.K. Corral outside Tombstone, Arizona, Wyatt, Virgil, and Morgan Earp, along with "Doc" Holliday, kill Billy Clanton, Frank McLowry, and Tom McLowry. This breaks up a gang headed by Clanton's brother Ike, who flees Tombstone. The townspeople, however, suspect the Earps and Holliday of murder. During the same year, Sheriff Pat Garrett shoots notorious criminal William Bonney, a.k.a. Billy the Kid, in Fort Sumner, New Mexico.

1883: Brooklyn Bridge is completed.

1889: Discontented southern farmers merge their farm organizations to form the Southern Alliance.

Event and Its Context

Ideology of the Producing Classes

On Thanksgiving Day 1869 six Philadelphia garment cutters met to disband their local craft union, which had struggled unsuccessfully to maintain wage rates. One veteran member, Uriah S. Stephens, proposed the creation of a new type of labor organization, and on 28 December 1869 they organized Local Assembly Number 1 of the Noble and Holy Order of the Knights of Labor. It emphasized education and cooperation as the means to escape the wage system, and took for its motto, "An injury to one is the concern of all." Wage earners—especially skilled workers—during the early years of the Gilded Age embraced a mix of cultural, political, and economic values that historians refer to as the "concept of the producing classes." They revered the freedom, egalitarianism, dignity of labor, and rewards of self-improvement as the principles that defined the American republic. Skilled workers saw themselves as valued citizens who contributed to the welfare of their communities; citizenship and work were intertwined. On the other hand, workers had fought recently for the Union to save the republic and abolish slavery, and they decried the consolidation of capital and its concomitant power that dictated to labor and treated workers as wage slaves.

Stephens, like many workers of the period, belonged to fraternal orders, and he advocated a secret organization steeped in the rituals and language of fraternal societies and nondenominational Christianity, believing it would foster loyalty and protect members from employer retribution, especially blacklisting. Consequently, initiates were required to swear an oath of secrecy against revealing the name, activities, and members of the order. The *Adelphon Kruptos* ("Secret Brotherhood"), the order's ritual book, combined elements of Masonic ritual with Scriptural passages and language. It was a "holy" organization, whose local assemblies met in "sanctuaries" rather than lodges. The language was softened after the resignation of Stephens, the first grand master workman (highest office) and author of the *Adelphon Kruptos*. Terence V. Powderly, his successor, served as the mayor of Scranton, Pennsylvania, an area that had been home to the secret and violent Molly Maguires. The Catholic Church pressured Powderly, an Irish Catholic, to remove oaths it believed could compromise the loyalty of lay church members. In 1882 the Knights toned down the language of the ritual and allowed local assemblies to make their existence public.

Although founded by garment cutters, Local Assembly Number 1 soon allowed "sojourners," nonvoting members from other trades, who it was hoped would create their own craft locals. Widespread unemployment during the depression of 1873–1877 made the recruitment of union members more difficult, and wage cuts sometimes pushed desperate workers to organize and strike. By 1875 the Knights had pushed beyond the Philadelphia area, organizing coal workers—both the skilled miners and mine laborers—in the anthracite fields in northeast Pennsylvania and in the bituminous region around Pittsburgh. In 1877 railroad workers and sympathizers across America erupted into spontaneous labor strikes brought on by the railroad companies' repeated wage cuts and antiunion activity. Some communities like Pittsburgh experienced large-scale

riots, which were put down by federal troops. Because of the 1877 strikes, some railroad workers in Pennsylvania joined the Knights. In 1878, 25 of the 35 delegates who came to Reading, Pennsylvania, for the first general assembly were from that state, while the other eight delegates came from neighboring states. Prior to the1880s membership was drawn primarily from a triangle bounded by Philadelphia on the south, Scranton on the north, and Pittsburgh on the west.

Knights of Labor and Strikes

The Knights' leadership counseled against labor strikes and, for arbitration, supported strikes only after members were locked out, and then only after sanctioned by the Knights' general executive board. Ironically, it was the successful strikes that spurred the Knights' growth. During the depression of 1883–1885, employers again cut wages to maintain profits. In 1883 the Telegraphers' National District Assembly Number 45 responded to a wage cut with the Knights' first nationwide strike. Meager financial support from the Knights forced the Telegraphers to capitulate to financier Jay Gould's Western Union and destroyed the union. In 1883–1884 Local Assembly Number 300, representing skilled window glass workers from across the United States, struck successfully against a wage cut. The Knights received credit for the victory, though the complete unionization of the industry made possible by the skilled nature of the glass workers' craft contributed far more than the Knights' insignificant financial support.

Joseph R. Buchanan, a typesetter and copublisher of a prolabor newspaper in Denver, joined the Knights in 1882. In 1884 the Union Pacific railroad cut the wages of Denver shop workers, who appealed to Buchanan for assistance. Buchanan quickly organized 25,000 railroad workers into the Union Pacific Employees' Protective Association, later becoming the Denver-based District Assembly Number 82. In the face of an organized workforce, the Union Pacific rescinded the wage cut.

In late 1884 and early 1885 the Missouri Pacific, Wabash, Kansas Pacific, and Texas and Pacific—all parts of the Gould-controlled Southwestern Railroad System—cut wages. The Southwestern railroad workers stuck in late February 1885 and, with support from Buchanan and the Union Pacific workers, forced the railroads to withdraw the reductions. In April and May 1885 the Wabash railroad discharged Knights' members and in June closed down its shops. Wabash workers struck on 16 June 1885 but received only reluctant support from the Knights' leadership. When the Wabash management refused to negotiate, the Knights' railroad workers ceased handling Wabash cars. Gould's Wabash capitulated on 3 September 1885.

The Great Upheaval of 1886

The optimism and militancy that characterized American workers at the beginning of 1886 sprang from the phenomenal growth of the Knights, general agitation for the eight-hour workday, and widespread working-class political activism. Many American workers hurriedly joined the Knights in the wake of its two victories over Gould, boosting membership from 111,000 in July 1885 to nearly 730,000 a year later. The Knights' executive board feared that workers were joining the organization just to receive support for labor strikes, so in January 1886 it called a 40-day moratorium on recruitment. At the zenith of the Knights' influence, local assemblies existed in both large and small communities in every section of the country.

The movement for the eight-hour workday enjoyed widespread support within the Knights and among workers in general. In 1884 the Knights wrote an article into their constitution that called on workers to refuse to work longer than an eight-hour day. The article implied the use of strikes, but Powderly advocated the political process to achieve a shorter workday. When the much smaller, struggling Federation of Organized Trades and Labor Unions set a deadline of 1 May 1886 for the eight-hour workday, many workers, including Knights, began to organize for a May Day strike.

The year 1886 ended with the American labor movement in retreat, including the Knights. In March 1886 Knights employed by the Texas Pacific railroad had struck after what they claimed was the arbitrary discharge of a member. Missouri Pacific workers also joined the strike. After local assemblies of railroad workers in Missouri voted to strike, the executive board of District Assembly 101 decided to strike without the approval or knowledge of Powderly and the general executive board. He countered by secretly issuing a circular to Knights that condemned strikes. After the circular became public, Martin Irons, the strike leader, asked Powderly to meet with Gould, who agreed to arbitrate with employees and rehire Knights members. Gould reneged after the strike was called off, resulting in the railroad workers going back on strike. When the strike was called off in early May, the Knights' momentum of 1885 came to a halt, and the organization lost credibility among workers.

On 1 May 1886 many Knights local assemblies participated in the strike for the eight-hour workday, and the Chicago stockyard workers were successful. On 4 May a rally to protest police violence against striking workers at the McCormick Harvester Company was held at Chicago's Haymarket Square. A bomb exploded in the midst of police trying to break up the protest. The incident was blamed on anarchists within the labor movement and became a major blow to support for organized labor. The meat packers took advantage of the backlash against labor by offering nine hours pay instead of ten for the eight-hour day. When the stockyard workers refused to accept the cut, employers returned to the ten-hour workday.

The Knights sent Thomas B. Barry, a member of the general executive board, to Chicago with orders not to involve the organization, although 75 percent of the workers belonged to the Knights. Powderly sent a communication to Barry calling for an end to the strike and threatening to revoke the charters of local assemblies that failed to comply. When this communication became public, it resulted in the defeat of the strike and a further erosion of workers' support for the Knights.

In late 1886 the American Federation of Labor was formed as a confederation of skilled trade unions and successor to the Federation of Organized Trades and Labor Unions. It competed directly for the loyalty of skilled workers who were increasingly at odds with the Knights' amorphous structure, its prohibition on strikes, and the costs and risks of organizing unskilled workers.

In the 1886 elections the Knights backed many political candidates, especially those from third parties. Labor-backed candidates ran for office in large cities such as New York and Chicago, mid-sized cities such as Richmond, Virginia, and Milwaukee, Wisconsin, and small towns, such as Rutland, Vermont, and Key West, Florida. They won some municipal, state, and congressional offices.

African Americans and Women

At a time when African American workers faced mounting racial segregation and exclusion from many craft unions, the Knights demonstrated their support for black workers, who represented about 10 percent of the membership, at the 1886 general assembly meeting in Richmond. New York City's District Assembly (Home Club), the order's second largest assembly, with 65,000 members, sent a delegation that included Frank J. Ferrell, an African American delegate. When hotels refused accommodations for Ferrell, the Home Club's delegation stayed in tents or boarded in African American homes. The general assembly opened with a welcome from Virginia's governor, Fitzhugh Lee. Ferrell followed with an introduction of grand master workman Powderly.

The Knights was the first American labor organization to admit women, although support for their inclusion was limited. The Knights' convention issued its first statement of principles in 1878, which included a plank "to secure for both sexes equal pay for equal work." In 1880—over the objections of many Knights, including the order's first grand master workman, Uriah Stephens—the Knights passed a resolution authorizing the admission of women. Growth was slow, but by 1886 between 50,000 to 65,000 women belonged to either mixed or all-female local assemblies. Prominent women in the Knights included Susan B. Anthony, Mary "Mother" Jones, Mary Lease, Leonora O'Reilly, Charlotte Smith, and Frances Willard. Leonora Barry joined the Knights in 1884, rose to the office of local master worker in 1885, led a successful strike, and attended the 1886 Richmond convention as one of 16 women among 658 delegates. Powderly appointed Barry to head the Department of Women's Work, where her main responsibility was to investigate abuses by employers. John Hayes, a treasurer and secretary-treasurer of KOL, was opposed to women in the order and pushed Barry to resign in 1890.

The Knights' Decline and Legacy

The Knights had fewer than 75,000 members when an alliance of socialists and farmers forced Powderly to resign in 1893. In 1895 Daniel DeLeon, a socialist in District Assembly 49, led many remaining workers out of the Knights and into the Socialist Trade and Labor Alliance. The Knights continued into the early twentieth century, but without any significant membership.

The order's producing-class ideology resonated with workers across Gilded Age America, which organized about 12,000 assemblies in 5,000 communities over the course of its history. In the mid-1880s the Knights used various means to challenge the rising influence of corporate America. On the one hand, their involvement in electoral politics suggests the reformist nature of an organization opposed to the rapidly changing social, economic, and political relationships that they believed undermined the rightful place of the producing class. On the other hand, their willingness to battle corporations over bread-and-butter labor issues suggests that they came to terms with their status as wage earners. Finally, the Knights' commitment to an inclusiveness that cut across the lines of skill, race, and gender left a legacy for succeeding labor unions.

Key Players

Barry, Leonora Marie Kearney (1849–1923): Barry, an Irish-born, unskilled clothing worker, joined a local assembly of women Knights in 1884. She was elected local master workman in 1885 and appointed general investigator for the Knights' women's department in 1886. She played a key role in the passage of Pennsylvania's first factory inspection act in 1889.

Barry, Thomas B. (1852–1888): Barry joined the Knights in the early 1880s, served as a Knights' organizer, and was elected to the Knights' executive committee in 1885. In 1886 he led Chicago stockyards workers in an unsuccessful strike for the eight-hour day. He was elected to the Michigan state legislature in 1884 on the Democratic-Greenback ticket.

Buchanan, Joseph Ray (1851–1924): Buchanan, a typesetter, newspaper reporter, and publisher, joined the Denver Knights in 1882 and became copublisher of the *Labor Enquirer*. He led a successful strike of Union Pacific railroad shop men in 1884, followed by two successful strikes against Jay Gould–controlled railroads in 1885. He was expelled from the Knights in 1886 over policy disagreements with Terence Powderly.

DeLeon Daniel (1852–1914): DeLeon, a Venezuelan-born teacher, lawyer, and leftwing political propagandist, immigrated to America in 1874 and joined District Assembly Number 49 (New York City) in 1888. A leader in the Socialist Labor Party, he viewed labor unions as vehicles for revolutionary politics. In 1895 he led a secessionist movement of leftists out of the Knights, who formed the Socialist Trade and Labor Alliance.

Gould, Jay (1836–1892): Gould, a Wall Street financier and "robber baron," controlled Western Union in 1883 when it defeated the Telegraphers in the Knights' first national labor strike. A victorious strike against Gould's Wabash railroad, in 1885, led to the Knights' phenomenal growth during 1885–1886. Gould's Southwestern Railroad System crushed a Knights' strike in 1886, precipitating a rapid decline in the organization's membership.

Hayes, John W. (1854–1942): Hayes, a train brakeman until the loss of an arm, joined the Knights in 1874, rose to prominence with the New Jersey Knights and led the telegraphers in a strike lost to Jay Gould's Western Union. He was elected as the Knights' general secretary (1882–1902) and grand master workman (1902–1906). His charges of corruption led Terence Powderly to resign as grand master workman in 1893.

Irons, Martin (1833–1900): Irons, a Scottish-born machinist, was a founder of District Assembly 101, a union of Missouri Pacific railroad workers. He led a strike against Jay Gould's Southwestern Railroad System that ended in defeat and contributed to a rapid decline in the Knights' membership starting in 1886.

Powderly, Terence Vincent (1849–1924): Powderly, a machinist, joined the Knights in 1876, serving as a leader in the Scranton, Pennsylvania, local and district assemblies. He succeeded Uriah Stephens, the Knights' founder, to the office of grand master workman in 1879 and held the post until defeated in 1893. In 1878 he was elected on the Greenback Labor party ticket to three two-year terms as the mayor of Scranton.

Stephens, Uriah Smith (1821–1882): Stephens, a reformer and abolitionist, was educated for the Baptist ministry but was forced by necessity to become a tailor. In 1862, while working in Philadelphia, he helped organize the Garment Cutters' Association. He cofounded the Knights in 1869, was elected master workman of District Assembly Number 1, and was the Knights' first elected grand master workman in 1879. He resigned in 1879.

See also: *American Federation of Labor; Haymarket Riot; Knights Break Color Line; Molly Maguires; Railroad Strike of 1877.*

BIBLIOGRAPHY

Books

Fink, Leon. *Workingmen's Democracy: The Knights of Labor and American Politics.* Urbana, IL: University of Illinois Press, 1983.

Grob, Gerald N. *Workers and Utopia: A Study of Ideological Conflict in the American Labor Movement, 1865–1900.* Evanston, IL: Northwestern University Press, 1961.

Phelan, Craig. *Grand Master Workman: Terence Powderly and the Knights of Labor.* Westport, CT: Greenwood, 2000.

Powderly, Terence. *The Path I Trod: The Autobiography of Terence V. Powderly.* New York: AMS, 1968.

———. *Thirty Years of Labor, 1859–1889.* New York: A. M. Kelley, 1967.

Ware, Norman Joseph. *The Labor Movement in the United States, 1860–1895: A Study in Democracy.* New York: D. Appleton, 1929.

Weir, Robert E. *Beyond Labor's Veil: The Culture of the Knights of Labor.* University Park, PA: Pennsylvania State University Press, 1996.

———. *Knights Unhorsed: Internal Conflict in a Gilded Age Social Movement.* Detroit: Wayne State University Press, 2000.

Periodicals

Birdsall, William C. "The Problem of Structure in the Knights of Labor." *Industrial and Labor Relations Review* 6 (July 1953): 532–546.

ADDITIONAL RESOURCES

Books

Allen, Ruth Alice. *The Great Southwest Strike.* Austin, TX: University of Texas Press, 1942.

Brundage, David. *The Making of Western Labor Radicalism: Denver's Organized Workers, 1878–1905.* Urbana, IL: University of Illinois Press, 1994.

Buhle, Paul. *From the Knights of Labor to the New World Order: Essays on Labor and Culture.* New York: Garland, 1997.

Garlock, Jonathan, ed. *Guide to Local Assemblies of the Knights of Labor.* Westport, CT: Greenwood, 1982.

Kealey, Gregory S., and Bryan D. Palmer. *Dreaming of What Might Be: The Knights of Labor in Ontario, 1880–1900.* New York: Cambridge University Press, 1982.

McLaurin, Melton A. *The Knights of Labor in the South.* Westport, CT: Greenwood, 1978.

Oestreicher, Richard Jules. *Solidarity and Fragmentation: Working People and Consciousness in Detroit, 1875–1900.* Urbana, IL: University of Illinois Press, 1986.

Rachleff, Peter J. *Black Labor in the South: Richmond, Virginia, 1865–1890.* Philadelphia: Temple University Press, 1984.

Voss, Kim. *The Making of American Exceptionalism: The Knights of Labor and Class Formation in the Nineteenth Century.* Ithaca, NY: Cornell University Press, 1993.

— Paul A. Frisch

L

La Follette Seamen's Act

United States 1915

Synopsis

Sailors and fishermen have historically faced grueling hours, hazardous conditions, and low wages. During the nineteenth century, they were also confronted with corporal punishment, poorly maintained vessels, and few labor rights. Despite union representation, seamen remained without a substantial voice in government and the courts. This changed in 1915 with the passing of the La Follette Seamen's Act.

In 1908 Andrew Furuseth became the president of the International Seamen's Union. He partnered with Senator Robert La Follette to create a bill devoted to changing important issues in the seafaring trades. However, like the oceans, politics are a fickle and ever-changing environment. It took years of sustained effort to see important legislation passed, but Furuseth and La Follette successfully championed the cause. With the passage of the La Follette Seamen's Act in 1915, the new legislation improved labor conditions and helped to protect the lives of America's seamen.

Timeline

1895: Brothers Auguste and Louis Lumière show the world's first motion picture—*Workers Leaving the Lumière Factory*—at a café in Paris.

1900: China's Boxer Rebellion, which began in the preceding year with attacks on foreigners and Christians, reaches its height. An international contingent of more than 2,000 men arrives to restore order, but only after several tens of thousands have died.

1905: Albert Einstein presents his special theory of relativity.

1910: Revolution breaks out in Mexico.

1915: A German submarine sinks the *Lusitania*, killing 1,195, including 128 U.S. citizens. Theretofore, many Americans had been sympathetic toward Germany, but the incident begins to turn the tide of U.S. sentiment toward the Allies.

1915: Italy enters the war on the side of the Allies, and Bulgaria on that of the Central Powers.

1915: At the Second Battle of Ypres, the Germans introduce a new weapon: poison gas.

1915: Turkey's solution to its Armenian "problem" becomes the first entry in a long catalogue of genocidal acts undertaken during the twentieth century. Claiming that the Armenians support Russia, the Turks deport some 1.75 million of them to the Mesopotamian desert, where between 600,000 and 1 million perish.

1915: D. W. Griffith's controversial *Birth of a Nation* is the first significant motion picture. As film, it is an enduring work of art, but its positive depiction of the Ku Klux Klan influences a rebirth of the Klan in Stone Mountain, Georgia.

1915: Albert Einstein publishes his General Theory of Relativity.

1917: On both the Western Front and in the Middle East, the tide of the war begins to turn against the Central Powers. The arrival of U.S. troops, led by General Pershing, in France in June greatly boosts morale, and reinforces exhausted Allied forces. Meanwhile, Great Britain scores two major victories against the Ottoman Empire as T. E. Lawrence leads an Arab revolt in Baghdad in March, and troops under Field Marshal Edmund Allenby take Jerusalem in December.

1919: Treaty of Versailles is signed by the Allies and Germany, but rejected by the U.S. Senate. This is due in part to rancor between President Woodrow Wilson and Republican Senate leaders, and in part to concerns over Wilson's plan to commit the United States to the newly established League of Nations and other international duties. Not until 1921 will Congress formally end U.S. participation in the war, but it will never agree to join the League.

Event and Its Context

The Perils of the Sea

As an inspiration to writers and artists, the sea is often romanticized. However, the experience of those who toil to earn a living on the sea is far from romantic. Indeed, for centuries seamen have endured dangers and hardships. With seemingly endless workdays, their living conditions aboard the ship were riddled with difficulty. Their sleeping quarters were extremely cramped, and the food they were given was neither enough nor was it acceptable in quality. To make matters worse, they were poorly paid and often had to tolerate unfair and brutal treatment from ship captains, who were rightly called "masters," given their complete authority over the crew.

Seafaring trades have always involved great risk to workers. Harsh weather poses a constant safety threat. Sailors are repeatedly lost at sea through collisions and rough waters. Accidents, even minor ones, can prove fatal, as medical attention can be days away. The annals of seagoing history are filled with ships "missing and presumed lost with all hands" (Bunker, 2002). Work at sea is not for the faint of heart.

Historically, seamen had little opportunity to protest their situation effectively, let alone organize into a union. They were too busy trying to survive. Mutinies against the terrible conditions they faced were settled by force, often at the end of a gun,

Robert M. La Follette. The Library of Congress.

and rarely to the seamen's advantage. Seamen choosing not to take the law into their own hands often found little satisfaction through the legal system, which often decided cases in favor of the captains or shipowners.

In the nineteenth century, a seaman who left the ship before the voyage's end faced dire consequences, as maritime nations imposed strict laws against such behavior. In fact, it was legal to use force, if necessary, to bring a seaman back on board. In the event a wayward seaman did not return on his own or was not found, "he automatically forfeited his pay and any belongings left on the ship" (Bunker, 2002). An unhappy sailor who decided to protest quickly got a reputation for being difficult, which thwarted his ability to find future work. Sailors wishing to form a union found themselves in an equally precarious position, because to organize a union required meetings on land and time away from the sea. This resulted in lost wages—wages they could ill afford to lose.

The Formation of the International Seamen's Union

Nonetheless, many seamen persevered and, over the years, participated in numerous strikes, requesting, among other things, higher wages and better living conditions aboard ship. Various unions were created; however, for the most part, they were dissolved in a relatively short period of time. Diverse opinions and divided energies sometimes caused problems, but small gains were made, although often on a regional basis only. By 1892 it became abundantly clear that a single powerful voice was needed in Congress to speak on behalf of the seamen—a voice calling for sweeping legislative changes. Therefore, in a wise strategic move, various union representatives from the Great Lakes, West Coast, and the Gulf of Mexico joined forces to form the National Seamen's Union of America, which later became the International Seamen's Union (ISU).

Elections were held, and Charles Hagen, a native German who had helped organize the Gulf Coast union, was chosen as the first president. A seasoned sailor and vocal activist, Thomas Elderkin had long sailed on the Great Lakes and was chosen the union's first secretary. James McLaren, a Nova Scotian from the West Coast with "shrewd energy and unswerving devotion to the sailors' cause" was chosen as the union's first national organizer (Bunker, 2002). A union of this size required a determination period to iron out its goals and direction. Then, in 1908 Norwegian-born Andrew Furuseth, a seasoned sailor and passionate activist, was elected president of the union. By coupling his no-nonsense approach with his deep-seated desire to help his fellow seamen, Furuseth became the respected voice that was heard within congressional halls and quoted in the press. Joined with him in the cause was Senator Robert M. La Follette of Wisconsin, who supported labor legislation because, in his opinion, "unions were battling the same enemies that menaced consumers and because consumers benefited directly from improvements in working conditions" (Eastland Memorial Society, 2002). Furthermore, La Follette thought it unjust that only a privileged few, most specifically powerful investment bankers, dominated the economy. He believed wholeheartedly in balancing the scales of justice so hardworking people were not held hostage by an unfair system.

The Importance of the La Follette Seamen's Act

While clearly a proponent of social justice laws, La Follette was a progressive Republican who did not support government sponsorship of big business. In addition, he sometimes found himself in disagreement with President Woodrow Wilson, who he thought "ignored the ideas of progressive Republicans and shaped most legislation in the Democratic caucus" (Eastland Memorial Society, 2002). However, Wilson and La Follette did have a meeting of minds over one important piece of legislation: the La Follette Seamen's Act of 1915. Designed to regulate the safety, living conditions, and food standards on ships, this groundbreaking legislation also reduced captains' power, defined seamen's legal status, and established rules of compensation.

Specifically, the act addressed the sailor's work schedule, outlining a maximum nine-hour workday in port. It called for a two-watch system for the deck and a three-watch system for the gang, which was intended to help improve safety and workload. The seamen's longtime complaints regarding cramped living quarters and too little food were rectified. A broader meal schedule was outlined, and the customary 72 cubic feet each sailor had for living space, which Furuseth described as "too large for a coffin, too little for a grave," was increased to at least 100 cubic feet (Bunker, 2002).

An interesting element of the act dealt with the need to improve communication and promote the hiring of American sailors, mandating that at least 75 percent of the crew be required to understand commands in English. In the eyes of many, this would also help to improve safety for all concerned. Additionally, the act heralded the idea that the number of lifeboats kept on each ship should be increased and special attention paid to their quality. Naturally, this garnered much support from the Boats for All movement, formed after the *Titanic* sank in 1912.

Aside from the pragmatic concerns affecting the everyday life of the sailor, unfairness in the legal system was addressed in the act. Creditors could no longer engage in the unscrupulous practice of coercion, which involved demanding a "mortgage" on a sailor's wages in exchange for lodging and food (Bunker, 2002). In addition, sailors who left a ship before the end of a voyage no longer faced prison terms for desertion, and corporal punishment aboard ships was banned.

Having spent many years passionately crusading for seafaring improvements, Furuseth had the ISU's full support and the public's attention. Couple that with the determination and persuasive talents of his longtime friend La Follette and the stamp of approval from the secretary of labor, and it wasn't long before many other congressmen were on board too, so to speak. Nonetheless, the bill met with resistance during the congressional hearings. For example, A. A. Schantz, president of the Detroit and Cleveland Navigation Company, testified that the addition of more lifesaving equipment to the shallow Great Lakes vessels would render them top-heavy and pose unnecessary passenger risk. None of the controversy, however, swayed Furuseth from the cause; he labored tirelessly, and finally, after a two-year battle in Congress, the bill was signed by Wilson on 4 March 1915.

The La Follette Seamen's Act was a crowning achievement for La Follette, who never gave up on the bill and truly believed it was in the best interest of both the passengers and the seamen. In fact, a tragic event illustrating its importance occurred in July 1915, just a few months before the act went into effect. The *Eastland*, owned by St. Joseph and Chicago Steamship Company, was granted a license to carry 2,500 passengers despite the fact that terms of the imminent act would have restricted the number of passengers to half that. Even though additional lifeboats were installed, there were not enough to save the 844 who drowned when the ship capsized. This event not only stressed the value of the act but also put a spotlight on the importance of an effective Steamship Inspection Service.

Conclusion

Sadly, by the early 1920s the shipping industry had suffered numerous losses, which resulted in companies going out of business and ships being sold at bargain prices to pay off debt. Some people blamed new legislation that governed the quality of ships and the improvement of seamen's working conditions for reducing the competitive ability of the United States shipping industry. As some owners clamored to reregister their fleets under the Panamanian flag, others saw little hope in the situation. Steamship companies saw a drop in passengers and income, as they were no longer allowed to overbook their vessels because of the passenger-to-lifeboat restriction. In addition, as the automobile gained in popularity, water travel began to lose its appeal, which affected the shipping industry as well.

By the 1930s the Great Depression had taken a substantial toll on the ISU. Internal politics weakened the union even further. Finally, it dissolved altogether, and a new union was formed—the Seafarers International Union, which still existed at the beginning of the twenty-first century.

Key Players

Furuseth, Andrew (1854–1938): Furuseth was a fiery, straightforward man with Norwegian roots who spent most of his life fighting for the rights of his fellow seamen. Known as the "Abraham Lincoln of the Seas," Furuseth was elected president of the International Seamen's Union (ISU) in 1908. In a lifelong friendship that proved rewarding for both, Andrew Furuseth and U.S. Senator Robert M. La Follette were committed to improving maritime labor. Furuseth worked tirelessly for two decades to see the La Follette Seamen's Act passed, having drafted much of its content.

La Follette, Robert M. (1855–1925). Beginning his career as a county district attorney, La Follette was quickly recognized for his oratory skills. He served three terms as governor of Wisconsin, having been elected on a platform that embraced tax reform, corporate regulation, and political democracy. In 1906 La Follette was elected to the U.S. Senate, where he supported the growth of trade unions and strongly believed that he was responsible for protecting the people against corporate tyranny. He and his wife, the feminist Belle La Follette, founded the *La Follette's Weekly Magazine*, which embraced the suffrage movement and racial equality.

BIBLIOGRAPHY

Books

La Follette, Robert M. *La Follette's Autobiography: A Personal Narrative of Political Experiences*. Madison, WI: The Robert M. La Follette Co., 1913.

Weintraub, Hyman. *Andrew Furuseth: Emancipator of the Seamen*. Berkeley, CA: University of California Press, 1959.

Other

Bunker, John. "A History of the SIU" [cited 2 February 2003]. <http://www.seafarers.org/about/history.xml>

Eastland Memorial Society. "Robert Marion La Follette (1855–1925)" [cited 2 February 2003]. <http://www.eastlandmemorial.org/lafollette.shtml>

ADDITIONAL RESOURCES

Unger, Nancy C. *Fighting Bob La Follette: The Righteous Reformer*. Chapel Hill, NC: University of North Carolina Press, 2000.

Weisberger, Bernard A. *The La Follettes of Wisconsin: Love and Politics in Progressive America*. Madison, WI: University of Wisconsin Press, 1994.

—Lee Ann Paradise

Terence V. Powderly. The Library of Congress.

Labor Day Established

United States 1882

Synopsis

Labor Day, a national holiday in the United States, takes place on the first Monday in September. The holiday honors the dignity of labor and celebrates the gains made by working people in their struggles for a better life. Although there have been controversies over the origins of the day, there is general agreement that it crystallized in the early 1880s and was embraced and celebrated by diverse forces in the labor movement. By the 1890s it had been recognized by a proliferating number of municipalities and states before being recognized by the federal government. Although it is a day of relaxation for many (as part of a "long weekend" that often allows for one final summer vacation), it has also been an annual "festival of rejoicing," according to Peter J. McGuire, a labor activist and founder of the American Federation of Labor (AFL), "to honor labor coming into its own." Labor Day was initiated by working people dedicated to uplifting their toiling brothers and sisters and "leading them to better conditions."

Timeline

1862: Though Great Britain depends on cotton from the American South, it is more dependent on grain from the North, and therefore refuses to recognize the Confederacy.

1867: Karl Marx publishes the first volume of *Das Kapital*.

1872: The title of Claude Monet's painting *Impression: Sunrise* gives a name to a new movement in art.

1878: Russo-Turkish War, begun in 1877, ends with the defeat of Turkey, which ceases to be an important power in Europe. The Treaty of San Stefano concluding the war is revised by the Congress of Berlin, which realigns the balance of power in southeastern Europe.

1882: Agitation against English rule spreads throughout Ireland, culminating with the assassination of chief secretary for Ireland Lord Frederick Cavendish and permanent undersecretary Thomas Burke in Dublin's Phoenix Park. The leader of the nationalist movement is Charles Stewart Parnell, but the use of assassination and terrorism—which Parnell himself has disavowed—makes clear the fact that he does not control all nationalist groups.

1882: British forces invade, and take control of, Egypt.

1882: Germany, Austria, and Italy form the Triple Alliance, which provides that if any of the three is attacked by France in the next five years, the others will come to its aid.

1882: John D. Rockefeller's Standard Oil trust, first major industrial monopoly, is established.

1882: German bacteriologist Robert Koch isolates the bacterium that causes tuberculosis.

1884: Due to isolationist policies, Japan's government had prohibited emigration, but this year it finally lifts the ban and allows citizens to immigrate to Hawaii, where many—having escaped the country illegally—already work as temporary laborers. Thereafter, Japanese will increasingly replace Chinese as workers in the United States, where a treaty limits Chinese immigration.

1888: Serbian-born American electrical engineer Nikola Tesla develops a practical system for generating and transmitting alternating current (AC), which will ultimately—and after an extremely acrimonious battle—replace Thomas Edison's direct current (DC) in most homes and businesses.

1891: French troops open fire on workers during a 1 May demonstration at Fourmies, where employees of the Sans Pareille factory are striking for an eight-hour day. Nine people are killed—two of them children—and sixty more are injured.

Event and Its Context

In the early 1960s, when unions in the United States generally seemed powerful, conservative, and self-satisfied, a liberal academic cynically commented that Labor Day "has lost practically all its significance, being no more than a holiday for everyone: a day of non-labor." In fact, the meaning of the day has varied from one time and place to another. In the early years of the twenty-first century, it remains a day of massive parades and picnics sponsored by the labor movement of certain U.S. cities. Just as there may be differences on the contemporary relevance of this holiday, the origins of Labor Day constitute the subject of scholarly wrangles.

Disputed History

Peter J. McGuire of the Carpenters Union has long been credited as being "the father of Labor Day," but more recently claims for that title have been made for Matthew Maguire of the Machinists. It has also been argued that both were involved, as both were members of the same Socialist Labor Party club that had decided to bring the motion to the New York Central Labor Union. This effort resulted in the great Labor Day parade, rally, and picnic in New York City on 5 September 1882.

The controversies do not end there. Typographical Union leader A. C. Cameron introduced an 1884 resolution into the Federation of Organized Trades and Labor Unions (predecessor of the American Federation of Labor) calling for Labor Day to be made a national holiday. The Knights of Labor—a much larger organization at that time—passed a similar resolution in the same year, and the AFL's "ownership" was challenged by Terence V. Powderly, leader of the Knights, who argued that the idea was a product of his organization. Some scholars agree, although it has been suggested that the concept of Labor Day was advanced by Powderly's left-wing opponents clustered in the Knights' District Assembly 49, in the secret "Home Club" led by French-born socialist-anarchist Victor Drury (with whom Matthew Maguire was presumably associated).

To add to the confusion, other historians argue that the New York event was not the first Labor Day. The honor has been awarded to Providence, Rhode Island and Pittsburgh, Pennsylvania.

Three Early Celebrations

On Wednesday, 23 August 1882—in what has been called "a dress rehearsal for New York's monster parade"—about 10,000 people converged in Providence for a parade involving about a thousand members of various craft unions and the massed strength of the Knights of Labor headed by a 25-piece band. This was accompanied by a rally (speakers included out-of-town guests Peter J. McGuire, Victor Drury, Robert Blissert of New York City's Central Labor Union, and prolabor journalist Louis F. Post). A picnic and baseball game took place after the parade.

A similar event had transpired two months earlier in Pittsburgh (on Saturday, 17 June 1882), under the auspices of Pittsburgh District Assembly 3 of the Knights of Labor, the Amalgamated Association of Iron and Steel Workers, and other trade unions. The Knights called it "a peaceable protest against the evils that exist against the many by and through the power of wealth possessed by the few." It is estimated that more than 100,000 people turned out for the parade, led by *National Labor Tribune* editor Thomas Armstrong, Andrew Burtt and Isaac Cline of the Glass Blowers Union, David R. Jones of the Mineworkers Union, John McLuckie who was a leader of the Amalgamated Association of Iron and Steel Workers (and would soon be elected mayor of Homestead), Alexander C. Rankin local grandmaster of the Knights of Labor, and Thomas "Beeswax" Taylor who was famous for writing the anthem "Storm the Fort, Ye Knights of Labor."

The first Labor Day celebration in New York City, on Tuesday, 5 September 1882, however, had the greatest national impact. The size of the parade itself has been estimated from

Peter J. McGuire. © Getty Images. Reproduced by permission.

10,000 to 30,000, with many more observing and joining in the picnic, the amusements in the park, the dancing and the fireworks that were also part of the labor festival. The multiethnic nature of the event (and of the working class) was reflected in the American, Irish, German, French flags being flown, as well as the prominent participation in the march of the all-black Wendell Phillips Labor Club. An estimated fifty labor figures on the reviewing stand at Union Square watched as workers carried banners proclaiming: "Labor Creates All Wealth," "We Must Crush Monopolies Lest They Crush Us," "A Fair Day's Pay for a Fair Day's Work," "Eight Hours of Work, Eight Hours of Rest, and Eight Hours for What We Will," and "Labor Will Be United."

Explaining the Origins of Labor Day

The German-American labor veteran and socialist Friedrich Sorge offered a general explanation that helps cut across much of the controversy. Sorge indicated that the origin of the holiday related to the need of German-speaking workers to compensate for the lack of holidays and Sunday observations with excursion to the countryside. At the end of the 1860s, the German trade associations and the First International transformed these outings into organized labor holidays by devoting part of the day to propagandizing for the labor press and organizations. Sorge also indicated that the English-speaking workers of the time were in the habit of staging large parades to support various causes, particularly the eight-hour movement: "In the 1880s both celebrations, the English speaking and the German speaking, were merged into one holiday during which the morning was devoted to the parade and the afternoon to entertainment."

In 1885 the New York Central Labor Union adopted a resolution that called for a special holiday that would stand as "a labor demonstration on the first Monday of each September," and invited "all central bodies of workers in the entire United States to join with us to carry out the present resolution in spirit and achievement."

An Official Holiday

By 1887 five states and many municipalities officially recognized Labor Day, and by 1894 the number had jumped to 23 states. In that year, Senator James Henderson Kyle of South Dakota's Populist Party and Amos J. Cummings, a prolabor Democrat from New York, introduced legislation to make the first Monday in September a legal holiday in Washington, D.C., in all U.S. territories, and for all federal employees. President Grover Cleveland—a probusiness Democrat who had just helped to crush the Pullman strike and was seeking to appear more attractive to working-class voters—signed the bill into law and made Labor Day a national holiday.

Key Players

Armstrong, Thomas A. (1840–1887): Armstrong was a major figure in the Pittsburgh labor movement, as a leader of the National Typographical Union, a founder of the National Labor Union, and member of the Knights of Labor. In 1874 he helped found the *National Labor Tribune*, serving as its editor until his death. In the wake of the 1877 rail strike he broke with the Republican Party and became a leading member of the Greenback Labor Party, running as its candidate for governor in 1882.

Blissert, Robert (1843–1899): Moving to the United States after participating in the London Tailor's Strike, Blissert, a socialist and Irish nationalist, became a prominent member of the International Workingmen's Association (First International) and the Knights of Labor. He was a founder and leader of the New York Central Labor Union.

Cameron, Andrew C. (1834–1890): Scottish-born son of a printer, in the United States Cameron played a central role in the National Typographical Union in Chicago. He was editor of the *Workingmen's Advocate* from 1860 to 1880 and then edited other trade journals.

Drury, Victor (1825–1918): A painter, writer, poet, and participant in the Paris uprising of 1848, Drury became a member of the First International in 1864. Coming to the United States in 1867, and influenced by a variety of socialist and anarchist thinkers, his political affiliations evolved from the Workingmen's Party and the Socialist Labor Party to the International Working Peoples Association. He also became influential in the Knights of Labor General Assembly 49, which in turn was dominated by the "Home Club," a secret radical faction of which Drury was a central member during the 1880s.

Maguire, Matthew (1850–1898): Maguire was a machinist and a leader of the Machinists and Blacksmith's International Union who lived at various times in New York, Brooklyn, and Patterson, New Jersey. He was active in the Knights of Labor and in the Socialist Labor Party (SLP). He was elected to the Patterson Board of Aldermen on the SLP ticket. In 1896 he was the SLP candidate for vice president of the United States.

McGuire, Peter J. (1852–1906): McGuire was an American-born worker whose initial involvement in socialist politics was as a member of the First International. McGuire left the SLP in the 1880s to become a founder and general secretary of the Brotherhood of Carpenters and Joiners and a founder of the AFL. He is often credited for being involved in the creation both of Labor Day (1882) and May Day (1886), although—as with Samuel Gompers—his socialist commitments faded with the passage of time.

Powderly, Terence V. (1849–1924): A member of the Machinists and Blacksmith's International Union, Powderly became the national grand master workman of the Knights of Labor in 1879. He developed a reputation as a labor moderate who preferred arbitration to confrontation between workers and employers and favored a variety of reforms and electoral remedies. Powderly was elected mayor of Scranton, Pennsylvania in 1878 as a candidate of the Greenback Labor Party. After losing his position in the Knights of Labor in 1893, he concentrated his efforts in the Republican Party and in 1897 was appointed U.S. Commissioner General of Immigration.

See also: *Eight-hour Day Movement; Knights of Labor.*

BIBLIOGRAPHY

Books

Filler, Louis. *A Dictionary of American Social Reform*. New York: Philosophical Library, 1963.

Fink, Gary, ed. *Biographical Dictionary of American Labor*. Westport, CT: Greenwood Press, 1984.

Foner, Philip. *History of the Labor Movement in the United States*, Vol. 2. New York: International Publishers, 1955.

Kaufman, Stuart B., ed. *The Samuel Gompers Papers, Volume 1: 1850–86*. Urbana: University of Illinois Press, 1986.

Krause, Paul. *The Battle for Homestead, 1880–1892: Politics, Culture, and Steel*. Pittsburgh, PA: University of Pittsburgh Press, 1992.

Molloy, Scott. "Rhode Island Hosted America's First Labor Day Parade." In *A History of Rhode Island Working People*, edited by Paul Buhle, Scott Molloy, and Gail Sansbury. Providence, RI: Regine Printing Co., 1983.

Sorge, Friedrich A. *Labor Movement in the United States*. Edited by Philip S. Foner and Brewster Chamberlin. Westport, CT: Greenwood Press, 1977.

Weir, Robert E. *Beyond Labor's Veil: The Culture of the Knights of Labor*. University Park: Pennsylvania University Press, 1996.

Periodicals

Erlich, Mark. "Peter J. McGuire's Trade Unionism: Socialism of a Trades Union Kind?" *Labor History* 24, no. 2 (spring 1983).

Grossman, Jonathan. "Who Was the Father of Labor Day?" *Monthly Labor Review* (September 1972).

Richards, Miles. "Thomas A. Armstrong, A Forgotten Advocate of Labor." *Western Pennsylvania Historical Magazine* 67 (October 1984).

Weir, Robert. "'Here's to the Men Who Lose!': The Hidden Career of Victor Drury." *Labor History* 36, no. 4 (fall 1995).

Other

Montgomery, David. "Labor Day and May Day." *Humanities and Social Sciences Online, H-Net Labor History.* September 6, 1995 [cited 16 July 2002]. <http://h-net.msu.edu>

—Paul Le Blanc

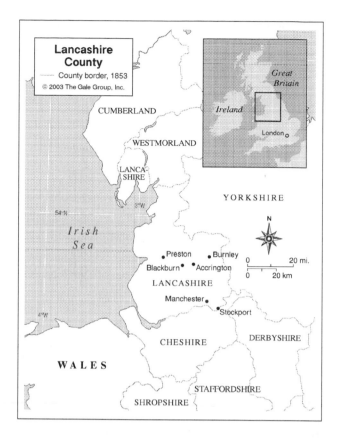

Lancashire Textile Strikes

Great Britain 1853–1854

Synopsis

In the late 1840s wages in the Lancashire cotton industry had been reduced by 10 percent. When prosperity improved, the workers were disappointed not to have their old rates reinstated. A two-month strike of spinners at Stockport in summer 1853 won back the 10 percent and was followed by other successes, but in Preston the Masters' Association announced a general lockout to begin in mid-October. It lasted 17 weeks, and when in theory the workers could have returned to work, most chose not to do so. An effective organization that raised funds, distributed relief payments, sustained morale, and influenced public opinion supported the locked-out "operatives." In February 1854 the mill owners began to bring in "blackleg" labor, which aroused resentment but resulted in few disturbances. In March 1854 prominent organizers and speakers were arrested on conspiracy charges, although the case was eventually dropped. The Preston strike ended on 1 May 1854, after a renewed depression of the industry had set in, without the owners conceding on the 10 percent wage increase. Although defeated, the struggle would survive in local collective memory and had made a forceful impression further afield.

Timeline

1831: Unsuccessful Polish revolt is waged against Russian rule.

1837: British inventor Isaac Pitman devises his shorthand system.

1842: Scientific and technological advances include the development of ether and artificial fertilizer; the identification of the Doppler effect (by Austrian physicist Christian Johann Doppler); the foundation of biochemistry as a discipline; and the coining of the word *dinosaur*.

1847: Patenting of the first successful rotary press, which replaces the old flatbed press, takes place in the United States.

1848: Scottish mathematician and physicist William Thomson, Lord Kelvin, introduces the concept of absolute zero, or the temperature at which molecular motion ceases. This value, -273°C, becomes 0K on his Kelvin scale of absolute temperature.

1851: Britain's Amalgamated Society of Engineers applies innovative organizational concepts, including large contributions from, and benefits to, members, as well as vigorous use of direct action and collective bargaining.

1852: Emigration from Ireland to the United States reaches its peak.

1852: France's Second Republic ends when Louis Napoleon declares himself Napoleon III, initiating the Second Empire.

1852: American inventor Elisha Graves Otis introduces the "safety" elevator, which has a safety brake to keep it from falling even if the cable holding it is completely cut.

1854: "The Charge of the Light Brigade" by Alfred Lord Tennyson and *Walden* by Henry David Thoreau are published.

1858: British explorer John Hanning Speke locates Lake Victoria, which he correctly identifies as the source of the Nile.

1862: American Richard Gatling invents the first practical machine gun.

Event and Its Context

In the county of Lancashire in northwest England, the manufacture of cotton was overwhelmingly dominant by the nineteenth century, employing tens of thousands in expanding towns. Some, like Preston, contained dozens of mills. The struggle between capital and labor was often on display in these towns. Lancashire had been the scene of noteworthy strikes in 1818, 1836, and 1842, and was a center of Chartist and 10-hour workday agitation and of pioneering efforts to form trade unions.

How It Started

The textile industry was vulnerable to fluctuations in trade. In 1847 employers imposed a general 10 percent wage reduction, which workers thought was a temporary measure. Within a few years the economic situation had eased, but the "Masters" did not restore the 10 percent and denied having made any promise to do so. Local strikes occurred in Preston in 1849, and by spring 1853 there were demands for higher wages in almost every cotton town.

In Stockport weavers called for an "advance" in March. Their spokesman, George Cooper, claimed their wages were lower than in other towns. The strike lasted from 9 June to 1 August 1853. When the weavers rejected an offer of 5 percent to weavers, and 10 percent to spinners and cardroom hands, the employers granted the 10 percent to all. Workers in Blackburn, Accrington, and Burnley won similar victories. By the end of the summer there were weekly mass meetings in Preston. Spinners and cardroom hands were campaigning for the 10 percent, and weavers were collecting for Stockport. On 5 August officials had the collectors arrested, supposedly at the instigation of Thomas Miller, a prominent mill owner. A meeting in Stockport on 14 August promised support from elsewhere if a strike should be needed at Preston. In September five youths were arrested and sentenced to prison for acting to enforce a levy for strike funds.

The cotton employers also had been organizing. In March, William Ainsworth took the lead in setting up the Preston Masters Association, which on 15 September announced a general lockout to begin in a month's time. At this stage only 8 or 10 firms in the town were in dispute, as the majority had conceded the 10 percent. Although processions were prohibited the same day, at an evening assembly the operatives declared themselves ready to take a stand. For both sides it was a crucial test: if Preston failed to get the 10 percent, the chances were wages would be rolled back elsewhere.

Organization and Survival

Before the lockout began on 15 October, the Preston operatives were mounting a campaign that built on methods tried out at Stockport. The workers engaged in local efforts to conduct the strike, raise and distribute relief funds, and promote public awareness and support. Committees for the different trades—weavers, spinners, and smaller numbers of cardroom hands and throstle-spinners—pooled their efforts. Open-air mass meetings publicized the mood of the rank-and-file and kept the strikers informed of developments. The two most prominent worker delegates, George Cowell and Mortimer Grimshaw, undertook a phenomenal program of adressing mass meetings, attending delegate meetings, and traveling on speaking tours.

Subscriptions came in from all over the country. The weavers were able to pay about half the normal working rate to over 7,000 people, with half as much to assistants and a comparable amount to spinners. Administrative expenses were scrupulously itemized and publicized in a weekly balance sheet. Levies on the few unaffected mills, collections in shops and public houses, and solidarity from other unions and trades all helped, as did public meetings, benefit concerts, and theatrical events in cities and towns from Scotland to London. Delegates visited Preston from within Lancashire, with Blackburn leading the support and contributing substantially to strike funds. The lockout ultimately affected 47,000 workers at 183 mills in the county by the end of October. A contemporary study by the Reverend John Clay gave the total number involved in the Preston lockout as 18,000: 11,800 women, over half adult and the rest teenaged; and 6,200 men, two-thirds adult and the rest aged 13 to 17. Women were present in meetings, crowds, clashes, and at least three as notable public speakers, but did not play a part proportionate to their numbers.

The operatives continued to seek negotiations and arbitration, but mill owners rejected peaceable overtures. A public notice on 1 November set the owners' terms for ending the lockout: abandon the 10 percent, accept lower pay at many mills, and put an end to the operatives' union. The next move was an offer to receive applications for employment and reopen if enough came forward; very few did.

Opposition and Defeat

The owners' position was strong nonetheless, amid signs that the cotton boom of the previous few years was over; the worsening economic situation meant that the closed mills would otherwise have been on short time, and stocks were plentiful. Food prices rose after a wet summer, which was followed by a severe winter. November brought setbacks: in Burnley spinners but not weavers got 10 percent and both were on a four-day week. The Preston weavers tried appealing to higher authority, sending a petition to Home Secretary Lord Palmerston on 21 November outlining the circumstances of the "unhappy dispute" and pleading for a reasonable solution. The eventual reply expressed sympathy and regret but indicated that there was no means of interposing to apply a remedy. The Board of Trade also refused to intervene.

In February 1854 the owners reopened the mills to try to force a return on their terms, so that the lockout became a strike. On the 23rd they decided to import labor from other parts of Britain and Ireland. The first contingent of "knobsticks" (i.e., blacklegs or scabs), a group of unemployed cotton hands, arrived at the end of the month. As a serious attempt to replace the strikers, the policy failed; by mid-March most mills were still closed. If, as the workers suspected, it was a move to provoke them, it had a measure of success. Pickets met and occasionally attacked the knobsticks. On 2 and 3 March a stone-throwing incident led to the reading of the Riot Act (warning gatherings to disperse), 100 police being brought from London, and the military being put on alert. The next day local officials prohibited all meetings in the borough. Generally, however, observers commended the operatives' restraint. There were perpetual complaints of police provocation steadfastly resisted.

Law and order was largely a matter for the local authorities, who could ban processions and meetings, and the masters were well represented on the town council. The system officially in place for relieving hardship was another opportunity to shape events, modified by the risk of precipitating disorder if conditions became intolerable, but the operatives largely avoided applying for relief. As union funds began to run out and deprivation took its toll, a few returned to work. Then, on 18 March the magistrates decided to charge strike leaders with conspiracy, and 11 were shortly arrested. Initially the public reaction was to fight on, but through April several groups seceded from the "10 percent and no surrender' position, until meetings on 30 April and 1 May proclaimed the end of the strike.

Significance

The Preston strike was remarkable not for the final outcome but for how long it lasted, what happened during it, and the notice it attracted at the time and afterwards. The struggle went beyond wages. The owners reaffirmed control of their property and reasserted authority in the mills; the workers not only developed valuable techniques for survival in struggle but excelled at winning hearts and minds. Theirs became a *cause célèbre* among labor movement luminaries such as Ernest Jones, who addressed a meeting at Preston and gave it extensive coverage in his *People's Paper*, and Karl Marx. Foremost among others who put in a good word for them was Charles Dickens, who had many positive things to say about the strikers and was exasperated by the owners' obstinacy. Preston provided the model for Coketown in Dickens' novel *Hard Times,* as it did for the mill town in Elizabeth Gaskell's *North and South.* Thus, albeit in fictionalized form, the Preston strike helped to shape cultural perceptions of the northern English working class. In real life the legacy of the strike may be less obvious, but there are signs that, although not the first, last, most widespread, or most violent such episode in the area, it did not by any means vanish from collective memory.

Key Players

Ainsworth, William (1807–1862): Son of a Unitarian cotton manufacturer, Ainsworth studied law at Glasgow University before going into the family business, which employed about 800 workers. He had a reputation for reducing wages, provoking frequent strikes, and prosecuting militants. Secretary of the Preston Masters' Association, he was also a borough and county magistrate and served on Preston town council.

Cooper, George (1824–1895): A weaver born in Stockport, Cooper campaigned against the loom tax (1847) and for the 10-hour day, the unemployed, and a weavers' union. He led the 1853 Stockport strike. He participated in the American Civil War, then returned to Lancashire and the cause of Parliamentary reform.

Cowell, George (c. 1800–?): Born near Preston, Cowell was a weaver, Methodist, and teetotaler known for his integrity. He was involved with Chartism and the 10-hour workday movement among other radical causes. After the Preston strike he became a tea and coffee dealer and continued to be active in the labor movement and the Lancashire Reform Union.

Grimshaw, Mortimer: Grimshaw came from Great Harwood in Lancashire and was a weaver who was allegedly blacklisted by local firms. He was secretary of the Short-Time Committee (1852–1853) in the "Jacobin village" of Royton, where he edited an anti-Whig election broadsheet. The demagogue "Slackbridge" in Dickens's *Hard Times* is said to have been based on Grimshaw.

Miller, Thomas (1811–1865): Miller married into the Horrocks cotton firm as had his father and later took over as sole proprietor of Horrocks, Miller & Co., which employed about 2,000 workers. Notorious for paying very low wages and imposing harsh discipline, he chaired the Preston Masters' Association and was a borough and county magistrate and alderman in local government.

See also: *Chartist Movement.*

BIBLIOGRAPHY

Books

Chapman, Stanley David. *The Cotton Industry in the Industrial Revolution.* London: Macmillan, 1972.

Dickens, Charles. "(On Strike) The Preston Spinners' Strike, 1853–1854: Dickens as Strike Reporter." In *Strikes: A Documentary History,* by Ruth Frow, Edmund Frow, and Michael Katanka. London: Charles Knight & Co. Ltd., 1971. Original work published 1854.

Dutton, H. I., and J. E. King. *Ten Percent and No Surrender: The Preston Strike, 1853–1854.* Cambridge: Cambridge University Press, 1981.

Neff, Wanda E. "The Textile Worker" In *Victorian Working Women: An Industrial and Literary Study of Women in British Industries and Professions, 1832–1850.* London: Frank Cass, 1966.

ADDITIONAL RESOURCES

Ashworth, Henry. *The Preston Strike: An Enquiry into its Causes and Consequences.* Manchester, UK: George Simms, 1854.

Howell, George. "Preston Strike." In *Labour Legislation, Labour Movements and Labour Leaders.* London: T. Fisher Unwin, 1902.

John L. McClellan Democratic senator from Arkansas (center holding paper), with members of Senate Labor Rackets Committee (l-r): Sam Ervin, Democratic senator from North Carolina; Carl Curtis, Republican senator from Nebraska; Barry Goldwater, Republican senator from Arizona; John F. Kennedy, Democratic senator from Massachusetts. AP/World Wide Photos. Reproduced by permission.

Jenkins, D. T. *The Industrial Revolution.* Volume 8: *The Textile Industries.* Oxford: Blackwell, 1994.

Morgan, Carol E. *Women Workers and Gender Identities, 1835–1913: The Cotton and Metal Industries in England.* London: Routledge, 2001.

Rose, Mary B. *The British and American Cotton Industries Since 1750.* Cambridge: Cambridge University Press, 2000.

Periodicals

Carnall E. "Dickens, Mrs. Gaskell and the Preston Strike." *Victorian Studies* 8 (1964–1965): 31–48.

Fielding K. "The Battle for Preston." *Dickensian* 50 (1954): 161.

Smith, Anne. "*Hard Times* and *The Times* Newspaper." *Dickensian* 69 (1973): 159.

        —Elizabeth A. Willis

Landrum-Griffin Act

United States 1959

Synopsis

The Labor-Management Reporting and Disclosure Act of 1959, commonly referred to as the Landrum-Griffin Act, regulates the internal affairs of labor unions. In particular, it protects union members from dishonest and abusive practices by the unions and their leadership. It incorporates a "bill of rights" that provides union members with equal rights to participate in union affairs, the right to freedom of speech and assembly, protection from excessive dues and assessments, the right to sue, and protection against improper disciplinary actions. Additionally, the act requires certain types of reports from unions, regulates union elections, and outlines the fiduciary responsibilities of union officers.

Timeline

1939: Britain and France declare war against Germany after the 1 September invasion of Poland, but little happens in the way of mobilization. Across the Atlantic, President Franklin D. Roosevelt proclaims U.S. neutrality, yet calls for a large defense budget ($1.139 billion) and declares a limited state of emergency. He also receives a letter from Albert Einstein discussing the feasibility of an atomic bomb.

1944: Nazis make their last major offensive in western Europe, and are defeated at the Battle of the Bulge in December.

1949: North Atlantic Treaty Organization (NATO) is established.

1952: Among the cultural landmarks of the year are the film *High Noon* and the book *The Invisible Man* by Ralph Ellison.

1955: Warsaw Pact is signed by the Soviet Union and its satellites in eastern Europe.

1959: Two new leaders appear on the scene in January as General Charles de Gaulle becomes the first president of France's Fifth Republic, and Fidel Castro takes control of Cuba after the collapse of the corrupt Batista regime. Initially, Castro denies that he is a communist, but as the year wears on and he replaces moderates with radicals such as Argentinean doctor Che Guevara, head of Cuba's national bank, his political leanings become more obvious.

1959: Alaska and Hawaii are added to the Union.

1959: Vice President Richard Nixon and Soviet leader Nikita Khrushchev engage in their famous "kitchen debate" in Moscow. Later in the year, Khrushchev visits the United States, signaling an improvement in U.S.-Soviet relations.

1964: Congress approves the Gulf of Tonkin resolution, giving President Johnson broad powers to prosecute the by now rapidly escalating war in Vietnam.

1969: Richard M. Nixon sworn in as president of the United States. In June he pulls 25,000 troops from Vietnam. From this point, America is no longer trying to win the war but to keep from losing it.

1973: Twin towers of the World Trade Center in New York City, built at a cost of $750 million, are completed. The 110-story buildings are the world's tallest, but by year's end they will be eclipsed by the Sears Tower in Chicago.

Event and Its Context

Background

By 1959 the public had long been concerned about reports of illegal and abusive labor union practices. At the turn of the twentieth century, investigations revealed a pattern of racketeering in unions representing the building trades, longshoremen, and Teamsters. Some officials in these unions were guilty of racial discrimination, mishandling of funds, extortion, violence, and graft. After World War II scrutiny of the labor unions intensified, largely because of gains that the unions had achieved through the legislative process—for example, the Wagner Act of 1935, which protected workers' rights to organize and bargain collectively—and because of the growing power of unions, whose membership swelled from 9 million in 1941 to 17 million in the 1950s.

The McClellan Report

This scrutiny began in earnest in 1954, when Congress launched an investigation of charges of improper administration of employee benefit plans. This investigation and the abuses that it exposed in some labor organizations led to the formation of the Senate Select Committee on Improper Activities in the Labor or Management Field, otherwise called the McClellan Anti-Racketeering Committee after its Senate chairman, Arkansas Democrat John L. McClellan. The committee began hearings on 26 February 1957, and over two years it held 270 days of public hearings, taking testimony from racketeers, mobsters, hoods, and union members who were fighting corruption in their unions. During these hearings the committee focused its attention on five unions: the Bakery and Confectionery Workers, the United Textile Workers, the Operating Engineers, the Allied Industrial Workers of America, and in particular the International Brotherhood of Teamsters, whose colorful and combative president, James "Jimmy" Hoffa, often engaged in sharp exchanges with McClellan. Testimony from 1,526 witnesses printed in 58 volumes produced a grim picture of fraud, abuse, racketeering, and corruption and prompted new calls for labor law reform. The chief legal counsel to the McClellan committee was Robert F. Kennedy, who gained experience he would put to use in combating abuses in organized labor as U.S. attorney general in the 1960s.

The McClellan hearings had three principal outcomes. First, the Teamsters Union was expelled from the AFL-CIO, and Hoffa was later convicted and sentenced to prison on charges of jury tampering and mail fraud. (Hoffa mysteriously disappeared in 1975 after he had been released from prison and attempted to regain control of the Teamsters.) Second, in 1957 the AFL-CIO, anticipating that the government would intervene in the affairs of labor, issued to its affiliates a series of six codes of ethical behavior. This step came too late, for in 1958 the third principal outcome of the hearings, the Select Committee's interim report, published the following findings:

- Rank-and-file union members had little voice in union affairs and were frequently denied secret ballots.

- Unions frequently abused their right to place local unions under trusteeship by imposing the trusteeship only to loot the local's treasury.

- Some management groups bribed union officials to get "sweetheart" contracts.

- Union funds were widely misused because of lack of inspection and audit.

- Unions used violence to keep union members in line.

- Employers took improper actions to influence employees in exercising their rights under the National Labor Relations Act.

- The unions misused picketing to extort money from employers or to otherwise influence them.

- Union leadership at high levels was infiltrated by criminals.

- There was a "no-man's land" in which employers and unions could resort neither to the National Labor Relations Board nor to state agencies for relief.

From these findings the McClellan committee recommended legislation that would do the following:

- Regulate and control pension, health, and welfare funds.

- Regulate and control union funds.

- Ensure union democracy.

- Curb activities of middlemen in labor–management disputes.

- Clarify the no-man's land in labor–management disputes.

In response to the McClellan report, the Senate, by a vote of 88 to 1, passed a labor reform bill, the Kennedy-Ives bill, in June 1958. The bill had been drafted by a blue-ribbon panel of labor attorneys, but it never made it to the floor of the House of Representatives, largely because it proposed controversial amendments to the Taft-Hartley Act, which organized labor had been trying to get repealed for over a decade. Congress then recessed for the year without having passed a bill.

The Legislative Debate

In the 1958 election, the Democratic Party made major gains in Congress, giving heart to union officials, who rightly believed that the party was largely prolabor. The Democratic leadership in the 86th Congress, however, accepted that it would have to intervene to clean up the unions—if for no other reason than to show the American public before the 1960 presidential election that it was competent to do the job. The public was indeed watching: a Gallup poll conducted in November 1958 revealed that the electorate felt that, other than integration in the public schools, Congress's most important job was to clean up racketeering and corruption in labor unions. Thus, when Congress reconvened in 1959, Senator John F. Kennedy introduced a revision of the Kennedy-Ives bill on 20 January. The effort to pass a bill gained momentum on 28 January, when President Dwight D. Eisenhower submitted to Congress a message outlining a 20-point program for eliminating abuses in labor-management relations and suggesting amendments to the Taft-Harley Act, many of which were regarded as promanagement. At this point the AFL-CIO miscalculated by refusing to accede to any compromises that would have ensured passage of the Kennedy-Ives bill, which contained a number of concessions to organized labor.

On 14 April the Senate Committee on Labor and Public Welfare reported out an amended bill called the Kennedy-Ervin bill, which passed in the Senate on 25 April by a vote of 90 to 1—primarily on the strength of an impassioned two-hour speech by McClellan in support of his amendment for a labor "bill of rights." Passage in the House of Representatives, though, was a more complicated affair. On 30 July the House Committee on Education and Labor reported out its own version of a labor reform law. Considerable debate ensued on the House floor over a number of competing bills, including the

Kennedy-Ervin bill; the Elliott bill, which labor favored because it was the least restrictive of the three; and the Landrum-Griffin bill, sponsored by representatives Phillip Landrum of Georgia and Paul Griffin of Michigan. On 6 August, Eisenhower delivered a radio and television address throwing his support to the Landrum-Griffin bill, which labor considered the most restrictive of the three bills. For several days the House and the Senate conferred, finally agreeing on a compromise bill on 2 September. Both the Senate and the House passed the conference version of the bill—the Senate by a vote of 95 to 2 and the House by a vote of 352 to 52—which President Eisenhower signed into law as the Labor-Management Reporting and Disclosure Act on 14 September 1959. This act was essentially the Landrum-Griffin bill, so the act is more commonly known by the names of its two congressional sponsors.

An Employee Bill of Rights

The centerpiece of the Landrum-Griffin Act is Title I, which provides a bill of rights for labor union members. Previously, a union member with a grievance against the union had to rely on contract law to seek redress. The courts tended to provide little relief, arguing that the "contract" in question was the union's constitution and bylaws and that if these documents did not touch on the issue raised by the member, there was little relief the court could provide. McClellan was convinced that effective union reform would be impossible without guaranteeing to union members rights similar to those granted to citizens by the U.S. Constitution. In his speech in Congress in April 1959, he said that "racketeering, corruption, abuse of power and other improper practices on the part of some labor organizations" was inevitable "unless the Congress of the United States has the wisdom and the courage to enact laws prescribing minimum standards of democratic process and conduct for the administration of internal union affairs."

Title I attempted to provide equal rights in a number of areas: nomination of candidates for office, voting, attendance at membership meetings, and participation in business transactions. It affirmed the right of union members to assemble freely with other members and to express their views without fear of reprisal, both at union meetings and at other places. It did not, however, attempt to dictate to the unions who they had to admit as members; racial discrimination, for example, continued to be permitted, and the courts upheld what is called *filial preference*, or the practice or admitting only the sons or close relatives of union members. Thus, Title I did not require the unions to admit members based on their qualifications and allowed the unions to establish in their constitution and bylaws "reasonable rules and regulations" over admission and participation. It also allowed the unions to establish reasonable procedures for conducting their affairs—for example, to keep dissident members from commandeering proceedings.

Additionally, Title I established standards to ensure that increases in union dues and fees reflected the desire of the majority of the membership; the purpose of this provision was to prevent unscrupulous union officials from assessing higher dues against the membership's will. It gave union members the right to sue the union after reasonable union procedures for redressing grievances had been exhausted. It established procedural safeguards to ensure that no member could be fined, disciplined, or expelled, except for nonpayment of dues, without written charges, time to prepare a defense, and a fair hearing. Finally, it obligated unions to provide members with a copy of any collective bargaining agreement.

The bill of rights articulated in Title I immediately met with a storm of protest. Labor organizations asserted that they could not function in a democratic fashion. Many labor union members were indifferent to the processes that took place in collective bargaining and cared only about the outcomes of those processes. Further, labor asserted that collective bargaining and "democracy" were often inconsistent and thus that unions had the right to impose on members the results of collective bargaining and that the members had to submit to those results. To back up their efforts, unions had to make and enforce rules to keep their membership in line. Recognizing these realities, the act stated that nothing in the law would "impair the right of a labor organization to adopt and enforce reasonable rules as to the responsibility of every member toward the organization as an institution and to his refraining from conduct that would interfere with its performance of its legal or contractual obligations."

Other Provisions

The Landrum-Griffin Act includes six additional titles.

Title II requires unions, union officers, and employers to submit annual reports of their financial affairs and administrative practices, as well as copies of their constitution and bylaws, to the U.S. secretary of labor. A union's initial report must provide information about membership qualifications, dues, audits, procedures for calling meetings, selection of officers, disciplinary procedures, strike authorization, and other matters. All of the information contained in these reports must be made available to the rank and file. Title II additionally imposes reporting requirements on employers, who must report, for example, any payment or loan made to a labor union or to employees with the purpose of causing those employees to persuade other members to not exercise their right to bargain collectively.

Title III regulates union trusteeships, by which national unions take over the affairs of subordinate unions to ensure order among them. The McClellan committee, however, discovered that some unions were imposing trusteeships to remove local officers who were opposed to the national union and to loot local union treasuries. Title III restricted trusteeships to those established to correct corruption and financial malpractice, to assure the performance of union contracts and of a bargaining representative's duty, to restore democratic processes, and to carry out the legitimate objects of the labor union.

Title IV regulates the conduct of union elections, including the frequency of elections, minimum election procedures, qualifications to run for union office, the conduct of campaigns, and procedures for removing union officers.

Title V outlines the fiduciary responsibilities of union officers. It makes it a federal crime to embezzle union funds and includes provisions for the recovery of assets. It requires officials with fiduciary responsibilities to be bonded. It limits the size of loans that unions can make to their personnel. It also prohibits communists and those convicted of certain crimes from holding office in the union for five years.

Finally, Title VI treats investigations and various miscellaneous matters, and Title VII consists of amendments to the Taft-Hartley Act, including provisions designed to settle questions of federal versus state jurisdiction (McClellan's no-man's land) and to regulate boycotts, picketing, and other matters.

Four Decades of Mixed Success

How successful has the Landrum-Griffin Act been? Although clearly the act has gone a long way toward curbing corruption in labor unions, many observers feel that it has not done enough, primarily because of lack of enforcement mechanisms. In 1979 Senator Robert Griffin, cosponsor of the act, lamented that the Department of Labor had "failed in the performance of its statutory duties" and had demonstrated a "studied reluctance" to enforce the act. In particular, some observers believe that Title I lacks teeth. Essentially, Congress forbade the U.S. secretary of labor from enforcing Title I, so there is no public remedy for violations. Any member who believes that his or her rights have been violated under Title I may bring suit, but few union members have the financial resources to engage in litigation. Further, if the basis of the employee's claim is that organized crime has infiltrated the union, that employee may be understandably hesitant to bring suit. Finally, an employee who brings such a suit could reasonably fear reprisals from fellow members whose position with regard to the union is different. Nonetheless, in the 15 years following passage of the act, more than 1,500 private suits were filed by union members alleging Title I violations.

In 2002 Deputy Secretary D. Cameron Findlay of the U.S. Department of Labor, in testimony before the House Subcommittee on Employer-Employee Relations, Subcommittee on Workforce Protections, and the Committee on Education and the Workforce, confessed that the Department of Labor had not done an effective job of enforcing the act. With regard to Title II, for example, Findlay pointed out that in 1998 more than 30 percent of required union filers were either late or did not file financial reports at all; that number rose to 34 percent in 2000. Additionally, the Labor Department's Office of Labor-Management Standards, which conducts audits of these financial reports, audited 1,583 in 1984 but only 238 in 2001. According to Findlay, 10 of the nation's largest unions have never been audited.

Key Players

Griffin, Robert Paul (1923–): Born in Detroit, Michigan, Griffin was admitted to the Michigan bar in 1950. After practicing law, he was elected as a Republican to the 85th Congress, where he served from 1957 to 1966. In May 1966 he was appointed to fill a Senate vacancy caused by the death of Patrick McNamara, and later that year he was elected to a full term. In 1972 he was reelected, but he lost his bid for reelection in 1978.

Landrum, Phillip Mitchell (1907–1990): Landrum was born in Martin, Georgia, where he was admitted to the bar in 1941 after serving as superintendent of a high school in Nelson, Georgia, from 1937. He ran unsuccessfully for Congress in 1942, but after World War II he was assistant attorney general of Georgia (1946–1947) and executive secretary to the governor of Georgia (1947–1948). He was then elected as a Democrat to the 83rd and 11 succeeding congresses (1953–1977).

McClellan, John L. (1896–1977): McClellan was born in Sheridan, Arkansas. He was admitted to the Arkansas bar in 1913 and practiced law until he entered politics in 1920 as city attorney in Malvern, Arkansas. In 1926 he was elected prosecuting attorney for the Seventh Judicial District of Arkansas. In 1934 he was elected to the U.S. House of Representatives, where he served two terms before launching an unsuccessful bid for a Senate seat. In 1942 he tried again, this time successfully, and he served in the Senate until his death. He gained public notice not only as chair of the Senate Select Committee on Improper Activities in the Labor or Management Field but also for leading a walkout of the McCarthy communist witch hunt hearings and, later, for investigating the activities of Jimmy Hoffa and Texas financier Billie Sol Estes.

See also: *Taft-Hartley Act; Wagner Act.*

BIBLIOGRAPHY

Books

Bellace, Janice R., and Alan D. Berkowitz. *The Landrum-Griffin Act: Twenty Years of Federal Protection of Union Members' Rights.* Labor Relations and Public Policy Series No. 19. Philadelphia: The Wharton School, University of Pennsylvania, 1979.

Gregory, Charles O. *Labor and the Law.* New York: W. W. Norton & Co., 1961.

Koretz, Robert F., ed. *Statutory History of the United States: Labor Organization.* New York, Chelsea House, 1970.

Lee, R. Alton. *Eisenhower and Landrum-Griffin: A Study in Labor-Management Politics.* Lexington, KY: University of Kentucky Press, 1990.

Taylor, Benjamin J., and Fred Witney. *Labor Relations Law,* 3rd ed. Englewood Cliffs, NJ: Prentice-Hall, 1979.

Other

Findlay, D. Cameron. Testimony before the House Subcommittee on Employer–Employee Relations, Subcommittee on Workforce Protections, and the Committee on Education and the Workforce. 10 April 2002 [cited 14 October 2002]. <http://edworkforce.house.gov/hearings/107th/wp/lmrda41002/findlay.htm>.

Interim Report of the Senate Select Committee on Improper Activities in the Labor or Management Field, Report No. 1417. 85th Congress, 1958.

—Michael J. O'Neal

La Semana Trágica: *See* **Tragic Week.**

Lawrence Textile Strike

United States 1912

Synopsis

The 1912 textile strike in Lawrence, Massachusetts, was one of the most heroic struggles and resounding victories of the U.S. working class and one of the most successful efforts of the Industrial Workers of the World (IWW). A distinctive characteristic was the diversity of the workforce: a variety of immigrant groups rallied to the strike, women played as decisive a role as the men, and children (many of whom were textile workers) played a powerful role as well. The strike rocked the nation. It is sometimes known as the "Bread and Roses" strike, thus associated with the stirring socialist-feminist anthem of that name written by James Oppenheim. Although there is scholarly controversy over whether that song was inspired by the Lawrence strike, it is obvious that the spirit of the Lawrence strike was consistent with that of the song: "Our lives shall not be sweated from birth until life closes; Hearts starve as well as bodies; give us bread, but give us roses!" The strike's outcome posed fundamental questions for the U.S. labor movement.

Timeline

1891: French troops open fire on workers during a 1 May demonstration at Fourmies, where employees of the Sans Pareille factory are striking for an eight-hour workday. Nine people are killed—two of them children—and 60 more are injured.

1897: In the midst of a nationwide depression, Mrs. Bradley Martin, daughter of Carnegie Steel magnate Henry Phipps, throws a lavish party at New York's recently opened Waldorf-Astoria Hotel, where she has a suite decorated to look like Versailles. Her 900 guests, dressed in Louis XV period costumes, consume sixty cases of champagne.

1902: Second Anglo-Boer War ends in victory for Great Britain. It is a costly victory, however, resulting in the loss of more British lives (5,774) than any conflict between 1815 and 1914. The war also sees the introduction of concentration camps, used by the British to incarcerate Boer civilians.

1905: Russian Revolution of 1905 occurs. Following the "bloody Sunday" riots before the Winter Palace in St. Petersburg in January, revolution spreads throughout Russia, in some places spurred on by newly formed workers' councils, or soviets. Among the most memorable incidents of the revolt is the mutiny aboard the battleship *Potemkin.* Suppressed by the czar, the revolution brings an end to liberal reforms, and thus sets the stage for the larger revolution of 1917.

1908: An earthquake in southern Italy and Sicily kills some 150,000 people.

1910: Revolution breaks out in Mexico, and will continue for the next seven years.

Protesting child textile workers of Lawrence parade down New York City street, 1912. © Corbis. Reproduced by permission.

1912: The First Balkan War, which results in the defeat of Turkey by the allied forces of Bulgaria, Serbia, Greece, and Montenegro, begins. A peace treaty the following year partitions the majority of remaining Turkish holdings in Europe between the victors.

1912: *Titanic* sinks on its maiden voyage, from Southampton to New York, on 14 April. More than 1,500 people are killed.

1912: New Mexico and Arizona are admitted to the Union as the forty-seventh and forty-eighth states, respectively— the last of the contiguous U.S. territories to achieve statehood.

1914: On 28 June in the town of Sarajevo, then part of the Austro-Hungarian Empire, Serbian nationalist Gavrilo Princip assassinates Austrian Archduke Francis Ferdinand and wife Sophie. In the weeks that follow, Austria declares war on Serbia, and Germany on Russia and France, while Great Britain responds by declaring war on Germany. By the beginning of August, the lines are drawn, with the Allies (Great Britain, France, Russia, Belgium, Serbia, Montenegro, and Japan) against the

Central Powers (Germany, Austria-Hungary, and Turkey).

1918: The Second Battle of the Marne in July and August is the last major conflict on the Western Front. In November, Kaiser Wilhelm II abdicates, bringing an end to the war.

1922: Inspired by the Bolsheviks' example of imposing revolution by means of a coup, Benito Mussolini leads his blackshirts in an October "March on Rome," and forms a new fascist government.

Event and Its Context

The textile mills of Lawrence attracted over the years a diverse, multiethnic labor force as waves of immigrant families were drawn into the area. By 1912 there was an impressive mixture of humanity working in the mills: 30,000 workers, composed of 25 ethnic groups speaking 45 languages. Working-class families constituted more than 60,000 inhabitants in an industrial city of about 80,000.

The average wage in the mills was notoriously low at 16 cents an hour, which—given periodic unemployment—yielded a yearly income of less than $500 in a period when it was estimated that an average family could not live on less than $900 a year. Consequently, a number of families had to have more than one family member, sometimes parents and children alike, working in the mills to earn enough money to make ends meet. Half of all children between the ages of 14 and 18 living in Lawrence worked in the mills. The average workweek was 60 hours, and conditions were such that "a considerable number of the boys and girls die within the first two or three years after beginning work," according to a knowledgeable local physician, who added: "Thirty-six out of every 100 of all men and women who work in the mill die before or by the time they are 25 years of age."

Unionization efforts in Lawrence had not succeeded in forging large organizations. Less than 2,500 workers in the Lawrence mills were union members. Most of them were distributed among 10 weak craft locals that represented more highly skilled workers including engineers and machinists, cotton and woolen yarn workers, loom-fixers, warp preparers, and mule-spinners. Only one of these craft unions—the 200-member Mule Spinners Union—had a national affiliation with the United Textile Workers of America in the American Federation of Labor (AFL). By this period, the dominant trend in the AFL involved a commitment to a "pure-and-simple" unionism that accepted the capitalist system and tended to dismiss efforts to organize unskilled workers (especially the new immigrants from areas outside of western Europe, such as the majority of Lawrence mill workers). One AFL official was quite explicit in his description of these workers as "an unassimilated and un-American element so large and so varied in its racial composition as to make it well nigh impossible to disseminate among these people the advantages of unionism."

The Industrial Workers of the World (IWW) had established a presence in Lawrence in 1906, building up IWW Local 20 as part of the National Industrial Union of Textile Workers with a base among Italian, French-Canadian, Belgian, and English-speaking workers. The *Outlook*, a conservative weekly, described the IWW viewpoint in a discussion of national IWW leader "Big Bill" Haywood: "Haywood does not want unions of weavers, unions of spinners, unions of loom-fixers, unions of wool-sorters, but he wants one comprehensive union of all textile workers, which in time will take over the textile factories, as the steel workers will take over the steel mills and the railway workers the railways." In his autobiography, the IWW leader proudly reproduced this description, which continued, "Haywood interprets the class conflict literally as a war which is always on, which becomes daily more bitter and uncompromising, which can end only with the conquest of capitalistic society by proletarians or wage workers, organized industry by industry."

Ironically, it was the implementation of a labor reform that sparked a massive uprising and general strike that closed the Lawrence mills. When that happened, only the IWW was in a position to provide leadership.

The Strike

In 1911 the Massachusetts state legislature passed a bill that was scheduled to go into effect on 1 January 1912. The bill stipulated that women and children under 18 years of age must not work more than 54 hours a week. In fact, 44.6 percent of the work force was female and 11.5 percent was younger than 18 years. The Lawrence mill owners decided to cut all their workers' hours to 54 per week. The employers ignored inquiries from the unions, including the IWW, regarding how this change would affect the employees' wages. Workers got their answer upon receipt of their pay envelopes.

"Short pay! Short pay!" came shouts in Polish as women workers walked off the job in one mill. Similar reactions spread among workers of other ethnic groups throughout many of the mills. Among the more numerous Italian workers, leaders arose who systematically moved to shut down all the mills by any means necessary and closed five mills before police intervened. On the following day, a young but seasoned IWW organizer named Joseph Ettor arrived to help forge this spontaneous mass uprising into the formidable working-class battalions that would be needed to confront the combined power of the employers, city government, police, and state militia. By the end of the first week, 14,000 workers were on strike.

Ettor emphasized to the workers that "you can hope for no success on any policy of violence," noting that "in the last analysis, all the blood spilled will be your blood," and that "violence necessarily means the loss of the strike." He added, "Remember, you are also armed . . . with your labor power, which you can withhold and stop production." He and his comrades repeatedly pointed out that "they cannot weave cloth with bayonets." Ettor emphasized the need for solidarity and that division among the ranks would ensure their failure. He stated, "Among workers there is only one nationality, one race, one creed. . . . Remember always that you are workers with interests against those of the mill-owners."

Ettor's effectiveness derived in part from the efforts of various activists from Lawrence and the New England area: IWW Local 20 president John Adamson, Angelo Rocco among the Italians, Louis Picavet and Joseph Bedard among the French

Canadians, Cyrille De Tollenaere among the Franco-Belgians, Ed Reilly among the Irish, Samuel Lipson among the Jews, and William Yates and Thomas Holliday among the English. Given the importance of women in the strike, the roles played by such militant workers as Anna Welzenbach, Rose Cardullo, and Josephine Liss were crucial.

Of the 30,000 textile workers in Lawrence, the great majority joined the IWW-led strike. These included 7,000 Italians, 6,000 Germans, 5,000 French Canadians, a mix of 5,000 English-speakers (U.S.-born, as well as Irish, Scottish, English, etc.), 2,500 Poles, 2,000 Lithuanians, 1,100 Franco-Belgians, 1,000 Syrians, and smaller numbers of Portuguese, Russians, Jews, Turks, Greeks, Letts, and others.

The workers elected a 12-person strike committee to coordinate daily efforts. The strike committee reported to a 56-person (later 60-person) general strike committee that met every morning and that represented the major nationalities involved in the strike. Behind each committee was a substitute committee intended to prevent disruption of strike activities in case of inevitable arrests and possible casualties during the strike. Ultimate decision-making power resided in the mass meetings of all strikers—men, women, and children—held on Saturdays and Sundays to communicate information on latest developments, to consider and vote on proposals of the general strike committee, to hear inspiring speeches and the native music of the various ethnic groups, and to join in singing stirring labor songs.

The strikers decided on four basic demands: (1) a 15 percent wage increase, (2) adoption of the 54-hour workweek, (3) abolition of the premium and bonus systems (connected to work speed-ups) and double pay for overtime, and (4) no discrimination against strikers for strike activities.

Effective Organization, National Attention, Victory

Big Bill Haywood noted that "the strikers handled their own affairs. . . . It was a democracy." A variety of subcommittees managed various aspects of the strike. In addition to mobilizing strikers to maintain mass picket lines, often confronting the police and militia, strikers devoted considerable effort to winning more workers to the strike and discouraging scabs from continuing to work. The strikers also managed six stores and 11 soup kitchens. The union sent out 120 relief investigators to determine the workers' needs. A fund-raising committee labored to secure about $75,000 in contributions needed to meet the expenses of the strike and to ensure that each family received between $2 and $5.50 for food each week, with an additional $1.50 every two weeks for fuel and clothing. Two volunteer doctors provided free medical care. Legal defense was provided to the many strikers who were arrested in the course of the strike. The committees also worked on the all-important matter of publicity to present the workers' case to the larger public. Vital cultural activities drew on the creative energies and lifted the spirits of the workers with music for the mass meetings, the poetry of such soulful and militant organizers as Arturo Giovannitti, as well as colorful and buoyant parades with banners and flags and song after song.

When Ettor and Giovannitti were arrested on trumped-up charges, other IWW militants—Haywood, Elizabeth Gurley Flynn, William Trautmann, and others—took their places. The

hulking, battled-scarred Haywood seemed to symbolize the rugged spirit of the American West and embraced the ethnic diversity of Lawrence, insisting, "They cannot break our ranks as long as we retain our unity." Elizabeth Gurley Flynn, a young and vibrant woman known as "labor's Joan of Arc," later recalled how the strikers rallied around the concept of solidarity, "a beautiful word in all the languages." In this multiethnic context, the call "workers unite" was an example of internationalism, Flynn noted. "It was also real Americanism—the first they had heard. 'One nation indivisible, with liberty and justice for all.' They hadn't found it here, but they were willingly fighting to create it."

A distinctive feature of the strike was the mass participation of working women. "We held special meetings for the women, at which Haywood and I spoke," Flynn noted. Rejecting "the old-world attitude of man as the 'lord and master,'" IWW organizers "resolutely set out to combat those notions. The women wanted to picket. They were strikers as well as wives and were valiant fighters."

The strike captured national attention thanks to its diversity and creative energy, its effectiveness and uncompromising militancy, and the fact that antistrike slanders, repression, and conspiracies on the part of Lawrence's "respectable" classes frequently backfired. Perhaps the most colossal blunder was a police assault on a demonstration by children. Working-class families in other cities and towns opened their homes to the working-class children of Lawrence for the duration of the strike. Reacting to the sympathetic publicity that this had created for the strikers, the authorities violently attacked and arrested a contingent of children who were en route to the train station on 24 February. Many witnesses, including journalists, were present at the debacle.

The resulting national scandal not only generated more sympathy for the strikers, but also generated a congressional investigation into the causes of the strike and the conditions of the workers, which further increased public sympathy for the strikers. Although the AFL did not rally to support the strike led by its radical competitor (in fact, the small local of the United Textile Workers denounced the strike and crossed the picket line), there was widespread labor support throughout the country and mounting political pressure on the mill owners to bargain with the strikers.

Pressure following "the children's affair" proved decisive. Negotiations began on 29 February, and within two weeks the parties forged an agreement that substantially raised wages and maintained the 54-hour week, with more modest increases for overtime work and a promise of no sanctions against strikers. The remarkable victory brought the strike to an end. The victory was "compounded" after a sustained defense campaign that involved a 24-hour sympathy strike when strike leaders Ettor and Giovannetti were found not guilty and released from jail on 24 November.

Aftermath and Legacy

The Lawrence strike was the outstanding victory of the IWW's history, and yet within a year its power among the workers had collapsed. Not all 1912 strikers were part of the IWW, but membership had swelled from less than 300 to 10,000 in that year—only to fall to 700 by 1913 and 400 by

1914. There were several factors at work. One key was the nature of the IWW itself. The article from the weekly *Outlook*, quoted proudly and extensively in "Big Bill" Haywood's book, described the basic IWW orientation this way: "Haywood places no trust in trade agreements [i.e., contracts between employer and employee], which, according to his theory, lead merely to social peace and 'put the workers to sleep.' Let the employer lock out his men when he pleases, and let the workmen strike when they please. . . . What he desires is not a treaty of industrial peace between two high contracting parties, but merely the creation of a proletarian impulse which will eventually revolutionize society."

Whereas most unions in this period, including the more radical of the AFL unions led by socialists, sought to reach and codify an understanding with the employers through contracts, the IWW chose a course of perpetual struggle. Yet, given the difficulty of mobilizing sufficient forces to sustain a victorious struggle, this approach increased its members' vulnerability. The union's enemies increased their efforts to undermine and dislodge the IWW in Lawrence after the 1912 victory. The absence of a contract, along with the IWW's uncompromising radicalism, made this easier.

A persistent barrage of anti-IWW propaganda with accusations of "un-Americanism" and "Godlessness" was not entirely ineffective, especially when accompanied by persistent efforts to pit ethnic groups against each other and to intimidate workers with petty and not-so-petty forms of repression and reprisal. Strong indications point to manipulation of the local labor market by employers so that during economic downturns Lawrence would be flooded by new immigrant waves, and those who had comprised the IWW's member base were forced to leave the area. Consequently, within two years none of the local 1912 strike leaders remained in any of the Lawrence mills.

Yet the legacy of Lawrence strike influenced workers in future strikes that rocked Lawrence in 1919 and the 1930s and in labor struggles elsewhere, especially as the CIO began to build mass industrial unions a quarter of a century later. "The strike had been a magnificent demonstration of solidarity," Haywood later reflected, "and of what solidarity can do for the workers."

Key Players

Ettor, Joseph (1885–1948): Born in Brooklyn and raised in San Francisco, Ettor worked on the railroad, in a lumber mill, in shipbuilding, and in cigarmaking before becoming a member of the Industrial Workers of the World (IWW) in 1906. He was an experienced organizer and strike leader by the time he came to Lawrence in 1912. In 1915 he became assistant secretary and general organizer of the IWW but left the organization in 1916 over sharp disagreements with IWW leader William Haywood. After 1925 Ettor abandoned radical politics and became a farmer and winemaker in California.

Flynn, Elizabeth Gurley (1890–1964): Born of radical Irish immigrants in Concord, New Hampshire, Flynn grew up in poverty in the South Bronx and joined the IWW in 1906. Her prominence in the organization ended in 1916 following differences with "Big Bill" Haywood, but she remained a member until 1928. She also helped to found the Workers

Defense League and the American Civil Liberties Union and was an early supporter of the International Labor Defense. Sympathetic to the communist movement for many years, she formally joined the U.S. Communist Party in 1938 and was one of its leading members until her death.

Giovannetti, Arturo (1882–1959): An Italian-born writer and orator, Giovannetti had upper-class origins but worked as a coal miner, bookkeeper, and teacher. He was influenced variously by Catholic, Protestant, Marxist, and anarchist thought and edited the socialist weekly, *Il Proletario*, while leading the Italian Socialist Federation of North America. He followed Joseph Ettor in breaking with the IWW in 1916. In later years he was associated with the International Ladies Garment Workers Union.

Haywood, William D. (1869–1928): Born in Salt Lake City, Haywood went to work in the copper mines at the age of 15, learning about industrial unionism and socialism from a member of the Knights of Labor. Becoming a member of the Western Federation of Miners in 1896, he became the union's secretary-treasurer in 1901. In 1905 he became a founder and the central leader of the IWW. Opposing U.S. entry into World War I, he was arrested under the Sedition Act. He sympathized with the Russian Revolution and fled to the Soviet Union in 1921, where he became part of the communist movement.

See also: *American Federation of Labor; Industrial Workers of the World.*

———

BIBLIOGRAPHY

Books
Buhel, Mari Jo, Paul Buhle, and Dan Georgakas, eds. *Encyclopedia of the American Left*, 2nd Edition. New York: Oxford University Press, 1998.

Cahn, William. *Lawrence 1912: The Bread and Roses Strike*. New York: Pilgrim Press, 1980.

Cannon, James P. *The First Ten Years of American Communism, Report of a Participant*. New York: Lyle Stuart, 1962.

Dubofsky, Melvyn. *We Shall Be All: A History of the IWW*. New York: Quadrangle Books, 1973.

Flynn, Elizabeth Gurley. *I Speak My Own Piece: Autobiography of "The Rebel Girl."* New York: Masses and Mainstream, 1955.

Foner, Philip S. *History of the Labor Movement in the United States,* Volume IV: *The Industrial Workers of the World, 1905–1917*. New York: International Publishers, 1965.

Haywood, William D. *Bill Haywood's Book: The Autobiography of "Big Bill" Haywood*. New York: International Publishers, 1929.

Kornbluh, Joyce L. *Rebel Voices: An IWW Anthology*. Chicago: Charles H. Kerr, 1988.

Thompson, Fred W., and Patrick Murfin. *The I.W.W.: Its First Seventy Years, 1905–1975*. Chicago: Industrial Workers of the World, 1976.

—Paul Le Blanc

Legalitarian Strike

Italy 1922

Synopsis

In the face of repeated fascist attacks and violence against trade unionists and left-wing militants (the so-called phenomenon of fascist *squadrismo*), the Italian Alliance for Labor, a coalition of the major Italian trade unions, decided to call for a general strike on 1 August 1922. In a climate of political instability in which the consensus was fragmented into a myriad of different parties, both the government headed by Ivanoe Bonomi and the one formed by Luigi Facta after the 1921 general election had proved passive and unable to stop the fascists. The organizers' intentions were to use the strike to restore legality (thus the title, "legalitarian strike") against the atmosphere of threat and intimidation that the fascists had been spreading before and after the general election. In fact, the strike was a failure and opened the way to power for Benito Mussolini, who, after the fascist "March on Rome," became prime minister in October later in the same year.

Timeline

1907: At the Second Hague Peace Conference, 46 nations adopt 10 conventions governing the rules of war.

1912: *Titanic* sinks on its maiden voyage, from Southampton to New York, on 14 April. More than 1,500 people are killed.

1917: In Russia, a revolution in March (or February according to the old Russian calendar) forces the abdication of Czar Nicholas II. By July, Alexander Kerensky has formed a democratic socialist government, and continues to fight the Germans, even as starvation and unrest sweep the nation. On 7 November (25 October old style), the Bolsheviks under V. I. Lenin and Leon Trotsky seize power. By 15 December, they have removed Russia from the war by signing the Treaty of Brest-Litovsk with Germany.

1919: With the formation of the Third International (Comintern), the Bolshevik government of Russia establishes its control over Communist movements worldwide.

1922: Great Britain establishes the Irish Free State as a dominion of the British Empire.

1922: With the centuries-old Ottoman Empire dissolved, Mustafa Kemal, a.k.a. Atatürk, overthrows the last sultan and establishes the modern Turkish republic.

1922: Union of Soviet Socialist Republics (U.S.S.R.) is formed.

1922: Published this year James Joyce's novel *Ulysses* and T. S. Eliot's poem *The Waste* Land will transform literature and inaugurate the era of modernism.

1925: European leaders attempt to secure the peace at the Locarno Conference, which guarantees the boundaries between France and Germany, and Belgium and Germany.

Benito Mussolini. AP/Wide World Photos. Reproduced by permission.

1927: Charles A. Lindbergh makes the first successful solo nonstop flight across the Atlantic, and becomes an international hero.

1932: When Ukrainians refuse to surrender their grain to his commissars, Stalin seals off supplies to the region, creating a manmade famine that will produce a greater death toll than the entirety of World War I.

Event and Its Context

Fascist Violence During the Bonomi and Facta Ministries and the Constitution of the Alliance for Labor

The Italian general election held in May 1921 elected a conspicuous number of fascist deputies for the first time and was a surprising success for the Fascist National Party (FNP) leaders. Together with the liberal democrats headed by Giovanni Giolitti, the political force that had governed Italy in the first two decades of the twentieth century, the fascists had formed the National Blocks. Giolitti's aim for this alliance (which was approved with several reservations within its own party) was twofold. First, he hoped that the National Blocks would put a stop to the growth of the Fascist Party by placing its candidates on the same ballot with more experienced and respected liberal politicians so as to diminish their chances of being elected. Second and more important, the Blocks represented a vast coalition of moderate and conservative forces that could appeal to the Italian bourgeoisie against the threat of the two main mass parties: the Italian Popular Party (PPI, of Christian-Democratic inspiration) and the Socialist Party. Yet the results went against Giolitti's expectations. The Socialist Party lost 34 seats but maintained a large parliamentary group of 122 deputies, many more than Giolitti had expected. In addition, the PPI gained seven deputies, increasing from 100 to 107 seats. The National Blocks took 275 seats, but the elected deputies for the Blocks were extremely heterogeneous and thus difficult for Giolitti to control. The fascists managed to elect 45 deputies, a striking result considering that this was the first political outing for many of their candidates. Two constituencies elected Benito Mussolini, and the fascist strategy to concentrate their votes on certain candidates paid off: the number of fascists elected to Parliament was almost double the number that Giolitti had expected in his more pessimist forecasts. The electoral campaign had been characterized by the intimidation and violence of fascist squads or *squadrismo* against socialist militants and trade union members. The Fascist Party was clearly entering its second phase: this was its offensive stage, following a period in the margins of the Italian political life after the humiliating results of the 1919 election.

In this climate of political fragmentation, King Vittorio Emanuele III appointed Bonomi as prime minister. His government was supported by a diverse coalition formed by parts of the National Blocks (on whose lists Bonomi himself had been elected) and by the PPI. The Bonomi ministry represented a serious moment of crisis for Italian institutions and was unable to face and to counteract effectively fascist violence, which continued almost undisturbed. Bonomi made several decisions designed to contain the aggressions of the squads, including restrictions on gun licenses and on the circulation of vehicles that were not allowed to transport groups of people. He also gave full powers to the *prefetti* (the local chiefs of police) to ban political organizations whose names and actions suggested that they were, in fact, military groups. Yet these measures had very limited success. In most areas, the behavior of the authorities was designed to keep the fascists in line and to use them against the communists where they were more active.

Less than six months after its formation, the Bonomi ministry was progressively embattled because of its own internal divisions and the opposition of the socialists. Several forces were trying to oppose the slow but determined rise in power of the fascists. On 9 February 1922 the railway section of the General Confederation of Labor (CGL, whose majority was linked to the Socialist Party) started negotiations with other labor forces to reach a common platform from which to counteract the violence of fascist squads. The talks ended on 20 February with the constitution of the Alliance for Labor, a political organization that included the CGL, the *Unione Italiano del Lavoro* (UIL), the Italian Anarcho-Syndicalist Union (USI), and the National Federation of Harbor Workers. Under the ideological and political direction of the socialist members of the CGL, one of the main goals of the alliance was, in the words of the socialist leader Pietro Nenni, "the alliance of proletarian forces, which aims to the restoration of civil liberties and common rights together with the defense of the general rights obtained by the working classes, both on economic and moral grounds."

The demise of the Bonomi ministry coincided with the birth of the alliance. This was already a defeat for the newly consti-

tuted alliance, whose socialist trade unionists were trying to persuade socialist deputies to support Bonomi in exchange for a program of restoring civil liberties. In spite of the opposition of Luigi Sturzo, one of the PPI's most charismatic leaders, the liberals, led by Facta, and the PPI supported the new government led by Facta. From its start, the Facta government was therefore a weak one. During his first two months as prime minister, Facta did not face serious crises. However, in May 1922 the beginning of the agricultural season and the first divisions within the ruling parties persuaded the fascists to intensify their campaign of intimidation throughout Italy. The aim of the fascists was clearly to erase the socialist organizations that were still resisting as well as to preempt any agreement between leftist labor organizations and Catholic and republican ones. There was a new dimension to this renewed fascist offensive. Thousands of armed militants would occupy villages and towns and then proceed with the methodical destruction of all working-class organizations. Facta proved completely unable to face this political cleansing.

The Legalitarian Strike

In June the CGL and the reformist minority of the Socialist Party tried unsuccessfully to push the more extremist and uncompromising majority of the party (the *massimalisti*) to open negotiations with Facta. The majority refused, following the same behavior that had led to the end Bonomi's ministry. In July the government resigned while the country fell prey to the violence of fascist squads. With the persistent clamor for and the imminent formation of a government open to the extreme right and to the fascists, the socialists decided to appeal to the masses. They hoped that the PPI and the other democratic forces would refuse to support any kind of government that was not openly antifascist. In July the Alliance for Labor declared several regional strikes that emanated more from the workers' frustration than from a coherent political plan.

The different working-class organizations were facing a vast crisis. The violence of the fascists had taken them by surprise, and in several areas it had successfully cut their links with the masses. Therefore, the situation was not particularly favorable for a general national strike. Yet the parliamentary group of the Socialist Party, including its reformist deputies, approved a motion on 28 July to support any type of action that aimed to restore the defense of freedom and the right to political organization. This was the beginning of the general strike, or "legalitarian strike" as socialist leader Filippo Turati called it. The same evening, the socialist-led Chamber of Labor in Rome declared that if the Alliance for Labor had not called for a general strike, they would have parted from it. On 1 August the Alliance proclaimed the general strike in defense of "political and trade-union rights, threatened by the rising reactionary factions," without specifying its duration. Even antifascist politicians judged the strike as a negative move, and Catholic working-class organizations refused to participate in it. Sturzo defined it as a "deadly moral and political mistake." Historians have been even harsher. In his much debated multivolume study on Mussolini, Renzo De Felice claimed that the 1922 general strike was the crucial event that defeated the already beleaguered Italian democracy, eliminating the last obstacles on Mussolini's way to power.

The strike ended the political negotiations for the creation of a new government. Facta received the task of forming his second ministry, which practically became a copy of the first one. However, the most important political consequence of the strike was to stop the detachment of the Italian bourgeoisie from fascism. The Italian bourgeoisie were looking with increasing concerns at the phenomenon of the *squadrismo* and its violence. Yet the general strike called by the alliance rekindled in the middle classes the anxiety about a "red" revolution, and fascism became once again the only possible means to eliminate the left from the political scene. The Fascist Party did not lose this chance to act as savior of the nation: on 1 August its leaders ordered all of the party's militants to be ready to be called to end the strike. They issued a 48-hour ultimatum, after which, their note claimed, they would replace the government in the protection of its citizens. Faced by this challenge, the alliance backed off and declared the end of the strike on 2 August. The fascists, however, were on the offensive and occupied several important working-class institutions and a number of important Council Houses (such as Milan's). The left was more divided than ever. Its leaders accused each other of causing the strike to fail, which produced a feeling of frustration in the working masses and pushed them toward the Fascist Party. The failure of the legalitarian strike represented the failure of Italian democracy. It was the necessary premise of the March on Rome, which would take place in October and would end with the appointment of Mussolini as prime minister.

Key Players

Facta, Luigi (1861–1930): The last prime minister of the Italian democratic era before the advent of fascism, Facta was the head of two weak governments that proved ineffectual in preventing the establishment of the fascist regime.

Mussolini, Benito (1883–1945): After starting his political career in the Socialist Party, from which Italy was expelled for its interventionist stance in World War I, Mussolini was the founder of the Fascist Nationalist Party and the organizer of the March on Rome. He proclaimed himself dictator in 1925, and his regime lasted until 1945. His reign was known as the *ventennio fascista* (20 years of fascism).

Turati, Filippo (1857–1932): Italian socialist leader belonging to the reformist current of the party. Turati advocated the gradual rise in power of the working classes rather than a proletarian revolution of a Soviet type.

BIBLIOGRAPHY

Books

De Felice, Renzo. *Mussolini il Fascista: La Conquista del Potere, 1921–1925*. Turin, Italy: Einaudi, 1966.
Giudice, Gaspare. *Mussolini*. Turin, Italy: UTET, 1969.
Veneruso, Danilo. *La Vigilia del Fascismo: Il Primo Ministero Facta Nella Crisi Dello Stato Liberale in Italia*. Bologna, Italy: Il Mulino, 1968.

—Luca Prono

William Lloyd Garrison. The Library of Congress.

Liberator Founded

United States 1831

Synopsis

Seeing slavery as an abomination to God and determined to force its immediate end in the United States, William Lloyd Garrison founded the nation's first militant antislavery newspaper, *The Liberator*, in 1831 in Boston, Massachusetts. The newspaper aimed to shame whites for their support of slavery by exposing northern links to bondage, by revealing the horrors of slave life, and by showing the cruelty behind the nascent movement to gradually end slave labor. Southerners banned Garrison's publication and blamed his relentless attacks on the institution of slavery for causing the violent Nat Turner-led slave revolt. Despite repeated attempts to suppress his newspaper, Garrison persevered to spark the rise of abolitionist sentiment in the North.

Timeline

1808: U.S. Congress bans the importation of slaves.

1812: The War of 1812, sparked by U.S. reactions to oppressive British maritime practices undertaken in the wake of the wars against Napoleon, begins in June. It lasts until December 1814.

1815: Napoleon returns from Elba, and his supporters attempt to restore him as French ruler, but just three months later, forces led by the Duke of Wellington defeat his armies at Waterloo. Napoleon spends the remainder of his days as a prisoner on the island of St. Helena in the south Atlantic.

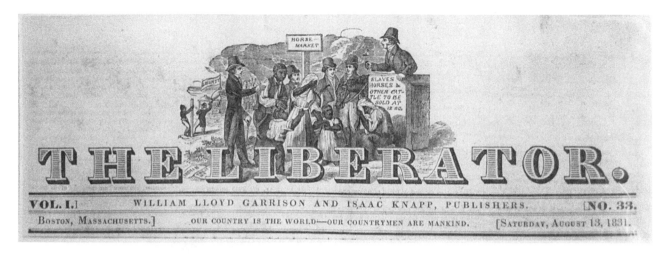

Masthead of *The Liberator*, published by William Lloyd Garrison. The Library of Congress.

1818: In a decisive defeat of Spanish forces, soldier and statesman Simón Bolívar leads the liberation of New Granada, which includes what is now Colombia, Panama, Venezuela, and Ecuador. With Spanish power now waning, Bolívar becomes president and virtual dictator of the newly created nation of Colombia.

1825: New York Stock Exchange opens.

1828: Election of Andrew Jackson as president begins a new era in American history.

1830: Mormon Church is founded by Joseph Smith.

1831: Young British naturalist Charles Darwin sets sail from England aboard the H.M.S. *Beagle* bound for South America, where he will make discoveries leading to the formation of his theory of evolution by means of natural selection.

1833: British Parliament passes the Slavery Abolition Act, giving freedom to all slaves throughout the British Empire.

1836: In Texas's war of independence with Mexico, the defenders of the Alamo, among them Davy Crockett and Jim Bowie, are killed in a siege. Later that year, Texas wins the Battle of San Jacinto and secures its independence.

1839: England launches the First Opium War against China. The war, which lasts three years, results in the British gaining a free hand to conduct a lucrative opium trade, despite opposition by the Chinese government.

1845: From Ireland to Russia, famine plagues Europe, killing some 2.5 million people.

Event and Its Context

In the years following the Revolutionary War, a small number of Americans began to agitate against slavery. To hold men, women, and children in bondage for life seemed to many to be contrary to the principles of liberty as embodied in the Declaration of Independence. Yet although a growing number of people opposed slavery, the idea of immediately ending the practice seemed absurd to all but a very few. A gradual end to bondage, antislavery forces argued, would preserve the social and economic stability of the South. Many of these reformers further expressed support for colonization, the gradual end of slavery through the immigration of blacks to Africa, in the belief that African Americans would forever be unable to compete equally with whites and that the best solution lay in the separation of the races.

William Lloyd Garrison

In this climate, William Lloyd Garrison began to gain notoriety. In the 1820s Garrison had attempted to start several newspapers in Massachusetts and Vermont, but all of the ventures had failed, partly because of Garrison's fiery writing style and willingness to provoke conflict. Always sympathetic to the underdog and familiar with black communities from the days of his poverty-stricken childhood, Garrison was a natural champion of the rights of the oppressed, but it appears that he became an abolitionist as the result of a job offer. In 1829 the Quaker abolitionist Benjamin Lundy invited Garrison to Baltimore to coedit *The Genius of Universal Emancipation*, and Garrison soon came to support Lundy's philosophy. A widely discussed libel suit, filed in 1830 by a slave trader who objected to being condemned for slave trading, quickly reversed the young editor's fortunes. Convicted and jailed for 49 days, Garrison publicized his martyrdom for the cause of abolition, then headed to Boston to start a new newspaper, *The Liberator*, first published on 1 January 1831.

Through the pages of *The Liberator*, Garrison pressed for equal treatment of the races, self-advancement through the acquisition of literacy and mechanical skills, united political action, and a thorough repudiation of slavery. Although Garrison shared the publishing duties with Isaac Knapp, a childhood friend and printer, the editorial voice of the paper was Garrison's alone. William Nell, an African American who would eventually write for the newspaper and become a prominent abolitionist in his own right, joined the enterprise as an errand boy. With the motto, "Our Country Is the World—Our Countrymen are Mankind," the newspaper appeared weekly without interruption for 35 years. It typically contained editorials, book reviews, poems, excerpts from the religious and temperance press, factual material on slavery, reports of meetings held to protect the slave trade or register opposition to colonization schemes, and letters from readers. The extraordinarily physical writing style employed in the newspaper made it impossible to evade the issue of slavery. In Garrison's hand, trumpets blared, statues bled, hearts melted, and slave apologists trembled as slavery became the question of the day.

Garrison wanted the newspaper to be a forum for black activists and a vehicle for a biracial political coalition. With money tight at first, Garrison worked odd jobs by day and produced the newspaper at night. Crucial support came from the black community, which provided 500 subscribers in *The Liberator*'s initial year. Given that copies of the paper were typically passed around and posted in reading rooms as well as barbershops, the actual readership of *The Liberator* was considerably greater than the subscription rolls indicated. The influence of *The Liberator* also extended past its actual readers. The paper had no agents and few subscribers south of Washington, D.C., yet the common practice of newspaper exchange put the periodical in the hands of southern editors who reprinted material from it accompanied by bitter condemnations that were picked up by other newspapers. These comments eventually reached Garrison, who commented and began the lively circle anew.

Insisting that slavery could not endure indefinitely in a Christian democratic society, Garrison sought to preserve the Union by removing an evil that, if allowed to grow, would inevitably produce a division of the states. He was determined to heat up the issue until the public felt ashamed of its connection to slavery and angry at granting political privileges to slaveholders. The masthead that Garrison chose for *The Liberator* reflected this desire to provoke as well as his ability to infuriate. Garrison pictured a slave auction in front of the nation's capitol with the flag of liberty blowing atop the building's dome. In 1838 he added to the masthead a second panel that depicted free labor and emancipation. In 1850 he combined the two vignettes with a medallion of Christ rebuking a master while elevating a slave. In response, John C. Calhoun, one of the most powerful men in the United States Senate and a die-hard proponent of slavery, attempted to ban from the mails newspapers with pictorial representations of slave labor.

Nat Turner

Other southerners soon joined Calhoun in expressing their rage at Garrison's provocations. When Nat Turner killed men, women, and children in a slave uprising in Virginia, terrified southerners blamed outside agitators for the bloodbath. Of these agitators, Garrison received the brunt of the blame. Although southerners demanded that northerners silence abolitionists before they succeeded at rending the social fabric of the slave states, supporters of slavery also took steps to stifle Garrison. In October 1831 the town of Georgetown near Washington, D.C., passed a law prohibiting African Americans from taking copies of *The Liberator* out of post offices. The penalty for such an act was a fine and 30 days in jail, plus the threat of being sold into slavery for four months if the fines went unpaid. A Raleigh,

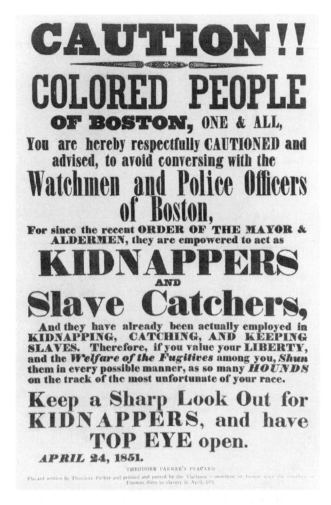

Abolitionist poster, Boston, Massachusetts. The Library of Congress.

North Carolina, grand jury indicted Garrison and Knapp for distributing incendiary matter, and the Georgia state legislature offered a $5,000 reward for anyone who arrested Garrison and brought him to the Peach State for trial on charges of seditious libel.

Colonization

Garrison habitually attacked racial prejudice and political hypocrisy. Because Garrison held that both these qualities could be found in the colonization scheme, he reserved his harshest attacks for its proponents. He charged that colonization had been designed by slaveholders to protect their system from serious criticism, a view that added greatly to his unpopularity. Although Garrison had hoped to use the newspaper to reach reform-minded leaders, the initial apathy of these prominent men turned into open hostility as the editor increased his attacks on colonizationists. When one minister opined about the dangers of immediate emancipation, Garrison responded that this was the first time that religious men had advised the gradual abolition of wickedness.

As Garrison kept clamoring, vigorous opposition to the growing abolition movement mounted in all parts of the nation.

The Missouri Compromise and the Limitations on the Expansion of Slavery

In 1819, when Missouri applied for admission to the Union, the United States had a balance of free states to slave states, with 11 of each. Slavery already existed in the Missouri Territory, and therefore Missouri asked to be admitted as a slave state. This infuriated New England abolitionists, but southern slaveholders were equally incensed at the suggestion of a ban on the importation of slaves as a precondition for Missouri's statehood.

To settle the problem—or at least to put it off a little longer—Congress in 1820 settled on a compromise. Because Maine had also requested admission to the Union, Missouri would enter as a slave state, and Maine as a free state, thus preserving the parity that existed. To limit the further expansion of slavery, Senator Jesse B. Thomas of Illinois drew an imaginary line at 36° 30' North latitude, Missouri's southern boundary. No territory located above that line could be admitted to the Union as a slave state, Thomas proposed, whereas any territory located below it could do so.

At the time when the Missouri Compromise was adopted, the only territories eligible to enter the Union as slave states were Florida and Arkansas. (The latter had been carved off of the southern part of Missouri, and contained part of modern-day Oklahoma.) Later these would join as slaveholding states, as would Texas, then still part of Mexico.

With the exception of a few zealous abolitionists, the people interested in limiting the spread of slavery did so not from humanitarian reasons. Rather, they were concerned that businesses might be hurt by competition with slave labor—and that the extra population of slaves would give slaveholding states an unfair advantage in the apportionment of congressional seats. At the time of its adoption, many wise minds recognized the Missouri Compromise for what it was—a mere stop-gap measure. "This is a reprieve only," said Thomas Jefferson. John Quincy Adams called it "the title page to a great tragic volume." The Missouri Compromise was overturned by the Kansas-Nebraska Act in 1854, which introduced popular sovereignty over the slavery issue and paved the way for further troubles.

Source: Glover Moore. *The Missouri Controversy, 1819–1821.* Lexington: University of Kentucky Press, 1953.

—Judson Knight

tionist meeting, dragged him through the streets, and barely missed lynching him.

Later that year, Garrison assisted the Quaker abolitionist Prudence Crandall in her attempt to open the first boarding school for African American women. An improvement in the condition of black citizens formed an essential element of Garrisonian abolitionist thinking. By reading *The Liberator*, Crandall had been convinced of the moral correctness of abolitionism and the need for better education of black students. The school, designed to instruct future teachers, came under heavy attack by critics who charged Crandall and Garrison with promoting miscegenation. In the face of all these attacks, Garrison remained serene in the belief that he was an instrument of God doing battle with Satan's minions. As he had declared in his opening editorial, "I will not retreat an inch and I will be heard."

Mission Accomplished

When the Civil War began, Garrison changed the motto of the newspaper to, "Proclaim Liberty throughout All the Land, to All the Inhabitants of the Land." He urged President Abraham Lincoln to emancipate all slaves and give compensation only to slaveholding loyal citizens. In 1865, when Congress passed the Thirteenth Amendment and abolished slavery, Garrison considered his life's ambition to have been filled. On 29 December 1865 he published the last issue of *The Liberator*.

Key Players

Crandall, Prudence (1803–1890): An educator, Crandall became the first advocate of desegregated schools when she enrolled black students at her Cranbury Female Seminary in Connecticut in 1832. In 1833 the school became a teacher-training institute exclusively for African American women. A mob attack forced its closure in 1834. Crandall left Connecticut and subsequently ran a school in Illinois before dying at her farm in Kansas.

Garrison, William Lloyd (1805–1879): An antislavery editor, Garrison sparked the abolition movement by publishing *The Liberator* and founding the American Anti-Slavery Society (AAS). With the abolition of slavery, Garrison shut down *The Liberator*, resigned from the AAS, and declared his retirement from the antislavery movement.

Knapp, Isaac (c. 1800–?): A printer and copublisher of *The Liberator*, Knapp ran the newspaper during Garrison's frequent absences. He became estranged from Garrison over differences in abolition strategy.

Lundy, Benjamin (1789–1839): An antislavery editor, Lundy spent much of his career attempting by political means to persuade southerners to end slavery. In 1821 he founded the *Genius of Universal Emancipation* in Mount Pleasant, Ohio, and subsequently published it in Greeneville, Tennessee (1822–1824), Baltimore (1824–1830), and Washington, D.C. (1830–1833). Besides encouraging a boycott of slave-produced goods, the newspaper focused on the interests of whites by emphasizing the unprofitability of slave labor and the danger of slave revolts.

Nell, William (1816–1874): Nell, a free-born African American, became an errand boy for *The Liberator* in 1831. In

In the slave states, abolitionists were threatened, harassed, and expelled. In cities across the North, mobs interrupted abolitionists' meetings, attacked their homes, and assaulted communities of free blacks. In Boston on an October night in 1835, an angry mob of whites threw a rope over Garrison as he left an aboli-

1840 he began writing articles for the newspaper and representing Garrison at various antislavery functions. He authored *Services of Colored Americans in the Wars of 1776 and 1812* (1851) and *Colored Patriots of the American Revolution* (1855).

Turner, Nat (1800–1831): Turner, a Virginia slave, led the first successful slave revolt in the United States, in August 1831. In the belief that God had chosen him to end slavery, Turner organized a band of slaves who killed more than 50 whites before being overcome by local, state, and federal troops. Prior to his execution, Turner granted an interview to a journalist that became the basis of the book *The Confessions of Nat Turner, the Leader of the Late Insurrection in Southampton, Va., as Fully and Voluntarily Made to Thomas R. Gray* (1831).

See also: *Abolition of Slavery: United States; Harpers Ferry Raid.*

BIBLIOGRAPHY

Books

Cain, William E., ed. *William Lloyd Garrison and the Fight Against Slavery: Selections from "The Liberator."* Boston: Bedford Books, 1995.

Mayer, Henry. *All on Fire: William Lloyd Garrison and the Abolition of Slavery.* New York: St. Martin's Press, 1998.

Stewart, James Brewer. *William Lloyd Garrison and the Challenge of Emancipation.* Arlington Heights, IL: Harlan Davidson, 1992.

ADDITIONAL RESOURCES

Books

Phillips, Wendell, and Francis Jackson Garrison. *William Lloyd Garrison, 1805–1879: The Story of His Life Told by His Children.* Boston: Houghton Mifflin, 1885.

Nye, Russel B. *William Lloyd Garrison and the Humanitarian Reformers.* Boston: Little, Brown, 1955.

—Caryn E. Neumann

Lloyd–La Follette Act

United States 1912

Synopsis

The Lloyd–La Follette Act was a civil service reform act passed by Congress under the sponsorship of Robert La Follette, a Progressive senator from Wisconsin. The act established

Robert M. La Follette. The Library of Congress.

procedures for the discharge of federal employees and guaranteed the right of federal employees to communicate with members of Congress, in effect making it the first protective legislation for "whistleblowers." The act also protected the right of federal employees to join unions.

Timeline

1891: French troops open fire on workers during a 1 May demonstration at Fourmies, where employees of the Sans Pareille factory are striking for an eight-hour workday. Nine people are killed—two of them children—and 60 more are injured.

1897: In the midst of a nationwide depression, Mrs. Bradley Martin, daughter of Carnegie Steel magnate Henry Phipps, throws a lavish party at New York's recently opened Waldorf-Astoria Hotel, where she has a suite decorated to look like Versailles. Her 900 guests, dressed in Louis XV period costumes, consume sixty cases of champagne.

1902: Second Anglo-Boer War ends in victory for Great Britain. It is a costly victory, however, resulting in the loss of more British lives (5,774) than any conflict between 1815 and 1914. The war also sees the introduction of concentration camps, used by the British to incarcerate Boer civilians.

1905: Russian Revolution of 1905 occurs. Following the "bloody Sunday" riots before the Winter Palace in St. Petersburg in January, revolution spreads throughout Russia, in some places spurred on by newly formed workers' councils, or soviets. Among the most memorable incidents of the revolt is the mutiny aboard the bat-

George Pendleton. The Library of Congress.

tleship *Potemkin.* Suppressed by the czar, the revolution brings an end to liberal reforms, and thus sets the stage for the larger revolution of 1917.

1908: An earthquake in southern Italy and Sicily kills some 150,000 people.

1910: Revolution breaks out in Mexico, and will continue for the next seven years.

1912: First Balkan War, which results in the defeat of Turkey by the allied forces of Bulgaria, Serbia, Greece, and Montenegro, begins. A peace treaty the following year partitions the majority of remaining Turkish holdings in Europe between the victors.

1912: *Titanic* sinks on its maiden voyage, from Southampton to New York, on 14 April. More than 1,500 people are killed.

1912: New Mexico and Arizona are admitted to the Union as the forty-seventh and forty-eighth states, respectively—the last of the contiguous U.S. territories to achieve statehood.

1914: On 28 June in the town of Sarajevo, then part of the Austro-Hungarian Empire, Serbian nationalist Gavrilo Princip assassinates Austrian Archduke Francis Ferdinand and wife Sophie. In the weeks that follow, Austria declares war on Serbia, and Germany on Russia and France, while Great Britain responds by declaring war on Germany. By the beginning of August, the lines are drawn, with the Allies (Great Britain, France, Russia, Belgium, Serbia, Montenegro, and Japan) against the Central Powers (Germany, Austria-Hungary, and Turkey).

1918: The Second Battle of the Marne in July and August is the last major conflict on the Western Front. In Novem-

ber, Kaiser Wilhelm II abdicates, bringing an end to the war.

1922: Inspired by the Bolsheviks' example of imposing revolution by means of a coup, Benito Mussolini leads his blackshirts in an October "March on Rome," and forms a new fascist government.

Event and Its Context

Civil Service Reform Before 1912

For its first century, the U.S. civil service operated under a "spoils system." Civil service jobs were a form of patronage extended by elected officials to their friends and political supporters. Incumbents in those jobs were usually expected to contribute both time and money to their patrons' political campaigns. While a political party was out of power, it geared up for the next election by recruiting supporters with promises of federal employment. Such a system led to massive inefficiency as civil service workers were usually swept out of office en masse when the opposing political party took power. This problem became particularly acute in the 1840s and 1850s as the rival Whigs and Democrats won every other election. Defenders of the system, including Andrew Jackson, argued that it ensured that civil service employees would diligently execute the policies of the administration that employed them.

Attempts to introduce civil service reform legislation began as early as 1865, but they lacked support both from legislators, who feared that it would disrupt party organization, and at the grass-roots level. During the Ulysses S. Grant and Rutherford B. Hayes administrations, however, support for reform began to grow. Hayes worked toward depoliticizing at least two agencies, the New York Customhouse and the New York Post Office. Matters came to a head on 2 July 1881, when President James A. Garfield was shot. The assassin was Charles J. Guiteau, a disturbed religious fanatic who was widely believed to be a disgruntled office seeker who blamed the president for his failure to gain an appointment as U.S. consul in Paris. Proponents of civil service reform took advantage of this belief to convince the public that the civil service system was responsible for the assassination.

During the summer of 1881, as Garfield lingered near death, delegates from 13 civil service reform organizations met to form the National Civil Service Reform League. This organization led the fight for reform, and out of its efforts came the Pendleton Civil Service Reform Act in 1883, sponsored by Democratic senator George H. Pendleton from Ohio. In creating a merit system and a competitive examination administered by a bipartisan Civil Service Commission, the act was a major step forward, but it was limited in its application. It dealt almost exclusively with entry into the civil service and barely touched on issues of tenure, promotion, and removal. Its only provision having to do with removal was to prohibit removal for refusal to contribute to a political fund or to render political service.

"Battling Bob" La Follette

During the 1890s Robert La Follette was a rising star in the Progressive firmament. A lawyer by trade, La Follette loved oratory and theater, and he put those talents to work throughout his political career. He served in the U.S. House of Representatives as a Republican from 1885 to 1891, and when he returned to his home in Wisconsin, he spent much of the decade on statewide public-speaking campaigns as the acknowledged leader of the growing agrarian revolt. His constant theme was that the "interests"—that is, corporations—were conspiring with the "bosses"—that is, the major political parties and their leaders— to exploit "the people," including small business owners, farmers, and workers. His growing popularity led in 1900 to the state governor's mansion on a platform that included a pledge to manage public resources in the public interest. One component of this pledge was that his administration was to be in the hands of nonpartisan civil servants.

The "Wisconsin Idea" brought La Follette nationwide attention, particularly among Progressives. With their sponsorship, "Battling Bob" was elected to the U.S. Senate in 1905, where he served for 20 years until his death. As a senator he did not put his name to many bills. Perhaps the most significant piece of legislation he sponsored was the La Follette Seamen's Act, which protected merchant seamen from exploitation and conditions amounting almost to involuntary servitude. To many people, however, he was the conscience of the Senate as he pushed uncompromisingly for legislation that he believed was in the interests of the people.

One bill to which La Follette did put his name was the Lloyd–La Follette Act, cosponsored by Representative James Lloyd, a Democrat from Missouri and House minority whip. The act, which became law on 24 August 1912, was part of the Post Office Department's appropriation bill for fiscal year 1913, but it later became part of the U.S. legal code. Authority to enforce the act was vested in the Civil Service Commission and the Office of Economic Opportunity until passage of the Civil Service Reform Act of 1978, which dissolved the Civil Service Commission and transferred its responsibilities to other federal agencies. Still today, the act, in combination with the administrative rules of the agencies that enforce it, provides the regulatory framework that controls the discharge of federal civil service employees.

The chief purpose of the Lloyd–La Follette Act was to protect federal civil servants from arbitrary discharge. Accordingly, it expanded on McKinley's Rule II by stating that persons employed in "classified civil service" could be removed "except for such cause as will promote the efficiency of said service and for reasons given in writing, and the person whose removal is sought shall have notice of the same and of any charges preferred against him."

The act, however, had at least two other purposes. First, it stated that "the right of employees . . . to petition Congress or a Member of Congress, or to furnish information to either House of Congress, or to a committee or Member thereof, may not be interfered with or denied." This provision was a response to gag orders issued by presidents Theodore Roosevelt and William Howard Taft prohibiting federal employees from petitioning Congress without authorization from their superiors. Thus, federal employees could now press wage and other demands directly to Congress.

Second, the act protected the right of civil servants to join employee organizations, including unions. In 1906 President

Roosevelt had issued an order under which federal employees were "forbidden . . . individually or through associations, to solicit an increase of pay or to influence or attempt to influence in their own interest any other legislation whatever." Under the Lloyd–La Follette Act, federal employees gained the right to organize and bargain collectively—but not to strike—without government interference, and they did so for more than two decades before the nation's industrial workers gained similar rights under the National Labor Relations Act of 1935. Ultimately, the Lloyd–La Follette Act paved the way for the formation of such federal unions such as the American Federation of Government Employees and the National Federation of Federal Employees.

Protection of Whistleblowers

Because it protects the rights of federal employees to communicate with Congress, the Lloyd–La Follette Act can be regarded as the first federal "whistleblowers' protection act," for presumably it allowed employees to expose corruption and malfeasance in the agencies and departments for which they worked. In the courts, application of the act turned into battles over the free speech protections of the First Amendment and due process considerations under the Fifth and Fourteenth Amendments.

A case in point is *Arnett v. Kennedy*, which the U.S. Supreme Court decided in 1974. Wayne Kennedy worked for the Office of Economic Opportunity (OEO) in Chicago. In 1972 the regional director of the OEO discharged him for "cause," including "reckless" charges Kennedy had made that the director had offered OEO funds as a bribe to a representative of a community action organization. Contending that his free-speech and due-process rights had been violated, Kennedy filed suit in federal district court, where he was joined by 18 other plaintiffs, who feared that under the Lloyd–La Follette Act they could be discharged for any off-duty public comments they might make. In ruling against Kennedy, the Court held that he was not entitled to any constitutional protections other than those afforded under the terms of the act and that the "cause" provision of the act was not impermissibly vague. The question of whether Kennedy's charges were true was never at issue; the sole issue was whether the Lloyd–La Follette Act gave the director the right to fire him.

In response to numerous and widespread charges of government waste and wrongdoing, Congress passed the Whistleblowers Protection Act of 1989, which, again, should have afforded protection to federal employees. Yet the federal government continues to wrestle with the issue. In 1997, for instance, the Senate, over the objections of the Clinton administration and the Justice Department, passed an intelligence authorization act that would have extended the protections of the Lloyd–La Follette Act to federal whistleblowers who revealed classified information to Congress without going through their superiors. The move came in response to at least two incidents. One involved a CIA analyst who was fired because of his intention to inform Congress about the true state of Pakistan's nuclear capability. The other involved a senior State Department official who was stripped of his security clearance because he informed a member of the House Intelligence Committee about CIA wrongdoing in Guatemala. A later, similar case involved an FBI forensic metallurgist whose superiors prohibited him from telling Congress that he had been pressured by law enforcement officials to endorse what turned out to be a false theory about the cause of the crash of TWA Flight 800 in 1996. In testimony before the Senate Subcommittee on Administrative Oversight, his attorneys argued that the FBI's gag order was a direct violation of the Lloyd–La Follette Act.

Key Players

La Follette, Robert M. (1855–1925): La Follette was born in Primrose, Wisconsin, and began his career as a lawyer. He was a U.S. congressman from 1885 to 1891, governor of Wisconsin from 1901 to 1906, and a U.S. senator from 1906 until his death. In the 1924 presidential election he received one-sixth of the vote as the Progressive Party candidate.

Lloyd, James Tighman (1857–1944): Lloyd was born in Canton, Missouri, and was a sheriff and prosecuting attorney before joining the U.S. House of Representatives (1897–1917), where as a Democrat he was minority whip for eight years. After leaving the House, he practiced law in Washington, D.C.

Pendleton, George (1825–1889): "Gentleman George" Pendleton was born in Cincinnati, Ohio, and served in the Ohio senate before serving in Congress (1857–1865). Later he was a U.S. senator (1879–1885) and ambassador to Germany (1885–1889). His wife, Alice, was the daughter of Francis Scott Key.

See also: *La Follette Seamen's Act; Wagner Act.*

BIBLIOGRAPHY

Books

Hanslow, Kurt L. *The Emerging Law of Labor Relations in Public Employment.* IRL Paperback No. 4. Ithaca, NY: New York State School of Industrial and Labor Relations, Cornell University, 1967.

La Follette, Belle Case, and Fola La Follette. *Robert M. La Follette,* 2 vols. New York: Macmillan, 1953.

Unger, Nancy C. *Fighting Bob La Follette: The Righteous Reformer.* Chapel Hill: University of North Carolina Press, 2000.

Other

Alvin J. Arnett, Director, Office of Economic Opportunity, et al. v. Wayne Kennedy et al. 416 U.S. 134; 94 S.Ct. 1633.

—Michael J. O'Neal

Lochner v. New York

United States 1905

Synopsis

In 1897, in response to wretched working conditions at bakeries in New York State, the state legislature enacted the New York Bakeshop Act, as part of the New York State Labor Law. Among other provisions, the act limited the hours that bakers could work. A bakery owner named Joseph Lochner from Utica, New York, subsequently challenged the Bakeshop Act in court, and the suit eventually made its way to the U.S. Supreme Court. The Supreme Court's upholding of Lochner's challenge to the New York Bakeshop Act became a landmark decision in support of *laissez-faire* economics and the newly invented legal doctrine of "substantive due process." It also touched off what is commonly known as the "Lochner Era," wherein the Court struck down many economic and labor regulations as violating the rights of businesses. The Lochner Era is viewed in many different ways today, but it is most commonly seen in a negative light, as an era during which the Court substituted its own political will and economic theories for those of legislatures.

Timeline

1885: Indian National Congress is founded. In the years that follow, the party will take the helm of India's independence movement.

1890: U.S. Congress passes the Sherman Antitrust Act, which in the years that follow will be used to break up large monopolies.

1895: Brothers Auguste and Louis Lumière show the world's first motion picture—*Workers Leaving the Lumière Factory*—at a café in Paris.

1898: United States defeats Spain in the three-month Spanish-American War. As a result, Cuba gains it independence, and the United States purchases Puerto Rico and the Philippines from Spain for $20 million.

1901: U.S. President William McKinley is assassinated by Leon Czolgosz, an anarchist. Vice President Theodore Roosevelt becomes president.

1903: Russia's Social Democratic Party splits into two factions: the moderate Mensheviks and the hard-line Bolsheviks. Despite their names, which in Russian mean "minority" and "majority," respectively, Mensheviks actually outnumber Bolsheviks.

1904: Russo-Japanese War, which lasts into 1905 and results in a resounding Japanese victory, begins. In Russia, the war is followed by the Revolution of 1905, which marks the beginning of the end of czarist rule; meanwhile, Japan is poised to become the first major non-western power of modern times.

1905: Russian Revolution of 1905 occurs. Following the "bloody Sunday" riots before the Winter Palace in St. Petersburg in January, revolution spreads throughout

Russia, in some places spurred on by newly formed workers' councils, or soviets. Among the most memorable incidents of the revolt is the mutiny aboard the battleship *Potemkin.* Suppressed by the czar, the revolution brings an end to liberal reforms, and thus sets the stage for the larger revolution of 1917.

1905: Albert Einstein presents his special theory of relativity.

1905: In the industrial Ruhr region in Germany, 200,000 miners go on strike.

1909: National Association for the Advancement of Colored People (NAACP) is founded by W. E. B. Du Bois and a number of other prominent black and white intellectuals in New York City.

1914: On the Western Front, the first battles of the Marne and Ypres establish a line that will more or less hold for the next four years. Exuberance is still high on both sides, but will dissipate as thousands of German, French, and British soldiers sacrifice their lives in battles over a few miles of barbed wire and mud. The Eastern Front is a different story: a German victory over Russia at Tannenberg in August sets the stage for a war in which Russia will enjoy little success, and will eventually descend into chaos that paves the way for the 1917 revolutions.

Oliver Wendell Holmes. The Library of Congress

Event and Its Context

Bakeries

During the late 1800s and early 1900s, baking as a profession, along with most of the American economy, had undergone macroeconomic shifts in the wake of the Civil War and the triumph of industrial capitalism that it heralded. Like most other workers, bakers were moving away from working for themselves and toward working for other people. A large number of bakeshops arose in New York State, due to the ease of opening such shops. There also appears to have been a large demand for bakeshop services as more and more people worked and lived in tenement buildings where doing one's own baking could be inconvenient.

The bakeries were often dark, dank, decrepit, and unsafe for workers and customers. Tuberculosis was rampant and bakeries almost certainly contributed to its spread. Contemporary accounts describe great mounds of dough resting on workers' sweaty bodies and knives being carried in their mouths.

Workers were made to work very long hours, in apparent violation of an 1867 eight-hour workday statute that provided for neither penalties nor enforcement of the requirement. In 1891 New York bakers went on strike for a 12-hour workday.

By 1895 the bakers' workweek appears to have stabilized at around 74 hours. This was long, even by the standards of the day, and bakers' working conditions were particularly odious. New York-based labor unions, especially in New York City, were concerned and sought to achieve safer working conditions and shorter hours by using collective bargaining and strikes, to little or no avail. As a general rule, the labor unions of the day were relatively suspicious of politics in general and of legislative action in particular and followed the bargaining strategy associated with Samuel Gompers, president of the American Federation of Labor.

Bakers' unions, however, appear never to have abandoned the legislative strategy, and their lobbying appears to have been behind New York State assembly member Arthur Audett's interest in the issue. In 1897 the legislature was preoccupied with a wholesale modification of New York State's General Laws (now known as the Consolidated Laws), which covered labor law in the state.

After dealing with the possible opposition of the Republican political boss Thomas C. Platt, Audett managed to add an article to the new labor law dealing specifically with labor, safety, and health conditions at bakeries (Article 8, "Bakery and Confectionary Establishments," informally known as the "New York State Bakeshop Act"). The Bakeshop Act consisted of three pages of a law that went on for several dozen. The bulk of the Bakeshop Act, Sections 111 through 115, outlined specific safety requirements. However, Section 110 specified that workers in bakeshops covered by the law could neither be required nor permitted to work more than 10 hours in one workday, nor more than 60 hours in one workweek. The act contained "flexibility" language that allowed more than 10 hours per day if compensatory time off was granted later in the week.

Bakers were never really happy about the law, but it took several years for a serious challenge against it to be mounted.

The Case

Joseph Lochner owned a small bakery in the upstate New York town of Utica. His first violation of Section 110 of the Bakeshop Act took place in 1902, and he violated it several times after that. He repeatedly appealed one of his convictions, which went to the Supreme Court in February 1905. At issue was whether or not the Bakeshop Act's limit on hours of labor

Thomas C. Platt. © Getty Images. Reproduced by permission.

was an improper use of the state's "police powers," a vaguely defined set of powers held by the states to regulate on behalf of their citizens' health, welfare, and morals. Police powers could, under certain conditions, override freedom of contract. Although the *Lochner* decision ultimately did little to define "police powers," it did help to establish the doctrine of "substantive due process," under which laws could be declared unconstitutional on their substance.

Lochner's apparently unlicensed attorney constructed a simple argument concluding that Section 110 of the labor law was contrary to the United States Constitution on three basic grounds:

- It did not apply uniformly to all bakeshops but only to those that met the specific definition in the law.

- Section 110 could not really be a health and safety law, as such issues were covered by other provisions of the Bakeshop Act.

- Section 110 was not a proper use of the state police power (this argument was vaguely constructed at best).

Lochner's attorney argued that these factors made this section of the New York State Bakeshop Act an impairment on Lochner's freedom of contract and that it violated the "due process" clause in the Fourteenth Amendment of the U.S. Constitution.

New York State, represented by State Attorney General Julius M. Mayer, constructed a monolithic argument; contextual

evidence suggests that Mayer was distracted by preparation for another case that he was to argue before the Court within a few months. Unless, Mayer argued, Lochner can show "no basis upon which the state court could rest its conclusion that the legislation in question was a proper exercise of the police power," such policy questions were up to the New York State legislature to decide, not the courts. In justifying the idea of such legislation to begin with, Mayer cited the state's interest in having "able-bodied men at its command when it desires." Neither side attempted to offer a specific definition of the "police powers" of the states.

The Decision

The majority opinion delivered by Justice Rufus Peckham simply concluded that Section 110 was an unfair and unwarranted limitation on freedom of contract and that it did not relate properly to public health or safety nor to the specific conditions of baking, and was therefore not a legitimate exercise of the state's police power. Somewhat oddly, Peckham specifically cited the fact that there was no means by which an emergency situation could override the hours limit (though Peckham failed to cite an example of a baking emergency). Peckham failed to develop a systematic legal test to determine what would and would not be a legitimate exercise of the police power.

Peckham went further, however, and insulted the legislature, suggesting that "other motives" than the public health and safety were behind the Bakeshop Act. Finally, Peckham argued that there was no empirical reason to enact such a law, as "common sense" dictated that baking was not a particularly dangerous profession.

Justice Harlan wrote the minority opinion. Harlan's minority opinion and Peckham's majority opinion agreed in the essentials. They agreed that the police power existed and that it was held by the states; they agreed further that it could override the implied freedom of contract in the Fourteenth Amendment's "due process" clause. Harlan, however, was willing to give the states the benefit of the doubt, and Peckham was not. Harlan argued that the burden of proof was on those who wished to repeal such laws, and that the presumption was in favor of the state legislatures. Peckham was unwilling to make that presumption. Harlan, further, had clearly done a good deal of reading on the subject of baking and came to the same conclusion as the New York State legislature: baking indeed *was* an abnormally dangerous profession, and it was conceivable that New York State could have had a legitimate public health rationale for enacting the law it did. Peckham, by contrast, fell back on "common sense" and offered no empirical evidence, nor did he display any knowledge on the subject of baking or of labor hazards in general.

Justice Oliver Wendell Holmes's dissenting opinion has entered the lexicon of American legal history to the point that Harlan's dissent is often seen as of secondary importance. However, apart from a bitter remark that the U.S. Constitution did not automatically legitimize the ideas of social theorist Herbert Spencer, the Holmes dissent amounted to a shorter and more strongly worded version of the Harlan dissent.

The Impact

As a general rule, the *Lochner* case is studied in the context of American legal rather than labor history. It is commonly seen in a negative light, as having ushered in the so-called Lochner Era, wherein the U.S. Supreme Court, using the "substantive due process" doctrine, sought to enforce a social Darwinist ideology and in so doing felt free to override state legislatures on what were essentially political questions. In relatively recent years, however, revisionist historians have attempted to argue that the Lochner Era represented not an imposition of the will of the Court on the will of the state legislatures, but rather a "restoration" of the American Constitution and American constitutional principles that had been under "assault" by the economic regulations enacted by the state legislatures. The conventional view, however, still seems to be the most commonly accepted one in most quarters.

Whatever view is taken, by the early to mid-1930s, when the Great Depression caused the courts to rethink *laissez-faire* capitalism and to uphold several economic and labor regulations, such as minimum wage and maximum hours laws, the Lochner Era was over.

Within the labor movement, the *Lochner* decision appears to have achieved relatively little notoriety or attention. This is probably because during the Lochner Era organized labor continued to organize workers, conduct strikes, and negotiate with employers for shorter working hours, higher wages, better working conditions, vacation time, and the like, just as they had always done. Within 30 years of the *Lochner* decision, many of the critical reforms for which labor had fought were enshrined in federal law, via the Fair Labor Standards Act.

Key Players

Audett, Arthur J.: Audett was a member of the New York State Assembly and primary author of the Bakeshop Act.

Holmes, Oliver Wendell (1841–1935): Holmes was a native of Boston, Massachusetts, and a graduate of Harvard University. He was a Theodore Roosevelt appointee to the U.S. Supreme Court from 1901 to 1932 and is an extremely important figure in American legal history. His notoriety in the *Lochner* decision comes chiefly from an extremely short and notably scathing dissent wherein he argued that the majority opinion was attempting to impose a social Darwinist ideology on the American Constitution. From a legal perspective, the other, less-cited dissent is of greater importance to the case itself, but it was Holmes's dissent that framed the continuing political and academic perception of the decision and its meaning.

Peckham, Rufus (1838–1909): Peckham was a native of Albany, New York, and a prominent lawyer affiliated with the Democratic Party. He was appointed by President Grover Cleveland to the U.S. Supreme Court in 1895 and served there until his death. Peckham had previously served as a judge in various New York State courts. He is best remembered for his *Lochner* decision.

Platt, Thomas C. (1833–1910): Platt was a native of Oswego, New York. He served in the U.S. House of Representatives from 1873 to 1877 and became a U.S. senator in 1881 but resigned almost immediately following a patronage dispute with then-President Garfield. He later served in the Senate from 1897 to 1909. In New York State, his prominence derived more from his prestige as a Republican political boss

Rufus Peckham. © The Library of Congress/Corbis. Reproduced by permission.

than from his various terms in elected office. His chief role in the *Lochner* matter was to allow Arthur Audett to persuade him to let the Bakeshop Act pass.

See also: *Fair Labor Standards Act.*

BIBLIOGRAPHY

Books

Bernstein, David E. *Only One Place of Redress: African Americans, Labor Regulations, and the Courts from Reconstruction to the New Deal.* Durham, NC: Duke University Press, 2001.

Friendly, Fred W., and Martha J. H. Elliott. *The Constitution: That Delicate Balance (Landmark Cases That Shaped the Constitution).* New York: McGraw-Hill Publishing Company, 1984.

Gillman, Howard. *The Constitution Besieged: The Rise and Demise of Lochner Era Police Powers Jurisprudence.* Durham, NC: Duke University Press, 1993.

Kens, Paul. *Judicial Power and Reform Politics: The Anatomy of Lochner v. New York.* Lawrence: The University of Kansas Press, 1990.

———. *Lochner v. New York: Economic Regulation on Trial.* Lawrence: The University of Kansas Press, 1998.

Padover, Saul K., and Jacob W. Landynski, eds. *The Living U.S. Constitution.* New York: New American Library, 1983.

Wall, Joseph F. "*Lochner v. New York*: A Study in the Modernization of Constitutional Law." In *American*

Industrialization, Economic Expansion, and the Law, edited by Joseph R. Frese and Jacob Judd. Tarrytown, NY: Sleepy Hollow Press, 1981.

Periodicals

Cohen, Julia E. "Lochner in Cyberspace: The New Economic Orthodoxy of 'Rights Management.'" *Michigan Law Review* 97 (November 1998).

Other

Lochner v. New York. 198 US 45 (1905).

—Steven Koczak

Lodz Uprising

Poland 1892

Synopsis

The city of Lodz in modern Poland came to prominence in the mid-nineteenth century as a textile production center. Part of the Kingdom of Poland, the city was the most important manufacturing center in the Russian Empire and the first truly industrial city in the region. Developed under the managerial expertise of capitalists from Prussia, Lodz also served as a cultural and economic crossroads of central Europe. It was in Lodz that organizers had their first successes outside of Warsaw in creating a socialist movement in Poland in the 1880s. On May Day in 1892, Lodz also witnessed a general strike and insurrection, one of the first in the Russian Empire. The protest, which was brutally suppressed in an action that ended in 46 deaths, involved at least 20,000 workers. In 1905 Lodz was once again the site of a general uprising against Russian authorities. Although this uprising began as a strike protest, it was fueled by Polish nationalism, which had been quietly gathering strength for generations. In later years one of the leading socialists to come out of Lodz, Jozef Pilsudski, would become the nation's first chief-of-state after its independence in 1919.

Timeline

1872: The Crédit Mobilier affair, in which several officials in the administration of President Ulysses S. Grant are accused of receiving stock in exchange for favors, is the first of many scandals that are to plague Grant's second term.

1877: In the face of uncertain results from the popular vote in the presidential election of 1876, the U.S. Electoral Commission awards the presidency to Rutherford B. Hayes despite a slight popular majority for his opponent, Samuel J. Tilden. The election of 1876 will remain the most controversial in American history for the next 124 years, until overshadowed by the race between George W. Bush and Al Gore in 2000.

1882: Agitation against English rule spreads throughout Ireland, culminating with the assassination of chief secretary for Ireland Lord Frederick Cavendish and permanent undersecretary Thomas Burke in Dublin's Phoenix Park. The leader of the nationalist movement is Charles Stewart Parnell, but the use of assassination and terrorism—which Parnell himself has disavowed—makes clear the fact that he does not control all nationalist groups.

1885: German engineer Karl Friedrich Benz builds the first true automobile.

1888: Serbian-born American electrical engineer Nikola Tesla develops a practical system for generating and transmitting alternating current (AC), which will ultimately—and after an extremely acrimonious battle—replace Thomas Edison's direct current (DC) in most homes and businesses.

1890: U.S. Congress passes the Sherman Antitrust Act, which in the years that follow will be used to break up large monopolies.

1891: French troops open fire on workers during a 1 May demonstration at Fourmies, where employees of the Sans Pareille factory are striking for an eight-hour workday. Nine people are killed—two of them children—and sixty more are injured.

1893: Henry Ford builds his first automobile.

1893: New Zealand is the first nation in the world to grant the vote to women.

1894: French army captain Alfred Dreyfus, a Jew, is convicted of treason. Dreyfus will later be cleared of all charges, but the Dreyfus case illustrates—and exacerbates—the increasingly virulent anti-Semitism that pervades France.

1896: First modern Olympic Games are held in Athens.

1900: The first zeppelin is test-flown.

Event and Its Context

A series of partitions by Poland's neighboring powers, Prussia, Austria (later Austria-Hungary), and Russia beginning in 1772 wiped Poland off the map after 1795. In the nineteenth century a series of uprisings—including major rebellions in 1830–1831, 1846, 1848, and 1863–1864—failed to reunite and free the country from foreign dominance. The rulers of the three partitions adopted various approaches to integrate the Polish territories into their empires. The multiethnic Austrian Empire, which shared the Roman Catholic religion with its Polish subjects, pursued a relatively lenient strategy that allowed local Polish landowners to govern without much interference. In the Prussian partition, deliberate policies to Germanize the region came into effect after 1848 and became oppressive after Prussian unification in 1871. In addition to prohibiting the use of the Polish language and the free practice of Catholicism, Prussian rulers began to buy up Polish lands for resettlement by Germans. In the Russian partition and the Kingdom of Poland, a puppet state set up under Russian dominance, similar cultural policies attempted to replace the Polish language with Russian and Catholicism with Russian Orthodoxy. The Polish nationalist November uprising in 1830–1831 and January uprising in 1863–1864 added to the political repression, which included mass executions and terms in Siberian exile for many of the rebels.

In the wake of the January uprising, a loose set of policies known as "Organic Work" came to dominate the thinking of Polish nationalists. Admitting the futility of using force against their oppressors, Polish leaders encouraged economic development as the best way to preserve Poland's cultural integrity until independence could be secured. In the Kingdom of Poland the abolition of tariffs with the Russian Empire in 1851 and the subsequent enactment of protectionist tariffs by the empire against Western countries in the 1860s supported the efforts toward development. Land reforms that ended feudalism in the 1860s also contributed by freeing up peasant labor to work in urban areas.

The Growth of Lodz

Long settled as an agricultural area, the town of Lodz was laid out in 1820 and within 10 years was home to over 1,000 families. Its first textile mill started production in 1823, and steam-powered looms started to produce cloth in 1839. By 1850 Lodz was the largest textile manufacturing center in the Kingdom of Poland. Ten years later, the town had a population of 32,000. Given that Lodz is often compared to Manchester, England, for its importance as a textile manufacturing center, Lodz's enterprises remained relatively small-scale until the 1870s. In 1870 its largest mills employed an average of 150 workers whereas in 1880 the largest cotton mills averaged 560 workers. The city experienced almost constant growth after 1850, although it was susceptible to cyclical downturns in the economy. One such depression in 1883–1884 put 2,000 Lodz mill hands, or about 20 percent of the town's working population, out of work. During the depression, 124 Lodz mills went out of business.

By far the largest number of employees in Lodz worked in the mills owned by Karl Wilhelm Scheibler, who came to Lodz in 1850. The son of a German cloth merchant and manufacturer, Scheibler was forced to flee Austria in 1848 and came to the Kingdom of Poland to work as a director of an uncle's mill. With the capital from his wife's dowry, Scheibler established his first mill at Lodz in 1855. Scheibler also began to build housing for his workers after 1865; eventually, Scheibler's buildings covered about one-seventh of the entire city of Lodz in the pre–World World I era. In the 1870s Scheibler owned and operated about 60 percent of the looms in the Kingdom of Poland.

Origins of Polish Socialism

The depression of 1883–1884 caused great distress for workers in Lodz, most of whom were the first generation to engage in urban wage work without relying on subsistence agriculture to see them through hard times. A working-class consciousness was slow to develop, although socialist organizers had attempted to make inroads in the city as early as 1878. In 1883 socialists under the banner of the Proletariat started to organize small workers' circles that eventually included as many as 200 of the region's mill workers. Faced with a largely illiterate workforce, organizers taught the tenets of socialism by adopting the framework of Catholic imagery, most notably by referring to Jesus Christ as the first socialist. Although the Proletariat was all but destroyed as a workers organization by the Russian regime in 1886, its attempt to create a form of Polish socialism outlived it and flourished in succeeding years.

Jozef Klemens Pilsudski. The Library of Congress.

The 1892 Uprising

Labor disturbances in Lodz were recorded as far back as 1861, when workers destroyed power looms. The misery of 1883–1884 and agitation by the Proletariat failed to stir workers to open protest, although authorities noted some instances of machinery breakage. After the economy recovered, the city continued to grow and by 1885 the textile industry employed over 23,000 workers. Worker dissatisfaction with conditions became more overt in the 1890s. In 1890 May Day demonstrations cropped up around the Kingdom of Poland and as many as 8,000 Lodz workers participated. Two years later May Day in Lodz once again occasioned demonstrations, which this time turned violent.

The uprising of 1892 began with a strike by the city's masons, which quickly gathered public support among other Lodz workers. On 1 May 1892 the strike and general demonstrations turned into a violent battle when about 20,000 strikers and their supporters began to battle with troops in the crowded streets. The soldiers crushed the uprising and killed 46 protesters. The

event appeared to be a fatal blow to working-class organization in the city; yet by the end of the year, former members of the Proletariat had formed the Union of Polish Socialists Abroad with other socialists from the Russian partition. The new organization quickly evolved into the Polish Socialist Party (*Polska Partia Socjalistyczna*, or PPS). Founded in Warsaw in 1893, the PPS had its greatest support in Lodz. Authorities banned the organization, which forced the PPS to operate in secret. It covertly published *Robotnik* (*The Worker*) from 1894 onward. The editor of *Robotnik*, Jozef Pilsudski, operated out of Lodz from 1899 to 1900 until his arrest by Russian authorities. Pilsudski later led Poland's military efforts in World War I and served as the independent nation's first chief-of-state in 1919.

In addition to its importance in forming the PPS, the labor history of Lodz also contributed to one of the outstanding works of Polish literature, Wladyslaw Reymont's *Ziemia Obiecana* (*The Promised Land*), published in 1899. Reymont grew up near Lodz and trained as a tailor until his alleged participation in the 1892 uprising led to his dismissal from the tailor's guild. *Ziemia Obiecana* depicted the dehumanizing aspects of industrialization on mill owners and workers and was twice made into films, the second time by leading Polish director Andrzej Wajda in 1975. Reymont received the Nobel Prize for literature in 1924.

The 1905 Uprising

Lodz witnessed another historic upheaval in 1905, a year in which the widely publicized violence of January's "Bloody Sunday" in St. Petersburg, Russia, stirred emotions. On 20 June 1905 workers at several of Lodz's largest textile mills walked off the job; they were met in the streets by bullets that killed as many as a dozen protesters. The workers' funerals inspired more protests and a call for a general strike, which took place on 22 June. The action quickly spiraled out of control as workers and anarchists threw up dozens of barricades around the city. Troops sent in to crush the rebellion killed as many as 300 during a day of violence, and up to 1500 were injured. The episode was the first urban revolt in the Russian Empire and foreshadowed similar future events during the Russian Revolution.

Key Players

Pilsudski, Jozef Klemens (1867–1935): Inspired by the Lodz Uprising, Pilsudski joined the Polish Socialist Party in 1892 and became editor of the party's newsletter, *Robotnik* (*The Worker*) in 1895. He settled in Lodz in 1899 and was arrested in 1900 by Russian officials for subversive activities. Pilsudski spent a brief time in prison and exile but reemerged as a leader of the socialist movement. While playing a key role in the battles against Russian authority during the Polish-Bolshevik War of 1918–1920, Pilsudski assumed the office of head of state from 1919 to 1922. He served as prime minister between 1926 and 1928 but continued to rule over Poland with increasing authoritarian overtones until his death in 1935.

Reymont, Wladyslaw (1867–1925): Reymont grew up in the small town of Kobiele Wielki, not far from Lodz. He trained and worked as a tailor but was expelled from his craft guild by Russian authorities who suspected him of taking part in the Lodz Uprising in 1892. Reymont turned to writing and published his first book in 1894. Inspired by his experiences in the industrial city of Lodz, Reymont wrote *Ziemia Obiecana* (*The Promised Land*) in 1899. Reymont won the Nobel Prize for literature in 1924, one year before his death. *Ziemia Obiecana* has been filmed twice, once during the silent era and the second time by Poland's great film director, Andrzej Wajda, in 1975.

Scheibler, Karl Wilhelm (1820–1881): The largest textile mill operator in Lodz, Scheibler took advantage of the tariff reductions between the Kingdom of Poland and the Russian Empire in the 1850s and the rail links from Lodz that began operating in 1866. Scheibler built the first company-owned housing for workers in Lodz at his complex in 1865–1868. By 1900 his family's textile operations were by far the largest in Lodz and among the largest in the world.

See also: *Bloody Sunday.*

BIBLIOGRAPHY

Books

Asherson, Neal. *The Struggles for Poland*. New York: Random House, 1987.

Davies, Norman. *God's Playground: A History of Poland*. Volume II: *1795–Present*. New York: Columbia University Press, 1982.

Gieysztor, Aleksander, et al. *History of Poland*. Warsaw: Polish Scientific Publishers, 1979.

Hobsbawm, Eric. *The Age of Empire, 1875–1914.* New York: Vintage Books, 1987.

Jedrzejewicz, Waclaw. *Pilsudski: A Life for Poland.* New York: Hippocrene Books, 1982.

Lukowski, Jerzy, and Hubert Zawadzki. *A Concise History of Poland.* Cambridge: Cambridge University Press, 2001.

Naimark, Norman A. *The History of the 'Proletariat': The Emergence of Marxism in the Kingdom of Poland, 1870–1887.* Boulder, CO: East European Quarterly, 1979.

Zamoyski, Adam. *The Polish Way: A Thousand-Year History of the Poles and Their Culture.* New York: Franklin Watts, 1988.

—Timothy G. Borden

London Workingmen's Association

Great Britain 1836

Synopsis

Some of the leading figures of working-class radicalism founded the London Workingmen's Association (LWMA) in 1836. The organization remained an exclusive body comprising skilled craftsmen who supported the political reform demands common to the radical movement. LWMA members also emphasized the deserving character of the respectable workingman and his worthiness for the vote. The group is chiefly remembered for its formative role in Chartism. A public meeting at the Crown and Anchor Tavern in February 1837 formalized the key radical demands that were later incorporated into the People's Charter that was drawn up by leading members of the Association in the following year. In London, more radical elements formed the London Democratic Association, which challenged the LWMA. More significantly, beyond the capital, the growing and more assertive working-class reform movement, which the LWMA had helped to establish, increasingly marginalized the LWMA. As the working-class character and radicalism of the Chartist movement developed, the LWMA's artisanal "respectability" was criticized as too moderate. The association was castigated, in particular, for its willingness to cooperate with middle-class reformers. Although many of its leaders became estranged from later Chartism, the LWMA's initial role and its representativeness as an exemplar of respectable working-class radicalism remain important.

Timeline

1812: The War of 1812, sparked by U.S. reactions to oppressive British maritime practices undertaken in the wake of the wars against Napoleon, begins in June. It lasts until December 1814.

1820: In the Missouri Compromise, Missouri is admitted to the Union as a slave state, but slavery is prohibited

Francis Place. © Hulton/Getty Images. Reproduced by permission.

in all portions of the Louisiana Purchase north of 36°30' N.

1828: Election of Andrew Jackson as president begins a new era in American history.

1833: British Parliament passes the Slavery Abolition Act, giving freedom to all slaves throughout the British Empire.

1834: American inventor Cyrus H. McCormick patents his reaper, a horse-drawn machine for harvesting wheat.

1836: Boer farmers embark on their "Great Trek" into the hinterlands of South Africa, forming the enclaves of Natal, Transvaal, and the Orange Free State.

1836: In Texas's war of independence with Mexico, the defenders of the Alamo, among them Davy Crockett and Jim Bowie, are killed in a siege. Later that year, Texas wins the Battle of San Jacinto and secures its independence.

1836: Charles Dickens publishes the earliest installments of *The Pickwick Papers,* his first novel.

1837: An Illinois mob slays abolitionist publisher Elijah P. Lovejoy.

1842: In *Sanitary Conditions of the Labouring Population of Great Britain,* British reformer Edwin Chadwick draws attention to the squalor in the nation's mill town slums, and shows that working people have a much higher incidence of disease than do the middle and upper classes.

1846: American inventor Elias Howe patents his sewing machine.

1848: Discovery of gold at Sutter's Mill in California starts a gold rush, which brings a tremendous influx of settlers—and spells the beginning of the end for California's Native Americans.

Event and Its Context

The roots of the LWMA lay in the radical movement that had developed by the end of the eighteenth century. Manhood suffrage, annual parliaments, and a secret ballot had formed the core of a radical reform program whose demands were a restoration of the supposed traditional rights of the "freeborn Englishman" that, it was claimed, had been usurped by a corrupt and greedy governing elite. Government repression and wartime patriotism extinguished the early activities of the radical movement in the 1790s, but after 1815 political agitation and organization revived powerfully in the period of economic depression and social unrest that culminated in the Peterloo Massacre of 1819.

Though protest declined in the 1820s, the fundamental grievances remained and working-class discontent revived once more in depressed economic conditions of the late 1820s and early 1830s. In the reform campaign that led to the 1832 Reform Bill, the National Union of the Working Classes, founded by Henry Hetherington and William Lovett, played a leading role in London. Members of the National Union formed the nucleus of both of the principal London radical organizations of the late 1830s. The 1832 act itself, passed by the Whig Government of Earl Grey, was deliberately and precisely designed to extend the vote to "solid" middle-class men of property while denying the vote to the "dangerous" working classes. Working-class radicals who participated in the cross-class protest movement that had forced reform, were bitter at the "great betrayal." In the aftermath of 1832, some workers looked to economic means of self-defense. The Grand National Consolidated Trades Union (GNCTU) that formed in 1834 existed for less than a year. Overall, its brief life owed more to practical trade union concerns than to the utopian ideas of Robert Owen. The union was strong, however, among the tailors and shoemakers of London, who saw in it a means of defending their livelihoods and craft prerogatives. Its collapse was instrumental in refocusing working-class radicalism in London back to political agitation.

The organizational genesis of the LWMA lay in the "War of the Unstamped." The Stamp Act, which was passed in 1815 and strengthened under the Six Acts of 1819, placed a 4 pence tax on newspapers and journals as a deliberate means of suppressing the circulation of the radical working-class press. Hetherington's *Poor Man's Guardian* and other radical journals of the day flouted the tax. The struggle against the duty (a "tax

on knowledge" according to radicals) became an important concern of London radicalism. In April 1836 the American middle-class radical, Dr. J. R. Black, instigated the formation of the Association of Workingmen to Secure and Cheap and Honest Press; Francis Place and William Lovett played vital role in securing artisanal support for the association. Its failure to strengthen the government's modest reform (which reduced the newspaper Stamp Duty to 1 penny) caused its founders to reformulate its objective more broadly to that of working-class self-improvement. In June 1836 they launched the LWMA.

The LWMA was initially an exclusively working-class body; full membership was limited to workingmen. It was exclusive also in that new enrollees had to be proposed by existing members and supported by the membership as a whole. It was designedly, therefore, an elite body, and membership stood at no more than 279 in 1839. Members were overwhelmingly literate and earnest men of the London trades, comprising many of the leading London radicals who had participated in previous campaigns for political reform, Owenism, trade union rights, and the unstamped press. The LWMA's chief aim was the political, moral, and social improvement of the "useful classes" and its primary activity was educational. Lectures, discussions, and readings formed the staple of the Association's regular program; members were welcome in the reading room, which was open daily. Education, however, was intended not only to convince the upper classes of the workingman's respectability but also to instill in the workingman himself a consciousness of his rights.

In February 1837 the LWMA organized a public meeting at the Crown and Anchor Tavern to adopt a petition for universal suffrage, annual parliaments, a secret ballot, equal electoral districts, and the abolition of the property qualification for members of Parliament (MPs). The meeting was a great success. In April LWMA members and sympathetic Radical MPs convened a joint meeting to agree a parliamentary bill. The LWMA's decision to send "missionaries" to the Midlands and Northern England to form provincial workingmen's association based on the London model helped to maintain the reform momentum. By the end of the year, 100 such bodies had been formed. In April 1838 Place and Lovett drew up the great unifying symbol of the nascent movement, the six-point Charter of radical demands (payment for MPs was added). With the support of the Birmingham Political Union and the adoption of LWMA's national reform petition to parliament in May, the essentials of Chartism were in place. Ironically, when delegates assembled in London in February 1839 at the Chartist National Convention, they were struck by the frigid atmosphere. Chartism was weak in London and the LWMA had failed to propagandize in the capital.

A split emerged between the LWMA and both more radical elements in London and the broader Chartist movement. In January 1837 George Julian Harney founded The East London Democratic Association (ELDA). Though not established in opposition to the LWMA, the focus of the ELDA's activity and politics was to create conflict between the two. The ELDA sought to recruit membership from among the unorganized poor of London's East End. The organization concerned itself with social and economic issues (notably the Poor Law) that were largely ignored by the independent craftsmen of the LWMA.

The ELDA was also suspicious of the links of the Workingmen's Association with middle-class radicals. Middle-class reformers were politically radical but economically liberal and were therefore hostile to trade unionism, which they saw as an infringement of the laws of the free market. The Glasgow cotton spinners strike in 1837 provided the litmus when it provoked Daniel O'Connell, radical Irish MP and ally of the LWMA, to attack trade unionism in a parliamentary debate. The LWMA (though unsympathetic to O'Connell's argument) refused to criticize him or to sanction a letter from Harney condemning his views. In March 1838, Harney resigned from the LWMA, denouncing its moderation and its emphasis on working-class self-improvement. The ELDA, renamed the London Democratic Association in August 1838, was revived as a deliberate rival to the LWMA.

A mutual antagonism developed between the self-conscious respectability of the LWMA and the coarser character of national Chartism. London's diverse and small-scale economy and its sheer size (population two million) impeded the growth of the more cohesive working-class consciousness that had developed particularly in Britain's industrial heartlands. In the Midlands and North, the 1834 Poor Law Amendment Act with its workhouses dubbed the "new Bastilles" by critics, had aroused fierce opposition and had provided the early political momentum of Chartist growth. In London, the new Poor Law had far less impact. The respectable tradesman radicals of the city lacked understanding of the emotions that the act had fired and deprecated the "extremist" rhetoric and threats of violence of northern-based leaders such as O'Connor, Oastler, and Stephens. The LWMA shared the radical belief in the popular right of self-defense against the oppressive violence of the state, but they opposed the sporadic violence of the anti-Poor Law Movement and disliked what they saw as the militancy of provincial Chartism.

Though the LWMA was able to secure the election of eight of its own supporters as delegates to the Chartist National Convention in 1839, by 1840 it was fading from significance. The growth of Chartist organizations in London increasingly eclipsed the LWMA as well as the London Democratic Association. The LWMA's leading lights, Lovett and Place, were marginalized from the Chartist mainstream by their gradualist and reformist temperament and by their stress on self-improvement as the means to working-class emancipation.

Key Players

Harney, George Julian (1817–1897): Harney was born in London and imprisoned three times for his role in the Unstamped Press in the 1830s. A member of the LWMA alienated by the body's moderation, he founded the London Democratic Association in 1838 and became a Chartist radical, advocating a general strike. He was arrested in 1839 and 1842, and then became an editor of the *Northern Star* in 1845. Active in international working-class politics and a convert to socialism, he published the *Red Republican* and Marx's *Communist Manifesto* in 1850.

Hetherington, Henry (1792–1849): Hetherington was a London radical best known as publisher of the *Poor Man's Guardian* and a leading campaigner for repeal of the Stamp

Duty. Disappointed by the 1832 Reform Act, he demanded further political reform as a member of the LWMA and a leader of early Chartism. A critic of O'Connor's leadership, Hetherington founded the People's Charter Union in 1849.

Lovett, William (1800–1877): A Cornish cabinetmaker who moved London aged 21, Lovett participated in most of the radical working-class movements of his time and supported Owenism, the National Union of the Working Classes, the Grand National Consolidated Trades Union, and the London Workingmen's Association. He played a significant role in the drafting of the People's Charter and was jailed in 1839 for seditious libel. Lovett's advocacy of working-class education and temperance isolated him from the mainstream of the movement and he retired from active politics after 1842 when he founded the National Association for Promoting the Political and Social Improvement of the People.

Oastler, Richard (1789–1861): A Tory paternalist employed as a land agent in Yorkshire, Oastler was horrified by child labor in the textile mills. In the 1830s he became the main spokesman of the Ten Hours movement to restrict factory hours and subsequently was leading opponent of the 1834 Poor Law. Jailed for debt between 1840–1844, he continued his campaign from prison and after his release.

Owen, Robert (1771–1858): Born in Wales, Owen was celebrated for his success as a humanitarian factory manager in New Lanark, Scotland. Owen argued that environment shaped character but his attempt to create an ideal cooperative community in New Harmony, Indiana in 1825 failed. Owen returned to found the National Equitable Labour Exchange in 1832 and the Grand National Consolidated Trades Union in 1834 as means of promoting working-class self-sufficiency but both collapsed. Owen continued to promote a communal socialism, later dubbed Utopian by Marx.

Place, Francis (1771–1854): A London tailor whose long career in radical politics began in the London Corresponding Society in 1794, Place played a leading role in the repeal of the Combination Laws (against trade unions) in 1824 and in the campaign for the 1832 Reform Act. A founder of the LWMA and drafter of the People's Charter, Place was linked with middle-class radicals through his Malthusianism (he wrote one of the earliest tracts on birth control in 1822), and his stress on working-class respectability and self-improvement divorced him from the Chartist mainstream but his perspective, conveyed in the mass of papers he left behind, influenced later historians.

See also: *Chartist Movement; Owen Model Communities; Peterloo Massacre.*

BIBLIOGRAPHY

Books

Bennett, Jennifer. "The London Democratic Association: A Study in London Radicalism." In *The Chartist Experience: Studies in Working-Class Radicalism and*

Culture, 1830–60, edited by J. Epstein and Dorothy Thompson. London and Basingstoke: The Macmillan Press, 1982.

Prothero, I. J. *Artisans and Politics.* Baton Rouge: Louisiana State University Press, 1979.

Periodicals

Rowe, D. J. "The Failure of London Chartism." *The Historical Journal* 11, no. 3 (1968): 472–487.

———. "The London Working Men's Association and the People's Charter." *Past and Present* (1967): 73–85.

ADDITIONAL RESOURCES

Books

Wright, D. G. *Democracy and Reform 1815–1885.* Harlow: Longmans, 1970.

—John Boughton

Longshoremen and Miners Strike

Chile 1907

Synopsis

The labor stoppage among the longshoremen and miners in Iquique, Chile, in the early twentieth century played a major role in the development of a working-class consciousness. Workers in the region viewed this labor mobilization as a source of their political and economic strength. This first sign of labor militancy involved nearly 10,000 workers. The major grievance by the workers was over wages and working conditions. The strike, however, became part of a larger series of worker mobilizations in which the government violently suppressed the workers, imprisoned the movement's leaders, and shut down the union halls. The repressive actions of the government, both during the strike and in the months after the mobilizations, caused deaths and injuries and proved instrumental for the workers on a national level by unifying the working class in challenging the long-ruling oligarchic Chilean government.

Timeline

1886: Bombing at Haymarket Square, Chicago, kills seven policemen and injures numerous others. Eight anarchists are accused and tried; three are imprisoned, one commits suicide, and four are hanged.

1891: Construction of Trans-Siberian Railway begins. Meanwhile, crop failures across Russia lead to widespread starvation.

1896: Nobel Prize is established.

1902: Second Anglo-Boer War ends in victory for Great Britain. It is a costly victory, however, resulting in the loss

Arturo Alessandri Palma. The Library of Congress.

of more British lives (5,774) than any conflict between 1815 and 1914. The war also sees the introduction of concentration camps, used by the British to incarcerate Boer civilians.

1904: The ten-hour workday is established in France.

1906: After disputes resulting from the presidential election in Cuba, various Cuban parties invite the United States, under the 1901 Platt Amendment (which limits the terms of Cuban independence), to restore order. American troops begin a three-year occupation of the country.

1906: German neurologist Alois Alzheimer identifies the degenerative brain disorder that today bears his name.

1906: An earthquake, the worst ever to hit a U.S. city, strikes San Francisco on 18 April. It kills some 2,500 people, leaves another 250,000 homeless, and destroys more than $400 million worth of property.

1906: The British Labour Party is founded.

1908: The Tunguska region of Siberia experiences a strange explosion, comparable to the detonation of a hydrogen bomb, whose causes will long be a subject of debate. Today many scientists believe that a comet caused the Tunguska event.

1912: *Titanic* sinks on its maiden voyage, from Southampton to New York, on 14 April. More than 1,500 people are killed.

1916: Battles of Verdun and the Somme on the Western Front. The latter sees the first use of tanks, by the British.

Event and Its Context

In the late nineteenth century, domestic politics favored the creation of a strong political labor movement in Chile. Specifically, Chile had a parliamentary system that allowed freedom of expression and labor mobilizations. This facilitated the rise of a multiparty system and the creation of organized labor associations. Nevertheless, worker mobilization was challenged by an oligarchic state, which, while preaching liberal and democratic ideas, practiced repressive measures against the working class. Chile witnessed numerous worker strikes in the years preceding the Iquique strike. In 1903 dockworkers declared a work stoppage in Valparaiso. In 1905 workers declared a general work stoppage in Santiago in what many rank-and-file workers called "the red week." In 1906 railway workers in the mining area of Antofogasta declared a work stoppage. Each of these strikes was significant in that the issues concerned basic living and working conditions, such as wages and housing.

In 1907 workers in the northern port city of Iquique staged a labor stoppage to protest low wages and deplorable working conditions. Skilled workers, primarily longshoremen and miners, participated in the action. Many of these workers belonged to the most militant labor organizations in the arid enclaves of northern Chile. As a result of a nationwide economic depression in 1907, the radical anarcho-syndicalists found the northern port city a fertile recruiting ground of discontented, unemployed skilled workers. The organizations in turn formed informal types of societies to care for its workers. Also known as *mancomunales*, or mutual aid societies, these regional organizations essentially served as recruiting centers for many workers. Indeed, many times they functioned as mutual aid societies, which allowed workers to borrow money and to seek financial aid and social assistance when needed. These associations proved beneficial for the many unemployed workers living in the area. Moreover, these associations played a major role in the labor mobilization of 1907.

The period leading up to the 1907 strike is critical to developing an understanding of the nature of the labor mobilization of 1907. From 1900 to 1907 Chile was plagued by political and labor turmoil. Some historians have estimated that between 1903 and 1907, workers called for work stoppages more than 200 times. In 1907 alone there were 20 strikes. The response by the government to these labor actions resulted in deportations and killings. For example, in a 1903 strike by dockworkers in Valparaiso, government shock troops killed more than 40 workers; in the 1906 railway strike, more than 150 workers may have been killed by government troops. The government's reaction to the strikers was perceived as repressive.

In 1907 skilled workers in Iquique, influenced by anarcho-syndicalist ideology and the violent protests of the previous 20 years, declared a general work stoppage in the booming port city metropolis. Many workers were disgruntled by the unequal and skewed pay structure in the mining camps. For years, American workers performing the same tasks as their Chilean counterparts received an average of twice the wage. Moreover, the high standards of living in early-twentieth-century Chile contributed to worker discontent as the price of consumer goods more than doubled between 1906 and 1907. Exacerbating the political and economic tensions was the fact that by the early twentieth century, American ownership of the nitrate industry, which produced raw materials for use in explosives and fertilizers, had reached unprecedented levels. Statistics vary, but between 1900 and 1940 approximately 55 percent of foreign trade derived from the prosperous nitrate industry. The majority of this trade involved British and American nitrate companies operating in the region. This alienated many workers in the region, particularly as the Americans received favorable economic and political treatment from the national government. Clearly, by 1907 the potent force of nationalism was increasing within the region. As labor contended with an increased nationalism among their rank-and-file members, they also had to deal with a national government that was becoming increasingly hostile and aggressive to the interests of a mobilized working class. Throughout 1907 the regime of Chilean president Pedro Montt embarked on a policy of increased repression of the striking longshoremen. Pressured by American capitalists to quell the workers, Montt mobilized the Chilean National Guard to attack the workers. As thousands of guardsmen entered the city, the longshoremen and their counterparts assumed a more aggressive stance. Union leaders expected the worst. In late 1907 the government sent the national army into Iquique to repress the strike, which was threatening production levels as well as the economic situation. As a result, over 100 workers were killed by government forces. Clearly, the government's response indicated weariness by American capitalists and the national elite in dealing with the impact of the strike. The impact of declining production levels, in concert with an economic depression, created problems for the government.

The workers met the government's response to the strike with indignation and shock. Union leaders demanded that the government cease the repression. When these calls went unheeded, union leaders had no alternative but to continue the strike. Labor unions continued the mobilization for a few more days until the government sent in shock troops to quell the conflict. Support for the workers during the strike was evident throughout the nation. Placards appeared in the streets of Santiago and Valparaiso, posted by members of the potent middle classes as well as other sectors of the working class. Government repression of the strike played a major role in eliciting public support of the strike and drawing public criticism. By the end of the strike, public favor became a serious issue for the Montt regime. The government's behavior toward the striking workers proved highly unpopular. However, for the workers, the action proved equally disastrous. Within months after the conclusion of the strike, most dockworkers' unions had been shut down by government decree. Most decrees cited a communist influence within the miners and dock unions as the major reason for the shutdown of the representative organizations. Essentially, the repressive actions of the Montt regime had destroyed the workers' movement in the booming port city. However, other organizations throughout Chile took heed of the actions of the port workers and called a general work stoppage within days of the final government clampdown.

Impact

The impact of the Iquique strike by the longshoremen is multifaceted. In the short term, the actions of the workers contributed to the decline of the working-class movement. The economic depression of 1907 stoked a decline in union membership as the nitrate companies began to dismiss many workers.

Many of these unemployed fled the region after the strike, finding their way to the streets of the major urban centers. However, in the long term, the strike played a major role in the definition of a working-class culture and identity among the Chilean working class. The brutal repression of the strike by the government, in concert with the actions of the unions, served as an example for many future labor leaders.

Luis Emilio Recabarren founded the Socialist Workers Party (POS) in 1909 with the goal of creating an open labor organization. He wanted to create a labor association that would embrace all aspects of labor. He cited the labor protests specifically of the Iquique strike. More important than Recabarren's efforts to unify the labor movement, however, was the impact of the massacre and strike on the Chilean national consciousness. The strong and vibrant Chilean middle class viewed the events of 1907 with severe disdain, as it revealed the contradictions of the so-called Parliamentary Republic. Many members of the middle class, like Arturo Allesandri, began to question the liberal and democratic rhetoric emanating from Santiago, the national capital, when the government's actions in the working-class centers indicated a growing repression. This pointed to stark contradictions within the liberal political model that had been established in Chile. The result was that Allesandri would emerge victorious in 1912 at the head of a coalition of working- and middle-class organizations.

Key Players

Alessandri Palma, Arturo (1868–1950): Alessandi led the middle class in the aftermath of the Iqueque massacre. He criticized the contradictions within the Chilean political system. He served as president of Chile from 1920 to 1924 and again in 1925.

Montt, Pedro (1848–1910): President of Chile during the Iquique strike, Montt called out the National Guard to repress the strike. He served as president of Chile from 1906 to 1910.

Recabarren, Luis Emilio (1876–1924): Recabarren was a key actor in the unification of the Chilean labor movement. After the Iquique strike, he left the Chilean Democratic Party and created the Socialist Workers Party, which later became the Chilean Communist Party (FOCh).

BIBLIOGRAPHY

Books
Collier, Ruth Berins, and David Collier. *Shaping the Political Arena: Critical Junctures, the Labor Movement and Regime Dynamics in Latin America.* Princeton, NJ: Princeton University Press, 1991.
De Shazo, Peter. *Urban Workers and Labor Unions in Chile,1902–1927.* Madison: University of Wisconsin Press, 1983.
Monteón, Michael. *Chile in the Nitrate Era: The Evolution of Economic Dependence, 1880–1930.* Madison: University of Wisconsin Press, 1982.

—Jaime Ramón Olivares

Loray Mill Strike

United States 1929

Synopsis

The Loray Mill Strike of 1929 is perhaps the most infamous strike in southern textile industry history, helping to build anti-unionism among workers that would last for most of the twentieth century. In 1928 the mill began introducing more efficient methods that significantly reduced the workforce, cut wages, and increased company profits. Workers at Loray were ripe for action when an organizer for the communist-backed National Textile Workers Union, Fred Beal, came to town in early 1929. When mill officials began firing workers who had contact with the union, Beal called a strike against Loray. What followed was a mini–class struggle between mill workers and the Gastonia establishment. Ideas of race, gender, religion, and class all came under attack. Before the incident ended, the local police chief, Orville Aderholt, and a popular female striker, Ella May Wiggins, had been killed. The trials that followed drew national and international attention. Ultimately, the strike failed and seven union men, including Beal, were convicted of conspiracy to murder the police chief. The men charged with Wiggins's death were acquitted.

Timeline

1914: On the Western Front, the first battles of the Marne and Ypres establish a line that will more or less hold for the next four years.

1919: Treaty of Versailles is signed by the Allies and Germany, but rejected by the U.S. Senate. This is due in part to rancor between President Woodrow Wilson and Republican Senate leaders, and in part to concerns over Wilson's plan to commit the United States to the newly established League of Nations and other international duties. Not until 1921 will Congress formally end U.S. participation in the war, but it will never agree to join the League.

1924: In the United States, Secretary of the Interior Albert B. Fall, along with oil company executives Harry Sinclair and Edward L. Doheny, is charged with conspiracy and bribery in making fraudulent leases of U.S. Navy oil reserves at Teapot Dome, Wyoming. The resulting Teapot Dome scandal clouds the administration of President Warren G. Harding.

1927: Charles A. Lindbergh makes the first successful solo nonstop flight across the Atlantic and becomes an international hero.

1929: The Lateran Treaty between the Catholic Church and Mussolini's regime establishes the Vatican City as an independent political entity.

1929: On "Black Friday" in October, prices on the U.S. stock market, which had been climbing wildly for several years, suddenly collapse. Thus begins the first phase of

Striking mill workers, Gastonia, North Carolina. AP/Wide World Photos. Reproduced by permission.

a world economic crisis and depression that will last until the beginning of World War II.

1929: Edwin Hubble proposes a model of an ever-expanding universe.

1931: Financial crisis widens in the United States and Europe, which reel from bank failures and climbing unemployment levels. In London, armies of the unemployed riot.

1933: Newly inaugurated U.S. president Franklin D. Roosevelt launches the first phase of his New Deal to put depression-era America back to work.

1935: Second phase of New Deal begins with the introduction of social security, farm assistance, and housing and tax reform.

1941: Japanese bombing of Pearl Harbor on 7 December brings the United States into the war against the Axis. Combined with the attack on the Soviet Union, which makes Stalin an unlikely ally of the Western democracies, the events of 1941 will ultimately turn the tide of the war.

1944: International Monetary Fund and World Bank are created at Bretton Woods Conference.

Event and Its Context

Gastonia, North Carolina, was at the heart of the South's textile industry in 1929, claiming more than a million spindles and the third largest textile center in the United States. Gastonia's Loray Mill was built in 1900 for $1 million and was by far the largest mill in the region. More than half of the initial capital came from New York investors. In 1919 the Jenckes Spinning Company of Pawtucket, Rhode Island, purchased the mill, making it the first mill in Gastonia to be owned and operated by northern capital. In November 1924 Jenckes merged with Manville, another New England company, creating the Manville-Jenckes Company.

Many of the seeds that produced the 1929 Loray Mill Strike were sown during the two years prior to the strike, when Manville-Jenckes brought in Gordon A. Johnstone as the new mill superintendent. Johnstone was a master of "stretch-out," production techniques, which increased productivity and profits for the company. Johnstone's approach to the mill workers was harsh and insensitive. During his time at Loray, Johnstone cut the total workforce from 3,500 to 2,200; initiated two 10-percent pay cuts; moved most of the female workers from salary to piecework; and raised workloads. He also fired skilled workers and replaced them with semiskilled and unskilled workers. Johnstone's efforts reduced worker wages by 25 to 50 percent. It also saved the company half a million dollars. In March 1928 weavers at the Loray Mill walked out. Their weekly income had dropped from between $30 and $35 to $15 and $18, and the number of looms they were required to operate had increased from between six and eight to between 15 and 18. In response, Jenckes replaced Johnstone with J. L. Baugh, who eased the pressure on workers but kept most of Johnstone's innovations in place.

Into this powder keg of worker dissatisfaction walked Fred E. Beal, the National Textile Workers Union (NTWU) representative. Coming south on a motorcycle, Beal initially stopped in Charlotte, where he began contacting textile workers. There he first learned of Gastonia's Loray Mill. Beal had been sent south by the NTWU secretary, Albert Weisbord, who believed the southern textile industry was ready for unionizing, and that once a strike began at one mill, it would quickly spread. The NTWU was a communist labor union born in the 1926 Passaic, New Jersey, textile strike and strengthened in the 1928 New Bedford, Massachusetts, strike, in which Beal had been one of the leading organizers. In Gastonia, Beal began forming a secret union organization among Loray Mill workers in March 1929. Recognizing both an opportunity and a challenge, Beal immediately asked Weisbord for assistance. The next NTWU organizer to arrive was Ellen Dawson, a veteran of the Passaic and New Bedford strikes.

On 30 March 1929 Beal and Dawson spoke to the first open meeting of Loray workers. In the crowd, Loray Mill spies noted the names of workers at the meeting. On the morning of 1 April, five Loray workers were fired for attending. That afternoon, workers voted to strike under the NTWU banner and marched to the mill, where they convinced most of the night shift not to report for work, effectively shutting down the mill. The following day the union presented its demands to Baugh, the mill's superintendent. The mill never negotiated with the union. On 3 April, after skirmishes between police and strikers, the Gasto-

nia mayor asked the governor to send the National Guard to surround the mill and protect the workers who wanted to go back to work. On 4 April, Beal, in an effort to prevent violence, directed strikers to stay away from the guardsmen.

By the second week of the strike, others representing the NTWU and related communist organizations began arriving in Gastonia. Among them were Vera Buch Weisbord and Amy Schechter, who became two of the most active organizers. On 9 April the governor reduced the National Guard contingent assigned to Loray. In response, Major A. L. Bulwinkle, a former congressman, convinced the sheriff to deputize local members of the American Legion. Under Bulwinkle's leadership, this group would become known as the Committee of One Hundred and actively participate in many of the violent acts of the following months. U.S. Labor Commissioner Charles Wood ruled out any chance of federal government mediation, claiming that the strike leaders were Bolsheviks trying to start a revolution.

By mid-April many of the Loray workers had abandoned the strike and returned work. To help the remaining strikers, the NTWU local established a small food warehouse, which became the focal point of the first violence. Shortly after midnight on 17 April, a mob of masked men, probably from the Committee of One Hundred, raided the warehouse, overpowered a handful of union guards, and destroyed the food supplies. National Guard troops, only a 100 yards away, did not arrive until after the vigilantes had disappeared, and then only to arrest the union guards.

On the same day, the NTWU organizer Ellen Dawson was arrested on charges that her U.S. citizenship had been obtained fraudulently. The same tactic had been used against her in New Bedford, forcing her to return to New Jersey. There the charges were ultimately dismissed, and the judge chastised the government for trying to deport an individual because of unpopular political beliefs. Although Dawson remained in the country, the action removed one of the NTWU's most effective organizers from Gastonia.

On 22 April approximately 500 workers marched through downtown Gastonia. They met a force of more than 50 deputies who used blackjacks, rifle butts, and bayonets to attack the marchers, many of them women. Thirty marchers, including Weisbord and Schechter, were arrested. At this point, the NTWU was able to spark strikes at several other mills in the region, building on the shoulders of a few dedicated union members. One was Ella May Wiggins, a single mother whose song-writing abilities provided inspiration for her fellow strikers.

By May, however, the strike at the Loray Mill was faltering. Most of the workers had returned to work, and the mill was running at near capacity. Baugh decided he no longer needed striking workers and began putting them out of their mill-owned houses. On 6 May the mill put 1,000 people out on the street. The union erected a tent city for workers still active in the strike.

On 7 June, Weisbord and Schechter led another march. As he often did, Beal remained at the union headquarters with his bodyguards. Again, police attacked the marchers. Most of the demonstrators scattered and returned to the tent city, followed by Gastonia police officers. Two of the police officers had been arrested a few hours earlier in the next county on charges of assault and drunkenness. At the tent city, both sides fired shots; who fired first remains unproven. Four police officers and one union man were shot. Police Chief Orville F. Aderholt died the next day. Vigilantes later raided the tent city, terrorizing the men, women, and children. Sixty people were jailed. Beal escaped but was arrested later in Spartanburg.

On 18 June, claiming union guards shot first, prosecutors charged 14 union people with murder. They included Beal, Weisbord, and Schechter. The subsequent trial drew national and international attention to Gastonia and was compared to the trial of Sacco and Vanzetti. A mistrial was declared when the prosecution, borrowing an idea from a contemporary movie, produced a life-size wax model of the dead police chief in the courtroom. According to locals, the shock drove one juror mad. Built secretly in the basement of the courthouse for a cost of $1,000, the wax model had caused janitors to report seeing the police chief's ghost in the weeks before the trial.

In the chaotic week that followed the mistrial, members of the Committee of One Hundred demonstrated throughout the area, and the union called another mass meeting. Ella May Wiggins and a group of NTWU members from Bessemer City were attacked on the way to the meeting, which, ironically, had been cancelled. Wiggins was killed. Seven men, including nonstriking employees of Loray Mill, were charged with her murder. Mill Superintendent Baugh bailed them out, and Major Bulwinkle led their defense team. All were acquitted.

At the second Aderholt murder trial, prosecutors limited the number of defendants to seven and reduced the charge to second-degree murder. Charges against Weisbord and Schechter were dropped. Beal remained the prime suspect. Ultimately, the remaining men were convicted and given sentences of from 5 to 20 years. While out on bail, most of the defendants escaped to the Soviet Union. Beal made two trips there before surrendering to North Carolina officials in 1939. He was pardoned in 1942 and returned to Massachusetts, where he died in 1954.

Key Players

Beal, Fred (1896–1954): Beal was an American communist labor organizer during the 1920s. He directed the National Textile Workers Union in the Gastonia Strike of 1929, where he was convicted of the murder of the local police chief. He escaped to the Soviet Union but returned to the United States disillusioned by Stalin's "workers' state." He wrote an autobiography, *Proletarian Journey* (1937). He surrendered to North Carolina authorities in 1939 and was pardoned after serving four years.

Dawson, Ellen (1900–?): A Scottish immigrant to the United States, Dawson was the National Textile Workers Union's national vice president and the second organizer to reach Gastonia in 1929. Known as the "Little Orphan of the Strikers," she came to the United States in 1921 and settled in Passaic, New Jersey. A weaver, she was active in strikes in Passaic and New Bedford.

Weisbord, Vera Buch (1895–1989): Weisbord was an American social activist who joined the Socialist Party in 1919 and was active in labor organizing. She was perhaps the most important woman organizer during the 1929 Loray Mill Strike in Gastonia. She and her husband, Albert Weis-

bord, moved to Chicago in the 1930s, where she remained active in labor causes throughout her life. She published an autobiography, *A Radical Life* (1977).

Wiggins, Ella May (1900–1929): Born in Tennessee, Wiggins was a textile worker, striker, songwriter, and mother. She was killed on the way to a union meeting during the 1929 Gastonia strike, and no one was convicted for her murder. She is buried in Bessemer City, North Carolina. Her tombstone reads, "She was killed carrying the torch of social justice."

BIBLIOGRAPHY

Books

Beal, Fred. *Proletarian Journey: New England, Gastonia, Moscow.* Freeport, NY: Books for Libraries, 1971.

Pope, Liston. *Millhands and Preachers: A Study of Gastonia.* New Haven, CT: Yale University Press, 1942.

Salmond, John A. *Gastonia, 1929: The Story of the Loray Mill Strike.* Chapel Hill, NC: University of North Carolina Press, 1995.

Weisbord, Vera Buch. *A Radical Life.* Bloomington, IN: Indiana University Press, 1977.

—David Lee McMullen

Lowell Industrial Experiment

United States 1823–1836

Synopsis

After 1823 a factory town grew up along the banks of the Merrimack River at Pawtucket Falls in Chelmsford, Massachusetts, which by 1836 had become the mill town of Lowell. The first planned industrial city in the nation, Lowell at this date had a population of 16,000 and employed more than 6,000 operatives in eight brick mills. A series of innovations in industrial organization and operation distinguished Lowell from earlier textile undertakings and made the town the center of the industrial revolution in the United States before the Civil War. The Lowell experiment also brought young, single, rural women into industrial employment in large numbers for the first time in American history and saw some of the nation's earliest labor protests among working women. The Lowell experiment prospered and set an example that was widely followed at first. With the entry into the market of large numbers of Irish immigrants after 1845, however, a new model of industrial employment emerged in Lowell, and textile manufacturing shed the unique aspects of the early decades. After the Civil War an immigrant-based labor force replaced the Lowell system and marked the end of this early experiment in industrial organization.

Merrimac Street, Lowell, Massachusetts, 1834. © Bettmann/Corbis. Reproduced by permission.

Timeline

1800: Italian physicist Alessandro Volta develops the voltaic cell, an early form of battery.

1803: English chemist and physicist John Dalton develops the first modern form of atomic theory.

1808: First performances of Beethoven's Fifth and Sixth symphonies take place.

1812: Napoleon invades Russia in June, but by October, his army, cold and hungry, is in retreat.

1818: Donkin, Hall & Gamble "Preservatory" in London produces the first canned foods.

1825: British Parliament enacts a law permitting workers to join together in order to secure regulation of wages and hours; however, other provisions in the law effectively deny the right to strike.

1826: French inventor Joseph-Nicéphore Niepce makes the first photographic image in history.

1828: Election of Andrew Jackson as president begins a new era in American history.

1829: Greece wins its independence after a seven-year war with Turkey.

1829: The last of the "penal laws" imposed by the English against the Catholics of Ireland since 1695 are overturned.

1830: French troops invade Algeria, and at home, a revolution forces the abdication of Charles V in favor of Louis Philippe, the "Citizen King."

1831: Young British naturalist Charles Darwin sets sail from England aboard the H.M.S. *Beagle* bound for South America, where he will make discoveries leading to the formation of his theory of evolution by means of natural selection.

Event and Its Context

The train of events that led to the emergence of a new system of industrial organization in Lowell began three decades earlier in the rise of the first successful cotton textile spinning factory in Pawtucket, Rhode Island, in December 1790. There the English immigrant Samuel Slater reconstructed the Arkwright water-powered spinning frame and established the first permanent spinning mill in the United States. The early workforce in the factory along the Blackstone River consisted of seven boys and two girls between the ages of seven and twelve. The operation combined carding and spinning operations, and the resulting cotton yarn was given out to women in neighboring families to be woven into cloth.

The Pawtucket firm of Almy, Brown, and Slater enjoyed considerable success in the 1790s, and over the next two decades the "Rhode Island model," as it came to be known, became a widespread feature of the landscape of southern New England. Small water-powered factories dotted the flowing streams of southern Massachusetts, Rhode Island, and eastern Connecticut. They employed whole families to produce yarn and put out the yarn to be woven by women in farming families in the surrounding countryside. Technological and organizational changes were limited, however, and few of the Rhode Island mills adopted power looms. Industrial production remained a subordinate element in what remained an overwhelmingly agricultural economy.

The early spinning mills of southern New England expanded rapidly in the years before 1815, sheltered in part by the cessation of English imports that came with the Embargo and Non-Intercourse Acts and the subsequent outbreak of the War of 1812. During the wartime boom, events in northern New England pointed toward more dramatic changes in the future. Just as Slater had earlier reconstructed the Arkwright spinning frame, in 1813 a Boston merchant, Francis Cabot Lowell, and a mechanic, Paul Moody, succeeded in building a power loom patterned after English models. Lowell then joined with others to obtain a charter from the state legislature to establish a cotton manufactory in Waltham, Massachusetts, that would combine spinning and weaving within a single factory. The Boston Manufacturing Company began operations in Waltham in 1814 and proved remarkably successful. It represented a radical departure from prevailing practice in textile mills of southern New England. Capitalized at $400,000, it was fully 10 times larger than the typical Rhode Island mill. Moreover, it integrated all the steps in the manufacturing process at a single location, eliminating the loss of time, labor, and materials associated with the putting out of yarn into rural homes. Commanding the American market in cheap coarse woven cloth, the company prospered and expanded its operations. Within a few years the firm was occupying all available waterpower space at its Charles River location.

In the fall of 1821 the owners of the Boston Manufacturing Company began a search for a larger waterpower site to permit expansion of their operations. They soon learned of an underutilized transportation canal, the Pawtucket Canal, which skirted the falls of the Merrimack River in East Chelmsford, some 27 miles north of Boston. The canal had been built in the 1790s but had fallen rapidly into disuse after 1804 with the completion of Middlesex Canal just a few miles upstream. The Middlesex Canal tapped the northern New England countryside, connecting Massachusetts and New Hampshire farmers to the growing Boston market, and would also permit easy transportation of bales of raw cotton and bolts of finished cloth between a rural factory and broader urban markets. The Boston Associates, as this group of merchant industrialists came to be called, quietly purchased a majority of the shares in the canal and most of the land between the canal and the Merrimack River. One of the Associates speculated at the time that they might "live to see the place contain twenty thousand inhabitants."

The group petitioned the legislature for a corporate charter, began work enlarging the Pawtucket Canal, and by the fall of 1823 the Merrimack Manufacturing Company was up and running in East Chelmsford, producing printed cotton cloth. Capitalized initially at $600,000, the new company was destined to dwarf its Waltham predecessor. The Associates soon moved the Waltham machine shop up to the new site and incorporated the Proprietors of Locks and Canals on the Merrimack River to develop and oversee the waterpower operations and to build and equip the new textile factories and expanding power canals that came to line the river.

The immediate success of the Merrimack Company and the expansionist vision of the Boston Associates led to the founding of new firms in rapid succession. The Hamilton Corporation (1825), the Appleton and Lowell corporations (1828), and Suffolk, Tremont, and Lawrence corporations (1831) followed one right after the other. By 1836 investment totaled more than $6.2 million in eight major firms that employed more than 6,000 workers. Industrial growth, in turn, led to urban growth. In 1820 the population of East Chelmsford had been about 200, but by 1826, when the community was incorporated as the town of Lowell, the population had reached 2,000. In 1836 Lowell became an incorporated city; its population of 16,000 made it the second largest city in Massachusetts.

As the mills grew apace in early Lowell, a new system of industrial organization took shape. Historians have subsequently called it the Waltham-Lowell system. A variety of characteristics distinguished this system and influenced the nation's economic development in the years before the Civil War. The Waltham-Lowell firms were all owned by a slowly expanding circle of Boston capitalists who shared officers, set common wages, shared data on production costs, and enforced common regulations on their workers. They were also fully integrated industrial enterprises that took raw cotton as input and produced bolts of finished cloth for sale on wholesale markets. They took full advantage of economies of scale, with a typical Lowell firm in the mid-1830s employing 1,000 workers, 20 times the number found in typical manufacturing firms in this period.

The recruitment, housing, and treatment of workers also distinguished Lowell from its southern New England competitors. Fully 85 percent of workers in the early years were young, single women recruited from the countryside surrounding Lowell. To house these women, Lowell companies built scores of boardinghouses. Furthermore, the companies paid these women monthly cash wages. Most other employers paid their workers with credit at a company store or settled wages perhaps four times a year. Finally, the mills established a set of common regulations that required that the women observe an evening curfew and regularly attend a house of worship. Workers who bridled at Lowell's paternalistic regime were often dismissed, and an intercompany blacklist (though only sporadically enforced) could make it difficult for a dismissed employee to find work elsewhere in Lowell.

Still, monthly cash wages that averaged $12 to $14 a month in the 1830s proved attractive to farmers' daughters with few other opportunities for self-support. The women were willing to relocate temporarily in Lowell, reside with their fellow operatives in company boardinghouses, and work six days a week, 12 hours a day, the standard work week for paid employment in the period. In addition, the social, cultural, and religious opportunities in Lowell proved attractive. Tens of thousands of young women came to Lowell for brief stints in the mills that rarely extended for more than three to five years. They could earn money, build up savings accounts, and either contribute to their families back home or bring some resources into their marriages. Their earnings from mill employment gave them a degree of economic and social independence that set them apart from New England women of earlier generations.

Though mill women preferred wages earned within the strictly regulated confines of New England factories over a less-driven dependence on their families back on hill-country farms, they did not accept uncritically all that went on in the mills. Periodically, in fact, Yankee women organized strikes in response to wage cuts or other management moves that they found contrary to their interests. The largest of these actions came in Lowell in February 1834 and October 1836, and an appreciation of these protests is crucial to an understanding of the system of industrial organization that emerged in early Lowell.

More than 800 women mill workers in Lowell "turned out"—went on strike—in February 1834 to protest a proposed wage reduction. Two weeks earlier, mill agents had posted identical broadsides in the mills notifying workers of the impending cuts. The broadsides stirred up "a good deal of excitement" among women operatives, and in mid-February women at one mill held a meeting during the noon hour and excluded a male watchman from their proceedings. The mill agent entered the room and attempted to dissuade the women from their course of action. Not succeeding in convincing the women to return to work, the agent dismissed the woman who seemed to be the ringleader, and a general "turn-out" ensued. The women marched from mill to mill securing additional participants. Their number reached 800—about a sixth of the female workforce in Lowell at this date—and, following a procession, the group rallied on the town common. According to a contemporary newspaper account, one of the leaders made a "flaming" Mary Wollstonecraft speech on the "rights of women and the iniquities of the 'monied aristocracy.'"

Viewing themselves as independent "daughters of freemen," the assembled women workers endorsed a set of demands. They would only return to work with their wages restored; they insisted that no strikers be singled out for punishment; they offered to provide monetary support to those strikers who lacked resources to return to their rural homes.

Millowners, however, were prepared for the turn-out. With the posting of the original announcements of the wage cut, agents lined up additional recruits to replace striking workers. Moreover, they demonstrated no inclination to accommodate the striking women. One agent probably reflected the general sentiment when he referred to the turn-out as an "amizonian [sic] display." Women turned out on a Saturday, were paid off on Monday, and by the end of the week, the mills were operating normally.

Although unsuccessful, this first strike in Lowell expressed the strong sense of independence among mill operatives in the 1830s. Women linked their actions expressly to the revolutionary republican tradition of their "Patriotic Ancestors." They viewed the millowners and agents as "Tories in disguise." They saw themselves as daughters of freehold farmers who were not dependent on their mill earnings for subsistence. If the mills would not hold up their end of the agreement that had drawn women into the mills, they would leave Lowell and return to their rural homes. This economic base permitted Yankee women workers a measure of independence not shared by immigrant operatives who succeeded them after 1845.

In October 1836 Yankee women turned out again. On this occasion an increase in the cost of room and board in company boardinghouses prompted the protest. The second turn-out was larger than the first, engaging 1,500 to 2,000 workers, fully a fourth of the female workforce in Lowell. The women formed a Factory Girls' Association, with "committees from the several corporations to make provisions for those who have not the means to pay their board." The association may also have provided stage fare for women who preferred to return to their rural homes to wait out the strike. A contemporary in Lowell, the Methodist minister Orange Scott, estimated that 2,000 women

left the city during the strike, an effective strategy to cripple production in the mills.

The strike was considerably more successful than its predecessor, and production in the mills was affected for several months. One agent complained in correspondence to his company's treasurer back in Boston that the decline in production was "no doubt the result of calculation and contrivance" on the part of the striking workers. Although perhaps a third of the women workers supported the strike, by drawing out all the operatives in a crucial step of the production process, the leaders of the strike were able to shut down production almost completely. As one local storekeeper commented at the time: "[It] was remarkable, that a few, probably less than half a dozen young women, should manage this whole affair with so much dexterity and correct judgement, that no power, or skill, could be successfully employed against them." The strike resulted in a compromise settlement as several firms rescinded the increases in the cost of room and board, and others did so for operatives paid on a daily basis.

The strikes of 1834 and 1836 were very much products of the new industrial organization that was adopted in Lowell. The early mills produced millions of yards of cotton cloth, but they also contributed to a new consciousness among Yankee working women. Bringing women together on the factory floor and in company boardinghouses, the Lowell system helped create a group consciousness that became evident in the two strikes. Women socialized one another at work and in their boardinghouses and responded with an unexpected sense of shared grievances when mill managers adopted policies that violated the women's expectations and sense of themselves.

A major depression hit the United States beginning in 1837, and the expansion of textile production across New England led to increasing competition for the mills in Lowell. Declining wages, deteriorating working conditions, and the refusal of the state to set limits on the hours of labor led Yankee women to leave mill employment in increasing numbers after 1845. Steadily, the influx of Irish immigrants changed the composition of the mill workforce in Lowell and across New England. By 1860 a majority of mill workers in Lowell were foreign born. Increasingly, immigrant newcomers resided in private homes and not "on the corporation." More children and more older women came to work in the mills. A family labor system evolved in Lowell and other mill towns of the Waltham-Lowell type so that by 1860 the differences that had once distinguished southern and northern New England mills became muted. The Lowell experiment quietly came to an end, and an industrial order came into existence that relied increasingly on an immigrant labor force.

Key Players

Bagley, Sarah G. (1820–1848): Bagley was a New Hampshire–born textile operative in Lowell who began working in Lowell in 1837 and became the leader of the Lowell Female Labor Reform Association that championed the 10-hour day for women mill workers between 1844 and 1847. Bagley organized petition campaigns, spoke at local labor rallies, edited a labor newspaper for a brief period, and testified before a state legislative committee. After her years in Lowell, Bagley married, lived in Albany and Brooklyn, and became a physician with an interest in women's and children's health.

Boott, Kirk (1790–1837): Former officer in the British army who served as the first agent of the Merrimack Manufacturing Company and then of the Proprietors of Locks and Canals, Boott was responsible for the physical development of the mills and the city in their early years and for the paternalist system of labor control that characterized the Lowell system that he dominated until his death in 1837.

Lowell, Francis Cabot (1775–1817): A Boston merchant who observed British textile mills and helped to reconstruct the first working power loom in the United States and one of the founders of the Boston Manufacturing Company in Waltham, Lowell died in 1817, and in 1826 his fellow Boston Associates named their infant mill town on the Merrimack after their visionary collaborator.

See also: *Factory Girls' Association.*

BIBLIOGRAPHY

Books

Dalzell, Robert F., Jr. *Enterprising Elite: The Boston Associates and the World They Made.* Cambridge, MA: Harvard University Press, 1987.

Dublin, Thomas. "Beginnings of Industrial America." In Thomas Dublin, *Lowell: The Story of an Industrial City, a Guide to Lowell National Historical Park and Lowell Heritage State Park, Lowell, Massachusetts.* Washington, DC: Produced by the Division of Publications, National Park Service. U.S. Dept. of the Interior, 1992.

———. *Farm to Factory: Women's Letters, 1830–1860,* 2nd. ed. New York: Columbia University Press, 1993.

———. *Women at Work: The Transformation of Work and Community in Lowell, Massachusetts, 1826–1860,* 2nd ed. New York: Columbia University Press, 1994.

Other

Lavender, Catherine. "Uses of Liberty Rhetoric among Lowell Mill Women." *Liberty Rhetoric and Nineteenth Century American Women.* College of Staten Island, CUNY. 1998, updated 19 April 1999 [cited 13 August 2002]. <http://www.library.csi.cuny.edu/dept/americanstudies/lavender/start.html>.

—Thomas Dublin

Lord Byron. The Library of Congress.

Luddites Destroy Woolen Machines

Great Britain 1811–1813

Synopsis

Enraged by job loss, low wages, exploitation, and the use of unapprenticed workers spawned by the advent of mechanization in the English textile industry, workers secretly entered factories to destroy the machines that displaced them. The Luddites (followers of the mythical Ned Ludd) were part of a decentralized, politically ambiguous, underground worker movement that rioted and resisted mechanization by destroying textile machinery throughout English industrial centers. While different Luddite groups defended different goals, the revolts drew Britain closer than ever toward violent class warfare and revolution. The government quelled the rebellions by executing workers, imprisoning them, or exiling them to penal colonies. While the movement was all but crushed in less than two years, the name *Luddite* has survived to become synonymous with those who oppose new technology.

Timeline

1790: Mutineers from the British H.M.S. *Bounty* settle on Pitcairn Island in the south Pacific.

1796: British engineer and inventor Joseph Bramah develops the first practical hydraulic press, a machine that will have numerous industrial applications

1799: French chemist and engineer Philippe Lebon introduces gas lighting.

1802: British Parliament passes the Health and Morals of Apprentices Act, an early piece of child-labor legislation, which prohibits the employment of children under nine years of age and limits a child's workday to 12 hours.

1807: American inventor Robert Fulton introduces the *Clermont,* the first practical steamboat, which begins service along the Hudson River in September.

1810: German art publisher Rudolph Ackerman invents the differential gear, which enables wheeled vehicles to make sharp turns.

1811: Worst earthquakes in U.S. history occur near New Madrid, Missouri, greatly altering the topography of a million-square-mile region.

1812: Napoleon invades Russia in June, but by October, his army, cold and hungry, is in retreat.

1813: Jane Austen publishes *Pride and Prejudice.*

1818: Donkin, Hall & Gamble "Preservatory" in London produces the first canned foods.

1824: French engineer Sadi Carnot describes a perfect engine: one in which all energy input is converted to energy output. The ideas in his *Reflections on the Motive Power of Fire* will influence the formulation of the Second Law of Thermodynamics, which shows that such a perfect engine is an impossibility.

1834: British mathematician Charles Babbage completes drawings for the "analytic engine," a forerunner of the modern computer that he never builds.

Event and Its Context

Death of a Cottage Industry

For hundreds of years, English weavers were considered fine craftsmen, working from home as independent contractors to produce high-quality stockings and lace for domestic and international markets. With the onset of the Industrial Revolution, self-managed laborers were forced into factories, where they were controlled by owners and the regimented schedules the owners imposed. Mechanization and cost cutting replaced artisanship with cheaply manufactured products of inferior quality. Since weavers were unable to purchase machines for themselves, the balance of power shifted in favor of factory owners. By 1811 hosiery manufacturers were forcing Midlands frame-knitters to rent the frames on which they worked, leaving a profit margin that kept the once prosperous workers in abject poverty.

The Luddite uprisings were preceded by years of deteriorating worker conditions. While mechanization had sparked exponential growth in cotton yarn spinning as early as the 1770s, weaving was still done by hand, thus prompting huge demand

for hand-loom weavers. By 1799 there were more than 200,000 of these artisans—a labor surplus that brought steadily decreasing wages and the gradual extinction of hand-loom weavers. By 1812, when the once well-paid weavers were "reduced to pauperism and the most dire distress," there were more than 30,000 hosiery frames in use in England. Adding to the misery were bad harvests that pushed grain prices beyond the purchasing power of most weavers. Moreover, after nearly two decades of war with Napoleon, a new war with the American colonies, and the subsequent export barriers, Britain saw the value of its woolen exports fall from £12 million to little more than £1 million annually.

Resistance to Mechanization

Even before 1812, a year of widespread machine destruction, Yorkshire croppers had been resisting the advent of machines in the woolen industry. Traditionally, finishing wool cloth was a two-part process carried out manually by "croppers," who raised the nap on newly woven wool by brushing with hand-held "teasles" and then cut or "cropped" by hand with huge, iron shears weighing up to 40 pounds. Technology brought direct competition in the form of the gig-mill (which used mechanically driven rollers to raise the nap on the woolen cloth) and the shearing-frame (which attached the shears onto a power-operated frame). The crude machine allowed two unskilled workers to do in a day a week's work performed by a skilled cropper. According to Luddite historian Steven Marcus, machine-breaking in the woolen district that year was "unquestionably aimed at preventing the movement of the woolen industry toward a factory system in which such machines would replace hand workers."

On 11 March 1811 a large crowd of framework-knitters gathered in the Nottingham marketplace calling for revenge on employers who had reduced payment for making stockings. By this time "wide machines," on which stockings were produced from one cut piece of material called a "cut-up," were rapidly making individual artisans superfluous through mass production. For weeks Nottingham employers had been receiving threatening letters from one General Ned Ludd and the Army of Redressers. Militia dispersed the crowd, but rioters went on to smash almost 60 knitting frames in Arnold that night. Over the next three weeks, several attacks took place nightly, with workers breaking into the factories of despised manufacturers to smash more than 200 stocking frames. One factory owner had 63 machines destroyed in a single night.

Luddite Tactics

The Luddites generally limited their attacks to the new machines that were displacing them, leaving the rest of the factories' infrastructures intact. In addition to factories, they attacked individual homes where the frames were in use.

They organized "in parties of from six to sixty," all following the supposed leader "Ned Ludd," also known as "General Ludd" or "King Ludd," who lived in Sherwood Forest. Ludd was most likely a fictional character around whom the rioters rallied, with the title being transferred to the acting leader of a particular raiding party. The groups acted at night, usually meeting in the forest outside towns before making their attacks. Luddites commonly wore disguises. While some workers stood guard in the streets or subdued owners with pistols, swords, firelocks, and other weapons, others entered houses with hammers and axes to destroy the frames. When the sabotage was complete, one would reportedly fire a shot and yell "Ned Ludd!" and the group would disband. With weeks of practice beforehand, the rioters could dismantle a frame secretly and in a question of minutes, without leaving any other trace of their presence.

Government Response

In the wake of the recent French Revolution and in fear of an English version, the government of Perceval Spencer ordered a large military force to Nottingham to weed out protest leaders. By mid-December, General Dyott's army of 900 cavalry and 1,000 infantry were aiding local militias in hunting down the Luddites. Despite the considerable monetary investment in a secret network of spies and informers bent on obtaining information about the Luddites, the rioters were able to keep their movements shrouded in secrecy, and proportionally few were caught. The Luddites met secretly at night, swore secret oaths, had secret greetings, and identified each other by numbers. In the very forests and hills that inspired the Robin Hood legend, Luddite sympathizers sang of a new hero: "Chant no more your old rhymes about bold Robin Hood/His feats I but little admire,/I will sing the Achievements of General Ludd/Now the Hero of Nottinghamshire."

The Movement Spreads

Popular support and relatively low capture rates emboldened the Luddites. In a new wave of attacks in November 1811, rioters carried out some actions in daylight. At least one raid occurred in sight of the military, and another, within 100 yards of troops. Despite a royal proclamation offering a £50 reward for information leading to the conviction of "any person or persons wickedly breaking the frames," the Luddites stepped up their attacks, and the movement spread. These "bands of famished operatives" reportedly plundered farmhouses of money and provisions, saying that "they would not starve while there was plenty in the land."

In 1812 rioters in Cheshire, Lancashire, Leicestershire, Derbyshire, and the West Riding of Yorkshire began destroying power cotton looms and wool shearing machines. In February and March the Luddites attacked factories in Halifax, Huddersfield, Wakefield, and Leeds. So secret and organized were the attacks that "the magistrates could not take upon themselves to apprehend the persons whom they suspect of having committed the outrages."

Amid Violence, Luddism Is Crushed

By 14 February 1812 the government was sufficiently alarmed to propose a bill making machine-breaking a crime punishable by death. Existing law allowed for those wrecking hosiery frames (but no other types of machinery) to be "transported" to a penal colony for 14 years. The bill passed the House of Commons within a week. One of the few members of the House of Lords to oppose the measure was the poet and writer Lord Byron, who spoke passionately in defense of the Luddites. Having recently returned from a trip to Nottingham and recognizing the "alarming extent" of the attacks, Byron declared on 27 February that they had risen from "circumstances of the most unparalleled distress. . . . They were not ashamed to beg, but there was none to relieve them." In March, Parliament passed the Frame-Breaking Act, which made machine-breaking a capital offense.

Despite death threats, attacks on property, and intimidation through arms, the Luddites avoided violence against people. The struggle turned bloody in April 1812, when mill owners started to defend their property. On 11 April some 200 Luddites led by a young cropper from Huddersfield named George Mellor attacked Rawfolds Mill in Yorkshire; armed guards forced back the rioters, killing two. Fourteen men would later be hanged for their involvement. A week later, Luddites killed William Horsfall, a large mill owner who reportedly swore he would ride "up to his saddle girths in Luddite blood." Hundreds of suspects were apprehended, 64 were indicted, and three were put to death. On 20 April nearly a thousand Luddites attacked the power loom mill of Emanuel Burton in Lancashire with sticks and rocks; this mill was also defended by well-armed private guards, who killed three rioters. The Luddites burned down Burton's house, after which the military returned to kill seven more of them.

The violence had escalated to the point that Parliament sent Lieutenant General Thomas Maitland and 35,000 men to stop the revolt. It was crushed by December. Luddite oaths of secrecy notwithstanding, Huddersfield magistrate Joseph Radcliff obtained a confession leading to the arrest of Luddite leaders. A special judicial commission held in January 1813 at York Castle found 24 men guilty. Seventeen were executed, 14 of those at the same time. Seven others were sent to Australia. There were occasional Luddite uprisings until 1817, but by 1813 the movement was all but broken.

Key Players

Lord Byron (1788–1824): Born George Gordon and later inheriting the title Baron Byron of Rochdale, he was a renowned English writer and advocate of social reform. In the House of Lords, Lord Byron was a vocal defender of the Luddites, arguing against the Frame-Breaking Act. In 1816 he penned "Song for the Luddites." In addition to his poetry and satire, he supplied frequent contributions to radical and progressive journals.

Ludd, Ned: Also called Edward Ludd, General Ludd, or King Ludd, this most likely fictional character was the proclaimed leader of the Luddites. There were numerous, conflicting legends surrounding the origin of the name. Several rioting workers were known to refer to themselves as Ned Ludd. On at least one occasion, workers marched with a straw figure meant to represent the mythical English leader.

Spencer, Perceval (1762–1812): A lawyer of noble origin and a loyal supporter of King George III, Spencer became prime minister of Britain in 1809 to oversee years of economic depression and labor unrest. Spencer was a supporter of the conservative Tory group and his rule was characterized by repression against the Luddites and the introduction of the Frame-Breaking Act. In 1812 a failed businessman shot Perceval upon entering the House of Commons, making him the only British prime minister ever to be assassinated.

BIBLIOGRAPHY

Books

Martineau, Harriet. *History of the Peace: Being a History of England from 1816 to 1854.* Boston: Walker, Wise, and Company, 1864–1866.

May, Thomas Erskine. *The Constitutional History of England Since the Accession of George the Third, 1760–1860.* London: Longman, Green, Longman, and Roberts, 1861–1863.

Young, Edward. *Labor in Europe and America.* United States Bureau of Statistics. Washington, DC: Government Printing Office, 1875.

Periodicals

Englander, David, and Taylor Downing. "The Mystery of Luddism." *History Today* 38 (March 1988).

Marcus, Steven. "Rebels Against the Future: The Luddites and Their War on the Industrial Revolution: Lessons for the Computer Age." *The New Republic* 214 (10 June 1996): 30.

Other

The Luddites. Spartacus Educational [cited 7 October 2002]. <http://www.spartacus.schoolnet.co.uk/PRluddites.htm>.

ADDITIONAL RESOURCES

Texts of the Nottinghamshire Luddites [cited 7 October 2002]. <http://campus.murraystate.edu/academic/faculty/kevin.binfield/luddites_sample.htm>.

—Brett Allan King

Ludlow Massacre

United States 1914

Synopsis

In the Colorado coalfields, miners labored for long hours under extremely dangerous conditions for comparatively little pay. When the miners attempted to organize under the auspices of the United Mine Workers, most of the coal companies in the southern part of the state refused to recognize the union, prompting workers to go out on strike in September 1913. The dispute soon degenerated into one of the most violent strikes in U.S. history, with both sides guilty of beatings and murder. Efforts by the newly formed U.S. Department of Labor failed to have any effect, since the companies were adamant about refusing to do anything that would imply union recognition. The Colorado National Guard came in to protect the mines, but as was typical of the era, the soldiers actually worked to break the strike. The militia, joined by strikebreakers and company guards, attacked the workers' tent colony at Ludlow on 20 April 1914. Gunfire and flames claimed the lives of 25 people, including 11 children. The strike ended shortly thereafter. The tragedy of Ludlow shocked the nation, with resulting public disgust contributing mightily to Progressive Era labor reforms.

Timeline

1894: Thousands of unemployed American workers—a group named "Coxey's Army" for their leader, Jacob S. Coxey—march on Washington, D.C. A number of such marches on the capital occurred during this period of economic challenges, but Coxey's march was the only one to actually reach its destination.

1899: The Second Anglo-Boer War, often known simply as the Boer War begins.

1904: The ten-hour workday is established in France.

1911: Turkish-Italian War sees the first use of aircraft as an offensive weapon. Italian victory results in the annexation of Libya.

1914: On 28 June in the town of Sarajevo, then part of the Austro-Hungarian Empire, Serbian nationalist Gavrilo Princip assassinates Austrian Archduke Francis Ferdinand and wife Sophie. In the weeks that follow, Austria declares war on Serbia, and Germany on Russia and France, while Great Britain responds by declaring war on Germany. By the beginning of August, the lines are drawn, with the Allies (Great Britain, France, Russia, Belgium, Serbia, Montenegro, and Japan) against the Central Powers (Germany, Austria-Hungary, and Turkey).

1914: On the Western Front, the first battles of the Marne and Ypres establish a line that will more or less hold for the next four years. Exuberance is still high on both sides but will dissipate as thousands of German, French, and British soldiers sacrifice their lives in battles over a few miles of barbed wire and mud. The Eastern Front is a different story: a German victory over Russia at Tannenberg in August sets the stage for a war in which Russia will enjoy little success, and will eventually descend into chaos that paves the way for the 1917 revolutions.

1914: The Panama Canal opens.

1914: U.S. Congress passes the Clayton Antitrust Act, and establishes the Federal Trade Commission.

1914: Intervening in Mexico's civil war to protect American financial assets and other U.S. interests, U.S. Marines occupy the city of Veracruz.

1916: Battles of Verdun and the Somme on the Western Front are waged. The latter sees the first use of tanks, by the British.

1920: League of Nations, based in Geneva, holds its first meetings.

1924: V. I. Lenin dies, and thus begins a struggle for succession from which Stalin will emerge five years later as the undisputed leader of the Communist Party, and of the Soviet Union.

Event and Its Context

Industrialization brought many benefits to the American working class. Jobs became plentiful as the demand for laborers dramatically grew, allowing even the unskilled with a poor command of English to find work. Incomes rose accordingly, but these benefits came at the cost of dangerous working conditions, diminished control over working conditions, and a growing sense of powerlessness. Industrial workers rarely saw an owner. The supervisor exercised almost complete control over the workers in his section, hiring, firing, and setting wages. Managers often compared workers to machines, paying them as little as possible for as much labor as possible. Worker's compensation was unknown and benefits for on-the-job deaths were rare. In this climate, labor trouble brewed and one of the most violent strikes occurred in the coalfields of southern Colorado.

On the east side of the Rockies, the coal seams occur in the foothills of the Sangre de Cristo Mountains. The coal from this area is particularly high-grade, low-sulfur bituminous and sub-bituminous. In the early nineteenth century, two southern Colorado counties, Las Animas and Huerfano, provided 60 percent of the state's total coal output and constituted the chief production area for coking coal west of the Mississippi River. This coking coal was primarily used by the steel industry, which supplied rails for the expanding U.S. rail network. Since the railroads needed to maintain a steady supply of coking coal, the southern field was heavily industrialized and dominated by a few large-scale corporate operations. The largest of these was the Colorado Fuel and Iron Company (CFI), which produced one-third of the state's coal output. In 1906 the *Engineering and Mining Journal* estimated that 10 percent of Colorado's population depended on CFI for a livelihood. The wealth and power of CFI and the other large coal operators, such as the Victor-American Fuel Company, allowed them to wield considerable political clout in Colorado. Their control over the government of Las Animas and Huerfano Counties was nearly total.

The Rockefellers

In 1903 CFI passed into the hands of John D. Rockefeller, who firmly believed that God had made him the richest man in the world as a reward for his worthiness. Rockefeller would receive $960,000 in dividends during the 11 years that he controlled the company, while the best miner only took home $696 annually. To Rockefeller and other followers of Social Darwinism, only the fittest survived in the world of business, and the subjugation of the weak was accepted as being part of the natural order. Like many other businessmen of his era, Rockefeller tempered this harsh philosophy with the Social Gospel notion that it was the duty of the wealthy to use their riches to advance social progress. Devout Baptists, both Rockefeller and his only son, John, Jr., gave away vast sums of money during their lives to a variety of worthy causes, but this philanthropy did not extend to their workers.

Although he had withdrawn from most of his father's businesses by 1910 to devote his energies to charitable endeavors, the younger Rockefeller became the majority stockholder in CFI and as such had the power to institute policy. Remaining in New York, about 2,000 miles from Colorado, Rockefeller relied on reports from the coal company managers, who repeatedly mentioned how well the workers were treated and how content they were with their situation. Rockefeller never personally investigated conditions in Colorado, as he later testified, and did not believe that the workers needed any help. Even after the strike had begun, he would insist that the miners had expressed

John D. Rockefeller, Jr. © Archive Photos Inc.
Reproduced by permission.

no dissatisfaction with their conditions and that outsiders imposed the troubles.

The Workers

In American mines, the accident rate was higher than that of any industrial nation in the world, and Colorado miners died at twice the national average. Cave-ins and poisonous gases claimed the lives of 618 coal diggers in Colorado between 1910 and 1913, leaving many of the families destitute. Coroners' juries typically absolved the coal companies of responsibility almost without exception. For example, in the years from 1904 to 1914, the juries picked by the sheriff of Huerfano County, Jeff Farr, found the coal operators to blame in only 1 case out of 95. The coroner's verdicts in the other cases show a similar refrain: "fall of rock, accident unavoidable," "fall of rock, due to his own negligence," "run over by a car... due to negligence of deceased," and "death by neglect on his part and no other." The average death benefit was around $700, but many families settled for less money. The attorney for one Colorado company told a widow to be satisfied with and thankful for a $20 coffin. The miners could do little to remedy this situation; workers were cheap and expendable. A bit of oft-repeated gallows humor among the miners held that the coal operators cared more about the well-being of the mules in the mines since they could not be replaced as inexpensively.

The workforce itself was largely immigrant labor from southern and eastern Europe, including many Greeks, Italians, Germans, Poles, Slavs, Serbians, Austrians, and Montenegrins. The wide range of languages, 24 by the United Mine Workers' (UMW) count, made it difficult for the miners to organize. Most of the miners lived in company towns, in company houses, and bought food and equipment with company-supplied scrip at

Coffins of victims of Ludlow Massacre pass in front of church, Trinidad, Colorado. © Bettmann/Corbis. Reproduced by permission.

company stores and alcohol at company saloons. Some were fired for refusing to pay the company's inflated prices. The doctors, priests, schoolteachers, and law enforcement were all company employees. The entries to the camps were gated and guarded by deputized armed guards. Despite evidence to the contrary, the coal operators argued that the miners were not employees, but independent contractors free to come and go as they pleased.

The men usually worked the mine two to a room cutting into the face of the seam between pillars of standing coal. Miners received their room assignments from a pit boss, who could assign to his favorites the rooms with the thickest coal seams, the ones with the least amount of water on the floor, or the ones that did not require much bending to reach the coal. Each miner was paid only by the ton of coal mined and not by the hour. The "dead work" that was crucial to digging the coal went unpaid. Dead work included taking away rock to get to the coal, removing coal dust, laying track for the cars, and placing timbers so that the ceiling would not collapse. Adding to the miners' grievances, a company man would weigh the collected coal, and many workers suspected the accuracy of the scale, a suspicion

enhanced by the company's aggression toward men who asked for a noncompany man to check the weight. Miners also complained of being forced to vote for company-approved candidates and about the blacklisting of miners who had joined the union.

The Strike Is Called

The UMW, the largest union in the United States, had spent a decade trying to organize Colorado. On 17 September 1913 the UMW president, John Lawson, announced that a strike would occur if the coal operators would not meet a list of seven demands: 1) a 10 percent increase on the tonnage rates; 2) an eight-hour workday; 3) payment for dead work; 4) the right to elect without any interference their own men to weigh coal; 5) the right to trade in any store, to choose their own boarding places, and choose their own doctors; 6) enforcement of Colorado mining laws and the abolition of the company guard system; 7) recognition of the union. The UMW gave the companies one week to accept the demands, by 23 September, and made preparations for a strike.

Expecting the workers to be evicted from the company towns, the UMW arranged for alternate housing and supplies. It leased land near the mouths of coal canyons, both to make it a shorter distance for mining families to move possessions and to have a strategically ideal site to harass strikebreakers attempting to enter the mines. The UMW supplied tents and ovens and also organized the strikers into colonies. The largest and most important tent colony, a 40-acre plot, was situated next to the railroad spur serving the coalfield's most valuable properties. This was Ludlow. It would become home to 1,200 miners and their families in 200 tents.

Coal company officials met the strike call with resounding silence. The operators refused to meet with UMW officials for fear of giving even token recognition to the union. Spies and company officials assured the younger Rockefeller that the miners were satisfied with their working conditions and would neither join the union nor heed the strike call. The campaign to terrorize miners into submission had given the operators a false sense of security. Fully aware that men who joined the union were fired, that union organizers risked beatings, and that spies were everywhere, comparatively few miners put their names on the union rolls. Meanwhile, a mass exodus of miners began, and by 22 September most of the coal diggers were idle. Approximately 95 percent of the workforce struck, consisting of about 11,232 of Colorado's 13,980 miners and their families. The surprised operators argued that the UMW had suddenly terrorized this huge mass of tranquil workers into subjection.

As expected, the striking miners who lived in the camps were evicted. On 23 September the striker families hauled their possessions through rain and snow out of the canyons to about a dozen UMW sites. At Ludlow, the miners erected a wooden stage for meetings and bedecked it with a U.S. flag. They marked out a baseball diamond and set up large tents for school, assembly, and recreation. Police squads were organized to keep the peace. From the union headquarters in Trinidad, the UMW paid benefits of $3 to each miner, $1 to each wife, and 50 cents for each child.

Mediation Fails

With Colorado coal crucial to the well being of the nation's industry, President Woodrow Wilson hoped for a quick solution to the turmoil. Unfortunately, the mediation effort by the newly formed Department of Labor failed. The federal mediator, Ethelbert Stewart, canvassed the situation and interviewed both sides, but he could not gain the trust of the operators. Deeply suspicious of William Wilson, the unionist labor secretary, the operators did not see what they could gain by dealing with his emissary. Rockefeller would later insist, when quizzed by a congressional committee headed by Representative Martin Foster, that by resisting the union he was helping miners determine the conditions under which they worked.

The mine operators adopted the position that most miners would return to their jobs if the state guaranteed protection from union intimidation. Seeking the commitment of state troops, they persuaded the county sheriffs of Las Animas and Huerfano to wire Colorado governor Elias Ammons for immediate assistance. Ammons hesitated, and then sent militia in October 1913 after the violence had escalated. The sympathies of the guard commander, General John Chase, would ensure that the militia would be used to break the strike rather than impartially keep the peace.

Violence

The strategic proximity of the tent colonies to railroad stations and canyon entrances served as a provocation to the private armies of the coal companies, while strikers were often enraged by the simple sight of a mine guard. The first to die was Bob Lee, a CFI deputy sheriff and the chief guard at the Segundo coking plants. A bully known for targeting the wives of miners, Lee stumbled upon a group of Greeks sabotaging a bridge two days after the walkout. As he chased the men and prepared to fire a rifle, one of the Greeks shot first, killing Lee instantly. The CFI blamed Lee's death on incendiary talk from the union organizer Mother Jones, who would subsequently spend three months in a Colorado jail without ever being charged with a crime. The white-haired, elderly Jones would leave Colorado just before the 1914 massacre.

As the number of murders and beatings increased, both sides began to stockpile arms and dynamite. Rockefeller was not informed that CFI men had purchased machine guns and armored a car known as the "Death Special." He also did not realize that CFI used eight searchlights with beams of five miles to survey the miners' camps each night and rob the families of sleep.

The Massacre

Excesses by the Colorado National Guard, including the attempted intimidation of congressional investigators, and the near bankruptcy of the state by the cost of maintaining troops, led to the removal of most of the militia by 17 April 1914. Only one unit of 34 soldiers remained, but it was joined by a newly formed unit of 100 mine employees who received no guard training or uniforms before going into action. Rockefeller was informed of this strike countermeasure.

Both sides expected an imminent attack when on 20 April 1914 Major Patrick Hamrock brought a mine company machine gun to a meeting with the Greek interpreter and union organizer Louis Tikas. The subsequent arrival of 20 mounted guardsmen led the Greeks to believe that an attack on their tent camp had begun. Soon the firing was general. Women and children were hustled into pits dug underneath tent floors for storage and shelter. One boy, attempting to get water for his sister, was shot through the head. The battle raged for 14 hours, during which bombs exploded and 177 militiamen pelted the tents with machine gun fire. Militiamen shot the unarmed Tikas in the back under unclear circumstances, either when he tried to escape or after ordering him to run. The arrival of a freight train gave many of the families the chance to use it as a barrier to flee. By evening the guardsmen were looting and setting tents afire. A group of two women and 10 children hiding in a pit died of smoke inhalation. The known fatalities at the end of the day were 25 people, including three militiamen and one uninvolved passerby.

The news of the massacre quickly spread, and a guerilla-style war began to rage along a 50-mile range from Trinidad to Walsenburg. For 10 days enraged miners destroyed buildings and battled with mine guards, leading to 14 more deaths. The fighting ceased when the governor requested federal intervention. In the first week of May, 2,000 federal troops arrived in Colorado. The strike dragged on for another seven months, until the union reached the end of its financial resources. The union declared defeat on 7 December 1914.

Legacy

The Ludlow Massacre focused national attention on the conditions in the Colorado coal camps, and on labor conditions throughout the United States. While facing public outrage, picketing, and death threats, the younger Rockefeller began to realize that unquestioning reliance on the company's management had not served him well. His efforts to improve his public image led to the development of the field of public relations.

Key Players

Jones, Mary Harris "Mother" (1837–1930): The Irish-born Jones began organizing for the United Mine Workers in 1894 and worked in a number of states, including Colorado. Active in other industries besides mining, she led the 1903 Children's Crusade to oppose child labor. Often harassed and jailed by state and local government officials, Jones was never convicted of any crime.

Rockefeller, John D., Jr. (1874–1960): Rockefeller Jr. held the majority share and a directorship in Colorado Fuel and Iron. Primarily a philanthropist, he donated vast sums of money during his lifetime to a wide range of causes including Christianity, conservation, higher education, and historic preservation. He also built Rockefeller Center in New York City.

Rockefeller, John D., Sr. (1839–1937): The founder of Standard Oil, Rockefeller Sr. is best known for obtaining a monopoly on the U.S. oil trade that was eventually broken up by the Supreme Court. In 1913 he established the Rockefeller Foundation for charitable works.

Tikas, Louis (1886–1913): Tikas, a Crete-born Greek who immigrated to the United States in 1906, helped to organize Colorado miners and served as a translator. He was shot and killed under suspicious circumstances at Ludlow.

See also: *United Mine Workers of America.*

BIBLIOGRAPHY

Books

Gitelman, Howard M. *Legacy of the Ludlow Massacre: A Chapter in American Industrial Relations.* Philadelphia: University of Pennsylvania Press, 1988.

Long, Priscilla. "The Women of the Colorado Fuel and Iron Strike, 1913–1914." In *Women, Work, and Protest: A Century of U.S. Women's Labor History,* edited by Ruth Milkman. London: Routledge and Kegan Paul, 1985.

McGovern, George S., and Leonard F. Guttridge. *The Great Coalfield War.* Boston: Houghton Mifflin, 1982.

Papanikolas, Zeese. *Buried Unsung: Louis Tikas and the Ludlow Massacre.* Salt Lake City: University of Utah Press, 1982.

Stein, Leon, and Philip Taft, eds. *Massacre at Ludlow: Four Reports.* New York: Arno, 1971.

Other

Colorado Coal Field War Project. 2000 [cited 14 February 2003]. <coloradodigital.coalliance.org/cfindex.html>.

ADDITIONAL RESOURCES

Books

Beshoar, Barron B. *Out of the Depths: The Story of John R. Lawson, a Labor Leader.* Denver: Colorado Historical Commission and Denver Trades and Labor Assembly, 1957.

Long, Priscilla. *Where the Sun Never Shines: A History of America's Bloody Coal Industry.* New York: Paragon Books, 1991.

Periodicals

Long, Priscilla. "The Voice of the Gun: Colorado's Great Coalfield War of 1913–1914." *Labor's Heritage* 1, no. 4 (1989): 4–23.

—Caryn E. Neumann

M

Maquiladoras Established

Mexico 1960s

Synopsis

Also known as "in-bond" plants or "twin" plants, *maquiladoras* are assembly plants in Mexico. Most of the maquiladoras are found along the border with the United States, although they are established throughout the country. Maquiladoras reflect shifts in global capitalism that emphasize production sharing. Increasingly, international corporations have divided the capital-intensive and technology-intensive aspects of production from those that are labor intensive. Unskilled assembly is done in developing countries, where wages are low, whereas skilled operations take place in developed countries that possess more skilled labor and technology.

In the maquiladora industry, firms from the United States and other foreign countries send component parts to Mexico. Mexican workers then assemble the product in the maquiladora plants. Once the product is assembled, it is exported back to the United States. Government regulations on both sides of the border help promote the industry. In Mexico, components, machinery, and supplies can be imported duty-free as long as the finished product is then reexported. In the United States, raw materials and components are not taxed when reentering the country. Tariffs apply only to the value added in Mexico.

The maquiladora industry began in the mid-1960s, when it concentrated along the border. The industry grew slowly at first. The economic collapse in Mexico during the 1980s and the devaluation of the peso greatly reduced the cost of labor in the country. This inexpensive labor force, in turn, made the maquiladora industry more competitive. By the 1990s there were more than 2,000 plants throughout Mexico, employing some 500,000 workers. These workers performed tasks that ranged from assembling electronic goods and automobiles to sorting grocery store coupons and shelling walnuts.

Timeline

1962: Publication of Rachel Carson's *Silent Spring* heightens Americans' awareness of environmental issues. A year later, *The Feminine Mystique* by Betty Friedan helps to usher in a feminist revolution.

1966: As a result of the Supreme Court's decision in *Miranda v. Arizona*, law officers are now required to inform arrestees of their rights.

1966: In August, Mao Zedong launches the "Great Proletarian Cultural Revolution," which rapidly plunges China into chaos as armed youths plunder the countryside, rooting out suspected foreign collaborators and anti-Chinese elements. Along with rifles and other weapons, these Red Guards are armed with copies of Mao's "Little Red Book."

1969: Assisted by pilot Michael Collins, astronauts Neil Armstrong and Edwin E. "Buzz" Aldrin become the first men to walk on the Moon on 20 July.

1970: President Nixon sends U.S. troops into Cambodia on 30 April. Four days later, National Guardsmen open fire on antiwar protesters at Kent State University in Ohio.

1973: Overthrow of Chile's Salvador Allende, the only freely elected Marxist leader in history, who dies in the presidential palace. According to supporters of the new leader, General Augusto Pinochet, Allende committed suicide, but Allende's supporters maintain that he was killed by Pinochet's troops.

1976: United States celebrates its bicentennial.

1978: U.S. Senate approves a measure presented by President Carter the year before, to turn the Panama Canal over to Panama by 2000.

1979: Nicaragua's president, General Anastasio Somoza Debayle, flees to Miami, and the Sandinista faction takes control of the government.

1982: Argentina invades the Falkland Islands, a British possession, and Great Britain strikes back in a ten-week war from which Britain emerges victorious.

1986: Seven astronauts die in the explosion of the U.S. Space Shuttle *Challenger* on 28 January.

1990: Though the Internet (originally the Arpanet) has existed for 21 years, it has not been very user-friendly and has remained the province of defense personnel and other specialists. This year, however, sees the beginnings of the World Wide Web, which will make the Net accessible to a broad range of users over the coming years.

1994: In a surprise upset, Republicans win control of both the House and the Senate, ending four decades of almost unbroken Democratic control. Georgia's Newt Gingrich becomes Speaker of the House.

1997: After 18 years out of power, the Labour Party, led by Prime Minister Tony Blair, wins control of the British government.

2001: On the morning of 11 September, terrorists hijack four jets, two of which ram the twin towers of the World Trade Center in New York City. A third plane slams into the Pentagon in Washington, D.C., and a fourth crashes in an empty field in Pennsylvania. The towers catch fire and collapse in a scene of horror witnessed by an audience of millions on live television. The death toll is approximately three thousand.

Adolfo López Mateos. The Library of Congress.

Event and Its Context

Origins of the Maquiladora Industry

The exact origins of the maquiladora industry are unclear. Before the 1960s, there already had been "free zones" along the Mexican-U.S. border, where laws regarding foreign investment were more relaxed. The establishment of maquiladoras grew out of a Mexican government program known as the *Programa Nacional Fronterizo* (PRONAF). The Mexican president Adolfo López Mateos established the program in 1961 to promote social and economic development along the border at the time that the Bracero Program, which had sent Mexican laborers to work in the United States, came to end. One of the key aspects of PRONAF was industrialization along the border. At first, PRONAF emphasized the production of goods for the Mexican market.

Later, Mexican government officials determined that the best course of action was to produce for the U.S. market. Sometimes credit for the ideas of maquiladoras is given to Richard Bolin, who conducted studies carried out by the industrial consulting firm Arthur D. Little de México. Further impetus came from Octaviano Campos Salas of the Mexican Ministry of Industry and Commerce. Campos Salas claimed that on a trip to Asia in 1964, he had observed the success of U.S. assembly plants, and he hoped that Mexico would become an alternative to Hong Kong and Taiwan. Mexico seemed uniquely qualified for such as role, with its 2,000-mile-long shared border and geographic proximity making transportation costs inexpensive.

Thus, in 1965 the Mexican government instituted the Border Industrialization Program (BIP) to create jobs by attracting foreign investment. This plan was to extend the "free zone" concept to the entire border region. The program allowed for the duty-free importation of machinery, equipment, and components to a zone within 20 kilometers of the border as long as these items were later reexported. The output of the assembly plants could not be sold in the Mexican market. The Mexican government hoped that the border would change from an underdeveloped region into a growth pole for the country.

Many Mexican workers also were hopeful when the government issued a new federal labor law on 1 May 1970. Maquiladora management was to implement the provisions of the new law within three years. It included paid vacations, mandatory Christmas bonuses, and employer-paid death, termination, and retirement compensation. The law was among the most progressive pieces of labor legislation in the developing world. Yet despite these potentially expensive mandated worker benefits, foreign firms continued to go to Mexico, and the number of assembly plants continued to increase.

In the United States, organized labor often opposed the maquiladoras, fearing that jobs would be lost. In part to dispel this fear, Bolin and others developed the concept of the twin plant, in which two facilities would exist, one on each side of the border. On the U.S. side, there would be a capital-intensive plant, while just across the border in Mexico there would be a plant for labor-intensive activities. Many envisioned that because they would be so close, the twin plants could share the same management, and transportation costs would be almost nonexistent. In reality, however, few true twin plants existed.

The early maquiladoras enjoyed some success. When the program began in the mid-1960s, Hong Kong assembled five times as many U.S. products as Mexico. By the end of the 1960s, Mexico processed twice as many goods that originated in the United States as Hong Kong. While wages in Mexico were, in fact, higher than in Asia, the low transport costs more than made up for the difference. By the end of the 1960s there were more than 100 maquiladora plants along the border, which employed more than 15,000 workers. While this figure was a small percentage of the workforce of the entire country, maquiladoras had become a major employer in the border region, where unemployment and underemployment were common.

The First Crisis in the Maquiladora Industry

The first crisis in the maquiladora industry came in 1974, resulting in the closure of plants and worker layoffs. Two factors caused the crisis. First, a recession in the United States in 1974 and 1975 hurt the maquiladoras, as demand decreased on the U.S. side of the border for many of the products assembled in Mexico. Second, maquiladora labor was becoming increasingly militant. Whereas at first the Mexican workers had been considered to be docile, they now were making more demands on management, including pay raises. If the cost of labor rose too high, Mexico would lose its competitive advantage. Indeed, some firms threatened to leave Mexico.

A series of steps ended this first crisis. First, the Mexican government and the maquiladora owners reached an agreement known as the Alliance for Production. Second, workers toned down their demands, fearing that if companies relocated, they would permanently lose their jobs. Third, in September 1976 the Mexican government devalued the peso, effectively lowering the cost of labor for foreign firms.

The Industry Recovers

A period of slow recovery followed until 1981. Between 1975 and 1981 the number of plants increased from about 450 to more than 600. In addition, the number of workers employed in the maquiladora industry nearly doubled, from about 67,000 to 131,000. This recovery was facilitated by a stronger U.S. economy and by the attitude of the new Mexican president, José López Portillo, who took office in 1976.

López Portillo's Alliance for Production was a new development strategy in which the government aided the maquiladora industry. The new president wanted to demonstrate that he would not follow the radical policies of his predecessor, Luís Echeverría Álavarez, but rather would help promote the industry. The government agreed to take such steps as financing industrial parks, and the plant owners promised to promote investment.

The government also changed its attitude toward labor. The previous administration had created the progressive 1970 labor code, but López Portillo slowly undid many of these reforms. The Mexican government now gave employers more freedom in their treatment of employees, making it easier to fire workers, extending the probationary period of employment from 30 to 90 days, and allowing room to alter wages and working conditions. Overall, in the late 1970s and early 1980s, labor was more disciplined by management, and the situation of laborers was made more difficult as the result of inflation and intensified production. Thus, they worked harder and earned less.

The Second Crisis in the Maquiladora Industry

A second crisis occurred in 1981–1982. There was another, though milder, recession in the United States that affected demand. Furthermore, in dollar terms the wages of Mexican maquiladora workers were rising once again. Indeed, they had surpassed those in Asian countries, such as Hong Kong, South Korea, and Taiwan. Many companies again threatened to pull out of Mexico. Once more the Mexican government decided that the solution was devaluation of the peso. This devaluation cut wages in dollar terms for the foreign companies. In addition, in a surprise move, López Portillo nationalized Mexico's banks and imposed exchange controls. Devaluations continued under the new president, Miguel de la Madrid Hurtado, who took office in 1982. These moves served to make the maquiladoras competitive once more.

Recovery and Expansion

The second crisis period was followed by another period of growth. The de la Madrid government continued to promote the industry, as seen in the August 1983 "Decree for the Promotion and Operation of the In-Bond Industry Export." Thus, by 1987 there were more than 1,000 plants employing more than 300,000 workers. By the late 1990s the maquiladora industry was booming. Between 1995 and 1999 employment in the industry grew by double-digit rates every year, reaching 1.1 million workers by 1999. The General Motors subsidiary Delphi, with plants in eight cities, had become Mexico's largest employer, with some 75,000 workers. Maquiladora workers sometimes earned as much as $1.90 an hour. While this wage was low compared with those in the United States, the Mexican average was about $3 per day.

Positive Aspects of the Maquiladoras

Proponents of the maquiladora industry point to a number of positive aspects. Some firms have been forced to close plants during hard economic times, but, in general, most of the companies have been stable. Such stability contributed to the creation of jobs in Mexico. Many advocates point to an overall high level of satisfaction among the maquiladora workers. Significant numbers of the workers are young women, who are able to secure regular paychecks and health insurance through their maquiladora jobs.

Originally a labor-intensive industry, maquiladoras have become increasingly capital intensive. Supporters also point to the transfer of skills and technology from industrialized countries to Mexico. In addition, the maquiladoras produce a significant amount of foreign exchange for Mexico. Moreover, recent changes have allowed the maquiladoras to sell their products in Mexico, thus contributing to the country's economic growth.

Negative Aspects of the Maquiladoras

While there is much support for the maquiladora industry, there are also numerous negative aspects. Opponents of the North American Free Trade Agreement (NAFTA), in particular, focus on various problems of the maquiladoras. A major criticism is that jobs are lost in the United States. Another significant concern is pollution in the border region, because Mexican environmental laws are not as strict as those in the Unites States. Other critics point to the treatment of the maquiladora labor force, claiming that the companies exploit the workers, especially the large female component of the workforce. In addition, companies often threaten to close or leave at the first sign of labor trouble, making workers hesitant to organize.

Yet another complaint is that the industry has remained isolated and has not become integrated into the larger Mexican economy. Some of these fears were borne out in the early years of the industry, because the maquiladoras did not create the backward linkages that Mexican officials had hoped for. It was only on a limited basis that Mexicans supplied goods and services to the plants. Instead, it was Mexicans involved in property development who prospered most, by providing land and factories to the foreign firms.

Furthermore, despite the claims of proponents, critics argue that there has been relatively little technology transfer from developing countries. Instead, developing countries such as Mexico become linked to an increasingly volatile world economy. It is the powerful international corporations that benefit, not the Mexican economy. Thus, some in Mexico have been concerned over what they see as U.S. economic imperialism.

Key Players

Bolin, Richard: Bolin played an important role in developing the maquiladora industry. While working for the industrial consulting firm Arthur D. Little de México, he carried out studies for the Mexican government. Bolin also was involved in the developing the twin plant concept for the border region.

Campos Salas, Octaviano: Campos Salas served as Mexico's commerce minister from 1964 to 1970 under President Gustavo Díaz Ordaz. Trained as an economist, he studied at the Universidad Nacional Autónoma de México as well as at the University of Chicago. During his term as commerce minister, Campos Salas was influential in setting the foundation for the maquiladora industry.

Echeverría Álvarez, Luís (1922–): Populist president of Mexico from 1970 to 1976, Echeverría Álvarez alienated many in the private sector because of his populist policies. Despite his emphasis on state-owned enterprises, he generally allowed the maquiladora industry to expand. The Echeverría administration implemented a labor code that greatly benefited the maquiladora workers.

López Mateos, Adolfo (1910–1969): After serving as secretary of labor, López Mateos was president of Mexico from 1958 to 1964. His administration was responsible for the implementation of an economic development program for the Mexico-U.S. border region that sparked the maquiladora industry. In general, López Mateos followed a moderate economic policy that contributed to the growth of Mexico's industrial infrastructure.

López Portillo, José (1920–): A Mexican lawyer who served as his country's president from 1976 to 1982, López Portillo took office at the start of an economic and political crisis, inheriting an unstable peso and high inflation. He attempted to reestablish a positive relationship with business interests in the wake of the Echeverría administration. To this end, he implemented the Alliance for Production, which had an important impact on the maquiladora industry.

See also: *North American Free Trade Agreement.*

BIBLIOGRAPHY

Fatemi, Khosrow, ed. *The Maquiladora Industry: Economic Solution or Problem?* New York: Praeger, 1990.

Grunwald, Joseph, and Kenneth Flamm. *The Global Factory: Foreign Assembly in International Trade.* Washington, DC: Brookings Institution, 1985.

Rockenbach, Leslie. *The Mexican-American Border: NAFTA and Global Linkages.* New York: Routledge, 2001.

Sklair, Leslie. *Assembling for Development: The Maquila Industry in Mexico and the United States.* San Diego: Center for U.S.-Mexican Studies, 1993.

Wilson, Patricia. *Exports and Local Development: Mexico's New Maquiladoras.* Austin: University of Texas Press, 1992.

—Ronald Young

March of the Mill Children

United States 1903

Synopsis

Mother Jones was a well-known labor firebrand and orator who, by 1903, had been increasingly concerned about the plight of working children. Child labor was rampant through many industries, including textiles and mining. Conditions were horrendous; many children were maimed, crippled, and killed yearly in accidents. Perhaps Jones's interest was motivated by her own background as a teacher or by her personal concern as a mother. Regardless, the abolition of child labor remained an important issue to her throughout her lifetime.

A powerful orator, Jones was called upon to speak at a Kensington, Pennsylvania, rally of more than 75,000 striking textile workers. Inspired by the numerous children among the workers, Jones decided to hold a march to raise awareness of child labor. She led nearly 400 children and adults through Pennsylvania and New Jersey to New York City. Although the march attracted media attention and some local support along the way, she encountered resistance to her requests to enter New York City and did not gain access to the president. Nonetheless, the Pennsylvania legislature passed laws the following year that limited child labor.

Timeline

1883: Foundation of the League of Struggle for the Emancipation of Labor by Marxist political philosopher Georgi Valentinovich Plekhanov marks the formal start of Russia's labor movement. Change still lies far in the future for Russia, however: tellingly, Plekhanov launches the movement in Switzerland.

1893: Henry Ford builds his first automobile.

1899: The Second Anglo-Boer War, often known simply as the Boer War, begins.

1903: Anti-Jewish pogroms break out in Russia.

1903: Henry Ford establishes the Ford Motor Company.

1903: Russia's Social Democratic Party splits into two factions: the moderate Mensheviks and the hard-line Bolsheviks. Despite their names, which in Russian mean "minority" and "majority," respectively, Mensheviks actually outnumber Bolsheviks.

1903: Polish-born French chemist Marie Curie becomes the first woman to be awarded the Nobel Prize.

1903: One of the earliest motion pictures, *The Great Train Robbery,* premieres.

1903: United States assumes control over the Panama Canal Zone, which it will retain until 1979.

1903: Wright brothers make their first flight at Kitty Hawk, North Carolina. Though balloons date back to the eighteenth century and gliders to the nineteenth, Orville Wright's twelve seconds aloft on 17 December mark the birth of practical human flight.

1906: The British Labour Party is founded.

1913: Two incidents illustrate the increasingly controversial nature of the arts in the new century. Visitors to the 17 February Armory Show in New York City are scandalized by such works as Marcel Duchamp's cubist *Nude Descending a Staircase,* which elicits vehement criticism, and theatergoers at the 29 May debut of Igor Stravinsky's ballet *Le Sacré du Printemps* (*The Rite of Spring*) are so horrified by the new work that a riot ensues.

Event and Its Context

Although Pennsylvania law prohibited children under the age of 13 from working, many children were compelled to work to help their families rather than attend school. Other states had child labor laws, but enforcement was not consistent and comprehensive protections were few. States were not effective in passing legislation even when child labor laws were suggested. No federal legislation existed.

Jones noted in her autobiography, "The [child labor] law was poorly enforced and the mothers of these children often swore falsely as to their children's age. In a single block in Kensington, 14 women, mothers of 22 children all under 12, explained it was a question of starvation or perjury. That the fathers had been killed or maimed at the mines."

Mill owners reaped financial benefit from this practice. They were apathetic because it was cheaper to employ children. Typical practice was to hire an entire family. Young children could also work faster and often better at tasks such as crawling beneath looms to lubricate machinery or spooling thread. Children often worked more than 60 hours a week for about $2.50. When children were maimed or killed on the job, there were always others willing to take their places.

Child labor was used in various industries throughout the United States, including paper mills, bottling plants, glass factories, and garment sweatshops. Children sold newspapers or worked in seafood processing plants, shucking oysters and peeling shrimp. Ironically, the majority of working children are reported to have wanted to go to work rather than suffer through school. Earning money gave them some measure of independence. Reformers interviewed one child who said he preferred work to being hit in school.

Mother Jones capitalized on a Philadelphia area textile strike to stage a child labor protest. She had been brought in as a speaker during the strike's third week. She arrived on 14 June 1903 in Kensington, where most of the 75,000 striking workers lived or worked. Mother Jones decided the time was right to organize the children. Of the strikers, an estimated 10,000 were children, most under 10.

Mother Jones took up the cause of the injustices of child labor and spoke out at various venues in and around Philadelphia in support of the strikers and especially the children, but it seemed none of the mill owners, wealthy area residents, or newspapers—those people who could change conditions by virtue of their standing in the community or access to the media—were taking notice.

On the morning of 7 July at a strike meeting, Mother Jones announced plans to organize a march from Philadelphia to New

Mary Harris "Mother" Jones. The Library of Congress.

York to draw attention to this matter. She told the strikers of her intent to gather at least 400 children and the same number of adults to help care for the children. Her goal was tripartite: to draw attention to child labor problems, rally support for the textile strike, and shame the capitalists.

Parents were concerned about the trip. Mother Jones had planned to have the entire "army" on foot, but relented, saying the marchers could ride in supply wagons and take public transportation when available. Some parents remained concerned. Nevertheless, about 300 to 400 people, both adults and children, participated. An estimated half of them were under the age of 16. Charles Sweeney, a union leader, helped Jones with the event. The participants congregated, then left Kensington at about 1 P.M. that day. Sweeney led the group, carrying a baton. Children playing instruments and other marchers followed. Some carried signs with slogans such as, "We only ask for Justice" and "We want to go to school." Behind the throng, a fleet of eight supply wagons carried donated food and the marchers' meager gear.

The march is often called the "March of the Mill Children," but others participated in addition to the children who were working in the mills. Many of those marching were mining children. Mother Jones had toured mines and factories and had seen first-hand the dangerous conditions that caused industrial accidents. Many of children on the march had been maimed or crippled by such accidents.

As Mother Jones had hoped, the media took interest in the march. Journalists traveled with the group. There are conflicting reports about the numbers of boys and girls, total participants, and how many completed the march. The marchers spent the first night at Torresdale Park on the outskirts of Philadelphia. The weather was unusually hot and had exacted a toll on the marchers by the time they reached Trenton, New Jersey. Many became exhausted or ill and were sent home. Some marchers behaved badly: children who were caught chasing a farmer's chickens were shipped back home. Mother Jones had to maintain decorum as the success of the march depended largely on the kindness of those along its route; the strike council had been unable to fund the march.

By 10 July the group was massed at Monument Park, a Trenton, New Jersey, park near the Delaware River. Mother Jones drew a crowd of 5,000 to hear her describe in vivid detail the conditions in which the children worked. Local citizens took up a collection and helped by providing hotel rooms and food.

An advance team arranged the civic receptions en route. Farmers donated produce and grocers provided foodstuffs to sustain the group. Even a caretaker at the estate of former president Grover Cleveland opened the barns to the children on a stormy night. Finding food was rarely a problem, but finding a direct route was becoming difficult, as some towns did not want the marchers coming through town. They were greeted enthusiastically in New Jersey cities including New Brunswick, Elizabeth, Newark, and Paterson.

As the march neared New York City, Mother Jones had an idea. Rather than a rally and pageant at Madison Square Garden, why not see the president? The ultimate destination was changed to the summer home of President Theodore Roosevelt in Oyster Bay, New York. "I decided to go with the children to see President Roosevelt to ask him to have Congress pass a law prohibiting the exploitation of childhood," she wrote. Jones was intent on getting Roosevelt's attention and federal legislation. She sent newspapers a series of open letters detailing the problems children faced in the workplace, which were published. Rumor abounded as to how Roosevelt would respond. Mother Jones was sure Roosevelt would meet with them. "We will approach the President as respectable people and feel sure that we will receive civil treatment."

The march reached New York City on 22 July. Local officials did not want the march in the city, and police commissioner refused to allow the marchers to enter the city. Outraged, Jones went to see New York City Mayor Seth Low. "The mayor was most courteous but he said he would have to support the police commissioner. I asked him what the reason was for refusing us entrance to the city and he said that we were not citizens of New York." Mother Jones pointed out to the mayor several instances in which foreign dignitaries were entertained at city expense. She swayed Low with the argument that the marchers were United States citizens and contributors to the gross national product and were therefore entitled to march through the city. Low relented. A police cordon accompanied the group to their rally destination on Twentieth Street, rather than Madison Square Garden.

The next day the marchers toured Coney Island, and Mother Jones gave a speech. Ultimately, she was unable to convince Roosevelt to meet with her. Despite this setback, Jones stated, "Our march had done its work. We had drawn the attention of the nation to the crime of child labor." Members of the Pennsylvania legislature took heed and in 1904 enacted laws restricting child labor. Jones continued to advocate the abolition of child labor throughout her life.

Key Players

Jones, Mary Harris "Mother" (*ca.* 1830–1930): Jones was born in Cork, Ireland but her precise birth year is not known. Some estimate that she "fudged" her age by as much as 15 years. Displaced by the potato famine, her family settled in Canada, where she worked as a teacher and dressmaker. After marrying an ironworker, she moved to Memphis. She lost her entire family—husband and four children—in the 1867 yellow fever epidemic. In 1871, after years of personal tragedy, she immersed herself in the labor movement. She gained a reputation as a hell-raising militant and was best known for her work supporting miners. Jones organized the week-long children's march in 1903 to draw attention to the need for laws to protect children.

Low, Seth (1850–1916): Born in New York, Low began his career as a merchant in Brooklyn. He became interested in civic affairs and politics beginning in 1878. Soon after, he became involved in the Young Republican Club and ran for mayor of Brooklyn in 1883; he won that term and a subsequent term. He was named president of Columbia College in 1889 after retiring from business. Low continued to be active in civic matters, including mediating labor disputes. In 1901 he was elected as mayor of greater New York. Low was mayor at the time of the children's march.

Roosevelt, Theodore (1858–1919): A descendant of one of the first families of New York, Roosevelt was a charismatic career politician. He was elected to the New York State Assembly in 1881. He was also New York police commissioner and assistant secretary of the navy. He resigned from the latter post to organize the First U.S. Volunteer Cavalry, commonly known as the Rough Riders, during the Spanish-American War. He continued in office as governor of New York and vice president under William McKinley. With the assassination of McKinley in September 1901, Roosevelt ascended to the presidency. He refused to meet with Jones and the marchers.

See also: *National Child Labor Committee.*

———————

BIBLIOGRAPHY

Books

Currie, Stephen. *We Have Marched Together: The Working Children's Crusade.* Minneapolis, MN: Lerner Publications Company, 1997.

Parton, Mary Field, ed. *Autobiography of Mother Jones.* Charles Kerr, 1925.

Other

Knebel, Jessica. Illinois Periodicals Online. "Mary Harris Jones, Labor's Advocate." *Illinois History*. December 1997 [cited 1 October 2002]. <http://www.lib.niu.edu/ipo/ihy971211.html>.

ADDITIONAL RESOURCES

Books

Steel, Edward, ed. *The Correspondence of Mother Jones.* Pittsburgh, PA: University of Pittsburgh Press, 1985.

Werstein, Irving. *Labor's Defiant Lady: The Story of Mother Jones.* New York: Thomas Y. Crowell, 1969.

—Linda Dailey Paulson

March on Washington Movement

United States 1941

Synopsis

In a 1941 effort to dramatize the situation of African Americans before President Franklin D. Roosevelt and the American public, A. Philip Randolph attempted to organize immense crowds to march on Washington, D.C. Randolph and his fellow March on Washington Movement activists demanded an end to segregation in the military and equal access to jobs in the national defense industry for black men and women who were habitually denied such jobs and subjected to other forms of discrimination. Although the activists abandoned the protest itself on condition of a deal with the president, the very threat of a march achieved its main goal: an executive order banning discrimination in national defense employment. It was in many ways the beginning of the modern civil rights movement. The movement's success set the stage for a hugely successful March on Washington in 1963 that would be imitated by many groups thereafter.

Timeline

1921: Washington Disarmament Conference limits the tonnage of world navies.

1925: European leaders attempt to secure the peace at the Locarno Conference, which guarantees the boundaries between France and Germany, and Belgium and Germany.

1931: Financial crisis widens in the United States and Europe, which reel from bank failures and climbing unemployment levels. In London, armies of the unemployed riot.

1936: Germany reoccupies the Rhineland, while Italy annexes Ethiopia. Recognizing a commonality of aims, the two totalitarian powers sign the Rome-Berlin Axis Pact. (Japan will join them in 1940.)

1941: German troops march into the Balkans, conquering Yugoslavia and Greece. (Bulgaria and Romania, along with Hungary, are aligned with the Nazis.)

Asa Philip Randolph. The Library of Congress.

1941: In a move that takes Stalin by surprise, Hitler sends his troops into the Soviet Union on 22 June. Like his hero Napoleon, Hitler believes that by stunning Russia with a lightning series of brilliant maneuvers, it is possible to gain a quick and relatively painless victory. Early successes seem to prove him right, and he is so confident of victory that he refuses to equip his soldiers with winter clothing.

1941: Japanese bombing of Pearl Harbor on 7 December brings the United States into the war against the Axis. Combined with the attack on the Soviet Union, which makes Stalin an unlikely ally of the Western democracies, the events of 1941 will ultimately turn the tide of the war.

1941: The United States initiates the Manhattan Project to build an atomic bomb and signs the Lend-Lease Act, whereby it provides aid to Great Britain and, later, the Soviet Union.

1941: Great films of the year include *The Maltese Falcon, Sullivan's Travels, Meet John Doe, How Green Was My Valley,* and a work often cited as one of the greatest films of all time: Orson Welles's *Citizen Kane.*

1946: Winston Churchill warns of an "Iron Curtain" spreading across Eastern Europe.

1951: Color television is introduced.

1956: First aerial testing of the hydrogen bomb at Bikini Atoll creates a blast so powerful—the equivalent of 10 million tons of TNT—that it actually results in the infusion of protons to atomic nuclei to create two new elements, einsteinium and fermium, which have atomic numbers of 99 and 100, respectively.

Event and Its Context

Unity in Inequality

The entry of the United States into World War II precipitated significant changes to the national labor market. With so many men fighting abroad, women joined in industry as part of the national war effort. Nonetheless, African Americans of both sexes continued to suffer intense discrimination both in and outside the workplace. More than 20 years after black Americans' full support in World War I had failed to bring full equality, "Jim Crow" laws banned black citizens from sharing facilities with whites in several states and in the nation's capital. In Washington, D.C., no black citizen could attend a theater (except local Jim Crow movie houses), eat in a public restaurant used by whites, sit next to a white passenger on a public bus, ride in a taxi driven by a white, or register in a hotel.

Despite calls for national unity in the fight against the Axis powers, both the domestic job market and the military continued to discriminate against African Americans. Moreover, government hiring practices kept black Americans from federal employment and from working in defense companies that received federal contracts. Throughout the war, the American armed forces were segregated. In a country that was awakening from economic hardships of the Great Depression, black workers were turned away from factory gates because of their race. In the view of labor and civil rights activists like A. Philip Randolph, such race-based discrimination was the cause for wealth disparities between black and white Americans. Randolph, along with other civil rights activists, called for a massive march of African Americans on Washington, D.C.

Black activists of the time asked why African Americans should fight in yet another foreign war when their own rights were not protected either at home or in the ranks of the military. Despite protests, black Americans in the U.S. Navy were generally confined to the messmen's branch. Soon after the war began, African American sailors on the U.S.S. *Philadelphia* were arrested for writing to the *Pittsburgh Courier* to expose the abuse and discrimination they faced on the ship. Whatever action the navy was to take and regardless of the consequences, the sailors wrote, "We only know that it could not possibly surpass the mental cruelty inflicted upon us on this ship." Despite a shortage of nurses, defense authorities were hesitant to accept black nurses to treat white troops, as doing so would be a violation of social norms. National Association for the Advancement of Colored People (NAACP) Graduate Nurses, headed by Mabel Staupers, were vocal protesters against racial policies in the Army Nurse Corps and in the military in general. A pamphlet by the Socialist Workers Party titled "The Negro and the U.S. Army" (by Eugene Varlin, c. 1940), asked what African Americans would get out of World War II. The pamphlet responded that "if the capitalist class remains the ruler of this country, the Negroes will get out this war what they got out of the last war—and maybe worse."

Taking People to the Power

The idea of taking the problems of the people to the seat of power was not entirely new. In 1894 Jacob Sechler Coxey's "army" of jobless men had marched on Washington to demand relief measures. In 1903 Mother Jones had led a march of underaged millworkers (many the victims of industrial accidents) to the New York home of President Theodore Roosevelt. From women demanding the vote to veterans demanding bonuses, a growing number of movements were claiming the capital for national public protests. The idea of a massive march of African Americans on the nation's capital, however, was the brainchild of Randolph, a man greatly respected in the African American community for his struggle to create the Brotherhood of Sleeping Car Porters. Randolph created the March on Washington Movement (MOWM) to demand "jobs and freedom" for African Americans. In particular, Randolph argued that "Negro America must bring its power and pressure to bear upon the agencies and representatives of the Federal Government to exact their rights" in the American armed forces and in national defense employment. "Winning Democracy for the Negro Is Winning the War for Democracy," stated MOWM literature. The movement had its national headquarters in the Theresa Hotel Building in New York City. Randolph served as national director, the office of executive secretary was held by E. Pauline Myers, and B. F. McLaurin served as national secretary.

One MOWM flyer summed up the movement's objectives in four points. The organization's foremost goal was to "crystallize the mass consciousness of grievances and injustices" suffered by African Americans as a means of rallying them behind a cause for which they would "gladly and willingly suffer and sacrifice." The second objective was to reeducate white America on the question of equality for black Americans. The movement also aimed to "enlist the support of liberal and Christian white America in an all-out struggle for unadulterated democracy at home as well as abroad." Finally, the MOWM was to operate by means of "mass maneuvers and demonstrations."

The MOWM was a wholly African American organization that excluded whites. Given a tendency toward solidarity among radical white activists, this was partly an effort to keep communists from entering the organization. It was also Randolph's attempt to appeal to lower-class African Americans and to promote self-confidence and a sense of black pride. He also placed emphasis on jobs, an issue that affected both urban black people in the industrial North and those in the rural South. At a time when young black activists were calling for "democracy in our time," the organization shunned judicial actions and backroom negotiations in favor of direct action. The idea of direct mass action derived from the principals of Indian pacifist Mahatma Gandhi, and as such, was to be nonviolent.

March on Washington Declared

On 15 January 1941 Randolph stated that "ten thousand Negroes" should march on Washington with the slogan, "We loyal Negro American citizens demand the right to work and fight for our country." The slogan was meant to counter any negative propaganda claiming that black Americans wanted to hurt the defense effort or jeopardize national unity. "On the contrary," said Randolph. "But certainly there can be no national unity where one-tenth of the population are denied their basic rights as American citizens." The plan was met with enthusiasm by the African American community, and many young militants invested themselves in the project with great fervor.

With the aid of NAACP executive secretary Walter White and National Youth Administration Negro Affairs director

Mary McLeod Bethune, Randolph forced Roosevelt to listen to MOWM demands. Roosevelt sent First Lady Eleanor Roosevelt and New York City mayor Fiorello La Guardia to negotiate with March on Washington leaders. Upon her return to Washington, the first lady told her husband that the movement leaders were steadfast in their plans and that only an order banning discrimination would avert the demonstration. Despite accusations from certain sectors that the president had deployed her to diffuse the march, the first lady urged him to act "for both moral and political reasons."

Eleanor Roosevelt was a vocal advocate of equal rights for people of all ethnic backgrounds. Her support for the NAACP when it was falsely considered a radical left-wing organization made her the subject of FBI investigations. Her article in *Negro Digest* (forerunner to *Ebony*), in which she stated that she would feel "bitterness" were she black and suffered similar discrimination, had critics labeling the magazine communist. Despite her support of desegregation and equal rights, Mrs. Roosevelt was not entirely convinced that the March on Washington was a good idea. The idea of tens of thousands of black demonstrators with nowhere to stay converging on a city of white police officers did not seem promising to her. Although she never publicly stated her opposition to the march, she did question its feasibility in private meetings. Despite minor differences, African American fighters for equal rights had an ally in the seat of power.

Nonetheless, "you can give her too much credit if you're not careful, by implying that she was the cause of the Negro movements of that time, the civil rights movements," journalist and commentator Vernon Jarrett recalled years later. "This came from black people themselves. They didn't need an Eleanor Roosevelt to protest."

On 18 June 1941 President Roosevelt and several defense ministers met with Randolph at the White House to discuss the March on Washington. Concerned about violence, the president called the march a "grave mistake" and personally urged the leaders to cancel it. He reportedly told the activists that he would not address demonstrators, in part because he sensed that Americans would resent any protest attempting to "coerce the Government and make it do certain things."

Also present at the half-hour meeting were La Guardia, White, and the first lady. When Randolph complained that black workers seeking employment at defense plants were being turned back simply because of their race, Roosevelt reportedly promised to call up the heads of the various defense plants and "have them see to it that Negroes are given the same opportunity to work in defense plants as any other citizen in the country." Randolph in turn requested "something concrete, something tangible, definite, positive, and affirmative." He wanted an executive mandate giving black workers the right to work in the plants. Roosevelt claimed that issuing an executive order for black workers would mean that other groups would show up at the White House to demand their own executive orders. Further, because "questions like this can't be settled with a sledge hammer," nothing could be done unless Randolph called off the strike. Randolph made it clear that he had no intention of calling off the strike but would march on the city with 100,000 African Americans.

As the group adjourned, it agreed to meet within a fortnight to study the president's proposal to set up a board "to receive and act upon complaints of racial discrimination in the defense program." The following day, La Guardia suggested creating a "Grievance Committee" and presented Roosevelt with the board's proposal for an executive order. The order was to include a nondiscriminatory policy in defense contracting and would require unions and government agencies to end discrimination.

Some of Roosevelt's defense collaborators had stated their belief that national defense was more important than reform. A week prior to the scheduled march, police and intelligence services were on the alert. Federal Bureau of Investigation (FBI) director J. Edgar Hoover warned both the attorney general and the solicitor general that the Communist Party could try to coopt the march to promote its own ideas. On 22 June, Nazi Germany invaded Soviet Russia. At the same time, the Washington press was reporting on a crime wave (which some attributed to the arrival of outsiders) and questioning how a nation with a chaotic capital could help restore international order. On 24 June the La Guardia committee presented the MOWM representatives with a draft of the executive order for their perusal. When they saw that the draft did not mention discrimination in government jobs, they quickly added a clause to that effect. Although Roosevelt's undersecretaries of war and navy expressed opposition to the order because it would hamper munitions contracts, the president rejected their advice.

A Labor and Civil Rights Victory

The proposed march was cancelled at the last moment because of the partial attainment of its objectives. On 25 June 1941 Roosevelt signed Executive Order 8802, establishing the Fair Employment Practice Committee (FEPC). The decree prohibited racial discrimination on the basis of "race, creed, color, or national origin" in the federal government and in any defense industries under government contract. The order was issued upon the condition that the march be called off. It was the first presidential decree since the Emancipation Proclamation on the rights of African Americans. According to James Farmer, founder of Congress of Racial Equality, Roosevelt could not take the chance that thousands of demonstrators would be in Washington "at a time when he was calling the United States the arsenal of democracy."

Although the president had agreed to have the FEPC ban discrimination in defense plants, he refused to consider Randolph's initial calls for an end to racial segregation in the military. The FEPC had the power to investigate and act against employment discrimination complaints. Roosevelt attempted to strengthen the FEPC with a full-time staff in 1943 after learning of noncompliance. Although the FEPC had no real enforcement capabilities, the FBI had the power to arrest anyone who thwarted the war effort. When Philadelphia transit workers went on strike against an FEPC desegregation order, FBI threats to arrest leaders ended the strike. By war's end, the number of African Americans with government jobs more than tripled to 200,000 and defense industry employment of black workers rose from 3 to 8 percent; most of these were menial jobs.

In keeping with Executive Order 8802, the National War Labor Board broke with standard practice to abolish the classifications "colored laborer" and "white laborer" and replaced them simply with "laborer," with one rate of pay. African American workers subsequently attained wage increases that achieved parity with white laborers.

By December 1941 the MOWM had become an all-black organization that was supported by dues-paying members. Building on the movement's initial victory, in 1942 Randolph organized a series of "colossal and dramatic" gatherings. That summer the movement "to help create faith by Negroes in Negroes" gathered 20,000 participants in New York, 12,000 in Chicago and 9,000 in St. Louis. The MOWM began to whither in 1943 but lasted until the late 1940s. Nonetheless, in 1948 the movement got President Harry Truman to sign Executive Order 9981, banning military segregation. In 1963 Randolph saw his dream come true. The March on Washington for Jobs and Freedom, organized by Randolph and Bayard Rustin, was the largest demonstration for racial and economic equality in U.S. history.

Key Players

Bethune, Mary McLeod (1875–1955): Bethune was vice president of the National Association for the Advancement of Colored People (NAACP). As director of Negro affairs in the National Youth Administration (1936–1944), she was an important force behind the March for Washington Movement's demand for fair employment practices.

La Guardia, Fiorello Henry (1882–1947): La Guardia was an American political reformer known for defending immigrants and workers. He served in Congress first in 1916, breaking to serve in World War I, and again from 1923 to 1933. His years as mayor of New York City (1933–1945) were credited with improving municipal efficiency and fighting corruption. During World War II he was director of the U.S. Office of Civilian Defense (1941–1942), helping Franklin Roosevelt resolve the threat of a March on Washington.

Randolph, Asa Philip (1889–1979): Randolph's struggle to organize the Brotherhood of Sleeping Car Porters, of which he was president, made him one of the most respected figures in black America. His fight for civil and economic justice was channeled largely through the March on Washington Movement, which he founded in 1941.

Roosevelt, Anna Eleanor (1884–1962): Roosevelt was an advocate of civil rights who took an active role in her husband's administration, serving as a "trusted and tireless reporter" for his causes. A vocal defender of equality for African Americans, she helped mediate between the president and the March on Washington activists.

White, Walter Francis (1893–1955): White, despite his blue eyes, fair skin, and blond hair, lived life as an African American and became a champion of civil rights. He was executive secretary of the NAACP from 1931 to 1955 and was a vocal opponent of lynching. During World War II he joined A. Philip Randolph to help ban discrimination in wartime industry.

See also: *Fair Employment Practice Committee; Jim Crow Segregation and Labor; March of the Mill Children.*

BIBLIOGRAPHY

Books

Kasher, Steven. *The Civil Rights Movement: A Photographic History, 1954–1968.* New York: Abbeville Press, 1996.

Kryder, Daniel. *Divided Arsenal: Race and the American State During World War II.* New York: Cambridge University Press, 2000.

Other

"A. Philip Randolph Exhibit." The George Meany Memorial Archives. George Meany Center for Labor Studies, National Labor College. 2001–2001 [cited 20 October 2002]. <http://www.georgemeany.org/archives/activist.html>.

"A. Philip Randolph: For Jobs and Freedom." PBS [cited 20 October 2002]. <http://www.pbs.org/weta/apr/aprprogram.html#marches>.

A. Philip Randolph Pullman Porter Museum [cited 20 October 2002]. <http://aphiliprandolphmuseum.com/evo_history5.html>.

African American Odyssey: The Depression, The New Deal, and World War II [cited 20 October 2002]. <http://memory.loc.gov/ammem/aaohtml/exhibit/aopart8.html>.

Eleanor Roosevelt and Human Rights Project. The Eleanor Roosevelt Research Papers, Department of History, George Washington University [cited 20 October 2002]. <http://www.gwu.edu/~erpapers/abouteleanor/q-and-a/glossary/fepc.htm>.

Federal Bureau of Investigation. "History of the FBI: World War II Period (late 1930s–1945)" [cited 20 October 2002]. <http://www.fbi.gov/libref/historic/history/worldwar.htm>.

Holloway, Kevin. Civil Rights: A Status Report. "World War II and Executive Order 8802" [cited 20 October 2002]. <http://www.ghg.net/hollaway/civil/civil27.htm>.

Holt Labor Library, Labor Studies and Radical History. "Pioneer Publishers 1940–1948." 2000 [cited 20 October 2002]. <http://www.holtlaborlibrary.org/pioneer.html>.

Lakewood Public Library. Women in History. "Mary McLeod Bethune Biography." 1 October 2002 [cited 20 October 2002]. <http://www.lkwdpl.org/wihohio/beth-mar.htm>.

March on Washington Movement. *How to Organize a Unit.* Pamphlet, c. 1941 [cited 20 October 2002]. <http://www.georgemeany.org/archives/3.6a.jpg>.

PBS Web site. *The American Experience.* Interview with Vernon Jarrett on "Eleanor's Commitment to African Americans" [cited 20 October 2002]. <http://www.pbs.org/wgbh/amex/eleanor/filmmore/reference/interview/jarrett07.html>.

"White, Walter (Francis)" [cited 20 October 2002]. <http://search.eb.com/blackhistory/micro/638/8.html>.

ADDITIONAL RESOURCES

Other

A. Philip Randolph Pullman Porter Museum. [cited 20 October 2002]. <http://www.aphiliprandolphmuseum.com>.

—Brett Allan King

Australia and New Zealand

— Provincial border, 1890
✪ National capital
• Other city
© 2003 The Gale Group, Inc.

Maritime Strike

Australasia 1890

Synopsis

On 15 August 1890 the Steamship Owners' Association told the Melbourne, Australia, branch of the Mercantile Marine Officers' Association that it would not negotiate a wage claim with the marine officers' union while it was affiliated to the Trades Hall Council. The marine officers objected to this condition and struck. Seamen, wharf laborers, and port workers followed the marine officers out on strike. The dispute came to be regarded as a conflict between the wider principle of the "closed shop" for unionists against "freedom of contract" for employers.

In 1890 there were seven Australasian colonies. Marine officers and seamen worked coastal and intercolonial routes between them. Unionism had begun to appear among the colonies. Employers could not easily—and perhaps did not want to—contain a maritime workers' strike in one colony. It was widely believed that the ship owners, who were themselves federating, had made secret financial preparations for an industrial showdown and that their behavior was provocative. At the same time, workers had affiliated to increasingly broader and more militant organizations. Tensions were high and the conditions ripe for industrial action.

The three-month Trans-Tasman industrial action began in August 1890 and involved at least 50,000 miners and transport and pastoral workers in New South Wales (NSW), Victoria, Queensland, and South Australia, and 8,000 in New Zealand. Most strikers went back to work in November because they could not afford to continue. Support from nonstriking unionists dwindled. The Illawarra miners were among the stragglers that returned to work in January 1891. Many industries around the Tasman Sea ground to a halt. The strike caused much bitterness over the use both of strikebreakers and police. Governments employed armed military troops and special police in all the major ports of Sydney, Melbourne, Newcastle, Adelaide, Brisbane, Auckland, Wellington, Lyttelton, and Dunedin. The strike coincided with the start of the "long depression" of the 1890s. Labor Party members won in subsequent elections starting in South Australia in January 1891. The Australian Labor Party did not form until Australian federation in 1901. The party's origins, however, date to 1891 and the formation of the NSW Labor Electoral League and the United Labor Party in South Australia. Between 1894 and 1919, Australasian state and national governments passed legislation that established a distinctive system of conciliation and arbitration. In the wake of the 1890 Maritime Strike, states established industrial tribunals for settling industrial issues and the sponsorship of trade unions. During this time, Australasia came to be regarded as a "social laboratory," as a raft of labor legislation was introduced.

Timeline

1870: Franco-Prussian War begins. German troops sweep over France, Napoleon III is dethroned, and France's Second Empire gives way to the Third Republic.

1876: Four-stroke cycle gas engine is introduced.

1880: South Africa's Boers declare an independent republic, precipitating the short First Anglo-Boer War.

1883: Foundation of the League of Struggle for the Emancipation of Labor by Marxist political philosopher Georgi Valentinovich Plekhanov marks the formal start of Russia's labor movement. Change still lies far in the future for Russia, however: tellingly, Plekhanov launches the movement in Switzerland.

1886: Bombing at Haymarket Square, Chicago, kills seven policemen and injures numerous others. Eight anarchists are accused and tried; three are imprisoned, one commits suicide, and four are hanged.

1888: Serbian-born American electrical engineer Nikola Tesla develops a practical system for generating and transmitting alternating current (AC), which will ultimately—and after an extremely acrimonious battle—replace Thomas Edison's direct current (DC) in most homes and businesses.

1890: U.S. Congress passes the Sherman Antitrust Act, which in the years that follow will be used to break up large monopolies.

1890: Police arrest and kill Sioux chief Sitting Bull, and two weeks later, federal troops kill over 200 Sioux at Wounded Knee.

1890: Alfred Thayer Mahan, a U.S. naval officer and historian, publishes *The Influence of Sea Power Upon History, 1660–1783,* which demonstrates the decisive role that maritime forces have played in past conflicts. The book will have an enormous impact on world events by encouraging the major powers to develop powerful navies.

1893: Henry Ford builds his first automobile.

1896: First modern Olympic Games are held in Athens.

1901: Federation of Australia is established.

Event and Its Context

The background to the Maritime Strike of 1890 lies in the rise of unionism and the formation of larger unions, economic depression, moral panic over sweating—a system of labor under which workers toiled for long hours in physically poor and morally dangerous conditions for low wages—concerns about colonial poverty, and awareness of the political possibilities in the Antipodes. Until recently these events have been regarded as connected both chronologically and causally.

Colonial expectations help to explain the strike, which casts a shadow over the myth of a colonial paradise. There was a hope, if not an illusion, that colonial Australasia was a working man's or working artisan's paradise. There are various versions of the paradise but they were all premised on New Zealanders' and Australians' relative wealth, prosperity, and working conditions. There were high wages, high demand for labor, and a high standard of living. Eight-hour days were enacted in various colonies between 1856 and 1896. Australasians had access to abundant rural land, although the majority of the population lived in cities and towns, where there were high rates of home ownership. By the late 1880s, Australasia seemed to be relatively equalitarian, with advanced democratic governments, votes for adult white men, secret ballots, and triennial parliaments that compensated members. Some regarded Australasia as a paradise for working women, too, as there were high marriage rates, early female suffrage, and protective labor legislation in some states.

There is debate over the extent to which Australasia was a colonial paradise. Historian James Belich argued that, although it fell far short of being a "worker's paradise," colonial life provided decent folk with opportunities for advancement. By the 1890s, however, Victoria suffered a sudden economic downturn; South Australia and New Zealand had been in economic depression for some time. Literate and transient people had emigrated halfway around the world because they wanted better lives. Discontent arose when their expectations were not met. The enthusiasm for unionism and the panic at allegations of outwork in the sweating crises in the late 1880s were reactions to the thought that "Old World" ills were following emigrants to the "New World." By the 1890s most of the Australasian population was native born or born in New Zealand or the Australian colonies. For the home-grown, the domestic ideology of the working man's paradise set the expectation level. Immigrants generally were content with the comparative view that Australasian wages and conditions were better than those they had left behind.

New Unionism and Colonial Class

Unions made their first appearances in the 1840s. Their standing was merely confirmed with legal recognition. Most of the provisions of the British Trade Union Acts of 1871 and 1876 and the Conspiracy and Protection of Property Act of 1875 were enacted in Australia and New Zealand; Western Australia was last to follow suit in 1902. Initially the unions were small groups of skilled male tradesmen in major regional centers. Membership dues were high and were used to fund benefits. The unions preserved standards by promoting apprenticeships and definitions of skill. Unionism in the 1880s was different in degree and possibly in kind: workplace relations changed as factories and export-related industries developed. Unionism became less exclusive and championed a range of issues, including the eight-hour workday, the restriction of child labor, the demand for time rates (as opposed to piecework), and the racist policies of the Australian and New Zealand governments. Earlier trickles of unionism became a flood in 1888. Between 1880 and 1890 the number of unions in New Zealand rose from 50 unions with 3,000 members to 200 unions with 63,000 members. This unionism was sudden, optimistic, and fragile.

The links between the labor movements in New Zealand and Australia were strong particularly among four Trans-Tasman occupational groups: the miners, the shearers, the wharfies, and the seamen. George Sangster, president of the Victorian Branch of the Seamen's Union of Austalasia, set a precedent when he was sent to New Zealand to establish a branch in 1880. Similarly, the Australian shearers' secretary, David Temple, and organizers J. A. Cook and James Slattery, crossed the Tasman Sea following the shearers' intercolonial seasonal labor market, to form branches of the Amalgamated Shearers' Union of Australasia in 1886. William Guthrie Spence was involved in both the miners' and shearers' unions the following year. The Denniston miners affiliated to the Amalgamated Miners' Association of Australasia in 1886 after the Australians provided financial support in a strike. In April 1890 a joint conference of Australian and New Zealand dockworkers in Sydney established a joint umbrella organization, the Amalgamated Wharf Labourers of Australasia.

The new unionists were keen to join new representative union coalitions. Trade and labor councils formed in the major cities between 1871 and 1882. Five intercolonial congresses convened between 1879 and 1890; the Australasian Labour Congress met in Sydney in 1885 and adopted a scheme for bringing all Australasian unions into one federation. A Maritime Labour Council formed in Melbourne on a platform of commitment to mutual cooperation and financial support. In 1885 a newly created Australian Maritime Council united the Seamen's Union of Australia and the Waterside Workers' Federation. The formation of the New Zealand Maritime Council in 1889 and its affiliation to the Australian council appeared a significant second step toward the Australasian dream that there would soon be a single, vast, and powerful federation of all the trade unions in Australasia. Councils of unskilled colonial-wide

unions used the language of collective class action as never before. John Lomas, the New Zealand council treasurer, was typical in stating that it was desirable to bring trade unions "under one head" to gain negotiated improvements of conditions and to avoid strikes if possible. John A. Millar, council secretary, told a mass meeting in Dunedin that "labor is one, and an injustice to one is an injustice to all."

Although shearers' leader W. G. Spence claimed that Australasian unionism made "no distinction of sex," it was indeed male dominated. Women had to seek a different avenue of redress than male unionists, often because of the exclusiveness of male unions. The position of women was a second major ingredient in the general social climate of 1890. The discovery of poverty and inequality seemed sudden. The number of women in industry increased considerably during the depression, particularly in clothing factories and workshops. Intercolonial competition contributed to contention. In 1887 Victoria raised the duty on cloth because of undercutting by New Zealand mills. Competition intensified, and clothing merchants and warehousemen in the major centers contracted out to small workshops. The Reverend Rutherford Waddell's 1888 sermon on the "sin of cheapness" prompted the Synod of the Presbyterian Church of Otago and Southland to pass a motion against the low wages and long hours in poor conditions of sweating. In 1888 the *Otago Daily Times* campaigned against the "sweating menace." The middle classes and liberals were outraged that women and girls might be subjected to the extreme conditions of sweating and supported the formation of Tailoresses' Unions and an official Sweating Commission. Similarly, the Victorian Anti-Sweating League was made up of men and women with links to Dr. Charles Strong's nonconformist Scots Church. A Working Women's Trade Union formed in Adelaide in 1890 in response to revelations of sweating. Unionism attained respectability. Middle-class liberals supported reform and encouraged unionism.

A Turning Point and Class Warfare?

Employers had won a complete victory in the Maritime Strike on both sides of the Tasman Sea. In Australia the maritime victory was followed by union defeats of the shearers in 1891 and 1894 and coal miners in 1894, 1895, and 1896. Nevertheless, the 1890 maritime strike appears to have been the impetus for formation of labor parties, election of labor representatives, passing of labor legislation, establishment of labor departments, and the institution of the industrial conciliation and arbitration system.

Indeed, historians have dwelt upon the question of the extent to which 1890 was a turning point. Union strategy appeared to shift from industrial power backed up by strikes to a focus on improving conditions through parliamentary power. The defeat of the Maritime Strike in 1890 (and the Australian shearers' strike in 1891) laid the framework for the entry of the labor movement into parliamentary politics. The NSW Labour Defence Committee summed up the union mood: "The time has come when trade unionists must use the parliamentary machine that in the past has used them." In June 1891, when the NSW Labour Electoral League adopted a platform to be endorsed by all candidates in that state, it gave rise to the nucleus of the Australian Labor Party. New Zealand elected a Liberal government

December 1890, with trade unions endorsing 38 candidates, half of whom were successful, including five "working men." These gains were offset by other circumstances. Formal arbitration followed a habit of informal arbitration in the region. Knights of Labour and trade union parliamentary committees predated the failure of the industrial muscle. No labor party formed in New Zealand until 1916. The formation of independent and viable labor parties, an arbitration system based on compulsion rather than voluntarism, and the passing of laws that transformed the Antipodes had been protracted developments. Even state involvement in alleviating unemployment, a practice known as "state socialism," has been shown to have been longstanding.

A second debate over the significance of the events of 1890 is the extent to which it is evidence of class warfare in the Antipodes. The historiography concentrates upon labor's defeats to show class formation. Keith Sinclair argued that "frightened conservatives heard the tramp of workers' boots, smelt the smoke and saw the flames of socialist revolt." Others heard only the sound of the "gumboots of cow-cockies entering a capitalist society" and their entrenchment in power that resulted from their victory. Certainly, William Lane wrote his ironic *The Working Man's Paradise* in 1892 and left Australia to try to form such a paradise in Paraguay. Verity Burgman pointed out that the "Maritime Strike acted in different ways upon different sections of the labor movement." She shows in some detail the extent to which the events of 1890 encouraged Socialist organization. The events surrounding 1890 indicate a divided working class, the beginning and end of large-scale Trans-Tasman industrial action (the New Zealand and Australian Workers' Unions conspicuously staggered on in formal federation until 1924), and nonindustrial solutions to social problems that prevailed throughout twentieth-century Australasia.

Key Players

Davis, Thomas Martin (1856–1899): English-born Davis, a seaman, arrived in Australia in 1876. He was elected secretary of the Federated Seamen's Union and was active in the local Maritime Council. He was a member of the NSW Labour Defence Committee and the Intercolonial Labour Conference, which attempted to coordinate strike action on a state and colonial basis during 1890. He was a member of the 1891 Royal Commission on Strikes. He was a founding member of the West Sydney Labor League in 1891, a successful candidate in the elections, and elected the first party whip.

Lane, William (1861–1917): English-born Lane arrived in Australia via Canada in 1885. He became a radical journalist and formed a Bellamy Society in Brisbane in 1887. He also wrote a Utopian novel, *Looking Backwards*, and coedited the *Boomerang*, a weekly labor newspaper. He was a leading figure in the formation of the Australian Labour Federation, which replaced the Brisbane Trades and Labour Council in 1889. He was the inaugural editor of *The Worker*. He left Australia in 1893 to found New Australia in Asunción, Paraguay, and then relocated to Cosme the next year. He abandoned the colony in 1899 and became the editor of a conservative Auckland newspaper, *New Zealand Herald*.

Lomas, John (1848–1933): English-born Lomas arrived in New Zealand in 1879. He was a coal miner, a Methodist lay preacher, and unionist. He was the inaugural president of the colony's first coal mining union in 1884. He launched the Amalgamated Miners' and Labourer's Association in 1885; it affiliated with the Amalgamated Miners' Association of Australia. He was elected treasurer of the Maritime Council in 1889. He contemplated entering parliament but he was recruited to the newly formed Department of Labour in 1891, becoming chief inspector of factories in 1907 and secretary of labour in 1912–1913.

Millar, John Andrew (1855–1915): Indian-born Millar arrived in New Zealand in 1870. He served his apprenticeship and became a ship's officer. He was elected the first full-time general secretary of the Federated Seamen's Union of New Zealand in 1887. He was secretary of the Maritime Council in 1889. He ran in the 1890 general election and was elected in 1893, becoming the Liberal-Labour leader in Parliament. He became a cabinet minister in 1909, first for railways and then labor. By 1913 he was voting with the conservative Reform party and gave his support to the repression of unionists in the 1913 general strike. He retired in 1914 and was appointed to the Legislative Council shortly before his death.

Spence, William Guthrie (1846–1926): Scottish-born Spence arrived in Australia in 1852. He was a gold miner who became involved in the Creswick Miners' Union, which affiliated to the Amalgamated Miners' Association, with Spence as its general secretary. Many ex-miners became shearers; in June 1886 Spence also helped to found the Australian Shearers' Union to serve both small landholders and itinerant laborers. The union's objective was to secure fair wage rates and "the adoption of just and equitable agreements between employers and employees." He supported the idea of an Australian Labour Federation and a combined industrial and political agenda. He founded the Australian Workers' Union of rural workers in 1894. He ran successfully in the first Australia federation elections in 1901 and held the seat of Darling for labor until 1917, then rose to postmaster general during World War I. He supported conscription and, after the Labor Party split over the issue, held a Nationalist federal seat for a term.

See also: *Dockers' Strike.*

BIBLIOGRAPHY

Books

Belich, James. *Making Peoples: A History of the New Zealanders.* Auckland, NZ: Allen Lane, the Penguin Press, 1996.

Bollinger, Conrad. *Against the Wind: The Story of the New Zealand Seamen's Union.* Wellington, NZ: New Zealand Seamen's Union, 1968.

Buckley, Ken and E. L. Wheelwright. *No Paradise for Workers: Capitalism and the Common People in Australia, 1788–1914.* Melbourne: Oxford University Press, 1988.

Fairburn, Miles. *The Ideal Society and its Enemies, 1850–1900.* Auckland, NZ: Auckland University Press, 1989.

Fry, Eric, ed. *Common Cause: Essays in Australian and New Zealand Labour History.* Sydney, Wellington, NZ: Allen and Unwin, 1992.

Hagan, Jim and Andrew Wells, eds. *The Maritime Strike: A Centennial Retrospective. Essays in Honour of E. C. Fry.* Wollongong: Five Islands Press in association with the University of Wollongong Labour History Research Group and the Australian Society for the Study of Labour History, 1992.

Lane, William. *The Workingman's Paradise: An Australian Novel.* Sydney: Sydney University Press, 1980. (First published under the name of John Miller.)

Martin, John E. "1890: A Turning Point for Labour." In *Pioneering New Zealand Labour History,* edited by Pat Welsh. Palmerston North, NZ: Dunmore Press, 1994: 21–51.

Roth, Bert. *Trade Unions in New Zealand.* Wellington, NZ: Reed Education, 1973.

Sinclair, Keith. *New Zealand Fabian: William Pember Reeves.* Auckland, NZ: Oxford University Press, 1965.

Spence, W. G. *Australia's Awakening, Thirty Years in the Life of an Australian Agitator.* Sydney and Melbourne: Worker Trustees, 1909.

Periodicals

Crawford, John. "Overt and Covert Military Involvement in the 1890 Maritime Strike and 1913 Waterfront Strike in New Zealand." *Labour History,* no. 60 (May 1991): 66–83.

Markey, Ray. "New Unionism in Australia, 1880–1900." *Labour History,* no. 48 (May 1985): 21–28.

Merritt, John. "W. G. Spence and the 1890 Maritime Strike." *Historical Studies* 15 (1973): 594–609.

Nairn, N. B. "The 1890 Maritime Strike in New South Wales." *Historical Studies* 10 (1961): 1–18.

Scates, Bruce. "Gender, Household and Community Politics: The 1890 Maritime Strike in Australia and New Zealand." *Labour History,* no. 61 (November 1991): 70–87.

Walker, R. B. "The Maritime Strikes in South Australia, 1887 and 1890." *Labour History,* no. 14 (1968): 3–12.

Other

Bennett, J. "The 1890 Maritime and the Triangular Relationship Between Britain, Australia and New Zealand." Master's thesis, University of Canterbury, 1985.

Merrett, I. A. "A Reappraisal of the 1890 Maritime Strikes in New Zealand." Master's thesis, University of Canterbury, 1969.

Salmond, J. D. "The History of the New Zealand Labour Movement from Settlement to the Conciliation and Arbitration Act 1894." Doctoral thesis, University of Otago, 1924 (published 1950).

—Melanie Nolan

Mass Strikes

United States 1934

Synopsis

Elected in 1932 on a platform of relief, reform, and recovery, President Franklin D. Roosevelt formulated a series of New Deal measures to address the economic crises of the Great Depression. One of the first pieces of New Deal legislation was the 1933 National Industrial Recovery Act (NIRA). A comprehensive initiative to create balance in the American economy, the NIRA suspended antitrust laws to allow businesses to coordinate production plans in return for a pledge to pay a minimum wage for a 40-hour workweek. Employers also had to allow their employees to form labor unions to engage in collective bargaining over labor contracts under Section 7(a) of the NIRA. Without an agency to oversee the collective bargaining process under the NIRA, however, employers routinely refused to recognize their employees' demands for representation through unions. Frustrated by the ambiguous federal response in enforcing the NIRA, workers and unionists in three cities—Toledo, Ohio; Minneapolis, Minnesota; and San Francisco, California—conducted major strikes to force union recognition by employers in those cities. Each of the strikes was at least partially successful in gaining union recognition, although the larger question of the enforcement of Section 7(a) of the NIRA remained ambiguous. In 1935 another landmark piece of New Deal legislation—the National Labor Relations Act, better known as the Wagner Act—left no doubt that workers had the right to organize labor unions without interference from their employers.

Timeline

1919: With the formation of the Third International (Comintern), the Bolshevik government of Russia establishes its control over communist movements worldwide.

1924: In the United States, Secretary of the Interior Albert B. Fall, along with oil company executives Harry Sinclair and Edward L. Doheny, is charged with conspiracy and bribery in making fraudulent leases of U.S. Navy oil reserves at Teapot Dome, Wyoming. The resulting Teapot Dome scandal clouds the administration of President Warren G. Harding.

1929: On "Black Friday" in October, prices on the U.S. stock market, which had been climbing wildly for several years, suddenly collapse. Thus begins the first phase of a world economic crisis and depression that will last until the beginning of World War II.

1931: Financial crisis widens in the United States and Europe, which reel from bank failures and climbing unemployment levels. In London, armies of the unemployed riot.

1934: Austrian chancellor Engelbert Dollfuss, who aligns his nation with Mussolini's Italy, establishes a fascist regime in an attempt to keep Austria out of the Nazi orbit. Austrian Nazis react by assassinating Dollfuss.

1934: Dionne sisters, the first quintuplets to survive beyond infancy, are born in Canada.

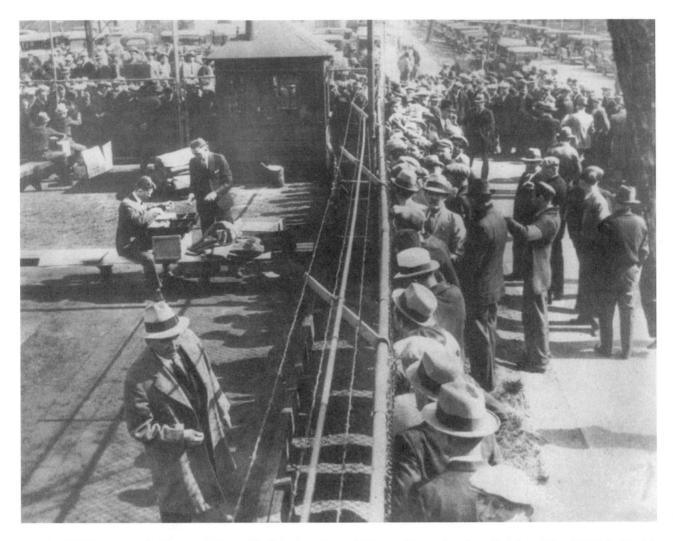

Striking UAW workers in line to receive strike benefits, General Motors Chevrolet plant, Toledo, Ohio. AP/Wide World Photos. Reproduced by permission.

1937: Japan attacks China, and annexes most of that nation's coastal areas.

1939: After years of loudly denouncing one another (and quietly cooperating), the Nazis and Soviets sign a non-aggression pact in August. This clears the way for the Nazi invasion of Poland, and for Soviet action against Finland. (Stalin also helps himself to a large portion of Poland.)

1942: Axis conquests reach their height in the middle of this year. The Nazis control a vast region from Normandy to the suburbs of Stalingrad, and from the Arctic Circle to the edges of the Sahara. To the east, the Japanese "Co-Prosperity Sphere" encompasses territories from China to Burma to the East Indies, stretching deep into the western Pacific.

1945: April sees the death of three leaders: Roosevelt passes away on 12 April; the Italians execute Mussolini and his mistress on 28 April; and Hitler (along with Eva Braun, propaganda minister Josef Goebbels, and Goebbels's family) commits suicide on 30 April.

1949: North Atlantic Treaty Organization (NATO) is established.

Event and Its Context

The NIRA and Section 7(a)

Although federal legislation before the New Deal had never barred workers from forming labor unions, neither did the government protect workers from retaliation or interference on the part of their employers for attempting to organize. While some skilled trades workers thus bargained for higher wages and improved benefits through their craft unions—often as part of the American Federation of Labor—unskilled workers in the mass-production industries such as automobiles, steel, and textiles were consistently frustrated in their unionization efforts. Throughout the 1920s successive Republican administrations had also scaled back Progressive Era reforms that had improved working conditions, while conservative federal courts issued injunctions to break strikes.

Striking Teamsters, Minneapolis, Minnesota, 1934. National Archives and Records Administration.

The election of Franklin D. Roosevelt to the presidency in 1932 promised to reverse the trends of the 1920s by injecting the federal government into labor relations on an unprecedented scale. Roosevelt had come to office with approximately 80 percent of the working-class vote on his pledge to provide relief to the poor, inaugurate recovery efforts for the economy, and pass reform legislation. Just three months into his first term, Roosevelt guided the National Industrial Recovery Act (NIRA) through Congress and signed it into law on 16 June 1933. Under a code of fair competition supervised by the National Recovery Administration (NRA), the NIRA temporarily suspended antitrust rules and allowed businesses to plan production on an industry-wide basis. In return, the NRA mandated a minimum wage set by industry and a 40-hour maximum workweek. From the start, the NRA's work was roundly criticized. Some in the business community resented the government's involvement in the private sector, while others argued that the NRA's reach did not go far enough in fundamentally restructuring the economy.

The NIRA provision that created the most controversy was Section 7(a). The section declared that "employees shall have the right to organize and bargain collectively through representatives of their own choosing, and be free from interference" by their employers in such efforts. The section also prohibited employers from forcing workers to join company-controlled unions or from firing them for joining independent labor unions.

Yet the NIRA did not specify penalties against employers for failing to follow Section 7(a), nor did it set up an administration to oversee the implementation of the article. Thus, while Section 7(a) seemed to place the weight of the government behind unionization for the first time in the country's history, it did little to clarify how workers could actually organize labor unions. In the wake of the NIRA's passage in June 1933, a new wave of labor unrest swept the country as business and labor tested the real impact of Section 7(a) in the workplace.

The Auto-Lite Strike

One of the first major strikes in 1934 to test the limits of Section 7(a) occurred in the auto-parts manufacturing city of Toledo, Ohio. A few workers at the Electric Auto-Lite plant had initially struck over union recognition for Local 18384 of the American Federation of Labor (AFL) from 23 to 28 February 1934. The action concluded when the company agreed to reinstate them; soon after, however, Auto-Lite management refused to recognize Local 18384 as a bargaining agent for the workers. On 13 April about 400 of the plant's 800 workers struck again; this time, they were joined by hundreds of other striking workers from other area factories as well as members of the Lucas County Unemployment League and the American Workers' Party, a Marxist organization led by A. J. Muste. The company responded by arming its plant with tear gas, machine guns, and a hastily assembled force of special deputies, in addition to a court injunction that limited the number of strikers around the plant to 25 picketers.

The company's strategy backfired. Defying the injunction to stay away from the plant, by the third week in May, up to 10,000 sympathetic Toledo residents protested at the plant each day. When someone in the factory threw a steel bracket at Auto-Lite striker Alma Hahn on 23 May 1934, the north-side working-class neighborhood that surrounded the factory erupted in four days of rioting. A force of about 1,350 National Guardsmen eventually silenced the Auto-Lite plant, but not before one striker and one protester were killed; about 200 others had been injured. Auto-Lite's management finally agreed to recognize the union after Ohio Governor George White refused to provide National Guard protection to allow the plant to operate. With an increase of five cents in wages and a minimum wage set at 35 cents, the plant reopened on 5 June 1934 with AFL Local 18384 as the recognized bargaining agent for the workers. The following year, after the establishment of the Congress of Industrial Organizations (CIO), Local 18384 became Local 12 of the United Auto Workers union and remained a powerful influence over the city's economic and political spheres.

The Teamsters' Strike

In Minneapolis, a strike led by Teamsters' Local 574 gripped the city between May and August 1934. After Teamsters' organizer Ray Dunne led a successful strike by coal-truck drivers in early February 1934, Local 574 signed up between 2,000 and 3,000 members and demanded union recognition, a wage hike, and overtime pay. Confronted by the antiunion Citizens' Alliance (CA), the union mustered public support for its position that proved decisive in the months to come. A series of battles at the city's public market on 21 and 22 May left two CA members dead; under pressure from Governor Floyed

Olson, who was sympathetic to the strikers, the employers' group signed an agreement to abide by Section 7(a) on 25 May. Almost immediately, the CA went back on its pledge to recognize Local 574 as a collective bargaining agent, and on 16 July 1934 the union's membership voted for another strike.

The second strike lasted for 36 days and brought crowds of up to 100,000 union supporters into Minneapolis. Another violent confrontation on 20 July left two strikers dead and 50 injured, prompting the governor to declare martial law six days later. Another month of negotiating under federal supervision finally produced a victory for Local 574, which gained undisputed recognition as a bargaining agent and a minimum wage for its members. Within two years of the strike, Local 574 represented members at 500 companies in the Minneapolis area, and the CA was effectively broken as a power in the city.

The Maritime Workers' Strike

The biggest of the three urban strike waves took place in San Francisco from May to July 1934 and culminated in a general strike from 16 to 19 July. A springtime strike by the International Longshoremen's Association (ILA) under the leadership of Harry Bridges had been averted through federal intervention, but the settlement left dockworkers unsatisfied with their wages, hours, hiring practices, and, most of all, lack of formal union recognition. On 9 May 1934 ILA members along the entire Pacific Coast (with the exception of Los Angeles) went on strike; in San Francisco, the Teamsters Union supported them by refusing to move cargo from the port.

As in Minneapolis, an employers' group—the Industrial Association of San Francisco (IASF)—took the lead in fighting the ILA. On 5 July 1934, in a battle instigated by the IASF with the support of the local police, two strikers were killed and dozens more were shot. In response, the ILA called for a general strike of San Francisco's workers. The resulting three-day strike shut down the city after 130,000 workers walked off the job on 16 July. Under pressure from NRA chief Hugh Johnson, the general strike was called off on 19 July, and the Teamsters went back to work two days later. The dockworkers followed them on 31 July, when the ILA agreed to federal arbitration of the initial strike's issues. The arbitration board issued a ruling on 12 October 1934 that granted the ILA most of its demands. Not only had it won recognition as a bargaining agent, it also gained joint control with employers over the hiring process, higher wages, and an overtime provision.

Together with a series of textile strikes in the Carolinas, the major urban strikes of 1934 demonstrated the problems in administering the vague clause of Section 7(a) of the NIRA. The NIRA itself was soon deemed irrelevant, however, when it was declared unconstitutional by the U.S. Supreme Court in 1935. In response, the Roosevelt administration fought to pass the National Labor Relations Act (often called the Wagner Act), which the president signed into law on 5 July 1935. Unlike the NIRA, the Wagner Act not only guaranteed the right of workers to bargain collectively, but also specified how that right would be enforced. It also created the National Labor Relations Board to issue injunctions over unfair labor practices, to oversee union elections, and to hear grievances between labor and management.

Key Players

Bridges, Alfred Renton ("Harry") (1901–1990): Head of the ILA in San Francisco in the 1930s, Bridges led the 1934 maritime workers' strike. In 1937 he founded the International Longshoremen's and Warehousemen's Union and worked as the West Coast director for the CIO in the 1940s. Born in Australia, Bridges became an American citizen in 1945.

Dunne, Vincent Raymond (1890–1970): A follower of the Trotskyite wing of the Communist Party, Dunne helped plan a February 1934 strike that empowered Teamsters' Local 574 in Minneapolis. He was also a leader in the subsequent 36-day trucking strike in July and August 1934, which decisively broke the power of the antiunion Citizens' Alliance in the city.

Johnson, Hugh Samuel (1885–1942): A graduate of the U.S. Military Academy, Johnson eventually reached the rank of brigadier general in the U.S. Army and helped to draft the first Selective Service Act in 1918. In 1933 Johnson was appointed to head the NRA, which had been created to implement the NIRA. After the Supreme Court declared the act unconstitutional in 1935, Johnson went on to lead another New Deal Agency, the Works Progress Administration.

Muste, A. J. (1885–1967): Born in Holland, Muste came to the United States with his family in 1891. Ordained a minister in the Dutch Reformed Church in 1909, he left for the Congregational Church in 1914 and declared himself a pacifist in opposition to World War I. The director of the AFL's Brockwood Labor College in the 1920s, Muste founded the Conference for Progressive Labor Action (CPLA) in 1929. The CPLA in turn spawned the American Workers Party in 1934, which played a pivotal role in assisting Toledo's Auto-Lite strikers. Muste continued to play a role in liberal and pacifist causes during the remainder of his life.

See also: *National Industrial Recovery Act; Stock Market Crash; Wagner Act.*

BIBLIOGRAPHY

Books

Bernstein, Irving. *Turbulent Years: A History of the American Worker, 1933–1941.* Boston: Houghton-Mifflin, 1971.

Cohen, Lizabeth. *Making a New Deal: Industrial Workers in Chicago, 1919–1939.* New York: Cambridge University Press, 1990.

Denning, Michael. *The Cultural Front: The Laboring of American Culture in the Twentieth Century.* New York: Verso, 1998.

Faue, Elizabeth. *Community of Suffering and Struggle: Women, Men, and the Labor Movement in Minneapolis, 1915–1945.* Chapel Hill, NC: University of North Carolina Press, 1991.

Hentoff, Nat. *Peace Agitator: The Story of A. J. Muste.* New York: A. J. Muste Memorial Institute, 1982.

Korth, Philip A., and Margaret R. Beegle, eds. *I Remember Like Today: The Auto-Lite Strike of 1934.* East Lansing, MI: Michigan State University Press, 1988.

Kraus, Henry. *Heroes of the Unwritten Story: The UAW, 1934–1939.* Urbana, IL: University of Illinois Press, 1993.

Nelson, Bruce. *Workers on the Waterfront: Seamen, Longshoremen, and Unionism in the 1930s.* Urbana, IL: University of Illinois Press, 1988.

Zieger, Robert. *The CIO, 1935–1955.* Chapel Hill, NC: University of North Carolina Press, 1995.

—Timothy G. Borden

McKees Rocks Strike

United States 1909

Synopsis

On 14 July 1909 unskilled and semiskilled Slavic workers staged a strike against the Pressed Steel Car Company of McKees Rocks, Pennsylvania, located near Pittsburgh. Strain between strikers (and their allies in the International Workers of the World or IWW) and the company (along with its replacement workers and state police forces) erupted in a riot on 22 August 1909. After six more weeks of minor skirmishes, the rioting culminated with the deaths of many people and the injury of many others. Although the steel manufacturing industry did not respond immediately to the riots with significant improvements to worker conditions, the McKees Rocks strike of 1909 is considered one of the more important incidents that eventually led to successful unionization efforts in the 1930s.

Timeline

1889: Flooding in Johnstown, Pennsylvania, kills thousands.

1893: Wall Street stock prices plummet on 5 May, precipitating a market collapse on 27 June. In the wake of this debacle, some 600 banks and 15,000 other businesses fail. The nationwide depression will last for four more years.

1898: Bayer introduces a cough suppressant, derived from opium, its brand name: Heroin.

1902: The *Times Literary Supplement,* a weekly review of literature and scholarship, begins publication in London.

1905: Russian Revolution of 1905 occurs. Following the "bloody Sunday" riots before the Winter Palace in St. Petersburg in January, revolution spreads throughout Russia, in some places spurred on by newly formed workers' councils, or soviets. Among the most memorable incidents of the revolt is the mutiny aboard the battleship *Potemkin.* Suppressed by the czar, the revolution brings an end to liberal reforms, and thus sets the stage for the larger revolution of 1917.

1909: Robert E. Peary and Matthew Henson reach the North Pole.

1909: National Association for the Advancement of Colored People (NAACP) is founded by W. E. B. Du Bois and a number of other prominent black and white intellectuals in New York City.

1909: William Cadbury's *Labour in Portuguese West Africa* draws attention to conditions of slavery in São Tomé and Principe.

1911: Revolution in Mexico, begun the year before, continues with the replacement of the corrupt Porfirio Diaz, president since 1877, by Francisco Madero.

1915: A German submarine sinks the *Lusitania,* killing 1,195, including 128 U.S. citizens. Theretofore, many Americans had been sympathetic toward Germany, but the incident begins to turn the tide of U.S. sentiment toward the Allies.

1919: With the formation of the Third International (Comintern), the Bolshevik government of Russia establishes its control over communist movements worldwide.

Event and Its Context

Slavic people came to the United States primarily from eastern and central Europe, most from the Balkan Peninsula, and from beyond the Ural Mountains in Russia. Slavic people at this time were generally grouped linguistically: the east Slavic branch consisted of Belarusian-, Russian-, and Ukrainian-speaking people; the west Slavic branch comprised Czech, Polish, Slovak, and Sorbian; and the south Slavic branch included Bulgarian, Macedonian, Serbo-Croatian, and Slovenian. Many of these Slavic people immigrated to the United States in the first half of the twentieth century for the express purpose of looking for a better way of life, and some of them eventually came to work in the coal mines and steel mills of Pennsylvania.

Anthracite to Steel

Large numbers of people of Slavic descent came to the steel mills of Pittsburgh, Pennsylvania, located in the western part of the state, by way of the anthracite coalfields in the eastern part of Pennsylvania. Conditions in these eastern coalfields were becoming increasingly difficult, and the Slavic peoples were looking primarily for better wages without the exposure to such terrible working conditions. They came to Pittsburgh as poor, illiterate people, with little industrial training and experience, yet they displayed courage, resourcefulness, and stability to their new employers.

Within a few years in the steel mills of Pittsburgh, the Slavic employees were considered strong, willing workers and were generally viewed by the steel management as some of the best workers available. The Slavic people had developed into strong manual laborers from backbreaking agricultural work in their native lands. The bulk of the unskilled labor around Pittsburgh—digging and carrying at factories, loading and unloading of raw materials on railroads and riverboats, heavy work at forges and foundries, and lifting in machine shops—was performed for the most part by Slavic workingmen. They also were involved in some of the worst accidents in the steel mills because of the strenuous and dangerous work that they often performed. A report of the National Croatian Society for 1905–1906 reported that out of a membership that averaged near 17,000 workers for that period, 95 men were killed by accident and 85 others were permanently disabled. In addition, 97 men died from consumption, a wasting disease traceable to the character of their work. Such was the general condition of the Slavic steel worker in 1909.

Working for the Pressed Steel Car Company

In 1909 many Slavic people worked for the Pressed Steel Car Company in the town of McKees Rocks (now a western suburb of Pittsburgh). Six years earlier, the Slavic workers had replaced English-speaking workers after those workers went out on strike, and the Slavic people agreed to perform the work at much lower wages than the English-speaking workers were paid. The new Slavic employees filled a variety of demanding positions, such as unskilled pressmen, punchers, riveters, and shearsmen; and semiskilled blacksmiths, carpenters, fitters, and painters. The Slavic pressmen, punchers, riveters, and shearsmen were paid by piecework at about $35 to $50 in a two-week pay period; the Slavic blacksmiths, carpenters, fitters, and painters received from $2.00 to $2.50 per day.

Slavic workers in the steel district had been unsuccessful in securing better worker rights from their employers, especially with regard to the safeguarding of their lives and welfare. One of the workers' specific complaints was the regular abuse of workers, especially immigrant workers, by foremen. The workers learned to join together as a group; they looked to the Industrial Workers of the World (IWW) for help at this time.

The Role of the IWW

The IWW, commonly called "The Wobblies," was one of the most revolutionary and often violent labor unions in the United States. The workers recognized it, however, as an association based on the old craft organizations (or "industrial unions") that included all the employees of an industry, whatever their occupation. The Slavic workers viewed the IWW as a solid ally in their opposition to the powerful steel capitalists.

The IWW was especially violent during the time period from 1906 to 1916, when it engaged in some of the fiercest fights between capitalists and laborers ever fought in the United States. The American Federation of Labor (AFL) sometimes joined the capitalists and governmental authorities in its opposition to the IWW. The AFL, one of the country's largest and most influential labor unions, often provided strikebreakers to be used against the IWW strikes.

McKees Rocks Strike

One of the more successful strikes led by the IWW was the one that occurred at McKees Rocks in 1909. The McKees Rocks strike was among the largest of the ethnic labor conflicts that occurred in the early twentieth century in the state of Pennsylvania. The steel companies in the state had chosen Slavic workers over other ethnic workers for their assumed submissiveness and because they were willing to work for less money than other ethnic groups. The factory owners also believed that Slavic workers would not agitate for better pay and conditions because the Slavs themselves were divided along ethnic lines. In all there were 14 distinct ethnic subdivisions of the Slavic workers. Poles, Czechs, Ukrainians, Russians, and other Slavic groups were divided by custom, language, and, sometimes religious beliefs and traditions.

The Slavic people's apparent passive acceptance of exploitative work and abusive treatment hid their determined ambition to better themselves. They had come to the United States believing that only there did they have a chance to improve their lot in life. Moreover, and contrary to their employers' initial views about Slavic workers, the various Slavic groups eventually demonstrated that they were capable of effective organization and resistance when the combination of poor working conditions and low pay became intolerable.

Beginning on 14 July 1909, the IWW led thousands of unskilled and semiskilled immigrant workers comprising 14 nationalities in a two-month violent strike against their employer, the Pressed Steel Car Company. The employees and the IWW also fought against the State Constabulary, whom they disrespectfully called "the Cossacks." Local authorities had called in the State Constabulary at the first signs of trouble. The Pennsylvania mine and mill owners had recently organized the State Constabulary, a specially trained group from the state police department, for the express purpose of maintaining stability during labor disturbances, resisting labor revolts, and taking command in emergencies. At the height of its effectiveness, the Pennsylvania Constabulary was considered the most violent and efficient antilabor police force in the United States.

The IWW, however, was a superior match for the Constabulary. On 22 August 1909, after nearly five weeks of continued strain that had built up between strikers, replacement workers, the company, and the Constabulary, a "Cossack" shot a striker, and a riot situation soon developed. The strike committee immediately informed the Constabulary commander that for every striker killed or injured by his men, a Constabulary man would also be killed or injured. The committee members emphasized that they were not especially concerned about who was selected for this retaliation. The angry strikers chanted: "Strike! Life for a life!"

After 11 weeks of minor skirmishes, a battle took place near the Pressed Steel Car Company plant between a mob of workers and the State Constabulary. After the riot subsided, about a dozen men from both sides had been killed and more than 50 men were wounded near a footbridge. The Constabulary could no longer control the streets and were backed into the factory property. This confrontation ended the violence on both sides for the remainder of the strike, which a few days later resulted in a victory for the workers. The strike was later described as an "industrial slaughterhouse."

Following the strike at McKees Rocks, the IWW stopped its practice of using violence in labor disputes. Instead it relied on sheer numbers when leading strikes. The police, the militia, and hired gunmen continued to use violence during the period 1910–1916 in ongoing efforts to stop strikes and free-speech campaigns. The Pennsylvania State Constabulary continued their brutality. Newspaper reports, such as one published in the *New York Call* (a socialist paper), that covered their violent actions often referred to the brutality of the Constabulary at the 1909 IWW strike in McKees Rocks.

Conclusion

Labor historians consider the McKees Rocks steel strike to be the first strike victory by Slavic workers in Pennsylvania. The strike demonstrated that unity was possible among the diverse Slavic ethnic groups—groups previously thought by management to be docile and incapable of uniting effectively. The success of the Pittsburgh-area Slavic workers in overcoming their ethnic divisions so as to conduct a successful strike is a testament to their will to obtain fair and equitable treatment from their employers.

The McKees Rocks strike in 1909 not only demonstrated that the Slavic workers could effectively organize, but also made it clear that they could do so under very adverse conditions. Intimidation by the steel plant owners and strikebreaking police were insufficient to hinder the workers' collective will. They also demonstrated the ability to attract attention and garner support from liberal and radical elements in the middle class (no doubt with the help of the radical IWW). However, despite continuing efforts and occasional successes, neither militant laborers nor progressive labor unions could stop the powerful organization of the steel industry in the early twentieth century. The working class of Pittsburgh would have to wait until the 1930s to have a successful union that consistently won concessions from the factory owners for working conditions, safety issues, and economic concessions including wages and retirement benefits. Pennsylvania labor historians often point to the Slavic workers and the McKees Rocks strike, along with other similar strikes of that time, as forerunners of the new unionization of the 1930s.

See also: *American Federation of Labor; International Workers of the World.*

BIBLIOGRAPHY

Books

Couvares, Francis G. *The Remaking of Pittsburgh: Class and Culture in an Industrializing City, 1877–1919.* Albany, NY: The State University of New York Press, 1984.

Dickerson, Dennis C. *Out of the Crucible: Steelworkers in Western Pennsylvania, 1875–1980.* Albany, NY: State University of New York Press, 1986.

Edwards, P. K. *Strikes in the United States: 1881–1974.* New York: St. Martin's Press, 1981.

Fitch, John A. *The Steel Workers.* New York: Arno, 1969.

Greene, Victor R. *The Slavic Community on Strike: Immigrant Labor in Pennsylvania Anthracite.* Notre Dame, IN: University of Notre Dame Press, 1968.

Greenwald, Maurine W., and Margo Anderson, eds. *Pittsburgh Surveyed: Social Science and Social Reform in the Early Twentieth Century.* Pittsburgh, PA: University of Pittsburgh Press, 1996.

—William Arthur Atkins

Philip Murray (left) and Walter Reuther. AP/Wide World Photos. Reproduced by permission.

Meany and Reuther Lead AFL, CIO

United States 1952

Synopsis

The ascension by George Meany to the presidency of the American Federation of Labor (AFL) and Walter Reuther to the presidency of the Congress of Industrial Organizations (CIO) marked the development of a more "modern" orientation, replacing what many considered to be outmoded traditions. A new generation of labor leaders replacing older leaders—AFL president William Green and CIO president Philip Murray— also helped facilitate the merger of the AFL and the CIO.

1932: Charles A. Lindbergh's baby son is kidnapped and killed, a crime for which Bruno Hauptmann will be charged in 1934, convicted in 1935, and executed in 1936.

1937: Stalin uses carefully staged show trials in Moscow to eliminate all rivals for leadership. These party purges, however, are only a small part of the death toll now being exacted in a country undergoing forced industrialization, much of it by means of slave labor.

1942: Declaration of the United Nations is signed in Washington, D.C.

1945: On 7 May, Germany surrenders to the Allied powers. Later in the summer, the new U.S. president, Harry Truman, joins Churchill and Stalin at Potsdam to discuss the reconstruction of Germany. (Churchill is replaced in mid-conference by Clement Attlee as Labour wins control of the British Parliament.)

1947: Marshall Plan is established to assist European nations in recovering from the war.

1949: Soviets conduct their first successful atomic test. This heightens growing cold war tensions, not least because the sudden acquisition of nuclear capabilities suggests that American spies are passing secrets.

1952: Among the cultural landmarks of the year are the film *High Noon* and the book *The Invisible Man* by Ralph Ellison.

1952: George Jorgenson travels to Copenhagen and returns as Christine Jorgenson. (This is not the first sex-change operation; however, it is the first to attract widespread attention.)

1955: Warsaw Pact is signed by the Soviet Union and its satellites in Eastern Europe.

1957: Soviets launch *Sputnik,* the world's first artificial satellite. This spawns a space race between the two superpowers.

1962: As the Soviets begin a missile buildup in Cuba, for a few tense days in October it appears that World War III is imminent. President Kennedy calls for a Cuban blockade, forcing the Soviets to back down and ultimately diffusing the crisis.

1967: Racial violence sweeps America's cities, as Harlem, Detroit, Birmingham, and other towns erupt with riots.

Event and Its Context

The men whom George Meany and Walter Reuther replaced had been stalwarts of American labor's mainstream and guardians of the deep division that had opened in labor's ranks during the Great Depression. Phil Murray and Bill Green had much more in common than dying within a dozen days of each other (on 9 and 21 November, respectively) in 1952. Both were warm and outgoing, deeply religious men who were utterly devoted to the labor movement and enjoyed considerable popularity. Both were born into mineworker families, and each entered the mines and union activity while still in his teens.

From Gompers to Green to Labor's Civil War

In the early 1920s, both Green and Murray had been supporters of United Mine Workers (UMW) leader John L. Lewis. Lewis played a key role in the rise of Green to the presidency of the AFL and in the rise of Murray to the presidency of the CIO. Both became bitter opponents of Lewis, though at different points in their careers. If anything, the points at which each man broke with John L. Lewis—far from narrowing the gap between them—helped to guarantee that Green and Murray would be sharply opposed to each other.

Green's rise into AFL presidency took place with the death of Samuel Gompers in 1924. As a UMW official, he had fa-

AFL Executive Council members, from left, David Dubinsky, vice president, William Green, president, and George Meany, vice president, Miami Beach. AP/Wide World Photos. Reproduced by permission.

vored industrial unionism and union involvement in broad efforts toward social reform, but he then embraced the dominant AFL orientation: narrow craft unionism and a "pure-and-simple" focus of only seeking to improve wages and conditions at the unionized workplace. His hostility to Lewis became open and uncompromising in 1935 when the UMW chieftain spearheaded the CIO rebellion for industrial unionism.

Murray supported Lewis's militant industrial unionism and swerve toward labor radicalism in the midst of the Great Depression, and after the formation of the CIO, Lewis appointed him to head the Steel Workers Organizing Committee, which evolved into the United Steel Workers of America. Lewis also chose Murray to succeed him as CIO president in 1940. Murray rejected Lewis' feud with President Franklin D. Roosevelt, his labor militancy during World War II, and his challenge to CIO authority when Lewis sought unity with the AFL to bring an end to what many saw as "labor's civil war."

For years Green had denounced the CIO's militancy as the "utterly subversive policies of minority domination and violence," claiming that many of its leaders were "moved by a con-

suming ambition to establish themselves as dictators," and alleging that "the CIO welcomes communist support and uses its methods." Green's most conciliatory note was urging wayward CIO unions to "come back into the House of Labor." According to George Meany, who became AFL secretary-treasurer in 1939, "Bill Green had done nothing for five years [before his death] but go around making speeches denouncing the group [the CIO] which was tearing us apart. He would always wind up that they should 'come back home.' That wasn't convincing anybody." It was certainly not convincing to Murray, whose break with his mentor Lewis was over preserving CIO integrity.

The federation led by Murray seemed qualitatively different from that led by Green. "CIO was an especially magical set of letters," remembered one 1930s militant. In 1938 labor journalist Edward Levinson described a crusade for a better world: "Around mammoth modern mills and at bleak old factories, on ships and on piers, at offices and in public gathering-places, men and women roared, 'CIO! CIO!' with the gathering velocity of a massed football cheer, with the difference that their goal was more and better bread for the family table and a greater sense of freedom in affairs economic, political, and social . . . . Labor was on the march as it had never been before in the history of the Republic." CIO staff member Shirley Quill's description of AFL union officials conveys profound cultural differences between the two federations: "The AFL leaders were . . . crafty, comfortable, conspicuously well-fed, successful powerbrokers in their own fiefdoms. They competently negotiated contracts covering wages, hours, working conditions and pensions, and stared blankly when such arcane subjects as discrimination, minority rights, seniority for women and voter registration appeared on the agenda."

Green's denunciations of the CIO drew bitterness from Murray: "He joined the procession of Wall Streeters and barons of the steel industry." Murray saw the leading representative of the AFL's younger layer as "some kind of loud-mouth bum from New York." In later years the target of this scorn, George Meany claimed that his relations with Murray were "quite friendly," but he added that a merger of the AFL and CIO would not have been possible as long as Murray was alive.

By the early 1950s great changes had been taking place within the cultures of both the AFL and the CIO, as well as in their larger social, economic, and political contexts. Meany and Reuther were better able to reflect and move within the altered realities. Significantly, neither had been personally involved in the original split between the AFL and CIO.

Red Menace and American Dream

The Great Depression had generated the mighty upsurge of labor radicalism that was the CIO. It had also pushed many workers and intellectuals toward left-wing activism. The growing Communist Party was able to point to—and secure support from—the allegedly "socialist" homeland of the USSR. Many left-wing activists, communists included, were employed by the less radical Lewis and Murray and helped build the organizations and victories of the CIO. The depression was not, however, overcome by heroic labor struggles. Franklin D. Roosevelt's New Deal social reforms beguiled masses of workers and labor activists but also failed to end the depression. It was instead massive government spending during World War II that skyrocketed the economy into prosperity and at the same time helped to increase government influence and controls over the labor movement.

Government involvement, under Roosevelt's liberal Democratic administration, had enabled the labor movement (in the form of unions) to grow and flourish so long as—occasional radical rhetoric aside—it would not become an anticapitalist force. In the postwar period, the success of labor's struggles would enable workers' buying power to help fuel the development of a buoyant consumer economy.

As the U.S. government moved to defeat the Axis powers in the war, it also prepared to establish what Henry Luce, the influential publisher of *Time, Life,* and *Fortune* magazines, termed in 1941 "the American Century." In the postwar period, the U.S. government sought to keep the labor movement enlisted in its foreign policy objectives of maintaining a prosperous U.S. capitalism by helping to preserve and rebuild a global capitalist economy in which the U.S. would be a central force. This would involve global containment of social revolutions and communism, culminating in the cold war.

Communism was associated—despite its revolutionary rhetoric and the idealism of many of its adherents—with the ruthless and sometimes murderous dictatorship of Joseph Stalin in the USSR, which facilitated the ability of the U.S. government to win many labor activists to its policy of probusiness anticommunism. Another factor was that the executive branch of the U.S. government—after the death of Roosevelt in 1945, and even after Republican Party congressional victories in 1946—continued to be in the hands of the relatively prolabor liberal wing of the Democratic Party under Harry Truman. Moreover, the long wave of economic prosperity that began at the end of World War II was having an impact on the lives of many workers who a decade earlier had been radicalized by hard times. A growing number of union leaders in both the CIO and the AFL were inclined to adapt to this powerful current.

This trend became clear in 1947 when congressional Republicans were able to push through the Taft-Hartley Act, which was designed to limit union power and eliminate labor radicalism. Among the restrictions it imposed were outlawing union tactics responsible for many previous union victories and prohibiting communists from serving as union officers. Although both had protested loudly against this "slave labor law," both the AFL and CIO leadership drifted into acquiescence once it was passed. In fact, many AFL leaders were almost exultant in signing the noncommunist affidavits that were required by the new law.

John L. Lewis—whose UMW had rejoined the AFL in 1946 and who remained a formidable figure in the ranks of organized labor—correctly predicted that the law's provisions would "make more difficult the securing of new members of this labor movement, without which our movement will become so possessed of inertia that there is no action and no growth." He challenged the AFL, at its 1947 national convention in San Francisco, to refuse to comply with the Taft-Hartley Act, including the requirement that all union officers sign noncommunist affidavits.

This was an incredible challenge to a federation whose youngest and most dynamic leader, 53-year-old secretary-treasurer George Meany, would later confess: "I never went on strike in my life; I never ran a strike in my life; I never ordered anyone else to run a strike in my life, never had anything to do with a picket line."

Yet it was Meany, the tough-minded organization man, who had the audacity to attack Lewis head-on. He denounced the UMW leader's proposal as impractical, argued that AFL leaders should be proud to sign noncommunist affidavits, and went on to "red-bait" Lewis' record as former head of the CIO. Lewis, he charged, had "made fellowship" with "stinking America-haters who love Moscow" and had been "a comrade to the comrades." Lewis pulled his union out of the AFL immediately after this convention. It was this attack that guaranteed Meany as Green's successor. "George 'elected himself' in San Francisco," commented Jay Lovestone, one of his key advisors. "Thereafter it was only a matter of time."

In the same year, Walter Reuther made his mark by "fighting communism" in the United Auto Workers (UAW). Reuther himself had been a left-wing activist for many years and an active member of the Socialist Party (until the late 1930s, when he switched to New Deal Democrats). He had played a key role in building the UAW and advancing the militant and socially conscious brand of unionism represented by the CIO. Labor journalist Len De Caux commented that "Walter was perceptive. He worked hard. He fought well. He deserved much credit—and he saw that he got it." Although Reuther once had been sympathetic to the "socialist experiment" in the USSR and on friendly terms with U.S. communists in the UAW, the combination of Stalinism and internal union politics, plus his own ambition, led to a shift.

Denouncing "the efforts of the Communist Party or any other outside groups or individual to interfere in the affairs of our union," Reuther aligned his campaign for UAW president with support for signing the noncommunist affidavits required by the Taft-Hartley Act. Trouncing the incumbents, he asserted as new UAW president that his union "understood that the alternative to a finish fight was communist control of our union." Not only did the dynamic, red-headed 40-year-old become a media celebrity, but he was catapulted into the central leadership of the CIO in time to play a leading role in the expulsion of "communist-led" unions from its ranks. A one-time supporter later complained that "UAW events moved swiftly toward a one-party state after Reuther's triumph in 1947," and another observed that Reuther had "fought under the banner of greater democracy for UAW members, and yet he became the instrument in the establishment of a tight restrictive union subject to the rule of one person." This was a growing trend throughout the CIO, however, and also characterized most AFL unions.

In 1948 a number of CIO unions openly opposed the reelection of U.S. President Harry Truman (supported by the CIO majority) and campaigned instead for Henry Wallace's left-liberal Progressive Party. In response, Philip Murray, who at first had sought to restrain Reuther's anticommunism, denounced "these so-called Left-Wingers" whose preference was "to be the satellites of Sovietism rather than to be loyal to their own country." Murray concluded, "There is no room in the CIO for communism." Eleven "left-wing" unions with a million members were kicked out. This was Reuther's line, and the UAW president came to be seen by many as Murray's obvious successor.

Death and Unity

The momentum of the CIO had visibly slowed by 1952, and the AFL, by that time twice the size of its once-dynamic challenger, was also stagnating. The success of the presidential campaign of Republican Dwight D. Eisenhower was both a defeat of the Democratic Party and a blow to Murray and Green. For the first time in two decades, the party in power had no obligations to organized labor, and the two union federations' greater-than-ever dependence on the federal government left them especially vulnerable to the potential antilabor shift. This anxiety haunted both men as they passed away.

Murray's death helped to save the career of a rival of Reuther's, David J. McDonald of the United Steel Workers of America. Seen by many as a pretentious opportunist with a taste for high living, McDonald was slated for removal from his position as secretary-treasure of the union by an increasingly critical Murray, who had earlier appointed him. Instead, McDonald was able to take over the Steelworkers' union presidency and had designs on the presidency of the CIO. Reuther was elected to the CIO presidency (by a narrow margin in a contest with

longtime CIO staffer Allan Haywood). An envious McDonald looked for ways to undermine his opponent's authority. "I didn't like Reuther, and I presume he felt the same way about me," he later asserted. (A less diplomatic comment of his referred to "that no good red-headed socialist bastard Reuther.") McDonald threatened to pull his union out of the CIO and used that threat as leverage to advance a rapid merger with the AFL.

Meany had no such difficulties when he took over the AFL presidency. His lack of "class struggle" credentials and his skills as a lobbyist and a tough-minded organization man blended well with the relative affluence and social conservatism that was then dominating the American scene. His fundamental outlook for the labor movement did not seem to differ substantially from Reuther's. That fact, plus the absence in either of an emotional stake for maintaining the division of CIO from AFL, contributed to the U.S. labor movement's rapid reunification.

Key Players

Green, William (1873–1952): An Ohio-born coal miner, Green rose through the ranks of the United Mine Workers of America to become its secretary-treasurer in 1913 and joined the AFL's executive council in the same year. In 1924 he succeeded Samuel Gompers as AFL president, a position Green held for the rest of his life.

Lewis, John L. (1880–1969): Born into a Welsh coal mining family in Iowa, Lewis worked in the mines and at other jobs until he became a full-time AFL organizer in 1910 and then secured employment as a statistician for the United Mine Workers of America in 1917. By 1919 he was UMW acting president, a position he would occupy on a permanent basis from 1920 to 1960, when he voluntarily retired. In 1935 he was centrally involved in the formation of the Committee for Industrial Organization inside the AFL, which led, after expulsion of its members, to the Congress of Industrial Organizations. Lewis was CIO president in both incarnations, a position he relinquished in 1940. In 1942 he withdrew the UMW from the CIO, then brought it back into the AFL briefly in 1946–1947, after which he maintained it independent of any labor federation.

Meany, George (1894–1980): Son of an Irish-American local president in the United Association of Journeymen and Apprentices of the Plumbing and Pipefitting Industry, Meany himself became a plumber in 1916. By 1922 he was business manager of what had been his father's local. He rose in the New York City Building Trades Council and became president of the New York State Federation of Labor in 1934 and a labor lobbyist influential in Democratic Party politics. In 1939 he became secretary-treasurer of the AFL and then took over the presidency of the federation in 1952. He played a central role in the merger of the AFL-CIO and served as its president from 1955 until 1979.

Murray, Philip (1886–1952): Born in Scotland, Murray came to the U.S. in 1902. He had been involved in mining and unions since the age of 16. An executive board member of the United Mine Workers of American beginning in 1912, he became a supporter of John L. Lewis in the 1920s and first vice president of the UMW during Lewis's presidency. When Lewis led the CIO, he made Murray the president of the Steel Workers Organizing Committee; Murray replaced Lewis as CIO president in 1940. When Murray broke with Lewis' policies, Murray was expelled as UMW vice president, but made his own distinctive mark as president of the CIO and the United Steel Workers of America.

Reuther, Walter (1907–1970): Son of a German-American socialist brewery worker, Reuther himself was drawn in the 1930s to radical activism and involvement in organizing the United Auto Workers, one of the most dynamic unions in the new CIO. Associated with its left wing in the late 1930s, he abandoned the Socialist Party to support the Democratic Party's New Deal coalition. A prominent anti-Communist in the 1940s, he helped break the left-wing influence in the UAW (of which he became president in 1947) and the CIO. Reuther served as CIO president from 1952 until the merger with the AFL, but remained UAW president until his untimely death.

See also: *AFL, CIO Merge; American Federation of Labor; CIO Anticommunist Drive; Congress of Industrial Organizations.*

BIBLIOGRAPHY

Books

Buhle, Paul. *Taking Care of Business: Samuel Gompers, George Meany, Lane Kirkland, and the Tragedy of American Labor.* New York: Monthly Review Press, 1999.

Cochran, Bert. *Labor and Communism: The Conflict that Shaped American Unions.* Princeton, NJ: Princeton University Press, 1977.

De Caux, Len. *Labor Radical, From the Wobblies to CIO: A Personal History.* Boston: Beacon Press, 1970.

Dollinger, Sol, and Genora Dollinger. *Not Automatic: Women and the Left in the Forging of the Auto Workers' Union.* New York: Monthly Review Press, 2000.

Dubofsky, Melvin, and Warren Van Tine, eds. *Labor Leaders in America.* Urbana: University of Illinois Press, 1987.

Goulden, Joseph C. *Meany, The Unchallenged Strong Man of American Labor.* New York: Atheneum, 1972.

Herling, John. *Right to Challenge: People and Power in the Steelworkers Union.* New York: Harper and Row, 1972.

Levinson, Edward. *Labor on the March.* Ithaca, NY: ILR Press, 1995.

Lichtenstein, Nelson. *Walter Reuther: The Most Dangerous Man in Detroit.* Urbana: University of Illinois Press, 1995.

Madison, Charles A. *American Labor Leaders,* 2nd edition. New York: Frederick Ungar, 1962.

Marquart, Frank. *An Auto Worker's Journal: The UAW from Crusade to One-Party Union.* University Park: Pennsylvania State University Press, 1975.

Preis, Art. *Labor's Giant Step: Twenty Years of the CIO.* New York: Pathfinder Press, 1972.

Quill, Shirley. *Mike Quill Himself: A Memoir.* Greenwich, CT: Devin-Adair, 1985.

Reuther, Victor G. *The Brothers Reuther and the Story of the CIO: A Memoir.* Boston: Houghton Mifflin Co., 1979.

Robinson, Archie. *George Meany and His Times: A Biography.* New York: Simon and Schuster, 1981.

Taft, Philip. *The AFL From the Death of Gompers to the Merger.* New York: Harper and Brothers, 1959.

Zieger, Robert H. *The CIO, 1935–1955.* Durham: University of North Carolina Press, 1995.

Other

Congress of Industrial Organizations. *Proceedings of 1949 Convention.*

—Paul Le Blanc

Mechanics' Union of Trade Associations

United States 1827

Synopsis

The Mechanics Union of Trade Associations (MUTA) was the first city central labor union in United States history. Begun when a strike for a 10-hour day by journeyman carpenters united with a wider movement led by a socialist shoemaker, MUTA came to represent at least 19 trade unions with more than 2,000 members. MUTA supported a library, sponsored the nation's first labor-run newspaper, regulated strikes, paid relief wages for striking workers, established work standards and pay-scales for journeymen in many different professions, and took an interest in local and federal political elections to help ensure that legislators were sympathetic to labor. Though MUTA lasted only two years, its influence in the politicization and empowerment of laborers was far-reaching: within a decade of its formation, similar unions were formed in every major city on the eastern seaboard, newspapers by and for working men were published throughout the country, and the Workingmen's Party it helped to materialize was a force in key elections of the early Jacksonian era.

Timeline

1802: Beethoven publishes his "Sonata quasi una fantasia," later nicknamed the "Moonlight Sonata."

1805: Britain's Royal Navy, commanded by Admiral Horatio Nelson, defeats the French at Trafalgar, thereby putting an end to Napoleon's hopes of dominating the seas.

1810: German art publisher Rudolph Ackerman invents the differential gear, which enables wheeled vehicles to make sharp turns.

1815: Congress of Vienna establishes the balance of power for post-Napoleonic Europe, and inaugurates a century of British dominance throughout most of the world.

1820: In the Missouri Compromise, Missouri is admitted to the Union as slave state, but slavery is prohibited in all portions of the Louisiana Purchase north of 36°30' N.

1821: Mexico declares independence from Spain.

1823: U.S. President James Monroe establishes the Monroe Doctrine, whereby the United States warns European nations not to interfere in the political affairs of the Western Hemisphere.

1825: New York Stock Exchange opens.

1826: French inventor Joseph-Nicéphore Niepce makes the first photographic image in history.

1828: Election of Andrew Jackson as president begins a new era in American history.

1830: French troops invade Algeria, and at home, a revolution forces the abdication of Charles V in favor of Louis Philippe, the "Citizen King."

1836: In Texas's war of independence with Mexico, the defenders of the Alamo, among them Davy Crockett and Jim Bowie, are killed in a siege. Later that year, Texas wins the Battle of San Jacinto and secures its independence.

Event and Its Context

Background

Philadelphia was one of the leading centers of master craftsmen and journeymen in the English-speaking New World, with mechanics and their families estimated to comprise one-half of the population of the city by the time of the American Revolution. Organization and agitation among laborers became increasingly frequent during the years that Philadelphia was the capital of the new nation. In 1786, while master printer Benjamin Franklin still lived in the city, the journeymen printers became the first profession to strike successfully when 26 members of their fraternal order spearheaded a stand-out to demand a minimum salary of $6 per week. In 1791 journeymen carpenters were less successful when they walked off their jobs demanding a workday from 6:00 A.M. to 6:00 P.M. (minus two hours for lunch) instead of the standard sun-up to sun-down schedule; the master builders were able to outlast their journeymen, but the warning of one master carpenter that "the contagion will soon be communicated to other artificers" proved quite accurate.

In 1794 the newly formed Federal Society of Cabinet and Chair Makers won a strike against their masters for higher minimum wages by receiving financial assistance not only from their fellow journeymen in other Philadelphia guilds but also from their fellow cabinet and chair makers in New York City. Emboldened by the success of their peers, the Federal Society of Journeymen Cordwainers (FSJC) of Philadelphia, founded in 1794, orchestrated three strikes by 1800 to require masters to hire only members of their union. FSJC members became the beneficiaries of the first known sympathy strike in American history when Philadelphia's boot-makers union joined them in a stand-out.

The first major legal blow against an individual Philadelphia union was struck against the FSJC in the trial of *Commonwealth v. Pullis*. The alleged intimidation tactics the cordwainers union had used against scabs (a term actually coined in its modern labor context by English cordwainers) during an 1805 strike landed eight of the society's leaders in court on conspiracy charges in January 1806. Thirteen witnesses testified before a jury composed of three master craftsmen and nine merchants that they had been the victims of physical intimidation and abuse by the society for their refusal to join and for working as shoemakers during one of the society's stand-outs. The defendants were represented by a pair of distinguished and high-priced Philadelphia attorneys, Caesar Rodney (nephew of the Declaration of Independence signer of the same name) and Walter Franklin, who based much of their defense on the inequity of a system in which a master cordwainer could earn $15,000 per year while the journeymen who earned him his wealth made only $50 per month. The jury found the society members guilty as charged, but Judge John Innskep imposed the relatively light sentence of an $8 fine per defendant plus court costs, all of which were defrayed by the FSJC.

The decade-long economic boom after the Philadelphia cordwainer's trial was a period of much manufacturing growth in and around the city and of relative peace on the labor front. The economy took a dramatic downturn beginning in 1817, caused largely by the repeal of the Embargo Act and the flood of cheap factory-made English goods into American harbors. In Philadelphia this was a time of massive layoffs and bankruptcies, with as many as one-fifth of Philadephia County's population of 100,000 unemployed by 1820. The sharp increase in poverty created desperation among the working class, and it was this rather than legislation that killed the unions. By the time prosperity returned in the early 1820s, most of the victories gained by unions over the past few decades had been lost by starving workers frantic for even subsistence wages on any terms.

William Heighton and the Founding of MUTA

Cheap manufactured goods were not the only English import to change the lives of American workingmen in the 1820s. The writings of the Ricardian socialists began to gain a serious foothold in American labor centers, albeit indirectly. Especially popular was John Gray's *Lecture on Human Happiness*, a treatise decrying the inequitable sharing of wealth between employers and employees and advocating the end of "that fountain head of evil" known as free market competition, a return to small self-governing communities, and a complete restructuring of a national government that heretofore sympathized with capital over labor. Ironically, Gray never gained an audience in England but his work became such a bestseller in Philadelphia that the 18-3/4 cent pamphlets of his essay sold out three printings in 1825 alone. Gray's *Lecture* and other lesser Ricardian-inspired writings became Holy Writ to a young English-born shoemaker named William Heighton who was living in Southwark, a Philadelphia suburb.

In 1827 the Mayor's Court, in the case of *Commonwealth v. Moore*, reversed the decision against the cordwainers union 21 years before by ruling that journeymen tailors who had gone on strike for higher wages were not guilty of conspiracy. Emboldened by this decision, and perhaps by the writings of Gray, the journeyman carpenters of Philadelphia, busier than ever in a city whose population grew by 20,000 that decade, renewed their generation-old demand for a 10-hour workday and higher wages. At the same time, a heavy Luddite sentiment began to sweep Philadelphia as journeymen were being replaced by lower-paid unskilled factory workers, and a serious plan was afoot to save even more money by using slave labor in the trades and factories (in spite of Philadelphia's pride in being the site of the first abolition society). A major labor crisis was developing in the city, and William Heighton quickly became its prophet.

The bright and outspoken Heighton had been growing in popularity with his fellow craftsmen and had begun giving informal lectures throughout the city, the print versions of which were widely circulated. Heighton's writing largely echoed (if not plagiarized) that of Gray, though he differed in one major aspect: whereas Gray called for a return to self-governing communities, Heighton believed in remaining in the cities and reforming them through economic pressure and block voting for candidates from the labor class. Heighton divided all citizens into producers and nonproducers, each with its own subdivisions, and attributed the bulk of poverty and unfair business practices to the fact that policymakers were almost invariably from one of the six subdivisions (theologians, jurists, military, commercial people, gentry, and legislators) of nonproducers and as such represented only the interests of their own class. In his surviving lectures, he made clear that he wanted nothing less than a peaceful but complete overthrow of the ruling capital class and an end to capitalist competition. To Heighton, Philadelphia was as good a place as any in which to begin his revolution for a socialist utopia.

In September 1827 Heighton's popularity was sufficient to convince 60 mechanics to pledge $1 apiece for his formation of the North Alley Mechanics Library Company, the funds used to purchase books and essays written for the labor classes. Two months later, Heighton delivered his most important lecture, later printed as *An Address, Delivered Before the Mechanics and Working Classes Generally, of the City and County of Philadelphia, of the Universal Church, in Callowehill Street, on Wednesday Evening, November 21, 1827, by the "Unlettered Mechanic."* ("Unlettered Mechanic" was, along with "Fellow-Labourer," one of the two pseudonyms Heighton used for most of his writings, and the *Address* was among the shorter titles for his publications.) At this eventful lecture, Heighton called upon all trade unions in Philadelphia to assemble a general convention, to send delegates of at least one in every 10 members to draw up a constitution for a new governing agency that would aid in furthering the cause of working classes and delivering them from "a life of barely subsistence," and to pool resources for a general fund that would assist striking workers and be used for the empowerment and enlightenment of all laborers through the development of their own publications and library.

Heighton's meeting transpired in December 1827 at the Widow Tyler's Tavern. Representatives from at least 10 of Philadelphia's trade unions attended and drafted a constitution with 23 articles and 16 bylaws for the first citywide labor union in American history. It was ratified the following month by at least 18 trade unions.

Powers and Responsibilities of MUTA

MUTA's constitution carried a preamble drafted by Heighton sometime in or before January 1828. Modeled loosely after the Declaration of Independence, with large measures of John Gray sprinkled liberally throughout, the preamble was equal parts manifesto and rant against the tyrannies of employers. Describing MUTA as an association "for the purpose of affording to each other mutual protection from oppression," it quickly gave way to an alternately eloquent and "unlettered" economic theory in which all wealth derived from "the bones, marrow, and muscles of the industrious classes" who "have a natural and unalienable right to reap the fruits of their own industry" and who, if paid more fairly, would create a major economic upswing. The preamble cried throughout about the evils of the "depreciation of the intrinsic value of human labour." It also asserted that the purpose of MUTA was not in any way to "injure or take the smallest unjust advantage" of employers, though it ultimately stated as an objective the toppling of "the capitalist, throned as he is, in the midst of his ill gotten abundance."

The articles and bylaws were of a more pragmatic nature. The first articles were concerned with financing the new association, calling for $50 loans by each of the participating trade unions and monthly dues of 10 cents apiece from each of the estimated 2,000 people represented by the unions in MUTA. The goal was to guarantee an income to the organization of at least $125 per month to be applied to the association's various purposes.

Probably of most interest to the workingmen represented were MUTA's policies and powers in the event of a general strike. The articles regulated that any constituent union wishing to strike would notify the president of the Mechanics' Association at least one week before the beginning of the stand-out. A special session of the delegates from all the unions would be called to hear the case for a stand-out, and if at least a two-thirds majority of those present agreed that the workers had just cause to strike, then the strikers would receive MUTA's endorsement and, more important, the strikers would receive monetary benefits.

In the event of an approved strike, the amount of money received by workmen depended upon several factors. Men who were required to leave the community during a strike were to receive travel expenses of from $3 to $6. Married men received $2 per week, plus additional sums to be provided by their own union for each of their dependents. Originally, married men had been forbidden to leave town during a strike, but this was quickly edited from the constitution.

The constitution also called for the North Alley Mechanics Library Company (whose collection by January 1828 was estimated at "about 100 volumes") to come under the auspices of MUTA. Ten mechanics were selected from the MUTA ranks to serve as its board of directors, whose primary responsibilities were to schedule debates and lectures in the room rented for the library and to oversee the establishment of a newspaper by and for workingmen.

Mechanics Free Press

Periodicals prior to the Jacksonian era were largely of necessity an elitist endeavor. Sold only in bookstores and through subscription, the average cost for a magazine or newspaper was $10 per year, an amount equal to a week's wages for most workers. Most publications were focused on trade, politics, and society, subjects that were, at least in Heighton's opinion, not representative of the interests of the working classes. Philadelphia had been home to at least two newspapers geared toward the working class, the *Journeymen's Mechanic Advocate* and *The Mechanic's Gazette*, but the publications had been for-profit interests owned by capitalists and neither fared well. The latter failed after only two months. Heighton sought to correct the situation and he used MUTA and the library that he had formed as the springboard for a new publication, *Mechanics Free Press*, a nonprofit publication to be produced with the co-operation of the printers union and written by and for laborers.

The first issue of *Mechanics Free Press* appeared in January 1828. Using as a logo the image of an eagle clutching arrows in one talon and flowers and fruit in the other, it carried the masthead, "A Journal of Practical and Useful Knowledge." Priced at $2 per year payable quarterly, the weekly paper consisted of four pages filled with editorials, most of them written by Heighton, on such issues as class struggle, education reform, socialism, and the need for a worker's political party. An odd hodgepodge of lighter fare included poetry, classifieds, and recipes. The paper was at least a limited success, boasting a circulation of 2,000 in an open letter to potential advertisers on 24 July 1830.

Mechanics Free Press received praise in other publications throughout the Northeast, including abolitionist newspapers (which was surprising, considering that the *Mechanics Free Press* never once attacked or even addressed slavery or the plight of free black laborers) and, ironically, in the elitist publication *The Deist*. More important, it was widely imitated, with the *New York Workingman's Advocate* appearing only a year after its initial issue.

Dissolution of MUTA

Most of the records and details of MUTA's meetings and administration have long disappeared from the historical record, so the reasons given for the union's disbanding in November 1829 are largely conjecture. Some of the theories, each probably at least to some degree correct, are monetary difficulties, political arguments among MUTA members, and Heighton's disillusionment with the labor movement.

Meager as were the allotments given to striking workers, MUTA approved at least four strikes including those by carpenters, bricklayers, painters, and glaziers. From what is known of the union's finances, these may have been sufficient to empty the organization's modest coffers. Although the *Mechanics Free Press* generated at least $4,000 per year at its height, the majority of the proceeds were used to cover the cost of publication.

The MUTA constitution stated clearly that "party politics shall be entirely out of the question" in the governing causes of the association, but MUTA immediately became linked to the rise of the Workingmen's Party, in which many of its members were involved and whose most enthusiastic trumpeter was the *Mechanics Free Press*. By 1829 the organization was extremely involved in politics and began to host regular political meetings to discuss nominations for various city and state offices. Dissent

ran high among the association's ranks and at least two political meetings degenerated into brawls, one of which was ended only after 20 mechanics attempted to throw MUTA chairman and hatter's union representative Michael Labarthe from a second-story window.

Meanwhile Heighton, whose zeal and energy had provided the vital spark for MUTA, became increasingly extreme in his views. He envisioned adding unions of unskilled workers to MUTA, a vision not shared by his journeymen peers. His embrace of radical socialism became stronger until he began to alienate many of his more moderate colleagues. The details are unknown, but he was no longer an active participant in MUTA by the November 1829 meeting, which chairman Labarthe announced would be the last.

MUTA was disbanded that month, and its funds were divided among its member unions. Heighton, angry and disillusioned with MUTA and the failure of the Workingmen's Party, left Philadelphia sometime in 1830, never again to be a force in labor or American socialist activities.

Legacy of MUTA

In spite of its short life, MUTA was not without success. In addition to representing at least 19 labor unions at its height, the organization inspired the creation of at least six new unions. By 1830 similar city central labor unions had followed MUTA's lead in New York City and Boston and would continue to grow and become more successful during the next decade. *Mechanics Free Press*, which survived until 1835, was also widely copied and influenced the next generation of labor writers.

Key Players

Gray, John (1799–1850): An unsuccessful merchant and Ricardian socialist in his native England, Gray authored the 1825 essay "Lecture on Human Happiness," which became a bestseller in America. He called for a return to small communities and an end to free-market enterprise, and he stressed that if employees were paid more, then it would be a major boon for the economy.

Heighton, William (1800–1873): Born in Oundle, Northhamptonshire, England, Heighton immigrated to the United States as a child and became a shoemaker as a young man. Though he was a voracious reader and writer of socialist literature, it is not believed that Heighton ever read the works of Ricardo or that he had a more than perfunctory education. After being the incarnation of the Philadelphia labor movement in the late 1820s, Heighton faded into obscurity, eventually becoming a farmer in New Jersey. He reemerged only briefly in 1865 to publish essays favoring radical reconstruction.

See also: *Workingmen's Party.*

BIBLIOGRAPHY

Books

Foner, Philip S. *William Heighton: Pioneer Labor Leader of Jacksonian Philadelphia*. New York: International Publishers, 1991.

Periodicals

Arky, Louis H. "The Mechanics' Union of Trade Associations and the Formation of the Philadelphia Workingmen's Movement." *Pennsylvania Magazine of History and Biography* 76 (April 1952): 142–176.

Pessen, Edward. "The Workingmen's Movement of the Jacksonian Era." *The Mississippi Valley Historical Review* 43 (December 1956): 428–443.

Saxton, Alexander. "Problems of Class and Race in the Origins of the Mass Circulation Press." *American Quarterly* 36 (summer 1984): 211–234.

Other

Morris, Richard B. "The Emergence of American Labor." U.S. Department of Labor. 2002 [cited 9 September 2002]. <http://www.dol.gov/asp/programs/history/chapter1.htm>.

Pessen, Edward. "Builders of the Young Republic." U.S. Department of Labor. 2002 [cited 9 September 2002]. <http://www.dol.gov/asp/programs/history/chapter2.htm>.

—Jonathan Darby

President Woodrow Wilson. The Library of Congress.

Mediation Commission, World War I

United States 1917–1918

Synopsis

When the United States entered World War I in 1917, it faced a mobilization crisis. Throughout the country, labor unrest was rampant and threatened the wartime supply of goods. In response, President Woodrow Wilson formed a Mediation Commission that he charged with traveling to the areas troubled by labor disputes and offering its services to help bring about settlements. The commission was formed to deal with the disputes in the Arizona copper mines and the timber industry of the Northwest, but it expanded to handle disputes in the telephone, transit, and meatpacking industries. The commission's efforts were generally successful, although it experienced failure with the meatpackers and in the timber industry. Usually, the grievances were similar and included such issues as the eight-hour workday, higher wages, collective bargaining, and a closed shop.

Timeline

1897: Zionist movement is established under the leadership of Theodor Herzl.

1902: Second Anglo-Boer War ends in victory for Great Britain. It is a costly victory, however, resulting in the loss of more British lives (5,774) than any conflict between 1815 and 1914. The war also sees the introduction of concentration camps, used by the British to incarcerate Boer civilians.

1905: Russian Revolution of 1905 occurs. Following the "bloody Sunday" riots before the Winter Palace in St. Petersburg in January, revolution spreads throughout Russia, in some places spurred on by newly formed workers' councils, or soviets. Among the most memorable incidents of the revolt is the mutiny aboard the battleship *Potemkin*. Suppressed by the czar, the revolution brings an end to liberal reforms and thus sets the stage for the larger revolutions of 1917.

1911: In China, revolutionary forces led by Sun Yat-sen bring an end to more than 2,100 years of imperial rule.

1915: A German submarine sinks the *Lusitania*, killing 1,195, including 128 U.S. citizens. Theretofore, many Americans had been sympathetic toward Germany, but the incident begins to turn the tide of U.S. sentiment toward the Allies.

1917: The intercepted "Zimmermann Telegram" reveals a plot by the German government to draw Mexico into an alliance against the United States in return for a German promise to return the southwestern U.S. territories taken in the Mexican War. Three months later on 6 April, in response to German threats of unrestricted submarine warfare, the United States declares war on Germany.

1917: On both the Western Front and in the Middle East, the tide of the war begins to turn against the Central Powers. The arrival of U.S. troops, led by General Pershing, in France in June greatly boosts morale and reinforces exhausted Allied forces. Meanwhile, Great Britain scores two major victories against the Ottoman Empire as T. E. Lawrence leads an Arab revolt in Baghdad in March, and troops under Field Marshal Edmund Allenby take Jerusalem in December.

1919: With the formation of the Third International (Comintern), the Bolshevik government of Russia establishes its control over communist movements worldwide.

1923: Conditions in Germany worsen as inflation skyrockets and France, attempting to collect on coal deliveries promised at Versailles, marches into the Ruhr basin. In November an obscure political group known as the National Socialist German Workers' Party attempts to stage a coup, or putsch, in a Munich beer hall. The revolt fails, and in 1924 the party's leader, Adolf Hitler, will receive a prison sentence of five years. He will only serve nine months, however, and the incident will serve to attract attention for him and his party, known as the Nazis.

1927: Stalin arranges to have Trotsky expelled from the Communist Party.

Event and Its Context

When the United States entered World War I on 6 April 1917, the country faced not only war but also growing labor unrest. The labor problems were not new, but with the United States depending on the materials from laborers to supply its armed forces, labor problems took on a new degree of urgency. In response, President Wilson created a commission to help arbitrate and allay misunderstandings between employees and employers. President Wilson's Mediation Commission was established on 19 September 1917 as part of a special branch of the Conciliation Service. The new commission was charged with helping to resolve labor problems in the West, especially in the Arizona copper mines, and in the Northwest to ensure an adequate supply for materials for the war effort. It was also asked to investigate the causes of labor unrest and recommend solutions.

William Wilson, the first secretary of labor, led the commission, which consisted of five others: Harvard professor of law Felix Frankfurter, business leaders Verner Z. Reed from Colorado and John L. Spangler from Pennsylvania, E. P. Marsh of the Washington State Federation of Labor, and John H. Walker of the Illinois Federation of Labor. The members of the commission traveled to the problem regions in the hopes of bringing about settlements between the workers and employers. The commission was unique because it was created by the gov-

ernment alone, not by an agreement between the government and organized labor. The commission was also responsible for providing assistance in developing agreements between labor and management. The original intent was for the commission to only travel to the copper mining and lumber regions, but soon problems in the telephone, transit, meatpacking, and oil industries demanded the commission's attention.

The conditions in the troubled areas varied greatly, but the problems that had caused the unrest were similar among the various industries. Generally, the problems included low pay, long hours, blacklisting of union members, and lack of collective bargaining. Each region, however, was different, and the commission was not always able to work out agreements between the parties. Further, union groups such as the Industrial Workers of the World (IWW) complicated the situation. The IWW, formed in 1905 by socialists and radical unionists, wanted to crush the more conservative American Federation of Labor (AFL) and lead the working class in a revolution to achieve an "industrial democracy." The Globe, Arizona, *Record* accused striking workers of being unpatriotic and disloyal and even made accusations that the IWW was subsidized by Germany. Embittered feelings over the IWW and strikers often led to violence. For example, more than 1,000 strikers in Arizona were deported; in Everett, Washington, several were killed during riots; and in Butte, Montana, labor leader Frank Little was lynched. Loyalty Leagues that developed in response to IWW further increased tension.

The most dramatic example of the commission's work was in the Arizona copper mines. Disputes there were particularly troublesome because the war effort depended heavily on the metals produced there. When the commission arrived in Arizona, it identified several serious problems. One of the biggest problems among the miners was language. The commission found 32 nationalities represented in one camp. The miners were unable to communicate effectively with each other or with their employers so as to organize or even to explain their grievances to management or the commission. The labor force was also migratory, and production in the mines suffered from a large turnover rate. Among other problems identified by the commission were absenteeism and the trade union movement.

In their discussions with the commission, the workers complained that the business was run autocratically. They wanted a way to ensure that they would be treated fairly. The miners wanted the mine owners to address concerns about wages, hours, and working conditions. The commission's findings prompted three recommendations. (1) The commission recommended the development of an orderly and impartial way to address the miners' grievances. The commission hoped that once they had a mechanism by which to voice grievances, the workers would agree not to strike during the course of the war. (2) The commission suggested that representatives be chosen from both the workers and employers to address working conditions, ensure that workers had the right to organize, and prohibit blacklisting. (3) The commission proposed that the employers should rehire former strikers who had been let go as a result of their protest. The commission's efforts in Arizona were mostly successful. Between 1 November 1917 and 21 October 1918, there were no strikes.

In the California oil fields, the disputes revolved around independent companies that refused to adopt an eight-hour workday and a minimum wage of $4.00 a day. The commission used Standard Oil's successful implementation of the eight-hour day as an example of success. The companies eventually accepted a plan similar to that of Standard Oil. The companies also agreed to hire members of the American Federation of Labor but refused to hire IWW members and refused a closed shop.

Another commission success was with the telephone dispute among workers, mostly women, in California, Oregon, Washington, Idaho, and Nevada. The main complaints centered on union recognition, wages, and a closed shop. The commission helped the parties reach an agreement on all three points.

By far the worst conditions that the commission witnessed were in the meatpacking industry. Among the complaints were long hours, blacklisting of union members, and lack of collective bargaining, but the most serious was low wages. Many meatpackers were still earning the same wage they had in 1904, only 18 cents an hour. Events reached a climax when packers refused to meet with representatives from the Amalgamated Meat Cutters and Butcher Workmen and called an industry-wide strike. The commission met separately with the meatpackers and with union representatives and arranged for collective bargaining. In arbitration, the workers also won an eight-hour day, wage increases, collective bargaining, and the right to join a trade union.

The commission suffered its first real failure at the hands of the timber operation management and the lumberjacks. Almost all of the men employed in the timber industry were described as "womanless, voteless, and jobless" men who worked intermittently in harsh frontier conditions. Further, their working and living conditions were very primitive. Loggers lived in lice-infested crowded barracks, had only cheap food, and were required to work regardless of the danger or weather conditions. These conditions made them especially receptive to the IWW, the group to offer the loggers help. The popular prejudices against the radical IWW worked to undermine their efforts to secure better working conditions, a $60 per month minimum wage, and a prohibition against blacklisting using "rustling" cards. A "rustling" indicated whether the worker had left his previous jobs on good terms, which would not be the case if he had been involved in a union.

In addition to striking, the lumberjacks used another tactic. A "strike on the job" involved workers intentionally slowing production through sabotage. For instance, often workers drove spikes into trees, which broke the saws. The operators, however, refused to budge on the issue of an eight-hour day unless southern mills also adopted an eight-hour day. The issue was complicated by the commission's own bias. The members of the commission who were affiliated with the AFL were unable to maintain impartiality. The commissioners did not question even one of the IWW members.

A few months after the commission's efforts failed, Colonel Brice P. Disque from the Spruce Division of the War Department, was able to arbitrate a settlement. Colonel Disque was sent west to investigate the poor supply of spruce, a key material for planes and ships, for the Division of Military Aeronautics. What he discovered was complete chaos. During his tour he heard a suggestion that a patriotic organization be created to win the support of the workers. After presenting his report and ideas to the secretary of war in Washington, Disque returned to Portland and organized the Loyalty Legion of Loggers and Lumbermen, or the "4 Ls." The legion proved successful and greatly decreased the IWW's influence in the timber industry.

In June 1918 the commission submitted a report to President Woodrow Wilson documenting its work and recommendations. The members of the commission also outlined what they believed were the four main causes of unrest in American industry. At the top of their list was the absence of a positive relationship between the employees and management caused by management's refusal to deal with employee organizations. The other three causes were a lack of a mechanism for employees to report grievances, ignorance of each side in attempting to understand the problems of the other side, and wage increases to match cost-of-living increases. To deal with these problems, the commission made several recommendations, including the elimination of all profiteering, establishing an eight-hour workday, the proactive management of grievances, and establishing some form of collective bargaining. The report itself remained an important document for labor in peace as well. Overall, the commission proved a success in bringing peace to various labor disputes in a time of crisis. It also brought to light a number of important issues such as the eight-hour day and collective bargaining.

The commission was unique because it was formed by presidential proclamation and not from an agreement with any labor unions. Its jurisdiction was not limited to any one place or one trade, thus establishing an important precedent for creating other agencies during crises such as the Great Depression, when the government would take on a referee function similar to that of the Mediation Commission. The creation of the commission addressed a weakness in the newly created Department of Labor, but because William Wilson was the chairman of the committee and the secretary of labor, his position and that of the Department of Labor was strengthened.

Key Players

Wilson, William Bauchop (1862–1934): The first secretary of labor (1913–1921), Wilson was a strong advocate of the eight-hour day, unions, workers compensation, child labor laws, and workplace safety. Among his other positions were secretary-treasurer of the United Mine Workers of America and in Congress.

Wilson, Woodrow (1856–1924): The 28th president of the United States, Wilson ran on a neutrality platform. Once elected, however, he was unable to keep the United States out of World War I. Wilson also sponsored laws outlawing child labor and creating an eight-hour work day for railroad workers.

See also: *American Federation of Labor; Department of Labor; Industrial Workers of the World; IWW Copper Strike.*

BIBLIOGRAPHY

Books

Bing, Alexander. *War-time Strikes and Their Adjustment.* New York: Arno and *The New York Times*, 1971.

Lombardi, John. *Labor's Voice in the Cabinet.* New York: AMS Press, 1968.

Periodicals

Overstreet, Daphne. "On Strike! The 1917 Walkout at Globe, Arizona." *Journal of Arizona History* 18 (summer 1977): 197–218.

Tyler, Robert L. "The United States Government as Union Organizer: The Loyalty Legion of Loggers and Timbermen." *The Mississippi Valley Historical Review* 47 (December 1960): 434–451.

Wilson, Marjorie Hayes. "Governor Hunt, the 'Beast' and the Miners." *Journal of Arizona History* 15 (summer 1974): 119–138.

Other

Sixth Annual Report of the Secretary of Labor for the Fiscal Year Ended June 30, 1918. Washington, DC: GPO, 1918.

—Lisa A. Ennis

Memorial Day Massacre

Chicago, Illinois, United States 1937

Synopsis

In March 1937 the Steel Workers Organizing Committee (SWOC) signed an agreement with U. S. Steel Corporation, the largest American steelmaker, that warranted an eight-hour workday and a 40-hour workweek. A group of smaller steel companies, the so-called Little Steel group, refused to sign the same agreement. This refusal led to bitter confrontation and violence. On Memorial Day 1937 strikers and their families joined with sympathizers in a demonstration in front of the Republic Steel plant in Chicago. In the violent riots that ensued, 10 strikers were killed and 40 were wounded. The police claimed that they had been attacked by demonstrators with clubs and bricks and that they had to respond with reasonable force to defend themselves and break up the mob. Accounts in newspapers, including the *Chicago Tribune*, fostered paranoia of an imminent communist revolution, describing the strikers as a trained military unit. To the contrary, the strikers argued that the police had started to shoot the peaceful demonstrators with no reason. Their version was validated by the investigation conducted by the La Follette Committee.

Timeline

1922: Published this year James Joyce's novel *Ulysses* and T. S. Eliot's poem *The Waste Land* will transform literature and inaugurate the era of modernism.

1927: American inventor Philo T. Farnsworth demonstrates a working model of the television, and Belgian astronomer Georges Lemaître proposes the Big Bang Theory.

1932: In German elections, Nazis gain a 37 percent plurality of Reichstag seats, raising tensions between the far right and the far left. On a "bloody Sunday" in July, communists in Hamburg attack Nazis with guns, and a fierce battle ensues.

1937: Italy signs the Anti-Comintern Pact, signed by Germany and Japan the preceding year. Like the two others before it, Italy now withdraws from the League of Nations.

1937: Japan attacks China and annexes most of that nation's coastal areas.

1937: Stalin uses carefully staged show trials in Moscow to eliminate all rivals for leadership. These party purges, however, are only a small part of the death toll now being exacted in a country undergoing forced industrialization, much of it by means of slave labor.

1937: In the middle of an around-the-world flight, Amelia Earhart and her plane disappear somewhere in the Pacific.

1937: Crash of the *Hindenburg* in Lakehurst, New Jersey, kills 36 and ends the brief era when rigid airships promised to be the ocean liners of the skies.

1937: Pablo Picasso paints his famous *Guernica* mural dramatizing the Nationalist bombing of a town in Spain. Thanks to artists and intellectuals such as Picasso and Ernest Hemingway, the Loyalists are winning the battle of hearts and minds, even if they are weaker militarily, and idealistic young men flock from America to join the "Abraham Lincoln Brigade." Yet as George Orwell later reveals in *Homage to Catalonia*, the lines between good and evil are not clear: with its Soviet backing, the Loyalist cause serves as proxy for a totalitarianism every bit as frightening as that of the Nationalists and their German and Italian supporters.

1942: Axis conquests reach their height in the middle of this year. The Nazis control a vast region from Normandy to the suburbs of Stalingrad, and from the Arctic Circle to the edges of the Sahara. To the east, the Japanese "Co-Prosperity Sphere" encompasses territories from China to Burma to the East Indies, stretching deep into the western Pacific.

1947: Marshall Plan is established to assist European nations in recovering from the war.

1952: Among the cultural landmarks of the year are the film *High Noon* and the book *The Invisible Man* by Ralph Ellison.

Event and Its Context

The Political Context of the Massacre: New Deal Labor Policies and the Steel Industry

The violent struggles of Memorial Day 1937 in Chicago cannot be understood separately from the more general tensions between labor and capital that characterized the historical peri-

Police hold back striking steelworkers, "Little Steel" Strike, Republic Steel Plant, South Chicago, Illinois. AP/World Wide Photos. Reproduced by permission.

od of the Great Depression. The New Deal industrial legislation tried to address these tensions. The massacre was itself part of the larger national strike against the Little Steel industries for the recognition of the workers' right to unionize and bargain collectively. The massacre had a crucial impact on the process of increasing unionism in American steel industries. Although the unions eventually called off the national strike of 1937 because of the demoralizing effect of the Chicago massacre and the death of other six union members in pickets throughout the country, the Little Steel companies finally surrendered in August 1941 under legal pressure and signed a contract that allowed collective bargaining.

The legal and political roots of the Memorial Day Massacre are in the legislative acts of the first New Deal, which attempted to cooperate with business in order to foster economic recovery. The National Industrial Recovery Act (NIRA), passed in 1933, tried to strike a balance between the requests of industrialists and workers. The act is the embodiment of the New Deal belief that national planning should replace individualistic and competitive business action. According to the act, the government would be the arbiter of economic competition between different

industrial groups, thus relinquishing a key principle of *laissez-faire* economy: minimal intervention by the state in economic matters. Under the patronage of the National Recovery Administration (NRA) set up by the act, rival companies decided to end ruthless competition and met with representatives of consumers and workers to draw up a code of fairer competition that raised prices by limiting production. To balance the allowances made to industries, section 7(a) of NIRA guaranteed workers their right to form unions and bargain collectively through representatives of their own choosing.

This atmosphere of cooperation between business and workers, however, was short-lived. In 1935 the Supreme Court unanimously declared the NIRA unconstitutional, claiming that it granted the federal government excessive authority to control businesses. This, together with joint attacks on other acts passed during the first New Deal, prompted Roosevelt and Congress to adopt a more aggressive stance toward industries that stood accused of putting their interests above national well-being. In the summer of 1935 Congress passed the Wagner Act (also known as the National Labor Relations Act), which reestablished the rights of workers as outlined in section 7(a) of the

Rioting after lockout of steel workers, Edger Thompson Works, Memorial Day Massacre, 1937. AP/World Wide Photos. Reproduced by permission.

NIRA. The new act also gave the NLRB the task of ensuring democratic union election and denouncing unfair labor practices carried out by industrialists, such as the firing of union members.

As a result of the Wagner Act, recruitment of union members increased steadily. The establishment of industrial unions led to a split between craft and industrial workers within the American Federation of Labor (AFL), which until then had been dominated by craft unions of skilled workers. The vice president of the AFL, John L. Lewis of the United Mine Workers, resigned and, together with other industrial unionists, formed the Committee for Industrial Organization (CIO) in November 1935. Because of the difficulties of advancing their demands experienced under the AFL, steelworkers were eager to defect and try the new approach to unionism that was espoused by the CIO. This approach urged all workers to organize in a single union and negotiate with management collectively rather than separately. Under CIO guidance, steelworkers were among the first to organize themselves in a union: the Steel Workers Organizing Committee (SWOC) formed in 1936. A year later, the United States Steel Corporation, the leading producer of steel (also known as "Big Steel"), recognized SWOC. The two parties signed an agreement recognizing SWOC as the bargaining agent for its members and establishing a common labor wage of $5 a day, with an eight-hour working day and paying workers time and one-half for overtime work.

Despite the fact that many companies signed the same agreement, a group of Little Steel firms that included Bethlehem Steel, Republic Steel, Inland Steel, and Youngstown Sheet and Tube refused to sign. Tom Girdler, the chairman of the board of Republic Steel, was particularly influential and vocal in his antiunion views. Confronted by this refusal, on 26 May 1937 SWOC called a strike against three of the Little Steel companies: Republic Steel, Inland Steel, and Youngstown Sheet and Tube. SWOC had just won a short strike with another steel company, Jones and Lauglin, and its leaders believed that they had the strength to close down the three companies. Most of the plants stopped production during the strike, and strikers set up picket lines to prevent any effort to reopen them. However, Republic Steel challenged strikers and refused to close down all its plants, going as far as housing nonunion workers within some plants, including the Republic Steel South Chicago Plant, so that the workers would not have to face the picket lines when going to work.

The Massacre to Stop Bolshevism: A Chronicle of the Memorial Day Massacre

Half of the 2,200 employees of the Republic Steel South Chicago Plant joined the strike on 26 May when the walkout began just after 3 P.M. The police intervened to stop the strikers' attempt to persuade other noncommitted workers to join the cause. When SWOC members tried to form a peaceful picket in front of the plant entrance, the police, led by Captain James Mooney, divided the demonstrators and arrested 23 people who had refused to obey their orders. The police action of breaking up this picket and forcing the activists to move to another location two blocks away from the plant clearly showed police support for Republic Steel.

Strike headquarters were established in Sam's Place, an abandoned tavern and dance hall six blocks northeast of the plant gate. The police further identified with the cause of Republic Steel by eating and sleeping in the plant. Meanwhile, Chicago mayor Edward J. Kelley announced in the *Chicago Tribune* that peaceful picketing would be permitted. Accordingly, strikers attempted to march again to the plant gate to strengthen the picket lines. The police confronted the strikers several blocks from the plant, and the strikers turned back without incident.

On 27 May demonstrators made another attempt to reinforce the pickets. Harsher police opposition confronted the marchers, a warning of what was to happen in the immediate future. At about 5 P.M., a group of several hundred strikers began to march to the plant gate. They encountered a stiffened police line that included reinforcements. The workers continued their march, and fighting broke out as a result. During the struggle several policemen took out their guns and discharged them into the air. This was a warning of the tragedy that was to occur on Memorial Day.

On 29 May, a Saturday, limited picketing took place at the plant. Nick Fontecchio, a local trade-unionist, called for a mass meeting at Sam's Place for Sunday in response to the violent behavior of the police. Strike leaders encouraged other local SWOC unions, in particular those from nearby closed-down plants, to send members to the meeting. The same day police captain James Mooney received an anonymous report that strikers would attempt to occupy the plant and throw out the nonunion workers the next day. Mooney took for granted the truthfulness of the report and ordered almost 300 policemen to be on duty at the Republic Steel plant on Sunday afternoon, thus setting the background for the unfolding of the massacre.

By 3:00 P.M. on 30 May, a crowd of around 1,500 strikers had gathered. It was a warm day, and many of the strikers and their supporters had brought along their wives and children to join in this almost festive gathering chaired by SWOC organizer Joe Weber. Speakers included Leo Krzycki, the regional director of SWOC, Nick Fontecchio, and Weber himself. They all addressed crucial labor issues of the day, especially the right to organize and picket. The workers approved some resolutions to send to government officials concerning police conduct at the Republic plant and decided to march to the plant and establish a mass picket.

When the march was agreed to, about 1,000 people went into formation behind two American flags. Instead of marching south down Green Bay Avenue, they turned onto a dirt road across an open prairie chanting, "CIO, CIO!" When the police realized the direction of the parade, they moved their position to across the dirt road. About 200 policemen stood in double file with their clubs drawn and watched the approaching marchers. The Republic mill had armed some of the officers with nonregulation clubs and tear gas.

The marchers met the police line and demanded that their rights to picket be recognized and that the police let them through. They were ordered to disperse, but the strikers persisted. The violent struggle was captured on a Paramount newsreel of the event, although the film was not released to the public at the time "on the grounds that such an unrelieved record of blood and brutality was liable to touch off more riots." Before the La Follette Committee investigating the responsibility for the massacre, cameraman Orlando Lippert testified that he was changing lenses when violence broke out. The reconstruction of events in the moments preceding the massacre relies on evidence presented during the hearings of the committee chaired by Senator Robert La Follette. The police were trying to prevent marchers from outflanking their line. As some strikers began to move back, a stick flew from the back of the line toward the police. Immediately, police threw tear gas bombs at the marchers. The next few moments were complete turmoil. Marchers threw more objects at the police. Acting without formal instructions, several policemen in the front line drew their revolvers and fired point blank at the marchers' ranks, the majority of whom were beginning to withdraw. The actual shooting only continued for 15 seconds, but the violence lasted for much longer. Using their clubs, the police beat anyone in their paths, including women and children. During this time, arrests were also made, and several injured were not even taken directly to local hospitals. As a result, four marchers were fatally shot and six were mortally wounded. Thirty others suffered gunshot wounds. Thirty-eight were hospitalized as a result of injuries from the beatings and 30 more required other medical care. It is noteworthy that all but four of the 54 gunshot wounds were to the victims' sides or backs; one was shot four times. There were minor police casualties with 35 reported injuries (no gunshot wounds), and only three needed overnight hospital care.

Although the immediate outcome of the massacre was negative for the demonstrators' cause, as the strike was called off, the SWOC filed a complaint with the NLRB that eventually led Republic Steel and other Little Steel Companies to give up unjust labor practices. Also, the La Follette Committee investigation of the massacre yielded several important conclusions. The committed stated that the police had no right to limit the number of peaceful pickets and that the march was not aimed at the invasion of the plant. The role played by the police was censored, and the report argued that the police should have stopped the march with limited violence: the force used by the police "was far in excess of that which the occasion required." "The provocation for the police assault," the report stated, "did not go beyond abusive language and the throwing of isolated missiles." Moreover, the report of the La Follette Committee found that the "treatment of the injured was characterized by the most callous indifference to human life and suffering. Wounded prisoners of war might have expected and received greater solicitude." Because of all this evidence, historians Bud and Ruth Schultz have argued that the "Memorial Day Massacre was the culmination of sixty years of assaults by the armed forces of the government" on labor organizations.

Competing Representations of the Memorial Day Massacre

After the riot, sympathetic strikers strongly objected to the police violence. On the other hand, the press, especially the *Chicago Tribune*, portrayed the marchers as communist conspirators who had essentially attacked the police and attempted to drive out nonunion workers. The conservative and antilabor *Tribune* distorted the demonstrators' decisions to cultivate paranoia of an imminent communist revolution: the next day's edition claimed that several "agitators went among the strikers convincing them that they were within their rights in invading the company's property." This was paired with a front-page article tellingly entitled, "Soviets Told CIO Leads To Bolshe-

vism," which claimed that the CIO was just a front organization for the Communist Party to recruit members. Quoting a pamphlet produced by communists the previous January, the newspaper claimed that "the communist party is mobilized behind the CIO and aims at a soviet dictatorship in America." The cartoon on the front page was also revealing of the indictment of strikers as dangerous revolutionaries willing to destroy the nation for their own selfish interests. Entitled "The Psychopath," the cartoon showed a fattish drunkard smashing to pieces "America's Household" together with its precious items, such as the "American Private Property" fish bowl, a "U.S. Constitutional Guarantees" cupboard, and a "U.S. Industry" door. The drunk is holding an axe called "Frenzy Against American Wealth," and his madness is provoked by the mirage of a dollar sign in the form of a snake. The *Tribune* thus gave the police an excuse for the massacre: as brutal as their act had been, the policemen fighting the demonstrators were to be considered as fighting dangerous Bolsheviks.

This landmark event in the history of unionism proved inspirational also for the American radical imagination. The events of Memorial Day Massacre were fictionalized in Meyer Levin's radical 1940 novel *Citizens* and were the subject of Philip Evergood's painting *American Tragedy* and of Frontier Film's *Native Land*. This artistic interest in the events of the Memorial Day Massacre clearly illustrates the connection between labor struggle and cultural representation typical of the 1930s and the early 1940s. As Michael Denning put it in *The Cultural Front*, his study of American Popular Front cultural politics, the many radical representations of the Memorial Day Massacre as well as of other labor struggles of the era "sought to inform and engage an audience and to memorialize the events as a mythic narrative." The events of Memorial Day Massacre may not have reached the mythic status that the "grapes of wrath" story attained in American popular culture. Yet, those events and their consequences are certainly crucial for an understanding of American trade unionism.

Key Players

Girdler, Tom M. (1877–1965): President of Republic Steel at the time of the Memorial Day Massacre, Girdler stated that he would close his mills and retire to tend the apple trees on his farm rather than meet with union representatives.

See also: *Committee for Industrial Organization; National Industrial Recovery Act; U.S. Steel Recognizes Steel Workers Organizing Committee; Wagner Act.*

BIBLIOGRAPHY

Books

Denning, Michael. *The Cultural Front: The Laboring of American Culture in the Twentieth Century.* London and New York: Verso, 1997.

Levin, Meyer. *Citizens.* New York: The Viking Press, 1940.

McDonald, David. *Union Man.* New York: E. P. Dutton & Co., 1969.

Schultz, Bud, and Ruth Schultz. *The Price of Dissent: Testimonies to Political Repression in America.* Berkeley: The University of California Press, 2001.

Sweeney, Vincent D. *The United Steelworkers of America: Twenty Years Later, 1936–1956.* United Steelworkers of America, 1956.

United Steelworkers of America Education Department. *Then and Now: The Road Between.* United Steelworkers of America, 1974.

Periodicals

"4 Dead, 90 Hurt in Steel Riot." *Chicago Tribune*, 31 May 1937, p. 1.

Day, Donald. "Soviets Told CIO Leads to Bolshevism." *Chicago Tribune*, 31 May 1937, p. 1.

"Five Chicago Steel Plants Shut; Ford CIO Fight." *Chicago Tribune*, 27 May 1937, pp. 1–2.

"Police Repulse Mob Attack on S. Chicago Mill." *Chicago Tribune*, 31 May 1937, pp. 1–2.

"South Chicago Mob Battles Police; 24 Hurt." *Chicago Tribune*, 29 May 1937, pp. 1–2.

Other

Bork, William. *Massacre at Republic Steel.* Illinois Labor Society. 1975 [cited 14 October 2002]. <http://www.kentlaw.edu/ilhs/republic.htm>.

Illinois Labor History Society. Film strip. *The Memorial Day Massacre of 1937.* 1975.

—Luca Prono

Vicente Lombardo Toledano. The Library of Congress.

Mexican Labor Confederations

Mexico 1912–1950

Synopsis

Three powerful trade union confederations dominated Mexican labor history in the twentieth century. The *Casa del Obrero* Mundial helped organize industrial workers from its founding in 1912 to its defeat in a general strike in 1916. The *Confederación Regional Obrera Mexicana* (CROM) ruled Mexican labor affairs from 1918 until its decline in the 1930s. The *Confederación de Trabajadores de México* (CTM) became part of Mexico's ruling political party from its inception in 1936, supplanting the CROM in the state-labor alliance. Within these organizations, three powerful leaders—Luis N. Morones, Vicente Lombardo Toledano, and Fidel Velázquez—shaped the history of the state-labor alliance in modern Mexico.

Timeline

1910: Vassily Kandinsky pioneers non-representational painting.

1912: *Titanic* sinks on its maiden voyage, from Southampton to New York, on 14 April. More than 1,500 people are killed.

1914: On 28 June in the town of Sarajevo, then part of the Austro-Hungarian Empire, Serbian nationalist Gavrilo Princip assassinates Austrian Archduke Francis Ferdinand and wife Sophie. In the weeks that follow, Austria declares war on Serbia, and Germany on Russia and France, while Great Britain responds by declaring war on Germany. By the beginning of August, the lines are drawn, with the Allies (Great Britain, France, Russia, Belgium, Serbia, Montenegro, and Japan) against the Central Powers (Germany, Austria-Hungary, and Turkey).

1918: The Second Battle of the Marne in July and August is the last major conflict on the Western Front. In November, Kaiser Wilhelm II abdicates, bringing an end to the war.

1922: Inspired by the Bolsheviks' example of imposing revolution by means of a coup, Benito Mussolini leads his blackshirts in an October "March on Rome" and forms a new fascist government.

1930: Naval disarmament treaty is signed by the United States, Great Britain, France, Italy, and Japan.

1942: At the Wannsee Conference, Nazi leaders formulate the "final solution to the Jewish question": a systematic campaign of genocide on a massive scale. By the time the Holocaust ends, along with the war itself, the Nazis will have killed some 6 million Jews, and as many as 6 million other victims in their death camps and slave-labor camps.

1948: Israel becomes a nation and is immediately attacked by a coalition of Arab countries. Despite being outnumbered, Israel will win the war in the following year—as it will win many another war against larger forces mobilized by its hostile neighbors.

1950: Senator Joseph McCarthy launches his campaign to root out communist infiltrators.

1955: Rosa Parks refuses to move from her seat near the front of a public bus in Montgomery, Alabama, and is arrested. The incident touches off a boycott of Montgomery's bus system, led by the Rev. Martin Luther King, Jr., which will last well into 1956.

Event and Its Context

Casa del Obrero Mundial

The Mexican Revolution (1910–1920) dramatically shaped the country's political and labor history. During the dictatorship of Porfirio Díaz (1876–1910), business owners and government officials easily destroyed trade unions and mutualist societies. The revolution that erupted when Francisco Madero challenged Díaz in 1910 radically transformed labor affairs. As successive governments fell apart under the weight of prolonged and widespread warfare, workers in key industries such as textiles, oil, electrical energy, and transportation successfully carried out strikes, built permanent trade unions, and began to implement collective bargaining.

In the midst of revolution, on 16 July 1912, Juan Francisco Moncaleano (Colombian anarchist and fugitive recently arrived from Havana), Luis Mendez, Jacinto Huitrón, and other artisans, workers, and anarchists founded the Casa del Obrero Mundial (Worldwide House of the Worker, or Casa) on the model of the *Escuela Racionalista* (Rationalist School) of Barcelona. Though not a union in itself, the Casa quickly became the leading national labor organization of the revolution, pursuing broadly anarcho-syndicalist goals. After Madero's assassination in 1913, a coalition led by wealthy landowner Venustiano Carranza, former bandit Pancho Villa, and radical land reformer Emiliano Zapata opposed the return of the Porfiristas to power. Upon the defeat of the old Porfirian general, Victoriano Huerta, the coalition fell apart. Carranza and his general, Alvaro Obregón, allied against Villa and Zapata. In February 1915 the leaders of the anarchist Casa signed an agreement with Carranza to contribute battalions of workers to the Constitutionalist cause, and Carranza promised support for labor's goals. Thus began the alliance of organized labor with the state.

In August 1916 the Casa led a major strike that Carranza ruthlessly suppressed, which effectively destroyed an organization that had come to depend on government despite its anarchist rhetoric. Nonetheless unions and labor militancy continued, as did efforts to build a powerful labor confederation. Even before the defeat of the Casa, the *Federación de Sindicatos Obreros del Distrito Federal* (Federation of Labor Unions of the Federal District) organized a meeting in Veracruz in March 1916 to unify the labor movement. The organization sent a mechanic from the Mexican Light and Power Company and a founding member of the *Sindicato Mexicano de Electricistas* (Mexican Union of Electricians), Luis N. Morones, to represent the capital's workers.

CROM

In February 1917 the soon-to-be victorious Constitutionalists drafted a new constitution, which included Article 123, the first labor code in Mexican history. Written by radicals against the wishes of the more elitist Carranza, the article legalized unions, protected strikers from being fired, and provided some of the strongest benefits and protections for labor in the Western Hemisphere. Legal protections for unions strengthened labor organizing. After a second national labor congress in Tampico in October 1917, an ally of Carranza, Governor Gustavo Espinosa Mireles, appointed an organizing committee that included Ricardo Treviño, a leader of the Industrial Workers of the World locals in the Tampico oil region, to plan for a third conference in March 1918. By then it was clear that the Casa would not recover its former influence and that the various groups allied under the Constitutionalist banner would form the nucleus of a postrevolutionary state. Unionists at the meeting, including former Casa members and anarchists, began work on 1 May 1918 and elected an executive committee that consisted of Huitrón, the former Casa leader, Morones, Treviño, and Teodoro Ramírez. The delegates capped the meeting by creating the *Confederación Regional Obrera Mexicana* (CROM) and installed Morones as the organization's general secretary.

Morones then created the Grupo Acción, a secret and disciplined group with great loyalty to Morones, which ran Mexican labor affairs in the 1920s. Morones understood that the Casa derived strength from its alliance with the state and collapsed when it challenged government. Having long combated anarchists in the labor movement, he worked to convince laborers that they had more to gain from a state-labor alliance than from an independent stance. In the unstable social and political climate of late revolutionary Mexico, the CROM quickly became one of the country's most powerful political actors.

In August 1919 Morones signed a secret pact with Carranza's former military leader and now political rival, Alvaro Obregón. He promised to support Obreón's presidential ambitions, and Obregón assured the CROM that it would have privileged access to government positions. Many of the anarchists who supported the CROM to that point then quit to form the rival *Confederación General de Trabajadores* (CGT). Morones meanwhile founded the political wing of the CROM, the Partido Laborista Mexicano (PLM), in August 1919. He used the PLM to support the electoral ambitions of his allies. When Obregón assassinated Carranza in 1920, Obregón's alliance with Morones and the PLM assured urban electoral support, with which he won election to the presidency later that year.

From 1920 to 1928 Obregón (1920–1924), Plutarco Elías Calles (1924–1928), and Morones dominated Mexican politics and the labor movement. When Obregón left office, he placed Calles in the presidency, but Obregón planned to run for reelection in 1928. Morones, the CROM, and the PLM gave full labor support to the two leaders. In return, an increasingly powerful federal government provided legal, financial, and sometimes military support to the CROM and the PLM against rivals such as the new Mexican Communist Party (PCM), the anarcho-syndicalist CGT, and conservative Catholic unions. Morones used that support to crush rival labor unions, expel dissidents from the CROM, and force businesses to accept his unions and their contracts.

The CROM was a national confederation of state labor federations, which in turn united local CROM unions organized by trade or by establishment. CROM-government labor policy supported the creation of national federations of unions by industry as well as the principle that contract terms negotiated by the union representing the largest number of workers in a factory or workplace, usually the CROM union, should apply to all workers there. Both policies increased membership in CROM unions, union dues collected by CROM officials, and political support for the new regime.

Obregón and Morones supported Calles' successful bid for the presidency in 1924. Calles repaid the favor by appointing Morones to the Ministry of Industry, Labor, and Commerce. Other CROM leaders became mayors, governors, senators, *diputados* (deputies), and heads of government offices. From his post atop the government's labor ministry, Morones could influence the recently established federal labor boards, whose decisions favored CROM over its rivals and often over business interests. In towns with a single powerful industry, CROM leaders became virtual local dictators. In Orizaba, an important mill town in Veracruz, the head of the local CROM, Eucario León, determined who worked and who did not, who obtained government concessions, and, sometimes, who lived and died. Antonio J. Hernández later exercised similar power in Atlixco. CROM leaders often employed hired gunmen to kill their enemies, unthreatened by local governments often run by them or their cronies. With state support, the national CROM claimed two million members in 1928. Though certainly exaggerated, the figure suggests the startling degree to which the organization thoroughly dominated the Mexican labor movement in the 1920s.

Morones and his friends earned great incomes from mandatory union dues, from government contracts and concessions, and from their political influence. Marjorie Ruth Clark, author of *Organized Labor in Mexico,* noted that "when a government department was placed in control of a CROM man, he made it known to every employee in that department that 'voluntary' contributions to the support of the Mexican Labor Party would be welcome and would be of material assistance in keeping the employee in the job." Most business owners understood that to settle a strike, cash would have to change hands. As Ernest Gruening, author of *Mexico and Its Heritage,* wrote, "The head of the Mexican labor movement, Luis N. Morones . . . owns many properties including a textile factory—though not in his own name. He lives lavishly. He sports not less than a half dozen automobiles. His *parrandas* [parties] staged every weekend in the suburb of Tlalpam are notorious for their orgiastic extravagance."

Some unions refused to join CROM, particularly large unions in critical economic sectors such as electrical power, railroads, and oil. In other sectors, the anarchist CGT, Catholic labor militants, and the PCM frequently competed with the CROM for control. Between 1921 and 1924 partisans of these organizations fought violent labor wars, but in the end CROM won.

The Casa collapsed when it fell out of favor with the state; a similar though slower fate befell the CROM. Alvaro Obregón ruled Mexico after the Carranza assassination, governing through local alliances with regional strongmen. Because electoral laws did not permit direct reelection to the presidency, he waited patiently while Calles served, then ran for office in 1928. His predecessors, Madero and Carranza, fell to assassins' bullets, and so did he when a Catholic militant shot him during a campaign dinner. Morones and CROM had not supported Obregón's reelection, so some of his supporters blamed the labor leader for the death of their former president.

Outgoing president Calles made two decisions that seriously affected the CROM. To avoid further assassinations, he decided to institutionalize the new ruling elite and founded the *Partido Nacional Revolucionario* (National Revolutionary Party, PNR) for that purpose. The move angered Morones, who held ambitions for his own PLM. He supported the presidential candidacy of Emilio Portes Gil, an opponent of CROM, in 1928. Losing support within the government, CROM began a slow decline as many regional federations begin to shift alliances. Portes Gil even supported the PCM's *Confederación Sindical Unitaria de México* (CSUM) as a rival to Morones. Vicente Lombardo Toledano and Fidel Velázquez led the dissident movement within the CROM. In 1931 Mexico's first federal labor law made unions more dependent on the state.

CTM

Lombardo was more of an intellectual than most Mexican labor leaders. He studied at the *Escuela Nacional Preparatoria* (National Preparatory School), earned a law degree from Mexico's National University in 1920 and a doctorate in 1933, and wrote some of the most significant texts on Mexican labor affairs. He began his labor career as secretary general of a Mexico City teachers union in 1920, then served on CROM's central committee from 1923 to 1932, though not in Grupo Acción. He was perhaps Morones's chief rival inside CROM, which he abandoned in September 1932 to form the *Confederación General de Obreros y Campesinos de México* (General Confederation of Workers and Farmers of Mexico, CGOCM) in 1933. The growing distance between the government and Morones and the success of dissidents like Lombardo and the Communist Party led to increasing dispersion of organized labor in the early 1930s, when there were 17 labor confederations and 2,800 individual unions.

In 1934 the PNR elected Lazaro Cárdenas to the presidency. Cárdenas sought a political base among farmers and urban workers, leading him to support efforts to unify the now fragmented labor movement. In 1935 former president Calles and Cárdenas suffered a public split, thus lending urgency to Cárdenas's attempts to gain labor's political support. In 1935 Lombardo organized a meeting of CGOCM, CSUM, and powerful unions in railroads and electrical power, forming the pro-

Cárdenas *Comité Nacional de Defensa Proletaria* (National Proletarian Defense Committee, CNDP). He then used the CNDP to organize the *Confederación de Trabajadores de México* (Mexican Workers' Union, CTM) in February 1936.

Lombardo became the CTM's first secretary general in 1936 and stayed in the post until 1941. His organization included unions and federations that were formally affiliated with the CGOCM (some of which supported Lombardo, and others Velázquez), the PCM-affiliated CSUM, and powerful national unions in railroads, electrical power, telephones, mining, and other sectors. Only the CROM and CGT unions stayed out. The old CROM dissident, Fidel Velázquez, became the first secretary of organization, 1936 to 1941, and in that post created state and local federations that were personally loyal to him. Quite the opposite of the intellectual Lombardo, Velázquez had worked in a dairy during the revolution. In 1923, with Alfonso and Justino Sánchez Madariaga, he founded a union of dairy workers that affiliated with CROM. Velázquez left CROM in 1929 to join those who supported Calles's project for an official party.

In March 1938 Cárdenas reorganized the PNR into the *Partido de la Revolución Mexicana* (Mexican Revolutionary Party, PRM), to represent four sectors: labor, popular, agrarian, and the military. Despite the withdrawal of the Miners Union in June 1936 and PCM opposition to labor joining the official party, the CTM claimed almost a million workers in 1938 and was the foundation of the PRM labor sector.

Close ties between Cárdenas and Lombardo assured labor support for Cárdenas's chosen successor as president, the more conservative Manuel Avila Camacho, who occupied the post from 1940 to 1946. Despite personal friendship between Avila Camacho and the Marxist Lombardo, the increasing ideological distance between an increasingly right-wing government and the admirer of the Soviet Union led to Velázquez replacing Lombardo as CTM secretary general in February 1941. Lombardo continued to head the *Confederación de Trabajadores de América Latina* (Union of Latin American Workers, CTAL) from 1938 to 1961.

Velázquez' closest allies were Fernando Amilpa, Jesús Yuren Aguilar, Alfonso Sánchez Madariaga, and Luis Quintero, together known as the *cinco lobitos*, or five little wolves. Like Velázquez, the five had worked in unions outside heavy industry. These unions required more government support than the industrial unions, undoubtedly shaping their views of the state-labor alliance.

The 1940s was a difficult period for urban labor in Mexico. Wartime inflation brought the sharpest decline in real wages in Mexican history, though both Communist and non-Communist unions of the CTM supported a pact with the government to suppress strikes and wage increases. In 1946 the strongly pro-United States and probusiness Miguel Alemán became Mexico's president (an office he occupied from 1946 to 1952) and transformed the official party into the Partido Revolucionario Institucional (Institutional Revolutionary party, PRI), which included only three sectors: labor, agrarian, and popular. The CTM tightened its control over the labor sector of the PRI while becoming an increasingly docile tool of an increasingly conservative government.

An antilabor government with a dependent Velázquez caused a crisis within the CTM. The PCM and the strong industrial unions began to oppose CTM leadership. The *lobitos* responded by expelling Lombardo from the organization in January 1948. In October of that year, President Alemán jailed the Communist leadership of the railroad union and imposed new leadership that was dependent on government and the army. Alemán then instituted similar measures to weaken previously independent national oil and mining unions.

The 1950s and Beyond

Velázquez had formally ceded the leadership of the CTM to Amilpa in 1947, but once Velázquez again became secretary general in 1950, only his death in 1997 would bring a new leader to the CTM. He retook the reins of power at a moment when the government had eliminated his strongest rivals within the organization, the independent national unions. From that point on the Mexican government both supported the CTM and also controlled it by allowing some national unions to remain outside the confederation and by permitting the existence of smaller, rival confederations. Nonetheless, the postwar CTM was the largest and most important member of the labor sector of the PRI and the largest and most powerful labor confederation in Mexico, bringing together about 1.6 million members and 4,200 unions by the end of the 1950s.

Although railroad, electrical, and telephone workers dared to confront government control of the labor movement in subsequent decades, the CTM stalwartly supported the regime, which in turn never abandoned its allies in the CTM bureaucracy. Many CTM unions required their members to belong to the PRI and to pay dues to both the union and the party, while the PRI-government assured that CTM leaders would defeat legal challenges from the rank and file. When the government began to abandon its protectionist policies after the economic crisis of 1976, and with enactment of the North American Free Trade Agreement (NAFTA) in 1994, the old industries that had been the heart of Mexican unionization inevitably declined, weakening both the PRI and organized labor. The slow decline of the CTM paralleled the fall of the PRI, which lost its first presidential election in history in 2000, only three years after the death of Fidel Velázquez, labor's leader during every PRI presidential victory between 1946 and 1994. While alive, Veázquez remembered the lesson he had learned from the Casa del Obrero Mundial and CROM: never disobey the state.

Key Players

Lombardo Toledano, Vicente (1894–1968): Lombardo Toledano was the founder and first secretary general (1936–1940) of *Confederación de Trabajadores de México* (Mexican Labor Confederation, CTM). He received his B.A. and Ph.D. from *Universidad Nacional Autónoma de México* (Independent National University of Mexico, UNAM), was interim governor of Puebla (December 1923), and a member of the Confederación Regional Obrera Méxicana (Mexican Regional Labor Union, CROM) central committee (1923–1932). A lawyer and intellectual, Lombardo Toledano wrote *La Libertad Sindical en México* (1926).

Morones, Luis N. (1890–1964): Morones was the founder and first secretary general of CROM. He was also founding member of the Sindicato Mexicano de Electricistas. Morones served as minister of industry, commerce, and labor in the government of Plutarco Elías Calles (1924–1928).

Velázquez Sánchez, Fidel (1900–1997): Velázquez Sánchez was the secretary general of CTM (1941–1947 and 1950–1997). Velázquez Sánchez founded the Unión de Trabajadores de la Industria Lechera (Milk Industry Workers' Union, 1923), which was affiliated with CROM.

See also: *North American Free Trade Agreement.*

BIBLIOGRAPHY

Books

Andrews, Gregg. *Shoulder to Shoulder? The American Federation of Labor, the United States, and the Mexican Revolution, 1910 to 1924.* Berkeley: University of California, 1991.

Ashby, Joe C. *Organized Labor and the Mexican Revolution Under Lazaro Cardenas.* Chapel Hill: The University of North Carolina Press, 1967.

Bortz, Jeffrey, and Stephen Haber, eds. *The Mexican Economy, 1870–1930: Essays on the Economic History of Institutions, Revolution, and Growth.* Stanford, CA: Stanford University Press, 2002.

Carr, Barry. *El Movimiento Obrero y la Politica en México, 1910–1929.* Mexico: Ediciones Era, 1981.

———. *Marxism and Communism in Twentieth Century Mexico.* Lincoln: University of Nebraska Press, 1992.

Clark, Marjorie Ruth. *Organized Labor in Mexico.* Chapel Hill: The University of North Carolina Press, 1934.

Cook, Maria Lorena. *Organizing Dissent: Unions, the State, and the Democratic Teachers' Movement in Mexico.* University Park: Pennsylvania State University Press, 1996.

Gruening, Ernest. *Mexico and Its Heritage.* New York: The Century Company, 1928.

Hart, John M. *Anarchism and the Mexican Working Class, 1860–1931.* Austin: University of Texas Press, 1978.

Knight, Alan. *The Mexican Revolution.* Lincoln: University of Nebraska Press, 1990.

LaBotz, Dan. *The Crisis of Mexican Labor.* New York: Praeger, 1988.

———. *Mask of Democracy: Labor Suppression in Mexico Today.* Boston: South End Press, 1992.

Middlebrook, Kevin J. *The Paradox of Revolution; Labor, the State, and Authoritarianism in Mexico.* Baltimore, MD: The Johns Hopkins University Press, 1995.

Ruiz, Ramon. *Labor and the Ambivalent Revolutionaries: Mexico, 1911–1923.* Baltimore, MD: The Johns Hopkins University Press, 1976.

Solís de Alba, Ana Alicia. *El Movimiento Sindical Pintado de Magenta: Productividad, Sexismo y Neocorporativismo.* Mexico: Editorial Itaca, 2002.

—Jeffrey Bortz

Milan Barricade Fights

Italy 1898

Synopsis

The early 1890s have been referred to as the Black Years in Italy because of the serious industrial and agricultural problems that confronted the country during that period. In the late 1890s economic conditions gradually began to improve. Grain shortages and higher bread prices that resulted from the Spanish-American war in 1898, however, became the focal point of discontent for workers and the population at large. During that year demonstrations took place in most of the large cities, particularly in the industrialized North, as part of a campaign to eliminate the tax on milling grain into flour. As the often violent demonstrations spread, the government began using force to suppress them. The most dramatic confrontation took place in Milan during May 1898, in what was called the Events of May (or, in Italian, *Fatti di Maggio*), when over a four-day period the military carried out a campaign to eliminate the demonstrators.

Timeline

1878: Thomas Edison develops a means of cheaply producing and transmitting electric current, which he succeeds in subdividing so as to make it adaptable to household use. The value of shares in gas companies plummets as news of his breakthrough reaches Wall Street.

1883: League of Struggle for the Emancipation of Labor is founded by Marxist political philosopher Georgi Valentinovich Plekhanov marks the formal start of Russia's labor movement. Change still lies far in the future for Russia, however: tellingly, Plekhanov launches the movement in Switzerland.

1888: Serbian-born American electrical engineer Nikola Tesla develops a practical system for generating and transmitting alternating current (AC), which will ultimately—and after an extremely acrimonious battle—replace Thomas Edison's direct current (DC) in most homes and businesses.

1891: French troops open fire on workers during a 1 May demonstration at Fourmies, where employees of the Sans Pareille factory are striking for an eight-hour workday. Nine people are killed—two of them children—and 60 more are injured.

1894: Thomas Edison gives the first public demonstration of his kinetoscope film projector, in New York City.

1898: United States defeats Spain in the three-month Spanish-American War. As a result, Cuba gains it independence, and the United States purchases Puerto Rico and the Philippines from Spain for $20 million.

1898: Chinese "Boxers," a militant group opposed to foreign occupation of their country, are organized.

1898: Marie and Pierre Curie discover the radioactive elements radium and polonium.

1898: Bayer introduces a cough suppressant, derived from opium, its brand name: Heroin.

1900: China's Boxer Rebellion, which began in the preceding year with attacks on foreigners and Christians, reaches its height. An international contingent of more than 2,000 men arrives to restore order, but only after several tens of thousands have died.

1904: The 10-hour workday is established in France.

1908: An earthquake in southern Italy and Sicily kills some 150,000 people.

Event and Its Context

During the 1880s and 1890s, Italy experienced accelerated growth in economic development and social urbanization, with an accompanying labor shift from agriculture to industry. These rapid developments brought about poor living conditions, massive housing shortages, and miserable employment conditions within the growing industrial cities of Italy, especially in Milan, which had become the largest Italian industrial city in the 1880s.

Before 1870 the only type of labor organizations permitted in Italy were mutual aid societies (*Societa di Mutuo Soccorso*). These local societies were widespread throughout industrial cities but were limited in providing help to members during times of distress, including sickness and unemployment. One such organization was the Consulate of Skilled Workers (*Consolato Operaio*), which was a collection of societies within the Lombardy region (surrounding Milan). In 1881 radical group members formed the Confederation of Lombardy Workers (*Confederazione Operaia Lombarda*), which actively placed pressure on management to improve working conditions.

Later Industrial Milan: 1877 to 1890

Beginning around 1877, considerable expenditure of domestic investment and foreign capital occurred in industry and construction within Milan as the factory system expanded. Milan, along with other industrial cities, saw increasing numbers of semiskilled and unskilled workers replacing the highly skilled craftsmen of the past. Even though the cost of living was declining, the proletariat began to take action against the widening social, economic, and political power exerted by the propertied class. Employers saw many conflicts and strikes as they continued to introduce new piece-rate systems, lower wages, and longer hours into their operations.

These economic conditions of the late 1870s favored the development of a moderate socialist movement in Italy. During this period the real beginnings of trade unions and worker political activities became established in Milan and across the industrial North.

Many Italian historians view the period from the 1880s through the 1890s as a crucial turning point for labor organizations as the older traditional craft organizations gave way to the new resistance leagues (*leghe di resistenza*), which were based on resisting oppressive employer trends involving mass production of goods. One of these leagues was the Milanese Italian Workers' Party, which was founded in 1882 by the Milan Consulate (*Consolato di Milan*), which itself was part of the Confederation of Lombardy Workers. The party was formed as a way to coordinate the activities of the numerous workers' leagues and associations that existed in Milan and in the Lombardy region. Its goal was to achieve direct representation for working people.

By the end of the 1880s, a new proletariat composed of industrial workers and laborers had mostly replaced the traditional Milanese workforce of artisans and craftsmen. This new worker class took over the leadership of the city's labor institutions, and its political viewpoints and values were represented in the programs of the Milanese Workers' Party.

Industrial Unions: 1891 to 1897

The new industrial unions that began to form at the end of the 1880s joined and sometimes took over the resistance leagues. These unions were based on the French labor market (*bourse du travail*) and were called the Chambers of Labor (*Camera del Lavoro*). The moderate socialist Osvaldo Gnocchi-Viani became the most active proponent in favor of the establishment of industrial unions in Italy. The first Chamber of Labor was organized in Milan in 1889 in response to a growing need for a class-conscious Italian labor movement. By 1893, with 14 local chambers already in existence, the first national congress of Chambers of Labor convened. By the end of the nineteenth century, more than 50 Chambers of Labor were operating with a membership of about 150,000 workers. Besides coordinating functions within local organizations, the chambers operated as an employment service and promoted education, organization, and labor dispute settlement. Many Italian labor historians describe the Chambers of Labor as a dynamic element of Italian trade unionism, one that played an important role in the history of the labor movement.

In the 1890s several crises arose that set the stage for the Milanese fighting of 1898. One such crisis was the fragile growth that Italy experienced in the 1880s, which was based on a banking system that was underdeveloped and highly speculative. As a result, from 1893 to 1894 a series of banking scandals and failures disrupted the Italian economy, raising concerns about Italy's capacity for industrialization.

Contributing to the country's crisis was a government attitude that the growing social and economic unrest in the labor market could be controlled and eliminated by force. After Francesco Crispi left office January 1891, Marquis Antonio Starrabba Di Rudinì took over from 1891 to 1892. The first ministry of Giovanni Giolitti followed from 1892 to 1893. In December 1893 Crispi returned to power and remained in office until March 1896. From that time until June 1898, the second Di Rudinì ministry governed Italy. General Luigi Pelloux succeeded Di Rudinì and governed until June 1900. Each leader used his coercive powers to control the laboring class.

At this same time the Italian labor movement was changing from a party focused exclusively on labor issues to one that emphasized both political and labor advocacy. The congress of the Italian Workers' Party met in Genoa on 14 August 1892 in response to continuing unemployment and high food prices that had prompted numerous worker demonstrations. It represented different types of workers' groups, including the recently organized Chambers of Labor. The dominant leaders of the congress were Filippo Turati of the Socialist League of Milan (*Lega Socialista Milanese*) and Giuseppe Croce of the Workers Party in Lombardy and Piedmont. The first resolution was to designate the Workers' Party as the Socialist Party of Italian Workers, which was renamed the Italian Socialist Party (*Partito Socialista Italiano*) in 1895. The Socialist Party was given the authority to improve the condition of the working classes through a campaign of political power, and the labor unions took on the job of improving hours, wages, and factory regulations. Because the word "election" was not specifically mentioned, revolutionary members felt that the use of violence and force was an acceptable means to their goals.

The Socialist Party was the central organization in the labor movement of the 1890s, as it fought to expand labor's role in Italian politics at the expense of the exclusive elites (such as landholders). Filippo Turati and Anna Kuliscioff based the party's ideology and political strategy on that of the Socialist League, which they had founded in Milan in 1889. Their brand of socialism was based on democratic and humanitarian traditions within socialism that provided them with the ability to gain broad support from both the Italian middle and working classes.

Discontent Spreads

The immediate cause of the crisis of the 1890s was the collapse of the industrial sector. Italy's adoption of high protective duties and tariffs on manufactured and agricultural products in 1897 worsened the collapse. The result was commercial recession, widespread bank failures, and heavy unemployment. When food prices rose dramatically following a poor harvest in 1897, protests spread quickly throughout Italy.

Workers no longer accepted conditions and events without protest. They could read, write, and think for themselves. Even though they were eating better food and buying more goods, workers were growing angrier about and less tolerant of the miserable conditions that persisted. Workers associated the government with burdensome taxes, depreciating currency, adverse trade imbalances, bank scandals, rumored political alliances with terrorist groups, and the siphoning of tariff monies to people in power.

The government did nothing to alleviate the near-starvation conditions that existed in Italy, especially in the rural South. The socialists exploited this condition, emphasizing that the government did not rescue the country from the unexpected rise in grain prices. By the end of 1897, renewed riots continued to show that the government was not curing or alleviating its social and economic problems. The climax of this upsurge of unrest took place in Milan from 6 to 9 May 1897. These four days are often considered the beginning of the violent times that led to the fights in Milan called the May Events (or *Fatti di Maggio*) in 1898.

January to April 1898

The Spanish-American war in 1898 continued to escalate grain prices. From January to April 1898, people in the regions of Marche, Apulia, and Sicily rioted. The protestors voiced their anger against grain dealers, who had raised wheat prices, and mayors and members of the communal councils, who had imposed additional taxes on flour.

In 1898 rural Italians began to pour increasingly into Milan (and other industrial cities) to look for work. These rural immigrants upset the city's social equilibrium. Additionally, the Milanese poor held justified grievances against the wealthier classes. Although the city furnished its people with excellent administration, local taxes burdened them excessively. Added to this, the city planned to expand its boundaries into the growing industrial suburbs. This contributed to worker unrest in those areas and spawned protests against the extension of Milan's heavy taxes on basic commodities to suburban areas.

By the end of April 1898, violence had spread. Crowds stormed bakery shops in Forlì, located in the southeastern region of Emilia-Romagna. Citizens fought with police near Ravenna (north of Forlì) and at Piacenza and Parma, both southeast of Milan. In response, the government alerted 80,000 reservists.

Barricade Fights in Milan: May 1898

On 5 May 1898 the police in Pavia (located south of Milan) fired into a group that had assembled to protest price increases in bread and killed a student, the son of a radical deputy from Milan. When the news reached Milan, the Socialist Party printed inflammatory handbills, which were distributed by a group of Pirelli plant workers. When the police interfered and arrested three of them, other workers intervened. The police, then outnumbered, withdrew to their barracks with one of the arrested men. Excitement escalated in the next several hours after authorities refused to release the man. Union leaders asked the workers to halt their aggression, but they refused. Additional workers gathered at the Stigler plant, and then advanced toward police barricades where soldiers, added as reinforcements, had positioned themselves. The police and soldiers eventually fired into the crowd, killing two workmen and wounding 14. A policeman also was killed before a rainstorm stopped the first round of violence.

On the next day, 6 May 1898, protesting workers from various factories stormed the streets. When cavalrymen rode toward them, demonstrators converted streetcars into barricades, and others broke windows and threw tiles from rooftops. The government declared martial law and ordered a military occupation to stop what it described as a revolution. More troops rushed to Milan. For three days, soldiers and police searched out demonstrators, sometimes killing them. On 9 May an artillery officer mistook beggars for rebels who had come for soup at a local monastery. Soldiers battered down the monastery walls in search of the protestors. The soldiers even pulled at the monks' beards, assuming they were disguised militants.

Afterwards: June to December 1898

The Milanese occupation was followed by the arrest of those held responsible for organizing the disorder, which included most of the leaders of the Socialist Party as well as leading Catholic opponents of the government. The activity in Milan was seen as the dramatic culmination of violent protests in other areas. The government pursued its repressive policy by shutting down the headquarters of any group suspected of having any responsibility for the demonstrations. Thousands were arrested and special military tribunals imprisoned more than 600. The government censored all newspapers and publications and forced the dissolution of unions and cooperatives.

Key Players

Turati, Filippo (1857–1932): Turati was an Italian political leader and an advocate of a moderate, nonviolent form of socialism. Turati cofounded the Italian Socialist Party in 1892. In 1926, threatened by the growing fascist movement, he fled the country, escaping in a boat to Corsica. From there, he traveled to Paris, where he spent the remainder of his life as the head of an antifascist coalition.

BIBLIOGRAPHY

Books

Geary, Dick. *Labour and Socialist Movements in Europe Before 1914*. New York: St. Martin's Press, 1989.

Goodstein, Phil H. *The Theory of the General Strike from the French Revolution to Poland*. Boulder, CO: East European Monographs, 1984.

Haimson, Leopold H., and Charles Tilly. *Strikes, Wars, and Revolutions in an International Perspective: Strike Waves in the Late Nineteenth and Early Twentieth Centuries*. Cambridge, UK: Cambridge University Press, 1989.

Roberts, David D. *The Syndicalist Tradition and Italian Fascism*. Chapel Hill: The University of North Carolina Press, 1979.

—William Arthur Atkins

Millworkers' Strike

United States 1934

Synopsis

An estimated 400,000 to 500,000 southern millworkers and their northern counterparts walked off the job in a general strike in September 1934. This is now often referred to as the Great Uprising of '34. That this strike was mobilized at all is worth noting. The southern United States has been historically opposed to unionism of any stripe. The millworkers themselves were typically unfamiliar with factory life as most had been farmers. The strikes led to violence and deaths and gained little in the way of concession for workers who walked out in hopes of securing higher wages, shorter workdays, and better conditions.

Timeline

1919: With the formation of the Third International (Comintern), the Bolshevik government of Russia establishes its control over communist movements worldwide.

1924: In the United States, Secretary of the Interior Albert B. Fall, along with oil company executives Harry Sinclair and Edward L. Doheny, is charged with conspiracy and bribery in making fraudulent leases of U.S. Navy oil reserves at Teapot Dome, Wyoming. The resulting Teapot Dome scandal clouds the administration of President Warren G. Harding.

1929: On "Black Friday" in October, prices on the U.S. stock market, which had been climbing wildly for several years, suddenly collapse. Thus begins the first phase of a world economic crisis and depression that will last until the beginning of World War II.

1931: Financial crisis widens in the United States and Europe, which reel from bank failures and climbing unemployment levels. In London, armies of the unemployed riot.

1934: Austrian chancellor Engelbert Dollfuss, who aligns his nation with Mussolini's Italy, establishes a fascist regime in an attempt to keep Austria out of the Nazi orbit. Austrian Nazis react by assassinating Dollfuss.

1934: Dionne sisters, the first quintuplets to survive beyond infancy, are born in Canada.

1937: Japan attacks China, and annexes most of that nation's coastal areas.

1939: After years of loudly denouncing one another (and quietly cooperating), the Nazis and Soviets sign a non-aggression pact in August. This clears the way for the Nazi invasion of Poland, and for Soviet action against Finland. (Stalin also helps himself to a large portion of Poland.)

1942: Axis conquests reach their height in the middle of this year. The Nazis control a vast region from Normandy to the suburbs of Stalingrad, and from the Arctic Circle to the edges of the Sahara. To the east, the Japanese "Co-Prosperity Sphere" encompasses territories from China to Burma to the East Indies, stretching deep into the western Pacific.

1945: April sees the death of three leaders: Roosevelt passes away on 12 April; the Italians execute Mussolini and his mistress on 28 April; and Hitler (along with Eva Braun, propaganda minister Josef Goebbels, and Goebbels's family) commits suicide on 30 April.

1949: North Atlantic Treaty Organization (NATO) is established.

Event and Its Context

Cities throughout the southern United States began courting the New England mill owners in the 1920s with various promises, not the least of which was cheap labor. Popular stereotypes portrayed the southern worker as docile and obedient and likely to accept any wages or conditions without question. Between 1923 and 1929, the number of textile workers in the region grew to a half million.

Work stoppages and protests initiated were typically confined to the isolated mill towns. These villages or towns were, in most cases, no more than company towns dotted with shacks. Working conditions throughout the Great Depression were terrible. The working poor often worked and lived in unsanitary

Police clash with striking mill workers, Bibb Manufacturing Company Mill, Macon, Georgia. AP/World Wide Photos. Reproduced by permission.

and unsafe places. Health problems, many induced by spending long hours in an environment in which the air was heavy with cotton lint, were common. Pellagra, a vitamin-deficiency disease resulting from the insufficiently varied diets that were often a byproduct of low wages, was common. As of 1926, working women in the mill towns typically worked 60 hours per week for about $1.81.

Textile workers were often subjected to stretch-outs, or schedule adjustments designed to increase production. During these periods, laborers were given more work to do in the same amount of time, often being asked to produce the same amount of yard goods. Mill owners typically demanded increased productivity from workers without increasing wages and attempted to undertake these increases with fewer workers. Health conditions did not improve. It was also common for workers to go an entire shift without so much as a meal break.

The United Textile Workers (UTW) and National Textile Workers Union (NTWU) had problems establishing local unions throughout the South, but the workers there had established their own independent unions. These homegrown unions,

which started becoming more effective around 1929, could be more responsive to local village conditions. The NTWU, which had attempted organizing campaigns in about 1931, was weak and considered radical.

Textile workers became increasingly dissatisfied with working conditions. The depression intervened to prevent more vocal protests when the workers were fed up with stretch-outs and poor wages. Strikes took place sporadically between 1929 and 1934. Some were effective, including one supported locally in South Carolina that involved 15 different mills. Another strike occurred in 1932 in the same region without the assistance of the UTW.

Another problem endemic in the region was protecting African American millworkers. The textile industry reflected the general condition in the South in segregating its workers.

The National Industrial Recovery Act of 1933 gave workers the right to strike. The Cotton Textile Institute, in an effort to circumvent the law, cajoled the NIRA into allowing it to chart its own independent board and thus established the Cotton Textile Code Authority. Mill owners had adopted a uniform

Striking textile workers, Astonia, North Carolina. AP/World Wide Photos. Reproduced by permission.

code, the Cotton Textile Code, that dictated working conditions. The first industry codes were enacted on 9 July 1933. These codes were designed to provide equitable conditions throughout the industry. They stipulated a minimum wage of 25 cents per hour, a workweek of 40 hours, abolition of child labor, wage differentials, and wages equivalent to 48 hours' earnings for 40 hours' work. The code increased the average wage to about $12 per week.

Complaints of code violations were to be brought before the Cotton Textile Industrial Relations Board—often referred to as the Bruere Board after its chairman, Robert Breure—but that rarely brought satisfaction. In fact, much of the time, the

board closed its eyes to stretch-outs or supported management decisions not to rehire strikers who sought to return to their jobs.

With the creation of the NIRA, southern textile workers had hoped for some reprieve. President Franklin D. Roosevelt, whom they supported, gave them hope with his talk of keeping the country working and productive through the economic hard times. The codes, however, failed to give the workers any relief. Mill owners decreased wages and cut hours. With the codes enacted, mill owners reduced the maximum possible wages back to the minimum required under the codes. The codes did not even address stretch-outs as workers had anticipated.

Norma Rae: Another Look at the Life of a Southern Millworker

The hugely successful 1979 motion picture *Norma Rae* depicted the life of a southern textile worker more than a generation after the Great Uprising of '34. As depicted in the film, conditions in the Alabama factory where Norma Rae (Sally Field) works are intolerable, and this leads her to organize the other workers. Field won an Academy Award for her portrayal of Norma Rae, which set the tone for Meryl Streep's performance in *Silkwood* (1983), Julia Roberts's in *Erin Brockovich* (2000), and numerous other films.

Source: Toplin, Robert Brent. *History by Hollywood: The Use and Abuse of the American Past.* Urbana: University of Illinois Press, 1996.

—Judson Knight

The depression brought soaring unemployment rates, and those who had work suffered dreadful conditions. In Georgia, for example, women workers had their pay cut capriciously for various infractions. Employees often had more work heaped upon them. They were also concerned with the mill owners circumventing the NIRA or "chiseling the code."

Throughout the United States, major strikes occurred in many industries. These prompted, if not encouraged, workers nationwide to consider strikes within their own plants. Some strikes occurred in the textile industry in the spring of 1934. These were nominal and had little lasting effect on conditions.

By May 1934 the manufacturers gained permission to cut production by 25 percent and so reduced workers' hours to 30 a week. There was no offsetting increase in wages. Women were hit hard by these reductions. According to Simon Bryant, some were subjected to sexual harassment by male supervisors: "Some male supervisors let female employees know that they could keep their jobs only in exchange for sexual favors or tolerance of lewd gestures and vulgar talk."

The union threatened to call a general strike. The government asked the union not to strike, and the union withdrew its threat. The code authority also discussed a move to shut down all textile manufacturers on 14 May. This would affect northern woolen and silk mills as well as the southern mills. Northern workers demanded a 30-hour week with 40 hours' pay. The UTW also gained representation within the NRA.

Workers in Alabama were not convinced that this would help them at all. On 17 July, 25,000 workers staged a walkout. Half of the strikers were women. This gained the action the support of the Women's Trade Union League (WTUL). It also enabled that union to establish a local in Birmingham, Alabama. This strike was pivotal in that the demands made by these workers were adopted by the UTW for its planned national strike.

The Strike Begins

The UTW convened an emergency national convention in August 1934. The vote was 571 to 10 in favor of a general strike. The action was called for 1 September. Although this strike is commonly associated with the southern United States, the general textile strike occurred throughout New England as well. The decision as to whether the cotton and woolen workers would be joined by the rayon and silk workers was left to the discretion of these other industries. As mentioned, demands of striking mill workers in Alabama were adopted for the national strike. These conditions included a maximum 30-hour workweek with a pay scale of $12 per week for unskilled laborers, $18 for semiskilled laborers, and $30 for the highly skilled mill workers. Workers also asked to be represented by the UTW in any bargaining and asked for an arbitration board to be appointed.

According to Janet Irons, "The day before it began the *New York Times* called it 'the gravest strike threat that has confronted the Roosevelt Administration.'" Roosevelt did not like strikes. On 6 September he appointed the Textile Board of Inquiry, with John G. Winant as its leader to mediate between the union and the mills.

The strike began in earnest on 3 September 1934. Because many of the striking mills were isolated and decentralized, the workers developed a tactic known as "flying squadrons." Groups of 200 to 1,000 workers jumped in cars and trucks and traveled to the remote mills to shut down the plants.

Early on the Associated Press reported that more than half of the 699,800 textile workers were on strike, but some estimates went as high as 65 percent. About 40 percent of the strikers were women. By 19 September 1934 there were 421,000 workers on strike. Although the mill strike is often called the largest single-industry strike in U.S. history, the some historians disagree and hold that the largest was the 1922 mine strike in which 612,000 workers were on strike.

In addition to flying squadrons, workers employed other tactics to call attention to their issues. In Macon, Georgia, for example, workers blockaded a train with their bodies. Squadrons often carried the American flag, believing that this would give them carte blanche to get past militia into the plants. Still, violence was common.

During the strike, mill owners leveraged law enforcement and public sentiment to attempt to break the strike. In cases in which the mill owners did not have the help of local or state law enforcement to quell worker unrest, vigilantes filled that role. Strikers were beaten, subjected to tear gas, kidnapped, or jailed. Even the Ku Klux Klan participated in the unrest. In some communities Klan members included supervisors who took their concerns about union organizing to their Klan meetings. The Klan harassed union members well after the strike, going so far as to leave their signature burning crosses on the lawns of some local leaders. Authorities in Atlanta imposed martial law and had strikers arrested and kept in internment camps. The National Guard was dispatched to mill towns in Connecticut and Rhode Island. These tactics generated confrontations.

Violence in Honea Path

Perhaps no incident blemished the strike more than that which occurred at Honea Path, South Carolina, site of the most overt antilabor violence of the strike. Located in Anderson County, the Chiquola Manufacturing Company mill was the area's largest employer and ran the community. The mayor of Honea Path was the mill superintendent.

Management recruited strikebreakers from neighboring areas. Some loyal workers crossed the picket lines. This continued for three days. Word reached the local sheriff that flying squadrons were en route to shut down the plant. The sheriff decided to deputize several people, mostly those still working in the mill.

The rumors had been correct. A flying squadron departed from Belton, 20 miles away, to Honea Path. On the morning of 6 September 1934, the crowd waiting to support the squadron was "singing gospel hymns and waving a gigantic American flag" outside the plant. Inside the mill building, law enforcement and mill employees were lying in wait. The mill whistle that called workers to the looms started the battle. Strikers and the flying squadron blocked the plant gate. Strikebreakers attempted to enter the mill. Soon, fist fights broke out. Gunfire started and reportedly lasted three minutes. The final tally was seven dead and 75 injured. Most of the injured had been shot in the back as they had tried to leave the scene.

The Chiquola Manufacturing Company refused to allow any churches in the community to have funeral services for the strikers. The 9 September services, held on the outskirts of town, attracted more than 10,000 people. A letter from Francis Gorman, union vice president, was read aloud at the services. He wrote, "Americanism does not mean shooting workers in the back and that is what has been done by the hirelings of the employers." Mill owners and middle-class residents feared what they saw as anarchy on the part of the strikers.

In addition to the seven deaths in South Carolina, two people were killed in Rhode Island and six in Georgia. Two of those six were killed in a gun battle in Trion, Georgia, that also injured another 15 people. Of all the deaths in the course of the strike, none was ever prosecuted.

Strike Ends in Disillusionment

In addition to the deaths and injuries, the mills fired other union leaders and evicted some from their company-owned houses. Those who had participated in the strike were blacklisted and never worked in the textile industry again.

Management also replaced some strikers. Some were forced to sign so-called yellow-dog contracts—an agreement in which a worker agrees never to join a union—if they were hired back at all. Eric Foner wrote, "Furious over the needless capitulation, the workers were even further alienated when they discovered that, despite the fact that both Roosevelt and Gorman had promised that all strikers would be rehired without discrimination, thousands of them were unable to get their jobs back." Some of the mills did not reopen immediately.

The board Roosevelt had assembled to discover what had been happening in the textile industry issued its report on 20 September. The document, which was not responsive to the strikers' demands, recommended leaving negotiations up to each individual mill. The board report did not require that striking workers be rehired, nor did it suggest that the mill owners recognize the UTW or any other union.

Gorman, at the insistence of Roosevelt, reluctantly asked striking workers to return to their jobs on 22 September 1934.

He had no alternative, having seen "force and hunger" compel workers to cross the picket lines. The union had few resources to assist the strikers. Strikers had apparently understood that they would get strike wages of $6 per week, but those payments never materialized. The promised relief of the New Deal also never arrived. Gorman had thought that the massive action would strengthen the union and improve conditions.

Strikers were disappointed and disillusioned in the aftermath of the strike. "Many of us did not understand fully the role of the Government in the struggle between labor and industry," wrote Gorman after the strike.

African American workers continued to fare poorly after the general strike. The UTW paid little heed to their needs, and its continuing discrimination against African American workers resulted in the establishment of separate unions by race. This defeated any solidarity the union had tried to cultivate.

The general strike of 1934 yielded little if anything in the way of improvement of conditions for the strikers and is generally regarded as unsuccessful. As Philip Taft noted, this labor action was "one of the least excusable in history. . . . The strike was called without adequate preparations and without a vote of the hundreds of thousands of workers who were called to join in the walkout." He stated that the union was squarely responsible for the defeat and that boasts of victory were hollow.

The Great Uprising of '34 remains the second largest worker walkout in U.S. history. Union membership in the UTW alone was 80,000 in 1935—significantly fewer than in 1934. The UTW remained one of the smallest AFL member unions. Following the strike, Roosevelt discarded the Cotton Textile Industrial Relations Board and replaced it with the Textile Labor Relations Board with Walter P. Stacy, a judge from North Carolina, as its chair. The new board had little impact on conditions. Despite the relative inaction of the Roosevelt government, the southern mill workers continued to be loyal to Roosevelt.

A legacy of the strike was an increase in already strong antiunion sentiment throughout the South. The violence against millworkers, the blacklists, and intimidation made any subsequent organization very difficult.

Key Players

Bruere, Robert W.: Bruere was chairman of the Cotton Textile Industrial Relations Board at the time of the 1934 general strike.

Gorman, Francis J. (1890–?): Born in a mill town in northern England, Gorman immigrated with his family to the United States to the mill town of Providence, Rhode Island. He went to work in the mills and was a United Textile Workers organizer. At the time of the strike, he was union vice president. He is known as a leader of the general strike for the UTW.

Love, J. Spencer (1893–1962): Founder of Burlington Mills, one of the many companies affected by the general strike, Love was born in New England and founded Burlington Mills upon his return from service in World War I. The company was named for his first mill.

McMahon, Thomas: President of the United Textile Workers at the time of the general strike and an advocate of industrial unionism, McMahon was one of the founding members of the Congress of Industrial Organizations the year after the strike.

Nord, Elizabeth (1902–1986): Born in Lancashire, England, Nord was the daughter of a coal miner and a weaver. The family moved to Pawtucket, Rhode Island when she was 10. She got her first job when she was 14 and attended night school. Nord was a weaver in the silk industry when she joined the union in 1928. She was a member of the Textile National Industrial Board and had been a leading organizer during the general strike, specifically in Blackstone Valley, Rhode Island. At the time of the strike she was the highest ranking woman in the UTW.

Sloan, George A. (1893–1955): Sloan was chairman of the Cotton Textile Code Authority at the time of the strike.

Winant, John G. (1889–1947): Born in New York, Winant eventually became governor of New Hampshire. He was appointed by President Franklin D. Roosevelt to head the Textile Board of Inquiry. He committed suicide in 1947.

See also: *Mass Strikes; National Industrial Recovery Act; National Women's Trade Union League; Stock Market Crash.*

BIBLIOGRAPHY

Books

Clayton, Bruce, and John Salmond, eds. *Debating Southern History: Ideas and Action in the Twentieth Century.* Lanham, MD: Rowman and Littlefield Publishers Inc., 1999.

Foner, Philip S. *Women and the American Labor Movement: From World War I to the Present.* New York: The Free Press, 1980.

Foner, Philip S., and Ronald L. Lewis, eds. *Black Workers: A Documentary History from Colonial Times to the Present.* Philadelphia: Temple University Press, 1989.

Galenson, Walter. *The CIO Challenge to the AFL: A History of the American Labor Movement 1935–1941.* Cambridge, MA: Harvard University Press, 1960.

Irons, Janet. *Testing the New Deal: The General Textile Strike of 1934 in the American South.* Urbana and Chicago: University of Illinois Press, 2000.

Lynd, Staughton, ed. *We Are All Leaders: The Alternative Unionism of the Early 1930s.* Champaign: University of Illinois Press, 1996.

Simon, Bryant. *Fabric of Defeat: The Politics of South Carolina Millhands, 1910–1948.* Chapel Hill: University of North Carolina Press, 1998.

Taft, Philip. *Organized Labor in American History.* New York: Harper and Row, 1964.

Waldrep, G. C. III. *Southern Workers and the Search for Community.* Champaign: University of Illinois Press, 2000.

Yellen, Samuel. *American Labor Struggles 1877–1934.* New York: Monad Press, 1936.

Periodicals

Hall, Jacquelyn Dowd, Robert Korstad, and James Leloudis. "Cotton Mill People: Work, Community, and Protest in the Textile South, 1880–1940." *The American Historical Review* 91, no. 2 (April 1986): 245–286.

Mitchell, George S. "The Labor Union Problem in the Southern Textile Industry." *Journal of Social Forces* 3, no. 4 (May 1925): 727–732

Phillips, William H. "Southern Textile Mill Villages on the Eve of World War II: The Courtenay Mill of South Carolina." *The Journal of Economic History* 45, no. 2 (June 1985): 269–275.

Wright, Annette C. "The Aftermath of the General Textile Strike: Managers and the Workplace at Burlington Mills." *Journal of Southern History* 60, no. 1 (February 1994): 81–112.

Other

"The Uprising of '34 Collection, 1987–1995." Georgia State University Special Collections Department [cited 21 September 2002]. <http://wwwlib.gsu.edu/spcoll/Collections/Labor/L1995-13.htm>.

—Linda Dailey Paulson

Miners' and General Strikes

Great Britain 1921, 1926

Synopsis

Industrial relations in the mining industry had long been fraught with contention. Miners' conditions improved during World War I and the immediate postwar period, when the mines were taken under government control and the demand for coal was high. However, an economic slump beginning in 1920 and the return of the mines to private ownership (despite an apparent promise to retain public control) created bitter industrial conflict. A national miners' strike in 1920 ended in compromise. Strike action against wage cuts and local pay bargaining in 1921 failed and was marked on "Black Friday" by the collapse of the Triple Alliance (of the unions of miners, transport workers, and rail workers) and its promise of joint industrial action. In 1925 the threat of joint union action helped resist wage cuts that were ultimately averted by a nine-month government subsidy. The renewed threat of cuts in 1926, enforced by a miners' lock-out, led to the General Strike of May 1926, which was coordinated by the Trades Union Congress (TUC) and involved some 1.8 million workers. Government resolution and the trade unions' lack of will or strategy to secure victory caused the strike to be called off after nine days. The strike failed to secure conditions acceptable to the miners, who held out for an additional seven months.

Timeline

1900: British Labour Party is founded.

1911: Revolution in Mexico, begun the year before, continues with the replacement of the corrupt Porfirio Diaz, president since 1877, by Francisco Madero.

Ernest Bevin. The Library of Congress.

1916: Battles of Verdun and the Somme occur on the Western Front. The latter sees the first use of tanks, by the British.

1918: The Second Battle of the Marne in July and August is the last major conflict on the Western Front. In November, Kaiser Wilhelm II abdicates, bringing an end to the world war.

1921: As the Allied Reparations Commission calls for payments of 132 billion gold marks, inflation in Germany begins to climb.

1921: Canadian scientists Frederick Banting and Charles Herbert Best isolate insulin, an advance that will alter the lives of diabetics and greatly reduce the number of deaths associated with the disease.

1924: V. I. Lenin dies, and thus begins a struggle for succession from which Josef Stalin will emerge five years later as the undisputed leader of the Communist Party, and of the Soviet Union.

1926: When a revolt breaks out in Nicaragua, U.S. Marines are sent to that country, where they will remain for the next seven years.

1929: On "Black Friday" in October, prices on the U.S. stock market, which had been climbing wildly for several years, suddenly collapse. Thus begins the first phase of a world economic crisis and depression that will last until the beginning of World War II.

1931: Financial crisis widens in the United States and Europe, which reel from bank failures and climbing unemployment levels.

1936: Germany reoccupies the Rhineland, while Italy annexes Ethiopia. Recognizing a commonality of aims, the two totalitarian powers sign the Rome-Berlin Axis Pact. (Japan will join them in 1940.)

Event and Its Context

By 1914 the coal industry employed 10 percent of the British workforce and lay at the heart of the industrial revolution. The industry's fragmented, complex structure gave rise to troubled industrial relations and provided ample grounds for confrontation between a management that was frequently perceived as obdurate and unsympathetic and a workforce with a powerful sense of community and status. A 10-month miners' strike had taken place in South Wales in 1910, followed by a national miners' strike in 1912. Further trade union militancy seemed imminent in 1914 during talks intended to create a Triple Alliance between mining, railway, and transport unions, but the First World War intervened.

Postwar Industrial Unrest

The war itself brought improved pay, a national minimum wage, and government control of the mines. In 1919, the Miners' Federation of Great Britain (MFGB) demanded a shorter working day, higher wages, and nationalization of the mines. The government temporized by establishing a Royal Commission under Justice Sankey and promised to observe its recommendations. The Sankey Commission was divided but, in its final reports published in June, a majority of commissioners (Sankey himself and the six labor representatives) favored nationalization. The government, however, rejected public ownership.

In 1920, the MFGB resumed its campaign for improved conditions, but a brief national miners' strike in October ended inconclusively as the result of a temporary agreement to match pay raises to increased output. In 1921, the economy fell into sharp downturn. The coal industry was particularly hard-hit by the slump in demand and by the flood of German coal that reached the world market as part of the Versailles reparations settlement. Britain's mines, hampered by inefficient organization and old-fashioned techniques, were unable to compete. The export price of British coal fell by 50 percent; by 1921 the government was spending £5 million a month to subsidize the industry. In February, the government announced that private control of the mines would resume on March 31. The mine owners announced drastic wage cuts and district agreements. The MFGB's refusal to accept these conditions led to the publication of lock-out notices that would come into effect on the day of decontrol.

The miners' union successfully called upon the aid of the Triple Alliance: transport and railway workers pledged to withdraw their labor on Friday, 15 April. In truth, support for sympathetic strike action was lukewarm and Alliance leaders, most notably Jimmy Thomas of the railwaymen, were seeking an escape clause. On the eve of the planned action, Frank Hodges, secretary of the MFGB, intimated to a meeting of MPs that the miners might be willing to accept district settlements provided that they were linked to the cost of living. Although Hodges

Striking British tradesman, 1921. © Hulton/Getty Images. Reproduced by permission.

was immediately repudiated by his executive, Alliance leaders used the opening to accuse the miners of unreasonable intransigence and withdraw strike notices. The debacle became known in labor movement mythology as Black Friday. The miners fought on for 11 weeks until they were forced to accept district settlements and wage cuts that ranged between 10 and 40 percent. Significantly, as many trade unionists had feared, the defeat of the miners heralded a sweeping round of wage reductions that affected some 6 million workers. The conflicts of 1921, therefore, played a crucial role in the origins of the much larger dispute that emerged in 1926. Industrial relations in the mining industry had been almost irreparably poisoned, and some union leaders concluded that it was only by effective concerted action that workers' wages and conditions as a whole could be defended.

Prelude to the General Strike

By 1925, 60 percent of British coal was being mined at a loss. Unemployment in the industry rose to nearly 18 percent. Mine owners announced that on 31 July, wages would be reduced by between 10 and 25 percent. The MFGB's resistance concentrated on securing joint union action. Little came of the July 1925 conference of Industrial Alliance of manufacturing and transport unions, but the TUC pledged full support to the miners at a meeting held on 10 July. The Transport and General Workers, led by Ernie Bevin, and the National Union of Railw-

aymen promised to back the miners by an embargo on coal movements. The Special Committee of the TUC, created to coordinate the unions' response to the coal crisis, issued orders for members to embargo coal starting on 30 July. On the same day, Conservative Prime Minister Stanley Baldwin stated his belief in the general need for wage reductions. Support and sympathy for the miners combined with union members' concerns for their own standards of living. On 31 July, at the eleventh hour, the government announced the creation of a Royal Commission to investigate the mining industry (to be led by Sir Herbert Samuel) and a nine-month subsidy to the mines pending its report. The labor movement celebrated the climb-down as Red Friday.

This action signaled a truce but not a settlement. Although many in the labor movement celebrated, other cautionary and more militant voices urged preparation for future conflict. The TUC created an Industrial Committee to liaise with the miners and take charge of the dispute, but meetings in October and December 1925 assumed no additional powers. The government, on the other hand, acted decisively. July 1925 brought the activation of the Supply and Transport Committee, which, under the 1920 Emergency Powers Act, granted plenary powers to 10 Civil Commissioners to maintain transport, food and coal supplies, and postal services. In September 1925, the Organization for the Maintenance of Supplies (OMS) was established to supply volunteer labor in the event of any general work stoppage. Though an unofficial body, it liaised closely with government.

British strikers, General Strike. © Hulton/Getty Images. Reproduced by permission.

The report of the Samuel Commission, when it came on 10 March 1926, disappointed all sides. It opposed the labor movement's nationalization scheme but supported state acquisition of mineral rights. The report proposed rationalization of the industry and favored improved welfare benefits for miners. It was adamant, however, that government subsidy must be ended and that wage cuts were unavoidable. The government was shy even of the limited state intervention that had been suggested. Coal owners opposed any infringement of their proprietorial prerogatives. Mineworkers stood by their slogan, "Not a penny off the pay, not a second on the day." Four days later, the owners stated their intention to implement wage cuts and district settlements and lock-out notices were posted to take effect on 1 May.

The TUC's Industrial Council reiterated its full support for the miners but, significantly for later developments, was wary of fully backing the MFGB's refusal of any wage cuts, increased hours, or district settlements. The implication was that some reduction in wages might be acceptable provided the rest of the Samuel Report was fully implemented. The miners, nevertheless, placed the conduct of the dispute under the TUC's control. The TUC continued to negotiate for a settlement, but Baldwin's comment to the press that longer hours were necessary and news of the government's preparations for a likely strike forced their hand. On 2 May, Baldwin called off last minute negotiations between the government and the TUC Industri-

al Council when he heard of unofficial action by *Daily Mail* print workers, who had refused to print an editorial that was hostile to the union cause.

The General Strike

The TUC strategy was to call out unions in two phases. Workers in transport, printing, building, metal, and chemical trades were to cease work at midnight on Monday, 3 May. A second phase, comprising engineering, shipbuilding, and power workers, was to follow on 12 May. The response was overwhelming; local organizers reported near unanimous support for the stoppage, both by the trades directly involved and often by workers who were not immediately affected. Nor were there any but isolated signs of the strike weakening as the dispute progressed, though these were a factor in the TUC's decision to halt the dispute. Most historians concur with the contemporary labor movement's claim that the strike demonstrated unprecedented class solidarity. In total, some 1.8 million workers participated in the strike over the course of the nine-day dispute.

Given the lack of detailed preparation, the labor movement also fashioned an impressive apparatus to coordinate its action by forming some 400–500 local organizing bodies. Local trades councils frequently played a leading role in these committees, which issued instructions, distributed permits for essential services, and generally sought to maintain workers' morale. A few of the more militant committees established Workers' Defence Corps.

The government, however, acted forcefully to maintain essential services. The Civil Commissioners implemented the plans already agreed upon and recruited volunteer labor with the aid of the OMS. Meanwhile, government propaganda painted the dispute as an attack on the Constitution and gave wide publicity to the pronouncements of Sir John Simon MP and Justice Astbury that the strike was illegal. Despite the aggressive rhetoric, relations between strikers and the forces of law and order were generally cordial, but the myth of a peaceful and "very British" conflict should be questioned in part. Troops were deployed to move food supplies, and clashes between pickets and police occurred in more militant areas. The government reported 1760 arrests during the strike.

Labour's parliamentary leadership, particularly Ramsay MacDonald, was equivocal in its support and the TUC itself wanted to bring the dispute to an early conclusion. Samuel was prevailed upon to act as an intermediary though he acknowledged that he acted with no governmental authority. The Samuel Memorandum published on 11 May was essentially a rehash of his Commission's previous report, but the TUC seized on the memorandum as the basis of a settlement and ignored the MFGB which, led by Herbert Smith and A. J. Cook, maintained its refusal to countenance wage cuts. On 12 May a TUC deputation met Baldwin to announce that the Strike had been called off. Baldwin, for his part, gave no assurances that the Samuel recommendations would be implemented.

The miners' struggle continued for an additional seven months. The government's repeal of the Seven Hours Act in July 1926 hardened feelings, and union members continued to refuse terms that involved degraded conditions. East Midlands union members formed a break-away "nonpolitical" union, and the hardships suffered by the mining communities impelled a slow drift back to work through October and November. In these circumstances, the MFGB's national conference on 19 November agreed to allow its member associations to negotiate local agreements (conforming in principle to national standards). The strike ended in abject failure with district settlements, longer hours, and wage cuts.

Impact

One immediate effect of the strike was the passing of the Trade Disputes and Trade Union Act of 1927. The act declared sympathetic and general strikes illegal, banned mass picketing, and forbade government employees to join "political" trade unions (those affiliated to the TUC or Labour Party). It also replaced *contracting-out* of the unions' political levy to the Labour Party by *contracting-in*; in other words, union members were now required to state expressly that they wished to pay the levy rather than the reverse. Union contributions to the Labour Party fell by about one-third, largely as a result of the inertia of union members rather than hostility to Labour as such. In fact, one of the effects of the Strike was to increase working-class support for Labour. The class-determined character of the General Strike and coal dispute and the apparently callous nature of government policy heightened Labour's appeal as a specifically working-class party. After the 1929 general election, Labour became the largest single party and formed its second government.

Trade union membership fell, particularly in those unions most closely involved in the dispute. Industrial action declined significantly in 1927 and 1928 as a result of the depletion of union funds and a decline in members' morale. By 1929, however, union finances were largely restored and the number of strikes increased. Generally, the union movement appeared to become more moderate and toned down left-wing rhetoric in the later 1920s. The TUC made moves to reduce communist influence in the unions. The Mond-Turner talks of 1928—headed by the Liberal MP and industrialist Sir Alfred Mond and Ben Turner, the textile workers' leader—adopted a more conciliatory industrial policy, though many in the union movement as a whole had long favored cooperation with employers.

Overall, the long-term impact of the General Strike was relatively slight. The British trade union movement was too solid and conservative to be shaken from long-established ideas and practices. The strike itself is best interpreted as an authentic expression of trade union values and tactics, albeit one radicalized by the troubled industrial relations of the time. The strike was an industrial dispute with undeniably political overtones, and its leaders and supporters (despite an active left-wing minority) were not motivated by revolutionary sentiments. It demonstrated and strengthened a powerful class identity among British workers, but working-class consciousness was, and remained, essentially moderate and reformist. The trade union movement continued to believe in its essentially defensive and economic role.

The Labour Party nationalized the mines in 1946, but the economics of the coal industry remained difficult. A year-long strike against pit closures occurred in 1984–1985, and in 1996 the government privatized a greatly reduced mining industry.

Key Players

Baldwin, Stanley (1867–1947): Baldwin was a Midlands industrialist, elected Conservative MP in 1906 and prime minister in 1923, 1924–1929 and 1935–1937. Baldwin's self-proclaimed moderation did not prevent him taking a strong line against the General Strike or passing the Trade Disputes Act, but working-class resentments contributed to his defeat in the 1929 general election.

Bevin, Ernest (1881–1951): Born in Bristol, Bevin was a farm laborer and van driver before becoming an official of the Dockers' Union. On the formation of the Transport and General Workers Union in 1921, Bevin was elected general secretary. He was also a generally moderate member of the General Council of the Trades Union Congress between 1925 and 1940. In 1940, Bevin became minister of labor in the wartime coalition government and was foreign secretary in the Labour Government from 1945 to 1951.

Cook, Arthur James (1885–1931): Born in mining village of Wookey, Somerset, Cook migrated to the South Wales coalfields where he became active in union politics. A founding member of the British Communist Party in 1920, he resigned when it criticized his acceptance of the 1921 strike settlement but remained, in his words, "a disciple of Karl Marx and a humble follower of Lenin." A fiery and emotional speaker, he became secretary of the MFGB in 1924. Mental exhaustion and physical ill health caused his early death in 1931.

Hodges, Frank (1887–1947): A miners' agent from South Wales, Hodges served as secretary of the MFGB between 1918 and 1924. Increasingly moderate and despised by the left for his role in Black Friday, he resigned his position on his appointment as a junior minister in the first Labour government. From 1927 to his death he was a member of the Central Electricity Board.

MacDonald, Ramsay (1866–1937): The illegitimate son of a Scottish maidservant and early member of the Fabian Society and Independent Labour Party, MacDonald became the secretary of the Labour Representation Committee. MacDonald was a Labour MP (1906–1918 and 1922–1931 and National Labour MP from 1931 to 1937) and was elected Labour leader in 1922. He served as prime minister in 1924 and 1929–31. MacDonald was an increasingly "respectable" moderate who opposed the 1926 General Strike and became leader of a "National" coalition government from 1931 to 1935.

Samuel, Herbert (1870–1963): Son of a wealthy banker, Liberal MP 1902–1918 and 1929–1935, and Liberal leader from 1931 to 1935, Samuel served as high commissioner for Palestine between 1920 and 1925. He was a reluctant participant in the coal dispute when called on by Stanley Baldwin to lead the Royal Commission into the industry in 1925.

Smillie, Robert (1857–1940): Born in Northern Ireland, Smillie and his family moved to central Scotland where he became a miner at age 17. A founder of the Lanarkshire Miners' Association, he was elected secretary of the Scottish Miners' Federation in 1894 and president of the Miners' Federation of Great Britain in 1912. Smillie pursued a radical line after World War I, calling for nationalization of the mines and workers' control, but the failure of the Triple Alliance in 1921 led to his resignation as MFGB president. He was Labour MP for the mining constituency of Morpeth from 1924 to 1929.

Smith, Herbert (1862–1938): A blunt Yorkshireman who entered the pits at age 10, Smith became an active socialist and trade unionist, rising through the South Yorkshire Miners' Association and serving as a miners' representative on the 1919 Sankey Commission to become president of the MFGB in 1922. Though increasingly moderate politically and opposed to communist influence within the trade union movement, he was seen as the most resolute of miners' leaders during the 1926 coal dispute.

Thomas, James (1874–1949): Thomas joined the railways in South Wales at age 15 and subsequently became an organizer for the Amalgamated Society of Railway Servants. Prominent in the formation of the National Union of Railwaymen in 1913, he became general secretary four years later. He was Labour MP for Derby from 1910 to 1931 but was a moderate in both union and parliamentary politics. A member of the Cabinet in Labour's First and Second Governments (1924, 1929–1931), Thomas supported MacDonald's formation of a National (coalition) government in 1931 but was forced to resign in 1936 for alleged corruption.

BIBLIOGRAPHY

Books

Clegg, H. A. *A History of British Trade Unions Since 1889.* Volume II, *1911–1933.* Oxford: Clarendon Press, 1985.

Farman, Christopher. *The General Strike, May 1926.* St. Albans: Panther, 1974.

Hutt, Allen. *The Post-War History of the British Working Class.* London: Victor Gollancz, 1937.

Phillips, G. A. *The General Strike: The Politics of Industrial Conflict.* London: Weidenfeld and Nicolson, 1976.

ADDITIONAL RESOURCES

Books

Laybourn, Keith. *The General Strike of 1926.* Manchester, New York: Manchester University Press, 1993.

Morris, Margaret. *The General Strike.* London: Journeyman, 1980.

—John Boughton

Miners' Strike

Germany 1889

Synopsis

During May 1889 nearly 100,000 German miners went on strike in the Ruhr Valley. They demanded wage increases and an eight-hour workday and raised other grievances. Faced with employer intransigence, some miners petitioned Kaiser Wilhelm II for a resolution of their dispute. Seeing this as an opportunity to enhance his authority, Wilhelm pressured the employers into negotiating a compromise with the miners. This exposed a rift between Wilhelm and Chancellor Otto von Bismarck, who had hoped to use the strike as an excuse to force more antisocialist legislation through the Reichstag, the German parliament. Despite being pushed into a settlement with the miners, the employers did not keep to the terms of the agreement and the miners failed to gain any lasting concessions. However, the strike had profound consequences for the development of the labor movement in the Ruhr Valley. Repeated conflicts between miners and mine owners occurred over the next two decades.

Timeline

1869: Black Friday panic ensues when James Fisk and Jay Gould attempt to control the gold market.

1874: Norwegian physician Arrnauer Gerhard Henrik Hansen discovers the bacillus that causes leprosy. This marks the major turning point in the history of an ailment (now known properly as Hansen's disease) that afflicted humans for thousands of years and was often regarded as evidence of divine judgment.

Wilhelm II. © Getty Images. Reproduced by permission.

1882: Agitation against English rule spreads throughout Ireland, culminating with the assassination of chief secretary for Ireland Lord Frederick Cavendish and permanent undersecretary Thomas Burke in Dublin's Phoenix Park. The leader of the nationalist movement is Charles Stewart Parnell, but the use of assassination and terrorism—which Parnell himself has disavowed—makes clear the fact that he does not control all nationalist groups.

1885: Belgium's King Leopold II becomes sovereign of the so-called Congo Free State, which he will rule for a quarter-century virtually as his own private property. The region in Africa, given the name of Zaire in the 1970s (and Congo in 1997), becomes the site of staggering atrocities, including forced labor and genocide, at the hands of Leopold's minions.

1887: John Emerich Edward Dalbert-Acton, a leader of the opposition to the papal dogma of infallibility, observes, in a letter to Cambridge University professor Mandell Creighton, that "Power tends to corrupt, and absolute power corrupts absolutely."

1889: Indian Territory in Oklahoma is opened to white settlement.

1889: Flooding in Johnstown, Pennsylvania, kills thousands.

1889: The 986-foot (300.5-m) Eiffel Tower, part of the Paris exposition, becomes the tallest structure in the world. It will remain so until the Chrysler Building surpasses it in 1930.

1889: Discontented southern farmers merge their farm organizations to form the Southern Alliance.

Germinal: The Miner's Life Profiled

Despite the fact that the nineteenth century saw the rise of organized labor, few important novels of the era depicted the lives—and the ideas—of workers in a sympathetic light. Among these few was *Germinal* (1885) by Emile Zola. Though he would later become a socialist, Zola did not view himself as an ally of the workers when he began his great work, but he did have a passion for realism (or "naturalism," as he called the literary movement that he founded), and sought to realistically chronicle the life of an entire class.

Inspired by Balzac's *Human Comedy,* Zola had set out to create a cycle of novels that examined the life of France in the latter half of the nineteenth century. Among these was *L'assomoir* (1877), which introduced readers to the character of Etienne Lantier, destined to become a leader of the Paris Commune in *La débâcle* (1892). Labor organizations criticized *L'assomoir* for what they considered an unflattering portrayal of workers, and though Zola had no interest in writing to please any constituency, it did concern him that he had neglected a movement that was changing society as labor was. He therefore set about to research the lives of workers firsthand for the writing on *Germinal.*

In his research, Zola descended mineshafts and delved into the dirty, dangerous world of the nineteenth-century miner. Only such direct experience could give him the insight required to write passages such as these:

"Of course he thought of himself as brave, yet an unpleasant emotion caused his throat to contract among the thundering of the carts, the clanking of the signals, the muffled bellowing of the megaphone, facing the continuously flying cables, unrolling and rolling up again at top speed on the spools of the machine. The cages rose and fell, slithering like some nocturnal animal, continually swallowing men that the hole seemed to drink down. It was his turn now. He was very cold."

Germinal eloquently illustrated the inhumanity of workers' lives, and particularly the lives of miners. Today it is regarded as the masterwork of one of the era's greatest writers, but even in its day, the influence of *Germinal* spread far and wide. Among those impressed by the book was Vincent Van Gogh, whose reading of Zola inspired much of the social criticism evident in paintings such as *The Potato Eaters.*

Source: Emile Zola. *Germinal.* Translated and with an introduction by Leonard Tancock. New York: Viking, 1954.

—Judson Knight

1891: Construction of Trans-Siberian Railway begins. Meanwhile, crop failures across Russia lead to widespread starvation.

1895: Guglielmo Marconi pioneers wireless telegraphy, which in the next three decades will make possible the use of radio waves for commercial broadcasts and other applications.

1899: Polish-born German socialist Rosa Luxembourg rejects the argument that working conditions in Europe have improved and that change must come by reforming the existing system. Rather, she calls for an overthrow of the existing power structure by means of violent international revolution.

Event and Its Context

Mining in the Ruhr Valley

The latter part of the nineteenth century brought enormous changes to the Ruhr Valley. Until the middle of the century, the Ruhr coal mines had been under government management. With legislation liberalizing the industry in the 1850s, the management of the mines passed into private hands. This produced a period of intense industrial expansion. By the turn of the century, the Ruhr Valley was the most heavily industrialized region of Europe, dominated by mining and steel. However, divisions of religion and ethnicity, combined with repression from both government and employers, helped to prevent the development of the labor movement in the Ruhr. Instead, the workforce had a reputation for being docile and obedient, and the miners seemed largely indifferent to social democracy. Workers' organizations were limited to social clubs and self-help associations, and the miners did not have a union. This was partly due to the control that the employers had over the industry. The Ruhr industrialists regarded their mines and factories as their personal fiefdoms. These men were the giants of German industry, and they were notorious for their arrogant and uncompromising resistance to any form of interference in their businesses. As the industrialist Emil Kirdof said, "Neither king nor emperor has any say in our workshops. We alone decide."

The Beginning of the Miners' Strike

Starting in 1888, an economic upturn occurred, and prices for coal began to rise after many years of depression. It was at this point that industrial unrest began. At this stage, action was spontaneous and largely unorganized. Meetings occurred throughout the early months of 1889 at the various pits, and miners sent lists of demands to mine owners. When no response was forthcoming, many younger miners stopped going to work in late April and the first days of May. Following violent confrontations between police and strikers at Gelsenkirchen on 5 May, authorities deployed troops. This action, the first official response to the miners' demands, angered the mining community, and the strike gathered momentum. Troops killed three people and wounded several others during a protest at one mine. In Bochum on 9 May, innocent bystanders were killed when troops opened fire on a crowd of strikers in the center of the town.

From the isolated and uncoordinated actions at various pits, a general strike developed. The tough stance taken by the authorities, in accordance with the policies of Chancellor Bismarck, had inflamed the situation and helped to unify the miners. At a conference on 10 May, delegates from each pit elected a central strike committee. By 13 May over 90,000 miners from a workforce of approximately 115,000—around 80 percent—were on strike. The strike began to spread to other mining regions as miners in the Saar district, Upper and Lower Silesia, Aachen, Lorraine, and Saxony went out. The number of strikers reached approximately 150,000. Considering that the previous largest strike in Germany had only involved 16,000 workers, this was industrial action on an unprecedented scale.

Strike Demands

The strikers' demands reflected a complex mix of grievances. At most pits, strikes began when the owners ignored requests for wage increases of around 20 to 25 percent. The issue of wage increases was in itself complex. Many indications suggest that the miners' incomes had been rising in the previous year; the Ruhr miners were the highest paid in the Reich. However, although incomes were rising, this was largely due to longer hours and extra shifts rather than to a substantial rise in actual wage rates. Wages also varied depending on the division of labor in the mines. The hewers, those who actually worked at the coal face, were paid according to how much coal they produced, and their wage rates were subject to monthly renegotiations; therefore, their wages were closely connected to the rise and fall in the market price of coal. Other workers, however, such as those who hauled the coal, were usually paid a set amount per shift. Their rates were more stable, which created frustrations during an economic upswing when the price of coal rose without a corresponding increase in wages. These workers were mostly younger men, without family responsibilities, so it was not surprising that they were the first to strike.

The other main demand was for an eight-hour shift. During the two previous decades, the length of the miners' working day had increased steadily. A large part of this involved unpaid traveling time. As mines became deeper, it could take a miner more than half an hour to get to and from the coalface. This meant that the working day had actually extended to more than 10 hours in some cases. In addition, miners complained about the unreasonable demands for overtime and extra shifts that were being placed upon them by management. Often, extended shifts were announced after the miners were already underground, which gave them no opportunity to refuse. The demand for the eight-hour day to include traveling time was closely linked to the issue of higher wages. For the hewers, who were paid by the amount of coal they produced, a shorter working day would result in a drop in income. Therefore, if the eight-hour day was won, wage increases were necessary to maintain their income at acceptable levels. As the strike progressed, the miners aired other grievances, most of which related to unfair work practices and poor treatment by management.

Kaiser Wilhelm II and the Miners

Despite the solidarity of the miners, it became apparent that most mine owners were not prepared to negotiate. A group of miners therefore decided to petition the kaiser, a traditional tactic in earlier generations of labor protest. Three miners, Ludwig Schroeder, August Siegel, and Fritz Bunte, traveled to Berlin on 14 May for an audience with Kaiser Wilhelm II. Wilhelm had only been in power for 10 months, and the miners' strike had revealed some profound differences between him and Bismarck. The so-called iron chancellor welcomed the miners' strike as an opportunity to frighten the liberal members of the Reichstag into supporting his demands for more repressive laws against socialism. Social unrest and instability resulting from the strikes could also provide Bismarck with an excuse to break with the German constitution and increase his own power. He was therefore totally against any kind of conciliation with the miners.

By contrast, the new kaiser saw the miners' strike as an opportunity to demonstrate his own authority. Unlike his predecessor, Wilhelm was not content to remain in Bismarck's shadow and took a direct interest in events as the strike unfolded. Wilhelm regarded the strike as largely the fault of the greed and exploitation of the mine owners. He was sympathetic to the petition from the miners, especially as it enabled him to play the part of the wise and benevolent ruler protecting his subjects. In the face of Bismarck's disapproval, Wilhelm ordered the mine owners to negotiate a compromise with the miners. Friedrich Hammacher, the moderate head of the mine owners' association, came to an agreement with the strikers that included wages increases and a true eight-hour day, including traveling time.

The mine owners rejected the Hammacher Protocol, however, and would only promise unspecified wage increases and an eight-hour day with no mention of traveling time. Strikers were confused about whether they should continue the protest. The strike collapsed in the last days of May, with the disarray of the movement exacerbated by police harassment and arrests. Although the Kaiser's intervention had wrung some concessions out of the owners, most failed to keep to the agreement, and the strike was unsuccessful in achieving the miners' main demands. As a result, sporadic and isolated strikes continued to occur throughout the rest of the year.

The Consequences of the 1889 Strike

The 1889 miners' strike increased the antagonism between the miners and their employers. One of its most important consequences was the formation of a miners' union, the *Alter Verband*, in the months after the strike. The experience of strike action had highlighted the need for a permanent organization to coordinate the miners' struggle for better wages, hours, and working conditions. The increased militancy of the Ruhr workers is also reflected in the gains made by the Social Democratic Party (SDP) in the region. In the 1887 Reichstag elections, the SPD candidate for Bochum received only 2 percent of the vote. In the 1890 election prominent leaders of the 1889 strike, such as Ludwig Schroeder, stood as SPD candidates and received around 15 percent of the vote. The strike was the culmination of a wave of industrial action that had proved the failure of Bismarck's oppressive Anti-Socialist Laws to prevent militant labor organization in the German Reich.

The strike also entrenched the hard-line position of the mine owners. They had been certain that they could crush the strike and so felt bitter about being forced to reach a settlement with the miners. The creation of the miners' union further convinced the owners that any compromise with the miners would be an admission of weakness that would inevitably lead to an erosion of their authority. The 1889 strike was therefore the first and last example of a negotiated industrial settlement in the mining industry before World War I. Successive strikes in the next two decades failed as employers refused to enter into collective agreements with workers or to recognize the right of unions to represent workers. The 1889 strike heralded a new era of industrial relations in the mining industry in which the battle lines between labor and capital were clearly drawn.

Key Players

Bismarck, Prince Otto von (1815–1898): German chancellor, Bismarck tried to use the 1889 miners' strike as an opportunity to force more antisocialist legislation through the Reichstag and increase his own power. He was therefore opposed to any conciliatory measures with the strikers. The strike exposed a rift between the chancellor and kaiser that eventually led to Bismarck's downfall in 1890.

Schroeder, Ludwig (1848–1914): German leader in the Ruhr mining community and miners' spokesman during the 1889 strike, Schroeder was one of three men who traveled to Berlin to petition the Kaiser. Despite this, Schroeder was a social democrat who later became the chairman of the *Alter Verband* and stood as a local candidate for the Social Democratic Party (SPD) during the 1890 election.

Wilhelm II (1859–1941): German emperor, Wilhelm II saw the 1889 miners' strike as an opportunity to stamp his authority on domestic policy and was therefore sympathetic to the petition from the miners. Because of his intervention, the mine owners were forced into a negotiated settlement with the miners.

BIBLIOGRAPHY

Books

Clark, Christopher. *Kaiser Wilhelm II*. London: Longman, 2000.

Crew, David F. *Town in the Ruhr: A Social History of Bochum*. New York: Columbia University Press, 1979.

Hickey, S. H. F. *Workers in Imperial Germany: The Miners of the Ruhr*. Oxford: Clarendon Press, 1985.

Moses, John A. *Trade Unionism in Germany From Bismarck to Hitler, 1869–1933*. Vol. 1, *1869–1918*. London: George Prior Publishers, 1982.

Reichard, Richard W. *From the Petition to the Strike: A History of Strikes in Germany, 1869–1914*. New York: Peter Lang Publishing, 1991.

Schneider, Michael. *A Brief History of the German Trade Unions*. Bonn, Germany: Verlag J. H. W. Dietz Nachf., 1991.

Spencer, Elaine Glovka. *Management and Labor in Imperial Germany: Ruhr Industrialists as Employers, 1896–1914*. New Brunswick, NJ: Rutgers University Press, 1984.

ADDITIONAL RESOURCES
Grebing, Helga. *History of the German Labour Movement.*
    Rev. ed. Leamington Spa, UK: Berg Publishers Ltd.,
    1985.

—Katrina Ford

Miners' Strike

South Africa 1922

Synopsis

In early 1922, white South African workers in the Witwatersrand gold mining region went on strike. The strike soon became a violent rebellion—sometimes known as the Rand Revolt—that pitted the white miners against the mine owners and the government. The workers' action was a response to the owners' plan to reduce wages and replace the well-paid white workers with cheaper black African workers. At first, the government attempted to get the two sides to negotiate, but neither side was willing to compromise. The strikers formed commandos. In response, the government sent in troops from the Active Citizens Force and declared martial law. The ensuing violence resulted in hundreds of injuries and deaths. Authorities arrested thousands of workers, and four were put to death. The negative reaction to the government's actions cost Prime Minister Jan Smuts and his South Africa Party the 1924 election.

Timeline

1907: At the Second Hague Peace Conference, forty-six nations adopt ten conventions governing the rules of war.

1912: *Titanic* sinks on its maiden voyage, from Southampton to New York, on 14 April. More than 1,500 people are killed.

1917: In Russia a revolution in March (or February according to the old Russian calendar) forces the abdication of Czar Nicholas II. By July, Alexander Kerensky has formed a democratic socialist government, and continues to fight the Germans, even as starvation and unrest sweep the nation. On 7 November (25 October old style) the Bolsheviks under V. I. Lenin and Leon Trotsky seize power. By 15 December they have removed Russia from the war by signing the Treaty of Brest-Litovsk with Germany.

1919: With the formation of the Third International (Comintern), the Bolshevik government of Russia establishes its control over communist movements worldwide.

1922: Inspired by the Bolsheviks' example of imposing revolution by means of a coup, Benito Mussolini leads his blackshirts in an October "March on Rome," and forms a new fascist government.

1922: Great Britain establishes the Irish Free State as a dominion of the British Empire.

Jan Christian Smuts. The Library of Congress.

1922: With the centuries-old Ottoman Empire dissolved, Mustafa Kemal, a.k.a. Atatürk, overthrows the last sultan and establishes the modern Turkish republic.

1922: Union of Soviet Socialist Republics (USSR) formed.

1922: Published this year James Joyce's novel *Ulysses* and T. S. Eliot's poem *The Waste Land* will transform literature and inaugurate the era of modernism.

1925: European leaders attempt to secure the peace at the Locarno Conference, which guarantees the boundaries between France and Germany, and Belgium and Germany.

1927: Charles A. Lindbergh makes the first successful solo nonstop flight across the Atlantic, and becomes an international hero.

1932: When Ukrainians refuse to surrender their grain to his commissars, Stalin seals off supplies to the region, creating a manmade famine that will produce a greater death toll than the entirety of World War I.

Event and Its Context

The Color Bar

The gold mining industry in South Africa—concentrated in the Witwatersrand region near Johannesburg—was the key to the entire economy and depended on two distinct labor markets. The majority of gold miners were black Africans, who worked for low wages and were often preferred by the nine owners, particularly during times of financial difficulty. There were also a smaller number of white workers who earned relatively high wages. For example, by 1921, there were approximately 180,000 black workers compared to about 21,000 white workers. Yet the total wages paid to white workers were twice those

Workers for a White South Africa

Surely one of the most unusual political slogans of all time, uniting as it does familiar themes of right and left, is this one, from the 1920s: "Workers of the world unite and fight for a white South Africa!" With these words, the Afrikaner National Party (which would later institutionalize Apartheid) made common cause with the nation's Labour Party, an organization of English-speakers, to protect white jobs.

The situation illustrates the truth that, while union activity has often been associated with the breaking of racial or ethnic barriers, this association is neither inherent nor universal. Analyzing the development of Apartheid as an ideology, and the contributions of the South African labor movement to that development, political scientist A. James Gregor wrote, "For the English-language community from which the entrepreneurial class was almost exclusively drawn, the influx of non-white labor was essential to the maintenance of an attractive profit structure. To the Afrikaner community, recently urbanized, the nonwhite influx constituted a persistent threat to their wage levels and traditions."

Source: A. James Gregor, *Contemporary Radical Ideologies: Totalitarian Thought in the Twentieth Century.* New York: Random House, 1968.

—Judson Knight

paid to the more numerous black workers. During World War I, wages for whites rose by 40 percent—on average, 15 times the amount black workers earned.

White workers' jobs were protected by the so-called color bar, which became the core of the dispute that led to the 1922 Rand Revolt. The "statutory" color bar legally protected some 7,000 jobs for white workers under the Mines and Works Act. Furthermore, the "conventional" color bar—custom, pressure from trade unions, and public opinion—protected the 14,000 jobs held by white miners. During World War I, however, the color bar eroded somewhat, as more black workers began to replace white workers in semi-skilled positions. In 1918, however, an agreement between employers and white miners halted this process of erosion. By 1921, the Chamber of Mines decided this agreement was no longer economically viable, leading to the 1922 strike and revolt.

Pre-1922 Strikes in the Gold Mines

In the years leading up to the 1922 Rand Revolt, there were a number of strikes and protests by both white and black workers in the South African gold mining industry. In 1907, white gold workers in the Transvaal struck against a plan to reduce their wages and hire cheaper African and Chinese labor. Prime Minister Louis Botha, however, suppressed this strike. White workers struck again in 1913, this time against working conditions as well as black competition. They demanded the right to establish trade unions and protection for their privileged position within the gold mines. This time, British imperial troops had to be brought in to keep the peace.

The next year there was yet another strike by white workers. This time the strike started among white railroad and port workers, who anticipated possible layoffs. The strike spread to the gold mines and soon became a national strike. Prime Minister Smuts sent in 10,000 troops of the newly created Active Citizens Force and declared martial law. Many strikers were arrested and nine leaders were deported, leading to the collapse of the strike. The 1914 incident led to the Riot Assemblies Bill, which gave the government and the police more power.

Crisis, Strike, and Revolt

In late 1921, the price of gold began to fall significantly. The Central Bank predicted that it would continue to fall. The Chamber of Mines claimed that, soon, 27 of the 38 mines in Witwatersrand would be operating at a loss. Under such conditions, the government of Prime Minister Jan Smuts felt compelled to intervene. Smuts convinced the Chamber of Mines, representing the owners, and the South African Industrial Federation, led by Archie Crawford and representing the workers, to begin meeting on 15 December. After a week, however, the two sides agreed to postpone the conference until 9 January 1922, because the Prime Minister was ill.

In the meantime, the Chamber of Mines announced that, starting on 1 February 1922, it would terminate the 1918 status quo agreement. This announcement meant that some 2,000 white gold miners could lose their jobs. To the chamber, the move was simply a reaction to rapidly falling gold prices. White workers, however, saw the move as an attack on them and went on strike in early January. They created an "Augmented Executive" to represent the various striking workers' unions. Smuts encouraged the unions to submit their case to a board of conciliation rather than strike. Although he convinced both sides to begin meeting on 13 January, within two weeks the talks collapsed in deadlock.

Neither side was willing to compromise, and soon what started as an industrial struggle turned into a political conflict. The Augmented Executive was especially unwilling to deal with the government. They accused the government of backing an attack on white workers. The strike leaders called on workers to back opposition political parties, to overthrow the government of Prime Minister Smuts, and to support a government that would promote the interests of white South Africans.

With the unofficial support of opposition parties, the strike leaders rejected government proposals. The Smuts government tried to get the two sides to negotiate an agreement during the first week of February, but with no settlement forthcoming, the government took a new approach. No longer willing to tolerate a work stoppage, Smuts demanded that the owners reopen the mines and encouraged the workers to go back to work. He also indicated that the government would provide police protection for scabs.

In the meantime, a small group of militant workers formed the Council of Action, which was influenced by communism. For example, its first secretary was W. H. Andrews, the founder of the South African Communist Party. The Council also urged workers of the world to fight for a white South Africa.

Some of the strikers also formed commando units of between fifty and five hundred workers, clearly an indication of Afrikaner tradition. Indeed, some 75 percent of the workers were Afrikaners. Many were also former soldiers. Led by Piet Erasmus, they operated independently of the Augmented Executive and the Council of Action. Soon they began drilling and started to put down scabbing. On 22 February, the government announced that commandos were unlawful assemblies and would be dispersed by the police, which led to conflicts between the police and the commandos, often resulting in arrests and even deaths.

The government now had to decide if it would declare martial law and use military force. Smuts had declared martial law before, in 1914, and many South Africans thought he was waiting for the opportunity to do so again. The prime minister would have to use the Active Citizen Forces to enforce martial law, but he was unsure if his order would be obeyed. There was still some hope that labor leaders such as Crawford and moderates in the Augmented Executive would settle the strike. However, by early March, the more militant workers seized control of the situation. On 6 March, the Council of Action and the commando leaders declared a general strike. While the general strike never really spread beyond the Rand, in the gold mining region, the strike turned into an uprising. The next day, violence began with attack on the police. There were also violent attacks on African miners.

The Government Response and the Aftermath of the Strike

On 9 March, the government mobilized the Active Citizen Force and on 10 March declared martial law. The soldiers did obey the government orders, and, after three days of fighting, they put down the rebellion. There were many deaths in the fighting. The government's Martial Law Commission reported that more than 150 people died in the uprising, although other estimates are somewhat higher. Some accused the police and military of using excessive force. Following the strike, authorities arrested thousands of strikers. Those accused of high treason and murder were to be tried in a special courts set up under the Riotous Assemblies Act of 1914, which were made up of Supreme Court judges but with no juries. Of the 46 men brought before the special courts, 18 were sentenced to death, although only four were actually put to death.

In the short term, the mine owners were victorious. Some white workers were laid off and wages were reduced. In the long term, however, the white workers achieved their goal; the color bar remained firmly in place, and one wanted to risk another rebellion. The situation led to the 1926 Mines and Works Amendment, under which black and Indian workers were excluded from the better jobs in the mining industry. In 1924, the Smuts government introduced the Industrial Conciliation Act to deal with disputes between workers and employers. It served to reduce tensions between the owners and white workers, but the black workers were excluded. There was also a political cost. Prime Minister Smuts's South Africa Party lost the 1924 elections. A coalition of the National and Labor Parties won a majority of seats in the Parliament, and National Party leader J. B. M. Hertzog became the new prime minister. The leaders of the coalition had promised to protect white South African workers.

Key Players

Andrews, William H. (1870–1950): Born in England, Andrews immigrated to South Africa in 1893. A leader of the 1922 strike who served on the Committee of Action. As a leader of the Communist Party, Andrews saw the strike as part of a global class struggle. He was among the more extremist strike leaders who favored a general strike. At the same time, Andrews urged the white miners not to fight with the black miners. During the strike, authorities arrested Andrews.

Crawford, Archie (1883–1924): Born in Scotland, Crawford went to South Africa in 1902, where he became an important labor leader. He founded the *Voice of Labor,* which he published from 1908 to 1912. In 1914, he was deported for his labor activities. Upon returning to South Africa, he was the leader of the South African Industrial Federation. During the 1922 strike, he was a moderate who favored wage cuts and negotiation with the government. More extreme elements among the white miners opposed him and often treated Crawford with contempt. He died in Johannesburg.

Erasmus, Piet (1884–?): Erasmus was the leader of the commandos during the 1922 revolt. Authorities arrested Erasmus and imprisoned him in the strike prisoners' camp. He was one of those tried by the special courts, which found him guilty of high treason and sentenced Erasmus to ten years in prison. He was released in 1924.

Smuts, Jan Christian (1870–1950): Smuts served as the prime minister of South Africa from 1919 to 1924 and again from 1939 to 1948. During the 1922 strike, Smuts at first attempted to get the owners and miners to negotiate a settlement. When this attempt failed, he decided to use force against the striking workers and declared martial law. The 1922 Rand Revolt hurt Smuts politically, as he and his South Africa Party lost the 1924 elections.

Thompson, Joe: Head of the South African Industrial Federation and the Augmented Executive, Thompson was among the moderate leaders of the workers who favored a softer line against the owners.

See also: *Miners' Strike, South Africa: 1946.*

BIBLIOGRAPHY

Books

Beck, Roger B. *The History of South Africa.* Westport, CT: Greenwood Press, 2000.

Hancock, W. K. *Smuts.* Cambridge, U.K.: Cambridge University Press, 1968.

Herd, Norman. *1922: The Revolt on the Rand.* Johannesburg, R.S.A.: Blue Crane, 1966.

Johnstone, Frederick A. *Class, Race, and Gold: A Study of Class Relations and Racial Discrimination in South Africa.* Lanham, MD: University Press of America, 1987.

Simons, Jack and Ray Simons. *Class and Colour in South Africa, 1850–1950.* London: International Defence and Aid Fund for Southern Africa, 1983.

Thompson, Leonard Monteath. *A History of South Africa.* New Haven, CT.: Yale University Press, 2001.

Walker, Ivan L. and Ben Weinbren. *2000 Casualties: A History of the Trade Unions and the Labour Movement in the Union of South Africa.* Johannesburg, R.S.A.: The South African Trade Union Council, 1961.

Wilson, Francis. *Labour in the South African Gold Mines, 1911–1969.* Cambridge, U.K.: Cambridge University Press, 1972.

—Ronald Young

Miners' Strike

South Africa 1946

Synopsis

In August 1946 the African Mine Workers Union (AMWU) in South Africa called a strike of black miners in the country's Witwatersrand gold producing region. The strike was the first widespread action taken by African workers since 1920. Nearly 100,000 black workers struck, completely or partially shutting down 13 mines. Despite the fact that in 1942 the government of prime minister Jan Smuts had declared all strikes by black workers to be illegal, the AMWU took an active role in demanding higher wages for black workers. When the government and the Chamber of Mines largely ignored the demands of the AMWU, the black workers struck. The government quickly used force to crack down on the strike. More than 1,200 people were injured and nine were killed. Authorities also arrested the strike leaders and dismissed some 70 workers. The defeat of the strike marked the end of the organization and unionization of black miners until 1982.

Timeline

1926: Britain is paralyzed by a general strike.

1931: Financial crisis widens in the United States and Europe, which reel from bank failures and climbing unemployment levels. In London, armies of the unemployed riot.

1936: The election of a leftist Popular Front government in Spain in February precipitates an uprising by rightists under the leadership of Francisco Franco. Over the next three years, war will rage between the Loyalists and Franco's Nationalists. The Spanish Civil War will prove to be a lightning rod for the world's tensions, with the Nazis and fascists supporting the Nationalists, and the Soviets the Loyalists.

1941: Japanese bombing of Pearl Harbor on 7 December brings the United States into the war against the Axis. Combined with the attack on the Soviet Union, which makes Stalin an unlikely ally of the Western democracies, the events of 1941 will ultimately turn the tide of the war.

1946: Winston Churchill warns of an "Iron Curtain" spreading across Eastern Europe.

1946: Three months after the first meeting of the United Nations General Assembly in London in January, the all-but-defunct League of Nations is officially dissolved.

1946: At the Nuremberg trials, twelve Nazi leaders are sentenced to death, and seven others to prison.

1946: The first true electronic computer, the Electronic Numerical Integrator and Computer (ENIAC), is built.

1951: Six western European nations form the European Coal and Steel Community, forerunner of the European Economic Community and the later European Union.

1956: Elvis Presley appears on Ed Sullivan's *Toast of the Town,* where he performs "Hound Dog" and "Love Me Tender" before a mostly female audience. Nationwide, 54 million people watch the performance, setting a new record.

1961: President Eisenhower steps down, warning of a "military-industrial complex" in his farewell speech, and 43-year-old John F. Kennedy becomes the youngest elected president in U.S. history. Three months later, he launches an unsuccessful invasion of Cuba at the Bay of Pigs.

Event and Its Context

Labor Shortage and the Mine Owners Response

Several causes precipitated the 1946 strike. One key cause was a labor shortage. The gold mining industry depended on African migrant workers from both within and outside of South Africa. Traditionally the migrants had been a stable and reliable source of labor and during the late 1930s, the number of South African migrant workers was up, as the Native Recruiting Corporation secured the labor of many workers.

During World War II, however, domestic sources of migrant labor declined as workers joined the military or took better paying urban factory jobs. The mine owners, therefore, looked to foreign sources of labor. The Witwatersrand Native Labor Association recruited workers from Mozambique and Central Africa. Nevertheless, these foreign workers could not make up for the labor shortage. Even more pressure was put on the mines, as there was also a shortage of white workers, many of whom had gone off to war. The "color bar" prevented black African workers from replacing these white workers in many positions. Therefore, mine owners had to find ways to increase productivity despite a lack of workers.

The mine owners took three main steps to increase output. First, starting in the late 1930s, the mine owners introduced more machines to replace traditionally labor intensive tasks. Mechanization helped to increase production and ore output increased by 10 percent per person per year. Yet, overall, mechanization was limited, as mine owners spent their capital more on expansion than on machines.

A second response was scientific management, which was led by J. S. Ford, the general manager at the Langlaagte mine. He argued that racism in the mining industry hurt productivity. He believed that African workers needed to be treated better and conditions should be improved. To achieve this, he called for standard practices and written training manuals.

Finally, tighter supervision was imposed on workers. Mine owners urged the managers to monitor more closely the underground work. There were both surface checking stations and underground native checkers that ensured that workers were putting forth maximum effort.

African Miners Respond: The Formation of the AMWU

All of these conditions made African workers unhappy and eventually led to the 1946 strike. As early as 1942 there were sit-down strikes and confrontations at some mines. In early 1943 miners at the Langlaagte mine complained about their working conditions. In the ensuing confrontation, some 500 miners were arrested. Owners and the police feared, however, that there would be even more problems if all of the workers were tried. The recently created African Mine Workers Union (AMWU) provided legal counsel for those on trial. All but eight leaders kept their jobs, which signaled a victory for the AMWU and give the organization credibility.

In 1941 Guar Radebe, a member of the Communist Party, established the Committee to Organize African Mineworkers. In 1942 this group became the AMWU. In the 1920s and 1930s the Communist Party had made some attempts to form trade unions of black miners. These efforts had met with little success. By the late-1930s blacks in other industries had begun to organize. When high inflation combined with low rainfall hit the country during World War II, many black miners began to join the AMWU.

The early leaders of the AMWU were President J. B. Marks and Secretary J. J. Majoro. At first, the AMWU attracted relatively few workers. Those who did join were mostly from mines near urban areas such as Johannesburg. By 1943 the AMWU had about 1,800 members out of some 300,000 African miners. Members were mainly mine clerks, who had to meet secretly.

In 1943 black miners began demanding higher wages. In response, the government formed the Witwatersrand Mine Natives' Wages Commission, more commonly known as the Lansdown Commission. Although the Lansdown Commission granted a small wage increase to the miners, it was less than wartime inflation.

The Dispute over Food and Wages

Another issue that contributed to the 1946 strike was food. Traditionally, mine management provided food to African miners at their compound dining halls. Owners could not realistically reduce food rations out of fear of riots. Instead they sought to modernize and rationalize food preparation to eliminate waste. A problem was that a series of poor harvests between 1943 and 1946 reduced the amount of corn available to mine owners. In addition, there were shortages of meat. Starting in early 1945 and into 1946, black gold miners initiated a series of sometimes violent food riots. The AMWU made this issue of food a key union issue. Soon, the AMWU and African miners were demanding to be able to provide their own food.

Yet another factor that led to the 1946 strike was a reduction in the profits earned by mine owners. By the mid-1940s their profits declined due to several problems. Labor shortages decreased production in some mines. At the same time, costs of operating mines were increasing. The costs of mine supplies and equipment were on the rise, as were the wages of white mine workers. At the same time, the world price of gold was stable and not based on the cost of production. Owners could not simply pass on their costs to the consumer.

In light of this situation, owners were not willing to increase wages for African miners. Once again, this led to a conflict with the AMWU. African wages had increased slightly in absolute terms but had declined in real terms. The AMWU was particularly upset over the implementation of the recommendations of the Lansdown Commission, which had called for wage increases for African mine workers. The Chamber of Mines, however, argued that the mine owners could not afford to pay such increases. The government thus agreed to pay the higher wages but paid only part of the recommended amount.

Unionization and Confrontation

In response to this situation, Marks and the AMWU decided to appeal to more workers. Thousands of African miners began to attend union meetings, which were watched carefully by police and management. The key issues discussed at these meetings were better wages, better food, and better living conditions. The labor leaders encouraged organization and unity of African workers through the union instead of relying on old ways of dealings with grievances such as destroying buildings or taking food from kitchens. At the same time, when such disturbances occurred, the AMWU often paid for the legal defense of the miners. The high point of this early organization came at the annual meeting in July 1944 in Johannesburg. Some 700 delegates from every mine on the Rand attended along with 1,300 rank-and-file members.

Soon, however, the government made union organization among African workers more difficult. In August 1944 the government issued Proclamation 1425, which prohibited organizations from meeting on mine property without permission. Because most of the compounds where the miners lived were surrounded by mine property, this law was a virtual ban on union meetings. Police dispersed any unauthorized meetings, and once again African miners had to rely on secretive meetings in Johannesburg.

Given the uncompromising attitude of the government and Chamber of Mines, AMWU leaders began to discuss the possibility of a general strike as the only alternative. By April 1946 numerous meetings and strikes on the mines and compounds made the demands for pay raises. The meetings and strikes sometimes became violent, with workers breaking ranks and throwing rocks and management calling in the police. These incidents in early 1946 were not organized directly by the AMWU, but rather were local and spontaneous.

In May 1946 the meeting of the AMWU was not well attended. This time, however, the union put a time limit on their demand for pay raises. The union leaders set a deadline of 4 August for mine owners to accept their demands. When the union met again on that date, Marks and Majoro explained to the workers that their demands had been ignored by both the Chamber of Mines and the government. Thus, AMWU leadership called for a strike to being on 12 August, and the workers approved.

On 12 August, African mine workers succeeded in shutting down seven mines completely and another five partially. According to the Department of Native Affairs, 21 out of a total of 47 mines were eventually affected. More than 70,000 workers were involved, about 25 percent of the total. To counter the strike by the African mine workers, authorities brought in some 1,600 police who used troop carriers borrowed from the military. These police often used force against the strikers, utilizing their batons, bayonets, and revolvers. Police arrested more than 1,000 workers, including leaders such as Marks. Some 1,200 African workers suffered injuries and nine miners were killed.

The strike was more widespread and successful than most thought it would be. It attracted workers from all job categories. In part, the AMWU succeeded in distributing its pamphlets. It was helped in this effort by other groups such as the Communist Party and the African National Congress. At the same time, many workers were only vaguely aware of the union. Instead, these miners relied on informal networks; grassroots organization at each mine compound was key.

Poor communications between the union and the workers also was significant. Finally, police violence and the early arrest of key leaders doomed the strike to failure. In the end, the government did not improve the situation of the African miners. Prime Minister Jan Smuts never thought the strike was based on legitimate grievances but rather had been caused by outside agitators. He felt that it was the government's duty to protect the African workers from such influences.

Key Players

Majoro, J. J.: Majoro was one of the principle leaders of the 1946 strike and served as first secretary of the AMWU. He worked as a clerk in the gold mines.

Marks, J. B. (1903–1972): Marks was a South African labor leader who served as the first president of the African Mine Workers' Union (AMWU). He also worked as the chairman of the South African Communist Party and was a member of the National Executive Committee of the African National Congress. Marks died in the Soviet Union.

Smuts, Jan Christian (1870–1950): Smuts served as the prime minister of South Africa from 1919 to 1924 and again from 1939 to 1948. Smuts' government cracked down on the organizational activities of the African miners in 1946, claiming that outside agitators were stirring up the black workers.

See also: *Miners' Strike, South Africa: 1922.*

BIBLIOGRAPHY

Books

Moodie, T. Dunbar. *Going for Gold: Men, Mines, and Migration.* Berkeley: University of California Press, 1994.
Simons, Jack and Ray Simons. *Class and Colour in South Africa, 1850–1950.* London: International Defence and Aid Fund for Southern Africa, 1983.

Periodicals

James, Wilmot G. "Grounds For a Strike: South African Gold Mining in the 1940s." *African Economic History* 16 (1987): 1–22.

Moodie, T. Dunbar. "The Moral Economy of the Black Miners' Strike of 1946." *Journal of Southern African Studies* 13, no. 1 (1986): 1–35.
O'Meara, Dan. "The 1946 African Mine Workers' Strike and the Political Economy of South Africa." *Journal of Commonwealth and Comparative Politics* 8 (1975): 146–173.

—Ronald Young

Minimum Wage Movement

United States 1910s–1930s

Synopsis

Long before a federal minimum wage was established, American workers in the 1910s and 1920s stepped up a decades-old struggle for a minimum wage law. One pivotal protest in 1912, a textile workers' strike demanding "fair pay for a day's work," made Massachusetts the first state in the United States to adopt a minimum wage law. By 1923, 15 states, Puerto Rico, and Washington, D.C., had instituted similar laws. Given that women were a vulnerable segment of the workforce, and most minimum wage legislation was limited to female workers, the struggle for a minimum wage was closely linked to the movement for women's rights. A key moment in the minimum wage struggle came with the 1923 Adkins decision, which equated the establishment of the minimum wage with price-fixing. That year the Supreme Court ruled 5–3 in the case of *Adkins v. Children's Hospital* that the minimum wage law of the District of Columbia was unconstitutional. The first federal minimum wage was finally established as part of the Fair Labor Standards Act of 1938.

Timeline

1910: Vassily Kandinsky pioneers non-representational painting.

1912: *Titanic* sinks on its maiden voyage, from Southampton to New York, on 14 April. More than 1,500 people are killed.

1914: On 28 June in the town of Sarajevo, then part of the Austro-Hungarian Empire, Serbian nationalist Gavrilo Princip assassinates Austrian Archduke Francis Ferdinand and wife Sophie. In the weeks that follow, Austria declares war on Serbia, and Germany on Russia and France, while Great Britain responds by declaring war on Germany. By the beginning of August, the lines are drawn, with the Allies (Great Britain, France, Russia, Belgium, Serbia, Montenegro, and Japan) against the Central Powers (Germany, Austria-Hungary, and Turkey).

1916: Battles of Verdun and the Somme are waged on the Western Front. The latter sees the first use of tanks, by the British.

1918: The Second Battle of the Marne in July and August is the last major conflict on the Western Front. In November, Kaiser Wilhelm II abdicates, bringing an end to the war.

1918: Upheaval sweeps Germany, which for a few weeks in late 1918 and early 1919 seems poised on the verge of communist revolution—or at least a Russian-style communist coup d'etat. But reactionary forces have regained their strength, and the newly organized Freikorps (composed of unemployed soldiers) suppresses the revolts. Even stronger than reaction or revolution, however, is republican sentiment, which opens the way for the creation of a democratic government based at Weimar.

1920: Bolsheviks eliminate the last of their opponents, bringing an end to the Russian Civil War. By then, foreign troops, representing a dozen nations that opposed the communists, have long since returned home.

1922: Inspired by the Bolsheviks' example of imposing revolution by means of a coup, Benito Mussolini leads his blackshirts in an October "March on Rome" and forms a new fascist government.

1924: V. I. Lenin dies, and thus begins a struggle for succession from which Josef Stalin will emerge five years later as the undisputed leader of the Communist Party, and of the Soviet Union.

1926: Britain is paralyzed by the General Strike.

1928: Stalin launches the first Five-Year Plan.

1930: Naval disarmament treaty is signed by the United States, Great Britain, France, Italy, and Japan.

Supreme Court justices Oliver Wendell Holmes, Jr. (right) and William Howard Taft, Washington, D.C. AP/ Wide World Photos. Reproduced by permission.

Event and Its Context

Early Progression Toward Minimum Wage Laws

The idea of a living wage is as old as the wage system itself. For individuals accustomed to controlling their own labor, having to answer to a boss in exchange for wages was tantamount to slavery. According to economist Oren M. Levin-Waldman, when wage laborers in the nineteenth century talked increasingly of a "living wage," they aimed not only for independence, "but to cast aside the perception of their work as slave labor." Following emancipation, when freed black slaves were hired as farm laborers under the wage system in the American South, many argued that "it was even more dehumanizing than slavery," wrote M. Langley Biegert. Men working for low wages "saw themselves as no different from prostitutes," and the concept of a living wage helped them "rise above the shameful image of a prostitute."

By the late nineteenth century, members of the "anti-sweating" movement (a fight against low wages paid to the "sweated" employees resulting from surplus labor in industrial economies) were vocal against subnormal pay. Some countries at that time began to legislate mandatory floors on hourly wages, thus guaranteeing a minimum standard of living for unskilled workers. New Zealand was the first to establish such legislation in 1894. The Australian state of Victoria followed in 1896. Great Britain became the first European nation to introduce a minimum wage in 1909, joined by several continental European nations in the following years. In the United States, where the movement for a minimum wage followed an 1877 railroad strike, the struggle heated up in the 1910s.

The minimum wage around this time was becoming an important part of progressive electoral platforms. In the 1911 and 1913 elections for Los Angeles City Council, for example, socialist candidates almost won with platforms calling for a "fair day's wage for a fair day's work." It was a textile workers' strike in Massachusetts, however, that drew national attention to and put human faces on the minimum wage struggle.

Strike for Three Loaves

Lawrence, Massachusetts' multiethnic workforce of more than 40,000 laborers worked for 16 cents an hour, averaging $8.75 a week, barely enough for rent and food. On 1 January 1912 the state forced mills to cut the workweek from 56 hours to 54; owners in such cases cut wages and sped up machines so workers did the same work for less pay. On 11 January women at Everett Mill walked out when they discovered short pay; on 12 January workers at Wood Mill shouted, "Short pay! Strike! All out!" and began destroying machinery. The pay cut

Workers at conveyor belt stations, California Fruit Company factory. © Hulton/Getty Images. Reproduced by permission.

amounted to about 32 cents per day, the cost of three loaves of bread. By noon some 11,000 millworkers in the area had joined the strike to demand "fair pay for a day's work."

The nine-week strike drew attention nationwide. The strike committee, organized by the Industrial Workers of the World (IWW), demanded among other things a 15 percent pay raise. Under the watch of state police and militia, strikers attacked anyone who tried to cross the picket line. By mid-January there were 25,000 strikers from 11 mills. A bloody 10 February clash between strikers and police led to congressional investigations. Bad nationwide press on factory conditions forced financially strained owners to meet strikers' demands. On 12 March the American Woolen Company offered a 5 percent minimum wage raise, with greater increases for the lowest-paid laborers. When other firms met the offer, workers voted on a date for returning to work, giving them time to negotiate pay raises at the remaining factories.

IWW leader Bill Haywood was in Lawrence to celebrate amidst the "shrill roar" of cheering workers. "Back and forth that spontaneous cry swept, not a concerted cheer at all, but the inarticulate cry of a crowd feeling deep emotion," reported the *Boston Globe* on 15 March. The Lawrence strike was credited with benefiting more than 250,000 workers and bringing greater attention to the minimum wage issue.

A Women's Movement

While male workers had long called for a living wage, the American minimum wage movement of the early twentieth century was inextricably linked to the struggle for women's rights. In the 1890s affluent women, appalled by the working conditions facing female department store workers, founded the National Consumers' League (NCL), a pioneer advocate of the minimum wage. Led by women but supported by both men and women of progressive, social democratic, and liberal tendencies, the turn-of-the-century NCL pioneered the idea of "ethical consumption," using consumer pressure to improve labor standards. The organization drafted a "white list" of department stores that treated their employees fairly and granted a minimum wage of $6 weekly for experienced saleswomen and $2 weekly for cash girls. The NCL spread its attention to manufacturing and other sectors, with special attention focused on the garment industry. By 1916 the NCL had some 15,000 members in 43 states.

According to Landon R. Y. Storrs in his book *Civilizing Capitalism,* the NCL was committed to improving the lot of all workers, but it was child labor and the abhorrent working conditions of women that most outraged them. Women usually earned "a fraction" of male wages, had less leisure time than men due to unpaid domestic duties, and were expected to be subservient to men. In general, noted Storrs, "dire need, combined with lack of union support and employer expectations of submissiveness, undercut wage-earning women's ability to protest these injustices."

The NCL soon came to realize the limits of voluntary compliance by employers and pushed for binding labor legislation nationwide. One vocal advocate for a minimum wage lobbying within the NCL was Molly Dewson (often called "Minimum Wage" Dewson), an early advocate of women's rights. Dewson joined the minimum wage movement in 1911 and, as executive secretary of the Minimum Wage Investigative Committee, attained national recognition for a report that led to the nation's first-ever minimum wage law. Under the leadership of the socialist and feminist Florence Kelley, the NCL drafted the law, which Massachusetts enacted in 1912. The NCL continued to push for minimum wage laws in other states.

Massachusetts Sets Precedent

The first minimum wage law in U.S. history was passed in 1912 in Massachusetts. This legislation contained numerous exceptions and applied only to women and children employed in specific industries. Some criticized it as effectively unenforceable, with public opinion being the only leverage workers had to force employers into compliance. That year, eight more states instituted similar laws. By 1923 the District of Columbia, Puerto Rico, and 15 states had enacted minimum wage laws. Despite talk of minimum wage laws as a component of the union struggle (a goal of labor unions was for men to earn wages high enough to support a family), some labor unions of the time opposed wage legislation for men. Union leaders feared that government enforcement of a minimum wage might lessen interest in union membership and thus jeopardize nationwide organizing campaigns among male workers. The American Federation of Labor, for example, favored a minimum wage for women but not for men.

Emile Hutchinson, in her 1919 study on the wages earned by industrial women, argued in favor of minimum wage legislation. "If an industry can maintain itself only by paying its workers less than a living wage," she said, "it is socially an unprofitable enterprise."

Equal Rights

In 1920 ratification of the Nineteenth Amendment to the U.S. Constitution gave women the right to vote. The amendment nonetheless contained no statement guaranteeing women "equal protection of the laws." This spurred a decades-long struggle for an Equal Rights Amendment (ERA), spearheaded by the National Woman's Party in 1921. Leading the opposition to the ERA was the NCL, which argued that the ERA would invalidate the guaranteed minimum wage and other labor laws protecting women.

The Nineteenth Amendment, despite constituting a significant advance in women's rights, was seen by some as a reason to invalidate minimum wage legislation favoring women. If women were now equal, the argument went, they should have the same rights as men to contract their services at the wages they saw fit. In the eyes of Clara Mortenson Beyer, secretary of the District of Columbia's Minimum Wage Board, this notion of freedom was "ludicrous" with "overworked, undernourished" women workers near the bottom of the industrial scale and largely unorganized. Rather than talk of freedom to choose jobs or freely bargain for hours and wages, "it would be more to the point to talk of the freedom of employers to exploit their workers," she wrote. More than half of all wage-earning women in the United States were not earning enough to live on. Until the day came that women needed fewer special protections than men, Beyer argued, it would be "little short of criminal to deny them the opportunity for reasonable leisure and a living wage, which legislation alone can obtain for them."

Supreme Court Antilabor Precedents

Ever since the first labor legislation was enacted, "employers have valiantly defended before the courts the freedom of contract and property rights of their workers. And, upon occasion, the judges take them seriously," wrote Beyer in 1923.

The late nineteenth and early twentieth centuries saw a wide body of labor legislation meant to protect workers. This time period also saw challenges to these laws, with varied results. Starting with the Slaughter-House cases in 1873, the United States Supreme Court generally took a laissez-faire approach to labor issues, arguing that workers and employers enjoyed freedom to negotiate their own contract terms and that the government should not intervene. The so-called Lochner Era (in which American courts tended to declare regulatory legislation unconstitutional and in violation of liberty of contract and due process established under the Fourteenth Amendment) would last until the late 1930s with the triumph of the New Deal.

Despite this general trend, there were some contradictory rulings during this period. In the case of *Holden v. Hardy,* the Supreme Court ruled in 1898 that a state could limit freedom of contract to restore equal bargaining power and to protect a worker's health. The Court's 1905 ruling in *Lochner v. New York,* however, used the arguments of freedom of contract and personal liberty to strike down a maximum-hours law for bakers. In 1908 the justices ruled in the case of *Muller v. Oregon* that a maximum-hours law for female laundry workers was acceptable given the "delicate physiology of women." According to Julie Novkov, author of *Constituting Workers, Protecting Women,* the case of *Adkins v. Children's Hospital* ushered in a fourth and final phase (1923–1937) of the Lochner era that she called "gendered rebalancing." Discussions of protective labor legislation over this period centered on female-specific laws and particular minimum wage laws.

Adkins v. Children's Hospital

While the aim of minimum wage legislation was to protect workers, workers themselves did not always support application of the legislation. Such was the case in the nation's capital, where the Minimum Wage Board ordered a local children's hospital to raise the wages of a group of women employees to the legal minimum. The U.S. Congress had on 19 September 1918 authorized the wage board to establish appropriate wages for women and children working in the District of Columbia. In the case of *Adkins v. Children's Hospital,* a District of Columbia hospital and some of its female workers had agreed upon wage rates and compensation "satisfactory to such employees, but which in some instances were less than the minimum wage fixed by an order of the board." When the hospital fired the women, a suit was brought before the Supreme Court to restrain the board from attempting to enforce the order. The suit argued that the district's order was unconstitutional and violated the due process clause of the Fifth Amendment.

On behalf of the appellants, Harvard law professor Felix Frankfurter tried unsuccessfully to defend the constitutionality of the minimum wage for women. Both the appellants and states supporting the minimum wage presented briefs claiming that minimum wage laws increased women's wages (which were often lower than the cost of living) and that minimum wage protection for women generally did not mean displacement by male workers.

Supreme Court Decision

In 1923 the U.S. Supreme Court overturned the District of Columbia's minimum wage law, which mandated a minimum wage for women working in hotels, restaurants, and hospitals. The minimum wage law, said the majority 5–3 opinion, constituted price-fixing and infringed unreasonably upon an individual's liberty to decide the price at which they would sell their labor. Moreover, the Court deemed that since the Nineteenth Amendment had given equality to women, they no longer needed labor legislation. Since there was no minimum wage for males, and they had the right to sell their labor at any price, women should also have "equal rights to work" for low wages without government intervention.

In the majority opinion, Justice George Sutherland (who nonetheless recognized "the physical differences" potentially warranting legislation of special work conditions for women) stated the following: "We cannot accept the doctrine that women of mature age . . . require . . . restrictions upon their liberty of contract which could not lawfully be imposed in the case of men under similar circumstances."

Justices Oliver Wendell Holmes, Jr., Edward T. Sanford, and William Howard Taft argued in their dissenting opinion that Congress had the authority to undo recognizable evils. "Pretty much all law consists in forbidding men to do some things that they want to do, and contract is no more exempt from law than other acts," wrote Holmes. Moreover, Holmes questioned the principle on which the Court could allow the establishment of maximum hours for female workers (as it did in *Muller v. Oregon*) yet deny the power to fix a minimum wage for their work. Holmes wrote that he would need "more than the Nineteenth Amendment to convince me that there are no differences between men and women, or that legislation cannot take those differences into account."

Critics called the Adkins decision the peak of a long period of antilabor protection sentiment on the nation's highest court.

Later Rulings

The Supreme Court later altered its position on the minimum wage. Despite striking down a minimum wage for female

laundry workers in the 1936 case of *Morehead v. New York,* the justices ruled in 1937, in *West Coast Hotel Company v. Parrish,* that some government intervention in labor contracts was not unconstitutional, effectively overturning *Adkins v. Children's Hospital.* With the Great Depression and the New Deal as a backdrop, views on the minimum wage came into greater favor; in June 1938 the Fair Labor Standards Act established the first federal minimum wage of 25 cents an hour.

Key Players

Beyer, Clara Mortenson (1892–1990): Beyer was the first secretary of the Minimum Wage Board of the District of Columbia, serving from 1919 to 1921. A specialist in labor issues, she served on the War Labor Policies Board in 1917.

Dewson, Mary Williams "Molly" (1874–1962): Dewson, a social worker, probation officer, and suffragist, joined the minimum wage movement in 1911. As executive secretary of the Minimum Wage Investigative Committee, she oversaw the report leading to the nation's first minimum wage law in 1912. She lobbied for a national minimum wage bill within the National Consumers' League and the Democratic Party.

Frankfurter, Felix (1882–1965): Frankfurter argued before the U.S. Supreme Court on the constitutionality of the District of Columbia's minimum wage rules for women. A professor at Harvard Law School (1914–1939), he was appointed to the Supreme Court in 1939 and served until 1962.

Holmes, Oliver Wendell, Jr. (1841–1935): A Massachusetts jurist and professor at the Harvard Law School, Holmes was a justice of the U.S. Supreme Court from 1902 to 1932, the oldest jurist ever to serve on the Court. He wrote the dissenting opinion in the case of *Adkins v. Children's Hospital.* On the Court he was known as the "Great Dissenter."

Kelley, Florence (1859–1932): Kelley was a socialist and feminist who headed the National Consumer's League from 1899 to 1932. She was an active proponent of minimum wage laws for women, but she opposed an Equal Rights Amendment on grounds it would invalidate protective legislation. Her coalition-building activities helped create federal labor agencies protecting women and children. Among her several books was *The Supreme Court and Minimum Wage Legislation.*

Sutherland, George (1862–1942): The English-born Sutherland immigrated to the United States in 1863. A lawyer, he served in both the Utah and the U.S. House of Representatives. As justice of the U.S. Supreme Court from 1922 to 1938, he wrote the majority opinion in the case of *Adkins v. Children's Hospital.* He was a consistent opponent of New Deal legislation.

See also: *Equal Rights Amendment and Protective Legislation; Fair Labor Standards Act; Industrial Workers of the World; Lochner v. New York; Muller v. Oregon.*

BIBLIOGRAPHY

Books

McWhirter, Darien A. "Sex Discrimination." In *Equal Protection*. Phoenix, AZ: Oryx Press, 1995.

Novkov, Julie. *Constituting Workers, Protecting Women: Gender, Law, and Labor in the Progressive Era and New Deal Years*. Ann Arbor, MI: University of Michigan Press, 2001.

Smith, Adam C. "The Power of the Dollar: Consumer Activism in the 20th Century: From the National Consumers' League to the Student Antisweatshop Movement." Master's thesis, Georgetown University, 2002.

Storrs, Landon R.Y. *Civilizing Capitalism: The National Consumers' League, Women's Activism, and Labor Standards in the New Deal Era*. Chapel Hill, NC: University of North Carolina Press, 2000.

Periodicals

Biegert, M. Langley. "Legacy of Resistance: Uncovering the History of Collective Action by Black Agricultural Workers in Central East Arkansas from the 1860s to the 1930s." *Journal of Social History* 32 (fall 1998): 73–99.

Shirley, Frank P. "Vote to Work in Six Mills." *Boston Globe,* 15 March 1912, p. 2.

Other

Bernstein, David. *Constituting Workers, Protecting Women.* IALHI News Service, International Association of Labour History Institutions. June 2002 [cited 7 November 2002]. <http://www.ialhi.org/news/i0206_4.html>

Chew, Robin. *Oliver Wendell Holmes, Jr., American Jurist* [cited 7 November 2002]. <http://www.lucidcafe.com/lucidcafe/library/96mar/holmes.html>

Equal Rights Debates in the 1920s: Biographic Sketches [cited 7 November 2002]. <http://womhist.binghamton.edu/era/bios.htm>

Felix Frankfurter [cited 7 November 2002]. <http://www.ripon.edu/faculty/bowenj/antitrust/frankfur.htm>

Fleming, Maria. *The Strike for Three Loaves.* Southern Poverty Law Center [cited 7 November 2002]. <http://www.splcenter.org/cgi-bin/goframe.pl?refname=/teachingtolerance/tt-11.html>

George Sutherland. Utah History Encyclopedia [cited 7 November 2002]. <http://www.media.utah.edu/UHE/s/SUTHERLAND,GEORGE.html>

A History of the Progressive Movement in Los Angeles: The Teens. Progressive Los Angeles Network [cited 7 November 2002]. <http://www.progressivela.org/history/teens.htm>

Kettering, Sharon. *The Supreme Court and the Minimum Wage Law for Women.* Georgetown University Law Center 2000 [cited 7 November 2002]. <http://data.law.georgetown.edu/glh/kettering.htm>

Labour Program (HRDC): Database on Minimum Wages. Human Resources Development Canada. 2001 [cited 7 November 2002]. <http://labour.hrdc-drhc.gc.ca/psait_spila/lmnec_eslc/eslc/salaire_minwage/intro/index.cfm/doc/english>

Levin-Waldman, Oren M. *The Minimum Wage in Historical Perspective: Progressive Reformers and the Constitutional Jurisprudence of "Liberty of Contract."* Working Paper No. 256. The Jerome Levy Economics Institute [cited 7 November 2002]. <http://www.levy.org/docs/wrkpap/papers/256.html>

———. *The Rhetorical Evolution of the Minimum Wage.* Working Paper No.280. The Jerome Levy Economics Institute. September 1999 [cited 7 November 2002]. <http://www.levy.org/docs/wrkpap/papers/280.html>

Mary Williams Dewson. Women's stories [cited 7 November 2002]. <http://writetools.com/women/stories/dewson_mary_williams.html>

Mary Williams (Molly) Dewson. The Eleanor Roosevelt Papers. The Eleanor Roosevelt and Human Rights Project [cited 7 November 2002]. <http://www.gwu.edu/~erpapers/abouteleanor/q-and-a/glossary/dewson-mary.htm>

Oliver Wendell Holmes, Jr., Associate Justice. Arlington National Cemetery [cited 7 November 2002]. <http://www.arlingtoncemetery.com/owholmes.htm>

—Brett Allan King

Molly Maguires

United States 1860–1879

Synopsis

Every movement has its legends, and none is more compelling or controversial in the American labor movement than the group of rough, preliterate Irish immigrants known as the Molly Maguires. Nineteen members of the group were hanged in all—10 of them on the "Day of the Rope," 21 June 1877. Their deeds and even their very existence have become the stuff of legend. The stories of the Molly Maguires merge unionism; acts of individual resistance and vengeance; cultural, political and religious organization; union-busting; and ethnic frictions against the desolate background of the Pennsylvania mining camps to create a complex and dramatic narrative that provokes controversy to the present day.

Timeline

1861: Within weeks of Abraham Lincoln's inauguration, the U.S. Civil War begins with the shelling of Fort Sumter. Six states secede from the Union, joining South Carolina to form the Confederate States of America (later joined by four other states) and electing Jefferson Davis as president. The first major battle of the war, at Bull Run or Manassas in Virginia, is a Confederate victory.

1862: Victor Hugo's *Les Misérables* depicts injustices in French society, and Ivan Turgenev's *Fathers and Sons* introduces the term *nihilism*.

Molly Maguire members on way to gallows, Pottsville, Pennsylvania. © Bettmann/Corbis. Reproduced by permission.

1863: World's first subway opens, in London.

1864: International Red Cross in Geneva is established.

1865: Civil War ends with the surrender of General Robert E. Lee to General Ulysses S. Grant at Appomattox, Virginia. More than 600,000 men have died, and the South is in ruins, but the Union has been restored. A few weeks after the Confederate surrender, John Wilkes Booth shoots President Lincoln while the latter attends a performance at Ford's Theater in Washington. Andrew Johnson is sworn is as president.

1868: Fourteenth Amendment to the U.S. Constitution, which grants civil rights to African Americans, is ratified.

1871: Boss Tweed corruption scandal in New York City.

1873: Financial panic begins in Vienna, and soon spreads to other European financial centers, as well as to the United States.

1874: As farm wages in Britain plummet, agricultural workers go on strike.

1876: General George Armstrong Custer and 264 soldiers are killed by the Sioux at the Little Big Horn River.

1876: Alexander Graham Bell introduces the telephone.

Event and Its Context

The invention in 1833 by Frederick W. Geisenheimer of a process for smelting iron with anthracite coal created an enormous demand for coal in the central counties of Pennsylvania. Coal production increased from one million tons in 1840 to 8.5 million tons in 1859. Combined with terrible famines and land seizures in Ireland, this circumstance created a wave of immigration. Two million Irish families, most of whom were from Donegal in the west of Ireland, came to the United States, and tens of thousands of the new immigrants settled in the coal counties. These immigrants brought with them a tradition of rebellion and organization into secret groups such as the Whiteboys and Ribbonmen, who protected the Irish tenant farmers from English landlords. A mythical Irish woman, Molly Maguire, was counted among those protectors of the downtrodden masses.

Conditions for these "papes," as the Irish immigrants were called, were desperate. In the mines, the Welsh and British performed the skilled mining work, which left the Irish with the hard, dangerous, and low-paid work of hauling the coal to the surface or sorting out the slag. In one period, 566 mine workers lost their lives in the mines. In Schuylkill County, near Pottsville, Pennsylvania, one-quarter of the workforce was children aged 7 to 16, mainly "breaker boys" who picked rock from the coal. The pit bosses were also British or Welsh; their ethnic slurs characterized the Irish as drunken, lazy, and superstitious and contributed to tensions in the coal fields.

The Irish mine workers lived in "patches," or small mining towns, and were paid in "bobtail check," or mine scrip, which could only be spent at the "pluck-me" stores. The workers' lives centered on two major foci: the Catholic Church parishes throughout the coal counties, and bodies of a cultural group called the Ancient Order of Hibernians (AOH) that were started by the workers and that were later alleged to be a concealment for "the terrorist activities of the Molly Maguires."

The principal representative of the mine owners was Franklin B. Gowen, who, on behalf of investors (many of whom were English), was consolidating an empire that included both railroads and coal mines. Gowen came to the coal counties in 1856 as the manager of a mine in Centralia and later bought a small

Molly Maguire victim attacked by gang. © Bettmann/Corbis. Reproduced by permission.

mine. When the mine went bankrupt, Gowen blamed the rising tide of unionism for driving out the small operators.

In 1862 the Civil War increased the demand for coal and decreased the miners available for the work. This spawned both another surge of immigration from Ireland and the first discussion by Gowen, the district attorney for Schuylkill County, of "a secret body of Irishmen" that he held were responsible for the unsolved murders of 17 men, 11 of them mine, or pit, bosses who had fired miners.

In a typical episode, a dispute arose on 14 June 1862, in Audenreid, Pennsylvania, during a celebration to raise more volunteers for the war effort. Frank Langdon, a pit boss often accused by the miners of shortweighting them, had a public dispute with a young miner named John Kehoe. Later that night, Langdon was stoned to death by "persons unknown." On 18 December 1878 the miner, then called "Black Jack" Kehoe and reputedly the head of the Molly Maguires, was hanged in Pottsville for Langdon's death.

Under pressure from Gowen, the Pennsylvania state legislature passed a most remarkable law. The Act of 27 February 1865, which Gowen himself wrote, was a reaction to Gowen's complaints that public officials were not protecting the property and interests of the mine operators. This law authorized the formation of private police forces, allowed the armed Coal and Iron Police to patrol the coal fields, and suspended constitutional guarantees. A deputy commission for the Pennsylvania Bureau of Labor Statistics reported in 1874 that the coal operators had created "absolute personal government in the midst of a republic."

A great concern was the organization in the coalfields of unions in the mines and on the Pennsylvania Railroad. The defeat of the Workingman's Benevolent Association (WBA) in the strike of 1870 and the subsequent Long Strike of 1875 were accompanied by waves of violence in which mines were dynamited and stores were burned. The lurid myth of "the avenging Mollies" spread.

On 1 September 1869 Gowen became president of the Reading Railroad, retaining his elected position as district attorney. He worked to control the coal fields by creating an association of operators called the Anthracite Board of Trade, which managed both the rates charged for coal and the wages paid to miners. The antiunion zeal of this board was so severe that Gowen doubled the freight rates for any mine operator who bargained with the WBA.

In the midst of the Panic of 1873—in which the country endured an economic crash followed by a severe depression—Gowen moved in another direction to wreck the organizations of the Irish miners. He confirmed with Allen Pinkerton, head of the Pinkerton Detective agency, a contract that would place dozens of "labor spies" in the coal fields. Pinkerton's agency was virtually bankrupt so this new line of work seemed both promising and enormously profitable, as Gowen paid an alleged $100,000.

Gowen and Pinkerton tried to place a tone of social improvement on this deal. According to Pinkerton, Gowen wanted "laboring men, of whatever creeds or nationalities, protected in their right to work to secure sustenance for their wives and little ones, unawed by outside influences."

The most famous—or infamous—spy and *agent provocateur* provided by the Pinkerton agency was another Irish immigrant named James McParlan. Adopting the pseudonym of James McKenna, he moved in January 1874 to Shenandoah, Pennsylvania, and rented a room from a miner named Michael "Muff" Lawler who was later to become a prosecution witness against the Molly Maguires. He also began to go out with a woman named Molly Malloy, the sister-in-law of James "Pow-

Meeting of striking coal miners, Molly Maguire Men. The Library of Congress.

der Keg" Kerrigan, who also became a public witness against the Molly Maguires in the trials of 1877. With an unlimited expense account provided by the Pinkerton agency and a boisterous personality, McParlan became immediately popular among the men. He was sworn in as a member of the AOH on 14 April 1874 by Alexander Campbell, who would be hanged on 21 June 1877 as a result of McParlan's testimony. Even though he was elected secretary of an AOH body, McParlan had great difficulty for several years finding any proof of the existence or activities of the Molly Maguires, a failure that threatened his income and the solvency of the Pinkerton Agency. Under pressure from Gowen after the Long Strike of 1875, however, McParlan miraculously discovered a series of "murderous plots."

In fact, violence became a characteristic of the coal field. The operators and their Coal and Iron Police were brutal to the miners, who responded with individual acts of retribution. The miners had brought from Ireland the practice of sending "coffin notices" to warn possible targets to leave the area. Sensationalistic and vindictive newspaper reports also contributed to the historical record. *The Daily Herald* in Shenandoah cried for vigilante actions and "lamp post elevation" against "these foreigners who come to this country and undertake to tamper with our free institutions."

The Catholic Church also announced its opposition to the Molly Maguires. Although some local priests supported the AOH, Bishop Wood, a close personal friend of Frederick Gowen, stated in *The Catholic Standard* on 17 October 1874, "The Molly Maguires is a society rendered infamous by its treachery and deeds of blood—the terror or every neighborhood in which it existed . . . the disgrace of Irishmen . . . the scandal of the Catholic Church."

According to McParlan's testimony, members of the Mollies protected their identities by trading executions with other chapters. The targets of these executions were coal company managers who had committed offenses such as firing and blacklisting of employees.

The most prominent individual murders involved a Tamaqua policeman named Benjamin Yost, who was allegedly targeted for arresting and beating a miner named Thomas Duffy. Yost was shot in Tamaqua as he extinguished a streetlight on 5 July 1875. Duffy, James Boyle, James Carroll, and Hugh McGehan, all members of the AOH body in Shenandoah, were hanged on 21 June 1877.

Alleged as an exchange for the murder of Yost, mine superintendent James P. Jones was also killed on 3 September 1875, for firing and blacklisting McGehan. After shooting Jones on a main street, Kerrigan and two compatriots were captured by a posse and jailed in Mauch Chunk. Kerrigan's betrayal of his friends at their trial led to the first capital conviction of a Molly Maguire, and both were hanged on 21 June 1877.

Another important assassination involved the murders of Thomas Sanger, a superintendent of a nonunion mine, and William Uren, a young Welsh miner, as they walked to work on 3 September 1875. For this crime, McParlan pointed to James Doyle, Tom Munley, Charles McAllister, and two brothers, Charles and James O'Donnell, who lived in a small area called Wiggans Patch. As an example of the conditions faced by the Irish miners, an armed vigilante mob assassinated Charles O'Donnell, his daughter, and young son, on 9 December 1875 near their house in Wiggans Patch. No one was ever arrested for this crime.

The inexorable "legal" attack on the Molly Maguires began on 18 January 1876, with the trial of Michael J. Doyle for the murder of James P. Jones. This trial, established a pattern for the series of show trials that would ultimately convict and sentence to death more than 20 miners. The commonwealth "borrowed" Franklin Gowen to serve as prosecutor and installed a jury of German-American citizens, who had difficulty understanding the testimony. More important, Gowen convinced "Powder Keg" Kerrigan to testify against his friends in exchange for mercy.

Doyle's immediate conviction on 1 February 1876 allowed Gowen to issue an additional 17 murder warrants for the murders of Yost, Sanger, and Uren. Kerrigan helpfully provided a 210-page confession, but the real damage was done when McParlan appeared in court to "finger" the Mollies. In the trial in May for the murder of Yost, both Kerrigan and McParlan testified for the prosecution. MacParlan appeared in court surrounded by Pinkerton bodyguards and spent almost a full day detailing the inner workings of the Molly Maguires, creating a hysteria in the area.

The convictions continued in the same pattern. Despite witnesses who testified that the accused men were elsewhere, the juries—from which all Catholics were excluded—voted consistently to convict. Gowen even indicted Alex Campbell, whose tavern was allegedly used for planning meetings, as "an accessory before the fact" in the murder of John P. Jones. The subsequent conviction of Campbell, on the flimsiest of evidence, was considered a major blow to the organization.

The most prominent target for Gowen, however, was Jack Kehoe, who had risen from poor immigrant miner to prosperous tavern owner and elected politician. Identified by McParlan as the head of the Molly Maguires, Kehoe was first tried with eight other men for the June 1875 murder of a Welsh miner.

The trial opened on 8 August 1876 with Gowen as the prosecutor and a jury of German-Americans. The trial has been called "the most highly publicized of all the trials staged in the anthracite region." Once again, Gowen relied on a defendant, named Frank McHugh, to betray his fellows in exchange for mercy. Four days later, the jury required only 20 minutes to find all of the other defendants guilty. The sentence was seven years in prison.

Convicting Kehoe on a capital offense was Gowen's final desire, and the trial for the murder of Frank Langdon provided

the opportunity. Even though all of the evidence was developed by the Coal and Iron Police, and no witness could place Kehoe at the scene of the beating, the jury convicted the "King of the Mollies" of first degree murder on 16 January 1877. Kehoe was sentenced to hang.

In January 1877, the annual report of the Reading Railroad gloated that "a landed estate of 250 square miles had to be taken from the control of an irresponsible trade-union and its inhabitants rescued from the domination of an oath-bound association of murderers."

Thursday, 21 June 1877, is known as "Black Thursday" or "Pennsylvania's Day of the Rope." On that day 10 of the convicted miners were hanged in a mass execution. Surrounded by weeping relatives, crowds of spectators under military guard, priests, newspaper reporters, and politicians, four men hanged in Mauch Chunk and six in Pottsville. As Alex Campbell was led from his cell, he pressed his hand to the wall of Cell 17; legend has it that his handprint is still visible as a sign of his innocence.

Subsequent executions stretched out over the next 19 months; following the denial of his handwritten appeal to Governor Hartranft, Jack Kehoe mounted the gallows in Pottsville on 18 December 1878.

Unionism suffered serious setbacks in the Pennsylvania coal fields, but ironically, Black Thursday was also when the strike against the B and O Railroad in Baltimore, the first national strike in the United States, gathered force.

The Mollies may have seemed a localized attack, but it was part of a well-coordinated campaign against unionism in the period following the Civil War. For decades, unions suffered the reputation of being descendants of the Molly Maguires as management and politicians attempted to discredit any workers' organization. Organizations that formed as secret bodies, such as the early Knights of Labor, also suffered from comparisons to the Molly Maguires. The Catholic Church, ever staunch in its condemnation of secret organizations, had become an enduring component of unionism. Terence V. Powderly, a Knights of Labor leader, devoted considerable efforts to enlist Cardinal James Gibbons to persuade the pope that the organization was legitimate and not a successor to the Molly Maguires.

The events of the coal fields also created the labor spy industry, which Pinkerton used to build his company back to prosperity. The most famous episode came during the Homestead Strike in 1892, when the Pinkertons were driven from the town. The Senate hearings, under the direction of Senator Robert La Follette in 1936, exposed the durability of the labor spy industry; in 1998 General Motors signed a $1.2 billion contract with the Pinkerton agency to provide plant security.

In many ways, the case of the Molly Maguires has never closed. For decades, their guilt was publicly accepted. When James McParlan returned to public view in 1906, however, and prepared a perjured witness named Harry Orchard in the trial of "Big Bill" Haywood, Charles Moyer, and George Pettibone for assassinating the governor of Idaho, all of McParlan's testimony in the Pennsylvania trials became suspect.

By the end of the twentieth century, the controversy over the Molly Maguires had come full circle. Under pressure from the grandchildren of John Kehoe, the Pennsylvania Board of

Pardons issued a posthumous pardon for Kehoe in January 1979. Governor Milton Shapp joined the Pennsylvania Labor History to issue a tribute to the Molly Maguires. A Hollywood production company, filming *The Molly Maguires* with Sean Connery as Jack Kehoe, rebuilt part of a mining village in Eckley, Pennsylvania, which now offers—in a kind of "terrorism to tourism" circle—tours of the mining camp and a history of its inhabitants, the Molly Maguires.

Key Players

Gowen, Franklin Benjamin (1836–1889): In 1869 Gowen became the president of the Reading Railroad, which controlled more than 100,000 acres of coal country. After destroying the Molly Maguires, he drove the Reading into bankruptcy. On 13 December 1889 he committed suicide in a Washington, D.C., hotel room, although newspapers tried to prove that he had been assassinated by a supporter of the Molly Maguires.

Kehoe, John (1837–1878): Also known as "Black Jack," Kehoe was born in County Wicklow, Ireland and emigrated to the United States with his parents and 10 siblings in 1849. He settled in Girardville as a politically ambitious "b'hoy" and ran a tavern called the Hibernia House. Elected high constable in the county and called "the King of the Mollies," Kehoe was tried for murder and hanged in December 1878. There are still divisions of the Ancient Order of Hibernians that are named for him.

McParlan, James (1844–1919): McParlan left County Armagh in 1860 and began to work for the Pinkerton Agency in 1873 to infiltrate the Molly Maguires. He continued working for the Pinkertons and became the head of the Denver office, then was involved in the Haywood–Moyer–Pettibone trial in Idaho. He died peacefully in Denver.

Pinkerton, Allen (1819–1884): Pinkerton developed the modern detective agency. After working as a deputy sheriff in Cook County, Illinois, he opened the agency in 1852 with the motto, "The Eye That Never Sleeps," which led competitors to describe themselves as "private eyes." He discovered a plot to assassinate President Abraham Lincoln and founded the Secret Service. With the help of seven ghost writers, he published 18 books on his agency, including one based upon James McParlan's reports. He retired from his agency in 1882 and died of a stroke on 1 July 1884.

See also: *Homestead Lockout; Knights of Labor; Panic of 1873; Railroad Strike of 1877; Workingman's Benevolent Association.*

BIBLIOGRAPHY

Books

Bimba, Anthony. *The Molly Maguires.* New York: International Publishers, 1970. Original work published 1932.

Broehl, Jr., Wayne G. *The Molly Maguires.* Cambridge, MA: 1964.

Dewees, F. P. *The Molly Maguires: The Origin, Growth and Character of the Organization.* New York: B. Franklin, 1969. Original work published 1877.

Gutman, Herbert G. "Trouble on the Railroads, 1873-1874." In *Work, Culture and Society in Industrializing America: Essays in American Working-class and Social History.* New York: Vintage Books, 1977.

———. "Two Lockouts in Pennsylvania, 1873–1874." In *Work, Culture and Society in Industrializing America: Essays in American Working-class and Social History.* New York: Vintage Books, 1977.

Kenny, Kevin. *Making Sense of the Molly Maguires.* New York: Oxford University Press, 1998.

Lens, Sidney. "The Molly Maguires." In *Strikemakers and Strikebreakers.* New York: Dutton, 1985.

Lewis, Arthur H. *Lament for the Molly Maguires.* New York: Harcourt, Brace & World, 1964.

Pinkerton, Alan. *The Mollie Maguires and the Detectives.* With a new introduction by John M. Elliott. New York: Dover, 1973. Original work published 1877.

Other

Ancient Order of Hibernians in America. 2002 [cited 1 August 2002]. <http://www.aoh.com>.

Budget Technologies. "The Molly Maguires." 21 October 2001 [cited 1 August 2002]. <http://www.budgettechnologies.com/mollymaguires/framesnu.html>.

The Molly Maguires. Feature film directed by Martin Ritt. 1970.

Schuylkill County Visitors Bureau. [cited 1 August 2002]. <http://www.schuylkill.orgs>.

—Bill Barry

Muller v. State of Oregon

United States 1908

Synopsis

Muller v. State of Oregon was an influential Supreme Court decision that asserted the right of the government to limit the workday for women. Using social science evidence, Louis Brandeis argued before the Court that women who worked long hours on the job suffered both physical and psychological problems. He emphasized the effect this had on their children, so that working for long hours outside the home adversely affected not only women workers themselves, but also their entire family.

Muller gave Congress the right to pass subsequent "protective" legislation that restricted the rights of women workers. This led in turn to the exclusion of women from certain kinds of occupations and employment opportunities. The *Muller* decision has never been overturned in the same way *Brown v. Board* of *Education of Topeka* overturned *Plessy v. Ferguson.* With the passage of the Civil Rights Act of 1964, legislators have since mitigated the restrictive and discriminatory intent the original legislation promoted.

Timeline

1889: Flooding in Johnstown, Pennsylvania, kills thousands.

1893: Wall Street stock prices plummet on 5 May, precipitating a market collapse on 27 June. In the wake of this debacle, some 600 banks and 15,000 other businesses fail. The nationwide depression will last for four more years.

1898: Bayer introduces a cough suppressant, derived from opium, its brand name: Heroin.

1902: The *Times Literary Supplement,* a weekly review of literature and scholarship, begins publication in London.

1905: Russian Revolution of 1905 occurs. Following the "bloody Sunday" riots before the Winter Palace in St. Petersburg in January, revolution spreads throughout Russia, in some places spurred on by newly formed workers' councils, or soviets. Among the most memorable incidents of the revolt is the mutiny aboard the battleship *Potemkin.* Suppressed by the czar, the revolution brings an end to liberal reforms, and thus sets the stage for the larger revolution of 1917.

1909: Robert E. Peary and Matthew Henson reach the North Pole.

1909: National Association for the Advancement of Colored People (NAACP) is founded by W. E. B. Du Bois and a number of other prominent black and white intellectuals in New York City.

1909: William Cadbury's *Labour in Portuguese West Africa* draws attention to conditions of slavery in São Tomé and Principe.

1911: Revolution in Mexico, begun the year before, continues with the replacement of the corrupt Porfírio Díaz, president since 1877, by Francisco Madero.

1915: A German submarine sinks the *Lusitania,* killing 1,195, including 128 U.S. citizens. Theretofore, many Americans had been sympathetic toward Germany, but the incident begins to turn the tide of U.S. sentiment toward the Allies.

1919: With the formation of the Third International (Comintern), the Bolshevik government of Russia establishes its control over communist movements worldwide.

Event and Its Context

Origins of Protective Legislation

America's cities rapidly industrialized following the Civil War. As a consequence of industrialization, people from rural areas of the United States as well as from foreign countries moved to these expanding urban centers at an alarming rate. They were abandoning the economic decline gripping rural

parts of the country and economic upheaval overseas; moreover, they were drawn to the many financial opportunities the cities offered. As a result of this increase in the urban population and workforce, many reformers of the time feared that the social fabric of society was unraveling. The target of this fear was the large number of women and children entering the workforce. Many reformers believed that single women, living away from home, could easily be dragged into moral degradation and sexual exploitation. As a result of this concern, reformers pressed federal, state, and local governments to enact legislation to protect women and children both in the workplace and at home.

This "protective legislation," while brimming with good intentions, in practice restricted the rights of children and women and led to government-sponsored discrimination rather than actual protection from exploitation. Men in the workplace, who were competing with women and children for jobs in the unskilled labor sector, welcomed this type of legislation. Employers preferred to hire women and children for unskilled labor, rather than men, because they worked for lower wages. By limiting the number of hours and types of jobs that women and children could attain, men hoped they could encourage more job opportunities and better negotiating positions for themselves.

Social Darwinism

By the late nineteenth century, social Darwinism was ingrained in American intellectual thought. Social Darwinism applied the ideas of natural selection, which Charles Darwin introduced in his 1859 work *On the Origin of Species,* to a social context. Based on this notion, many Progressive Era reformers became "race" advocates out of fear that this era of "moral uncertainty" would denigrate the white race. Reformers during this time felt they had to control the behavior of white women in order to preserve the future of the common culture and civilization of white Americans. Thus, these reformers were not concerned about the moral dilemmas facing women of color; indeed, social Darwinists saw no moral conflict in curbing civil liberties in order to prevent perceived denigration of the white race.

Additionally, social Darwinists had a paternalistic outlook toward gender roles in American society. They believed that adult women were like children and that it was the role of adult men in society to protect them from the viciousness of American life. Like children, women could not be expected to make serious, informed decisions about their own well-being. In fact, the belief that women were incapable of making decisions outside the domestic realm was the primary argument for restricting the right to vote to adult, generally white, men.

Liberty of Contract Doctrine

Before the era of the minimum wage, courts tacitly defined the complex relationships among workers, management, and government through the "liberty of contract doctrine." Courts took a laissez-faire attitude when it came to the role of government in determining labor negotiations between workers and management. They believed that government had no right to abridge the rights of workers to negotiate issues related to working conditions, wages, and hours. However, the courts believed that government could interfere in the individual freedom of workers and management if there was a real threat to public safety. The courts spelled out this policy through a series of labor decisions in the late nineteenth and early twentieth centuries.

Thomas M. Cooley (1824–1898), a famous legal scholar of the time, published *A Treatise on the Constitutional Limitations Which Rest upon the Legislative Power of the States of the American Union,* which addressed the liberty of contract doctrine. Cooley noted that the liberty of contract doctrine was sex-based and recommended that it be applied only to adult men, not to women. Influenced by social Darwinism, Cooley believed that women legally had the same status as children and the mentally deficient.

Progressive Era Reform

Many reformers in the late nineteenth century were influenced by the tenets of social Darwinism. They believed that women in the workplace represented a threat to racial progress in the United States. Reformers believed that work diverted white women away from marriage and motherhood and that they would be educated in skills that would not help them to become better homemakers, which was considered their prime function. Reformers explained that women on the job learned masculine tasks and had no opportunity to develop their feminine attributes. Thus, in the event they decided to marry, they would find themselves unattractive to men and unprepared for marriage. Additionally women, particularly young ones, who either gained financial independence or offered economic assistance to their families or households were very real threats to male authority. Reformers believed that it was better for all women to stay at home and remain dependent on their fathers and husbands so that the patriarchal hierarchy would not be challenged.

Racism ran rampant through the policies these reformers promoted. The more race-conscious reformers feared that young white women would be exposed to women of color in the workplace. As a result of this workplace "race mixing," reformers believed that white women would learn immoral behavior, which in turn would denigrate white civilization. While these reformers may have genuinely believed that they were trying to uplift white women, they had no interest in reforming the circumstances of women of color in the workplace.

Reformers organized groups such as the Working Women's Protective Union, the Working Girl's Society, and the Travelers Aid Society to shield women from the moral horrors of the workplace. Settlement houses also promoted these reform agendas and tried to educate immigrants and rural women moving to the city about the evils of urban life. These organizations and reformers stepped into the fray by using the liberty of contract exception against women workers. They believed that by identifying the specific ways in which women in the workplace posed a threat to civilization, they could influence local and state governments to address legislation to direct how and for how long women could work outside their homes. They convinced local and state governments to set aside the liberty of contract doctrine in favor of enacting laws that directed the lives of working women. A favorite policy of these organizations was to limit the number of hours women were allowed to work.

State Legislatures

Many of these reformers were successful in convincing state legislatures to enact laws to restrict the number of hours women could work. Massachusetts was the first state to address this issue. In 1842 the state legislature passed a law limiting the number of hours children could work and then, five years later, added women to the measure. Men, however, were never added to the legislation. Under pressure from the reformers at Hull House, a settlement house in Chicago, Illinois, that state passed a measure in 1893 to limit the number of hours women could work in factories to just eight per day. By 1902 Washington, New York, Nebraska, and Pennsylvania had all passed laws limiting the number of hours women could work in industry. Women workers challenged most of the laws in these states.

Previous Court Challenges

Women who objected to these laws challenged them in courts based on the liberty of contract doctrine. *Commonwealth v. Hamilton Manufacturing Company* was the first challenge to the minimum-hour law for women. Without making specific references to women in their decision, the Massachusetts Supreme Court ruled in 1876 that this law did not violate the rights of workers, since it only applied to one employer at a time. Therefore, if a woman worked two jobs, she could work the minimum number of hours for both employers. Additionally, the court recognized that the Massachusetts law was a health regulation.

One victory for women who objected to these laws was *Ritchie v. People,* which targeted the Illinois minimum-hour law. The Illinois Supreme Court struck down the law in 1895 for two reasons. In 1872 the state legislature had passed a law that guaranteed women "freedom of occupation." Secondly, the state's minimum-hour law used the terminology "he/she," instead of singling out men or women specifically. Thus, since men were technically part of the original legislation, the law violated the liberty of contract doctrine. Although this court decision was a victory for white women who desired to work outside the home, it was hollow for the opponents of minimum-hour laws. Even though the court struck down the law, the decision still recognized that women in the workplace represented a threat to the social welfare of society. Consequently, the Illinois court case became not an affirmation for equal rights but a condemnation of poor legal phrasing.

In 1900 *Commonwealth v. Beatty* made its way to the Pennsylvania Supreme Court. This case was important because for the first time the courts publicly recognized the liberty of contract doctrine as pertaining only to adult males. The court referred to the *Holden v. Hardy* decision, which affirmed the right of the state of Utah to impose an eight-hour workday on miners who worked underground. *Holden* recognized the right of the government to dismiss the liberty of contract doctrine when the health of the workers was at risk. The Pennsylvania court applied this principle to *Commonwealth v. Beatty* by recognizing women not only as potential mothers but also as sharing legal status that was identical to that of their children. Thus the court affirmed the idea that women are biologically distinct from men and are therefore incapable of performing certain types of dangerous or physically demanding work or of working long, exhausting hours. The court noted that it was the responsibility of the government to shield women from these dangers in the workplace. This case was important because it would set the legal precedent identifying the inherent differences between men and women.

Finally, an important case that set the stage for *Muller* was *Lochner v. New York*. The United States Supreme Court heard the *Lochner* case in 1905. *Lochner* challenged a New York law that restricted the number of hours a baker could work. Many legislators believed that because baking conditions were hazardous and unsanitary, the baking industry posed a risk to workers. Lawyers challenged the law by preparing briefs indicating that medical authorities believed that baking conditions posed no threat to workers. The Court was so moved by the evidence contained in the brief that they declared the law unconstitutional. Although this decision represented a victory for the liberty of contract doctrine, it did not translate into a victory for gender equality. In their decision, the justices only referred to bakers as "men" and used the masculine pronoun when referring to the bakers affected by the Court's decision. Clearly, the judges felt that the *Lochner* decision did not apply to women; their conscious references to men and men alone sent a message that this verdict had no relevance to minimum-hour laws directed toward women.

Curt Muller and Mrs. E. Gotcher

The Oregon legislature passed a law in 1903 that limited the length of time a woman in the laundry industry and factories could work to 10 hours per day. Curt Muller owned the Grand Laundry in Portland. He required an employee, Mrs. E. Gotcher, to work for more than 10 hours on 4 September 1905. On the basis of the state law, Muller was indicted, convicted, and fined $10.00; the Oregon Supreme Court upheld his conviction. Believing that the *Lochner* decision applied to his case, he appealed his conviction to the United States Supreme Court.

The Brandeis Brief

Advocates for minimum-hour laws rallied to defend the Oregon statute. Florence Kelley of the National Consumer's League convinced Louis Brandeis to take the case on behalf of the state of Oregon. He, along with Helen Marot, Josephine Goldmark, and other women from the National Consumer League, prepared the evidence used to argue the case. Taking a page from the *Lochner* trial, Brandeis and his associates prepared what became know as the "Brandeis brief." Similar to the brief used to argue the *Lochner* case, Brandeis and his associates developed medical, sociological, and other professional evidence to suggest that women who worked long hours placed their health and the health of their families at risk. Although this argument had been tried in earlier litigation, the Brandeis brief was much longer, provided much more evidence, and contained more professional voices than the *Lochner* brief. Presentation of the Brandeis brief was, in fact, the first time in U.S. history that a lawyer tried a case with factual and expert testimony alone rather than relying on previous court decisions or interpretations of law.

Initially, Brandeis argued that certain types of work posed certain dangers to women, and he presented four reasons that women's labor should be regulated. First, women were biologically different from men and in many regards physically weaker

than men. Second, adversity in the workplace might have an impact on the reproductive capabilities of women. Third, the health of a child might be in jeopardy if a mother chose to work. Fourth, too much time spent at work meant that a woman had less time to spend at home taking care of her family. Only one of Brandeis's points affected women directly; the rest of them affected women's families or potential children.

Muller and his attorney, William D. Fenton, argued that the Oregon law violated the equal rights of both men and women in the workplace. He noted that whatever dangers the workplace posed to women, men were subject to the same dangers. Thus if the law did not apply to men and women equally, it violated the constitutional guarantee of "equal protection." He hoped that the court would recognize the precedent set with both the *Ritchie* and *Lochner* decisions.

The Supreme Court Decision

The Supreme Court rendered a unanimous decision. Associate Justice David J. Brewer wrote the opinion. According to Brewer's opinion, the Court recognized the physical difference between the sexes and maintained the opinion that women were of the same legal status as children. He frequently made references to the earlier Court decisions in regard to minimum-hour laws. The Court even believed that this decision would stand for some time, because Brewer noted that if women eventually won the right to vote, their legal status would not change.

Impact

The *Muller* verdict had a far-reaching impact for all workers and future landmark lawsuits in the United States. *Muller* introduced the techniques employed in the Brandeis brief to courtrooms across the country, and they became a popular way to present evidence for most of the twentieth century. The National Association for the Advancement of Colored People utilized the techniques employed in the Brandeis brief when they presented their case for *Brown v. Board of Education of Topeka*. The *Muller* decision also allowed government to exercise control over women in the workplace. As the twentieth century progressed and the demand for gender equality became more vocal, the overt sexism in these laws diminished, and many of them were voided by the Civil Rights Act of 1964, which also addressed discrimination based on race and sex.

Key Players

Brandeis, Louis (1856–1941): Brandeis was a famous lawyer who tried high-profile and controversial cases. He accepted and relished in cases that had social reform implications, such as *Muller v. State of Oregon*. Later, President Woodrow Wilson appointed him to the U.S. Supreme Court, where he served from 1916 to 1939.

Brewer, David J. (1837–1910): Brewer, an associate justice of the U.S. Supreme Court (1889–1910), was appointed to the High Court bench by President Benjamin Harrison. He delivered the unanimous opinion in the *Muller v. State of Oregon* case.

Goldmark, Josephine Clara (1877–1950): Goldmark was a social scientist and journalist. She was a social and labor reformer interested in preserving labor laws that protected women and children. She helped her brother-in-law, Louis Brandeis, gather evidence to argue *Muller* successfully before the Supreme Court.

Kelley, Florence (1859–1932): Kelley was a social reformer who advocated for the federal government to take a role in labor reform. She supported numerous efforts for protective legislation regarding women and children in the workplace. She was director of the National Consumer League and a founder of the National Women's Trade Union League. She was instrumental in convincing Louis Brandeis to take the *Muller* case and helped to research and write the information contained in the Brandeis brief.

Marot, Helen (1865–1940): Marot was a social scientist and labor reformer. She was an activist for women and children who were in the workforce. She helped gather evidence and write the Brandeis brief for the *Muller* case.

See also: *Civil Rights Act of 1964; Lochner v. New York; Working Women's Protective Union.*

BIBLIOGRAPHY

Books

Abramovitz, Mimi. *Regulating the Lives of Women: Social Welfare Policy from Colonial Times to the Present.* Boston, MA: South End Press, 1988.

Dalrymple, Candice. *Sexual Distinctions in the Law: Early Maximum Hour Decisions of the United States Supreme Court, 1905–1917.* American Legal and Constitutional History. New York: Garland, 1987. (Originally Ph.D. diss., University of Florida, 1979.)

Johnson, Elaine Gale Zahnd. "Protective Legislation and Women's Work: Oregon's Ten-Hour Law and the *Muller v. Oregon* Case, 1900–1913." Ph.D. diss., University of Oregon, 1982.

Woloch, Nancy. *Muller v. Oregon: A Brief History with Documents.* Boston, MA: Bedford Books of St. Martin's Press, 1996.

Periodicals

Acker, James R. "Thirty Years of Social Science in Supreme Court Criminal Cases." *Law and Policy* 12 (fall 1990): 1–23.

Allen, Ann. "Women's Labor Laws and the Judiciary: Reaction to Progressive Philosophy." *Proceedings of the South Carolina Historical Association* 65 (1985): 75–85.

Duncanson, Ian W. "Seen from Afar: An Outsider's Response to the Hurst Symposium." *Law and History Review* 18 (fall 2000): 181–185.

Englander, Susan. "The Science of Protection: Gender-Based Legal Arguments for the Ten-Hour Workday." *UCLA Historical Journal* 14 (1994): 33–52.

Erickson, Nancy S. "*Muller v. Oregon* Reconsidered: The Origins of a Sex-Based Doctrine of Liberty of Contract." *Labor History* 30 (winter 1989): 228–250.

Urofsky, Melvin I. "Myth and Reality: The Supreme Court and Protective Legislation in the Progressive Era." *Journal of Supreme Court History: Yearbook of the Supreme Court Historical Society* (1983): 53–72.

Other

Muller, Plaintiff in Error, v. the State of Oregon. Decided February 24, 1908 [cited 16 November 2002]. <http://www.tourolaw.edu/patch/Muller/>.

Muller v. State of Oregon 1908. Women in American History. Encyclopaedia Britannica. 1999 [cited 16 November 2002]. <http://search.eb.com/women/articles/Muller_v_Oregon.html>.

—Robert Cassanello